new zealand official yearbook 2008

Te Pukapuka Houanga Whaimana
o Aotearoa 2008

106th edition

Statistics
New Zealand
TATAURANGA AOTEAROA

David Bateman

Statistics New Zealand

For further information about statistics, and for help finding or using the statistical information available on the Statistics New Zealand website, contact the information centre:

Email   info@stats.govt.nz
Phone toll-free 0508 525 525
Phone   +64 4 931 4600
Fax   +64 4 931 4610
Website   www.stats.govt.nz

Acknowledgements

The *New Zealand Official Yearbook 2008* was produced by Statistics New Zealand, with the assistance of many individuals and the organisations listed in the 'Contributors and related websites' section at the end of each chapter. The department thanks them and the following:

Statistics New Zealand

Project editor Sarah Brazil

Senior editors Jan Schrader, Sarah Brazil

Editors Heather McLay, Désirée Patterson

Production editor Heather McLay

Illustrations editor and photographer Jarrad Mapp

Technical support Shirley Dixon

Other

Graphics and typesetters Totem Communications Ltd

Cover Shelley Watson/Sublime Design

Indexer Jill Gallop

Liability

Statistics New Zealand has made every effort to obtain, analyse, and edit the information and statistics used in the *New Zealand Official Yearbook 2008*. However, Statistics New Zealand gives no warranty that the information or data supplied contains no errors, and will not be liable for any loss or damage caused by the use, directly or indirectly, of material contained in the Yearbook.

Publication materials

This Yearbook is printed on 9lives satin paper, which is manufactured from 55 percent recycled fibre (made up of 30 percent pre-consumer and 25 percent post-consumer recycled fibre) and 45 percent virgin fibre from Forest Stewardship Council (FSC) certified, well managed forests, and is elemental chlorine free (ECF) bleached. The paper mill holds an FSC chain of custody certificate and is both ISO 14001 and ISO 9001 accredited. The ink used in this publication is 100 percent vegetable based, mineral oil free, and based on 100 percent renewable resources.

New Zealand Official Yearbook 2008
ISSN 0078-0170
ISBN 978-1-86953-717-3

Published in 2008 by David Bateman Ltd, 30 Tarndale Grove, Rosedale, North Shore City 0632, New Zealand.

Printed by PrintLink, Wellington, New Zealand.

Preface

The *New Zealand Official Yearbook* has provided a comprehensive statistical picture of life in New Zealand for more than 100 years. The 106th edition celebrates and continues this tradition, providing a wide-ranging picture of New Zealand society in 2008, based on the latest information available.

Recent Yearbooks have carried a theme, and the 2008 edition has an environmental focus, with conserving the natural environment as the unifying theme throughout the Yearbook. This theme provides a common thread for many of the sidebar stories, which enhance the main content of the Yearbook by elaborating or highlighting significant related events, achievements, or trends.

This environmental focus is timely – 2008 is the United Nations' International Year of Planet Earth, and on 5 June 2008 New Zealand hosted World Environment Day, in partnership with the United Nations' Environment Programme.

There is growing public interest in the state of our natural environment and the importance of conservation issues generally. People, organisations, and governments are working individually and collectively to reduce our impact on the planet.

The 2008 Yearbook is printed on '9lives paper', a Forest Stewardship Council certified paper, manufactured with a 55 percent recycled fibre content. The inks used in printing the Yearbook are vegetable-based.

Internationally there is a rising expectation for improved environmental statistics and reporting. In late 2007 the Ministry for the Environment released the second national state of the environment report *Environment New Zealand 2007*.

Statistics New Zealand has been an active contributor over the past two years to the Joint UNECE/OECD/Eurostat working group on Statistics for Sustainable Development. The working group's *Report on Measuring Sustainable Development* will provide a base for statistical reporting in this area in coming years. This framework will be used to update Statistics New Zealand's *Monitoring Progress Towards a Sustainable New Zealand*, to be published again in mid-2009.

On behalf of Statistics New Zealand, I thank the nearly 300 businesses, government departments, non-government organisations, academic institutions and individuals for their time, effort and goodwill in providing and updating contributions to the *New Zealand Official Yearbook 2008*. Their high level of cooperation with the Yearbook, along with the contributions from respondents to all our surveys, ensures the continuing high quality of New Zealand's official statistics.

Geoff Bascand
Government Statistician

The New Zealand flag

The New Zealand flag is the symbol of the realm, government and people of New Zealand. The flag features, on a royal blue background, a Union Jack in the first quarter and four five-pointed red stars of the Southern Cross on the fly. The stars have white borders. The flag's royal blue background represents the blue sea and clear sky surrounding New Zealand, while the stars of the Southern Cross emphasise New Zealand's location in the South Pacific Ocean. The Union Jack gives recognition to New Zealand's historical foundations and the fact that the country was once a British colony and dominion. The flag, previously known as the New Zealand Ensign, was declared the National Flag of New Zealand under the Flags, Emblems and Names Protection Act 1981.

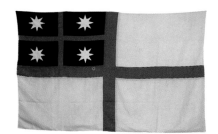

Te Hakituatahi o Aotearoa – 1835
The First Flag of New Zealand

The flag features, on a white field, a red St George's Cross. In the upper quarter next to the staff, on a blue field, a smaller St George's Cross is depicted in red, severed from the blue by a narrow border (fimbriation) of black half the width of the red, and, in the centre of each blue quarter, a white eight-pointed star. For a detailed history of Te Hakituatahi o Aotearoa, see chapter 3: Government.

The New Zealand coat of arms

One of the few specific changes to flow on from the granting of dominion status in 1907 was the right for New Zealand to have its own coat of arms. The design was approved by royal warrant on 26 August 1911. Before then, the United Kingdom coat of arms (featuring a lion and a unicorn on either side of a shield and crown) was used. This design still adorns the top of the pediment on the Old Government Buildings in Lambton Quay, Wellington.

The 1911 coat of arms was revised in 1956, following further constitutional changes when the country became the 'Realm of New Zealand' instead of the 'Dominion of New Zealand'. The British lion holding aloft the Union Jack was replaced by St Edward's Crown, which was worn by Queen Elizabeth II at her coronation. At the same time, the dress of the figures at the side of the shield was revamped, some Victorian-looking scroll work at the base of the design was replaced by two ferns, and the motto 'Onward' was replaced with 'New Zealand'.

The shield itself remained unchanged. The first quarter features four stars, representing the Southern Cross. The three ships in the centre of the shield symbolise the importance of New Zealand's sea trade. In the top right quarter, a fleece represents the farming industry. The wheat sheaf in the third quarter represents the agricultural industry, while the crossed hammers in the fourth quarter represent the mining industry. Supporters on either side of the shield are a Māori chieftain holding a taiaha (Māori war weapon) and a European woman holding the New Zealand flag. Above the arms is the St Edward's Crown. The crown symbolises the fact that the Queen is Queen of New Zealand under the New Zealand Royal Titles Act 1953.

The New Zealand Coat of Arms is protected under the Flags, Emblems and Names Protection Act 1981. Use of the coat of arms is restricted to the government and may not be used by private individuals or organisations.

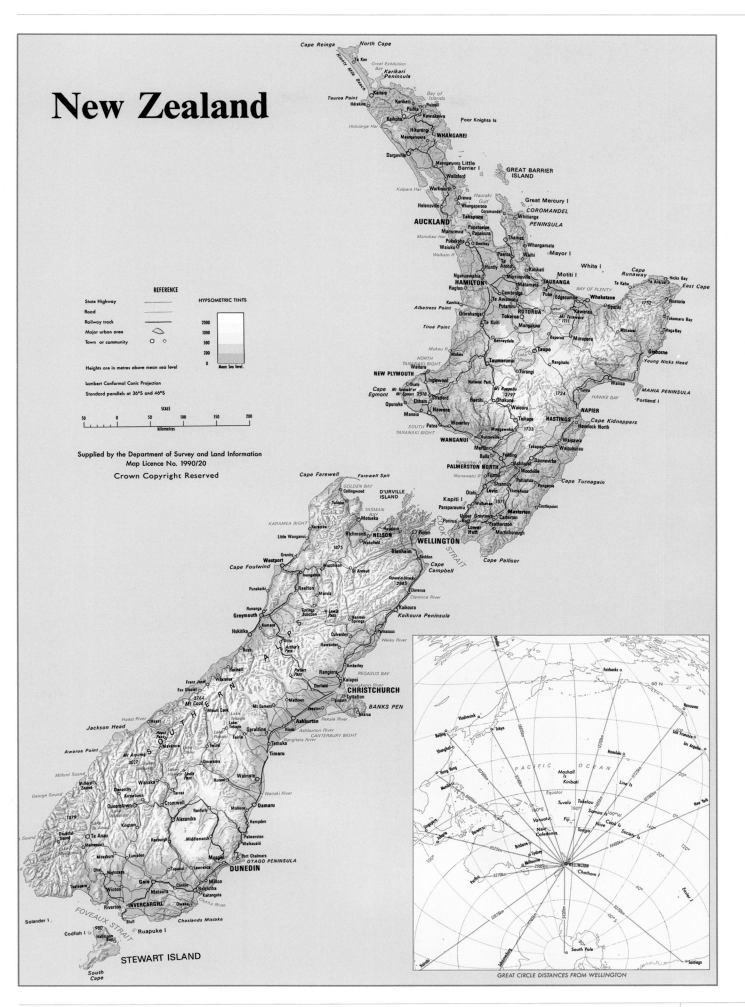

New Zealand

Contents

1 Geography
Physical features	1
Geology and soils	3
Climate	7
Wildlife and vegetation	12
Time zone	14

2 History
A brief history of New Zealand	15
Chronology of New Zealand events	22

3 Government
Constitution	29
Parliament	32
State sector	42
Local government	51

4 International relations and defence
Relations with other countries	57
Assistance to developing countries	65
Involvement in international organisations	67
New Zealand territories	69
Defence	71

5 Population
Population growth	83
Distribution of population	90
Components of population change	95
Composition of the population	103

6 Social framework
Social diversity	105
Citizenship	109
Immigration	110
Māori society	116
Pacific peoples	121
Asian population	124
Human rights	126

7 Social development
Ministry of Social Development	129
Work and Income	130
Child, Youth and Family	137

8 Health and safety
Organisation of health services	141
Health service benefits and subsidies	148
Public health	149
Hospitals	159
Causes of death	160
Accidents	162
Accident insurance	167
Emergency management	168
Occupational safety and health	170

9 Education
Curriculum	173
National Qualifications Framework	174
Administration of education	175
Government funding	178
Māori education	182
Early childhood education	182
Compulsory education	184
Tertiary education	186
International students	191
Sector statistics	192

10 Justice and law
Legal system	195
Criminal justice	201
Corrections system	208
New Zealand Police	215

11 Communications
Communications	219
Internet use	220
Broadcasting	222
Telecommunications	224
Television broadcasting	228
Radio broadcasting	230
Newspapers and magazines	233
Advertising	235
Postal services	236

12 Arts and cultural heritage
Taonga tuku iho	239
Heritage	241
Library services	243
Literature	246
Performing arts	247
Film and video	250
Censorship	251
Copyright	253
Administration	254

13 Leisure and tourism
Physical recreation and sport	259
Outdoor leisure activities	263
Racing and gaming	266
Tourism	268

14 Labour market	Labour relations	275	Unemployment	284
	Labour force	281	Employment assistance	287
	Employment	282	Income	288

| 15 Science and technology | Science and technology | 293 | Research agencies | 298 |
| | Investment in research, science and technology | 294 | Technology services | 302 |

| 16 Land and environment | Land and environment | 307 | Land resources and ownership | 321 |
| | Environmental and resource management | 313 | Public conservation land | 326 |

17 National economy	National economy	331	International accounts	348
	Prices	334	Business statistics	355
	National accounts	339		

18 Agriculture	Current situation and trends	357	Dairy produce	366
	Pastoral agriculture	359	Pigs, poultry, eggs and bees	368
	Meat	361	Horticulture	370
	Wool	364		

| 19 Forestry and fishing | Forestry | 375 | Fisheries | 381 |
| | Forest products and timber | 378 | Seafood industry | 385 |

20 Energy and minerals	Building a sustainable energy future	387	Gas	396
	Energy	390	Coal	397
	Electricity	391	Renewables	399
	Oil	394	Minerals	401

| 21 Manufacturing | Manufacturing | 405 | | |

| 22 Housing and construction | Housing | 413 | | |
| | Building and construction | 419 | | |

| 23 Transport | Shipping | 425 | Railways | 431 |
| | Civil aviation | 428 | Road transport | 433 |

| 24 Commerce and services | Commercial framework | 443 | Retail trade and services | 452 |
| | Controls on trading | 448 | Insurance and superannuation | 454 |

25 Overseas trade	Development and administration of trade	457	Imports	466
	Exports	459	Trading partners	470
			Overseas cargo	476

| 26 Money and banking | Financial institutions | 479 | | |
| | Money | 485 | | |

27 Public sector finance	Central government finance	489		
	Taxation	496		
	Assets and liabilities	504		

Glossary		507		
Abbreviations		513		
Weights and measures		514		
Index		515		

The Clutha River, in Central Otago, looking from Luggate towards Tarras.

GNS Science

New Zealand's mountain chains have been built by the folding and displacement of the earth's crust along faults. This photo looks back towards the Southern Alps from the West Coast, over Omoeroa Bluff and the Omoeroa River mouth.

1 | Geography

Physical features

New Zealand lies in the south-west Pacific Ocean and consists of two main and a number of smaller islands. Their combined area of 267,707 square kilometres is similar in size to Japan or the British Isles. Table 1.01 gives the size of the islands that make up New Zealand.

The main North and South Islands are separated by Cook Strait, which, at its narrowest point, is 20 kilometres wide.

The North and South Islands lie on an axis running from north-east to south-west, except for the low-lying Northland peninsula.

The administrative boundaries of New Zealand extend from 33 degrees to 53 degrees south latitude and from 160 degrees east to 173 degrees west longitude.

In addition to the main and nearby islands, New Zealand also includes the small outlying Chatham Islands (two of which are inhabited), 850 kilometres east of Christchurch; Raoul Island, in the Kermadec Group, 930 kilometres north-east of the Bay of Islands; and Campbell Island, 590 kilometres south of Stewart Island.

New Zealand also has jurisdiction over the territories of Tokelau and the Ross Dependency.

Table 1.01

Land area of New Zealand[1]	
	Size (sq km)
North Island	114,154
South Island	150,416
Stewart Island/Rakiura	1,681
Chatham Islands	963
Raoul Island	34
Campbell Island/Motu Ihupuku	113
Offshore islands[2]	346

(1) Includes all internal waterways (lakes and rivers). (2) Includes all offshore islands 20 square kilometres or larger, except those listed separately.

Source: Land Information New Zealand

Geographical extremes of New Zealand

Highest point	Aoraki/Mt Cook (3,754m)
Lowest point	Bottom of Lake Hauroko (462m below sea level)
Largest lake	Taupō (606sq km)
Deepest lake	Hauroko (462m)
River with greatest flow	Clutha (650cu m/sec)
Longest glacier	Tasman (29km)
Deepest cave	Nettlebed, Mt Arthur (889m)
Town furthest from sea	Cromwell (120km approx)
Coastline length	18,252km
Width at its widest point	450km

Source: Land Information New Zealand

Young River landslide – a new lake?

Instruments in the southern part of the New Zealand seismograph network detected a large landslide falling in the north branch of Young River in Mount Aspiring National Park at 4:40am on 29 August 2007. The landslide blocked the river and a new lake began to fill. It was first seen in mid-September by helicopter pilot Harvey Hutton, when the lake was mostly full. The new dam survived its most dangerous period of initial overflow on 7 September 2007.

The new lake – as yet unnamed – has an area of 100 hectares and a maximum depth of about 60 metres, dammed behind a landslide of about 10 million cubic metres.

Most lakes dammed by landslides prove to be very temporary features, with few surviving longer than a few years. Only time will tell if the new lake becomes a permanent addition to New Zealand's lakes.

Source: GNS Science

New Zealand is more than 1,600 kilometres long, 450 kilometres across at its widest part, and has a long coastline (more than 18,000 kilometres) for its area. The coast is very indented in places, providing many natural harbours.

The country is also very mountainous, with about three-quarters of the land 200 metres or more above sea level.

In the North Island, the main ranges run generally north-east to south-west, parallel to the coast, from East Cape to Cook Strait, with further ranges and four volcanic peaks to the north-west.

The South Island is much more mountainous than the North Island, with the Southern Alps, a massive mountain chain, running nearly the length of the island. There are many outlying ranges to the Southern Alps in the north and the south-west of the South Island. New Zealand has at least 223 named peaks higher than 2,300 metres. Table 1.02 lists the highest mountains and peaks in both the North and South Islands.

There are 360 glaciers in the Southern Alps. The largest are, on the east, the Tasman (29 kilometres in length), Murchison (13 kilometres), Mueller (13 kilometres), Godley (13 kilometres) and Hooker (11 kilometres), and on the west, the Fox (15 kilometres) and the Franz Josef (13 kilometres).

New Zealand's rivers (see table 1.03) are mainly swift and difficult to navigate. They are important as sources of hydroelectric power, and artificial lakes have been created as part of major hydroelectric schemes.

New Zealand's artificial lakes created by the South Island's hydroelectric schemes are included in table 1.04, which lists the country's principal lakes.

Table 1.02

Principal mountains and peaks

Mountain or peak	Elevation (metres)	Mountain or peak	Elevation (metres)
North Island		Lendenfeld Peak	3,194
Ruapehu	2,797	Graham	3,184
Taranaki or Egmont[1]	2,518	Torres Peak	3,160
Ngāuruhoe	2,287	Sefton	3,151
Tongariro	1,967	Haast	3,114
		Elie De Beaumont	3,109
South Island		La Perouse	3,078
Aoraki/Cook[2]	3,754	Douglas Peak	3,077
Tasman	3,497	Haidinger	3,070
Dampier	3,440	Minarets	3,040
Silberhorn	3,300	Aspiring/Tititea	3,033
Malte Brun	3,199	Glacier Peak	3,002
Hicks (St Davids Dome)	3,198		

(1) Taranaki or Egmont was gazetted by the New Zealand Geographic Board in 1986 as the mountain's dual name. (2) GNS Science photogrametrically confirmed the height of Aoraki/Cook as 3,754 metres after a slip from the peak in 1991.

Source: Land Information New Zealand

Table 1.03

Principal rivers[1]

North Island rivers	Length (km)	South Island rivers	Length (km)
Flowing into the Pacific Ocean		**Flowing into Cook Strait**	
Rangitaiki	193	Wairau	169
Waihou	175		
Mōhaka	172	**Flowing into the Pacific Ocean**	
Ngāruroro	154	Clutha/Mata-Au	322
		Taieri	288
Flowing into the Tasman Sea		Clarence	209
Waikato	425	Waitaki	209
Whanganui	290	Waiau	169
Rangitīkei	241	Waimakariri	161
Manawatū	182		
Whangaehu	161	**Flowing into Foveaux Strait**	
Mōkau	158	Mataura	240
		Waiau	217
		Ōreti	203
		Flowing into the Tasman Sea	
		Buller	177

(1) More than 150 kilometres in length from the mouth to the farthest point in the river system, irrespective of name, including estimated courses through lakes.

Source: Land Information New Zealand

Table 1.04

Principal lakes[1]					
	Maximum depth (metres)	Area (sq km)		Maximum depth (metres)	Area (sq km)
North Island					
Taupō (Taupō Moana)	163	606	Manapōuri	444	139
Rotorua	45	81	Hāwea	384	152
Wairarapa	3	77	Tekapō	120	96
Waikaremoana	248	50	Benmore (artificial)	120	75
Tarawera	87	41	Hauroko	462	71
Rotoiti	94	34	Ōhau	129	59
Waikare	2	34	Poteriteri	..	44
			Brunner (Moana)	109	41
South Island			Coleridge	200	37
Te Ānau	417	344	Monowai	161	32
Wakatipu	380	295	Aviemore (artificial)	62	28
Wānaka	311	201	Dunstan (artificial)	70	27
Ellesmere (Te Waihora)	2	197	Rotoroa	152	24
Pukaki	99	172	McKerrow/Whakatipu Waitai	121	23

(1) Greater than 20 square kilometres in area.

Symbol: .. not available.

Sources: NIWA (depths) and Land Information New Zealand (areas)

New Zealand caves

Name	Area	Depth (metres)	Year first measured
Deepest			
1 Nettlebed Cave	Mt Arthur	889	1986
2 Ellis Basin system	Mt Arthur	775	1991
3 Bulmer Cavern	Mt Owen	749	1988
4 HH Cave	Mt Arthur	721	1984
5 Bohemia Cave	Mt Owen	713	1994
6 Incognito/Falcon	Mt Arthur	540	1991
7 Viceroy Shaft	Mt Owen	440	1999
8 Deep Thought	Mt Owen	422	2007
9 Twin Traverse	Mt Arthur	400	2001
10 Greenlink-Middle Earth	Tākaka Hill	394	1983
11 Windrift	Mt Arthur	362	1985
12 Legless	Tākaka Hill	362	2000
13 Harwood Hole	Tākaka Hill	357	1959
14 Gorgoroth	Mt Arthur	346	1972
15 Rotapot	Mt Owen	341	2001

	Area	Surveyed length (metres)
Longest		
1 Bulmer Cavern	Mt Owen	50,125
2 Ellis Basin system	Mt Arthur	28,730
3 Nettlebed Cave	Mt Arthur	24,252
4 Megamania	Buller	14,800
5 Honeycomb Hill Cave	Oparara	13,712
6 Gardner's Gut	Waitomo	12,197
7 Bohemia Cave	Mt Owen	9,300
8 Mangawhitikau system	Waitomo	8,054
9 The Metro/Te Ananui	Charleston	8,000
10 Aurora-Te Ana-au	Te Ānau	6,400
11 Mangaone Cave	Gisborne	6,300
12 Greenlink System	Takaka Hill	6,228
13 Moonsilver Cave	Upper Tākaka	5,900
14 Waitomo headwaters system	Waitomo	5,618
15 Millars Waterfall	Waitomo	5,150

Source: New Zealand Speleological Society

Geology and soils

New Zealand is in an area of the world characterised by active volcanoes and frequent earthquakes. The 'ring of fire', as this area is known, forms a belt that surrounds the Pacific Ocean and is the surface expression of a series of boundaries between the plates that make up the earth's crust.

The boundary between the Indo-Australian and the Pacific plates runs through New Zealand, and processes from their collisions have had a profound effect on New Zealand's size, shape and geology.

Landscape

Mountain building in New Zealand between about six million years ago and the present is primarily responsible for the landscape of today.

Mountain chains have been built by the folding and displacement of the earth's crust along faults, or by the flexing of crustal plates, due to sediment loading and unloading. As a result of this activity, well-preserved tilted blocks bounded by fault scarps (steep faces hundreds or even thousands of metres high) are visible in the landscape of some regions.

Ongoing movement of the Pacific and Indo-Australian plates is responsible for continued earth strain in New Zealand, and this results in periodic rupture of faults, with several of these causing major earthquakes in the last hundred years.

GNS Science

Coastal erosion is visible at Cape Turnagain in the Wairarapa. Erosion, enhanced by climate, has transformed the landscape, carving detailed patterns of peaks, ridges, valleys and gorges.

Earthquake fatalities since 1843[1]

Date	Location	Magnitude[2]	Deaths
1843 (July 8)	Wanganui	7.5	2
1848 (Oct 17)	NE Marlborough (aftershock)	6.0[3]	3
1855 (Jan 23)	SW Wairarapa	8.2	8
1882 (date unknown)	Kapiti Coast	5–6	3
1901 (Nov 16)	Cheviot	6.8	1
1913 (Apr 12)	Masterton	5.6	1
1914 (Oct 7)	East Cape	6.6	1
1929 (June 17)	Murchison	7.7	15
1931 (Feb 3)	Hawke's Bay	7.8	261
1968 (May 24)	Inangahua	7.2	2
Total deaths			**297**

(1) Information on deaths due to earthquakes before 1843 is not available. (2) Richter scale. (3) Estimate.

Source: GNS Science

Erosion, enhanced by climate, has transformed the landscape, carving detailed patterns of peaks, ridges, valleys and gorges. Deposits of debris have built up to create alluvial plains, shingle fans and other constructed forms.

At the coast, waves have eaten back headlands and built beaches, spits and bars. Glaciers have carved the sea-filled valleys of Fiordland and have occupied most valleys of the South Island, many of which now have lakes held in by terminal moraines. Sea level changes accompanied the formation, and later the melting, of global glacial ice. These changes affected the erosion and the formation of rivers, and were responsible for the creation of many prominent river terraces.

Volcanic activity during the past few million years has played an important part in shaping the landscape of the central North Island. The largest volcanic outpourings of late geological times were in the region between Tongariro National Park and the Bay of Plenty coast.

The most recognisable volcanoes in New Zealand, all of which are 'active', include Ruapehu, Tongariro, Ngāuruhoe, White Island, and Taranaki or Egmont.

Other major volcanoes are less obvious, but have even more dramatic impacts on the landscape. These are the caldera-forming volcanoes that are now occupied by large central North Island lakes. Lakes Taupō, Rotorua and Tarawera can be thought of as upside-down volcanoes.

Small volcanic cones, such as One Tree Hill, Mt Eden and Rangitoto, are an important part of the Auckland landscape. These are dormant, but the volcanic field is still regarded as posing a significant hazard.

Earthquakes

Living in New Zealand means living with earthquakes. There is an almost continuous belt of earthquake activity around the edge of the Pacific Ocean that affects the geological stability of many countries on the Pacific Rim, particularly New Zealand, the west coast of the United States, Chile, Peru, Japan and the Philippines.

New Zealand's level of earthquake activity is similar to that of California, but slightly lower than that of Japan. A shallow magnitude 8 earthquake occurs in New Zealand about once a century, a shallow magnitude 7 earthquake about once a decade, and a shallow magnitude 6 earthquake about once a year.

New Zealand has many earthquakes because it straddles the boundary between two of the earth's great tectonic plates – the Pacific plate in the east and the Indo-Australian plate in the west. These two plates are converging obliquely at different rates – about 30 millimetres a year in Fiordland, increasing to about 50 millimetres a year at East Cape in the North Island.

The plates converge in different ways. In the North Island and the northern South Island, the Pacific plate sinks below the Indo-Australian plate. Earthquakes originating within the subducting Pacific plate are less than 60 kilometres deep along the eastern coast and become deeper westward. In Fiordland and the region to the south, the Indo-Australian plate subducts beneath the Pacific plate, so earthquake sources are shallow in the west and become deeper eastward.

Between these two subduction zones, the crust of both plates is too buoyant to subduct, so convergence is accommodated by uplift, which has created the Southern Alps, and horizontal movement along the Alpine Fault. This has resulted in parts of Nelson and western Otago, adjacent five million years ago, now being 450 kilometres apart.

Earthquakes in New Zealand, 2006–07

This map shows earthquakes felt in New Zealand during 2006 and 2007. Moderate earthquakes are capable of causing damage to household contents and fittings, whilst significant earthquakes can damage structures.

Of note is the magnitude 6.8 earthquake offshore from Gisborne in December 2007, which badly damaged some buildings within the central business district of the city. The other significant earthquakes occurred off the Fiordland coast in mid-October 2007, fortunately well away from populated centres, with only minor damage and inconvenience. Also of interest, Aucklanders were shaken on 21 February 2007 by a magnitude 4.5 earthquake centred in the Hauraki Gulf. Following an earlier 'swarm' of earthquakes during 2005, the region near Matatā in the Bay of Plenty experienced another swarm, beginning in late 2006 and continuing through 2007. The largest earthquake in this swarm was of magnitude 4.7 on 30 September 2007.

Green – minor   Yellow – moderate   Red – significant

Source: GNS Science

Shallow earthquakes are the most numerous and originate within the earth's crust, which has an average thickness of 35 kilometres in New Zealand. Crustal earthquakes are responsible for almost all damage to property and occur widely throughout New Zealand.

In the Taupō volcanic zone, from White Island to Ruapehu, swarms of small earthquakes of similar magnitude are common, and are associated with the area's active volcanism. Although the number of such shocks can be alarming, they rarely cause major damage.

Earthquake risk The worst disaster in New Zealand that can reasonably be expected within a generation is a 7.5 magnitude earthquake on the segment of the Wellington fault within the city. It has a 12 percent probability of occurring within the next 30 years and would affect 200,000 residential properties, from Palmerston North to Nelson, as well as roads, bridges and dams, and services such as electricity, water and sewerage.

GNS Science runs national and regional earthquake and volcano monitoring networks. A major upgrade of monitoring equipment began in 2001 with the Earthquake Commission providing core funding over 10 years. The project, known as GeoNet, is being undertaken by GNS Science on a not-for-profit basis for the national good. GeoNet equipment at sites throughout New Zealand is linked to GNS Science data centres via satellite, cellular and radio networks, permitting more rapid and reliable determinations of the location and magnitude of all significant earthquakes and volcanic activity within the New Zealand region. GeoNet information is made available to civil defence and emergency management authorities and international earthquake centres, and also underpins current and emerging research on geological hazards.

New Zealand scientists undertake a large body of research aimed at improving the understanding of, and ways to mitigate, seismic and volcanic risk in New Zealand. Mitigation measures include improved engineering design of buildings and infrastructure, better prepared communities, and better regional planning.

The GeoNet website (www.geonet.org.nz) provides public access to information about hazards, including earthquake bulletins and volcano alerts. It also provides access to fundamental datasets, such as GPS Rinex files, earthquake hypocentres and instrument waveform data. This data is freely available to the research community.

The year of the lahar

On 18 March 2007, the long-awaited break-out from Ruapehu's summit crater lake finally occurred. Volcanic eruptions (in 1995 and 1996) had emptied the lake, and deposited a natural dam of ash and rocks across the former outlet area. Eleven years later, the refilling lake breached this fragile barrier.

Approximately 1.3 million cubic metres of warm acidic water poured from the lake in less than two hours. As it rushed down the steep gorge of the upper Whangaehu River, the natural outlet path, it dragged along several times its volume in older lahar deposits and landslide debris, becoming a debris flow within 7 kilometres. The flow reached Tangiwai — the site of a rail disaster caused by a similar break-out lahar in 1953 – after two hours. The peak discharge was estimated to be at least 25 percent larger than the previous event.

The successful triggering of the state-of-the-art eastern Ruapehu lahar warning system (ERLAWS) ensured there was no loss of human life and only minimal property damage.

Policy work initially led by the Department of Conservation provided advice to the ministers of Conservation and Civil Defence, who then made decisions based on maximising public safety in the long term, not just for one predicted lahar. As a result of these decisions, the alarm system and a stopbank were installed in 2001/02, and the State Highway 49 bridge over the Whangaehu lahar path was raised and strengthened in 2004/05.

The result is a warning and response system and a national infrastructure that is now prepared for lahars no matter how or when they are triggered. The unpredictable lahars generated by a small eruption on 25 September 2007 (see story on Ruapehu eruption) showed how important long-term preparedness is.

In addition to the emergency management response, a comprehensive science plan, led and coordinated by GNS Science, Massey University, and several other national and international research groups in the lead-up to the lahar, enabled a dataset of unprecedented quality and volume to be collected. Fixed equipment included a time-lapse still camera overlooking the lake, which captured the sequence of dam failure, and vibration. Water level and water quality sensors were installed at other key points downstream. Mobile observer teams collected additional time series measurements of the lahar's properties as it travelled towards the coast.

Detailed analysis of instrumental records and deposit characteristics is ongoing, but early results are already reshaping ideas of lahar behaviour at New Zealand's most active onshore volcano.

The eastern Ruapehu lahar warning system (ERLAWS) ensured there was no loss of life and only minimal damage when the long awaited break-out from Ruapehu's crater lake finally occurred on 18 March 2007.

Source: Department of Conservation

Volcanic hazards

The New Zealand region is characterised by both a high density of active volcanoes and a high frequency of eruptions. Volcanic activity in the New Zealand region occurs within the North Island and offshore to the north-east in the Kermadec Islands. In the past 150 years, more people have been killed by volcanoes than by earthquakes, yet the scale and style of historically-recorded volcanic activity is dwarfed by events known to have occurred in the past 2,000 to 5,000 years.

Volcanism in New Zealand is confined to five areas in the North Island – the Bay of Islands, Whangarei, Auckland, a zone extending from White Island to Ruapehu, and Taranaki or Egmont. The area from White Island to Ruapehu is known as the Taupō Volcanic Zone and is by far the most frequently active. There are three major types of volcano in New Zealand:

- *Volcanic fields,* such as Auckland, where each eruption builds a single small volcano (eg Mt Eden), that does not erupt again. The next eruption in the field occurs at a different place, the site of which cannot be predicted until the eruption is imminent.
- *Cone volcanoes,* such as Taranaki or Egmont and Ruapehu, where a succession of small eruptions occurs from roughly the same point on the earth's surface. The products of successive eruptions accumulate close to the vent to form a large cone, which is the volcano itself. The site of future eruptions can generally be predicted.
- *Caldera volcanoes,* such as Taupō and Rotorua. Eruptions at these volcanoes are occasionally so large that the ground surface collapses into the 'hole' left behind. For example, Lake Taupō infills a caldera formed in two episodes about 1,800 and 26,000 years ago.

The Taupō Volcanic Zone contains four frequently active cone volcanoes (Ruapehu, Tongariro, Ngāuruhoe and White Island) and two of the most productive caldera volcanoes (Taupō and Ōkataina) in the world.

Casualties Deaths due directly or indirectly to volcanic activity (and associated hydrothermal explosions) represent the biggest single source of fatalities from natural disasters in New Zealand since 1846.

Table 1.05 lists deaths in volcanic areas of New Zealand since 1846. Economic loss due to volcanism, however, has been low compared with that from earthquakes or flooding. The cost of the 1995 and 1996 eruptions of Ruapehu has been estimated at $130 million.

An assessment of the size and style of volcanic eruptions in the geologically recent past, coupled with consideration of the economic development of New Zealand, especially in the central North Island, shows that the record since 1846 represents only a fraction of the type and size of hazard posed by New Zealand volcanic activity.

Table 1.05

Deaths in volcanic areas since 1846[1]

Year	Location (eruption)	Cause/hazard	Fatalities
1846	Waihi (Lake Taupō)	Debris avalanche/mudflow from thermal area	60[2]
1886	Tarawera Rift	Large volcanic eruption	›108
1903	Waimangu (Tarawera)	Hydrothermal explosion	4
1910	Waihi (Lake Taupō)	Debris avalanche/mudflow from thermal area	1
1914	White Island	Debris avalanche from crater wall	11
1917	Waimangu (Tarawera)	Hydrothermal explosion	2
1953	Tangiwai (Ruapehu)	Lahar and flood from crater lake	151
2006	Raoul Island	Phreatic explosion[3]	1
	Total		**›338**

(1) Information about death in volcanic areas before 1846 is not available. (2) Estimate. (3) Explosion caused by the heating and expansion of underground water.

Source: GNS Science

Surveillance All the active volcanoes in New Zealand are monitored as part of the GeoNet project funded by the Earthquake Commission. This provides a near real-time understanding of volcanoes.

Volcanologists use three primary techniques to establish the status of an active volcano:

- *Monitoring of volcanic earthquakes* This is done using closely-spaced networks of seismometers, designed to detect movement of magma (molten rock) below the surface and allow assessment of the possible onset and timing of eruptive activity. There are five volcano-seismic networks in New Zealand (Auckland, Bay of Plenty-Rotorua, Taranaki, Tongariro and Taupō). The Auckland and Taranaki networks are operated by regional councils.
- *Monitoring of ground deformation* This is done using precise geodetic surveys. The concept is that if magma is moving upwards before an eruption it will cause the volcano to swell (ie the ground surface to rise) and this swelling can be detected. Most of this work is done using continuous GPS installations on the volcanoes. The lakes at Taupō and Tarawera are also used as giant spirit levels to detect height changes.
- *Monitoring of volcanic gases* Magma at depth in the earth contains gases (carbon dioxide, together with various compounds of sulphur, chlorine and fluorine) dissolved in it. As the magma rises to shallow levels before an eruption, these gases are released and come to the surface via fumaroles. The temperatures and the abundance of the gases and their relative proportions give information on the state of the magma and how close to the surface it is.

In a volcanic crisis, practical steps can be taken to mitigate risk and lessen the threat to life, but this requires accurate recognition of the onset of a crisis.

This recognition in turn depends on a knowledge of the background or 'normal' levels of seismicity, ground movement and gas flux at the volcano, coupled with real-time determination of any significant changes from normal levels of activity.

The GeoNet active volcano surveillance programme helps define these background levels.

Climate

Summaries of New Zealand's climate extremes compiled by the National Institute of Water and Atmospheric Research Ltd (NIWA) contain detailed descriptions of the most extreme weather events recorded in the country.

The maps in Figure 1.01 (page 9) show mean annual figures struck over a 30-year period, to create what are referred to as 'climate norms'. The next 'normal' period for calculating mean annual figures will be 1981 to 2010.

The climate of New Zealand is largely influenced by:

- its location in a latitude zone where the prevailing wind flow is westerly
- its surrounding ocean environment
- its mountains, especially the main mountain chain, which modify weather systems as they pass eastwards, and which also provide a sheltering effect on the leeward side.

Day-to-day weather is mostly determined by a series of anticyclones and troughs of low pressure in the westerlies. Consequently, New Zealand's weather is changeable, typically with short periods of settled or unsettled weather. At times, the westerly regime breaks down and there are cold, southerly outbreaks, with snow in winter and sometimes spring; or northerly intrusions of warm,

Unlocking secrets of deep sea volcanoes

The vast majority of New Zealand volcanoes lie offshore, extending in a line north-eastwards from White Island, off the Bay of Plenty coast. These volcanoes form part of the Kermadec arc, which extends about 1,300 kilometres towards Tonga.

Some of these volcanoes are larger than Mt Ruapehu. There are at least 30 major ones, with many more smaller volcanic edifices along the arc. In the southern end of the arc the volcanoes are predominantly cones, like Ngāuruhoe. Further north, they commonly form caldera volcanoes, like White Island, although much larger. (The Macauley and Monowai calderas both span at least 10 kilometres, about the size of Wellington harbour.) The volcanoes range in height from around 120 metres beneath the sea surface at the top of Rumble III, to 1,850 metres to the bottom of the caldera at Brothers volcano.

Investigation of these volcanoes began in the late 1980s. Over the last five years, research expeditions have surveyed all of the major volcanoes, using multi-beam mapping.

Between 1999 and 2004, three New Zealand/American expeditions focused on spatially delineating and chemically characterising hydrothermal 'plumes', the metal-rich smoke that discharges from vents on the sea-floor. These surveys showed that about 70 percent of the volcanoes are host to hot springs, with most of the vents located at, or near, the volcano summits.

In late 2004, the Japanese submersible Shinkai 6500 made the first of four dives on Brothers volcano. Scientists found chimneys up to eight metres tall, many of which were discharging hydrothermal fluids of up to 300 degrees Celsius. The scientists also found a wealth of animal life associated with the venting, including long-necked barnacles, shrimps, limpets, crabs and tube worms.

In early 2005, a more extensive expedition using the American submersible Pisces V discovered a diverse

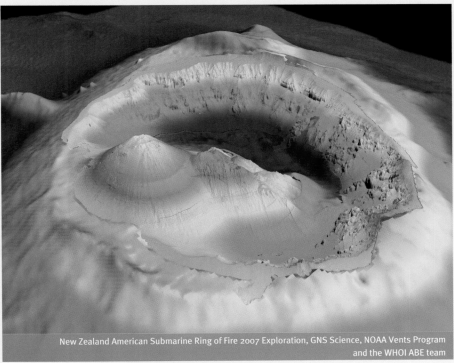

New Zealand American Submarine Ring of Fire 2007 Exploration, GNS Science, NOAA Vents Program and the WHOI ABE team

The deep-sea robot ABE created this map of the active underwater Brothers volcano, in the Kermadec arc, north-east of New Zealand.

range of geological and geochemical environments, and new species of animals.

More recently, the July–August 2007 NZ/German/US ROVARK cruise employed an autonomous underwater vehicle, known as ABE, to map Brothers volcano at a resolution of around one metre (compared with a resolution of 25 metres in earlier expeditions).

This is the first time anywhere in the world that a submarine arc volcano like Brothers has been mapped and surveyed for hydrothermal venting at such a detailed scale.

These vent sites will provide scientists with insights into the poorly understood world of sea floor hot springs associated with submarine volcanoes.

Source: GNS Science

Ruapehu eruption

Mt Ruapehu erupted on Tuesday, 25 September 2007 at 8.26pm. It produced two lahars, a moderate eruption column about 5 kilometres in height, and ash and rock falls across the summit of the volcano.

A record of the air blast from the eruption showed that the initial explosion lasted for no more than one minute and occurred at the start of the eruption sequence. The explosion was preceded by about 10 minutes of minor earthquake activity. This initial activity was too small, and of too short a duration, to provide a useful warning of the impending eruption.

A ballistic (rockfall) apron extended north from the crater lake. Typically ash travels further than the heavier ballistics, however in this case the ballistic rocks were ejected with sufficient force to out-travel the lighter ash material. Many of the ballistic rocks formed impact craters, while others later melted their way into the snow and ice. The ballistics consisted of various rock types – material from old andesitic flows (from the 1945, 1995 and 1996 eruptions), a variety of tephra, and vent-fill debris. Unfortunately, a climber in a shelter on the summit at the time of the eruption was seriously injured by ballistic rocks.

Scientists from GNS Science and Massey University analysed the lahar deposits. The Whakapapa ski field lahar travelled approximately 1 kilometre down the ski field to the north-west, reaching an altitude of 2,100 metres. The deposit was about 30 metres wide and consisted of grey ashy snow, with fragments of rime ice and scattered rocks. Initial estimates suggest the lahar travelled at 20–30 kilometres per hour. A snow slurry lahar also travelled down the Whangaehu River to the east, as far as the Wahianoa Aqueduct 24 kilometres downstream, and leaving a deposit approximately 80 metres wide and 1–3 metres thick near the Round-the-Mountain track bridge, 7 kilometres from the crater lake. This was quite a different lahar from the dam break lahar in March 2007 – it was much smaller and had a higher proportion of snow and ice, rather than mud and rock.

The eruption was similar to the 1969, 1975 and 1988 eruptions. All evidence indicated the eruption was hydrothermal in nature. Before the eruption the lake temperature was 13 degrees Celsius. Six weeks after the eruption, the temperature had risen to 32 degrees, most likely as a result of new hotter water from the vent area being injected into the lake.

Sources: GNS Science and Department of Conservation

Dean Treml

As part of a Global Day of Action on climate change, the 'Be The Change' campaign hosted a Climate Rescue Carnival, which involved over 350 of those who visited the carnival spelling out "Climate SOS" at Western Park in Auckland on 8 December 2007.

moist air when tropical depressions move southwards into New Zealand latitudes in the summer. The main mountain chain, the Southern Alps, is a major barrier to weather systems approaching from the west. Consequently, there is a marked contrast between the climates of regions west and east of the mountains. This contrast is much greater than north–south climatic differences. Surrounding oceans have a moderating effect on temperatures in most northern and western regions. However, inland and eastern areas can experience large temperature variations.

High temperatures usually occur in the east in warm, north-westerly wind conditions. These high temperatures are often followed by sudden falls in temperature, as cold fronts move up the east coast of both islands. Many parts of New Zealand are subject to extremes of wind, occasionally causing damage to buildings and forests, and rain, as depressions with their fronts pass close to, or over, the country. The rugged terrain is an important factor in enhancement of wind strength and/or rainfall.

Climate change

The *Fourth Assessment Report* of the Intergovernmental Panel on Climate Change (IPCC) in 2007 concluded that "warming of the climate system is unequivocal". Evidence includes increases in global average air and ocean temperatures, widespread melting of snow and ice, and a rising global mean sea level. The 2007 report said it is "very likely" (more than 90 percent likely) that most of the global warming since the mid-20th century is due to rising greenhouse gas concentrations from human activities. This is a stronger conclusion than in 2001 when the IPCC used the word "likely" (more than 66 percent likely).

The *Fourth Assessment Report* predicted increases in global mean temperatures in the period 1990–2100 of between 1.1 and 6.4 degrees Celsius, and global mean sea level increases of between 18 and 59 centimetres. It said that even if greenhouse gas emissions cease entirely, the global average temperature will rise by another 0.6 degrees Celsius. Projected sea level changes do not include the effects of rapid dynamic changes in ice sheet flow from Greenland and Antarctica.

The report said changes could also be expected in some extreme weather and climate events, including "very likely" increases in the frequency of hot extremes, heatwaves, and heavy rainfall. What the warming climate will mean in detail for New Zealand and the South Pacific is still the subject of investigation by scientific researchers.

The report found that the most vulnerable sectors for New Zealand are natural ecosystems, water security, and coastal communities. The main impacts are:

- *Projected climate changes* Temperatures in New Zealand are likely to increase faster in the North Island than in the South Island, but generally less than global average temperatures. Annual rainfall is projected to increase in the west of the country and to decrease in many eastern regions.

  In the long term, rising seas are expected to increase erosion of vulnerable beaches and breach coastal protection structures more often. By 2050, there is very likely to be increasing loss of high-value land, faster road deterioration, degrading of beaches, and loss of landmarks of cultural significance.

- *Primary production* Up to about 2050, enhanced growing conditions from higher carbon dioxide concentrations, longer growing seasons and less frost risk are likely to benefit agriculture, horticulture, and forestry over much of New Zealand, provided adequate water is

Figure 1.01

Climate norms

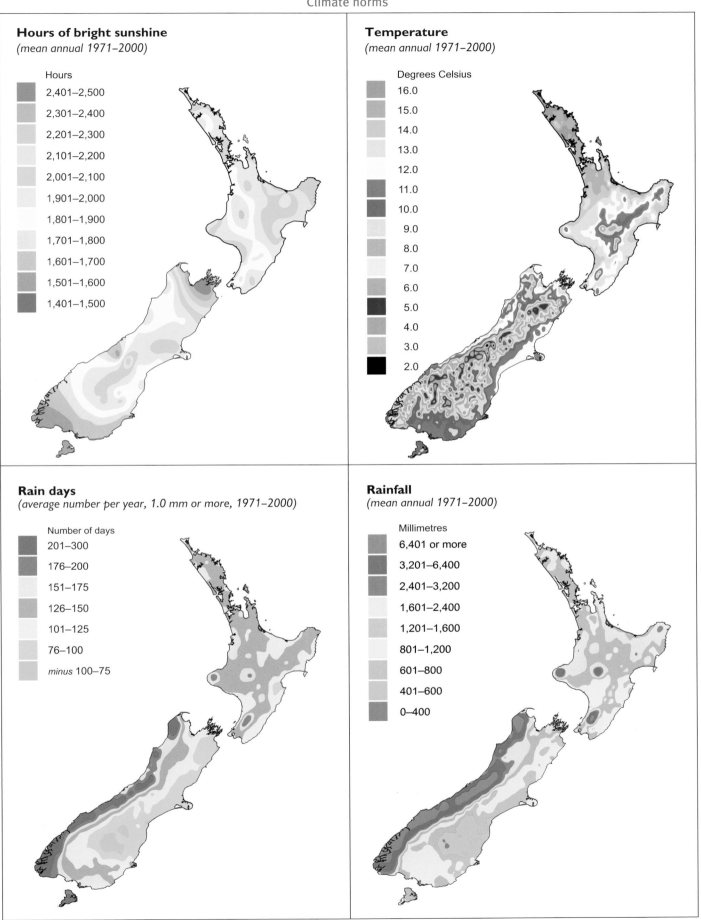

Hours of bright sunshine
(mean annual 1971–2000)

Hours
- 2,401–2,500
- 2,301–2,400
- 2,201–2,300
- 2,101–2,200
- 2,001–2,100
- 1,901–2,000
- 1,801–1,900
- 1,701–1,800
- 1,601–1,700
- 1,501–1,600
- 1,401–1,500

Temperature
(mean annual 1971–2000)

Degrees Celsius
- 16.0
- 15.0
- 14.0
- 13.0
- 12.0
- 11.0
- 10.0
- 9.0
- 8.0
- 7.0
- 6.0
- 5.0
- 4.0
- 3.0
- 2.0

Rain days
(average number per year, 1.0 mm or more, 1971–2000)

Number of days
- 201–300
- 176–200
- 151–175
- 126–150
- 101–125
- 76–100
- *minus* 100–75

Rainfall
(mean annual 1971–2000)

Millimetres
- 6,401 or more
- 3,201–6,400
- 2,401–3,200
- 1,601–2,400
- 1,201–1,600
- 801–1,200
- 601–800
- 401–600
- 0–400

Source: NIWA

available. But by 2050, agriculture and forestry production is likely to be reduced over parts of eastern New Zealand due to increased drought and fire. The range and incidence of many pests and diseases are likely to increase, and areas suitable for particular crops are projected to change.

- *Native ecosystems* The structure, function, and species composition of many natural ecosystems are very likely to change. The impacts of climate change are likely to be significant by 2020, and are virtually certain to exacerbate existing stresses such as invasive species and habitat loss. The projected rate of climate change is very likely to exceed the rate of evolutionary adaptation in many species. The IPCC identified alpine zones in the Southern Alps as a 'hotspot' where vulnerability to climate change (eg loss of plant and animal species, glacier shrinkage, reduced snow cover) is likely to be high by 2050.

- *Urban environment, transport and energy* The main threat to the urban environment comes from possible increases in heavy rainfall, which would put pressure on drainage and stormwater systems and increase the risk of flooding in some areas. Warmer conditions would substantially reduce home heating costs, leading to reduced electricity demand during the peak winter season, but possibly increased demand for air conditioning during summer. Wetter conditions on the West Coast could eventually increase hydroelectricity production in winter.

- *Health* Higher temperatures are expected to reduce winter illnesses and lead to higher death rates during summer. Warmer temperatures and increased rainfall variability are likely to increase the intensity and frequency of summertime food-borne and water-borne diseases.

The year's weather in 2007

New Zealand's weather for 2007 was marked by too much rain in many places, and record low rainfalls in some locations.

Rainfall during the year was less than 60 percent of average rainfall in parts of Marlborough, Canterbury and Central Ōtago, with some places experiencing their driest year on record. Parts of the south and east, Bay of Plenty and Wellington had one of their sunniest years on record too.

Table 1.06

Projected changes in annual mean temperature and precipitation[1]
Between 1980–1999 and 2080–2099

Region	Temperature (°C)	Precipitation (%)
Northland, Auckland	+0.6 – +5.9	-28 – +9
Western North Island from Waikato to Wellington	+0.6 – +5.6	-11 – +15
Eastern North Island from Bay of Plenty to Wairarapa	+0.6 – +5.5	-22 – +11
Nelson, Marlborough, Canterbury plains	+0.6 – +5.1	-14 – +16
Canterbury foothills, West Coast, Otago, Southland	+0.7 – +5.0	-12 – +34

(1) Projected changes encompass the range of results from 12 global climate models for six greenhouse gas emission scenarios.

Source: NIWA

There were numerous heavy rainfall events during 2007, nine of which produced floods. Here, a tractor is rescuing equipment from storm water at Maraekākaho, near Hastings in July 2007.

Table 1.07

Summary of New Zealand climate extremes
At 31 December 2007

Rainfall

Period	Amount (mm)	Location	Date
Highest			
10 minutes	34	Tauranga	17 April 1948
1 hour	109	Leigh	30 May 2001
12 hours	473	Colliers Creek (Hokitika catchment)	22 January 1994
24 hours	682	Colliers Creek (Hokitika catchment)	21–22 January 1994
48 hours	1,049	Waterfall, Cropp River (Hokitika catchment)	12–13 December 1995
1 calendar month	2,927	Waterfall, Cropp River (Hokitika catchment)	December 1995
1 calendar year	16,617	Waterfall, Cropp River (Hokitika catchment)	January–December 1998
365 days	18,442	Waterfall, Cropp River (Hokitika catchment)	29 October 1997–1998
Lowest			
3 months	9	Cape Campbell	January–March 2001
6 months	52	Cape Campbell	Nov 2000–April 2001
12 months	167	Alexandra	Nov 1963–Oct 1964
Longest rainless period			
71 days	0	Wai-iti, Marlborough	From 8 Feb 1939

Temperature

	Temperature (°C)	Location	Date
Highest air temperature			
North Island	39.2	Ruatōria	7 February 1973
South Island	42.4	Rangiora	7 February 1973
Lowest air temperature			
North Island	-13.6	Chateau Tongariro	7 July 1937
South Island	-21.6	Ophir	3 July 1995
Lowest grass minimum	-21.6	Lake Tekapō	4 August 1938

Sunshine

	Hours	Location	Date
Highest in one year			
North Island	2,588	Napier	1994
South Island	2,711	Nelson	1931
Highest in one month			
North Island	335	Taupō	January 1950
South Island	336	Nelson	December 1934
Lowest in one year			
North Island	1,357	Palmerston North	1992
South Island	1,333	Invercargill	1983
Lowest in one month			
North Island	27	Taumarunui	June 2002
South Island	35	Invercargill	June 1935

Wind gusts

	Speed (km/h)	Location	Date
North Island	248	Hawkins Hill, Wellington	6 November 1959 and 4 July 1962
South Island	250	Mt John, Canterbury	18 April 1970

Source: NIWA

Taranaki tornadoes

One of the most significant extreme weather events of 2007 was the extraordinary swarm of damaging tornadoes that wreaked havoc throughout Taranaki over 4 and 5 July, as active frontal bands crossed the country from the Tasman Sea.

The first tornado hit the central business district in New Plymouth at about 1pm on 4 July. The tornado was reported as 10 metres high, 15 metres wide, and described as "a dark column, with a huge amount of noise, including thunder and lightning". Damage was severe, with a large section of roof lifted off the PlaceMakers store. More than 50 staff and customers were in the building at the time. Several other shops and houses were damaged, as were cars.

The following day, Taranaki was hit by at least seven damaging tornadoes. A state of emergency was declared in the New Plymouth District. There was a swath of damage along a 140 kilometre front, and temporary supplies and accommodation had to be found for affected residents. At least 7,000 homes throughout the region were without electricity after lightning strikes and damage to power lines. The worst-hit town was Ōākura, where about 50 houses were damaged, of which 80 percent were destroyed. In Ōpunake, eight people were trapped in a motor vehicle surrounded by damaged, but live, power lines. Many other areas were also affected. Total damage from the tornadoes in Taranaki was estimated at $7 million.

On average, Taranaki experiences one damaging tornado a year and a more destructive tornado once in four years – well above the national average, and on a par with Auckland and the Bay of Plenty. New Plymouth District is the part of Taranaki most at risk.

Source: NIWA

The national average temperature of 12.7 degrees Celsius during 2007 was close to normal. This was a result of some warm months being offset by some cooler months. For New Zealand as a whole, there were five warmer than normal months (March, May, July, August and December), and five cooler than normal months (January, April, June, October and November). All other months had mean temperatures close to the climatological average. May had a mean temperature of 12.4 degrees Celsius (1.7 degrees above normal) and was the warmest nationally since reliable records began in the 1860s.

In 2007 there was a swing from an El Niño to a La Niña climate pattern. The start of the year was dominated by a weakening El Niño in the equatorial Pacific. From September onwards La Niña conditions had developed in the tropical Pacific, with a noticeable increase in the frequency and strength of westerlies over New Zealand in October, and then a significant drop in windiness from November. Moderate to strong La Niña conditions had developed by the end of the year. Overall more anticyclones (highs) occurred over New Zealand.

Notable weather features in various parts of the country were: disastrous floods in Northland; drought conditions in the east of the North Island (with the exception of one storm that caused major flooding in Hawke's Bay on 17–18 July); an unprecedented swarm of tornadoes in Taranaki; destructive windstorms in Northland and in eastern New Zealand in October; and hot spells.

There were numerous heavy rainfall events during 2007, nine of which produced floods. Notable snowfall events occurred on relatively few occasions. There were 14 damaging tornado events for New Zealand during the year. Other features were early autumn and late spring hot spells, two severe hailstorms, and seven damaging electrical storms.

Wildlife and vegetation

The islands of New Zealand separated from their nearest neighbours more than 80 million years ago. They stretch across 24 degrees of latitude from the subtropical to the subantarctic, making New Zealand a slender archipelago with an extraordinary natural heritage, born from its biological and geological isolation.

Some of the original inhabitants endured times of turbulent change and violent upheaval, evolving and adapting to become part of a unique natural biota (animal and plant life of a region). Other species died out (either nationally or regionally), unable to compete or survive environmental disturbances such as ice ages. For example, coconut palms were once found in New Zealand, and kauri, now mainly confined to the north of the North Island, used to grow as far south as Canterbury.

Over the years, the earliest inhabitants were joined by other plants and animals carried across the oceans by wind and current.

Fauna

The pre-human environment was notable for the absence of snakes, land mammals (apart from three species of bat) and many of the flowering plant families. Whole orders and families were found only in New Zealand, including tuatara, moa and kiwi, all of the native lizards, and nearly 200 species of native earthworms.

Many remarkable plants, insects and birds evolved to fill ecological niches normally occupied by mammals. Others diversified to fill new territories created by sea-level fluctuations and land uplift.

With no mammalian predators on the ground, but avian predators everywhere, flightlessness was not a handicap, nor was size. Moa (11 species, some up to three metres tall) became extinct in pre-European times, but many other large flightless birds still remain, including kiwi, the nocturnal kākāpō (the only flightless parrot in the world) and weka (of the rail family).

Flightless insects are numerous, including many large beetles and 70 or so species of the cricket-like weta, found only in New Zealand.

New Zealand, with 84 species, has the most diverse seabird fauna of any country. Nearly half of all native bird species depend on the ocean for food – the feeding zones of some extending as far south as the Antarctic continent. New Zealand's extensive coastline and many islands offer a huge range of habitat, from estuaries and mud-flats, to rocky cliffs and boulder banks.

The ocean is marvellously rich. There are well over 1,200 different species of fish in the waters around New Zealand, and as many as 15 more are discovered every year as a result of research in previously unsampled areas. There are also various species of seals, dolphins and porpoises. Twenty-nine species of whale have been recorded, and three of the largest (sperm, humpback and right) regularly migrate to New Zealand waters in spring and autumn.

Flora

The most widespread and complex type of forest in New Zealand is a podocarp (conifer) broadleaf association. It is generally found at lower altitudes and is characterised by a variety of species, a stratified canopy, and an abundance of vines and epiphytic plants.

Beech and kauri forests, by contrast, are much simpler in structure. New Zealand's beech species have close relatives in Australia and South America, and the five different types of species in New Zealand have exploited habitats from valley floor to mountain tops. Kauri, true forest giants, dominate only in the warmer climes to the north.

Some of the most specialised plants are those occupying the alpine zone. A remarkable 25 percent of all New Zealand's plants can be found above the treeline. Ninety-three percent of all alpine plants are found only in New Zealand, compared with 80 percent for the rest of the higher plant species. Snow tussock herbfields are one of the most distinctive elements in this cold, windswept environment. Remarkably long-lived, some larger specimens may be several centuries old. Like beech trees, they seed infrequently, but in profusion.

A definitive feature of New Zealand's land-based plants and animals is their degree of specialisation and narrow habitat requirements (eg takahē – tussock grasslands; blue duck – fast flowing rivers and streams), and their evolution in the absence of mammalian predators (for birds) or browsers (for plants).This specialisation, and adaptations which make New Zealand's wildlife so unique, render them extremely vulnerable to introduced predators, such as rats and cats; competitors, such as deer and possums; and loss of habitat.

Hector's dolphins

Department of Conservation

South Island Hector's dolphin spyhopping.

Hector's dolphins are among the world's smallest marine dolphins. They are found only in the inshore waters of New Zealand.

Two sub-species exist: the South Island Hector's dolphin, which is found around the South Island of New Zealand, and the Maui's dolphin, which is found off the west coast of the North Island.

Maui's dolphin, with an estimated 111 left in the wild, is not only New Zealand's rarest dolphin, but one of the rarest globally. The dolphin is listed internationally as 'critically endangered', which means there is a high risk of it becoming extinct in the near future. This small population of dolphins is thought to have been isolated from their more numerous relatives, the South Island Hector's dolphins, for thousands of years. Maui's dolphin used to be known as the North Island Hector's dolphin. But recent research showed the North and South Island dolphins are separate sub-species that are physically and genetically distinct.

Distribution of the South Island Hector's dolphins is patchy. Populations are concentrated between Haast and Farewell Spit in the west, around Banks Peninsula in the east, and Te Waewae Bay and Porpoise Bay/Te whanangā aihe in the south.

South Island Hector's dolphins are the only dolphins in New Zealand with a well-rounded black dorsal fin. Their bodies are a distinctive grey, with white and black markings and a short snout. The adult dolphins don't often exceed 1.5 metres in length and weigh between 40 and 60 kilograms. Males are slightly smaller and lighter than females.

Females reach sexual maturity between seven and nine years of age. They produce just one calf every two to three years, making population increase a very slow process. Most females only have four or five calves in a lifetime. Calving usually occurs between November and mid-February, and calves stay with their mothers for up to two years. South Island Hector's dolphins live to a maximum of about 20 years.

Like other dolphins, South Island Hector's dolphins use echolocation to find their food. They send out high frequency 'clicks' that bounce off surrounding objects and fish, giving the dolphins a detailed picture of their surroundings. This sonar is not used all the time, which may be one of the reasons why the dolphins get caught in nets.

Hector's and Maui's dolphins are known to Māori by other names, including tutumairekurai, aihe, papakanua, upokohue, tukuperu, tūpoupou and hopuhopu.

Source: Department of Conservation

Otago Daily Times

Toroa – Māori for albatross – was the 500th royal albatross chick to hatch at Taiaroa Head/Pukekura on the Otago Peninsula, the only mainland breeding colony of albatross in the southern hemisphere. He hatched on 26 January 2007 and is the first chick to be formally named by the Minister of Conservation.

Introduced vegetation and wildlife

The arrival of people in New Zealand heralded times of rapid change.

Introduction of exotic plants and animals (intentionally or accidentally) and modification of habitat radically affected native species' populations.

In the pre-1800 period, following the arrival and expansion of Māori, forest cover was reduced and 34 species became extinct, including moa, the adzebill and the flightless goose.

In the much shorter post-1800 period of European settlement, the forest area was further reduced to around 25 percent of the land, nine more bird species became extinct, and many more were threatened.

Since 1840, more than 80 new species of mammals, birds and fish, and more than 1,800 plant species have been introduced, in many places totally changing the landscape and ecology.

Daylight saving period extended

New Zealand Daylight Saving, which provides an extra hour of sunlight in the evenings, began a week earlier in 2007, after the government extended the period.

When first introduced in 1974, daylight saving started on the last Sunday in October and ended on the first Sunday in March. The period was extended by five weeks in 1990, to start on the first Sunday in October and finish on the third Sunday in March.

In 2007, the daylight saving period was further extended to start on the last Sunday in September, and finish on the first Sunday in April.

The change followed public debate generated by the end of daylight saving in March 2006. The earlier start also avoids clashing with the beginning of the fourth school term, which has caused disruptions for schools and families in the past. The government will monitor the impact of the extension on New Zealanders and on parts of the economy, such as the energy sector, to see if there are long-term sustainable benefits.

Source: Department of Internal Affairs

Time zone

One uniform time is kept throughout mainland New Zealand. This time is 12 hours ahead of Co-ordinated Universal Time and is called New Zealand Standard Time. It is an atomic standard maintained by the Measurement Standards Laboratory (MSL), part of Industrial Research Ltd, Lower Hutt.

In November 1868, New Zealand became one of the first countries in the world to adopt standard time – 11.5 hours ahead of Greenwich Mean Time. In 1941, as a wartime measure, clocks were advanced half an hour and this was made permanent in 1945 by the Standard Time Act, which set time at 12 hours ahead of GMT or Universal Time. A new time scale based on the readings of atomic clocks, known as Co-ordinated Universal Time (UTC), was adopted internationally in 1972.

New Zealand Standard Time (NZST) is currently defined in the Time Act 1974 as meaning 12 hours in advance of UTC, with the time for the Chatham Islands set 45 minutes in advance of NZST.

One hour of daylight saving, called New Zealand Daylight Time (NZDT), which is 13 hours ahead of UTC, is observed during the summer months. Chatham Islands time is always 45 minutes ahead of that kept in New Zealand.

Contributors and related websites

Department of Conservation – www.doc.govt.nz

Department of Internal Affairs – www.dia.govt.nz

GNS Science – www.gns.cri.nz

Industrial Research Ltd – www.irl.cri.nz

Land Information New Zealand – www.linz.govt.nz

Metservice – www.weather.co.nz

New Zealand Speleological Society – caves.org.nz

NIWA – www.niwa.cri.nz

Ref: B-139-014 Alexander Turnbull Library

Pai Mārire (Hauhau) supporters determine the fate of their prisoners through karakia (prayer). Formed in 1862, this first organised expression of Māori Christianity, founded on the principle of pai mārire (goodness and peace), grew from conflict over land in Taranaki. Painting by Herbert Meade, 1865.

2 | History

A brief history of New Zealand

Discovery and migration

New Zealand has a shorter human history than any other country. The precise date of settlement is a matter of debate, but current understanding is that the first arrivals came from East Polynesia in the 13th century. It was not until 1642 that Europeans became aware the country existed.

The original Polynesian settlers discovered the country on deliberate voyages of exploration, navigating by ocean currents, winds and stars. The navigator credited in some traditions with discovering New Zealand is Kupe. Some time later, the first small groups arrived from Polynesia. Now known as Māori, these tribes did not identify themselves by a collective name until the arrival of Europeans when, to mark their distinction, the name Māori, meaning 'ordinary', came into use.

The early settlers lived in small hunting bands. Seals and the large flightless moa bird were their main prey, until moa were hunted to extinction.

In the South Island, hunting and gathering remained the main mode of survival, but the kūmara (sweet potato) and yams the Polynesians brought with them grew well in the warmer North Island. Extensive kūmara gardens supported relatively large settlements. But even in the north, birds, fish and shellfish were important in the Māori diet. In some northern areas, larger populations put pressure on resources. The Polynesian dog and rat came with the early arrivals, but the domestic pigs and chickens of the islands did not, for reasons not fully understood.

In favourable conditions, Māori lived reasonably well. Their life expectancy was low by modern standards, but probably comparable with that of Europeans in the same era. The Māori population before European contact may have reached 100,000.

Māori passed on rich and detailed history and legends orally. Society was organised around groups that traced their descent from common ancestors. Reciting whakapapa (genealogies) was an important way to communicate knowledge. The concepts of mana (status) and utu (reciprocity) were central to the culture, and led to widespread warfare. But the violence was usually episodic. For most of the time, Māori lived not in fortified pā, but in unprotected settlements or seasonal camps.

The greatest achievements of Māori material culture were carving wood for important buildings and canoes, and fashioning stone into tools and ornaments. Warfare did not inhibit regular trade in desirable stones and foods, and was itself a means by which resources were appropriated.

STAETEN LANDT Bezylt en Ontdekt met de Scheepen Heemskerk en de Zeehaen onder het Commande van den E.ABEL TASMAN. in den Iaare 1642. Den 13 December.

Aldus vertoont zich het Drie Koningen Eyland, als gy het aen de Noort West Zyde op 40. Vademen van uw heeft.

Ref: PUBL-0105-004, Alexander Turnbull Library

An engraving by Frederik Ottens, from drawings made by Isaac Gilsemans on Tasman's voyage to New Zealand in December 1642. Abel Tasman's ships the Zeehaen *and the* Heemskerck *are close to Three Kings Islands, with two Māori men against the skyline.*

European discovery

In 1642, Dutch explorer Abel Tasman made the first confirmed European discovery of New Zealand. He charted the country's west coast from about Hokitika up to Cape Maria van Diemen. Subsequently, a Dutch map maker gave the name Nieuw Zeeland to the land Tasman had discovered. A surprisingly long time (127 years) passed before another European reached New Zealand.

James Cook visited New Zealand in 1769, on the first of three voyages. He circumnavigated and mapped both main islands and returned to Britain with reports about the country's inhabitants and resources.

For 50 years after Sydney was founded in 1788, New Zealand was an economic and cultural outpost of New South Wales, and most of the earliest European settlers came from Sydney. In the late 18th century, sealers and whalers began visiting, and by the early 19th century some began to settle, some to farm. During these years, New Zealand was part of a Pacific-wide trade system and New Zealand goods were sold in China.

The first European 'town' grew at Kororāreka when whalers began calling into the Bay of Islands for food and water. From the 1790s, Māori produced pork and potatoes for this trade. The other main area of early interaction between Māori and others was the Foveaux Strait sealing grounds. The presence of traders drew Māori to particular locations. Having a European living among them gave some tribal groups an advantage in the race to acquire European goods, especially firearms.

A Sydney chaplain, Samuel Marsden, founded the first Christian mission station in the Bay of Islands in 1814. By 1840, more than 20 stations had been established. From missionaries, Māori learnt not just about Christianity, but also about European farming techniques and trades, and how to read and write. The missionaries also transcribed the Māori language into written form. In the 1830s, French missionaries brought Catholicism to Māori.

Christianity would become important for Māori, but they were slow to convert. Muskets, traded for flax and potatoes, had a greater impact in the 1820s and 1830s than religion, and escalated killings in tribal conflicts. The Ngā Puhi tribe, led by Hongi Hika, devastated southerly tribes, and Ngāti Toa, under Te Rauparaha, attacked Ngai Tahu in the South Island. But diseases introduced by Europeans caused more fatalities than firearms did.

British sovereignty

In the 1830s, the British Government came under increasing pressure to curb lawlessness in New Zealand to protect British traders, and to forestall the French, who also had imperial ambitions. The missionaries, for their part, wanted to protect Māori from the effects of European settlement.

In 1833, James Busby was sent to the Bay of Islands as British Resident. At Busby's instigation, northern chiefs adopted a flag in 1834 and signed a declaration of independence in 1835. Seven years after Busby's arrival, at Waitangi on 6 February 1840, William Hobson, New Zealand's first governor, invited assembled Māori chiefs to sign a treaty with the British Crown. The treaty was taken all round the country, as far south as Foveaux Strait, for signing by local chiefs, and eventually more than 500 signed.

Under the treaty, Māori ceded powers of government to Britain in return for the rights of British subjects and guaranteed possession of their lands and other 'treasures'. In later years, differences of interpretation between the English and Māori texts complicated efforts to redress breaches of the treaty.

British sovereignty was proclaimed over New Zealand on the basis of Māori consent, though the South Island was initially claimed on the basis of discovery.

In the 19th century, the British and the French were rivals in the Pacific. The French had only minor interests in New Zealand, but the myth persists that the South Island escaped being French only because in the scramble to colonise Akaroa the British got there first. By the time the French settlers and their naval escort reached New Zealand, the whole country was securely British. Governor Hobson, learning the French were heading for Akaroa, did send Captain Stanley of the *Britomart* to demonstrate British sovereignty. However, there was never any chance Cook Strait would become, like the English Channel, a passage between English and French-speaking regions.

Even before the Treaty of Waitangi had been signed, the New Zealand Company, inspired by the colonial promoter Edward Gibbon Wakefield, had despatched British settlers to Wellington. In the next two years, the company also founded Wanganui, Nelson and New Plymouth. Otago was founded in 1848 and Canterbury in 1850, both by New Zealand Company affiliates. Auckland, capital of the new Crown colony, grew independently.

By the 1850s, most of the interior of the North Island had been explored by Europeans. Māori guides usually showed European explorers the way and New Zealand's first Anglican bishop, George Selwyn, travelled widely. Much of the mountainous interior of the South Island was not explored until gold miners arrived in the 1860s.

When British settlers sought self-government, the British Parliament passed the New Zealand Constitution Act of 1852, setting up a central government with an elected House of Representatives and six provincial governments. The settlers soon won the right to responsible government (with an executive supported by a majority in the elected assembly). But the governor, and through him the Colonial Office in London, retained control of 'native' policy.

War, expansion, depression

In the 1840s, there were clashes between Māori and Pākehā (Europeans). In Marlborough's Wairau Valley in 1843, a dispute over land erupted, leading to bloodshed. The war in the north (1845–46) began when Hone Heke cut down the flagpole flying the British flag at Russell. There were also troubles in the 1840s over land in Wellington and Wanganui. In the 1850s, disputes between Māori over the sale of land to Europeans kept Taranaki in ferment.

Until the late 1850s, the government managed to purchase enough land to meet settler demands. But many Māori became increasingly reluctant to sell their land, which tribes owned collectively. The Māori King movement, under the leadership of Wiremu Tamihana, grew in part out of Māori resistance to land sales. Potatau Te Wherowhero was elected the first Māori King in 1858. The flashpoint was Taranaki. The refusal of Wiremu Kingi Te Rangitake to sell land at Waitara led to war in 1860. The efforts of Māori to retain their land were depicted by the settlers as a challenge to British sovereignty.

Māori resistance was effectively crushed after Governor George Grey took war to the Waikato in 1863–64. Two chiefs, Te Kooti and Titokowaru, prolonged war through the 1860s, but by 1872 the wars over land had ended. Large areas of land were confiscated from 'rebellious' tribes. A Native Land Court gave land titles to individual Māori, to facilitate sales to Pākehā.

After the wars, many Māori drew back from contact with European settlers. Most lived in isolated rural communities. Māori land continued to pass into Pākehā hands, usually by sale through the Native Land Court. In the 1870s, the village of Parihaka became the centre of a peaceful protest, led by the prophet Te Whiti-o-Rongomai, against occupation of confiscated land in Taranaki. In 1881, government forces invaded Parihaka in an attempt to crush this resistance.

While progress in the North Island was held back by war, the South Island forged ahead on the proceeds of wool and gold. Sheep were turned loose on South Island grasslands, and after gold had been discovered in Otago in 1861, and then on the West Coast, settlers flooded in. Six years later, the discovery of gold at Thames boosted the town of Auckland. Wool ensured that Canterbury became the wealthiest province, and gold made Dunedin the largest town.

Towards the end of the 1860s, gold production fell and wool prices slipped. A new boost to growth came in 1870 when Colonial Treasurer Julius Vogel proposed a loans-funded programme of public works, including the building of railways, and assisted immigration.

The population increased dramatically. The 1871 Census (non-Māori) recorded a total of about 250,000; 10 years later this had grown to half a million. Vogel's policies, like those of Wakefield before him, were based on a belief that New Zealand would grow only if people and capital could be attracted. This stimulated a sense of a single nation rather than separate settlements, and led to the abolition of the provinces in 1876.

The aftermath of Vogel's borrowing was an economic depression that lasted into the 1890s. Despite a brief boom in wheat, prices for farm products sagged and the market for land became depressed. Hard times led to urban unemployment and sweated labour in industry. The country lost people through emigration, mostly to Australia.

Scarcely had depression gripped the country than future prosperity was anticipated with the first successful shipment of frozen meat to England in 1882. Exporting meat (frozen) and butter and cheese (chilled) became possible. After dealing with initial setbacks in refrigerated shipping, New Zealand became a British farm. With an economy based on agriculture, the landscape was transformed from forest to farmland.

Liberal to Labour

The watershed election of 1890 put the Liberals, New Zealand's first 'modern' political party, into power. From 1893 to 1906, the government was headed by 'King Dick' Seddon. The Liberals cemented in place New Zealand's 'family farm' economy by subdividing large estates, buying Māori land in the North Island, and offering advances to settlers. Buoyant markets for New Zealand's farm products ensured the success of these policies. The Minister of Lands, John McKenzie, championed the family farm. Farming progressed, especially in the north, and by 1901, more than half the European population was living north of Cook Strait for the first time since the 1850s.

The Liberal Government reinforced an established pattern of State involvement in the economy and regulation of society. Its old-age pensions and workers' dwellings anticipated the welfare state. In 1893, after campaigns led by women like suffragist Kate Sheppard, New Zealand became the first country in the world to give women the vote.

Ref: Eph-F-MEAT-Gear-018 Alexander Turnbull Library

Frozen meat exports to Britain started in 1882, from Dunedin. These labels are from tinned meat, exported from Wellington's Gear Meat Company, 1890–1920.

Ref: G-75160-1/2 Alexander Turnbull Library

Wellington's Oriental Bay around 1922.

New Zealand's close economic ties with Britain reinforced the loyalty of New Zealanders to an empire that secured their place in the world. The loyalty found expression in the despatch of troops to fight for Britain in South Africa in 1899. A self-confident nationalism was also evident, and New Zealand declined to join the Australian Federation of 1901.

Liberal rule ended in 1912, when William Massey led the Reform Party to power, promising State leaseholders they could freehold their land.

When World War I broke out, New Zealand rallied to England's aid. Thousands of New Zealanders served, and died, overseas. The 1915 landing at Gallipoli in Turkey was a coming of age for the country and established the potent tradition of ANZAC (Australian and New Zealand Army Corps) – a pride in New Zealand's military achievement and its special relationship with Australia. New Zealand troops also fought and died on the Western Front.

After some prosperous years in the later 1920s, the worldwide Great Depression hit New Zealand hard. Export prices collapsed. Farmers faced difficulties over their mortgages and urban unemployment soared. Discontent erupted in riots. A coalition government, dominated by Gordon Coates, failed to lift the country out of depression.

Organised labour flexed its muscle in the 1890 maritime strike, and in the Waihi and watersider strikes of 1912–13. Setbacks on the industrial front turned the labour movement towards political action. The Labour Party, founded in 1916, made uneven gains through the 1920s, then was swept into power under Michael Joseph Savage in 1935 by an electorate disillusioned with how the conservative coalition government had handled the depression. When Savage died in 1940, Peter Fraser became prime minister.

In power, the Labour Party, aided by an economic recovery already underway when it was elected, revived the economy further by pragmatic rather than doctrinaire socialist policies. The Reserve Bank of New Zealand was taken over by the State in 1936, spending on public works increased and a State housing programme began. The Social Security Act 1938 dramatically extended the welfare state.

With the outbreak of World War II, New Zealand troops again fought overseas in support of the United Kingdom. The fall of Singapore shook New Zealanders' confidence that Britain could guarantee the country's security. During the war in the Pacific, the United States protected New Zealand against Japan. Labour remained in power through World War II and in 1945, Peter Fraser played a significant role in the conference that set up the United Nations. But the party had lost the reforming zeal of the previous decade and its electoral support ebbed after the war.

In the early 1950s, New Zealand troops fought in Korea. Later, in the 1960s, concern to keep on side with this new protector prompted the National Government of Keith Holyoake to send troops to Viet Nam, despite popular protests.

The later 20th century

After Labour lost power in 1949, the conservative National Party ruled the country until 1984, interrupted by two single-term Labour governments, in 1957–60 and 1972–75. National Party Prime Minister Sidney Holland used the bitter 1951 waterfront strike to consolidate his power by calling a snap election.

Te Ara – encyclopedia on the web

Te Ara – The Encyclopedia of New Zealand, the first national encyclopedia in the world designed for the world wide web, was launched by Prime Minister Helen Clark in February 2005. When completed, *Te Ara* (the pathway), will provide a comprehensive introduction to New Zealand – its people, its natural environment, its history and its culture and society.

Te Ara is a multi-media experience drawing on photographs, cartoons, sounds, television footage, films and maps to display the cultural richness of New Zealand.

The encyclopedia is being prepared in stages. The first theme, launched in 2005, is 'the New Zealanders'. This includes entries on all those peoples who settled New Zealand – from English, Scots and Irish, to Dalmatians, Samoans and Chinese. It also has an introduction to the country's major Māori tribes, and an entry on the evolution of New Zealanders as a people. All entries on the tribes of New Zealand are available in both the Māori language and English.

The second theme 'Earth, Sea and Sky' went live in June 2006. This covers the shaping forces of New Zealand – the climate, the seas around New Zealand, and the huge geological forces which through earthquakes and volcanoes have carved the landscapes.

The third theme, 'the Bush' appeared in September 2007, focusing on the indigenous flora and fauna of New Zealand – birds, insects, plants and fish.

Since December 2005, *Te Ara* has launched nine of 22 guides to different regions of New Zealand, found in the 'Places' theme.

Te Ara also includes a complete digitised version of the official 1966 *Encyclopaedia of New Zealand* and eight brief entries providing an overview of New Zealand. The entries link to individual biographies in the prize-winning *Dictionary of New Zealand Biography*.

Te Ara is designed to appeal to people of all ages and interests – with a short story on each entry for primary school children, through to original documents and links to additional sources for those who wish to explore further. *Te Ara* has drawn on some of the country's finest scholars and writers and is compiled by the Ministry for Culture and Heritage.

Source: *Te Ara – The Encyclopedia of New Zealand*

Ref: G-49251-1/4 Alexander Turnbull Library

Crowds line Wellington's Lambton Quay to welcome the crew of HMS Achilles *in 1940.*

New immigrants, still mainly British, flooded in while New Zealand remained prosperous by exporting farm products to Britain. The country's culture remained based on Britain's. In 1953, New Zealanders took pride that countryman Edmund Hillary gave Queen Elizabeth II a coronation gift by reaching the summit of Mt Everest.

Britain joined the European Economic Community in 1973. New Zealand had already diversified its export trade, but the loss of an assured market for farm products was a blow.

The first oil shock of 1973 contributed to the fall of the Labour Government in 1975, led by Norman Kirk until his death. After the second oil shock of 1978, the National Government of Robert Muldoon tried to keep New Zealand prosperous by so-called 'think big' industrial and energy projects, and farm subsidies. The economy faltered as the fall of oil prices in the early 1980s made these schemes unsound. Inflation and unemployment mounted.

The fourth Labour Government was elected in 1984. The Minister of Finance, Roger Douglas, was an ardent advocate of economic liberalisation. He removed most controls over the economy, privatised many State enterprises and called aspects of the welfare state into question. Many saw these measures as an assault on New Zealand's egalitarian traditions. In foreign affairs, Labour's anti-nuclear policy ruptured relations with the United States.

The National Government of 1990–99 pursued similar policies to Labour's, passing the controversial Employment Contracts Act, which opened up the labour market and diminished the power of trade unions. The Government also mounted a more sustained attack on the welfare state, most obviously by cutting benefits.

From 1996, under a new voting system (mixed member proportional representation), minority or coalition governments became the norm but National and Labour remained the major parties.

Māori in the 20th century

Most Māori continued to live in remote rural communities until World War II. But Māori society was dynamic. The Kotahitanga movement of the late 19th and early 20th centuries was evidence of Māori resilience. So were the land development work of Apirana Ngata and the revitalisation of the Māori King movement by Te Puea Herangi. In the early 1920s, Wiremu Ratana founded the Ratana Church.

Post-World War II Māori migration into the cities, together with Māori anger at their economic deprivation and concern about loss of mana (status) and continuing loss of land, pushed race relations and the place of the Treaty of Waitangi into the forefront of national life.

For many, sporting contacts with apartheid South Africa became a touchstone of race relations. During the 1981 Springbok rugby tour, New Zealand experienced divisive unrest. After the tour, attention turned to domestic race relations and to the need for New Zealanders to have a better understanding of the Treaty of Waitangi.

Māori became more assertive. Some, alleging breaches of the Treaty of Waitangi, wished to reclaim Māori sovereignty. The Waitangi Tribunal was set up in 1975 to consider their claims and to address grievances. In 1985, the tribunal was empowered to look at breaches of the treaty since 1840, rather than since 1975.

A Māori cultural renaissance, including efforts to foster the Māori language in the early 1980s, increased awareness that New Zealand society was bicultural. At the same time, more immigrants were arriving. Almost before it had been properly acknowledged that New Zealand was bicultural, it became multicultural – first in the composition of its population, more slowly in how it ran its national life. The country's new Pacific island and Asian citizens were testament to the fact that it was no longer, culturally or economically, the offshore island of Europe it had seemed to earlier generations.

"I SIMPLY WENT OUT AND BOUGHT A FEW MORE – NOW I HAVE ONE FOR EVERY STICKER IN THE WEEK"

Ref: B-135-684 Alexander Turnbull Library

Cartoonist Nevile Lodge's comment on the Government's introduction of stickers for carless days in 1979 after significant oil price increases.

Sir Edmund Hillary 1919–2008

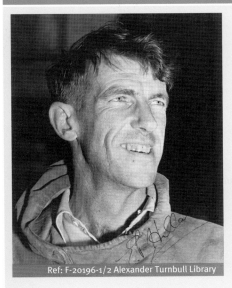

Ref: F-20196-1/2 Alexander Turnbull Library

When Sir Edmund Hillary died in January 2008, New Zealand lost its most admired citizen. He'd been a Kiwi hero and role model for the more than 50 years since he and his climbing mate Sherpa Tenzing Norgay stood on the top of the world, Mt Everest, in 1953.

It was being the first to reach Mt Everest's summit that brought the young beekeeper's name into public consciousness. However, this wasn't all that endeared him to New Zealanders – he saw himself as an ordinary bloke who liked a challenge, was a modest humanitarian, didn't 'show-off', and regularly chatted to those seeking an autograph on their five-dollar note, which bore his picture.

Born in 1919, Ed Hillary's childhood was spent south of Auckland at Tuakau. The gangly teenager discovered the allure of the mountains when on a school trip to Mt Ruapehu, and became increasingly aware of his physical energy, strength, stamina and drive through tramping, and later through his enthusiastic response to the Southern Alps. During the war years he climbed peak after peak, learning from the best mountain guides.

After further testing himself in Europe and the Himalayas, Hillary was invited to join a 10-man British team to Mt Everest led by John Hunt. Chosen as the 'end links' on the climb, it was Hillary and Tenzing who stepped up into history on 29 May 1953.

His famous comment to fellow New Zealand climber George Lowe after reaching the summit was typical Hillary understatement, "Well George, we knocked the bastard off".

The knighthood immediately bestowed by New Zealand's new queen, Elizabeth II, didn't sit easily with Hillary 'the ordinary man'. But he learnt to value the fund-raising opportunities that being Sir Ed offered. He used his fame to benefit the Sherpa people by developing the Himalayan Trust, which since 1964 has built schools, hospitals, bridges and airstrips in the Mt Everest region. Sir Ed was often a hands-on participant in construction.

An expedition in 1960 to search for the fabled Himalayan yeti and a 1977 jet-boat journey up India's Ganges river 'from the ocean to the sky', were fitted around his writing, speaking and tireless fundraising work.

Hillary's personal life was shattered when his wife Louise and daughter Belinda died in a plane crash in Nepal in 1975. Yet he pulled through, and joy returned through his work as New Zealand's High Commissioner to India from 1985–89, with long-time friend June Mulgrew whom he later married.

Although Everest was the pinnacle of Hillary's mountain climbing, he's almost as well-known for establishing Scott Base, home to countless New Zealand Antarctic researchers, and driving red tractors to the South Pole in the summer of 1957–58 – against instructions. Sir Ed's task was to lay supply depots for Sir Vivian Fuchs' attempt to cross Antarctica, then return to Scott Base, but he pushed on, becoming the first to reach the pole overland since Scott's ill-fated 1912 journey. Kiwis chuckled.

Sir Ed was often honoured. In 1987 he became one of the first 20 members of the Order of New Zealand, the country's highest honour. In 1995 he was appointed to Britain's oldest and highest order of chivalry, being made Knight Companion of the Most Noble Order of the Garter, the first non-Briton appointed for other than vice-regal or political achievements.

He has also been commemorated in the names of New Zealand schools and organisations and holds many honorary degrees and medals. In 2003, the 50th anniversary of the Everest climb brought him honorary citizenship of Nepal.

Sir Edmund Hillary was loved by many in Nepal – those he most directly helped to acquire services and education that New Zealanders take for granted. They called him Baba Sahib. But this tall man with a big heart was also loved by his fellow citizens. He enshrined the nation's view of what a hero is and what everyone can aspire to. "In this unique egalitarian society of ours we are all heroes as long as we play our part," historian Tony Simpson said. Sir Ed did this in bucket loads.

His own assessment of his life on his 85th birthday was typically modest, "What a fortunate person I have been!".

Sources: www.nzherald.co.nz; www.stuff.co.nz

Chronology of New Zealand events

c1300 Archaeological evidence indicates Polynesian settlement of New Zealand established by this date.

1642 Dutch explorer Abel Janszoon Tasman discovers a land he calls Staten Landt, later named Nieuw Zeeland.

1769 British explorer James Cook makes first of three visits to New Zealand, taking possession of the country in the name of King George III.

1790s Sealing, deep-sea whaling, flax and timber trading begins, with some small temporary settlements. First severe introduced epidemic among Māori population.

1791 First visit by a whaling vessel, the *William and Ann*, to Doubtless Bay.

1806 First Pākehā (European) women arrive in New Zealand.

1814 British missionary Samuel Marsden makes first visit to New Zealand. Anglican mission station established. Sheep, cattle, horses and poultry introduced.

1815 First Pākehā child, Thomas Holloway King, born in New Zealand.

1819 Raids on Taranaki and Te Whanganui-a-Tara regions by Ngā Puhi and Ngāti Toa people led by chiefs Patuone, Nene, Moetara, Tuwhare and Te Rauparaha.

1820 Ngā Puhi chief Hongi Hika visits England, meets King George IV and secures supply of muskets.

1821 Musket wars begin with raids by Hongi Hika and Te Morenga on southern iwi and continue throughout the decade.

1822 Ngāti Toa migration south to Cook Strait region, led by Te Rauparaha, begins.

1823 Wesleyan Missionary Society mission established. First Church of England marriage between Pākehā and Māori – Phillip Tapsell and Maria Ringa.

1824 Te Heke Niho-Puta migration of Taranaki iwi to the Kapiti Coast. Rawiri Taiwhanga in Bay of Islands sells dairy produce and other food supplies to visiting ships.

1827 Te Rauparaha's invasion of the South Island from Kapiti begins.

1831 Whaling stations established at Tory Channel and Preservation Inlet.

1833 James Busby arrives in the Bay of Islands to take up appointment as British Resident in New Zealand.

1834 United Tribes' flag adopted by some 25 northern chiefs at Busby's suggestion.

1835 Declaration of Independence by the 'United Tribes of New Zealand' signed by 34 northern chiefs.

1837 New Zealand Association formed in London, becoming the New Zealand Colonisation Society in 1838 and the New Zealand Company in 1839, under the inspiration of Edward Gibbon Wakefield. William Colenso completes printing the New Testament in Māori, the first book printed in New Zealand.

1838 Bishop Pompallier founds Roman Catholic mission at Hokianga.

1839 William Hobson instructed to establish British rule in New Zealand, as a dependency of New South Wales. Colonel William Wakefield, of the New Zealand Company, arrives on the *Tory* to purchase land for settlement.

1840 Treaty of Waitangi signed at Bay of Islands and later around most of the country. British sovereignty proclaimed. Hobson becomes first governor and sets up executive and legislative councils. New Zealand Company settlers arrive at Port Nicholson, Wellington. French settlers land at Akaroa. Local Māori initially provide food for these and later settlements.

1841 European settlements established at New Plymouth and Wanganui. Capital shifted from Russell to Auckland.

1842 Main body of settlers arrive at Nelson.

1843 Twenty-two European settlers and four Māori killed at a confrontation at Tua Marina, near Wairau, in Marlborough. Robert FitzRoy becomes governor.

1844 New Zealand Company suspends colonising operations due to financial difficulties.

1845 Hone Heke begins war in the north. George Grey becomes governor. Half of all adult Māori are at least partly literate.

1846 War in the north ends with capture of Ruapekapeka. Fighting between Māori and Pākehā around Wellington. Te Rauparaha captured by Grey. First New Zealand Constitution Act passed. Heaphy, Fox and Brunner begin exploring the West Coast. First steam vessel, HMS *Driver*, arrives in New Zealand.

1848 Settlement founded by Scottish Otago Association. Provinces of New Ulster and New Munster established. Coal discovered at Brunner on the West Coast. Earthquake centred in Marlborough damages most Wellington buildings.

1850 Canterbury settlement founded.

1852 Second New Zealand Constitution Act passed creating general assembly and six provinces with representative government.

1853 Idea of a Māori King canvassed by Tamihana Te Rauparaha and Matene Te Whiwhi. Many Māori agree not to sell any more land – 32 million acres have been bought by the government in the past five years.

1854 First session of general assembly opens in Auckland.

1855 Governor Thomas Gore Browne, appointed in 1854, arrives. Severe earthquake both sides of Cook Strait.

1856 Henry Sewell forms first ministry under responsible government and becomes first premier. Edward Stafford forms first stable ministry.

1858 New Provinces Act passed. Te Wherowhero installed as first Māori King, taking name Pōtatau I.

1859 First session of new Hawke's Bay and Marlborough provincial councils. Gold discovered in Buller River.

Ref: A-195-015 Alexander Turnbull Library

An ink drawing by William Fox showing Port Lyttelton with Canterbury's first four ships, and emigrants landing from the Cressy, *December 1850.*

The fowl house in which we spent the night 10th June 1886

Ref: G-23412-1/1 Alexander Turnbull Library

Two men outside the chicken coop they took shelter in during the 1886 eruption of Mt Tarawera.

1860   Waitara dispute develops into general warfare in Taranaki. Te Wherowhero dies and is replaced as Māori King by his son, Tawhiao. Kohimaramara Conference of Chiefs.

1861   Grey begins second governorship. Gold discovered at Gabriel's Gully and Otago goldrushes begin. First session of Southland provincial council. Bank of New Zealand incorporated at Auckland.

1862   First electric telegraph line opens – from Christchurch to Lyttelton. First gold shipment from Dunedin to London.

1863   War resumes in Taranaki and begins in Waikato when General Cameron crosses the Mangatawhiri Stream. New Zealand Settlements Act passed to effect land confiscation. First steam railway in New Zealand opened.

1864   War in the Waikato ends after battle of Orakau. Māori defeat British at Gate Pa, Tauranga. Land in Waikato, Taranaki, Bay of Plenty and Hawke's Bay confiscated. Gold discovered in Marlborough and Westland. Arthur, George and Edward Dobson are the first Pākehā to cross what becomes known as Arthur's Pass.

1865   Seat of government transferred from Auckland to Wellington. Native Land Court established. Māori resistance continues. Auckland streets lit by gas for first time.

1866   Cook Strait submarine telegraph cable laid. Cobb and Co coaches start running from Canterbury to the West Coast.

1867   Thames goldfield opens. Four Māori seats established in Parliament. Lyttelton railway tunnel completed. Armed constabulary established.

1868   Māori resistance continues through campaigns of Te Kooti Arikirangi and Titokowaru. New Zealand's first sheep breed, the Corriedale, developed.

1869   New Zealand's first university, the University of Otago, established.

1870   Last imperial forces leave New Zealand. Julius Vogel's public works and immigration policy begins. New Zealand University Act passed, establishing a federal system that lasts until 1961. Vogel announces national railway construction programme; more than 1,000 miles constructed by 1879. First rugby match in New Zealand played at Nelson. Auckland to San Francisco mail service begins.

1871   Deer released in Otago.

1872   Te Kooti retreats to the King Country and Māori armed resistance ceases. Telegraph communication links Auckland, Wellington and southern provinces.

1873   New Zealand Shipping Company established.

1876   Abolition of the provinces and establishment of local government by counties and boroughs. New Zealand–Australia telegraph cable established.

1877   Education Act passed, establishing national system of primary education.

1878   Completion of Christchurch to Invercargill railway.

1879   Triennial Parliaments Act passed. Vote is given to every male aged 21 and over. Kaitangata mine explosion, 34 people die. Annual property tax introduced.

1881   Parihaka community forcibly broken up by troops. Te Whiti, Tohu Kakahi and followers arrested and imprisoned. Wreck of SS *Tararua*, 131 people die. Auckland and Christchurch telephone exchanges open.

1882   First shipment of frozen meat leaves Port Chalmers for England on the SS *Dunedin*.

1883   Te Kooti pardoned; Te Whiti and other prisoners released. Direct steamer link established between New Zealand and Britain.

1884   King Tawhiao visits England with petition to Queen Victoria and is refused access. First overseas tour by a New Zealand rugby team, to New South Wales. Construction of King Country section of North Island main trunk railway begins.

1886   Mt Tarawera erupts and Pink and White Terraces destroyed, 108 people die. Oil discovered in Taranaki.

1887   New Zealand's first national park, Tongariro, is presented to the nation by Te Heuheu Tukino IV. Reefton becomes first town to have electricity. First inland parcel post service.

1888   Birth of writer Katherine Mansfield.

1889   Abolition of non-residential or property qualification to vote. The first New Zealand-built locomotive completed at Addington.

1890   Maritime strike involves 8,000 unionists. 'Sweating' commission on employment conditions reports. First election on a one-man one-vote basis.

1891   John McKenzie introduces the first of a series of measures to promote closer land settlement. John Ballance becomes premier of first Liberal Government.

1892   First meeting of national Kotahitanga Māori Parliament. The Kingitanga sets up its own Kauhanganui Parliament.

1893   Right to vote extended to women. Richard John Seddon succeeds Ballance. Liquor licensing poll introduced. Elizabeth Yates becomes New Zealand's first woman mayor, of Onehunga. Banknotes become legal tender.

1894   Compulsory arbitration of industrial disputes and reform of employment laws. Advances to Settlers Act. Clark, Fyfe and Graham are the first to climb Mt Cook.

1896   Brunner mine explosion, 67 people die. Census measures national population as 743,214.

1897 First of series of colonial, and later imperial, conferences in London.	**1919** Women eligible for election to Parliament. Massey signs Treaty of Versailles. First official airmail flight from Auckland to Dargaville.	**1940** Savage dies and is succeeded by Peter Fraser. Sidney Holland becomes leader of opposition. Conscription for military service. German mines laid across Hauraki Gulf.

1897 First of series of colonial, and later imperial, conferences in London.

1898 Old Age Pensions Act passed. First cars imported to New Zealand.

1899 New Zealand army contingent sent to South African war. First celebration of Labour Day.

1900 Māori Councils Act passed. Public Health Act sets up Department of Public Health in 1901.

1901 Cook and other Pacific islands annexed. Penny postage first used.

1902 Pacific cable begins operating between New Zealand, Australia and Fiji.

1903 Richard Pearse achieves semi-controlled flight near Timaru.

1905 The 'Originals' rugby team tours Britain and becomes known as the All Blacks.

1906 Seddon dies and is succeeded by William Hall-Jones as prime minister.

1907 New Zealand constituted as a dominion. Fire destroys Parliament Buildings.

1908 Auckland to Wellington main trunk railway line opens. Ernest Rutherford awarded Nobel Prize in Chemistry. New Zealand's population reaches 1 million.

1909 'Red' Federation of Labour formed. SS *Penguin* wrecked in Cook Strait, 75 people die. Compulsory military training introduced. Stamp-vending machine invented and manufactured in New Zealand.

1912 William Massey becomes first Reform Party prime minister. Waihi miners strike. Malcolm Champion New Zealand's first Olympic gold medallist (as a member of the Australasian 200 metre freestyle relay swimming team).

1913 Waterfront strikes in Auckland and Wellington.

1914 World War I begins and German Samoa occupied. New Zealand Expeditionary Forces despatched to Egypt. Huntly coal mine disaster, 43 people die.

1915 New Zealand forces take part in Gallipoli campaign. Reform and Liberal form National War Cabinet. Britain announces its intention to purchase all New Zealand meat exports during war.

1916 New Zealand troops transfer to Western Front. Conscription introduced. Labour Party formed.

1917 Battle of Passchendaele – about 1,000 New Zealanders die. Six o'clock public house closing introduced.

1918 World War I ends. Influenza epidemic kills an estimated 8,500. Prohibition petition (242,001 signatures) presented to Parliament.

1919 Women eligible for election to Parliament. Massey signs Treaty of Versailles. First official airmail flight from Auckland to Dargaville.

1920 Anzac Day established. New Zealand gets League of Nations mandate to govern Western Samoa. First aeroplane flight across Cook Strait.

1921 New Zealand division of Royal Navy established.

1923 Otira tunnel opens. Ross Dependency proclaimed. Katherine Mansfield dies.

1926 National public broadcasting begins under auspices of Radio Broadcasting Co Ltd.

1928 United Party wins general election. Kingsford-Smith completes first trans-Tasman flight.

1929 Depression deepens. Earthquake in Murchison-Karamea district, 15 people die. First health stamps issued.

1930 Unemployment Board set up to provide relief work.

1931 Newly formed coalition under George Forbes wins general election. Hawke's Bay earthquake, 261 die. Substantial reductions in public service wages and salaries.

1932 Compulsory arbitration of industrial disputes abolished. Unemployed riot in Auckland, Dunedin and Christchurch. Reductions in old age and other pensions.

1933 Elizabeth McCombs becomes first woman MP. Distinctive New Zealand coins first issued.

1934 First trans-Tasman airmail.

1935 First Labour Government elected under Michael Joseph Savage. Air services begin across Cook Strait.

1936 Reserve Bank of New Zealand taken over by State. State housing programme launched. Guaranteed prices for dairy products introduced. National Party formed from former Coalition MPs. Inter-island trunk air services introduced. Jean Batten's record flight from England. Standard working week reduces from 44 to 40 hours for many workers.

1937 Federation of Labour unifies trade union movement. Royal New Zealand Air Force set up as separate branch of armed forces.

1938 Social Security Act establishes revised pensions structure and the basis of a national health service. Import and exchange controls introduced.

1939 World War II begins. Second New Zealand Expeditionary Force formed; Māori Battalion organised on tribal lines. Bulk purchases of farm products by Great Britain. HMS *Achilles*, on loan to New Zealand, takes part in Battle of the River Plate.

1940 Savage dies and is succeeded by Peter Fraser. Sidney Holland becomes leader of opposition. Conscription for military service. German mines laid across Hauraki Gulf.

1941 Japan enters the war. Māori War Effort Organisation set up. Pharmaceutical and general practitioner medical benefits introduced.

1942 Economic stabilisation. New Zealand troops in Battle of El Alamein. Food rationing introduced. Women mobilise for essential work.

1943 New Zealand troops take part in invasion of Italy.

1944 Australia-New Zealand Agreement provides for cooperation in the South Pacific.

1945 War in Europe ends 8 May; in the Pacific on 15 August. New Zealand signs United Nations charter. Māori Social and Economic Advancement Act passed. National Airways Corporation founded.

1946 Family benefit of £1 a week becomes universal. Bank of New Zealand nationalised.

1947 Statute of Westminster adopted by New Zealand Parliament. First public performance by National Orchestra. Mabel Howard the first woman cabinet minister. Fire in Ballantyne's department store, Christchurch, 41 die.

1948 Protest campaign against exclusion of Māori players from 1949 rugby tour of South Africa. Polio epidemic closes schools. Mts Ruapehu and Ngāuruhoe erupt. Meat rationing ends.

1949 Referendum supports compulsory military training. National Government elected. New Zealand gets first four navy frigates.

1950 Naval and ground forces sent to Korean War. Legislative Council abolished. Wool boom. Empire Games in Auckland.

1951 Prolonged waterfront dispute – state of emergency proclaimed. ANZUS Treaty signed by United States, Australia and New Zealand. Māori Women's Welfare League established.

1952 Population passes 2 million.

1953 First tour by a reigning monarch, Queen Elizabeth II. Edmund Hillary and Sherpa Tensing Norgay first to climb Mt Everest. Railway disaster at Tangiwai, 151 die. World sheep-shearing record set by Godfrey Bowen.

1954 New Zealand signs South-east Asia Collective Defence Treaty. New Zealand gains seat on United Nations Security Council. Social Credit gets 10 percent of vote in general election, but no seat in Parliament.

Ref: WA-48833 Alexander Turnbull Library

Auckland Harbour Bridge under construction in 1958. The bridge opened in 1959.

1955 Pulp and paper mill opens at Kawerau. Rimutaka rail tunnel opens.

1956 New Zealand troops deployed in Malaya.

1957 Walter Nash leads second Labour Government. Last hanging. Scott Base established in Antarctica. Court of Appeal constituted. Dairy products gain 10 years unrestricted access to Britain. Compulsory military training abolished.

1958 'Pay as you earn' tax introduced. Arnold Nordmeyer's 'Black Budget'. First geothermal electricity generated at Wairakei.

1959 Antarctic Treaty signed with other countries involved in Antarctic scientific exploration. Auckland's harbour bridge opens.

1960 Regular television programmes begin in Auckland. National Government elected. Government Service Equal Pay Act passed.

1961 New Zealand joins the International Monetary Fund. Capital punishment abolished.

1962 Western Samoa becomes independent. Sir Guy Powles becomes first ombudsman. New Zealand Māori Council established. Cook Strait rail ferry service begins. Taranaki gas well opens. Olympic gold medallist Peter Snell establishes mile and half-mile world athletic records.

1964 Marsden Point oil refinery opens near Whangarei. Cook Strait power cables laid.

1965 Free trade (NAFTA) agreement negotiated with Australia. New Zealand combat forces support United States troops in Viet Nam amid public protests. Self-government for Cook Islands.

1966 International airport officially opens at Auckland. Te Atairangikaahu becomes first Māori Queen.

1967 Referendum extends hotel closing hours to 10pm. Decimal currency introduced. Lord Arthur Porritt becomes first New Zealand-born governor-general. Breath and blood tests introduced for suspected drinking drivers.

1968 Inter-island ferry *Wahine* sinks in Wellington Harbour, 51 die. Inangahua earthquake, three die.

1969 Vote extended to 20-year-olds. National Government wins fourth election in a row. First output from Glenbrook steel mill.

1970 Natural gas from Kapuni supplied to Auckland.

1971 New Zealand secures continued access of butter and cheese to the United Kingdom. Nga Tamatoa protest at Waitangi celebrations. Tiwai Point aluminium smelter begins operating. Warkworth satellite communications station opens.

1972 Labour Government led by Norman Kirk elected. Equal Pay Act passed.

1973 Great Britain becomes member of European Economic Community (EEC). Naval frigate protests against French nuclear testing in Pacific. New Zealand's population is 3 million. Rugby tour by South Africa cancelled. Colour television introduced.

1974 Prime Minister Norman Kirk dies. Commonwealth Games held in Christchurch. Vote given to 18-year-olds.

1975 National wins election; Robert Muldoon becomes prime minister. Māori march against land loss. Waitangi Tribunal established.

1976 Matrimonial Property Act passed. Pacific island overstayers deported. EEC quotas for New Zealand butter set until 1980. Metric system of weights and measures introduced. Subscriber toll dialling begins.

1977 New Zealand's 200-mile exclusive economic zone established. Bastion Point occupied by Māori land protesters.

1978 National Government re-elected.

1979 Air New Zealand plane crashes on Mt Erebus, Antarctica, 257 die. Car-less days introduced to reduce petrol use.

1980 Saturday trading partly legalised. Eighty-day strike at Kinleith pulp and paper mill.

1981 South African rugby team's tour brings widespread disruption.

1982 Closer Economic Relations (CER) agreement signed with Australia. First kōhanga reo established. Wage, price and rent freeze imposed – lasts until 1984.

1983 Visit by nuclear-powered United States Navy frigate *Texas* sparks protests. Official Information Act replaces Official Secrets Act. New Zealand Party founded.

1984 Labour Party wins snap general election. Finance Minister Roger Douglas begins deregulating economy. Te Hikoi ki Waitangi march and disruption of Waitangi Day celebrations. Auckland's population exceeds that of the South Island. Government devalues New Zealand dollar by 20 percent.

1985 Anti-nuclear policy means visit by American warship USS *Buchanan* refused. Greenpeace vessel *Rainbow Warrior* bombed by French agents in Auckland harbour. New Zealand dollar floated. Author Keri Hulme wins Booker Prize for *The Bone People*. First case of locally-contracted AIDS reported. Waitangi Tribunal given power to hear Māori land grievances back to 1840.

1986 Homosexual Law Reform Bill passed. Royal Commission favours MMP electoral system. Soviet cruise ship, the *Mikhail Lermontov*, sinks in Marlborough Sounds. Goods and services tax (GST) introduced. First visit to New Zealand by a pope.

1987 Share prices plummet 59 percent in four months. Labour wins general election. Māori Language Act makes Māori an official language. Anti-nuclear legislation enacted. First Lotto draw. New Zealand's first heart transplant performed. New Zealand wins first rugby World Cup.

1988 More than 100,000 unemployed. Bastion Point land returns to Māori ownership. Electrification of North Island's main trunk line completed. New Zealand Post closes 432 post offices. Fisheries quota package announced for Māori iwi.

1989 Prime Minister David Lange suggests formal withdrawal from ANZUS. Jim Anderton founds NewLabour Party. Lange resigns; Geoffrey Palmer becomes prime minister. Reserve Bank Act sets bank's role to maintain price stability. Sunday trading begins. Māori Fisheries Act passed.

1990 New Zealand celebrates its sesqui-centennial. Māori leaders inaugurate National Congress of Tribes. Dame Catherine Tizard becomes first woman governor-general. National Party has landslide victory; Jim Bolger becomes prime minister. One and two cent coins withdrawn. Commonwealth Games in Auckland. Telecom sold for $4.25 billion. Welfare payments cut.

1991 Welfare payments cut further. Alliance Party formed. Employment Contracts Act passed. Number of unemployed exceeds 200,000. New Zealand troops join multi-national force in Gulf War. Avalanche reduces Aoraki/Mt Cook's height by 10.5 metres.

1992 Government and Māori negotiate Sealord fisheries deal. Public health system reformed. State housing commercialised. New Zealand has seat on United Nations Security Council.

1993 New Zealand First Party launched. National wins election without majority; Opposition MP Peter Tapsell becomes Speaker of the House, giving National a majority. Referendum favours MMP electoral system.

1994 Government commits 250 soldiers to peacekeeping in Bosnia. Government proposes $1 billion cap for final settlement of Treaty of Waitangi claims. New Zealand's first casino opens in Christchurch. First fast-ferry passenger service begins across Cook Strait.

1995 Team New Zealand wins yachting's America's Cup. Occupation of Moutua Gardens, Wanganui. Renewed French nuclear testing results in New Zealand protest flotilla and navy ship *Tui* sailing for Mururoa Atoll. Commonwealth Heads of Government meeting in Auckland. New Zealand soldiers return from Bosnia.

1996 First MMP election brings National/New Zealand First coalition government. First legal sports betting through Totalisator Agency Board.

1997 Government signs $170 million settlement with Ngai Tahu. Prime Minister Bolger resigns after National Party coup while he is overseas; replaced by New Zealand's first woman prime minister, Jenny Shipley.

1998 Auckland city businesses hit by month-long power cut. New Zealand women's rugby team, the Black Ferns, become world champions. Coalition government dissolved; National becomes minority government.

1999 New Zealand sends peacekeepers to East Timor. Auckland hosts APEC world leaders' conference. Former prime minister Mike Moore becomes World Trade Organisation head.

Labour forms government in coalition with Alliance party and with support of the Greens, who enter Parliament for the first time with seven seats. Legal drinking age lowered – from 20 to 18 years.

2000 Air New Zealand gains ownership of Ansett Australia. Team New Zealand beats Italy's *Prada* 5-0 to retain the America's Cup. Labour Government abolishes knighthoods. Dr Alan MacDiarmid wins Nobel Prize for Chemistry for his part in the discovery and development of conductive polymers.

2001 New Zealand's largest company, Fonterra, forms from New Zealand Dairy Group and Kiwi Dairies. Qantas New Zealand and Ansett collapse. Government injects $550 million to keep Air New Zealand flying following a $1.4 billion loss – the largest in New Zealand's corporate history. Government disbands RNZAF combat wing. Bill English becomes leader of the National Party. Yachtsman Sir Peter Blake murdered by pirates on the Amazon.

2002 Labour wins election; forms coalition government with Progressive Coalition, and a special arrangement with United Future. Rakiura, New Zealand's 14th national park covering about 85 percent of Stewart Island, opens. Three New Zealanders among 185 killed in Bali terrorist bombing. *The Fellowship of the Ring*, first film in *The Lord of the Rings* trilogy directed by New Zealand's Peter Jackson, wins four Oscars.

2003 New Zealand loses America's Cup to Swiss challenger *Alinghi*, skippered by Russell Coutts, previously of Team New Zealand. Population reaches 4 million. National elects Don Brash as leader.

2004 *The Return of the King* film wins 11 Oscars. Controversial Foreshore and Seabed Act passed following a hikoi (march) of thousands of protestors. Tariana Turia resigns as Labour MP; re-elected eight weeks later as Māori Party's first MP. Supreme Court replaces London-based Privy Council as New Zealand's court of final appeal. Unknown World War I warrior from Somme battlefield returned, to rest at Wellington's National War Memorial.

2005 Titahi Bay golfer Michael Campbell wins US Open. Former Prime Minister David Lange dies. Labour has one-seat election night lead; forms Government in coalition with Jim Anderton's Progressives, and United Future. Green Party co-leader Rod Donald dies. Naval frigate *Wellington* scuttled off Wellington's south coast, as a diving attraction. New Zealand wins right to host 2011 rugby World Cup.

Ref: EP/1981/3106/17a Alexander Turnbull Library

Protesters against the 1981 Springbok rugby tour clash with supporters outside Eden Park in Auckland.

2006 Dame Te Ātairangikaahu, Māori Queen for 40 years, dies; her son becomes King Tūheitia. Lowest road toll (391) since 1960. Icebergs float past Otago. Trade Me online auction site sold to media company. John Key topples Don Brash as National Party leader. Government regulates to 'unbundle' the telecommunications copper-wire network. Canterbury has heaviest snowfall since 1945; Wellington's spring is windiest in 40 years.

2007 Government introduces 20 hours free early childhood education, four weeks annual leave for workers, and KiwiSaver. Lowest unemployment level since late 1970s; oil prices and the dollar at highest levels. Country debates 'smacking' children before the Crimes (Substituted Section 59) Amendment Bill passes. Willie Apiata is first New Zealander awarded Victoria Cross since World War II. South Island population passes 1 million. Nation 'mourns' sporting 'almost-but-not-quite' experiences – the yachting America's Cup, netball World Championship, and rugby and cricket world cups.

The Dominion Post

The casket carrying the Māori Queen Dame Te Ātairangikaahu travels by waka down the Waikato river to Taupiri mountain for burial. Dame Te Ata was the sixth monarch of the Kingitanga movement, and ruled for 40 years.

History of conservation

When Captain Cook visited New Zealand between 1769 and 1777 he introduced exotic plants, and animals such as pigs, rats and goats. With the arrival of European settlers in the early 1800s land clearing progressively destroyed much of the indigenous forest. By the 1860s concern was growing about a loss of birdlife and forest.

Premier Julius Vogel made several attempts to pass laws controlling deforestation, but with limited success.

The introduction of mustelids (ferrets, stoats and weasels) to fight a rabbit plague in the 1880s devastated the native bird population. In the early 1890s, birds were relocated to 'pest-free' island sanctuaries in an attempt to avoid likely extinctions. Native birds were also badly affected by the Victorian passion for collecting.

Horonuku Te Heuheu, paramount chief of Ngāti Tūwharetoa, gifted Mts Tongariro, Ngāuruhoe and Ruapehu to the Crown in 1887. The peaks became the centre of Tongariro National Park in 1894, one of the world's first national parks. The 1903 Scenery Preservation Act allowed the Crown to protect existing reserves and create new ones.

Interest in outdoor activities and the natural environment grew in the early 20th century. The Native Bird Protection Society (later the Royal Forest and Bird Society of New Zealand) formed in 1913, while the Royal Commission on Forestry report of 1923 led to widespread exotic tree planting, to counter rapid native timber depletion.

Public pressure about the loss of kauri forest created the Waipoua Forest Sanctuary in the late 1940s. Rivalry between the Lands and Survey Department (which managed national parks) and the Forest Service (which controlled forested land) led to the first forest park being established in 1954, for both commercial and recreational use.

By 1965 there were 10 national parks, mainly in mountainous areas not wanted for agriculture, and over 1,300 reserves – including the sub-Antarctic islands and small areas of bush.

The National Party included conservation in its 1960 election manifesto, then set up the Nature Conservation Council in 1962.

Meantime, the public had begun to challenge the inevitable environmental damage of infrastructure development – in 1969 the Save Manapouri campaign was formed to counter the government's agreement to raise the lake's level to create power for an aluminium smelter. For the first time a major development was opposed, successfully, on environmental grounds.

The 1970s saw more conservation concern when South Island beech forest logging for wood pulp was proposed. In 1977, the Maruia Declaration was submitted to the Government as a public petition demanding legal recognition of native forests and an end to logging.

Debate over the ecological versus economic value of native lowland forest grew between 1975 and 1985. Protesters hoisted themselves into trees in a central North Island forest, attempting to stop milling. Eventually new national parks containing lowland forest were created – Whanganui (1986) and Paparoa (1987).

The Department of Conservation was set up in 1987 to oversee the management of parks and reserves, and protect inland waters and native wildlife, while the Resource Management Act 1991 ensured conservation issues must be considered in all future development plans.

In the 1990s, emphasis shifted from saving individual species to looking at the whole range of native plants and animals and their habitats. This led to the *New Zealand Biodiversity Strategy* (2000), aimed at restoring the country's ecosystems and biodiversity.

Ref: EP/1970/2201/12A
Alexander Turnbull Library

The Save Manapouri petition is prepared for Parliament by Royal Forest and Bird Protection Society staff. The petition, presented on 26 May 1970, contained 264,857 signatures.

Today the public is widely engaged in volunteer conservation work – for example in replanting, possum control, or caring for parks. There is increased vigilance at entry ports to inhibit the arrival of biological invaders from overseas. And by 2006, 31 marine reserves had been created.

Source: *Te Ara – The Encyclopedia of New Zealand*

Contributors and related websites

Archives New Zealand – www.archives.govt.nz

Dictionary of New Zealand Biography – www.dnzb.govt.nz

History Group, Ministry for Culture and Heritage – www.nzhistory.net.nz

National Library of New Zealand – www.natlib.govt.nz

New Zealand Archaeology – www.nzarchaeology.org

New Zealand Electronic Text Centre – www.nzetc.org

Statistics New Zealand – www.stats.govt.nz

Te Ara – The Encyclopedia of New Zealand – www.teara.govt.nz

Treaty of Waitangi – www.treatyofwaitangi.govt.nz

Jarrad Mapp

A member of the public uses one of the new recycling bins installed outside Wellington's railway station in 2008. The Ministry for the Environment is working with local government to trial public-place recycling bins in the Far North, Wellington, Kaikoura, and Christchurch.

3 | Government

Constitution

New Zealand is a constitutional monarchy and has had a parliamentary government since 1856. Queen Elizabeth II has the title Queen of New Zealand. The constitution is concerned with the establishment and composition of the legislative, executive and judicial branches of government, their powers and duties, and the relationship between these branches.

New Zealand's constitutional history can be traced back to the signing of the Treaty of Waitangi in 1840. The treaty was an agreement between the British Crown and Māori in which Māori gave the Crown rights to govern, and the Crown guaranteed Māori full protection of their interests and status, and full citizenship rights.

Five years earlier, on 28 October 1835, an assembly of the Confederation of Chiefs of the United Tribes of New Zealand had proclaimed the country independent and signed a Declaration of Independence.

New Zealand's Constitution Act 1986 brought together important statutory constitutional provisions and clarified rules relating to the governmental hand-over of power. Other sources of New Zealand's constitution include the Electoral Act 1993, the Imperial Laws Application Act 1988 (which lists United Kingdom statutes still in force in New Zealand), Standing Orders of the House of Representatives, constitutional conventions, New Zealand legislation, and decisions of the courts.

Table 3.01 lists the Sovereigns of New Zealand since the signing of the Treaty of Waitangi in 1840.

The Crown and the governor-general

The Governor-General of New Zealand is the Crown's representative in New Zealand, and exercises the royal powers derived from statute and the general law.

The powers of the governor-general are set out in the Letters Patent 1983 and it is for the courts to decide on the limits of these powers. One of the governor-general's main constitutional functions is to arrange for the leader of the majority party in Parliament to form a government.

The Crown is part of Parliament and the governor-general's assent is required before bills can become law. However, the governor-general is required by constitutional convention and the Letters Patent, to follow the advice of ministers. In extraordinary circumstances, the governor-general can reject advice if he or she believes a government is intending to act unconstitutionally.

Table 3.01

Sovereigns of New Zealand				
Monarch	Accession	Died	Age	Reigned (years)
House of Hanover				
Victoria	1837[1]	1901	81	63
House of Saxe-Coburg				
Edward VII	1901	1910	68	9
House of Windsor				
George V	1910	1936	70	25
Edward VIII[2]	1936	1972	77	
George VI	1936	1952	56	15
Elizabeth II	1952	...	...	...

(1) Queen Victoria became New Zealand's queen in 1840.
(2) Abdicated; reigned 325 days.
Symbol: ... not applicable

Source: Statistics New Zealand

The Hon Anand Satyanand, PCNZM, QSO

The New Zealand Herald

The Governor-General of New Zealand is the Hon Anand Satyanand. His previous roles as a lawyer, judge and ombudsman have given him a wide perspective on the workings of government, its relationship with citizens, and the needs of individuals. The Hon Anand Satyanand has also been involved in a range of community, cultural and sporting groups, and maintains a keen interest in international affairs and New Zealand's relationships with other countries.

Born and raised in Auckland, where he attended Richmond Road Primary School in Ponsonby, and Sacred Heart College at Glen Innes, the Hon Anand Satyanand graduated with a law degree from Auckland University in 1970. After 12 years practising in Auckland, including work with the Crown Solicitor's Office, he became a district court judge, serving in Palmerston North, Waitakere, Otahuhu and Auckland.

In 1995, the Hon Anand Satyanand was appointed an ombudsman, completing two five-year terms in February 2005. In this role, he dealt with complaints about unfairness on the part of government officials, assessed governance processes, and worked in the freedom of information area.

Throughout his career, the Hon Anand Satyanand has contributed to professional legal education in New Zealand and internationally. He has written extensively and been published in his specialist areas, and has also been a regular contributor to the Commonwealth Secretariat-funded ombudsman training programme.

Since completing his terms as an ombudsman, the Hon Anand Satyanand has reviewed the New Zealand Banking Ombudsman Scheme, and served as chairman of the Confidential Forum for Former In-patients of Psychiatric Hospitals, and as Registrar of Pecuniary Interests of Members of Parliament.

The Hon Anand Satyanand was born in Auckland on 22 July 1944 and raised in New Zealand. His grandparents migrated from India to Fiji at the turn of the 20th century, and his parents moved to New Zealand from Fiji following completion of their education. He and his wife Susan were married in 1970, and they have three adult children.

Source: Government House

This is known as the reserve power. The Sovereign appoints the governor-general on the prime minister's recommendation, normally for a term of five years. Table 3.02 lists the vice-regal representatives of New Zealand since the signing of the Treaty of Waitangi.

Table 3.02

Vice-regal representatives of New Zealand		
Representative[1]	Assumed office	Retired
Dependency		
Lieutenant-governor		
Captain William Hobson, RN	30 Jan 1840	3 May 1841
Crown colony		
Governor		
Captain William Hobson, RN	3 May 1841	10 Sep 1842
Captain Robert Fitzroy, RN	26 Dec 1843	17 Nov 1845
Captain George Grey	18 Nov 1845	31 Dec 1847
Governor-in-chief		
Sir George Grey, KCB	1 Jan 1848	7 Mar 1853
Self-governing colony		
Governor		
Sir George Grey, KCB	7 Mar 1853	31 Dec 1853
Colonel Thomas Gore Browne, CB	6 Sep 1855	2 Oct 1861
Sir George Grey, KCB	4 Dec 1861	5 Feb 1868
Sir George Ferguson Bowen, GCMG	5 Feb 1868	19 Mar 1873
Rt Hon Sir James Fergusson, Bt	14 Jun 1873	3 Dec 1874
Marquess of Normanby, GCB, GCMG, PC	9 Jan 1875	21 Feb 1879
Sir Hercules George Robert Robinson, GCMG	17 Apr 1879	8 Sep 1880
Hon Sir Arthur Hamilton Gordon, GCMG	29 Nov 1880	23 Jun 1882
Lieutenant-General Sir William Francis Drummond Jervois, GCMG, CB	20 Jan 1883	22 Mar 1889
Earl of Onslow, GCMG	2 May 1889	24 Feb 1892
Earl of Glasgow, GCMG	7 Jun 1892	6 Feb 1897
Earl of Ranfurly, GCMG	10 Aug 1897	19 Jun 1904
Lord Plunket, GCMG, KCVO	20 Jun 1904	7 Jun 1910
Dominion		
Lord Islington, KCMG, DSO, PC	22 Jun 1910	2 Dec 1912
Earl of Liverpool, GCMG, MVO, PC	19 Dec 1912	27 Jun 1917
Governor-general		
Earl of Liverpool, GCB, GCMG, GBE, MVO, PC	28 Jun 1917	7 Jul 1920
Admiral of the Fleet Viscount Jellicoe, GCB, OM, GCVO	27 Sep 1920	26 Nov 1924
General Sir Charles Fergusson, BT, GCMG, KCB, DSO, MVO	13 Dec 1924	8 Feb 1930
Viscount Bledisloe, GCMG, KBE, PC	19 Mar 1930	15 Mar 1935
Viscount Galway, GCMG, DSO, OBE, PC	12 Apr 1935	3 Feb 1941
Marshal of the Royal Air Force Sir Cyril Louis Norton Newall, GCB, OM, GCMG, CBE, AM	22 Feb 1941	19 Apr 1946
Realm		
Lieutenant-General the Lord Freyberg, VC, GCMG, KCB, KBE, DSO	17 Jun 1946	15 Aug 1952
Lieutenant-General the Lord Norrie, GCMG, GCVO, CB, DSO, MC	2 Dec 1952	25 Jul 1957
Viscount Cobham, GCMG, TD	5 Sep 1957	13 Sep 1962
Brigadier Sir Bernard Fergusson, GCMG, GCVO, DSO, OBE	9 Nov 1962	20 Oct 1967
Sir Arthur Espie Porritt, BT, GCMG, GCVO, CBE	1 Dec 1967	7 Sep 1972
Sir (Edward) Denis Blundell, GCMG, GCVO, KBE, QSO	27 Sep 1972	5 Oct 1977
Rt Hon Sir Keith Jacka Holyoake, KG, GCMG, CH, QSO	26 Oct 1977	27 Oct 1980
Hon Sir David Stuart Beattie, GCMG, GCVO, QSO, QC	6 Nov 1980	10 Nov 1985
Rt Rev Hon Sir Paul Alfred Reeves, GCMG, GCVO, QSO	20 Nov 1985	29 Nov 1990
Hon Dame Catherine Anne Tizard, GCMG, GCVO, DBE, QSO	13 Dec 1990	3 Mar 1996
Rt Hon Sir Michael Hardie Boys, GNZM, GCMG, QSO	21 Mar 1996	21 Mar 2001
Hon Dame Silvia Cartwright, PCNZM, DBE, QSO	4 April 2001	4 Aug 2006
Hon Anand Satyanand, PCNZM, QSO	23 Aug 2006	...

(1) Honours are specified only if held on retirement from office.
Symbol: ... not applicable

Source: Government House

Parliamentary tradition

Since 1856, New Zealand has been a constitutional monarchy with a parliamentary system of government. The government cannot act effectively without Parliament, because it cannot raise or spend money without parliamentary approval. For most categories of expenditure, this approval takes the form of an annual vote of funds to the government. Parliament has to be assembled regularly and has the opportunity to hold the government to account.

Electoral system

Since 1996, New Zealand has had a mixed member proportional (MMP) electoral system. Voters have two votes – one electorate vote and one party vote.

Electorate votes are used to elect Members of Parliament (MPs) to represent local areas. Party votes are used to allocate extra seats to political parties so that the make-up of Parliament reflects the support for these parties across the country.

Otago Daily Times

Electorate officer Sue Skelt stands on the boundary between the Clutha-Southland and Waitaki electorates, in the middle of the Roaring Meg river.

For the 2005 election, New Zealand was divided geographically into 62 general and seven Māori electorates. The political parties were subsequently allocated 52 party seats after party votes were counted, and the number of seats in Parliament increased by one to 121. Table 3.03 shows seats won by each political party since 1949, and the total number of seats available, at general elections.

Table 3.03

							United		
Election	National	Labour	NZ First	Alliance	ACT	Green	Future	Other	**Total**
1949	46	34	...	...	...	...	...	0	**80**
1951	50	30	...	...	...	...	...	0	**80**
1954	45	35	...	...	...	...	...	0	**80**
1957	39	41	...	...	...	...	...	0	**80**
1960	46	34	...	...	...	...	...	0	**80**
1963	45	35	...	...	...	...	...	0	**80**
1966	44	35	...	...	...	...	...	1[1]	**80**
1969	45	39	...	...	...	...	...	0	**84**
1972	32	55	...	...	...	...	...	0	**87**
1975	55	32	...	...	...	...	...	0	**87**
1978	51	40	...	...	...	...	...	1[1]	**92**
1981	47	43	...	...	...	...	...	2[1]	**92**
1984	37	56	...	...	...	...	...	2[1]	**95**
1987	40	57	...	...	...	...	...	0	**97**
1990	67	29	...	...	...	...	...	1[2]	**97**
1993	50	45	2	2	...	...	...	0	**99**
1996	44	37	17	13	8	...	...	1[3]	**120**
1999	39	49	5	10	9	7	...	1[3]	**120**
2002	27	52	13	0	9	9	8	2[4]	**120**
2005	48	50	7	0	2	6	3	5[5]	**121**

(1) Social Credit/Democrats. (2) NewLabour. (3) United. (4) Progressive Coalition. (5) Progressive 1 seat, Māori 4 seats.

Symbol: ... not applicable

Source: Office of the Clerk of the House of Representatives

Electorate boundaries are redrawn by the Representation Commission after each population census. The number of electorates can change as the population increases or decreases.

The Māori electoral option follows every census and gives people of Māori descent the opportunity to choose whether to be on the Māori, or the general, electoral roll. Once electors have chosen which roll to be on, they cannot change until the next Māori electoral option takes place.

The New Zealand electoral system is set out in the Electoral Act 1993. This Act is the only statute in New Zealand with entrenched provisions. This means that either 75 percent of MPs, or a majority of voters in a referendum of all registered voters, must agree to make changes to these provisions. Normally, a simple majority of MPs is all that is required to make changes to legislation.

Te Hakituatahi o Aotearoa

The principal reason behind the creation of Te Hakituatahi o Aotearoa, the First Flag of New Zealand, was to provide essential protection for trading ships built in New Zealand.

In 1830, the *Sir George Murray*, a New Zealand-built ship, was seized in Sydney, together with its cargo of flax and timber (which were confiscated), for sailing without a flag signalling national identity.

In October 1832, Paratene Te Manu and other chiefs met with King William IV in England and were given the right to fly a flag. In 1833, James Busby, the British Resident at the Bay of Islands, wrote to the Colonial Secretary suggesting a national flag for New Zealand should be adopted. He considered the Māori chiefs should have a say as to the choice of flag.

Three flags were made in Sydney and brought to New Zealand on the *HMS Alligator* and, on 20 March 1834, representatives of Te Runanga Kohuiarau (the Confederation of Chiefs of the United Tribes of New Zealand) chose one.

The flag was subsequently hoisted up a flagpole and declared the 'Flag of the Confederation of Chiefs of the United Tribes of New Zealand and the Crown of England'.

The chosen flag was described as a red cross of St George on a white field, with a blue field in the upper corner (upper canton) next to the staff. The blue field was pierced by four white eight-point stars, and also contained another red cross with a narrow black border (see page IV).

The flag was dispatched to England for approval by King William IV, who subsequently directed the Admiralty to recognise and protect any vessel bearing this flag. On 19 August 1835, the New South Wales Parliament gazetted a notice recognising this flag as the national flag of New Zealand. The flag gave recognition and protection to New Zealand vessels trading abroad until February 1840.

When New Zealand became a member of the British Empire with the signing of the Treaty of Waitangi, the Union Flag Notice recognised the Union Flag as New Zealand's national flag.

In the mid-1840s, Hone Heke cut down the flagpole flying the Union Flag at Russell/Kororāreka, in the Bay of Islands, in protest over the removal of Māori chiefs' rights to trade and designate customs duties. The first flag has important historical significance for New Zealand because today's formal trading arrangements had their beginnings at the time of the flag's origin.

Whenever flags are flown on a ship, there are four positions in which they can be flown. The number one position is at the gaff (reserved for the New Zealand flag), number two is at the masthead (for the governor-general's flag or the Royal Standard or for Te Hakituatahi o Aotearoa), number three should be flown on the cross-arm on the port side (Te Hakituatahi o Aotearoa if the number two position is occupied), and the number four position is for an iwi/hapu (tribe/subtribe) flag or other flag.

Today Te Hakituatahi o Aotearoa is flown daily at Waitangi in the Bay of Islands. This tradition is attributed to the late Lt. Col. Sir James Henare, of Ngāti Hine. As the nation continues into the 21st century and discussion continues about a new New Zealand flag, it is more than fitting that we recognise the earliest flag.

Source: Dr Henare R Broughton

Speaker of the House of Representatives

Speakers are elected by the House of Representatives at the opening sitting of each parliament and normally holds office until the dissolution of that Parliament.

Speakers of the House of Representatives

Speaker	Political party	Term(s)
Sir Charles Clifford	...	1854–60
Sir David Monro	...	1861–70
Sir Francis Dillon Bell	...	1871–75
Sir William Fitzherbert	...	1876–79
Sir George O'Rorke	...	1879–90
William Steward	Liberal	1891–93
Sir George O'Rorke	Liberal	1894–1902
Sir Arthur Guinness[1]	Liberal	1903–13
Sir Frederic William Lang	Reform	1913–22
Sir Charles Statham	Independent	1923–35
William Barnard	Labour	1936–43
Frederick William Schramm	Labour	1944–46
Robert McKeen	Labour	1947–49
Sir Matthew Oram	National	1950–57
Robert Macfarlane	Labour	1958–60
Sir Ronald Algie	National	1961–66
Sir Roy Jack	National	1967–72
Alfred Allen	National	1972
Stanley Whitehead	Labour	1973–75
Jonathan Hunt (acting)	Labour	1975
Sir Roy Jack[1]	National	1976–77
Richard Harrison (acting)	National	1977
Sir Richard Harrison	National	1978–84
Sir Basil Arthur[1]	Labour	1984–85
Sir Gerry Wall	Labour	1985–87
Sir Kerry Burke	Labour	1987–90
Robin Gray	National	1990–93
Hon Peter Tapsell[2]	Labour[3]	1993–96
Hon Doug Kidd[2]	National	1997–99
Rt Hon Jonathan Hunt	Labour	1999–05
Hon Margaret Wilson[2]	Labour	2005–08

(1) Died in office. (2) 'Hon' before elected Speaker. (3) During National party administration.

Note: The title Honourable was granted to speakers in 1856. Other titles are shown only if they were held while the individual was in office as speaker. Dates shown include the period between dissolution and the start of the next Parliament, if the speaker held office in successive Parliaments.

Symbol: ... not applicable

Source: Office of the Clerk of the House of Representatives

House of Representatives debating chamber. Speaker Hon Margaret Wilson presides, while Deputy Prime Minister Hon Dr Michael Cullen addresses the house.

Parliament

House of Representatives

The power to make laws lies at the heart of New Zealand's parliamentary system. This power is vested in the Parliament of New Zealand by the Constitution Act 1986.

Parliament consists of the Crown (normally represented by the governor-general) and an elected House of Representatives. The principal functions of Parliament are to enact laws, to supervise the government's administration, to vote for the supply of funds, to provide a government, and to redress grievances by way of petition.

The Constitution Act 1986 forbids the Crown from taxing citizens without express parliamentary approval. Under standing orders, private members are also able to initiate proposals involving expenditure or taxation. However, the government has an absolute right to veto such proposals if they would have more than a minor impact on the government's finances.

Perhaps the most important privilege of the House of Representatives is that of freedom of speech, guaranteed by the Bill of Rights 1688 and claimed by the speaker after the governor-general has confirmed office.

A session of Parliament is the period during which the house sits, usually the full parliamentary term of three years. The house meets after an election in answer to a summons from the governor-general. Sessions of Parliament are marked by a formal opening, when the government's legislative programme is described in the Speech from the Throne, read by the governor-general in the absence of the Sovereign. The session is terminated by the governor-general bringing Parliament to an end, usually just before a general election.

Unless there is a new session in the second and third years of the parliamentary term, the prime minister's statement at the start of business reviews public affairs, and outlines the government's legislative and other policy intentions for the year ahead.

The speaker, elected by the house, is the principal presiding officer. The speaker maintains order in proceedings and ensures standing orders are complied with. The speaker is assisted by the clerk of the House of Representatives, who records all proceedings of the house and of any committee of the house, and provides advice on parliamentary law and custom.

The first session of the 48th New Zealand Parliament was called following the general election on 17 September 2005, and began sitting on 7 November 2005.

Salaries and allowances of parliamentarians are set by the Remuneration Authority and are shown in table 3.04.

Role of parties Until 1993, under the first past the post (FPP) system of electoral representation, the House of Representatives was characterised by the presence of two large dominant parties, with the majority party forming the government and the minority party the opposition. This has given way to multi-party representation under the mixed member proportional (MMP) system of electoral representation, adopted after two referendums, one indicative (1992) and one binding (1993).

Table 3.04

Parliamentary salaries and allowances

Position	Yearly salary payable from 1 July 2007 ($)
Members of the executive	
Prime minister	375,000
Deputy prime minister	264,500
Cabinet minister	233,000
Minister with portfolio outside cabinet	195,700
Minister without portfolio	169,400
Parliamentary under-secretary	150,000
Officers of the House of Representatives	
Speaker of the House of Representatives	233,000
Deputy speaker	162,750
Assistant speaker	139,000
Chairperson of a select committee	139,000
Deputy chairperson of a select committee	130,300
Leaders of non-government parties	
Leader of the opposition	233,000
Other party leaders (depending on number of MPs)	139,000 +
Deputy leader of party with 25 MPs or more (depending on number of MPs)	160,400 +
Whips	
Senior government whip (depending on number of MPs)	143,120 +
Other whips (depending on number of MPs)	139,000 +
Junior whip of party with 25 MPs or more	139,000
Other members of Parliament	
Member of Parliament	126,200
Expenses allowance	
Prime minister	19,000
Speaker	17,750
Other members of Parliament	14,280

Source: Remuneration Authority

The four general elections held since 1996 have indicated that under MMP it is unlikely that a single party can command an absolute majority in the house and form a government on its own account. The party caucus (a meeting of each party's members of Parliament in closed session at regular intervals) has become a primary means of developing policies and tactics.

Party representation The general election on 17 September 2005 resulted in the formation of a Labour-led minority coalition government. The Labour Party entered into a coalition agreement with the Progressive Party, which included the leader of the Progressive Party being a Cabinet minister.

Agreements were also made between the minority coalition government and two other parties – United Future and New Zealand First. Both parties promised to provide confidence and supply to the Labour/Progressive government for the term of the Parliament. It was also agreed that the leaders of United Future and New Zealand First would be appointed to ministerial positions outside Cabinet.

The new ministry was sworn in on 19 October 2005. A cooperation agreement was entered into by the Government with the Green Party, which provided for consultation on the broad outline of the legislative programme, on key legislative measures on which support was needed, on major policy issues, and on broad budget parameters.

The fourth House of Representatives elected under MMP in 2005 consisted of:

- Labour – 50 seats (31 electorate, 19 party list)
- National – 48 seats (31 electorate, 17 party list)
- New Zealand First – 7 seats (7 party list)
- Green – 6 seats (6 party list)
- Māori – 4 seats (4 electorate)
- United Future – 3 seats (1 electorate, 2 party list)
- ACT New Zealand – 2 seats (1 electorate, 1 party list)
- Progressive – 1 seat (1 electorate).

An overhang of one seat resulted from the Māori Party winning more seats from electorate votes than was representative of its share of all party votes.

Table 3.05 (overleaf) lists members of the 48th Parliament House of Representatives, the party they belong to, their previous occupation, and whether they are list or electorate members.

Table 3.05

House of Representatives, 48th Parliament

Prime Minister	Rt Hon Helen Clark
Leader of the Opposition	Dr Don Brash; John Key (from 27 November 2006)
Speaker	Hon Margaret Wilson
Deputy Speaker	Hon Clem Simich
Clerk of the House	D G McGee (until 1 November 2007); Mary Harris (since 10 December 2007)

Member[1]	Year of birth	Previous occupation	Electorate/list	Party
Anderton, Hon Jim	1938	Company director	Wigram	Progressive
Ardern, Shane	1960	Farmer	Taranaki-King Country	National
Auchinvole, Chris	1945	Manager	List	National
Barker, Hon Rick	1951	Trade unionist	List	Labour
Barnett, Tim	1958	Voluntary sector manager	Christchurch Central	Labour
Bennett, David	1970	Farmer	Hamilton East	National
Bennett, Paula	1969	Manager	List	National
Benson-Pope, Hon David	1950	Teacher	Dunedin South	Labour
Beyer, Georgina[2]	1957	Mayor	List	Labour
Blue, Dr Jackie	1956	Medical practitioner	List	National
Blumsky, Mark	1957	Mayor	List	National
Borrows, Chester	1957	Police officer, lawyer	Whanganui	National
Bradford, Sue	1952	Community development worker	List	Green
Brash, Dr Don[3]	1940	Governor of Reserve Bank of New Zealand	List	National
Brown, Peter	1939	Company director	List	NZ First
Brownlee, Gerry	1956	Teacher	Ilam	National
Burton, Hon Mark	1956	Community education organiser	Taupo	Labour
Carter, Hon Chris	1952	Electorate secretary	Te Atatū	Labour
Carter, Hon David	1952	Businessman, farmer	List	National
Carter, John	1950	Local government officer	Northland	National
Chadwick, Steve	1948	Nurse, midwife	Rotorua	Labour
Chauvel, Charles[4]	1969	Lawyer	List	Labour
Choudhary, Dr Ashraf	1949	University lecturer	List	Labour
Clark, Rt Hon Helen	1950	University lecturer	Mt Albert	Labour
Clarkson, Bob	1939	Commercial property developer	Tauranga	National
Coleman, Dr Jonathan	1966	Medical practitioner	Northcote	National
Collins, Judith	1959	Lawyer	Clevedon	National
Connell, Brian	1956	Farmer	Rakaia	National
Copeland, Gordon[5]	1943	Financial administrator	List	Independent
Cosgrove, Hon Clayton	1969	Public relations executive	Waimakariri	Labour
Cullen, Hon Dr Michael	1945	University lecturer	List	Labour
Cunliffe, Hon David	1963	Management consultant	New Lynn	Labour
Dalziel, Hon Lianne	1960	Trade unionist	Christchurch East	Labour
Dean, Jacqui	1957	Professional actor	Otago	National
Donald, Rod[6]	1960	Voluntary sector administrator	List	Green
Donnelly, Hon Brian[7]	1949	School principal	List	NZ First
Dunne, Hon Peter	1954	Deputy chief executive officer	Ōhariu-Belmont	United Future
Duynhoven, Hon Harry	1955	Teacher	New Plymouth	Labour
Dyson, Hon Ruth	1957	Employment consultant	Banks Peninsula	Labour
English, Hon Bill	1961	Farmer	Clutha-Southland	National
Fairbrother, Russell	1944	Lawyer	List	Labour
Fenton, Darien	1954	Trade unionist	List	Labour
Field, Taito Phillip[8]	1952	Trade unionist	Māngere	Labour
Finlayson, Christopher	1956	Lawyer	List	National
Fitzsimons, Jeanette	1945	Organic farmer, consultant	List	Green
Flavell, Te Ururoa	1955	Lecturer	Waiāriki	Māori
Foss, Craig	1963	Banker	Tukituki	National
Gallagher, Martin	1952	Teacher	Hamilton West	Labour
Goff, Hon Phil	1953	University lecturer	Mt Roskill	Labour
Goodhew, Jo	1961	Nurse	Aoraki	National
Gosche, Hon Mark	1955	Trade unionist	Maungakiekie	Labour
Goudie, Sandra	1952	Farmer	Coromandel	National
Groser, Tim	1949	Diplomat	List	National
Guy, Nathan	1970	Farmer	List	National
Harawira, Hone	1955	Manager	Te Tai Tokerau	Māori
Hartley, Ann[9]	1942	Real estate agent	List	Labour
Hawkins, Hon George	1946	Teacher	Manurewa	Labour
Hayes, John	1948	Diplomat	Wairarapa	National
Henare, Hon Tau	1960	Advisory officer	List	National
Hereora, Dave	1956	Trade unionist	List	Labour
Hide, Rodney	1956	Economic consultant	Epsom	ACT
Hobbs, Hon Marian	1947	Teacher	Wellington Central	Labour
Hodgson, Hon Pete	1950	Veterinarian	Dunedin North	Labour
Horomia, Hon Parekura	1950	Farmer	Ikaroa-Rāwhiti	Labour

Table 3.05 continued

House of Representatives, 48th Parliament

Member[1]	Year of birth	Previous occupation	Electorate/list	Party
Hughes, Darren	1978	Executive secretary	Ōtaki	Labour
Hutchison, Dr Paul	1947	Medical practitioner	Port Waikato	National
Jones, Dail[10]	1944	Lawyer	List	NZ First
Jones, Shane	1959	Manager	List	Labour
Kedgley, Sue	1948	Author, city councillor	List	Green
Key, John	1961	Investment banker	Helensville	National
King, Colin	1951	Shearer, manager	Kaikōura	National
King, Hon Annette	1947	Chief executive officer	Rongotai	Labour
Laban, Hon Winnie	1955	Family therapist	Mana	Labour
Locke, Keith	1944	Bookshop manager	List	Green
Mackey, Moana	1974	Biochemist	List	Labour
Maharey, Hon Steve	1953	University lecturer	Palmerston North	Labour
Mahuta, Hon Nanaia	1970	Archivist librarian	Tainui	Labour
Mallard, Hon Trevor	1954	Executive assistant	Hutt South	Labour
Mapp, Dr Wayne	1952	University law lecturer	North Shore	National
Mark, Ron	1954	Businessman, army officer	List	NZ First
McCully, Hon Murray	1953	Public relations consultant	East Coast Bays	National
Moroney, Sue	1964	Trade unionist	List	Labour
Norman, Russell[11]	1967	Executive secretary	List	Green
O'Connor, Hon Damien	1958	Tourism operator	West Coast-Tasman	Labour
Okeroa, Hon Mahara	1946	Regional director	Te Tai Tonga	Labour
Paraone, Pita	1945	Public servant	List	NZ First
Parker, Hon David	1960	Biotechnology businessman	List	Labour
Peachey, Allan	1949	Teacher	Tāmaki	National
Peters, Rt Hon Winston	1945	Lawyer	List	NZ First
Pettis, Jill	1952	Education administrator	List	Labour
Pillay, Lynne	1950	Trade unionist	Waitakere	Labour
Power, Simon	1969	Lawyer	Rangitīkei	National
Rich, Katherine	1967	Businesswoman	List	National
Ririnui, Hon Mita	1951	Minister of religion	List	Labour
Robertson, H V Ross	1949	Industrial engineer	Manukau East	Labour
Roy, Eric	1948	Farmer	Invercargill	National
Roy, Heather	1964	Gallery contractor	List	ACT
Ryall, Hon Tony	1964	Accountant	Bay of Plenty	National
Samuels, Hon Dover	1939	Company director	List	Labour
Shanks, Katrina[12]	1969	Accountant	List	National
Sharples, Dr Pita	1941	University lecturer	Tāmaki Makaurau	Māori
Simich, Hon Clem	1939	General manager	List	National
Sio, Su'a William[13]	1960	City councillor	List	Labour
Smith, Hon Dr Lockwood	1948	Managing director	Rodney	National
Smith, Hon Dr Nick	1964	Engineer	Nelson	National
Soper, Lesley[14]	1954	Trade unionist	List	Labour
Stewart, Barbara	1952	Training and development manager	List	NZ First
Street, Maryan	1955	Teacher, trade unionist	List	Labour
Sutton, Hon Jim[15]	1941	Farmer	List	Labour
Swain, Hon Paul	1951	Trade unionist	Rimutaka	Labour
Tanczos, Nandor[16]	1966	Business owner/director	List	Green
Te Heuheu, Hon Georgina	1942	Consultant, advocate Treaty issues	List	National
Tisch, Lindsay	1947	Management consultant	Piako	National
Tizard, Hon Judith	1956	Electorate secretary	Auckland Central	Labour
Tolley, Anne	1953	Bed and breakfast operator	East Coast	National
Tremain, Chris	1966	Businessman	Napier	National
Turei, Metiria	1970	Lawyer	List	Green
Turia, Tariana	1944	Iwi development worker	Te Tai Hauāuru	Māori
Turner, Judy	1956	Teacher	List	United Future
Wagner, Nicky	1953	Company director	List	National
Wall, Louisa[17]	1972	Programme manager	List	Labour
Wilkinson, Kate	1957	Lawyer	List	National
Williamson, Hon Maurice	1951	Planning analyst	Pakuranga	National
Wilson, Hon Margaret	1947	University lecturer	List	Labour
Wong, Pansy	1955	Accountant	List	National
Woolerton, R Doug	1944	Farmer	List	NZ First
Worth, Dr Richard	1948	Lawyer	List	National
Yates, Dianne[18]	1943	Education officer	List	Labour

(1) Names are given by which individual members prefer to be addressed. (2) Resigned 16 February 2007. (3) Resigned 6 February 2007. (4) Replaced Jim Sutton 1 August 2006. (5) Independent member from 16 May 2007. (6) Died 6 November 2005. (7) Resigned 14 February 2008. (8) Independent member from 14 February 2007. (9) Resigned 28 February 2008. (10) Replaced Brian Donnelly 16 February 2008. (11) Replaced Nandor Tanczos 1 July 2008. (12) Replaced Don Brash 8 February 2007. (13) Replaced Dianne Yates 1 April 2008. (14) Replaced Georgina Beyer 20 February 2007. (15) Resigned 30 July 2006. (16) Replaced Rod Donald 15 November 2005, resigned 26 June 2008. (17) Replaced Ann Hartley 1 March 2008. (18) Resigned 28 March 2008.

Source: Office of the Clerk of the House of Representatives

Legislative procedure The legislative procedure in New Zealand starts when proposed laws are presented to the House of Representatives in the form of draft laws known as 'bills'. The classes of bills are:

- Government bills – introduced by a minister and dealing with matters of public policy
- Members' bills – introduced by a Member of Parliament who is not a minister and dealing with matters of public policy
- Local bills – promoted by local authorities to give them special powers or to validate actions they may have taken, and which affect particular localities
- Private bills – promoted by individuals or bodies (such as companies or trusts) for their particular interest or benefit.

All types of bills follow a similar procedure in the house, with every bill being required to be 'read' three times. A local bill or a private bill must also comply with prescribed preliminary procedures, which include advertising the bill before it is introduced into the house. The number of members' bills that may be introduced and proceed at any one time to first reading is limited to four. These are chosen by ballot.

Under standing orders, the leader of the house informs the clerk of the house that the government intends to introduce a government bill. A member's bill or a local bill is introduced after notice has been given and announced to the house. A private bill is introduced by presenting a petition for the bill to the house. The bill is then set down for first reading on the third sitting day following.

Debate on the first reading is limited to 12 speeches of up to 10 minutes in the case of a government bill, while for a member's bill, private bill or local bill there may be two 10-minute speeches and eight five-minute speeches, with the member in charge having a five-minute right of reply.

After its first reading, a bill is referred to a select committee of the house for consideration, unless it is an appropriation bill, an imprest supply bill, or a bill that has been accorded urgency for its passing. The consideration of bills by a select committee provides an opportunity for the public and interested bodies to make submissions. Committees also scrutinise estimates, financial reviews and petitions. A committee must finally report to the house on a bill within six months of the bill being referred to it (unless the business committee extends that time). In its report recommending amendments to a bill, the committee must distinguish between those adopted unanimously by the committee and those adopted by a majority. After the select committee's report is presented, the bill is set down for a second reading on the third sitting day following.

The second reading of a bill is directed to the principles and objects of the bill. At the conclusion of debate, the house decides whether to accept the amendments that only a majority in the select committee recommended. (Unanimous recommendations are automatically accepted when a bill passes its second reading.) The house then votes on whether the bill should be read a second time.

The bill is set down for consideration in a committee of the whole house on the next sitting day (unless the business committee decides that the bill does not require consideration in committee). In committee, the bill is considered in detail, normally part by part. Once a bill has been fully considered by the committee, it is reported to the house with any amendments. The bill is then set down for third reading next sitting day.

Debate on the third reading is limited to 12 speeches of 10 minutes each. At the third reading stage, the bill is voted on for the final time. A bill that has been passed by the house is forwarded to the governor-general for the Royal Assent. The bill then becomes an Act of Parliament and part of the law of New Zealand.

Televising the house

On 28 June 2007, the House of Representatives adopted new rules relating to television coverage. This follows consideration of the matter by Parliament's Standing Orders Committee. In 2003 the committee had recommended that an in-house facility for televising in Parliament be developed.

On 17 July 2007, remote-controlled television cameras began to film all proceedings of the house – this amounts to approximately 17.5 hours in a sitting week. SKY television has been broadcasting the house's question time each sitting day, from footage provided by Television New Zealand (TVNZ). TVNZ and TV3 are allowed to continue using their own cameras for question time and debates.

With the advent of the in-house facility, proceedings can be viewed on an internal television system or through live streaming on the parliamentary website

– www.parliament.nz. On the first two days there were almost 6,500 visitors to the live broadcast page, peaking during question time. A broadcast-quality live feed of the images was made available to television broadcasters.

Television broadcasting rules were also reviewed. The rules had been in operation since 1990 (when permission was first given for television broadcasters to film) and were reiterated in September 2000. The committee considered that some relaxation of the rules on coverage would enable television to present a fuller experience of Parliament, to sustain interest, and to give a more accurate impression of how the house works.

The revised rules continue to require cameras to focus on the member who has the speaker's call until the member's speech is concluded, but the director may vary the camera angle to add interest to the coverage – for example, a wide angle shot of the debating chamber.

Reaction shots are now allowed, such as a member listening to the reply to a question, or of an interjector (if the member speaking engages with that interjector). The default shot is to be on the speaker or presiding officer, particularly in cases of disorder on the floor or interruptions from the public gallery.

Broadcasts or rebroadcasts are to comply with normal broadcasting standards. Reports that use extracts must be fair and accurate. Coverage of proceedings cannot be used for political advertising or election campaigns, for satire, ridicule or denigration, or for commercial sponsorship or advertising. A breach of these conditions may result in the privilege of filming proceedings being withdrawn, but a breach may now also be treated as a contempt.

Source: Office of the Clerk of the House of Representatives

The New Zealand Herald

Nelson City councillor, Mark Holmes, hands over a 40,000+ signature petition (to extend the hours of daylight saving) to United Future leader Peter Dunne. The petition was successful – daylight saving was extended three weeks by the New Zealand Daylight Time Order 2007.

Executive government

The executive functions of government in New Zealand are carried out by ministers of the Crown. All ministers are members of the Executive Council, and most ministers are members of Cabinet. By constitutional convention, ministers are responsible to the House of Representatives for their official actions, and are required by the Constitution Act 1986 to be a Member of Parliament (MP).

New Zealand's head of state, Queen Elizabeth II, has delegated her executive authority to the governor-general, who is her representative in New Zealand. The governor-general plays an important role in many of the formal procedures associated with government.

After a general election, a government is formed by the party or grouping of parties that has the confidence of the House of Representatives. The governor-general invites the leader to become prime minister and lead a government. On the advice of the prime minister, the governor-general appoints a number of MPs as members of the Executive Council and as ministers. Ministers are generally responsible for certain areas of government administration (portfolios).

Cabinet and the Executive Council

The Cabinet and the Executive Council have separate functions. The Executive Council is a formal body with formal functions, whereas Cabinet is an informal body with deliberative functions. All ministers are members of the Executive Council, but not all ministers are members of Cabinet.

The Cabinet is the highest decision-making body of government. It is the main vehicle by which major policy issues, legislative proposals, and government appointments are considered and decided on. It also coordinates the work of ministers.

The Cabinet has a system of committees that examine subjects in detail before they are considered by the full Cabinet.

Proceedings of Cabinet are informal and confidential, and decisions are usually made by consensus. Members of Cabinet accept collective responsibility for decisions. This convention ensures that decisions are usually supported publicly by all members of Cabinet.

Orders in council, made by the governor-general on the advice and with the consent of the Executive Council, are the main vehicles for law-making by the executive. In particular, authority to make statutory regulations is delegated by Parliament to the governor-general, in council.

The governor-general presides over, but is not a member of, the Executive Council. He or she takes formal actions, such as making regulations or significant appointments, on the basis of a recommendation tendered by a minister, and consented to by the Executive Council.

The Cabinet Office provides support services for the Cabinet and its committees. The secretary of the Cabinet is also clerk of the Executive Council.

The makeup of the Executive Council at 5 November 2007 is shown in table 3.07 (overleaf).

The Rt Hon Helen Clark

Office of the Prime Minister

The first woman to be elected Prime Minister of New Zealand, Helen Clark was born in Hamilton in 1950. She grew up on a Waikato farm and was educated at Epsom Girls' Grammar School (Auckland) and the University of Auckland. It was there, in 1971, that she joined the Labour Party. She graduated MA (Hons) in 1974. From 1973 to 1975, Clark was a junior lecturer in political studies at Auckland University, becoming a lecturer in 1977. After unsuccessfully contesting the Piako seat in 1975, she was elected Labour Member of Parliament for Mt Albert in 1981.

Clark convened the Government Caucus Committee on External Affairs and Security from 1984 to 1987 and was Minister of Conservation and Minister of Housing from 1987 to 1989. She became Minister of Health in January 1989 and Minister of Labour and deputy prime minister in August of that year. She chaired the Cabinet Social Equity Committee and served on seven other cabinet committees. Clark has also chaired two select committees – foreign affairs and defence, and disarmament and arms control.

Following the Labour Government's defeat in October 1990, Clark became deputy leader of the opposition. Three years later, on 1 December 1993, she succeeded Mike Moore as Labour's parliamentary leader and as leader of the opposition. When Labour formed a government after the second MMP election on 27 November 1999, Clark became prime minister. She is now also Minister for Arts, Culture and Heritage, and for the Security Intelligence Service. In 2005, she became the first Labour Prime Minister to win three elections.

She has had a long involvement with politics. As well as serving for many years on the Labour Party's executive, Clark has been president of the Labour Youth Council, an executive member of the party's Auckland-regional council, secretary of the Labour Women's Council and a member of the policy council. She has also represented the party at Socialist International congresses and conferences overseas.

In 1986, Clark was awarded the annual peace prize of the Danish Peace Foundation for her work in promoting international peace and disarmament. In 2008 she was named one of six 'champions of the Earth' by the United Nations Environmental Programme, for her efforts to address to the global impact of climate change.

She is married to Peter Davis and her leisure activities include reading, music and theatre, and hiking and cross-country skiing.

Source: Office of the Prime Minister

Table 3.06

Premiers and prime ministers of New Zealand

Premier/Prime minister[1]	Political party	Term(s) of office
Premiers		
Henry Sewell	...	7 May 1856–20 May 1856
William Fox	...	20 May 1856–2 Jun 1856
Edward William Stafford	...	2 Jun 1856–12 Jul 1861
William Fox	...	12 Jul 1861–6 Aug 1862
Alfred Domett	...	6 Aug 1862–30 Oct 1863
Frederick Whitaker, MLC	...	30 Oct 1863–24 Nov 1864
Frederick Aloysius Weld	...	24 Nov 1864–16 Oct 1865
Edward William Stafford	...	16 Oct 1865–28 Jun 1869
William Fox	...	28 Jun 1869–10 Sep 1872
Edward William Stafford	...	10 Sep 1872–11 Oct 1872
George Marsden Waterhouse, MLC	...	11 Oct 1872–3 Mar 1873
William Fox	...	3 Mar 1873–8 Apr 1873
Sir Julius Vogel, KCMG	...	8 Apr 1873–6 Jul 1875
Daniel Pollen, MLC	...	6 Jul 1875–15 Feb 1876
Sir Julius Vogel, KCMG	...	15 Feb 1876–1 Sep 1876
Sir Harry Albert Atkinson, KCMG	...	1 Sep 1876–13 Oct 1877
Sir George Grey, KCB	...	13 Oct 1877–8 Oct 1879
John Hall	...	8 Oct 1879–21 Apr 1882
Frederick Whitaker, MLC	...	21 Apr 1882–25 Sep 1883
Sir Harry Albert Atkinson, KCMG	...	25 Sep 1883–16 Aug 1884
Sir Robert Stout, KCMG	...	16 Aug 1884–28 Aug 1884
Sir Harry Albert Atkinson, KCMG	...	28 Aug 1884–3 Sep 1884
Sir Robert Stout, KCMG	...	3 Sep 1884–8 Oct 1887
Sir Harry Albert Atkinson, KCMG	...	8 Oct 1887–24 Jan 1891
John Ballance	Liberal	24 Jan 1891–d 27 Apr 1893
Rt Hon Richard John Seddon	Liberal	1 May 1893–d 10 Jun 1906
Prime ministers		
William Hall-Jones	Liberal	21 Jun 1906–6 Aug 1906
Rt Hon Sir Joseph George Ward, Bt, KCMG	Liberal	6 Aug 1906–28 Mar 1912
Thomas MacKenzie	Liberal	28 Mar 1912–10 Jul 1912
Rt Hon William Ferguson Massey	Reform	10 Jul 1912–10 May 1925
Sir Francis Henry Dillon Bell, GCMG, KC, MLC	Reform	14 May 1925–30 May 1925
Rt Hon Joseph Gordon Coates, MC	Reform	30 May 1925–10 Dec 1928
Rt Hon Sir Joseph George Ward, Bt, KCMG	United	10 Dec 1928–28 May 1930
Rt Hon George William Forbes	United	28 May 1930–22 Sep 1931
	Coalition	22 Sep 1931–6 Dec 1935
Rt Hon Michael Joseph Savage	Labour	6 Dec 1935–d 27 Mar 1940
Rt Hon Peter Fraser, CH	Labour	1 Apr 1940–13 Dec 1949
Rt Hon Sidney George Holland, CH	National	13 Dec 1949–20 Sep 1957
Rt Hon Sir Keith Jacka Holyoake, GCMG, CH	National	20 Sep 1957–12 Dec 1957
Rt Hon Walter Nash, CH	Labour	12 Dec 1957–12 Dec 1960
Rt Hon Sir Keith Jacka Holyoake, GCMG, CH	National	12 Dec 1960–7 Feb 1972
Rt Hon John Ross Marshall	National	7 Feb 1972–8 Dec 1972
Rt Hon Norman Eric Kirk	Labour	8 Dec 1973–d 31 Aug 1974
Rt Hon Wallace Edward Rowling	Labour	6 Sep 1974–12 Dec 1975
Rt Hon Sir Robert David Muldoon, GCMG, CH	National	12 Dec 1975–26 Jul 1984
Rt Hon David Russell Lange	Labour	26 Jul 1984–8 Aug 1989
Rt Hon Geoffrey Winston Russell Palmer	Labour	8 Aug 1989–4 Sep 1990
Rt Hon Michael Kenneth Moore	Labour	4 Sep 1990–2 Nov 1990
Rt Hon James Brendan Bolger	National	2 Nov 1990–12 Oct 1996
	Coalition	12 Oct 1996–8 Dec 1997
Rt Hon Jennifer Mary Shipley	Coalition	8 Dec 1997–10 Dec 1999
Rt Hon Helen Elizabeth Clark	Labour/Alliance	10 Dec 1999–15 Aug 2002
	Labour/Progressive	15 Aug 2002–19 Oct 2005
	Labour/Progressive	19 Oct 2005–

(1) Honours are specified only if held on retirement from office.

Symbol: ... not applicable

Source: Cabinet Office

Table 3.07

New Zealand Executive Council
At 5 November 2007

Governor-general
His Excellency the Honourable Anand Satyanand, PCNZM, QSO

Executive Council
The Executive Council comprises all ministers. The governor-general presides over meetings of the council, unless he or she is unavailable.

The Cabinet
1 Rt Hon Helen Clark, Prime Minister, Minister for Arts, Culture and Heritage, Minister responsible for Ministerial Services, Minister in Charge of the New Zealand Security Intelligence Service, Minister Responsible for the Government Communications Security Bureau.
2 Hon Dr Michael Cullen, Deputy Prime Minister, Minister of Finance, Attorney-General (includes responsibility for the Serious Fraud Office) Minister in Charge of Treaty of Waitangi Negotiations, Leader of the House.
3 Hon Jim Anderton, Minister of Agriculture, Minister for Biosecurity, Minister of Fisheries, Minister of Forestry, Minister Responsible for the Public Trust, Associate Minister of Health, Associate Minister for Tertiary Education.
4 Hon Phil Goff, Minister of Defence, Minister of Corrections, Minister of Trade, Minister for Disarmament and Arms Control, Associate Minister of Finance.
5 Hon Annette King, Minister of Justice, Minister of Police, Minister of Transport, Minister Responsible for the Law Commission.
6 Hon Pete Hodgson, Minister for Economic Development, Minister for Tertiary Education, Minister of Research, Science and Technology.
7 Hon Parekura Horomia, Minister of Māori Affairs, Associate Minister for Social Development and Employment, Associate Minister of Education, Associate Minister of State Services, Associate Minister of Fisheries.
8 Hon Chris Carter, Minister of Education, Minister Responsible for the Education Review Office, Minister for Ethnic Affairs.
9 Hon David Cunliffe, Minister of Health, Minister for Communications and Information Technology.
10 Hon Trevor Mallard, Minister for the Environment, Minister of Labour, Minister of Broadcasting, Minister for State Owned Enterprises, Associate Minister of Finance.
11 Hon Ruth Dyson, Minister for Social Development and Employment, Minister for Senior Citizens, Minister for the Community and Voluntary Sector, Minister for Disability Issues.
12 Hon Lianne Dalziel, Minister of Commerce, Minister for Food Safety, Associate Minister of Justice.
13 Hon David Parker, Minister of State Services, Minister of Energy, Minister for Land Information, Minister Responsible for Climate Change Issues.
14 Hon Nanaia Mahuta, Minister of Customs, Minister of Local Government, Minister of Youth Affairs, Associate Minister for the Environment, Associate Minister of Tourism.
15 Hon Clayton Cosgrove, Minister of Immigration, Minister for Sport and Recreation, Minister for Small Business, Minister for the Rugby World Cup, Associate Minister of Finance, Associate Minister of Justice.
16 Hon Rick Barker, Minister of Internal Affairs, Minister of Civil Defence, Minister for Courts, Minister of Veterans' Affairs, Associate Minister of Justice.
17 Hon Damien O'Connor, Minister of Tourism, Minister for Rural Affairs, Associate Minister of Health.
18 Hon Steve Chadwick, Minister of Conservation, Minister of Women's Affairs, Associate Minister of Health.
19 Hon Maryan Street, Minister for Accident Compensation Corporation, Minister of Housing, Associate Minister for Economic Development, Associate Minister for Tertiary Education.
20 Hon Shane Jones, Minister for Building and Construction, Associate Minister in Charge of Treaty of Waitangi Negotiations, Associate Minister of Immigration, Associate Minister of Trade.

Ministers outside Cabinet
21 Hon Judith Tizard, Minister of Consumer Affairs, Minister Responsible for Archives New Zealand, Minister Responsible for the National Library, Associate Minister for Arts, Culture and Heritage, Associate Minister of Commerce, Associate Minister of Transport.
22 Hon Harry Duynhoven, Minister for Transport Safety, Associate Minister of Energy.
23 Hon Mita Ririnui, Minister of State, Associate Minister of Corrections, Associate Minister in Charge of Treaty of Waitangi Negotiations, Associate Minister of Forestry, Associate Minister of Health.
24 Hon Luamanuvao Winnie Laban, Minister of Pacific Island Affairs, Associate Minister for Social Development and Employment, Associate Minister of Trade, Associate Minister for Economic Development.
25 Hon Mahara Okeroa, Minister of State, Associate Minister for Social Development and Employment, Associate Minister for Arts, Culture and Heritage, Associate Minister of Conservation.
26 Hon Darren Hughes, Minister of Statistics, Deputy Leader of the House, Associate Minister for Social Development and Employment.

Ministers outside Cabinet from other parties with confidence and supply agreements
Rt Hon Winston Peters, Minister of Foreign Affairs, Minister for Racing, Associate Minister for Senior Citizens.
Hon Peter Dunne, Minister of Revenue, Associate Minister of Health.

Source: Cabinet Office

World Environment Day

On 5 June 2008, New Zealand hosted World Environment Day, in partnership with the United Nations Environment Programme (UNEP).

The theme for World Environment Day 2008 was Kick the Carbon Habit – with a focus on moving towards a low-carbon economy and lifestyle. The Ministry for the Environment was the lead government agency coordinating the event for the New Zealand Government, alongside UNEP.

This was the first time New Zealand has hosted the internationally celebrated event since it was established in 1972. World Environment Day is observed annually in more than 100 countries, and is one of the most popular days on the United Nations calendar.

The ministry's annual Green Ribbon Awards marked the start of the celebrations two days before World Environment Day. The 2008 award categories reflected the areas in which New Zealanders contribute to reducing the impact of climate change.

Other events marking the celebration were:

- a symposium on leadership in climate change solutions
- an Auckland business and science leaders' breakfast, discussing the challenges and opportunities presented to business by climate change
- the Art for the Environment Exhibition at the Museum of New Zealand (Te Papa) with works from renowned international artists
- an exhibition at Wellington's Waitangi Park from the UNEP's international photographic competition on the environment
- an international children's painting exhibition at Te Papa.

Source: Ministry for the Environment

The New Zealand Herald

Shortland Street actor, Adam Rickitt, encourages Auckland University students to enrol to vote. Eligible voters must be listed on the electoral roll to be allowed to vote in a general or local body election.

Parliamentary elections

People 18 years and over have the right to vote in New Zealand's parliamentary elections. Enrolment as an elector is compulsory, but voting is not. To qualify for enrolment a person must:

- be at least 18 years old
- be a New Zealand citizen or permanent resident
- have lived continuously in New Zealand for at least a year at some time
- have lived continuously for one month or more in the electorate in which they want to enrol.

Māori and people of Māori descent may choose to enrol for either a Māori, or a general electorate, but may make the choice at certain times only. Māori may make the choice the first time they enrol, or at the five-yearly Māori electoral option exercise. The most recent Māori electoral option was in 2006.

Electoral rolls are maintained by the Electoral Enrolment Centre, a division of New Zealand Post.

The Chief Electoral Office, a division of the Ministry of Justice, is responsible for conducting parliamentary elections and referendums. Returning officers are responsible for arranging voting facilities and staff, and conducting elections in their electorates. In an election year, a returning officer is appointed for each electorate.

Only people enrolled before an election are qualified to vote. Voting is by secret ballot. Most electors cast their vote at a polling place in their electorate on polling day, but they may cast a special vote at a polling place outside their electorate if necessary.

Electors can also cast their vote at an advance-voting place or by post if they are unable to attend a polling place on election day due to illness, or if they will be travelling outside their electorate, or because of their religious beliefs.

Voters overseas can cast their vote by downloading their voting papers from the Internet and faxing or posting them back to New Zealand.

A preliminary count of ordinary votes is available for each electorate on election night, and final results are normally available a fortnight later, once special and overseas votes have been counted. Voting patterns in recent general elections are shown in table 3.08.

There were 2,847,396 electors on the master roll for the 2005 general election. A total of 2,304,005 votes were cast, representing a turnout of 80.92 percent. This was an increase on the 2002 election, where turnout was 76.98 percent. The highest turnout in recent elections was 93.71 percent in 1984. Figure 3.01 shows the percentage of enrolled voters voting in general elections.

Electoral boundaries

The boundaries of electorates are revised every five years, based on electoral population figures from the Census of Population and Dwellings. The new boundaries come into effect at the end of the parliamentary term during which the revision is finalised.

Table 3.08

Voting patterns 1981–2005

Year	Vote type	Electors on master roll	Valid votes	Informal votes[1]	Special votes disallowed[2]	Percentage of electors who voted
1981	...	2,034,747	1,801,303	8,998	50,263	91.4
1984	...	2,111,651	1,929,201	7,565	42,032	93.7
1987	...	2,114,656	1,831,777	11,184	40,433	89.1
1990	...	2,202,157	1,824,092	10,180	42,843	85.2
1993	...	2,321,664	1,922,796	11,364	43,932	85.2
1996	party	2,418,587	2,072,359	8,183	54,633	88.3
	electorate	...	2,061,746	18,796	..	..
1999	party	2,509,365	2,065,494	19,887	41,884	84.8
	electorate	...	2,047,473	37,908	..	..
2002	party	2,670,030	2,031,617	8,631	15,156	77.0
	electorate	...	1,995,586	26,529	33,289	..
2005	party	2,847,396	2,275,629	10,561	17,815	80.9
	electorate	...	2,235,869	24,801	43,335	..

(1) A vote that doesn't clearly indicate the voter's intention. (2) Because they voted in the wrong electorate, 18,133 voters in 2002 and 25,520 voters in 2005 had their electorate votes disallowed, but their party vote allowed.

Symbols: .. figure not available ... not applicable

Source: Chief Electoral Office

Figure 3.01

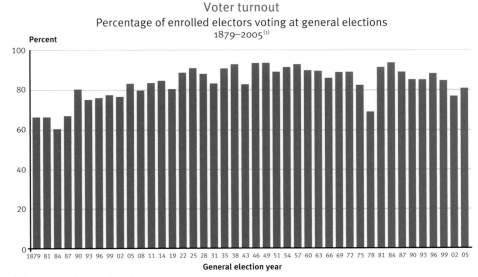

Voter turnout
Percentage of enrolled electors voting at general elections
1879–2005[1]

(1) Excludes Māori population before 1951.

Source: Chief Electoral Office

Electoral boundaries are defined by the Representation Commission, which consists of a chairperson, four officials (the surveyor-general, the government statistician, the chief electoral officer, and the chairman of the local government commission) and two members nominated by Parliament to represent the government and the opposition.

When determining boundaries for Māori electoral districts, the commission is joined by the chief executive officer of Te Puni Kōkiri, and two Māori representatives nominated by Parliament to represent the government and the opposition. After proposed boundaries have been drawn up and published, objections and counter-objections are considered by the commission, which then makes a decision on final boundaries.

Under the Electoral Act 1993, the South Island is allocated 16 general electorates. The number of general electorates for the North Island and the number of Māori electorates are then calculated so that their electoral populations are approximately the same as those for South Island general electorates.

The commission is required to consider community relationships, communication facilities, topographical features, and any projected variation in the general electoral population of the electorates when determining boundaries.

Based on the South Island population, the South Island general electorate quota for the 2008 general election was 57,562, resulting in 47 North Island general electorates (quota 57,243), and seven Māori electorates (quota 59,583).

Figure 3.02

Māori electoral districts as defined by the Representation Commission
September 2007

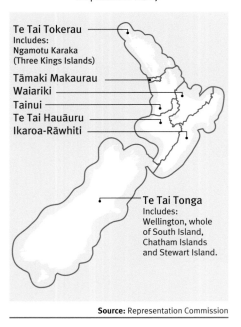

Te Tai Tokerau
Includes:
Ngamotu Karaka
(Three Kings Islands)

Tāmaki Makaurau
Waiariki
Tainui
Te Tai Hauāuru
Ikaroa-Rāwhiti

Te Tai Tonga
Includes:
Wellington, whole
of South Island,
Chatham Islands
and Stewart Island.

Source: Representation Commission

All electorates are allowed 5 percent above or below their electoral population quota. Figures 3.02, and 3.03 show Māori and general electoral districts for the 2008 general election.

Figure 3.03

General electoral districts as defined by the Representation Commission
September 2007

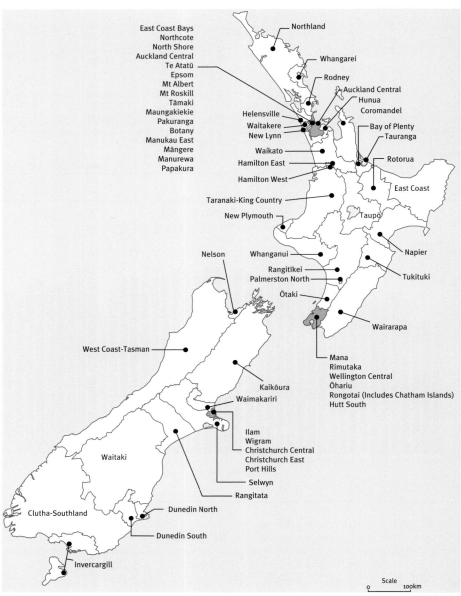

East Coast Bays
Northcote
North Shore
Auckland Central
Te Atatū
Epsom
Mt Albert
Mt Roskill
Tāmaki
Maungakiekie
Pakuranga
Botany
Manukau East
Māngere
Manurewa
Papakura

Northland
Whangarei
Rodney
Auckland Central
Hunua
Coromandel
Helensville
Waitakere
New Lynn
Bay of Plenty
Tauranga
Waikato
Rotorua
Hamilton East
Hamilton West
East Coast
Taranaki-King Country
Taupō
New Plymouth
Nelson
Whanganui
Napier
Rangitīkei
Palmerston North
Tukituki
Ōtaki
Wairarapa
West Coast-Tasman
Mana
Rimutaka
Wellington Central
Ōhariu
Rongotai (Includes Chatham Islands)
Hutt South
Kaikōura
Waimakariri
Ilam
Wigram
Christchurch Central
Christchurch East
Port Hills
Selwyn
Rangitata
Waitaki
Dunedin North
Clutha-Southland
Dunedin South
Invercargill

Scale
0   100km

Source: Representation Commission

State sector

State sector is the common term for all organisations whose financial situation and performance is reported in the annual financial statements of the government.

The state sector includes all state services – Crown-owned or Crown-controlled agencies – through which executive government carries out many of its roles and functions.

State services includes: all public service departments; other departments not part of the public service; Crown entities (except tertiary education institutions); organisations listed in schedule 4 of the Public Finance Act 1989; and the Reserve Bank of New Zealand.

In addition to state services, the state sector includes tertiary education institutions, offices of parliament, state-owned enterprises, and some departments that are not part of the state services.

Ministry of Justice

Courts Minister, Rick Barker, with 40 reams of paper – the quantity saved every week by Police and councils now filing infringement notices electronically.

State services

Public-service departments are those departments listed in schedule 1 of the State Sector Act 1988. At 31 October 2007, there were 35 public-service departments (these are called 'departments' in terms of the Act, irrespective of their individual label of department, ministry or any other title):

- Archives New Zealand – www.archives.govt.nz
- Crown Law Office – www.crownlaw.govt.nz
- Department of Building and Housing – www.dbh.govt.nz
- Department of Conservation – www.doc.govt.nz
- Department of Corrections – www.corrections.govt.nz
- Department of Internal Affairs – www.dia.govt.nz
- Department of Labour – www.dol.govt.nz
- Department of the Prime Minister and Cabinet – www.dpmc.govt.nz
- Education Review Office – www.ero.govt.nz
- Government Communications Security Bureau – www.gcsb.govt.nz
- Inland Revenue Department – www.ird.govt.nz
- Land Information New Zealand – www.linz.govt.nz
- Ministry for Culture and Heritage – www.mch.govt.nz
- Ministry for the Environment – www.mfe.govt.nz
- Ministry of Agriculture and Forestry – www.maf.govt.nz
- Ministry of Defence – www.defence.govt.nz
- Ministry of Economic Development – www.med.govt.nz
- Ministry of Education – www.minedu.govt.nz
- Ministry of Fisheries – www.fish.govt.nz
- Ministry of Foreign Affairs and Trade – www.mfat.govt.nz
- Ministry of Health – www.moh.govt.nz
- Ministry of Justice – www.justice.govt.nz
- Ministry of Māori Development – www.tpk.govt.nz
- Ministry of Pacific Island Affairs – www.minpac.govt.nz
- Ministry of Research, Science and Technology – www.morst.govt.nz
- Ministry of Social Development – www.msd.govt.nz
- Ministry of Transport – www.transport.govt.nz
- Ministry of Women's Affairs – www.mwa.govt.nz
- National Library of New Zealand – www.natlib.govt.nz
- New Zealand Customs Service – www.customs.govt.nz
- New Zealand Food Safety Authority – www.nzfsa.govt.nz
- Serious Fraud Office – www.sfo.govt.nz

Environmental programme for state sector

Govt[3] is a programme led by the Ministry for the Environment to encourage government agencies to become more sustainable, and deal with climate change.

Fifty-four agencies have signed up to the Govt[3] programme, including all core government agencies. Govt[3] is about adopting sustainable ways of working, and sharing practical action between agencies in the public and private sectors.

Through the Govt[3] programme, and other initiatives, agencies are:

- reducing their greenhouse gas emissions
- reducing their resource use, including kilometres travelled
- buying sustainable products
- improving energy efficiency in their buildings, transport options, office consumables, and equipment
- reducing their waste, and recycling more.

The government spends about $20 billion a year, and is responsible for over 30 percent of the buildings in New Zealand. It also has an impact on the environment – for example, through its large workforce, owned and leased buildings, IT needs, paper use, and vehicle fleet. The Govt[3] programme provides practical and measurable ways that government can influence sustainable choices.

Source: Ministry for the Environment

- State Services Commission – www.ssc.govt.nz
- Statistics New Zealand – www.stats.govt.nz
- The Treasury – www.treasury.govt.nz

At 30 June 2007, the number of full-time-equivalent staff employed in public-service departments was 42,047, compared with 38,032 at 30 June 2005, and 33,118 at 30 June 2003. When reform of the state sector began in the 1980s, about 70,000 people were permanent employees in government departments. Many of these have shifted to Crown entities, state-owned enterprises or the private sector. The public service today is characterised by relatively small departments, which have defined roles in policy advice, service delivery, regulatory or funding functions. Some bigger departments perform a combination of roles.

Non-public-service departments are agencies which are departments in terms of the Public Finance Act 1989, but are not listed in schedule 1 of the State Sector Act 1988. Consequently they are not part of the public service. At 31 October 2007, there were four such departments:

- New Zealand Defence Force – www.nzdf.mil.nz
- New Zealand Police – www.police.govt.nz
- New Zealand Security Intelligence Service – www.nzsis.govt.nz
- Parliamentary Counsel Office – www.pco.parliament.govt.nz.

Crown entities are organisations included in one of the five categories defined in section 7 of the Crown Entities Act 2004: Statutory entities (further subdivided into Crown agents, autonomous Crown entities, and independent Crown entities), Crown entity companies, Crown entity subsidiaries, and school boards of trustees. The fifth category is tertiary education institutions, which are Crown entities but are not included in the state services.

Crown entities make up a significant part of the state services and include a wide variety of corporations, Crown companies, and subsidiaries. The Crown Entities Act 2004 provides for the establishment and accountability of Crown entities, their operations, and reporting and financial obligations. At 31 October 2007, Crown entities in the state services included:

- 83 statutory entities – 46 Crown agents, 21 district health boards, 22 autonomous Crown entities, and 15 independent Crown entities
- 12 Crown entity companies, including nine Crown research institutes
- approximately 200 Crown entity subsidiaries
- approximately 2,465 school boards of trustees.

Organisations listed in schedule 4 of the Public Finance Act 1989 are those agencies included in the state services for which the full governance, accountability and reporting obligations of the Crown Entities Act 2004 would not be suitable. They include reserves boards, fish and game councils, and a small number of trusts and other organisations.

Reserve Bank of New Zealand is a stand-alone organisation included in the state services. It does not come under any other specific category or type of organisation within the state services.

Other state sector organisations

Non-state-service departments Two departments are considered to be outside the state services because their roles are supportive of the legislative branch of government, rather than of executive government. They are part of the state sector as departments under the Public Finance Act 1989:

- Office of the Clerk of the House of Representatives – www.clerk.parliament.govt.nz
- Parliamentary Service – www.ps.parliament.govt.nz.

Offices of Parliament The Office of the Ombudsmen, the Office of the Controller and Auditor-General, and the Office of the Parliamentary Commissioner for the Environment are not part of the executive branch of government, as their primary function is to provide a check on executive use of power and resources.

Tertiary education institutions These institutions are one of the five categories of Crown entities defined in the Crown Entities Act 2004, but are explicitly excluded from the definition of state services in the State Sector Act 1988. At 30 October 2007, there were 31 tertiary education institutions: eight universities, 20 polytechnics/institutes of technology, and three wānanga (Māori tertiary institutions).

State-owned enterprises (SOE) These are companies listed in schedule 1 of the State-Owned Enterprises Act 1986, that operate on commercial lines and are companies under the Companies Act 1993. Their objective is to be as profitable and as efficient as a comparable business not owned by the Crown, and to be socially responsible. The government may purchase services from SOEs, but generally will do so on the same basis as other purchasers. The government's interest in SOEs is substantially in their ownership. The government's interest in SOEs is supported by the Crown Company Monitoring Advisory Unit, a unit attached to the Treasury. At 31 October 2007, there were 17 state-owned enterprises:

- Airways Corporation of New Zealand Ltd – www.airways.co.nz
- Animal Control Products Ltd – www.pestoff.co.nz

- AsureQuality Ltd − www.asurequality.co.nz
- Electricity Corporation of New Zealand Ltd
- Genesis Power Ltd − www.genesisenergy.co.nz
- Kordia Group Ltd − www.kordiasolutions.com
- Landcorp Farming Ltd − www.landcorp.co.nz
- Learning Media Ltd − www.learningmedia.co.nz
- Meridian Energy Ltd − www.meridianenergy.co.nz
- Meteorological Service of New Zealand Ltd − www.metservice.com
- Mighty River Power Ltd − www.mightyriverpower.co.nz
- New Zealand Post Ltd − www.nzpost.co.nz
- New Zealand Railways Corporation − www.nzrailcorp.co.nz
- Quotable Value Ltd − www.qv.co.nz
- Solid Energy New Zealand Ltd − www.coalnz.com
- Timberlands West Coast Ltd − www.timberlands.co.nz
- Transpower New Zealand Ltd − www.transpower.co.nz

Air New Zealand Limited (www.airnewzealand.co.nz) is also included in the annual financial statements of the government, for disclosure purposes, as if it were a state-owned enterprise.

State services commissioner

The state services commissioner is central to New Zealand's politically neutral public service. The commissioner is appointed by the governor-general on the recommendation of the prime minister.

The commissioner has two separate roles. As holder of a statutory office, the commissioner acts independently in a range of matters concerning the operation of the public service, state services and the wider state sector. As chief executive of the State Services Commission, the commissioner is also responsible to the Minister of State Services for the commission's functions and duties, capability, and performance.

The office of state services commissioner follows on from the Public Service Commission, which was established in 1912 to employ all public servants, and to protect the public service from political interference, preserving its political neutrality. The commissioner no longer employs all public servants, but still employs the chief executives of public service departments, and so continues to act as a buffer between ministers and the public service. The commissioner also undertakes a variety of functions relating to departmental performance. These include:

- promoting and developing policies and standards for personnel administration and equal employment opportunities in the public service
- promoting and developing senior leadership and management capability in the public service
- providing advice on management systems, structures and organisations within the public service and Crown entities
- setting minimum standards of integrity and conduct for the public service, most Crown entities, and some other agencies
- advising the government on the structure of the state sector, including the allocation of functions among agencies.

The State Services Commission, with the support of other central agencies and the government, launched development goals for New Zealand's state services in March 2005. The goals were developed following new state sector legislation, and they focus on performance and quality within the state services as a whole. The commission is responsible for driving the goals' work programmes following on from the goals.

Crown Company Monitoring Advisory Unit

The Crown Company Monitoring Advisory Unit (CCMAU) was formed in 1993 to provide commercially-oriented advice on the Crown's ownership-interest in limited liability companies.

CCMAU advises and supports the Minister for State Owned Enterprises and the Minister for Crown Research Institutes. Other ministers also receive advice from CCMAU regarding the Crown's ownership interest in Crown entities such as Television New Zealand Ltd, Radio New Zealand Ltd, Animal Control Products Ltd, and three airport companies. Advice to the Minister of Finance is provided by the Treasury directly, while the Treasury and CCMAU also prepare joint reports for ministers.

One of CCMAU's primary functions is to provide advice on corporate intent targets and to monitor the performance of Crown companies against those targets. Other functions include providing advice on company restructuring, expansion, diversification and divestment plans; managing ownership issues; and identifying prospective directors and promoting best corporate governance practice of Crown companies. CCMAU, while independent for advice purposes, is attached to the Treasury for administrative purposes.

Controller and auditor-general

The controller and auditor-general (the auditor-general) is an officer of Parliament, appointed by the governor-general under the Public Audit Act 2001. The position is independent of the executive government and only the governor-general, on advice from the House of Representatives, can end the auditor-general's tenure.

The constitutionally important 'controller' function, as set out in the Public Finance Act 1989, provides independent assurance to Parliament that the expenses and capital expenditure of government departments and offices of Parliament have been incurred for lawful purposes, and are within the scope, amount, and period of the appropriations or other authority granted by Parliament.

The auditor-general audits the financial statements of government departments, local authorities, and most government-controlled corporations, boards and companies, and plays a key part in ensuring adequate accountability by these public entities.

The auditor-general also conducts performance audits to assess whether public entities are carrying out their activities effectively and efficiently, and are complying with their statutory obligations. If shortcomings are discovered during an audit, the principal recourse of the auditor-general is to report to the management of the entity, to a minister, or to Parliament and its select committees.

Official information

The Official Information Act 1982 requires the government to release official information when asked, whether or not that information is damaging to the government. Some information is exempted under the provisions of the Act.

The Act is based on the principle that information should be made available unless there is good reason for withholding it. The purpose of the Act is to:

- increase the availability of official information
- ensure corporations can access official information relating to themselves (access by individuals to their information is now governed by the Privacy Act 1993)
- protect official information when it is in the public interest and preserve individual privacy.

With the exception of the Parliamentary Counsel Service, the Official Information Act 1982 covers all government departments, state-owned enterprises, and a range of statutory bodies. It does not include courts, tribunals (in relation to their judicial function), or some judicial bodies. All local authorities and statutory boards are covered under either the Official Information Act 1982 or the Local Government Official Information and Meetings Act 1987.

Criteria to be considered when deciding whether information should be withheld include:

- the security, defence or economic international relations of New Zealand
- the maintenance of law and order
- the effective conduct of public affairs
- trade secrets and commercial sensitivity
- personal privacy and the safety of any person.

Protection of personal privacy may be overturned if it is in the public interest to make the information available.

New Zealand parliamentary ombudsmen are able to investigate and review decisions made about a request for official information. If the request has been unreasonably refused, an ombudsman can order that the information be released.

Ombudsmen

The New Zealand parliamentary ombudsmen are impartial and independent authorities that review government. Parliament has implemented initiatives to strengthen and protect the independence of ombudsmen and to help the ombudsmen to gain credibility with the public. These initiatives are:

- ombudsmen have the special status of 'officer of Parliament'
- ombudsmen are appointed by the governor-general, on the recommendation of the House of Representatives, not by the government
- ombudsmen and their staff are not public servants
- ombudsmen may report directly to Parliament
- a special multi-party committee of Parliament (Officers of Parliament Committee) that considers and recommends, directly to Parliament, the names of prospective ombudsman appointees, and the financial requirements of the ombudsmen's office.

Ombudsmen investigate and form opinions on complaints about an act, omission, decision or recommendation – relating to a matter of administration – by any central, regional or local government department or organisation. An ombudsman may also initiate an investigation.

A committee of the House of Representatives can refer a petition to an ombudsman to investigate and report on. The prime minister can, with the consent of the chief ombudsman, refer any matter (other than a matter concerning a judicial proceeding) to an ombudsman for investigation and report.

Ombudsmen provide information and guidance on the application of the Protected Disclosures Act 2000 to an employee who has made, or is considering making, a protected disclosure.

On 21 June 2007 the ombudsmen became responsible for examining and monitoring the conditions and treatment of people detained in prisons, in health and disability places of detention, in youth justice residences, and those detained under the Immigration Act 1987.

Table 3.09 shows the results of complaints to the ombudsmen.

Table 3.09

Complaints to the ombudsmen
By outcome
Year ending 30 June 2007

Outcome	Ombudsmen Act 1975	Official Information Act 1982	Local Government Official Information and Meetings Act 1987
Declined , no jurisdiction	84	5	0
Declined under ombudsman's discretion	267	58	17
Discontinued, inquiry not warranted	269	49	23
Resolved in course of investigation	249	180	70
Sustained, recommendation made	5	5	1
Sustained, no recommendation made	25	10	2
Not sustained	160	171	14
Formal investigation not undertaken, but explanation, advice or assistance given	6,226	294	69
Complaints transferred to			
Privacy Commissioner	11	27	7
Health and Disability Commissioner	4	0	0
Police Complaints Authority	0	1	0
Administration closed	2	1	0
Still under investigation at 30 June	536	289	59
Total	**7,754**	**1,090**	**262**
Total 2006	8,293	754	172

Source: Office of the Ombudsmen

Privacy commissioner

The Office of the Privacy Commissioner Te Mana Matapono Matatapu is independent of the executive and of Parliament. One of the main purposes of the office is to promote and protect individual privacy.

The Privacy Act 1993 establishes 12 information privacy principles and four public-register privacy principles. The principles apply to both the public and private sectors, but do not overrule other laws governing the use of personal information.

Information privacy principles cover the collecting, securing, using and disclosing of personal information; access to and correction of personal information; and assigning and using unique identifiers. Public-register privacy principles place some controls on the availability of public register information and its subsequent use.

The privacy commissioner observes, and reports on, issues that affect the way personal information is handled. The commissioner examines new legislation, and appears before parliamentary select committees that are considering new bills.

The privacy commissioner has the power to issue codes of practice that modify privacy principles. These codes replace the principles in particular contexts. Two major industry codes issued by the commissioner are the Health Information Privacy Code 1994, and the Credit Reporting Privacy Code 2004.

The commissioner oversees the operation of public sector information-matching programmes that government agencies use to compare databases of personal records (to establish, for example, entitlement to services, or instances of benefit fraud). The Act requires that an affected individual be given notice before adverse action is taken as a result of a match.

The Office of the Privacy Commissioner investigates complaints about breaches of privacy. If a complaint cannot be settled, or parties reconciled, using low-level dispute resolution, the commissioner may refer it to the Director of Human Rights Proceedings, who may bring proceedings before the Human Rights Review Tribunal. In the year ending 30 June 2007, the privacy commissioner referred 15 complaints to the Director of Human Rights Proceedings. Alternatively, aggrieved people may bring proceedings before the tribunal on their own behalf. The tribunal has the power to award remedies, including declarations, orders, damages and costs.

The Official Information Act 1982 and the Local Government Official Information and Meetings Act 1987 require the ombudsmen to consult with the commissioner on official information access requests where privacy is a possible ground for withholding information. In the year ending 30 June 2007, 25 formal consultations under the two acts were completed. Table 3.10 (overleaf) details complaints made to the privacy commissioner in recent years.

The New Zealand Herald

Former All Blacks captain Tana Umaga receiving the insignia of a Companion of the Queen's Service Order in 2006.

Table 3.10

Complaints to the privacy commissioner					
Year ending 30 June					
	2003	2004	2005	2006	2007
New complaints received	928	934	721	636	640
Complaints current at start of year	1,039	1,052	818	569	455
Number of complaints under process	1,967	1,986	1,539	1,205	1,095
Number of complaints closed during year	915	1,168	970	752	701
No jurisdiction	23	56	40	26	15
Complaints resolved without final opinion	747	848	683	500	524
Final opinion	145	264	247	220	140

Source: Office of the Privacy Commissioner

The New Zealand Royal Honours system

The New Zealand honours system recognises achievements, and services to New Zealand.

The Honours Secretariat, part of the Cabinet Office, administers the New Zealand Royal Honours System. Honours lists are issued at the new year, on the observance of the Queen's birthday and in special lists. Approximately 350 honours are available each year, although fewer may be recommended.

The Order of New Zealand is New Zealand's highest honour. It was instituted in 1987, to recognise outstanding civil or military service to the Crown and people of New Zealand.

Ordinary membership is limited to 20 living people. Members may use the letters ONZ after their name. The order does not confer a title.

The New Zealand Order of Merit recognises those who have performed exemplary service to the Crown and nation, in any field; or have become distinguished by their prominence, talents, contributions or other merits. The five levels of the order are, principal companions (PCNZM), distinguished companions (DCNZM), companions (CNZM), officers (ONZM), members (MNZM).

In 2000, the Queen approved the discontinuation of titles (knights and damehoods) within the order. The New Zealand Order of Merit replaced the various British state orders of chivalry (eg the orders of the Bath, St Michael and St George, British Empire, the Companion of Honour, and the honour of knighthood).

The Queen's Service Order recognises voluntary service to the community, and service through elected or appointed office. It ranks as a fourth-level order and has no title. Those appointed to the order are styled 'companions' and may use the letters QSO after their name. The ordinary membership is limited to 30 appointments a year.

In 2007 the Queen approved changes to the order, including the removal of the subdivisions ('for community service') and ('for public services'), and for the governor-general to be appointed to the order in his or her own right.

Associated with the order is the Queen's Service Medal, which ranks as a sixth-level award. The medal is also for those who have given voluntary service to the community, and service through elected or appointed office. Those awarded the medal may use the letters QSM after their name.

The New Zealand Gallantry Awards were instituted in 1999 to recognise military and support personnel who perform acts of gallantry while involved in war and operational service (including peacekeeping). There are four levels of gallantry awards: Victoria Cross for New Zealand (VC), New Zealand Gallantry Star (NZGS), New Zealand Gallantry Decoration (NZGD), and the New Zealand Gallantry Medal (NZGM).

The New Zealand Bravery Awards were instituted in 1999 to recognise the actions of people who save or attempt to save the life of another person, in the course of which they place their own safety or life at risk. There are four levels of bravery awards: New Zealand Cross (NZC), New Zealand Bravery Star (NZBS), New Zealand Bravery Decoration (NZBD), and the New Zealand Bravery Medal (NZBM).

The New Zealand Antarctic Medal was instituted as a New Zealand Royal Honour in 2006 and may be awarded to individuals, or members of a New Zealand programme in the Antarctic region, who make an outstanding contribution to exploration, scientific research, conservation, environmental protection, or knowledge of the Antarctic region; or support New Zealand's objectives or operations in the Antarctic region. Those awarded the medal may use the letters NZAM after their names.

The New Zealand Distinguished Service Decoration was instituted as a New Zealand Royal Honour in 2007 to recognise distinguished military service by regular, territorial and reserve members of the New Zealand Defence Force. Those awarded the decoration may use the letters DSD after their names.

Source: Honours Secretariat

Bill of rights

The New Zealand Bill of Rights Act 1990 is intended to provide minimum standards to which public decision making must conform. It emphasises New Zealand's formal commitment to fundamental civil and political rights, and affirms New Zealand's obligations under the International Convention on Civil and Political Rights.

The Act is designed to protect individuals and corporations from the actions of the State. It specifically applies to any acts by the legislative, executive and judicial branches of government; or by a person or body performing a public function, power or duty.

The attorney-general is required to notify the House of Representatives about any provision in any bill introduced into the house that appears to be inconsistent with the Act. The Ministry of Justice advises departments on the consistency of policy proposals and government bills with New Zealand's human rights laws, and advises the attorney-general on a bill's consistency with the Act. The Crown Law Office is responsible for providing advice to the attorney-general on bills from the Ministry of Justice.

An individual or legal body can go to court if they believe the Act has been breached. The Act has no remedy provision, but under common law the courts have provided remedies for infringement of the rights and freedoms identified in the Act.

The Human Rights Act 1993 provides for a publicly-funded complaints process in respect of breaches of the right to be free from discrimination section of the New Zealand Bill of Rights Act 1990. Individuals can lodge a complaint with the United Nations Human Rights Committee if the domestic options for a human rights complaint have been exhausted.

Human rights

The Human Rights Act 1993 makes it unlawful to discriminate in: employment; access to places, vehicles and facilities; provision of goods and services; provision of land, housing and other accommodation; and access to education.

Other forms of discrimination made unlawful by the Act include racial disharmony, racial harassment, sexual harassment, and victimisation. Both the public and private sectors are subject to the Act. There are 13 prohibited grounds of discrimination – sex, marital status, religious belief, ethical belief, colour, race, ethnic or national origin, disability, age, political opinion, employment status, family status, and sexual orientation. The Act also defines a number of circumstances where discrimination is not unlawful.

The Human Rights Commission, which from 2002 has included the former Office of the Race Relations Conciliator, is an independent Crown entity. Its primary functions are to:

- promote respect for, and an understanding and appreciation of, human rights
- encourage harmonious relations between individuals and among the diverse groups in New Zealand society
- mediate disputes relating to unlawful discrimination.

The commission has developed a national plan of action for human rights. The commission also promotes a better understanding of the human rights aspects of the Treaty of Waitangi, and their relationship with domestic and international human rights law.

The Tuhoe hikoi (walk) arrives at Parliament to protest against the Police raids carried out on 15 October 2007 under anti-terror legislation.

Human rights complaints about government activities that are taken to the commission – other than employment, and sexual and racial harassment – are tested against the anti-discrimination standard set out in the Act. This provides that government or public sector activities that discriminate will be exempt if they are reasonable, lawful, and demonstrably justifiable in a free and democratic society.

Complaints of discrimination about government activities may also be taken to court under the New Zealand Bill of Rights Act 1990.

The commission acts as a first contact for those who wish to make a discrimination complaint, and assists parties to resolve complaints, using either mediation or other low-level means of resolving disputes.

The commission works with parties to try to reach a settlement, which may include an apology, an agreement not to discriminate in the future and/or compensation.

If lower-level dispute resolution is not appropriate or possible, a complainant may approach the Director of Human Rights Proceedings for possible litigation assistance. Complainants may also take their own litigation, or engage their own legal counsel and take their case to the Human Rights Review Tribunal.

If the tribunal upholds a complaint, a wide range of remedies is available, such as damages, and orders of specific performance. The remedies vary according to whether the complaint is about private sector activities, or government policy or practices.

When a complaint concerns legislation or validly-made regulations (and is not about the discriminatory application of legislation), and the complaint is upheld, the sole remedy available is a declaration of inconsistency. While this does not invalidate the legislation, the responsible minister is required to bring the tribunal's declaration to the attention of the House of Representatives, along with the Executive Council's response.

Parties can appeal to the High Court to overturn tribunal decisions.

Parliamentary commissioner for the environment

The parliamentary commissioner for the environment (PCE) is an independent officer of Parliament with wide-ranging powers to investigate environmental concerns. The office was set up under the Environment Act 1986. The PCE has discretion to:

- review the system of agencies and processes established by the government to manage New Zealand's natural and physical resources
- investigate public authorities' environmental planning and management, and advise them on remedial action
- investigate any matter where the environment may be or has been adversely affected
- at Parliament's request, report on any petition, bill, or other matter that may have a significant effect on the environment
- at Parliament's direction, inquire into any matter that has had or may have a substantial and damaging effect on the environment
- undertake and encourage collection and reporting of information about the environment
- encourage preventive measures and remedial actions to protect the environment.

In investigating and reporting on environmental matters, the PCE can obtain information (protecting the confidentiality of that information where appropriate), report findings, and make recommendations. However, the PCE does not have the power to make any binding rulings or to reverse decisions made by public authorities.

Major reports released during the year 2006/07 included *Get smart, think small: Local energy systems for New Zealand*; *Wind power, people, and place*; *Healthy, wealthy and wise* on the links between energy use and health and well-being; and *Changing behaviour: Economic instruments in the management of waste*.

In the year ending 30 June 2007, the PCE responded on 217 occasions to requests for information and advice, and to issues of concern raised by individuals and groups.

Table 3.11

Reports and papers by the parliamentary commissioner for the environment

	Year ending 30 June				
	2003	2004	2005	2006	2007
Investigation reports	81	90	92	92	88
Information transfer papers or presentations	147	185	155	123	185
Total	**228**	**275**	**247**	**215**	**273**

Source: Parliamentary Commissioner for the Environment

Public Trust

The Public Trust Office is a Crown entity, founded in 1873 to provide a stable, independent and impartial trustee organisation. Its purpose is to help New Zealanders take care of their interests through the provision of trustee and financial services.

Public Trust also cares for overseas assets and property under various statutes, acts as trustee-guardian for minors and protected persons, and acts as a trustee of last resort. Its key priorities are:

- administering estates of deceased people
- wills and enduring powers of attorney advice and preparation
- establishing and administering trusts
- agency and asset management services
- providing financial and investment products and services
- corporate and other trustee services
- managing investment funds.

Local government

New Zealand's system of local government is largely separate from central government. Local government has a subordinate role in the constitution – its powers are conferred by Parliament.

Under the Local Government Act 2002, the purpose of local government is to enable democratic local decision-making and action, to promote the social, economic, environmental and cultural well-being of communities.

Local authorities fall into three categories: regional, territorial and special purpose authorities. Boundaries of regions, cities and districts are usually defined by the Local Government Commission or the Minister of Local Government. Many territorial authorities contain communities administered by community boards, but these are not separate local authorities. Six special purpose authorities are constituted under their own acts.

Local authorities have their own sources of income, independent of central government, with the main source (other than income from trading activities) being local taxes on land property – rates. Rates are set by local authorities themselves, subject to the Local Government (Rating) Act 2002.

Laws that apply to local authorities, and a range of other public bodies, include the Local Government Act 2002, the Local Government Official Information and Meetings Act 1987, the Local Authorities (Members' Interests) Act 1968, and the Local Electoral Act 2001. Local authorities derive their functions and powers not only from local government legislation, but also from numerous other acts, such as the Resource Management Act 1991, the Transit New Zealand Act 1989 and the Building Act 2004.

Local authorities can promote legislation to government about matters affecting their local area that they are not already empowered to deal with. When permanent or major additional powers are sought, a local bill must be prepared for Parliament to consider. If this is enacted, it becomes a local act, and applies only to the body or bodies that promoted it.

Local authorities are required to give public notice and receive public submissions before making certain important decisions. They may also come under the scrutiny of ombudsmen, the auditor-general and the parliamentary commissioner for the environment. Any decision by a local authority may be reviewed by appeal to the High Court. Decisions made under the Resource Management Act 1991 can be appealed to the Environment Court.

The Minister of Local Government may appoint a review authority when it is considered there has been serious mismanagement by a local authority, and can require the local authority to implement the review authority's recommendations.

Local government organisation

New Zealand has 12 regional councils, 73 territorial authorities, 143 community boards, and six special authorities. Table 3.12 (overleaf) lists regional councils, territorial authorities and numbers of councillors.

The Local Government Act 2002 recognises the diverse communities in New Zealand, their separate identities and values. It encourages participation by local people in local government. Local authorities are required to conduct their affairs in an open and proper manner, and to adequately inform local communities of their activities. Emphasis is placed on setting objectives and measuring performance.

Local authorities must separate their regulatory and non-regulatory activities. Local authorities are permitted to privatise their trading activities and may put the delivery of services out to competitive tender as an alternative to using in-house business units.

The Act lets regional councils and territorial authorities carry out activities they consider appropriate for their region or district in the context of the purpose of local government. Prior to 2002, local authorities were permitted to carry out only those activities specifically allowed by statute.

Regional councils are directly elected, set their own rates, and have a chairperson elected by their members. Their main functions relate to:

- the Resource Management Act 1991 and the Soil Conservation and Rivers Control Act 1941
- the control of pests and noxious plants
- harbour regulations and marine pollution control
- regional aspects of civil defence
- an overview of transport planning
- control of passenger transport operators.

Some regional councils have other functions, such as those formerly undertaken by land drainage boards.

Territorial authorities in New Zealand include 16 city councils, 56 district councils and the Chatham Islands Council. Territorial authorities are directly elected, set their own rates, and have a mayor elected by the people. They have a wide range of functions, including: land use consents under the Resource Management Act 1991, noise and litter control, roading, water supply, sewage reticulation and disposal, rubbish collection and disposal, parks and reserves, libraries, land subdivision, pensioner housing, health inspection, liquor licensing, building consents, parking controls, and civil defence.

New cities can either be constituted by an Order in Council giving effect to a decision of the Local Government Commission, or be constituted by a reorganisation scheme that forms a new district with a population of at least 50,000, that is predominantly urban, is a distinct entity, and is a major centre of activity within the region.

Kai to Compost

Mark Coote

Kai to Compost is a food-waste collection service for businesses and apartment dwellers in Wellington. The council provides 120–240 litre wheelie bins to participants. The food waste is mixed with green waste and used to produce compost, which is then sold to local gardens, orchards and vineyards.

By separating food waste from general rubbish, the service aims to minimise the environmental problems caused by food in landfills. Anaerobic decomposition in the landfill is slow and produces methane, a potent greenhouse gas. Keeping food out of the landfill is important for resource recovery, and removing food waste from the general rubbish collection means businesses don't need their general rubbish collected so often.

Wellington City Council secured funding from the Ministry for the Environment's Sustainable Management Fund to trial the Kai to Compost programme in 2006. The success of the trial has prompted the council to expand the service in the Wellington central city, on a user-pay basis. If this next stage is successful, it could lead to a permanent operation.

The Kai to Compost service, and composting at home, create a useful resource for gardeners, and help towards the council's goal of a carbon-neutral Wellington.

Source: Wellington City Council

Table 3.12

Territorial authorities and councillors
At 30 November 2007

City/district	Number of councillors[1]	Council type	City/district	Number of councillors[1]	Council type
Ashburton	13	District	Northland	8	Regional
Auckland	20	City	North Shore	16	City
Auckland	13	Regional	Opotiki	7	District
Buller	11	District	Otago	11	Regional
Carterton	9	District	Otorohanga	8	District
Central Hawke's Bay	9	District	Palmerston North	16	City
Central Otago	11	District	Papakura	9	District
Chatham Islands	9	Council	Porirua	14	City
Christchurch	14	City	Queenstown-Lakes	11	District
Clutha	15	District	Rangitikei	10	District
Dunedin	15	City	Rodney	13	District
Environment Bay of Plenty	13	Regional	Rotorua	13	District
Environment Canterbury	14	Regional	Ruapehu	12	District
Environment Southland	12	Regional	Selwyn	11	District
Environment Waikato	12	Regional	Southland	13	District
Far North	10	District	South Taranaki	13	District
Franklin	13	District	South Waikato	11	District
Gisborne[2]	15	District	South Wairarapa	10	District
Gore	12	District	Stratford	10	District
Greater Wellington	13	Regional	Taranaki	11	Regional
Grey	9	District	Tararua	9	District
Hamilton	13	City	Tasman[2]	14	District
Hastings	15	District	Taupo	11	District
Hauraki	14	District	Tauranga	11	City
Hawke's Bay	9	Regional	Thames-Coromandel	9	District
Horizons[3]	12	Regional	Timaru	11	District
Horowhenua	11	District	Upper Hutt	11	City
Hurunui	11	District	Waikato	14	District
Hutt City	13	City	Waimakariri	11	District
Invercargill	13	City	Waimate	9	District
Kaikoura	8	District	Waipa	13	District
Kaipara	9	District	Wairoa	7	District
Kapiti Coast	12	District	Waitakere	15	City
Kawerau	9	District	Waitaki	9	District
Mackenzie	7	District	Waitomo	7	District
Manawatu	11	District	Wanganui	13	District
Manukau	18	City	Wellington	15	City
Marlborough[2]	14	District	West Coast	7	Regional
Masterton	11	District	Western Bay of Plenty	13	District
Matamata-Piako	12	District	Westland	11	District
Napier	13	City	Whakatane	11	District
Nelson[2]	13	City	Whangarei	14	District
New Plymouth	15	District			

(1) Figures include mayors. (2) Unitary authority (city or district council and regional council responsibilities). (3) Trading name of Manawatu/Wanganui Regional Council.

Source: Local Government New Zealand

Quality urban design commitment

Good urban design enhances the economic, environmental, cultural, and social dimensions of towns and cities. The New Zealand Urban Design Protocol is a voluntary commitment to specific urban design initiatives. It was launched by the Government in 2005, as part of the Sustainable Development Programme of Action under the 'sustainable cities' action area. Organisations that have signed up include central and local government, the property sector, design professionals, and professional institutes.

The protocol identifies seven essential design qualities:

- context – viewing buildings and spaces as part of the whole town or city
- character – reflecting and enhancing the distinctive character, heritage and identity of the urban environment
- choice – ensuring diversity and choice for people
- connections – enhancing the way different networks link together for people
- creativity – encouraging innovative and imaginative solutions
- custodianship – ensuring design is environmentally sustainable, safe and healthy
- collaboration – communicating and sharing knowledge across sectors, professions and communities.

The protocol includes a toolkit, to help signatory organisations apply quality urban design to their projects.

Each organisation must appoint a design champion – someone influential at a senior level who will promote urban design, and challenge existing approaches within the organisation.

The organisations commit to developing and monitoring a set of actions specific to their organisation, then reporting back to the Ministry for the Environment within six months. These actions are grouped into research and analysis, community participation and raising awareness, planning and design, and implementation.

Source: Ministry for the Environment

Unitary authorities are territorial authorities that also have regional powers. Legislation in 1989 prevented any unitary authorities being established, other than in Gisborne. However, an amendment in 1992 not only created three more unitary authorities (Marlborough District, Tasman District and Nelson City), but made it possible for others to be created by submitting proposals to the Local Government Commission.

Community boards advocate for the community and are a way for the territorial authority to consult with the community. Community board powers are delegated by the territorial authority. Those powers cannot include levying rates, appointing staff, or owning property. Community boards can be partly elected by the community and partly appointed by the territorial authority from among its own members, or be entirely elected. Community boards can be established anywhere in New Zealand to serve any number of inhabitants. They may be established on the initiative of a given number of electors of the territorial authority, through a reorganisation scheme. Community boundaries often coincide with those of wards (divisions of the district for electoral purposes). Boards have between four and 12 members.

Special purpose local authorities were greatly reduced in number following local government reform in 1989. Catchment boards, harbour boards, pest destruction boards, and land drainage boards disappeared, with their functions reallocated either to regional councils or, to a lesser extent, territorial authorities.

Categories remaining include scenic and recreation boards. There are also some unique authorities, such as the Aotea Centre Board of Management, the Canterbury Museum Trust Board, the Council of the Auckland Institute and Museum, the Otago Museum Trust Board, the Masterton Lands Trust, and the Greytown Lands Trust.

Peter Salmon QC, chairman of the Royal Commission on Auckland Governance, with hundreds of submissions about how the Auckland region should be governed in the future.

Local government elections

All regional council, territorial authority, special purpose local authority, and community board elections, as well as those for district health boards, are conducted at the same time. Local government elections are held on the second Saturday in October every third year. The next elections will be in 2010.

Electorates are known as 'wards' in the case of territorial authorities and 'constituencies' in the case of regions. Territorial authorities can decide whether members will be elected by the electors of wards, from the district as a whole, or a mixture of both. Regions must be divided into constituencies.

At least once every six years, in the year before an election, regional and territorial authorities are required to review the number of council or board members, the number and size of their electorates, and whether or not community boards should be established. The purpose of the review is to give effective representation to communities, and fair representation to electors. The review process provides for objections and appeals by the public. When necessary, final decisions are made by the Local Government Commission.

Voting procedures Although postal voting is now universal, a territorial authority may decide whether an election is to be conducted by attendance at a polling booth or by post. The method of casting a vote is similar to that for parliamentary elections. The surnames of candidates are printed on the ballot paper and electors place a tick after the name of the candidate they wish to vote for. The voting system currently used is 'first past the post', except for district health boards, and nine local authorities, which use the single transferable vote (STV) system – in which voters rank candidates in the order of preference. Other local authorities have the option of using STV at future elections.

Local authority franchise Every parliamentary elector is automatically qualified as a residential elector of a local authority, if the address at which the person is registered on the electoral roll is within the district of the local authority. Ratepayers who are not residents are entitled to enrol and vote in any region, district or community that they pay rates in. Rolls are compiled by territorial authorities. Information for the residential electoral roll is obtained from the parliamentary electoral database, and the ratepayer roll is compiled from enrolment forms received from ratepayers.

Membership of local authorities Any person who is a New Zealand citizen and a parliamentary elector may be elected to a regional council, territorial authority, or community board. In 1992, a prohibition was introduced on a person being a candidate for both a regional council and a territorial authority, or community board, within that region. Vacancies may be filled either by an election or by appointment, depending on the timing of the vacancy.

Remuneration Most boards and councils pay their chairperson or mayor an annual salary, while other members are paid a combination of a meeting allowance and an annual salary. Maximum and minimum salary and allowance levels are set by the Remuneration Authority. The council or board decides the actual rate within those limits.

Local Government Commission

The Local Government Commission consists of three members, including a chairperson appointed by the Minister of Local Government.

The commission hears and determines:

- appeals against local authority decisions on proposed boundary alterations
- appeals and complaints relating to a local authority's ward and membership proposals following a representation review
- proposals for the constitution of communities.

The commission considers and processes proposals to join or create districts or regions. The commission may also carry out investigations of particular matters affecting local government and report on them to the Minister of Local Government.

The commission is required to review and report to the Minister of Local Government on the operation of the Local Government Act 2002, and the Local Electoral Act 2001. It must report to the minister as soon as practicable after local elections.

Local government finance

Most of New Zealand's local authorities separate their activities into regulatory-type functions and trading activities. To support this, councils have set up business units that compete with outside businesses for council contracts, such as those involving roading, works and maintenance, and refuse collection.

In addition to business units, councils often have a shareholding in electricity supply companies, as well as companies which operate ports, airports and bus transport.

The total value of the non-trading activities of all local authorities is shown in table 3.13.

Table 3.13

Local authority statistics – non-trading activities[1]
Year ending 30 June

	2002	2003	2004	2005	2006
	\$(million)				
Rates	2,301	2,440	2,620	2,779	3,010
Regulatory income and petrol tax	227	242	275	302	310
Government grants and subsidies	444	483	556	661	684
Investment income	420	279	302	307	308
Sales of goods and services and all other income	748	809	874	948	1,056
Total operating income	4,140	4,252	4,626	4,996	5,367
Employee costs	884	951	1,030	1,098	1,174
Interest paid	141	141	142	158	184
Depreciation	770	829	890	957	1,075
Purchases and other expenditure	1,997	2,106	2,309	2,534	2,787
Total operating expenditure	3,792	4,026	4,370	4,747	5,220
Surplus before non-operating items	348	225	256	249	148
Additions to fixed assets	1,598	1,725	1,938	2,134	2,323
Disposal of fixed assets	97	235	125	235	177

(1) Covers all activities of local authorities not classified as trading activities, eg local government administration, provision of water supply, roading, parks and reserves, town planning and regulation.

Note: Figures may not add up to stated totals due to rounding.

Source: Statistics New Zealand

National anthems

New Zealand has two national anthems: 'God Defend New Zealand' and 'God Save the Queen'.

God Defend New Zealand is a poem written by Thomas Bracken and set to music composed by John J Woods. It was first performed in public on Christmas Day 1876 and formally adopted as the national hymn in 1940.

In 1977, with the permission of Queen Elizabeth II, the government adopted both God Defend New Zealand and God Save the Queen as national anthems of equal status, to be used as appropriate to the occasion.

Māori and English texts of God Defend New Zealand:

1. E Ihowā Atua,
O ngā iwi mātou rā,
Āta whakarongona;
Me aroha noa.
Kia hua ko te pai;
Kia tau tō atawhai;
Manaakitia mai
Aotearoa.

2. Ōna mano tāngata
Kiri whero, kiri mā,
Iwi Māori Pākehā
Rūpeke katoa,
Nei ka tono ko ngā hē
Māu e whakaahu kē,
Kia ora mārire
Aotearoa.

3. Tōna mana kia tū!
Tōna kaha kia ū;
Tona rongo hei paku
Ki te ao katoa
Aua rawa ngā whawhai,
Ngā tutu a tata mai;
Kia tupu nui ai
Aotearoa.

4. Waiho tōna takiwā
Ko te ao mārama;
Kia whiti tōna rā
Taiāwhio noa.
Ko te hae me te ngangau
Meinga kia kore kau;
Waiho i te rongo mau
Aotearoa.

5. Tōna pai me toitū;
Tika rawa, pono pū;
Tōna noho, tāna tū;
Iwi nō Ihoa.
Kaua mōna whakamā;
Kia hau te ingoa;
Kia tū hei tauira;
Aotearoa.

1. God of Nations at Thy feet,
In the bonds of love we meet,
Hear our voices, we entreat,
God defend our free land.
Guard Pacific's triple star
From the shafts of strife and war,
Make her praises heard afar,
God defend New Zealand.

2. Men of every creed and race,
Gather here before Thy face,
Asking Thee to bless this place,
God defend our free land.
From dissension, envy, hate,
And corruption guard our State,
Make our country good and great,
God defend New Zealand.

3. Peace, not war, shall be our boast,
But, should foes assail our coast,
Make us then a mighty host,
God defend our free land.
Lord of battles in Thy might,
Put our enemies to flight,
Let our cause be just and right,
God defend New Zealand.

4. Let our love for Thee increase,
May Thy blessings never cease,
Give us plenty, give us peace,
God defend our free land.
From dishonour and from shame,
Guard our country's spotless name,
Crown her with immortal fame,
God defend New Zealand.

5. May our mountains ever be
Freedom's ramparts on the sea,
Make us faithful unto Thee,
God defend our free land.
Guide her in the nation's van,
Preaching love and truth to man,
Working out Thy glorious plan,
God defend New Zealand.

Contributors and related websites

Cabinet Office – www.dpmc.govt.nz/Cabinet

Chief Electoral Office – www.elections.govt.nz

Crown Company Monitoring Advisory Unit – www.ccmau.govt.nz

Department of the Prime Minister and Cabinet – www.dpmc.govt.nz

Government House – www.gov-gen.govt.nz

Honours Secretariat – www.dpmc.govt.nz/honours

Local Government Commission – www.lgc.govt.nz

Local Government New Zealand – www.localgovtnz.co.nz

Ministry for Culture and Heritage – www.mch.govt.nz

Ministry for the Environment – www.mfe.govt.nz

Ministry of Justice – www.justice.govt.nz

Office of the Clerk of the House of Representatives – www.parliament.govt.nz

Office of the Controller and Auditor-General – www.oag.govt.nz

Office of the Ombudsmen – www.ombudsmen.govt.nz

Office of the Parliamentary Commissioner for the Environment – www.pce.govt.nz

Office of the Privacy Commissioner – www.privacy.org.nz

Parliamentary Counsel Office – www.pco.parliament.govt.nz

Parliamentary Service – www.parliament.govt.nz

Prime Minister's Office – www.primeminister.govt.nz

Public Trust – www.publictrust.co.nz

State Services Commission – www.ssc.govt.nz

Statistics New Zealand – www.stats.govt.nz

Wellington City Council – www.wellington.govt.nz

New Zealand Defence Force

Timor-Leste children at a local orphanage in Dili chat with Private Tai. Since 1999, New Zealand has provided strong support for the development of an independent and stable Timor-Leste, through peacekeeping, development assistance, and diplomacy.

4 | International relations and defence

Relations with other countries

The New Zealand Government began stationing diplomatic representatives overseas in 1943. Today, New Zealand has 50 overseas posts, with multiple accreditations allowing New Zealand representatives to cover 119 countries. The most recently opened overseas posts are an embassy in Cairo, Egypt, set up in October 2006, and a consulate-general in Guangzhou, China, which opened on 26 April 2007.

The government interacts with other governments and international institutions through the Ministry of Foreign Affairs and Trade Manatū Aorere (MFAT). The ministry's mission is to advance and protect New Zealand's security and prosperity interests abroad. MFAT is responsible for providing the government with policy advice on New Zealand's foreign affairs, trade and security interests. It represents and advocates for New Zealand's views and positions to other countries and in international institutions and negotiations, and manages New Zealand's foreign affairs and trade relations with other countries. It also provides consular services to New Zealanders abroad.

The ministry is formally responsible for the administration of Tokelau, although Tokelauan institutions have had administration powers since 1994. MFAT also manages New Zealand's constitutional relationships with the Cook Islands and Niue. These relationships involve New Zealand's residual responsibilities for the external affairs and defence of both states, when requested, and providing necessary economic and administrative assistance to Niue.

New Zealand's International Aid and Development Agency (NZAID) is a semi-autonomous body within the ministry. It was established in 2002 and is responsible for managing the delivery of New Zealand's official development assistance programme.

MFAT consults and works closely with other government departments and agencies in pursuing New Zealand's interests abroad. It coordinates a whole-of-government approach for advancing national interests and national identity abroad.

A key area of collaboration is in the area of furthering economic transformation, where MFAT works to strengthen international connections and increase trade by encouraging the flow of investment, skills and technology to New Zealand. New Zealand Trade and Enterprise (NZTE) is a particularly important partner in promoting the government's external policies for economic transformation and sustainability.

MFAT operates and administers a network of 50 diplomatic and consular posts to represent and pursue New Zealand's interests overseas. People at these posts perform services on behalf of all government departments, and provide a platform to support their overseas activities. Around 112 staff from other government departments and agencies currently work alongside ministry staff at overseas posts. NZTE also operates nine consular offices in conjunction with the ministry.

The ministry's overseas posts offer assistance to New Zealanders overseas, whether travelling in official or private capacities. MFAT maintains a website, www.safetravel.govt.nz, which provides travel advice and other consular information for New Zealanders.

Figure 4.01

Overseas representation

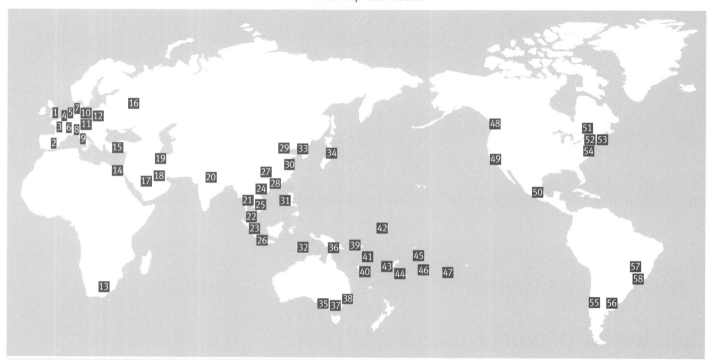

1 London, United Kingdom	**12 Warsaw, Poland**	**20 New Delhi, India**	**42 Tarawa, Kiribati**
Ireland	Estonia	Bangladesh	Marshall Islands
Nigeria	Latvia	Nepal	Federated States of Micronesia
2 Madrid, Spain	Lithuania	Sri Lanka	Palau
Holy See	**13 Pretoria, South Africa**	**21 Bangkok, Thailand**	**43 Suva, Fiji**
Morocco	Botswana	Cambodia	Nauru
3 Paris, France	Kenya	Myanmar	Tuvalu
Algeria	Lesotho	Laos	**44 Nuku'alofa, Tonga**
4 Brussels, Belgium	Mauritius	**22 Kuala Lumpur, Malaysia**	**45 Apia, Samoa**
Luxembourg	Mozambique	Brunei Darussalam	American Samoa
5 The Hague, The Netherlands	Namibia	**23 Singapore**	**46 Niue**
Denmark	Swaziland	Maldives	**47 Rarotonga, Cook Islands**
Finland	Tanzania	**24 Ha Noi, Viet Nam**	**48 Vancouver, Canada**
Norway	Zambia	**25 Ho Chi Minh City, Viet Nam**	**49 Los Angeles, United States**
Sweden	Zimbabwe	**26 Jakarta, Indonesia**	**50 Mexico City, Mexico**
6 Geneva, Switzerland	**14 Cairo, Egypt**	**27 Guangzhou, China**	El Salvador
(permanent mission)	**15 Ankara, Turkey**	**28 Hong Kong (SAR)**[1]	Guatemala
7 Hamburg, Germany	Israel	Macau (SAR)[1]	Venezuela
8 Milan, Italy	Jordan	**29 Beijing, China**	**51 Ottawa, Canada**
9 Rome, Italy	**16 Moscow, Russia**	Mongolia	Barbados
Bosnia	Kazakhstan	**30 Shanghai, China**	Guyana
Croatia	Kyrgyz Republic	**31 Manila, Philippines**	Jamaica
Cyprus	Turkmenistan	**32 Dili, Timor-Leste**	Trinidad and Tobago
Greece	Ukraine	**33 Seoul, Republic of Korea**	**52 New York, United Nations**
Malta	Uzbekistan	Democratic People's Republic	**53 New York, United States**
Portugal	**17 Riyadh, Saudi Arabia**	of Korea	**54 Washington, United States**
Slovenia	Bahrain	**34 Tokyo, Japan**	**55 Santiago, Chile**
10 Berlin, Germany	Kuwait	**35 Melbourne, Australia**	Colombia
Austria	Oman	**36 Port Moresby, Papua New Guinea**	Peru
Czech Republic	Qatar	**37 Canberra, Australia**	**56 Buenos Aires, Argentina**
Hungary	United Arab Emirates	**38 Sydney, Australia**	Paraguay
Slovakia	**18 Dubai, United Arab Emirates**	**39 Honiara, Solomon Islands**	Uruguay
Switzerland	**19 Tehran, Iran**	**40 Noumea, New Caledonia**	**57 Brasilia, Brazil**
11 Vienna, Austria	Afghanistan	**41 Port Vila, Vanuatu**	**58 Sao Paulo, Brazil**
	Pakistan		

(1) Special Administrative Region.

Source: Ministry of Foreign Affairs and Trade

Figure 4.01 shows where the Ministry of Foreign Affairs and Trade has diplomatic and consular representation. Cities where New Zealand has a diplomatic mission are numbered and listed in bold. Countries listed under a mission are accredited to that mission – the head of the mission is New Zealand's representative to that country also.

The Pacific

New Zealand enjoys a close association with Pacific island nations. New Zealand has 10 diplomatic missions and consulates in the region and accreditation to a further six states and territories.

Special relationships exist between New Zealand and the Cook Islands, Niue and Tokelau. Cook Islanders, Niueans and Tokelauans are New Zealand citizens. The Cook Islands became a self-governing state in free association with New Zealand in 1965 and Niue followed in 1974. Tokelau is a non-self-governing territory of New Zealand.

Trade with Pacific countries is important to New Zealand. Exports totalled $1,056 million in the year ending 30 June 2007. Imports totalled $218 million, an increase of 36 percent on the previous year, largely as a result of increased oil imports from Papua New Guinea.

Imports from Pacific countries have duty-free access on a non-reciprocal basis to both New Zealand and Australian markets under the South Pacific Regional Trade and Economic Cooperation Agreement. Efforts are being made to promote imports from the Pacific, with increased NZAID support for the Pacific Islands Trade and Investment Commission, based in Auckland.

Pacific Islands Forum New Zealand has developed extensive links with Pacific regional organisations. It was a founding member of the South Pacific Forum, formed in 1971 to promote regional cooperation, particularly in trade and economic development. Renamed the Pacific Islands Forum in 1999, it now comprises 16 Pacific countries and provides an opportunity to discuss regional and international issues of interest to the region, such as regional security, environmental issues, fisheries, and economic development. Pacific Islands Forum countries meet annually at heads of government level, with meetings throughout the year at ministerial and official levels to consider specific issues.

An important aspect of the forum's work is the annual Forum Economic Ministers' Meeting. Since the first meeting in 1995, ministers have agreed on an action plan covering accountability principles, public sector reform initiatives, tariff reform and investment reform. Forum trade ministers also meet at least once every two years to advance regional trade initiatives.

The Pacific Agreement on Closer Economic Relations covers all Pacific Islands Forum countries, including Australia and New Zealand. It aims to develop closer trade and economic integration arrangements in the Pacific region.

The Pacific Island Countries Trade Agreement is a free trade agreement among Pacific Islands Forum countries. It came into force in 2003, but only became operational from 2007. As a result of the delays, the schedule to eliminate tariffs on intra-regional trade now extends out to 2021.

Fisheries management The importance of fisheries as an economic resource in the Pacific led to the September 2000 completion of the Convention on the Conservation and Management of Highly Migratory Fish Stocks in the Western and Central Pacific Ocean. Work is currently underway on a further multilateral agreement, the South Pacific Regional Fisheries Management Agreement, which will cover non-highly migratory fish species in the region. Pacific leaders also recognised the significance of fisheries for the region by issuing the Vava'u Declaration on Pacific Fisheries Resources at the 2007 Pacific Islands Forum in Tonga.

Other regional organisations that New Zealand is a member of include:

- the Forum Fisheries Agency – assists members with management and conservation of the region's marine resources
- the Secretariat of the Pacific Community – helps promote economic and social development in the region through work in agriculture, marine resources, health, socio-economic and statistical services, and community education
- the South Pacific Regional Environment Programme – focuses on protection and management of environmental resources
- the Pacific Forum Line – facilitates regional trade through improved shipping links
- the South Pacific Applied Geoscience Commission – assists in assessment, exploration and development of mineral and other non-living resources.

New Zealand has other links with the Pacific that cover official development assistance, defence, and disaster coordination. The France, Australia, and New Zealand arrangement (FRANZ) is an important element in the provision of rapid emergency assistance to the region in the event of natural disasters, such as tropical cyclones.

Aid The Pacific is also the area of New Zealand's primary aid focus. About $205 million – approximately half of NZAID's budget – goes towards development assistance in the Pacific region.

New Zealanders volunteer in environmental projects abroad

For over 45 years, Volunteer Service Abroad (VSA) has been linking New Zealanders with organisations and communities in Africa, Asia and the Pacific to help create positive change.

The management of natural resources has been an important focus, as poverty often leads people to exploit their environment in their struggle to survive. Environmental projects that VSA volunteers engage in typically revolve around ensuring proper management of scarce non-renewable resources. Often this requires finding other ways for people who are dependent on the local environment to earn a living, while ensuring they, their children, and their children's children are provided for into the future.

An example is the work VSA volunteers have been doing with the Binh Dinh Fisheries Department in Viet Nam. Over-fishing and pollution are problems within the Con Shim Marine Sanctuary area, which supports around 7,400 people. These people struggle to provide for their basic needs, using the only resource at their disposal. Solutions like planting mangroves, setting up tourism initiatives, and villager education programmes have helped curb the degradation.

Another fishing project involving VSA volunteers has been in the Solomon Islands. The transition from subsistence to a subsistence-plus-cash economy, and a rapidly increasing population means traditional use of the sea and its produce is under threat. A project with the WorldFish Center in Gizo has seen village 'growers' on remote islands use environmentally friendly aquaculture techniques to cultivate giant clams for the international marine ornamental clam and coral market. This way, they can earn a livelihood and preserve 'wild' stocks.

In 2007, 12 percent of VSA's assignments had an environmental focus.

Other sectors VSA is involved in include education and training, health, community and economic development, and agriculture. Assignments are generally for two years. VSA works with organisations in 13 countries in Africa, Asia and the Pacific, and has around 100 volunteers in the field at any one time.

Source: Volunteer Service Abroad

NZAID has extensive relationships with countries in the Pacific and provides significant support for regional organisations, such as the Secretariat of the Pacific Community and the University of the South Pacific. Under its current Pacific strategy, regional programmes are divided into broad themes of:

- strengthening governance
- achieving broader-based growth and improved livelihoods
- improving health and education
- reducing vulnerability.

Security issues In the Pacific, security issues are characterised by internal and external security challenges stemming from factors including ethnic differences, economic disparities, land disputes, and transnational crime. New Zealand has been involved extensively in regional efforts to resolve these security challenges, especially in Bougainville and the Solomon Islands. In Bougainville, New Zealand committed personnel to the Peace Monitoring Group (1998–2003) and the Bougainville Transitional Team (2003). New Zealand also contributes police and military personnel, as well as civilian staff, to the Regional Assistance Mission to the Solomon Islands.

Regional cooperation in security matters has been centred on the Pacific Islands Forum and its regional security committee. The Biketawa Declaration, made by forum leaders in 2000, assigned the forum's secretary-general a specific role in monitoring possible sources of conflict, and in developing methods of dispute settlement and conflict avoidance to prevent them from developing into open conflict.

Australia

New Zealand's closest partnership is with Australia. The relationship is central to New Zealand's trade and economic interests, its defence, security and foreign policy interests, and to the country's overall economic and social well-being. New Zealand is represented in Australia by a high commission in Canberra and consulates-general in Sydney and Melbourne.

The political framework for managing the relationship includes regular dedicated meetings between the New Zealand and Australian prime ministers, meetings between the ministers of foreign affairs, finance, and defence, and the annual Closer Economic Relations Ministerial Forum for key trade and economic ministers.

Complementing these meetings, around 80 business and community leaders from both countries – including relevant senior ministers and opposition spokespeople – meet annually at the Australia New Zealand Leadership Forum.

Trans-Tasman travel arrangement (TTTA) This arrangement enables New Zealand citizens to travel, live and work in Australia, and Australian residents to receive similar access to New Zealand. A social security agreement negotiated with Australia, covering superannuation and severe disability, has been in effect since 2002. This preserves the ability of New Zealanders to live and work in Australia (and vice versa) under the TTTA, while allowing both governments to determine their own policies regarding access to all other social welfare benefits. More than 469,000 New Zealanders live in Australia and about 62,000 Australians live in New Zealand. More than a million New Zealanders and 900,000 Australians cross the Tasman on short-term visits each year.

Trade Australia is New Zealand's most important trading partner. New Zealand is Australia's number one market for highly-manufactured goods and the fifth-largest individual export market.

The Australia New Zealand Closer Economic Relations (CER) trade agreement, signed in 1983, and its associated arrangements and agreements, governs most trade and economic relations between the two countries. CER agreements on free trade on goods and a protocol on services provide for free trade in nearly all service sectors.

The CER also addresses a range of non-tariff trade matters, such as customs requirements, standards, business law regulations, and occupational registration requirements. The CER includes mutual recognition principles relating to the sale of goods and the registration of occupations, and an 'open skies' aviation market agreement. An Australia New Zealand Food Standards Code has been in effect since 2002. In August 2007, the Government announced that it would initiate World Trade Organization dispute settlement proceedings to address the long-running issue of access for New Zealand apples to the Australian market.

A major focus in the relationship now is on creating a seamless trans-Tasman business environment. Significant progress on this includes an agreement to coordinate business law, signed in 2000 and updated in 2005, and a cooperation protocol signed on 31 July 2007 between the New Zealand Commerce Commission and the Australian Competition and Consumer Commission on competition and consumer policy issues.

Security Australia is also New Zealand's closest and most important security partner. The alliance with Australia remains central to New Zealand's defence policies. Both governments are committed to achieving the highest possible level of cooperation with each other, while acknowledging the need for each to meet its own defence priorities. Australia and New Zealand have worked together closely and effectively in deployments in Timor-Leste, Bougainville and the Solomon Islands.

New Zealand Red Cross

New Zealand Red Cross delegate, Peter Cameron, distributes aid to people displaced by severe flooding in Jakarta, Indonesia, in February 2007.

Asia

New Zealand invests considerable resources in developing closer political relations with Asian neighbours and it is represented by a network of offices in Bangkok, Beijing, Dili, Guangzhou, Ha Noi, Ho Chi Minh City, Hong Kong, Jakarta, Kuala Lumpur, Manila, New Delhi, Seoul, Singapore, Shanghai and Tokyo.

Cultural ties have grown rapidly. New Zealanders are coming into increasingly close and frequent contact with Asia and its people, through short-term visitors (tourists, students and business people) and through immigration from the region to New Zealand. New Zealanders of Asian ethnicity make up 9 percent of the total population and many ethnic communities maintain active links and connections with Asia.

The Government's 'Seriously Asia' fund aims to build links with rising Asian leaders and those well placed to influence public opinion. Long term, the trend towards closer integration in the Asian region and the possibility of a future East Asia community is of particular significance to New Zealand. New Zealand's intentions to strengthen its engagement with Asia have been outlined in the Government's white paper on New Zealand's relations with Asia, *Our Future with Asia*.

Trade New Zealand's economic links with the region have grown rapidly. In the year ending 30 June 2007, Asia was home to 11 of New Zealand's top 20 markets for goods exports. The region takes nearly 40 percent of New Zealand's exports by value, totalling more than $11.7 billion for the June 2007 year.

Trade in tourism and education services has been increasing rapidly, especially with the large economies of North Asia. Japan remains New Zealand's most important market in Asia, but China has emerged as a significant economic player in its own right and is now New Zealand's fourth-largest trading partner. South and South-East Asia represent emerging markets for New Zealand. There are also significant flows of direct investment between Asia and New Zealand.

New Zealand has finalised trade agreements with Singapore, Thailand and Brunei and signed a free trade agreement with China in April 2008. It is presently negotiating a bilateral trade agreement with Malaysia and, along with Australia, has been jointly negotiating with the Association of South-East Asian Nations.

Aid Asia is currently New Zealand's second priority for official development assistance (after the Pacific). Assistance is channelled directly through a variety of programmes such as English language training, human resources development and capacity building, and disaster relief, as well as through regional agencies.

Asia New Zealand Foundation This organisation helps to promote closer ties with Asia by supporting a broad range of cultural, academic and business engagement, including an extensive research programme. It receives funding from the New Zealand Government and corporate donors.

Association of South-East Asian Nations (ASEAN) New Zealand already has a long-standing relationship with ASEAN (Malaysia, Indonesia, the Philippines, Singapore, Thailand, Brunei Darussalam, Laos, Viet Nam, Myanmar and Cambodia). In 1975, New Zealand was one of the first countries to enter a 'dialogue partner' relationship with ASEAN, and New Zealand participates annually in the ASEAN Post-Ministerial Conference, where key international and regional issues are discussed. In 2005, New Zealand formally acceded to the ASEAN Treaty of Amity

Liberating trade in the Asia-Pacific region

Leaders at the 2007 APEC meeting in Sydney.

New Zealand was a founding member of Asia Pacific Economic Cooperation (APEC). The 21 member economies support more than 2.6 billion people, and account for almost half of world trade and around 56 percent of global gross domestic product.

APEC promotes trade and investment liberalisation, business facilitation, and economic and technical cooperation. In recent years, APEC has taken on a complementary human security dimension, aimed largely at securing trade and travel within the region from the effects of terrorism. It has also reinvigorated its work programme on structural reform, which addresses behind-the-border barriers to trade, and given attention to other pressing regional and global issues such as climate change.

All members have committed themselves to achieving APEC's 'Bogor Goals' of free and open trade and investment by 2010 for industrialised economies, and by 2020 for developing economies. Progress is monitored by reviews of each economy's individual action plan. A review of New Zealand's plan in 2007 showed it had made strong progress, having achieved 11 of the 13 Bogor Goals and being on track to achieve the remaining two.

Annual APEC summits provide a forum for leaders to meet and address important regional economic, political, and security issues. At the Sydney summit in 2007, member economies pressed for an early and successful conclusion to the World Trade Organization's Doha Round, launched the region's first joint Declaration on Climate Change, Energy Security and Clean Development, and endorsed a range of steps to promote regional economic integration, including the possibility of a free-trade area for the Asia-Pacific region.

Source: Ministry of Foreign Affairs and Trade

and Cooperation, signalling a commitment to closer engagement with ASEAN, and with Asia more generally.

New Zealand's participation in the inaugural East Asia Summit in Malaysia in 2005 was a further step towards building a deeper, more inclusive relationship with the region. The summit is made up of the 10 ASEAN nations, plus China, Japan, the Republic of Korea, New Zealand, Australia and India. Although it is one of the newest groupings in Asia, its annual leaders' summit has already become a major event in the regional calendar. Within the summit countries, a comprehensive economic partnership for East Asia has been proposed.

Asia Pacific Economic Cooperation (APEC) New Zealand is an active player in APEC, a grouping formed in 1989 that draws together 21 economies from around Asia and the Pacific rim. APEC summits are held annually at leaders' level and its trade facilitation efforts enjoy wide support. Some APEC members are promoting an Asia-Pacific free-trade region.

Security The ASEAN Regional Forum provides ministers from throughout the Asia-Pacific region with an opportunity to focus collectively on regional security issues. New Zealand is also a member of the Five Power Defence Arrangements, which brings together Malaysia, Singapore, the United Kingdom, Australia and New Zealand.

An important component of New Zealand's contribution to security in the region is its long-standing commitment to assist Timor-Leste, the youngest nation in the Asia-Pacific region. Since 1999 New Zealand has provided strong support for the development of an independent and stable Timor-Leste, through peacekeeping, development assistance and diplomatic efforts.

Americas

United States Shared values between New Zealand and the United States underpin close government and private sector contacts across a broad range of bilateral, regional and multilateral activities. The United States is one of New Zealand's key economic partners. It is one of New Zealand's three most important export markets and a major source of imports and investment. In multilateral trade discussions, the two countries advocate similar open market philosophies.

There is close cooperation in Antarctica and on Antarctic and Southern Ocean issues, including safeguarding the environment, supporting the Antarctic Treaty system, and scientific research into key issues like climate change. In the Pacific, New Zealand and the United States are working increasingly closely on issues of stability, security and governance. Both countries have common interests in countering terrorism and its proliferation in the Asia-Pacific region and elsewhere.

Canada New Zealand and Canada enjoy a positive and close relationship, based on shared Commonwealth, United Nations, Asian and Pacific interests. The two countries cooperate closely on a range of issues, including disarmament, international peacekeeping and security, policies in the Asia-Pacific region, and international economic matters. Canada is also an important market for New Zealand's agricultural products.

Latin America New Zealand aims to increase links between New Zealand and Latin America in three broad areas – political and diplomatic, economic and trade, and cultural – and focuses on six priority countries: Argentina, Brazil, Chile, Mexico, Peru and Uruguay.

New Zealand has a Trans-Pacific Strategic Economic Partnership agreement with Chile (as well as Singapore and Brunei), signed in July 2005. A report by the New Zealand-Mexico joint experts group, presented in November 2006, identified ways to advance trade and economic liberalisation between the two countries.

Working holiday agreements with Chile, Argentina, Uruguay and Mexico have increased cultural links considerably. Latin American countries also cooperate with New Zealand in a range of multilateral areas, including trade, the environment, Antarctica, disarmament and fisheries.

Cuba established an embassy in Wellington in October 2007. Argentina, Brazil, Chile, Mexico and Peru also have embassies in New Zealand, while Guatemala, Uruguay and Venezuela are cross-accredited to New Zealand.

Caribbean New Zealand's relationship with the Caribbean is based largely on membership of the Commonwealth, of which many Caribbean states are members. Beyond this, New Zealand's relationship with the Caribbean is supported by direct cultural links, such as tourism.

European Union

The European Union (EU) is a major political and economic entity and a significant player in world affairs. It accepted two more countries in January 2007, to become a community of 27 member states.

New Zealand's relationship with the EU was given renewed encouragement with the adoption of the Joint Declaration on Relations and Cooperation between the EU and New Zealand in September 2007. The declaration sets out the directions in which the relationship has moved, and establishes new areas of cooperation, including trade talks, increased cooperation on environment and climate change issues, science and technology cooperation, and research and educational exchanges.

New Zealand, the EU, and its member states, cooperate on many international issues, particularly at the multilateral level. Political consultations are held twice a year, at ministerial level, with the revolving EU presidency and the European Commission. Contact with the European Commission in Brussels, and also with the European Parliament, is critical to maintaining New Zealand's profile in Europe.

New Zealand also has important relationships with the EU's individual member states, including strong historical ties with the United Kingdom. Enlargement of the EU in May 2004 and January 2007 to encompass states in Eastern Europe has resulted in increased contacts between New Zealand and these countries.

New Zealand has accreditations to all 27 member states. A New Zealand embassy was opened in Warsaw in January 2005 in order to further support development of relationships with new member states in central Europe. New Zealand has eight bilateral embassies/high commissions in EU countries: in Berlin, Brussels, The Hague, London, Madrid, Paris, Rome and Warsaw. There are consulates in Hamburg and Milan, and a number of honorary consulates in other European cities.

Trade The EU is New Zealand's second-largest trading partner. It is the largest market for a broad range of primary produce, including sheepmeat, wool, butter, kiwifruit, apples and venison. Successful negotiations in the Uruguay round on the General Agreement on Tariffs and Trade improved the volume and overall stability of New Zealand's access to the EU market.

Russia and the Commonwealth of Independent States

New Zealand cooperates with Russia on a range of international issues in multilateral and regional bodies such as the United Nations, the Asia Pacific Economic Cooperation organisation, and the Association of South-East Asian Nations Regional Forum. It is heavily involved in negotiations for Russia to join the World Trade Organization. New Zealand has an embassy in Moscow, which is also accredited to Kazakhstan, the Kyrgyz Republic, Turkmenistan, Ukraine and Uzbekistan. An honorary consulate in Vladivostok covers New Zealand's interests in the Russian far-east.

Middle East and North Africa

Developments centred on the Middle East continue to have global strategic implications. Al Qa'ida's attacks on the United States on 11 September 2001 prompted the US-led invasion and occupation of Afghanistan and the US-led invasion and occupation of Iraq.

New Zealand has embassies in Egypt (Cairo), Saudi Arabia (Riyadh), Turkey (Ankara) and Iran (Tehran), with cross accreditations to Afghanistan, Bahrain, Israel, Jordan, Kuwait, Oman, Qatar and the United Arab Emirates. The New Zealand consulate-general in Dubai is also the regional office for New Zealand Trade and Enterprise. In North Africa, New Zealand is accredited to Morocco from its embassy in Madrid, and to Algeria from its embassy in Paris.

Revenues from buoyant oil prices, boosted by continuing strong world demand, continue to feed investment in infrastructure development, and demand for goods and services in the region.

Trade and economic interests New Zealand's trade with the Middle East and North Africa has been boosted in recent years, on the back of high oil and food prices. The region is a valuable

Culverts are delivered for water supply reconstruction in Afghanistan. The New Zealand Defence Force has been involved in security and development in Afghanistan since 2001.

Corporal Apiata honoured for courageous action

In 2004, while on operations with other members of the New Zealand Special Air Service Group in Afghanistan, Corporal Willie Apiata, with utter disregard for his own safety, rescued a critically injured soldier while under heavy fire, and carried the injured man to a safe location where he could receive life-saving medical attention. Corporal Apiata then re-armed himself and joined a counter-attack that repelled the attacking force.

In 2007, Corporal Apiata was awarded the Victoria Cross for his extraordinary act of gallantry.

The Victoria Cross was introduced in 1856, during the reign of Queen Victoria, to recognise valour in the face of an enemy by any member of the armed forces. It takes precedence over all other honours and awards.

Corporal Apiata is the first to be awarded the Victoria Cross for New Zealand, which was introduced in 1999. Although it is now awarded outside the British honours system, the New Zealand decoration remains identical to the traditional award. Corporal Apiata's Victoria Cross is also the first to be awarded to a serving member of the SAS anywhere in the Commonwealth.

Source: New Zealand Defence Force

market for dairy, meat, wool, manufactured goods and services, and an important source of crude oil, polymers and fertilisers.

In the year ending 30 June 2007, New Zealand's exports to the Middle East totalled $1.187 billion, while imports for the same period were $1.870 billion. In North Africa, New Zealand's exports for the year ending 30 June 2007 totalled $455.58 million, while imports for the same period were $191 million. The growing importance and potential of trade in the region is reflected by the opening of negotiations towards a free trade agreement with the Cooperation Council of the Arab Gulf States. The demand for New Zealand education services has grown significantly. The region remains a major potential source and site for investment.

Security New Zealand personnel have served with the United Nations Truce Supervisory Organization in Israel, Egypt, Jordan, Lebanon and Syria since 1954 and with the Multinational Force and Observers in the Sinai since 1981. New Zealand Defence Force personnel also serve with the International Security Assistance Force in Afghanistan and with United Nations (UN) missions in Afghanistan, Iraq and Lebanon.

Afghanistan New Zealand maintains a strong commitment to restoring peace and security in Afghanistan. New Zealand supported the Bonn Process under which Afghanistan was returned to constitutional democratic government, and continues to support the partnership between the Afghanistan Government and the international community under the Afghanistan Compact. It has been involved in security and development efforts in Afghanistan since late 2001, supporting both the NATO-led International Security Assistance Force (ISAF) and Operation Enduring Freedom. New Zealand helps provide security to Bamyan Province (200 kilometres west of Kabul) through command of the provincial reconstruction team there. It also contributes officers to ISAF headquarters and the UN Assistance Mission in Afghanistan. Police training and mentoring is provided in Bamyan, and army training in Kabul. NZAID runs a mix of national and provincial assistance programmes, with a focus on human rights, alternative rural livelihoods, education and health care. New Zealand assistance for 2001–07, both military and development, totals more than $160 million. The deployment has been extended to September 2009.

Arab-Israeli conflict New Zealand continues to strongly support efforts to find a lasting solution to the Arab-Israeli conflict. New Zealand takes a balanced and constructive approach, encouraging dialogue, and supporting efforts towards a just, enduring and comprehensive peace settlement. New Zealand continues to advocate for an Israeli and a Palestinian state, coexisting side-by-side in peace and security, in line with relevant UN Security Council resolutions. New Zealand contributes $1 million annually to the UN Relief and Works Agency for Palestinian Refugees in the Near East (UNRWA). In 2007 NZAID also contributed $1 million to UNRWA's emergency appeal.

Iraq New Zealand did not support the 2003 military invasion of Iraq, but along with many other members of the international community, it backs UN-mandated processes to restore stability, security and able government to Iraq. New Zealand has contributed emergency humanitarian relief and other assistance (total value to 2007 was $24 million) to Iraq, mostly in recent years through the UN Development Programme trust fund, but also through the 2003–04 deployment of an New Zealand Defence Force light engineering group to carry out humanitarian and reconstruction tasks near Basra. In addition, New Zealand contributed $1 million in 2007 for UN relief assistance to Iraqi refugees, and another $700,000 to the International Red Cross.

Sub-Saharan Africa

New Zealand's official relations with Sub-Saharan Africa are mainly with the Commonwealth countries of southern and eastern Africa, with South Africa being the most significant.

New Zealand has one diplomatic mission in Sub-Saharan Africa – the New Zealand High Commission in Pretoria, South Africa. This is accredited to 10 other southern and eastern African countries: Botswana, Kenya, Lesotho, Mauritius, Mozambique, Namibia, Swaziland, Tanzania, Zambia and Zimbabwe. The New Zealand High Commission in London is responsible for relations with Nigeria.

Aid There is a strong humanitarian focus to many of New Zealand's relationships in Sub-Saharan Africa. New Zealand has a long-standing involvement in development in Africa through its official development assistance programme, which focuses on primary and non-formal education, rural development, and primary health care.

There is also provision for short-term technical assistance and support for New Zealand non-government organisations, including Volunteer Service Abroad. During 2006, $20 million was spent in the region on development assistance, including scholarships.

Security As part of peace-building operations in Africa, New Zealand has three defence force personnel at the United Nations mission in Sudan.

Trade Sub-Saharan Africa accounts for only a small proportion of New Zealand's global trade. Exports to the region were valued at around $516 million in the year ending 30 June 2007. Among major exports to the region were dairy, fish, and other food products, casein, and electrical equipment. South Africa and Mauritius were New Zealand's most important markets in the region. Imports in the year ending 30 June 2007 totalled $314 million, with petroleum products, iron and steel, vehicles and parts, tobacco, coffee, and wine the major items.

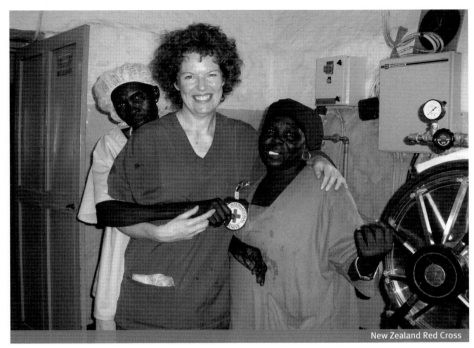
New Zealand Red Cross

Red Cross nurse Wendy Hetrick at the Juba Teaching Hospital in southern Sudan, where the International Red Cross is phasing out support as the region transitions to peace. Resources will then be concentrated in Darfur and other areas of Sudan where communities remain under threat from violence and armed conflict.

Assistance to developing countries

NZAID

New Zealand's Agency for International Development (NZAID) Nga Hoe Tuputupu-mai-tawhiti is the agency responsible for delivering New Zealand's official development assistance. It also advises ministers on development assistance policy and operations.

Reflecting the government's commitment to being a good international citizen and neighbour, NZAID aims to help eliminate poverty through development partnerships. NZAID's geographical focus is the Pacific region where New Zealand has close historic and cultural links. The agency also works in Asia, Africa and Latin America.

Established in 2002, NZAID places a high priority on building strong partnerships. It concentrates its development assistance on activities that contribute to eliminating poverty by creating safe, just and inclusive societies; fulfilling basic needs; and achieving environmental sustainability and sustainable livelihoods.

NZAID is a semi-autonomous body within the Ministry of Foreign Affairs and Trade. Its management is tailored to its core business and it has separate government funding.

NZAID's total budget allocation in the 2007/08 financial year takes New Zealand's expected overseas development aid to 0.3 percent of gross national income, with a commitment to move this to 0.35 percent by 2010/11. Table 4.01 (overleaf) shows NZAID's spending on programmes for 2006/07.

Pacific programme

While poverty is a global problem, development indicators show significant challenges in the Pacific region. Just over half of primary-school aged children go to school in the Solomon Islands; 20 percent of the population in Vanuatu have no access to health care services; and Papua New Guinea has the lowest living standards of any country in the Pacific, with many basic needs not met.

New Zealand is a Pacific nation and links with its neighbours are long standing and far reaching. As a small island nation, New Zealand understands many of the issues faced by its neighbours and by spending over half its aid in the Pacific, New Zealand is in a position to play a significant role in assisting Pacific countries address their development challenges.

NZAID's Pacific programme is focused where the need is greatest, with prioritised programmes in Vanuatu, Papua New Guinea and the Solomon Islands, where poverty is more severe and pervasive. NZAID also has major development partnerships with Fiji, Samoa, Tonga, Cook Islands, and Kiribati, and provides assistance to Niue and Tokelau that reflects New Zealand's constitutional commitments and close social ties.

Gifts that keep giving

Buying friends and loved ones a goat for Christmas instead of the usual socks and chocolates proved a popular choice for New Zealanders in 2007. Kiwis bought more than 22,000 gifts from international development agency Oxfam New Zealand's alternative gift-giving scheme – Oxfam Unwrapped.

There are more than 50 gifts to choose from, specially selected to help people in developing countries work themselves out of poverty.

Friends and loved ones receive a card detailing the present bought for them, and the donation goes to those who need it most.

New Zealanders took to the concept in 2007, with a 46 percent increase in Oxfam Unwrapped sales from the previous year. The most popular gifts included: chickens and ducks, which can provide a family with an income from the sale of eggs and organic fertiliser; goats, which can produce up to seven litres of fresh milk a week and whose manure helps to grow crops; and the planting of 25 trees to furnish communities with food, shelter, and warmth. School books, donkeys, and baby buffalos also made it onto the most wanted list.

But it isn't just about Christmas presents. Oxfam Unwrapped is becoming a popular alternative for Valentine's Day and birthdays, as well as wedding registries for couples who already have a kitchen full of platters.

Tearfund's Gift for Life, and Wish List by Save The Children, offer similar gift options to help communities and families in developing countries around the world.

Source: Oxfam

Table 4.01

Spending on NZAID programmes
Year ending 30 June 2007

Programme	Spending $(million)	Percent of total
Pacific	162.43	49
Global	80.42	24
International agencies	64.17	19
New Zealand agencies	23.21	7
Total	**330.23**	**100**

Note: Figures may not add up to stated totals due to rounding.

Source: NZAID

NZAID supports the work of key regional agencies in the Pacific, including the Pacific Islands Forum Secretariat, the University of the South Pacific, the Secretariat for the Pacific Community, the Pacific Applied Geoscience Commission, the Pacific Regional Environment Programme, the Forum Fisheries Agency, and the South Pacific Board for Educational Assessment.

Asia programme

Asia is home to two-thirds of the world's poorest people. New Zealand's programmes in the region are targeted where they can make the greatest difference. South-East Asia is NZAID's major geographic focus outside the Pacific. The agency focuses on sustainable rural livelihoods in the region, including a strong emphasis on trade and development, and human resources development. Programmes in South-East Asia are closely aligned to partner government priorities and are delivered through direct support to government agencies and multilateral organisations. In 2006/07 close to $50 million was targeted to six bilateral partners – Indonesia, Viet Nam, Timor-Leste, Philippines, Cambodia, Laos – and linked regional programmes.

Latin America programme

NZAID's engagement in Latin America focuses on rural livelihoods and indigenous peoples in the central Andean Highlands and rural development in Central America. The main development partners are United Nations agencies, local and New Zealand non-government organisations (NGOs). NZAID also supports small local governance initiatives in Argentina, Chile and Brazil.

Africa programme

As well as providing support through international agencies and NGOs, to address development and humanitarian needs throughout Africa in 2006/07, NZAID managed a targeted development programme in southern Africa, covering South Africa, Tanzania, Zambia, Zimbabwe, Kenya, Mozambique, Namibia and Swaziland. The priority focus was youth oriented HIV/Aids healthcare, basic education and governance initiatives, working mainly through UN agencies and local NGOs on the ground.

Humanitarian assistance

Crises can arise for many reasons including natural disasters, conflict, or collapse of governmental systems. NZAID's first priority in humanitarian crises is to save lives, reduce suffering, and maintain human dignity, during and in the aftermath of the emergency.

The principals that NZAID follows when taking humanitarian action involve:

- following international humanitarian law and international human rights conventions
- ensuring that it assists longer-term development opportunities
- ensuring that assistance is fair and equitable
- working together with the local government and partners to make sure that decisions are reached in a participatory way
- strengthening local capacity and ownership
- monitoring how effective the action is, in order to improve future actions.

New Zealand agencies

NGOs play a crucial role in sustainable development and addressing humanitarian needs worldwide. NZAID provides support to the work carried out by New Zealand NGOs and their partners overseas through two major programmes – the Humanitarian Action Fund and Kaihono-hei-Oranga-Hapori o te Ao Partnerships for International Community Development (KOHA-PICD). NZAID also provides core funding for the Council for International Development (the umbrella body for New Zealand development NGOs), Volunteer Service Abroad, the Development Resource Centre and Trade Aid.

International agencies

NZAID engages with the multilateral system in collective action aimed at eliminating poverty and realising human rights for all. New Zealand support for international development bodies, including UN agencies and financial organisations such as the Asian Development Bank and the World Bank, is delivered under NZAID's multilateral programmes.

New Zealand contributes funding to UN agencies to enable development and humanitarian assistance for poor people in countries outside of the Asia/Pacific region. The assistance focuses on reproductive and sexual health, women's and children's issues, supporting refugees, and helping countries to meet basic needs.

NZAID's support prioritises engagement with 10 key agency partners that share New Zealand's priorities and policy settings. NZAID also prioritises certain issues for discussion in international meetings. These issues include gender, human rights, HIV/Aids, and aid effectiveness.

Involvement in international organisations

United Nations

New Zealand was a founding member of the United Nations (UN) in 1945 and successive New Zealand governments have continued to strongly support it. The UN is the major global forum for maintaining peace and security, strengthening relations among countries, encouraging international cooperation aimed at solving economic and social problems, establishing and strengthening an international legal framework, and promoting respect for human rights.

The range and complexity of the functions of the UN and its specialised agencies have grown steadily during the years. New Zealand concentrates on areas where it can play a useful role in matters directly affecting New Zealand interests, and where it can support efforts to secure lasting peace and security.

New Zealand is a strong advocate of international law and is actively engaged in the global debate on peace and security issues, disarmament, conflict prevention, sustainable development, the environment and the promotion of human rights, decolonisation, and reform of the UN organisation itself.

Contributions to the UN Each member's contribution is based on its capacity to pay. In 2006/07, New Zealand contributed $7.6 million in annual dues to the UN plus $16.9 million for the peacekeeping budget and $1 million for international tribunals. New Zealand's contribution for 2007 was 0.256 percent of the UN budget. Contributions to the UN's specialised agencies vary, according to scales agreed to by members of each agency.

Human rights During the 62nd session of the General Assembly in 2007, New Zealand played a pivotal role as a co-author of a resolution on the death penalty. It worked with other strongly abolitionist countries from all regions of the world to produce a resolution that calls on countries to implement a global moratorium on executions as a concrete step towards the total abolition of the death penalty. New Zealand also co-sponsored country-specific resolutions at the 2007 assembly relating to human rights situations of particular concern. These included Iran, the Democratic People's Republic of Korea, and Myanmar.

During 2007, New Zealand submitted its fifth periodic report under the Convention Against Torture, and its fifth report under the International Covenant on Civil and Political Rights. New Zealand also presented its seventeenth report to the Committee on the Elimination of Racial Discrimination and its sixth report to the Committee on the Elimination of All Forms of Discrimination Against Women in August 2007 (these two reports were first submitted in 2006).

The Convention on the Rights of Persons with Disabilities was adopted at the 61st session of the General Assembly in December 2006. New Zealand played a lead role in negotiating this convention and signed it on 30 March 2007.

In 2006, New Zealand announced that it was standing for the UN Human Rights Council for the period 2009–12.

The International Court of Justice This is the principal judicial organ of the UN. Its function is to decide, in accordance with international law, cases that are submitted to it by states. A New Zealand judge, Sir Kenneth Keith, was the first New Zealander to be elected to it as one of its 15 members, in November 2005.

Specialised agencies and related intergovernmental organisations Many subsidiaries, specialised agencies, and related agencies, work with the UN and each other to achieve shared goals. New Zealand is a member of the major specialised agencies, including:

- the Food and Agricultural Organization (FAO) – aims to raise nutrition levels and improve food production and distribution, thereby contributing towards an expanding world economy and humanity's freedom from hunger
- the International Labour Organization (ILO) – seeks to achieve important advances in working and living conditions
- the World Health Organization (WHO) – aims to advance international health
- UN Educational, Scientific and Cultural Organization (UNESCO) – seeks to develop the interconnected fields of education, science and culture.

In October 2007, New Zealand completed a term on the UNESCO World Heritage Committee, which is responsible for implementing the World Heritage Convention for the protection of natural and cultural heritage. New Zealand is a member of the WHO Executive Board, for the 2007–10 term.

New Zealand fully participates in the work of the International Atomic Energy Agency, which promotes the development and transfer of peaceful nuclear technologies, builds and maintains a global nuclear safety regime, and assists in global efforts to prevent the proliferation of nuclear weapons. It is similarly active in the Comprehensive Nuclear-Test-Ban Treaty Organization, and the Organisation for the Prohibition of Chemical Weapons.

Interfaith and inter-cultural dialogue

New Zealand has been actively engaged in regional and multilateral interfaith and inter-cultural initiatives such as the Asia-Pacific Regional Interfaith Dialogue and the UN's Alliance of Civilisations. These initiatives aim to encourage respect for diversity and strengthen social cohesiveness for a more peaceful and secure region and world. Such initiatives can help address radicalisation and terrorist recruitment and are an important element of New Zealand's counter-terrorism efforts.

The Asia-Pacific Regional Interfaith Dialogue is co-sponsored by New Zealand, Australia, Indonesia and the Philippines. New Zealand hosted the third dialogue in Waitangi in May 2007, following on from the two previous meetings: Yogyakarta, Indonesia, in December 2004 and Cebu, the Philippines, in March 2006.

The Asia-Pacific Regional Interfaith Dialogue brings together representatives of the major faith and community groups of 15 countries from South-East Asia and the adjacent South Pacific. The dialogue explores how the people in the region can cooperate and communicate better to build understanding and respect for people of different religious faiths. It focuses the region's attention on the need for inclusion and respect within our own diverse communities, so that no faith community feels marginalised or excluded. Its basic principle is that no religion should be used as a basis or justification for intolerance, fanaticism and terrorist activity.

New Zealand is a strong supporter of the Alliance of Civilisations (AOC) initiative launched by the UN Secretary-General in 2005. The AOC initiative is increasingly recognised as the focal point of multilateral efforts to build bridges between cultures and societies and to strengthen trust and cooperation. The report of the AOC's high-level group identified practical actions that states can take to improve relations between faiths, societies and cultures, particularly between Islam and western societies.

In May 2007, New Zealand convened a symposium in Auckland on the AOC. The symposium participants included prominent leaders, thinkers, faith leaders and experts from the Asia-Pacific region and elsewhere, including three members of the AOC's high-level group. The symposium focused regional attention on the AOC report's recommendations, particularly in the four 'fields of action' – education, youth, media and migration – and identified possibilities for follow-up action by countries in the region.

Source: Ministry of Foreign Affairs and Trade

World Trade Organization

The World Trade Organization (WTO) is the only international organisation that deals with rules of trade among nations. It acts as a single institutional framework over the General Agreement on Tariffs and Trade (which has been in force since 1948), and over the multilateral agreements that resulted from the Uruguay round of trade negotiations between 1986 and 1994.

The WTO provides a code of rules and a forum in which its 152 member countries can discuss trade problems, and negotiate and enlarge world trading opportunities. It is based on principles that the trading system should be:

- Without discrimination – WTO members must treat all members as favourably as any other country. This principle is particularly important for countries such as New Zealand, since it ensures that larger countries cannot adopt discriminatory trade policies (except for preferential free trade areas and customs unions). Imported products must not be treated less favourably than domestic products with respect to internal taxes, regulations and other requirements.
- Freer – barriers such as tariffs should come down progressively through negotiations.
- Predictable – businesses should be confident that trade barriers, including tariffs, non-tariff barriers and other measures, will not be raised arbitrarily. This is achieved by members making binding commitments not to raise trade barriers beyond current levels.
- Transparent – the WTO discourages less transparent instruments, such as quotas and import licensing, in favour of protection in the form of tariffs.
- More competitive – the WTO discourages unfair practices, such as export subsidies, and dumping products below cost to gain market share.
- More beneficial to less developed countries – developing countries are allowed more time to adjust, with greater flexibility and special privileges to help them in their development objectives.

The highest decision-making level in the WTO is the ministerial conference, which meets every two years. The 2002 ministerial conference in Doha, Qatar, launched a new round of negotiations with the aim of concluding them by 1 January 2005. The new round was termed the Doha Development Agenda, to acknowledge the importance of development issues to the achievement of further trade liberalisation.

Key provisions in the Doha declaration included agreement to improve market access for agricultural and non-agricultural products and services, new mandates to negotiate to reduce fishing subsidies, and recognition of the relationship between WTO trade rules and multilateral environmental agreements. The declaration also referred to the work of the International Labour Organization, and to avoiding mandates that could weaken critical WTO disciplines, such as the Sanitary and Phytosanitary Agreement.

Real progress on the Doha Round was not evident until the first half of 2004, when a political process produced breakthroughs in agriculture that led to a 'framework' agreement being adopted in Geneva in July 2004. This included advances on export subsidy elimination in agriculture, and progress across a range of other issues. The declaration did not meet the 2005 deadline for completion but intensive negotiations continued.

Talks among the so-called G6, the United States, EU, Brazil, India, Japan and Australia, broke down in mid 2006 and the WTO Director General suspended Doha negotiations. Negotiations were restarted following an informal meeting among trade ministers in the margins of the World Economic Forum meeting in Davos, Switzerland, in January 2007, and have continued since then. In July 2007, enough progress had been made to allow the chairs of the key negotiating groups on agriculture and non-agricultural market access to issue draft negotiating texts.

Commonwealth

The 53 member countries of the Commonwealth represent close to two billion people (about 30 percent of the world's population), from a broad range of cultures, faiths and traditions. The capacity of this diverse association to speak with a single voice on shared Commonwealth values – including a strong commitment to democracy, good governance and the rule of law – makes it a unique voice in world affairs.

Meetings of the Commonwealth Heads of Government (CHOGM), every two years, set the direction of the Commonwealth, with routine activities performed by the Commonwealth secretariat in London. The secretary-general and the secretariat, based in London, pursue the Commonwealth's twin goals of democracy and development.

New Zealand was a founding member of the Commonwealth in 1931, and in the 2007/08 year was the sixth-largest contributor to the Commonwealth Secretariat budget. New Zealand actively promotes the Commonwealth's core beliefs and principles.

The Commonwealth Games have been held in New Zealand three times, and New Zealand hosted the 1995 CHOGM in Auckland. A key achievement of the Auckland CHOGM was the establishment of the Commonwealth Ministerial Action Group (CMAG), which acts as the Commonwealth's watchdog on democracy and governance. New Zealand served on CMAG from 1995–99, and was again appointed as one of the nine members of CMAG at Kampala CHOGM in November 2007.

Former New Zealand Minister of Foreign Affairs and Trade, Rt Hon Don McKinnon, was appointed Commonwealth Secretary-General in 1999 and was re-elected for a second term in 2003. When his term concluded in March 2008, he was succeeded by H E Kamalesh Sharma of India.

Since 1992, New Zealanders have participated in numerous missions to observe elections in member countries, including Zimbabwe in 2000 and 2002, Pakistan in 2002, Nigeria in 2003, Sri Lanka in 2004, the Solomon Islands in 2004, Bougainville in 2005 and Lesotho in 2006.

Organisation for Economic Co-operation and Development

New Zealand joined the Organisation for Economic Co-operation and Development (OECD) in 1973. The OECD is a forum for democratic and market-oriented economies to study and develop economic, social, environment and development policies, with the ultimate aim of fostering prosperity and sustainable development.

The OECD works on almost all of the key economic, social and development issues on the international agenda. Its work programme includes projects on growth and innovation, agricultural policy reform, employment and social inclusion, sustainable development, ageing populations, education, information and communications technology, health care issues, and global trade liberalisation. Its staff are among the world's leading authorities in many of these areas.

Based in Paris, the OECD has 30 members: Australia, Austria, Belgium, Canada, the Czech Republic, Denmark, Finland, France, Germany, Greece, Hungary, Iceland, Ireland, Italy, Japan, Republic of Korea, Luxembourg, Mexico, Netherlands, New Zealand, Norway, Poland, Portugal, the Slovak Republic, Spain, Sweden, Switzerland, Turkey, the United Kingdom and the United States. In May 2007, the OECD invited Chile, Estonia, Israel, Russia and Slovenia to begin negotiations towards becoming members of the OECD. The OECD has extensive cooperation programmes with key non-member countries, including Brazil, China, India, Indonesia, and South Africa, and regionally focused programmes, including the Middle East and Africa.

Also of central importance is its programme of outreach with non-government organisations, to explain how the OECD's goals and activities are designed to promote the economic well-being of all citizens in both developed and developing countries.

New Zealand is a member of the International Energy Agency, an autonomous body within the OECD framework. The primary focus of the agency is oil security among members, but its programme embraces a wide range of energy issues. New Zealand is also a member of the Financial Action Task Force, an independent body housed in the OECD, dedicated to combating money laundering and terrorist financing.

New Zealand territories

Tokelau

Tokelau consists of three small atolls in the South Pacific – Atafu, Fakaofo and Nukunonu – with a combined land area of 12 square kilometres and a population of 1,466 (2006 Census). The central atoll, Nukunonu, is 92 kilometres from Atafu and 64 kilometres from Fakaofo. It is 480 kilometres north of Samoa.

The British Government transferred administrative control of Tokelau (then known as the Union Islands) to New Zealand in 1926. Formal sovereignty was transferred to New Zealand in 1948 by an act of the New Zealand Parliament. New Zealand statute law, however, does not apply to Tokelau unless it is expressly extended. In practice, no New Zealand legislation is extended to Tokelau without consent.

Governance Tokelau is listed as a non-self-governing territory and is on the schedule of territories under supervision of the United Nations Special Committee on Decolonisation. The Administrator of Tokelau is appointed by the Minister of Foreign Affairs and Trade and is responsible for the administration of the executive government of Tokelau. Under a programme of constitutional change agreed in 1992, the role of Tokelau's political institutions has been re-defined and expanded. In 1994, the administrator's powers were formally delegated to the General Fono (National Parliament), and the Council of Faipule (now the Council for Ongoing Government) when the General Fono is not in session.

In 1996, the formal step of devolving legislative power was taken. The Tokelau Amendment Act 1996, by the New Zealand Parliament, allowed the General Fono to exercise rule-making power. This power has been used primarily to manage major economic activities in Tokelau and for financial management of Tokelau's accounts.

The faipule are leaders of their respective villages (one on each atoll), and the ministerial portfolios they hold represent an extension of their formal responsibility. Traditionally, each village has been largely autonomous. The Tokelau Village Incorporation Regulations 1986 gave legal recognition to each village and granted it independent law-making power.

Ministry of Foreign Affairs and Trade

The ballot box arrives on the atoll of Atafu, Tokelau, for the 2006 referendum on self-governance.

In 2004, as part of the Modern House of Tokelau project, the administrator's powers were transferred from the General Fono to the three village councils (taupulega). The aim was to put in place a governance system that was functional in the local setting, blending the modern with the traditional. The challenge was to devise a structure which properly established the village as the focus of social and economic activities, that delivered services within the village, and that integrated traditional decision-making processes with modern advice and support.

In October 2003, the General Fono instituted a number of constitutional and law changes, which included renaming the Council of Faipule to Tokelau Council for Ongoing Government. The new council has six members, the three faipule and the three pulenuku (village mayors). The position of Ulu o Tokelau (leader of Tokelau) will continue to rotate on a yearly basis among the three faipule.

Public services A review of Tokelau public services carried out in 2003/04 shifted responsibility for public services away from the national office in Apia, Samoa, back to the three atolls. The office in Apia has been restructured to enhance its capability to deliver services on a national basis, and to provide a liaison point for international issues.

Finance Tokelau runs its own budget, and although it is currently heavily dependent on New Zealand for economic support, Tokelau has its own trust fund (now standing at just over $28.3 million). It is looking at ways of increasing its own revenue-earning capacity in areas such as fisheries licensing, handicrafts, tourism, and stamps and coins.

Self-determination Tokelau has in recent years been moving steadily towards an act of self-determination based on the Niue and Cook Islands form of self-government in free association with New Zealand. With the administrative powers formerly exercised by New Zealand having been transferred progressively to Tokelau, it is, in most practical respects, self-governing.

In 2005, New Zealand and Tokelau completed a draft Constitution for Tokelau and a draft Treaty of Free Association that could form the basis for a formal act of self-determination. In February 2006, Tokelau, under United Nations (UN) supervision, voted on whether to become self-governing in free association with New Zealand or retain its current status. Sixty percent of registered voters were in favour of self-government, but the vote did not produce the required two-thirds majority – the benchmark set by the General Fono. In October 2007, Tokelau held a second referendum, under UN supervision, and again the vote failed to produce the two-thirds majority required for a change in Tokelau's status.

Ross Dependency

The Ross Dependency consists of the land, permanent ice-shelf, and islands of Antarctica below 60 degrees south and between 160 degrees east and 150 degrees west. New Zealand's Antarctic territory includes the Ross Ice Shelf, the Balleny Islands, Scott Island, and the landmass and islands within these longitudes to the point where they meet at the South Pole.

The land is almost entirely covered by ice and is uninhabited except for the people who are conducting or supporting scientific research programmes. New Zealand operates a permanent scientific research station, Scott Base, on Ross Island in the dependency.

New Zealand has exercised jurisdiction over the dependency since 1923, when an Imperial Order-In-Council, made by the King in Executive Council in London, granted executive and legislative power to the New Zealand Governor-General in respect of the dependency.

New Zealand actively participates in the Antarctic Treaty System, which consists of the 1959 Antarctic Treaty and associated agreements. The treaty system serves to coordinate relations between states with respect to Antarctica, and its primary purpose is to ensure Antarctica is used for peaceful purposes only and that it does not become the scene or object of international discord. It designates Antarctica as "a natural reserve, devoted to peace and science"; promotes international scientific cooperation; and bans mining, nuclear testing and the dumping of nuclear waste, and the deployment of military personnel (except in support of peaceful purposes) in Antarctica.

Membership of the treaty system has grown from the 12 original signatories of the Antarctic Treaty (of which New Zealand was one) to 46 parties, 28 of which have consultative or decision-making status. Treaty parties meet regularly to consider issues within its framework, such as scientific and logistical cooperation and environmental protection measures, as well as the regulation of human activities in Antarctica, such as tourism.

People or groups going to the Ross Dependency, or who are departing for Antarctica from New Zealand (whatever their nationality), are required to submit an Environmental Impact Assessment under the Antarctica (Environmental Protection) Act 1994 to the Minister of Foreign Affairs. Permits must also be obtained for certain Antarctic activities. Official expeditions of governments that are parties to the Antarctic Treaty are exempt from these requirements.

Fishing in the Ross Sea must be consistent with conservation measures adopted by the Commission for the Conservation of Antarctic Marine Living Resources, based in Hobart, Australia. New Zealand has conducted exploratory fishing for toothfish in the Ross Sea since 1997.

Defence

The Governor-General of New Zealand is commander-in-chief in and over New Zealand. Authority over New Zealand's armed forces, however, is vested in the government – responsibility for defence matters within the government is held by the Minister of Defence.

The defence portfolio encompasses both the Ministry of Defence Manatū Kaupapa Waonga and the New Zealand Defence Force Te Ope Kaatua o Aotearoa. The chief of the defence force and the secretary of defence (the chief executive of the Ministry of Defence) are both accountable to the Minister of Defence.

The Ministry of Defence is responsible for policy, and advice on funding for defence activities, major capability procurement and repair. The secretary of defence is the government's principal civilian adviser on defence policy matters. The ministry also conducts evaluations of the performance of the New Zealand Defence Force.

New Zealand's armed forces consist of the Royal New Zealand Navy, the New Zealand Army, and the Royal New Zealand Air Force. These regular forces, together with territorial, reserve and civilian personnel, constitute the New Zealand Defence Force.

The chief of the defence force is both the commander and chief executive of the New Zealand Defence Force and is the government's principal military adviser on defence matters. The chief of defence force is responsible for the New Zealand Defence Force's management of resources, the general conduct of the New Zealand Defence Force, and chairs the meetings of the executive leadership team and chiefs of service committee.

The role of the chiefs of the navy, army, and air force, is to raise, train and maintain their respective services.

The commander of the joint forces in New Zealand exercises operational control of forces assigned to the headquarters of the joint forces, and commands all New Zealand Defence Force operations and exercises, as directed by the chief of the defence force.

The military and civilian advisory roles are complementary, with considerable overlap on defence, security, and capability issues. Close cooperation and consultation is required between the Ministry of Defence and the New Zealand Defence Force. The office of chief executives brings the secretary of defence and the chief of defence force together to discuss policy issues of mutual interest. The executive governance boards oversee major New Zealand Defence Force capital equipment and infrastructure projects.

The government funds defence through the Ministry of Defence and the New Zealand Defence Force. The two organisations' expenditure is consolidated in table 4.02 (overleaf).

Table 4.03 compares New Zealand's defence expenditure with international expenditure for 2000–06. Table 4.04 shows defence force personnel numbers 1998–2007.

Anzacs at Gallipoli

On 25 April 1915, New Zealand troops, as part of the Australian and New Zealand Army Corps (ANZAC), landed at Gallipoli at a place now known as Anzac Cove. A larger British force landed at the tip of the peninsula.

The allies hoped to seize Gallipoli and open the Dardanelles for an attack on the Turkish capital, Constantinople. Their ultimate aim was to force the Ottoman Empire out of the war and to open a supply line to Russia.

The Anzacs were to play a key role in this plan. Thwarted in their initial attempt to seize and hold the high ground above the landing place, they soon found themselves confined to a small area around Anzac Cove, which was dominated by strong Turkish positions on higher ground.

August 1915 saw the last great attempt to break the military deadlock with fresh landings and an attempt by the allies to capture the heights above Anzac Cove. The New Zealand troops' objective was to seize control of Chunuk Bair, a high point in the Gallipoli Peninsula's Sari Bair mountain range. After the Mounted Rifles seized the foothills of the Sari Bair range, the New Zealand Infantry Brigade attacked the heights. The Wellington Infantry Battalion managed to capture Chunuk Bair early on 8 August, but suffered severe casualties when the Turks counter-attacked. Of the 760-strong battalion, only 70 soldiers remained unwounded or only slightly wounded. The Wellingtons were relieved late that night. Further Turkish attacks on 10 August recaptured Chunuk Bair.

The exhausted New Zealand force had suffered more than 1,700 casualties in a few days. One New Zealander, signaller Cyril Bassett, was awarded the Victoria Cross for repeatedly repairing telephone wires under heavy fire.

The shattered New Zealand Infantry Brigade was shipped to the island of Lemnos for rest in September, returning to Gallipoli in November to fight again until the campaign was abandoned. Anzac Cove was evacuated in December.

Of the 8,556 New Zealanders who served in the campaign, 2,515 were killed in action, 206 died of disease and other causes and a further 4,752 were wounded. New Zealand memorials on Twelve Tree Copse, Lone Pine, Hill 60 and Chunuk Bair commemorate the fallen. Australia suffered 26,000 casualties in the campaign, Britain 120,000 and France 27,000.

The Gallipoli experience contributed to the realisation that New Zealanders had acquired their own national identity. Ormond Burton, a veteran of the campaign, wrote in 1935 that: "For us of New Zealand the fighting at Anzac must always remain in the nature of an epic. It was a tragedy that moved through terror and exultation and triumph to failure and defeat... but the way men died on Chunuk is shaping the deeds yet to be done by the generations yet unborn who will fill this land of ours in the great days to come."

On 25 April 1916, one year after the landing at Anzac Cove, the first Anzac Day was commemorated. In 1920, 25 April was set aside as the day to commemorate those killed at Gallipoli and in the other theatres of World War I.

Large numbers of New Zealanders take part in Anzac Day commemorations, both in New Zealand and at Gallipoli, and a trip to Gallipoli has become a national pilgrimage for many New Zealanders.

Source: New Zealand Defence Force

Table 4.02

Defence expenditure
Year ending 30 June

Item	2004	2005	2006	2007
	$(000)			
Personnel costs	561,887	576,119	616,823	649,744
Operating costs	461,666	443,561	492,849	532,538
Depreciation	229,678	232,669	235,801	290,608
Capital charge	289,139	281,894	316,264	346,845
Total output expenses	**1,542,370**	**1,534,243**	**1,661,737**	**1,819,735**
Other expenses[1]	72,000	-3,266	0	1,665
Remeasurement expenses[1]	0	0	0	90,484
Total expenses[2]	**1,614,370**	**1,530,977**	**1,661,737**	**1,911,884**
Less				
Other revenue	(17,202)	(17,037)	(16,552)	(17,339)
Profit on sale of assets[3]	(25,483)	(40,762)	0	(1,765)
Net operating surplus/(deficit)	(46,296)	63,468	61	(85,968)
Revenue Crown-provided	**1,525,389**	**1,536,646**	**1,645,246**	**1,806,812**

(1) Non-cash technical adjustments. (2) Non-departmental expenditure for social development activities (not included in the table) was: in 2004, $12,311; in 2005, $9,850; in 2006, $10,153; in 2007, $10,283. (3) Funds recovered by New Zealand Defence Force for long-term working capital.

Sources: New Zealand Defence Force, Ministry of Defence

Table 4.03

International comparison of defence expenditure
As proportion of gross domestic product

Country	2000	2001	2002	2003	2004	2005	2006
	Percent						
United States[1]	3.2	3.1	3.4	3.8	4.0	4.0	3.8
United Kingdom[2]	2.5	2.4	2.4	2.4	2.3	2.5	2.3
Australia[3]	1.8	1.9	2.3	2.3	2.6	1.9	1.9
Sweden[3]	2.2	2.9	1.9	1.8	1.7	1.5	1.4
Canada[2]	1.2	1.1	1.2	1.2	1.2	1.2	1.2
New Zealand[4]	1.0	1.0	1.0	0.9	1.1	0.9	1.0

(1) Year ending 30 September; US budget definition differs from NATO definition. (2) Year ending 31 March. (3) Year ending 30 June. (4) Using NATO definition, excluding GST, capital charge and war pensions.

Source: New Zealand Defence Force

Table 4.04

Defence personnel
At 30 June

Year	Navy	Army	Air Force	Total	Civilians (NZDF and Ministry of Defence)
1998	2,104	4,431	2,991	**9,526**	2,195
1999	2,080	4,417	2,885	**9,382**	1,912
2000	1,967	4,513	2,786	**9,266**	1,936
2001	1,893	4,580	2,624	**9,097**	1,877
2002	1,911	4,492	2,194	**8,597**	1,879
2003	1,969	4,388	2,245	**8,602**	1,923
2004	1,953	4,479	2,249	**8,681**	2,025
2005	1,910	4,438	2,266	**8,614**	2,092
2006	1,998	4,563	2,388	**8,949**	2,253
2007	2,034	4,580	2,437	**9,051**	2,321

Sources: New Zealand Defence Force, Ministry of Defence

Defence policy

The Government's defence policy is to have a modern, professional, and well-equipped defence force with the military capabilities to meet New Zealand's objectives. The five key objectives for New Zealand's defence policy are to:

- defend New Zealand and to protect its people, land, territorial waters, exclusive economic zone, natural resources, and critical infrastructure
- meet New Zealand's alliance commitments to Australia by maintaining a close defence partnership in pursuit of common security interests
- assist in the maintenance of security in the South Pacific and to provide assistance to New Zealand's Pacific neighbours
- play an appropriate role in the maintenance of security in the Asia-Pacific region, including meeting New Zealand's obligations as a member of the Five Power Defence Arrangements

- contribute to global security and peacekeeping through participation in the full range of United Nations operations, and other appropriate multilateral peace support and humanitarian relief operations.

While New Zealand may not face a direct military threat from another country in the foreseeable future, the security of the country and its citizens is threatened by non-military groups, such as terrorists, international criminals, and resource poachers.

Deployment of New Zealand Defence Force personnel to trouble spots around the world demonstrates New Zealand's commitment to international peace and security. Since 2002/03, defence force personnel have been deployed to Afghanistan, and the Arabian Gulf region, in the international fight against terrorism. Hundreds of other defence force personnel are deployed to Timor-Leste and the Solomon Islands.

New Zealand Defence Force personnel were also deployed to longer-standing commitments in the Middle East, the Balkans, North-East and South-East Asia, and Africa.

Disarmament

New Zealand's voice on disarmament and arms control is listened to with respect, due to its role in creating the United Nations (UN), its opposition to nuclear testing, the establishment of a nuclear-free New Zealand, and practical contributions to UN peacekeeping and de-mining operations.

New Zealand also cooperates with other like-minded countries to exert influence. An example is its membership of the New Agenda Coalition (Brazil, Egypt, Ireland, Mexico, New Zealand, South Africa and Sweden) – a strong advocate for multilateral progress towards nuclear disarmament. New Zealand is also deeply involved with international efforts to stop the illicit arms trade, and to regulate conventional weapons.

The Ministry of Foreign Affairs and Trade's international security and disarmament division is responsible for policy and treaty implementation. It prepares advice for the Minister for Disarmament and Arms Control, represents New Zealand at international meetings, and ensures that New Zealand's international legal obligations are implemented at the national level. The division is also responsible for issuing export permits for items on New Zealand's list of strategic goods.

Overseas-based ministry officers, including an ambassador for disarmament, are involved in negotiations and activities with disarmament organisations, mainly in Geneva, Vienna, New York and The Hague.

The government values the views of New Zealand's non-government peace and disarmament groups, whose representatives join official delegations to international meetings to contribute their advice and perspective on the pursuit of New Zealand's disarmament goals.

New Zealand Defence Force personnel discuss how to disarm a smoke projectile near the village of Bint Jubayl on the Israeli/Lebanese border in February 2008.

Wellington conference on cluster munitions

New Zealand hosted an international conference in Wellington from 18–22 February 2008 that advanced discussions on a new treaty on cluster munitions. Over 100 countries, as well as representatives from civil society and UN agencies, attended the conference, which took place within the framework of the 'Oslo Process'.

The Oslo Process was launched in February 2007 and it committed states to conclude a new international treaty on cluster munitions by the end of 2008. The objectives of the new treaty would be to prohibit cluster munitions that cause unacceptable harm to civilians; and to establish a framework for co-operation and assistance for survivors, clearance of land contaminated by cluster-munition remnants and the destruction of stockpiles.

The key outcome of the conference was the Wellington Declaration, which contained a decision to conclude negotiations on a new convention on cluster munitions at a diplomatic conference that was held in Dublin in May 2008. Eighty-two countries endorsed the declaration at the conclusion of the conference, which underlined the political momentum towards a new convention. More countries endorsed the declaration subsequently. Countries needed to take this step to be able to formally participate in the Dublin Conference.

Cluster munitions are area weapons that normally comprise a canister containing a number of sub-munitions or bomblets. They have caused severe harm to civilians in conflict areas where they have been used. While designed to explode on impact, many of the sub-munitions in cluster munitions fail and become a serious hazard. Civilians have been killed or injured by sub-munitions which remain, sometimes many years after the conflict.

Cluster munitions were used in the 2006 conflict in Southern Lebanon, following which an estimated one million unexploded cluster munitions contaminated the territory. The New Zealand Defence Force sent teams of ordnance experts to help clear these unexploded sub-munitions in the aftermath of the conflict.

Source: Ministry of Foreign Affairs and Trade

A statutory body, the Public Advisory Committee on Disarmament and Arms Control, was established under the New Zealand Nuclear Free Zone, Disarmament and Arms Control Act 1987 to:

- advise the Minister of Foreign Affairs and Trade on disarmament and arms control
- advise the prime minister on implementation of the Act
- publish reports on disarmament and arms control matters and on implementation of the Act
- make recommendations for grants from the Peace and Disarmament Education Trust, established from Rainbow Warrior compensation funds, and grant funding from the UN Disarmament and Education Implementation Fund.

The committee has nine members, including the Minister for Disarmament and Arms Control, who is the chair. The other eight are appointed by the Minister of Foreign Affairs and Trade for three-year terms.

Royal New Zealand Navy

The chief of the Royal New Zealand Navy Te Taua Moana o Aotearoa exercises full command of the navy. The operational elements of the fleet are commanded by the commander of joint forces in New Zealand through the maritime-component commander, based at the headquarters of the joint forces, at Trentham. The deputy chief of navy, based in Wellington, is responsible to the chief of the navy for the navy's 'raise, train and maintain' functions.

The naval base at Devonport, Auckland, (known as HMNZS *Philomel*), consists of the navy's main naval barracks, wharf facilities, and administrative units; the naval hospital; and the naval supply and armament depots. The base also contains the naval dockyard, an engineering and support facility managed by a private company under contract. HMNZS *Wakefield* is the administrative unit in the Wellington area. There are four Royal New Zealand Naval Volunteer Reserve units in the main centres: HMNZS *Ngapona* in Auckland, HMNZS *Olphert* in Wellington, HMNZS *Pegasus* in Christchurch and HMNZS *Toroa* in Dunedin. There is also a port headquarters in Tauranga (attached to HMNZS *Ngapona*).

Table 4.05 lists the navy's ships and helicopters, while table 4.06 shows navy personnel.

Figure 4.02

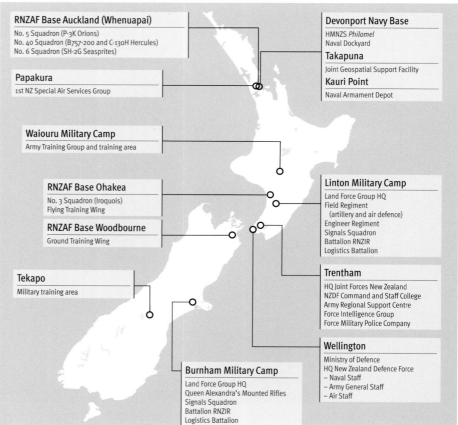

Principal defence force locations

RNZAF Base Auckland (Whenuapai)
No. 5 Squadron (P-3K Orions)
No. 40 Squadron (B757-200 and C-130H Hercules)
No. 6 Squadron (SH-2G Seasprites)

Papakura
1st NZ Special Air Services Group

Waiouru Military Camp
Army Training Group and training area

RNZAF Base Ohakea
No. 3 Squadron (Iroquois)
Flying Training Wing

RNZAF Base Woodbourne
Ground Training Wing

Tekapo
Military training area

Burnham Military Camp
Land Force Group HQ
Queen Alexandra's Mounted Rifles
Signals Squadron
Battalion RNZIR
Logistics Battalion

Devonport Navy Base
HMNZS *Philomel*
Naval Dockyard

Takapuna
Joint Geospatial Support Facility

Kauri Point
Naval Armament Depot

Linton Military Camp
Land Force Group HQ
Field Regiment
  (artillery and air defence)
Engineer Regiment
Signals Squadron
Battalion RNZIR
Logistics Battalion

Trentham
HQ Joint Forces New Zealand
NZDF Command and Staff College
Army Regional Support Centre
Force Intelligence Group
Force Military Police Company

Wellington
Ministry of Defence
HQ New Zealand Defence Force
 – Naval Staff
 – Army General Staff
 – Air Staff

Source: New Zealand Defence Force

Royal New Zealand Navy sailors perform a haka as the project protector vessel, HMNZS Otago, is launched at a Melbourne shipyard in November 2006. The ship will be involved in patrolling, surveillance, search and rescue, humanitarian and peacekeeping assistance, and training.

Nautical surveying

The Joint Geospatial Support Facility provides geospatial intelligence to support New Zealand Defence Force planning for military operations. Its products include marine, topographical and aviation maps and charts, and 3D digital models.

The unit also contributes to the national charting programme coordinated by Land Information New Zealand by producing nautical charts and providing other services in the interests of navigational safety.

Hydrographic survey work is undertaken in inshore areas by the detached hydrographic survey unit, using the survey motorboat *Adventure*.

In 2006, the hydrographic and oceanographic vessel, HMNZS *Resolution*, completed the hydrographic survey of shipping routes for sea lanes in Hawke's Bay, and conducted rapid environmental assessments for amphibious operations around New Plymouth and the Marlborough Sounds.

Source: New Zealand Defence Force

Table 4.05

Navy vessels

2007

Ship/helicopter type	Name	Force
ANZAC-class frigates	*Te Kaha*	Naval combat
	Te Mana	
Multi-role vessel	*Canterbury*	Naval support
Logistics (fleet replenishment)	*Endeavour*	Naval support
Offshore patrol vessels	*Otago*	Naval patrol
	Wellington	
Inshore patrol vessels	*Rotoiti*	Naval patrol
	Pukaki	
	Taupo	
	Hawea	
Survey ship	*Resolution*	Hydrographic support
Diving support ship	*Manawanui*	Diving support
Training tender	*Kahu*	Sea training
Mine counter measures support vessel	*Kiwi*	Training, mine countermeasures
Kaman Super Seasprite SH-2G (NZ) helicopter (x5)	*Seasprite*	Naval aviation

Source: New Zealand Defence Force

Table 4.06

Navy personnel

At 30 June

Category	2001	2002	2003	2004	2005	2006	2007
Regular force (all ranks)	1,893	1,918	1,978	1,953	1,910	1,998	2,034
Volunteer reserve (all ranks)	385	357	354	317	327	291	287
Total uniformed	**2,278**	**2,275**	**2,332**	**2,270**	**2,237**	**2,289**	**2,321**
Civilian employees	434	444	441	436	40	387	378
Total navy	**2,712**	**2,719**	**2,773**	**2,706**	**2,277**	**2,676**	**2,699**

Source: New Zealand Defence Force

New Zealand Army

The New Zealand Army Ngati Tumatauenga is organised, equipped, and trained to respond to lower-level contingencies in the Asia-Pacific region, or contribute to a collective force, including a United Nations force. It can provide a flexible range of units and sub-units for deployments of up to a battalion group in size.

The chief of the army, under the chief of the defence force, has full command of the army. The chief of army is assisted in discharging his statutory command requirements by the army general staff. The army general staff has both a policy formulation and a policy implementation role.

The land-component commander, under the commander of the joint forces in New Zealand, commands the operational elements of the army. The land-component commander is assigned operational command of the second land force group, primarily based at Linton, and the third land force group, primarily based at Burnham. This position also commands all regular and territorial force units, except for those elements assigned to the land training and doctrine group. The land training and doctrine group, primarily based in Waiouru, reports directly to the army general staff and is responsible for most of the individual training conducted within the army.

Army specialist units, based at Auckland and Trentham, include a special air service group and a military police company, and are commanded by the land-component commander.

Table 4.07 lists army headquarters and units and table 4.08 shows army personnel.

Table 4.07

Army headquarters and units
2007

Headquarters/unit	Location	Role
Auckland and Northland battalion group	Auckland	Territorial force
New Zealand special air service group	Auckland	Special forces
Hauraki battalion group	Tauranga	Territorial force
Army depot	Waiouru	Training
Headquarters – Army training group	Waiouru	Command
Land operations training centre	Waiouru	Training
Officer cadet school	Waiouru	Training
Wellington and Hawke's Bay battalion group	Napier	Territorial force
Wellington, West Coast and Taranaki battalion group	Wanganui	Territorial force
Battalion Royal New Zealand infantry regiment	Linton	Combat
Engineer regiment	Linton	Combat support
Field regiment	Linton	Combat support
Headquarters – Land force group	Linton	Command
Health services battalion	Linton	Combat service support
Logistics battalion	Linton	Combat service support
Signals squadron	Linton	Combat support
Force intelligence group	Trentham	Combat support
Force military police company	Trentham	Combat service support
Trentham regional support centre	Trentham	Static support
Army general staff	Wellington	Command
Battalion Royal New Zealand infantry regiment	Burnham	Combat
Canterbury, Nelson, Marlborough and West Coast battalion group	Burnham	Territorial force
Field troop	Burnham	Combat support
Headquarters – Land force group	Burnham	Command
Logistics battalion	Burnham	Combat service support
Queen Alexandra's mounted rifles	Burnham	Combat
Signals squadron	Burnham	Combat support
Otago and Southland battalion group	Dunedin	Territorial force

Source: New Zealand Defence Force

Table 4.08

Army personnel
At 30 June

Category	2001	2002	2003	2004	2005	2006	2007
Officers	742	735	732	729	746	775	804
Other ranks	3,838	3,757	3,656	3,750	3,692	3,788	3,712
Total regular force	**4,580**	**4,492**	**4,388**	**4,479**	**4,438**	**4,563**	**4,516**
Territorial force (all ranks)	2,159	2,158	2,031	1,856	1,888	1,912	1,826
Total uniformed	**6,739**	**6,650**	**6,419**	**6,335**	**6,326**	**6,475**	**6,342**
Civilians	643	779	687	684	706	745	693
Total army	**7,382**	**7,429**	**7,106**	**7,019**	**7,032**	**7,220**	**7,035**

Source: New Zealand Defence Force

Royal New Zealand Air Force

The Royal New Zealand Air Force (RNZAF) provides a maritime patrol force, a fixed wing transport force, and a rotary wing transport force. The chief of the air force, supported by the air staff, commands the air force.

The air-component commander within the headquarters of the joint forces commands the RNZAF's deployable operational units. The broad range of activities carried out to raise, train and maintain the operational units of the air force is provided under the direction of the air staff. Operational flying units are based at the Auckland and Ohakea RNZAF bases. The Ohakea base also hosts primary and advanced flying training, while most ground training is done at the Woodbourne base, near Blenheim.

RNZAF logistics services are coordinated by the air staff, with specific aircraft maintenance and supply support performed by operational squadrons and base logistics units. Much of the depot-level repair and overhaul work is contracted to private companies in New Zealand and overseas. Air force training aircraft are maintained and supported by private contractors.

Table 4.09 lists air force aircraft, and table 4.10 shows air force personnel for 2001–07.

Table 4.09

Air force aircraft		
	2007	
Aircraft	RNZAF base	Force
P-3K Orions (x6)	Auckland	Maritime patrol force
Boeing 757-200s (x2)	Auckland	Fixed wing transport force
C-130H Hercules (x5)	Auckland	Fixed wing transport force
SH-2G (NZ) Super Seasprites (x5)	Auckland	Naval helicopter force
Bell UH-1H Iroquois (x14)	Ohakea	Rotary wing transport force
Bell 47G Sioux (x5)	Ohakea	Flying training
CT-4E Air Trainers (x13)	Ohakea	Flying training
Beechcraft King Air B200s (x5)	Ohakea	Flying training

Source: New Zealand Defence Force

Table 4.10

Air force personnel							
At 30 June							
Category	2001	2002	2003	2004	2005	2006	2007
Officers	571	509	508	523	541	577	600
Other ranks	2,053	1,714	1,718	1,726	1,725	1,811	1,837
Total regular force	**2,624**	**2,223**	**2,226**	**2,249**	**2,266**	**2,388**	**2,437**
Territorial force (all ranks)	176	157	155	32	28	25	191
Total uniformed	**2,800**	**2,380**	**2,381**	**2,281**	**2,294**	**2,413**	**2,628**
Civilians	411	390	412	402	376	408	379
Total air force	**3,211**	**2,770**	**2,793**	**2,683**	**2,670**	**2,821**	**3,007**

Source: New Zealand Defence Force

International defence relationships

The Five Power Defence Arrangements Concern about security arrangements in South-East Asia led to the establishment, in 1971, of the Five Power Defence Arrangements (FPDA), involving New Zealand, Australia, Singapore, Malaysia and the United Kingdom. The arrangements are consultative and aim to contribute to the security of Malaysia and Singapore and to the long-term stability of the region. Members take part in exercise programmes that increase the ability of the five countries' armed forces to operate with each other. Defence ministers and defence chiefs meet regularly and there is a range of other exchanges.

The exercises and contacts which New Zealand has with FPDA partners are an important part of the New Zealand Defence Force's training programme and has expanded significantly in recent years. The FPDA continues to evolve to meet the challenges of the changing security environment, with attention now being given to combating non-traditional threats such as maritime terrorism, piracy, and people smuggling. Scenarios based around these threats are being introduced into exercises.

Mutual assistance programme Most South Pacific countries, some members of the Association of South-East Asian Nations (ASEAN), and Timor-Leste participate in the New Zealand Defence Force's mutual assistance programme. Through training cooperation and advisory assistance, the programme contributes to the effectiveness of defence forces and law enforcement agencies in the South Pacific region. From time to time, the programme also supports development projects in the South Pacific by using the engineering and trade skills of the armed forces. Training is provided in New Zealand, and training and technical teams are deployed overseas. Military instructors are attached to other armed forces in the Cook Islands, Samoa, Tonga, Vanuatu, and Malaysia, for up to two years.

Australia A close defence relationship with Australia in support of common interests for a secure and peaceful region is a key policy objective for the government. Both countries share a strong commitment to the security and stability of the Asia-Pacific region, as reflected in combined efforts in recent years in Bougainville, Timor-Leste, and the Solomon Islands. The security relationship between Australia and New Zealand is embodied by the policy of closer defence relations, adopted in 1991 and realised through a programme of cooperative activities designed to give the relationship practical effect.

Confronting the threat of terrorism

International terrorism is one of the greatest challenges to peace and security that societies face today. While the threat of a direct attack against New Zealand remains low, New Zealanders were victims in the attacks in the United States in 2001, in Bali in 2002, and in the London bombings in 2005. New Zealand's dependence on international trade, and love of travel, means New Zealand interests are very much at stake in the fight against terrorism.

New Zealand is committed to regional and international counter-terrorism cooperation, and to improving its counter-terrorism capability, within the rule of law and fundamental human rights.

New Zealand has implemented counter-terrorism measures required by the UN Security Council and other international bodies, both through legislation and by strengthening border security, intelligence capability and financial infrastructure. New Zealand also contributes militarily to international efforts against terrorist infrastructure in Afghanistan, and to maritime operations in the Persian Gulf and Arabian Sea.

Counter-terrorism has become an important agenda item for many of the regional forums in which New Zealand participates. It works with its partners to strengthen the region's counter-terrorism capacity in areas such as border, transport and financial security.

New Zealand works with Pacific island countries to assist them to meet UN Security Council counter-terrorism requirements. New Zealand helps them to implement necessary legislation, establish effective border control operations, and meet their reporting obligations. Central to New Zealand's efforts is the Pacific Working Group on Counter-Terrorism, which New Zealand has convened and chaired for the last three years. The working group provides an opportunity for Pacific island countries to receive up-to-date information on international counter-terrorism and to coordinate technical assistance projects. New Zealand also provides technical advice and supports a variety of capacity building projects.

New Zealand also works with ASEAN countries to help build regional counter-terrorism capacity. This includes cooperative projects with the region's three counter-terrorism training centres.

Source: Ministry of Foreign Affairs and Trade

New Zealand Defence Force

Air Loadmaster Sergeants McQueen and Hodges launch a package over the drop zone during Exercise Skytrain. New Zealand and New Caledonian aircraft were involved in this RNZAF tactical low-level flying exercise, based out of Napier airport in January 2007.

ANZUS The ANZUS security treaty between Australia, New Zealand and the United States came into force in 1952. The United States, however, is unwilling to accept restrictions on access to New Zealand ports for nuclear-powered or nuclear-armed ships of the United States Navy and the ANZUS Council has not met since 1984.

Other military liaisons To facilitate exchanges on military matters, defence representatives are posted to many of New Zealand's overseas diplomatic missions, with some accredited to more than one country. New Zealand has defence representatives in Australia; Canada; China; Fiji/Samoa/ Tonga; Indonesia/Timor-Leste; Malaysia/Brunei; Cook Islands/Niue; Papua New Guinea/ Vanuatu/ Solomon Islands; Philippines; Japan; Korea; Saudi Arabia/Qatar/Bahrain/United Arab Emirates/ Oman/Kuwait/Afghanistan; Singapore; Thailand/Laos/Cambodia/Viet Nam; United Kingdom/ Germany/France/Belgium/Italy/Ireland; and the United States.

Military representatives are also accredited to multilateral bodies, including New Zealand's United Nations New York mission, and the headquarters of the Integrated Area Defence System in Malaysia. A representative in the United Kingdom is accredited to the European Union and the North Atlantic Treaty Organisation. In addition, a number of countries have military representatives attached to their diplomatic missions in Wellington, or accredited to, but not resident in, New Zealand.

Armed forces overseas at 31 August 2007

United Nations Truce Supervisory Organization (UNTSO) New Zealanders have been serving as UN military observers with UNTSO since 1948. UNTSO was formed to supervise the various truces stemming from the first Arab-Israeli War. These days the main purpose of the organisation is to monitor the various armistices and peace agreements, and use its positive influence to mediate between the disputing parties.

Groups of UNTSO observers are also attached to the UN Disengagement Force on the Golan Heights and the UN Interim Force in Lebanon. NZDF personnel are mainly based in Damascus, Tiberias, Nahariya, and at UNTSO headquarters in Jerusalem. They usually work at observation posts between frontline regular forces on both sides of international borders. They are not normally involved with the continuing clashes between Israeli and Palestinian forces in the occupied territories of the Gaza Strip and the West Bank.

New Zealand observers are drawn from all three services and may include female and territorial force officers. The Cabinet reviews New Zealand's contribution to this mission periodically.

East Timor/Timor-Leste In 1999, the Indonesian Government agreed to hold a vote in East Timor to decide its future. New Zealand military personnel and civilian police have participated in various UN missions in East Timor since then to halt violence and to support stability in the region. Most troops were withdrawn in 2002.

A mutual assistance programme with Timor-Leste was established in 2005, to provide a framework for training assistance in the longer term. Following unrest in 2006, New Zealand recommitted a large number of personnel, together with Australia, to a combined joint task force. Currently, 180 NZDF personnel are deployed to Timor-Leste.

Afghanistan In the Afghanistan summer, 122 New Zealand Defence Force personnel are deployed as the New Zealand provincial reconstruction team in the province of Bamyan in central Afghanistan; approximately 80 are deployed during the winter. Three other personnel are attached to the International Security Assistance Force headquarters in Kabul. Another defence force officer works as a military liaison officer to the UN Assistance Mission to Afghanistan. Two personnel serve at the headquarters of the Combined Forces Command Afghanistan and Coalition Joint Task Force 76. Two more New Zealand Defence Force personnel assist in training the Afghan National Army as part of the Kabul-based United Kingdom Afghan National Army training team. Three staff officers are based at central command headquarters in Florida to provide planning advice and support for the New Zealand personnel contributing to Operation Enduring Freedom in Afghanistan. Contingents drawn from the New Zealand special air service group were deployed to Afghanistan, but the last returned in 2005.

Regional Assistance Mission to the Solomon Islands (RAMSI) The mission was deployed following a request from Solomon Islands' Prime Minister Kanaleeza in July 2003 for assistance in restoring security, particularly on the islands of Guadalcanal and Malaita. RAMSI is an Australian-led mission comprising Australian, Papua New Guinean, Fijian, New Zealand and Tongan officials, elements of the Australian and New Zealand defence forces and police officers from Australia, New Zealand and Pacific countries. New Zealand initially contributed 230 personnel to RAMSI, although the mission was later scaled down. The New Zealand Defence Force deployed a 30-strong platoon and a three-person National Support Element between November 2004 and February 2005, and another infantry platoon in 2006. Currently, there are 44 defence force personnel in the Solomon Islands.

Multinational Force and Observers (MFO) This force, in Sinai, was established in 1981 to verify compliance with the terms of the 1979 peace treaty between Egypt and Israel. Eleven countries contribute to the MFO, including New Zealand, whose 26-strong contingent provides a training and advisory team, a heavy transport section, engineers, and staff officers.

Arabian Gulf Six New Zealand Defence Force personnel are based in the Arabian Gulf to provide logistical support to defence force operations in the region.

The Republic of Korea Three New Zealand officers serve with the UN Command Military Armistice Commission in the Republic of Korea.

Sudan Two New Zealand military observers and one staff officer are serving with the UN Mission in Sudan.

Iraq After the return to New Zealand in September 2004 of the 61 New Zealand Defence Force personnel attached to a British Engineer Regiment in Basra, only one officer remains in Iraq, as a military liaison adviser with the UN Assistance Mission in Iraq.

Former Yugoslavia The New Zealand Defence Force deployed personnel to different parts of the former Yugoslavia for peacekeeping for many years. One officer remains in Kosovo (at the Headquarters of the UN Mission in Kosovo), but all other missions have finished.

Casualties There have been five fatalities among New Zealand Defence Force personnel serving in UN observer and peacekeeping missions since the defence force began participating in such missions.

Community assistance

New Zealand Cadet Forces Community-based youth groups, the cadet forces include the Sea Cadet Corps, the New Zealand Cadet Corps and the Air Training Corps. In 2006/07, the New Zealand Defence Force supported 103 cadet units with a total strength of 3,671 cadets and 330 officers. These groups receive assistance from the New Zealand Defence Force and support from the Sea Cadet Association of New Zealand, the Cadet Corps Association of New Zealand, the Air Training Corps Association of New Zealand, community organisations, and the Royal New Zealand Returned and Services Association.

Limited Service These volunteer training courses have been run by the army since 1995; additional staffing support has been provided by the navy and air force since 1998. The programme offers 144 positions on five courses each year, and provides unemployed volunteers, between the ages of 17 and 25, with six weeks of residential motivational training in a military cultural environment, teaching outdoor activities and general life skills.

Disaster relief The New Zealand Defence Force provides assistance to civil authorities following natural disasters in New Zealand, the Pacific and South-East Asia. Assistance can include surveying damage; transporting relief, food and medical supplies; and providing medical, engineering and communications services.

Assistance was provided during the civil defence emergency declared during the floods in Northland in July 2007 (and also during the 2004 and 2005 floods in Eastern Bay of Plenty, Manawatu/Rangitikei, and Tauranga).

The defence force can also be called on for post-cyclone damage assessment, and delivery of supplies in the Pacific and in Asia (for example, following the Boxing Day 2004 tsunami). Army engineers, usually working through New Zealand's Agency for International Development, may be used for limited reinstatement of some infrastructure.

New Zealand Defence Force

Ship navigator Lieutenant Rendall plots coordinates on HMNZS Te Kaha. Te Kaha is one of two ANZAC class frigates, which patrol New Zealand waters and the South Pacific region and participate in naval exercises with New Zealand's military partners.

Fisheries protection New Zealand's 200-mile exclusive economic zone is patrolled by the air force's P-3K Orions and navy vessels. Information from surveillance patrols is passed to the Ministry of Fisheries, and fisheries officers are sometimes carried on board aircraft or ships when patrols are conducted. The air force conducted numerous patrols in the New Zealand and South Pacific exclusive economic zones during 2006/07 and also patrolled the Southern Ocean. Navy fisheries protection and border surveillance patrols are expected to increase as two new offshore and four new inshore patrol vessels are introduced into service.

Search and rescue All three New Zealand defence force services maintain a search and rescue capability. Naval and air units are on 24-hour standby, and provide personnel and advice to Rescue Coordination Centre New Zealand when needed. The navy and air force assist in sea searches, while the army and the air force assist the New Zealand Police in land searches and rescues. The air force also carries out emergency medical evacuations throughout New Zealand, the South Pacific and Antarctica. In 2006/07, the air force recorded 176 Orion and Iroquois search and rescue flight hours, which was less than half the 373 hours flown in 2005/06.

Operation Antarctica New Zealand Defence Force personnel support Operation Antarctica in terminal and logistic support operations. Up to 70 personnel are based at Harewood in Christchurch, and at McMurdo Station and Scott Base in Antarctica for varying periods during the Antarctic summer season from September to February. In 2006/07, RNZAF aircraft carried 110 passengers and more than 101,000 kilograms of freight to Antarctica.

Border surveillance The navy and air force support the New Zealand Customs Service in maintaining border security and reducing the risks that may arise as a result of the movement of people, goods and craft into and out of New Zealand. On request, the defence force will also patrol the exclusive economic zones of other South Pacific Forum countries.

Patrol flights in the South Pacific are carried out for military surveillance and economic-zone protection purposes. Unclassified results of these flights are shared with Pacific island countries and the Forum Fisheries Agency. Seats on these flights are frequently made available for Pacific island governments to allocate. All patrols are coordinated with Australian and French military authorities.

The New Zealand Defence Force's liaison with the New Zealand Customs Service will increase in importance as the navy's new offshore and inshore patrol vessels are introduced into service.

Other assistance The New Zealand Defence Force provides assistance to other government agencies and to the community. Assistance includes mail drops for Department of Conservation staff on outlying islands, ceremonial support for state occasions, helicopter and logistic support to the New Zealand Police, assistance with fire fighting, and explosive ordnance disposal.

Inspector-general of intelligence and security

The inspector-general of intelligence and security helps the prime minister oversee and review the Security Intelligence Service and the Government Communications Security Bureau. The inspector-general's focus is on the lawfulness of each organisation's activities, and that any complaints are independently investigated. The inspector-general is appointed by the governor-general on the recommendation of the prime minister following consultation with the leader of the opposition.

The New Zealand Security Intelligence Service

The New Zealand Security Intelligence Service (NZSIS) provides the government with intelligence and advice on national security issues within the terms of the New Zealand Security Intelligence Service Act 1969. The service is a civilian organisation governed by statute. The director of security, appointed by the governor-general, is responsible to the Minister in Charge of the New Zealand Security Intelligence Service for its efficient and proper working.

The NZSIS:

- obtains and evaluates intelligence relevant to security (this includes collecting and assessing domestically focused security intelligence, and the provision of foreign intelligence reports to meet New Zealand's foreign intelligence requirements)
- communicates the intelligence to those whom the director considers appropriate, in the interests of security
- advises the government about matters relevant to security
- cooperates with other organisations in New Zealand and overseas that can assist the service
- makes security-related recommendations on immigration and citizenship matters
- conducts enquiries and makes recommendations on security clearances for particular individuals
- gives advice on protective measures relevant to security.

Security involves protecting New Zealand from acts of espionage, sabotage, and subversion, whether or not the acts are directed from, or intended to be committed in, New Zealand. Security also involves protecting New Zealand from activities of foreign organisations or people that are clandestine, deceptive, threaten the safety of anyone, or have a negative impact on New Zealand's international or economic well-being.

The service aims to identify foreign capabilities, intentions or activities, within or relating to New Zealand, that impact on New Zealand's international or economic well-being; and to prevent any terrorist act or activity.

The NZSIS may not enforce security, or investigate people only because they take part in legal protest activities or disagree with the government of the day, nor can it do anything for the purpose of harming or furthering the interests of any political party.

The inspector-general of intelligence and security may enquire into any matter relating to the service's compliance with the law. The inspector-general may enquire into a complaint by any New Zealand person who considers that they have been adversely affected by any act, omission, practice, policy or procedure of the NZSIS. The service is also overseen by the Intelligence and Security Committee of Parliament.

Government Communications Security Bureau

The Government Communications Security Bureau (GCSB) provides information, advice and assistance to the New Zealand Government, government departments and organisations. The GCSB is responsible to the prime minister.

The operations of the GCSB are governed by the Government Communications Security Bureau Act 2003. The GCSB is subject to oversight and review by the inspector-general of intelligence and security.

The GCSB protects information that is processed, stored, or communicated by electronic or similar means. The GCSB formulates communications security and computer security policy. It promotes standards and provides material, advice, and assistance to government departments and authorities (including the New Zealand armed forces), on matters relating to the security and integrity of official information – the loss or compromise of which could adversely affect national security.

The GCSB provides advice to government departments and authorities about official information that, although unrelated to national security, requires protection for privacy, safety, and commercial reasons, or to protect the functions of government. It also provides technical security services to defend against eavesdropping and other forms of technical attack against New Zealand Government premises worldwide.

The GCSB warns, guides, and coordinates the national response to information-technology-based threats to New Zealand's critical infrastructure (ie power, telecommunications, emergency services, banking and finance, transport, and government).

GCSB collects foreign signals intelligence to meet the national intelligence requirements of the New Zealand Government.

The GCSB head office is in Wellington and it operates two communications stations, at Tangimoana, near Palmerston North, and Waihopai, near Blenheim.

External Assessments Bureau

The External Assessments Bureau produces intelligence assessments of events and trends overseas that are likely to influence New Zealand's foreign relations and external interests. Part of the Department of the Prime Minister and Cabinet, the bureau supports informed decision-making by the government.

The bureau employs about 30 staff, who identify, collate, evaluate and analyse information collected from a range of sources and prepare assessments and reports on political, economic, biographic, strategic and scientific matters.

Table 4.11 shows annual expenditure on the three intelligence and security agencies.

Table 4.11

	Expenditure on intelligence and security agencies		
	Year ending 30 June		
Year	External Assessments Bureau	New Zealand Security Intelligence Service	Government Communications Security Bureau
		$(000)	
1996	2,121	9,964	19,498
1997	2,216	9,968	18,496
1998	2,274	10,514	18,506
1999	2,287	10,583	19,083
2000	2,292	11,500	21,289
2001	2,462	10,956	19,327
2002	2,541	11,690	20,116
2003	2,709	13,376	23,216
2004	3,129	15,655	29,154
2005	3,079	17,206	29,754
2006	3,058	22,433	37,977
2007	3,162	28,399	42,077

Sources: External Assessments Bureau, New Zealand Security Intelligence Service, Government Communications Security Bureau

Contributors and related websites

Department of the Prime Minister and Cabinet – www.dpmc.govt.nz

Government Communications Security Bureau – www.gcsb.govt.nz

Ministry of Defence – www.defence.govt.nz

Ministry of Foreign Affairs and Trade – www.mfat.govt.nz

New Zealand Army – www.army.mil.nz

New Zealand Defence Force – www.nzdf.mil.nz

New Zealand Security Intelligence Service – www.nzsis.govt.nz

NZAID – www.nzaid.govt.nz

Office of the Inspector General of Intelligence and Security

Royal New Zealand Air Force – www.airforce.mil.nz

Royal New Zealand Navy – www.navy.mil.nz

Statistics New Zealand – www.stats.govt.nz

Volunteer Service Abroad – www.vsa.org.nz

The ethnic mosaic of New Zealand's population is changing, with the Māori, Asian and Pacific populations making up a growing proportion of the overall population. Some pupils from Aorangi Primary School in Christchurch in 2008 – Samantha Jory-Smart (left), 7, Hassain Raja, 9, Poutiriao McDowell, 6, Fatima Zawari, 10, Chris Choi, 8, and Diana Elisara, 10.

5 | Population

Population growth

The population of New Zealand reached 500,000 in 1880, boosted by the introduction of government-assisted immigration. The first million mark was passed in 1908, following economic recovery from the depression of the 1880s and 1890s. In the aftermath of World War II, the growth rate climbed dramatically, compared with stagnation in the early 1930s, as the baby boom and increased immigration took effect.

The second million was reached in 1952, 44 years after the first million, and the third was reached only 21 years later, in 1973. Nearly 20 percent of the population growth during this period came from net migration. New Zealand's estimated resident population reached 4 million 30 years later in 2003. Nearly all the population growth between 3 and 4 million was due to natural increase (an excess of births over deaths), with migration not contributing significantly.

Figure 5.01 (overleaf) tracks New Zealand's historical and projected population and growth from 1961 to 2061.

Future demographic trends

Future population trends are uncertain because demographic changes affect, and in turn are influenced by, social, economic, political and other circumstances. Despite the inherent uncertainty, demographic projections provide relatively robust and useful information for several reasons.

Firstly, despite the range of influences that can impact on it, population change is fundamentally driven by births, deaths and net migration (arrivals minus departures).

Secondly, birth and death rates are generally consistent over several years, especially for larger geographical areas, barring major catastrophes, wars or epidemics.

Thirdly, three-quarters of people who will live in New Zealand in 20 years time have already been born. With the uncertainty of the births component removed, only migration or death can change the existing population.

Some broad future trends and structural changes can be identified. For example, population ageing and sub-replacement fertility in New Zealand have raised the prospect of slower population growth in coming decades. Sub-replacement fertility means that the population will not replace itself in the long-run, without migration.

The Dhue family has seven boys – Jesse (left), 14, Presley, 4, Taylor, 11, Bodhi, 12, Dylan, 16, Staeski, 7 months, with father Spencer Dhue, and Britten, 2, with mother Tina Dhue. At the time of the 2006 Census, 20,556 women stated that they had given birth to seven or more children.

Figure 5.01

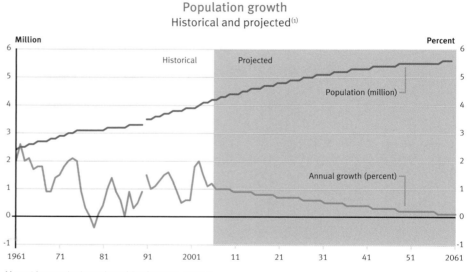

(1) 2006-base projections released October 2007, series 5.
Note: The break in data between 1990 and 1991 denotes a change from the de facto population concept to the resident population concept.

Source: Statistics New Zealand

The entry of large baby boom cohorts into retirement ages from 2011 will result in an increasing number of people aged 65 years and over. New Zealand's workforce will take on an older profile.

Projections also point to greater ethnic diversity in the future, with the broad Māori, Pacific and Asian populations all expected to increase their share of the New Zealand population.

Within the national scene, there will be contrasting population changes, with further concentration of population likely in the northern North Island. Given the narrowing gap between births and deaths, more and more areas will be relying on migration from other areas of New Zealand, or from overseas, if they want to maintain (let alone increase) their population. For many areas, this would require a reversal of recent migration flows.

Fertility has been below replacement level for most of the past few decades and is likely to remain so. However, New Zealand's population will continue to grow steadily but slowly for some time. This is because the current age structure has a built-in momentum for further growth, while international migration generally contributes more arrivals than departures. Slow growth aside, there will be profound shifts in population composition, including further ageing of the population, a burgeoning population aged 65 years and over, growing ethnic diversity, and geographic redistribution of the population.

Table 5.01

New Zealand population
By census

Year[1][2]	Census date	Population	Increase from previous census		Average annual increase (percent)
			Number	Percent	
1858	24 December	115,461	...	...	...
1874	1 March	344,985	...	...	...
1878	3 March	458,007	113,022	32.76	7.33
1881	3 April	534,030	76,023	16.60	5.10
1886	28 March	620,451	86,421	16.18	3.06
1891	5 April	668,652	48,201	7.77	1.50
1896	12 April	743,214	74,562	11.15	2.13
1901	31 March	815,862	72,648	9.77	1.90
1906	29 April	936,309	120,447	14.76	2.75
1911	2 April	1,058,313	122,004	13.03	2.52
1916	15 October	1,149,225	90,912	8.59	1.50
1921	17 April	1,271,667	122,442	10.65	2.27
1926	20 April	1,408,140	136,473	10.73	2.06
1936	24 March	1,573,812	165,672	11.77	1.13
1945	25 September	1,702,329	128,517	8.17	0.83
1951	17 April	1,939,473	237,144	13.93	2.37
1956	17 April	2,174,061	234,588	12.10	2.31
1961	18 April	2,414,985	240,924	11.08	2.12
1966	22 March	2,676,918	261,933	10.85	2.11
1971	23 March	2,862,630	185,712	6.94	1.35
1976	23 March	3,129,384	266,754	9.32	1.80
1981	24 March	3,143,307	...	...	...
1986	4 March	3,263,283	119,976	3.82	0.76
1991	5 March	3,373,926	110,643	3.39	0.67
1996	5 March	3,618,303	244,377	7.24	1.41
2001	6 March	3,737,277	118,974	3.29	0.65
2006	7 March	4,027,947	290,670	7.78	1.51

(1) Omits censuses of 1851, 1861, 1864, 1867 and 1871 as censuses of the Māori population were not taken in these years.
(2) Figures from 1981 onwards are census usually resident population counts, replacing census night population counts used previously.
Note: All figures are randomly rounded to base 3.
Symbol: ... not applicable

Source: Statistics New Zealand

Projected population

A number of population projection series are produced to illustrate a range of possible population scenarios. Projections given in this chapter draw on series 5 of the 2006-base national population projections released in October 2007. Series 5 assumes that: New Zealand women will average 1.9 births each in the long-run (below the 2.1 births required for the population to replace itself without migration); life expectancy at birth will increase to reach 84.5 years for males and 88.0 years for females in 2061; and there will be a long-run net migration gain of 10,000 people annually from 2010.

Given this scenario, the New Zealand population is projected to reach 5.09 million in 2031 and 5.57 million in 2061. The 5 million population mark is projected to be reached in 2028.

The pace of growth is not likely to be uniform. The New Zealand population grew at an average rate of 1.4 percent a year between 1951 and 2006. The population is projected to grow by an average of 1.0 percent a year between 2006 and 2011. Growth is expected to slow during the remainder of the projection period – to 0.6 percent in 2031 and to 0.1 percent in 2061.

The age structure of New Zealand's population is undergoing significant changes as a result of changing fertility patterns and increasing longevity. Overall, the population will take on an older profile. The median age (half the population is older, and half younger, than this age) of New Zealand's population increased from 26 years in 1971 to 36 years in 2006. According to projection series 5, half the population will be 40 years and older by 2027, and half the population will be 44 years and older by 2061.

Population ageing can be regarded as an inevitable dimension of the 'demographic transition' – the shift from high fertility rates and high mortality rates to low mortality rates and low fertility rates. Population ageing is often wrongly attributed to the post-war baby boom. The changes in fertility rates, birth numbers and the age structure during the baby boom have delayed the general ageing of New Zealand's population, although these changes will also make population growth among older age groups more pronounced after 2011.

Table 5.02 (overleaf) shows New Zealand's projected population according to series 5 (a mid-range scenario), and figure 5.02 shows the historical and projected age distribution of the population.

Population projected to pass 5 million

New Zealand's estimated resident population reached 4 million in 2003. New Zealand's first million was reached in 1908 and the second million was reached 44 years later in 1952. It took only 21 years to add the third million in 1973 – the fastest million achieved in New Zealand's history. The fourth million took 30 years to reach.

Nearly all the population growth from 3 to 4 million was due to natural increase (excess of births over deaths). Net migration did not contribute significantly to overall population growth during this period, although it had a significant impact on population composition, with departures exceeding arrivals for some ages, and arrivals exceeding departures for other ages.

Between 2001 and 2006, New Zealand experienced relatively rapid population growth, averaging 1.5 percent a year. This was partly due to high net migration gains compared with historic New Zealand levels, estimated at a net migration gain of 160,000 people between 30 June 2001 and 30 June 2006. However, population growth was about 1.0 percent in the year ended 30 June 2007, with net migration contributing about 10,000 people and natural increase about 34,000 people.

Projections suggest that New Zealand will have much slower population growth in the future, mainly because of the impact of population ageing on birth and death numbers. Various projection series are produced to illustrate a range of possible population scenarios. Series 5 (a mid-range scenario) assumes that: New Zealand women will average 1.9 births each in the long-run; life expectancy at birth will increase to reach 84.5 years for males and 88.0 years for females in 2061; and there will be a long-run annual net migration gain of 10,000 people from 2010.

Under this scenario, natural increase is projected to decline to 18,000 people in 2031 and to zero in the mid-2050s. As a result, the population is projected to reach 5 million in the late 2020s, before increasing slowly to 5.57 million in 2061. For the population to reach 6 million by 2061, New Zealand would need a sustained net migration gain of about 15,000 a year (assuming long-run fertility rates of 1.9 births per woman). Although annual net migration has exceeded 30,000 in recent years, the external migration balance has also fluctuated widely, with several periods of net migration loss.

Alternatively, New Zealand's population would reach 6 million by 2061 if women average 2.1 births each (and net migration averaged 10,000 a year). Only occasionally in the past few decades have fertility rates reached that level, although they were at that level in 2007.

Source: Statistics New Zealand

Figure 5.02

Age distribution of population[1]
1961–2061

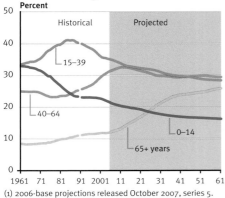

(1) 2006-base projections released October 2007, series 5.

Note: The break in data between 1990 and 1991 denotes a change from the de facto to the resident population concept.

Source: Statistics New Zealand

Counting the population

Statistics New Zealand has adopted the 'estimated resident population' concept as a standard for producing official population estimates and projections.

This concept is viewed as a more accurate estimate of the population normally living in an area than the 'census usually resident population count'. The estimated resident population of New Zealand includes all residents present in New Zealand and counted by the census (census usually resident population count), residents who are temporarily overseas (who are not included in the census), and an adjustment for residents missed or counted more than once by the census (net census undercount). Visitors from overseas are excluded.

Source: Statistics New Zealand

Table 5.02

New Zealand population projections[1] (2006–base)

	2006	2011	2021	2031	2041	2051	2061
Population by age group (years) at 30 June				**(000)**			
All ages	4,185	4,393	4,771	5,090	5,325	5,481	5,571
0–14	888	895	918	903	903	910	907
15–39	1,464	1,481	1,539	1,576	1,583	1,581	1,583
40–64	1,321	1,432	1,498	1,519	1,568	1,637	1,640
65+	512	585	817	1,091	1,272	1,353	1,441
Components of population change (year ending 30 June)				**(000)**			
Births	58	61	59	59	60	59	59
Deaths	27	30	34	41	50	57	62
Net migration	11	10	10	10	10	10	10
Annual population change	51	41	35	28	20	12	7
				Years			
Median age[2] (at 30 June)	36	37	39	41	43	44	44
Dependency ratio (at 30 June)			**Per 100 people aged 15–64**				
0–14[3]	32	31	30	29	29	28	28
65+[4]	18	20	27	35	40	42	45
0–14 and 65+[5]	50	51	57	64	69	70	73

(1) 2006-base projections released October 2007, series 5. (2) Half the population is younger, and half older, than this age. (3) The number of people aged 0–14 years per 100 people aged 15–64 years. (4) The number of people aged 65+ years per 100 people aged 15–64 years. (5) The number of people aged 0–14 and 65+ years per 100 people aged 15–64 years.

Note: Figures may not add up to stated totals, due to rounding.

Source: Statistics New Zealand

Age groups

The number of children (those aged 0–14 years) is expected to increase from 890,000 in 2006 to 900,000 in 2013, and then remain relatively stable between 900,000 and 920,000 over subsequent decades (under projection series 5). The small projected fluctuations will reflect birth numbers in preceding years.

As a result, children will account for only 16 percent of the population by 2061, compared with 21 percent in 2006.

By contrast, the population aged 65 years and over is projected to almost double from 510,000 in 2006 to 1 million in the late 2020s, and continue increasing to reach 1.44 million in 2061.

In the mid-2020s, the number of people aged 65 years and over is expected to surpass the number of children. From the late 2040s, over 25 percent of the population will be aged 65 years and over, compared with 12 percent in 2006 (see figure 5.02).

Within the 65-and-over age group, there will be about 360,000 people aged 85 years and over in 2061, more than six times the 2006 total of 58,000 people.

Allan, 89, and Hazel, 86, Hagan of Waikouaiti celebrate their 60th wedding anniversary. In 2061, it is projected that there will be about 360,000 people aged 85 years and over, more than six times the 2006 total of 58,000 people.

The working-age population (those aged 15–64 years) is projected to increase from 2.78 million in 2006 to 3.08 million in 2026, before increasing more slowly to 3.22 million in 2061. Most of the increase will be in the older half of this age group (40–64 years), as the large number of people born during the 1950s to early 1970s move through these ages. In 2006, the population aged 15–39 was 11 percent larger than the population aged 40–64. After 2010, the younger and older working-age groups will be similar in number.

In 2006, there were 5.4 people in the working-age group for every person aged 65 years and over. This ratio is expected to drop substantially to 3.2 people in 2026 and to 2.2 people in 2061. In the mid-1960s, the ratio was 7.1 people.

Educational ages The population in the various educational age groups is projected to fluctuate, as it has in the past. The fluctuations mainly reflect changes in births in preceding years, and although the number of future births is uncertain, the fluctuations have potentially significant impact on the demand for teachers and other educational resources. The projected numbers below refer to the New Zealand resident population in each age group, rather than the numbers in primary, secondary and tertiary education.

The primary-school-age population (5–12 years) peaked in 1975 at about 500,000 and then dropped to 400,000 in 1989. By 2006 the population had reached 475,000. It is projected to drop to 466,000 in 2009–10, before increasing to about 500,000 in 2018–19.

The trend in the secondary-school-age population (13–17 years) is similar to that for the primary-school-age population, except that the peaks and troughs lag behind those of the primary-school-age population by about six years. The secondary-school-age population is projected to drop from 320,000 in 2006–07 to about 300,000 in the late 2010s. By the mid-2020s, the numbers are expected to return to 320,000.

Peaks and troughs in the tertiary-age population (18–22 years) lag those of the secondary-school-age population by about five years. The tertiary-age population is projected to increase from about 300,000 in 2007 to peak at 326,000 in 2012. A similar peak will be reached again around 2029.

Figure 5.03

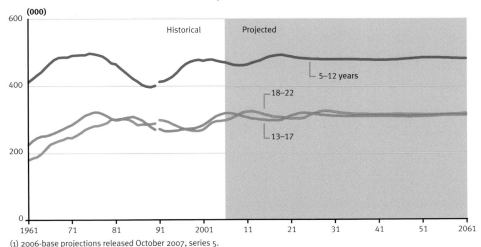

Population in educational age groups[1]
1961–2061

(1) 2006-base projections released October 2007, series 5.

Note: The break in data between 1990 and 1991 denotes a change from the de facto population to the resident population concept.
Source: Statistics New Zealand

Rounding and random rounding

Rounding of numbers is the technique of replacing a given number with another number called the rounded number. When used in tables, rounding may create a discrepancy between the total shown and the total of the individual items in the table.

Data is rounded for ease of use, or for confidentiality reasons. Quite different techniques are used in each case.

Rounding of numbers – for ease of use

It is often necessary to round numbers when making statistical calculations, where it might not be possible, practical, or reasonable to record numbers to the last digit. Statistical series are often rounded in publications to make them easily understood and readily comparable with other data. Such practices are quite acceptable, providing that an adequate level of accuracy is retained.

The chosen rounding interval determines selection of the rounded number.

For example: a rounding interval of 0.1 means rounding to one decimal place, so that 12.223 becomes 12.2. A rounding interval of 10 means rounding to the nearest multiple of 10, so that 1,222.3 becomes 1,220.

Rules are in place to ensure that any long-run bias in rounded numbers is avoided.

Random rounding – for confidentiality reasons

Since the 1981 Census, Statistics New Zealand has used a confidentiality assurance technique of randomly rounding census statistics to base 3. This enables the greatest possible amount of census data to be released without compromising the privacy of individual responses.

Random rounding to base 3 means that all table cell values, including row and column totals, are rounded as follows: zero counts and counts that are already multiples of three are left unchanged. Other counts are randomly rounded to one or other of the two nearest multiples of three. The figure that the original figure is rounded to is determined randomly, using fixed probabilities. For example, the number nine is left unchanged, whereas the number eight could be rounded to either six or nine.

Because rounding is done separately for each cell in a table, the rows and columns do not necessarily add up to the published row and column totals. However, the effect of this rounding on the accuracy of census statistics for practically any proposed use is insignificant.

Source: Statistics New Zealand

Ethnic and cultural diversity

Ethnic population information presented in this chapter is based on the concept of self-identification. Each ethnic group includes people who identify with that ethnic group, either solely or in conjunction with other ethnic groups. It excludes people who have ancestry but do not identify with that ethnic group. Some people identify with two or more ethnic groups, so the broad European, Māori, Pacific and Asian populations are not mutually exclusive.

New Zealand has been ethnically and culturally connected to Polynesia for at least 1,000 years. Its population and cultural heritage 200 years ago was wholly that of Polynesia, but it is now dominated by cultural traditions that are mainly European, especially those from the United Kingdom.

In 2006, about 77 percent of New Zealanders identified with a European ethnicity and/or 'New Zealander'. The indigenous Māori ethnic group makes up the next-largest group of the population (about 15 percent in 2006). The other main ethnic groups are Asian and Pacific peoples, who made up 10 and 7 percent, respectively, of the estimated resident population in 2006.

The Dominion Post

Jaquintin Putaura, 9 (left), Metusela Robati, 2, TC Robati, 9, and Enuake Robati, 10, a cultural group from the northern Cook Islands, perform at the festival of the elements in Porirua as part of 2008 Waitangi celebrations. New Zealand's Pacific and Māori populations are projected to have higher growth rates, due to higher fertility rates and numbers in the main childbearing ages.

The ethnic and cultural composition of New Zealand has been shaped and reshaped by three main demographic processes – international migration, natural increase and intermarriage. Of these processes, international migration has had the most pronounced effect.

All four broad ethnic populations are projected to experience growth between 2006 and 2026. Under a mid-range scenario, the Asian population is projected to have the largest growth over this period, an increase of 380,000 (3.4 percent a year).

The Pacific and Māori populations will experience increases of 180,000 (2.4 percent a year) and 190,000 (1.4 percent a year), respectively, while the European population will increase by 220,000 (0.3 percent a year).

The higher Asian growth rate is mainly driven by the assumed levels of net migration. By comparison, the higher Māori and Pacific growth, relative to the New Zealand population overall, is largely driven by higher fertility rates and numbers of people in the main childbearing ages.

The European/'New Zealander' share of the New Zealand population is projected to fall to 69 percent by 2026 – a reflection of the slower growth rate of the European population compared with the growth rate of the total New Zealand population.

By contrast, the share of the population belonging to the Māori, Asian and Pacific ethnic groups is projected to increase, to 17, 16 and 10 percent, respectively, by 2026. Diversity in fertility and migration patterns means the various ethnic groups will follow different paths to population ageing in future decades.

Table 5.03

Ethnic population projections[1]				
Proportion of New Zealand population by broad age group				
	European[2]	Māori	Asian	Pacific
Age group (years)	Percent			
2006[3]				
Under 15	73	24	9	12
15–39	71	17	13	8
40–64	81	10	8	5
65+	91	5	4	2
All ages	77	15	10	7
2026[4]				
Under 15	64	29	18	18
15–39	65	19	18	12
40–64	69	12	17	7
65+	82	7	10	3
All ages	69	17	16	10

(1) People who identify with more than one ethnic group are included in each ethnic population, so percentages add up to more than 100. (2) European or Other (including New Zealander) ethnic group. (3) Estimated resident population of each ethnic group at 30 June 2006. (4) 2006-base ethnic population projections released April 2008, series 6, compared with 2006-base New Zealand population projections released October 2007, series 5.

Source: Statistics New Zealand

With a median age of 38 years in 2006, the European population has a much older age structure than the Māori (23 years) and Pacific (22 years) populations. Despite ageing, the median age of the Māori (25 years) and Pacific populations (23 years) in 2026 will still be lower than the median age of the total New Zealand population (40 years).

Table 5.03 shows projected changes in New Zealand's population proportions by ethnicity and age group, and table 5.04 shows ethnic population projections for 2026.

Table 5.04

Ethnic populations and projections[1][2]
2006–2026

	European[3]	Māori	Asian	Pacific	Total New Zealand
Population			**(000)**		
2006[4]	3,213	624	404	302	**4,185**
2026	3,429	818	788	482	**4,939**
Average annual population change			**percent**		
2006–2026	0.3	1.4	3.4	2.4	**0.8**
Median age[5]			**years**		
2006	38	23	28	22	**36**
2026	43	25	36	23	**40**

(1) People who identify with more than one ethnic group are included in each ethnic population, so figures do not add up to stated totals. (2) 2006-base ethnic population projections released April 2008, series 6, and 2006-base New Zealand population projections released October 2007, series 5. (3) European or Other (including New Zealander) ethnic group. (4) Estimated resident population of each ethnic group at 30 June 2006. (5) Half the population is older, and half younger, than this age.

Source: Statistics New Zealand

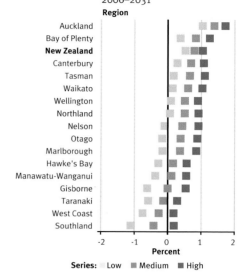

Figure 5.04

Projected average annual population change
By regional council area
2006–2031

Series: Low ■ Medium ■ High

Source: Statistics New Zealand

Regional populations

Under the medium (mid-range) projection series, 12 of New Zealand's 16 regional council areas (regions) will be home to more people in 2031 than in 2006. Ten regions will experience population growth throughout the entire projection period.

The populations of Hawke's Bay and Manawatu-Wanganui are projected to increase between 2006 and 2026, and then decrease for the remainder of the projection period. The Gisborne region is projected to increase between 2006 and 2021 and then decrease, so that its population in 2031 will be similar to that in 2006. The population of Taranaki is projected to increase between 2006 and 2016 before decreasing.

The West Coast and Southland are projected to have fewer residents in 2031, compared with 2006.

The low projection series for each region results in 7 of New Zealand's 16 regions having more people in 2031 than in 2006. With the high projection series, all 16 of New Zealand's regions will be home to more people in 2031 than in 2006.

Population growth is projected to slow in all 16 regions between 2006 and 2031, in the low, medium and high projection series. This slowing of growth is due to declining natural increase (births minus deaths).

Births are projected to decline in most regions, reflecting the assumed decrease in fertility rates combined with fewer women in the childbearing ages. In contrast, deaths are projected to increase in all regions, as the population in the older ages increases.

The Auckland region is projected to account for 62 percent of New Zealand's population growth between 2006 and 2031, with an increase of 560,000 people (from 1.37 million to 1.93 million (medium series)). The Auckland region would then be home to 38 percent of New Zealand's population in 2031, compared with 33 percent in 2006.

Natural increase is projected to account for almost two-thirds of the growth, with the remainder due to net migration gains. Under the low, medium and high projection series, Auckland's annual population growth will average 1.0, 1.4 and 1.7 percent, respectively.

There is considerable variation likely in population growth rates within the cities and districts of each region, largely because of differences in age structures, fertility levels, and migration patterns.

Figure 5.04 shows projected regional population changes by regional council area between 2006 and 2031 under the low, medium and high projection series.

Distribution of population

There has been a trend in the geographic distribution and redistribution of New Zealand's population in the past 150 years towards an increasing degree of urbanisation and, in particular, a concentration of people in the main urban centres.

North Island and South Island distribution

Following the end of the gold boom in the South Island in the 1870s, the proportion of people living in the South Island began to steadily decrease. From the 1896 Census onward, the census night population of the North Island has exceeded that of the South. Since that time, the North Island's population has continued to grow at a greater rate, and its share of the New Zealand total population has continued to increase.

At the time of the 1956 Census, 69 percent of New Zealanders lived in the North Island. This rose to more than 72 percent by 1976, and in 2006 it had risen to 76 percent.

Many influences have contributed to the population difference between the islands – for example, the North Island has had a higher birth rate and most overseas migrants choose to settle in the North Island.

Table 5.05 shows the estimated population of New Zealand from 1885 to 2007, while table 5.06 lists the North Island, the South Island, and total New Zealand populations from 1858 to 2006.

Table 5.05

Estimated population
1885–2007

Year	At 31 December	Mean for year ended 31 December	Year	At 31 December	Mean for year ended 31 December	Year	At 31 December	Mean for year ended 31 December
	Estimated de facto population			Estimated de facto population			Estimated de facto population	
1885	619,300	613,900	1927	1,450,400	1,439,000	1969	2,804,000	2,780,100
1886	631,400	624,300	1928	1,467,400	1,456,100	1970	2,852,100	2,819,600
1887	645,300	638,300	1929	1,486,100	1,473,400	1971	2,898,500	2,864,200
1888	649,300	647,300	1930	1,506,800	1,493,000	1972	2,959,700	2,915,600
1889	658,000	653,700	1931	1,522,800	1,514,200	1973	3,024,900	2,977,100
1890	667,500	662,700	1932	1,534,700	1,527,100	1974	3,091,900	3,041,800
1891	676,100	671,800	1933	1,547,100	1,539,600	1975	3,143,700	3,100,100
1892	692,400	684,200	1934	1,558,400	1,551,500	1976	3,163,400	3,131,800
1893	714,300	703,300	1935	1,569,700	1,562,200	1977	3,166,400	3,142,600
1894	728,100	721,200	1936	1,584,600	1,575,200	1978	3,165,200	3,143,500
1895	740,700	734,400	1937	1,601,800	1,590,000	1979	3,163,900	3,137,800
1896	754,000	746,300	1938	1,618,300	1,606,800	1980	3,176,400	3,144,000
1897	768,900	761,500	1939	1,641,600	1,628,500	1981	3,194,500	3,156,700
1898	783,300	776,100	1940	1,633,600	1,637,300	1982	3,226,800	3,180,800
1899	796,400	789,800	1941	1,631,200	1,630,900	1983	3,264,800	3,221,700
1900	808,100	802,200	1942	1,636,400	1,639,500	1984	3,293,000	3,252,800
1901	830,800	821,100	1943	1,642,000	1,635,600	1985	3,303,100	3,271,500
1902	851,100	840,900	1944	1,676,300	1,655,800	1986	3,313,500	3,277,000
1903	875,600	863,400	1945	1,727,800	1,694,700	1987	3,342,100	3,303,600
1904	900,700	888,200	1946	1,781,200	1,759,600	1988	3,345,200	3,317,000
1905	925,600	913,100	1947	1,817,500	1,798,300	1989	3,369,800	3,330,200
1906	956,500	943,300	1948	1,853,900	1,834,700	1990	3,410,400	3,362,500
1907	977,200	966,800	1949	1,892,100	1,871,700			
1908	1,008,400	992,800	1950	1,927,700	1,909,100			
1909	1,030,700	1,019,500	1951	1,970,500	1,947,600		Estimated resident population[1]	
1910	1,050,400	1,040,500	1952	2,024,600	1,996,200	1991	3,516,000	3,495,800
1911	1,075,300	1,063,900	1953	2,074,700	2,048,800	1992	3,552,200	3,533,000
1912	1,102,500	1,088,900	1954	2,118,400	2,094,900	1993	3,597,900	3,573,600
1913	1,134,500	1,118,500	1955	2,164,800	2,139,000	1994	3,648,200	3,621,600
1914	1,145,800	1,140,200	1956	2,209,200	2,182,800	1995	3,706,700	3,675,800
1915	1,152,600	1,149,200	1957	2,262,800	2,232,500	1996	3,762,300	3,733,900
1916	1,150,200	1,149,200	1958	2,316,000	2,285,800	1997	3,802,600	3,782,600
1917	1,147,400	1,148,900	1959	2,359,700	2,334,600	1998	3,829,200	3,815,800
1918	1,158,100	1,152,800	1960	2,403,600	2,377,000	1999	3,851,200	3,837,300
1919	1,227,200	1,192,700	1961	2,461,300	2,426,700	2000	3,873,000	3,860,100
1920	1,257,600	1,242,400	1962	2,515,800	2,484,900	2001	3,916,200	3,887,000
1921	1,292,700	1,276,700	1963	2,566,900	2,536,900	2002	3,989,500	3,951,200
1922	1,318,900	1,305,100	1964	2,617,000	2,589,100	2003	4,061,600	4,027,700
1923	1,343,000	1,328,200	1965	2,663,800	2,635,300	2004	4,114,300	4,088,700
1924	1,370,400	1,352,600	1966	2,711,300	2,682,600	2005	4,161,000	4,136,000
1925	1,401,200	1,384,400	1967	2,745,000	2,727,700	2006	4,211,400	4,186,900
1926	1,429,700	1,413,700	1968	2,773,000	2,753,500	2007	4,252,600	4,230,700

(1) Population estimates for 1991 onwards are based on the resident population concept, replacing the de facto population concept previously used. Resident population estimates are not strictly comparable with census usually resident population counts, as they include adjustments for census undercount and New Zealand residents temporarily overseas.

Source: Statistics New Zealand

Table 5.06

New Zealand's population[1]
By census[2]

Census	North Island[3]	South Island[4]	Total population
1858	87,150	28,311	115,461
1874	155,472	189,513	344,985
1878	199,524	258,483	458,007
1881	234,648	299,382	534,030
1886	290,010	330,441	620,451
1891	321,246	347,403	668,652
1896	377,955	365,259	743,214
1901	431,472	384,390	815,862
1906	521,898	414,411	936,309
1911	610,599	447,714	1,058,313
1916	695,397	453,828	1,149,225
1921	791,919	479,751	1,271,667
1926	892,680	515,460	1,408,140
1936	1,018,038	555,774	1,573,812
1945	1,146,315	556,014	1,702,329
1951	1,313,871	625,602	1,939,473
1956	1,497,363	676,698	2,174,061
1961	1,684,785	730,200	2,414,985
1966	1,893,327	783,594	2,676,918
1971	2,051,364	811,269	2,862,630
1976	2,268,393	860,991	3,129,384
1981	2,306,667	836,643	3,143,307
1986	2,412,660	850,623	3,263,283
1991	2,520,348	853,578	3,373,926
1996	2,718,189	900,114	3,618,303
2001	2,829,801	907,476	3,737,277
2006	3,059,427	968,520	4,027,947

(1) Figures from 1981 onwards are census usually resident population counts, replacing the census night population counts previously used. (2) Omits censuses of 1851, 1861, 1864, 1867 and 1871 as censuses of the Māori population were not taken in these years. (3) Includes the population of Kermadec Islands and people on oil rigs. (4) Includes the populations of the Chatham Islands and Campbell Island.
Note: All figures randomly rounded to base 3.

Source: Statistics New Zealand

Internal migration

The movement of people within and between regions is an important determinant of New Zealand's population distribution. Overall, New Zealanders are a mobile people and, while the majority of movement is within regions, there is significant movement between regions.

In addition to affecting the size of the population, inter-regional migration also influences age structures, fertility levels and population growth rates within regions.

Table 5.07 shows population movements in to and out of regions between the 2001 and 2006 Censuses.

Table 5.07

Migration between regions
2001–2006

Region	Population[1]	Migration in	Migration out	Net migration
Northland	138,198	18,726	17,172	1,554
Auckland	1,209,165	59,304	75,966	-16,662
Waikato	355,044	47,754	42,228	5,526
Bay of Plenty	239,112	34,701	28,821	5,880
Gisborne	40,848	4,884	6,405	-1,521
Hawke's Bay	137,343	15,168	15,957	-789
Taranaki	97,263	9,267	11,520	-2,253
Manawatu-Wanganui	207,666	26,901	29,571	-2,670
Wellington	418,578	39,519	38,946	573
Tasman	41,727	8,760	6,999	1,761
Nelson	40,365	7,968	9,531	-1,563
Marlborough	40,188	7,179	6,813	366
West Coast	29,430	4,749	5,175	-426
Canterbury	489,369	40,467	32,364	8,103
Otago	183,165	26,238	21,756	4,482
Southland	84,837	8,913	11,268	-2,355

(1) Census usually resident population count of all people aged five years and over, 2006.
Note: Confidentiality rules have been applied to all cells in this table, including randomly rounding to base 3.

Source: Statistics New Zealand

Urban and rural distribution

New Zealand is a highly urbanised country, with 86 percent of the census usually resident population count living in urban areas at the time of the 2006 Census.

Table 5.08

	Urban and rural populations[1]				
	Urban			Rural	
Census[2]	Number	Percent		Number	Percent
Non-Māori population					
1881	194,982	40.1		291,237	59.9
1886	245,613	42.9		327,327	57.1
1891	270,342	43.4		352,098	56.6
1896	307,293	44.0		391,734	56.0
1901	350,202	45.6		417,597	54.4
1906	424,614	48.1		458,796	51.9
1911	505,599	50.4		496,779	49.6
1916	585,306	53.9		501,258	46.1
1921	681,987	56.2		530,853	43.8
Total population					
1926	953,172	68.0		448,500	32.0
1936	1,065,228	67.9		503,886	32.1
1945	1,227,069	72.2		472,077	27.8
1951	1,406,517	72.7		527,079	27.3
1956	1,600,809	73.8		568,806	26.2
1961	1,840,203	76.4		569,217	23.6
1966	2,119,086	79.3		553,023	20.7
1971	2,328,876	81.5		528,609	18.5
1976	2,614,119	83.6		511,005	16.4
1981	2,682,906	85.4		460,401	14.6
1986	2,780,151	85.2		481,467	14.8
1991	2,884,668	85.5		488,604	14.5
1996	3,091,659	85.5		524,976	14.5
2001	3,204,294	85.8		531,888	14.2
2006	3,463,188	86.0		563,931	14.0

(1) From 1881–1921, 'urban' is based on boroughs and cities, and 'rural' is based on counties (including town districts). From 1926–2006, 'urban' is based on urban areas and towns with over 1,000 people, and 'rural' is the remainder. (2) Figures from 1981 onwards are census usually resident population counts, replacing census night population counts used previously.
Note: Confidentiality rules have been applied to all cells in this table, including randomly rounding to base 3.

Source: Statistics New Zealand

Main urban areas

Seventy-two percent of the 2006 Census usually resident population count lived in main urban areas (places with 30,000 or more people). With the exception of Wanganui, all main urban areas experienced population growth, between 2001 and 2006, along with most secondary urban areas (places with between 10,000 and 29,999 people). Between 1996 and 2001 most secondary urban areas had experienced a decrease in population.

Table 5.09

	Population of largest urban areas								
	At selected censuses								
Urban area	1886[1]	1911[1]	1936	1961	1986[2]	1991[2]	1996[2]	2001[2]	2006[2]
Auckland	33,162	102,675	226,365	448,365	816,927	878,220	991,812	1,074,450	1,208,094
Christchurch	29,655	80,193	133,515	220,509	295,749	303,411	325,251	334,107	360,768
Wellington	25,944	70,728	159,357	249,531	323,421	324,147	334,002	339,927	360,624
Hamilton	1,200	3,543	20,097	50,505	138,645	146,148	158,043	166,128	184,908
Dunedin	23,244	64,236	85,608	105,003	107,331	107,526	110,793	107,088	110,997
Tauranga	1,149	1,347	5,808	24,660	62,370	70,257	82,149	95,664	108,882
Palmerston North	2,607	10,992	24,372	43,185	66,951	70,239	73,860	72,681	76,032
Hastings	1,503	6,285	17,919	32,490	56,718	57,267	58,584	59,211	62,118
Nelson	7,314	8,235	13,494	25,320	43,725	45,879	50,691	53,688	56,367
Napier	7,680	11,736	19,170	32,715	52,524	52,122	54,300	54,534	56,286
Rotorua	…	2,391	8,898	25,068	48,855	50,772	52,953	52,608	53,766
New Plymouth	3,093	5,238	18,597	32,388	47,370	47,655	48,873	47,763	49,281
Whangarei	…	2,664	9,867	21,789	44,097	44,406	45,963	46,107	49,080
Invercargill	8,250	15,858	25,911	41,088	52,818	51,540	49,404	46,305	46,773
Wanganui	4,902	14,703	25,749	35,694	40,512	41,100	41,097	39,423	38,988
Kapiti	…	1,068	5,367	12,306	23,040	27,345	30,288	33,672	37,347
Gisborne	2,193	8,196	15,879	25,065	32,019	31,401	32,607	31,722	32,529
Blenheim	3,093	3,771	5,037	11,955	22,998	23,799	25,752	26,592	28,527
Timaru	3,753	11,280	18,771	26,424	28,692	27,786	27,171	26,745	26,886
Pukekohe	…	…	…	…	14,220	15,324	16,917	18,825	22,518
Taupo	…	…	…	…	16,260	17,163	19,227	20,364	21,291
Masterton	…	5,181	9,096	15,120	19,353	19,770	19,686	19,497	19,497

(1) Excludes Māori. (2) Figures from 1986 onwards are census usually resident population counts, replacing census night population counts used previously.
Note: Confidentiality rules have been applied to all cells in this table, including randomly rounding to base 3. **Symbol:** … not applicable.

Source: Statistics New Zealand

Population of local government areas

Table 5.10 shows the estimated resident population of New Zealand's regions and table 5.11 (overleaf) gives the estimated populations of territorial authority areas (cities and districts).

Table 5.10

Estimated resident population of regions
At 30 June

Region[1]	Estimated resident population[2]			Population change 2006–2007	
	2001	2006	2007	Number	Percent
North Island					
Northland	144,400	152,700	153,800	1,170	0.8
Auckland	1,216,900	1,371,000	1,394,000	23,020	1.7
Waikato	369,800	395,100	398,600	3,460	0.9
Bay of Plenty	246,900	265,300	267,700	2,390	0.9
Gisborne	45,500	46,000	45,900	-40	-0.1
Hawke's Bay	147,300	152,100	152,500	460	0.3
Taranaki	105,700	107,300	107,200	-90	-0.1
Manawatu-Wanganui	227,500	229,400	229,000	-330	-0.1
Wellington	440,200	466,300	470,300	4,050	0.9
Total North Island	**2,944,300**	**3,185,100**	**3,219,200**	**34,090**	**1.1**
South Island					
Tasman	42,400	45,800	46,100	350	0.8
Nelson	42,900	44,300	44,400	170	0.4
Marlborough	40,700	43,600	44,000	410	1.0
West Coast	31,100	32,100	32,200	160	0.5
Canterbury	496,700	540,000	546,900	6,890	1.3
Otago	188,300	199,800	201,700	1,860	0.9
Southland	93,300	93,200	93,000	-190	-0.2
Total South Island	**935,400**	**998,800**	**1,008,400**	**9,640**	**1.0**
New Zealand[3]	**3,880,500**	**4,184,600**	**4,228,300**	**43,730**	**1.0**

(1) Based on 2007 regional council boundaries. (2) Resident population estimates are not strictly comparable with census usually resident population counts, as they include adjustments for census undercount and New Zealand residents temporarily overseas. (3) Includes the population of Kermadec Islands, Chatham Islands Territory, and people on oil rigs. These are not included within regional council areas.
Note: Figures may not add up to stated totals, due to rounding.

Source: Statistics New Zealand

Urban and rural changes

New Zealand is among the most urbanised societies in the world, with 86 percent of the usually resident population living in an urban area at the time of the 2006 Census.

Main urban areas (places with 30,000 people or more) account for 72 percent of the population, with a further 6 percent in secondary urban areas (places with between 10,000 and 29,999 people). The remaining 22 percent of the population live in minor urban areas (8 percent), rural centres (2 percent), and other rural areas (12 percent).

Urbanisation was a feature of much of the history of the first half of the 20th century, largely driven by social and economic changes, such as mechanisation of agriculture, the shift of growth from south to north, and the growth of urban production industries. Alongside urbanisation, the population of urban areas swelled with the inflow of people from overseas. Much of the growth of secondary urban areas came from rural populations leaving the land, whereas the relatively slower growth of main urban areas was more connected with immigration from overseas.

Following World War II, returning troops, many of rural origin, resettled initially with their families in local urban areas, frequently moving on to larger cities for work. Post-war resettlement of displaced European families added to the urban populations, though some also came to assist rural labour shortages and some came as farmers. By mid-century, almost three-quarters of the population were urban dwellers.

In the second half of last century, continued immigration and slower growth of rural populations gradually increased the urban share of the population. Changes in source countries of migrants and a trend towards globalisation increasingly changed the urban/rural landscape to a more metropolitan focus, with the growth of service industries based in the largest cities, especially in Auckland. Recent trends are for immigrants and returning New Zealanders to be more likely to settle in a main urban area, with 93 percent of people who were overseas at the time of the 2001 Census living in an urban area at the time of the 2006 Census (84 percent lived in main urban areas), with the majority living in Auckland.

While the urban share of the population has increased only very slowly over the last quarter century, the exchange of people within and between areas has been dramatic. Between 2001 and 2006, the main urban areas grew by nearly 238,000 people. This period saw the addition of 289,400 people from overseas, including returning New Zealanders, but this was offset by the loss of a similar number of people moving overseas. Over this period, main urban areas lost around 134,600 people to other area types, but gained 133,200 from other area types, with large net outflows from Auckland, but significant gains for other major cities, such as Tauranga and Hamilton.

Rural areas also grew by over 31,000 people. Rural areas gained just over 9,000 people from internal migration, compared with a net loss for main urban areas of more than 1,300 people. Rural areas are not necessarily in remote locations. Much of the rural population growth follows from the popularity of life-style blocks, and similar developments, in areas classified as rural, but which are in close proximity to urban areas. Many rural areas have lost population and radically changed their character, with transformation of farming in recent years, especially in the dairy industry.

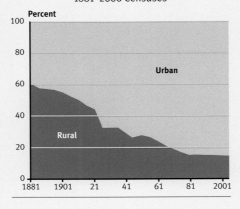

Urban drift
Proportions of urban and rural population
1881–2006 Censuses

Source: Statistics New Zealand

Table 5.11

Estimated resident population of territorial authority areas at 30 June

Territorial authority area[1]	Estimated resident population[2]			Population change 2006–2007	
	2001	2006	2007	Number	Percent
Far North district	56,400	57,500	57,800	210	0.4
Whangarei district	70,000	76,500	77,500	930	1.2
Kaipara district	17,950	18,550	18,600	30	0.1
Rodney district	78,500	92,400	94,700	2,220	2.4
North Shore city	194,200	216,900	220,200	3,320	1.5
Waitakere city	176,200	195,300	198,400	3,090	1.6
Auckland city	388,800	428,300	433,200	4,920	1.1
Manukau city	298,200	347,100	354,800	7,730	2.2
Papakura district	42,300	46,900	47,700	790	1.7
Franklin district	53,300	60,900	62,200	1,310	2.2
Thames-Coromandel district	25,800	26,700	26,800	100	0.4
Hauraki district	17,250	17,600	17,650	40	0.2
Waikato district	41,300	45,400	46,000	590	1.3
Matamata-Piako district	30,300	31,200	31,200	50	0.2
Hamilton city	120,900	134,400	136,600	2,150	1.6
Waipa district	40,000	43,700	44,200	550	1.3
Otorohanga district	9,590	9,310	9,250	-60	-0.7
South Waikato district	24,200	23,200	22,900	-310	-1.3
Waitomo district	9,780	9,680	9,600	-80	-0.8
Taupo district	32,500	33,400	33,500	40	0.1
Western Bay of Plenty district	39,300	43,300	43,900	590	1.4
Tauranga city	93,300	106,700	108,800	2,120	2.0
Rotorua district	66,900	68,100	68,000	-130	-0.2
Whakatane district	34,100	34,500	34,400	-40	-0.1
Kawerau district	7,290	7,150	7,070	-70	-1.0
Opotiki district	9,490	9,200	9,140	-60	-0.6
Gisborne district	45,500	45,900	45,900	-40	-0.1
Wairoa district	9,260	8,720	8,580	-140	-1.6
Hastings district	69,600	73,200	73,600	430	0.6
Napier city	55,200	56,800	56,900	150	0.3
Central Hawke's Bay district	13,200	13,250	13,250	20	0.1
New Plymouth district	68,400	71,100	71,400	300	0.4
Stratford district	9,110	9,120	9,090	-30	-0.3
South Taranaki district	28,400	27,200	26,800	-360	-1.3
Ruapehu district	15,000	14,050	13,800	-250	-1.8
Wanganui district	44,400	43,800	43,600	-220	-0.5
Rangitikei district	15,500	15,150	15,050	-110	-0.7
Manawatu district	28,200	29,000	29,100	110	0.4
Palmerston North city	75,200	78,500	78,800	320	0.4
Tararua district	18,350	18,050	17,950	-140	-0.8
Horowhenua district	30,600	30,600	30,500	-30	-0.1
Kapiti Coast district	43,600	47,500	48,000	550	1.2
Porirua city	49,500	50,600	50,700	140	0.3
Upper Hutt city	37,700	39,700	40,000	330	0.8
Lower Hutt city	99,100	101,300	101,500	280	0.3
Wellington city	171,100	187,700	190,500	2,780	1.5
Masterton district	23,200	23,200	23,100	-80	-0.4
Carterton district	7,000	7,260	7,300	40	0.5
South Wairarapa district	8,940	9,120	9,140	20	0.2
Tasman district	42,400	45,800	46,100	350	0.8
Nelson city	42,900	44,300	44,400	170	0.4
Marlborough district	40,700	43,600	44,000	410	1.0
Kaikoura district	3,580	3,730	3,750	30	0.8
Buller district	9,860	9,940	9,960	20	0.2
Grey district	13,200	13,550	13,600	60	0.5
Westland district	7,990	8,620	8,690	70	0.9
Hurunui district	10,150	10,750	10,800	20	0.2
Waimakariri district	37,900	44,100	45,100	1,030	2.3
Christchurch city	335,300	361,800	365,700	3,870	1.1
Selwyn district	28,300	35,000	36,400	1,400	4.0
Ashburton district	26,000	28,000	28,400	370	1.3
Timaru district	42,800	43,800	43,900	110	0.2
Mackenzie district	3,790	3,900	3,920	20	0.5
Waimate district	7,220	7,380	7,420	40	0.5
Chatham Islands territory	750	650	640	0	-0.5
Waitaki district	20,500	20,700	20,700	10	0.0
Central Otago district	14,750	17,050	17,450	360	2.1
Queenstown-Lakes district	17,850	24,100	25,400	1,320	5.5
Dunedin city	119,300	122,300	122,500	170	0.1
Clutha district	17,550	17,200	17,200	-10	-0.1
Southland district	29,400	29,200	29,100	-110	-0.4
Gore district	12,750	12,400	12,300	-110	-0.9
Invercargill city	51,100	51,600	51,600	20	0.0
New Zealand[3]	**3,880,500**	**4,184,600**	**4,228,300**	**43,730**	**1.0**

Source: Statistics New Zealand

(1) Based on the 2007 territorial authority area boundaries. (2) Resident population estimates are not strictly comparable with census usually resident population counts, as they include adjustments for census undercount and New Zealand residents temporarily overseas. (3) Includes the population of inlets, ships, oil rigs, and Bays-Waiheke, Kermadec, Mayor, Motiti and White Islands, which are not included within territorial authority areas.
Note: figures may not add up to stated totals, due to rounding.

Components of population change

Population change has two main components, natural increase (the excess of births over deaths) and net migration (the difference between arrivals and departures).

Figure 5.05 shows New Zealand's population change from 1867 to 2007 and contributions made by natural increase and net migration.

Figure 5.05

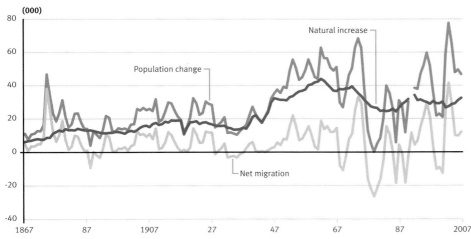

Components of annual population change
Natural increase[1] and net migration[2]
Year ending 31 March

(1) Up to 1990, based on number of registered births and deaths. From 1992, based on estimated number of births and deaths by period of occurrence. (2) Total migration (used in estimating the de facto population) up to 1990; permanent and long-term migration (used in estimating resident population) from 1991 onwards.

Source: Statistics New Zealand

Fertility

Changing levels of fertility over the years have played a major role in determining the size and structure of New Zealand's population. Figure 5.06 (overleaf) shows the significant changes in the fertility rate (births per woman) in New Zealand from 1916 to 2006. In 1935, the fertility rate in New Zealand fell to 2.2 births per woman. This was attributed to fewer and later marriages, and limitation of family size within marriage. With demobilisation of forces after World War II and the resulting increase in marriages and births, the fertility rate reached 3.6 births per woman in 1947.

Other features of the years following World War II were New Zealanders marrying younger and marriage becoming almost universal. By 1961, half of all women were married before the age of 22, compared with barely one-quarter married by that age in the early 1940s. These trends were reinforced by early childbearing and the shortening of intervals between births.

The median age of women having their first child fell from 25.4 years in 1945 to 22.8 years in 1964. Fewer couples remained childless or had only one child. The net result was soaring birth numbers, up from 27,000 in 1935 to about 42,000 in 1945, and to 65,000 in 1961. About 1.13 million New Zealanders were born between 1946 and 1965.

At its peak in 1961, the total fertility rate exceeded 4.3 births per woman, and significantly exceeded figures for other developed nations. The upward trend was reversed in the early 1960s just as suddenly as it had begun, which has prompted demographers to suggest that the 'baby boom' was merely a temporary diversion from a long-term downward trend.

The turnaround coincided with introduction of the oral contraceptive pill in the early 1960s, but the 'cause-and-effect' relationship is not clear-cut. It is possible that increased acceptance and use of the pill helped sustain the downward trend.

By the mid-1970s, the post-World War II rise in fertility had ended. The total fertility rate fell below the 'replacement level' (2.1 births per woman) in 1978, and then to a low of 1.9 births per woman in 1983. This drop had a great impact on the annual number of births.

Despite a substantial increase in the number of prospective mothers caused by the 'baby boomers' entering prime reproductive ages, births dropped from around 64,000 in 1971 to around 50,000 in 1982.

Table 5.12 (overleaf) shows fertility trends and patterns from 1881 to 2006.

Information about genetic origins

Since 2005, the office of Births, Deaths and Marriages (BDM) has administered the Human Assisted Reproductive Technology (HART) register, which will enable donor offspring – people born from donated embryos, sperm or eggs – to get information about their genetic origins.

In accordance with the Human Assisted Reproductive Technology Act 2004, the HART register holds information about donors, donor offspring, and guardians who have been involved in treatment at fertility clinics using donated embryos, sperm or eggs.

Only those donations made on or after 22 August 2005 that result in a birth will automatically be included on the register. However, people who donated sperm, eggs or embryos before 22 August 2005, and people who were born as a result of those donations (and their guardians), can choose to provide information for the register.

Access to information is generally restricted to the people named on the register, or the guardians of offspring under the age of 18.

Source: Department of Internal Affairs

Table 5.12

Fertility trends and patterns
Year ending 31 December

Year	Live births	Crude birth rate[1]	Fertility rate[2]	Gross reproduction rate[3][4]	Net reproduction rate[4][5]
1881[6]		38.00	..	..	..
1886[6]		33.14	..	..	..
1891[6]		29.01	..	..	..
1896[6]		26.35	..	..	..
1901[6]		26.34	..	..	..
1906[6]		27.08	..	..	..
1911[6]		25.99	..	..	..
1916[6]	28,509	25.94	..	..	..
1921	29,623	23.24	3.08	..	..
1926	29,904	21.15	2.88	..	..
1931	28,867	19.06	2.56	..	..
1936	28,395	18.03	2.30	1.04	0.97
1941	39,170	24.02	2.93	1.37	1.27
1946	47,524	27.01	3.45	1.59	1.47
1951	49,806	25.57	3.60	1.64	1.58
1956	56,531	25.90	3.98	1.84	1.77
1961	65,390	26.95	4.31	2.03	1.96
1966	60,003	22.37	3.41	1.66	1.61
1971	64,460	22.51	3.18	1.55	1.51
1976	55,105	17.60	2.27	1.09	1.07
1981	50,794	16.09	2.01	0.98	0.96
1986	52,823	16.12	1.96	0.96	0.94
1991	59,911	17.14	2.09	1.01	1.00
1996	57,280	15.34	1.96	0.95	0.93
1997	57,604	15.23	1.96	0.96	0.94
1998[7]	55,349	14.51	1.89	0.92	0.90
1999	57,053	14.87	1.97	0.96	0.95
2000	56,605	14.66	1.98	0.96	0.95
2001	55,799	14.36	1.97	0.97	0.95
2002	54,021	13.67	1.89	0.92	0.91
2003	56,134	13.94	1.93	0.94	0.93
2004	58,073	14.20	1.98	0.97	0.95
2005	57,745	13.96	1.97	0.96	0.95
2006	59,193	14.14	2.01	0.98	0.97

(1) Live births per 1,000 estimated mean population. (2) The average number of live births that a woman would have during her life if she experienced the age-specific fertility rates of that year. (3) The average number of daughters that a woman would have during her life if she experienced the age-specific fertility rates of that year. (4) Figures before 1966 exclude the Māori population. (5) The average number of daughters that a woman would have during her life if she experienced the age-specific fertility and mortality rates of that year. (6) Excludes the Māori population. (7) Births and fertility rates for 1998 are lower than expected because of a small change to the way in which births were registered during 1998.
Note: Birth and fertility rates for 1991 onwards are based on the resident population concept, replacing the de facto population concept used previously.
Symbol: .. figure not available

Source: Statistics New Zealand

Figure 5.06

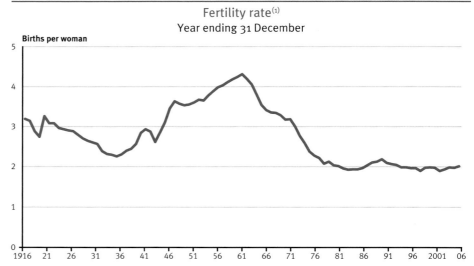

Fertility rate[1]
Year ending 31 December

(1) The average number of live births that a woman would have during her life if she experienced the age-specific fertility rates of a given period (usually a year). The figure for 1998 is lower than expected because of small change to the way in which births were registered during 1998.

Source: Statistics New Zealand

New mother Patricia Heffernan cuddles her day-old daughter, Hannah. The median age of women having their first child rose steadily from 23 years in 1964 to 28 years in 2006.

Number of births[1] per woman aged 15 years and over
Census usually resident population count

Number of births[1]	Number of women
0	461,217
1	177,138
2	374,001
3	253,293
4	121,239
5	49,188
6	22,041
7	9,843
8	4,884
9	2,616
10+	3,213
Object to answering	45,717
Response unidentifiable	4,515
Response outside scope	156
Not stated	109,728
Total births	**1,638,783**

(1) This refers to live births only.

Note: This data has been randomly rounded to protect confidentiality. Individual figures may not add up to the stated total.

Source: Statistics New Zealand

Table 5.13 (overleaf) provides a summary of vital statistics for the New Zealand population from 1950 to 2006.

After 1983, there was a minor resurgence in the fertility rate, to 2.18 births per woman in 1990, but the rate soon dropped to 2.04 (below replacement level) in 1993. Since then the fertility rate has fluctuated around 1.96. This level of fertility is slightly below the level required for the population to replace itself without migration.

The median age of women having their first child rose steadily from 22.8 years in 1964 to 28.5 years in 2003, and dropped slightly to 28.2 years in 2006. In 2002, the 30–34-year age group replaced the 25–29-year age group as the most common for childbearing.

Figure 5.07 shows the median age of childbearing for New Zealand women from 1966 to 2006, based on all live births.

Figure 5.07

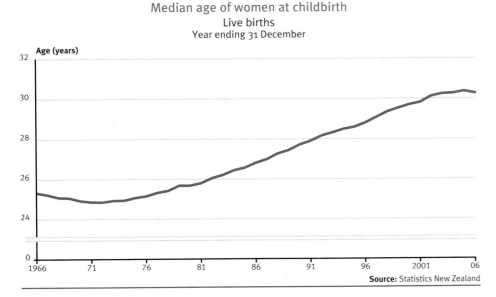

Median age of women at childbirth
Live births
Year ending 31 December

Source: Statistics New Zealand

The dynamics of the fertility decline and of current low fertility levels are complex. Increased use of contraceptives, increased participation of women in the labour force, rising divorce rates, and general economic conditions have probably all, directly or indirectly, contributed.

Demographic measures for 2000–2002 indicate a significant ethnic difference in fertility, with the birth rate for Pacific, Māori, European and Asian women at 2.9, 2.6, 1.8 and 1.7 births, respectively.

Top 20 male and female names
For children born 2006–2007

Rank	2006	2007
Male names		
1	Jack	Jack
2	Joshua	James
3	Daniel	Joshua
4	William	Daniel
5	Samuel	William
6	Jacob	Oliver
7	Thomas	Samuel
8	Benjamin	Benjamin
9	Ryan	Ethan
10	Liam	Ryan
11	Oliver	Jacob
12	Ethan	Liam
13	James	Thomas
14	Luke	Lucas
15	Matthew	Luke
16	Noah	Noah
17	Caleb	Riley
18	Max	Jayden
19	Jayden	Matthew
20	Logan	Alexander
Female names		
1	Charlotte	Ella
2	Ella	Sophie
3	Sophie	Olivia
4	Emma	Emma
5	Olivia	Charlotte
6	Emily	Emily
7	Grace	Lily
8	Jessica	Grace
9	Hannah	Hannah
10	Lily	Isabella
11	Isabella	Jessica
12	Lucy	Ruby
13	Chloe	Amelia
14	Ruby	Lucy
15	Georgia	Madison
16	Paige	Chloe
17	Amelia	Brooke
18	Maia	Ava
19	Zoe	Mia
20	Madison	Paige

Source: Department of Internal Affairs

Patterns of marriage and family formation have changed radically, with a shift away from early marriage and childbearing, toward later marriage and delayed parenthood. Between 1971 and 1986, the first-marriage rate for women aged 20–24 dropped by about two-thirds, from 314 to 113 marriages per 1,000 never-married women.

By 2006, the first-marriage rate for women aged 20–24 had dropped to 32 per 1,000. Men and women who were marrying for the first time in 2006, were, on average, marrying about seven years later than those who married for the first time in 1971. In 2006, the median age for women at first marriage was 28.2 years, and 30.0 years for men. This compares with 20.8 and 23.0 years, respectively, in 1971.

A growing proportion of New Zealanders are remaining single through their twenties. The substantial postponement of marriage has been partly offset by the growth of de facto relationships (cohabitation outside marriage). Such relationships may be either a prelude to, or a substitute for, formal marriage.

The Aucklander

Becca Duffy (left), 18, with her daughter Charlie, 17 months, and Natalie Jury, 18, with her son Dontay, aged two. The teen mums visit groups to talk about their experiences of sex education at school. Awareness-raising by peers is a way of reducing the number of unplanned teen pregnancies. In 2006, the fertility rate for New Zealand teenagers was 28 births per 1,000 women aged 15–19 years. This compares with a fertility rate of 119 births per 1,000 women aged 30–34 years, and 105 births for women aged 25–29.

Table 5.13

Vital statistics
Year ending 31 December

Year	Live births	Deaths	Natural increase(1)	Median age at death Male	Female
	Number			Years	
1950	49,331	18,084	31,247	68.0	69.7
1955	55,596	19,225	36,371	68.9	72.1
1960	62,779	20,892	41,887	69.8	74.0
1965	60,047	22,976	37,071	69.0	74.7
1970	62,050	24,840	37,210	68.5	75.0
1975	56,639	25,114	31,525	68.6	74.9
1980	50,542	26,676	23,866	70.4	75.7
1985	51,798	27,480	24,318	71.4	77.2
1990	60,153	26,531	33,622	72.0	77.7
1991	59,911	26,389	33,522	71.8	78.1
1992	59,166	27,115	32,051	72.4	78.7
1993	58,782	27,100	31,682	72.9	78.8
1994	57,321	26,953	30,368	73.2	79.2
1995	57,671	27,813	29,858	73.3	79.3
1996	57,280	28,255	29,025	73.5	79.7
1997	57,604	27,471	30,133	73.5	80.1
1998(2)	55,349	26,206	29,143	73.8	79.9
1999	57,053	28,122	28,931	74.5	80.6
2000	56,605	26,660	29,945	74.8	80.5
2001	55,799	27,825	27,974	75.0	81.3
2002	54,021	28,065	25,956	75.5	81.4
2003	56,134	28,010	28,124	75.7	81.5
2004	58,073	28,419	29,654	76.2	82.0
2005	57,745	27,034	30,711	75.8	82.0
2006	59,193	28,245	30,948	76.3	82.3

(1) Live births minus deaths. (2) Births are lower than expected because of a small change to the way in which births were registered during 1998.

Note: Figures from 1991 onwards are based on the resident population concept, replacing the de facto population concept used previously.

Source: Statistics New Zealand

Births, deaths, marriages and civil unions

Herald on Sunday

The civil union ceremony celebration of Chris Carter and Peter Kaiser in February 2007. There were 316 civil unions of New Zealand residents registered in 2007, of which 80 percent were same-sex unions.

Births, Deaths and Marriages (BDM) registers and maintains birth, death, marriage and civil union information, and issues certificates and electronic printouts. BDM also appoints marriage and civil union celebrants.

Births All births in New Zealand must be registered. Hospitals, doctors or midwives must notify BDM of the birth within five working days, and the child's guardians must register the birth within two months. There is no fee for this service, but a fee applies for providing birth certificates.

Deaths All deaths in New Zealand must be notified to BDM. The funeral director or other person in charge of the burial or cremation must notify BDM within three working days of the burial or cremation. There is no fee for registering a death, but a fee applies for providing death certificates.

Marriages Anyone wishing to marry in New Zealand must give notice to a registrar of marriages. A marriage licence is normally issued no earlier than the third day after the day the notice was given, and is valid for three months. Marriages can be conducted by a registrar at a registry office or by a marriage celebrant at any other place. Where a couple are in a civil union and are eligible to marry, they may do so without formally dissolving their civil union. Same-sex couples may not marry in New Zealand. Fees apply for a marriage licence, registry office marriages, and marriage certificates.

Civil unions Anyone wishing to enter into a civil union must give notice to a registrar of civil unions. Same-sex or opposite sex couples may enter into a civil union in New Zealand. A civil union licence is issued no earlier than the third day after the day the notice was given and is valid for three months. A married couple may change the form of their relationship to a civil union without formally dissolving their marriage. Civil unions can be conducted by a registrar at a registry office or by a civil union celebrant at any other place. Fees apply for a civil union licence, registry office civil unions, and civil union certificates.

Marriage celebrants BDM appoints marriage celebrants under the Marriage Act 1955. The list of marriage celebrants is published in the *New Zealand Gazette* annually and on the Department of Internal Affairs (DIA) website, where names are added or removed throughout the year. Marriage celebrants must apply each year to renew their appointment.

Civil union celebrants BDM appoints civil union celebrants under the Civil Union Act 2004. The list of civil union celebrants is published in the *New Zealand Gazette* annually and on the DIA website, where names are updated throughout the year. Civil union celebrants must apply each year to renew their appointment.

Certificates Birth, death, marriage and civil union certificates and printouts can be ordered from BDM.

Source: Department of Internal Affairs

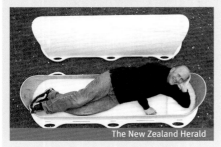
Mortality

A temperate climate, low population density, lack of heavy industry, and good nutrition have given New Zealand a comparative advantage over other nations in terms of health. Ongoing advances in living standards, medical knowledge, technology, and health services continue to increase life expectancy.

Nevertheless, life expectancy rates for the total New Zealand population mask the fact that Māori life expectancy rates are much lower than for non-Māori, and that New Zealand life expectancy rates have been overtaken by some other countries, as shown in table 5.15.

A large part of longevity improvement in New Zealand occurred before 1930 and was due to the saving of life at younger ages. Allowing for higher Māori mortality, the infant mortality rate fell steadily from more than 100 deaths per 1,000 live births in the late 19th century to about 50 deaths per 1,000 births in the 1920s. As table 5.14 shows, the infant mortality rate (under the age of one year) has continued to drop, from 22.76 deaths per 1,000 in 1961, to 5.07 deaths per 1,000 in 2006.

Table 5.14

	Death rate[1] By age group and sex Year ending 31 December									
	Age group (years)									
Year	Under 1[2]	1–4	5–14	15–24	25–34	35–44	45–54	55–64	65–74	75+
Male										
1901[3]	78.60	6.81	1.89	3.52	3.97	6.16	11.94	23.12	50.59	141.67
1921[3]	53.10	4.78	1.85	2.44	3.56	5.55	9.61	19.96	46.17	128.60
1941	43.65	4.39	1.36	2.53	2.93	3.95	9.20	21.13	47.45	140.17
1961	25.86	1.35	0.49	1.28	1.47	2.67	7.37	19.70	47.40	125.90
1981	13.01	0.95	0.35	1.53	1.35	2.26	6.57	17.30	43.39	114.11
2001	6.14	0.33	0.20	1.08	1.20	1.56	3.26	9.04	26.86	87.33
2002	5.62	0.39	0.20	0.90	1.12	1.59	3.39	8.84	24.95	86.79
2003	5.69	0.34	0.19	0.93	1.14	1.59	3.38	8.40	23.81	84.34
2004	5.68	0.30	0.17	0.91	0.96	1.52	3.28	7.84	22.98	84.29
2005	5.82	0.27	0.17	0.99	1.01	1.62	3.09	7.79	20.52	76.09
2006	5.72	0.28	0.16	0.88	0.98	1.39	3.07	7.79	20.63	77.85
Female										
1901[3]	63.87	5.50	1.64	3.58	4.72	6.70	10.62	19.44	43.32	127.98
1921[3]	42.31	4.49	1.31	2.34	3.38	4.46	8.00	14.88	36.81	120.23
1941	35.75	3.84	1.20	1.94	2.44	3.50	6.90	15.04	38.61	118.74
1961	19.50	1.16	0.35	0.54	0.87	1.95	4.59	11.23	29.92	104.72
1981	10.22	0.64	0.23	0.67	0.64	1.51	3.94	9.19	23.73	84.67
2001	4.44	0.33	0.18	0.41	0.51	0.90	2.47	6.30	15.68	72.37
2002	5.48	0.32	0.13	0.39	0.56	0.96	2.29	6.02	15.70	72.44
2003	4.14	0.36	0.12	0.46	0.49	0.97	2.41	5.69	15.41	70.82
2004	5.47	0.24	0.11	0.40	0.47	0.96	2.41	5.68	14.79	72.15
2005	4.36	0.26	0.15	0.39	0.45	0.95	2.24	5.25	13.15	67.63
2006	4.39	0.23	0.10	0.36	0.42	0.94	2.25	5.16	13.73	70.52
Total										
1901[3]	71.40	6.17	1.77	3.55	4.33	6.40	11.37	21.63	47.87	135.71
1921[3]	47.82	4.64	1.58	2.39	3.47	5.10	8.85	17.59	41.90	124.84
1941	39.81	4.12	1.28	2.22	2.67	3.72	8.02	18.16	43.06	129.00
1961	22.76	1.26	0.42	0.92	1.18	2.31	5.99	15.43	37.71	113.84
1981	11.65	1.56	0.29	1.11	0.99	1.89	5.29	13.15	32.67	95.41
2001	5.30	0.33	0.19	0.75	0.84	1.22	2.86	7.65	21.07	78.11
2002	5.55	0.35	0.17	0.65	0.83	1.27	2.83	7.42	20.16	78.01
2003	4.93	0.35	0.16	0.70	0.80	1.27	2.89	7.03	19.46	76.14
2004	5.58	0.27	0.14	0.66	0.70	1.23	2.84	6.75	18.73	76.97
2005	5.11	0.26	0.16	0.70	0.72	1.27	2.66	6.51	16.70	71.03
2006	5.07	0.26	0.13	0.62	0.69	1.16	2.65	6.46	17.06	73.50

(1) Per 1,000 mean estimated population. (2) Per 1,000 live births. (3) Excludes the Māori population.
Note: Live births for 1901–1961 include late registrations, while those from 1981 onwards exclude late registrations. Death rates for 1991 onwards are based on the resident population concept, replacing the de facto population concept used previously.

Source: Statistics New Zealand

Significant ethnic differences exist in mortality rates. According to 2000–02 complete period life tables, a newborn girl could expect to live 81.1 years, and a newborn boy could expect to live 76.3 years. For Māori, life expectancy was 73.2 years for newborn girls and 69.0 years for boys.

Higher Māori death rates at ages 45–79 account for about three-quarters of these differences, and this partly reflects different rates of smoking and diabetes, as well as socio-economic differences. For example, the 2006 Census reported that 42 percent of Māori aged 15 and over were regular smokers, compared with 21 percent of the total population.

Women live longer than men and experience lower death rates at all ages, although men have closed the gap in recent decades. A century ago, women could expect to outlive men by about 2.5 years. By 1950–52, the female advantage had increased to 4.1 years, and by 1975–77 it was 6.4 years. However, the male-female difference narrowed to 4.8 years in 2000–02, and further to 4.1 years in 2004–2006.

Figure 5.08

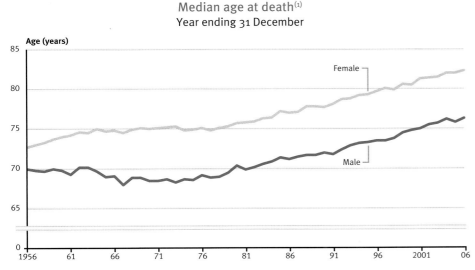

Median age at death[1]
Year ending 31 December

(1) Half the population dying is younger, and half older, than this age.
Note: Figures before 1991 refer to deaths registered in New Zealand of people resident in New Zealand and people visiting from overseas. Figures from 1991 onwards refer to deaths registered in New Zealand of people resident in New Zealand.
Source: Statistics New Zealand

External migration

New Zealand has traditionally been a country of immigration, although its intake has been small compared with immigration flows to New World countries such as Australia, Canada and the United States. The end of World War II saw economic stability and the reintroduction, in 1947, of an assisted/free passage scheme to attract working-age industrial and agricultural labour from the United Kingdom.

Agreements were also negotiated to accept young non-British European migrants, and refugee immigration was allowed on humanitarian grounds. This led to the settlement of nearly 4,000 Indo-Chinese refugees in New Zealand during 1978–82. Historical and regional considerations also led to establishment of immigration quotas for small Pacific island countries.

The Government adopted a new immigration policy in 1974 that ended unrestricted immigration from the United Kingdom and Ireland, and provided for the selection of immigrants from all sources on the same criteria. The reciprocal trans-Tasman travel agreement, which allows free movement of residents between Australia and New Zealand, was not changed. The right of free entry into New Zealand was also maintained for the people of the Cook Islands, Niue and the Tokelau Islands, who are regarded as New Zealand citizens.

As a result of these initiatives, and further policy changes in the 1980s and 1990s, immigrants in post-war years have come from a wider range of countries than before.

Between the 1947 and 1967 March years, New Zealand recorded a net gain of about 281,000 permanent and long-term migrants (people whose stated intention is to stay in New Zealand) . In each of the 21 years, net migration was positive; for 16 of those years, the net gain was more than 10,000. During this period, annual immigrants increased from 8,106 in 1947 to 38,999 in 1967, while annual emigrants increased from 6,051 to 21,128.

Net migration between 1968 and 2007 was volatile, with 17 years of net outflows and 23 years of net inflows. The economic recession of the late 1960s led to a significant drop in immigration, and an upturn in emigration, which resulted in a net outflow of 7,386 people during 1968–70.

There were net migration gains in each of the next six years, with a total gain over this period of 83,149 people. As a result of the 1974 immigration policy changes and the end of the assisted passage scheme in 1975, immigration from the United Kingdom decreased, and Australia became the biggest source and destination country for migrants.

Between 1976 and 1979, the annual number of emigrants almost doubled, to 81,008, with nearly two-thirds of this increase being departures to Australia. Departures exceeded arrivals for each year between 1977 and 1982, with a total net loss of 156,704 people.

Table 5.15

Life expectancy at birth
International comparisons

Country	Period	Male	Female
		Years of life	
New Zealand	**1901–05**[1]	**58.1**	**60.6**
Australia	1901–10	55.2	58.8
Denmark	1901–05	52.9	56.2
Japan	1899–1903	44.0	44.8
Norway	1901–05	54.0	56.9
United Kingdom	1906	48.0	51.6
New Zealand	**1950–52**	**67.2**	**71.3**
Australia	1953–55	67.1	72.8
Denmark	1951–55	69.8	72.6
Japan	1950–52	59.6	63.0
Norway	1951–55	71.1	74.7
United Kingdom	1951	66.2	71.2
New Zealand	**1960–62**	**68.4**	**73.8**
Australia	1960–62	67.9	74.2
Denmark	1961–62	70.4	74.4
Japan	1960	65.3	70.2
Norway	1961–65	71.0	76.0
United Kingdom	1961	67.8	73.7
New Zealand	**1970–72**	**68.5**	**74.6**
Australia	1971	68.3	74.8
Denmark	1971–72	70.7	76.1
Japan	1970	69.3	74.7
Norway	1971–75	71.4	77.7
United Kingdom	1971	68.8	75.0
New Zealand	**1980–82**	**70.4**	**76.4**
Australia	1981	71.4	78.4
Denmark	1981–82	71.4	77.4
Japan	1980	73.4	78.8
Norway	1981–85	72.7	79.4
United Kingdom	1980–82	70.8	76.8
New Zealand	**1990–92**	**72.9**	**78.7**
Australia	1991	74.4	80.3
Denmark	1991–92	72.5	77.9
Japan	1990	75.9	81.9
Norway	1991–95	74.4	80.4
United Kingdom	1990–92	73.2	78.7
New Zealand	**2000–02**	**76.3**	**81.1**
Australia	2000–02	77.4	82.6
Denmark	2001–02	74.7	79.2
Japan	2000	77.7	84.6
Norway	2001–05	76.9	81.9
United Kingdom	2000–02	75.6	80.4
New Zealand	**2005–07**[2]	**78.1**	**82.2**
Australia	2004–06	78.7	83.5
Denmark	2006–07	75.9	80.5
Japan	2006	79.0	85.8
Norway	2006	78.1	82.7
United Kingdom	2004–06	76.9	81.3

(1) Excludes the Māori population.
(2) Abridged period life table.

Source: Statistics New Zealand

Table 5.16

				External migration Year ending 31 March						
	Total			Permanent and long-term			Short-term			
Year	Arrivals	Departures	Net	Arrivals	Departures	Net	Arrivals	Departures	Net	
				Five-year totals						
1900	93,037	84,398	8,639	..	..	..	..	..	..	
1905	141,678	99,501	42,177	..	..	..	..	..	..	
1910	190,772	146,783	43,989	..	..	..	..	..	..	
1915	202,087	165,286	36,801	..	..	..	..	..	..	
1920	98,473	90,532	7,941	..	..	..	..	..	..	
1925	199,791	151,285	48,506	..	..	..	..	..	..	
1930	192,606	167,346	25,260	53,988	16,081	37,907	138,618	151,265	-12,647	
1935	111,933	118,076	-6,143	13,466	14,830	-1,364	98,467	103,246	-4,779	
1940	171,424	159,514	11,910	22,871	19,267	3,604	148,553	140,247	8,306	
1945	35,003	32,414	2,589	6,597	9,241	-2,644	28,406	23,173	5,233	
1950	158,637	135,439	23,198	51,487	30,020	21,467	107,150	105,419	1,731	
1955	306,837	239,148	67,689	116,510	37,419	79,091	190,327	201,729	-11,402	
1960	395,218	347,021	48,197	115,308	51,169	64,139	279,910	295,852	-15,942	
1965	737,703	676,137	61,566	156,462	75,055	81,407	581,241	601,082	-19,841	
1970	1,278,867	1,273,409	5,458	155,008	127,814	27,195	1,123,859	1,145,595	-21,736	
1975	2,506,714	2,400,234	106,480	274,842	196,993	77,849	2,231,872	2,203,241	28,631	
1980	3,793,483	3,874,575	-81,092	204,867	319,964	-115,097	3,588,616	3,554,611	34,005	
1985	4,772,257	4,766,993	5,264	213,059	247,712	-34,653	4,559,198	4,519,281	39,917	
1990	7,359,340	7,394,389	-35,049	226,420	306,653	-80,233	7,132,920	7,087,736	45,184	
1995	9,773,429	9,711,641	61,788	280,508	220,473	60,035	9,492,921	9,491,168	1,753	
2000	13,519,016	13,462,491	56,525	337,781	303,480	34,301	13,181,235	13,159,011	22,224	
2005	18,000,320	17,815,512	184,808	419,038	326,420	92,618	17,581,282	17,489,092	92,190	
				Annual totals						
1997	2,726,897	2,689,118	37,779	76,896	55,948	20,948	2,650,001	2,633,170	16,831	
1998	2,651,737	2,649,814	1,923	62,928	60,221	2,707	2,588,809	2,589,593	-784	
1999	2,755,895	2,769,847	-13,952	56,580	66,779	-10,199	2,699,315	2,703,068	-3,753	
2000	2,919,755	2,917,606	2,149	61,089	70,076	-8,987	2,858,666	2,847,530	11,136	
2001	3,218,995	3,214,037	4,958	66,465	79,065	-12,600	3,152,530	3,134,972	17,558	
2002	3,336,555	3,269,158	67,397	88,365	62,730	25,635	3,248,190	3,206,428	41,762	
2003	3,481,498	3,417,540	63,958	98,671	57,079	41,592	3,382,827	3,360,461	22,366	
2004	3,702,754	3,668,348	34,406	87,473	59,495	27,978	3,615,281	3,608,853	6,428	
2005	4,261,006	4,246,399	14,607	78,064	68,051	10,013	4,182,942	4,178,348	4,594	
2006	4,342,084	4,334,698	7,386	80,125	70,386	9,739	4,261,959	4,264,312	-2,353	
2007	4,413,238	4,391,457	21,781	82,531	70,450	12,081	4,330,707	4,321,007	9,700	

Symbol: .. figure not available

Source: Statistics New Zealand

By 1984, the number of emigrants had fallen to 34,147. More people arrived in New Zealand than left in 1983 and 1984, giving small gains to the country of 3,180 and 6,558 people, respectively.

The turnaround was short-lived, however. During the remainder of the 1980s, the number of departures resumed an upward movement, primarily driven by people moving to Australia. The peak year was 1989, with 70,941 emigrants, giving a net outflow of 24,708 people for that year. Although arrivals also increased over the period, departures exceeded arrivals for each year from 1985 and 1990, with a total net loss of 88,317 people.

The 1990s saw a return to net migration gains, with arrivals exceeding departures from 1991 to 1998. The total net gain over the eight years was 113,522 people. During this period, arrivals increased steadily, from 49,010 in 1992 to a peak of 80,288 in 1996, before dropping back. Migrants from Asia made a significant contribution to these changes.

Fewer arrivals combined with more departures resulted in another period of net outflows between 1999 and 2001, with a total loss of 31,786 people through migration.

Between 2001 and 2003, there was a decrease of over 20,000 in the annual number of departures, mainly due to fewer people moving to Australia. This coincided with arrivals increasing to 98,671 in 2003, resulting in a net migration gain of 41,592 people that year – the highest recorded for a March year.

The increase in arrivals was driven predominantly by arrivals from Asia (many of whom were students), and from the United Kingdom. The main contributor to a subsequent decrease in arrivals in 2004 and 2005 was a drop in the number of arrivals from Asia.

Although permanent and long-term departures increased again between 2003 and 2007, net migration remained positive. Over the 2002–2007 period, there was a net gain of 127,038 permanent and long-term migrants.

During the past two decades, there have been consistent net migration gains from Asia, but consistent net losses to Australia.

Composition of the population

Age and sex

The age and sex profile of a population represents the cumulative effect of past changes in the dynamics of population growth – fertility, mortality and migration.

At the time of the 2006 Census, there were slightly more females than males in the New Zealand population. This contrasts with early colonial days, when there was a large surplus of males, especially young males. Each census has seen the sex ratio draw closer to parity, with two exceptions – when there was a temporary excess of females during World War I and, again, during World War II. In 1968, females again outnumbered males, and the ratio of females to males has increased steadily since then.

The 2006 Census showed there were 1,965,618 males and 2,062,329 females usually resident in New Zealand, representing a ratio of 95 males to 100 females. There is a preponderance of females among the older population (those aged 65 years and over), with 81 males to 100 females in 2006. At ages below 65 years, the sex ratio was 98 males to 100 females.

Figure 5.09 shows crude birth and death rates, and figure 5.10 shows the age and sex distribution of the New Zealand population at ten-year intervals from 1976 to 2006.

Changes in the age structure of New Zealand's population in the past 100 years largely reflect the 'roller coaster' movements in the birth rate, with small and large birth cohorts moving through the age structure. However, migration gains and losses (dominated by people of younger and middle working ages) have added significantly to these structural changes.

Figure 5.09

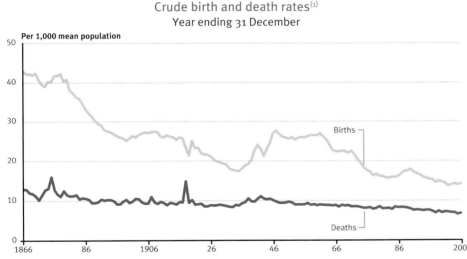

Crude birth and death rates[1]
Year ending 31 December

(1) Excludes the Māori population until 1921.
Note: Figures from 1991 onwards are based on resident population concept, replacing the de facto population concept used previously.

Source: Statistics New Zealand

Warm weather draws holidaymakers to the Christchurch beach Taylors Mistake in early January 2008. The age structure of the population is undergoing significant changes as a result of changing fertility patterns and increased longevity. Overall, New Zealand's population will take on an older profile.

Figure 5.10

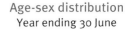

Age-sex distribution
Year ending 30 June

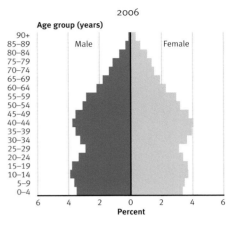

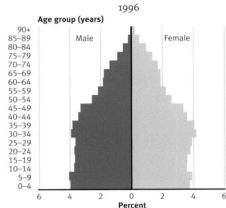

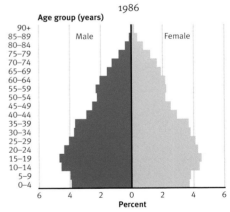

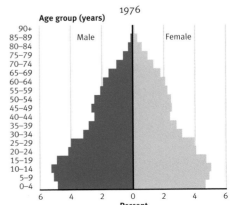

Source: Statistics New Zealand

The five-yearly Census of Population and Dwellings carried out by Statistics New Zealand is the country's biggest official survey. The 2006 Census was the first time respondents were given the option of completing their census forms online. Internal and public trials were carried out in the months before census day to ensure that the system was not only simple to use, but also maintained the confidentiality and privacy of information. The online option included forms in both Māori and English.

Approximately 7 percent of all 2006 Census forms were completed online. This represents nearly 400,000 census dwelling or individual forms. The online census forms were well received, both by respondents who used them and by the media. A Research New Zealand survey showed that 97 percent of those who were surveyed and had filled out the online forms, found it easy to do so.

The Internet option will be available for the 2011 Census, however, every household will still have the option of using paper forms. Although it is likely that the proportion of households who have Internet access will continue to grow, there will still be respondents who do not have Internet access, or who prefer to complete paper forms.

Source: Statistics New Zealand

The baby boom lifted the proportion of children in the population to 33 percent in 1961, with nearly half of the population aged under 25 at that time. The subsequent sharp decline in fertility, increased longevity, and the movement of the baby boom 'bulge' into working ages, caused a major realignment of the age structure. The median age of the population rose by 7.8 years between 1981 and 2006, from 28.1 years to 35.9 years.

At the 2006 Census, there were 867,576 children under the age of 15 usually resident in New Zealand (up from 846,600 in 1981). They made up 22 percent of the population (down from 27 percent in 1981). The 15–64-year age group increased by more than half a million between 1981 and 2006, to number 2,664,768 at the 2006 Census.

The greatest change in the age structure of the population is at the older ages. Since 1981, the number of people aged 65 and over has increased by more than one-and-a-half times (from 309,792 to 495,600), and the number aged 80 and over has more than doubled (from 53,538 to 128,904).

Contributors and related websites

Births, deaths and marriages – www.bdm.govt.nz

Department of Internal Affairs – www.dia.govt.nz

Ministry of Education – www.minedu.govt.nz

Statistics New Zealand – www.stats.govt.nz

The Aucklander

Ben Lee (left), Daniel Lee, and Jae Ahn are a group of Korean New Zealanders who have been voluntarily weeding and tidying up Stancich Reserve, North Shore, for the past 10 years. They had hoped to build a Korean style garden as part of the reserve, but the North Shore City Council's parks department was concerned that this would introduce exotic plants into a native reserve.

6 | Social framework

Social diversity

Information in this chapter is based on the census 'usually resident population count' – a count of all people who usually live in New Zealand and were present in New Zealand on the night of the census. It excludes visitors from overseas and New Zealand residents who were temporarily overseas on census night.

Ethnicity

Ethnicity is a key variable used to explain differences in social characteristics, social well-being, and social change.

The population census has traditionally been the main source of national statistics on ethnicity in New Zealand. Since 1991, people have been asked to identify which ethnic group, or groups, they belong to, and multiple responses are counted.

The 2006 Census showed that New Zealand's ethnic make-up continues to change.

Although the total European grouping, including New Zealand European, remained the largest of the major ethnic groups in 2006, it reduced from 80 percent of the population in 2001, to 67.6 percent in 2006 (2,609,592 people). The main reason is that, for the first time, 'New Zealander' responses were counted separately from the European category. In 2006, 11.1 percent of the total population (429,429 people) gave 'New Zealander' as their only or as one of their responses, making this the third-largest category in the census.

The Māori ethnic group is the second largest, with 14.6 percent of the total population (565,329 people) – an increase of 7.4 percent (39,048 people) since 2001. The Asian ethnic group increased 48.9 percent between censuses, increasing from 238,176 people in 2001, to reach 354,552 in 2006. Those identifying with the Pacific ethnic group increased 14.7 percent from the 2001 Census, to 265,974 people in 2006. The Korean, Arab, Croatian, Iraqi, and South African ethnic groups also made significant population gains between 2001 and 2006.

In the 2001 Census, 9.0 percent of New Zealand's population identified with more than one ethnic group. However, in 2006 this figure increased to 10.4 percent. The 2006 Census results showed that young people were far more likely to list multiple ethnicities. Of people aged under 15 years, 19.7 percent identified with more than one ethnic group, compared with 3.5 percent of those aged 65 years and over.

Ethnicity definition

The census has collected race or ethnicity information about the New Zealand population for most of its census-taking history. The Statistics Act 1975 mandated a statutory question about ethnicity on the personal or individual form for each census.

The following definition is used by Statistics New Zealand to measure ethnicity:

Ethnicity is the ethnic group, or groups, that people identify with, or feel they belong to.

It is a measure of cultural affiliation, as opposed to race, ancestry, nationality, or citizenship. Ethnicity is self-perceived and people can belong to more than one ethnic group. An ethnic group is made up of people who have some or all of the following characteristics:

- a common proper name
- one or more elements of common culture, which need not be specified, but may include religion, customs, or language
- unique community of interests, feelings, and actions
- a shared sense of common origins or ancestry
- a common geographic origin.

Ethnicity is identified by the person themselves whenever possible. Ethnicity identification can change over time because of personal reasons and external circumstances. It may also change in the context of where, how, and when it is collected.

Source: Statistics New Zealand

Table 6.01 shows changes in the ethnic make-up of the New Zealand population between the 2001 and 2006 Censuses. Table 6.02 compares the age structure of New Zealand's major ethnic groups.

Table 6.01

Ethnic group	2001 Census Number of people	2001 Census Percentage[1]	2006 Census Number of people	2006 Census Percentage[1]	Change between censuses (percent)
Ethnic groups (total responses)					
European	2,871,432	80.1	2,609,592	67.6	-9.1
Māori	526,281	14.7	565,329	14.6	7.4
Pacific peoples	231,798	6.5	265,974	6.9	14.7
Asian	238,179	6.6	354,552	9.2	48.9
Middle Eastern/Latin American/African[2]	24,084	0.7	34,746	0.9	44.3
Other Ethnicity					
New Zealander	...	...	429,429	11.1	...
Other 'Other' Ethnicity	801	--	1,494	--	86.5
Not elsewhere included[3]	150,636	...	167,784	...	...
Total New Zealand resident population	3,737,277	100.0	4,027,947	100.0	7.8
Selected ethnic groups (total responses)					
New Zealand European	2,696,724	75.2	2,381,076	61.7	-11.7
Māori	526,281	14.7	565,329	14.6	7.4
Samoan	115,017	3.2	131,103	3.4	14.0
Chinese	105,057	2.9	147,570	3.8	40.5
Indian	62,187	1.7	104,583	2.7	68.2
Cook Island Maori	52,569	1.5	58,011	1.5	10.4
Tongan	40,716	1.1	50,481	1.3	24.0
British and Irish					
British not further defined	16,572	0.5	27,189	0.7	64.1
English	35,082	1.0	44,202	1.1	26.0
Scottish	13,785	0.4	15,039	0.4	9.1
Irish	11,706	0.3	12,648	0.3	8.0
Welsh	3,411	0.1	3,771	0.1	10.6
Other British and Irish	1,917	0.1	1,977	0.1	3.1
Total British and Irish	77,523	2.2	100,668	2.6	29.9
Dutch	27,507	0.8	28,641	0.7	4.1
Niuean	20,148	0.6	22,473	0.6	11.5
Korean	19,026	0.5	30,792	0.8	61.8
South African	14,913	0.4	22,893	0.6	53.5
Filipino	11,091	0.3	16,938	0.4	52.7
Japanese	10,023	0.3	11,910	0.3	18.8
Fijian	7,041	0.2	9,861	0.3	40.1
Tokelauan	6,204	0.2	6,819	0.2	9.9
Sri Lankan	7,014	0.2	8,310	0.2	18.5
Arab	2,856	0.1	2,607	0.1	-8.7
Iraqi	2,145	0.1	3,222	0.1	50.2

(1) The percentage of the population that specified an ethnicity. (2) Middle Eastern, Latin American and African was introduced as a new category for the 2006 Census. Previously Middle Eastern, Latin American and African responses were allocated to the Other category. (3) Includes response unidentifiable, response outside scope, and not stated.
Note: The number of responses is greater than the total population, as multiple responses are counted. This data has been randomly rounded to protect confidentiality. Individual figures may not add up to totals, and values for the same data may vary in different tables.
Symbols: ... not applicable -- figure too small to be expressed

Source: Statistics New Zealand

Table 6.02

Major ethnic groups
By age group
2006 Census

Age group (years)	European	Māori	Pacific peoples	Asian	MELAA[1]	Other ethnicity[2]
	Percentage of ethnic group population					
0–4	6.6	11.7	13.1	6.7	9.7	6.1
5–14	14.0	23.6	24.6	15.0	17.8	12.9
15–24	13.1	17.9	18.2	21.9	19.6	9.5
25–34	11.9	13.7	13.9	17.0	18.9	12.7
35–44	14.7	13.4	12.8	16.9	17.0	17.4
45–54	13.6	9.9	8.5	12.1	10.0	17.2
55–64	11.0	5.6	5.0	5.9	4.2	13.7
65–74	7.6	2.9	2.6	3.3	1.8	6.9
75–84	5.6	1.0	1.0	1.0	0.8	2.8
85+	1.9	0.2	0.2	0.2	0.2	0.7
Total	**100.0**	**100.0**	**100.0**	**100.0**	**100.0**	**100.0**

(1) Middle Eastern, Latin American and African. (2) Includes 'New Zealander' responses.
Note: Figures may not add up to stated totals, due to rounding.

Source: Statistics New Zealand

Country of birth

The increasing diversity of New Zealand's population is reflected in the number of people born overseas. In 2006, of the people who usually live in New Zealand, 77.1 percent were born there, down from 80.5 percent in 2001 (see table 6.03).

Between 2001 and 2006, New Zealand's overseas-born population rose by 180,915 people, an increase of 25.9 percent. Much of this increase occurred in Auckland – in 2006, over one-third (37.0 percent) of Auckland's population was born overseas, and over half (51.8 percent) of the entire overseas-born population of New Zealand live in Auckland.

Areas that overseas-born people came from are changing. In 2001, almost one-third (32.2 percent) were born in the United Kingdom and Ireland – historically New Zealand's most significant source of migrants – but by 2006, the proportion had decreased to 28.6 percent. In contrast, the proportion of people born in Asia increased from 25.5 percent in 2001 to reach 28.6 percent in 2006, and for the first time, equalled the proportion born in the United Kingdom and Ireland. A 100.8 percent increase in the number of people born in the People's Republic of China – from 38,949 people in 2001 to 78,117 in 2006 – was the main contributor to the increase.

The Indian-born population more than doubled, from 20,889 in 2001 to 43,341 in 2006, an increase of 107.5 percent. The number born in the Republic of Korea increased 60.6 percent, to 28,806. Another significant increase was in the South African-born population, which increased from 26,061 in 2001 to 41,676 in 2006, a 59.9 percent increase.

Significant proportions of New Zealand's immigrant population are relatively recent arrivals in the country. In 2006, almost one-third (32.3 percent) of overseas-born residents had lived there less than five years, while a further 17.0 percent had lived here between five and nine years.

Figure 6.01

Overseas-born New Zealanders by birthplace

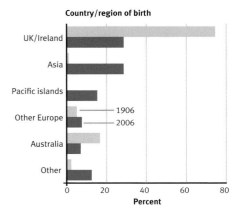

Note: Figures may not add up to 100 due to rounding.

Source: Statistics New Zealand

Who responded as 'New Zealander'?

In the 2006 Census, 429,429 people gave 'New Zealander' as the only or as one of their responses to the ethnicity question on the individual form. This represents 11.1 percent of New Zealand's total population, and compares with 2.4 percent in 2001. The number of New Zealander responses has been growing with each census since 1986.

The *Profile of New Zealander Responses, Ethnicity Question: 2006 Census* (see www.stats.govt.nz) provides background and analysis on some of the differences and similarities between New Zealander responses and other response categories.

In the 2006 Census, the people who identified as New Zealander:

- cover all ages, and are more likely to be male
- make up a larger proportion of the population in the South Island than the North Island
- are most often born in New Zealand.

In contrast to the total population, those identifying as New Zealander:

- have an older median age
- tend to have more educational qualifications, and higher incomes
- are less likely to be of Māori descent
- smoke less than the total population
- are more likely to live in a rural area.

Although the 2006 Census recorded a change in response to the New Zealander category, other collections of official statistics do not show a similar pattern. The way information is collected, the population it is collected from, and the context the collection takes place in, can all affect the way people respond to ethnicity questions.

Trends in ethnic group responses over time are affected by both changes in the actual ethnic make-up of the population, and changes in the ways that people choose to report their identity.

Source: Statistics New Zealand

Table 6.03

Country of birth[1][2]

Country of birth	2001 Census Number of people	2001 Census Percentage[1]	2006 Census Number of people	2006 Census Percentage[1]	Change between censuses (percent)
New Zealand	2,890,869	80.5	2,960,217	77.1	2.4
Australia[3]	56,259	1.6	62,742	1.6	11.5
Samoa	47,118	1.3	50,649	1.3	7.5
Fiji	25,722	0.7	37,749	1.0	46.8
Tonga	18,051	0.5	20,520	0.5	13.7
Cook Islands	15,222	0.4	14,697	0.4	-3.4
Other Oceania and Antarctica	11,877	0.3	12,246	0.3	3.1
Total Oceania and Antarctica	**3,065,121**	**85.4**	**3,158,814**	**82.3**	**3.1**
United Kingdom and Ireland	225,123	6.3	251,688	6.6	11.8
Netherlands	22,242	0.6	22,101	0.6	-0.6
Germany	8,382	0.2	10,761	0.3	28.4
Other Europe[4]	28,923	0.8	35,205	0.9	21.7
Total Europe	**284,670**	**7.9**	**319,755**	**8.3**	**12.3**
Iraq	4,848	0.1	6,024	0.2	24.3
Iran	1,980	0.1	2,793	0.1	41.1
Egypt	1,179	--	1,344	--	14.0
Other North Africa and Middle East	4,164	0.1	6,372	0.2	53.0
Total North Africa and Middle East	**12,174**	**0.3**	**16,533**	**0.4**	**35.8**
Malaysia	11,460	0.3	14,547	0.4	26.9
Philippines	10,137	0.3	15,282	0.4	50.8
Other South-East Asia	23,595	0.7	28,437	0.7	20.5
China, People's Republic of	38,949	1.1	78,117	2.0	100.6
Korea, Republic of	17,934	0.5	28,806	0.8	60.6
Taiwan	12,486	0.3	10,764	0.3	-13.8
Hong Kong	11,301	0.3	7,683	0.2	-32.0
Japan	8,622	0.2	9,573	0.2	11.0
India	20,889	0.6	43,341	1.1	107.5
Other North-East, Southern and Central Asia	10,401	0.3	14,583	0.4	40.2
Total Asia	**165,774**	**4.6**	**251,133**	**6.5**	**51.5**
North America	21,114	0.6	26,742	0.7	26.7
Central and South America	4,395	0.1	7,638	0.2	73.8
Total Americas	**25,509**	**0.7**	**34,380**	**0.9**	**34.8**
South Africa	26,061	0.7	41,676	1.1	59.9
Other sub-Saharan Africa	10,152	0.3	17,442	0.5	71.8
Total Africa	**36,213**	**1.0**	**59,118**	**1.5**	**63.3**
Not specified/born at sea	147,816	...	188,211	...	27.3
Total	**3,737,277**	**...**	**4,027,947**	**...**	**7.8**

(1) All figures are for the census usually resident population, and calculations are made based on the number of people who specified a country of birth. (2) Categories in this table are for major groups and selected categories, where the total number of responses exceeded 1,000. All remaining categories have been grouped as 'Other...'. (3) Includes Australian External Territories. (4) The data includes counts of people who reported being born in Yugoslavia.

Note: This data has been randomly rounded to protect confidentiality. All totals are randomly rounded to base 3. Individual figures may not add up to totals, and values for the same data may vary in different tables.

Symbols: ... not applicable -- figure too small to be expressed.

Source: Statistics New Zealand

Religious affiliation

Results from the 2006 Census showed that New Zealand is becoming increasingly more secular, with 34.7 percent of the people who responded to the religious affiliation question indicating that they had 'no religion', compared with 29.6 percent in the 2001 Census. This continues a steady trend from the last three censuses.

Christianity (including Māori Christian) remained the dominant religion, with over 2 million people, or 55.6 percent of those who answered the religious affiliation question. This compares with the 2001 Census, when 60.6 percent of people affiliated with Christianity.

The five largest Christian denominations in 2001 remained the largest in 2006, with some denominations increasing and some decreasing. Compared with 2001, Anglican affiliation decreased 5.1 percent; Catholic increased 4.7 percent; Presbyterian, Congregational and Reformed affiliations decreased 7.0 percent; Christian not further defined decreased 3.1 percent; and Methodist increased 1.0 percent.

Between 2001 and 2006, some smaller Christian denominations had larger increases in affiliation. Most significantly, in 2006, the number of people affiliating with Orthodox Christian religions increased 37.8 percent; Evangelical, Born Again and Fundamental affiliation increased 25.6 percent; and affiliation with Pentecostal religions increased 17.8 percent. Of the people of Māori ethnicity who answered the religious affiliation question, 11.1 percent identified with a Māori Christian religion, such as Rātana or Ringatū.

The three most common non-Christian religions in 2006 were the Hindu, Buddhist and Islam/ Muslim religions, which made up 1.7 percent, 1.4 percent and 1.0 percent of total responses, respectively. There were also more than 90 religious groups that together made up less than 1 percent of the population. Those who objected to answering the religious affiliation question decreased from 6.9 percent in 2001 to 6.5 percent in 2006.

Changes to the question on religious affiliation from 2001 onwards mean direct comparisons cannot be made with censuses before 2001. Previous censuses collected only one response for religious affiliation, whereas in 2001 and 2006, people were able to give up to four responses.

Table 6.04

Religious affiliation (total responses)

Religious affiliation	2001 Census	2006 Census
Anglican	584,793	554,925
Catholic	486,012	508,437
Presbyterian, Congregational and Reformed	431,547	400,839
Christian not further defined	192,165	186,234
Methodist	120,705	121,806
Pentecostal	67,239	79,155
Māori Christian	63,597	65,550
Hindu	39,798	64,392
Baptist	51,426	56,913
Buddhist	41,634	52,362
Latter-day Saints	39,912	43,539
Islam/Muslim	23,631	36,072
Spiritualism and New Age	16,062	19,800
Brethren	20,406	19,617
Jehovah's Witness	17,826	17,910
Adventist	14,868	16,191
Evangelical, Born Again and Fundamentalist	11,019	13,836
Orthodox	9,588	13,194
Salvation Army	12,618	11,493
Judaism/Jewish	6,636	6,858
Lutheran	4,314	4,476
Other Christian	3,558	3,798
Church of Christ and Associated Churches of Christ	3,270	2,988
Protestant not further defined	2,784	3,954
Uniting/Union Church and Ecumenical	1,389	1,419
Asian Christian	195	195
Other	18,783	24,191
No religion	1,028,052	1,297,104
Object to answering	239,244	242,609
Total people[1]	**3,468,813**	**3,743,655**

(1) Total number of people who specified at least one religious affiliation or objected to answering the question.
Note: All totals are randomly rounded to base 3.

Source: Statistics New Zealand

Citizenship

New Zealand's citizenship legislation is contained in the Citizenship Act 1977, the Citizenship (Western Samoa) Act 1982, and Citizenship Regulations 2002. All citizenship legislation and policy is administered by the Department of Internal Affairs. The principal legislation – the 1977 Act – includes the Cook Islands, Niue, Tokelau, and the Ross Dependency in the definition of New Zealand for purposes of New Zealand citizenship.

Under the Act, a person may be a New Zealand citizen by birth in New Zealand, or by grant, or by descent from a parent who is a New Zealand citizen (but not by descent). British subjects resident in New Zealand throughout 1948 may also apply for confirmation of citizenship.

Citizenship by birth Most people born in New Zealand after 1 January 1949 are New Zealand citizens by birth. From 1 January 2006, children born in New Zealand (or in the Cook Islands, Niue or Tokelau) can acquire New Zealand citizenship at birth only if at least one of their parents is either a New Zealand citizen or entitled to be in New Zealand (or in the Cook Islands, Niue or Tokelau) permanently. This entitlement generally includes Australian citizens, and persons entitled to be in Australia permanently. A child born in New Zealand is a New Zealand citizen by birth if they would otherwise be stateless.

Citizenship by descent Most people born outside New Zealand after 1 January 1949 to a parent who is a New Zealand citizen but not by descent have a claim to citizenship by descent (although there are some limitations on this). New Zealand's citizenship legislation also contains provisions for those adopted by New Zealand citizens.

Grant of citizenship Migrants to New Zealand who wish to make New Zealand their home may apply for a grant of citizenship. They must be 16 years or older, of full capacity, and must submit an application form and fee. Applicants must satisfy the Minister of Internal Affairs that they:

- have been present in New Zealand for the five years immediately preceding their application
- are entitled to remain in New Zealand permanently (most applicants are required to have permanent residence status)
- are of good character
- have a sufficient knowledge of the English language, and of the responsibilities and privileges attached to New Zealand citizenship
- intend to continue to live in New Zealand, or to work overseas in Crown service or for a New Zealand resident or established organisation.

The Citizenship Act 1977 contains special provisions for those whose parents are citizens by descent, for minors, for those who would otherwise be stateless, and for people with special circumstances.

The Citizenship (Western Samoa) Act 1982 provides for the grant of citizenship to Samoan citizens. To be granted citizenship under this Act, a person must be able to prove that they: either were in New Zealand at any time on 14 September 1982 (the day before the commencement of this Act); or have lawfully entered New Zealand after that date, and have an entitlement to remain in New Zealand permanently (most applicants will be required to have permanent residence status).

Otago Daily Times

Dunedin mayor Peter Chin chats with new New Zealanders Ramachandra Keertipati (left), Swetha Keertipati, and Smitha Keertipati, after they received their certificates of New Zealand citizenship at a ceremony in 2007.

Language

New Zealand is largely a monolingual nation, with 80.5 percent of people speaking only one language. However, the number of people who can speak two or more languages has continued to increase. The number of bilingual or multilingual people increased 19.5 percent between the 2001 and 2006 Censuses, to 671,658 people. As expected, people in the Pacific, Asian and MELAA (Middle Eastern, Latin American, and African) ethnic groupings had a much higher proportion of their populations speaking more than one language than did the New Zealander category and the European group.

After English (spoken by 95.9 percent of people), the most common language in which people could have a conversation about everyday things was Māori, spoken by 4.1 percent (157,110 people). New Zealand Sign Language, New Zealand's third official language after English and Māori, was able to be used by 24,090 people (0.6 percent). In comparison, the 2001 Census showed that English was spoken by 96.1 percent, Māori by 4.5 percent and New Zealand Sign Language by 0.8 percent of the population.

New Zealand's changing ethnic composition and the impact of migration between 2001 and 2006 was reflected in the increasing diversity of languages spoken. During that period, the number of people able to speak Hindi almost doubled, from 22,749 to 44,589. Those able to speak one or more of the Chinese languages increased from 76,992 to 108,378, speakers of Korean increased from 15,873 to 26,967, and speakers of Afrikaans increased from 12,783 to 21,123.

Languages spoken (total responses)[1][2]

Languages spoken	2001 Census	2006 Census
English	3,425,301	3,673,626
Māori	160,527	157,110
Samoan	81,033	85,428
NZ Sign Language	27,285	24,090
Other	384,858	509,358
None (eg too young to talk)	76,053	75,570
Total people stated	3,563,796	3,830,757
Total people, not elsewhere included[3]	181,302	204,177
Total population	**3,737,277**	**4,027,947**

(1) All figures are for the census usually resident population. (2) Includes all of the people who stated each language spoken, whether as their only language or as one of several languages. Where a person reported more than one language spoken, they have been counted in each applicable group. (3) Includes response unidentifiable, response outside scope, and not stated.
Note: This data has been randomly rounded to protect confidentiality. Individual figures may not add up to totals.

Source: Statistics New Zealand

Applicants aged 14 and over who are approved for citizenship are required to attend a citizenship ceremony to swear allegiance to New Zealand and Queen Elizabeth II as Head of State. After this, the grant of citizenship is complete and a citizenship certificate is provided.

New Zealand citizens may be deprived of their citizenship if they act in a manner contrary to the interests of New Zealand, or if citizenship was obtained by fraud, false representation, or wilful concealment of relevant information. A citizen cannot be deprived of citizenship if citizenship was acquired by mistake, or if depriving them would leave them stateless. New Zealand citizens may choose to renounce citizenship if they hold citizenship of another country.

Figure 6.02 shows the number of citizenship applications granted from 1962 to 2007, while table 6.05 shows the country of birth of approved citizenship applicants in 2006 and 2007.

Figure 6.02

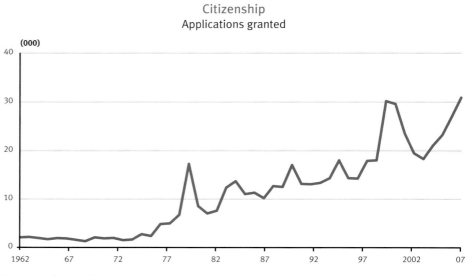

Citizenship
Applications granted

Note: Data is for year ending 31 March to 1993; year ending 30 June from 1994.

Source: Department of Internal Affairs

Immigration

Immigration legislation and policy are administered by Immigration New Zealand (INZ), part of the Department of Labour.

The role of INZ is to increase the economic capacity of New Zealand through immigration, and to position New Zealand as an international country with immigration-related interests and obligations. INZ has branches overseas and throughout New Zealand.

The Ministry of Foreign Affairs and Trade processes applications for temporary entry to New Zealand on behalf of INZ in some countries where INZ is not represented.

Residence

People who want to migrate permanently to New Zealand can apply under one of the three streams of the New Zealand residence programme: skilled/business, family sponsored, or international/humanitarian. Each stream has a number of categories. For 2006/07, the immigration programme's residence approval target was between 47,000 and 52,000 people.

Residence applications are considered on the basis of whether principal applicants meet policy criteria set by the government. Principal applicants may include their partners and dependent children in their application. All applicants must meet health and character requirements, and all migrants over the age of 16 in the skilled migrant, entrepreneur, and in most investor categories must meet a minimum standard of English. This standard can be satisfied by either meeting the specified score in the International English Language Testing System (IELTS), or by showing other evidence of English language ability. Skilled migrants must have an average of 6.5 on the IELTS scale across the four skill areas (speaking, writing, listening and reading). For business migrants the requirements vary, depending on which category they apply under. Non-principal applicants who do not meet the standard may still be granted residence, provided they purchase, in advance, English language tuition to be taken up once they arrive in New Zealand.

Skilled/business residence stream

The skilled/business residence stream consists of the skilled migrant, work-to-residence, and business categories. The business category includes active investor migrants, entrepreneurs, and employees of businesses relocating to New Zealand. In 2006/07, there were 28,140 people

Table 6.05

Citizenship approvals
By country of birth
Year ending 31 December

Country of birth[1]	2006	2007	Country of birth[1]	2006	2007	Country of birth[1]	2006	2007
Afghanistan	368	254	Guatemala	0	3	Peru	27	23
Albania	8	3	Guinea	1	0	Philippines	1,123	1,166
Algeria	9	14	Guyana	4	0	Pitcairn Island	0	1
American Samoa	22	22	Haiti	0	1	Poland	44	52
Angola	1	2	Honduras	1	5	Portugal	2	6
Argentina	68	51	Hong Kong	166	174	Qatar	2	4
Armenia	5	6	Hungary	32	33	Republic of Ireland	37	28
Australia	146	149	Iceland	2	1	Rhodesia	24	31
Austria	12	16	India	4,331	5,177	Rhodesia and Nyasaland	2	4
Azerbaijan	4	2	Indonesia	139	164	Romania	364	233
Bahamas	2	1	Iran	232	237	Russia	319	268
Bahrain	4	15	Iraq	738	500	Rwanda	0	8
Bangladesh	117	110	Ireland	24	33	Samoa	1,205	1,237
Barbados	1	1	Isle of Man	3	1	Saudi Arabia	37	33
Belarus	9	14	Israel	83	49	Scotland	284	331
Belgian Congo	1	0	Italy	19	31	Serbia	2	16
Belgium	4	11	Jamaica	2	6	Serbia and Montenegro	19	1
Belize	0	2	Japan	40	37	Seychelles	3	5
Bermuda	2	1	Jordan	68	56	Sierra Leone	2	6
Bhutan	0	1	Kazakhstan	26	9	Singapore	124	119
Bolivia	8	6	Kenya	65	103	Slovakia	12	18
Bosnia-Herzegovina	10	10	Kiribati	2	4	Slovenia	2	13
Botswana	11	19	Korea	1,638	1,448	Solomon Islands	9	8
Brazil	66	54	Kuwait	73	46	Somalia	237	167
British Virgin Islands	1	0	Kyrgyzstan	3	3	South Africa	2,802	3,131
Brunei	6	7	Laos	11	6	South Vietnam	1	0
Bulgaria	63	52	Latvia	7	5	South West Africa	2	5
Burma	13	9	Lebanon	16	23	Southern Rhodesia	42	43
Burundi	1	4	Lesotho	0	1	Spain	10	13
Cambodia	388	300	Liberia	2	0	Sri Lanka	435	480
Canada	96	121	Libya	2	5	St Kitts and Nevis	1	0
Central Africa	1	0	Lithuania	0	2	St Lucia	0	1
Channel Islands	27	33	Luxembourg	0	1	St Vincent and the Grenadines	0	1
Chile	16	19	Macau	4	7	Sudan	38	76
China	3,886	3,077	Macedonia	44	48	Swaziland	1	3
Colombia	17	40	Madagascar	3	1	Sweden	36	31
Congo	4	1	Malawi	2	13	Switzerland	51	54
Costa Rica	1	2	Malaya	0	2	Syria	33	26
Croatia	30	14	Malaysia	330	449	Tahiti	2	0
Cuba	2	0	Maldives	5	3	Taiwan	429	373
Cyprus	5	6	Malta	8	3	Tajikistan	0	5
Czech Republic	9	8	Mauritius	13	9	Tanganyika	1	0
Czechoslovakia	6	2	Mexico	6	17	Tanzania	12	16
Democratic Republic of the Congo	0	2	Moldova	7	7	Thailand	252	212
Denmark	7	5	Mongolia	3	1	The Netherlands	139	145
Djibouti	4	1	Montenegro	3	1	Tibet	1	0
Dominica	1	1	Morocco	9	9	Togo	0	1
Dutch East Indies	0	1	Mozambique	1	3	Tonga	191	259
East Germany	1	0	Myanmar	35	34	Trinidad and Tobago	6	1
East Timor	1	2	Namibia	35	23	Tunisia	3	1
Ecuador	2	2	Nauru	3	5	Turkey	38	33
Egypt	86	104	Nepal	37	30	Tuvalu	9	10
England	2,464	3,085	Netherlands Antilles	0	4	USA	346	401
Eritrea	4	22	New Caledonia	4	3	Uganda	6	7
Estonia	0	3	New Zealand	1	6	Ukraine	104	66
Ethiopia	71	103	Nigeria	39	34	United Arab Emirates	64	55
Falkland Islands	1	0	Norfolk Island	1	2	Uruguay	6	3
Federation of Rhodesia and Nyasaland	0	1	North Korea	1	1	USSR	33	38
Fiji	1,692	1,722	Northern Ireland	42	61	Uzbekistan	13	20
Finland	10	8	Northern Mariana Islands	1	1	Vanuatu	0	4
France	77	55	Northern Rhodesia	7	8	Venezuela	6	12
French Equatorial Africa	0	1	Norway	4	2	Vietnam	214	215
French Polynesia	2	2	Nyasaland	0	1	Wales	105	124
Georgia	7	12	Oman	21	23	Western Samoa	163	208
Germany	129	153	Pakistan	251	297	Yemen	3	1
Ghana	11	8	Palestine	1	1	Yugoslavia	90	45
Gibraltar	0	2	Palestinian Administered Area	7	6	Zambia	82	89
Greece	8	6	Papua New Guinea	14	15	Zimbabwe	771	864
Guam	1	1	Paraguay	1	0	**Total**	**29,123**	**29,905**

(1) Countries are shown as stated on individuals' applications. This results in duplication of some countries, which may be listed by both their current and former names.

Source: Department of Internal Affairs

approved for residence under the skilled/business stream. This represented 60 percent of all approvals. Of these, 26,874 applications were approved under the skilled migrant and work-to-residence categories, and the other 1,266 were approved under the business category.

Skilled migrant The skilled migrant category focuses on the active recruitment of applicants with the skills that New Zealand needs.

Potential migrants submit expressions of interest, and information from this is used to score points for a number of employability and capacity-building factors. They must meet a pre-set number of points in order to enter a pool of potential residence applicants. They are then invited to apply for residence, based on their ranking in the residence pool and other point factors, and subject to them meeting health, character, English language, and initial verification requirements. Principal applicants invited to apply must be no older than 55 years. Applications for residence are assessed against government residence policy, and the applicant's ability to settle and contribute to New Zealand.

A person who can demonstrate their ability to settle in New Zealand successfully – by having skilled employment, an offer of skilled employment in New Zealand, or a New Zealand post-graduate qualification – may qualify for residence. A person who has potential but does not have these attributes will be interviewed to gather more information. Either a residence or a work-to-residence visa/permit may be issued to these people.

Work to residence This category provides a pathway to residence for holders of permits granted under three specific work policies – talent accredited employers; talent arts, culture and sports; and the long-term skill shortage list.

Active investor migrant This category changed when a new policy came into effect in November 2007, replacing the 2005 Investor category. It has three subcategories:

- General (active) investor category – under this category, points for age, business experience, and lawfully earned or acquired investment funds may be claimed. Applicants first lodge an expression of interest to enter a pool from which they may be invited to apply for residence. A number of policy requirements must be met – including the principal applicant being no older than 54 years, having a minimum of four years' business experience, and investing a minimum of NZ$2.5 million in New Zealand for four years. The IELTS standard for the English language requirement is two band scores of 5 or more.

- Professional investor category – this category has the same requirements relating to business experience and lawfully earned or acquired investment funds as the general (active) investor category, but it is not points based, so does not require an invitation to apply for residence. Professional investors must be no older than 64 years. They must invest a minimum of NZ$10 million, of which NZ$2 million is to be actively invested in one or more new or existing lawful enterprises that undertakes significant economic activity in New Zealand, and results in the principal applicant acquiring at least a 10 percent shareholding. The IELTS standard for the English language requirement is two band scores of 4 or more.

- Global investor category – this category also has the same requirements relating to business experience and lawfully earned or acquired investment funds as the general (active) investor category, but again, it is not points based, so does not require an invitation to apply for residence. It requires a minimum investment in New Zealand of NZ$20 million for four years, of which NZ$5 million is to be actively invested in one or more new or existing lawful enterprises that undertakes significant economic activity in New Zealand, and results in the principal applicant acquiring at least a 10 percent shareholding. The global investor category has no age or English language requirements.

Entrepreneur People who have successfully established a business that benefits New Zealand – and have been self-employed in New Zealand in that business for at least two years – can be granted residence under this category. Successful establishment means the applicant has established, purchased, or made a substantial investment in a profit-making business operating in New Zealand. The business must also benefit New Zealand, and may meet this criterion if it creates employment, revitalises an existing business, enhances New Zealand's export markets, or introduces new skills or technologies to New Zealand.

Employees of businesses relocating to New Zealand This category is available on a case-by-case basis to essential employees of businesses relocating to New Zealand who do not qualify for residence under any other category.

Family-sponsored residence stream

Thirty percent of approvals were allocated to the family-sponsored residence stream for 2006/07, and 14,705 applications were approved. The family-sponsored stream allows migrants in a variety of close relationships with New Zealand citizens or residents to be sponsored for residence. In general, sponsors must have held New Zealand residence for at least three years immediately before sponsorship, and must sign a declaration that they will provide accommodation and financial support for the first two years of the migrant's residence in New Zealand. Sponsors of parents must meet a minimum income requirement. Financially-dependent children under the age of 25 may also be sponsored. Adult children and siblings who have no parents or siblings in their home country are eligible to be sponsored for residence, along with their dependants, providing they have a job offer in New Zealand, and meet a minimum income requirement.

Partnership policy To qualify for residence under this policy, applicants have to prove they have been living in a genuine and stable relationship with a New Zealander for 12 months or more at the time of application, whether or not they are in a marriage or de facto relationship (whether opposite or same sex).

International/humanitarian residence stream

The international/humanitarian residence stream includes the refugee quota and other refugee-linked categories, such as refugee status, and the refugee family support category. Other categories include the Pacific access category, the Samoan quota, ministerial exceptions to policy, a category for victims of domestic violence, and various miscellaneous categories.

Refugees New Zealand is committed to working with the international community to help resolve refugee problems. The Department of Labour manages the refugee quota programme, which allows up to 750 refugees to settle in New Zealand each year. It consists of a number of categories, including women at risk, medical/disabled, protection and emergency. In 2006/07, the 748 people approved for residence through the programme included refugees from Myanmar (Burma), Afghanistan, Sudan, and the Democratic Republic of Congo.

All refugees attend a six-week orientation programme at the Department of Labour's Mangere Refugee Resettlement Centre. The department locates and maintains sponsors who assist refugees to settle in the community following their induction. Refugees accepted under the quota are granted residence permits on arrival in New Zealand. This means they are entitled to live in New Zealand permanently, and to enjoy the rights of New Zealand residents in matters such as education, health, employment, and social welfare.

New Zealand also considers claims for refugee status from people who arrive in New Zealand seeking asylum. Claims are assessed under the 1951 United Nations Convention and 1967 Protocols relating to the status of refugees. The refugee status branch of INZ assesses claims in the first instance. In 2006/07, there were 62 successful refugee status claimants. The number of refugee status claims in New Zealand has reduced substantially in recent years. If a claim is declined, the claimant may appeal to the Refugee Status Appeals Authority.

Pacific access The Pacific access category enables up to 250 people from Tonga, 75 people from Tuvalu, and 75 people from Kiribati to be granted residence each year. Applicants must be citizens of their country, meet English language, health, and character requirements, and have an offer of employment in New Zealand.

Samoan quota Up to 1,100 Samoan citizens may be granted residence in New Zealand each year under the Samoan quota. English language, health, and character requirements must be met, and the principal applicant must have an offer of employment in New Zealand.

Domestic violence policy The domestic violence policy enables ex-partners of New Zealand citizens or residents to apply for residence when their relationship has ended as a result of domestic violence, and they are unable to return to their home country, for cultural or social reasons, and would not have (or be able to get) independent support (eg financial) in their home country.

Promoting ethnic perspectives

The Office of Ethnic Affairs Te Tari Matawaka was established in 2001 as part of the Department of Internal Affairs. It is responsible for the provision of policy advice, information, and liaison services to the Minister for Ethnic Affairs. The office also provides information and referral services, and administers the telephone interpreting service Language Line.

The office was established to ensure that people from smaller ethnic communities (those who do not identify as Anglo-Saxon, Celtic, Māori or Pacific peoples) can be seen, heard, included and accepted in New Zealand society.

Ethnic peoples include refugees, migrants, and their New Zealand-born descendants. The office monitors issues affecting these communities, and develops, or contributes to the development of, policies and initiatives affecting them. Its role is to:

- provide high-quality evaluation, evidence-informed policy analysis, and advice to ministers, to support their decision making
- provide high-quality ministerial support and services
- be the primary repository of knowledge and information on ethnic community matters
- help local and central government to communicate with ethnic communities
- help ethnic people to access government services through the Language Line telephone interpreting service
- publish material that promotes intercultural understanding, and discussion of ethnic issues in the wider community.

Source: Office of Ethnic Affairs

The Aucklander

Gadir Maklaf (left) and his parents, Fauzia Zahroon and Moayed Sowadi, came to New Zealand from Iraq as refugees. Every year 750 refugees are able to settle in New Zealand under the refugee programme.

Sources of migration

United Kingdom nationals accounted for 26 percent of the 46,964 people approved for residence in New Zealand in 2006/07. Twelve percent of those approved for residence were from China, 9 percent were from India, and 8 percent were from South Africa.

In 2006/07, categories in the skilled/business residence stream made up 60 percent (28,140 people) of all approvals, and a further 30 percent (14,705 people) were granted residence under the family-sponsored stream. In the same period, 10 percent of residence approvals were allocated to the international/humanitarian stream, and 4,119 people were granted residence.

Temporary entry

All travellers arriving in New Zealand, including New Zealand citizens, must produce a valid passport or another form of recognised travel document.

With the exception of New Zealand citizens (including people born in the Cook Islands, Niue and Tokelau), Australian citizens, and a small number of people exempt under the Immigration Act 1987, everyone entering New Zealand is required to obtain a permit to remain in New Zealand. The main categories for temporary permits are outlined below.

Visitors People may enter New Zealand as visitors if they are tourists, visiting friends or relatives, studying for less than three months, playing sport or performing in cultural events without pay, or making short business trips. A visitor's permit is usually granted for an initial period of three months, and may be extended for up to a further six months.

More than 50 countries have been granted visa waivers, so citizens of these countries do not need to apply for a visitor's visa before they travel to New Zealand (they are granted a visitor's permit at the border). Visitors from countries without visa waivers need to apply for a visitor's visa before travelling to New Zealand.

Visitors must have sponsorship or sufficient funds to support themselves while they are in New Zealand, and must have an outward ticket or some other travel arrangement.

Students International students from visa-required countries must apply for a visa before travelling to New Zealand to study. If the course of study is less than 12 weeks, they may be granted a visitor's visa. If the course of study is more than 12 weeks, they may be granted a student visa. Students from visa-waived countries who are intending to study for a period of less than 12 weeks may enter New Zealand as visitors and be granted a visitor's permit. If they are enrolled in a course of study for a period of more than 12 weeks, they must apply for a student visa before entering New Zealand.

Students must show they have been offered a place at a recognised educational institution. They must have: evidence that course fees have been paid, a guarantee of accommodation, the ability to support themselves, and a return ticket (or the funds to buy one). During their studies, student permit holders must attend classes and make satisfactory progress.

Students may be granted permission to work for up to 20 hours a week if certain conditions are met. Students undertaking a full-time course of 12 months or more may be allowed to work full time during the summer holiday period.

Students who have successfully completed a New Zealand qualification that would gain points under the skilled migrant category are eligible for a 12-month open work permit. Students who have graduated from a course of at least three years duration, or who have completed a New Zealand qualification that would qualify for points under the skilled migrant category, may be granted a work permit for up to two years if they have an offer of employment relevant to their course or qualification. A permit of up to three years may be granted if this is necessary in order to gain membership or registration with a New Zealand professional organisation. Partners of students undertaking particular courses may be eligible for an open work permit for the duration of the student's course of study.

Guardian This policy allows the legal guardian of a young international student to live with and care for the child, while they study in New Zealand. The guardian visa applies to legal guardians of children aged 17 and under who are enrolled for years 1 to 13 at a New Zealand school. The guardian visa is linked to the child's student visa and can be renewed annually. Only one legal guardian in each family is eligible for a guardian visa.

Work-related entry

Anyone who wishes to work in New Zealand (except New Zealand or Australian citizens or residents) must have a work permit. The policy allows people to enter New Zealand for a variety of work-related purposes. Some policies allow employers to recruit temporary workers from overseas to meet particular or seasonal skill needs that cannot be met from within New Zealand. Other policies allow partners of New Zealand citizens or residents to participate in the labour market. Work permits are also issued to young people (those aged 18–30 years) participating in working holiday schemes that New Zealand has established with a number of countries, and to people applying through work-to-residence policies.

For immigration purposes, 'work' is defined as an activity for which the person receives 'gain or reward', which can include not only money, but also accommodation and food. A work permit is still required if payment is made by an overseas employer.

Manawatu Standard

Setu Sua, a Samoan worker on a temporary work permit picks asparagus on Lewis Farms, one of the biggest producers of asparagus in New Zealand, which covers 70 hectares near Foxton in Manawatu. For the past three years, farm owner Geoff Lewis has arranged for up to 30 workers to come from Samoa to help with the harvest, as it has become increasingly difficult to find local staff.

Recognised seasonal employer policy In 2007, the recognised seasonal employer policy was introduced to facilitate the recruitment of overseas workers by employers in the horticulture and viticulture sectors, when labour demand exceeds the available New Zealand workforce, and employers have made reasonable attempts to train and recruit New Zealanders. Employers must meet a number of 'good employer' requirements to become a recognised seasonal employer, and if approval to recruit overseas is granted, preferential access is given to workers who are citizens of eligible Pacific countries.

Immediate skills shortage list INZ publishes this regionally-based labour market skills shortage list to facilitate work visa and permit applications from employers where there appears to be a skills shortage. This list is updated six-monthly.

In 2002, new work permit categories that provide a pathway for gaining residence in New Zealand were introduced. These categories allow people who are interested in applying for residence in New Zealand to work for up to two years before lodging their application for residence. These categories include the long-term skills shortage list, and talent visas. Holders of work permits under these policies may be eligible for residence after two years, if they meet all policy requirements including, in most cases, an offer of ongoing employment with a minimum base salary.

Long-term skills shortage list Applicants are eligible for a work permit under this category if they have an offer of employment for an occupation that is on the long-term skills shortage list, and they have the necessary qualifications, training or experience, and registration (if required) to undertake the offer of employment. The employment offer must be for at least 24 months, be full time, and comply with all relevant New Zealand employment laws.

Talent (accredited employer) Businesses operating in New Zealand can apply to become accredited employers with INZ. Accredited employers are able to recruit workers directly from overseas to fill skill shortages, provided those workers meet immigration criteria.

Talent (arts, culture and sports) Under this category, a person who has an international reputation, a record of excellence in their field, and who will enhance the quality of New Zealand's accomplishments and participation in that field, may be granted a work permit. An applicant must be sponsored by a New Zealand organisation of national repute.

Working holiday schemes These schemes generally allow 18–30-year olds from partner countries to spend 12 months in New Zealand and undertake temporary work. The schemes also allow young New Zealanders to work overseas under reciprocal agreements. At March 2008, New Zealand had schemes with 27 countries.

Long-term business visa Work permits may be granted to business people interested in either applying for residence under the entrepreneur category, or establishing a business in New Zealand without living permanently in New Zealand. A satisfactory business plan must be submitted, and applicants must have sufficient funds to finance their proposed business, and to support themselves and their families. English language requirements were introduced for this category of applicants in November 2002.

A long-term business visa is issued for nine months. By the end this period, in order to be granted an extension to their visa for a three-year term (including the initial nine months), applicants must provide evidence of having transferred the investment funds for the business to New Zealand, and of taking reasonable steps to establish the business.

Removal and deportation

The Immigration Act 1987 requires all people in New Zealand, other than New Zealand citizens, to hold a permit or be exempt from holding a permit. The Act provides for residence to be revoked by the Minister of Immigration on certain grounds. People who do not hold a permit or an exemption are deemed to be unlawfully in New Zealand and may be removed.

Any person may appeal against removal on humanitarian grounds to the Removal Review Authority within 42 days of becoming unlawfully present in New Zealand. People removed from New Zealand are not eligible to return for five years after the date of their departure.

The Act provides for deportation of people who threaten national security or are suspected terrorists, or are criminal offenders who are residents of New Zealand. Such people may appeal on humanitarian grounds to the Deportation Review Tribunal, an independent tribunal administered by the Ministry of Justice. If the tribunal dismisses an appeal, the deportation order remains in place. A further appeal, only on a point of law, may be made to the High Court of New Zealand. Anyone deported from New Zealand is not permitted to return without special permission from the Minister of Immigration.

Māori society

Demography

In most surveys collecting data about ethnicity, including the Census of Population and Dwellings, ethnicity is self-perceived and people can, and do, identify with more than one ethnic group. People are counted as having Māori ethnicity if they identify with the Māori ethnic group as one of their ethnicities.

Statistics based on ethnicity are widely used for analysing Māori population growth and distribution, and are relevant to many requirements of users. However, a different concept, based on Māori descent, is used to measure the Māori electoral population.

Figure 6.03

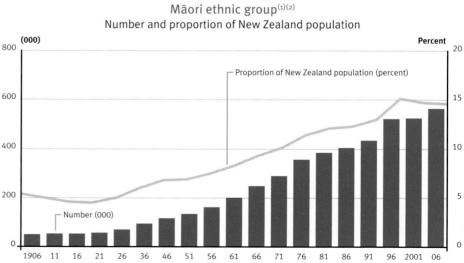

Māori ethnic group[1][2]
Number and proportion of New Zealand population

(1) Information on Māori ethnicity is unavailable prior to 1991. Information about Māori collected in the censuses prior to 1991 was on the basis of descent/origin. (2) Prior to 1991 the subject population is the census night population count, which includes overseas visitors. From 1991 onwards, the subject population is those in the census usually resident population count who stated an ethnicity, and does not include overseas visitors.
Note: There was no census in 1931 and 1941.

Source: Statistics New Zealand

Age distribution Table 6.06 compares the Māori ethnic group population at the 2001 and 2006 Censuses by age group. Apart from the impact of births, deaths and migration, inter-ethnic mobility (changes in ethnic identification over time) is also an important factor in Māori population change.

The 2006 Census showed that the Māori ethnic group was significantly younger in age structure than the total population – 35.4 percent of the Māori population was aged under 15 years, compared with 21.5 percent of the total population. By contrast, only 4.1 percent of the Māori population was aged 65 and over, compared with 12.3 percent of the total population. These differences mainly reflect the higher historical fertility (in terms of birth rates) and the lower life expectancy of the Māori ethnic group, relative to the total population.

Figure 6.03 shows the Māori ethnic group population as a proportion of the total New Zealand population in the census years from 1906 to 2006.

Table 6.06

Māori ethnic group[1]
By age group

Age group (years)	2001 Census Number of people	Percentage	2006 Census Number of people	Percentage	Change between censuses (percent)
0–4	67,560	12.8	66,423	11.7	-1.7
5–9	66,114	12.6	66,771	11.8	1.0
10–14	62,805	11.9	66,726	11.8	6.2
15–19	49,530	9.4	58,533	10.4	18.2
20–24	42,093	8.0	42,771	7.6	1.6
25–29	40,164	7.6	38,106	6.7	-5.1
30–34	39,252	7.5	39,456	7.0	0.5
35–39	38,322	7.3	38,598	6.8	0.7
40–44	32,859	6.2	37,272	6.6	13.4
45–49	25,092	4.8	31,905	5.6	27.2
50–54	19,473	3.7	24,192	4.3	24.2
55–59	13,827	2.6	18,627	3.3	34.7
60–64	11,550	2.2	12,816	2.3	11.0
65–69	7,938	1.5	10,155	1.8	27.9
70–74	5,070	1.0	6,510	1.2	28.4
75–79	2,688	0.5	3,807	0.7	41.6
80+	1,941	0.4	2,652	0.5	36.6
Total	**526,281**	**100.0**	**565,329**	**100.0**	**7.4**

(1) Māori ethnic group census usually resident population count.
Note: Figures may not add up to stated totals, due to rounding.

Source: Statistics New Zealand

Female-to-male ratio In the 2006 Census, females outnumbered males in the Māori ethnic group. There were 290,466 Māori females and 274,860 Māori males, representing a sex ratio of 105.7 females to every 100 males.

Regional distribution Changes in the regional distribution of the Māori ethnic group between the 2001 and 2006 Censuses are shown in table 6.07 (overleaf). People of Māori ethnicity continue to be concentrated in the North Island, and more especially in Northland, Auckland, Waikato and Bay of Plenty. The Māori population in the North Island and South Island increased 6.6 and 13.3 percent, respectively, between the 2001 and 2006 Censuses. The Otago and Canterbury regions showed the largest percentage increases between the two censuses. Redistribution of the Māori population between 2001 and 2006 was the result of variations in the relative levels of natural increase (births minus deaths) in the regions, and the impact of both internal and external migration flows.

Dynamics of population change Māori have a substantially higher rate of natural increase than the total population, partly because of their more youthful age structure and higher birth rate. The birth rate for Māori women fell rapidly during the 1960s and 1970s and, as a consequence, the gap between their birth rate and that of the total population narrowed, from a two-child difference in 1962 to less than one child in 2006. Nevertheless, the Māori birth rate of 2.7 births per woman in 2006 remains higher than that for all women (2.0 births per woman). Births to non-Māori mothers and Māori fathers also contributed to Māori population growth.

Treaty of Waitangi

The Treaty of Waitangi Te Tiriti o Waitangi was signed at Waitangi on 6 February 1840. While the treaty has always been recognised within Māori society as an affirmation of rights and highly valued as a taonga (treasure) and a sacred pact, this has not always been the case for governments or the courts.

However, in 1987, a ruling by the Court of Appeal ensured that the treaty moved from being 'a simple nullity', as it was described in 1877, to exerting an important influence over much of government activity.

The Māori King movement

The New Zealand Herald

The new Māori King, Te Arikinui Tūheitia Paki, is welcomed on to Houmaitawhiti Marae at Okere Falls, near Rotorua, on 25 September 2006.

In May 2008 Māori gathered at Ngaruawahia to celebrate the 150th anniversary of the formation of the Kingitanga, or Māori King movement. The current king, Te Arikinui Tūheitia Paki, is the seventh Māori monarch. He took the throne in August 2006, following the death of his mother, Te Arikinui Dame Te Atairangikaahu. She was the longest serving Māori monarch, having celebrated the 40th jubilee of her coronation on 23 May 2006.

The Kingitanga movement began in the 1850s, some years after the arrival of Europeans, in an attempt to halt sales of land and promote Māori authority in New Zealand. A number of tribes supported the movement, but it became centred on the Waikato region and people. The desire to retain land was a central concern of the movement.

The position of Māori monarch, which was established in May 1858, is a non-constitutional role with no legal power in New Zealand, but it is a symbolic role invested with a high degree of mana (prestige).

In principle, the position is not hereditary. The monarch is appointed by the leaders of the tribes involved in the Kingitanga movement on the day of the previous monarch's funeral. To date, all Māori monarchs have been direct descendants of Pōtatau Te Wherowhero, the first Māori king, and each monarch since then has been succeeded by a son or daughter. However, after any reign ends, there is the potential for the mantle to be passed to someone from another family or tribe, if the chiefs of the various tribes are in agreement.

The Kingitanga movement has expanded since its establishment, and is widely recognised and respected by Māori in many parts of New Zealand.

Source: www.tvnz.co.nz

Table 6.07

Māori ethnic group[1]
By region

Region	2001 Census		2006 Census		Change between censuses (percent)
	Number of people	Percentage	Number of people	Percentage	
North Island					
Northland	40,734	7.7	43,527	7.7	6.9
Auckland	127,626	24.3	137,133	24.3	7.4
Waikato	72,822	13.8	76,572	13.5	5.1
Bay of Plenty	63,654	12.1	67,662	12.0	6.3
Gisborne	19,365	3.7	19,758	3.5	2.0
Hawke's Bay	32,088	6.1	33,555	5.9	4.6
Taranaki	14,559	2.8	15,798	2.8	8.5
Manawatu-Wanganui	39,267	7.5	42,288	7.5	7.7
Wellington	51,123	9.7	55,437	9.8	8.4
Total	**461,235**	**87.6**	**491,730**	**87.0**	**6.6**
South Island					
Tasman	2,778	0.5	3,063	0.5	10.3
Nelson	3,219	0.6	3,612	0.6	12.2
Marlborough	3,891	0.7	4,275	0.8	9.9
West Coast	2,547	0.5	2,916	0.5	14.5
Canterbury	31,635	6.0	36,669	6.5	15.9
Otago	10,545	2.0	12,270	2.2	16.4
Southland	10,038	1.9	10,422	1.8	3.8
Total	**64,650**	**12.3**	**73,230**	**13.0**	**13.3**
Area outside region[2]	393	0.1	369	0.1	-6.1
Total New Zealand	**526,281**	**100.0**	**565,329**	**100.0**	**7.4**

(1) Maori ethnic group census usually resident population count. (2) Includes Chatham Islands.
Note: Figures may not add up to stated totals, due to rounding.

Source: Statistics New Zealand

The ruling confirmed the special relationship between Māori and the Crown as one of an ongoing partnership, requiring the partners to act reasonably and with the utmost good faith towards each other.

Waitangi Tribunal

The Waitangi Tribunal Te Rōpū Whakamana i te Tiriti o Waitangi, established under the Treaty of Waitangi Act 1975, is a permanent commission of inquiry. Its main functions are to inquire into, and make findings and recommendations to the Crown on claims by Māori relating to the Treaty of Waitangi.

The tribunal consists of up to 16 members appointed by the governor-general for up to three years, and a chairperson, who is either a judge or retired judge of the High Court of New Zealand or the chief judge of the Māori Land Court. The chairperson may appoint a judge of the Māori Land Court as deputy chairperson and assign Māori Land Court judges to preside over particular inquiries.

Members are appointed for their expertise in matters likely to come before the tribunal. Membership of the tribunal reflects partnership in the Treaty of Waitangi through balanced representation of Māori and New Zealanders of European descent.

In exercising any of its functions, the Waitangi Tribunal has exclusive authority to determine the meaning and effect of the Treaty of Waitangi, as embodied in the English and Māori texts, and to decide upon issues raised by the differences between them.

The tribunal may inquire only into claims by Māori concerning legislation, acts, omissions, policies, and practices of the Crown that are alleged to have caused prejudice to the claimants, and that are claimed to be inconsistent with the principles of the Treaty of Waitangi.

Claims fall into three broad categories:

- historical claims (for example, past government actions)
- contemporary claims (for example, current government policies or practices)
- conceptual claims (for example, ownership of natural resources).

The tribunal must register any claim that complies with the Act, but may refuse to inquire into claims it considers frivolous or vexatious.

The tribunal does not settle claims – it makes recommendations to the government on how claims might be settled. Generally, the tribunal has the authority to make recommendations only.

In most instances, its recommendations do not bind the Crown, claimants, or third parties, and nearly all claims are settled by negotiation with the government. However, in certain limited situations, the tribunal does have binding powers. These include powers to order the return of former State-owned enterprise, railway, education, or Crown forest land that has been memorialised (which makes them available to the tribunal). However, in no other circumstances can the tribunal recommend or order the return of private land.

The tribunal's process is flexible and inquisitorial. It is not required to follow court rules of evidence, and it can adapt its procedures as it sees fit. For example, the tribunal can adopt the protocols of the marae (meeting place) at which a hearing is taking place.

All evidence is presented in public, hearings are open to all, and the tribunal's reports are published.

The tribunal has given priority to hearing historical claims, which are defined as those alleging grievances that arose before September 1992. The government set a statutory deadline of 1 September 2008 for the submission of new historical claims.

From 1975 to 31 December 2007, the tribunal registered 1,428 claims. Of these, 949 claims were under inquiry or had received tribunal reports. They range from small claims submitted by individuals, up to comprehensive claims on behalf of large iwi- or hapū-based (tribe and sub-tribe) groups.

The tribunal inquires into most historical and contemporary claims on a joint district basis. At 31 December 2007, the tribunal had reported on or started inquiries in 27 of the tribunal's 37 districts. These covered 89 percent of the national territory. In several other districts, the principal claimant groups had completed or were negotiating with the Crown for the settlement of their claims.

Office of Treaty Settlements Te Tari Whakatau Take e pā ana ki te Tiriti o Waitangi was established on 1 January 1995, to give better focus to government objectives to resolve historical claims under the Treaty of Waitangi. The office has the following major functions:

- to provide policy advice to the Minister in Charge of Treaty of Waitangi Negotiations on specific treaty claims, and generic issues that impact on these claims
- to negotiate and implement settlement of specific claims
- to acquire, manage, and dispose of Crown-owned property for purposes related to treaty claims.

For administration and financial management purposes, the office is attached to, but funded separately from, the Ministry of Justice, and has its own Vote Treaty Negotiations allocation. At the beginning of 2007, the office was dealing with about 25 claimant groups at the pre-negotiation, negotiation, or implementation stage.

Te Puni Kōkiri

Te Puni Kōkiri Ministry of Māori Development is the Crown's principal adviser on relationships between Māori and the Crown, and guides Māori public policy by advising the government on policy affecting Māori well-being and development.

Te Puni Kōkiri's strategic outcome is 'Māori succeeding as Māori'. This outcome strives to achieve a sustainable level of success for Māori as individuals, in organisations, and in collectives.

The purpose of Te Puni Kōkiri is to 'realise Māori potential'. Te Puni Kōkiri has developed the Māori Potential Approach, an innovative, forward-looking policy approach that aims to better position Māori to realise the potential of their collective resources, knowledge, skills, and leadership capability to improve their overall quality of life.

Māori organisations

Māori Trustee has been in existence since 1921 and is now governed by the Māori Trustee Act 1953. It is independent of the Crown and is accountable to landowners and the Māori Land Court. The Māori Trustee exists to:

- protect and enhance the interests of Māori clients and their resources
- manage the adverse effects of fragmented and multiple ownership of Māori land
- provide fair, proper, and prudent administration and management of clients' assets within the principles and obligations of trusteeship and agency.

In helping Māori to manage their land and assets, the Māori Trustee:

- acts as either a trustee or an agent for owners of Māori land, usually in leasing the land
- collects and pays rent and other income to owners
- invests trust moneys
- keeps landowners informed about how their land is managed
- regularly publishes an unclaimed moneys list.

New Zealand Māori Council Te Kaunihera Māori is constituted under the Māori Community Development Act 1962, and is a founding member of the World Indigenous People's Council. Some of the functions of the council are to:

- consider and discuss matters that are relevant to the social and economic advancement of Māori

Treaty of Waitangi claim process

Each negotiation of a Treaty of Waitangi claim is different, reflecting the particular characteristics and interests of the claimant group. Most negotiations, however, progress through the following stages:

- Before negotiations begin, claimant groups need to establish that a breach of the treaty has occurred. To achieve this, claimants may go to the Waitangi Tribunal to have their claim heard or to do their research.
- In the pre-negotiations stage, a claimant group establishes a mandate from its members to negotiate with the Crown, and settles with the Crown the terms under which it will negotiate. A negotiated settlement will address multiple claims lodged at the Waitangi Tribunal.
- The negotiations stage covers discussions between a claimant group and the Crown over the basic elements of a settlement. These include the form of a historical account, the form of an apology, and the types of cultural and commercial redress that are appropriate.
- The next stage is the agreement in principle (previously called a heads of agreement), which is a broad agreement between the claimant group and the Crown as to what will make up a treaty settlement, including the total quantum, or fiscal value, of the settlement.
- Once the Crown and the claimant group's negotiators agree on the fine detail of the settlement, the two parties initial a deed of settlement. This is the Crown's formal offer of settlement and is subject to ratification by all members of the claimant group, usually through hui (meetings) and a postal ballot. If the deed of settlement is ratified by a clear majority of the claimant group, the deed will be signed and becomes binding. A bill is prepared to give effect to the settlement.
- This bill is then introduced into parliament and passes through the normal parliamentary process (including referral to a select committee) before becoming law. A representative, transparent, and accountable governance entity needs to be established and ratified in order to receive the settlement redress.
- Implementation is the final stage of the process.

Twenty-one deeds of settlement had been signed by November 2007, settling multiple claims covering more than half of New Zealand's land area and over 25 percent of the Māori population.

Source: Office of Treaty Settlements

- consider, and as far as possible act on, any measures that will conserve and promote harmonious and friendly relations between Māori and other members of the community
- promote, encourage, and assist Māori to conserve, improve, and advance their physical, economic, industrial, educational, social, moral, cultural, and spiritual well-being through self-reliance, sound economic management, and pride in themselves
- collaborate with and assist government departments and other organisations and agencies in development of employment, education, training, housing, and health care for Māori people.

As a statutory body, the council is accountable to the government for its funding. The council is based on the 946 marae (rural or urban Māori centres) throughout New Zealand. It represents 17 district Māori councils, which nominate three delegates to attend full council meetings. The council also includes representatives from the Māori Women's Welfare League and Māori wardens. The executive committee consists of the chairperson of each district council. The council is the only national Māori body with a statutory framework that recognises non-iwi-based representation. Apart from the urban councils, each district council is tribally represented and the council promotes the traditional social infrastructure of whānau (family) and hapū (subtribe).

Māori Congress Te Whakakotahitanga o ngā Iwi o Aotearoa was officially launched in July 1990, after three national Māori leaders – the late Sir Hepi Te Heuheu, the late Dame Te Ātairangikaahu (the Māori Queen) and the late Mrs Te Reo Hura – sought to create a national body under which iwi (tribes) could gather to share, consolidate and advance their positions. Objectives of the congress include:

- advancement of all Māori people
- exercise by each iwi of tino rangatiratanga (self-determination)
- provision of a national forum for iwi representatives to address economic, social, cultural and political issues within tikanga Māori (Māori custom)
- promotion of constitutional and legislative arrangements enabling Māori to control their development and exercise self-determination.

While acknowledging the strengths and autonomy of each iwi, the Māori Congress provides a forum at which matters of national importance affecting all iwi and, indeed, all Māori, can be debated within a Māori context. By standing apart from government, both in terms of direction and funding, it offers Māori people an opportunity to consider options and strategies for social, economic and cultural advancement. With its wide iwi base, the congress provides a source of collective Māori opinion from which policies acceptable to it can develop. The congress is led by two presidents, and has three elected officers. Membership includes five delegates from 45 participating iwi.

Māori Women's Welfare League Te Rōpū Wāhine Māori Toko i te Ora is a national voluntary organisation that aims to promote the well-being of Māori women and their families. The league has a nationwide network of 165 branches, with a membership of 3,000. It has been actively involved with Māori families and communities since 1951, improving health, housing, education, welfare, justice, and economic development for Māori people.

Māori wardens were established by the Maori Community Development Act 1962. Māori wardens are volunteers who provide services such as maintaining security for territorial local authorities, businesses and hospitals; addressing truancy issues and removing children and young people from risk situations; dealing with issues of drug and alcohol misuse; helping whānau in need; working at the courts and other parts of the justice sector; and walking and patrolling the streets. They are usually people of high standing in the Māori community. Their approach is based on rangimārie (peace), aroha (compassion), and kōrero (persuasion). Knowledge of taha Māori (Māori ways) and pride in Māori identity guides the way the wardens operate.

Te reo Māori

Te reo Māori is the language of the indigenous people of New Zealand and an official language of the country. Legislation that led to declaring Māori as an official language of New Zealand was passed in 1987.

Māori Language Commission Te Taura Whiri i te Reo Māori was established by the Māori Language Act 1987 to promote the Māori language and its use as an official language of New Zealand – as a living language, and as an ordinary means of communication.

The Māori language renaissance, which began about 30 years ago, has fostered many Māori language initiatives to revitalise te reo Māori, including kōhanga reo (Māori language immersion preschool movement), kura kaupapa Māori and wharekura (Māori language immersion primary and secondary schools), and whare wānanga (Māori tertiary institutions). There are also 21 Māori radio stations, and a Māori television service, which began in 2004. New Zealand's first 100 percent Māori language television channel, Te Reo, was launched in March 2008.

Kōhanga reo is a whānau (family) base where Māori language, values and customs are naturally acquired by preschool children from kaumātua (elders), whānau, kaimahi (staff), and kaiako (teachers).

The kōhanga reo movement's aim is that through the example of the whānau, children learn aroha (love, compassion), manaakitanga (caring, hospitality) and whānaungatanga (family

The Napier Mail

Children from Hawke's Bay Te Kōhanga Reo o Te Ara Hou explore the workings of a worm farm with whānau workers. The kōhanga (language nest) gives preschoolers an opportunity to watch their food scraps being recycled, while learning about natural processes and the environment. Worm farms are an excellent way to teach the principle of 'kaitiakitanga' – showing responsibility and guardianship for natural and physical resources.

responsibilities) through the medium of Māori language. The movement provides a variety of courses and training programmes that can be accessed by whānau through their own kōhanga reo. These courses are whānau-based and have been designed to improve whānau skills and knowledge, not only in te reo and tikanga Māori, but also in learning and teaching, administration, and management of the kōhanga reo operation.

In 2007, there were approximately 500 kōhanga reo attended by 9,500 children throughout New Zealand.

Pacific peoples

Demography

Population statistics for the Pacific ethnic group are compiled on the basis of self-identification. People are counted in the Pacific ethnic group if they indicate one or more Pacific ethnicities in response to the census ethnicity question.

The Pacific ethnic group includes people of Samoan, Cook Island Maori, Niuean, Tokelauan, Fijian, Tuvaluan, and other Pacific ethnicities (eg Hawaiian and Tahitian). People may identify themselves as belonging to more than one Pacific ethnicity. While they are counted in each ethnicity when considering ethnicities within the broad Pacific ethnic group, they are counted only once in the Pacific ethnic group.

Age distribution Table 6.08 (overleaf) compares the Pacific population at the 2001 and 2006 Censuses on an age group basis. The increase of 34,176 (14.7 percent) in the Pacific population between the 2001 and 2006 Censuses was partly a result of significant natural increase (an excess of births over deaths).

At the time of the 2006 Census, the Pacific population was considerably younger in age structure than the total population, with 37.7 percent of Pacific peoples under the age of 15, compared with 21.5 percent of the total population. By contrast, only 3.8 percent of Pacific people were aged 65 and over, compared with 12.3 percent of the total population. In the past, people of Pacific ethnicities in New Zealand had a different age structure from that of the Māori ethnic group. This difference was mainly the result of Pacific peoples' consistently high net migration levels, especially for the younger working-age group (15–24 years) during the 1970s. However, since 1996, with a large increase in intermarriage, the ageing of Pacific people, and relatively high fertility rates, their age structure has become almost identical with that of Māori.

Two other features affect the Pacific population. Firstly, in the past three decades, the number of Pacific people born in New Zealand has increased significantly, to reach 60 percent in 2006 – the result of growth in the population of reproductive age. Secondly, an increasingly large proportion of children and teenagers identify themselves as being of both Pacific and Māori ethnicities. More than 25 percent of all children under the age of five who belong to the Pacific ethnic group also belong to the Māori ethnic group.

Who are New Zealand's Pacific peoples?

The 2006 Census showed that the seven largest Pacific ethnic groups in New Zealand are: Samoan, making up the largest proportion (49 percent of all Pacific people in New Zealand), Cook Island Maori (22 percent), Tongan (19 percent), Niuean (8 percent), Fijian (4 percent), Tokelauan (3 percent), and Tuvaluan (1 percent).

All seven Pacific ethnic groups have very youthful populations, with a large proportion aged under 15 years, and only a very small proportion over 65 years. This distinctive age structure contributes to many of the differences between Pacific peoples and the total New Zealand population, which has an older age structure.

Around three-quarters of New Zealand's Cook Island Maori, Niuean and Tokelauan populations were born in New Zealand. New Zealand-born Samoans and Tongans accounted for 60 percent and 56 percent of their respective populations. Fijians and Tuvaluans had the lowest New Zealand-born proportions (44 percent and 37 percent, respectively).

Pacific language retention varied, with Tuvaluans being the most likely to speak their own language, at 71 percent, followed by Samoans (63 percent) and Tongans (61 percent). Cook Island Maori, Niueans, Fijians, and Tokelauans had significantly lower rates, Cook Island Maori having the lowest, at 16 percent. Around one-quarter of Niueans and Fijians were able to speak their own Pacific language.

Fijians have the highest proportion of adults with a formal educational qualification (secondary school or post-school qualification), at 82 percent. Samoans have the next-highest proportion (69 percent). The other groups range from 55 percent (Cook Island Maori) to 64 percent (Tongans). The comparable figures for the total Pacific and total New Zealand populations are 65 percent and 75 percent, respectively.

All Pacific ethnic groups have a high proportion of people stating a religious affiliation. Highest are the Tuvaluans and the Tongans with 96 percent and 90 percent, respectively, followed by 86 percent of Samoans and Tokelauans, 82 percent of Fijians, and 70 percent of both Cook Island Maori and Niueans. In all groups, except Fijians, 96–98 percent of the affiliations were with a Christian denomination. Among Fijians, 87 percent were affiliated to a Christian denomination.

All seven Pacific ethnic groups continue to live mainly in urban areas, and only the Tokelauan group did not have the majority residing in the Auckland region, with 51 percent living in the Wellington region.

For all Pacific ethnic groups, those in the younger age groups are more likely to belong to more than one ethnic group.

Table 6.08

Pacific ethnic group[1]
By age group

Age group (years)	2001 Census Number of people	Percentage	2006 Census Number of people	Percentage	Change between censuses (percent)
0–4	32,775	14.1	34,848	13.1	6.3
5–9	30,480	13.1	33,597	12.6	10.2
10–14	26,889	11.6	31,896	12.0	18.6
15–19	21,486	9.3	27,690	10.4	28.9
20–24	19,782	8.5	20,721	7.8	4.7
25–29	17,976	7.8	18,918	7.1	5.2
30–34	17,778	7.7	18,129	6.8	2.0
35–39	16,011	6.9	18,075	6.8	12.9
40–44	12,753	5.5	16,089	6.0	26.2
45–49	10,131	4.4	12,687	4.8	25.2
50–54	7,977	3.4	10,047	3.8	25.9
55–59	5,667	2.4	7,611	2.9	34.3
60–64	4,461	1.9	5,577	2.1	25.0
65–69	3,150	1.4	4,290	1.6	36.2
70–74	2,241	1.0	2,715	1.0	21.2
75–79	1,269	0.5	1,716	0.6	35.2
80+	975	0.4	1,359	0.5	39.4
Total	**231,798**	**100.0**	**265,974**	**100.0**	**14.7**

(1) Pacific ethnic group census usually resident population count.
Note: Figures may not add up to stated totals, due to rounding.

Source: Statistics New Zealand

Regional distribution More than two-thirds of New Zealand's Pacific population live in the Auckland region. While all regions experienced growth in their Pacific populations between the 2001 and 2006 Censuses, in the Auckland region the Pacific population grew by 23,253 (15.0 percent) during the five-year period.

Table 6.09

Pacific ethnic group[1]
By region

Region	2001 Census Number of people	Percentage	2006 Census Number of people	Percentage	Change between censuses (percent)
North Island					
Northland	2,943	1.3	3,702	1.4	25.8
Auckland	154,680	66.7	177,933	66.9	15.0
Waikato	10,524	4.5	11,796	4.4	12.1
Bay of Plenty	5,463	2.4	6,465	2.4	18.3
Gisborne	1,137	0.5	1,299	0.5	14.2
Hawke's Bay	4,710	2.0	5,265	2.0	11.8
Taranaki	1,059	0.5	1,365	0.5	28.9
Manawatu-Wanganui	5,031	2.2	5,892	2.2	17.1
Wellington	32,283	13.9	34,752	13.1	7.6
Total	**217,833**	**94.0**	**248,472**	**93.4**	**14.1**
South Island					
Tasman	222	0.1	336	0.1	51.4
Nelson	594	0.3	711	0.3	19.7
Marlborough	408	0.2	642	0.2	57.4
West Coast	186	0.1	282	0.1	51.6
Canterbury	8,622	3.7	10,923	4.1	26.7
Otago	2,646	1.1	3,141	1.2	18.7
Southland	1,278	0.6	1,461	0.5	14.3
Total	**13,950**	**6.0**	**17,496**	**6.6**	**25.4**
Area outside region[2]	15	0.0	6	0.0	-60.0
Total New Zealand	**231,801**	**100.0**	**265,974**	**100.0**	**14.7**

(1) Pacific ethnic group census usually resident population count. (2) Includes Chatham Islands territory.
Note: Figures may not add up to stated totals, due to rounding.

Source: Statistics New Zealand

Migration to New Zealand

Cook Islands The Cook Islands gained independence in free association with New Zealand in 1965. Its people retained the right of free entry to New Zealand and significant emigration began in the 1950s, and increased during the 1960s and 1970s. The most common destinations were Auckland and Wellington. Smaller numbers of migrants settled in other parts of New Zealand, mostly in the main urban areas. The 2006 Census recorded 58,011 Cook Island Maori living in New Zealand.

The New Zealand Herald

Niuean Tifa Ikitoelagi dances with other women at the Niuean village during the Pasifika Festival at Western Springs, Auckland. More than 22,000 Niueans lived in New Zealand in 2006, most of them in Auckland.

Fiji At the time of the 2006 Census, there were 9,861 Fijians living in New Zealand, an increase of 40.1 percent since 2001. New Zealand-born Fijians made up 43.5 percent of the Fijian population in 2006, while 51.7 percent of Fijians born overseas had been living in New Zealand for less than 10 years. Nearly 60 percent of Fijians lived in the Auckland urban area, with the next-largest concentration, 9.5 percent, in the Wellington urban area. Figure 6.04 shows the pattern of Pacific migration from 1987 to 2007.

Niue achieved self-government in free association with New Zealand in 1974 and Niueans were granted right of free entry, residence, and New Zealand citizenship. Among New Zealand's attractions for Niueans is a more settled way of life. Niue is particularly vulnerable to natural disasters, such as drought and cyclones, and cyclones in 1959, 1960, and 2004 had devastating effects. In 2006, there were over 22,000 Niueans living in New Zealand, most of them in Auckland.

Samoa Samoa's 13 islands are divided into Samoa and American Samoa. The six islands east of the 171st meridian were annexed by the United States in 1899. New Zealand assumed control of Western Samoa at the start of World War I, and retained it until 1962, when Western Samoa became independent. Western Samoa is now known as Samoa. Emigration from the islands picked up in the mid 1960s and continues largely through the process of chain migration. Rapid population growth, a decline in export prices for cocoa and copra, a banana crop disease, and a major cyclone in 1966 were persuading factors for migrants. The Treaty of Friendship signed at Western Samoa's independence ensured emigrants would not have to register in New Zealand as aliens. Samoans constitute the largest group of Pacific peoples living in New Zealand – more than 130,000 at the 2006 Census. Most live in Auckland.

Figure 6.04

Net Pacific migration to New Zealand[1]
Year ending 31 March

(000)

(1) Permanent and long-term migrants with a country of last or next permanent residence within Melanesia, Micronesia and Polynesia.

Source: Statistics New Zealand

Tokelau The small island group of Tokelau was declared a British Protectorate in 1889. New Zealand took over administration on behalf of Britain in 1925 and it became part of New Zealand's territory in 1948, with full political independence being gained in 1994. The 10 square kilometres of Tokelau's three atolls have few natural resources, apart from lagoons, coconut palms and the ocean. The atolls are also vulnerable to cyclones. After a devastating cyclone in 1966, the New Zealand Government set up a resettlement scheme that involved about 500 people, half the Tokelauan population. These people voluntarily left Tokelau and resettled in urban Porirua and forest-industry towns such as Rotorua. In 2006, there were close to 7,000 Tokelauans living in New Zealand and only about 1,500 in Tokelau.

Tonga The Kingdom of Tonga is an independent nation. Population pressures have forced it to adopt emigration as an official policy. In 1970, a scheme was initiated under which Tongans were allowed to migrate to New Zealand temporarily to work in unskilled jobs in the processing industry. Many also went to Australia and to the United States. In 2006, more than 50,000 Tongans were living in New Zealand, most of them in Auckland.

Asian population

Demography

The population of the Asian ethnic group in New Zealand increased markedly between 1996 and 2006. People are counted as belonging to the Asian ethnic group if they give any Asian ethnicity in response to the census ethnicity question. People may identify themselves as belonging to more than one Asian ethnicity. While they are counted in each ethnicity when considering the ethnicities within the broad Asian ethnic group, they are counted only once in the Asian ethnic group. Figure 6.05 shows the pattern of Asian migration from 1981 to 2007.

Figure 6.05

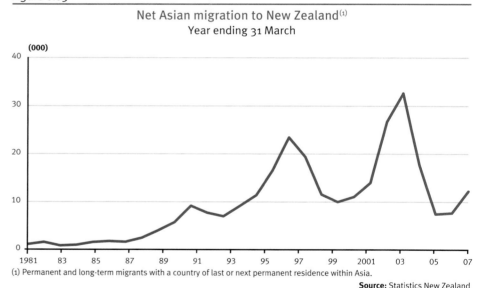

Net Asian migration to New Zealand[1]
Year ending 31 March

(1) Permanent and long-term migrants with a country of last or next permanent residence within Asia.

Source: Statistics New Zealand

Asian ethnicities Even though most Asian ethnicities increased significantly between 2001 and 2006, each group's share of the total Asian population changed only marginally. In 2006, people of Chinese ethnicities were the largest subgroup within the Asian ethnic group (with a share of 41.6 percent) and they experienced the largest numerical increase in their population, from 105,057 people in 2001 to 147,570 in 2006. People of Indian ethnicities (29.5 percent of the Asian ethnic group in 2006), experienced a similar numerical increase, from 62,187 people to 104,583 between 2001 and 2006, but had the highest percentage increase, at 68.2 percent. People of Korean ethnicity were the third largest group, accounting for 8.7 percent (30,792 people) of the Asian ethnic group in 2006.

Age distribution Between 2001 and 2006, the population of the Asian ethnic group increased by nearly 50 percent, from 238,176 people to 354,552. This represents an average growth rate of 9.8 percent a year, compared with 1.6 percent for the total New Zealand population. Net migration was a major contributor to this population growth. This growth also had a significant impact on the overall age structure of the Asian group. At the time of the 2006 Census, 73.8 percent of the Asian ethnic group were of working age (15–64 years), compared with 66.2 percent for the total population. By contrast, only 4.5 percent of Asians were aged 65 and over, compared with 12.3 percent of the total population.

Regional distribution The Asian ethnic group continues to be concentrated in the Auckland, Wellington and Canterbury regions. Between the 2001 and 2006 Censuses, the Auckland region experienced the largest growth in its Asian population in numerical terms, while Marlborough experienced the largest growth in percentage terms (65.1 percent). The Auckland region's Asian population increased more than 80,000, to reach 234,219 people in 2006, and represented 71.0 percent of the national increase of 116,376 people between 2001 and 2006.

Table 6.10

Asian ethnic group[1]
By age group

Age group (years)	2001 Census Number of people	Percentage	2006 Census Number of people	Percentage	Change between censuses (percent)
0–4	18,378	7.7	23,910	6.7	30.1
5–9	18,381	7.7	25,053	7.1	36.3
10–14	19,521	8.2	27,987	7.9	43.4
15–19	27,102	11.4	32,076	9.0	18.4
20–24	24,018	10.1	45,621	12.9	89.9
25–29	17,979	7.5	32,232	9.1	79.3
30–34	19,947	8.4	27,882	7.9	39.8
35–39	22,722	9.5	29,163	8.2	28.3
40–44	19,806	8.3	30,747	8.7	55.2
45–49	15,690	6.6	24,870	7.0	58.5
50–54	11,520	4.8	18,012	5.1	56.4
55–59	7,161	3.0	12,525	3.5	74.9
60–64	6,192	2.6	8,403	2.4	35.7
65–69	4,434	1.9	6,987	2.0	57.6
70–74	2,589	1.1	4,602	1.3	77.8
75–79	1,485	0.6	2,445	0.7	64.6
80+	1,254	0.5	2,037	0.6	62.4
Total	**238,176**	**100.0**	**354,552**	**100.0**	**48.9**

(1) Asian ethnic group census usually resident population count.
Note: Figures may not add up to stated totals, due to rounding.

Source: Statistics New Zealand

Table 6.11

Asian ethnic group[1]
By region

Region	2001 Census Number of people	Percentage	2006 Census Number of people	Percentage	Change between censuses (percent)
North Island					
Northland	1,998	0.8	2,580	0.7	29.1
Auckland	151,602	63.7	234,219	66.1	54.5
Waikato	12,021	5.0	18,204	5.1	51.4
Bay of Plenty	5,202	2.2	7,824	2.2	50.4
Gisborne	621	0.3	741	0.2	19.3
Hawke's Bay	2,937	1.2	3,513	1.0	19.6
Taranaki	1,500	0.6	2,154	0.6	43.6
Manawatu-Wanganui	6,564	2.8	8,121	2.3	23.7
Wellington	27,819	11.7	36,477	10.3	31.1
Total North Island	**210,264**	**88.3**	**313,833**	**88.5**	**49.3**
South Island					
Tasman	369	0.2	567	0.2	53.7
Nelson	861	0.4	1,065	0.3	23.7
Marlborough	387	0.2	639	0.2	65.1
West Coast	243	0.1	345	0.1	42.0
Canterbury	19,431	8.2	29,169	8.2	50.1
Otago	5,769	2.4	7,779	2.2	34.8
Southland	849	0.4	1,149	0.3	35.3
Total South Island	**27,909**	**11.7**	**40,713**	**11.5**	**45.9**
Area outside region[2]	C	C	C	C	C
Total New Zealand	**238,176**	**100.0**	**354,552**	**100.0**	**48.9**

(1) Asian ethnic group census usually resident population count. (2) Includes Chatham Islands territory.
Note: Figures may not add up to stated totals, due to rounding.
Symbol: C confidential

Source: Statistics New Zealand

Human rights

Human Rights Commission

The Human Rights Commission Te Kāhui Tika Tangata is an independent Crown entity, which has a range of functions to perform under the Human Rights Act 1993. The commission's four major functions are to:

- advocate and promote respect for, and an understanding and appreciation of, human rights in New Zealand society
- encourage maintenance and development of harmonious relations among individuals, and among the diverse groups in New Zealand society
- lead, evaluate, monitor, advise, analyse, and liaise on equal employment opportunities
- respond to enquiries from members of the public about discrimination
- facilitate the resolution of disputes alleging discrimination in the most efficient, informal, and cost-effective manner possible.

The commission is required to act independently in performing its statutory functions and duties, and in exercising its statutory powers. The Act provides for the positions of Chief Commissioner, Equal Employment Opportunities Commissioner, Race Relations Commissioner, and no more than five part-time human rights commissioners.

The commission has offices in Auckland, Wellington and Christchurch.

Dispute resolution The commission has the function of mediating disputes relating to unlawful discrimination on the grounds of sex (including pregnancy) and sexual harassment; marital status (including being in a civil union); religious belief; ethical belief; colour; race; ethnic or national origins; disability; age; political opinion; employment status; family status; and sexual orientation in the following areas of government or public sector activities: employment; access to education; access to public places, vehicles and facilities; provision of goods and services; provision of land, housing and accommodation; industrial and professional associations, qualifying bodies, and vocational training bodies; and partnerships.

In the year ending 30 June 2007, the commission received 5,796 enquiries and complaints. Of these, 1,665 had an unlawful discrimination component. The rest were predominantly about other human rights matters. Outcomes achieved through the dispute resolution process include encouraging parties towards self-help (where appropriate), increasing the parties' understanding of human rights standards, apologies, participation in policy reviews, and financial compensation. Where a settlement cannot be reached, complainants may take their case to the Human Rights Review Tribunal, and seek legal representation from the Director of Human Rights Proceedings.

Equal Employment Opportunities Trust

The Equal Employment Opportunities (EEO) Trust was established in 1991 by the Government and the private sector to promote EEO principles and best practice in the workplace. Trustees are representative of both public and private sectors.

The EEO Trust raises awareness of the business benefits of developing versatile workplaces that employ people on the basis of merit. The annual EEO Trust Work and Life Awards recognise organisations and individuals who champion work/life balance.

Women's issues

New Zealand women were the first in the world to win the right to vote in national elections (in 1893).

Today, women's rights have wide legislative protection, but despite this, inequalities still exist. For example, women are still paid less on average than men, and they are more likely to be victims of sexual and family violence.

The government is working to eliminate these inequalities, and to ensure that there are no barriers for women to contribute to social, economic, and environmental outcomes for New Zealand. This work is guided by the Action Plan for New Zealand Women – a five-year, whole-of-government plan launched in 2004.

The plan has three high-level outcomes:

- improving the economic independence of women – to help ensure they have enough money to care for themselves and those who depend on them
- greater work/life balance in New Zealand – to help women balance work, family/whānau, and community roles
- improved well-being for all New Zealand women – focusing on preserving women's general well-being, including their safety, security, housing, and physical and mental health.

The Ministry of Women's Affairs monitors progress on implementing the plan.

Family issues

Property (Relationships) Act 1976 In 2001, the Matrimonial Property Act 1976 was renamed the Property (Relationships) Act 1976, and was amended to provide for division of property when a married or de facto couple separates, or when one of the partners in a married or de facto relationship dies. The 1976 Act was further amended in 2005 to include civil union couples.

Domestic Violence Act 1995 The Domestic Violence Act 1995 aims to deliver greater protection for victims of domestic violence. The Act provides for a single protection order that protects against a wide range of behaviour amounting to physical, sexual, or psychological abuse. The order involves certain statutory provisions, including a prohibition on any form of violence, and restricting the possession of firearms. It includes special conditions that a court can impose to suit the circumstances of the particular case. The order also contains flexibility around certain provisions, such as the non-contact provision, so that the applicant can agree to live with the respondent. The other conditions still apply, and the applicant can change their mind at any time. The Act places particular emphasis on providing programmes for victims and their children, and mandatory programmes for respondents to protection orders.

The Act applies to married and de facto spouses, same-sex partners, family and household members, and those in close personal relationships. The Act also recognises that abuse can occur not just in relationships between domestic partners, but also in wider family groups.

Youth issues

The Ministry of Youth Development Te Manatū Whakahiato Taiohi aims to make a real difference in the lives of young people in New Zealand. It was created on 1 October 2003 and is administered by the Ministry of Social Development. It brought together the former Ministry of Youth Affairs and the youth policy functions of the Ministry of Social Development.

From 2005, the ministry developed a small regional presence across New Zealand to enable it to support and achieve positive outcomes for young people at a local level. The ministry's five key functions are:

- providing young people with a central point of contact within government so they can express their views and interests
- providing government with advice on how to improve outcomes for young people
- working with other government agencies, local government, and the youth development sector to improve services and opportunities for young people
- funding services to provide at-risk young people with support in their local communities
- building and sharing an evidence base about youth development in New Zealand.

Participation projects for young people A key role of the Ministry of Youth Development is to ensure that young people's diverse voices and interests are known to government to support the best possible decision making on behalf of all young people in New Zealand. Since its establishment, the ministry has increased young people's involvement in consultation, advice, project development, and decision making within the ministry and government.

Human rights in New Zealand

In March 2005, the Human Rights Commission published a national action plan for the better protection and promotion of human rights in New Zealand. *The New Zealand Action Plan for Human Rights/Mana ki te Tangata* identified what needed to be done over a five-year period so that the human rights of everyone who lives in New Zealand are better recognised, protected, and respected.

The commission's *2006–07 Statement of Intent and Service Performance* was shaped by the priorities identified in the action plan. It confirms the commission's emphasis on a comprehensive approach to human rights and race relations, rather than a merely reactive response to problems as they arise. It highlights the commission's active engagement with a wide range of organisations, groups, and communities to build a nationwide understanding of, and respect for, human rights and responsibilities.

The commission's programme of work is structured under the following themes, which support the priorities identified in the action plan:

- the human rights environment
- disabled people
- race relations
- the right to work
- human rights and the Treaty of Waitangi
- international connectedness.

Source: Human Rights Commission

Ministry of Youth Development

Voices rose, and order was called during a fiery session in the House of Representatives during Youth Parliament 2007. The 121 Youth MPs from around New Zealand met at Parliament to debate topics that included binge drinking and the young driving age, and inflation and the housing market.

The ministry's youth participation channels provide young people with opportunities to give input into key policy areas, government reviews, and service delivery.

Youth Development Strategy Aotearoa This strategy sets out a vision, supported by principles and goals, for all New Zealand young people aged 12–24 years. In particular it provides a framework for government and non-government agencies to develop policies that impact on young people, and guide the design of services and programmes for youth.

Through Services for Young People, the ministry supports organisations that provide vulnerable young people with tangible outcomes, through innovative and creative youth development services.

Existing services engage young people through positive relationships, connection to the outdoor environment, and opportunities for participants to give back to local communities. Curriculum components of programmes target specific needs of participants, including educational qualifications, alcohol and drug management, health, and relationship issues.

The Youth Development Partnership Fund allows the ministry and territorial authorities to work together to provide opportunities for young people. A key objective of the fund is to increase achievement of positive social, economic and well-being outcomes for young people by providing opportunities to develop valuable work, life and learning skills.

Youth Parliament Every three to four years, the Youth Parliament provides young people with an opportunity to learn about how parliament works. They have their views heard by the actual Members of Parliament (MPs), who each select a Youth MP for the Youth Parliament experience.

Youth MPs take part in all the work that real MPs do, such as debating in the house, reviewing legislation, asking ministers questions, and select committee meetings.

Running alongside the Youth Parliament is a Youth Press Gallery, which gives aspiring young journalists a taste of political reporting.

The next Youth Parliament is expected to be in 2010.

Contributors and related websites

Department of Internal Affairs – www.dia.govt.nz

Equal Employment Opportunities Trust – www.eeotrust.org.nz

Human Rights Commission – www.hrc.co.nz

Immigration New Zealand – www.immigration.govt.nz

Māori Language Commission – www.tetaurawhiri.govt.nz

Ministry of Justice – www.justice.govt.nz

Ministry of Women's Affairs – www.mwa.govt.nz

Ministry of Youth Development – www.myd.govt.nz

Office of Ethnic Affairs – www.ethnicaffairs.govt.nz

Office of Treaty Settlements – www.ots.govt.nz

Statistics New Zealand – www.stats.govt.nz

Te Kohanga Reo – www.kohanga.ac.nz

Te Puni Kōkiri Ministry of Māori Development – www.tpk.govt.nz

Waitangi Tribunal – www.waitangi-tribunal.govt.nz

Youth Parliament – www.youthparliament.govt.nz

The New Zealand Herald

Roger and Teresa van Kuylenberg with seven of the eight grandchildren that they raise, Patrick (left), 11, Mathias, 3, Takawai, 11, Phoenix, 6, Teresa, 7, Cairo, 3, and 18 month-old Faith, during their day out at the grandparents raising grandchildren day, held at Chelsea Primary School in Auckland in 2008.

7 | Social development

Social development is a process of coordinated social change, which promotes the well-being of the population as a whole and of disadvantaged groups within it.

Social development aims to promote well-being across a range of areas, such as social assistance, health, education, employment, care, and protection, and takes a whole-of-life approach to improving outcomes.

Successful social development involves:

- ensuring that social and economic interventions are sustainable and mutually reinforcing
- supporting individuals, families and communities to develop and deliver their own solutions, focusing on their strengths, needs and issues
- working with the private sector, local authorities, communities, and the voluntary sector to develop unified local services
- regularly monitoring New Zealanders' well-being, ensuring there is flexibility to respond to regional and local needs.

Ministry of Social Development

The Ministry of Social Development was established on 1 October 2001, bringing together the policy advice and research functions of the Ministry of Social Policy and the income support and employment services of Work and Income.

The ministry's aims include building strong and healthy families, supporting young people, helping people achieve economic independence, developing well-being within communities, and contributing to a growing and resilient economy.

The ministry works closely with other social sector agencies, including health, education and housing, to improve all areas of people's lives. The ministry's framework covers children and young people, working-age people, older people, families, and communities.

The ministry undertakes social research and evaluation, gives cross-sectoral policy advice to the government, delivers income support and employment services through Work and Income, and delivers services to students through StudyLink. Family and Community Services – part of the ministry – leads and coordinates community-based services to families.

Helping people move into work

The Ministry of Social Development's focus is on helping people to gain the skills that lead to sustainable employment, providing effective support to keep them in work, and making sure that work leaves them and their families better off.

The ministry, through Work and Income, offers support and a range of services to help people make the transition to, and remain in, employment.

Planning services help people looking for work to create a definite pathway to employment. Planning includes the development of "job seeker agreements" for people receiving the Unemployment Benefit, and "personal development and employment plans" for other people who will be able to move into employment in the future. These plans, developed in agreement with each client, set concrete goals to help people with their job search.

People seeking work may be able to get help to gain the skills required to move into employment, pay some of the costs associated with seeking work, and stay in employment when a suitable job has been secured. Eligibility to access this assistance has recently been broadened to include people with ill-health, the disabled, and sole parents.

Some of the services and assistance for people seeking employment include job search assistance, development services, self-employment assistance, upskilling assistance, work experience, wage subsidies, Training Incentive Allowance, and Course Participation Assistance. The range of services and assistance offered for people seeking work is designed to ensure each person is in the best position to move into employment when appropriate. Work and Income also offers seminars and services specifically designed to meet the needs of certain client groups.

People moving into employment may be able to access such assistance as Seasonal Work Assistance, New Employment Transition Grants, and Transition to Work Grants. This assistance can help with some of the costs associated with actively seeking employment, moving into employment, and remaining there.

Work and Income employs people in specialist roles to help job seekers secure and remain in suitable, sustainable employment. These roles include work brokers and specialised employment coordinators, who liaise with employers to help fill vacancies. Work and Income also offers In-work Support to some people who have moved into employment, to help them remain there.

Source: Ministry of Social Development

The ministry also administers Child, Youth and Family, the Ministry of Youth Development, the Office for Disability Issues, the Office for the Community and Voluntary Sector, and the Office for Senior Citizens.

Policy, research and evaluation

The Ministry of Social Development's strategic social policy group monitors and reports on the social well-being of New Zealanders, and delivers policy advice to the government on cross-sectoral policy issues.

The sector policy group delivers policy advice on: the care and protection of children and young people; social assistance and employment; positive ageing and retirement; disability issues; and family and community development.

The Centre for Social Research and Evaluation researches key social policy issues, provides evidence to support policy development, and evaluates the effectiveness of government policies and programmes.

Work and Income

Work and Income, a service line of the Ministry of Social Development, provides income support and employment services for more than 1 million New Zealanders a year, and employs approximately 4,400 people in 190 locations.

The average number of applications for main benefits and pensions per working day is about 1,800. (Applications for supplementary benefits by people receiving a main benefit, and lump sum grants and benefit advances, are not included.) This total includes applications for all benefits, including the Orphan's Benefit and the Unsupported Child's Benefit, non-beneficiaries receiving a supplementary benefit, Unemployment – Student Hardship, New Zealand Superannuation, and the Veteran's Pension.

Work and Income pays a wide range of benefits, supplementary benefits and pensions.

Benefits paid in the year ending 30 June 2007 included:

- Caring benefits – Domestic Purposes Benefit (Sole Parent), Domestic Purposes Benefit (Caring for the Sick or Infirm) and Domestic Purposes Benefit (Woman Alone)
- Incapacity benefits – Sickness Benefit and Invalid's Benefit
- Work-related benefits – Independent Youth Benefit and Unemployment Benefit
- Miscellaneous benefits – Emergency Benefit, Unsupported Child's Benefit, Orphan's Benefit and Widow's Benefit
- Military service pensions – Veteran's Pension, War Disability Pension and dependant's allowance
- New Zealand Superannuation
- Supplementary benefits and lump sum assistance payments – Accommodation Supplement, Childcare Subsidy, Out of School Care and Recreation (OSCAR) Subsidy, Disability Allowance, Funeral Grant, Special Benefit, Special Needs Grant, Training Incentive Allowance, advance payments of income support, and recoverable assistance available to people not receiving benefits or pensions.

Weekly rates of income support at 1 April 2007 are shown in table 7.01.

The Aucklander

Barbara Stone set up a food bank 17 years ago, but it has now turned into a cashless supermarket. People come in and get what they want, after being referred by social workers.

Table 7.01

Income support weekly[1] rates[2]
At 1 April 2007

Type of income support	Net weekly payment[3] ($)
Unemployment Benefit/Sickness Benefit[4]	
Single, aged 18–19 years, at home	118.98
Single, aged 18–19 years, away from home	148.73
Single, aged 20–24 years	148.73
Single, aged 25 years and over	178.49
Married couple (each partner)[5]	148.73
Sole parent	255.65
Invalid's Benefit	
Single, aged 16–17 years	180.54
Single, aged 18 years and over	223.10
Married couple (each partner)[5]	185.92
Sole parent	293.08
Domestic Purposes Benefit	
Woman alone	185.92
Sole parent	255.65
Domestic Purposes Benefit – Caring for the Sick or Infirm[6]	
Single, aged 16–17 years	180.54
Single, aged 18 years and over	223.10
Married couple (each partner)[5]	175.61
Sole parent	293.08
Emergency Maintenance Allowance	
Aged 16–17 years, at home	118.98
Aged 16–17 years, away from home	255.65
Aged 18 years and over	255.65
Widow's Benefit	
Single	185.92
Sole parent	255.65
Orphan's Benefit and Unsupported Child's Benefit	
Child, aged under 5 years	117.76
Child, aged 5–9 years	135.42
Child, aged 10–13 years	144.24
Child, aged 14 years and over	153.05
Independent Youth Benefit	
Single, aged 16–17 years	148.73
New Zealand Superannuation and Veteran's Pension	
Single, living alone	277.06
Single, sharing	255.74
Married person[5]	213.12
Married couple (both qualify)[5]	426.24
Married couple with non-qualifying spouse (each partner)[5]	203.22

(1) Prior to 1 July 2007, some people may have received fortnightly payments at double the indicated rates. Since that date, all benefits have been paid weekly. (2) Rates shown are maximum amounts. For income-tested benefits, the amount a person actually receives will depend on their income from other sources. (3) From 1 April 2005, the child component of benefits (that is the additional payment included for one or more children) was removed from benefit payments and included in Working for Families Tax Credits. (4) From 1 April 2006, all people receiving Sickness Benefits have been paid at the same rate, regardless of when their benefit was granted. (5) 'Married' includes people who are married, living as married, or in a civil union. (6) Only the caregiver receives payment.

Source: Ministry of Social Development

Income adjustment People receiving an Invalid's Benefit, Widow's Benefit, any Domestic Purposes Benefit, Sickness Benefit or Unemployment Benefit have any income they earn above $80 per week (or $4,160 per year) charged against their benefit payment.

These benefits may also be subject to an initial stand-down period of up to two weeks.

The levels at which all benefits are paid are adjusted annually, in line with movement in the consumers price index (CPI). In addition, the CPI-adjusted rate for New Zealand Superannuation and Veteran's Pension is compared with average wage levels, to ensure the after-tax payment rate for couples is between 65 and 72.5 percent of the after-tax average ordinary time weekly wage.

Basic income exemptions People receiving the Unemployment Benefit, Sickness Benefit or Independent Youth Benefit, and non-qualified spouses of people receiving New Zealand Superannuation, have their weekly benefit reduced by 70 cents for each dollar of gross weekly income they earn above $80.

People receiving Invalid's Benefit, Widow's Benefit or any Domestic Purposes Benefit have their benefit reduced by 30 cents for every dollar earned between $80 and $180 a week, and by 70 cents per dollar earned above $180 a week.

Unemployment Benefit This benefit is available to people who are not in full-time employment, are capable of and willing to undertake full-time work, and are taking reasonable steps to obtain employment. An Unemployment Benefit is also available to people who are not full-time students, but are engaged in full-time, employment-related training programmes.

At the end of June 2007, there were 23,159 working-aged people receiving an Unemployment Benefit, 16,593 fewer than at the end of June 2006. There were 6,099 working-aged people in

Extra financial help for families

Working for Families, a package implemented progressively since October 2004, is designed to make it easier to work and raise a family.

Under the programme, extra financial support is available for nearly all families (with children) earning under $70,000 a year, many families (with children) earning up to $100,000 a year, and some larger families earning more.

Working for Families is delivered by Work and Income and Inland Revenue. The phase of implementation introduced on 1 April 2006 involved an in-work payment for eligible families in lieu of the Child Tax Credit.

Changes have also been made to make housing more affordable. The Accommodation Supplement has increased, and is available to more working families and to many people without children.

Subsidies for pre-school and out-of-school care have increased significantly, and are now available to more parents earning higher incomes.

Source: Ministry of Social Development

training and receiving an Unemployment Benefit at the end of June 2007, 533 more than at the end of June 2006.

Domestic Purposes Benefit This benefit is available to parents caring for children without the support of partners, to people caring at home for someone who would otherwise be receiving hospital care, and, in some circumstances, to older women living alone.

At the end of June 2007, there were 96,467 working-aged people receiving a Domestic Purposes Benefit, 5,174 fewer than at the end of June 2006.

Widow's Benefit This benefit is available to women whose husbands, civil union partners, or de facto partners have died. At the end of June 2007, 6,287 working-aged people were receiving the Widow's Benefit, 714 fewer than at the end of June 2006.

Invalid's Benefit This benefit is available to people aged 16 years and over who are either totally blind, or permanently and severely restricted in their capacity for work.

At the end of June 2007, 77,301 working-aged people were receiving an Invalid's Benefit, 1,952 more than at the end of June 2006.

Sickness Benefit This benefit is generally available to people aged 18 and over who cannot work due to sickness, injury, disability or pregnancy. It can also be paid when a person is employed, but is losing earnings through sickness or injury; or is working at a reduced level. At the end of June 2007, 48,063 working-aged people were receiving a Sickness Benefit, 991 more than at the end of June 2006.

Family assistance

Working for Families Tax Credits These tax credits are provided to low- to middle-income families with dependent children. They are paid to income earners through Inland Revenue and Work and Income New Zealand. People receiving benefits, who live with dependants, get the Family Tax Credit.

Childcare Subsidy This subsidy provides financial assistance to low -to middle-income families with dependent children aged under five years, to help pay the costs of preschool childcare services. In the year ending June 2007, there were 58,051 approved applications for Childcare Subsidies, 4,949 more than in the year ending June 2006.

The increased use of Childcare Subsidies largely reflects the increased eligibility for this subsidy, which was part of the Working for Families package.

OSCAR Subsidy The OSCAR (Out of School Care and Recreation) Subsidy provides financial assistance with the costs of OSCAR-approved childcare before and after school, and for approved school holiday programmes. It is available to low- to middle-income families with dependent children aged five to 13 years. In the year ending June 2007, 27,621 applications for an OSCAR Subsidy were approved, 5,792 more than in the year ending June 2006.

The increased use of OSCAR Subsidies largely reflects the increased eligibility for this subsidy which was part of the Working for Families package.

Orphan's Benefit This benefit is available to carers of children whose parents cannot support the child because they are deceased, are ill or incapacitated, or cannot be found. This benefit is non-taxable.

The Aucklander

Josie Pouwhare, who was born blind, is attending a course to learn touch typing at the New Zealand Foundation of the Blind. The foundation also offers employer awareness training and assistance, along with support and resources for employers and employees.

At the end of June 2007, 382 people were receiving an Orphan's Benefit, five more than at the end of June 2006.

Unsupported Child's Benefit This benefit is available to carers of children whose parents are, because of a family breakdown, unable to either care for the child, or provide fully for the child's support. This benefit is non-taxable.

At the end of June 2007, 7,205 people were receiving an Unsupported Child's Benefit, 80 more than at the end of June 2006.

Child Disability Allowance This is a non-taxable allowance paid to the parent or guardian of a seriously disabled child who requires constant care and attention.

There were 39,145 children covered by the Child Disability Allowance at the end of June 2007, 2,938 more than at the end of June 2006. Over the year ending June 2007, 10,019 applications for the allowance were granted, 344 more than in the year to June 2006.

Other assistance

Disability Allowance This is an income-tested allowance paid to people with additional, ongoing costs arising from a disability or a personal health need.

At the end of June 2007, 231,214 people were receiving a Disability Allowance, 3,494 more than at the end of June 2006. In the year to June 2007, 77,679 applications were granted for Disability Allowances, 255 more than in the year to June 2006. People may receive a Disability Allowance for themselves or on behalf of one or more dependants.

Community Services Card This is an entitlement card that people on low- to middle-incomes can use to reduce the cost of doctor fees and prescription charges.

At the end of June 2007, there were 924,092 cardholders, 89,432 fewer than at the end of June 2006. Decreased use of Community Services Cards reflects in part the progressive rollout of Primary Health Organisation funding, which has meant that fewer people need a card to access subsidised health care.

Special Needs Grant This is a one-off payment made in an emergency situation where the need cannot be met in any other way, and where the person has insufficient financial resources to meet the need. A client does not have to be receiving a benefit to qualify for a Special Needs Grant. In the year ending June 2007, 363,279 grants were made, 30,112 fewer than in the previous June year. Table 7.02 provides more details.

Special Benefit and Temporary Additional Support A Special Benefit provides financial assistance for people who have ongoing, essential costs that exceed their income and who are in hardship because of this.

Temporary Additional Support replaced the Special Benefit on 1 April 2006, and offers assistance for a maximum of 13 weeks. It is paid as a last resort to help clients with their regular essential living costs that cannot be met from their chargeable income and other resources.

Removing barriers for disabled people

The Office for Disability Issues promotes the New Zealand Disability Strategy's vision of a non-disabling, inclusive society, where disabled people can say they are highly valued and can fully participate. The strategy provides a framework for policy and services that impact on disabled people. It also calls for a change in thinking about and behaviour towards disabled people.

Disabled New Zealanders are a diverse group, representing all sectors of society and a wide range of impairment types. Many disabled people experience multiple disadvantages in their everyday lives, and are excluded from places and activities most New Zealanders take for granted.

The office is located within the Ministry of Social Development, and takes a whole-of-government, strategic approach to its work. Key roles undertaken by the office include: leading strategic policy development across government; encouraging an understanding of disabled people by other agencies, along with inclusion of a disability perspective in their policy development; monitoring and reporting progress in implementing the New Zealand Disability Strategy; and building strong relationships with the disability sector.

Source: Ministry of Social Development

Table 7.02

Special needs grants[1]
Year ending 30 June 2007

	Number	Amount ($)
Recipient's income type		
Domestic Purposes Benefit[2]	123,616	15,403,217
Unemployment Benefit[3]	49,949	5,837,067
Invalid's Benefit	50,378	5,843,052
Sickness Benefit[4]	52,681	5,785,194
Low-income earner[5]	74,328	11,776,594
New Zealand Superannuation	9,803	1,314,787
Widow's Benefit	2,377	285,850
Veteran's Pension	147	24,412
Total	**363,279**	**46,270,173**
Reason for grant		
Food	272,100	25,545,873
Other emergency	18,636	4,307,039
Medical, in rest home	43,582	10,485,397
Education	2,456	510,477
Health-related	11,828	1,012,816
Re-establishment	11,953	3,810,472
Benefit stand downs	987	110,349
Goods or services	271	25,669
Miscellaneous	1,466	462,081
Total	**363,279**	**46,270,173**

(1) Includes recoverable and non-recoverable Special Needs Grants. Excludes benefit advances and payments made under the recoverable assistance programme. (2) Includes Sole Parent, Caring for Sick or Infirm, Woman Alone, and Emergency Maintenance Allowance. (3) Includes Unemployment Benefit, Hardship, Training, Training – Hardship, Hardship – Students, Independent Youth Benefit, and Emergency Benefit. (4) Includes Sickness Benefit and Hardship. (5) Includes Accommodation Supplement, Childcare Subsidy, OSCAR Subsidy, Disability Allowance, Child Disability Allowance, Orphan's Benefit, and Unsupported Child's Benefit.

Source: Ministry of Social Development

Community contribution to conservation

A recent study into the contribution of community groups to conservation identified 362 groups across the country that work with the Department of Conservation (DOC) to achieve conservation benefits.

A survey of 201 of the groups showed that together they contributed $15 million annually in combined income, voluntary hours, and in-kind contributions. The groups contributed a total income of over $12 million to their work, of which over half came from non-government sources, such as sponsorship and donations. Over 6,000 volunteers from these groups contributed almost 175,000 hours of voluntary work, valued at over $2.1 million (based on an hourly wage of $12.15). They also brought in-kind contributions of $894,000, from donated or discounted goods, equipment, supplies and the costs of travel.

The study also assessed some of the conservation and wider benefits of the community groups' work. The groups were involved in a wide range of activities, with the most common being ecological restoration, recreational/visitor services, education and species recovery, pest control, and awareness and publicity.

More than half of the groups said other benefits from working with DOC were: building strong relationships and networks; contributing to a greater sense of community; gaining greater access to technical assistance; gaining skills and knowledge; and raising awareness and support for their work.

Conservation activity – main purpose	People involved (percent)
Habitat/ecosystem restoration	21
Developing/maintaining visitor or recreational facilities	18
Species recovery/conservation	14
Pest/weed/predator control	12
Beautifying, protecting or caring for a site	9
Education, research or monitoring	7
Community involvement and understanding	6
Historic restoration/preservation	4
Other activity	9

In New Zealand approximately 3,000 community groups are involved in ecological restoration project, with 362 of these groups and iwi working in partnership with DOC. Nearly 8,000 individual volunteers participate in DOC volunteer programmes, with 19,393 work-day equivalents contributed each year.

Source: Department of Conservation

Good jobs and good workers

Regional labour market teams are working with communities, industries, employers and other organisations to identify labour market needs.

Enterprising Communities Advisors are part of these teams. Their role is to help not-for-profit organisations create community-based enterprises that provide local employment opportunities for those disadvantaged in the labour market.

Industry Partnership Advisors are also part of the regional labour market teams. They work with employers, training providers, and other government agencies to provide targeted training that assists those disadvantaged in the labour market.

'Straight2Work' industry partnerships highlight where skill shortages are happening and what training will fill the gaps. In the year ending 30 June 2007, Work and Income had 39 industry partnerships under this programme. Successful outcomes are good jobs for New Zealanders that meet the labour demands of industries.

Source: Ministry of Social Development

At the end of June 2007, 40,919 people were receiving a Special Benefit or Temporary Additional Support, 8,414 fewer than at the end of June 2006.

Advance payment of benefit This is available to people receiving benefits, to help them pay for one-off, essential needs they would otherwise be unable to afford.

StudyLink services

StudyLink, a service of the Ministry of Social Development, connects people with the information they need to make informed decisions about student finances and other study-related issues, and provides financial support to students.

StudyLink provides services to over 200,000 clients, with staff located in 44 sites nationwide.

The Student Allowance is a weekly payment that helps students with living costs while they study full time. It is money that does not need to be paid back.

The Student Loan can help with study costs. It is a loan that needs to be paid back, so it is important that students only borrow what they need.

StudyLink also offers two scholarships: the Step Up and Bonded Merit scholarships. They also offer advice on what other scholarships are available for students.

Along with offering financial assistance in the form of Student Allowance, Student Loan, scholarships, and extra help with costs, StudyLink offers 'StudyWise' consultations to Student Loan borrowers and delivers 'On Course' presentations to senior secondary school students.

In addition, StudyLink offers advice and support for students in a range of circumstances, including those with childcare costs, those with ongoing medical and disability costs, and students who are unable to find work during breaks from study.

StudyLink offers online application for Student Allowance and Loans, and enables students to manage their own information online with 'MyStudyLink'. More information about the Student Allowance, Student Loan, scholarships and the full range of extra support that StudyLink can offer can be found on the StudyLink website, www.studylink.govt.nz.

In 2007 StudyLink:

- responded to over 1 million calls
- managed around 230,000 Student Loan, 90,000 Student Allowance, 12,000 Unemployment Benefit – Student Hardship, and 4,000 scholarship applications
- paid about $390 million in Student Allowances and $1.1 billion in Student Loans.

Table 7.03

People receiving income support and pensions
1940–2007[1]

	Benefit type										Pension			
Year[2]	Unemployment[3]	Unemployment – Training[4]	Sickness[5]	Invalid's	Miner's	Domestic Purposes[6]	Widow's	Orphan's and Unsupported Child's	Family[7]	Transitional Retirement[8]	New Zealand Superannuation[9]	Veteran's[10]	War[11]	Total
1940	4,053	...	2,565	11,811	988	...	10,174	330	11,053	...	93,262	...	3,485	137,721
1945	198	...	4,233	12,205	783	...	10,965	421	24,251	...	158,332	...	54,083	265,471
1950	12	...	4,931	9,476	636	...	14,198	366	254,920	...	186,512	...	56,398	527,449
1955	19	...	4,277	8,110	481	...	12,197	300	298,370	...	199,236	...	56,497	579,487
1960	312	...	4,064	8,024	353	...	13,049	277	343,193	...	204,036	...	59,676	632,984
1965	208	...	4,681	7,951	184	...	14,529	316	376,824	...	214,659	...	57,576	676,928
1970	983	...	5,876	8,342	98	...	15,663	315	408,397	...	241,772	...	51,698	733,144
1975	2,894	...	7,830	9,414	45	17,231	16,738	376	452,389	...	289,348	...	46,920	843,185
1980	20,850	...	7,504	5,647	21	37,040	16,120	413	460,897	...	405,834	...	39,296	993,622
1985	38,419	...	9,627	21,464	11	56,548	13,557	365	455,961	...	459,813	...	31,537	1,087,302
1990	139,625	9,453	19,511	27,824	6	94,823	12,676	5,239	446,373	...	495,500	3,428	25,424	1,279,882
1995	139,387	11,655	34,037	39,686	...	104,027	9,007	4,280		7,327	469,239	6,380	25,748	850,773
2000	155,405	3,755	32,294	55,392	...	108,939	9,104	5,799	...	8,856	453,401	7,248	24,056	864,249
2001	141,083	3,766	33,620	59,812	...	107,821	8,900	6,075	...	9,012	446,706	7,425	23,435	847,655
2002	125,942	3,990	36,380	64,529	...	108,009	8,774	6,332	...	5,118	450,435	7,587	22,722	839,818
2003	111,906	4,291	39,902	68,507	...	109,295	8,659	6,789	...	2,110	457,278	7,872	22,242	838,851
2004	81,238	4,474	44,128	72,342	...	109,526	8,413	7,051	...	...	464,624	8,465	21,732	821,993
2005	62,453	4,369	45,646	74,796	...	106,330	7,795	7,279	...	...	475,215	8,871	21,128	813,822
2006	51,553	5,571	47,559	77,046	...	102,331	7,181	7,502	...	...	488,825	9,472	21,103	818,143
2007	34,219	6,104	48,587	79,077	...	97,111	6,471	7,587	...	...	502,717	10,065	20,866	812,804

(1) Since 1975, hardship assistance has been included in figures for related statutory benefits. (2) Prior to 1990, the year ending 31 March; from 1990 onwards, the year ending 30 June. (3) Includes Unemployment Benefit and Hardship, Independent Youth Benefit, and Emergency Benefit. From 1 July 2001, includes Hardship – Student. (4) Includes Unemployment Benefit and Hardship paid to people in training. (5) Includes Sickness Benefit and Hardship. (6) Includes Sole Parent, Care of Sick or Infirm, Woman Alone, and Emergency Maintenance Allowance. (7) Family Benefit was abolished from 1 April 1991. Statistics for 1985 and 1990 are of uncertain accuracy. (8) The Transitional Retirement Benefit was abolished on 1 April 2004. (9) Superannuation and age-related benefits are combined up to 1975, National Superannuation from 1976–1990, Guaranteed Retirement Income from 1990–1992, and New Zealand Superannuation since 1994. This includes non-qualified spouses since 1996. (10) From 1996, includes non-qualified spouses, but excludes clients receiving War Pension. From 1 July 1999, Veteran's Pensions have been funded from Vote Veterans' Affairs – Work and Income. (11) Includes pensions paid to surviving spouses and other dependants. From 1 July 1999, War Pensions have been funded from the Vote Veterans' Affairs Work and Income allocation.

Symbol: ... not applicable

Source: Ministry of Social Development

Training Incentive Allowance This allowance helps people meet the costs associated with attending recognised occupational or work-related courses that provide specific work skills. The allowance is available to people receiving Widow's Benefit, Invalid's Benefit, Emergency Maintenance Allowance, or any Domestic Purposes Benefit. In the year ending December 2006, 16,523 Training Incentive Allowances were granted, 2,692 fewer than in the previous June year.

Hospital rate of payment Income support clients with no dependent children receive their full income support payments for the first 13 weeks of hospitalisation. Following 13 weeks of hospitalisation, they receive a reduced hospital rate. The benefit rate is not reduced for clients with dependent children.

Table 7.03 shows the number of benefits and pensions in place since 1940, while table 7.04 shows income support and pension expenditure for the same period.

Support of children by non-custodial parents

Child support Responsibility for collection of child support payments from non-custodial parents rests with Inland Revenue. The aim of collecting payments is to ensure that parents contribute to the support of their children.

New Zealand Superannuation

At 1 April 2007, New Zealand Superannuation provided $277.06 a week (after tax at the 'M' rate) for a single person living alone, and $426.24 a week for a married couple (or $406.44 if one spouse did not qualify for New Zealand Superannuation).

Recipients are required to pay tax on their superannuation payments.

The qualifying age for New Zealand Superannuation has been 65 years since 1 April 2001. A 10-year residency requirement also applies to applicants in order to qualify for New Zealand Superannuation.

At the end of June 2007, there were 502,717 people receiving New Zealand Superannuation, 13,892 more than at the end of June 2006.

War pensions

War pensions and concessions are available for those who served in World War I and II, Korea, Operation Grapple (1950s British nuclear tests), Malaya, Viet Nam, Mururoa (1970s French nuclear tests), the Gulf, Angola, Bosnia, Sierra Leone, East Timor, Afghanistan, the Solomon Islands and Iraq.

Table 7.04

Expenditure on income support and pensions
1940–2007[1]

	Benefit type										Pension		
Year[2]	Unemployment[3]	Unemployment – Training[4]	Sickness[5]	Invalid's	Miner's	Domestic Purposes[6]	Widow's	Orphan's and Unsupported Child's	Family[7]	Transitional Retirement[8]	New Zealand Superannuation[9]	Veteran's[10]	War[10]
							$(000)						
1940	869	...	418	1,884	185	...	1,572	30	505	...	13,036	...	4,286
1945	56	...	704	2,145	149	...	1,971	47	2,810	...	18,974	...	8,405
1950	21	...	2,017	2,795	240	...	4,320	62	29,702	...	34,627	...	10,517
1955	11	...	2,554	3,233	257	...	5,329	58	36,358	...	58,002	...	15,860
1960	380	...	3,439	4,237	226	...	7,832	79	63,584	...	85,502	...	22,939
1965	197	...	3,914	4,830	153	...	10,215	110	65,925	...	110,314	...	27,862
1970	1,465	...	6,073	6,093	99	...	13,742	150	72,318	...	155,822	...	30,929
1975	5,155	...	15,887	13,665	84	30,156	27,967	381	153,175	...	365,803	...	49,944
1980	66,077	...	33,236	40,924	76	169,449	53,342	778	220,854	...	1,334,115	...	92,529
1985	274,689	...	72,550	105,724	72	460,385	78,495	1,004	284,167	...	2,743,512	...	95,438
1990	1,235,056	56,460	229,568	260,751	68	1,136,718	114,888	24,742	284,444	...	4,774,676	1,147	103,770
1995	1,335,229	93,584	352,167	463,598	...	1,300,173	81,258	20,557	...	79,167	5,083,119	57,217	91,050
2000	1,663,822	45,201	384,680	700,385	...	1,590,813	91,592	35,413	...	112,384	5,227,598	73,801	101,277
2001	1,536,340	40,575	385,680	761,656	...	1,575,974	89,008	38,567	...	114,108	5,442,012	78,354	102,709
2002	1,418,622	37,593	415,683	843,535	...	1,588,381	88,958	41,593	...	86,567	5,600,488	83,605	105,214
2003	1,287,730	37,942	460,209	926,515	...	1,634,477	90,265	47,081	...	42,013	5,798,873	87,625	108,862
2004	1,090,885	42,544	518,943	996,639	...	1,716,917	90,252	50,991	...	9,679	6,059,395	95,803	112,886
2005	838,901	43,196	571,866	1,057,376	...	1,725,624	87,424	55,827	...	...	6,269,743	103,890	117,565
2006	716,072	47,686	612,367	1,097,936	...	1,682,154	82,446	64,624	...	...	6,615,876	112,335	128,303
2007	592,137	60,253	640,912	1,155,312	...	1,634,412	77,534	70,579	...	...	7,021,582	125,207	139,804

(1) Expenditure is on a cash basis to 30 June 1994 and on an accrual basis thereafter, net of taxation except for New Zealand Superannuation, and includes expenditure on selected supplementary benefits paid to clients receiving the benefits shown. (2) Prior to 1990, the year ending 31 March; from 1990 onwards, the year ending 30 June. (3) Includes Unemployment Benefit, Hardship paid to unemployed people, Independent Youth Benefit and Emergency Benefit. From 1 July 2001, includes Hardship – Student. (4) Includes Unemployment Benefit and Hardship paid to people in training. (5) Includes Sickness Benefit and Hardship. (6) Includes Sole Parent, Care of Sick or Infirm, Woman Alone, and Emergency Maintenance Allowance. (7) The Family Benefit was abolished from 1 April 1991. (8) The Transitional Retirement Benefit was abolished on 1 April 2004. (9) Superannuation and age-related benefits are combined up to 1975. National Superannuation was in place from 1976–1990, Guaranteed Retirement Income from 1990–1992, and New Zealand Superannuation since 1994. This includes the rest home subsidy and other supplementary payments before 1994. (10) From 1 July 1999, the Veteran's Pension and the War Disability Pension have been funded from the Vote Veteran's Affairs – Work and Income allocation.

Symbol: ... not applicable

Source: Ministry of Social Development

Helping New Zealanders prepare financially for retirement

The Retirement Commission was established in 1993 to promote public education about retirement income issues and to monitor the effects of retirement income policies. It helps New Zealanders prepare financially for retirement through education and information programmes.

Sorted

The commission's website (www.sorted.org.nz) is designed to help New Zealanders make well-informed financial decisions. Designed to meet the needs of diverse age groups, ranging from children to those nearing or in retirement, Sorted provides a personalised, confidential approach to financial planning.

Using calculators and other interactive tools, Sorted allows people to enter their details to find answers to their money-management questions. It covers setting financial goals, budgeting, saving, managing debt, mortgages, student loans, investing, retirement planning, and includes a section to help children learn about money.

Financial education for young people

The commission has a strong focus on developing financial skills from an early age, so young New Zealanders can make well-informed financial decisions. The commission has drafted a financial education curriculum for schools and will work with the Ministry of Education to develop teaching resources and professional development programmes for teachers, with the aim of the curriculum being rolled out in schools from 2009.

Workplace financial education

The commission is running a workplace financial education programme to help employees make informed decisions on participation in KiwiSaver or other savings options, in the context of their wider personal financial situation.

Research and monitoring

The commission monitors the effects of retirement income policies in New Zealand, and undertakes research into retirement income issues. It also monitors levels of public awareness, knowledge, attitudes and behaviours related to retirement planning.

Retirement villages

The commission monitors the Retirement Villages Act 2003 and approves panel members for disputes.

The commission received funding of $6.43 million (GST exclusive) for the year ending 30 June 2007.

Source: Retirement Commission

The New Zealand Herald

Veterans stand to attention during the Anzac Day dawn service at the Cenotaph in Wellington in 2007.

Routine service in New Zealand before 1 April 1974 is also included. Since then, service personnel have been covered under accident compensation provisions.

The War Pensions Act 1954 is administered by the Secretary for War Pensions, who is also Director of Veterans' Affairs New Zealand. Payments are provided from the Vote Veterans' Affairs – Social Development allocation, and the processing and payment of pensions is carried out by Work and Income.

Decisions on eligibility for war pensions are made by war pension claims panels, acting under delegation from the secretary. Each claims panel consists of a nominee from the Royal New Zealand Returned and Services Association and an employee of Veterans' Affairs New Zealand.

Veteran's Pension This pension is available to ex-service personnel with a significant disability. The pension is paid at the same rate as New Zealand Superannuation and is taxable. At the end of June 2007, 10,065 people were receiving a Veteran's Pension, 593 more than at the end of June 2006.

War Disablement Pension This pension provides tax-free compensation for people who served in the armed forces and who suffer from a disability or disabilities related to that service. War pensions are increasingly related to the ageing of the population, and numbers receiving these pensions have remained relatively constant in recent years. At the end of June 2007, 15,441 people were receiving War Disablement Pensions, 489 fewer than at the end of June 2006.

Other war pension provisions In addition to War Disablement Pensions, the war pensions programme provides pensions for surviving spouses and additional allowances and concessions for clients receiving War Disablement Pensions. At the end of June 2007, 5,325 surviving spouses and other dependants were receiving war pensions, 252 more than at the end of June 2006.

Social security agreements

New Zealand has social security agreements with Australia, Canada, Denmark, Greece (the Hellenic Republic), the Republic of Ireland, Jersey and Guernsey, the Netherlands, and the United Kingdom.

The main purposes of the agreements are to encourage the free movement of labour and to ensure that when a person has lived or worked in more than one country, each of those countries takes a fair share of responsibility for meeting the costs of that person's social security coverage.

The agreements are becoming part of the basic infrastructure of the global village, enabling people to move about the world for short or long periods, either to work or to be with family, without jeopardising their social security coverage. By entering into such agreements, New Zealand is better able to attract skills, specialist knowledge and technical know-how from overseas. A widening network of agreements also provides more options for New Zealanders who wish to live overseas in their retirement.

General portability Under the general portability provision, people eligible to receive New Zealand Superannuation or a Veteran's Pension in their own right may receive 50 percent of the payment while living outside New Zealand, provided they are not living in a country that has a social security agreement with New Zealand. Applications under this provision must be made while applicants are living in New Zealand.

Special portability arrangement People leaving New Zealand to live in certain Pacific countries can receive a rate of New Zealand Superannuation or Veteran's Pension based on the length of their New Zealand residence since the age of 20.

People with 10 years' New Zealand residence since the age of 20 receive 50 percent of New Zealand Superannuation or Veteran's Pension.

People with between 10 and 20 years' New Zealand residence since the age of 20 are entitled to an additional 5 percent of New Zealand Superannuation or Veteran's Pension for each year of residence over 10 years. People with over 20 years' residence are entitled to the full rate.

At the date of application, applicants must be living and be present in New Zealand and intending to live in the Pacific country for 52 weeks or more. Pacific countries covered by the arrangement are American Samoa, the Cook Islands, the Federated States of Micronesia, Fiji, French Polynesia, Guam, Kiribati, Marshall Islands, Nauru, New Caledonia, Niue, Northern Mariana Islands, Palau, Papua New Guinea, Pitcairn Island, Samoa, Solomon Islands, Tokelau, Tonga, Tuvalu, Vanuatu, and Wallis and Fortuna.

Child, Youth and Family

Child, Youth and Family provides direct services for children and young people in need of care and protection, for children and young people who have committed offences, and for people involved in adoption processes.

Child, Youth and Family's vision is to have safe children and young people in strong families and responsive communities.

Child, Youth and Family was established on 1 October 1999, following the integration of two Department of Social Welfare business units – the Children, Young Persons and Their Families Service and the New Zealand Community Funding Agency. From 1 July 2006, Child, Youth and Family became a service line of the Ministry of Social Development.

Child, Youth and Family has statutory responsibility for children and young people whose family circumstances put them at risk of abuse and neglect, offending behaviour, or poor life outcomes. Child, Youth and Family is guided by the objectives and principles of the Children, Young Persons and Their Families Act 1989, and also by other legislation, including the Adoptions Act 1955, Adult Adoption Information Act 1985, Adoption (Intercountry) Act 1997, and the Care of Children Act 2004.

Care and protection

Table 7.05 shows the number of care and protection notifications received and the number assessed as requiring further investigation and action by a social worker. All cases accepted for investigation are assigned a criticality rating, or response category, at time of intake.

In the year ending 30 June 2007, 75,326 notifications involving children and young people under the age of 17 were received, of which 46,776 required further action. In the previous June year, there were 66,210 notifications, with 49,063 requiring further investigation.

After investigation, findings are classified and recorded under the categories of sexual abuse, physical abuse, emotional abuse, neglect, behavioural/relationship problems, self-harm/suicidal behaviour, or abuse not found.

Case management When, through investigation, it is decided that Child, Youth and Family needs to remain involved with a child or family, direct services may be provided through family/whānau agreements, care agreements, family group conference plans, or court plans.

Family/whānau agreements When a family agrees there is a problem to address, family/whānau agreements are negotiated by a social worker. These agreements may be for up to three months, must be formally reviewed, and may be renewed for one further three-month period. There were 4,383 family/whānau agreements signed in the June 2007 year, compared with 3,442 agreements in 2006, 3,010 agreements in 2005, and 2,528 agreements in 2004.

Table 7.05

Care and protection notifications
Year ending 30 June

Action	2003	2004	2005	2006	2007
Care and protection notifications received	31,781	43,314	53,097	66,210	75,326
Notifications for further investigation	27,394	36,066	43,460	49,063	46,776
Critical – immediate response time (same day)	3,045	4,302	4,725	4,999	4,318
Very urgent (same day to one calendar day)	1,656	2,354	2,621	2,833	2,391
Urgent (same day to six calendar days)	14,963	20,277	25,832	29,119	26,374
Low urgency (same day to 27 calendar days)	7,730	8,410	8,187	9,411	10,824

Source: Child, Youth and Family

Supporting families and communities

Family and Community Services, part of the Ministry of Social Development, was established in July 2004 to lead and coordinate government and non-government actions to support families and communities. Its work contributes to families being strong and communities being connected.

Family and Community Services focuses on prevention and early intervention, to build the capability and resilience of families and communities. It does this by:

- supporting social cohesion and participation in communities
- helping families and communities to access the information and develop the knowledge they need to thrive, and building community capability and capacity
- supporting families to be resilient and free from violence.

Source: Ministry of Social Development

Table 7.06

Abuse and neglect investigation findings[1]
Year ending 30 June

Year	Sexual abuse	Physical abuse	Emotional abuse	Neglect	Behavioural/ relationship problems	Self-harm/ suicidal	Abuse not found	Total
2003	1,288	2,002	2,282	2,939	3,328	128	14,238	**26,205**
2004	1,187	2,035	2,807	3,212	3,589	104	16,682	**29,616**
2005	1,466	2,477	4,889	4,366	4,573	179	24,414	**42,364**
2006	1,291	2,336	6,142	4,199	4,657	172	26,011	**44,808**
2007	1,194	2,274	8,256	4,486	4,461	138	22,921	**43,730**

(1) Figures represent the number of findings, not the number of clients. Due to multiple findings, some clients are counted across more than one category.

Source: Child, Youth and Family

Family group conferences and court orders When a family/whānau agreement is not considered appropriate, intervention may occur through the statutorily-defined process of a family group conference. Child, Youth and Family manages family group conference plans and court orders to provide care for children, while working towards their return to parents, family or whānau. These may include custody orders, plans resulting from family group conferences, counselling orders and support orders. There were 9,243 referrals for family group conferences in the year ending June 2007, and 9,179 new and reconvened family conferences were held.

There are more family group conference plans than court orders, as a means of managing young people who come to the notice of Child, Youth and Family. Family group conferences encourage participation in the resolution of care and protection issues and often avoid the need for court involvement. The plans must be reviewed by reconvening the conference or by a less formal process.

Emergency action The Children, Young Persons and Their Families Act 1989 provides measures for securing the safety of a child through warrant action by social workers or the Police, or through temporary care agreements with parents, to provide immediate care for a child while longer-term solutions are explored.

Youth justice services

There has been a new youth justice structure in place since July 2007, along with new youth justice teams. Child, Youth and Family has established 25 new dedicated youth justice teams of social workers, coordinators, and practice advisors, who are led by youth justice managers.

The new structure and teams:

- change how youth justice works and focus on addressing the unique factors that lead young people to offend

The New Zealand Herald

The Rapana family (from left) Noelene, Hannah (aged four), John, Jacob (aged two), and Maria (aged 12). The family, who live in Papamoa in the Bay of Plenty, are part of The Incredible Years project, an education and mentoring programme that focuses on raising families in constructive ways without violence.

- focus on addressing issues that lead young people to commit crime, particularly serious violent crime

- allow youth justice to provide a range of services that will address both young people's offending behaviour and the context in which they offend

- help youth justice to more effectively address re-offending, particularly as re-offending often involves more serious crimes.

Stakeholder collaboration Youth justice believes that solutions to offending exist in the community. Within the new structure, youth justice services will work alongside the youth justice sector and the community to develop an in-depth understanding of local issues, and to bring together the necessary support systems to prevent re-offending.

Youth justice managers have been aligned to youth court boundaries and work closely with their local youth court judges.

Youth justice family group conferences Family group conferences are convened to address the offending behaviour of children and young people, as well as addressing re-offending. They bring together, in a statutorily-defined forum, members of the offender's family or whānau, law enforcement officers, and victims, to agree how the young offender will be held accountable, and to agree on appropriate intervention plans.

Care services Two main placement options are used in New Zealand for children and young people requiring alternative care. These are either based in a home environment (extended family, caregivers, family home, special purpose family home, specialist or group homes) or in a residential care centre (short- or extended-term local or national residences).

International research indicates that family-based placements are more effective than other forms of placement. Children and young people are more likely to return to their usual caregivers, and are less likely to be re-abused, if they are placed in family-based care, rather than in non-kin-based care. The Children, Young Persons and Their Families Act 1989 shifted the emphasis away from longer-term, extended-care placements towards restoring usual caregiving arrangements. When alternative placements are necessary, emphasis is put on making a placement, whenever possible, within the child's extended family or community.

Residential care Child, Youth and Family residences provide care and protection and youth justice programmes for children and young people aged eight to 16 years. Admission to a residence only happens when there are no other practical alternatives, or when a child's continued presence in the community is a threat to their own safety, or the safety of others. There are currently seven residences around New Zealand.

Table 7.07

Youth admissions to national residential facilities
Year ending 30 June

Type of admission	2003	2004	2005	2006	2007
Care and protection	...	...	...	109	135
Youth justice	...	...	...	307	299
Total admissions	**751**	**714**	**654**	**416**	**434**

Symbol: ... not applicable

Source: Child, Youth and Family

Adoption assessment, placement and information services

The adoption information and services unit of Child, Youth and Family is responsible for statutory adoption services. Child, Youth and Family became a service of the Ministry of Social Development on 1 July 2006.

Local and inter-country adoption services include education, preparation and assessment of prospective adoptive applicants, counselling of birth parents, approval of placements, supervision, and reporting to the New Zealand Family Court.

Post-adoption services for birth and adoptive families are provided when requested, or referrals made.

Table 7.08

Access to adoption information

Action	1996	1997	1998	1999	2000	2001	2002	2003	2004	2005	2006
Original birth certificates issued to adopted people	1,580	1,925	1,446	1,356	1,230	1,030	943	902	800	785	679
Original vetoes from adopted people	17	30	22	8	1	4	0	6	2	3	12
Renewal vetoes from adopted people	51	13	4	5	6	8	0	9	1	1	4
Cancelled vetoes from adopted people	17	0	2	3	5	1	2	2	1	0	0
Birth parent applications for identifying information	650	534	450	392	325	303	285	269	254	246	145
Original vetoes from birth parents	126	60	22	15	4	2	1	5	3	4	62
Renewal vetoes from birth parents	351	77	19	11	13	13	10	11	23	46	0
Cancelled vetoes from birth parents	10	2	6	1	1	1	5	0	0	1	0

Sources: Child, Youth and Family; Department of Internal Affairs

Free information and help on any issue

Citizens Advice Bureaux (CAB) have been serving New Zealand communities for over 35 years through provision of information, advice and advocacy.

From 93 sites around the country, the CAB provides free, confidential and independent information and help to individuals. The sites are staffed by 2,700 trained volunteers, making the CAB one of New Zealand's largest voluntary organisations. It provides information to clients from a comprehensive database, which includes local and national information, and from an extensive range of information resources.

In the year to June 2007 CABs assisted with approximately 644,000 enquiries from the public.

Trained CAB volunteers can help people with information on almost any topic or issue, including education and training information, legal services, employment rights, housing and tenancy, budgeting, health and welfare, consumer rights, personal and family matters, community groups, finance and tax.

With one of the largest referral databases in the country, if the CAB cannot assist people directly, they will find someone who can. Many also provide free legal services, links to free budgeting services and have justices of the peace available at regular times.

The CAB has a diverse volunteer base, which includes bilingual and multilingual volunteers, as well as a multilingual information service, which provides the full CAB service in 26 languages.

The experience and information the CAB gains from its work with clients means that the organisation is a window on the community and therefore well positioned to identify systemic social issues. The CAB uses this experience and information in a manner that protects the confidentiality of its clients, to advocate for socially-just legislation, policy and practice.

Volunteering with the CAB provides an opportunity to connect with local communities, develop new skills, meet new people, and work on a variety of interesting issues.

CAB can be accessed via a toll-free line 0800 367 222 and through its website, www.cab.org.nz.

Source: New Zealand Association of Citizens Advice Bureaux

Table 7.09

Adoptions by New Zealand citizens
Year ending 30 June

	2003	2004	2005	2006	2007
Adoption of New Zealand children by	**323**	**275**	**314**	**294**	**213**
Non-relatives	81	108	113	87	60
One parent and spouse	71	54	56	73	69
Relatives	71	65	71	65	70
Foster parents	2	8	8	4	3
Adoption type not recorded[1]	98	40	66	65	11
Adoption of foreign children	**316**	**387**	**262**	**417**	**406**
In New Zealand court to non-relatives	13	12	12	18	11
In New Zealand court to relatives	38	36	41	43	42
In overseas court (section 17 Adoption Act 1955)	265	339	209	356	353
Total adoptions granted or recognised by New Zealand	**639**	**662**	**576**	**711**	**619**

(1) A registration may occur in a different financial year from the adoption report, therefore the total number of adoptions may not equal the sum of the adoption reports for the same period. Any disparity is included under 'adoption type not recorded'.

Source: Child, Youth and Family

Other social services

Community services funding Community providers are funded each year by Child, Youth and Family to provide a variety of social services from non-departmental budget allocations. Child, Youth and Family is responsible for allocation and management of funding and support to iwi (tribal) and community-based social and welfare services in accordance with government policies and criteria. Table 7.10 shows budget allocations for contracted social services from 2004 to 2007.

Table 7.10

Community services funding
Year ending 30 June

Allocation	2004	2005	2006[1]	2007[1][2]
	\$(000)			
Information and advice	1,426	1,429	915	...
Education and prevention services	9,605	9,876	8,199	5,771
Family well-being services	51,851	55,684	41,092	38,962
Counselling and rehabilitation services	15,109	15,966	10,470	10,963
Emergency and special purpose housing and associated services	995	1,006	900	...
Strengthening providers and communities	8,925	6,679	6,500	5,011
Total	**87,911**	**90,640**	**68,076**	**60,707**
Other expenses incurred by Child, Youth and Family				
Contingency and innovations fund	365	365	365	365
Stronger communities action fund	1,916	1,916	...	...

(1) Figures for 2006 and 2007 exclude GST. (2) From 1 July 2006, the funding of community services is grouped into four, rather than six categories.
Symbol: ... not applicable

Source: Child, Youth and Family

Contributors and related websites

Child, Youth and Family – www.cyf.govt.nz

Department of Conservation – www.doc.govt.nz

Department of Internal Affairs – www.dia.govt.nz

Family and Community Services – www.familyservices.govt.nz

Ministry of Social Development – www.msd.govt.nz

New Zealand Association of Citizens Advice Bureaux – www.cab.org.nz

Office for Disability Issues – www.odi.govt.nz

Retirement Commission – www.sorted.org.nz

Studylink – www.studylink.govt.nz

Veterans' Affairs New Zealand – www.veteransaffairs.mil.nz

The Dominion Post

Michelle Bussey, a case manager at Accident Compensation Corporation (ACC), sees the results of injuries and accidents and says it has made her more cautious than most. She holds safety equipment used in the workplace. Ninety percent of ACC claimants (excluding serious claims such as car accidents and head injuries) are back at work within 70 days.

8 | Health and safety

Organisation of health services

The New Zealand health system is made up of public, private and voluntary sectors, which interact to provide and fund health care. Seventy-eight percent of health care is publicly funded, with out-of-pocket payments and private insurance being the other main contributors.

Ministry of Health

The Ministry of Health Manatū Hauora is the government's primary advisor on health policy and disability support services. The ministry aims to ensure that the health and disability system works for all New Zealanders. The ministry consists of eight directorates with defined responsibilities, each led by a deputy director-general: corporate services; health and disability national services; health and disability systems strategy; information; Māori health; population health; sector accountability and funding; and sector capability and innovation.

For more information about each of the directorates, visit the Ministry of Health website, www.moh.govt.nz.

District health boards

New Zealand's 21 district health boards (DHBs) are Crown entities and have both funding (planning and funding health services for their populations) and provider (delivery of hospital and related services) roles.

Established under the New Zealand Public Health and Disability Act 2000, the statutory objectives of DHBs are to: improve, promote and protect the health of communities; promote integration of health services, especially primary and secondary care services; and promote effective care or support for those in need of personal health services or disability support services.

Boards are also responsible for promoting the independence, inclusion and participation in society of people with disabilities, and of reducing health outcome disparities among various population groups.

Boards are expected to show a sense of social responsibility, to foster community participation in health improvement, and to uphold the ethical and quality standards expected of providers of services, and public sector organisations.

The boards work with all health-care provider organisations to ensure specified health services are provided, and to balance each community's needs for health and disability services.

Crown-owned public hospitals are the main providers of secondary health-care services. Primary and community-based care comes from private/non-government providers, such as general practitioners, Māori providers, and disability support providers.

Boards have seven elected members, and up to four members appointed by the Minister of Health. DHB elections are held every three years, at the same time as local government elections, using a single transferable voting system. In addition to the governing board, each DHB must have three statutory advisory committees. Each board has a separate operating charter, and a set of accountabilities and reporting requirements.

The 21 DHBs and their constituencies are:

- Northland – Far North, Whangarei, Kaipara
- Waitemata – Rodney, North Shore, Waitakere
- Auckland – Auckland north-west and gulf, Auckland north-east, Auckland south
- Counties Manukau – Manukau, Mangere, Manurewa, Franklin, Papakura
- Waikato – Thames-Coromandel, Waikato, Hamilton, South Waikato
- Bay of Plenty – Western Bay of Plenty, Tauranga, Whakatane
- Lakes – Rotorua north, Rotorua south, Taupo
- Tairawhiti – Gisborne, Tairawhiti
- Hawke's Bay – Wairoa, Hastings, Napier-Chatham Islands, Central Hawke's Bay
- Taranaki – New Plymouth, Taranaki north, Taranaki south
- Whanganui – Wanganui, Waimarino, Rangitikei
- MidCentral – Manawatu, Palmerston North, Tararua, Horowhenua
- Wairarapa – Masterton, Carterton, South Wairarapa
- Hutt Valley – Lower Hutt central, Lower Hutt harbour, Wainuiomata
- Capital & Coast – Kapiti Coast, Porirua, north-west and south-east Wellington, Lambton
- Nelson Marlborough – Tasman, Richmond, Nelson, Marlborough, Blenheim
- West Coast – Buller, Grey, Westland
- Canterbury – North Canterbury, Christchurch, Mid-Canterbury
- South Canterbury – Timaru, Temuka-Pleasant Point, Mackenzie-Geraldine, Waimate
- Otago – Waitaki, Central Otago, Clutha, Dunedin north, Dunedin south
- Southland – Queenstown-Lakes, Southland, Gore, Invercargill.

Crown Health Financing Agency (CHFA) This agency is the Crown provider of long-term debt finance to DHBs. The range of loan facilities available to boards is similar to that offered by private banks. CHFA loans are available to refinance boards' private bank debt, or to finance new capital work projects.

The CHFA offers property advice and a land disposal service to help DHBs to dispose of surplus property. Formerly the Residual Health Management Unit, the CHFA is the legal successor to area health boards and manages a range of residual functions, assets and liabilities transferred from area health boards to the CHFA in 1993. The CHFA operates under provisions of the New Zealand Public Health and Disability Act 2000.

Health advisory committees

National Advisory Committee on Health and Disability (National Health Committee) This committee provides the Minister of Health with independent advice on a broad spectrum of health and disability issues. Their website is: www.nhc.health.govt.nz.

The Public Health Advisory Committee, a subcommittee of the National Health Committee, provides the minister with independent advice on public health issues.

National Advisory Committee on Health and Disability Support Services Ethics This committee is responsible for providing the Minister of Health with advice on ethical issues of national significance in respect of any health and disability matter, including research and health services. The committee is also required to determine nationally-consistent ethical standards across the health and disability sector.

Child and Youth Mortality Review Committee (CYMRC) This is an independent ministerial committee that reviews deaths of children and young people aged from four weeks to 24 years. The committee reports to the Minister of Health at least annually on how to reduce the number of preventable deaths in this age group.

Data is collected through a network of local agents of the CYMRC, which review deaths and submit additional information to the ministry-funded mortality database. A particular focus of the committee has been sudden unexpected death in infancy. The Ministry of Health funds the committee and provides secretariat support. Their website is: www.cymrc.health.govt.nz.

Ethics Committee on Assisted Reproductive Technology The committee's main function is to consider and determine applications for assisted reproductive procedures or human reproductive research. Their website is www.ecart.health.govt.nz.

Quality Improvement Committee Since the beginning of 2007, the National Health Epidemiology and Quality Assurance Committee (EpiQual) has been operating as the Quality Improvement Committee. This statutory committee is independent and reports directly to the minister on matters relating to quality in health care. The committee has been focusing on a range of key priorities for the health-care sector. The Ministry of Health funds the committee and provides secretariat support. Their website is: www.qic.health.govt.nz.

Cancer Control Council The council is responsible for making sure New Zealand's Cancer Control Strategy is turned into action. The council is an independent advisory body appointed by the Minister of Health. It gives strategic advice directly to the minister, as well as to the wider cancer control community. The council works with all the bodies involved in controlling cancer, to reduce both the incidence and impact of cancer in New Zealand and the inequalities that surround it.

The council's key tasks are to:

- monitor and review implementation of the Cancer Control Strategy
- provide independent strategic advice to the Minister of Health, the Director-General of Health, DHBs and non-government organisations, on matters related to cancer control
- foster collaboration and cooperation between bodies involved in cancer control
- foster and support best practice in, and an evidence-based approach to, improvements in the effectiveness of cancer control
- set up links with overseas cancer control agencies.

The council's members are drawn from across the cancer control field – from primary prevention, screening and early detection, through to palliative care and research. Their website is: www.cancercontrolcouncil.govt.nz.

Advisory Committee on Assisted Reproductive Technology This committee, established under the Human Assisted Reproductive Technology Act 2004, is responsible for issuing guidelines and advice to the Ethics Committee on Assisted Reproductive Technology. The committee is also responsible for providing advice to the Minister of Health on options for regulation of assisted reproductive procedures and research.

Health Information Strategy Action Committee This is a discretionary advisory committee, established under the New Zealand Public Health and Disability Act 2000, and is responsible for providing the Minister of Health with advice on a national framework for the development of health information standards.

Health and Disability Ethics Committees A multi-region committee and six regional ethics committees provide independent ethical review of health and disability research and innovative practice that will be conducted in New Zealand, to safeguard the rights, health and well-being of consumers and research participants.

Perinatal and Maternity Mortality Review Committee This committee was established in 2005 under the New Zealand Public Health and Disability Act 2000, to review perinatal and maternal deaths and report to the Minister of Health. The aim is to reduce the number of deaths, and to encourage continuous quality improvement through promotion of quality assurance programmes.

Radiation Protection Advisory Council The council is a statutory body established under the Radiation Protection Act 1965 to advise and make recommendations to the Minister of Health and to the Director-General of Health about the use of ionizing radiations.

New Zealand Blood Service

The New Zealand Blood Service (NZBS) ensures the supply of safe blood and blood products. It is also responsible for all aspects of the national blood transfusion service, from collection of blood from volunteer donors to transfusion of blood products within the hospital environment – 'vein to vein' transfusion.

In addition to its core activities, NZBS provides related services, including matching of patients and donors prior to transplantation, and provision of tissue banking services.

Health research

Health Research Council of New Zealand (HRC) The HRC was established under the Health Research Council Act 1990, and is the Crown agency responsible for management of the government's investment in public-good health research in New Zealand. The Act requires the HRC to set guidelines for health research ethics and to accredit regional ethics committees.

Ownership of the HRC resides with the Minister of Health. The HRC is also responsible for advising the Ministry of Health and administering funds in relation to national health research policy. The HRC's statutory functions include fostering recruitment, education, training, and retention of those engaged in health research in New Zealand.

Health and air pollution study

The Health and Air Pollution in New Zealand (HAPiNZ) study is a large-scale investigation of the health effects of air pollution, its causes, and associated costs. The study was published in 2007 and involved 2.7 million people in 67 urban areas throughout the country.

The largest impact of New Zealand's urban air pollution (with the highest cost) is premature mortality, caused by long-term exposure to fine particles. These particles are emitted by combustion sources, mainly home heating, but also from vehicles and industrial sources. The study has also linked carbon monoxide with increased rates of mortality and illness.

Health effects from air pollution can include premature death, bronchitis, respiratory or cardiac hospital admissions, cancer, and restricted activity days (days missed from work and days when activities are restricted due to illness). Those whose health was most affected by air pollution were older people (particularly those aged over 65 years), infants (particularly those aged under one year), asthmatics and people with bronchitis, people with other respiratory problems, and people with other chronic diseases, such as heart disease.

Air pollution from home heating, vehicles and industry causes almost 1,100 premature deaths in New Zealand each year, around 1,500 extra cases of bronchitis and related illnesses, and 700 extra hospital admissions for respiratory and cardiac illnesses. The cost of health problems related to air pollution is estimated to be $1.14 billion annually.

Since the study started in 2003, a number of government initiatives to improve New Zealand's air pollution have been undertaken.

These include:

- the introduction of the national environmental standards for air quality
- emissions and efficiency regulations for design standards for domestic wood burners (the number one source of fine particle air pollution in New Zealand)
- regulations banning activities that discharge significant quantities of dioxins and other toxics in the air, such as the burning of tyres and oil
- the introduction of emission standards for vehicles entering the New Zealand fleet
- the reduction of sulphur in diesel from around 2,500ppm to 50ppm, and the reduction of benzene in petrol to 1 percent from 1 January 2006.

The HAPiNZ study was a jointly funded initiative between the Health Research Council of New Zealand, the Ministry for the Environment, and the Ministry of Transport. The project was also supported by the Ministry of Health, the Auckland Regional Council (ARC), and Environment Canterbury, with data also provided by all the other regional councils. The $1 million study ran over four years and will inform a number of other related projects and policy developments.

Source: Health Research Council

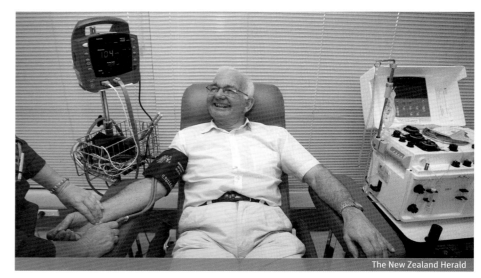

The New Zealand Herald

Blood donor Graeme Thomas has his blood pressure taken. Graeme has donated blood more than 450 times and has made the highest number of donations in New Zealand. Although 80 percent of people will need blood or blood products during their lifetime, only 4 percent currently roll up their sleeves and donate. Approximately 3,000 donations are needed each week to meet hospital needs.

The HRC aims to improve human health by promoting and funding health research. The HRC funds a broad spectrum of health research, including biomedical, public health, Māori and Pacific peoples' health, and clinical research. HRC funding is largely through the Vote Research, Science and Technology allocation, with funding for ethics policy advice coming from the Vote Health allocation. Total government funding for the HRC's work in 2006/07 was $77.90 million.

The Malaghan Institute of Medical Research Established in Wellington in 1979 as an independent medical research institute, the Malaghan Institute is a charitable trust dedicated to the relief of human suffering through scientific research into the causes, nature and treatment of disease. Formerly the Wellington Cancer and Medical Research Institute, it was renamed in 1986 to recognise the contribution of Len and Ann Malaghan.

More than 50 full-time Malaghan Institute scientists carry out research into cancer, asthma, arthritis, multiple sclerosis and infectious diseases, including tuberculosis and RSV (a respiratory infection most serious in children aged under 12 months). The institute has a commitment to educating, fostering, and developing scientists, which it regards as essential to the continuing success of scientific research in New Zealand. To that end, the institute sponsors programmes for doctoral candidates and summer internships for university students. The Malaghan Institute is funded by contestable research grants, contributions from corporate sponsors, bequests and donations.

Health expenditure (public)

As shown in table 8.01, public health expenditure (this includes expenditure on public health by the Ministry of Health, Accident Compensation Corporation, other government departments, and local authorities) in New Zealand was $12,013 million in 2005/06, the latest year for which figures are available. Expenditure by the Ministry of Health of $10,302 million represented 18 percent of estimated appropriations for government for the year ending 30 June 2006.

Table 8.01

Health expenditure[1] Year ending 30 June										
Sector	1997	1998	1999	2000	2001	2002	2003	2004	2005	2006
	$(million)[2]									
Public										
Ministry of Health	6,786	7,072	7,505	7,715	8,025	8,514	8,752	9,124	9,733	10,302
ACC and other govt	684	792	881	979	1,132	1,226	1,355	1,283	1,455	1,630
Local authorities	57	56	72	71	74	76	81	68	64	82
Subtotal	**7,526**	**7,920**	**8,458**	**8,764**	**9,231**	**9,816**	**10,188**	**10,475**	**11,253**	**12,013**
Private										
Households	1,415	1,563	1,582	1,619	1,891	1,906	1,906	2,306	2,447	2,553
Insurance	613	612	634	661	697	680	702	684	688	724
Not for profits	28	32	36	38	38	37	40	99	153	144
Subtotal	**2,057**	**2,207**	**2,252**	**2,317**	**2,626**	**2,623**	**2,648**	**3,088**	**3,287**	**3,420**
Total	**9,583**	**10,127**	**10,710**	**11,082**	**11,857**	**12,439**	**12,836**	**13,563**	**14,540**	**15,433**

(1) Consumers price index-deflated, non-health items excluded. (2) Expressed in 2005/06 dollars.
Note: Figures may not add up to stated totals, due to rounding.

Source: Ministry of Health

Regulation of health service professionals

The health service workforce is made up of a large number of professions and occupations. The Health Practitioners Competence Assurance Act 2003 seeks to protect the health and safety of members of the public by providing mechanisms to ensure that registered health practitioners are competent and fit to practise their professions. The following practitioners are provided for under the Act:

Doctors The Medical Council of New Zealand is a statutory body, with a primary purpose of protecting public health and safety by ensuring that doctors are competent and fit to practise medicine.

Registration of a doctor by the council is evidence that a doctor has met a certain standard. In addition to registration, the council has responsibilities in the areas of doctor education, standards, conduct and health.

The main functions of the council are:

- registration – the council registers all doctors working in New Zealand. Doctors who complete medical training outside New Zealand or Australia must show they meet certain standards by examination and/or assessment before registration is granted. Doctors with recognised postgraduate qualifications and training are registered in recognised branches of medicine (and are sometimes called specialists).

- medical education – this involves accreditation of New Zealand medical schools, courses and curricula, in association with the Australian Medical Council. The council approves 'runs' in hospitals that are suitable for the education, training and experience of interns in their seventh year, the mandatory period before general registration. It also promotes vocational and continuing medical education in New Zealand and accredits societies and colleges responsible for postgraduate or higher training.

- health – the council manages the rehabilitation and continued monitoring of doctors who, because of some mental or physical health problem, may not be fit to practise for a period of time.

- professional standards – legislation provides for the council to review the competency or performance of doctors and to implement remediation as appropriate, including, if necessary, imposing conditions on annual practising certificates or registration. The council also ensures doctors maintain their competency to practise through continuing medical education, peer reviews, and individual audits to overcome any knowledge or skill gaps.

Complaints about doctors may be received by either the Medical Council of New Zealand or the Health and Disability Commissioner (HDC), but all complaints must be referred to the HDC. The HDC may refer complaints back to the Medical Council and the council must assess the complaint promptly and consider what action should be taken, including referral to a Professional Conduct Committee. Under the Health and Disability Commissioner Act 1994, the HDC must notify the Medical Council of any investigation directly involving a doctor.

The number of practising doctors at 30 June 2006 was 11,398. The Medical Council's website is: www.mcnz.org.nz.

Oral health practitioners The Dental Council of New Zealand regulates all oral health practitioners. This includes dentists, clinical dental technicians, dental technicians, dental therapists and dental hygienists. The Dental Council has constituted four committees, known as workforce boards, to manage the registration of practitioners and liaison with educational establishments on training and examination requirements.

The Office of the Health and Disability Commissioner (HDC) is the initial recipient of complaints about health-care practitioners, including oral health practitioners. The HDC may refer a complaint back to the Dental Council under the Health and Disability Commissioner Act 1994. The council will assess the complaint and decide what action, if any, to take. There are a number of options available to the council, including whether to: review the practitioner's competence or fitness to practise; refer the complaint for investigation by a professional conduct committee; establish an individual recertification programme; or send an educational letter to the practitioner concerned.

The Dental Council issues annual practising certificates, which certify that the practitioner is competent and fit to practise. Where public safety issues arise, the council may appoint a competence review committee – consisting of two of the practitioner's peers and a layperson. The competence review aims to ensure practitioners are practising at the required standard and may require them to undertake further education or assessment.

Disciplining of oral health practitioners is carried out by the Health Practitioners Disciplinary Tribunal (HPDT). The HPDT can impose penalties, including fines and suspension or cancellation of a practitioner's registration.

There are two main training providers for oral health practitioners. The University of Otago offers degree programmes for dentists, dental technicians, clinical dental technicians, dental therapists and dental hygienists. The Auckland University of Technology offers a degree programme for dental therapists and dental hygienists and a pre-degree certificate in dental assisting.

Protecting the rights of health services consumers

The Health and Disability Commissioner promotes and protects the rights of health and disability services consumers and facilitates the fair, simple, speedy and efficient resolution of complaints.

A code of health and disability services consumers' rights gives 10 rights to users in New Zealand. These include the right to be treated with respect, care and skill; the right to information and to give informed consent; freedom from discrimination or coercion; and the right to make a complaint. Corresponding responsibilities are placed on service providers.

The code applies to all health and disability services, public or private, whether paid for or not. It does not cover issues of access, funding, or entitlement to services.

The Health and Disability Commissioner Act 1994 provides the commissioner with a range of options for addressing complaints about breaches of the code. These include: mediation; formal investigation; referral to the provider, to an independent advocate, or to another agency; or taking no further action.

Status of complaints to the Health and Disability Commissioner
Year ending 30 June

	2005	2006	2007
Open at year start	347	313	279
New during year	1,124	1,076	1,289
Closed during year	1,158	1,110	1,273
Open at year end	313	279	295

Source: Health and Disability Commission

The Aucklander

Dr Nikki Turner offers her services to the City Mission by giving free check-ups. The mission provides a range of social and health services to marginalised Aucklanders, including the homeless, elderly, families in crisis, people with dependencies, and people living with HIV/Aids.

At 31 March 2007, the following numbers of oral health practitioners were registered and practising:

- 1,966 dentists
- 167 clinical dental technicians
- 191 dental technicians
- 675 dental therapists
- 400 dental hygienists.

Nurses The Nursing Council of New Zealand is the health regulatory authority responsible for nurses in New Zealand. The council's primary concern is public safety.

The council registers nurses; sets minimum standards for registration; issues practising certificates; sets standards for, approves and monitors nursing programmes at educational institutions; conducts examinations; ensures maintenance of professional standards and continuing competence of nurses; assesses, investigates and prosecutes complaints about nurses; and deals with health issues that affect nurses' ability to practise safely.

The council aims to act in a manner that is proactive and responsive to relevant national and international trends that influence the practice of nursing. At 31 March 2007, 44,520 New Zealand nurses held practising certificates.

Midwives The Midwifery Council is concerned with registration and education of midwives, setting standards for practice, issuing practising certificates, ensuring midwives maintain competence, and (in conjunction with the Health and Disability Commissioner) addressing matters involving the competence and discipline of registered midwives.

A direct entry, three-year Bachelor of Midwifery programme is offered at five institutions throughout New Zealand. Students must complete the programme, pass a national examination, and meet required standards of fitness for practise and competencies for entry to the register, before being registered.

Overseas-qualified midwives who meet a separate set of requirements are able to be registered in New Zealand. All midwives wishing to hold practising certificates must engage in a recertification programme in each three-year period, in order to maintain competence. This requires completion of compulsory and elective clinical and theoretical courses and engagement in professional development. At 1 April 2007, there were 13,412 registered midwives, with approximately 2,500 holding practising certificates.

Psychologists The Psychologists Board promotes education and training in the profession, and reviews and promotes the competency of registered psychologists. It sets standards of clinical and cultural competence and ethical conduct. Maintenance of an accurate register of psychologists is one of the board's key responsibilities. The board also investigates complaints against psychologists. At 31 March 2007 there were 1,732 psychologists holding annual practising certificates, an increase of 107 over the previous year.

Physiotherapists The Physiotherapy Board protects the health and safety of the New Zealand public by providing mechanisms to ensure that physiotherapists are competent and fit to practise. At 1 October 2007, 3,770 physiotherapists held annual practising certificates.

Occupational therapists The Occupational Therapy Board of New Zealand is responsible for registering and overseeing occupational therapy practitioners. Three-year, full-time degree courses for occupational therapists are conducted at Auckland University of Technology and at Otago Polytechnic. At 31 March 2008, there were 2,043 registered occupational therapists holding current practising certificates.

Dietitians The Dietitians Board prescribes qualifications, accredits programmes and institutions, and oversees and registers dietitians. A 15-month postgraduate training course for dietitians is conducted at the University of Otago, the prerequisite qualification being a three-year Bachelor of Science degree in Human Nutrition or a Bachelor of Consumer and Applied Science from the University of Otago. At 31 March 2006, there were 1,174 registered dietitians, with 430 holding annual practising certificates.

Optometrists and dispensing opticians The Optometrists and Dispensing Opticians Board is concerned with registration and conduct of optometrists and dispensing opticians. Optometrists are trained at the University of Auckland in a five-year, full-time degree course. Dispensing opticians are trained through a two-and-a-half-year correspondence course. At 31 March 2007, there were 821 registered optometrists, with 541 holding annual practising certificates. There were also 163 registered dispensing opticians, with 133 holding annual practising certificates.

Podiatrists The Podiatrists Board registers qualified podiatrists and sets standards for education through audit and accreditation, and for professional competence through its re-certification framework programme. The Auckland University of Technology offers a three-year Bachelor of Health Science (Podiatry) degree, which is the only New Zealand qualification recognised for registration. The board issues annual practising certificates and acts on complaints against members of the profession. At 31 March 2007, there were 273 registered podiatrists holding an annual practising certificate.

Chiropractors The Chiropractic Board is concerned with registration, education and professional conduct of registered chiropractors. The board conducts registration examinations twice a year and successful candidates are considered for registration by the board. The board also issues annual practising certificates and acts on complaints against members of the profession. At October 2007, there were 345 chiropractors registered and holding an annual practising certificate.

Pharmacists The Pharmacy Council of New Zealand is the regulatory authority responsible for pharmacists' registration, competence and fitness to practise. Entry to the pharmacy profession can be gained through a four-year degree course at either the University of Auckland or the University of Otago, followed by one year's practical training as an intern pharmacist. Recognition of pharmacy qualifications exists between New Zealand and Australia. Other routes of entry are available for pharmacists with qualifications gained in other countries. At 30 June 2007, there were 3,900 registered pharmacists, with 2,889 holding an annual practising certificate.

Medical radiation technologists The Medical Radiation Technologists Board is concerned with registration, education, and the conduct of those practising medical radiation technology.

There are five scopes of practice of medical radiation technology: diagnostic imaging general; radiation therapy; nuclear medicine; ultrasound imaging; and magnetic resonance imaging. The first two require undergraduate degrees, while the other three require postgraduate qualifications.

Students study diagnostic imaging general at UNITEC in Auckland, the Universal College of Learning, and the Christchurch Polytechnic Institute of Technology. Those studying radiation therapy undertake a three-year course at the University of Otago's Wellington School of Medicine and Health Sciences.

At 31 March 2007, 2,008 medical radiation technologists held annual practising certificates. Excluding those in training, the number in each scope of practice was as follows: diagnostic imaging general, 1,464 people; magnetic resonance imaging, 38 people; nuclear medicine, 44 people; radiation therapy, 238 people; and ultrasound, 256 people.

Medical laboratory scientists and technicians The Medical Laboratory Science Board deals with training, registration and the conduct of people who practise medical laboratory science, and it has approved two scopes of practice – medical laboratory scientists and medical laboratory technicians.

The University of Otago, Massey University and Auckland University of Technology offer a Bachelor of Medical Laboratory Science degree. The board has also approved a graduate diploma route to registration as a medical laboratory scientist.

The New Zealand Institute of Medical Laboratory Science offers two qualifications leading to registration as a medical laboratory technician. These are the Qualified Medical Laboratory Technician examination and the Qualified Phlebotomy Technician examination.

At 31 March 2007, there were 3,308 registered medical laboratory scientists. Of these, 1,538 were licensed to practise. There were also 1,794 registered medical laboratory technicians, of these 1,232 were licensed to practise.

Osteopaths The Osteopathic Council is concerned with registration, conduct and certification of the competency of osteopaths.

Osteopaths are required to complete a Master of Osteopathy degree from the Auckland University of Technology or successfully complete an Osteopathic Council examination in order to seek registration. There were 330 registered osteopaths at 31 March 2007.

Health service benefits and subsidies

General practitioner subsidies Nearly all New Zealanders are enrolled with a general practice that is part of a primary health organisation (PHO). Funding is based on a PHO's population, rather than a payment for each service. General practitioners set their own fees.

In recent years, cheaper doctor visits through PHOs were progressively rolled out to people, based on their age group. The increased funding has resulted in fee reductions (compared with unsubsidised charges) of approximately $25 for those over the age of six, while doctor visits for children under six continue to be free.

Where people receive care outside a PHO, previous subsidies still apply – $35 for children under six; $15 for older children and low income or high-use adults; and $20 for low income or high-use older children. Services for children and influenza vaccines for high-need adults are free.

Hospital treatment Inpatient, outpatient and day treatment in New Zealand public hospitals is free to all people eligible for publicly-funded health services. Services related to public hospital treatment, such as pharmaceuticals and x-rays, are also free, as are inpatient, outpatient and day treatment in public psychiatric hospitals. Mental health services, including pharmaceuticals, are free to day patients or outpatients, including those who are patients of community mental health teams on community treatment orders.

Pharmaceutical benefits All people eligible for publicly-funded health services are entitled to a wide range of medicines, approved appliances, and materials included in the pharmaceutical schedule. These are usually supplied at a small cost. The pharmaceutical schedule is a list of drugs and services subsidised by the government. Special mechanisms ensure people get access to non-schedule drugs in exceptional circumstances. The government sets a standard maximum pharmaceutical charge of $15 an item.

People who are enrolled in Access PHOs (primary health organisations in socio-economically deprived areas), and those under the age of 24 or over 65 are entitled to higher government subsidies on pharmaceuticals. The standard charge for this group is $3 for a prescription item that is on the schedule.

Individuals or families pay the pharmaceutical charge for the first 20 pharmaceutical items from 1 February each year. After 20 items, an individual or a family is eligible for a pharmaceutical subsidy card, which allows the cardholder and named family members to pay a lower amount for prescriptions. Community services cardholders do not pay a prescription charge after 20 items, until the following 1 February.

Maternity services Eligible women in New Zealand receive free pregnancy, childbirth, and postnatal care from general practitioners or midwives through benefits paid by the Ministry of Health. Some women choose to receive primary maternity care from a specialist obstetrician and may then be charged above the rate provided by the benefit. If clinical reasons require involvement of a specialist obstetrician, the service is available free from public hospitals.

Approximately 96 percent of births take place in hospitals, but midwives may provide care to women who choose to have their babies at home. All maternity hospitals are licensed under the Hospitals Act 1957 and the Ministry of Health is responsible for ensuring regulations regarding buildings, equipment, and staff are observed.

Home nursing and home help This service is free when provided by a registered nurse or midwife employed by a district health board (DHB) or an approved organisation. Subsidies are available to organisations that provide domestic help, in appropriate cases, to older people or families with young children. DHBs also provide home help as part of a range of services to reduce the need for hospital or residential home care, and as a temporary follow-up to hospital care.

Equipment and modifications services These services are available to enable people with long-term disabilities to participate in activities in and around their home, and in the wider community. Equipment includes, but is not limited to, hearing aids, cochlear implants and other equipment that improves communication; wheelchairs and other mobility devices; and equipment that assists daily living, such as shower chairs. Subsidies are available for items such as artificial eyes and wigs. Modifications are made to houses and motor vehicles, and there may be assistance for vehicle purchase.

Specific eligibility conditions apply for each type of support, and in some cases access may be prioritised. In some cases, items are subsidised rather than fully funded, or there may be part charges.

HealthPAC (health payments, agreements and compliance) HealthPAC is a business unit of the Ministry of Health that makes government subsidy payments to health professionals on behalf of the Ministry of Health and DHBs. It also administers contracts between vendors and health professionals, and monitors payments to ensure taxpayer money is being spent appropriately.

Contractual agreements apply to all primary care-based transactions subsidised by the government, such as visits to the doctor, pharmaceutical prescriptions, and maternity, immunisation and disability services.

HealthPAC handles around $4.3 billion in payments a year, involving around 70 million items. Confidential aggregated payment-related information from HealthPAC is used by the Ministry of Health for health reports and planning.

PHARMAC A Crown entity reporting to the Minister of Health, PHARMAC's main role is to manage New Zealand's Pharmaceutical Schedule – the list of more than 2,000 subsidised prescription drugs and related products, and to manage expenditure on prescription medicines on behalf of DHBs, who hold the funding.

The schedule, which is updated monthly, records the price of each drug, the subsidy it receives from public funds, and the guidelines or conditions under which it is subsidised. In 2006/07, 11 new medicines were added to the schedule, compared with 14 in 2005/06.

DHBs spent $599 million on pharmaceuticals (drug cost ex-manufacturer) in the year ending 30 June 2007, up $35 million (6.2 percent) on the previous year. In the same period, the number of prescriptions grew by 11.8 percent. This controlled increase in spending reflects PHARMAC's ability to negotiate lower prices, which offsets volume growth and spending on new pharmaceuticals.

PHARMAC also promotes the optimal use of prescription medicines and manages the purchasing of some pharmaceuticals used in hospitals. It is also able to engage in research.

Public health

Public health services are generally those provided to populations rather than to individuals, or those provided to individuals that require population-wide planning, such as population-based screening, or development of an immunisation register.

Public health supports a population health approach, which takes into account all factors that determine health, and systematically plans how these will be tackled and how inequalities can be reduced. Public health services account for 1.9 percent of health services funded through the Vote Health allocation.

The Ministry of Health is responsible for providing policy and strategic advice on public health issues and services, for monitoring the state of health of the population, for developing and enforcing public health legislation, for developing public health strategies, and for planning and funding public health services. Staff working on public health issues are located in a number of the ministry's directorates. The Director of Public Health provides overall professional leadership, and also undertakes various statutory and international roles.

Twelve public health units based in district health boards (DHBs) provide health promotion, health protection and disease prevention services to all 21 DHB districts.

Public health activities are also carried out by local authorities, who have a role in improvement, promotion and protection of public health, and are charged with developing long-term plans, with a focus on community public health. Around 200 non-government providers also provide complementary public health services at a national, regional and local level.

Safe drinking water

Safe drinking water is an essential prerequisite for public health. If a community's drinking water supply becomes contaminated by pathogenic organisms, a large number of people can be infected quickly, and this can lead to the spread of infectious diseases in pandemic proportions.

Chemical contamination of drinking water also has to be guarded against, although this is less common in New Zealand than contamination by pathogenic organisms is. Although direct health risks from chemicals in New Zealand are lower than for contamination by pathogens, there is public concern about chemical contamination.

The Health (Drinking Water) Amendment Act, passed in October 2007, makes most of the (previously voluntary) elements of the current Ministry of Health drinking water strategy subject to legal duties. It brings New Zealand into line with the Bonn Charter for Safe Drinking Water, and encourages the introduction of integrated water resource management.

The Act is probably the first in the world to require all water suppliers servicing more than 500 people to produce and implement public health risk management plans for their supplies. It also requires all water suppliers to take all practicable steps to comply with the drinking water standards for New Zealand.

The Act is complemented by a Drinking Water Assistance Programme that provides free technical assistance to all water suppliers serving fewer than 5,000 people, and may provide funding assistance to these water suppliers if they do not meet the standards, or their risk management plan identifies significant public health risks related to the supply.

The Ministry of Health informs the public about the safety of both public and privately-owned community drinking water supplies, using a system that grades water supplies from A1 (completely satisfactory) to E (completely unsatisfactory).

Table 8.02

Subsidised prescriptions Year ending 30 June		
Year	Number of prescriptions	Government expenditure[1] $(million)
1997	21,902,649	542
1998	22,471,870	550
1999	21,850,759	502
2000	21,742,171	517
2001	21,484,187	516
2002	21,943,895	504
2003	22,337,364	510
2004	24,272,384	534
2005	26,941,947	565
2006	28,550,543	564
2007	31,923,044	599

(1) Drug expenditure is ex-manufacturer. Expenditure figures exclude distribution and dispensing costs. Any payments by patients have not been deducted. Figures exclude GST and are not adjusted for inflation.

Source: PHARMAC

Marketing healthy lifestyles

Otago Daily Times

Sun smart year 1 pupils Chloe Hill (left), Brianna Romeril and Jasper Bloomfield try out the playground on their first day at Queenstown Primary School.

The Health Sponsorship Council (HSC) Te Rōpū Whakatarairanga Hauora is a Crown entity established in 1990 with a focus on marketing health and healthy lifestyles to New Zealanders. The HSC is government-funded through a purchasing agreement with the Ministry of Health. Three ongoing areas of focus are sun safety, tobacco control, and healthy eating.

SunSmart
HSC's SunSmart campaign reminds people to protect themselves from the harmful effects of the sun – to use sunscreen, wear loose clothing to cover up, wear sunhats and sunglasses, and keep out of the sun between the hours of 11am and 4pm.

The SunSmart campaign has recently focused on parents protecting their children from overexposure of the skin to ultraviolet radiation. The key message for the summer of 2008 – "Never let your children get sunburnt".

Smokefree and Auahi Kore
Through the Smokefree and Auahi Kore programmes, the HSC encourages New Zealanders not to start smoking, to reduce children's exposure to second-hand smoke, to reduce children's exposure to smoking behaviour in outdoor and recreational settings, and to reduce smoking-related inequalities.

Key initiatives include: raising awareness about not smoking in cars; celebrating world smokefree day; Smoking Not *Our* Future (an aspirational campaign targeting young people through high-profile media and music personalities); support for the key youth music events (Smokefreerockquest and Smokefree Pacifica Beats); and the Auahi Kore programme, which uses Māori images and messages to reduce the uptake of smoking among young Māori.

Feeding our Futures
In order to make an effective contribution to reducing the burden of disease associated with obesity, attention has focused on preventing obesity in children before they reach adolescence. The Feeding our Futures programme provides parents with simple nutrition tips, and encourages positive eating behaviours.

Initial messages focused on: eating together regularly as a family; encouraging children to get involved with meal preparation; and promoting the message that water or milk should be the first choice for children's drinks.

These were followed by a further three messages: kids learn better when they eat fruit and vegetables; make at least half your meal vegetables; and help kids to snack the healthy way – snacks don't need to come in packets.

Source: Health Sponsorship Council

The Aucklander

Waitakere College student Alana Bulling (right) drinks filtered water from a water fountain, while Santana Bagnall drinks water from a bottle. The college is one of 12 schools in New Zealand chosen as part of a government-led health initiative, Mission On – one of their projects is filtered water fountains.

Gradings are determined by the extent to which the supply and distribution complies with drinking water standards, and whether adequate barriers to contamination are in place.

The *Register of Community Drinking Water Supplies in New Zealand* lists community drinking water supplies that serve 25 or more people for 60 or more days a year. The Act requires all community drinking water supplies to be registered. The register provides information on public health gradings and whether any chemical contaminants are present at concentrations that could potentially be of public health significance.

The quality of community water supplies is assessed by qualified drinking-water assessors and the results published in an annual review.

Misuse of drugs

A wide range of drugs capable of being misused, including illegal drugs, prescription drugs and restricted substances, are controlled by the Misuse of Drugs Act 1975, the Misuse of Drugs Regulations 1977, and associated legislation.

It is an offence to obtain, manufacture, possess, consume, supply, or offer to supply controlled drugs unless authorised under the Act. Illegal dealing in any class of controlled drug is subject to penalties varying from fines to imprisonment.

Controlled drugs are divided into three classes depending on their assessed level of harm. Heavier penalties are provided for offences involving Class A drugs, such as heroin, cocaine and methamphetamine. Penalties for drugs in Class B and Class C are progressively less. Many Class B and C drugs, such as morphine and pethidine, are legitimately used for medical and scientific purposes.

Cannabis plants, fruit and seeds are included in Class C. Substances manufactured from cannabis plants are classified B. Benzylpiperazine (BZP) was reclassified from a restricted substance to a Class C drug in April 2008.

Rapid emergence of potentially dangerous 'designer' drugs necessitated a quicker way to control these drugs. In 2000, Parliament amended the Misuse of Drugs Act 1975 to create a more rapid and evidence-based process for classifying drugs. The amendment clarified the basis of drug classification to relate to risk of harm to individuals and society arising from the drug. The risks range from Class A (very high) and Class B (high) to Class C (moderate risk). An expert advisory committee was established to assess the relative risk of various drugs and to make classification recommendations to the Minister of Health.

A review of the Misuse of Drugs Act 1975 has been announced and the Law Commission will be working closely with the Ministries of Health and Justice, and other interested agencies and groups on this.

National drug policy *The National Drug Policy 2007–2012* (2007) sets out the Government's policy for tobacco, alcohol, illegal drugs, and other drugs, within a single framework. The overarching principle is 'harm minimisation', which involves a coordinated set of initiatives across government agencies under a three-pronged approach:

- supply control (limiting availability of drugs through, for example, legislation and law enforcement)

- demand reduction (reducing the desire to use drugs through initiatives such as education programmes)
- problem limitation (mitigating harm from drugs through treatment services).

Other principles include: evidence-informed policy; whole-of-government approach; partnerships with non-government stakeholders; and reducing inequalities. The NDP, led by the Ministry of Health, provides a basis for priority setting, inter-sectoral decision-making and strategic alignment. The national drug policy website is www.ndp.govt.nz.

National Drug Intelligence Bureau To ensure that drug policy is based on sound information, the Ministry of Health, the New Zealand Customs Service and the New Zealand Police have maintained the National Drug Intelligence Bureau since 1972.

Alcohol

Alcohol is the most commonly-used recreational drug in New Zealand, with the most recent survey results showing 81 percent of people aged 12–65 had consumed alcohol in the last 12 months. While most people drink without harming themselves or others, the misuse of alcohol by some results in considerable health, social, and economic costs to individuals, families, and the wider community. Alcohol abuse can lead to physical and mental health problems, dependence, injury and death on the roads, drownings, violence, fetal abnormalities, absenteeism, and impaired work performance.

Figure 8.01

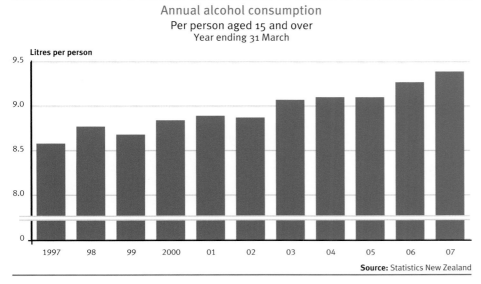

Annual alcohol consumption
Per person aged 15 and over
Year ending 31 March

Source: Statistics New Zealand

Ministry of Transport figures indicate that alcohol was a contributing factor in about 28 percent of fatal road accidents and 14 percent of injury accidents in 2006. In annual terms, the social cost of alcohol misuse in New Zealand has been estimated at between $1.5 and 2.4 billion.

The 2004 New Zealand Health Behaviours Survey – Alcohol Use found that one in four New Zealanders aged 12–65 years who had consumed alcohol in the previous year, reported consuming amounts on a typical drinking occasion that are potentially hazardous and harmful.

Although less likely to be drinkers, Māori and Pacific peoples who drank were more likely to have potentially hazardous drinking patterns than other ethnic groups, and young people who drank were also likely to have hazardous drinking patterns. Fifty-six percent of those aged 12–17 had consumed alcohol in the last 12 months, and of these, two in five reported consuming large amounts of alcohol on a typical drinking occasion.

Recognising the potential for harm, the sale and supply of alcohol is regulated and policies and programmes are in place to reduce alcohol-related harm. These include regular advertising campaigns to alert people to the dangers of drinking then driving; pregnant women being advised of the potential harm to unborn babies of drinking during pregnancy; and liquor bans in some areas to enhance public safety.

Alcohol and other drug issues are one of the priority areas for action identified in the *New Zealand Health Strategy* (2000). Alcohol is one of the substances covered by the National Drug Policy, which aims to minimise harm from alcohol, tobacco and other drugs.

Tobacco

Smoking is the greatest single preventable cause of premature death in New Zealand. Each year about 4,700 New Zealanders die from cancers, cardiovascular disease, chronic obstructive pulmonary disease, and other diseases caused by smoking. There is also considerable evidence of harm to adults and children from exposure to second-hand smoke in homes, workplaces and enclosed public places.

Problem gambling

In March 2007, the Health Sponsorship Council (HSC) Te Rōpū Whakatarairanga Hauora launched a new social marketing campaign: Problem gambling – our communities, our families, our problem.

Tens of thousands of New Zealanders' lives are affected by excessive gambling. Problem gambling can lead to, or is associated with: relationship breakdown, divorce and separation; decreased work productivity; strained or ruined friendships; crime; depression; suicide; alcohol and drug abuse, and other health problems; debt and loss of assets; violence in the home; isolation from a person's culture, family and community; neglect of children; and poverty.

The HSC wants to increase awareness and knowledge of the harm associated with gambling and encourage people to find out how to address gambling problems – for families/whānau and communities to see and acknowledge that problem gambling affects us all.

The programme's key activities are:

- implementing national communications strategies to increase awareness and understanding of gambling-related harm
- implementing strategies to prevent and minimise problem gambling
- maintaining and developing relationships at national, regional and community levels and working collaboratively with partner agencies within the problem gambling sector to ensure consistent messages about gambling, and appropriate responses to people seeking information about, or support for, gambling-related harm
- planning the next stage of the campaign, informed by research.

For more information, visit www.ourproblem.org.nz.

Source: Health Sponsorship Council

Table 8.03

Cigarette smoking status
Usual residents aged 15 years and over
2006 Census

Smoking status	Number of people
Regular smoker	597,792
Ex-smoker	637,293
Never smoked regularly	1,653,924
Response unidentifiable	106,347
Not stated	165,015
Total	**3,160,371**

Source: Statistics New Zealand

Jarrad Mapp

Under new regulations about the sale of cigarettes, 30 percent of the front and 90 percent of the back of packets are now covered in graphic warnings, which include images of gangrenous toes, rotting teeth and gums, diseased lungs and smoking-damaged hearts. Cigarette packets also carry the Quitline logo and freephone number and other information about quitting smoking. These regulations came into force on 28 February 2008 and all retailers were required to comply by 1 August 2008.

Smokers who die from tobacco-related causes lose, on average, 13 years of life compared with non-smokers.

The prevalence of smoking in New Zealand is decreasing. The 2006 New Zealand Tobacco Use Survey results show that 23.5 percent of those aged 15–64 currently smoke, and the 2006 Census showed that 20.7 percent of people aged 15 and over smoke on a daily basis. These figures represent a large decline in smoking since 1990 (when 28 percent of people smoked) and 1983 (when 33 percent smoked).

Increases in the prevalence of smoking by secondary school students in the 1990s have been reversed, with a strong downward trend apparent between 1999 and 2006 for both males and females.

The prevalence of smoking among adult Māori and Pacific peoples remains high, 45.8 percent and 36.2 percent, respectively, in 2006.

Annual tobacco consumption per adult (15 years and over) continues to track downwards, from 1,971 cigarettes in 1990 to 999 cigarettes in 2004. There was a slight increase in 2005, to 1,033 cigarettes per adult.

The success of New Zealand's smoking cessation programmes has been achieved through a mix of legislation, taxation, health promotion, and cessation support.

Figure 8.02

Annual tobacco consumption
Per person aged 15 and over
Year ending 31 December

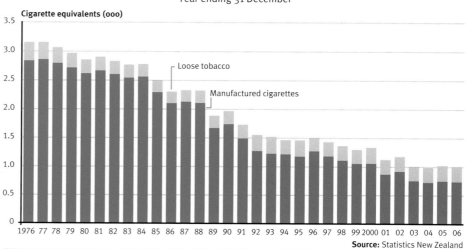

Source: Statistics New Zealand

An amendment to the Smoke-free Environments Act 1990, which reduced exposure to environmental tobacco smoke by extending the scope of smoke-free workplaces to include bars, restaurants, cafes and clubs, took effect during 2004. The amendments also restricted further access by minors to tobacco products and placed restrictions on the display of tobacco products at point of sale.

Communicable disease control

Medical practitioners are required under the Health Act 1956 to notify medical health officers of notifiable disease cases they suspect or diagnose. Since December 2007 medical laboratories are also required to notify test results that indicate a notifiable disease.

Notification data is recorded on a computerised database in each public health service and is used to guide local control measures. The data is, in turn, collated and analysed at national level by the Institute of Environmental Science and Research on behalf of the Ministry of Health.

The Ministry of Health monitors the prevalence of communicable diseases, manages national coordination of responses to disease outbreaks, and is responsible for the national immunisation schedule and the control of communicable diseases through designated officers.

The ministry is also responsible for policy development, promulgation of regulations and fulfilment of the new disease-reporting requirements, based on the International Health Regulations, 2005.

Changes to the national immunisation schedule in 2008 Immunisation provides protection from or resistance to infectious diseases. The Ministry of Health's National Immunisation Programme improves health by reducing diseases, such as hepatitis B, measles, and influenza, through the use of vaccines.

The national immunisation schedule is the series of vaccines that are offered free to babies, children and adolescents. Some vaccines are also provided for adults. Pneumococcal vaccine was added to the schedule on 1 June 2008.

Pneumococcal vaccine protects against the most common strains of the pneumococcal bacteria that cause severe disease. Severe pneumococcal disease can cause meningitis, blood poisoning and pneumonia. All babies are at risk of severe pneumococcal disease.

The addition of the pneumococcal vaccine to the schedule means that from 1 June 2008 all New Zealand babies have access to free immunisations that protect them against 11 serious diseases. The schedule is reviewed every two years to make sure New Zealanders receive safe and effective vaccines.

Table 8.04

Recommended immunisation schedule[1] from 1 June 2008	
Age	Disease protected against (vaccine name)
6 weeks[2]	diphtheria, tetanus, whooping cough, polio, hepatitis B, haemophilius influenzae type b (Infanrix-hexa)
	pneumococcal (Prevenar)
	meningococcal B (MeNZB)
3 months	diphtheria, tetanus, whooping cough, polio, hepatitis B, haemophilius influenzae type b (Infanrix-hexa)
	pneumococcal (Prevenar)
	meningococcal B (MeNZB)
5 months	diphtheria, tetanus, whooping cough, polio, hepatitis B, haemophilius influenzae type b (Infanrix-hexa)
	pneumococcal (Prevenar)
	meningococcal B (MeNZB)
10 months	meningococcal B (MeNZB)
15 months	haemophilius influenzae type b (Hiberix)
	pneumococcal (Prevenar)
	measles, mumps, rubella (MMRII)
4 years	diphtheria, tetanus, whooping cough, polio, (Infanrix-IPV)
	measles, mumps, rubella (MMRII)
11 years[3]	diphtheria, tetanus, whooping cough (Boostrix)
45 years	diphtheria, tetanus (ADT)[3]
65 years	diphtheria, tetanus (ADT)[3]
	influenza[4] (Vaxigrip or Fluvax)

(1) Effective from 1 January 2008. (2) Hepatitis B vaccine and hepatitis B immunoglobulin is also given at birth to babies of a mother who is a carrier of hepatitis B, and bacille calmette-gurin is offered to babies who will be living in households where there are recent immigrants from high risk countries, or people with current or past history of tuberculosis. The rubella vaccine (as MMR vaccine) is available for susceptible women. (3) Administration is not funded for these vaccines. (4) The influenza vaccine is also funded for people of all ages with certain chronic medical conditions.

Source: Ministry of Health

Food safety and quality

The New Zealand Food Safety Authority (NZFSA) protects and promotes public health by ensuring safe and suitable food supply, and facilitates access to markets for New Zealand food and food-related products.

It also administers legislation covering food manufactured and sold on the domestic market (both local and imported); primary production and processing of animal products and official assurances related to their export; export of plant products; and controls surrounding registration and use of agricultural compounds and veterinary medicines.

The authority's market access activities focus on negotiating conditions and certification requirements with countries importing New Zealand's animal and plant products. This includes managing bilateral agreements, trading partner relationships and equivalency negotiations.

NZFSA works to secure market access at various levels. At a multilateral level, it works with international bodies such as the World Organization for Animal Health and the International Plant Protection Convention. These are multinational groups of the World Trade Organization that review international standards for trade in food and other agricultural products. NZFSA's role is to ensure that rules are science and risk-based, and reflect New Zealand's needs.

Under the Food Act 1981, NZFSA is responsible for the development of food safety standards and for ensuring labelling and composition standards developed for both Australia and New Zealand by Food Standards Australia New Zealand (FSANZ) meet New Zealand's needs.

NZFSA is responsible for compliance and enforcement of food legislation and for investigation of food complaints, while the Ministry of Health manages communicable disease, including identification of food-borne illness.

Cancer control

Cancer is a major health issue for New Zealanders. One in three will have some experience of cancer, either personally or through a relative or friend. The number of people who develop cancer is rising, with much of this increase being due to an increasing and ageing population. Currently, about 17,000 New Zealanders develop cancer each year, while about 7,500 die as a result of cancer.

Reducing the incidence and impact of cancer is one of 13 population health objectives in the *New Zealand Health Strategy* (2000).

The cancer control programme is an organised approach to reducing the community burden of cancer through prevention, screening and early detection, treatment, support and rehabilitation, and palliative care.

The *New Zealand Cancer Control Strategy* (2003) outlines the goals of the strategy, which are to:

- reduce the incidence of cancer through primary prevention
- ensure effective screening and early detection to reduce incidence and mortality
- ensure effective diagnosis and treatment to reduce morbidity and mortality
- improve the quality of life for those with cancer, and their family or whānau, through support, rehabilitation and palliative care
- improve delivery of services across the continuum of cancer control through effective planning, coordination and integration of resources and activity, monitoring, and evaluation
- improve effectiveness of cancer control in New Zealand through research and surveillance.

The *New Zealand Cancer Control Strategy Action Plan 2005–10* was published in March 2005. The Cancer Control Council was appointed in 2005 by the Minister of Health to monitor implementation of the plan and provide the minister with independent advice.

Services for older people

Most older people are fit and well, and live independent lives. However, with advancing age, older people become increasingly high users of health and disability support services, such as home support and residential care.

People are now entering residential care later but with a higher level of dependency than in the past. The average age of entry to aged residential care is 82.3 years.

In terms of government expenditure, the most significant services used specifically by older people are: residential care; home-based support; assessment, treatment and rehabilitation; environmental support; and carer support. Public expenditure on these services is estimated to be $1,160 million in 2007/08.

DHBs are responsible for planning and funding health and disability services for older people, except for environmental support services, which are funded directly by the Ministry of Health.

In 2006/07 approximately 27,100 people received aged residential care, funded to a greater or lesser extent by DHBs, at a cost of approximately $690 million (excluding GST). This did not include contributions made by residents.

Approximately $145 million was spent by DHBs on home-based support services for older people in 2006/07. DHBs also spent $180 million on assessment, treatment and rehabilitation services, and $35 million on carer support.

In Budget 2007, the Government increased annual funding of aged residential care by $37.5 million and home-based support services by $20.3 million. In addition, $32 million per year was provided to DHBs for inflation and volume increases for these services.

The Health of Older People Strategy, released in 2002, provides a framework for future service development for older people. Key directions in the strategy are an integrated approach to service planning and provision, and a greater emphasis on community-based services to support older people to remain at home with a good quality of life.

Not for profit organisations

Not for profit organisations make valuable contributions to aspects of public health. The Vote Health allocation, through a variety of contracts and other agreements, funds a wide range of independent service providers and related organisations, including the Royal New Zealand Plunket Society, the New Zealand Family Planning Association, the National Heart Foundation and the New Zealand AIDS Foundation.

Mental health

The Ministry of Health has responsibility for leading implementation of the National Mental Health Strategy contained in *Looking Forward* (1994) and *Moving Forward* (1997) and the Government's most recent policy direction for mental health and addiction, *Te Tāhuhu – Improving Mental Health 2005–2015: The Second New Zealand Mental Health and Addiction Plan* released in June 2005.

Implementation of the strategy has been supported by growth in public funding – from $465 million (excluding GST) in 1997/98 to $1,021 million (excluding GST) in 2006/07. Growth in funding has been accompanied by significant growth in services, 74 percent of which are community based, with inpatient services making up the remainder.

Services provided by non-government organisations receive 29 percent of funding for community-based services.

New Zealand's 21 DHBs have responsibility for planning, funding and ensuring provision of mental health and addiction services.

Te Tāhuhu – Improving Mental Health sets out Government policy and priorities for mental health and addiction for the 10 years to 2015, and provides an overall direction for investment in the area. Based on an outcomes framework, it broadens government interest in the mental health of all New Zealanders, while continuing to place an emphasis on those most severely affected by mental illness and addiction. It covers the spectrum of interventions, from promotion and prevention, to primary care and specialist services.

Te Puāwaitanga: Māori Mental Health National Strategic Framework (2002) was developed to assist and provide detailed guidance for the mental health sector and DHBs on the planning and delivery of services for Māori, recognising the importance of cultural identity as an essential component of mental health care.

Building on Strengths: a new approach to promoting mental health in New Zealand/Aotearoa (2002) outlines a national approach to mental health promotion, with the aim of providing education and guidance on mental health promotion, along with planned priority actions for promotional activities.

The 'Like Minds, Like Mine' programme continues to counter stigma and discrimination, and promote social inclusion of people who experience mental illness. More information is at www.likeminds.org.nz.

Suicide

Suicidal behaviour is a significant and preventable public health issue in New Zealand. It is a major cause of death and injury and a significant contributor to social and health costs. In 2004, the total cost (economic and non-economic) of suicide and attempted suicide was estimated at $1.6 billion.

Every year approximately 500 people die by suicide, and approximately 10 times that number are hospitalised for intentional self-harm. The three-year moving average rate of suicide for 2003–05 was 13.2 deaths per 100,000 people. This is a decrease of 19 percent from the 1996–98 peak of 16.3 deaths per 100,000 people, and continues the downward trend of recent years.

Males consistently have a higher rate of suicide than females, with approximately three male suicides to every female suicide. However, females have a higher rate of hospitalisation for intentional self-harm than males, with two females being hospitalised for every male hospitalisation.

The subgroups with the highest rates of suicide were: males; Māori (as opposed to non-Māori); those aged 15–44 years; and those residing in the most socio-economically deprived areas of New Zealand.

Research suggests that over their lifetime, 15.7 percent of New Zealanders will report experiencing ideas about suicide, 5.5 percent will make a suicide plan, and 4.5 percent will make a suicide attempt.

There is a broad range of factors involved in the development of suicidal behaviours, such as: the presence of a mental health problem (for example depression or an alcohol or drug disorder); social isolation and discrimination; family disadvantage; exposure to trauma, such as family violence, sexual abuse, or bullying; having a friend or family member die by suicide; having ready access to the means of suicide; experiencing adverse life events, such as financial or legal problems or a relationship loss; and the inability to manage life stressors and bounce back from adversity. Most often suicide results from an accumulation of risk factors.

Because there are multiple contributing factors to suicide, no single initiative is likely, on its own, to make a significant difference, and there are no 'quick fixes'. Reducing the rate of suicide in New Zealand requires sustained action, from a number of sectors over a long period of time.

In 2006 the Government released the *New Zealand Suicide Prevention Strategy 2006–2016*, which will guide prevention efforts nationally. As a companion to the strategy, the *New Zealand Suicide Prevention Action Plan 2008–2012* (2008) outlines in more detail a programme of action to achieve the aims of the strategy. This strategy is led and coordinated by the Ministry of Health, with input from other government agencies whose sectors have a role in suicide prevention.

The Ministry of Health's suicide prevention website is: www.moh.govt.nz/suicideprevention.

Disability support services

The 2006 New Zealand Disability Survey estimates that 1 in 10 New Zealanders rely on some form of disability support to help them live their everyday life. This includes support with housework and personal care, support for education and employment, and support to move around the community. Much support is provided directly by paid and unpaid caregivers, but it can also include equipment, and home and motor vehicle modifications.

While most support is provided by family, friends and other people in the community, people with disabilities can also receive support through government agencies. In 2005/06, government agencies spent $2.7 billion on long-term disability supports (that is supports that are required for more than six months). More than half the total expenditure on disability supports was through the Vote Health allocation, with other significant expenditure being through the Vote Social Development and Vote Education allocations, and the Accident Compensation Corporation.

Within the Vote Health allocation, the Ministry of Health spent $699 million (excluding GST) on disability supports for people with long-term physical, intellectual and sensory disabilities (mostly people aged under 65 years); and DHBs spent $905 million (excluding GST) on disability supports for older people with disabilities and people with psychiatric disabilities. DHBs also funded health services for people with disabilities.

Any person wishing to access long-term disability supports (funded by the Vote Health allocation) has their needs assessed, after which a service coordinator develops a package of care to meet a person's identified needs. In most cases, the supports people receive are 'in-kind' supports, although a small number receive direct funding that they can use to purchase supports themselves. Of expenditure by the Ministry of Health, about 42 percent was spent on community residential care. The other key areas of expenditure were environmental support services (10 percent), home support (9 percent), high and complex services (9 percent), caregiver support (3 percent), assessment, treatment and rehabilitation (3 percent) and respite care (2 percent).

Family health

The Ministry of Health, DHBs, health professionals, government, and non-government agencies all promote good health of New Zealand families. A strong primary health-care system is central to improving the health of New Zealanders and, in particular, tackling inequalities in health and reducing hospital admissions.

The Government has made considerable investment to ensure better access to primary health care. For example, the Under-6s initiative offers a premium to primary health-care organisation practices that agree to provide free standard consultations to children aged under six. At 1 January 2008, 70 percent of children aged under six were receiving free standard consultations through practices participating in the Under-6s initiative, or very low cost access scheme.

Sexual and reproductive health

The Government has declared its commitment to development of a comprehensive sexual and reproductive health strategy, including HIV/Aids prevention and control.

Nearly all sexually transmitted infections (STIs) that are reported on in New Zealand have increased in recent years. STIs, such as syphilis, genital herpes and gonorrhoea, can facilitate the spread of HIV infection. Some STIs, for example chlamydia, gonorrhoea and genital warts, are associated with severe, long-term effects, such as infertility, ectopic pregnancy and cancer.

In 2001, phase one of the *Sexual and Reproductive Health Strategy* was released. It provides the overall vision, principles, obligations, strategic context and strategic directions for achieving good sexual and reproductive health for all New Zealanders. It highlights the need to increase knowledge about safer sex and to provide information on sexual health, the risk of STIs and HIV, prevention, and early diagnosis and treatment.

Māori health

As a population group, Māori have, on average, the poorest health status of any ethnic group in New Zealand. The Government and the Ministry of Health have made it a key priority to improve Māori health outcomes and reduce health inequalities.

At a structural level, factors such as education, income, and housing have the potential to affect health outcomes, and their uneven distribution is a key cause of health inequalities.

Health and disability services therefore have a role, not only in the crucial work of addressing the health needs of the populations they serve, but also in identifying the role of the wider determinants of health (like education, income and housing), and in designing services that respond to existing inequalities.

He Korowai Oranga: Māori Health Strategy (2002) provides the strategic direction to achieve whānau ora: Māori families supported to achieve their maximum health and well-being. The strategy recognises that action is required along four pathways: working across sectors; effective service delivery; Māori participation; and whānau (family), hapū (subtribe), and iwi (tribe) development. The strategy also acknowledges the importance of action in the health and disability sector being underpinned by a solid evidence base.

Accompanying *He Korowai Oranga* was an action plan for 2002–05, and *Whakatātaka Tuarua: Māori Health Action Plan 2006–2011* (2006). These publications outline specific actions to achieve whānau ora. In *Whakatātaka Tuarua*, four focus areas have been identified over the five-year period. These are:

- building quality data and monitoring Māori health
- developing whānau-based models
- ensuring Māori participation in the workforce and in governance
- improving primary health care.

Research supports that improving Māori health outcomes and reducing inequalities will benefit not only Māori, but all New Zealanders.

Women's health

The Ministry of Health provides policy advice on a range of issues of particular relevance to women. These include contraception, sexual and reproductive health, infertility, pregnancy and childbirth, abortion services, and breast and cervical cancer screening.

Women's health services are provided by DHBs, health professionals, and a large number of community and consumer groups.

Cervical screening International evidence suggests morbidity and mortality from invasive cervical cancer can be reduced with an organised screening programme aimed at detecting and treating pre-cancerous changes to the cervix. New Zealand's National Cervical Screening Programme was established in 1990 and is targeted at women aged 20–69. In 2007, 70 percent of eligible women had been screened within the past three years as recommended by the programme. Cervical cancer incidence and mortality rates have both halved since the introduction of the screening programme.

National breast cancer screening programme Established in 1998, the BreastScreen Aotearoa (BSA) programme provides two-yearly mammographic screening and follow-up assessment and treatment services to women. In July 2004, the programme was expanded to include all women aged 45–69 years. By 30 June 2006, BSA had screened 326,674 women in two years, an increase of 32 percent on the number screened in the June 2002–04 years. Breast cancer is the leading cause of cancer deaths in New Zealand women. Between 1998 and July 2006, BSA detected breast cancer in 5,510 women.

Child health

The Ministry of Health's *Child Health Strategy* (1998) continues to provide direction to the health and disability sector on overall improvement in child health and disability outcomes. The strategy recognises that a comprehensive approach is required in order to improve outcomes, involving:

- greater focus on health promotion
- disease prevention and early intervention
- better coordination of resources
- development of a national child health information strategy
- development of the child health workforce

Cervical cancer vaccine

New Zealand girls aged 12 to 18 years are being offered a free vaccine to prevent the most common infections that can lead to cervical cancer.

Cervical cancer is caused by human papillomavirus (HPV). HPV is a common virus that is spread through skin-to-skin contact. Some types of HPV infection can cause cell changes that may lead to cervical cancer, and these types are spread through sexual contact.

Most women who develop HPV infections clear the virus naturally and do not develop cervical cancer. About four out of five people have HPV infection at some time in their lives. There is no treatment for HPV infections, but there is treatment for the health problems that HPV can cause (such as warts, abnormal changes to cervical cells, and cancers).

Immunisation with the Gardasil vaccine can protect against the two HPV types that cause 7 out of 10 cervical cancers and 9 out of 10 cases of genital warts, provided a person has not already been infected. The HPV vaccine only prevents HPV infection, it does not treat infection. Therefore, for best protection, girls need to be vaccinated before they are likely to be exposed to HPV, which means before they start having any sexual contact.

New Zealand's HPV immunisation programme started in September 2008, and has been initially offered to girls born in 1990 and 1991 who are not at school, through their family doctor or practice nurse. The next stage of the programme will see younger girls in the 12–18-year age group offered the vaccine at school, starting in early 2009. The vaccine offer will be ongoing for year 8 girls (aged 12–13 years) through nurses in schools.

The HPV programme aims to reduce cervical cancer in New Zealand by protecting girls against HPV infection. Currently, around 160 New Zealand women each year are diagnosed with cervical cancer, and 60 women die from cervical cancer each year.

Cervical cancer is one of the most preventable of all cancers. A woman's best protection against developing cervical cancer is having regular cervical smear tests, between the ages of 20 and 69 years, which can reduce her risk of developing cervical cancer by 90 percent.

As with all vaccines, people need to be properly informed about the potential risks. Gardasil has been licensed for use in more than 100 countries, including New Zealand, Australia, the United States, and the United Kingdom.

Source: Ministry of Health

Figure 8.03

Infant mortality[1]
Death of infants under the age of one year
Year ending 31 December

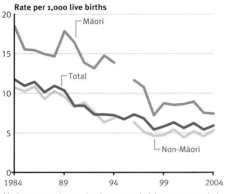

Rate per 1,000 live births

Māori

Total

Non-Māori

(1) Due to a change in the way ethnicity was recorded, 1995 figures are not directly comparable with those before and after.

Source: New Zealand Health Information Service

• improved child health research and evaluation
• leadership in child health.

The strategy emphasises the need to reduce inequalities in health and disability outcomes by focusing on: Māori children, Pacific children, children whose families experience multiple social and economic disadvantages, and children with high health and disability support needs.

DHBs and the Ministry of Health purchase a comprehensive range of health services, including high-quality secondary and tertiary pediatric services, primary care, and well-child services that focus on disease prevention and health promotion. Individual boards are developing strategies incorporating local concerns and demographics.

New Zealand also has a comprehensive and free well-child service, which includes newborn screening; developmental, vision and hearing screening for children aged under five years; and immunisation. Well-child services for this age group are offered by a range of providers, including hospitals, Plunket, and Māori and Pacific providers. The service recommends examination by family doctors at about six weeks of age, and whenever there is anxiety over acute or chronic illness or development.

The infant mortality rate was 5.1 deaths per 1,000 live births in 2006, continuing the reduction that began in the early 1990s, following release of the New Zealand Cot Death Study.

Youth Health Action Plan This plan was published in 2002, following extensive consultation with the health, social services and education professions, and with young people. The plan identifies the need to improve young people's mental and physical health, with special reference to Māori and Pacific youth, and to those with disabilities and chronic illness. Participation by young people in development of policy, programmes, and the running of health services was emphasised.

Oral health

New Zealand's oral health service includes a Community Oral Health Service that provides care primarily for children from birth to year 8 at school. Publicly-funded oral health services are also available from year 9 to the age of 18. Major hospitals provide dental services for in-patient and other special groups.

Emergency dental care for low-income adults is provided by some hospital dental services, and by contracts with private dentists in some DHBs.

Community Oral Health Service The Community Oral Health Service has replaced the School Dental Service. The free community-based service is characterised by prevention and early intervention from birth to year 8 at school. Care includes examination, disease prevention measures, fillings, and oral health education.

Oral health services from year 9 to the age of 18 years are free. These services are usually provided by private dentists who are contracted by DHBs, but in some areas adolescents will be able to attend a Community Oral Health Service.

The Community Oral Health Service is funded by DHBs. Treatment requiring a general anaesthetic is performed at a hospital. Orthodontic treatment and some other specialist services can only be obtained privately.

Two-year-old Farah Thien (left) eating fruit alongside her sister Fendi (aged 14) and brother Harris (aged 12) at their home. Fruit and vegetables are an important part of children's diets. Programmes such as "5+ a day" and Healthy Eating – Healthy Action Oranga Kai – Oranga are some of the high-profile initiatives to raise awareness about the importance of good nutrition.

Dental research The bulk of dental research in New Zealand is undertaken by the School of Dentistry at the University of Otago. Health Research Council-funded dental research is undertaken by a number of researchers.

Fluoridation More than 60 percent of New Zealanders on reticulated water supplies live in areas with fluoridated water. Water fluoridation is a proven measure to reduce dental decay. The benefit of fluoridation in preventing dental decay is greatest for those in low socio-economic groups, for Māori, and for children. In 2006, 57 percent of five-year-olds living in fluoridated areas showed no dental decay, compared with 48 percent of five-year-olds in non-fluoridated areas.

Hospitals

In the year ending 30 June 2007, there were 558,543 inpatient and day-case medical and surgical discharges from publicly-funded district health board (DHB) hospitals in New Zealand.

This number does not include directly-purchased Accident Compensation Corporation elective cases, maternity cases, and short stay accident and emergency cases.

Outpatients

Most people who attend a hospital are 'ambulatory' (not confined to a bed) and do not require constant hospital care. These people receive treatment in outpatient and community settings.

In the year ending 30 June 2007, 937,008 people attended a specialist medical or surgical clinic at a hospital for diagnosis, treatment and pre- and post-operative care, typically on two or more occasions.

In the same year, health professionals assessed, treated and rehabilitated approximately 204,640 patients in clinical and home-based settings; 52,480 people attended educational programmes for diabetes and cardiac conditions; 19,412 patients received dialysis treatment; and 365,000 people received specialist outpatient dental treatment.

Length of stay in public hospitals The length of time spent by inpatients in hospital continues to fall, reflecting long-term trends. If day-case patients are excluded, the average length of stay, at 30 September 2007, was 4.08 days. This is shorter than the average stay of 4.18 days recorded five years previously (30 September 2002).

Shorter hospital stays are the result of advances in medical technology, such as new medical treatments and more effective drugs; improved community and follow-up care; and more effective hospital administration.

Table 8.05

Hospital-based outpatient and community services
Year ending 30 June

Service	Number of unique patients[1]		Number of discharges	
	2006	2007	2006	2007
Allied health[2]	108,410	125,905	379,396	401,938
Community services[3]	93,471	78,735	931,086	650,167
Blood products[4]	2,897	3,292	9,284	8,427
Chemotherapy	5,972	10,368	43,496	62,075
Outpatient dental[5]	381,296	365,000	147,863	95,626
Dialysis[6]	14,726	19,412	154,950	221,223
Emergency department events	543,660	640,118	716,529	846,560
Education-related programmes (incl training)	42,626	52,480	107,257	46,221
Radiotherapy	5,659	9,011	90,412	142,084
Scopes[7]	41,352	44,640	46,256	47,839
Spinal procedures[8]	357	361	442	447
Medical specialist (first assessment)	141,268	145,544	148,710	157,086
Surgical specialist (first assessment)	232,554	243,275	240,922	258,196
Total first assessments	**373,822**	**388,819**	**389,632**	**415,282**
Medical specialist (subsequent assessment)	224,527	235,356	468,859	482,143
Surgical specialist (subsequent assessment)	295,228	312,833	527,175	560,639
Total subsequent assessments	**519,755**	**548,189**	**468,859**	**1,042,782**
Total assessments	**3,027,580**	**3,223,338**	**4,871,128**	**5,438,735**

(1) Accuracy of counts is limited by the accuracy of health care user identification (National Health Index). (2) Refers to treatment by professionals such as dietitians and physiotherapists. Excludes treatment in support of inpatient and other outpatient events. (3) Includes domiciliary, disability, or health older people (HOP) service areas. HOP was introduced in 2006, as part of a rehabilitation service, which is an alternative to inpatient or outpatient care. (4) Includes blood transfusions and blood products such as Factor VIII. Excludes transfusions occurring as part of inpatient or other outpatient attendances. (5) Includes school and adolescent dental services and special services for children and adolescents. (6) Renal medicine excludes dialysis training such as CAPD, haemodialysis, and in-centre self-managed dialysis training. (7) Minor diagnostic procedures performed on a day-patient or outpatient basis. Excludes scopes performed as part of an inpatient stay. (8) Inpatient events that are recorded separately because they are excluded from the national minimum dataset.

Source: Ministry of Health

Planning for a pandemic

An influenza pandemic can occur when a new strain of influenza virus emerges that people have no natural immunity to. If this new virus is able to spread easily from person to person, it could trigger a pandemic by quickly spreading around the world. The Ministry of Health has been planning for a pandemic for some time. A pandemic action plan was first developed in 1999, and the plan has been regularly reviewed and updated.

In 2005, there was heightened international awareness of the potential for an influenza pandemic, when a circulating avian influenza virus (H5N1) infected some people who had been in close contact with sick birds. In response, the ministry engaged with the health sector and other government agencies to evolve the pandemic plan into an all-of-government plan for managing an influenza pandemic.

The health sector worked to ensure there are plans in place to manage a pandemic at the national, regional and local level. National working groups have also considered a range of non-health issues, such as potential school closures, border management, maintenance of critical infrastructure (including the supply of food and water), and law and order. The publication of the *New Zealand Influenza Pandemic Action Plan* in 2006 was the result of this work.

In 2007, the ministry ran a national all-of-government exercise to put the plan into practice, and identify areas for improvement. This major exercise is informing the future pandemic planning of the ministry, the health sector, and other agencies.

The ministry has prepared information packs and brochures advising on ways to minimise the spread of a virus among the public and health workers, and the steps people can take to protect and care for their families. In the event of a pandemic, these steps include keeping at least a metre from other people, covering coughs and sneezes, and washing and drying hands often. They also include forward planning measures, such as building up an emergency supplies kit.

The Government has a large stockpile of clinical and non-clinical supplies for use in a pandemic. Contractual arrangements are also in place for supplies of vaccine, which can be manufactured once the pandemic strain is identified by the World Health Organization.

Source: Ministry of Health

The Aucklander

Norman Reynolds donated a defibrillator to St Heliers Village Association, and 10 local shop owners have been trained to use it. Portable defibrillators can resuscitate a person who has had a cardiac arrest. Improvements in defibrillator design mean trained non-medical people can respond to emergencies effectively.

Causes of death

Malignant neoplasm (cancer), ischaemic heart disease, and cerebrovascular disease were the leading causes of death in New Zealand in the year ending 31 December 2004, the most recent year for which statistics are available.

Collectively, they accounted for almost 60 percent of all deaths. Cancer was the cause of 28.0 percent of deaths, ischaemic heart disease 22.0 percent, and cerebrovascular disease 9.8 percent.

Table 8.06

| | Major causes of death 2002–2004 | | | | | |
| | Number of deaths | | | Rate per million people | | |
Cause of death	2002	2003	2004	2002	2003	2004
Malignant neoplasm	7,800	7,932	8,023	1,978.6	1,978.3	1,974.9
Diabetes mellitus	805	847	843	204.2	211.2	207.5
Chronic rheumatic heart disease	150	148	123	38.1	36.9	30.3
Hypertensive disease	219	247	283	55.6	61.6	69.7
Ischaemic heart disease	6,287	6,196	6,313	1,594.8	1,545.3	1,554.0
Other forms of heart disease	1,293	1,293	1,205	328.0	322.5	296.6
Cerebrovascular disease	2,829	2,692	2,806	717.6	671.4	690.7
Disease of artery, arteriole or capillary	558	461	508	141.5	115.0	125.0
Influenza and pneumonia	462	412	465	117.2	102.8	114.5
Bronchitis, emphysema and asthma	209	205	175	53.0	51.1	43.1
Other disease of respiratory system	1,712	1,742	1,827	434.3	434.5	449.7
Disease of the liver	140	132	134	35.5	32.9	33.0
Peptic ulcer	95	88	82	24.1	21.9	20.2
Congenital anomaly	200	188	178	50.7	46.9	43.8
Conditions of perinatal mortality	172	137	150	43.6	34.2	36.9
Transport accidents	531	582	520	134.7	145.2	128.0
Intentional self-harm	466	517	488	118.2	128.9	120.1
Other injury and poisoning	699	704	702	177.3	175.6	172.8
All other diseases	3,733	3,538	3,811	947.0	882.4	938.1
Total	**28,360**	**28,061**	**28,636**	**7,194.1**	**6,998.5**	**7,048.9**

Source: New Zealand Health Information Service

Cancer

In 2004 (the latest year for which statistics are available), 95.4 percent of cancer deaths occurred at age 45 years and over, with 70.4 percent occurring at 65 years and over.

Table 8.07 compares male and female deaths from malignant cancer.

Table 8.07

Deaths from malignant cancer
By sex and age group
Year ending 31 December 2004

Age group (years)	Males			Females		
	Number	Rate per 100,000 people	Percentage of total deaths	Number	Rate per 100,000 people	Percentage of total deaths
Under 5	2	1.4	0.0	1	0.7	0.0
5–14	7	2.3	0.2	10	3.4	0.3
15–24	11	3.7	0.3	11	3.8	0.3
25–44	126	22.3	3.0	204	33.9	5.3
45–64	986	212.7	23.6	1017	214.8	26.4
65+	3,041	1,414	72.9	2,607	962.5	67.7
Total	**4,173**	**208.8**	**100.0**	**3,850**	**186.5**	**100.0**
Total in 2003	4,233	214.7	100.0	3,699	181.5	100.0

Source: New Zealand Health Information Service

Fetal and infant mortality

The term perinatal death covers fetal deaths at 20 or more weeks gestation or 400 grams birthweight, and infant deaths within seven days of birth (early neonatal deaths). A late neonatal death occurs when a live-born infant dies after seven days but before 28 days after birth. A post-neonatal death is when a live-born infant dies after 28 days but before the first year of life is completed. An infant death is the death of a live-born infant before the first year of life is completed.

Table 8.08

Fetal and infant mortality rates
By ethnic group
Year ending 31 December 2005[1]

Category of death	Māori		Pacific peoples		Other		Total	
	Number	Rate[2]	Number	Rate[2]	Number	Rate[2]	Number	Rate[2]
Total fetal[3]	**160**	**9.3**	**64**	**10.2**	**327**	**9.2**	**551**	**9.3**
Infant								
Early neonatal[4]	47	2.8	24	3.8	77	2.2	148	2.5
Late neonatal[5]	10	0.6	5	0.8	20	0.6	35	0.6
Post-neonatal[6]	57	3.4	14	2.2	40	1.1	111	1.9
Total infant	**114**	**6.7**	**43**	**6.9**	**137**	**3.9**	**294**	**5.0**

(1) Figures for 2005 are provisional. (2) Rate per 1,000 recorded pregnancies or live births. (3) Deaths at before 20 weeks or under 400 grams birth weight. (4) Fetal deaths at 20 or more weeks gestation or 400 grams birth weight, and infant deaths within seven days of birth (early neonatal deaths). (5) When a live-born infant dies after seven days but before 28 days after birth. (6) Infant death after 28 days but before the first year of life is completed.

Source: New Zealand Health Information Service

Table 8.09

Infant mortality rates for selected OECD[1] countries
Deaths per 1,000 live births

	2000	2001	2002	2003	2004	2005
Australia	5.2	5.3	5.0	4.8	4.7	5.0
Austria	4.8	4.8	4.1	4.5	4.5	4.2
Germany	4.4	4.3	4.2	4.2	4.1	3.9
Greece	5.4	5.1	5.1	4.0	4.1	3.8
Iceland	3.0	2.7	2.3	2.4	2.8	2.3
Japan	3.2	3.1	3.0	3.0	2.8	2.8
New Zealand	**6.1**	**5.3**	**5.6**	**4.9**	**5.6**	**5.1**
Portugal	5.5	5.0	5.0	4.1	3.8	3.5
Switzerland	4.9	5.0	5.0	4.3	4.2	4.2
United Kingdom	5.6	5.5	5.2	5.3	5.0	5.1

(1) Organisation for Economic Co-operation and Development.

Source: OECD Health Division

Abortion

Abortion is permitted by New Zealand law under the Contraception, Sterilisation and Abortion Act 1977 in circumstances where strict criteria are met. The criteria are that continuation of the pregnancy would result in serious danger (excluding the danger normally associated with childbirth) to the life, or to the physical or mental health of the woman or girl; or that there is a substantial risk that the child, if born, would be so physically or mentally abnormal as to be seriously handicapped.

The grounds are stricter when the gestation of the pregnancy is more than 20 weeks. Then, an abortion will be authorised only to save the life of the mother, or to prevent serious, permanent injury to her physical or mental health. The Crimes Act 1961 sets out when an abortion would be unlawful.

The Contraception, Sterilisation and Abortion Act 1977 sets out the referral procedure where a woman seeks an abortion. It also sets out the criteria for determining a case. If, after consideration of a case, two certifying consultants establish that the case meets the criteria of the Act, they will each issue an authorising certificate.

The Act also created a three-member Abortion Supervisory Committee. The committee's functions include keeping provisions of the Act under review, granting licences to institutions (both private and public) to perform abortions, appointing certifying consultants, and collating and disseminating information relating to the performance of abortions in New Zealand. The committee also appoints counselling advisors to monitor counselling services for women seeking advice about their pregnancy.

Table 8.10

Abortions[1]
By age group
Year ending 31 December

Age group (years)	2001	2002	2003	2004	2005	2006
11–14	66	78	89	85	92	105
15–19	3,240	3,602	3,757	3,758	3,718	3,978
20–24	4,728	5,124	5,670	5,528	5,203	5,314
25–29	3,450	3,450	3,619	3,501	3,491	3,530
30–34	2,555	2,676	2,800	2,644	2,520	2,497
35–39	1,730	1,715	1,846	1,916	1,773	1,777
40–44	593	686	692	721	687	691
45+	48	49	38	58	47	42
Total	**16,410**	**17,380**	**18,511**	**18,211**	**17,531**	**17,934**
Total abortion rate[2]	594.9	621.3	648.2	628.7	600.8	608.2

(1) New Zealand-registered induced abortions. (2) The average number of abortions that 1,000 women would have during their life if they experienced the age-specific abortion rates of a given period (usually a year). It excludes the effect of mortality.

Source: Abortion Supervisory Committee

International comparisons International comparisons are affected by both statistical coverage and laws relating to induced abortion, so differences between New Zealand and other countries' abortion rates should be interpreted with care. International data for 2006 is not available, so comparisons have generally been made using 2005 data. In 2005, the general abortion rate (abortions per 1,000 women aged 15–44 years) for New Zealand was 19.7 per 1,000. The Netherlands (8.6), Scotland (11.9), Denmark (14.3), Norway (15.2), and England and Wales (17.8) had lower rates. In Australia (19.3 in 2004), Sweden (20.2) and the United States (20.8 in 2003), the abortion rate was similar to that of New Zealand.

Accidents

Road crashes

Motor vehicle crashes involving death or personal injury are required by law to be reported to the Police. During the year ending 31 December 2006, there were 11,291 reported crashes, resulting in 391 fatalities and injuries to 15,174 individuals.

Table 8.11

Motor vehicle crashes resulting in injury or death
By classification
Year ending 31 December

Classification	2005				2006			
	People killed	Serious injuries	Minor injuries	**Total**	People killed	Serious injuries	Minor injuries	**Total**
Overtaking or lane change	26	121	441	**588**	22	116	413	**551**
Head on (not overtaking)	136	453	1,032	**1,621**	107	415	1,149	**1,671**
Lost control or ran off road on straight	42	308	1,237	**1,587**	37	298	1,289	**1,624**
Lost control or ran off road while cornering	103	637	2,586	**3,326**	99	677	2,865	**3,641**
Collision with obstruction	3	75	351	**429**	6	92	373	**471**
Rear end	7	78	1,427	**1,512**	6	94	1,446	**1,546**
At intersections or driveways								
Turning versus same direction	13	90	573	**676**	6	82	641	**729**
Crossing, no turn	15	133	865	**1,013**	11	156	990	**1,157**
Crossing, vehicle turning	11	121	957	**1,089**	18	136	950	**1,104**
Vehicles merging	1	40	230	**271**	2	42	272	**316**
Right turn against	5	145	930	**1,080**	16	157	884	**1,057**
Vehicles manoeuvring	4	80	510	**594**	7	83	511	**601**
Pedestrian crossing road	17	184	591	**792**	28	212	589	**829**
Pedestrian – other	11	39	99	**149**	18	36	105	**159**
Miscellaneous	11	27	91	**129**	8	33	68	**109**
Total	**405**	**2,531**	**11,920**	**14,856**	**391**	**2,629**	**12,545**	**15,565**

Source: Ministry of Transport

Figure 8.04

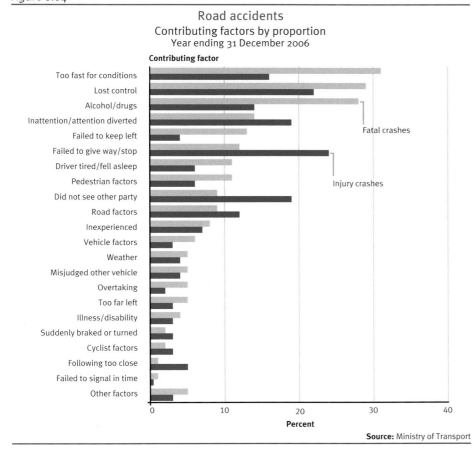

Road accidents
Contributing factors by proportion
Year ending 31 December 2006

Source: Ministry of Transport

Road Safety to 2010 (2003) provides the strategic direction for road safety in New Zealand and describes the result the Government wants to achieve by 2010 – to reduce road deaths to no more than 300 a year.

The government's key priorities for road safety include engineering safer roads, reducing speed, combating drink driving, dealing with serious offenders, encouraging the use of seat belts, improving safety for pedestrians and cyclists, improving the vehicle fleet, and providing new and better-targeted education initiatives.

Road safety is built around engineering, education and enforcement, and this requires coordination among agencies such as the Ministry of Transport, Transit New Zealand, Land Transport New Zealand, the Ministry of Education, the New Zealand Police, and local authorities. The National Road Safety Committee and a number of other bodies, including local road safety committees, provide advice and coordination for road safety partners.

Figure 8.05

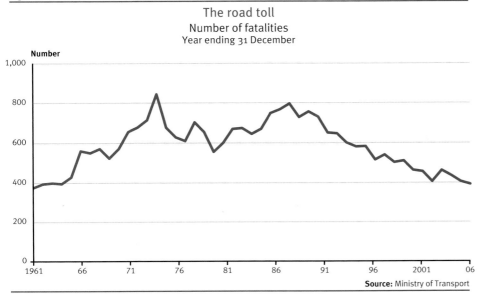

The road toll
Number of fatalities
Year ending 31 December

Source: Ministry of Transport

There has been considerable progress in reducing road deaths – the road toll was 766 in 1986, 514 in 1996 and 391 for 2006. This was the lowest number of fatalities since 1960.

Table 8.12

Fatalities and injuries in motor vehicle crashes
By age group
Year ending 31 December

Age group (years)	Fatalities[1]					Injuries				
	2002	2003	2004	2005	2006	2002	2003	2004	2005	2006
Under 5	8	10	10	8	6	204	198	157	180	192
5–9	8	8	10	10	11	386	363	355	337	368
10–14	15	9	5	13	8	639	650	567	630	593
15–19	54	73	81	84	61	2,506	2,541	2,575	2,678	2,850
20–24	47	56	56	49	41	1,867	1,978	1,862	2,057	2,139
25–29	38	41	27	27	20	1,265	1,236	1,180	1,212	1,318
30–34	37	45	33	20	29	1,152	1,253	1,134	1,131	1,185
35–39	27	40	24	20	26	1,082	1,074	991	1,092	1,062
40–44	22	28	34	35	33	947	1,013	1,007	1,045	1,068
45–49	19	25	26	27	30	719	761	826	832	919
50–54	29	20	16	25	21	619	685	615	678	709
55–59	18	15	30	13	11	471	532	521	576	613
60–64	15	18	13	13	17	396	401	394	383	408
65–69	13	16	12	14	13	306	302	294	300	301
70–74	15	14	16	11	11	261	254	258	284	290
75–79	15	14	16	11	16	226	223	238	235	253
80+	18	22	18	20	31	253	258	265	260	302
Age unknown	7	7	8	5	6	619	650	651	541	604
Total	**405**	**461**	**435**	**405**	**391**	**13,918**	**14,372**	**13,890**	**14,451**	**15,174**

(1) Killed immediately or died within 30 days of accident.

Source: Ministry of Transport

Table 8.13

Road crash casualties and rates

Year	Fatalities	Fatality rate[1]	Injuries	Injury rate[1]	Total casualty rate[1]
1996	514	13.8	14,796	398	**412**
1997	539	14.4	13,375	356	**370**
1998	501	13.2	12,412	328	**341**
1999	509	13.4	11,999	316	**329**
2000	462	12.1	10,962	286	**298**
2001	455	11.8	12,368	321	**333**
2002	405	10.3	13,918	353	**364**
2003	461	11.5	14,372	359	**370**
2004	435	10.7	13,890	342	**353**
2005	405	9.9	14,451	353	**363**
2006	391	9.4	15,174	367	**376**

(1) Per 100,000 people.

Source: Ministry of Transport

Table 8.14

International comparison of motor vehicle fatality rates[1]
Year ending 31 December

Country	2004			2005		
	Fatality number	Fatality rate[2]	Fatality rate per 10,000 vehicles	Fatality number	Fatality rate[2]	Fatality rate per 10,000 vehicles
United States	42,636	14.5	1.8	43,443	14.7	1.8
New Zealand	**435**	**10.7**	**1.5**	**405**	**9.9**	**1.3**
France	5,530	9.2	1.5	5,318	8.8	1.4
Canada	2,725	8.5	1.4	..	..	..
Australia	1,583	7.9	1.2	1,639	8.1	1.2
Germany	5,842	7.1	1.1	5,361	6.5	1.0
Japan	8,492	6.7	1.0	7,931	6.2	1.0
United Kingdom	3,368	5.6	1.0	3,336	5.5	1.0
Norway	259	5.7	0.9	224	4.9	0.8
Sweden	480	5.4	0.9	440	4.9	0.9

(1) Data is for countries that contribute data to the International Road Traffic and Accident Database and is the most recent available. (2) Per 100,000 people.

Symbol: .. figures not available

Source: Ministry of Transport

Otago Daily Times

New Zealand Fire Service trainer Dean Ligtenburg oversees the extraction of Randy, a fully-jointed dummy, from a tricky situation. Mr Ligtenburg was training members of the Queenstown and Frankton Fire Brigades in the skills needed to get crash victims out of cars as quickly as possible. Firefighters attended 3,055 rescues and medical emergency incidents in the year ending 30 June 2007.

Water accidents

Water Safety New Zealand is responsible for water safety education in New Zealand. Formed in 1949, Water Safety New Zealand represents the interests of 36 aquatic sports, recreational, and community organisations. It is funded by the New Zealand Lottery Grants Board and through sponsorship of specific programmes by organisations such as the Accident Compensation Corporation.

Water Safety New Zealand helps meet the water safety needs of the community through education, information and statistics, research and advice, and consultancy. The organisation also supports and funds educational activities by member organisations, such as Surf Life Saving New Zealand, the Coastguard Boating Education, the New Zealand Outdoor Instructors' Association, and the New Zealand Underwater Association.

Table 8.15

Drownings by activity type							
Year ending 31 December							
Activity type	2000	2001	2002	2003	2004	2005	2006
Recreational							
Land-based fishing	5	10	14	8	11	13	6
Non-powered boat	8	13	11	7	9	8	3
Powered boat	14	10	13	11	7	6	8
Sailing	2	1	2	1	1	2	0
Underwater	10	4	8	10	2	6	6
Swimming	10	9	13	18	14	12	13
Water sport/recreation	8	6	3	8	9	4	6
Subtotal	**57**	**53**	**64**	**63**	**53**	**51**	**42**
Non-recreational							
Accidental immersion	33	32	41	30	25	26	26
Flood/civil emergency	1	0	1	0	1	0	0
Rescuing others	4	2	5	1	3	2	1
Commercial fishing	4	3	1	1	5	3	0
Subtotal	**42**	**37**	**48**	**32**	**34**	**31**	**27**
Other							
Aircraft	0	0	0	0	1	0	2
Homicide	3	2	0	0	1	0	1
Other commercial	4	0	0	0	0	3	2
Road vehicle	10	15	12	18	17	19	6
Suicide	16	14	15	12	16	16	9
Subtotal	**33**	**31**	**27**	**30**	**35**	**38**	**20**
Total drownings	**132**	**121**	**139**	**125**	**122**	**120**	**89**
						Source: Water Safety New Zealand	

General accidents

External causes Accidents, poisoning and violence caused 6.0 percent of deaths from all causes in New Zealand in 2004 (the latest New Zealand Health Information Service statistics available), compared with 6.4 percent in 2003, 6.0 percent in 2002, and 5.9 percent in 2001.

Table 8.16

Deaths from external causes
Year ending 31 December

Cause	2002 Number	2002 Rate[1]	2003 Number	2003 Rate[1]	2004 Number	2004 Rate[1]
Transport accident	531	134.7	582	145.2	520	128.0
Intentional self-harm	466	118.2	517	128.9	488	120.1
Accidental fall[2]	304	77.1	337	84.0	354	87.1
Accidental drowning[3]	74	18.8	60	15.0	58	14.3
Accidental poisoning	42	10.7	46	11.5	49	12.1
Assault	69	17.5	56	14.0	47	11.6
Exposure to smoke, fire and flames	31	7.9	19	4.7	22	5.4
Firearm accident	2	0.5	7	1.7	2	0.5
Undetermined	30	7.6	32	8.0	30	7.4
Other external causes	147	37.3	147	36.7	140	34.5
Total	**1,696**	**430.2**	**1,803**	**449.7**	**1,710**	**420.9**

(1) Per million people. (2) Includes falls aboard ships and from horseback. (3) Includes drowning from water transport.

Source: New Zealand Health Information Service

Males accounted for 66.1 percent of deaths from external causes in 2004 (the latest New Zealand Health Information Service statistics available). Males aged 15–24 had the highest number of deaths for any age group, with transport accidents being the most common cause of death, followed by intentional self-harm.

Table 8.17

Deaths from external causes
By sex and age group
Year ending 31 December 2004

Age group (years)	Transport accident M	Transport accident F	Intentional self-harm M	Intentional self-harm F	Assault M	Assault F	Undetermined M	Undetermined F	Accidental fall M	Accidental fall F	Accidental drowning M	Accidental drowning F	Exposure to smoke, fire or flames M	Exposure to smoke, fire or flames F	Firearm accident M	Firearm accident F	Accidental poisoning M	Accidental poisoning F	Other external cause M	Other external cause F	Total M	Total F
0–14	16	10	4	2	4	5	0	1	1	1	7	6	3	2	1	1	1	0	13	11	50	39
15–24	107	48	83	30	6	0	4	4	12	0	8	2	1	0	6	3	0	0	5	0	232	87
25–34	50	23	76	19	5	4	2	1	8	1	9	0	2	0	7	1	1	0	13	0	173	49
35–44	58	15	84	20	7	1	3	1	10	0	8	2	2	0	10	6	0	0	15	4	197	49
45–54	42	16	48	17	6	3	3	4	9	1	4	0	1	0	4	4	0	0	8	5	125	50
55–64	41	18	40	12	3	0	2	1	9	7	4	1	0	2	1	2	0	0	7	7	107	50
65–74	23	11	17	6	1	0	1	2	22	14	3	2	1	2	0	0	0	0	9	10	77	47
75+	29	13	27	3	2	0	1	0	96	163	2	0	1	5	1	2	0	0	11	22	170	208
Total	**366**	**154**	**379**	**109**	**34**	**13**	**16**	**14**	**167**	**187**	**45**	**13**	**11**	**11**	**30**	**19**	**2**	**0**	**81**	**59**	**1,131**	**579**
Total in 2003	411	171	376	141	38	18	26	6	157	180	48	12	7	12	25	21	7	0	95	52	1,190	613

Source: New Zealand Health Information Service

Injury prevention

Injury prevention activities are guided by the *New Zealand Injury Prevention Strategy* (2003), which is led by the Accident Compensation Corporation (ACC). The strategy sets out a number of priority action areas for 2005–08. These include injury prevention strategies for motor vehicle crashes, suicide and deliberate self-harm, falls, workplace injuries, assault, and drowning and near drowning. The Ministry of Health and a number of other agencies fund injury prevention activities throughout New Zealand.

The Ministry of Health has been the lead agency for the suicide and deliberate self-harm priority area since July 2005. In July 2006, the Ministry of Health released the national all-age suicide prevention strategy, *New Zealand Suicide Prevention Strategy 2006–2016*. While the ministry leads and coordinates the strategy, the prevention of suicide requires input from other government and non-government agencies. The ministry's five-year plan, the *New Zealand Suicide Prevention Action Plan 2008–2012* (2008), translates the high-level goals of the strategy into specific actions.

The Ministry of Health also funds a number of public health-focused regional and national injury prevention programmes that contribute to other priorities under the *New Zealand Injury Prevention Strategy*. These programmes can include those that prevent intentional injuries, and those that prevent unintentional injuries.

Initiatives aimed at preventing unintentional injuries include falls prevention and child safety programmes, and community injury prevention programmes. Those initiatives for preventing intentional injuries include programmes to reduce physical, emotional and sexual violence in families, schools, communities, and marae, through education and by changing the social norms that tolerate violence. The ministry also runs the Violence Intervention Programme, under which health professionals routinely screen women aged over 16 for experience of family violence and provide support and referrals where necessary.

Accident insurance

Nearly 35 years ago New Zealand was the first country to introduce comprehensive 24-hour, no-fault personal accident insurance cover for people injured in accidents.

Legislation creating the accident compensation scheme took effect on 1 April 1974, replacing a statutory workers' compensation scheme, compulsory third-party motor vehicle accident insurance, and a criminal injuries compensation scheme. This scheme also removed the common law right to sue for damages, in return for support for all people injured, regardless of fault.

Essentially, the scheme covers all New Zealand residents, New Zealand residents temporarily overseas, and overseas visitors in New Zealand.

The scheme is managed by a statutory corporation, the Accident Compensation Corporation (ACC).

The scheme has been amended from time to time, mainly to keep its entitlements in line with social changes. The Injury Prevention, Rehabilitation and Compensation Act, which came into effect from 1 April 2002, reintroduced lump sum payments for injuries that resulted in permanent impairment, required ACC to develop a code of claimant rights, and made a number of changes to entitlements for injured people.

Accident Compensation Corporation

The Accident Compensation Corporation (ACC) is a Crown entity with a board of directors appointed by the Minister for the Accident Compensation Corporation. A service agreement between the board and the minister specifies ACC's desired outcomes and objectives, and acts as an accountability mechanism.

In the year ending 30 June 2007, ACC processed almost 1.8 million claims (an increase of 5 percent over the previous year) from injured people in New Zealand, and paid $2.4 billion in total claims costs. Through good care and high-quality programmes, injured people return to productive life as quickly as possible. In 2007, rehabilitation rates for new compensation claims were high – with 65 percent of injured people returning to productive life within three months, 83 percent within six months, and 92 percent within a year.

Services The main services ACC provides to injured people are:

- retrieval from accident scene – when ambulance or air transport is necessary
- physical rehabilitation – including cost of some public hospital and private hospital treatment; contribution to costs of the primary health-care provider (such as general practitioners) for consultation and treatment relating to minor injury; and some contribution to cost of travel for treatment
- compensation for loss of earnings – weekly payments of up to 80 percent of a claimant's pre-injury income for the period during which the claimant is unable to work as a result of the accident (abated compensation is available if the claimant is able to resume work on reduced earnings)
- vocational support – through the provision of retraining to enable claimants to return to their previous employment, or to take up alternative employment
- personal support – designed to make living with the results of an accident more comfortable (this can include payment of an independence allowance, modification of homes and vehicles for those with lasting incapacity, and a range of care services for those unable to manage the normal routine of daily life)
- lump sum compensation – a one-off payment to compensate for permanent impairment resulting from injury (this lump sum is paid in addition to any other entitlements or assistance a claimant may receive from ACC, with the payment amount dependent on the level of permanent impairment).

Funding ACC is funded by all New Zealanders, with the funding reserves policy moving in 1998 from a 'pay-as-you-go' basis to a 'fully-funded' basis. This change required ACC to set levies today, which will cover the full future cost of each claim, and to establish reserves to meet the full future entitlement of people injured in the past. This brought ACC into line with usual insurance practice, and means that each generation pays the cost of its own accidents, rather than passing the cost on to future generations.

ACC receives income from:

- earners – who pay levies based on their earnings, collected with PAYE (pay as you earn) tax
- motor vehicle owners and users – who pay a levy as part of their annual motor vehicle licence fee, and a petrol levy
- the government – on behalf of non-income earners
- employers and the self-employed
- investment earnings – on funds held to cover claims costs.

Costs Injury costs are assigned to one of six accounts:

- The work account meets the cost of all work-related injuries to employees and the self-employed. The account is funded from levies paid by employers based on industry risk, and earnings-related levies paid by self-employed people.
- The residual claims account covers the continuing cost of work-related injuries sustained before 1 July 1999, and non-work injuries to earners occurring before 1 July 1992 for all earners, including the self-employed. The account is funded by employers, and from levies on the self-employed.
- The earners' account covers the cost of non-work injuries (including injuries sustained at home, and during sport and recreation) occurring to all earners, including the self-employed, after 1 July 1992. The account is funded from earners' levies paid through PAYE and from earnings-related levies on the self-employed.
- The non-earners' account meets the cost of all injuries to people who are not in the paid workforce: students, beneficiaries, older people and children. This account is funded by contributions from government.
- The motor vehicle account covers the costs of all personal injuries involving motor vehicles on public roads. It is funded from petrol excise duty and a levy collected with the motor vehicle relicensing fee.
- The treatment injury account meets the cost of treatment injuries from medical or surgical procedures. The account is funded from the earners' or non-earners' accounts, depending on the earning status of the injured person.

In the year ending 30 June 2007, ACC's income from levies and investments was $4.1 billion, and total expenditure including movement in claims liability was $3.8 billion.

Table 8.18

	ACC claims registered					
	By ACC account					
	Year ending 30 June					
Account	2002	2003	2004	2005	2006	2007
Non-earners	723,108	725,476	717,896	734,046	781,414	817,198
Earners	458,864	497,808	529,645	529,631	561,866	612,094
Employers/other insurer	158,103	165,404	167,388	169,978	169,024	167,222
Self-employed work	49,153	48,306	45,086	44,678	42,374	39,162
Motor vehicle	34,896	36,704	39,561	40,941	43,083	44,130
Medical misadventure	663	690	823	893	2,563	3,964
Residual claims	853	609	1,592	946	1,229	2,225
Total	**1,425,640**	**1,474,997**	**1,501,991**	**1,521,113**	**1,601,553**	**1,685,995**

Source: Accident Compensation Corporation

Emergency management

Ministry of Civil Defence and Emergency Management

The Ministry of Civil Defence and Emergency Management Te Rākau Whakamarumaru leads the way in making New Zealand and its communities resilient to hazards and disasters. The overarching strategy for achieving this is through a risk-management approach to the four 'Rs' – reduction, readiness, response and recovery.

This approach starts with recognising hazards, and the vulnerability of communities and infrastructure to those hazards. By addressing the possible effects of these hazards, the focus can move to measures for reducing risks and managing the potential impact.

The ministry aims to put the right tools, knowledge and skills in the hands of those responsible for designing and implementing solutions at the local level. It does this by working closely with local government, utilities, and emergency services involved in civil defence emergency management.

The New Zealand Herald

The control room of the Western Bay of Plenty Civil Defence headquarters in Tauranga during a civil defence exercise that simulated a tsunami in the Pacific, generated by an earthquake near Chile.

Fire protection

Fire protection involves fire safety and operational firefighting. These services are managed nationally by the New Zealand Fire Service on behalf of the New Zealand Fire Service Commission. The primary emphasis on fire safety is determined by legislation in the Fire Service Act 1975.

New Zealand Fire Service Commission The commission is responsible for ensuring statutory requirements set out in the Fire Service Act 1975 are met. The commission consists of five members appointed by the government, and is the national purchasing and policy-setting agency. Established under the Forest and Rural Fires Act 1977 as the National Rural Fire Authority, the commission is today responsible for coordinating 112 rural fire authorities operating in areas outside the designated fire districts (in which operational firefighting is provided by the New Zealand Fire Service).

The net cost of funding the commission, after allowing for miscellaneous income, is met by a levy on insured property collected by the insurance industry. For the year ending 30 June 2006, the levy total was $254.28 million, compared with $249.04 million in the year ending 30 June 2005.

New Zealand Fire Service The service aims to reduce the incidence and consequence of fires. It has an operating structure designed to deliver decision-making, response and resources to frontline operations. Senior managers are specifically responsible for fire safety, and enhancement of fire safety technology. Eight fire regions are responsible for fire safety programmes, fire fighting resources, and the training and operational efficiency of brigades within their fire districts.

Table 8.19

Incidents attended by fire brigades Year ending 30 June					
	2003	2004	2005	2006	2007
Fires					
Structure fire	6,880	6,591	6,486	6,110	6,269
Mobile property fire	3,218	3,152	3,295	3,492	3,485
Vegetation fire	4,771	4,359	4,198	4,874	5,545
Chemical, flammable liquid or gas fire	79	132	139	121	125
Miscellaneous fire	7,870	7,796	7,731	8,950	10,076
All fires	**22,818**	**22,030**	**21,849**	**23,547**	**25,500**
Fatalities from fires	41	43	24	28	32
Hazardous emergencies	2,541	2,928	2,816	2,961	3,336
Incidents relating to mobile property/accidents	5,975	5,396	5,823	5,909	6,636
Rescues and medical emergencies	1,100	3,029	2,773	3,092	3,055
Assist other emergency services	3,607	2,863	3,802	3,715	3,876
Other incidents	2,324	2,805	2,299	2,606	2,621
Natural disasters					
Flood	523	1,172	1,347	745	698
Wind-storm, tornado, cyclone, etc	46	759	482	457	412
Other natural hazard emergencies	6	68	29	22	38
False alarms					
Good intent calls	6,637	4,744	4,678	4,738	6,368
False alarm	19,383	21,289	20,246	19,945	20,535
All incident types	**64,960**	**67,083**	**66,144**	**67,737**	**73,075**

Source: New Zealand Fire Service

Work-related injuries

Injury is the leading cause of premature death and disability in New Zealand. Collecting and analysing injury data from different agencies, including the Accident Compensation Corporation (ACC) and the Ministry of Health, is a key role for Statistics New Zealand in its government-appointed role as injury information manager.

Injuries that occur in the workplace have been analysed by Statistics New Zealand since 2001. The latest results, derived from ACC data, revealed that 235,200 claims for work-related injury and disease were made in 2006. These claims were made by 216,900 workers, and show an incidence rate of around 126 claims per 1,000 full-time equivalent workers (FTEs). Approximately, three-quarters of claims were lodged by males.

The 2006 figures indicate the continued domination of three industry groups: agriculture, forestry and fishing; manufacturing; and construction, which together accounted for approximately 40 percent of all claims, with respective injury rates of 177, 165 and 152 per 1,000 FTEs. The majority of claims requiring rehabilitation or compensation payments, and more than half of the 81 claims for fatalities, were lodged for injuries that occurred in these industries. These three industries are associated with physically demanding work.

Source: Statistics New Zealand

Otago Daily Times

Firefighter Wayne Hamilton demonstrates the effect of pouring a cup of water on a fat fire in the New Zealand Fire Service's portable kitchen. The cooking mishap, which finished with a great ball of fire, was part of a demonstration in Dunedin's Octagon by the Fire Service. The portable kitchen is made of stainless steel and was developed in Christchurch by a team of firefighters.

Thirty of 348 fire districts are served mainly by career firefighters, with some stations being augmented by volunteers, while the remaining 318 districts are staffed by volunteers. Nationally in 2006, there were 1,665 career firefighters, compared with 1,621 in 2005 and 1,575 in 2004.

There were more than 7,500 volunteers and 3,000 volunteer rural firefighters in 2006, numbers similar to the previous year. There were 507 support staff in 2006 (including those at communications centres in Auckland, Wellington and Christchurch).

The New Zealand Fire Service has the responsibility of fighting fires in all urban fire districts and, without compromising its ability to fight fires, it can also respond to other emergencies at which its fire fighting resources can be used.

Occupational safety and health

Primary responsibility for the provision of occupational safety and health policy advice and services rests with the Department of Labour.

Maritime New Zealand and the Civil Aviation Authority have designated responsibility for administration and enforcement of legislation in their respective sectors, while the commercial vehicle investigation unit of the New Zealand Police undertakes investigation and enforcement of work-related incidents on public roads. The Accident Compensation Corporation (ACC) also plays a major role in workplace injury prevention.

The principal legislation is the Health and Safety in Employment Act 1992, the object of which is to promote prevention of harm in the workplace.

To achieve this, the Act:

- defines hazards and places of work
- promotes excellence in health and safety management
- imposes enforceable duties on those responsible for work, and those who do the work
- provides for making regulations and codes of practice for dealing with particular hazards or types of work
- encourages employee participation and a cooperative approach to workplace health and safety between employers and employees.

The Act sets out the responsibilities of employers, employees, contractors, and others who exercise control over places of work. It provides for detailed guidance material to be created by either mandatory regulations, or by codes of practice approved by the Minister of Labour, after consultation with industry.

Table 8.20

Fatal accidents investigated by the Occupational Safety and Health Service
By industry
Year ending 30 June

Industry	2000	2001[1]	2002[1]	2003[1]	2004[1]	2005	2006
Agriculture and hunting	17	17	25	22	15	24	17
Forestry and logging	4	7	2	7	9	1	7
Construction	17	8	12	14	6	5	14
Other[2]	18	7	34	30	32	17	27
Total	**57**	**39**	**73**	**73**	**62**	**47**	**65**

(1) Includes bystanders killed as a result of workplace accidents – 2001 (0), 2002 (5), 2003 (16) and 2004 (8). (2) Includes fatalities in extractive industries, such as mining – 2001 (2), 2002 (5), 2003 (1), 2004 (1), 2005 (1) and 2006 (1).

Source: Department of Labour

Approved codes are not mandatory, but outline an acceptable regulatory standard of workplace health and safety practice for the particular area covered. Other subject-specific best-practice guidelines are also developed by the Department of Labour, in conjunction with industry.

The Department of Labour focuses on supporting safe and healthy workplace practices and reducing work-related illness, injury and deaths through:

- working with other government agencies in promoting and supporting health and safety in the workplace
- providing information and advice to help workplaces self-manage health and safety
- identifying changes and risks in workplaces through environmental scoping
- promoting research and influencing society's attitudes towards workplace health and safety
- investigating workplace accidents and complaints and enforcing health and safety legislation.

The department also inspects workplaces for compliance with the law, and regulates agents who certify safety-critical equipment. The department investigates all workplace fatalities.

As the designated enforcement agency for workplaces under the Hazardous Substances and New Organisms Act 1996, the department works closely with emergency services, local authorities and defence forces in the area of explosives and dangerous goods, and work-related hazardous substances.

The department has 20 regional offices delivering services to workplaces, and had a total of 155 health and safety inspectors and occupational medicine specialists for the year ending June 2007.

During 2006/07, the department completed 3,778 forums and information visits, and 5,144 workplace assessments. A total of 9,746 health and safety complaints, incidents or fatalities were notified, with 4,761 investigations being opened in response.

In 2006/07 investigations led to the start of 97 prosecutions, and 80 convictions (some of which followed prosecutions begun in previous years). This compares with 80 prosecutions and 79 convictions in 2005/06, and 110 prosecutions and 119 convictions in 2004/05.

Revenue is gathered through a levy on employers and self-employed people, collected alongside ACC levies. For 2006/07, the Health and Safety in Employment Levy was 5 cents per $100 of wages paid. The Government's budgeted Crown funding to administer the Act for the 2006/07 year was $32.185 million.

Contributors and related websites

Accident Compensation Corporation – www.acc.co.nz

Dental Council of New Zealand – www.dentalcouncil.org.nz

Department of Labour – www.dol.govt.nz

Health and Disability Commissioner – www.hdc.org.nz

Health Research Council of New Zealand – www.hrc.govt.nz

Health Sponsorship Council – www.hsc.org.nz

Malaghan Institute of Medical Research – www.malaghan.org.nz

Medical Council of New Zealand – www.mcnz.org.nz

Medical Laboratory Science Board – www.mlsboard.org.nz

Medical Radiation Technologists Board – www.mrtboard.org.nz

Midwifery Council of New Zealand – www.midwiferycouncil.org.nz

Ministry of Civil Defence and Emergency Management – www.civildefence.govt.nz

Ministry of Health – www.moh.govt.nz

Ministry of Justice – www.justice.govt.nz

Ministry of Transport – www.transport.govt.nz

New Zealand Fire Service Commission – www.fire.org.nz

New Zealand Food Safety Authority – www.nzfsa.govt.nz

New Zealand Health Information Service – www.nzhis.govt.nz

New Zealand Psychologists Board – www.psychologistsboard.org.nz

Nursing Council of New Zealand – www.nursingcouncil.org.nz

Occupational Therapy Board of New Zealand – www.otboard.org.nz

Osteopathic Council of New Zealand – www.osteopathiccouncil.org.nz

PHARMAC – www.pharmac.govt.nz

Pharmacy Council of New Zealand – www.pharmacycouncil.org.nz

Physiotherapy Board of New Zealand – www.physioboard.org.nz

Registration Boards Secretariat Ltd – www.regboards.co.nz

Statistics New Zealand – www.stats.govt.nz

Water Safety New Zealand – www.watersafety.org.nz

Workplace Health and Safety – www.osh.govt.nz

the moment of our birth...Cycle, recycle, send it round and round. Purify the water clean th...

Tiakina te taiao

ENVIROSCHOOLS

Pukehou School

Students at Pukehou School in Hawke's Bay in front of the environment wall they painted, and holding the flag presented to the school when it became one of five green-gold enviroschools in 2006. New Zealand had 533 enviroschools in 2007.

9 | Education

Curriculum

The New Zealand Curriculum is a statement of official policy relating to teaching and learning in English-medium New Zealand schools. It sets the direction for student learning and provides guidance for schools as they design and review their curriculum. A parallel statement, Te Marautanga o Aotearoa, was launched in 2008 and serves the same function for Māori-medium schools.

The curriculum includes a set of principles that guide what is important and desirable in teaching and learning. These principles underpin all school decision making, put students at the centre of teaching and learning, and affirm New Zealand's unique identity. They are:

- high expectations
- learning to learn
- Treaty of Waitangi
- cultural diversity
- inclusion
- community engagement
- coherence
- future focus.

The curriculum also includes a set of values that students will be encouraged to follow. These include: excellence, innovation, inquiry and curiosity, diversity, equity, community and participation, ecological sustainability, integrity and respect.

The curriculum specifies eight learning areas: English, the arts, health and physical education, learning languages, mathematics and statistics, science, social sciences and technology.

The New Zealand Curriculum provides the framework and a common direction for all schools. It gives schools the scope, flexibility and authority they need to design and shape their own curriculum so that teaching and learning is meaningful and beneficial to their particular communities of students. The design of each school's curriculum then allows teachers to set a classroom curriculum that responds to the particular needs, interests and talents of individuals and groups of students in their classes.

National Qualifications Framework

The National Qualifications Framework (NQF) brings qualifications for senior secondary education, industry training and tertiary education into one system.

Coordinated and administered by the New Zealand Qualifications Authority (NZQA), the NQF is based on nationally-agreed unit standards, achievement standards and national qualifications. Each standard belongs to one of 10 framework levels, has a credit value associated with it, and may be used to meet the requirements of registered national qualifications.

National certificates awarded at levels 1–7 include the senior secondary education qualifications, the National Certificate of Educational Achievement (NCEA) at levels 1–3.

National diplomas are awarded at levels 5–7. There is provision for the award of national graduate diplomas and certificates at levels 6 and 7; national bachelor's degrees at level 7; national postgraduate diplomas and certificates, and national bachelor's degrees with honours, at level 8; national master's degrees at level 9; and doctorates at level 10. However, at December 2006, only national certificates, national diplomas and a national postgraduate certificate had been registered on the NQF.

The NQF enables students to continue their studies and trade training wherever they wish – at school, university, polytechnic, private or government training establishment, wānanga, or in the workplace. Each student receives a record of achievement – a personalised list of credits achieved. NZQA updates the learner's record of achievement when results are received from accredited organisations.

National certificates and national diplomas are developed by industry training organisations or other approved standard-setting bodies. Training for these qualifications occurs on the job, off the job, or in a mixture of these, depending on the qualification.

The Dominion Post

Wellington student John Stewart (16 years) has a thoughtful response to receiving his NCEA results in January 2008. Secondary students' qualifications include NCEA at levels 1–3.

National certificates (and in a few cases national diplomas) have replaced trade certificates and advanced trade certificates in nearly every industry.

In the year ending 30 June 2007, a total of 162,582 NQF qualifications were awarded.

National Certificate of Educational Achievement

The National Certificate of Educational Achievement (NCEA) is designed to acknowledge achievement across a range of learning fields, particularly those identified in the New Zealand Curriculum. It also acts as a learning goal; and attests to a student's ability to participate in and benefit from further study, thereby promoting lifelong learning.

NCEA allows recognition of a broad range of student achievement, such as performance ability, research measurement and laboratory skills.

Success in NCEA is assessed against nationally-agreed standards of achievement. These standards have been developed in line with both English and Māori language curriculums to ensure equity of access to the qualification.

NCEA shows differences between 'achieving the standard', 'achieving the standard with merit' and 'achieving the standard with excellence'. Candidates working towards NCEA are also able to work towards other national certificates and qualifications.

NCEA Level 1 holders have typically shown themselves able to work at directed activities, with limited responsibility for decisions about the organisation of their work. The qualification is available mainly to year 11 school students. It is awarded to those credited with a minimum of 80 credits at level 1 or above who have met literacy and numeracy requirements – a minimum of eight credits from specified literacy subfields and/or listed standards, and a minimum of eight credits from specified numeracy subfields and/or domains.

NCEA Level 2 is designed to help access the foundation skills required for employment. At level 2, students have typically shown themselves able to integrate knowledge and skills to solve familiar problems; find and use available sources of information; and work in directed activity. The qualification also provides a base for further study and knowledge. This qualification is mainly available to year 12 school students. It is awarded to those credited with at least 80 credits, of which a minimum of 60 credits are at level 2 or above, from achievement standards and/or unit standards anywhere on the National Qualifications Framework.

NCEA Level 3 is designed to enable access to the skills required for employment. Students certificated at level 3 have typically shown themselves able to integrate knowledge and skills to solve unfamiliar problems; access, analyse and use available sources of information; and work independently in undirected activity. The qualification also provides a more advanced foundation for further study and knowledge. Level 3 is available mainly to year 13 school students. It is awarded to those credited with at least 80 credits at level 2 or above, of which a minimum of 60 credits are at level 3 or above, from achievement standards and/or unit standards anywhere on the National Qualifications Framework (NQF).

New Zealand Scholarship is an award, not a qualification, that extends the best secondary school students and enables top scholars to be identified and acknowledged. New Zealand Scholarship candidates are expected to have completed a full year of study of courses at level 3 of the NQF. New Zealand Scholarship holders will have demonstrated high-level critical thinking, abstraction and generalisation, and an ability to integrate, synthesise and apply knowledge, skills, understanding and ideas to complex situations. Depending on the subject, students will also have displayed effective communication, original or sophisticated solutions, performances or approaches, critical evaluation, and flexible thinking in unfamiliar or unexpected situations. Substantial monetary awards are made for individual performances of a high level in each subject, overall high performance in three scholarship subjects, and outstanding performance in at least two scholarship subjects. Students who receive the Premier Award are identified from those students who demonstrate outstanding performance in at least three scholarship subjects.

Administration of education

Ministry of Education

The Ministry of Education Te Tāhuhu o te Mātauranga is responsible for advising government on matters relating to early childhood education, compulsory schooling, tertiary education and training, and for implementing government education policy.

The Ministry of Education is committed to building and supporting a world-leading education system that equips all New Zealanders with the knowledge, skills and values to be successful citizens in the 21st century. Its focus is on:

- increasing participation in high quality early childhood education
- building strong early foundations in primary schooling with an emphasis on literacy and numeracy, in particular for Māori and Pasifika students and students with special education needs

- increasing presence and engagement in secondary schooling and ensuring that more school leavers have meaningful qualifications
- ensuring tertiary education is high quality and relevant, and that research supports the realisation of New Zealanders' goals and national social development.

The ministry has around 3,350 employees located in 51 sites. The secretary of education and six deputy secretaries are based in the national office in Wellington. Deputy secretaries are responsible for: strategy and performance, people and business capability, schooling, early childhood and regional education, special education, and Māori.

Special education The Education Act 1989 states that all children from five years of age are able to attend their local school full time (when school is open) until the end of the year in which they turn 19. Students with a section 9 agreement can stay at school to the end of the year they turn 21.

The government's five-year action plan, *Better Outcomes for Children*, aims to improve outcomes for all students with special educational needs. This involves being at early childhood and school education facilities, and participating in learning that helps them achieve.

Students with special education needs include children and young people with disabilities, learning difficulties, communication or behavioural difficulties, and sensory or physical impairment.

Best practice encourages schools and early childhood centres to work closely with students, their families, whānau, communities and specialists to identify needs and make the best decisions to meet these needs.

Future needs A key planning role for the Ministry of Education is assessing the need for new schools and classrooms. The primary school (5–12-year-olds) roll peaked at 487,000 in 2003 and has been declining since then. The decline was expected to stop in 2008, with growth to follow. The secondary school (13–17-year-olds) roll is growing and in 2007 there were 1,636 more full-time equivalent students than in 2006. While these are national figures, there are significant local variations, with some areas in heavy decline and others sustaining long-term growth (Auckland in particular). Ten new schools are opening in 2008 and 2009, in response to demographic changes and roll growth. An additional 200 classrooms are planned to meet increased school rolls. Eleven new school sites will be purchased, and existing school sites extended to cater for future roll growth.

Education Review Office

The Education Review Office Te Tari Arotake Mātauranga (ERO) is a government department that reports publicly on the quality of education and the care of students in schools and early childhood services. ERO findings help parents, educators, managers and others make decisions and choices.

ERO's chief review officer accredits review officers to carry out reviews. There are approximately 150 review officers in nine local offices, a national evaluation unit that reviews kura and kōhanga reo (Māori-medium education), and a Pacific evaluation unit.

In an education review, ERO investigates and reports to boards of trustees, early childhood service managers and the government on the quality of education provided for students in individual services and schools.

School and early childhood service reviews are scheduled, on average, once every three years. The review schedule is based on previous performance and current risk analysis – reviews are more frequent in cases such as low quality performance, or where there are major risks to students and their safety. ERO's reports on individual schools and services are available to the public. They can be obtained from the individual school or service, from any ERO office, or from the ERO website.

ERO also publishes national reports that evaluate specific educational issues, using information from its reviews. National reports cover areas such as curriculum, assessment, principals and teachers, early childhood education, management, school types, cluster reports, and good practice.

New Zealand Qualifications Authority

The overall role of the New Zealand Qualifications Authority Mana Tohu Mātauranga o Aotearoa (NZQA) is to be the independent expert organisation that administers robust National Qualifications Framework (NQF) assessment systems, and provides reliable quality assurance systems – in accordance with its statutory accountabilities.

This allows New Zealand qualifications to be accepted as credible and robust, nationally and internationally.

NZQA's main functions are to:

- develop and maintain a comprehensive, flexible and accessible NQF
- oversee the setting of standards for qualifications
- ensure that assessment procedures adopted by accredited providers are fair, consistent, and in keeping with the required standard

- ensure New Zealand qualifications are recognised overseas and overseas qualifications are recognised in New Zealand

- administer national secondary school examinations.

NZQA is one of six government agencies that work together to achieve educational outcomes in New Zealand. The Ministry of Education monitors NZQA's performance as a Crown entity.

New Zealand Teachers' Council

The New Zealand Teachers' Council Te Pouherenga Kaiako o Aotearoa is a Crown entity established under the Education Standards Act 2001. It maintains an online register of teachers who meet the requirements of the Act, are of good character, are fit to be teachers, are satisfactorily trained to teach, are satisfactory teachers in practice, and who hold a current practising certificate.

Teacher registration is compulsory for teachers employed as supervisors in early childhood centres and in private and state schools. Teachers are issued with a practising certificate valid for three years. There were 87,000 teachers with current practising certificates at 1 December 2007, compared with 85,000 in June 2005 and 67,000 two years earlier. Renewal of practising certificates depends on teachers demonstrating they remain satisfactory teachers. Teachers not meeting registration requirements can be employed temporarily, with a limited authority to teach.

Names of teachers who have their registrations cancelled, or have conditions placed on renewal of their practising certificates, are listed on the council's publicly accessible web register.

The council operates reciprocal registration with Australia under the Trans-Tasman Recognition Agreement, and maintains links with the General Teaching Council for Scotland and other teacher registration bodies overseas.

The council is primarily funded from practising certificate fees paid by teachers.

Other administrative bodies

Boards of trustees All state and state-integrated schools are governed by boards of trustees. Boards include three to seven parent representatives, the principal of the school and a staff representative. Parent representatives are elected by parents of students enrolled at the school. Where there are students enrolled full time in year 9 or above, a student representative must also be elected to the board. Boards may co-opt additional members to ensure, for instance, that there is a gender balance and that the board reflects the ethnic and socio-economic diversity of the student body of the school. The proprietors of state-integrated schools may appoint up to four representatives to their boards.

Boards of trustees work in partnership with their communities, principals, staff and the government to ensure the best possible educational outcomes for their students. In consultation with its community, each board develops a school charter, which communicates the vision and direction of the school, its goals for the long and short term, and its approach to meeting legal responsibilities. Boards are accountable for meeting objectives in their charter and for managing funds they receive from the government to run the school. They are required to present an annual report to their community and the Ministry of Education in April/May of each year.

Tertiary councils Under the Education Act 1989, tertiary institutions (universities, polytechnics and wānanga) are governed by councils. Council members represent business, industry, local authorities, universities, women's and ethnic groups, as well as other educational and community interests. The council of each university is the governing body.

New Zealand Register of Quality Assured Qualifications Te Āhurutanga provides a comprehensive list of all quality-assured qualifications (40 credits and over). It includes all qualifications on the National Qualifications Framework, as well as those developed by tertiary education organisations.

Key purposes of the register, administered by the New Zealand Qualifications Authority, are to:

- identify all quality-assured qualifications in New Zealand

- ensure that all qualifications have a purpose and relate to each other in a way students and the public can understand

- maintain and enhance learners' ability to transfer credits by establishing a common system of credit

- enhance and build on the international recognition of New Zealand qualifications.

Register requirements ensure consistency of description across all quality-assured qualifications, regardless of whether they are awarded by a school or university, are academic or vocational, or are a six-month or three-year qualification. The public face of the register is the website: www.kiwiquals.govt.nz.

Education and the non-profit sector

Hundreds of thousands of New Zealanders volunteer for or receive services from non-profit organisations. Within the education group such organisations include playgroups, private schools and private tertiary providers, and groups teaching English to speakers of other languages.

The *Non-profit Institutions Satellite Account: 2004*, released in 2007, provides a measure of the quantity and economic value of activities undertaken by non-profit organisations.

Education and research organisations provided 16 percent of the total non-profit institution contribution to New Zealand's gross domestic product (GDP). This is a small percentage when contrasted with other comparable countries, but is due mainly to the majority of New Zealand's education institutions being within the government sector. In 2004, the entire education sector contributed $5.65 billion to GDP, with non-profit education and research providing $495 million (9 percent).

Volunteering played a significant role for education groups, with 77 percent of institutions not employing paid staff in 2004. More than half the organisations in this group were in support roles such as parent teacher or home and school associations.

Education and research non-profit institutions also employ many people. Nearly half the early childhood education organisations had paid staff, while the top 10 primary and secondary schools employed more than 2,200 people.

Source: Statistics New Zealand

A selection of publications from Learning Media Ltd. The organisation is a major publisher of resources in te reo Māori and five Pasifika languages.

Learning Media Ltd

Learning Media Ltd Te Pou Taki Kōrero is a state-owned enterprise whose services and products contribute significantly to education in New Zealand and internationally.

Learning Media designs and delivers many of the educational resources the Ministry of Education provides to New Zealand teachers and students, as well as creating and implementing key professional development programmes. It is a major publisher of resources in te reo Māori and five Pasifika languages.

Learning Media also produces educational resources in a variety of media for other New Zealand public and private sector organisations. The company has built a significant global presence and exports to Canada, the United States, Australia, Europe and the Pacific.

Government funding

Table 9.01 shows that government spending on education from 1996/97 to 2005/06 increased steadily, both in dollar terms and generally as a proportion of government expenses. There was a small decrease in 2006/07.

Early childhood education

Early childhood education funding is payable to chartered early childhood service providers. To be chartered, a service must be licensed under the Education (Early Childhood Centres) Regulations 1998, or comply with the Education (Home-based Care) Order 1992.

Table 9.01

	Government expenditure on education				
	1996/97–2006/07				
Year	Education expenses[1]	Gross domestic product[2]	Education expenses as a percentage of GDP	Total government expenses[3]	Education expenses as a percentage of government expenses
	$(million)		%	$(million)	%
1996/97	4,817	99,034	4.9	31,708	15.2
1997/98	5,162	101,592	5.1	32,852	15.7
1998/99	5,337	104,689	5.1	34,367	15.5
1999/2000	5,712	111,025	5.1	34,536	16.5
2000/01	6,136	118,349	5.2	36,699	16.7
2001/02	6,473	125,795	5.1	37,970	17
2002/03	7,016	132,730	5.3	41,749	16.8
2003/04	7,585	142,746	5.3	41,608	18.2
2004/05	7,930	150,990	5.3	46,234	17.2
2005/06	9,914	156,325	6.3	50,238	19.7
2006/07	9,289	166,714	5.6	49,900	18.6

(1) Education expenses from 1997/98 exclude GST on Crown spending. Figures are from The Treasury. (2) The expenditure measure of GDP in current prices. (3) Total government expenses from 1997/98 exclude GST on Crown spending.

Sources: Ministry of Education, Statistics New Zealand, The Treasury

To receive government funding, a service must be open continuously for at least 2.5 hours a day. Each service can claim funding for up to six hours per child-place each day, to a maximum 30 hours per child-place a week.

The funding subsidy is not intended to cover the full cost of providing early childhood education. Parents are expected to contribute to the cost of services through fees, donations or fundraising activities.

The early childhood education funding system, introduced in April 2005, ensures the subsidy rates accurately reflect the costs of providing early childhood education. Funding rates for teacher-led, centre-based services depend on whether the service is all-day or sessional (all-day funding rates are higher because of higher staff-to-child ratio requirements), the proportion of registered teacher hours, and the age of children attending. Funding rates for teacher-led, home-based care and parent/whānau-led services depend on whether they meet the standard or quality requirements, and the age of the children attending.

Free ECE funding, introduced in July 2007, covers the average cost of providing the good standard of early childhood education required by regulations. This includes staff costs, equipment and resources, property and all other operating costs.

Other funding streams available to early childhood education services are:

- equity funding (available for chartered community-based early childhood services that meet criteria set out by the Ministry of Education)
- an annual top-up for isolated services (available to those generating $5,000 to $20,000 in funding subsidy and equity funding between 1 June and 31 May each year)
- incentive and support grants to help meet the costs of teachers becoming registered (available to teacher-led services)
- the Discretionary Grants Scheme ($16.239 million for 2007/08), an annual scheme designed to increase participation in early childhood education services by providing capital assistance to eligible community-based groups. Funding is allocated to projects that address participation through creating new or retaining existing places in licensed services
- establishment grants that contribute to certain operational costs associated with establishing a new licensed service, or services that are extending a building to increase their licensed child-places.

Compulsory schooling

Compulsory schooling is funded for state and state-integrated schools at levels adequate to ensure delivery of the curriculum to all students entitled to attend school. State and state-integrated schools receive funding from the Ministry of Education for operational funding, staffing entitlement, school property, and school transport assistance. Expenditure is controlled by each school's board of trustees, with the board's financial management audited by the Audit Office.

Private schools receive a government subsidy and charge student fees.

All schools are reviewed by the Education Review Office for their provision of education, management and governance.

Operational funding Operational funding levels vary according to school type, student numbers and year levels, and the school's property profile. State and state-integrated schools receive operational funding on an entitlement and a targeted basis. Many boards of trustees choose to supplement this resourcing with funds raised by the local community to provide for extra activities and staffing. Schools may also receive the following targeted funding entitlements:

- Māori language resourcing – funding depends on the level of Māori immersion in the programme
- for educational achievement – funds to address barriers to learning associated with socio-economic factors, based on the school's roll and the location of students' homes
- for isolation – to recognise the additional costs of accessing goods and services needed to operate an isolated school and to deliver the curriculum
- careers information grant – to provide school-based careers information for secondary students
- Secondary Tertiary Alignment Resource (STAR) – for senior programmes in area and secondary schools
- special education grant and learning support funding – to assist with support for students with moderate special education needs.

Supplementary funding is also available to support students with verified high and very high special education needs, and for students needing English for speakers of other languages programmes.

Staffing entitlement Schools receive a formula-driven entitlement to employ teachers. This provides schools with a measure of security and stability, enabling them to make long-term decisions about students' curriculum and pastoral care needs. Above this entitlement, additional staffing is provided in response to specifically identified needs. Teachers' salary funding is managed centrally and accessed through the Ministry of Education's education service payroll.

Students adopt waterways

Adopt a Stream coordinator Sally Smith and Albany students test the local water's oxygen content.

Auckland's Watercare Services Ltd (Watercare) runs Adopt a Stream, a free community education programme that encourages school students to learn about the water cycle, conduct water quality experiments, and assess the quality of local waterways.

In 2007 more than 5,900 students took part in the programme, which is aimed at students aged 10 to 14 years. The programme aligns with levels 2–4 of the science curriculum, with links to mathematics, English, social studies and technology.

Adopt a Stream is popular with students and teachers. They work with classroom materials to identify freshwater macro invertebrates (bugs), and carry out pH and nitrate testing and turbidity (water clarity) analysis. Some teachers extend the programme to include planting programmes, creative writing and art projects with a water theme.

Watercare's programme coordinator Sally Smith says the students are very engaged through the Adopt a Stream programme. "They learn about their local waterways and gain an awareness of water-related environmental issues. Students get hands-on, practical science experience which not only integrates with the curriculum, but applies directly to their local environment and illustrates how water quality and ecology directly affect their lives."

For more information, visit www.watercare.co.nz.

Watercare is the bulk water and wastewater service provider for the greater Auckland area. It is jointly-owned by the city and district councils of Auckland, Manukau, Waitakere, North Shore, Papakura and Rodney.

Source: Watercare

Children from Te One School on the Chatham Islands wave from their school bus as it heads towards Owenga to drop them home. Around 100,000 students in New Zealand use a school bus each day.

School property New Zealand's state school property portfolio consists of about 2,300 schools and 938 houses. There are also more than 300 state-integrated schools. Although part of the state network, these schools are not owned by the Ministry of Education, but by individual proprietors, mainly representing the Catholic church. Proprietors may charge attendance fees to finance capital work, whereas this is the responsibility of the Ministry of Education for full state schools.

Of the full state school portfolio, 70 percent of schools are in urban areas and 30 percent in rural areas. There are nearly 21,000 individual buildings, of which 90 percent were constructed after 1950. Replacement value of the portfolio, excluding state-integrated schools, is $11.5 billion. Managing state school property is a shared responsibility between the ministry and each school's board of trustees.

The ministry represents the owner, provides advice to both schools and the government on property management policies, and allocates capital funding to schools for property-related works. The ministry also maintains a database of all land and buildings, arranges insurance, town-planning designations, building warrants of fitness, the sale of surplus property, and administers housing for some teachers and caretakers.

Boards of trustees for both state and integrated schools manage the daily needs of schools. This involves ensuring all building, health and safety laws are met, as well as planning and implementing property-related works to maintain and improve the teaching and learning environment. Boards of trustees own approximately 1,100 houses.

School transport Students who travel long distances to school in areas where there is no public transport may be entitled to use a government-subsidised school bus, or get financial help for transport. Around 100,000 students use school buses each day. Another 5,000 students receive transport allowances because they cannot use a school bus or need to travel long distances to do so.

Bus operators are contracted to the Ministry of Education and to schools. Approximately 1,600 school bus services carry students to and from school each day. Another 800 services transport some primary school students to technology classes at other schools during the day.

Special education students also receive transport assistance, usually in the form of taxis.

School boarding bursaries Boarding assistance is available to students who need to live away from home in order to receive their education. The annual value of a school boarding bursary is $2,725, paid to the school in equal amounts at the end of each term.

Tertiary education

Significant changes to the tertiary funding system were put in place in 2006/07, with most tertiary funding being determined through the Tertiary Education Commission's decisions on the level of investment in tertiary organisations' plans. The total funding available for allocation is capped.

Private training establishments (PTEs) In 2007 the Government provided $121 million in student component funding to 204 private providers, to subsidise tertiary tuition costs for more than 19,700 full-time equivalent students. The role of PTEs is to provide education that complements public providers.

StudyLink

StudyLink, a service of the Ministry of Social Development, connects people with information they need to make informed decisions about student finances and other study-related issues. It also supplies financial support to students. StudyLink provides services to over 200,000 people.

Along with financial assistance in the form of student allowance, student loans, scholarships and extra help with costs, StudyLink offers StudyWise consultations to loan borrowers. These consultations help students make wise study choices and ensure they consider all options for financing their studies.

Student allowance is a weekly payment that helps students with living costs while they study full time. It's money that doesn't need to be paid back. A student loan helps with study costs and needs to be paid back.

StudyLink also offers two scholarships, the Step Up and Bonded Merit scholarships, and offers advice on other scholarships available.

To ensure students' applications are managed quickly and efficiently StudyLink offers an online service for allowance and loan applicants. Students can also manage their own information online. Both services are accessed through the StudyLink website.

In addition, StudyLink offers advice and support for students about issues such as childcare costs, ongoing medical and disability costs, or being unable to find work during study breaks.

More information about student allowances, student loans, scholarships and the extra support that StudyLink offers is at www.studylink.govt.nz.

StudyLink also delivers presentations to senior students in around 95 percent of New Zealand secondary schools. These help to: support students make informed tertiary study decisions, illustrate the realities of being a student, identify ways for students to fund their study, explain what StudyLink does, and show the consequences of borrowing to pay for study.

StudyLink works closely with students, and in cooperation with education providers, student bodies and other agencies, to ensure students get the information they need and the financial support they are entitled to.

Table 9.02

Student allowance and accommodation benefit
By number of students and amount paid
Year ending December 2003–07

	2003	2004	2005	2006	2007
Number of students					
Student allowance	64,036	60,826	56,806	59,431	62,479
Accommodation benefit	50,446	48,143	43,644	45,068	45,976
Total students	64,053	60,958	56,811	59,459	62,505
Total payments ($million)					
Student allowance	350.6	341.1	318.0	341.4	357.7
Accommodation benefit	42.0	42.6	44.0	48.7	50.8
Average payments ($)					
Student allowance	5,474	5,608	5,597	5,744	5,724
Accommodation benefit	833	885	1,007	1,081	1,104

Source: Ministry of Social Development

Table 9.03

Student loans, repayments, administration fees
By number of students and amount paid
Year ending 31 December 2003–07

	2003	2004	2005	2006	2007
Number of students					
Fees	144,678	145,549	143,406	156,236	160,855
Course related costs	101,664	98,506	94,782	103,553	103,651
Living costs	79,373	77,507	73,668	80,921	87,175
Repayments and refunds	38,278	42,079	38,421	43,257	46,968
Administration fees	150,754	150,899	149,447	162,211	166,315
Total students	156,250	157,032	154,411	167,420	173,791
Total payments ($million)					
Fees	593.9	589.6	609.8	688.7	736.1
Course related costs	95.1	92.4	89.4	98.4	98.2
Living costs	297.7	293.0	282.5	311.3	337.5
Repayments and refunds	51.2	58.2	55.5	60.0	70.9
Administration charges	7.7	7.7	7.6	8.3	8.5
Average payments ($)					
Fees	4,105	4,051	4,253	4,408	4,576
Course related costs	936	938	943	950	948
Living costs	3,751	3,780	3,835	3,847	3,871

Source: Ministry of Social Development

StudyLink staff are located in 44 sites nationwide, with a central processing centre in Palmerston North, a contact centre in Lower Hutt, a national office in Wellington and outreach offices around New Zealand.

In 2007, StudyLink handled over 1 million calls, and managed applications for about 230,000 student loans, 90,000 student allowances, 12,000 unemployment benefit student hardship allowances, and 4,000 scholarship applications. It also paid out about $390 million in student allowances and $1.1 billion in student loans.

Rural Education Activities Programme

The Rural Education Activities Programme is a community-managed package of educational resources operating in 13 rural communities: the Far North, Eastern Bay of Plenty, Tairawhiti (East Coast), the Central Plateau, Central King Country, Ruapehu, Tararua (Southern Hawke's Bay), Wairarapa, Marlborough, Buller, Westland, Central Otago and Southland.

Each programme provides educational support and assistance across all education sectors, from early childhood, through primary and secondary education, to adult and community education.

Activities in the adult and community education sector include access to information about adult learning opportunities and assistance with meeting adult education needs identified by the community, as well as information and advice on community development, piloting new learning methods, and managing projects and programmes.

In January 2005, the Tertiary Education Commission took over Rural Education Activities Programme funding for adult and community education from the Ministry of Education. The ministry continues to fund the early childhood, primary and secondary sectors covered by the programme.

Māori education

By 2021, the Māori population will be 30 percent greater than the 2001 figure, and Māori will make up more than 16 percent of the total New Zealand population.

Most Māori students are in mainstream (English medium) education, although there is a steadily increasing number in kaupapa Māori (Māori medium) education – in early childhood, school and tertiary learning environments.

The government has a range of initiatives to improve Māori education outcomes. Ensuring Māori students participate and achieve to their full potential in the education system involves:

- building strong learning foundations for Māori in quality early childhood education
- supporting provision of Māori language learning options such as kōhanga reo, kura kaupapa Māori and bilingual education
- ensuring that Māori students can be successful in mainstream education
- developing strong partnerships between schools, students, parents, whānau (family), iwi (tribe) and community
- recognising the importance of whānau in supporting children's and young people's education.

In 2007, *Ka Hikitia – Managing for Success: The draft Māori Education Strategy 2008–2012* was released for consultation. In this context, 'ka hikitia' means stepping up the performance of the education system to ensure Māori students enjoy success.

The draft outlines plans to improve Māori education, drawing on research, and feedback from iwi partners and interested groups. There are four focus areas: early childhood education and the first school years, young people in learning, Māori language learning, and the ministry's leadership role. The final strategy document was due for release in 2008.

Māori Education Trust

The Māori Education Trust was set up in 1961 to encourage more Māori into tertiary education, and improve Māori educational achievement by providing financial assistance to Māori students.

The trust achieves this objective by administering and co-sponsoring scholarships for Māori attending secondary and tertiary (undergraduate and postgraduate) courses, both in New Zealand and overseas. Income for scholarships comes from two dairy farms, investment interest, and fee-based service contracts with other organisations, including the Ministry of Education.

Early childhood education

Early childhood education (ECE) is non-compulsory education and care provided for infants, toddlers and young children before they begin school. It is available to children under the age of six years. ECE is provided by education and care services, kindergartens, playcentres, home-based services, kōhanga reo (Māori medium) and Pasifika services.

All ECE services must be licensed and chartered, chartered (home-based services), or licence-exempt. Licensing ensures that minimum quality standards are maintained. A charter contains objectives and practices about the learning opportunities provided by the service.

Since 31 December 2007, teacher-led, centre-based early childhood services have needed at least 50 percent of their regulated staff to hold a recognised ECE qualification. Home-based care networks must have a coordinator who has a Diploma of Teaching (ECE) or equivalent qualification.

The main licence-exempt providers are playgroups, including groups with a focus on Māori immersion, Pasifika ECE services and general playgroups.

Participation in ECE is vital to ensuring young children get the best possible start in life. The Ministry of Education is working with a 10-year strategic plan – *Pathways to the Future: Ngā Huarahi Arataki*, released in 2002.

Figure 9.01 shows the percentage of children enrolled in each type of early childhood education.

Kindergartens are education and care centres run by a kindergarten association. All kindergarten teachers must be registered teachers and hold at least a Diploma of Teaching (ECE). Most kindergartens offer services to children aged between two-and-a-half and five years. Older children attend morning sessions five days a week, and younger children attend afternoon sessions three days a week. Some kindergartens offer all-day sessions and may take children under two years.

Each kindergarten is run by a committee of parents and community people. The committee reports to its kindergarten association. Kindergartens usually ask for a parent donation or fee. At 1 July 2007, there were 43,695 children enrolled in 618 licensed kindergartens.

Playcentres have parents, whānau and caregivers who directly support their children's early learning. Most playcentres are licensed and/or chartered services that offer learning through play for children from birth to school age. Each playcentre sets its own session times and children attend up to five sessions a week. People become members of a playcentre when they enrol their child. They are then involved in running the centre and taking part in the daily programme.

Each centre is linked to a regional association, which belongs to the New Zealand Playcentre Federation. Parents, whānau and caregivers are encouraged to work towards a playcentre qualification. Playcentres usually charge fees. At 1 July 2007, there were 14,664 enrolments in 466 licensed playcentres.

Kōhanga reo build children's and parents' knowledge of te reo Māori (language) and tikanga (culture), with whānau being closely involved in the child's learning and development. Children can be part of the kōhanga reo total immersion environment, where te reo is the only language used, from birth to six years of age.

Parents are responsible for managing and operating their kōhanga reo, within guidelines set by Te Kōhanga Reo National Trust Board, and are encouraged to take part in the daily programme. Kōhanga reo have a whānau contribution system, which may vary according to the needs of the whānau. This contribution can be koha – donations for food and/or paying fees. At 1 July 2007, there were 9,236 enrolments in 470 licensed kōhanga reo.

Parents as First Teachers (PAFT) is based on programmes developed in the United States. PAFT programmes provide regular home visits by early childhood educators to parents with children – from birth to three years. The programmes were built on the belief that parents are their children's most important teachers. By helping parents feel good about this role, they will become more confident, and participate more effectively in the development and education of their children. Core elements of the programme include individual support, through structured learning on child development, and the fostering of early learning.

Programmes are funded directly by the government, cover most regions of New Zealand, and involve around 8,000 families. A range of organisations are contracted to provide PAFT programmes.

Pasifika Early Childhood Education Services offer programmes based on the values and languages of Pasifika cultures. The services cover Samoan, Cook Islands Maori, Niuean, Tongan, Tokelauan, Tuvaluan and Fijian nationalities. Services include licence-exempt groups (playgroups) meeting once or twice a week, to licensed and chartered education and care centres meeting all day, five days a week. Programmes have high parental involvement and emphasise language development, both in Pacific languages and English, and increased parental knowledge about early childhood care and education.

Nearly all Pasifika Early Childhood Education Services are community owned and operated. At 1 September 2007, there were 96 licensed Pasifika education and care centres, mostly in the Auckland region.

Education and care services are licensed and/or chartered early childhood centres offering all-day or part-day services. Education and care services include crèche, workplace, and childcare centres that are run by either community or private owners. Some services are based on a specific culture, or around certain education beliefs or methods, such as the Montessori or Rudolph Steiner centres.

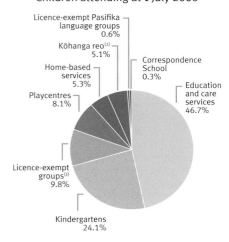

Figure 9.01

Early childhood education
Children attending at 1 July 2006

- Licence-exempt Pasifika language groups 0.6%
- Kōhanga reo(2) 5.1%
- Home-based services 5.3%
- Playcentres 8.1%
- Licence-exempt groups(1) 9.8%
- Kindergartens 24.1%
- Correspondence School 0.3%
- Education and care services 46.7%

(1) Includes unlicensed playcentres; excludes licence-exempt Pasifika language groups. (2) Licensed and developing.
Source: Ministry of Education

20 hours free

From July 2007, three and four-year-olds enrolled in a participating teacher-led early childhood education (ECE) service, or kōhanga reo with a suitably qualified teacher, can receive up to 20 hours free early childhood education (Free ECE). Some five-year olds with special educational needs can also receive Free ECE.

Teacher-led services are those required to have a qualified and registered early childhood teacher in charge, including kindergartens, crèches, day care and home-based services. Teacher-led services are eligible because they usually have higher costs than parent-led services.

There were more than 65,000 Free ECE enrolments at 1,703 services (62 percent of eligible providers) when Free ECE started on 1 July 2007. By January 2008, this had increased to 79,186 enrolments at 2,138 services. At 3 December 2007, 45 kōhanga reo had received Free ECE funding from the Ministry of Education, and another 30 indicated they had begun offering Free ECE.

Free ECE is not based on income or whether a parent works outside the home. Children can receive up to six hours of Free ECE a day, up to 20 hours per week. This can be with more than one service. Although no fees are charged for this time, donations may still be requested and services can charge for hours outside Free ECE. For any extra hours, parents may be eligible for Work and Income's childcare subsidy to help cover costs.

ECE services can also ask for an optional charge payment, to cover services they offer which are above regulation requirements – such as hot lunches, a visiting teacher or sunscreen. Parents can choose whether or not to purchase these optional extras.

The government is funding Free ECE because it believes that quality ECE builds a lifelong foundation for successful learning. Although New Zealand has had high ECE participation rates, three- and four-year-old children have attended for an average of only around 14 to 17 hours per week. By reducing the cost to families, Free ECE encourages parents to enrol their children or increase their time in early childhood education.

Statistics New Zealand estimates that the overall cost of ECE to parents fell 34 percent between the June and December 2007 quarters, following the introduction of Free ECE.

For the Government, Free ECE is "the most significant expansion of the education system since the rollout of free secondary education by the first Labour Government in the 1930s."

Source: Ministry of Education

Minister of Māori Affairs Parekura Horomia reads to four-year-old Ethan Walker at Pikipiko Clyde Quay Kindergarten in Wellington. Free ECE gave many three- and four-year-old children up to 20 hours free early childhood education from July 2007.

The Dominion Post

Teachers in charge must be registered teachers holding a Diploma of Teaching (ECE) or similar early childhood teaching qualification. At 1 July 2007, 60 percent of usual teaching staff at teacher-led services were qualified. Depending on the centre, children may be accepted from birth to school age. In most services, children need to be enrolled for a set period of time.

Education and care services usually charge fees. Parents, whānau or caregivers can be involved with management committees, or as voluntary helpers or fundraisers. At 1 July 2007, there were 91,733 enrolments in 1,932 licensed education and care services.

Home-based education and care services involve a caregiver providing education and care for small groups of young children in their home as part of a chartered home-based education and care network. Caregivers provide full-day or part-day education and care. They may also provide emergency care. A registered teacher (coordinator) from the network supports the caregiver's work and the child's learning programme. The coordinator also helps parents choose the right caregiver for their child and visits the home-based caregiver regularly to check on the child's safety, well-being and learning progress.

Home-based care services usually charge fees. At 1 July 2007, there were 11,073 children enrolled across 227 licensed home-based networks.

Playgroups are licence-exempt, community-based, non-profit services run by groups of parents who meet to provide early childhood education for their children. Funded community playgroups are exempt from licensing, but must meet criteria set by the Ministry of Education. Active parental participation is required at all sessions. Many licence-exempt groups work with Ministry of Education staff to develop the learning programmes they offer.

There were 18,058 children enrolled in 608 playgroups at 1 July 2007.

Compulsory education

Compulsory education in New Zealand is divided into primary, intermediate and secondary schooling.

Primary schools cater for children from the age of five (year 0) to the end of year 6. Children in years 7 and 8 may either go to a separate intermediate school, or to part of a primary, secondary or composite/area school. Secondary schools usually provide for students from year 9 until the end of year 13. Adult students who return to school enter in the year of the majority of their subjects. Composite/area schools, usually based in rural areas, combine primary, intermediate and secondary schooling at one location.

A child aged between five and six years, starting primary school for the first time between July (when the school roll is counted) and the end of that school year, is classed as year 0. Children who begin school for the first time between 1 January and before the July roll count, are classed as year 1. Children who start school for the first time after the age of six, are placed in the same year as other children of the same age.

Primary schools are required to be open for at least 394 half days each year and secondary schools for at least 380 half days. The New Zealand school year is divided into four terms of approximately even length.

Table 9.04 shows the level of highest achievement, the ethnicity and the sex of secondary school leavers in 2006.

Choices in schooling

While most students in New Zealand attend state-funded schools, parents or caregivers and students have the choice of a number of schooling options.

State schools are co-educational (both sexes) at primary and intermediate level, but some offer single-sex education at secondary level. Lessons are based on the New Zealand Curriculum. Some state schools offer special programmes for adult students, or run community education classes.

Integrated schools are those that used to be private but have become part of the state system. They teach the New Zealand Curriculum, but keep their own special character (usually a philosophical or religious belief) as part of their school programme. Integrated schools receive the same government funding for each student as state schools, but as their buildings and land are privately owned, they charge attendance fees to meet property costs.

Kura kaupapa Māori are state schools where teaching is in the Māori language (te reo Māori) and is based on Māori culture and values. The curriculum is the same as at other state schools. Kura kaupapa cater for students from years 1–8 or years 1–13. The schools build on kōhanga reo (Māori language early childhood education centres) learning. A key goal of kura kaupapa is to produce students who are equally skilled in both Māori and English.

Independent schools (or private schools) are governed by their own independent boards, but must meet certain standards in order to be registered. Independent schools may be either co-educational or single sex. They charge fees, but also receive government funding.

Boarding schools may either be independent or part of a state-funded school. All charge boarding fees.

The Correspondence School Te Kura ā Tuhi is a national state school funded by the Ministry of Education and administered by a board of trustees. The school has around 14,000 students on its roll at any one time. It provides early childhood, primary, secondary and special education programmes for full-time and part-time students across New Zealand and overseas.

Home-based schooling is available for parents and caregivers who want to educate their children at home. Parents and caregivers need approval from the Ministry of Education and must educate their children at least as regularly and as well as at a registered school. Home-based schooling

Table 9.04

Secondary school leavers in 2006
By level of highest attainment, ethnic identification, and sex

Highest attainment	European Male	European Female	Māori Male	Māori Female	Pasifika Male	Pasifika Female	Asian Male	Asian Female	Other Male	Other Female	Total Male	Total Female
NZ Scholarship award or NQF qualification at level 4 or higher	70	21	2	14	0	0	55	16	1	2	128	53
NCEA level 3 or other level 3 NQF qualification	5,320	7,822	571	872	245	442	1,230	1,470	187	208	7,553	10,814
Year 13: Cambridge International Exams, International Baccalaureate, Accelerated Christian Education, or other overseas awards	405	217	13	8	9	2	252	96	20	5	699	328
30+ credits at level 3 or above	1,743	1,614	407	516	298	432	361	298	62	76	2,871	2,936
NCEA level 2 or other level 2 NQF qualification	3,088	2,712	732	831	475	401	252	220	81	72	4,628	4,236
Year 12: Cambridge International Exams, International Baccalaureate, Accelerated Christian Education, or other overseas awards	50	42	5	1	1	0	17	11	0	0	73	54
30+ credits at level 2 or above	1,532	987	603	559	300	324	165	119	77	54	2,677	2,043
NCEA level 1 or other level 1 NQF qualification	1,400	1,053	450	470	116	104	57	63	23	20	2,046	1,710
40+ credits at any level including literacy & numeracy for NCEA level 1	680	497	311	368	103	112	35	13	19	16	1,148	1,006
40+ credits at any level without literacy & numeracy for NCEA level 1	838	485	390	292	199	140	65	31	27	20	1,519	968
Year 11: Cambridge International Exams, International Baccalaureate (prep year), Accelerated Christian Education, or other overseas awards	18	14	0	1		0	3	0	0	0	21	15
14–39 credits at any level including literacy & numeracy for NCEA level 1	151	100	91	103	19	21	18	3	4	5	283	232
14–39 credits at any level without literacy & numeracy for NCEA level 1	695	529	423	411	212	123	61	28	23	21	1,414	1,112
1–13 credits at any level	450	392	302	326	111	77	53	17	19	12	935	824
No formal attainment	1,271	964	837	889	209	168	86	75	38	32	2,441	2,128
Total	**17,711**	**17,449**	**5,137**	**5,661**	**2,297**	**2,346**	**2,710**	**2,460**	**581**	**543**	**28,436**	**28,459**
Number of students with university entrance included in total	5,531	7,562	511	758	198	360	1,514	1,492	196	198	7,950	10,370

Source: Ministry of Education

parents and caregivers are given an annual grant to help with the cost of learning materials and can choose to purchase teaching services from the Correspondence School. Home-schooled children account for approximately 1 percent of total New Zealand school enrolments.

Designated character schools are state schools that teach the New Zealand curriculum, but have been allowed to develop their own set of aims, purposes and objectives to reflect their particular values.

Special schools are state schools that provide education for students with special education needs. The curriculum is the same as at other state schools. New Zealand has eight residential special schools.

Assessment of students

Assessment information gathered about the progress and achievement of students is used to improve the quality of teaching programmes. Most information comes from ongoing classroom assessment.

Strengths and weaknesses identified as a result of assessment are shared with students and parents. Parents are also entitled to ask for meetings with teachers to talk about their child's progress.

Achievement by primary students across New Zealand is monitored by assessing around 3 percent of 8- and 12-year-olds each year. The National Education Monitoring Project covers all New Zealand curriculum learning areas on a four-year rolling cycle. At secondary school level, results from the National Certificate of Educational Achievement are used to provide national information about student achievement. A sample of New Zealand students also participates in international assessment studies to measure achievement levels against those of other OECD countries.

Tables 9.06 and 9.07 show results for students in NCEA level 3 and Scholarship in 2006.

Tertiary education

After finishing compulsory schooling, many New Zealanders continue their education at tertiary level. The tertiary sector encompasses adult and community education, industry training, foundation education (basic skills usually acquired at school), and study at tertiary institutions such as universities, polytechnics, wānanga (Māori tertiary institutions) and private training establishments. Ministry of Education figures for 2006 showed around 703,000 New Zealanders participating in formal tertiary education. This included 176,600 in industry training and

Table 9.05

Secondary school leavers in 2006
By year level, ethnicity and sex

Year level	European Male	European Female	Māori Male	Māori Female	Pasifika Male	Pasifika Female	Asian Male	Asian Female	Other Male	Other Female	Total Male	Total Female
Year 9	16	6	12	14	2	2	0	0	1	0	31	22
Year 10	303	137	172	171	33	24	11	6	7	3	526	341
Year 11	2,420	1,629	1,231	1,117	284	210	93	56	34	32	4,062	3,044
Year 12	4,496	3,705	1,534	1,698	509	415	299	246	99	75	6,937	6,139
Year 13	10,289	11,788	2,103	2,560	1,407	1,663	2,259	2,114	420	421	16,478	18,546
Year 14	139	144	70	66	45	23	42	33	14	10	310	276
Year 15	48	40	15	35	17	9	6	5	6	2	92	91
Total	**17,711**	**17,449**	**5,137**	**5,661**	**2,297**	**2,346**	**2,710**	**2,460**	**581**	**543**	**28,436**	**28,459**

Source: Ministry of Education

Table 9.06

NCEA level 3 results in 2006
By learning area

Learning area	All standards	Unit standards	Achievement standards	Achieved	Merit	Excellence
	Number of students			% of students		
Language and languages	101,599	15,466	86,133	52.32	30.33	17.35
English	84,602	14,796	69,806	56.32	29.99	13.69
Te reo Māori	4,006	507	3,499	50.13	27.04	22.84
Other languages	12,991	163	12,828	31.14	33.06	35.8
Mathematics	122,905	17,930	104,975	52.46	35.42	12.12
Science	92,579	12,043	80,536	56.65	26.58	16.77
Technology (eg design, generic computing)	41,681	32,717	8,964	54.35	28.68	16.97
Social sciences (eg geography, history, social studies)	88,883	20,090	68,793	55.26	30.11	14.63
Arts (eg practical art, drama performance)	34,745	2,384	32,361	43.93	32.43	23.64
Health & physical education	41,320	18,578	22,742	56.32	29.41	14.26
Specialist studies (eg hospitality, travel & tourism)	12,403	12,403	0	...	...	...

Symbol: ... not applicable

Source: NZQA

modern apprenticeship programmes, 28,600 in targeted training and 491,000 in other formal tertiary education.

The number in industry training was up 116 percent on those involved in 2000. Enrolments in targeted training programmes, which provide employment-related skills for people seeking work, fell 23 percent between 2000 and 2006 in response to falling unemployment. Other formal enrolments by domestic students rose more than 48 percent in the same period.

Qualifications gained are part of the 10-level New Zealand Register of Quality Assured Qualifications. The register provides a common basis for the level, name and size of qualifications. It helps students transfer between qualifications, enabling people to build their skills over a lifetime.

In December 2006, the Government released the *Tertiary Education Strategy 2007–12* and the *Statement of Tertiary Education Priorities 2008–10*. The strategy has a sharp focus on the expected contribution of the tertiary education system to the Government's national goals. It also describes how the tertiary education system is expected to contribute to lifelong learning – creating and applying knowledge to drive innovation, and connecting tertiary education organisations with the communities they serve.

The Statement of Tertiary Education Priorities 2008–10 articulates priorities for implementing the strategy, indicating areas in which the sector needs to make a focused effort. These are shown in the priority outcomes of:

- increasing educational success for young New Zealanders – more achieving qualifications at level 4 and above by age 25
- increasing literacy and numeracy levels for the workforce
- increasing the number achieving advanced trade, technical and professional qualifications, to meet regional and industry needs
- improving research connections and linkages to create economic opportunities.

The Tertiary Education Commission was established in January 2003 under the Education (Tertiary Reform) Amendment Act 2002. It is responsible for funding post-compulsory education and training offered by universities, polytechnics, colleges of education, wānanga, private training establishments, foundation education agencies, industry training organisations, and adult/community education providers. The Tertiary Education Commission invests, within the funding available, in a broad range of quality, relevant education and research that fits within tertiary education organisations' distinctive contributions.

Initiatives to improve the affordability of tertiary education and increase student access to tertiary education include the policy that limits increases to course fees. In addition, since 1 April 2006 student loans have been interest-free for borrowers living in New Zealand.

Table 9.07

New Zealand Scholarship results in 2006
By subject

Subject	Level 3 students taking subject	Percentage receiving Scholarship	Number achieving Scholarship	Outstanding Scholarship
Accounting	2,894	3.0	75	12
Art history	1,728	3.2	48	7
Biology	7,742	2.9	191	30
Chemistry	6,388	3.3	189	21
Chinese	164	13.4	20	2
Classical studies	4,915	3.2	142	16
Drama	1,491	3.0	38	6
Economics	4,355	3.1	119	17
English	12,852	3.0	346	38
French	748	3.6	25	2
Geography	5,961	3.0	151	29
German	380	5.5	19	2
Graphics	1,582	3.1	44	5
History	5,383	2.8	140	10
Japanese	814	3.6	25	4
Latin	23	17.4	3	1
Mathematics with calculus	6,981	3.1	197	21
Media studies	2,371	2.7	57	6
Music studies	875	3.2	25	3
Physical education	3,612	2.2	66	12
Physics	6,345	2.8	162	17
Science	699	3.2	20	2
Spanish	238	3.8	8	1
Statistics and modelling	12,533	3.0	325	49
Te reo Māori	428	3.7	14	2
Technology	920	2.1	14	5
Visual arts	5,585	3.0	148	18
Total	...	...	**2,611**	338

Symbol: ... not applicable

Source: NZQA

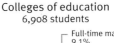
Figure 9.02

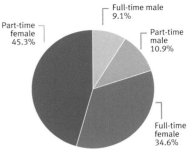
Tertiary attendance 2006
Colleges of education
6,908 students
- Full-time male 9.1%
- Part-time male 10.9%
- Full-time female 34.6%
- Part-time female 45.3%

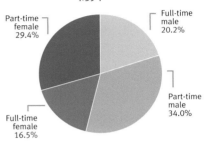
Polytechnics
214,394 students
- Full-time male 20.2%
- Part-time male 34.0%
- Full-time female 16.5%
- Part-time female 29.4%

Universities
165,571 students
- Full-time male 29.8%
- Part-time male 13.1%
- Full-time female 36.8%
- Part-time female 20.3%

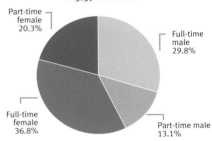
Wānanga
48,842 students
- Full-time male 10.8%
- Part-time male 20.1%
- Full-time female 23.1%
- Part-time female 46.0%

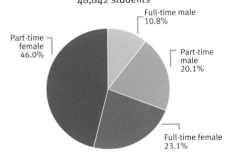
Private tertiary education
80,432 students
- Full-time male 21.8%
- Part-time male 16.9%
- Full-time female 28.1%
- Part-time female 33.3%

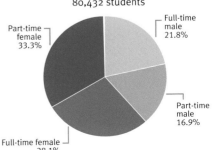

Note: Percentages may not total 100 due to rounding.
Source: Ministry of Education

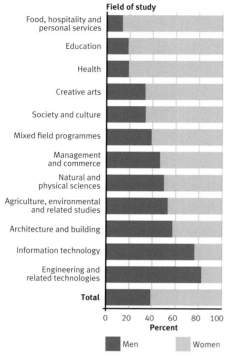

Figure 9.03

Sex ratio of bachelor's degrees[1]
By selected field of study
Completed in 2006

Men   Women

(1) Completed at public tertiary education institutions.

Source: Ministry of Education

There have been improvements in the way public tertiary education institutions collaborate and coordinate to offer more effective and diverse education services. These include mergers between tertiary education institutions, and the development of accords and working alliances between education institutions and industry bodies.

Universities

There are eight universities in New Zealand – Auckland University of Technology, Lincoln University, Massey University, Victoria University of Wellington, the University of Auckland, the University of Canterbury, the University of Otago and the University of Waikato.

Universities are controlled by their own councils, established under legislation that maximises their autonomy, consistent with normal requirements of accountability for public funding.

Each university sets its own academic programmes, which are subject to external quality assurance, and each university council sets dates for terms or semesters.

Councils, which represent the interests of staff, students and the community, set the strategy of the institution, employ the chief executive officer and oversee management of the university. Councils are also responsible for approving course regulations and for maintaining the equivalences of courses for degrees and other qualifications.

Over the 10 years to 2006, the universities absorbed the six colleges of education, which were responsible for training teachers.

Polytechnics

Polytechnics and institutes of technology provide a diverse range of academic, vocational and professional programmes, including trade training. They cover an increasing number of subjects at various levels of specialisation.

There are 20 polytechnics in New Zealand – Northland Polytechnic, UNITEC New Zealand, Manukau Institute of Technology, Waikato Polytechnic, Bay of Plenty Polytechnic, Waiariki Institute of Technology, Tairawhiti Polytechnic, Eastern Institute of Technology, Western Institute of Technology, Universal College of Learning, Whitireia Polytechnic, The Open Polytechnic of New Zealand, Wellington Institute of Technology, Nelson Marlborough Institute of Technology, Tai Poutini Polytechnic, Christchurch Polytechnic Institute of Technology, Aoraki Polytechnic, Otago Polytechnic, Telford Polytechnic and Southland Institute of Technology.

Wānanga

Wānanga (Māori tertiary institutions) provide tertiary education and training while helping students apply knowledge of ahuatanga Māori (Māori tradition), in accordance with tikanga Māori (Māori custom). Te Wānanga o Aotearoa in Te Awamutu, Te Wānanga o Awanuiarangi in Whakatane, and Te Wānanga o Raukawa in Otaki are governed in the same way as other tertiary institutions.

The Open Polytechnic of New Zealand

The Open Polytechnic of New Zealand He Wharekura-tini Kaihautu o Aotearoa is the country's only broad-based national polytechnic, and is the specialist tertiary institution in open and distance learning. In 2006, it had 570 equivalent full-time staff and 31,908 enrolled students. Nearly all students are part-time learners.

The Open Polytechnic is a major educator of adult learners and people in the workforce. A large proportion of students are in paid employment, studying in their own time to enhance job and career opportunities. The polytechnic's flexible service also ensures access to vocational learning for people otherwise unable to study due to distance, disability or personal circumstances.

The polytechnic works closely with many industry training organisations to enrol a large group of industry trainees. It also provides staff training and development services to organisations.

The Open Polytechnic is internationally recognised, and in 2004 received the Commonwealth of Learning's Award for Institutional Excellence in Distance Education. In New Zealand it received the Supreme Vero Award for Excellence in Business Support (2005) for its contribution to business education and training, and in 2007 won the Education Provider category in the same awards.

The polytechnic offers more than 1,300 courses and 150 programmes, from national certificate to diploma and degree level. It consults closely with industry and other interested groups to ensure qualifications are directly related to present and future workplace requirements. All degrees are approved by the New Zealand Qualifications Authority.

As well as supporting individual learners, the Open Polytechnic has led major collaborative projects contributing to e-learning development in New Zealand's tertiary education sector.

Canterbury University graduate Siatua Faletanoai-Evalu speaks after receiving his Pacific Achievers' award from the Prime Minister, Helen Clark in 2007. New Zealand has eight universities.

Private training establishments

Private training establishments (PTEs) provide post-school education and training, and are operated by a wide range of companies, trusts and other entities. The PTE sector is diverse – in size, location, ethnicity, culture and areas of education expertise. This enables flexibility and responsiveness.

At December 2007, there were 756 PTEs registered with the New Zealand Qualifications Authority (NZQA).

NZQA assures the quality of education services provided by PTEs. This is regardless of whether the PTE receives state funding, or students receive loans or allowances. Student fees are protected through the Student Fee Protection Policy.

Career Services

Career Services Rapuara assists all New Zealanders to maximise their potential by encouraging and supporting them to make informed career and learning decisions.

Career Services works with other government agencies and organisations advising them on incorporating career information into their work, based on research evidence and practical industry experience.

Career Services' consultants work with clients to identify skills, investigate career and training options, develop career plans, teach interview and job search techniques, and prepare CVs.

The Career Services website provides free, impartial and up-to-date information on jobs, industries, training, qualifications and the labour market. This resource is also supported by Pathfinder, a

Table 9.08

Enrolments at tertiary institutions
By field of study, level of study and sex
2006

Field of study	Post-graduate Female	Post-graduate Male	Bachelor's degree Female	Bachelor's degree Male	Diploma Female	Diploma Male	Certificate Female	Certificate Male	Total Female	Total Male
Management and commerce	3,713	3,983	20,607	18,395	11,790	7,802	43,035	20,295	75,861	48,605
Society and culture	4,892	2,890	22,469	12,588	9,236	4,025	29,534	14,777	63,837	33,161
Mixed field programmes	2,518	2,424	4,304	3,280	2,334	1,731	25,116	20,116	33,899	27,319
Engineering and related technologies	308	1,104	1,130	5,553	907	4,971	3,158	29,868	5,418	39,945
Agriculture, environmental and related studies	274	249	764	850	413	656	9,000	30,851	10,102	31,616
Education	2,188	621	10,750	2,242	8,522	2,081	5,115	3,326	26,025	8,157
Health	4,694	1,050	12,877	3,321	3,422	586	5,168	2,441	25,573	7,239
Information technology	123	372	727	2,872	998	2,914	12,211	6,435	13,883	12,109
Natural and physical sciences	1,679	1,571	8,215	8,511	381	306	968	428	11,098	10,695
Creative arts	526	389	7,015	3,727	3,385	2,317	3,141	1,819	13,835	8,074
Architecture and building	67	81	957	1,373	677	1,963	1,382	10,012	3,050	13,091
Food, hospitality and personal services	0	0	258	91	1,988	869	7,846	2,966	9,623	3,806
Total enrolments	**20,982**	**14,734**	**90,073**	**62,803**	**44,053**	**30,221**	**145,674**	**143,334**	**292,204**	**243,817**
Adjustment for multiple enrolments	57	46	2,331	1,818	1,020	626	8,713	6,258	26,803	18,193
Total students	**20,925**	**14,688**	**87,742**	**60,985**	**43,033**	**29,595**	**136,961**	**137,076**	**265,401**	**225,624**

Source: Ministry of Education

free, online career guidance programme. Pathfinder generates career options based on the profile an individual compiles by completing a range of activities and questionnaires.

In the year to 30 June 2006, more than 626,000 people accessed career information and advice from Career Services, and more than 6,600 received government-funded career guidance and planning assistance.

Vocational qualifications

National diplomas are qualifications based on standards and are registered on the National Qualifications Framework (NQF). All framework qualifications must meet the requirements of the New Zealand Register of Quality Assured Qualifications.

All framework standards and national qualifications are developed by subject experts within a standard setting body.

Standard setting bodies which develop NQF standards include:

- industry training organisations, which develop industry-related unit standards and national qualifications

Table 9.09

Qualifications completed
By award level, education sector and sex
2006

Award level	Institutes of technology and polytechnics Female	Male	Colleges of education Female	Male	Universities Female	Male	Wānanga Female	Male	Private training establishments Female	Male	Total Female	Male
Doctorate	0	0	0	0	320	321	0	0	0	0	320	321
Master's degree	90	42	9	1	2,143	1,667	13	7	56	84	2,311	1,796
Honours or postgraduate certificate/diploma	418	79	34	8	3,709	2,319	11	5	550	318	4,641	2,691
Bachelor's degree	2,884	1,383	937	254	14,074	9,542	290	90	264	258	18,405	11,500
Diploma	4,017	2,523	605	505	1,381	1,036	917	408	3,570	2,454	10,473	6,917
Certificate	15,422	15,193	133	7	2,093	1,274	12,636	5,390	11,690	5,790	41,339	27,374
Total qualifications completed	**22,831**	**19,220**	**1,718**	**775**	**23,720**	**16,159**	**13,867**	**5,900**	**16,130**	**8,904**	**77,489**	**50,599**
Adjustment for multiple completions	613	381	11	4	477	325	328	110	396	248	2,793	1,460
Total students	**22,218**	**18,839**	**1,707**	**771**	**23,243**	**15,834**	**13,539**	**5,790**	**15,734**	**8,656**	**74,696**	**49,139**

Source: Ministry of Education

Table 9.10

Qualifications completed
By field of study, award level and sex
2006

Field of study	Doctorate Female	Male	Master's degree Female	Male	Honours or postgraduate certificate/ diploma Female	Male	Bachelor's degree Female	Male	Diploma Female	Male	Certificate Female	Male	Total Female	Male
Natural and physical sciences	0	1	332	267	438	402	1,581	1,555	62	58	39	47	2,438	2,303
Information technology	0	0	17	34	20	68	197	631	349	1,027	1,937	1,139	2,498	2,847
Engineering and related technologies	1	0	46	189	48	151	232	1,067	117	450	680	3,878	1,112	5,662
Architecture and building	0	0	8	14	13	17	178	236	124	134	123	1,307	444	1,679
Agriculture, environmental and related studies	0	0	62	49	37	41	187	210	89	190	1,824	5,400	2,169	5,863
Health	0	2	259	65	1,435	291	2,577	602	1,015	153	2,588	1,010	7,744	2,034
Education	6	5	230	62	386	104	3,599	810	2,135	764	1,322	212	7,608	1,948
Management and commerce	0	0	525	659	796	801	4,237	3,634	2,496	1,764	9,639	3,804	17,244	10,462
Society and culture	33	30	711	360	1,325	718	4,307	2,208	2,182	1,253	11,450	5,675	19,380	9,917
Creative arts	3	1	116	93	99	72	1,574	798	1,135	912	1,550	749	4,444	2,600
Food, hospitality and personal services	0	0	0	0	0	0	72	11	677	165	2,870	1,100	3,454	1,228
Mixed field programmes	277	282	5	5	49	35	255	155	160	87	8,378	3,530	9,100	4,085
Total qualifications completed	**320**	**321**	**2,311**	**1,797**	**4,646**	**2,700**	**18,996**	**11,917**	**10,541**	**6,957**	**42,400**	**27,851**	**77,635**	**50,628**
Adjustment for multiple completions	0	0	0	1	5	9	591	417	68	40	1,061	477	2,939	1,489
Total students	**320**	**321**	**2,311**	**1,796**	**4,641**	**2,691**	**18,405**	**11,500**	**10,473**	**6,917**	**41,339**	**27,374**	**74,696**	**49,139**

Source: Ministry of Education

The Dominion Post

Apprentice mechanic 18-year-old Frances Tunley at her Kapiti coast workplace in 2007. After a one-year polytech course, she has up to three more years study to complete her automotive technician apprenticeship.

- Māori qualifications services within the New Zealand Qualifications Authority (NZQA), which develops unit standards and national qualifications for the classification field 'Māori' (eg Reo Māori)
- national qualifications services within NZQA, which develops unit standards and national qualifications for generic skills
- Ministry of Education, which develops the New Zealand curriculum-based achievement standards and the National Certificate of Educational Achievement.

New Zealand certificates in engineering (NZCE) have been replaced by national diplomas. The last date for the award of NZCE is December 2008. Certificates required students to complete three years' suitable work experience. NZQA was responsible for maintaining the national database of results, evaluating and approving work experience, and certification of the qualification.

New Zealand certificates Many certificates have now been replaced by national diplomas. Courses for certificate qualifications are no longer available, but subjects may be completed through recognition of prior learning. A diploma can be awarded when a student completes requirements for the qualification – usually work experience.

New Zealand Diploma in Business (NZDipBus) is a generic business qualification, endorsed by a number of industries, including accounting, marketing, tourism, banking and management. Courses are available at accredited tertiary education providers. Most papers are one semester (half-year) long and are completed through full- or part-time study.

NZQA is the owner of the NZDipBus and is responsible for: establishing and maintaining regulations for the qualification, maintaining a database of results and issuing results notices, maintaining national records, developing and maintaining prescriptions, managing the national external moderation system, and certifying the qualification. Accredited training providers may award the NZDipBus in conjunction with NZQA.

Other qualifications A wide range of other vocational qualifications are available, including those developed and administered by polytechnics and other tertiary training providers; national bodies, such as the New Zealand Institute of Management and the Royal New Zealand Air Force; and private training providers. Responsibility for all aspects of these qualifications lies with the appropriate bodies, which are quality-assured by NZQA or a delegated quality-assurance organisation.

International students

A New Zealand educational institution enrolling international students must be a signatory to the Code of Practice for the Pastoral Care of International Students.

The code sets requirements for education providers which protect and promote the interests, welfare and safety of international students. This includes minimum requirements for recruitment and enrolment of students, and standards for accommodation and support services. The Ministry of Education implements the code.

Education providers are also required to ensure that international students have adequate medical and travel insurance cover.

International students intending to enrol with a New Zealand education institution or private training establishment should ensure that their chosen courses and providers are approved by the New Zealand Qualifications Authority (NZQA). This information is available from KiwiQuals, a database list of all quality-assured qualifications in New Zealand, on the NZQA website, www.nzqa.govt.nz.

Information for international students about New Zealand courses of study, academic entry requirements and costs is available at www.newzealandeducated.com.

Other information channels are New Zealand government offices in the student's home country, or direct contact with the educational institution a student wishes to attend.

Students require a visa for any course of study longer than three months. Student visas and permits are issued for the period for which fees have been paid.

Educational institutions set their own academic entrance requirements and fees. Some allow payment of annual fees by instalment. International students are not entitled to New Zealand student allowances or loans.

Table 9.11

International students studying in New Zealand[1][2]
1999–2007

Category	1999	2000	2001	2002	2003	2004	2005	2006	2007
Primary and secondary students[3]	6,030	8,150	11,330	16,010	18,080	15,050	11,984	10,363	10,869
Tertiary students[4]	11,728	16,628	26,333	38,476	47,186	50,442	47,351	42,589	..
Students at English language providers[5] and on study tours	21,000	23,400	31,500	47,000	74,800	..	..	..	..
Total	**38,758**	**48,178**	**69,163**	**101,486**	**140,066**	**65,492**	**59,335**	**52,952**	..

(1) All figures independently rounded. (2) Regardless of length of stay. (3) Ministry of Education, at 1 July. (4) Ministry of Education, full year data. (5) Survey of English Language Providers, year ending 30 June for 1999 and 2000, year ending 31 March from 2001.

Symbol: .. not available

Sources: Ministry of Education, Statistics New Zealand

Sector statistics

Table 9.12

Full-time equivalent teaching staff at educational institutions
At 1 July

Institution type	2000	2001	2002	2003	2004	2005	2006
Licensed early childhood services							
Kindergartens	1,617	1,643	1,644	1,663	1,673	1,672	1,672
Playcentres (includes unpaid adults on duty)	1,251	1,182	1,174	1,204	1,218	1,203	1,199
Education and care services – regular and casual	7,854	8,212	8,734	9,362	9,875	10,327	10,914
Home-based services – coordinators	271	258	265	307	305	293	264
Correspondence School	20	25	29	32	33	29	22
Kōhanga reo	..	..	..	..	..	..	..
Primary schools							
State	22,957	23,362	23,358	23,611	23,583	23,357	23,738
Private	401	452	465	450	464	446	450
Composite schools							
State	1,406	1,485	1,572	1690	1,795	2,007	2,043
Private	937	959	1,016	1,093	1,186	1,294	1,270
Secondary schools							
State	15,083	15,374	15,596	16,488	17,279	18,044	18,473
Private	512	596	615	651	732	709	703
Special schools							
State	663	743	764	801	834	909	930
Private	..	..	..	...	...	..	...
Correspondence School							
Primary and secondary	299	318	290	290	285	244	210
Tertiary education providers – academic staff							
Public tertiary education institutions							
Polytechnics	4,035	3,999	4,323	4,223	4,405	4,362	4,396
Colleges of education	505	475	485	491	450	228	200
Universities	5,936	6,103	6,365	6,562	6,678	7,112	7,030
Wānanga	156	237	526	781	987	865	665
Private tertiary education providers	3,290	3,753	4,119	4,186	4,187	3,916	3,884

Symbols: .. not available ... not applicable

Source: Ministry of Education

Table 9.13

Formal educational institutions and students enrolled
At 1 July

Institution type	2005 Number	2005 Students	2006 Number	2006 Students
Early childhood education				
Licensed early childhood education services				
Kindergartens	618	44,920	619	44,435
Playcentres	482	15,059	474	14,888
Education and care services	1,754	83,889	1,842	86,059
Casual education and care (no regular roll)	41	...	41	...
Home-based services	201	9,770	202	9,802
Kōhanga reo	501	10,070	486	9,493
Correspondence School	1	813	1	577
Total licensed	3,598	164,521	3,665	165,254
Licence-exempt early childhood education services				
ECD[1] funded playgroups	641	18,042	667	17,476
ECD[1] funded ngā puna kohungahunga	49	519	41	289
ECD[1] funded Pacific peoples language groups	106	1,864	93	1,179
ECD[1] funded playcentres	31	436	22	167
Kōhanga reo	11	146	8	89
Total licence-exempt	838	21,007	831	19,200
Total early childhood education	**4,436**	**185,528**	**4,496**	**184,454**
Compulsory education				
Primary schools				
State full primary	1,101	168,611	1,092	167,903
State contributing	795	211,531	798	210,590
State intermediate	121	58,466	121	57,448
Private primary and intermediate	42	5,838	40	5,829
Total primary	**2,059**	**444,446**	**2,051**	**441,770**
Composite schools				
State composite	101	25,707	100	25,221
State Correspondence School	1	6,632	1	5,873
Private composite	46	15,509	47	15,806
Total composite	**148**	**47,848**	**148**	**46,900**
Secondary schools				
State years 9–15	239	206,448	238	206,133
State years 7–15	94	53,268	96	54,903
Private years 7–15 and years 9–15	19	7,996	18	8,260
Total secondary	**352**	**267,712**	**352**	**269,296**
Special schools				
State	46	2,735	46	2,747
Private	1	15	0	0
Other Vote: Education	1	34	1	48
Total compulsory schooling	**2,607**	**762,790**	**2,598**	**760,761**
Home schooling	...	**6,428**	...	**6,298**
Tertiary education providers[2]				
Public tertiary education institutions				
Polytechnics	20	118,020	20	116,601
Universities	8	139,151	8	136,363
Colleges of education	2	5,686	2	5,518
Wānanga	3	33,027	3	27,500
Total public providers	33	295,884	33	285,982
Private tertiary education providers	480	54,969	323	59,761
Total tertiary	**513**	**350,853**	**389**	**345,743**

(1) Early childhood development. (2) Counts only institutions with formally enrolled students.

Symbol: ... not applicable

Source: Ministry of Education

Table 9.14

	Education 1875–2006										
Year[1]	Early childhood education providers[2]	Students (000)	Primary schools[3][4]	Students (000)	Secondary schools[5][6]	Students	University students[8]	Polytechnic students[7][8]	College of education students[8] (000)	Wānanga students[8]	Private training establishment students[8]
1875	..	..	830	54.2	4	..	...	...	...	...	...
1880	..	..	1,171	95.2	14	1.6	211	...	...	...	...
1885	..	..	1,363	116.5	24	2.6	442	...	...	...	...
1890	..	..	1,566	134.1	22	2.1	596	...	...	...	...
1895	..	..	1,831	145.8	24	2.5	742	...	...	...	...
1900	..	..	2,157	149.4	86	6.9	805	...	...	...	...
1905	..	..	2,192	158.1	86	6.9	1,153	...	211	...	...
1910	..	..	2,508	179.6	94	9.1	1,862	...	380	...	...
1915	..	..	2,765	210.8	129	11.5	2,039	...	390	...	...
1920	..	..	2,777	225.3	131	15.4	3,822	...	680	...	...
1925	..	..	2,995	247.3	181	23.2	4,442	...	1,271	...	...
1930	..	..	3,045	252.6	209	31	4,801	...	1,155	...	...
1935	..	..	2,950	232.3	216	31.9	5,101	...	429	...	...
1940	..	..	2,656	243.3	234	36.1	5,528	...	1,457	...	...
1945	..	..	2,874	252.5	248	46.9	8,425	...	1,431	...	...
1950	..	..	2,377	304.6	269	53.7	11,515	...	2,684	...	...
1955	..	..	2,423	365.4	313	80.8	10,851	...	2,847	...	...
1960	..	..	2,517	425	354	111.4	15,809	7,663	3,828	...	...
1965	..	27.8	2,594	472.9	376	157.9	22,145	29,074	4,790	...	...
1970	..	41.1	2,595	516.7	386	186.8	31,908	43,204	7,587	...	...
1975	1,098	54.8	2,542	525.3	408	219.7	35,499	56,098	8,004	...	...
1980	1,208	56.9	2,595	507.9	394	226.3	43,933	73,067	5,919	...	...
1985	1,389	60.7	2,641	452.4	403	230.9	59,123	76,054	2,703	...	...
1990	2,890	118.4	2,460	420.4	400	230.2	78,919	56,771	5,766	...	...
1995	3,824	159.4	2,368	448.2	430	236.6	104,389	95,664	10,156	726	...
2000	4,175	174.2	2,268	484.2	456	245.5	122,727	87,436	12,045	2,972	39,173
2001	4,213	171.3	2,256	484.1	462	249.9	125,668	87,965	10,884	11,278	51,666
2002	4,228	175	2,235	488.7	464	259.7	132,396	95,782	10,788	27,535	53,385
2003	4,280	180	2,224	492.9	469	268.8	137,007	98,072	10,828	41,200	49,897
2004	4,374	184.5	2,171	488.1	500	276.6	138,583	117,514	11,107	41,644	59,158
2005	4,436	185.5	2,107	485.1	500	277.7	168,333	212,634	6,990	62,200	83,556
2006	4,496	184.5	2,098	482.8	500	278.0	165,571	214,394	6,908	48,842	80,432

(1) Year ending 31 December until 1925, then at 1 July. Figures from 1994 on revised and not comparable with previous years. (2) Figures include only playcentres and kindergartens until 1990, then include childcare, kōhanga reo and Pasifika language groups. (3) Includes year 1–8 students at all schools. (4) Includes full primary, contributing, intermediate and special schools. Special schools can contain year 9–15 students. (5) Includes year 9–15 students at all schools. (6) Includes secondary and composite schools and Correspondence School. Some schools also have year 1–8 students. (7) Prior to 1990, figures included all students attending polytechnic. From 1990, only those attending on 31 July. (8) From 2005, all tertiary figures are full year.

Symbols: .. not available ... not applicable

Source: Ministry of Education

Contributors and related websites

Career Services Rapuara – www.careers.govt.nz

Education Review Office – www.ero.govt.nz

Learning Media Ltd – www.learningmedia.co.nz

Māori Education Trust – www.maorieducation.org.nz

Ministry of Education – www.minedu.govt.nz

Ministry of Social Development – www.msd.govt.nz

New Zealand Qualifications Authority – www.nzqa.govt.nz

New Zealand Teachers' Council – www.teacherscouncil.govt.nz

Statistics New Zealand – www.stats.govt.nz

Tertiary Education Commission – www.tec.govt.nz

The Correspondence School – www.correspondence.school.nz

The Open Polytechnic of New Zealand – www.openpolytechnic.ac.nz

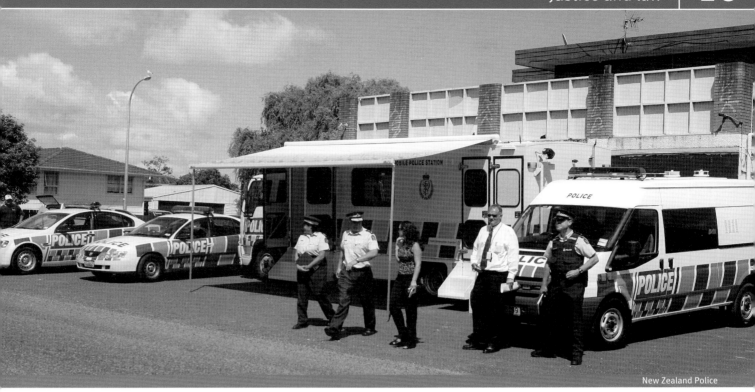

New Zealand Police

Counties Manukau's new Mobile Police Station (MPS) at the scene of a serious crime. The MPS operates as the base from which foot and vehicle patrols are deployed.

10 | Justice and law

Legal system

New Zealand is an independent state, with both a constitutional monarchy and a parliamentary democracy. The Queen, as Head of State, is the source of legal authority, but she and her representative, the Governor-General of New Zealand, act on the advice of the democratically-elected government in all but the most exceptional circumstances.

New Zealand has inherited from the United Kingdom the 'Westminster' system of parliamentary government and, as part of that system, the doctrine of the separation of powers. The doctrine provides that the three branches of government – Parliament, the Executive and the Judiciary – have different functions, which act as a check on the others.

Parliament has the function of the formal act of law-making, which is carried out through scrutinising, amending and passing bills that are introduced by government ministers or individual members of Parliament.

The Executive determines government policy, is responsible for the administration of law, and carries out all the powers and functions of organised central government through ministers directly, and through the public service and other bodies.

The Judiciary makes binding determinations of disputes between private individuals, and between individuals and the State, including determining the application and meaning of relevant laws.

Judges are appointed by the governor-general on the advice of the attorney-general. No person may be appointed as a judge unless he or she has held a practising certificate as a barrister or solicitor for at least seven years. Usually, those appointed to the judiciary have practised law for longer than seven years.

Judges in the Supreme Court of New Zealand, the New Zealand Court of Appeal, and the New Zealand High Court can only be removed from office by the governor-general, acting on advice from the House of Representatives, on the grounds of misbehaviour or incapacity. District court judges may be removed from office by the governor-general on the grounds of inability to perform or misbehaviour.

The passing of the Judicial Conduct Commissioner and Judicial Conduct Panel Act 2004 established a statutory complaints process for complaints about judges.

Ministry of Justice

The Ministry of Justice administers legislation and provides services to contribute to safer communities and a fairer, more credible, and more effective justice system by:

- developing robust policy advice that influences the direction of justice in New Zealand
- supporting an efficient and accessible court system
- providing effective services to support independent judicial decision making
- settling Treaty of Waitangi claims in a fair and durable way
- managing parliamentary elections and referendums effectively, to maintain public confidence in electoral processes
- working with communities to enhance safety and well-being.

The Ministry of Justice delivers the following services on behalf of the government:

- administration, case management, and support services for the Supreme Court of New Zealand, the New Zealand Court of Appeal, the New Zealand High Court, and district courts, including the Family Court and Youth Court
- administration, case management, and support services to specialist jurisdictions, including the Māori Land Court, the Māori Appellate Court, the Environment Court, the Employment Court, and a range of authorities, committees and tribunals
- administration, inquiry management, and support services to the Waitangi Tribunal; negotiations for settlement of historical claims arising from the Treaty of Waitangi; and management of land for use in settlements
- administration of parliamentary elections, by-elections, and referendums
- collection and enforcement of court-imposed monetary penalties and infringement fines, and enforcement of civil court orders.

The ministry provides policy advice to a number of ministers and select committees, and works with a range of non-government organisations in crime prevention and other activities. This work includes:

- providing policy advice to the Minister of Justice, the Minister in Charge of Treaty of Waitangi Negotiations, the Minister for Courts, the Minister Responsible for the Law Commission, and the attorney-general
- providing briefings and advice to ministers and Cabinet to assist in the development of government policy and changes to legislation
- providing support and advice to a number of parliamentary select committees, including the Justice and Electoral, Law and Order, and Māori Affairs select committees
- facilitating input into the justice system from the public, by managing consultation during legislation development and reform
- working directly with a range of non-government agencies in crime prevention and other activities, such as partnerships with territorial authorities and iwi (tribes), and providing funding directly to support local initiatives.

The ministry has a mandate to lead the justice sector and to coordinate processes that ensure a collaborative, outcome-focused approach.

In leading the sector, some of the ministry's activities are: research and evaluation, advising on sector outcomes, linking cross-sector strategies, strengthening knowledge and information flows across the sector, and coordinating the sector's annual budget process.

Hierarchy of courts

The Supreme Court of New Zealand is the country's court of final appeal. The Chief Justice of New Zealand presides over the court.

Below the Supreme Court is the New Zealand Court of Appeal, then the New Zealand High Court and district courts, which are the main courts that exercise general criminal and civil jurisdiction.

There are also a number of courts and tribunals that have jurisdiction over specific areas of law, with rights of appeal to one or more of the four main courts.

Supreme Court of New Zealand

Established in 2003, the Supreme Court is New Zealand's court of final appeal. It can hear appeals across almost all areas of law. While the right to appeal to the United Kingdom-based Judicial Committee of the Privy Council was abolished from 1 January 2004, certain appeals that were active before this date continue to be determined by the Privy Council.

The Supreme Court consists of the Chief Justice and up to five other judges. It is located in Wellington. A new building to house the Supreme Court is under construction, and is expected to be completed in 2009. At May 2008, the Chief Justice was Rt Hon Dame Sian Elias.

New Zealand Court of Appeal

The Court of Appeal hears civil and criminal appeals from proceedings heard in the High Court, and indictable criminal proceedings in district courts.

Matters appealed to the High Court from a district court can be taken to the Court of Appeal with leave, if they are considered to be of sufficient significance to warrant a second appeal.

The Court of Appeal may hear appeals against pre-trial rulings in criminal cases. The court also hears appeals on questions of law from the Employment Court.

The Court of Appeal is New Zealand's principal intermediate appellate court, and is located in Wellington. Its full-time membership is eight appellate judges and a president. At May 2008, the president was Hon Justice William Young.

New Zealand High Court

The High Court has jurisdiction over serious crimes, civil claims involving more than $200,000, judicial reviews of administrative action, admiralty proceedings, and appeals from tribunals and lower courts, including district courts.

Judges of the High Court include the Chief Justice of New Zealand, 48 judges (including judges of the Supreme Court and the Court of Appeal) and seven associate judges. They are led by the Chief Judge of the High Court, who is responsible to the Chief Justice of New Zealand for administration of the court. At May 2008, the Chief High Court Judge was Hon Justice Randerson.

Judges are based in Auckland, Wellington and Christchurch and travel on circuit to centres throughout the country. Associate judges of the High Court supervise the court's preliminary processes in most civil proceedings and have jurisdiction to deal with summary judgement applications, company liquidations, bankruptcy proceedings and some other types of civil proceedings.

District courts

District courts hear the majority of criminal offences, and civil claims up to $200,000. There are 63 district courts throughout New Zealand. There are 133 district court judges, including the principal judges and judges of the Environment Court. In addition to the judges there are 52 disputes tribunal referees and approximately 400 justices of the peace. The District Courts Act 1947 sets jurisdiction for district courts.

Justices of the Peace are persons of good standing in the community who administer documentation and justice. They are appointed by the governor general, on the recommendation of a Member of Parliament. Ministerial duties include witnessing documents, certifying copies, and taking declarations, affidavits or affirmations. Judicial duties include hearing summary offences, presiding over preliminary hearings, conducting traffic courts, hearing bail applications and requests for remands and adjournments, and issuing search warrants.

Specialist courts

New Zealand has a number of courts with specialist functions.

Employment courts hear cases concerned with the employment of employees by employers, and injunctions arising out of unlawful strikes, lockouts, and pickets. Judges of the court must have held a practising certificate as a barrister or solicitor for not less than seven years. The court consists of a chief judge and at least two other judges.

Normally, the court's jurisdiction is exercised by a judge sitting alone, but on occasions of appropriate significance, it will sit as a full bench of at least three judges. The Employment Court exercises jurisdiction under the Employment Relations Act 2000, the State Sector Act 1988, and other acts. Support for the Employment Court transferred from the Department of Labour to the Ministry of Justice on 1 December 2004.

Family courts are a specialist division of the district courts. They aim, wherever possible, to help people sort out their own problems through counselling, conciliation, and mediation. It deals with family and relationship matters, including: adoption, care of children, care and protection of children who are abused or neglected, inter-country child abduction, consents for minors to marry, protection from domestic violence, separation, divorce, matrimonial/relationship property, compulsory mental health assessment and treatment, protection of personal and property rights for people who are incapacitated, claims for maintenance and support, and bequests from estates.

Family court proceedings are not open to the public. The Care of Children Act 2004 established the right of 'accredited' news media organisations to attend family court hearings. It also sets important limitations on media coverage. There are 58 family courts, with 43 warranted judges, throughout New Zealand. Family courts, which administer 15 acts, were established under the Family Courts Act 1980.

Youth courts are part of the district court structure. They hear all criminal cases where the alleged offender is aged 14–16 years – except for charges of murder, manslaughter, or when a young person chooses to have a jury trial. There are 50 warranted youth court judges. Proceedings

Judicial salaries and principal allowances

The salaries of judges are determined annually by the Remuneration Authority under the Remuneration Authority Act 1977. The Judicial Salaries and Allowances Determination (No. 2) 2006 set the following rates:

Judicial salaries and principal allowances
Effective 1 October 2007

Position	Salary payable $	Principal allowance payable $
Chief Justice	412,000	7,900
Judge of the Supreme Court	385,000	6,500
President of the Court of Appeal	385,000	6,500
Judge of the Court of Appeal	361,000	5,600
Chief High Court Judge	360,000	5,600
Judge of the High Court	345,000	5,600
Chief District Court Judge	345,000	5,000
Principal Family Court Judge	298,000	5,000
Principal Youth Court Judge	280,000	5,000
Principal Environment Court Judge	280,000	5,000
District Court Judge	260,000	4,100
Chief Judge of the Employment Court	327,000	5,600
Judge of the Employment Court	295,000	4,700
Chief Judge of the Māori Land Court	295,000	5,000
Deputy Chief Judge of the Māori Land Court	279,000	4,700
Judge of the Māori Land Court	260,000	4,100
Associate Judge of the High Court	260,000	4,100

Note: A principal allowance for the Chief High Court Judge for secondary residential accommodation in Wellington has been determined, subject to certain conditions. The maximum yearly rate of the allowance payable is $20,000.

Source: Remuneration Authority

Māori Land Court, Ministry of Justice

In December 2007, the Minister of Māori Affairs, Parekura Horomia, announced the appointment of two new judges to the bench of the Māori Land Court. The swearing-in ceremony of judges Stephen Clark and Craig Coxhead took place at Rangiaowhia Marae in Hamilton, in January 2008.

are not open to the public. Media can attend, however specific conditions apply. The court was established under the Children Young Persons and Their Families Act 1989.

Māori Land Court makes decisions on applications relating to the ownership, occupation, utilisation, and development of Māori land. The court also hears applications under new jurisdictions arising from the Māori Fisheries Act 2004, the Foreshore and Seabed Act 2004, and the Māori Commercial Aquaculture Claims Settlement Act 2004. The court has eight judges, including a chief judge and a deputy chief judge. The court was established under the Native Lands Act 1865, and continued under Te Ture Whenua Māori Act 1993.

Māori Appellate Court hears appeals from orders or preliminary determinations of the Māori Land Court, as well as cases stated by the Māori Land Court, the High Court, and the Waitangi Tribunal. Any three or more Māori Land Court judges have power to act as the Māori Appellate Court. The court was established under the Native Land Court Act 1894, and continued under Te Ture Whenua Māori Act 1993.

Environment Court considers appeals about regional and district statements and plans, and appeals from resource consent applications for land use, subdivision, water or discharge permits, or a combination of those. The Environment Court was constituted under the Resource Management Amendment Act 1996. The court has specialist judges, who are also district court judges and environment commissioners. The court has registries in Auckland, Wellington, and Christchurch. Sittings are held throughout the country, usually with one judge and two commissioners.

Coronial Services of New Zealand employs coroners – judicial officers appointed under the Coroners Act 2006. The role of the coroner is to establish the cause and circumstances of sudden or unexplained deaths, and deaths in other special circumstances. As part of their inquiry, the coroner may authorise post-mortem examinations. They may also make recommendations or comments on ways of avoiding future deaths.

Tribunals

More than 100 tribunals, authorities, committees, or related boards exist in New Zealand to deal with matters such as environmental planning, abortion supervision, taxation reviews, deportation reviews, land valuations, and occupational licensing.

Disputes tribunals are a division of district courts, and were established under the Disputes Tribunals Act 1988. They resolve disputes up to a value of $7,500, or $12,000 by agreement of the parties. Disputes referees preside over each tribunal.

Human Rights Review Tribunal hears civil proceedings brought by individuals or by the Director of Human Rights Proceedings, for alleged breaches of the Privacy Act 1993, the Human Rights Act 1993, and the New Zealand Bill of Rights Act 1990. It also hears proceedings brought by the Office of the Health and Disability Commissioner under the Health and Disability Commissioner Act 1994. The tribunal has a chairperson – a barrister or solicitor of the High Court of not less than five years' practice – who sits with two members appointed from a panel of not more than 20.

Tenancy Tribunal adjudicators make decisions on disputes up to a value of $12,000 brought to the Tenancy Tribunal by landlords or tenants in relation to residential tenancies. The tribunal was established under the Residential Tenancies Act 1986.

Waitangi Tribunal is a permanent Commission of Inquiry. It makes recommendations on claims brought by Māori, relating to actions or omissions of the Crown that allegedly breach promises made in the Treaty of Waitangi. It also examines and reports on proposed legislation referred to it by the House of Representatives or a minister of the Crown, and makes recommendations or determinations about certain Crown forest land, railway land, state-owned enterprise land, and land transferred to educational institutions.

The tribunal has a chairperson who is either a High Court judge, a retired High Court judge, or the chief judge of the Māori Land Court, and a deputy chairperson who is a judge of the Māori Land Court. It also has up to 16 members, appointed by the governor-general on the recommendation of the Minister of Māori Affairs. The tribunal was established by the Treaty of Waitangi Act 1975.

Law Commission

Established by the Law Commission Act 1985, the Law Commission Te Aka Matua o te Ture is an independent, government-funded organisation, which reviews areas of the law that need updating, reforming, or developing.

The commission helps ensure that laws provide effectively for the current and future needs of New Zealand's changing society. Its goal is to achieve law that is just, principled, and accessible, and that reflects the heritage and aspirations of the people of New Zealand.

Under the Act, up to six commissioners (one of them the president) can be appointed by the governor-general on the recommendation of the Minister Responsible for the Law Commission.

The commission is funded through the Vote Justice allocation, and employs legal researchers, librarians, and support staff.

Legal Services Agency

The Legal Services Agency is a Crown entity established by the Legal Services Act 2000. The agency replaced the Legal Services Board, and its task is to promote access to justice for those who have the greatest need and least capacity to pay for legal services. It does this by administering, funding, or sponsoring a range of legal services, including:

- legal advice and representation through legal aid, duty solicitor, and Police detention legal assistance schemes
- community legal services, such as those provided by community law centres
- production of information and educational resources, targeting those with unmet legal needs
- research into the unfulfilled legal needs of communities and how those needs might be met.

The agency is assisted by a public advisory committee, which advises on community concerns about legal aid, access to legal aid, unmet legal needs, community law centre funding, legal information and law-related educational needs, and areas in need of research.

Criminal legal aid This aid is available to anyone who has been charged with a criminal offence. In some cases, it is also available for people appearing before the New Zealand Parole Board.

Duty solicitors The duty solicitor scheme ensures that lawyers are available 'on duty' at every district court in the country. Duty lawyers provide free legal help on the first day in court for anyone who has been charged with a criminal offence, and doesn't have their own lawyer. The duty lawyer can explain the charge, and will advise on pleas, bail, and the sentencing options available to the court. They also help people to apply for legal aid.

Police detention legal assistance (PDLA) The PDLA scheme enables anyone who is arrested or held by the police to obtain free confidential legal advice from a lawyer. Advice may be provided by a lawyer over the telephone or in person. The scheme ensures that section 23 of the New Zealand Bill of Rights Act 1990 is given practical effect. This says that people detained for questioning "have the right to consult and instruct a lawyer without delay, and to be informed of that right". Young people can use the PDLA scheme – there is no minimum age.

Civil legal aid This aid applies to all family and civil matters encompassing the Waitangi Tribunal and other civil proceedings, including refugee, accident compensation, and employment matters.

Grants and payments In the year ending 30 June 2007, 79,397 legal aid grants were made, and legal aid payments totalled $107.4 million. Payments made can relate to grants approved in previous years. Of these payments, $51.7 million was spent on criminal cases (private providers $48.9 million, public defender service $2.8 million), $28.3 million on family law cases, $12.6 million on Waitangi Tribunal matters, and $6.5 million on civil actions. A further $7.8 million was spent on the duty solicitor scheme, and $0.5 million on the Police Detention Legal Assistance scheme. Legal aid repayments totalled $9.9 million.

Legal aid is demand-driven. Once an entitlement to assistance is established, aid must be provided, and no direct control can be exercised over the number of applications submitted.

Community law centres These centres provide legal services to those in communities with unmet legal needs, particularly those who cannot afford to pay for legal services. The centres provide free legal advice and sometimes representation, law-related education, and legal information, and may work on law reform. The centres are funded mostly from a special

Helping those who cannot afford a lawyer

The legal aid scheme in New Zealand grants legal aid to people who are eligible, for representation in criminal and civil proceedings. Civil legal aid encompasses family, Waitangi Tribunal, and other civil proceedings, including refugee, Accident Compensation Corporation (ACC), and employment matters.

Legal aid is granted by the Legal Services Agency to those who do not have the means to meet their legal costs. Applicants do not have to be New Zealand citizens or residents, and special rules apply for those under the age of 20. A lawyer or a community law centre worker may help the person to apply for legal aid.

The agency assesses eligibility for civil and family legal aid on the following grounds:

- whether proceedings are covered by section 7 of the Legal Services Act 2000
- the applicant's disposable income and assets
- the reasonableness of taking the case (for civil and family proceedings)
- the prospect of applicants succeeding in the proceedings they are taking or defending.

Eligibility for criminal legal aid is assessed on the basis of:

- whether proceedings are covered by section 6 of the Legal Services Act 2000
- whether or not applicants have sufficient financial resources to fund their own representation
- the gravity (potential penalties if found guilty) of the offence the applicant has been charged with.

The legal aid system is based on the principles of access to justice, the concept that a person is innocent until proven guilty, and the right of everybody to be defended in court.

When criminal legal aid is granted, the agency appoints a legal aid lawyer from a list of approved lawyers. A person may choose their own lawyer, as long as the lawyer is based in the location where the case is to be heard, is able to appear at court when needed, is willing to take the case, and is registered as a legal aid lawyer.

A contribution to the costs of legal aid may be required. This is based on a calculation which considers income, assets, and expenditure. The Legal Services Agency may ask for this to be paid in a lump sum, in instalments, or when a house or other property is sold.

Decisions on legal aid may be referred back to the agency for reconsideration, or be reviewed by the independent Legal Aid Review Panel.

Source: Legal Services Agency

fund (administered by the New Zealand Law Society), which earns revenue from interest income from nominated lawyers' trust accounts, plus some government funding. There were 27 centres in 2007.

Public Advisory Committee The Legal Services Agency's Public Advisory Committee represents a range of groups, including women, Māori, Pacific peoples, young people, older people, people with disabilities, consumers, community law centres, the legal profession, refugees, and migrants.

The committee provides advice to the agency on a number of matters, including feedback and concerns about legal aid schemes and other services funded or delivered by the agency, unmet legal needs, funding of community law centres, research, and law-related education.

Jury service

Jury service is an extremely important part of the justice system and democracy. The contribution of jurors is very much needed, valued, and appreciated.

A jury is a group of 12 people who have been chosen at random to sit in a court trial, hear the evidence, and reach a verdict. Its job is to decide what facts have been proved, apply the law to the facts with guidance on the law from the judge, and return a proper verdict.

A jury list for each court is made up by random selection from electoral rolls in the court area. People's names are then selected at random from the jury list, and those people are summonsed. Members of parliament, members of the Judiciary, those involved in certain justice-related occupations, and people who have been sentenced to certain prison terms are not eligible to serve on a jury.

Crown Law

Crown Law is a government agency providing legal advice and representation services to the government, particularly in areas of criminal, public, and administrative law. Its two primary objectives are to ensure that:

- the operations and responsibilities of the Executive arm of government are conducted lawfully
- the government is not prevented, through legal process, from lawfully implementing its policies, and discharging its governmental responsibilities.

The Solicitor-General of New Zealand is chief executive of Crown Law, and is the chief legal adviser to the government, subject to any views expressed by the attorney-general. In this capacity, the solicitor-general is the government's chief advocate in the courts. In addition, the solicitor-general is responsible for conducting the prosecution of indictable crime, and also has a number of specific statutory duties and functions.

Crown Law is organised into three practice groups, which bring together specialist teams enabling clients to address key issues about:

- constitutional advice and litigation, including Treaty of Waitangi matters and constitutional conventions
- the conduct of Crown prosecutions, including advice on international human rights obligations, the bill of rights, and criminal appeals
- public law arising out of the exercise and control of governmental power and public sector governance.

The criminal process group is responsible for the supervision and conduct of the nationwide network of Crown solicitors. Crown solicitors, who are private legal practitioners in the main centres of New Zealand, conduct prosecutions for indictable crime on behalf of the Crown. Crown solicitors are appointed by the governor-general on the recommendation of the attorney-general.

Serious Fraud Office

The Serious Fraud Office Te Tari Hara Tāware (SFO) is a specialist department established by the Serious Fraud Office Act 1990, to facilitate the detection, investigation, and expeditious prosecution of serious and/or complex fraud offending.

At 30 June 2007, SFO had a staff of 33, consisting of forensic accountants, investigators, prosecutors, and support staff. Multi-disciplinary teams are used in the investigation and prosecution of cases.

To determine whether an offence involves serious or complex fraud, the Act provides that the director may, among other things, consider: the suspected nature, consequences, and scale of the fraud; the legal, factual and evidential complexity of the matter; and any relevant public-interest considerations. The director's decision to investigate or take proceedings is discretionary, and not subject to review.

During the 2006/07 financial year, 65 complaints were received and 23 full investigations were concluded. Of these, 11 resulted in prosecution, some with multiple offenders. In addition,

12 investigations were completed, but did not proceed to prosecution. Thirty-three cases remained at the full investigation stage at 30 June 2007.

Nineteen prosecutions were concluded during the year ending 30 June 2007 (some of which began before the 2006/07 year). Several involved a number of defendants. Convictions were obtained in 16 of the 19 cases. One prosecution was stayed after two jury trials failed to produce a verdict.

Four appeals against conviction and sentence were heard in the 2006/07 year. Three of these were dismissed.

The SFO's statutory powers are the most extensive in the area of criminal investigation in New Zealand. They require any person whose affairs are being investigated, or any other person the director has reason to believe may have relevant information or documents, to appear before the SFO to answer questions and produce such documents for inspection.

In the year ending 30 June 2007, 1,135 notices were issued under these powers (873 requiring documents or information, and 262 requiring people to attend interviews), compared with 859 in the previous year. Seven search warrants were executed, compared with five in the year before. Government funding for the year to 30 June 2007 was $5.5 million.

Criminal justice

The most serious crimes in New Zealand are defined in the Crimes Act 1961, the International Crimes and International Criminal Court Act 2000, and the Misuse of Drugs Act 1975. Other acts, such as the Aviation Crimes Act 1972 and the Maritime Crimes Act 1999, also outline serious indictable offences.

The Summary Offences Act 1981 covers a wide variety of less serious (summary) offences, including offences against public order, such as disorderly behaviour and fighting in a public place, and offences against people or property, such as common assault and wilful damage.

Convictions

A conviction is the most frequent outcome of a prosecution. The proportion of prosecutions that resulted in a conviction decreased slightly in the decade to 2006. In 1997, 69 percent of prosecutions resulted in conviction, but by 2000 the proportion had fallen to 66 percent. In 2000–03, the proportion remained at 66 percent, before decreasing slightly to 65 percent in 2004–06.

Total convictions The number of convictions decreased each year between 1998–2002. However, numbers increased again from 2003–06.

Figure 10.01 shows the types of offence as a proportion of all convictions from 2002 to 2006.

Table 10.01

	Offences[1] 1878–2007[2]		
Year	Recorded	Resolved	Percent resolved
1878	14,157	..	..
1880	17,837	16,723	93.8
1885	18,955	17,723	93.5
1890	13,115	12,177	92.8
1895	14,010	12,435	88.8
1900	18,358	17,131	93.3
1905	20,249	19,251	95.1
1910	25,106	23,949	95.4
1915	28,412	27,096	95.4
1920	26,106	24,718	94.7
1925	30,470	28,668	94.1
1930	37,214	33,690	90.5
1935	33,168	30,601	92.3
1940	45,009	41,619	92.5
1945	34,000	27,965	82.3
1950	35,383	..	..
1955	63,550	..	..
1960	102,792	66,857	65.0
1965	132,311	73,294	55.4
1970	165,859	94,785	57.1
1975	233,644	115,671	49.5
1980	349,193	166,535	47.7
1985	435,640	182,849	42.0
1990	488,886	201,942	41.3
1995	506,359	211,956	41.9
2000	432,354	174,611	40.4
2001	424,286	182,137	42.9
2002	436,315	182,468	41.8
2003	447,146	195,502	43.7
2004	426,149	191,988	45.1
2005	396,018	174,937	44.2
2006	426,469	188,511	44.2
2007	426,584	190,705	44.7

(1) Figures before 1995 may not be comparable with previous figures because they represent all offences, including traffic.
(2) Figures prior to 2000 are for a calendar year. Figures from 2000 are for the year ending 30 June.
Symbol: .. figure not available

Source: New Zealand Police

Figure 10.01

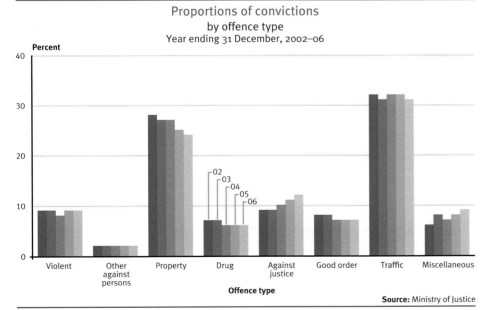

Proportions of convictions by offence type. Year ending 31 December, 2002–06

Source: Ministry of Justice

Violent offences The number of convictions for violent offences generally showed a decreasing trend from 1997–2002, from 15,683 to 14,427, before increasing each year for the next four years, reaching 17,059 in 2006. In each year to 2006, violent offences averaged between 8 and 9 percent of all convictions. Table 10.03 (overleaf) shows the number of convictions for violent offences for 1997–2006.

Restorative justice services

Restorative justice is a process that focuses on the people affected by a crime. While the victim's needs are a primary concern, offender restoration is a priority. Offenders are made accountable at face-to-face meetings with the victim. Support people help the parties achieve reconciliation and reintegration.

The Ministry of Justice continues to support the provision of restorative justice services to a number of courts around New Zealand. The ministry contracts 30 providers to offer restorative justice to victims and adult offenders.

Restorative justice is successfully used in a wide range of cases from serious and moderate levels of offending, to low level offending and diversion cases.

If a victim has been personally affected by an offence, and the offender pleads guilty, a judge can refer the case to a restorative justice provider to see whether the process should take place. A meeting only goes ahead where the offender and the victim agree to meet, and after careful consideration of its appropriateness.

The restorative justice meeting is relatively informal, and involves the offender and the victim, their support people, and one or two facilitators. The meeting may include one or two community representatives, who can talk about the effect of the offending on the community. The victim and offender discuss what happened, describe the consequences of the offence, and consider steps that the offender can take to repair harm caused, and to avoid re-offending.

Where the restorative justice process takes place before sentencing, a report on the meeting, including any agreements reached, is given to those involved in the case. The Sentencing Act 2002 requires judges to take restorative justice processes into account during sentencing.

With less serious offending, the case may be adjourned for the offender to complete agreements made in the restorative justice meeting. These frequently include reparative measures, such as voluntary payments to the victim, and rehabilitative measures, such as attending therapeutic programmes. In cases that are accepted for the Police Adult Diversion Scheme, successful completion of agreements results in the charge being withdrawn. In other cases, the court receives a report about the completion (or non-completion) of the agreements, which is taken into account during sentencing.

Evaluations of restorative justice in New Zealand show that:

- victims and offenders feel positive about the process
- victims and offenders are more involved in dealing with the offending
- victims have a better understanding of why the offence occurred and the likelihood of recurrence
- victims feel more positively about the criminal justice system
- restorative justice can help to reduce re-offending.

Source: Ministry of Justice

Table 10.02

Convictions
By type of offence
Year ending 31 December

Offence type	1997	1998	1999	2000	2001	2002	2003	2004	2005	2006
Violent	15,683	16,131	15,287	14,577	14,692	14,427	15,224	15,585	16,606	17,059
Other against persons	3,496	3,706	3,686	3,682	3,702	3,771	4,164	4,240	4,472	4,628
Property	53,674	53,295	51,178	49,635	48,715	47,546	49,021	49,849	46,444	47,263
Drug	12,997	14,168	14,021	13,649	12,555	12,272	12,359	11,643	10,923	11,326
Against justice	14,819	15,685	15,306	15,465	15,017	14,972	16,034	19,083	21,381	23,840
Good order	9,918	10,527	11,030	11,579	12,389	12,839	13,987	13,938	13,343	15,009
Traffic	60,511	62,226	58,817	57,025	56,584	54,541	55,847	59,308	59,809	63,360
Miscellaneous	9,706	10,101	9,437	7,663	9,296	10,150	13,516	13,474	14,533	19,032
Total	**180,804**	**185,839**	**178,762**	**173,275**	**172,950**	**170,518**	**180,152**	**187,120**	**187,511**	**201,517**

Source: Ministry of Justice

Violent sex offences Convictions for violent sex offences (rape, unlawful sexual connection, attempted sexual violation, and indecent assault) averaged just under 1,500 a year from 1997–2006. In 2006, there were 1,548 convictions for violent sex offences.

The number of rape convictions decreased from 253 in 1998 to 131 in 2000. Convictions increased to 213 in 2003, and then fluctuated around 200 from 2004–06. In the decade to 2006, convictions for unlawful sexual connection averaged 353 each year. In the same decade, convictions for attempted sexual violation and indecent assault averaged 49 and 900 per year, respectively.

Non-sexual assaults The number of convictions for non-sexual assaults increased by 11 percent between 1997–2006. The number of 'male assaults female' convictions decreased from 3,335 in 1997, to 2,625 in 2002, before increasing each year for the next four years, reaching 3,587 in 2006. Table 10.02 shows annual convictions by type of offence from 1997–2006.

Assaults on children Convictions for assaults on children aged less than 14 years, under section 194(a) of the Crimes Act 1961, were relatively stable between 1997–2002, at approximately 290 convictions per year. The number decreased to 253 in 2003 – the lowest figure recorded in the decade to 2006. In 2004, convictions rose to 312, and then fell to 269 in 2006.

Assault The number of convictions in the two most serious categories of assault – grievous assault and serious assault – generally increased by 32 percent and 43 percent, respectively, in the decade to 2006. Convictions for minor assault generally decreased, from 4,432 in 1997, to 3,815 in 2006.

Table 10.03

Convictions for violent offences
Year ending 31 December

Offence type	1997	1998	1999	2000	2001	2002	2003	2004	2005	2006
Murder	39	24	25	31	19	31	24	27	21	28
Manslaughter[1]	28	45	28	23	31	30	35	56	21	29
Attempted murder	19	5	6	9	11	16	5	16	5	6
Kidnapping/abduction	112	149	81	106	114	117	176	117	111	169
Rape	210	253	207	131	169	168	213	174	200	222
Unlawful sexual connection	279	349	361	311	384	343	414	338	339	414
Attempted sexual violation	58	56	58	42	59	36	48	42	53	42
Indecent assault	947	1,054	968	794	818	957	935	780	874	870
Aggravated burglary[2]	102	83	77	71	76	67	69	86	87	57
Aggravated robbery	582	555	523	424	366	349	398	388	477	433
Robbery[3]	258	278	233	170	152	172	207	206	245	273
Grievous assault[4]	1,209	1,335	1,258	1,320	1,303	1,296	1,372	1,465	1,608	1,597
Serious assault[5]	3,031	3,239	3,090	3,247	3,364	3,341	3,458	3,807	4,098	4,335
Male assaults female[6]	3,335	3,145	3,043	2,916	2,916	2,625	2,870	3,100	3,561	3,587
Assault on a child[7]	298	294	304	280	294	291	253	312	287	269
Minor assault[8]	4,432	4,516	4,245	3,959	3,848	3,763	3,800	3,777	3,782	3,815
Threaten to kill/do GBH[9]	602	633	641	628	626	697	771	772	698	773
Cruelty to a child[10]	17	17	40	21	23	19	27	28	20	16
Other violence	125	101	99	94	119	109	149	94	119	124
Total	**15,683**	**16,131**	**15,287**	**14,577**	**14,692**	**14,427**	**15,224**	**15,585**	**16,606**	**17,059**

(1) Includes convictions for manslaughter that involved the use of a motor vehicle. (2) The definitions of burglary and aggravated burglary were amended in 2003, and the new definitions came into force on 1 October 2003. (3) Includes both robbery and assault with intent to rob. (4) Mostly assault with a weapon, wounding with intent, and injuring with intent, but also includes aggravated wounding or injury, disabling, committing a dangerous act with intent, acid throwing, and poisoning with intent to cause grievous bodily harm. These offences have maximum penalties of at least five years' imprisonment. (5) Mostly common assault under the Crimes Act 1961, but also includes assault with intent to injure, injuring by an unlawful act, and aggravated assault (including assault on a police officer or a person assisting the police under the Crimes Act 1961). These offences have maximum penalties of at least five years' imprisonment. (6) Offences under section 194(b) of the Crimes Act 1961. These are likely to be mostly domestic-related assaults. These offences could have been included in the 'serious assault' category, as they have a maximum penalty of two years' imprisonment. However they have been presented separately to show trends in domestic-related assaults. These offences are the best available proxy for such offences, given that the data does not include information on victim-offender relationships. (7) Assault on a child under the age of 14 years under section 194(a) of the Crimes Act 1961. (8) Mostly common assault under the Summary Offences Act 1981, but also includes assault on a police or prison officer, or on a person assisting the police, under the same Act. These offences have a maximum penalty of six months' imprisonment. (9) Threaten to kill or do grievous bodily harm. (10) Offences under section 195 of the Crimes Act 1961.

Source: Ministry of Justice

Robbery The number of convictions for robbery has fluctuated between 1997–2006, around an annual average of 219. Convictions for aggravated robbery peaked at 582 in 1997, and dropped each year after that to 349 in 2002. Numbers rose again, then dropped to 433 in 2006.

Other convictions Convictions for threatening to kill or do grievous bodily harm showed a general upward trend between 1997–2006, with 773 convictions in 2006 – 28 percent higher than the 602 recorded in 1997. Convictions for non-violent sexual offences fell by 28 percent between 1997–2001, and then rose by 47 percent between 2001–06, reaching 610 convictions in 2006.

Table 10.04

Convictions for other offences against the person
Year ending 31 December

Offence type	1997	1998	1999	2000	2001	2002	2003	2004	2005	2006
Non-violent sexual[1]	579	492	474	495	415	447	468	453	573	610
Obstructing/resisting[2]	2,269	2,493	2,405	2,376	2,289	2,377	2,556	2,553	2,574	2,718
Intimidation[3]	466	477	549	560	618	653	772	933	1,097	1,082
Other against persons	182	244	258	251	380	294	368	301	228	218
Total	**3,496**	**3,706**	**3,686**	**3,682**	**3,702**	**3,771**	**4,164**	**4,240**	**4,472**	**4,628**

(1) Mainly unlawful sexual intercourse or committing an indecent act with or upon another person, committing an indecent act in a public place, or obscene exposure in a public place. Sex offences reported in the violent offences category are not included in the figures for this category. (2) Obstructing or resisting a police officer, traffic officer, or other official. (3) Mostly offences under section 21 of the Summary Offences Act 1981. Excludes threatening to kill or do grievous bodily harm, which is classified as a violent offence.

Source: Ministry of Justice

Drug offences In 2006, 73 percent of drug convictions involved cannabis. As table 10.05 shows, between 1997–2006, annual convictions for drug offences fluctuated around an average of 12,600. Six percent of all convictions in 2006 were for drug offences.

Table 10.05

Convictions for drug offences
Year ending 31 December

Offence type	1997	1998	1999	2000	2001	2002	2003	2004	2005	2006
Use cannabis	6,459	6,970	6,761	6,131	5,541	4,988	4,856	4,279	4,040	4,121
Deal in cannabis	3,708	3,977	3,916	3,884	3,589	3,305	3,125	2,675	2,189	2,196
Other cannabis[1]	1,730	2,172	2,255	2,186	2,183	2,072	2,240	2,093	1,942	1,933
Use other drug	444	412	493	676	544	668	733	851	808	1,030
Deal in other drug	496	415	405	459	403	772	631	575	610	660
Other drug[1]	160	222	191	313	295	467	774	1,170	1,334	1,386
Total	**12,997**	**14,168**	**14,021**	**13,649**	**12,555**	**12,272**	**12,359**	**11,643**	**10,923**	**11,326**

(1) Mostly offences relating to the possession of pipes, needles, syringes or other drug-related utensils. The category also includes offences where the offender permitted their premises or motor vehicle to be used for a drug offence, or where the offender made a false statement in relation to the Misuse of Drugs Act 1975.

Source: Ministry of Justice

Property offences The second largest group of charges resulting in a conviction is property offences. In 2006, 23 percent of all convictions were for offences against property. Convictions for property offences fell by 12 percent between 1997–2006. Numbers showed a slightly decreasing trend each year between 1997–2002, increased slightly in the following two years, and then decreased again in 2005, to reach the lowest value in the decade (46,444). In 2006, convictions for property offences increased again, but the number was still lower than earlier in the decade.

Table 10.06

Convictions for property offences
Year ending 31 December

Offence type	1997	1998	1999	2000	2001	2002	2003	2004	2005	2006
Burglary[1]	6,719	6,374	5,938	6,339	5,502	5,711	5,424	6,398	6,481	6,087
Theft	13,208	13,793	13,720	13,246	14,145	13,921	14,269	14,276	14,170	14,644
Receiving stolen goods	3,084	3,374	3,000	3,010	2,827	2,437	2,611	2,729	2,509	2,683
Motor vehicle conversion	2,793	2,538	2,431	2,173	2,053	2,093	2,130	2,110	1,967	2,127
Fraud[2]	18,661	17,124	15,078	14,394	14,220	12,765	13,629	13,550	11,078	10,770
Arson	198	313	209	170	198	213	212	219	238	209
Wilful damage[3]	4,800	5,087	5,156	5,232	5,065	5,103	5,285	5,551	5,802	6,724
Other property[4]	4,211	4,692	5,646	5,071	4,705	5,303	5,461	5,016	4,199	4,019
Total	**53,674**	**53,295**	**51,178**	**49,635**	**48,715**	**47,546**	**49,021**	**49,849**	**46,444**	**47,263**

(1) The definition of burglary was amended in 2003, and the new definition came into force on 1 October 2003. (2) Includes fraud, false pretences, forgery, and crimes involving deceit. The Crimes Amendment Act 2003 removed any references to 'fraud' from the Crimes Act 1961, and inserted sections referring to 'crimes involving deceit'. (3) Includes intentional damage under section 269 of the Crimes Act 1961 and wilful damage under section 11 of the Summary Offences Act 1981. (4) Mostly unlawfully interfering with, or getting into/onto, a motor vehicle or motorcycle, misleading a social welfare officer, providing misleading information to obtain a benefit/finance, possessing instruments for burglary or conversion, or unlawfully taking a bicycle.

Source: Ministry of Justice

Most of the decrease in property offences during the decade was due to a decrease in the number of convictions for fraud, which fell by 42 percent in the decade to 2006, from 18,661 in 1997, to 10,770 in 2006. This does not necessarily mean a decline in the number of offenders convicted of fraud, as many face a large number of charges – the total number of fraud charges can change considerably without the number of people involved changing appreciably.

Motor vehicle conversion In 2006, there were 2,127 convictions for motor vehicle conversion, down 24 percent compared with 1997.

Traffic convictions Convictions for driving causing the death or injury of another person tended to decrease between 1998–2002, but then increased in the next four years, reaching 1,675 convictions in 2006, back to the same level as in 1998.

For 2005–06 the average annual number of convictions for driving with excess alcohol was approximately 23,700. This was an increase from 2000–04, when the annual average number of convictions had dropped to around 21,700, from an average of 24,200 for 1997–99.

Between 1998–2002, the number of convictions for driving while disqualified decreased considerably, down from 11,605 to 6,861. From 2002–06, the number of convictions increased to 8,787, but the number was still 24 percent lower than in 1998.

Convictions for reckless or dangerous driving showed a generally increasing trend across the decade, from 2,611 in 1997, to 5,084 in 2006, an increase of 95 percent. This category includes offences related to unauthorised street or drag racing. Legislation making this an offence was introduced in May 2003 with the Land Transport (Unauthorised Street and Drag Racing) Amendment Act 2003.

In 2006, there were 7,441 convictions for careless driving; this was 23 percent lower than the figure for 1997.

Traffic offences As table 10.07 shows, the number of convictions for all traffic offences decreased from 60,511 in 1997, to 54,541 in 2002. In the next four years, the numbers increased, to reach 63,360 in 2006, the highest number in the decade. In the decade to 2006, traffic offences (at 31 percent) made up the largest group of charges resulting in conviction.

Table 10.07

Convictions for traffic offences
Year ending 31 December

Offence type	1997	1998	1999	2000	2001	2002	2003	2004	2005	2006
Driving causing death or injury[1]	1,556	1,679	1,575	1,446	1,422	1,403	1,528	1,572	1,631	1,675
Driving with excess alcohol[2]	24,672	24,819	23,101	21,601	22,363	20,811	21,078	22,589	23,061	24,240
Driving while disqualified	10,746	11,605	10,451	7,862	7,399	6,861	7,036	7,734	8,017	8,787
Reckless/dangerous driving	2,611	2,881	2,939	2,691	2,773	3,014	3,468	4,226	4,625	5,084
Careless driving	9,639	10,248	9,177	8,417	7,961	8,248	7,529	7,481	7,654	7,441
Other traffic	11,287	10,994	11,574	15,008	14,666	14,204	15,208	15,706	14,821	16,133
Total	**60,511**	**62,226**	**58,817**	**57,025**	**56,584**	**54,541**	**55,847**	**59,308**	**59,809**	**63,360**

(1) Charges involving driving with excess alcohol, reckless or dangerous driving, or careless driving, where death or injury occurred. This data does not distinguish between charges resulting in injury and charges resulting in death. A small number of people who kill a person while driving a motor vehicle will be charged with manslaughter rather than driving causing death (see table 10.03). (2) Mostly charges where the person was driving with excess alcohol, but also includes charges where the offender refused to supply a blood specimen, or was convicted for driving under the influence of drink or drugs. Charges where a person was driving with excess alcohol and caused death or injury are recorded in the first category in this table.

Source: Ministry of Justice

Offences against administration of justice As shown in table 10.08, the number of convictions for offences against the administration of justice increased (by 61 percent) in the decade to 2006, with a particularly large increase between 2003–06. The 2006 figure of 23,840 was the highest recorded in the decade. Offences against the administration of justice accounted for 12 percent of all convictions in 2006, compared with 8 percent in 1997.

Protection orders The number of breaches of protection orders increased by 73 percent between 1997–99, from 1,223 to 2,117. Between 1999–2006, the number of convictions stabilised, averaging 2,240 a year.

Offences against good order There was a strong increasing trend for these offences in the decade to 2006, rising 51 percent – from 9,918 in 1997 to 15,009 in 2006 – as shown in table 10.09. Convictions for disorderly behaviour, and for possession of an offensive weapon nearly doubled in the decade, reaching 8,592 and 2,285, respectively, in 2006. Convictions for trespassing offences also showed an increasing trend, up from 2,997 in 1997, to reach 3,466 in 2006.

Miscellaneous offence convictions The wide variety of offences included in this category means it is difficult to explain annual fluctuations in the total number of convictions for these offences. Legislative amendments to the Dog Control Act 1996 led to large decreases in the number of convictions under this Act, as shown in table 10.10 (overleaf). Legislative amendments to the Sale of Liquor Act 1989 also led to large decreases in the number of convictions under this Act between 2000–02. Convictions then increased substantially between 2003–06, after convictions for breaching local liquor bans were included in this offence category. Before April 2003, these had been incorporated within the category of other miscellaneous offences.

Table 10.08

Convictions for offences against the administration of justice
Year ending 31 December

Offence type	1997	1998	1999	2000	2001	2002	2003	2004	2005	2006
Breach of community work[1]	...	...	...	...	...	522	5,251	7,925	9,064	10,518
Breach of periodic detention[2]	7,318	7,532	7,011	6,623	6,257	5,551	1,090	340	130	65
Breach of community service[3]	326	282	220	246	219	277	144	28	16	10
Subtotal	**7,644**	**7,814**	**7,231**	**6,869**	**6,476**	**6,350**	**6,485**	**8,293**	**9,210**	**10,593**
Breach of supervision	634	601	553	502	577	500	566	744	1,062	1,185
Breach of release conditions[4]	180	202	199	235	267	309	567	939	1,241	1,427
Failure to answer bail[5]	3,959	4,013	4,124	4,285	4,307	4,393	5,104	5,745	6,220	7,263
Breach of protection/ non-molestation order	1,223	1,881	2,117	2,257	2,360	2,027	2,254	2,264	2,381	2,249
Escape custody[6]	380	424	406	372	292	285	332	322	370	340
Obstructing/perverting the course of justice	155	152	132	143	115	128	149	174	205	182
Other against justice	644	598	544	802	623	980	577	602	692	601
Total	**14,819**	**15,685**	**15,306**	**15,465**	**15,017**	**14,972**	**16,034**	**19,083**	**21,381**	**23,840**

(1) Community work was introduced on 30 June 2002 by the Sentencing Act 2002. (2) The sentence of periodic detention was abolished by the Sentencing Act 2002 from 30 June 2002. (3) The sentence of community service was abolished by the Sentencing Act 2002 from 30 June 2002. (4) Failure, without reasonable excuse, to comply with any condition of release from prison. (5) Failure by a person on bail to appear in court at a specified time and place. (6) Mostly refers to escapes from custody in a penal institution, or escapes from police custody. Also includes a small number of charges for escaping custody from some other type of institution, such as a psychiatric hospital.

Symbol: ... not applicable

Source: Ministry of Justice

Characteristics of convicted offenders Male offenders accounted for 82 percent of all convictions in 2006 (where the offender's gender was known). Forty-five percent of all convictions in 2006 (where the offender's ethnicity was known) involved Europeans, 43 percent Māori, 9 percent Pacific peoples, and 3 percent involved offenders of other ethnicities.

Of all convictions in 2006 (where the offender's age was known), 21 percent involved teenagers, 38 percent were in their twenties, 21 percent were in their thirties, and 19 percent were aged 40 years and over.

Table 10.09

Convictions for offences against good order
Year ending 31 December

Offence type	1997	1998	1999	2000	2001	2002	2003	2004	2005	2006
Riot	7	2	5	23	15	6	4	15	3	0
Unlawful assembly	69	40	21	23	17	30	53	72	51	34
Possessing an offensive weapon	1,259	1,417	1,417	1,310	1,444	1,537	1,650	1,780	1,955	2,285
Offensive language	598	650	699	681	645	581	551	493	386	420
Disorderly behaviour[1]	4,661	5,130	5,645	6,149	6,933	7,151	8,114	7,968	7,451	8,592
Trespassing	2,997	3,028	3,006	3,135	3,092	3,288	3,393	3,400	3,307	3,466
Other against good order	327	260	237	258	243	246	222	210	190	212
Total	**9,918**	**10,527**	**11,030**	**11,579**	**12,389**	**12,839**	**13,987**	**13,938**	**13,343**	**15,009**

(1) Mostly refers to behaving in a disorderly or offensive manner (section 4 Summary Offences Act 1981), disorderly or threatening behaviour (section 3 Summary Offences Act 1981), or fighting in a public place (section 7 Summary Offences Act 1981).

Source: Ministry of Justice

Sentencing for all offences

Throughout the decade ending 2006, 8–10 percent of convicted cases resulted in a custodial sentence. In 2006, 10,469 cases resulted in a custodial sentence.

Of all cases resulting in custodial sentences across the decade, between 21–32 percent resulted in short prison sentences of three months or less (excluding corrective training).

Cases with prison sentences of more than three months and up to two years made up between 51–65 percent of all cases resulting in custodial sentences during the decade.

In each year during the decade, less than 1 percent of all cases that resulted in imprisonment received a custodial sentence of more than 10 years (including life imprisonment and preventive detention).

The average custodial sentence length imposed (including life imprisonment and preventive detention) increased from 13.5 months in 1997, to 15.7 months in 2003. Between 2004–06, the average custodial sentence length imposed was 14 months.

In 2006, 90 percent of cases resulting in custodial sentences involved male offenders.

Dealing with young offenders

Section 21 of the Crimes Act 1961 states that "no person shall be convicted of an offence by reason of any act done or omitted when under the age of 10". Similarly, section 22 of the Crimes Act 1961 states that "no person shall be convicted of an offence by reason of any act done or omitted when of the age of 10 but under the age of 14, unless he knew either that the act or omission was wrong, or that it was contrary to the law".

Consequently, Police often take action other than apprehension when dealing with young offenders. Police data on the apprehension of children should not be used to make quantitative inferences about levels or trends in offending by children.

Apprehension of children[1] and young persons[2]
Year ending 30 June

Type of resolution	2005	2006	2007
Finalised by warning	9,375	11,436	11,299
Youth Aid alternative action	22,216	17,235	15,329
Referred for family group conference or youth court	6,921	11,706	11,165
Resolved by other means	1,383	2,237	1,204
Total cleared	**39,895**	**42,614**	**38,997**
Offences dealt with per Youth Aid officer	235	237	223
Offences referred to family group conference per officer	41	65	64
	Percent		
Offenders dealt with by police only	82.7	72.6	71.4
Offenders dealt with by family group conference	17.3	27.4	28.6

(1) Aged 10, 11, 12 or 13 years on the day of the alleged offence. (2) Aged 14, 15 or 16 years on the day of the alleged offence.

Source: New Zealand Police

Making sure fines are paid

Collections is an operational business unit of the Ministry of Justice. Collections field staff operate with the powers, functions and responsibilities of deputy registrars or bailiffs of district courts to carry out four distinct responsibilities:

- collection and enforcement of fines, including court-imposed fines, lodged infringements, reparation, court costs and fees

- enforcement of civil judgment orders on behalf of judgment creditors where payment has been ordered by the court

- service of court documents

- administration of summary instalment orders.

The effective collection of fines and civil debts helps to enhance the credibility of fines as a sentencing option, increases public regard for the administration of justice, and fosters respect for, and compliance with, the law.

Collections seeks compliance with the requirement for the public to pay outstanding fines and reparation in a number of ways, including:

- 'attachments' on wages or benefits, requiring the employer or the Ministry of Social Development to pay a portion of the money owing in outstanding reparation or fines

- seizing and selling property of people owing fines or reparation to pay what is owed

- deducting money from fine defaulters' bank accounts

- issuing a charging order against property (including land) that prevents the sale of property without first discharging the 'charge' against it

- intercepting ('garnish') money being paid to a fines defaulter to use that money to pay the reparation or fine

- intercepting, and possibly arresting, serious fines and reparation defaulters at airports when they enter or leave New Zealand.

From 1 July 2007 to 31 March 2008, $172.7 million in fines was collected. Collections also collected or placed under arrangement to pay within four months 80.3 percent of court-imposed fines, and actioned 89.2 percent of civil enforcement applications within 28 days.

Source: Ministry of Justice

Table 10.10

Convictions for miscellaneous offences
Year ending 31 December

Offence type/ Act breached	1997	1998	1999	2000	2001	2002	2003	2004	2005	2006
Arms Act[1]	880	952	921	857	705	737	808	884	846	1,015
Dog Control Act	1,641	885	592	432	491	346	551	286	347	305
Tax Act[2]	2,471	2,464	2,105	2,269	3,773	4,161	5,313	5,181	5,994	7,510
Liquor-related[3]	957	1,200	1,181	223	190	251	1,242	3,221	2,927	4,821
Fisheries Act[4]	319	714	455	750	762	719	792	847	623	496
Other miscellaneous[5]	3,438	3,886	4,183	3,132	3,375	3,936	4,810	3,055	3,796	4,885
Total	**9,706**	**10,101**	**9,437**	**7,663**	**9,296**	**10,150**	**13,516**	**13,474**	**14,533**	**19,032**

(1) Excludes a small number of offences prosecuted under this Act that were categorised as violent offences or other offences against the person. (2) Offences under the Income Tax Act 1976, the Income Tax Act 1994, the Goods and Services Tax Act 1985, or the Tax Administration Act 1994. (3) Includes convictions under the Sale of Liquor Act 1962 and the Sale of Liquor Act 1989 as well as convictions under section 38(3) of the Summary Offences Act 1981 (minors drinking in a public place) and, from April 2003, convictions for breaches of local liquor bans under section 709A(8) of the Local Government Act 1974. (4) This category covers convictions under the Fisheries Act 1983 and related regulations, eg commercial fishing regulations and freshwater fisheries regulations. (5) Includes a wide variety of offences such as breaches under: the Health and Safety in Employment Act 1992, the Insolvency Act 1967, the Resource Management Act 1991, the Films, Videos, and Publications Classification Act 1993, the Building Act 1991, the Telecommunications Act 1987, the Medicines Act 1981, and the Conservation Act 1987.

Source: Ministry of Justice

Of cases resulting in imprisonment in 2006 (where the offender's ethnicity was known), Māori accounted for 53 percent, 37 percent involved Europeans, 7 percent involved Pacific peoples, and 3 percent involved offenders of other ethnicities.

Of cases resulting in custodial sentences in 2006, 41 percent involved offenders in their twenties, while 12 percent involved teenagers (mainly aged 17–19 years).

Offenders in their thirties and those aged 40 years and over accounted for 26 and 20 percent, respectively, of cases where a custodial sentence was given in 2006.

Between 25 percent and 35 percent of all convicted cases in each year of the decade resulted in the imposition of community-based sentences. This percentage showed a decreasing trend after 1999, with the average figure for 2004–06 (25 percent) representing the lowest of the decade.

The use of monetary penalties as the most serious sentence fluctuated between 47 and 52 percent of all convicted cases during the decade.

Table 10.11

Sentencing for all offences[1][2]
Year ending 31 December

Sentence type	1997	1998	1999	2000	2001	2002	2003	2004	2005	2006
Custodial	8,102	8,255	8,177	7,886	7,805	7,930	8,497	10,353	10,553	10,469
Community work[3]	...	...	...	...	...	12,693	25,073	24,839	24,998	27,196
Periodic detention[4]	19,510	21,340	20,481	18,395	18,461	8,791	...	...	...	...
Community service[4]	7,812	8,525	8,226	7,124	6,764	3,073	...	...	...	...
Community programme[4]	430	379	287	203	207	54	...	...	...	...
Supervision	5,037	5,004	4,550	4,024	3,367	2,312	1,894	2,014	2,347	2,243
Monetary[5]	47,515	47,165	47,326	47,215	48,028	48,507	50,733	52,918	50,650	53,207
Deferment[6]	3,233	3,560	3,502	3,590	3,606	3,612	4,134	4,831	4,916	5,345
Other[7]	808	983	1,116	1,125	1,135	1,226	1,295	1,878	1,897	2,061
Conviction and discharge[8]	4,068	4,994	4,982	5,945	6,233	6,141	6,960	12,184	12,573	12,253
Total	**96,515**	**100,205**	**98,647**	**95,507**	**95,606**	**94,339**	**98,586**	**109,017**	**107,934**	**112,774**

(1) The system used to log cases was updated in 2004. This has caused changes in the figures and trends in cases that are observed up to and following 2004. In particular, any changes in the number of cases in 2004 may not represent a true change in offender patterns. Caution should therefore be used when making inferences based on any change between 2003 and 2004. (2) Only the most serious sentence imposed is shown for cases where more than one sentence was imposed. (3) Community work was introduced from 30 June 2002 by the Sentencing Act 2002. (4) Sentence abolished from 30 June 2002 by the Sentencing Act 2002. (5) Monetary penalties include fines and reparation. (6) To come up for sentence if called on, or a suspended prison sentence. Suspended prison sentences were abolished from 30 June 2002 by the Sentencing Act 2002. (7) Mainly cases that resulted in disqualification from driving, or an order under section 34 of the Criminal Procedure (Mentally Impaired Persons) Act 2003 for treatment or care of the offender in a psychiatric hospital or secure facility. Deportation orders are also included in this category. (8) Conviction and discharge under section 20 of the Criminal Justice Act 1985, or section 108 of the Sentencing Act 2002.

Symbol: ... not applicable

Source: Ministry of Justice

Proceeds of crime

Apart from his role in company liquidations and bankruptcies, the official assignee has certain statutory responsibilities under the Proceeds of Crime Act 1991.

The High Court may order that assets be placed in the custody and control of the official assignee. This is to ensure that assets are not depleted or destroyed while a criminal trial is pending, or a further application under the Act is to be heard.

If the court orders forfeiture of a criminal's property, or that restrained property must be sold to satisfy a fine, the official assignee takes the necessary steps to realise those assets, and to transfer proceeds to the Crown.

In the year ending 30 June 2007, the official assignee, in relation to proceeds of crime matters, returned $1,445,766 to the Crown, compared with $1,012,205 in the 2006 year, and $1,235,991 in 2005.

In March 2007, the government introduced the Criminal Proceeds (Recovery) Bill, to repeal and replace the Proceeds of Crime Act 1991. The Bill expands the proceeds of crime regime considerably, chiefly by introducing a civil forfeiture regime. The official assignee will continue to have responsibility for the custody and control of restrained property under the new regime, and for realising forfeited property.

Victim Support

Victim Support is a community, not-for-profit organisation providing a nationwide, 24-hour, seven-day-a-week support service for victims of crime and trauma.

Of those receiving support, 90 percent are victims of crime. Other victims include families and survivors where there has been a serious transport accident, a sudden death, a suicide attempt or completion, or a natural disaster.

A range of support services, based on the victim's needs, are provided by trained volunteer support workers. These include: crisis intervention at the time of an incident, where practical and emotional support is offered; advice on other services and agencies available to the victim; provision of information about police investigations and judicial processes; and ongoing support as needed, particularly throughout the criminal justice process. This latter support includes: assisting the victim to prepare a victim impact statement; attending court with the victim; supporting victims who have agreed to participate in a restorative justice conference or family group conference; and supporting victims who wish to participate in a parole hearing.

Other services available to victims include free counselling for families and close friends of victims of a homicide; financial assistance for victims who wish to attend a High Court trial, or to present a submission at a parole hearing; and advice on assistance with improving home security for low-income people who have been victims of repeat burglaries.

The main funding for Victim Support comes from government contracts for services, grants, sponsorship and donations, and national and local fund-raising activities. Victim Support also receives funding from the Vote Justice allocation, which contributes to the cost of providing core services for victims of crime.

Victim Support works closely with the Police, who provide office accommodation and facilities. There are 71 Victim Support offices throughout New Zealand, grouped into 12 districts. Table 10.12 provides details of Victim Support activities for the years ending 30 June 2001 to 2006.

Table 10.12

Victim Support operation and funding Year ending 30 June						
	2001	2002	2003	2004	2005	2006
Victim Support groups	66	67	67	67	63	70
Staff employed (full-time equivalent)	53	53	53	62	78	93
Contacts made with victims	212,443	140,659	187,211	163,026	127,692	135,427
Volunteer workers	1,326	1,311	1,304	1,352	1,428	1,670
Hours of service given by volunteers	134,700	73,284	80,137	73,321	55,134	49,877
Ministry of Justice funding ($million)	1.2	1.7	1.9	2.5	3.4	3.4
Funding for victim assistance schemes ($)	583,000	653,000	653,000	653,000	653,000	653,000

Source: New Zealand Council of Victim Support Groups

Crime reduction

The Crime Reduction Strategy, introduced in 2001, establishes priorities for preventing and reducing crime. The strategy targets: family violence, including child abuse; other violence, including sexual abuse; burglary; theft of and from cars; organised criminal activity; serious traffic offending; youth offending and reoffending.

The strategy emphasises a partnership approach among government agencies, local government, and communities. Target groups include victims (particularly repeat victims), Māori, Pacific peoples, at-risk families, and those affected by drugs, alcohol, or gambling.

In June 2004, the Ministry of Justice's Crime Prevention Unit (CPU) launched an action plan to reduce community and sexual violence.

The CPU also implemented changes to the funding of local government activities to prevent community crime. From 1 July 2004, funding has been provided to territorial authorities, according to criteria determined by their crime prevention needs, including the size of population and crime rates. Metropolitan and provincial authorities are funded directly on the basis of a crime prevention plan designed to meet local needs. Smaller and rural authorities are funded on the basis of approved crime prevention projects.

The CPU has crime prevention partnership agreements with four iwi (tribes), and also funds crime prevention projects and programmes directly through individual contracts. The biggest contracted programmes are community-managed restorative justice programmes, community youth programmes run in conjunction with the Police, and neighbourhood-based safety programmes.

The appropriation for community crime reduction and prevention initiatives in the 2006/07 financial year was $5.950 million, compared with $6.538 million in the previous financial year.

Corrections system

The Department of Corrections' core responsibility is to manage the New Zealand corrections system and in doing so, to protect the public and reduce reoffending.

The department (also referred to as 'Corrections') ensures that custodial sentences (imprisonment), and community-based sentences and orders imposed by the courts and the New Zealand Parole Board, are administered in a safe, secure, humane and effective way.

Protecting the public involves ensuring compliance with sentences and orders, and providing information to the courts and parole board to assist them in their decision making. Reducing reoffending involves provision of targeted rehabilitative and reintegrative interventions to change offending behaviour.

The department operates:

- 20 prisons
- three community probation and psychological services regions, managing more than 1,500 staff in more than 140 locations nationwide. These staff include probation officers, psychologists and programme facilitators
- 13 prison-based special treatment units – six drug and alcohol units, five Māori focus units, one violence prevention unit, and two sex offender units.

The Department of Corrections consists of eight groups and services, headed by a chief executive who is responsible to the Minister of Corrections for the broad direction of the department's work, goal and objective setting, policy advice formulation, effective implementation of major policy decisions, determining the department's priorities, and effective administration of the organisation.

Contracted facilities and services

Prisoner escort and courtroom custodial services The Department of Corrections has a contract with Chubb New Zealand Ltd to provide prisoner escort and courtroom custodial services in the Northland and Auckland regions. This includes escorting prisoners between corrections facilities, courts, and forensic psychiatric units, and court custody of prisoners appearing for judicial purposes. In the rest of New Zealand, prisoner escort and courtroom custodial services are provided by the Police and prison services officers.

Community Probation and Psychological Services

Each year, Community Probation and Psychological Services (CPPS) manages close to 72,000 sentences and orders, such as home detention and community-based sentences. CPPS has a key role in providing information and assessment reports to assist the courts in their sentencing function. It provides information to judges and the New Zealand Parole Board to inform sentencing and release decisions.

CPPS programme facilitators deliver a range of targeted rehabilitation programmes to offenders and prisoners to address their offending behaviour. CPPS psychologists treat offenders, conduct research, develop intervention programmes, and provide detailed reports about offenders to the court and parole boards. They also provide training and education for other Corrections staff and research programmes.

They operate from 10 offices nationwide, and at three special treatment units – Te Piriti, for child sex offenders (Auckland Prison); Kia Marama, for child sex offenders (Rolleston Prison); and the Violence Prevention Unit (Rimutaka Prison).

Over 2008–09, the department will also offer three special treatment unit programmes for high risk offenders – the Karaka Unit at Waikeria Prison is already operating and Matapuna at Christchurch Men's Prison will open in 2009. Puna Tatari at Spring Hill, in the Waikato, has special treatment and drug treatment units from September 2008.

At 30 June 2007, the Department of Corrections employed 89 psychologists. Department psychologists delivered close to 30,000 consultation hours to CPPS and Prison Services for the 2006/07 year.

CPPS manages offenders subject to sentences and orders in the community – community work, community detention, supervision, intensive supervision, extended supervision, home detention, parole, post-detention conditions, and release on conditions.

Community sentences

A new sentencing hierarchy was introduced on 1 October 2007. It is based on the degree of restriction on the offender's liberty and the level of supervision provided in each sentence. The level of monitoring, supervision and restriction of an offender increases as they move up the hierarchy. Imprisonment is the most severe penalty, and the sentence of 'convict and discharge' is the least severe.

In sentencing an offender, the court has a range of non-custodial sentences available and the opportunity to combine sentencing options. In order of severity, community-based sentences available are:

Community work sentences require offenders to do up to 400 hours of unpaid work for non-profit organisations. Community-work offenders contribute more than two million hours of free labour a year.

Supervision is a rehabilitative community-based sentence. Offenders can be sentenced to supervision for between six months and one year. Offenders will have standard, and possibly special, conditions imposed under supervision. They report to a probation officer, who will explain the requirements and conditions of the sentence, including how often they have to report.

Intensive supervision is a rehabilitative community-based sentence. It requires offenders to address the causes of their offending, with intensive oversight from a probation officer. Offenders can be sentenced to intensive supervision for between six months and two years.

Community detention requires the offender to comply with an electronically-monitored curfew imposed by the court. Offenders can be sentenced to detention for up to six months. Curfews can total up to 84 hours per week, with the minimum curfew period being two hours.

Home detention is the most severe sentence below imprisonment. It is intended for offenders who would otherwise receive a short sentence of imprisonment, and for whom community-based sentences are not deemed appropriate.

Home detention requires an offender to remain at an approved residence at all times, under electronic monitoring and close supervision by a probation officer. It can help offenders maintain family relationships, keep working or actively seek work, attend training or rehabilitative programmes. Sentences may range from 14 days to 12 months.

In addition to the above sentences, CPPS manages the following two sentences and orders:

Extended supervision is aimed at managing the long-term risks posed by child sex offenders in the community. Extended supervision is an order imposed by the court that allows the highest-risk child sex offenders to be monitored in the community for up to 10 years after their release from prison. It is expected to significantly reduce the rate of reoffending.

Extended supervision is combined with special conditions imposed by the parole board. These can include curfews, reporting, electronic monitoring, and off-limit areas.

Parole involves release into the community under the management of a probation officer. The Parole Act 2002 allows offenders serving sentences of more than two years to be considered by the New Zealand Parole Board for parole.

People on parole are released from prison under strict conditions laid down by law. Often they will be moved to a community-based programme designed to deal with their offending-related problems. They must report regularly to a probation officer, who will monitor their progress and adherence to conditions imposed as part of parole.

Table 10.13

Community-based sentences					
Year ending 30 June					
Sentence	2003	2004	2005	2006	2007
Community work	27,936	28,043	27,928	28,400	31,387
Supervision	5,059	4,928	5,301	5,565	6,359
Home detention	1,575	1,950	1,515	1,293	1,517
Parole	1,923	1,308	1,132	1,244	1,451
Post-release conditions	1,461	3,457	4,652	4,819	4,867
Extended supervision orders[1]	...	...	21	48	38

(1) Introduced by the Parole (Extended Supervision) Amendment Act 2004.

Symbol: ... not applicable

Source: Department of Corrections

Increased prison capacity

In 1997, the Department of Corrections established the Regional Prisons Development Programme (RPDP) to construct four new regional prisons, and add approximately 1,600 new beds to the prison system by the end of 2007.

- The Northland Region Corrections Facility (350 beds) opened on time and within budget in March 2005.

- The Auckland Region Women's Corrections Facility (286 beds) in Manukau, which opened in June 2006, is at full capacity, having completed its prisoner build-up in January 2007.

- The 335-bed Otago Corrections Facility at Milburn, south of Dunedin, opened in May 2007, and reached full capacity in November 2007.

- The 650-bed Spring Hill Corrections Facility in north Waikato opened in September 2007.

The new facilities are low-rise and mainly single-level, with groups of cells set out in clusters over a large area. Local communities, especially tangata whenua (indigenous people), were involved in the design and establishment process.

Regional prisons enable prisoners to be kept closer to their families/whānau, provide as near to a normal environment as possible, and maximise the benefits of modern management practices. These elements aim to reduce reoffending.

While new prisons have been important, the expansion of cell capacity at existing sites has also been critical to meeting increasing prisoner numbers. A total of 773 beds have been added to existing sites since 2004.

By the end of 2007, more than 2,370 new beds had been added to the prison system.

A number of improvements have also been made to prison security:

- 65 percent of all prisons now have a single point of entry to restrict contraband

- 35 percent of all prisons have centralised visiting, to restrict the entry of contraband

- 65 percent of all prisons have a central control room facility, to enhance surveillance and improve prison operation and staff safety

- prison escapes have fallen by 84 percent in the 10 years to December 2007.

Source: Department of Corrections

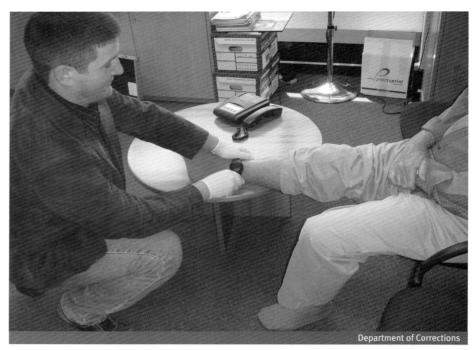

Department of Corrections

If a prisoner is granted permission to reside at home, through a home detention sentence, the electronic monitoring anklet will show that he or she is on the property they are confined to.

Figure 10.02

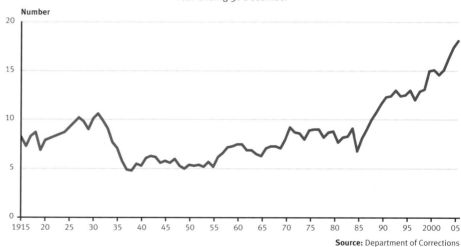

Prison inmates
Per 10,000 people
Year ending 31 December

Source: Department of Corrections

Prison Services

Prison Services is the part of the Department of Corrections responsible for running New Zealand's 20 prisons. It is responsible for providing safe, secure, and humane prison services, which contribute to reducing re-offending. It manages the sentence needs of each offender, including rehabilitation and reintegration.

Prison Services manages prisoners' security, with two key priorities. The first focuses on community safety, ensuring prisoners are securely contained in prison for the duration of their sentence. The second concentrates on encouraging prisoners to address the factors that drive their criminal lifestyle, and take steps to change their offending behaviour.

The 20 prisons/corrections facilities are managed within three regions, with a national office in Wellington. Prisons are listed in table 10.14.

Prisoners with different security classifications are held at each institution. Fifteen prisons are receiving institutions, while Auckland, Spring Hill, Tongariro, Wellington and Rolleston do not receive directly from courts. The cost per prisoner per day increased from $188.71 in the 2005/06 financial year to $209.97 in the 2006/07 year.

Detention in a corrections facility

Prison Services administers and manages custodial sentences imposed on offenders sentenced to imprisonment. Prison Services also manages remand offenders waiting on court appearances or sentencing.

At the time of sentencing, a judge may impose release conditions (both standard and special) on offenders sentenced to terms of imprisonment of 12 months or less, and must impose standard conditions on those sentenced to more than 12 months, but not more than 24 months. The courts may also impose special conditions on these offenders. Courts may defer the start of a person's prison sentence for up to two months. They can also impose a minimum non-parole period on any offender sentenced to more than 24 months, if satisfied that the circumstances of the offence are sufficiently serious.

The New Zealand Parole Board must impose standard conditions on offenders at their statutory release date, to take effect for six months beyond that date. The parole board may also impose special conditions to apply for the same length of time.

Murder The Sentencing Act 2002 reformed the law regarding sentencing for murder. Previously, a conviction for murder automatically resulted in a sentence of life imprisonment. Under the 2002 Act, there is still a strong presumption in favour of that, but the court may impose a determinate sentence, if satisfied that life imprisonment would be 'manifestly unjust' in the circumstances.

If the court chooses not to impose life imprisonment, it must give reasons in writing. If an offender is sentenced to life imprisonment, the court must also impose a minimum non-parole period of at least 10 years. In cases where there are specified aggravating factors, such as unusual callousness or a vulnerable victim, the court must impose a minimum non-parole period of at least 17 years, unless the court considers that to be 'manifestly unjust'.

Preventive detention This sentence can be imposed for a range of sexual and violent offending. The Sentencing Act 2002 lowered the age of eligibility for preventive detention from 21 to 18 years, and increased the range of offences for which preventive detention can be imposed. When the court imposes this sentence, it must also impose a minimum non-parole period of at least five years. Under previous legislation, the minimum non-parole period had to be at least 10 years.

Victims' rights Victims of certain offences can apply under the Victims' Rights Act 2002 to receive specified information about offenders serving a sentence of imprisonment, either in prison or under home detention, or who have been released on parole. Victims are also entitled to information about a prisoner's sentence (including any programmes they have undertaken and completed,

Table 10.14

Corrections facilities At 11 December 2007	
Prison/corrections facility	Capacity
Male prisons	
Waikeria	1,031
Rimutaka	1,044
Christchurch	920
Auckland	681
Hawke's Bay	666
Spring Hill	650
Tongariro/Rangipo	601
Wanganui	538
Mt Eden	527
Auckland Central Remand	412
Northland Region	366
Otago	335
Rolleston	320
Manawatu	290
Invercargill	180
Wellington	140
New Plymouth	112
Female prisons	
Arohata	154
Auckland Region Women's	286
Christchurch Women's	138
Source: Department of Corrections	

Reducing energy costs in New Zealand prisons

Corrections' energy manager Cees Ebskamp inspecting solar panels at Waikato's new Spring Hill Corrections Facility, which has the largest solar water heating system in the country.

As New Zealand's third-largest government department, and one with a major ecological footprint, Corrections has a key role to play in achieving the Government's goal of building a sustainable nation. It's a role they take seriously.

Corrections' 20 prison sites make it one of the country's biggest users of hot water. Where it is cost-effective to do so, water-saving devices and methods, and solar panels are installed. These supplement other energy sources for hot water, to reduce CO2 emissions and save energy costs.

The Spring Hill Corrections Facility in the Waikato, and Christchurch Men's Prison are good examples of how effective solar panels can be. Spring Hill's 36 solar panels generate about 40 percent of the hot water needed for one of its large accommodation blocks. It is currently the largest solar water heating system site in New Zealand.

The decision to add solar panels to one of the accommodation blocks was made towards the end of the design phase of the new prison, which was completed late in 2007. The performance of this pilot system will be monitored, with a view to re-configuring if required, and installing solar panels on other blocks at a later stage.

At Christchurch Prison, 97 square metres of solar panels supplement the LPG-fired (liquefied petroleum gas) boiler, to produce the 7,000 litres of hot water required daily for the laundry.

For the past two years, recycled water from Wanganui Prison's sewage treatment ponds has nourished trees, shrubs and plants grown in the prison's onsite nursery. ESR (Environmental Science and Research) gave Corrections the thumbs up for its innovative and safe recycling of Wanganui Prison's sewage water. Tests for impurities showed the recycling process was working exceptionally well.

The prison's sewage water is passed through several ponds, filtered, stored, and ultra-violet treated, before being sprayed through heavy droplet sprinklers, designed to stop it blowing away on windy days. Great care is taken not to use the water on edible plants, and to ensure that the watering system only operate after everyone has left the nursery at the end of the day.

Early indications suggest that, thanks to the recycling scheme, water use per prisoner has decreased by about 10 percent. Water recycling at other prisons is being actively considered.

Source: Department of Corrections

and their security classification), to help them prepare their submission. All applications are verified by Police, and sent to the government agency responsible for notification.

The Department of Corrections notifies registered victims about offenders' information, such as their escape or death in custody, release to work, temporary release, or impending release date. The parole board is responsible under the Parole Act 2002 for notifying registered victims of impending parole hearings and of the victim's right to make submissions to the board. The board also notifies registered victims of the outcome of the board's hearings and, if the offender is released, any conditions on release that specifically relate to the registered victim or to submissions they have made to the board.

Parole eligibility and final release

New Zealand Parole Board The board is an independent statutory body that considers when offenders can be released on parole. It can also recall offenders to prison, on application by the Department of Corrections. The board is made up of full-time and part-time members appointed from the community and the judiciary. It operates in panels of three, with a district court judge convening each panel.

The parole board's paramount consideration, as set out in the Parole Act 2002, must be the safety of the community. The board considers the likelihood of further offending, and the possible nature and seriousness of this prospect. An offender does not apply for parole, it is a legal entitlement.

Determinate sentences Prisoners serving finite terms of imprisonment of 24 months or less are not eligible for parole, but are released automatically after serving half of their sentence. Prisoners serving finite terms of imprisonment of more than 24 months are eligible for parole after serving one-third of their sentences, unless the court has imposed a minimum non-parole period longer than this. A non-parole period can be for 10 years, or two-thirds of the total sentence, whichever is the lesser. When offenders are eligible for parole, their suitability for parole will be considered once a year, although further hearings can be postponed for up to two years. Prisoners must be released on their statutory release date, if not granted parole before then.

Indeterminate sentences Prisoners sentenced to preventive detention are subject to a minimum period of imprisonment specified by the court, which must be for a term of at least five years. When offenders are eligible for parole, their suitability for parole will be considered once a year, although further parole hearings can be postponed for up to three years.

Prisoners serving life sentences for murder are normally eligible for parole after serving 10 years of their sentences, unless the court has imposed a minimum period of imprisonment longer than this. However, where there are unusual mitigating factors, the court may decide to impose a determinate sentence, rather than life. When offenders are eligible for parole, their suitability for parole will be considered once a year, although further parole hearings can be postponed for up to three years.

Prisoners

Prisoner numbers The number of prisoners in New Zealand prisons has been increasing steadily. On 10 December 2007, there were 7,771 prisoners (7,319 males and 452 females) with 6,068 sentenced prisoners and 1,703 prisoners remanded in custody. By comparison, on 29 December 2005, there were 7,420 prisoners (6,965 males and 455 females) – 6,076 sentenced prisoners and 1,344 prisoners remanded in custody.

Age and ethnicity At 30 March 2008, Māori made up 49.6 percent of the prison population (3,770), and 45.1 percent of those serving community sentences (14,135). Pacific peoples accounted for 11.6 percent of the prison population (882), and 9.2 percent of those serving community sentences (2,902).

At 30 March 2008, 44.5 percent of all Māori prisoners were serving sentences for violent offences, compared with 48.5 percent of Pacific prisoners, and 26.5 percent of European prisoners. Among Māori prisoners, 27.3 percent were aged under 25 years, compared with 29.5 percent of Pacific prisoners, and 19.0 percent of European prisoners.

Pacific peoples accounted for 9.3 percent of offenders on community sentences and orders. The statistics are boosted by the high proportion of offenders aged 15–24 years – the group most likely to come into contact with Corrections.

However, Pacific peoples have some of the lowest recidivism and reimprisonment rates. Of prisoners released in 2005/06, only 18.7 percent of offenders in this ethnic group were reimprisoned 12 months after release, compared with 24.9 percent of European offenders, and 31.2 percent of Māori offenders.

Table 10.15 shows that over 40 percent of all prisoners were under 30 years old. The highest proportion of both male (18.0 percent) and female (19.8 percent) prisoners were in the 20–24-year age group. Those aged 40 years and over accounted for 28.6 percent of male and 27.1 percent of female prisoners.

Major offence As table 10.16 shows, 34.4 percent of male prisoners were imprisoned for violence offences (excluding sexual violence). The next-largest groups were property offenders (22.7 percent), and sex offenders (20.4 percent).

Table 10.15

Sentenced prisoners by age group and sex
At 30 June 2007

Age group (years)	Female Number	Female Percent	Male Number	Male Percent	Total Number	Total Percent
14–16	1	0.2	17	0.3	18	0.3
17–19	26	6.3	414	6.9	440	6.8
20–24	81	19.8	1,086	18.0	1,167	18.1
25–29	68	16.6	991	16.4	1,059	16.4
30–34	69	16.8	899	14.9	968	15.0
35–39	51	12.4	884	14.6	935	14.5
40–49	86	21.0	1,122	18.6	1,208	18.7
50–59	19	4.6	421	7.0	440	6.8
60+	6	1.5	182	3.0	188	2.9
Age unknown	3	0.7	19	0.3	22	0.3
Total	**410**	**100.0**	**6,035**	**100.0**	**6,445**	**100.0**

Note: Individual figures may not add up to stated totals due to rounding.

Source: Department of Corrections

Female prisoners were most likely to have been imprisoned for violence (35.9 percent) and for property offences (32.2 percent). Of all those imprisoned for drug offences, 65 women represented 15.9 percent of all female prisoners, while 594 men represented 10 percent of all male prisoners.

Sentence length As shown in table 10.17, the most common sentence length for women was 6–12 months, while for men, it was 3–5 years. The 65 women serving sentences for drug offences made up 15.9 percent of all female prisoners, while the 594 men sentenced made up 9.8 percent of all male prisoners. There were 23 women (5.6 percent) serving indeterminate sentences (life or preventive detention), while 567 men (9.4 percent) were imprisoned for an indeterminate length of time.

Table 10.16

Sentenced prisoners by major offence and sex
At 30 June 2007

Offence	Female Number	Female Percent	Male Number	Male Percent	Total Number	Total Percent
Violence	147	35.9	2,071	34.3	2,218	34.4
Sexual violence	8	2.0	1,308	21.7	1,316	20.4
Against property	132	32.2	1,333	22.1	1,465	22.7
Involving drugs	65	15.9	594	9.8	659	10.2
Traffic	40	9.8	558	9.2	598	9.3
Miscellaneous	18	4.4	171	2.8	189	2.9
Total	**410**	**100.0**	**6,035**	**100.0**	**6,445**	**100.0**

Note: Individual figures may not add up to stated totals due to rounding.

Source: Department of Corrections

Table 10.17

Custodial sentence length imposed by sex
At 30 June 2007

Sentence	Female Number	Female Percent	Male Number	Male Percent	Total Number	Total Percent
Up to 3 months	10	2.4	58	1.0	68	1.1
3–6 months	12	2.9	159	2.6	171	2.7
6–12 months	77	18.8	561	9.3	638	9.9
1–2 years	70	17.1	790	13.1	860	13.3
2–3 years	76	18.5	978	16.2	1,054	16.4
3–5 years	74	18.0	1,237	20.5	1,311	20.3
5–7 years	31	7.6	619	10.3	650	10.1
7–10 years	31	7.6	605	10.0	636	9.9
10 years and over	6	1.5	461	7.6	467	7.2
Indeterminate[1]	23	5.6	567	9.4	590	9.2
Total	**410**	**100.0**	**6,035**	**100.0**	**6,445**	**100.0**

(1) Indeterminate length means either life or preventive detention.

Note: Individual figures may not add up to stated totals due to rounding.

Source: Department of Corrections

Offending history In table 10.19 (overleaf), the number of previous sentences served by prisoners gives an indication of the extent of offending careers. For female prisoners, 60 percent had no previous sentences, but 33.6 percent had between one and five previous sentences, and 6.4 percent had more than six previous sentences. For male prisoners, these proportions were 38.0, 44.3 and 17.6 percent, respectively. Thirty-three men had between 21–50 previous sentences.

Table 10.18

NZQA[1] units and credits achieved by prison inmates
2006/07

Activity	Units achieved	Credits achieved
Engineering		
Concrete products	450	1,635
Asset maintenance	486	1,041
Light engineering	337	940
Other engineering	66	106
Garages	19	29
Subtotal	1,358	3,751
Internal services		
Catering	2,305	5,180
Sundry internal services	116	258
Laundry	271	980
Subtotal	2,692	6,418
Land-based		
Grounds	277	664
Nurseries	533	2,474
Farms	894	2,700
Subtotal	1,704	5,838
Timber and textiles		
Contract gangs	35	134
Joinery	289	474
Processing	121	227
Textiles	450	991
Forests	917	2,517
Subtotal	1,812	4,343
Total	**7,566**	**20,350**

(1) New Zealand Qualifications Authority.

Source: Department of Corrections

Table 10.19

	Previous periods in custody by sex					
	At 30 June 2007					
	Female		Male		Total	
Number	Number	Percent	Number	Percent	Number	Percent
0	246	60.0	2,294	38.0	2,540	39.4
1	59	14.4	919	15.2	978	15.2
2	33	8.0	671	11.1	704	10.9
3–5	46	11.2	1,089	18.0	1,135	17.6
6–10	20	4.9	752	12.5	772	12.0
11–20	6	1.5	277	4.6	283	4.4
21–50	0	0.0	33	0.5	33	0.5
Total	410	100.0	6,035	100.0	6,445	100.0

Note: Individual figures may not add up to stated totals due to rounding.

Source: Department of Corrections

Inmate employment In October 2007, 45.5 percent of the prison population and 56.8 percent of sentenced prisoners were engaged in employment or training. A total of 3,755 prisoners were engaged in work activities – 1,799 in business-like industries, 147 in the Release to Work programme, 27 in trade and technical training, and 1,782 in unit-based activities.

- Business-like industries – more than 140 business-like industries operate in prisons nationwide. They aim to provide work environments that match, as closely as possible, comparable industry environments.
- Work parties – low security, supervised groups of prisoners work for councils, communities, or businesses outside the prison. Contracts include forestry, horticulture, farming, construction, and grounds maintenance.

Prisoners grow job skills in farms and gardens

An eco-barn full of weaners at Christchurch Prison. The award-winning piggery is expanding and will eventually house 15,000 pigs for bacon and pork. In 2007, the prison won first and third places in the pork section of the Freshpork Carcass Competition, which was open to all South Island farmers.

The last prison census in 2003 revealed that 52 percent of New Zealand prisoners had no qualifications, and only 45 percent had been involved in paid work before entering prison. Research has shown that prisoners who find employment when released are less likely to reoffend, making our communities safer.

Corrections Inmate Employment (CIE) is a committed programme aimed at improving prisoners' employment skills, training, and formal qualifications, while they serve their sentences. To do this, CIE evaluates market trends to identify accessible industries in need of qualified workers.

Around 2,000 prisoners are employed in CIE work programme sectors which include: internal services, engineering, timber and textiles, the primary sector, and the Release to Work programme.

The primary sector is a significant area of employment, with around 500 prisoners employed in agricultural and horticultural work. This sector operates two dairy farms, three dry stock farms, one piggery, two sheep farms, six nurseries, and three organic gardens.

The dairy farming industry accounts for around 20 percent of the nation's export income. Corrections can help address a shortfall in the number of skilled dairy farm workers. Prison dairy farms offer prisoners practical training and experience, putting them in good stead for securing jobs in the industry on release.

Corrections' largest dairy farm is at Waikeria Prison. With 1,000 hectares and a herd of 3,200 cows, it produces up to 1.3 million kilograms of milk solids a year. The farm at Otago Corrections Facility, established in 2007, runs about 400 dairy cows on 130 hectares. From

here, replacement calves are trucked to Christchurch Prison, where prisoners have the opportunity to train as qualified calf rearers.

Calves and heifers from Waikeria Prison's dairy farm are raised on dry stock farms based at Spring Hill Corrections Facility, Tongariro/Rangipo, and Hawke's Bay prisons. When the heifers are 18 months old and in calf, they return to Waikeria for inclusion in the milking herd.

The Waikeria and Otago farms, along with the three dry stock farms, employ a total of around 180 prisoners. The farms are integrated to operate as one business.

The organics industry is also thriving, with the export market being worth around $100 million a year.

Rolleston Prison's garden yields 150 tonnes of crops a year and employs 18 prisoners. The garden at Christchurch Prison employs up to 12 prisoners, while the garden at the new Christchurch Women's Prison employs four prisoners to grow seedlings. The two men's prisons produce quality organic vegetables that are sold and distributed nationally by Fresh Direct.

Prisoners receive training from qualified instructors while working towards an NZQA National Certificate in Horticulture (level 2). Giving prisoners the chance to achieve practical qualifications is a key part of CIE's work. Classroom-based training is available for prisoners who are unable to work in prison industries because of their security classification. As their classification lowers, they will be able to put the theory into practice within a prison industry.

Corrections has two sheep farms – one at Christchurch Prison, with 800 hectares and grazing 4,000 sheep, and another at Tongariro/Rangipo, with 2,500 hectares and grazing 10,000 sheep. Between them, the farms employ for more than 30 prisoners.

The CIE piggery, which won awards in the 2007 Freshpork Carcass competition, provides employment for another 20 prisoners, who farm approximately 800 sows for breeding, and fatten between 15,000 and 16,000 pigs a year.

Source: Department of Corrections

- Release to work – low security prisoners approaching the end of their prison sentence are sometimes eligible to work for an approved employer, with a view to maintaining their employment on release. Such prisoners must meet strict eligibility criteria and demonstrate that they are highly motivated to work.

- Industry training – prisoners can undertake industry training (within the prison environment) through the New Zealand Qualifications Authority (NZQA) framework, to gain unit standards or industry-certified national certificates. Table 10.18 (on page 213) shows the number of units and credits achieved by prison inmates for the year to 30 June 2007.

- Unit-based activities – prisoners are employed in the cleaning and care of their unit, community work parties, and other constructive activities.

Earnings Modest earnings are paid to prisoners who work, or are involved in some reintegrative programmes. Amounts vary, depending on the nature of the work or activity, and the standard of performance. Money is banked in a personal trust account, and prisoners can spend it on personal items through a weekly shopping system. Any person who has been in custody for more than 31 days is eligible, on release, for the Steps to Freedom grant administered by the Ministry of Social Development. The grant is up to $350, but the amount of money in a prisoner's trust account on final release is deducted from the grant.

Punishments A prisoner charged with an offence against prison discipline appears before an authorised staff member or a Visiting Justice. If the prisoner is found guilty, a penalty may be imposed. Serious criminal offences by prisoners are referred to the Police for investigation.

New Zealand Police

National administrative and operational control of the New Zealand Police is vested in the Commissioner of Police. Police National Headquarters in Wellington provides policy advice and support to the government through the Minister of Police, and to the country's 12 police districts.

Each district is managed by a district commander, with a number of service centres throughout New Zealand providing administrative support to districts.

Police are responsible for enforcing the criminal law, principally through the Crimes Act and the Summary Offences Act, but also through various other statutes such as the Arms Act, the Sale of Liquor Act, the Gambling Act, the Misuse of Drugs Act, the Children Young Persons and Their Families Act, the Police Act, and the Transport Act.

Trained police prosecutors undertake summary prosecution, in district courts, of criminal offences investigated by the police.

At 30 June 2007 there was a full-time equivalent force of 7,891 sworn officers (506 more than at 30 June 2005). There were also 2,770 non-sworn, full-time equivalent personnel (up 424 on the 2005 figure).

Figure 10.03 shows the New Zealand population per sworn officer from 1916–2006.

Figure 10.03

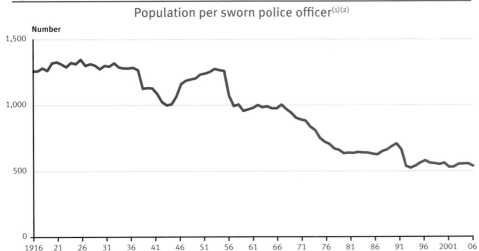

Population per sworn police officer[1][2]

(1) Based on mean population for the year ended 31 December. Numbers are expressed as full-time equivalents. (2) Years ending 31 December until 1976, years ending 31 March from 1977 to 1989, years ending 30 June from 1990.

Note: Until 1977, the number of sworn police was based on 'establishment' (authorised) numbers. From 1977, police numbers are actual sworn officers. From 1989 onwards, police recruits and those on leave without pay, or on parental leave without pay are excluded. From 1992, numbers include traffic safety personnel following their merger with Police.

Sources: New Zealand Police, Statistics New Zealand

New Zealand's Wiki Policing Act 2008

In March 2006, the Government agreed to a comprehensive review of the legislative arrangements for policing in New Zealand. To allow New Zealanders to have a say in shaping future police legislation, both traditional and innovative communication and consultation methods were adopted. Electronic communication and engagement channels were important features.

The development of a 'wiki' to consult about ideas for a new Policing Act was seen as a natural step, providing an electronic channel for capturing views not only from citizens in New Zealand, but also expatriate New Zealanders, and other international persons interested in policing and law making. An 'open wiki' with no password or registration was preferred because of its ability to generate dynamic, user-created content.

(A wiki is a collaborative website that users can easily modify via the Internet, typically without restriction. It allows anyone to edit, delete or modify content that has been placed on the site.)

To start the process, the review team decided that providing an outline of a possible Policing Act would be both provocative and useful. By doing this, participants could have a feel for the scope of the proposals, and would know where to start in putting forward their ideas, or in reacting to the suggestions already made. This approach seems to have been successful.

The wiki act website received over 26,000 visits, with the majority coming from referrals through links in online news stories. Interest in the wiki act was international, particularly after an article appeared on the main BBC web page. Foreign language articles about the wiki act also appeared in mainstream media in numerous countries.

The open wiki closed on 30 September 2007, with the resulting conversation being edited and reopened as a document of record on 1 October 2007.

Overall, the wiki act produced hundreds of constructive edits. It yielded at least three positive outcomes: a number of fresh ideas were raised; awareness of the review, and engagement in it, was significantly increased; and while not a direct objective of the review, a deeper discussion developed about government use of web-based technologies, online social networking spaces, and the process of law making.

Source: New Zealand Police

Investigating complaints against Police

In November 2007, Parliament renamed the Police Complaints Authority the Independent Police Conduct Authority, to re-emphasise its independence from the Police and from political direction. The authority exists to provide robust review of police conduct in the public interest. In particular, its task is to receive complaints of misconduct or neglect of duty, and to investigate incidents involving death or serious harm in which police staff are involved. The authority is a board presided over by a serving High Court judge appointed by the governor-general.

Complaints can be made to the authority, the Police, an ombudsman, or a registrar of a district court. The authority has power to investigate complaints itself, oversee complaints, and review complaints investigated by the Police and then sent to the authority. All complaints against police conduct, wherever laid, are ultimately dealt with by the authority.

In the year ending June 2007, a total of 3,525 complaints were received from 2,016 individual complainants, compared with 2,829 from 1,741 individual complainants in the previous year. Of the complaints received in 2007, 432 (348 in 2006) were withdrawn, refused, or did not qualify for the authority's jurisdiction, leaving 3,093 (2,481 in 2006) accepted for investigation. Of these, 112 (96 in 2006) were sustained or partly sustained, 341 (207) were conciliated, 326 (356) not sustained, and 239 not pursued. Investigation of 2,075 complaints remained incomplete at 30 June 2007.

Source: Independent Police Conduct Authority

Table 10.20

Reported assaults on police
Year ending 30 June

Year	Assaults involving weapons (firearms)	Total
1998	71 (23)	1,924
1999	57 (13)	1,878
2000	59 (19)	1,965
2001	66 (18)	1,997
2002	92 (30)	2,150
2003	88 (31)	2,072
2004	75 (30)	2,053
2005	87 (37)	1,869
2006	84 (22)	2,123
2007	88 (31)	2,248

Source: New Zealand Police

Police operations

Armed offenders squads Police maintain 17 armed offenders squads of specially-trained and equipped officers throughout New Zealand. In the year ending 30 June 2007, armed offenders squads were deployed 620 times. The squads work with police negotiators and other specialist police support staff.

Special Tactics Group This group consists of selected members of armed offenders squads from Auckland, Wellington and Christchurch. It receives specialised training to enable it to deal with incidents beyond the capability of armed offenders squads. The group was deployed 32 times during the 2006/07 year.

Search and rescue There were 1,513 police-controlled search and rescue operations during the year ending 30 June 2007, which searched for and/or rescued over 1,770 people. The comparable activity in 2005/06 was 1,411 searches and more than 2,960 people being assisted.

National Drug Intelligence Bureau As shown in table 10.21, there were significant reductions in seizures in the year ending 31 December 2007 – for methamphetamine, cocaine, LSD, GHB/GBL (Fantasy type drugs), cannabis plants/leaf, and pseudoephedrine.

There are several explanations which, in part, illustrate the reasons for the decreases recorded in 2007 compared with 2006.

- Since methamphetamine seizures in 2006 were characterised by one significant seizure of 95,000 grams, the 39,304 gram total seized in 2007 illustrates an overall increasing trend. New Zealand faces continuing challenges from both domestically manufactured methamphetamine and imported crystal methamphetamine.
- Cocaine seizures in 2006 were elevated by a series of significant border interceptions of cocaine destined for the Australian market.
- LSD seizures in 2006 spiked upwards, but in 2007 have returned to the levels experienced in earlier years.
- GHB/GBL (Fantasy) seizures in 2006 were dominated by one significant seizure of 200,000ml.
- Cannabis plant seizures in 2007 show a continued overall decline since 2002. The statistics do not reflect a reduction in either the known supply of, or demand for, cannabis, which continues to be widely available throughout New Zealand.
- Cannabis leaf seizures in 2007 also show a decline compared with 2006.

There was a further reduction in seizures of MDMA (Ecstasy) in 2007, down from a peak of 266,175 tablets in 2003. However, MDMA remains popular in New Zealand.

In 2007, a total of 190 clandestine drug laboratories were detected and dismantled. A significant reduction has been recorded in seizures of pseudoephedrine/ephedrine tablets (the active ingredient used in the manufacture of methamphetamine) in 2007 compared with 2006.

Drug seizure data alone does not necessarily reflect known drug use or prevalence in New Zealand.

Table 10.21

Drug seizures[1]
By substance
Year ending 31 December

Substance	2002	2003	2004	2005	2006	2007
Amphetamine (grams)	1,517	419	2,146	694	237	746
Cannabis leaf (kgs)	618	819	625	777	752	524
Cannabis oil (grams)	1,342	1,373	8,266	1,406	2,978	912
Cannabis plants (number)	197,873	179,416	189,389	170,104	144,039	126,688
Cocaine (grams)	267	7,060	30,270	14,112	32,955	25
Ecstasy/MDMA (tablets)	256,350	266,175	115,256	28,736	8,769	3,123
Fantasy/GHB/GBL(millilitres)	5,170	9,941	118,818	22,919	202,294	5,131
Heroin (grams)	10	1,466	385	89	13	4
Khat/*Catha edulis* (grams)	..	16,787	30,456	18,347	54,329	3,988
LSD (trips)	431	6,966	745	1,529	3,483	1,031
Methamphetamine (grams)	7,720	3,632	28,460	30,693	121,838	39,304
Psilocybin (grams)	1,192	426	1,666	1,766	648	846
Psilocybin (mushrooms)	87	370	616	728	397	263
Pseudoephedrine and ephedrine (tablets)	254,987	830,320	2,159,017	2,321,645	2,718,869	1,806,452

(1) Combined New Zealand Police and New Zealand Customs Service.
Symbol: .. figure not available

Source: National Drug Intelligence Bureau

Police Infringement Bureau The Police Infringement Bureau administers the Speed Camera Programme and the Community Roadwatch Programme. It is the national processing centre for police-issued infringement offence notices, and also has an adjudication function in connection with these notices.

Police began speed camera operations in 1993, and since 1994 have delivered 74,000 hours of speed camera activity per year. Camera sites are selected by road safety and community groups who, together with Police, identify areas with a history of speed-related accidents. 'Anywhere/anytime' cameras were introduced as part of the government's *Road Safety to 2010* package in December 2003. From April 2004, signs indicating speed camera zones were removed, to encourage drivers to remain within the speed limits over their whole journey.

Criminal Investigation Branch This branch of the Police is dedicated to investigating and solving serious crime, and targeting organised crime and recidivist criminals. The job of the branch is to investigate serious crimes, such as homicides, aggravated violence, sexual offending, drug offences, crimes against society, and fraud. Law enforcement teams in each police district target crime 'hot spots'.

Modern policing tools assist most of the complex crime enquiries. A criminal investigation database is used to record and organise information gathered during serious crime investigations. Intelligence-led policing and analytical computer tools are increasingly used to help Police detect and suppress crime. Crime mapping is a tool that presents information on where certain crimes are being committed, while link charting enables detectives to plot the relationship between criminals and their activities.

Police dogs A comprehensive network of police dogs and handlers is maintained throughout New Zealand. During the year ending 30 June 2007, police dog teams were deployed to 31,729 calls for service, leading to the apprehension of 6,373 suspects. In the 2006/07 year, Police worked with 117 general-purpose dogs, seven narcotics-detector dogs, three firearms-detector dogs, and three explosives-detector dogs. Ten of the general-purpose dogs were also trained in search and rescue and victim recovery (cadaver), and 30 of the general-purpose dogs were trained to work with armed offenders squads.

Youth Education Service (YES) This service is the New Zealand Police's national strategy to deliver crime prevention programmes to schools and school communities. The mission of YES is to promote individual safety with school students and the wider school community, and to reduce the level at which these groups become either the perpetrators or the victims of road crashes, crime, and anti-social behaviour. YES promotes a curriculum for schools that has four themes:

- crime prevention and social responsibility programmes focused on reducing the opportunity for young people to be involved in anti-social behaviour, or to commit crime
- drug education programmes
- road safety education, through school traffic safety teams and the RoadSense and RoadSafe Series programmes
- violence prevention, for example, Keeping Ourselves Safe (personal safety) and Kia Kaha (anti-bullying).

There were 112 full-time equivalent youth education officers throughout New Zealand at 30 June 2007.

Youth Aid Under the Children, Young Persons and Their Families Act 1989, the Police must follow the principle that, unless the public interest requires otherwise, criminal proceedings are not instituted against children or young persons if there is an alternative means of dealing with the matter. This aims to limit the number of young people who go on to the formal youth justice process.

Police Youth Aid currently diverts about 80 percent of young offenders out of the formal youth justice process by way of warnings, cautions, and alternative actions. There were 174.5 full-time equivalent Youth Aid staff throughout New Zealand at 30 June 2007.

Youth development Police employ 58 people nationally in district-based youth development programmes. The programmes use mentoring approaches to develop the supportive capacity of young offenders' families.

A mix of sworn police officers and non-sworn caseworkers provides holistic wrap-around services that help to shape family dynamics, and work to ensure offenders and their siblings are prevented from engaging in cycles of victimisation, offending, and reoffending. Police also manage a number of external contracts with community provider agencies that target youth offending and general violence.

Community policing Nearly 200 community constables are located throughout New Zealand. In the 2006 Budget the government agreed that an additional 250 community police would be provided by 2009. Their role will include a proactive focus on identifying and solving community crime and safety-related problems, to reduce real crime and road trauma, and increase community safety and reassurance. Community constables are helped by government, non-government, and community groups and organisations.

Some of the new community police will be focused on geographic communities (including rural); some on communities of interest such as youth, or on problems such as alcohol or graffiti; and some will be working in teams.

Thirty staff were allocated in 2006/07 to demonstration projects in Central, Wellington and Canterbury districts, and to setting up the National Community Policing Group. A further allocation of 120 staff in the districts was approved for 2007/08. The final 100 are being allocated in 2008/09.

New Zealand Police overseas

The four primary roles of the New Zealand Police International Service Group (ISG) are:

- furthering New Zealand's law enforcement interests internationally
- supporting New Zealand's foreign policy objectives in the Pacific region and beyond
- contributing to peace support and peacekeeping operations
- contributing to disaster and emergency response, security liaison, and other tasks as required.

The work of ISG has an emphasis on the south and west Pacific region, and south-east and north Asia. There is a strong focus on developing and managing relationships with foreign counterparts – establishing formal relationships where beneficial. The ISG aims to develop New Zealand Police's profile internationally while balancing the impact on domestic policing.

At June 2007, the Police had 86 staff serving in policing capacities in 14 countries (numbers peaked at 126 in 2006). This included eight police liaison posts staffed by nine senior officers – in Bangkok, Sydney, Canberra, Washington, London, Jakarta (2 officers), Suva and Beijing. There were 72 staff in operational roles on five overseas deployments. These included the: European Union Police Mission in Afghanistan (3), Bougainville Community Policing Project (5), Regional Assistance Mission in the Solomon Islands (35), United Nations Integrated Mission in Timor-Leste (25), and Joint Programme of Assistance to Tonga Police (4). A further five staff were deployed on international secondments, including the Solomon Islands Police Force executive staff (3), Niue Chief of Police (1), and an attachment to the Joint Inter-agency Task Force (West), in Honolulu (1).

In addition, the ISG manages a number of long-term programmes and short-term projects that provide capacity-building assistance to South-East Asian and Pacific police services.

Source: New Zealand Police

Corporal Whitney Benoit (second from left) from the Royal Canadian Mounted Police (RCMP) visits the New Zealand Police dog breeding programme in 2007. With her, from left, are: Constable Mike Calvert and Peyton; Sergeant Mark Sanford; Senior Constable Mike Hore and Phagan; and Constable Matt Hay and Quade. Peyton and Phagan are from the 'P' litter and sons of Buddy, the dog whose semen was donated to the RCMP.

Community support groups The involvement of communities in identifying community crime and safety-related problems, and working alongside Police to assist in the creation of safer, more caring communities is fundamental to the New Zealand approach. Police work closely with partners, providing and receiving information from independent community groups, such as Neighbourhood Support New Zealand, and Community Patrols of New Zealand. Police also work closely with Victim Support, Women's Refuge, and other violence intervention, road safety, youth development, and health groups interested in reducing crime and victimisation, and making communities safer.

Contributors and related websites

Crime Prevention Unit – www.justice.govt.nz/cpu/

Crown Law Office – www.crownlaw.govt.nz

Department of Corrections – www.corrections.govt.nz

Independent Police Conduct Authority – www.pca.govt.nz

Law Commission – www.lawcom.govt.nz

Legal Services Agency – www.lsa.govt.nz

Ministry of Justice – www.justice.govt.nz

New Zealand Council of Victim Support Groups – www.victimsupport.org.nz

New Zealand Police – www.police.govt.nz

Serious Fraud Office – www.sfo.govt.nz

Volunteer Chris Ballantyne sorts computers at the free community computer recycling day held in Wellington in 2006. The equipment was disassembled and the components recycled, with only 3 percent going to landfill.

11 | Communications

In New Zealand, and around the world, information, broadcasting and telecommunication technologies are converging. These technologies play a key role in enhancing the lives of individuals and communities, and in accelerating economic growth.

The rapid expansion of the Internet has probably caused more social and economic change than any other aspect of information and communication technology (ICT). However, as full participation by local, national, and international communities becomes increasingly dependent on access to ICT and on having the skills to make use of it, the need to ensure 'digital inclusion' is a constant challenge.

New Zealand's small size, geographic isolation and technologically-aware population have all contributed to the widespread and rapid uptake of ICT, particularly in relation to Internet access. At 31 March 2007, there were 57 Internet service providers (ISPs) operating in New Zealand, with around 1.46 million active subscribers, providing a wide range of services, including dial-up and broadband access, and voice over Internet protocol (VoIP). New Zealand's relatively cheap dial-up Internet access facilitated the rapid adoption and diffusion of Internet use. It may, however, also have been responsible for a slower uptake of broadband services, since the expense of the latter is still comparatively high.

Several competing telecommunications companies in New Zealand offer an extensive range of ICT services, including television, telephony and Internet access. The Government has actively encouraged such competition, and, in recent years, has introduced regulations requiring the unbundling of the local loop and the operational separation of the telecommunications provider Telecom New Zealand Ltd.

The Government has implemented a wide range of ICT initiatives in e-government, health, commerce and education. The *2005 Digital Strategy*, a whole-of-government strategy provided a unifying framework for ICT-related policies and initiatives.

The strategy identifies three key enabling conditions – content, confidence and connection – necessary to facilitate the transition to a 'knowledge-based society', allowing all New Zealanders to access and use appropriate, affordable digital technologies to find the information they need. The strategy also focuses on building partnerships between the key user groups – individuals and their communities, businesses and government.

In line with OECD guidelines, Statistics New Zealand, in collaboration with the Ministry of Economic Development, has developed a suite of surveys to measure the impact of ICT across the economy. These surveys include ICT use and uptake for businesses, government and households, with an ICT supply survey and a twice-yearly ISP census survey.

The Digital Strategy

In 2005, the Government released the *2005 Digital Strategy*, with a vision to create a digital future for all New Zealanders, using information and communication technology (ICT) to enhance our lives. The strategy provides a framework for a greater understanding of how New Zealanders could think about and use digital technology for individual and national benefits.

The three enabling conditions are:

- **content** – to unlock New Zealand's stock of content and provide all New Zealanders with seamless, easy access to the information that is important to their lives, businesses and cultural identity
- **confidence** – to provide all New Zealanders with the digital skills and confidence to find and use the information they need, and to ensure that telecommunications and the Internet in New Zealand are reliable and secure
- **connection** – New Zealand will be in the top half of the OECD for broadband uptake by 2010.

A considerable amount of work has been undertaken since the launch of the strategy. Over 70 government initiatives are under way, including two contestable funds for communities and regions throughout New Zealand. Close to $40 million in funding for 120 community-based projects has been made available to regions, communities and partnerships throughout New Zealand, through the Broadband Challenge Fund and the Community Partnership Fund.

Significant progress has been made to reform the regulatory environment for telecommunications to improve conditions for investment and competition, including the telecommunications stocktake, changes to the Telecommunications Act 2001, local-loop unbundling, and the operational separation of Telecom.

The strategy has recently been refreshed to keep up with advances in technology and to align more closely with the Government's strategic objectives of economic transformation, national identity, and sustainability. Inter-sector collaboration and partnership, which have been features of the original strategy, have a stronger focus in the refresh.

The *Digital Strategy 2.0* was released for public submission on 31 March 2008, with the final document released on 30 June 2008. For more about the strategy, visit www.digitalstrategy.govt.nz.

Source: Ministry of Economic Development

Internet use

The government was indirectly involved in establishing the Internet through its funding of universities and other research institutions, but commercial Internet services in New Zealand have been developed entirely by the private sector.

Responsibility for domain name registrations in the .nz domain (for example, stats.govt.nz) lies with InternetNZ (formerly the Internet Society of New Zealand).

The Māori Internet Society, established with help from the Māori Language Commission (among others), promotes a strong Māori presence on the Internet, and has successfully established the .maori.nz Internet domain name.

In general, there are minimal restrictions on New Zealand organisations registering a domain name in the .nz domain.

At 30 September 2007, there were 300,397 active registrations in the .nz domain. During the month of September 2007, 7,263 new domain names were created, compared with 6,900 in September 2006. In the same month, there were 12 active registrations in the .maori.nz domain and 16 in the .geek.nz domain. There are four moderated second-level domains in the .nz domain name space – .govt.nz, .iwi.nz, .cri.nz and .mil.nz.

Following a decision made early in 2005, InternetNZ has implemented a dispute resolution service for .nz domain names, based on the Nominet UK system, which has been in place successfully for a number of years. The dispute resolution service provides an alternative-to-court action, giving parties another mechanism to resolve disputes.

Of New Zealand's 1.46 million Internet subscribers at 31 March 2007, 84.9 percent were residential (household) subscribers, who provided 73.1 percent of the revenue. Business/government subscribers accounted for 15.1 percent of subscribers and provided 26.8 percent of the revenue. In the six months to September 2007, the number of broadband subscribers overtook the number of dial-up subscribers.

Figure 11.01

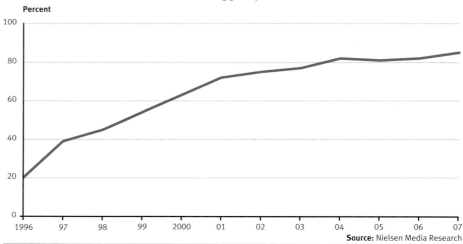

Growth in Internet access
Proportion of New Zealanders with Internet access at any location
Year ending 30 September

Source: Nielsen Media Research

E-government

The information and communication technology branch of the State Services Commission (SSC) is responsible for implementing the Government's vision to enable all New Zealanders to use information and communication technology (ICT) to access government information and services, and to participate in democratic processes.

The E-government Strategy is the whole-of-government approach to transforming how agencies use technology to deliver services, provide information, and interact with people, as they work to achieve the outcomes sought by Government. Government agencies will use technology to provide complete services for both simple and complex transactions. These might be handled by agencies on their own or in conjunction with others. The strategy anticipates that by 2020, people's engagement with government will have been transformed, as increasing and innovative use is made of the opportunities offered by network technologies.

All government agencies are using the Internet, including websites, to provide ready access to government information and services. Technology is also being used to group services at a single point of entry, making online access to services more convenient, allowing multiple transactions on one site. Customers forming a company online can register for goods and services tax (GST) and apply for an IRD number at the same time. These numbers are returned to the customer and all changes immediately updated between Inland Revenue and the Companies Office.

The government portal, www.newzealand.govt.nz, enables convenient public access to government information and services in one place, without needing to know in advance which agency provides the resources. The portal searches not only government web pages, news and images, but also some government information sets that are not available on the World Wide Web.

The business portal, www.business.govt.nz, groups business services at a single point of entry, providing information and tools designed to help people start, manage or grow their business, and deal with the day-to-day challenges along the way. It brings together government and non-government business-related information.

Agencies are increasingly sharing electronic data through the use of the Internet and CDs. In June 2007 there were 44 active authorised information-matching programmes out of an estimated 76 authorised programmes permitted by the Privacy Commissioner. This compares with an estimated 21 authorised programmes in June 1998.

Widespread adoption of information-sharing standards, such as the e-government interoperability framework (e-GIF) developed by the SSC, is helping to make information-sharing easier and less expensive for agencies. The use of the e-GIF is mandatory for all public service departments. Updated web standards released in 2007 are an important part of ensuring that online government information and services are accessible to everyone. They give government agencies clarity and direction on how to use the Internet to deliver information and services.

The SSC is developing infrastructure to help agencies integrate information and services. The ongoing development of a whole-of-government network infrastructure supports information-sharing across agencies and reduces the transaction burden on the end-user. The government logon service and the identity verification service will provide government agencies with a high level of confidence as to the identity of the online user, place people in control of their transactions, and protect their privacy. The government shared network is a high-speed inter-agency network that enables State-sector agencies to share information securely and more cost-effectively.

Indications are that e-government is welcomed by New Zealanders, with Nielsen NetRatings research showing that government websites (as a group) are in the top six websites accessed by New Zealanders. The two main reasons for visiting government websites are to find information and to download a form or brochure. An increasing number of government forms can be fully completed online, and the number of sites where people can carry out an online transaction with government is growing. Fifty-six percent of all government organisations' websites contained interactive information (for example, online forms), 28 percent had dynamic information (for example, webcams) and 26 percent offered online transaction services.

Figure 11.02

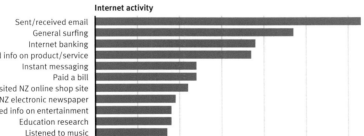

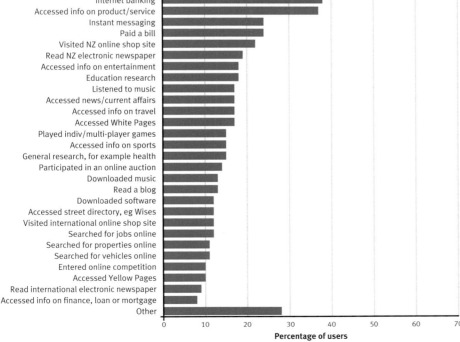

Type of Internet activities
Measured over four weeks of quarter ending 31 December 2007

Internet activity

Percentage of users

Source: Nielson Media Research

Computer and e-waste recycling

Electronic waste (e-waste) is one of the fastest growing waste streams around the world. Rapid technical advances mean that the average computer has a lifespan of less than five years. The problem arises at the end of its useful life and is compounded by the hazardous nature of the waste. Computers contain substances such as lead, mercury, cadmium, hexavalent chromium and brominated flame retardants.

In New Zealand, most redundant electronic equipment is being landfilled. There is no legislation or industry-related body coordinating an effort to deal with e-waste, although the Waste Minimisation Bill is currently on its second reading in Parliament. The lack of available data on the amount of e-waste generated makes it hard to determine the extent of the problem. However, e-Waste in New Zealand, a report by the Computer Access NZ Trust, quoted that approximately 830,000 new computers were sold in New Zealand in 2005. There are also an estimated 10 million cathode ray tubes (CRTs) currently in use in New Zealand or stored awaiting disposal.

Small scale refurbishment and recycling is happening at a local level, where individuals are making huge efforts to extend the usable life of equipment. Organisations, such as The Ark Recycling, RCN in Auckland, and ReMarkit Solutions in Wellington, will take old computers for refurbishment and reuse in schools and charitable organisations. The public can expect a small charge for this service. Dell has initiated a recycling programme in Auckland, Wellington and Christchurch.

Three Auckland companies have solved the problem of hazardous waste in the disposal of old televisions and computer monitors, or CRTs. In true Kiwi do-it-yourself style, Auckland companies RCN & Associates Ltd; the Abilities Group; and Rose Engineering have teamed up to develop a process, and have locally designed and built equipment for the environmental disposal of end-of-life computer monitors and televisions. These contain many toxic materials, including lead, barium, cadmium, mercury and arsenic.

During the CRT disposal process all the partners play a part. The monitors or televisions are dismantled and broken down into their components. This results in plastic, copper, aluminium and steel all being recycled. The printed circuit boards are further processed environmentally at an ISO-certified disposal centre, which deals with dangerous wastes environmentally.

The tube then goes through a number of processes, including the separation of the lead-bearing glass. This glass is consolidated and exported to a lead smelter and used as flux in the smelting of lead.

The Ark is an Auckland-based company that recovers computers from industry, refurbishes them, and sells them at low cost to schools. Over the past three years, the Ark has taken in over 8,000 computers. They have put 3,000 refurbished units into schools, have dismantled approximately 3,000 for parts and have an inventory of about 2,000 in their warehouse. At 25–30kg per complete computer, they have diverted between 200 and 240 metric tonnes of potential waste from landfill.

For more information, visit www.zerowaste.co.nz.

Source: Zero Waste New Zealand Trust

E-commerce

New Zealand has a highly competitive information and communication technology (ICT) market, with a range of equipment and software companies supplying both the domestic market and niche markets overseas. Total sales of ICT goods and services were valued at $17,643 million in 2005/06. Of these sales, 90.9 percent ($16,033 million) were solely domestic and 9.1 percent ($1,610 million) were to export markets. This represents a 7.9 percent increase in total sales, with domestic sales rising 6.9 percent and export sales rising 19.9 percent from sales in 2004/05.

In 2005/06, sales of ICT services increased 7 percent to reach $9,518 million, while sales of ICT goods (including published software) increased 9.1 percent to $8,125 million. Sales of telecommunications and program distribution services increased 5.8 percent, to reach $5,803 million. Additionally, sales of Internet access and Internet telecommunication services increased 32.5 percent to reach $595 million in 2005/06.

In 2005/06, export sales of ICT goods were 78.3 percent ($1,260 million) of the total export value ($1,610 million), while ICT services accounted for 21.7 percent ($350 million) of the total. The highest value exported commodity category is electronic devices and equipment, which increased from $97 million in 2004/05 to $523 million in 2005/06. This represents 32.5 percent of the total value of exports in 2005/06.

Spam is a term generally used in relation to unsolicited and unwelcome electronic messaging, normally in the form of unsolicited bulk emails that market products. Spam uses up network resources and the productive time of computer users, is a vehicle for viruses and scams, and undermines user confidence in the use of electronic communications.

The government has adopted a multilateral strategy to combat spam, which includes legislation in the form of the Unsolicited Electronic Messages Act 2007; self-regulation in the form of industry codes of practice; technical measures, education and awareness-raising for users; and international cooperation. The Unsolicited Electronic Messages Act prohibits the sending of commercial electronic messages (as defined by the Act) without the consent of the recipient, which may be express, inferred or deemed. The Act is enforced by the Department of Internal Affairs.

Industry codes of practice have been developed by service providers for text messaging and email. The Direct Marketing Association has also developed a code of practice for e-marketing.

Broadcasting

Broadcasting policy

The Government has given renewed priority to the role of broadcasting in contributing to the nation's culture and identity, and to the promotion of a well-informed participatory democracy. Broadcasting is also undergoing rapid technological change, presenting the sector with new opportunities and challenges.

In July 2000, the Government formulated a set of broadcasting content objectives that guided subsequent decisions, such as reorientation of Television New Zealand's (TVNZ) direction and the allocation of non-commercial spectrum. The objectives are designed to:

- ensure that all New Zealanders have reasonable and regular access to broadcasting that represents the uniqueness and diversity of New Zealand life, recognising that the histories and stories of whānau (family), hapū (subtribe) and iwi (tribe) are integral to any description of that life
- meet the information and entertainment needs of as many interests as reasonably possible, including those that cannot be met by commercial broadcasting
- contribute to public awareness of, and participation in, the political and social debates of the day
- provide for minority interests and increased choice
- encourage innovation and creativity in broadcasting, while aiming to continually increase audience satisfaction with the quality of content.

One of the most significant changes resulting from these objectives was the Television New Zealand Act 2003, which transformed TVNZ from a state-owned enterprise into a Crown company. Its charter sets out, in broad terms, the kind of programming it is to provide. The Act requires TVNZ to keep a balance between giving effect to the public broadcasting objectives embodied in the charter and maintaining its commercial performance. In 2006/07, the Government granted direct funding of $24,808 million to TVNZ for charter purposes.

In February 2005, the Government published a broadcasting programme of action setting out a series of priority areas for broadcasting policy to the end of the decade. The programme encompasses work on the funding of broadcasting, the future role of public broadcasters, the transition to digital transmission, and the enhancement of regional broadcasting, among other tasks.

The Ministry for Culture and Heritage's policy work on New Zealand's transition to digital television contributed, in May 2007, to the launch of the Freeview satellite service – a consortium of free-to-air broadcasters whose founding members are TVNZ, MediaWorks, Māori Television and Radio New Zealand.

A new policy framework to guide the development of regional and community broadcasting policy was established. Its goals are to enable a range of broadcasting services, content and formats for regional, local and community, and minority audiences, including ethnic minorities, communities of interest and students. The framework promotes local and diverse broadcasting in ways that are accessible to audiences both culturally and technically, as well as future-proofed for long-term developments affecting broadcasting.

Broadcasting Commission (NZ On Air)

The role of NZ On Air is to promote cultural and social objectives in broadcasting that are seen as unlikely to receive sufficient commercial provision. Members of the commission are appointed by the Minister of Broadcasting. The statutory objectives of NZ On Air are to:

- reflect and develop New Zealand identity and culture by promoting programmes about New Zealand interests and by promoting Māori language and culture
- maintain and, where considered appropriate, extend radio coverage to New Zealand communities that otherwise would not receive a commercially-viable signal
- ensure programmes are available to provide for the interests of women, youth, children, people with disabilities, and minorities in the community, including ethnic minorities, and encourage broadcasts that reflect the diverse religious and ethical beliefs of New Zealanders
- encourage the archiving of programmes likely to be of historical interest to New Zealand.

NZ On Air fulfils these objectives by providing funds for the broadcasting, production and archiving of programmes. When allocating funds for programme production, NZ On Air is required to take into account such factors as availability of other sources of funding, likely audience size, and the likelihood of a programme being broadcast.

NZ On Air's activities are funded by the government under the Vote Culture and Heritage allocation. In the 2005/06 financial year, NZ On Air spent $70.04 million on production of television programmes, and $27.32 million on National Radio and Concert FM. It also spent $4.83 million on New Zealand music projects, $1.16 million on broadcasting archives and more than $820,000 on a variety of programmes for commercial radio.

Broadcasting Standards Authority

The Broadcasting Standards Authority is a Crown entity set up by the Broadcasting Act 1989, reporting to Parliament through the Minister of Broadcasting.

The authority's mission is to support fairness and freedom in broadcasting through impartial complaints determination and research, and through stakeholder engagement.

The authority does not deal with complaints about advertisements, except for party political and parliamentary candidate advertising on radio and television during the lead-up to an election.

The authority consists of four members, one of whom is appointed after consultation with broadcasters and another who is appointed after consultation with public interest groups.

Soccer superstar David Beckham tackles the media after the Wellington Phoenix FC versus LA Galaxy game at Wellington's Westpac Stadium in 2007.

Māori broadcasting funding agency Te Reo Whakapuaki Irirangi, operating as Te Mängai Pāho, was established in 1993, with statutory functions set out in the Broadcasting Act 1989 and the Broadcasting Amendment Act 1993.

Te Mängai Pāho is required to promote Māori language and culture by making funds available, on terms and conditions it thinks fit, for broadcasting and the production of programmes to be broadcast.

Te Mängai Pāho consists of up to seven members appointed by the Minister of Communications in consultation with the Minister of Māori Affairs. Eleven staff work from a Wellington office.

Te Mängai Pāho's main functions are to:

- purchase programming for broadcast on television and radio, targeted at the promotion of Māori language and culture
- develop funding policies that encourage a diverse range of programmes, to assist revitalisation of Māori language
- monitor Māori language content of programmes purchased
- consult with Māori broadcasters, Māori interest groups, Māori audiences and government agencies on the most appropriate way to promote Māori language and culture through broadcasting.

Te Mängai Pāho is funded by Crown appropriation. For the year ending 30 June 2008, $40.3 million (GST exclusive) was allocated to Māori television programming. Of this, approximately 40 percent was committed for direct funding of the Māori Television channel, which began transmission on 28 March 2004.

The balance is available for television programmes destined for national broadcasters, such as Māori Television, TV ONE, TV2, TV3, and Prime.

The appropriation for radio funding is $10.7 million (GST exclusive) for the year ending 30 June 2008, divided between the 21 iwi radio stations (which provide a minimum of eight hours of Māori language content each day), service providers for the running of the radio network distribution system, and providers of a range of programmes to supplement local Māori radio programming.

Radio funding is also applied to capacity building within the Māori radio industry, as well as the production of music singles and music albums in the Māori language.

Source: Te Mängai Pāho

Of the 156 decisions issued by the authority in the year ending 30 June 2006, 19 were upheld in part or in total, 127 were not upheld, four were interlocutory and six were unable to be determined. Of the complaints upheld, 11 related to balance, fairness and accuracy standards and three related to matters of good taste and decency (including language).

Māori broadcasting

Under the Radio Communications Act 1989, frequencies suitable for radio and television were reserved throughout New Zealand for the promotion of Māori language and culture.

From 1989 to 1994, NZ On Air provided public funding for operating and capital costs of iwi radio stations and for the production of Māori programmes broadcast on network television.

The Broadcasting Amendment Act 1993 established the Māori broadcasting funding agency Te Reo Whakapuaki Irirangi, which operates as Te Mängai Pāho. Te Mängai Pāho has the function of promoting Māori language and Māori culture by making funds available for broadcasting and the production of programmes to be broadcast.

On 1 January 1995, Te Mängai Pāho assumed primary responsibility for allocation of public funding for Māori broadcasting. This includes the purchase of Māori language programming broadcast on national television and Māori language content from 21 iwi radio stations. Māori radio programming is also purchased from programme providers through contestable funding rounds and the programmes made available to Māori stations by means of a nationwide radio programme distribution service. Te Mängai Pāho also funds the production of music singles and albums in the Māori language.

In 2001, the Government confirmed its intention to establish a Māori television channel, and the Māori Television Service Act was passed in 2003. The channel, known as Māori Television, began transmission on 28 March 2004 on free-to-air digital and UHF frequencies.

The principal function of the television service is to promote te reo Māori me nga tikanga Māori (Māori language, culture and heritage) through provision of a high-quality, cost-effective Māori television service, in both Māori and English, which informs, educates and entertains, and in doing so enriches New Zealand's society, culture and heritage.

Television programme funding is provided by Te Mängai Pāho through direct funding to Māori Television (for in-house production and acquisitions), and through contestable funding to other broadcasters and independent production houses (for programmes destined for Māori Television or the other national networks). In the year ending 30 June 2008, appropriation for Te Mängai Pāho's broadcasting funding was $40.3 million for television and $10.7 million for radio.

New Zealand's first 100 percent Māori language television channel, Te Reo, was launched on 25 March 2008.

Telecommunications

The level of telecommunications service in New Zealand is comparable with most other OECD countries. Market penetration is high, with more than 96 percent of households taking up fixed-line telephone services and 80 percent of individuals having had personal use of a mobile phone in the 12 months to the December 2006 quarter.

Telecom New Zealand Ltd, provider of the most extensive range of telecommunication services throughout the country, was established as a state-owned enterprise in 1987, following the break-up of the New Zealand Post Office. The telecommunications market was opened fully to competition in 1989, and up until 2001 the telecommunications sector was subject to relatively light-handed regulatory control. During this time, the government relied on competition to drive efficiency in telecommunications markets, within the bounds of general competition law.

In 2000 a ministerial inquiry into telecommunications recommended changes to the New Zealand telecommunications regulatory regime, to better meet government policy objectives. Subsequently, the regulatory regime was reformed with the passing of the Telecommunications Act 2001, which established an industry-specific telecommunications regulatory regime in New Zealand. This included setting up a Telecommunications Commissioner in the Commerce Commission, who administers regulated telecommunication services that include network interconnection, telephone number portability and wholesale telecommunication services.

The commissioner's key functions are to resolve disputes over regulated services, to report to the Minister of Communications on the desirability of regulating additional services, and to calculate and allocate the net cost of telecommunication service obligations (TSO).

In 2005, a stocktake of the New Zealand telecommunications sector was undertaken, and consequently the Telecommunications Act was amended in 2006.

Telecom's major competitors are TelstraClear and Vodafone, although there are several other small telecommunications operators in New Zealand who primarily use Telecom's fixed-line network or offer wireless solutions. Telecom and Vodafone provide cellular mobile phone services, with their networks providing extensive coverage within New Zealand. There is particularly high use of prepaid phones and SMS (short message service) messaging in New Zealand.

Given New Zealand's small population and relatively large geographic area, the more advanced telecommunication services (for example higher broadband speeds) are more available in urban areas. Nevertheless, 93 percent of the population has access to broadband via the fixed-line network, with satellite access available to all.

Regulatory bodies

The Commerce Commission is the independent regulatory body with the authority to enforce competition law in New Zealand. The Ministry of Economic Development provides advice to the government on telecommunications policy issues, manages the radio spectrum, and carries out some regulatory functions relating to communications. The ministry administers the Telecommunications Act 2001, Postal Services Act 1998, and Radiocommunications Act 1989.

Regulated services

There are two levels of access regulation provided for in the Telecommunications Act 2001 – designated services and specified services. Both are services for which there is an enforceable obligation on an access provider to supply service in accordance with any prescribed conditions. Designated services include pricing principles, while specified services exclude pricing principles.

Declared regulated services are as follows:

Designated access services, which include

- interconnection with Telecom's fixed public switched telephone network (PSTN)
- interconnection with fixed PSTN other than Telecom's
- retail services offered by means of Telecom's fixed network
- residential local access and calling service offered by means of Telecom's fixed network
- bundle of retail services offered by means of Telecom's fixed network
- retail services offered by means of Telecom's fixed network as part of bundle of retail services.

Designated multi-network services, which include:

- local telephone number portability service
- cellular telephone number portability service.

Specified services, which include:

- national roaming
- co-location on cellular mobile transmission sites.

Telecommunications service obligations

The Telecommunications Act 2001 provides for telecommunications service obligations (TSO) instruments for the supply of telecommunications services to meet social objectives.

The Kiwi Share TSO between the Crown and Telecom New Zealand controls the supply of local residential telephone services. The Kiwi Share TSO requires that a price-capped local telephone service (including an option for unlimited non-chargeable local calls) be available to residential users.

The Kiwi Share TSO commits Telecom to:

- not increasing in real terms the standard line rental, provided that the overall profitability of Telecom's fixed business is not unreasonably impaired
- the standard line rental for customers in rural areas being no higher than for customers in urban areas
- local residential telephone service being as widely available as it was in December 2001
- 99 percent of residential telephone lines being capable of supporting a connect speed of at least 9.6 kbps
- a range of specific service quality standards
- reporting of service performance to the Crown and the Telecommunications Commissioner.

A TSO instrument has been established for a telecommunications relay service to meet the communications needs of people who are deaf, hearing impaired, and speech impaired. The service was launched in November 2004.

The TSO framework is currently being reviewed. This review will focus on:

- TSO requirements for the supply of telephone and Internet access services
- TSO role in the supply of emergency call services
- TSO role in the supply of rural broadband services

Household access to phones, fax and Internet[1]
2006 Census

Type of access	Number of responses
None	28,407
Cellphone/mobile phone	1,034,526
Telephone	1,277,325
Fax machine	362,040
Internet	843,738
Response unidentifiable	3,123
Not stated	57,342
Total responses	3,606,501
Total number of households	1,454,175

(1) Private occupied households reporting more than one means of access to telecommunications have been counted in each stated category. The total number of responses will therefore be greater than the total number of households.

Source: Statistics New Zealand

Unbundling the local loop

The local loop is the copper telephone wire that runs from a Telecom telephone exchange to an end-user's premises. Unbundling the local loop will allow other telecommunications providers to use Telecom's copper network to deliver services to their own customers. Many OECD countries have done this already and in many of those countries local loop unbundling has changed the competitive landscape.

In November 2007, the Commerce Commission released its unbundled copper local loop standard terms determination. The commission's determinations are complete commercial arrangements that will allow competitors to take the services from Telecom without the need for any separate agreements.

The determination contains a 15-month implementation plan, starting from the determination date. It involves a soft launch, unbundling up to five exchanges between January and April 2008, and up to 15 further exchanges per quarter for the next year.

The Commerce Commission believes that unbundling the local loop is an important component in achieving its objective of promoting competition for the long-term benefits of end users. It expects that consumers will benefit from better prices, greater choice, and access to more innovative products.

Source: Commerce Commission

- rules for the application of TSO levies on the industry to recover charges for services supplied under TSO instruments.

Recent changes to the regulatory regime

In December 2005, the Government commenced a stocktake of the New Zealand telecommunications sector. The purpose of the stocktake was to consider developments in the telecommunications sector as a whole over the medium term (three to five years).

As a result of the stocktake, a package was announced in May 2006 that included:

- requiring unbundling of the local loop and sub-loop copper-wire lines between telephone exchanges and homes and businesses
- regulatory action, such as information disclosure, accounting separation of Telecom's business operations, and an enhanced Commerce Commission monitoring role to ensure improved competition
- removing constraints on the existing regulated unbundled bit-stream service (UBS) ensures Internet service providers (ISPs) can offer better and cheaper broadband at upload speeds faster than 128kbps
- encouraging investment in alternative infrastructure, such as fibre, wireless and satellite networks by measures including a review of public sector investment in telecommunications infrastructure, to encourage a whole-of-government approach
- developing a rural package and expansion of the Digital Strategy Broadband Challenge Fund (a fund established to assist development of open access networks to offer affordable broadband).

The Telecommunications Amendment Bill was passed in December 2006, and since its introduction the Commerce Commission has initiated standard term determination processes for the following sub-loop related services (in addition to already regulated services that were rolled over in 2007):

- unbundled copper local loop from Telecom's distribution cabinets
- backhaul from Telecom's distribution cabinet to the exchange
- co-location services at Telecom's distribution cabinets.

The Commerce Commission also recommended regulation of mobile termination, however, the minister rejected this recommendation. Both Telecom and Vodafone have separately provided deeds setting out binding commitments related to mobile termination that they are willing to implement if mobile termination services are not regulated.

In September 2007, the Minister of Communications made a determination of further requirements, additional to those already set out in the Telecommunications Act 2001, with which Telecom's three-way operational separation plan must comply. The Minister of Communications received Telecom's draft separation plan in October 2007, which was amended following public consultation. In December 2007, the minister released an amending determination updating this determination of requirements for Telecom's operational separation and called for public submissions on Telecom's amended separation plan.

Telecommunications relay service (TRS) was established under the TSO framework of the Telecommunications Act 2001. The TRS was launched in November 2004, and is designed to meet the telephone communication needs of deaf, deaf-blind, hearing impaired and speech-impaired people. Sign language became the third official language of New Zealand (after English and Māori) when the New Zealand Sign Language Act 2006 was passed.

Telecom Corporation of New Zealand Ltd The Telecom group provides a full range of Internet, data, voice, mobile and fixed-line calling services to customers in New Zealand and in Australia. Telecom has been privately owned since September 1990 and listed on stockmarkets in New Zealand, Australia and New York. It has 50,000 New Zealand shareholders, representing about 28 percent of its total shareholders, with a further 28 percent in Australia.

Telecom has New Zealand's most extensive telecommunications network and directly employs almost 7,000 staff in New Zealand. Telecom provides trans-Tasman solutions through Gen-i, and owns AAPT/PowerTel – the third-largest telecommunications provider in Australia.

Telecom has been investing increasing amounts in its New Zealand operations and its forecast capital expenditure for 2007/08 is $865 million. Recent New Zealand capital expenditure was $701 million for 2006/07 and $620 million for 2005/06. Investments include a new W-CDMA mobile network and faster broadband technology.

Telecom's network was one of the earliest in the world to be digitised and is now being transitioned to a next-generation Internet protocol-based network. The new network will deliver voice, video and data services over one connection. About 20,000km of fibre-optic cable already forms a central part of Telecom's network.

At 30 September 2007, Telecom had more than 2 million mobile connections, 1.4 million fixed-line residential customers in New Zealand and 694,000 broadband customers (including residential, business, wholesale and mobile broadband connections). Telecom Wholesale had 192,000 access lines and 188,000 broadband connections.

In late 2006 Telecom announced a new partnership with Yahoo! to form a joint venture called Yahoo!Xtra. In March 2007, Telecom sold its Yellow Pages Group business to a private equity consortium for $2.24 billion.

TelstraClear Ltd is a voice and data company providing innovative products and services to the business, government, wholesale and residential sectors. TelstraClear has a customer base of around 400,000, made up of residential users around New Zealand, and business clients in every major central business district and in more than 30 regional centres. TelstraClear Ltd is wholly owned by Telstra Corporation Ltd, Australia's largest telecommunications company.

Vodafone New Zealand is New Zealand's leading mobile operator, providing a wide range of services, including voice and data solutions, to more than 2.3 million customers.

Vodafone Group acquired its New Zealand business (previously known as BellSouth New Zealand) in November 1998. At the time of purchase, BellSouth had 138,000 customers.

At 31 December 2007, Vodafone New Zealand had 2.3 million customers and a 52 percent share of connections in the New Zealand mobile market. Vodafone has more than 1,500 mobile phone sites around New Zealand making up its GSM digital network, covering 97 percent of the population. Since its arrival in New Zealand, Vodafone has brought competition to the mobile market and introduced a raft of products and services for business and consumers, including prepay, TXT, PXT, video PXT, the BlackBerry™ handheld device, and international voice and data roaming.

In August 2005, Vodafone launched its new 3G network, which supports real-time, face-to-face video calling, full-track music downloads to mobile, mobile television and the high-speed Vodafone mobile connect datacard. Vodafone has extended that service with 3G broadband, offering New Zealanders an affordable, viable alternative to fixed-line options.

Vodafone has invested more than $2 billion in New Zealand since 1998 and supports a wide range of community, sporting and charitable initiatives, including the Vodafone New Zealand Foundation. Vodafone employs around 1,600 people, with most based in Auckland.

TUANZ the Telecommunications Users' Association of New Zealand (TUANZ) recognises the value of effective and efficient use of information technology in business, and is committed to leading the innovative use of e-commerce in New Zealand. The purpose of TUANZ is to lead informed and sophisticated usage of technology-based communications by New Zealand businesses.

Broadband (high-speed Internet) data services share the characteristics of high speed and being 'always on' (that is, users do not need to establish specific connections to a service provider, apart from an initial set-up). Almost nationwide broadband coverage is available either through terrestrial wire and wireless services, accounting for approximately 95 percent (predominantly DSL), or via satellite technologies. Residential uptake has been relatively low compared with other OECD countries, but is accelerating quickly as prices reduce, following decisions made by the Telecommunications Commissioner with regard to regulating an unbundled bit-stream service (UBS).

Non-analog (broadband) became the main connection technology in the six months to September 2007, when the number of broadband connections overtook the number of analog (dial-up) connections for the first time, with 829,300 broadband subscribers and 675,800 dial-up subscribers.

Jarrad Mapp

Text messaging is the most widely used mobile data service on the planet, with over 70 percent of all mobile phone users worldwide (or 1.9 billion out of 2.7 billion phone subscribers) at the end of 2006 being active users of text messaging.

Broadband subscribers continued to increase over this period, up 14.4 percent, but this growth rate was slower than the 28.6 percent increase recorded in September 2006, and the 18.5 percent increase in March 2007. Subscribers with dial-up connections fell 8.6 percent in the six months to September 2007.

A number of relatively small, localised wireless operators have entered the telecommunications market offering broadband wireless services using general user radio licence spectrum (2.4 and 5 GHz bands). In addition, there are many private or semi-private networks using the general user licence spectrum. Since operators are not required to obtain permits or to register services, the number of such networks is not known.

Advanced network The New Zealand Government has committed to development and construction of an advanced network for New Zealand. The network will be made up of an optical network 'backbone' linking research and educational institutions in Auckland, Hamilton, Palmerston North, Wellington, Christchurch and Dunedin, with regional connections to Hawke's Bay, Nelson and Rotorua. Its members will include New Zealand's tertiary education institutions, Crown research institutes and the National Library.

The advanced network is focused on the specific needs of the research, education and innovation communities. The network will deliver at least 1 gigabit/second data to research institutions, with backbone speeds expected to exceed 40 gigabits/second within a few years.

High performance computing centres There are several centres in the North Island, and the Canterbury Development Corporation is developing a proposal for another in the South Island. The National Institute of Water and Atmospheric Research (NIWA) has a CRAY 3TE parallel supercomputer (Maui) with 17.6 terabytes of storage capacity. When first installed in 1999, it was ranked as the 64th most powerful computer in the world. It has very-high-speed interconnection between 32 powerful microprocessors and its theoretical peak performance is 638 gigaflops (638 x 109 operations a second). It is mainly used for modelling climate, ocean, fisheries and the atmosphere.

The University of Auckland has an IBM eServer POWER4-based supercomputer, the Regatta H 32 processor with 32 gigabytes of operating memory. It is mainly used for biological modelling and bioengineering, such as that used for the Physiome Project, the world's first accurate computer model of a human heart – it behaves like a human heart when subjected to chemical or electrical changes, drugs or other influences.

The New Zealand Supercomputing Centre (NZSC) in central Wellington is one of the world's largest commercially-available supercomputing clusters, and is a joint venture between Weta Digital and Telecom subsidiary Gen-i. The servers were originally set up for use by Weta Digital to help create special effects for *The Lord of the Rings* films. The NZSC can provide up to 5.6 teraflops of pure processing power for high-intensity computing applications and projects.

Victoria University of Wellington (VUW) has implemented a computational grid consisting of 175 Unix workstations any or all of which can be brought to bear on a single problem, such as gravitational lens and random evolution modelling. VUW is in the process of expanding the grid to include 900 Windows workstations located in various student computing suites. Sun's Grid Engine has been used to implement the Unix Grid and Condor has been used to build the Windows-based grid. Globus will be used to integrate the two into a single computational resource.

Television broadcasting

Television New Zealand (TVNZ) is a Crown entity company under the Crown Entities Act 2004. TVNZ is New Zealand's largest free-to-air public broadcaster. It operates under a charter incorporated into the Television New Zealand Act 2003.

TVNZ operates four channels, TV ONE and TV2, and another two digital-only channels, TVNZ 6 and TVNZ 7, which are broadcast through the Freeview platform.

TVNZ also runs an online 'catch-up TV' service called TVNZ ondemand, which makes some popular television shows and some shows that have screened in the past week available to download and view. Most of the locally made content is free to download, while most of the international content has a cost, and therefore a licence has to be purchased to download it.

About 90 percent of TVNZ's revenue is gained through commercial activity, such as advertising, licensing and merchandising, and hiring out production resources. Approximately 10 percent of its revenue comes from government sources.

The TVNZ charter provides a guide to its broadcasting responsibilities and makes it clear that TVNZ's role is to reflect and explore what it means to be a New Zealander.

As a Crown entity incorporated under the Companies Act 1993, it has a board of directors appointed by the company's shareholding ministers – the Minister of Broadcasting and the Minister of Finance. Day-to-day management of the company is delegated to the chief executive officer. TVNZ's editorial independence is enshrined in legislation (the Television New Zealand Act 2003) and freedom from political influence is a fundamental principle.

Freeview

Freeview was established by New Zealand's free-to-air broadcasters including TVNZ, TVWorks (owners of TV3 and C4), Māori Television and Radio New Zealand, to offer free digital-quality television programmes (after a one-off purchase of a digital receiver and, if required, a satellite dish or UHF aerial installation).

Digital transmission is a change to the way television and radio signals are broadcast. Digital signals use less bandwidth, so more channels and better quality pictures and sound can be provided. Until now, the pictures on television seen by the majority of New Zealanders have been by analogue transmissions. The existing analogue services will be switched off in the next 6–10 years.

As well as better television reception, Freeview offers access to National Radio and to interactive television content, like the eight-day electronic programme guide – Freeview Guide.

The Freeview satellite service covers all of New Zealand and offers access to TV ONE, TV2, TV3, C4, Māori TV, TVNZ 6, TVNZ 7, TVNZ Sports Extra, Stratos, Parliament TV, CUE TV, Te Reo, Radio New Zealand National, Radio New Zealand Concert and George FM.

A high-definition service Freeview|HD™ was launched in April 2008 in nine major centres (Auckland, Hamilton, Tauranga, Napier, Hastings, Palmerston North, Wellington, Christchurch and Dunedin), covering 75 percent of New Zealand homes.

For more information visit: www.freeviewnz.tv.

Source: Freeview NZ

Table 11.01

	Hours of local content on network television[1]						
Year	TV ONE	TV2	TV3	Prime	Māori TV	C4	**Total**
1996	2,407	1,255	1,404	...	...	...	**5,066**
1997	2,638	1,324	1,639	...	...	...	**5,601**
1998	3,503	1,307	1,487	...	...	...	**6,297**
1999	3,516	1,334	1,292	...	...	...	**6,142**
2000	3,544	1,158	1,484	...	...	...	**6,186**
2001	3,587	1,298	1,305	...	...	...	**6,190**
2002	4,003	1,758	1,439	...	...	...	**7,200**
2003	3,586	1,742	1,347	...	...	...	**6,675**
2004	3,401	1,603	1,420	...	...	...	**6,424**
2005	3,551	1,523	1,381	571	...	...	**7,025**
2006	3,492	1,270	1,300	863	2,323	1,008	**10,256**

(1) From 2004, local content on television is measured on an 18-hour clock (6am to midnight) basis. Prior to this, a 24-hour clock was used.

Symbol: ... not applicable

Source: NZ On Air

TVNZ earned $375.2 million in operating revenue in 2006/07, mostly from advertising ($312.8 million) and commercial production funding ($27.7 million). The remainder ($34.7 million) came primarily from government sources, including charter funding, New Zealand On Air, and Te Māngai Pāho.

TV3 is a free-to-air television station that primarily targets viewers aged 18–49. With strong emphasis on news, current affairs, and quality local and international entertainment programming, it is the leading privately-owned free-to-air television station in New Zealand.

TV3 began operating and was floated in 1989, when New Zealand's broadcast industry was deregulated. After a shaky start, it was placed in receivership in 1990, and was then de-listed in 1991. The company remained in receivership until the Government relaxed restrictions on foreign ownership in December 1991, allowing the Canadian broadcaster CanWest Global Group to buy 20 percent of TV3. Over the course of the next few years, CanWest gradually bought more of the station, until it gained 100 percent ownership in November 1997.

Over the next 10 years, CanWest continued its move into New Zealand media ownership, launching TV4 (now C4) and purchasing the companies and stations that now make up the RadioWorks stable. It also launched the new media section of the company, known as NetWorks.

On 29 July 2004, the MediaWorks IPO (Initial Public Offering) took place. At this time, CanWest MediaWorks (NZ) Limited acquired the New Zealand radio and television businesses of the CanWest Global Group (RadioWorks and TVWorks). Thirty percent of its interest was sold to the investing public.

Between 2004 and 2007, TV3 launched the current affairs show *Campbell Live* and the breakfast television show *Sunrise*, as well as securing the rights to the 2007 Rugby World Cup. This was also a period of growth for *3 News*.

On 15 June 2007, Ironbridge Capital, a leading independent Australasian private equity group (through its subsidiary HT Media), purchased CanWest's controlling 69.99 percent share in MediaWorks. Over the course of the next month, Ironbridge continued to accumulate additional shares, and on 20 July 2007 it announced an arrangement with Brook Asset Management to acquire its 8.7 percent stake in the company. This pushed the ownership over the 90 percent threshold necessary to make it compulsory for the outstanding shareholders to sell. The parent company, now known simply as MediaWorks NZ, was consequently de-listed from the New Zealand Stock Exchange.

Prime Television (Prime) acquired 34 UHF licences covering all major cities and towns in New Zealand in 1997, and started broadcasting in August 1998. Prime is a free-to-air terrestrial broadcaster, with its main office in Auckland, and regional sales offices in Hamilton, Tauranga, Wellington, Christchurch and Dunedin. An initial potential reach of 65 percent of the population expanded to 71 percent by the end of 2001, and to more than 90 percent by November 2003. In March 2002, Prime began broadcasting an entertainment-based programme schedule following a joint-venture agreement with Nine Network of Australia, departing from its initial British programming line-up. In February 2006, the Commerce Commission approved a $30.26 million takeover of Prime by SKY.

SKY Network Television Ltd (SKY) is primarily a pay television company. It began broadcasting in May 1990 using scrambled UHF channels. At 31 December 2007, SKY had 720,919 subscribers. SKY's UHF signal reaches more than 83 percent of New Zealand households. In December 1998, SKY launched its digital direct broadcast satellite service, which reaches all of the estimated 1.5 million households that have a television.

SKY broadcasts more than 100 entertainment channels on its digital satellite platform and four on its UHF terrestrial platform. SKY owns and operates 11 of its channels, including SKY sports channels, the Box, Vibe, the Rugby Channel and SKY movie channels. In February 2006, the Commerce Commission approved a $30.26 million takeover bid by SKY for the free-to-air channel operated by Prime Television.

Most popular television programmes
2007

Rank	Programme	Channel	Percentage of people aged 5+
1	AB v FRA Rugby World Cup Live	TV3	28.2
2	ENG v RSA Rugby World Cup Final	TV3	21.8
3	Dancing With the Stars	TV ONE	20.5
4	Fair Go Ad Awards 2007	TV ONE	18.6
5	Ice (documentary)	TV ONE	17.9
6	ENG v FRA Rugby World Cup Live	TV3	17.0
7	AB v ITA Rugby World Cup Live	TV3	16.7
8	Fair Go	TV ONE	16.4
9	Mucking In	TV ONE	16.3
10	Piha Rescue	TV ONE	16.3
11	AB v POR Rugby World Cup Live	TV3	16.2
12	Border Security	TV ONE	16.1
13	Coastwatch	TV ONE	15.4
14	National Bank Country Calendar	TV ONE	15.1
15	AUS v NZ Netball World Cup Final	TV ONE	14.7
16	Sunday (PM)	TV ONE	14.6
17	Rapid Response	TV ONE	14.5
18	ONE News	TV ONE	14.2
19	Location Location Location	TV ONE	14.2
20	This is Your Life	TV ONE	14.1

Source: Statistics New Zealand

More New Zealand channels broadcasting New Zealand content

NZ On Air measures New Zealand programmes screened on television. Its annual *Local Content Report* tracks the hours of New Zealand-made programming broadcast across the country's free-to-air television channels. The survey has been carried out annually since 1990, with Māori Television included for the first time in 2006.

The 2006 report shows local content is quickly spreading to new channels. Over 10,000 hours of New Zealand programmes screened on New Zealand's six free-to-air channels in 2006. Total first-run content increased to just under 8,000 hours, with TV ONE and Māori TV screening the most local content (first run and repeat).

Total first-run local content hours increased by 2,201 hours, but total hours (including repeats) dropped slightly on the three main free-to-air channels (TV ONE, TV2 and TV3) from 6,455 hours to 6,061 hours. The hours were made up on other channels – Prime TV, Māori TV and C4.

Overseas programmes cost a fraction of their production cost to buy. The quantity of local programmes able to be supported by a broadcaster indicates whether they are seen as strategically important by that channel and if the broadcaster is committed to a range of New Zealand stories.

The report also showed that first-run documentary hours on the mainstream channels had dropped, but total documentary hours increased due to Māori TV. First-run drama and comedy increased on TV ONE, and children's programming increased on TV2. First-run information programming increased on TV ONE, TV2 and TV3.

Overall results:

- Of the six free-to-air channels measured, TV ONE screened the most first-run local content (46 percent) and Prime the lowest (12 percent).
- In prime time, Māori TV screened the most local content (first-run and repeat) at 62 percent, TV ONE screened 60 percent (61 percent in 2005), TV2 screened 22 percent (26 percent in 2005), and TV3 screened 42 percent (46 percent in 2005).
- TV ONE screened the highest first-run hours of news, documentary and information.
- TV2 screened the most drama hours.
- C4 screened the most entertainment hours (mostly music) and Prime the most free-to-air sports hours.
- SKY Television screened 14,000 pay TV hours (mostly sport and music), up from 12,641 hours in 2005.

The report is available from: www.nzonair.govt.nz.

Source: NZ On Air

Trackside broadcasts live racing, race results and programmes about racing on a nationwide basis, using UHF and satellite frequencies. It is owned by the New Zealand Racing Board.

Non-commercial television The government has reserved UHF frequencies nationwide for the provision of non-commercial (community access) television services. Since 1998, the Ministry of Economic Development, latterly on the recommendation of the Ministry for Culture and Heritage, has offered licences for non-commercial use to broadcasters in the Far North, Whangarei, Auckland, Waikato, Bay of Plenty, Wellington, the Wairarapa, the East Coast, Christchurch and Oamaru regions. Many of these stations are getting national exposure on the Freeview and SKY satellite services via the Stratos network. In Budget 2005, public funding was made available for regional television for the first time, and funding support was significantly increased for non-commercial local radio. This funding is channelled through NZ On Air.

Regional and local television services A number of small regional television services operate throughout New Zealand, providing schedules with diverse programmes, including music television and mixed local and international news and entertainment. Other services provide information about local events and attractions, targeted primarily at tourists.

Local television services operating in 2007 included Te Hiku TV (Kaitaia), Family Television Network (Warkworth), Triangle Television (Auckland), Shine TV (Auckland), Family TV (Waikato), ITV Live (Matamata), Family TV (Rotorua), East Coast Television (Gisborne), Tararua Television (Tararua), Triangle Television (Wellington), Channel 61 (Taupo), TV Hawke's Bay (Hawke's Bay), Canterbury Television (Christchurch), 45 South Television (Oamaru), Channel 5 (Queenstown), Channel 9 (Dunedin), and Cue TV (Invercargill).

Radio broadcasting

The radio broadcasting sector consists of: public radio service Radio New Zealand; two major private owners of radio networks; other private stations; a publicly-funded Pacific radio service, Niu FM; a series of non-profit community stations; student radio stations; and a network of 21 iwi radio stations.

Radio New Zealand broadcasts over three nationwide networks: Radio New Zealand National, Radio New Zealand Concert, and the AM Network, which relays parliamentary proceedings. Radio New Zealand International (RNZI) is the overseas shortwave service, broadcasting to the South Pacific and beyond, while Radio New Zealand News provides comprehensive, up-to-the-minute news and current affairs information.

In November 2001, the Government gave priority to reserving frequencies for:

- National Radio to be simulcast on reserved FM frequencies. Concert FM to migrate to a designated group of frequencies in the upper FM band. Following a decision that Concert FM will not now make use of these frequencies, they remain in reserve pending future decisions on the nature of youth radio services.

Green television

Award winning WA$TED! presenters and eco-experts Francesca Price and Tristan Glendinning show there's a pot of cash to be made by saving the environment.

Two New Zealand-based environmental television shows started in 2007 – *Kaitiaki*, Māori Television's inside look at environmental issues from a uniquely Māori perspective, and *WA$TED!*, an award winning show that follows individual households challenged to embrace a greener approach to living, saving money and the planet.

Kaitiaki is a half-hour weekly programme produced by Auckland-based Kiwa Media that showcases the ways in which whānau (family), hāpu (subtribe) and iwi (tribe) are working as active kaitiaki (guardians) of the environment. Each episode looks at a single environmental issue in depth and begins to explore the causes of the problem. Inevitably, there's never an easy solution but *Kaitiaki* looks to the community for sustainable answers.

On *WA$TED!* two eco-experts visit households and look at daily lives of the householders and the resulting impact on our planet. They explore areas for improvement; provide advice, resources and financial incentives; and challenge householders to reduce their eco-footprint.

The show has been an international success, screening in over 10 countries worldwide, with the United States, Canada, Spain, Portugal and Denmark making their own versions.

Source: Fumes NZ Ltd

- Establishment of a national service for promotion of Māori language and culture. Further decisions on the use of these frequencies are pending.
- Establishment of a national service for Pacific peoples in New Zealand. The National Pacific Radio Trust (NPRT) is a private trust established under the Charitable Trusts Act 1957. NPRT is responsible for providing a national Pacific radio network, which is broadcast as Niu FM. In early 2007, NPRT merged with Radio 531pi and established the media network Pacific Radio News.

Radiocommunications The radio spectrum is an important resource managed by the Crown, through the Ministry of Economic Development, on behalf of the people of New Zealand. The efficient use of this resource to support telecommunications and broadcasting services is essential to the functioning of a modern economy.

The main legislative vehicle for managing the radio spectrum in New Zealand is the Radiocommunications Act 1989, which provides for a market-based system of spectrum management, with up to 20-year tradable spectrum access rights.

Some classes of licences remain under an administrative licensing regime. In 2007, amendments to regulations introduced a five-year notice period before such licences could be revoked, with provision for a shorter period (as long as a suitable transition plan is developed in consultation with licensees).

Allocation by tender/auction The Radiocommunications Act 1989 heralded a new era for radio spectrum management, enabling use of market-driven allocation mechanisms for distribution of spectrum rights. Radio spectrum was initially sold in 1989 and 1990 using a second-price tender system, then later by first-price tender. In 1996, an Internet-based computer system was developed for the sale of spectrum by auction. There were seven rounds of tenders and nine auctions between 1989 and 2007.

From 2003, Government policy on the renewal of spectrum rights determined that, subject to a case-by-case review five years before expiry, right-holders would be offered renewal at a fair market value.

Frequencies auctioned included bands suitable for UHF television, AM and FM radio broadcasting, mobile telephony (including 3G) and wireless broadband telecommunications. Once spectrum rights have been sold by the Crown, the purchaser has the right, subject to any such conditions as acquisition caps, conditions of ownership, or use-or-lose provisions that may be attached to the rights, to resell and transfer them to other parties.

Other allocation methods The administrative licensing regime that existed before 1989 still exists in many bands. These bands are planned for various services, and licences are available on application by people wanting to use these frequencies in accordance with these plans. Examples include land mobile and various public safety and civil aviation agencies. Spectrum rights will begin to expire from 2010–2011 and, in 2003, the Government agreed on a policy regarding renewal of commercial rights.

The policy creates a presumption that current right-holders will receive an offer for the renewal of their rights for a further 20 years at a price to be determined by a price-setting formula being developed by the Ministry of Economic Development. Finally, not all use of the spectrum is on an individually-licensed basis. There are also spectrum 'public parks', which anyone may use in accordance with terms of the corresponding general user licence. These are often used for consumer devices, such as garage door openers.

Radio New Zealand (RNZ), a Crown entity established by the Radio New Zealand Act 1995, is the country's public service radio broadcaster. The Act established the Radio New Zealand Charter, which sets out the company's broadcasting functions. RNZ receives annual funding of about $30 million (including GST) from NZ On Air to maintain and enhance its services. Funding for Radio New Zealand International, which broadcasts primarily to the Pacific region, is provided through the Ministry for Culture and Heritage.

RNZ operates three non-commercial radio networks (Radio New Zealand National, Radio New Zealand Concert and the AM Network), a shortwave service (Radio New Zealand International), a news service (Radio New Zealand News and Current Affairs) and Radio New Zealand Sound Archives Ngā Taonga Kōrero. Radio New Zealand National and Radio New Zealand Concert began to be carried by SKY Television's digital satellite in 2000, and the networks are also carried on the new Freeview platform introduced in 2007.

- Radio New Zealand National focuses primarily on news and information, with a mix of features, drama and entertainment programmes. Broadcasting 24 hours a day, the network reaches most New Zealanders on the AM band, and on FM in all main metropolitan centres and in several provincial areas, and also via satellite through SKY and Freeview.
- Radio New Zealand Concert is Radio New Zealand's fine music network, broadcasting a programme of mainly classical music and spoken features about music 24 hours a day on the FM band.
- The AM Network broadcasts all sittings of Parliament from transmitters in Auckland, Napier, Wellington, Christchurch and Dunedin. When not used for Parliament, the network is leased out.

Broadcasting to the Pacific and the world

Introduction of a digital short-wave transmitter in 2006 enabled Radio New Zealand International (RNZI) to provide high-quality broadcast of news bulletins and programmes for re-broadcasting by 14 Pacific radio stations in 11 countries.

The digital transmitter works alongside RNZI's analogue transmitter on the Rangitāiki Plains, in the middle of the North Island. As well as being heard throughout the Pacific, RNZI's 24-hour broadcasts can, at times, also be heard in North America, Europe, Asia and the Middle East.

The RNZI service is funded through the Ministry for Culture and Heritage and is run as part of Radio New Zealand. The service has 12 full-time staff in Wellington and draws on 20 correspondents in 13 Pacific countries.

RNZI also provides daily programmes for Radio Australia and for the World Radio Network, which broadcasts across Europe, North America, Asia and Africa. European listeners can also hear RNZI on the VT Merlin DRM service.

The station broadcasts bulletins of Pacific, world, New Zealand, business and sports news, along with Samoan, Tongan, Cook Island Maori, Niuean and Solomon Island Pijin bulletins. Daily current affairs programmes cover Pacific politics, business and economic issues, social issues and entertainment.

RNZI rebroadcasts Radio New Zealand National – part of New Zealand's nationwide public broadcasting network – for several hours each day to listeners in the Pacific. In return, RNZI supplies Radio New Zealand National with Pacific news and programmes.

Radio New Zealand International's website is www.rnzi.com.

Source: Radio New Zealand International

State of nation in sound

Sound Archives Ngā Taonga Kōrero is a wholly-owned subsidiary of Radio New Zealand and is funded by NZ On Air. It holds New Zealand's most significant collection of broadcast radio archives.

The collections amount to thousands of hours of radio broadcast recordings relating to all aspects of New Zealand's history, society and bicultural heritage, dating from the early 1930s to the present day. These include recordings of peoples' memories dating much further back, for example to the eruption of Mt Tarawera in 1886. With topics as diverse as ancient waiata (songs) and discussions of the current state of politics, Sound Archives selects and preserves broadcasts from both the public and private radio sectors that capture the state of the nation in sound.

The archive is also a living entity, continuing to take in today's broadcasts that will reflect present-day trends, tastes and values for future generations. About 1,200 hours of new recordings are archived each year, capturing the diversity of material broadcast by all networks and stations.

The collections, held in Christchurch and Auckland, are widely used by the general public, researchers, television and film-makers, academics and educators, production companies, students and musicians. Copies of recordings from Sound Archives can be supplied, subject to copyright restrictions. Charges are on a cost-recovery basis and licensing fees may be payable, depending on the intended end use of the archival audio. The Sound Archives website is www.soundarchives.co.nz.

Source: Sound Archives

Radio Tainui

Renee Haumaha, a breakfast announcer on air for Radio Tainui in Ngaruawahia. Radio Tainui is one of 21 iwi stations delivering programming for Māori audiences. It broadcasts 24 hours a day, seven days a week.

- Radio New Zealand International is the country's international shortwave service, providing news and information programmes to listeners in the Pacific 24 hours a day. Radio New Zealand International's 100-kilowatt signal is beamed to the South Pacific, but can be heard by listeners as far away as Japan, North America, the Middle East and Europe.

- Radio New Zealand News and Current Affairs provides news coverage, current affairs and specialist reporting for Radio New Zealand National and Radio New Zealand Concert. International news services, correspondents overseas, and reporters throughout New Zealand deliver news to listeners throughout the day.

- Radio New Zealand Sound Archives Ngā Taonga Kōrero is a subsidiary of Radio New Zealand, which gained archive status under section 90 of the Copyright Act in 1994, allowing material broadcast by any New Zealand network or station to be archived without breaching copyright. This enabled Radio New Zealand Sound Archives Ngā Taonga Kōrero to become a national collection, representing all broadcast radio providers in New Zealand, as well as preserving existing collections largely created during the era of state-owned radio.

The Radio New Zealand website was redesigned in 2005 and now carries live streaming, audio on demand and podcast services, allowing programmes to be accessed worldwide.

The Radio Network of New Zealand Ltd (TRN) owns 123 radio stations, operating in 26 markets across New Zealand.

TRN was formed following the sale of Radio New Zealand Commercial (a state-owned enterprise) by the New Zealand Government in 1996. TRN is a wholly-owned subsidiary of Australian Radio Network (ARN). Shareholders in ARN are Clear Channel Communications (US) and APN News & Media (Australia).

TRN's programme brands are Classic Hits (26 stations), Newstalk ZB (25 stations), Radio Sport (19 stations), ZM (18 stations), Radio Hauraki (14 stations), Coast (12 stations), Easy Mix (four stations), Flava (three stations) and Hokonui Gold (one station).

TRN stations reach a listening audience of 1.327 million New Zealanders aged 10 and over on a weekly basis. TRN is a joint venture partner in The Radio Bureau, which represents nearly all of the radio industry to advertising agencies and their clients.

Non-commercial radio broadcasting The Crown has reserved AM and FM radio frequencies throughout New Zealand for use by non-commercial broadcasters. AM frequencies have been reserved in all communities with populations of 10,000 or more. Broadcasters may have access to reserved spectrum for non-profit, community purposes. Licences are allocated to appropriate community organisations, who are responsible for ensuring that all interested groups have access to airtime on the frequencies. Access radio stations operating on reserved frequencies provide airtime on a non-profit basis to a range of minority groups in the community. In 2005/06, and also 2006/07, there were 11 access radio stations in New Zealand. All were assisted by NZ On Air, whose funding for access radio was $2.29 million in 2005/06, and $2.34 million in 2006/07.

Applications for frequencies are received by the Ministry of Economic Development and allocated on the advice of the Ministry for Culture and Heritage.

Newspapers and magazines

New Zealand has a high number of daily newspapers in relation to its population. There are 23 daily newspapers, with 15 of these being afternoon papers published in provincial towns and cities. According to figures released by the Audit Bureau of Circulations, Auckland-based *The New Zealand Herald* had the largest audited net circulation of a daily newspaper in 2007, with a circulation of 195,681. The biggest provincial paper in 2007 was Hamilton's *Waikato Times*, with an audited net circulation of 41,430. Other daily newspapers have circulations ranging from about 2,000 to nearly 100,000.

The majority of daily newspapers are owned by two major publishing groups, Fairfax New Zealand Ltd and APN New Zealand Ltd. Between them, these groups account for just over 90 percent of

Figure 11.03

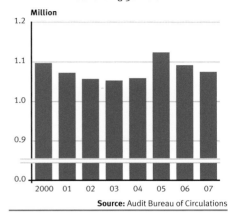

Total newspaper circulation
Daily and Sunday papers
Year ending 31 March

Source: Audit Bureau of Circulations

Table 11.02

Newspaper circulation
At 31 March

Paper (date founded)	2002	2003	2004	2005	2006	2007
Dailies						
The New Zealand Herald – Auckland (1863)	210,841	210,910	211,490	204,549	200,309	195,681
The Dominion Post[1] – Wellington (2002)	101,511	99,089	99,123	98,232	98,251	98,326
The Press – Christchurch (1869)	92,713	91,111	92,436	92,458	92,465	90,030
Otago Daily Times – Dunedin (1861)	44,352	44,546	45,400	44,928	43,246	43,469
Waikato Times – Hamilton (1872)	41,121	40,970	41,009	41,017	41,083	41,430
The Southland Times – Invercargill (1862)	30,840	29,928	29,557	29,567	29,571	29,059
Hawke's Bay Today – Hastings (1998)	31,665	30,079	30,197	30,073	28,037	26,946
Taranaki Daily News – New Plymouth (1857)	26,784	26,687	26,749	26,754	26,506	26,522
Bay of Plenty Times – Tauranga (1872)	22,726	23,285	22,726	23,919	24,038	23,179
Manawatu Standard – Palmerston North (1880)	20,840	20,357	20,566	20,576	20,578	20,165
The Nelson Mail (1866)	18,274	18,312	18,425	18,437	18,445	17,497
The Northern Advocate – Whangarei (1877)	15,319	15,112	15,321	14,890	14,987	15,012
The Timaru Herald (1864)	14,308	14,360	14,329	14,335	14,114	14,120
Wanganui Chronicle (1856)	14,059	13,103	12,483	12,652	12,486	12,532
The Daily Post – Rotorua (1885)	11,955	11,979	12,120	12,063	12,056	11,796
The Marlborough Express – Blenheim (1866)	10,113	10,173	10,296	10,362	10,371	10,381
The Gisborne Herald (1874)	8,623	8,573	8,620	8,631	8,586	8,667
Wairarapa Times-Age – Masterton (1878)	7,713	7,585	7,619	7,664	7,698	7,276
Ashburton Guardian (1879)	5,497	5,554	5,525	5,460	5,529	5,670
The Greymouth Evening Star (1866)	4,266	4,219	4,303	4,289	..	4,883
The Oamaru Mail (1876)	3,644	3,464	3,545	3,561	3,517	3,446
Daily Chronicle[2] – Levin (1893)	3,789	37,892	37,892	2,868	..	2,661
The Westport News (1872)	2,010	..	2,016	..	..	1,998
Sundays						
Sunday Star Times (1994)	202,511	203,901	209,143	203,647	200,991	181,127
Herald on Sunday (2004)	...	...	...	101,355	93,193	91,521
Sunday News (1963)	108,869	110,136	110,759	101,279	95,546	90,857

(1) Formed by the integration of *The Evening Post* (1865) and *The Dominion* (1907). (2) Formerly *The Horowhenua-Kapiti Chronicle* – Levin.

Symbols: .. figure not available ... not applicable

Source: Audit Bureau of Circulations

Table 11.03

Magazine circulation[1]

	2002	2003	2004	2005	2006	2007
AA Directions (quarterly)	542,219	540,395	573,864	548,327	546,968	546,407
SkyWatch (monthly)	358,589	390,571	416,290	455,411	492,408	504,882
TV Guide (weekly)	225,648	222,931	217,492	203,456	195,072	189,215
New Zealand Woman's Day (weekly)	141,781	147,124	142,610	151,074	152,609	136,702
New Zealand Woman's Weekly (weekly)	97,013	101,397	97,769	102,542	98,847	98,738
Reader's Digest NZ (monthly)	101,756	92,258	85,036	88,267	93,934	95,872
Straight Furrow (monthly)	80,006	85,231	85,009	84,741	84,801	87,288
AgTrader (monthly)	77,723	85,241	84,665	81,036	83,047	85,911
Australian Woman's Weekly NZ (monthly)	92,627	98,888	97,342	93,698	85,014	83,834
Rural News (fortnightly)	84,607	86,134	87,854	85,888	84,203	81,585
Cuisine (alternative months)	79,760	76,977	75,810	71,030	64,103	64,761
New Zealand Listener (weekly)	76,844	76,171	75,177	73,034	71,508	63,902
NZ House & Garden (monthly)	80,669	79,299	77,655	75,619	65,215	62,598
New Idea (weekly)	54,427	57,408	58,591	61,484	65,440	62,315
Next (monthly)	63,070	67,471	66,836	70,606	63,747	58,052
That's Life (weekly)	44,366	45,640	46,134	44,919	45,411	45,739
Your Home & Garden (monthly)	50,382	50,073	47,179	46,769	41,510	38,511
New Zealand Gardener (monthly)	50,619	45,094	38,196	37,734	34,745	35,332
Little Treasures (alternative months)	46,184	43,974	45,196	45,581	40,190	34,208
Family Times (quarterly)[2]	41,558	41,996	42,795	180,596	199,131	199,640

(1) Audit period of selected magazines: January–June. (2) From 2005, *Family Times* appears in four metropolitan editions, with aggregated circulation. Circulation figures for 2007 are Auckland *Family Times* (98,480), Wellington *Family Times* (43,054), Christchurch *Family Times* (44,843) and Dunedin *Family Times* (13,263).

Source: Audit Bureau of Circulations

New Zealand's aggregate daily newspaper circulation of about 720,000. The largest independent newspaper is the *Otago Daily Times* in Dunedin.

At 31 March 2007, there were three Sunday newspapers – the *Sunday Star Times* and *Sunday News*, both published by Fairfax New Zealand, and the *Herald on Sunday*, published by APN New Zealand. All three newspapers are distributed nationwide, with a collective circulation of about 360,000. The *Sunday Star Times* had the largest audited net circulation of a Sunday newspaper, with a circulation of 181,127 in 2007.

Daily and Sunday newspapers are widely read. On a typical day, nearly 1.6 million New Zealanders aged 15 years and over read a newspaper.

There are also approximately 120 community newspapers in New Zealand, the majority of which are tabloid in format. Many of these are owned by the two big newspaper publishing groups, or by publishers of other newspapers outside the groups. Some are owned by individuals or small companies. More than 6,000 magazines are available on a regular basis in New Zealand, 650 of which are published in New Zealand.

New Zealand Press Association (NZPA) Through international agreements with Reuters, Australian Associated Press and other news organisations, the cooperatively-owned NZPA provides an international and domestic news service to all daily and Sunday newspapers. A major change in 2005 was that the NZPA newswire was no longer exclusive to daily and Sunday newspapers, but available for sale to broadcast and electronic media as well.

New Zealand Press Council is a self-regulatory body founded in 1972 with the primary function of investigating and adjudicating complaints against newspapers and other publications. Its constituent members are the Newspaper Publishers Association (NPA) and the New Zealand Engineering, Printing and Manufacturing Union (EPMU). The council consists of an independent chairperson, five members representing the public, and five members representing the industry. Two of the five industry representatives are nominated by the NPA, two are nominated by the EPMU and one by magazine publishers. A panel, which includes the chief ombudsman, appoints public members.

The principal objectives of the Press Council are to:

- consider complaints against the editorial content of newspapers and other publications (a separate body deals with complaints against advertising)
- promote freedom of speech and freedom of the press in New Zealand
- maintain the New Zealand press in accordance with the highest professional standards.

The council may also consider complaints about the conduct of people and organisations towards the press.

The council does not set standards for newspapers, but from time to time it issues recommendations to editors in general terms. To make a complaint to the council, complainants are first required to complain in writing to the editor of the publication concerned. This allows the editor the opportunity of righting a possible wrong. If complainants are still not satisfied, they can then approach the council.

Eventual third place winners (from left) Max Gunn (13), Alison Macharg (13), and Caleb Dawson-Swale (14) of Wakatipu High School, scan the Otago Daily Times *for answers at the September 2007* Otago Daily Times *social studies quiz for schools in the Central Otago Region.*

Table 11.04

New Zealand Press Council statistics
Year ending 31 December

	2003	2004	2005	2006
Decisions issued	**52**	**45**	**41**	**32**
Upheld	14	9	4	6
Upheld with dissent	0	0	0	1
Part upheld	5	3	4	2
Part upheld with dissent	0	0	0	2
Not upheld with dissent	2	0	0	0
Not upheld with dissent on casting vote of chairman	0	0	0	1
Not upheld	31	33	33	19
Declined	0	0	0	1
Not adjudicated	**27**	**30**	**39**	**23**
Mediated/resolved	3	3	3	0
Withdrawn	2	1	5	2
Withdrawn at late stage	2	1	1	1
Not followed through	9	12	11	6
Out of time	2	0	2	2
Not accepted	2	2	2	0
Outside jurisdiction	0	3	7	2
In action at end of year	7	8	8	10
Total complaints	**79**	**75**	**80**	**55**

Source: New Zealand Press Council

There is no charge for the council's service. In circumstances where legally actionable issues may be involved, complainants are required to provide a waiver that, having referred the matter to the council, no legal proceedings will be taken against the newspaper or journalist concerned. The council is funded entirely by the industry.

Table 11.06

Advertising expenditure
By consumer sector
Year ending 31 December 2007

Section	Total media ($000)
Leisure and entertainment	334,063
Retail	285,483
Foodstuffs	268,107
Government departments, services and community	209,649
Automotive	178,138
Investment, finance and banking	155,501
Toiletries and cosmetics	153,422
Home improvements	103,480
Pharmaceuticals and health	101,950
Travel	94,219
Beverages	84,185
Household electrical products	83,657
Household furnishings	82,420
Telecommunications	80,239
Computers	77,524
Clothing	61,368
Business services	44,633
Real estate	39,341
Agricultural	27,297
Insurance	8,518
Total	**2,473,192**

Source: Nielsen Media Research

Advertising

Approximately 1,000 people are employed in New Zealand advertising agencies and 2,500 in advertising-related services. Advertising revenue also contributes to the employment of another 10,000 people in the publishing, radio and television industries. Mainstream media advertising for the year ending December 2006 totalled $2.2 billion.

At the beginning of 2007, there were approximately 200 advertising agencies, most of them New Zealand-owned, but with 25 percent (mostly larger agencies) affiliated to multinationals by total or part ownership.

Industry organisations and self-regulation The Communication Agencies Association of New Zealand (CAANZ) is an incorporated body representing the interests of members on issues affecting the advertising industry and agencies. There are 65 member agencies that collectively represent 80 percent of agency billings in New Zealand, with combined turnover of approximately $900 million.

Table 11.05

Advertising expenditure in media[1]
Year ending 31 December

Media	2002 Expenditure $(million)	2002 Share (percent)	2003 Expenditure $(million)	2003 Share (percent)	2004 Expenditure $(million)	2004 Share (percent)	2005 Expenditure $(million)	2005 Share (percent)	2006 Expenditure $(million)	2006 Share (percent)
Newspapers[2]	628	40.1	689	37.1	790	38.1	830	37.2	810	36.4
Television	516	33.0	592	31.9	643	31.1	666	29.9	641	28.8
Radio	203	13.0	224	12.1	247	11.9	256	11.5	269	12.1
Magazines	173	11.0	194	10.4	223	10.7	260	11.7	251	11.3
Unaddressed mail	..	..	56	3.1	59	2.8	72	3.2	79	3.6
Outdoor and cinemas combined	37	2.4	47	2.5	51	2.5	11	0.5	10	0.4
Addressed mail[3]	..	..	35	1.9	34	1.6	34	1.5	35	1.6
Online	..	..	8	0.4	15	0.7	56	2.5	64	2.9
Cinema only	8	0.5	12	0.6	13	0.6	44	2.0	65	2.9
Total	**1,565**	**100.0**	**1,857**	**100.0**	**2,075**	**100.0**	**2,229**	**100.0**	**2,224**	**100.0**

(1) All cash advertising revenue, plus agency commission where applicable. (2) Includes daily and community newspapers. (3) Addressed advertising mail is an actual return for 2004. The 2003 figure is an estimate.

Note: Figures may not add up to stated totals, due to rounding.

Symbol: .. figure not available

Source: CAANZ

The Association of New Zealand Advertisers (ANZA) represents the interests of advertisers and has 100 members. ANZA administers two pre-placement vetting systems – one for liquor advertising and one for therapeutic advertising.

The advertising industry has a self-regulatory system managed by the Advertising Standards Authority (ASA) and the Advertising Standards Complaints Board. The authority's function is to promulgate codes of practice and develop policies on advertising standards. The board's function is to adjudicate on complaints and advise the ASA on codes and public issues.

Postal services

The Postal Services Act 1998 permitted full competition in all areas of the postal services market. All mail must carry a mark to identify the postal operator that carried it.

Postal operators have the right to open mail in certain circumstances (for example, so it can be returned to the sender when an address is illegible). They also have the right to erect letterboxes.

To carry out a business involving carriage of letters, a person or company must be registered as a postal operator with the Ministry of Economic Development. At 23 November 2007, there were 27 registered postal operators.

New Zealand Post Ltd

Under a deed of understanding with the government, New Zealand Post is required to meet certain social obligations, including maintaining a minimum number of delivery points and postal outlets, maintaining five- or six-day a week delivery to 99.88 percent of delivery points, and providing competitors with access to its network on terms and conditions no less favourable than those offered to equivalent customers.

New Zealand Post is designated as New Zealand's 'postal administration' to the Universal Postal Union (UPU) and has the exclusive right to issue New Zealand stamps.

New Zealand Post is a state-owned enterprise, which has been operating in a deregulated postal environment since 1998. The Postal Services Act of that year removed New Zealand Post's monopoly on the standard letter, allowing full competition in postal services. The price of standard letter postage was reduced from 45 cents to 40 cents on 2 October 1995 and was maintained at that level until 5 April 2004, when it returned to 45 cents. On 1 June 2007, the price was increased to 50 cents. The price of postage in New Zealand compares favourably with many overseas countries and, in real terms, the price of postage is significantly cheaper than before the introduction of competition in 1998.

New Zealand Post's service delivery – the independent measure of mail delivered on time – was 95.5 percent for the year to 30 June 2007, putting its service standards among the best in the world.

While it continues the tradition of carrying and delivering letters and parcels, New Zealand Post has responded to customers' growing communications needs by providing electronic solutions to residential, business and international markets.

Its business activities include letters, courier services, banking and financial transactions, mail and stamp production, as well as data processing and electronic billing, commerce and messaging.

Table 11.07

Mail delivery points Year ending 30 June						
	2002	2003	2004	2005	2006	2007
Residential	1,253,693	1,243,613	1,258,302	1,319,017	1,330,303	1,335,999
Private box and bag	181,999	189,244	202,278	205,642	6,330	216,330
Rural delivery	177,727	180,495	191,363	200,673	206,299	208,892
Business	57,314	59,508	58,270	114,773	83,941	67,748
Other	23,837	25,096	14,752	13,501	13,306	13,306
Total	**1,694,570**	**1,697,956**	**1,724,965**	**1,853,606**	**1,845,029**	**1,842,275**

Source: New Zealand Post

Table 11.08

Postal outlets Year ending 30 June					
Outlet	2003	2004	2005	2006	2007
PostShops (including franchises)	315	323	323	325	325
Post Centres	697	698	672	667	663
Stamp resellers	2,735	2,647	1,601	1,620	1,622
Total	**3,747**	**3,668**	**2,596**	**2,612**	**2,610**

Source: New Zealand Post

Recent performance New Zealand Post reported a net profit of $70.2 million after tax for the 2006/07 financial year, compared with $68.7 million in 2005/06, $137.2 million in 2004/05, and $36.5 million in 2003/04.

Mail services

Inland services Fast post or standard post can be used in New Zealand to send letters up to 20 millimetres thick and up to 1 kilogram in weight. Fast post targets next working day delivery between major towns and cities, with standard post delivery targets of next working day delivery across town, and two-to-three working days across New Zealand.

Packet post is used to send parcels up to 1.5 kilograms either fast post or standard post. Parcel post is used for parcels up to 25 kilograms, with delivery targets of next working day for delivery across town, and two-to-three working days nationwide. Other services include BoxLink, registered post, business mail centres, and postage included envelopes. In December 2004, New Zealand Post and DHL announced the formation of Express Couriers Limited, a 50:50 joint venture encompassing the express and logistics units of New Zealand Post and the brands Pace, CourierPost and Contract Logistics. In July 2007, Roadstar Transport was added to the family, providing palletised freight services.

New Zealand Post also provides bulk mail services (starting at 300 same-sized items) which include volume post, GoFlexible and print post, and offers direct mail services through the mail marketing services division. New Zealand Post subsidiary the Letterbox Channel handles delivery of unaddressed mail (circulars).

Overseas services New Zealand Post International operates several overseas mail and courier services. International express is a premium track-and-trace courier service delivering to more than 220 countries, with next-day delivery to Australian main cities and targeting delivery within days to the rest of the world. It includes built-in compensation cover and additional cover options.

International economy courier is a recently-launched cost-effective courier service to selected key destinations around the world. The delivery target is in two to six working days and includes built-in compensation cover and additional cover options.

International air offers air mail delivery in approximately one to two weeks, with built-in compensation cover and the option of additional cover and/or track and trace facilities to selected countries.

Table 11.09

Stamp issues
1 January 2006 – 30 June 2008

Date of issue	Issue name	Denomination
2006		
4 January	Year of the Dog	45c, 90c, $1.35, $1.50, $2.00
3 February	75th Anniversary of the Hawke's Bay Earthquake	45c x 20
1 March	Tourism 2006	$1.50 x 6
21 April	80th Birthday of Her Majesty the Queen	$5.00
3 May	Personalised Stamps	45c x 7, $1.50, $2.00 x 2
5 July	Scenic – Renewable Energy	45c, 90c, $1.35, $1.50, $2.00
2 August	Children's Health	$1.35, $1.50, $2.00
6 September	Gold Rush	45c, 90c, $1.35, $1.50, $2.00
4 October	Christmas Stamps	45c x 6, 90c, $1.35, $1.50, $2.00
1 November	Summer Festivals	45c, 90c, $1.35, $1.50, $2.00
1 November	2006 Ross Dependency	45c, 90c, $1.35, $1.50, $2.00
2007		
2 February	Year of the Pig	45c, 90c, $1.35, $1.50, $2.00
7 March	New Zealand Native Wildlife	45c, 90c, $1.35, $1.50, $2.00
24 April	2007 Centenaries	50c & $1.00, 50c & $1.50, 50c & $2.00, 50c & $2.50
9 May	Scenic definitives	5c, 10c, 20c, 50c, $1.00, $2.50, $3.00
6 June	Southern Skies	50c, $1.00, $1.50, $2.00, $2.50
4 July	Classic Kiwi	50c x 20
1 August	Clever Kiwis	50c, $1.00, $1.50, $2.00, $2.50
5 September	Royal Diamond Wedding Anniversary	50c, $2.00
5 September	Health, Annual Collector Pack	50c x 2, $1.00
3 October	Christmas	50c, $1.00, $1.50, $2.00, $2.50
7 November	2007 Ross Dependency	50c, $1.00, $1.50, $2.00, $2.50
2008		
9 January	Underwater Reefs	50c, $1.00, $1.50, $2.00
2 February	Fish and Game	$10.00
7 February	Year of the Rat	50c, $1.00, $1.50, $2.00
5 March	Weather Extremes	50c x 2, $1.00, $1.50, $2.00, $2.50
2 April	ANZAC	50c x 2, $1.00, $1.50, $2.00, $2.50
2 May	Kingitanga	50c, $1.50, $2.00
7 May	Prince Caspian	50c, $1.00, $1.50, $2.00
4 June	Matariki	50c x 2, $1.00, $1.50, $2.00, $2.50

Source: New Zealand Post

Weather extremes

Drought, wind, storm, flooding, snow storm and heat – the "Weather Extremes" set was issued in 2008, the International Year of Planet Earth. New Zealand Post's stamp issue highlights the diverse New Zealand weather experience.

Source: New Zealand Post

International economy offers cost-effective delivery to anywhere in the world within approximately three to five weeks.

Retail network New Zealand Post's retail network at 30 June 2007 consisted of 325 PostShops (including franchises), with postal services available at a further 663 Post Centres. There were also 1,622 stamp resellers. More than 140 different payments, to 80 different agencies, can be made through the retail network. In 2005/06, 85 percent of adult New Zealanders used at least one agency service through the retail network. New Zealand Post processed around 20 million financial transactions on behalf of the 80 agencies, collecting $3.1 billion in payments.

Stamp issues

New Zealand Post's stamp unit produces around 12 commemorative stamp issues each year and up to three definitive stamp issues. Table 11.09 (previous page) lists stamps issued from 1 January 2006 to 30 June 2008.

A variety of products, including commemorative coins on behalf of the Reserve Bank of New Zealand, are sold by mail order through the Philatelic Bureau at Wanganui, at stamp sales centres, through PostShops, and from the stamps website www.stamps.co.nz.

Contributors and related websites

Broadcasting Standards Authority – www.bsa.govt.nz

Commerce Commission – www.comcom.govt.nz

Communication Agencies Association of New Zealand – www.caanz.co.nz

Department of Internal Affairs – www.dia.govt.nz

Freeview NZ – www.freeviewnz.tv

InternetNZ – www.internetnz.net.nz

Māori Television – www.maoritelevision.com

Ministry for Culture and Heritage – www.mch.govt.nz

Ministry of Economic Development – www.med.govt.nz

New Zealand Audit Bureau of Circulations – www.abc.org.nz

New Zealand Post – www.nzpost.co.nz

New Zealand Press Council – www.presscouncil.org.nz

Nielsen Media Research – www.nielsenmedia.co.nz

NZ On Air – www.nzonair.govt.nz

Radio Network – www.radionetwork.co.nz

Radio New Zealand – www.radionz.co.nz

Radio New Zealand International – www.rnzi.com

SKY Network Television – www.skytv.co.nz

Sound Archives – www.soundarchives.co.nz

State Services Commission – www.ssc.govt.nz

Te Māngai Pāho – www.tmp.govt.nz

Telecom – www.telecom.co.nz

Telecommunications Users' Association of New Zealand – www.tuanz.org.nz

Television New Zealand – www.tvnz.co.nz

TelstraClear – www.telstraclear.co.nz

TV3 Network – www.tv3.co.nz

Vodafone – www.vodafone.co.nz

Hocken Collections

The painting, Josepha from Les Martinique, *by New Zealand artist Sydney Lough Thompson, is returned to storage at the University of Otago's Hocken Collections by curator Anna Peterson. The collections include 13,610 paintings and more than 1 million photographs.*

12 | Arts and cultural heritage

Successive governments have recognised the value of culture for individuals, communities and the country as a whole. Increasing recognition by government of the strategic and intrinsic importance of arts, culture and heritage has been reflected in increased investment in these activities. Central government spending on culture, adjusted for inflation, rose from $388 million in 1990/91 to $675 million in 2003/04, an increase of 73 percent. A small and increasingly diverse population and the relative absence of private patronage make this government assistance necessary if all New Zealanders are to have access to meaningful cultural experiences.

New Zealanders actively engage with their culture. The Cultural Experiences Survey in 2002 provided a snapshot of New Zealanders' cultural activity, which included listening to popular music, visiting museums and art galleries, visiting marae and buying original art works and craft objects. Around 93 percent of the population aged 15 and over had participated in at least one cultural activity, and there was a very high level of interest in New Zealand content, including theatre, music and literature. These cultural activities and experiences are essential in the development of strong, but overlapping cultural identities, and promote a cohesive society that accepts and encourages diversity.

The development of creative talent and cultural industries also enhances economic growth. Worldwide, the creative, cultural and heritage sectors are key growth industries for the 21st century, and New Zealand is following this trend. Between 1996 and 2001, the number of people in paid cultural employment in New Zealand rose 17 percent, almost three times the growth in total employment over the same period. From 1997 to 2001 cultural activity contributed an average of $3.0 billion a year to GDP, or 3.1 percent of New Zealand's total industry contribution.

Taonga tuku iho

Ngā taonga tuku iho nō ngā tūpuna, or the treasures handed down by our ancestors, make New Zealand's cultural heritage unique, and successive governments have made special provision to support them.

The government does this through a number of agencies, including the Museum of New Zealand Te Papa Tongarewa which actively promotes the significance of Māori cultural heritage through its collections and programmes.

The government also provides capital funding, from time to time, to regional museums that have nationally significant Māori taonga collections.

The Māori Heritage Council (part of the New Zealand Historic Places Trust) registers and protects wāhi tapu (sacred places), provides assistance to whānau (families), hapū (subtribes) and iwi (tribes) to preserve heritage resources, and makes recommendations on archaeological sites.

Te Waka Toi fulfils Creative New Zealand's statutory responsibility to recognise in the arts the role of Māori as tangata whenua ('people of the land').

The Māori Arts and Crafts Institute, based at Te Puia (Rotorua), trains students in traditional skills, such as carving and weaving, and promotes Māori culture.

The Māori Language Commission Te Taura Whiri i te Reo Māori promotes the use of Māori as a living language and encourages Māori-English bilingualism as a valued part of New Zealand culture.

Te Māngai Pāho provides broadcasting funding for production of Māori language television programmes, Māori music and the national network of Māori radio stations. Māori Television provides a high-quality bilingual broadcasting service. The first 100 percent Māori television channel, Te Reo, was launched in March 2008.

The government also supports Te Matatini Society Inc, which focuses on Māori performance arts, including national kapa haka competitions, the South Pacific Arts Festival and the biennial Te Matatini National Festival.

Further support for taonga tuku iho comes from the Lottery Grants Board, which allocates profits to community enterprises, including restoration of marae.

The Protected Objects Act 1975 regulates the export of antiquities, including taonga, and provides protection for newly-discovered artefacts.

Te Puia

A student at the New Zealand Māori Arts and Crafts Institute at Te Puia, Rotorua, carves a tekoteko (figure). For 38 years, students have been learning traditional crafts here, keeping stories alive. Today, students study full time for three years at the carving school.

Heritage

Museum of New Zealand

The Museum of New Zealand Te Papa Tongarewa (Te Papa) is New Zealand's national museum. Since opening on the Wellington waterfront in February 1998, it has established a national and international reputation as New Zealand's 'must-see' visitor attraction. Ten years later, in February 2008, more than 14 million visits had been made to Te Papa.

Te Papa's founding concept was developed through an extensive national consultative process and was adopted by the Government in 1990. It introduced: unified collections, the narratives of culture and place, the idea of forum, the bicultural partnership between tangata whenua ('people of the land') and tangata tiriti ('people of the treaty'), and a multidisciplinary approach to delivering a national museum for diverse audiences.

Its mission, to be a forum for the nation to explore and preserve its unique cultural and natural heritage, is underpinned by the principles of the bicultural partnership; being a waharoa (entry) to exploring and reflecting on cultural identity; acknowledging and recognising the role of communities in the care, management and understanding of taonga (treasures) and collections; speaking with authority; being committed to providing excellent services; and being commercially positive.

The museum contains 19 major long-term exhibitions, and features innovative and exciting exhibitions that draw on the richness of its collections and bring the best of the rest of the world to New Zealand.

Permanent exhibitions include Bush City, an outdoor space that recreates distinctive aspects of the New Zealand landform and its associated plant life, and Toi Te Papa: Art of the Nation, a celebration of New Zealand's rich and diverse artistic heritage featuring over 300 artworks from Te Papa's collection.

Te Papa is the only museum in the world with its own living, functioning marae, Rongomaraeroa, Te Marae ō Te Papa Tongarewa.

Central to Te Papa's existence are its collections, spanning five main areas: art, natural history, New Zealand history and heritage, Pacific, and taonga Māori. Te Papa has particularly rich collections of New Zealand plants and animals, taonga Māori, and Pacific treasures.

As the national museum, Te Papa operates services for audiences and communities outside its premises. These include National Services Te Paerangi, through which Te Papa works with other museums, iwi (tribes) and related organisations on projects to build capacity and sustain the services they provide in their local communities.

Other services include Te Papa Press, touring exhibitions, a collections loans service, a programme of iwi partnership projects, and the Te Papa website.

Te Papa's presence has changed tourist visitor patterns to Wellington. Of 1.35 million visits to Te Papa in the 2006/07 year, more than 30 percent of domestic visitors were from outside Wellington city and 46 percent of visitors were from overseas. The ethnic pattern of Te Papa's New Zealand visitors is similar to that of the total population.

Te Papa's funding is from central government (55 percent), local government (5 percent) and self-generated funding from sponsors and commercial enterprises (40 percent).

Art galleries and museums

There are between 500 and 600 public museums and art galleries in New Zealand, ranging from small volunteer-run museums housing collections primarily of local importance, to larger institutions providing guardianship to collections of regional, national and international significance. As well as allowing access to their collections through exhibitions and public programmes, museums conduct research within their collecting areas, produce resources, give support to their communities, and provide educational services. Many museums are working on digitisation programmes aimed at making their collections more accessible to the wider public while ensuring their long-term care.

Many art galleries and museums are partly funded by local government. Funding for capital works may be provided by the Ministry for Culture and Heritage under the regional museums policy for capital construction projects, and by the Lottery Grants Board, community trusts, electricity trusts or other funding bodies.

New Zealand Historic Places Trust

The New Zealand Historic Places Trust Pouhere Taonga (NZHPT) is New Zealand's national historic heritage agency. The trust is established under the Historic Places Act 1993 and is an autonomous Crown entity governed by the Crown Entities Act 2004. Its board of trustees is assisted by the Māori Heritage Council, ensuring that the NZHPT reflects a bicultural view in exercising its powers and functions.

Living Heritage – our past for our future

Living Heritage is an online bilingual (Māori/English) initiative that enables New Zealand schools to develop and publish an online resource, based on a heritage treasure in their community. Students create their own websites, using their study of local heritage to tell stories and contribute to the preservation of New Zealand history and culture.

Students have investigated the history of local areas and schools, notable people in the community, interesting landmarks, flora and fauna, and environmental issues.

The Living Heritage project started in 2001. In 2007, 82 schools registered to take part and 14 completed sites were published on the Living Heritage website.

The project is supported by 2020 Communications Trust, the National Library of New Zealand, CWA New Media and the New Zealand Government's Digital Strategy Community Partnership Fund 2006–08. CWA New Media provides technical support for schools throughout their projects, and facilitates the online publication of the school's website. The National Library hosts the completed resources in a digital repository that will be preserved forever.

In 2007, Te Kura Kaupapa Māori o Te Ara Whānui in Lower Hutt published the first Living Heritage website in te reo Māori.

The New Zealand National Commission for UNESCO has created a Living Heritage award to celebrate the achievements of schools that are helping to preserve our past using digital media. Cannon's Creek School in Porirua, Central School in New Plymouth, and Franz Josef Glacier School received UNESCO awards in 2007.

The 2020 Communications Trust researched the Living Heritage project in 2007. Findings clearly demonstrated the project's success in connecting teachers, students and schools with their communities, and in enhancing students' and teachers' ICT skills. The project has created a permanent online record of local heritage information which can be added to as a growing digital collection.

Source: www.livingheritage.org.nz

The NZHPT is funded by government through the Vote Arts, Culture and Heritage allocation.

The NZHPT's role in identifying, protecting, preserving and conserving historical and cultural heritage is extensive. This role includes:

- leadership on heritage issues important to New Zealand
- assisting Māori communities to identify and recognise wāhi tapu (sacred sites) and restore historic marae-related buildings and structures
- management, administration and control of 46 nationally-significant heritage properties
- establishment and maintenance of the register of historic places, historic areas, wāhi tapu and wāhi tapu areas
- administration of archaeological authorities with regard to activities that may destroy, damage or modify archaeological sites
- statutory advocacy for the protection of historic and cultural heritage, including issuing heritage orders and negotiating and executing heritage covenants
- providing grants or advances to property owners for restoration and protection of heritage places under the National Heritage Preservation Incentive Fund
- providing and distributing advice and information on protection and conservation of heritage places.

The NZHPT national office is in Wellington, with regional offices in Auckland, Wellington and Christchurch, and area offices in Kerikeri, Tauranga and Dunedin. The NZHPT has approximately 26,000 members who elect branch committees. Branches work closely with the trust's area managers, coordinators and the community to raise awareness of heritage issues, and provide opportunities for participation in heritage-related activities.

Māori communities are increasingly concerned with, and active in, the protection and management of their heritage. The NZHPT provides conservation and funding advice, and practical training, to support whānau (families), hapū (subtribes) and iwi (tribes) in managing their heritage.

The NZHPT is custodian of a portfolio of nationally important heritage properties such as the Kerikeri Stone Store, Pompallier at Russell, Alberton in Auckland, Te Pōrere redoubts near Turangi, Old St Paul's in Wellington, the Timeball Station in Lyttelton, and Totara Estate near Oamaru.

New Zealand's rich archaeological resource includes shipwrecks, historic pā and villages, battle sites, rock art sites, stone walls, gardens, whaling stations and gold mining landscapes. The NZHPT administers a process to protect archaeological sites, and it is unlawful to disturb a site without their approval. Where a site is to be destroyed, damaged or modified, NZHPT ensures that significant information is retained and documented in a credible, consistent and coherent way.

Incentive funds are critical to achieve positive heritage outcomes, by assisting private owners to maintain historic buildings and structures. The NZHPT administers the National Heritage Preservation Incentive Fund ($500,000 annually) to encourage conservation of nationally significant heritage in private ownership.

Protection of antiquities and archaeological and traditional sites New Zealand has legal provisions to protect items and sites of historical and cultural significance. The Antiquities Act 1975, administered by the Ministry for Culture and Heritage, includes provisions controlling the sale of Māori artefacts in New Zealand. Artefacts found after 1976 are deemed to be Crown

Kevin L Jones

Remains of the Māori pā (fortified place) site at Maungakiekie/One Tree Hill, in Auckland. Pā are protected by the Historic Places Act 1993.

property. There are export controls on culturally significant items: Māori artefacts; chattels relating to European discovery, settlement or development of New Zealand; written and printed matter; works of art, reproductions, prints, films and sound recordings; specimens of animals, plants and minerals; meteorites; remains of extinct fauna; and shipwreck items. The Historic Places Act 1993 defines an archaeological site as a place associated with pre-1900 human activity, where there may be evidence relating to the history of New Zealand. The Act makes it unlawful for any person to destroy, damage or modify the whole or any part of an archaeological site (including archaeological investigations) without an archaeological authority from the NZHPT.

Archives New Zealand

Archives New Zealand has three roles:

- to preserve and provide access to the archived records of government
- to ensure government records are created and maintained
- to provide leadership and advice to the New Zealand recordkeeping and archiving community.

Archives are important, both as the raw material for the history of New Zealand and for ensuring citizens can hold the government to account for its actions. In addition, a verifiable record provides the government with the protection that comes from its citizens trusting it to be truthful and accountable in its dealings.

Archives New Zealand stores, arranges, describes, and gives access to records from government agencies (past and present), and provides standards and advice to government agencies regarding best practice in recordkeeping. It has repositories and reading rooms in Dunedin, Christchurch, Wellington and Auckland. The Wellington repository includes the Constitution Room, which houses some of New Zealand's most significant documents, including the Treaty of Waitangi, the Women's Suffrage Petition and the Declaration of Independence.

In its leadership role, Archives New Zealand advises and assists local bodies and community groups in the care, preservation and disposal of their records.

It is also responsible for administration of the Public Records Act 2005 and the National Register of Archives and Manuscripts. Archives New Zealand has partnerships with other repositories to promote awareness and use of archives generally, and to support development of professional skills in recordkeeping and archiving throughout New Zealand.

New Zealand Cartoon Archive

The New Zealand Cartoon Archive was founded by Ian F Grant as a result of researching his cartoon history of New Zealand, and launched on April Fool's Day (1 April) 1992.

The archive's purpose is to collect historical and contemporary New Zealand editorial cartoons and to promote the collection to the New Zealand public. Cartoon images are increasingly used by teachers, researchers, writers, publishers and film makers.

The New Zealand Cartoon Archive is New Zealand's principal cartoon collection. It holds more than 30,000 cartoons – originals and copies – given by cartoonists and their relatives, collectors, politicians and organisations. The collection includes the work of more than 60 local and expatriate New Zealand cartoonists.

Since 1992, it has been receiving copies (and some originals) of cartoons that appear in New Zealand newspapers and periodicals. Many are now received electronically.

In 2005, the New Zealand Cartoon Trust, which had run the cartoon archive for its first 13 years, was wound up. The archive was fully integrated into the Alexander Turnbull Library, retaining its name and identity within the drawings and prints department.

The collection is indexed on the National Library's Tapuhi website. The archive also has several hundred cartoon images on the National Library's Timeframes website.

By December 2007, the archive had curated 14 cartoon exhibitions, most touring to several New Zealand centres, and published five books.

Library services

National Library of New Zealand

The National Library of New Zealand Te Puna Mātauranga o Aotearoa was established in 1965 by an act of Parliament, which also incorporated the Alexander Turnbull Library into the National Library.

The National Library of New Zealand (Te Puna Mātauranga o Aotearoa) Act 2003 replaced the earlier Act and confirmed the Crown's undertaking to preserve, protect, develop and make accessible the collections of the Alexander Turnbull Library forever. It also created an independent advisory body to the government – the Library and Information Advisory Commission.

Documentary heritage of New Zealand preserved

Under legal deposit legislative provisions, the National Library of New Zealand is required to receive two copies of every publication produced in New Zealand.

The Legal Deposit Office records the titles, and the publications go to the Alexander Turnbull Library as part of New Zealand's documentary heritage and to the National Library for lending purposes.

Since 1961, the National Library has maintained the New Zealand National Bibliography, the authoritative record of New Zealand publishing in book, periodical and non-book formats (such as videos, art prints, sound cassettes and CDs). In 2006/07 the Legal Deposit Office acquired 4,072 electronic resources.

New Zealand publications received by Legal Deposit Office

Year	New monograph (book) titles	New serial titles
1994	4,400	764
1995	4,412	546
1996	4,563	889
1997	5,084	968
1998	5,575	954
1999	4,814	704
2000	5,083	423
2001	4,552	576
2002	4,960	770
2003	4,937	828
2004	5,089	720
2005	4,536	1,705
2005/06	4,910	642
2006/07	4,488	678

Note: Years are to 31 December, except for 2005/06 and 2006/07, which are to 30 June.

Items added to the national bibliography include the publications above, and others added to the National Library collections.

Additions to national bibliography

Year	Number of items
1994	5,487
1995	6,246
1996	7,693
1997	10,466
1998	14,680
1999	8,017
2000	7,438
2001	8,402
2002	7,280
2003	8,375
2004	9,159
2005	8,974
2006/07	8,568

Note: Years are to 31 December, except for 2006/07, which is to 30 June.

Source: National Library of New Zealand

In its general collections the library holds 308 e-books, 22,341 e-serials, 910,555 books, 26,735 print serial titles (of which 8,135 are current), 12 main microform collections, 10,790 audio-book titles, and 586,000 items in the schools collections.

Family history, music and children's literature are strengths within the collections.

The Alexander Turnbull Library has more than 350,000 books, mostly relating to New Zealand and the Pacific. There are 44,000 rare books, dating mainly from before 1801. Special collections include works by John Milton and Katherine Mansfield. There are 54,000 maps, and more than 140,000 items of printed ephemera (including 17,000 posters). The national newspaper collection is approximately 1,600 metres in total, and there are more than four kilometres of serials/magazines.

The library holds over eight kilometres of manuscripts and archives; in excess of three million photographs, negatives, and albums; more than 78,000 paintings, drawings, prints, and cartoons; and approximately 40,000 discs, tapes, and cassettes – recording music and oral history. There are about 124,000 microfilm reels.

The National Library provides access to its general collections on site and by lending to other libraries through the interloan system. Alexander Turnbull Library collections are not available for borrowing, but material can be selected and used in special areas of the library. Some items, such as microform copies of serials, newspapers, books and manuscripts, and some oral history interviews and other unpublished sound recordings, may be available through inter-library lending.

With a programme of exhibitions and public events, the library's gallery provides access to, and interpretation of, the heritage collections held by the Alexander Turnbull Library.

Access to the records of most collections is available through the Internet.

Services available from the National Library include:

- Collection and reference services – under the 2003 Act, publishers are required to deposit copies of every publication produced in New Zealand, including electronic published material. The library lists these publications in the *New Zealand National Bibliography*, published monthly and often used by buyers to order new titles. The general collection includes the family history area, where people trace their family tree using books, CD-ROMs and microfiche information from New Zealand and overseas.

- Te Puna – the web-based gateway to the library's online collections, catalogues and directories.

- School services – located in 13 centres around the country, this service is available to all New Zealand schools. School services provides advisory support on school library management and development through courses, seminars and consultancy services. Curriculum information service provides reference services and loans of curriculum-related resources to teachers and home-schoolers, from the schools collection and online information resources.

- Services to Māori – helps Māori gain optimum use of the library's resources and services.

- National Preservation Office – the National Library and National Archives established New Zealand's National Preservation Office Te Tari Tohu Taonga in 1997. This provides an advisory service, including training in preservation management and conservation assessments.

- Print disabilities service – provides audio books (cassettes and CDs) to people with print disabilities who cannot independently access information in a print form.

The Alexander Turnbull Library Part of the National Library of New Zealand, the Alexander Turnbull Library holds collections of books, photos, manuscripts and archives, letters, drawings and prints, music, newspapers, maps and sound recordings that document the history of New Zealand and the Pacific. Other significant holdings are the major research collection on John Milton and his times, a selection of illuminated manuscripts, and New Zealand's largest collection of early printed books and fine printing. The library was started by Alexander Horsburgh Turnbull, a wealthy Wellington merchant who died in 1918 and bequeathed to the nation 55,000 volumes, as well as manuscripts, photographs, paintings and sketches collected during his lifetime.

Oral History Centre The many different voices of New Zealanders are recorded by the Alexander Turnbull Library's Oral History Centre. The recordings provide valuable information about language, accent, inflection, emphasis and tone. The centre conducts weekly or monthly interviews with people such as leading politicians or the long-term unemployed. With more than 12,000 hours of spoken recording on disc, reel and cassette tape, the Alexander Turnbull Library has the most extensive collection of oral history recordings in the country.

Parliamentary Library

The Parliamentary Library provides information, research and reference services for Parliament as required by the Parliamentary Service Act 2000. Services include providing desktop access to electronic resources such as legislative, statistical, legal and news databases.

The library's print collection of more than 500,000 volumes is strongest in economics, politics, public administration, law, social sciences and statistics. A complete set of New Zealand parliamentary publications is maintained. As a result of longstanding exchange and depository arrangements, the library has a significant number of international official publications. These become part of the International Documents Collection, which includes publications from other countries and inter-governmental agencies (eg the United Nations).

The International Documents Collection is available for public use, as is the Parliamentary Information Service, which responds to public enquiries on all aspects of the New Zealand Parliament. Research papers written by library staff are available on Parliament's website at www.parliament.nz/en-NZ/PubRes/Research.

In 2008, the Parliamentary Library celebrated its 150th anniversary. The building, opened in 1899, is a striking example of 19th century Gothic architecture. It was extensively refurbished and earthquake strengthened between 1992 and 1996.

Hocken Collections

Founded in 1910 through a gift from Dr T M Hocken, Dunedin physician, bibliographer and collector, the Hocken Collections contain major research collections about New Zealand, the Pacific and early Australia.

Administered in trust by the University of Otago, the library includes more than 231,150 books and periodicals, 2,750 linear metres of newspapers, 12,930 sound recordings, 2,350 pieces of sheet music, 440 videos, 16,220 microforms, 11,040 maps, 1,079,250 photographs, 17,670 posters, and 13,610 paintings, including modern works of art.

Archives and manuscripts total 8,113 linear metres and are rich in sources for early missionary history; literary study; Otago businesses, local government, education, health, sport, community organisations and churches; and the University of Otago.

Public libraries

The library needs of the majority of New Zealanders are met through public libraries provided by local authorities. Most cities and districts provide a coordinated library service to the whole district's population. There may be a number of service points, which could include a central district or city library.

At the end of 2006, there were more than 400 libraries in New Zealand – covering public, specialist, commercial, government and educational needs.

Other libraries

There are more than 60 libraries in tertiary education institutions, including very significant research collections at the universities. These collections are recorded in Te Puna, the national catalogue, and underpin New Zealand's inter-library loan and document delivery systems.

There is provision for a library or library room in every New Zealand school.

Developments in information technology, including easy access to the Internet, have enabled much more intensive use of remote electronic databases, and the sourcing of material from external databases and collections.

Children listen to Dame Kate Harcourt reading at the Wellington Public Library. Most cities and districts provide a library service to residents.

Source: Booksellers New Zealand

Best of the Bestsellers 2007

The following titles appeared most often on the Bestsellers lists for the 12 months to November 2007.

This list summarises the number of times each title appeared as a bestseller and does not necessarily represent a ranking in terms of total copies sold, or the position at which a title appeared.

Over a 12-month period, 25 lists are prepared in the adult and 12 in the children and teen categories.

Title	Appearances
New Zealand fiction for adults	
Mister Pip Lloyd Jones (Penguin Books)	25
The Bone People Keri Hulme (Picador)	14
The Denniston Rose Jenny Pattrick (Black Swan)	13
New Zealand non-fiction for adults	
Edmonds Cookery Book revised edition (Hachette Livre NZ)	23
100 Great Ways To Use Slow Cookers & Crockpots Simon & Alison Holst (Hyndman Publishing)	14
New Zealand Aotearoa Craig Potton (Craig Potton Publishing)	11
International fiction for adults	
The Memory Keeper's Daughter Kim Edwards (Penguin/Viking)	19
The Lovely Bones Alice Sebold (Picador)	12
Bad Luck and Trouble Lee Child (Bantam Press)	11
International non-fiction for adults	
The Secret Rhonda Byrne (Simon & Schuster)	21
A Short History of Nearly Everything Bill Bryson (Black Swan)	19
Scar Tissue Anthony Kiedis (Little, Brown)	17
Titles for children and teens	
Eldest: Inheritance Trilogy Christopher Paolini (Corgi)	5
Perky the Pukeko Michelle Osment (Little Friends Publishing)	5
Hairy Maclary and Friends Lynley Dodd (Puffin Books)	4
Harry Potter and the Deathly Hallows JK Rowling (Bloomsbury)	4
Where the Wild Things Are Maurice Sendak (Red Fox)	4
The Gruffalo Julia Donaldson and Axel Scheffler (Macmillan)	4

More than 200 specialist libraries and information centres serve government departments, businesses and other organisations.

A cooperative inter-library lending system allows resource sharing among libraries.

Literature

New Zealand Society of Authors

The New Zealand Society of Authors (PEN NZ Inc) is the principal advocate for the professional interests of writers, protecting basic rights to freedom of expression, working to improve income and conditions, and promoting New Zealand writing and literary culture.

Membership is open to anyone interested in writing. The society had 1,260 members at 31 December 2007.

The society provides professional development leaflets, contracts, publications, programmes and communications services. It also represents writers on boards and committees of industry partners in publishing, bookselling and audience development, and with Creative New Zealand and government departments.

New Zealand was one of the first English-speaking countries to compensate writers for lost royalties on books held in public libraries, and the society continues to advocate on their behalf.

The society's mentor and manuscript assessment programmes provide emerging writers with qualified professional feedback on their writing, while contract and publishing advisory services provide advice on all aspects of the publishing process.

The society maintains an involvement with International PEN, which works on behalf of writers whose lives and freedoms are endangered.

PEN NZ Inc has representatives on: the Montana New Zealand, and New Zealand Post book awards management committees, Whitireia Polytechnic, Creative New Zealand's audience and market development reference group, the Robert Burns Fellowship selection committee, the Copyright Council, and the Coalition of Creative Unions and Guilds. It has members on the board of Copyright Licensing Ltd, which distributes fees to authors and publishers for institutional photocopying of their work. It has close ties with the Australian and United Kingdom's societies of authors.

The society administers four awards: the Ashton Wylie Charitable Trust Awards, the Foxton Fellowship, the Janet Frame Memorial Award and the Lillian Ida Smith Award, and provides the three Best First Book Awards (fiction, poetry and non-fiction) at the Montana New Zealand Book Awards each year.

New Zealand Authors' Fund

Administered by Creative New Zealand, the New Zealand Authors' Fund compensates authors for loss of earnings when their books are held by public libraries. Every year, approximately $1.5 million is distributed among more than 1,600 New Zealand writers.

Booksellers New Zealand

Booksellers New Zealand is committed to fostering a strong, efficient and professional book industry by increasing the sales of books, developing industry knowledge, and assisting with business operating costs.

As the trade organisation representing the majority of booksellers and publishers in the country, Booksellers New Zealand undertakes national book promotions.

The organisation also generates opportunities for debating industry issues, lobbies government, and ensures industry awareness and visibility. It works closely with other arts sector groups, book organisations, the media and sponsors.

Booksellers New Zealand organises the Montana New Zealand book awards, Montana Poetry Day, the New Zealand Post book awards and festival, and is a sponsor of NZ Book Month.

The Montana New Zealand book awards recognise excellence and provide recognition for the best books published annually in New Zealand. In 2007, the winners were: *Mister Pip* by Lloyd Jones (Montana Medal for Fiction), *Eagle's Complete Trees and Shrubs of New Zealand* by Audrey Eagle (Montana Medal for Non-Fiction), *The Sound of Butterflies* by Rachael King (New Zealand Society of Authors Hubert Church Best First Book of Fiction Award), *Secret Heart* by Airini Beautrais (New Zealand Society of Authors Jessie Mackay Best First Book of Poetry Award), and *Furniture of the New Zealand Colonial Era: An Illustrated History 1830–1900* by William Cottrell (New Zealand Society of Authors E H McCormick Best First Book of Non-Fiction Award).

The New Zealand Post Book Awards for Children and Young Adults recognise the best in books for children and teens. In 2007, *Illustrated History of the South Pacific* by Marcia Stenson won New Zealand Post Book of the Year and was also the winner of the non-fiction category. The young adult fiction category was won by *Genesis* by Bernard Beckett, and the junior fiction category by

Janice Marriott's *Thor's Tale. Kiss! Kiss! Yuck! Yuck!* written by Kyle Mewburn and illustrated by Ali Teo and John O'Reilly won the Children's Choice Award, and the Best First Book Award went to *The Three Fishing Brothers Gruff* by Ben Galbraith.

Booksellers New Zealand also administers Radio New Zealand's weekday book reviews, produces a fortnightly bestsellers list and the trade magazine *Booksellers News*, along with a weekly electronic newsletter to booksellers and publishers.

Each year, Booksellers New Zealand updates the Premier New Zealand Bestsellers list of books that have sold at least 5,000 copies.

Book publishing

It is estimated there are around 600 book publishers in New Zealand, with most being New Zealand-owned and employing one or two people.

A survey commissioned by the Book Publishers Association of New Zealand showed there were 2,394 new book titles published in New Zealand in 2007. Education was the largest category, followed by technical/professional, and general non-fiction and children's books.

Total New Zealand publishing industry turnover in 2007 was $266 million, of which $36 million came from export sales. New Zealand titles generated turnover of $127 million in 2007, against $117 million from sales of imported published titles. The 21 largest companies generated the bulk of revenue.

Of the publishers surveyed, 36 percent considered their businesses to be growing.

Performing arts

New Zealand Music Commission

The New Zealand Music Commission was established in June 2000 as a government-funded charitable trust, to facilitate growth in the New Zealand music industry through specific projects such as New Zealand Music Month.

One of its main functions is to help the information flow within the industry, which it does through its website. Here, music companies can register, gain information about projects, and get advice on matters such as tours, media and taxation.

The commission also promotes New Zealand music internationally. Outward Sound is a programme that assists music industry practitioners to develop an international market.

New Zealand Symphony Orchestra

The New Zealand Symphony Orchestra (NZSO), founded in 1946, is the country's leading professional orchestra. It has 90 players and performs over 100 concerts annually. Touring within New Zealand looms large for the orchestra – while all its main symphonic programmes are presented in Auckland and Wellington, the orchestra also visits some 30 other towns and cities each year.

Robert Catto

The New Zealand Symphony Orchestra's new musical director, Pietari Inkinen, conducts the orchestra in 2007. The NZSO performs over 100 concerts each year.

Wind powers art

Leon Van den Eijkel and Allan Brown's wind-powered Urban Forest *sculpture near Wellington's airport.*

Wellington is well known for its access to the wind. Since 2001 this has worked to the city's benefit through the installation of four sculptures that are influenced by the wind. Sited along the route to the airport, they move and light up with greater or less intensity as the wind blows.

Kon Dimopoulos' *Pacific Grass* has 1,500 'characters' whose movements are choreographed by the wind, while Phil Price's needle gauge-like *Zephyrometer* sways as the strength and direction of the wind changes. *Tower of Light* by Andrew Drummond converts wind speed to light in coloured neon rings – the faster the wind, the more rings are lit.

In 2007, artist Leon van den Eijkel and engineer Allan Brown's *Urban Forest* was installed. The stacks of brightly coloured cubes respond to the wind by spinning.

All sculptures are clearly visible to passing cars and pedestrians. They are sponsored by Meridian Energy, assisted by the Wellington City Council and the Wellington Sculpture Trust. Two more sculptures are appearing during 2008.

New Plymouth, home of kinetic artist the late Len Lye, also has public wind-powered sculpture. One of Lye's works is a 45-metre wind wand situated by the coast. The wand bends and sways over 20 metres and at night a small globe at the end glows red.

Sources: www.sculpture.org.nz, Meridian Energy

In 2005 the NZSO undertook a highly successful tour that included performances at the BBC Proms in the United Kingdom, at the Concertgebouw (Amsterdam), and the World Expo at Aichi in Japan.

Pietari Inkinen became the NZSO's music director in January 2008, succeeding James Judd who is now music director emeritus. Other conductors who worked with the NZSO in the past decade are: Alexander Lazarev, Dimitri Sitkovetsky, David Atherton, Yan Pascal Tortelier and Edo de Waart. Recent international soloists include musicians Lynn Harrell, Lang Lang, Hilary Hahn, Vadim Repin and Steven Isserlis, and singers Jonathan Lemalu and Dame Kiri Te Kanawa.

The NZSO has an extensive catalogue of CD recordings. As part of a commitment to promote music by New Zealand composers, the NZSO records at least one CD of New Zealand music annually. The orchestra has a recording repertoire which includes Elgar, Ries, Beethoven, Bernstein, Copland, Lilburn, Sculthorpe, Bridge, Akutagawa, Mendelssohn, Honegger, Liszt and Vaughan Williams. Over half a million CDs have been sold in the last decade. Douglas Lilburn's *Orchestral Works* was chosen for the Editor's Choice section of *Gramophone* magazine in 2006.

National Youth Orchestra

Since 1959, the National Youth Orchestra has each year brought together about 100 young instrumental musicians aged 13–25 years for an intensive week of rehearsal, culminating in a public concert.

Live auditions, which take place nationally during April, are independently assessed by NZSO principals. The principals also assist with teaching workshops and coaching during the six days of pre-concert preparation.

Many members of the National Youth Orchestra later become NZSO and regional orchestra players. Others develop careers overseas as orchestral players, soloists, chamber musicians and teachers.

The National Youth Orchestra is administered and funded by the NZSO.

Chamber Music New Zealand

Chamber Music New Zealand is the major presenter of chamber music concerts in New Zealand. International and New Zealand artists perform in Celebrity Season concerts in nine centres, with additional concerts in 22 smaller cities and towns. There were more than 150 concerts and events in 2007.

With almost 60 years' experience, Chamber Music New Zealand has strong ties with artist management and concert presenters worldwide. While this offers the opportunity to tour the best of both established and emerging international ensembles, there is also a strong commitment to develop New Zealand musicians and composers.

In 1987, Chamber Music New Zealand established the New Zealand String Quartet, a professional, full-time quartet which has an international reputation.

Chamber Music New Zealand organises contests for secondary school students in both instrumental performance and composition. Many contestants have subsequently enjoyed distinguished international careers. The 2007 contest attracted more than 520 groups, involving 2,020 young musicians from throughout New Zealand.

Ticket sales are the major source of Chamber Music New Zealand's funding, with the rest coming from grants from Creative New Zealand and sponsorship.

New Zealand Choral Federation

The New Zealand Choral Federation Te Kotahitanga Manu Reo o Aotearoa (NZCF) is an incorporated society representing 390 member choirs. It has a governance board and management group.

The NZCF, whose Māori name means 'the assembly of the chorus of birds of New Zealand', promotes choral music in all forms and aims to ensure that the experience of singing in a group is available to all New Zealanders. Its long-term goal is to develop a unique New Zealand 'voice', a distinctive choral sound which amalgamates the singing traditions of Māori, Polynesian and western music.

Formed in 1985, NZCF provides advisory and information services on all group singing matters, and is the link to the International Federation for Choral Music. NZCF income is from membership fees, events management, sponsorship and Creative New Zealand.

The NZCF has developed a 'family' of national events to promote group singing and raise its profile. These events encourage participation and promote excellence in group singing from an early age through the Kids Sing (young voices' awards), the Big Sing (secondary school choral festivals) and the Classic Sing (community choirs' festival.) In 2007, 238 choirs from 212 schools entered the secondary school festivals, with 20 choirs at the national final in Christchurch.

The NZCF also holds the Sing Aotearoa Festival every three years, a multi-cultural, multi-art event first held in 1990 to commemorate the 150th anniversary of the signing of the Treaty of Waitangi. Sing Aotearoa brings together singers, writers, composers and dancers for an intensive weekend of workshops, performances, forums and cultural exchange with international music educators.

Royal New Zealand Ballet

The Royal New Zealand Ballet is one of New Zealand's largest performing arts organisations, with 32 dancers, and 25 staff in artistic support, production, marketing and management.

Established in 1953, it is the oldest professional ballet company in Australasia.

With a strong classical base, and a healthy attitude towards innovation, the company presents an eclectic repertoire of choreographic styles – from 19th century classics to 21st century contemporary works. Through these productions, the Royal New Zealand Ballet aims to inspire and challenge both the artists and audiences.

Dancers of the Royal New Zealand Ballet possess physical strength and versatility, and a well-developed sense of individuality. New international and New Zealand choreography expresses these qualities, and features prominently in the company's repertoire.

The Royal New Zealand Ballet tours New Zealand more extensively and frequently than any other major performing arts organisation. In 2007, more than 100,000 people attended performances in 50 centres across the country. International tours have taken the ballet to the United States, Europe, Asia and Australia.

In 2008, the company marked the 50th anniversary of one of its most-loved performers, Sir Jon Trimmer.

The company receives 40 percent of its income directly from central government through the Vote Arts Culture and Heritage allocation, and 60 percent from box office sales and sponsorship.

New Zealand School of Dance

Founded in 1967, the New Zealand School of Dance provides comprehensive full-time training for about 65 young dancers a year. Based in Wellington, the school offers a two-year Certificate in Dance Performance and a three-year Diploma in Dance Performance. Students come from New Zealand, Australia and a few other countries.

The school has a close relationship with national and international professional dance companies and students are often seconded to companies as part of their training. Students are also able to work with a number of artists-in-residence and international tutors each year, and they present two performance seasons. The school also offers junior associate and regional associate programmes for aspiring young dancers.

The New Zealand School of Dance shares Te Whaea National Dance and Drama Centre with Toi Whakaari: New Zealand Drama School.

The New Zealand School of Dance is funded by the Tertiary Education Commission, and from tuition fees, sponsorships and grants. Fees for 2008 were $4,230.

Toi Whakaari: New Zealand Drama School

Te Kura Toi Whakaari O Aotearoa: New Zealand Drama School, established in 1970, is the premier training ground for entertainment professionals in New Zealand. Nearly 500 graduates have gone on to successful careers in theatre, television, film, radio and performance, both in New Zealand and internationally.

The Wellington-based tertiary institution offers students the following courses: Master of Theatre Arts in Directing, Bachelor of Performing Arts (Acting or Management), Bachelor of Design for Stage and Screen, Diploma and Advanced Diploma in Entertainment Technology, Diploma in Costume Construction – for theatre, film and allied industries.

The school is funded by the Tertiary Education Commission, tuition fees, sponsorship and grants. In 2007, annual fees ranged from $4,850 to $5,350.

New Zealand Opera Ltd

New Zealand Opera Ltd was formed in 2000 with the merging of the National Opera of Wellington and Auckland's Opera New Zealand.

The company's aim is to provide a high calibre arts experience through theatrical productions that engage the audience and create excitement about the art form.

In its first eight years, the company has significantly increased its audience throughout the country, through both main city and national touring productions. Productions have included several New Zealand premieres and involved talented New Zealand opera performers and creative teams, as well as international artists. Integral to the company's productions are the Auckland and Wellington-based Chapman Tripp Opera Choruses. The company also collaborates with regional orchestras and festivals around New Zealand.

In 2008 the company staged Puccini's *La Bohème* and Janáček's *Jenufa*, and took Humperdinck's *Hansel and Gretel* on a national tour.

The company actively seeks to develop and nurture young talent through the new three-tier internship structure: The PricewaterhouseCoopers Dame Malvina Major Emerging Artists, and

Screen industry revenue remains steady

Total gross revenue for the New Zealand screen industry for 2006 was $2,542 million, similar to the 2005 figure of $2,602 million. The number of businesses working in the screen industry was 2,052, down from 2,058 in 2005. Production and post-production services was again the most significant sector, accounting for $1,206 million, although this was down 6.8 percent from the 2005 figure of $1,294 million.

The international contribution to gross revenue for the screen production industry decreased 30.7 percent in 2006, down from $592 million in 2005 to $410 million. This was largely driven by a 37.7 percent reduction in revenue received from the United States, although this remains the highest international contributor at $325 million. Asian countries as a group are now the second-largest international contributor, providing $26 million ($15 million in 2005).

The overall number of businesses working in the screen production industry in 2006 was up only 1.2 percent. However, there were 234 businesses indicating both screen production company and contractor activity, up from 144 businesses in 2005.

Feature films and short films remained the largest sub-sector for screen production companies, at $333 million. However, this was a 33.7 percent decrease compared with 2005. Gross revenue for contractors increased 22.4 percent in 2006, to $412 million.

Source: Statistics New Zealand

Neil McKenzie

New Zealand Opera Ltd at a performance of Lucia di Lammermoor *in 2007. The eight-year-old company helps develop young singers through a new internship structure.*

Young Artists programmes, and The NBR New Zealand Opera Resident Artists programme. Development training focuses on all aspects of building a career in opera, including voice and performance, with regular tuition from leading opera professionals.

Opera Outreach is an initiative designed to make opera more accessible to young people. This is achieved by hosting creative workshops that give school students the chance to create and perform in their own opera or musical drama, and by having school children attend final dress rehearsals of each opera season.

Film and video

New Zealand Film Commission

The New Zealand Film Commission (NZFC) finances distinctly New Zealand films, with the aim of reaching significant New Zealand audiences and producing high returns on investment, in both cultural and financial terms.

More than 200 feature films have been made in New Zealand since the commission was established in 1978. Approximately 100 of these have had NZFC finance and five have also had finance from the New Zealand Film Fund.

Recent successes at international film festivals include *Black Sheep* (Toronto, and San Sebastian in Spain), and *Eagle vs Shark* (in the United States and Europe). Two short films were honoured with official selection at the 2007 Cannes Film Festival. It was the fourth consecutive year that a NZFC-supported short film was in competition – *Run* received a Special Mention from the jury.

The NZFC also administers the Large Budget Screen Production Grant. Aimed at attracting large-budget film and television production to New Zealand, the incentive has been in place since 2003, and provides a rebate on production expenditure over a certain value.

The functions, powers and duties of the NZFC are defined in the New Zealand Film Commission Act 1978. The budget comes from the Lottery Grants Board, central government (through the Ministry for Culture and Heritage), and from film investments and sales. The budget varies year by year according to public funding and returns on film investments.

Distribution and exhibition

Film-going peaked at 40.6 million admissions in 1960/61, but declined dramatically after the introduction of television in 1961 and later, of home videos.

However, as figure 12.01 shows, cinema admissions were showing steady growth in recent years, from 6.6 million in 1992 to a latter-day peak of more than 18.3 million in 2003, before dropping to around 15.3 million in 2006.

According to Motion Picture Distributors' Association figures, box office takings in 2006 were $146.4 million, compared with $146.8 million in 2005 and $152.8 million in 2004.

New Zealand Film Archive

The New Zealand Film Archive Ngā Kaitiaki O Ngā Taonga Whitiāhua has three principal functions – to collect, protect and project New Zealand's moving image heritage.

Established in Wellington in 1981, the archive's collections reflect the breadth of New Zealand's moving image history, from the earliest days of cinema to contemporary film, video and digital productions. The film and video collection includes features and short films, newsreels, documentaries, home movies, music videos, broadcast programmes, commercials and video art.

The archive also maintains the national television collection on behalf of NZ On Air. This collection represents a diverse range of broadcasters and programming, including television news, drama, documentaries, game shows, music videos, infomercials, youth programming and sport.

The documentation collection has promotional, critical and historical materials from 1896 onwards. The collection also includes stills, posters, scripts, clippings, programmes, publicity material, production records and files, personal records, storyboards, props and costumes, animation cels, taped interviews and equipment.

The New Zealand Film Archive's catalogue is described on its website at www.filmarchive.org.nz.

While based in central Wellington, the archive has a national focus. In addition to a library, screenings and exhibitions in Wellington, the archive has an Auckland branch, and video access sites in art galleries and museums in Whangarei, Hamilton, New Plymouth, Palmerston North, Otaki, Christchurch and Dunedin.

The archive receives public funding through the Vote Arts, Culture and Heritage allocation, and the New Zealand Lottery Grants Board, New Zealand Film Commission and NZ On Air.

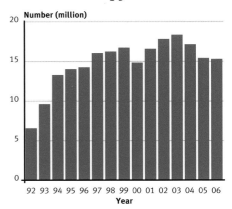

Figure 12.01

Cinema admissions
Year ending 31 December

Note: 1997 and 2003 include 53 weeks.
Source: Motion Picture Distributors' Association

Censorship

The Films, Videos, and Publications Classification Act 1993 covers a range of media, and defines a 'publication' as:

- any film, book, sound recording, picture, newspaper, photograph, photographic negative, photographic plate or photographic slide
- any print or writing
- a paper or other thing that has printed or impressed upon it, or otherwise shown upon it, one or more (or a combination of one or more) images, representations, signs, statements or words

Top 12 films at the box office

Over the past five years, more New Zealanders than ever are watching local feature films whose production was supported by the New Zealand Film Commission (NZFC).

During 2006/07 *Out of the Blue* and *Black Sheep* attracted more than 200,000 cinema-goers, and an estimated one million people watched *Sione's Wedding* and *The World's Fastest Indian* on DVD. TV premieres of *The World's Fastest Indian*, *In My Father's Den*, *Perfect Strangers* and a repeat screening of *Whale Rider* were seen by 1 million New Zealanders. The broadcast of *The World's Fastest Indian* out-rated screenings of high profile Hollywood titles.

Although largely shot in New Zealand by New Zealand-based or expatriate directors, global blockbusters such as *King Kong* and *The Lord of the Rings* are not included in the top 12 as they are not funded by the NZFC.

Top 12 New Zealand films
New Zealand box office
To 31 August 2007

Film	Director	Amount ($)	Year
The World's Fastest Indian	Roger Donaldson	7,043,000	2005
Once Were Warriors	Lee Tamahori	6,795,000	1994/95
Whale Rider	Niki Caro	6,400,000	2003
Sione's Wedding	Chris Graham	4,075,000	2006
What Becomes of the Broken Hearted?	Ian Mune	3,200,991	1999
Footrot Flats	Murray Ball	2,420,000	1986/87
Goodbye Pork Pie	Geoff Murphy	1,600,000	1981
In My Father's Den	Brad McGann	1,500,000	2004
Scarfies	Robert Sarkies	1,259,626	1999
Out of the Blue	Robert Sarkies	1,127,151	2006
Heavenly Creatures	Peter Jackson	1,012,500	1994/95
River Queen	Vincent Ward	1,008,545	2005

Source: New Zealand Film Commission

Ken George

Crew of New Zealand feature film Black Sheep *filming at Titahi Bay near Wellington in 2007.*

- a thing (including, but not limited to, a disc, or an electronic or computer file) on which is recorded or stored information that, by the use of a computer or other electronic device, is capable of being reproduced or shown as one or more (or a combination of one or more) images, representations, signs, statements or words.

Film is further defined as including cinematographic film, video recordings, DVDs, computer games and any other material record of visual moving images.

Administration The Act established the following bodies:

- Office of Film and Literature Classification – an independent Crown entity with censors, classification officers, an information unit and support staff. The office classifies publications likely to be restricted or objectionable, provides information on the classification system to the public, and conducts research.

- The Film and Video Labelling Body – an industry-based body responsible for rating unrestricted films and videos and issuing labels. New Zealand ratings may be based on those assigned by Australian or British authorities. Ratings are consumer guides, not legal restrictions. If a film is likely to be restricted, or if the labelling body is having difficulty assigning a rating, the film is referred to the Office of Film and Literature Classification. The body submits publications to the office on behalf of distributors.

- Film and Literature Board of Review – consists of members of the public appointed by the governor-general on the recommendation of the Minister of Internal Affairs. The Act provides for the original applicant, the owner, maker, publisher or authorised distributor, or any other person the Secretary for Internal Affairs allows, to submit a publication for a review of its classification. The board re-examines the publication, without considering the decision of the Office of Film and Literature Classification. The president of the board can also make a decision on any application for an interim restriction order on any publication, preventing a publication being available before the board issues its decision. The board is an independent statutory body supported by the Department of Internal Affairs.

Classification The Films, Videos, and Publications Classification Act 1993 established a legal test that considers whether availability of a publication would be injurious to the public good. This test is applied before deciding if restriction is required, and if so, at what level – to people over a certain age (up to 18 years), to a person or class of persons, or to a specified purpose. It can ban a publication and can also place no restriction on one. Publications classified by the Office of Film and Literature Classification deal with sex, horror, crime, cruelty or violence.

After classification, films are labelled by the Film and Video Labelling Body. Films rated G (suitable for general audiences) have green labels. Yellow labels (PG and M) are issued for unrestricted films recommended for a certain age or group. A PG rating means that younger persons may require parental guidance. An M rating recommends a film for mature audiences 16 years and over. Red labels signify a restricted film. Computer games fall under the definition of films, and the Act requires that films intended for supply to the public must be labelled. However, games are exempt from labelling unless they are likely to be restricted – those with restricted content must be classified. Publications other than films are not required to be labelled before being supplied to the public. However, distributors or publishers can ask to submit publications such as magazines and books for classification. If the chief censor grants leave, the Office of Film and Literature Classification will classify the material as unrestricted, restricted or objectionable. In addition to labelling, display conditions may be imposed.

Publications can also be submitted to the Office of Film and Literature Classification by the Secretary for Internal Affairs, the Comptroller of Customs, Commissioner of Police or anyone else the chief censor allows. The chief censor can also 'call in' publications. Classifications assigned are legally enforceable. Under the Act, it is illegal to possess or supply an objectionable publication, whether or not the publication has been classified. It is illegal to supply or exhibit a restricted publication to people under the age of the restriction.

Enforcement The Department of Internal Affairs enforces the Act. It aims to increase compliance with New Zealand's censorship laws by ensuring that the film and video industry, magazine distributors and shops adhere to the Office of Film and Literature Classification decisions. Inspectors check compliance, to ensure that restricted material is correctly labelled and displayed, and objectionable material is not available. The unit also inspects New Zealand websites. It is the primary agency for monitoring, investigating and prosecuting offences involving objectionable material – across all publication formats.

The unit investigates the making and distribution of child pornography on the Internet, with strong links to overseas law enforcement agencies. Staff regularly exchange intelligence on offenders. The New Zealand Police are also inspectors of publications under the Act, with the same powers as censorship compliance inspectors. The New Zealand Customs Service ensures that material imported into New Zealand complies with the law. Customs may refer material it seizes to the Office of Film and Literature Classification.

Copyright

Copyright in New Zealand is based on the Copyright Act 1994, and administered by the Ministry of Economic Development.

The Copyright (New Technologies and Performers' Rights) Amendment Bill amends the Act to clarify the application of existing rights and exceptions in the digital environment and to take account of international developments.

Copyright protection in New Zealand exists automatically on the creation of any original literary, dramatic, musical or artistic work (including photographs), sound recording, film, broadcast, cable programme and typographical arrangement of published editions. Computer programs are protected under 'literary work'.

No registration is necessary (or possible), nor is any other formality required to secure copyright protection.

Duration of copyright For literary, dramatic, musical and artistic works (including photographs), copyright continues for the lifetime of the author, plus 50 years after the year the author dies. For sound recordings and films, copyright generally continues for 50 years after the year in which they were made, or made available (whichever is later). For broadcasts and cable programmes, copyright continues for 50 years after they were made (broadcasts), or included in a service (cable programmes). Copyright in typographical arrangements of published editions is for 25 years after they were first published. Shorter periods apply to works that are industrially applied.

Ownership of copyright The first owner of copyright is usually the work's author – the person who created the work. However, if this person created the work in the course of employment, then the employer is the first owner. For some work (such as sound recordings, films, photographs and computer programs), if the author was commissioned to make the work, the first owner is the commissioner. For works commissioned or created by an employee, the parties can vary the first ownership rule. Ownership can also be assigned in writing to another person. The commissioning rule is under review.

Jarrad Mapp

New Zealand School of Dance student Allan Anderson. Copyright protection exists automatically when an original artistic work is created.

Moral rights Authors and directors have certain 'moral rights' in addition to the economic rights provided under the Copyright Act. These include the rights to be identified as the author of a work, to object to derogatory treatment of the work, and to not have a work falsely attributed to them. Moral rights cannot be assigned to another person except on the death of the author.

Exclusive rights of copyright owners The copyright owner has the exclusive right to do, and authorise others to do, 'restricted acts' in relation to the work or an adaptation of the work in New Zealand. These include rights to make copies; issue copies to the public, including the rental of films, computer programs and sound recordings; perform, play or show the work in public; broadcast the work or include the work in a cable service; and make an adaptation of the work. Copyright is infringed when someone does this without the permission of, or a licence from, the copyright owner.

Exceptions to copyright Exceptions to exclusive rights, called 'permitted acts', allow copyright works to be used without the permission of the copyright owner. These include fair dealing for criticism, review, and news reporting; fair dealing for research and private study; recording broadcasts or cable programmes for listening or watching at another time; and backing-up computer programs. Libraries, archives and educational institutions have specific exceptions.

Performers' rights Performers have certain limited rights to control exploitation of their performances where they have not given consent. This includes, for example, the right to control the recording, broadcast or inclusion in a cable programme of a live performance. Protected performances include dramatic, musical and variety performances, and readings and recitations of literary works. Protection is provided for 50 years from when the performance takes place.

Enforcement of copyright Action for copyright infringement in New Zealand is generally through civil action by the owner. Remedies include damages, injunctions, or an order for delivery up. Criminal offences apply to certain commercial activities and can result in fines up to $150,000, or five years imprisonment.

Copyright Tribunal The role of the Copyright Tribunal is to resolve disputes regarding licences or proposed licences for the copying, performing or broadcasting of copyright works.

Protection overseas New Zealand is a signatory to various international copyright agreements. Participation in these agreements means that when an original work is created in New Zealand, it is also automatically protected in countries that are signatories to these agreements. And original works created in other countries are protected in New Zealand.

Administration

Ministry for Culture and Heritage

The Ministry for Culture and Heritage is one of many agencies through which government manages its involvement with culture. Its role is "to help make culture visible and accessible".

Other organisations also supply services to the Crown. For example, Te Puni Kōkiri, Archives New Zealand, and the National Library provide cultural advice and services to government in

Brian Harris

Tyne Cot cemetery in Belgium, where 520 New Zealanders are buried, and 1,166 are listed on the memorial to the missing among 34,857 World War I Commonwealth casualties. The Ministry for Culture and Heritage helps care for the war graves through the Commonwealth War Graves Commission.

their areas of responsibility. However, the Ministry for Culture and Heritage is government's key advisor across the broad range of culture and heritage issues.

The ministry serves the government of the day by implementing and overseeing its cultural support programme. It advises on the programme's shape, which includes identifying new opportunities to contribute to cultural and other objectives.

The ministry advises on funding, legislation, organisational arrangements and implementing cultural initiatives. It also supplies input to other government work where a cultural perspective is desirable.

The ministry administers the funding of, and monitors and supports the work of, cultural and broadcasting agencies that deliver government-funded cultural services. These range from major Crown entities, such as the Museum of New Zealand Te Papa Tongarewa and NZ On Air, to small, independent, single-focus organisations like the Antarctic Heritage Trust. The ministry monitors the performance of each agency to confirm that government funding is used to support agreed outcomes, and assists with agency planning and development.

The Ministry for Culture and Heritage also researches and produces online and published work on New Zealand history, and war veterans' oral history. It produces websites to provide easily-accessible cultural content, and support cultural activities: the Dictionary of New Zealand Biography (www.dbnz.govt.nz), New Zealand History Online (www.nzhistory.net.nz), New Zealand Culture Online (www.nzlive.com), and Te Ara – the Encyclopedia of New Zealand (www.teara.govt.nz).

The ministry manages and maintains a number of heritage properties, including the National War Memorial, the Tomb of the Unknown Warrior and war graves throughout the country. It also commissions new memorials, such as those in Korea (2005) and London (2007).

It administers laws aimed at protecting objects and symbols of national identity, and promoting New Zealand's heritage, including the Protected Objects Act 1975, the Flags, Emblems and Names Protection Act 1981 and the Waitangi Day Act 1976.

The ministry is also the lead agency for the Cultural Diplomacy International Programme, in collaboration with the Ministry of Foreign Affairs and Trade, New Zealand Trade and Enterprise and Tourism New Zealand. This programme aims to establish and maintain a cultural presence in key overseas regions or countries, to boost New Zealand's profile, and economic, trade, tourism, diplomatic and cultural interests.

The ministry's statement of intent for the four years from 2007 outlines four key priorities: advancing digital and online delivery of cultural content, developing new symbols of nationhood, promoting New Zealand internationally through culture, and enhancing the performance of other agencies that contribute to a strong sense of cultural and national identity.

The Ministry for Cultural and Heritage's budget for 2007/08 was $15.03 million.

Indicators to monitor cultural sector

Cultural Indicators for New Zealand: 2006 provides a wide-ranging snapshot of the country's cultural activity. The report identifies specific indicators that can be used to monitor the health of New Zealand's cultural sector. These indicators are grouped around five theme areas that broadly reflect outcomes the government seeks to achieve for the cultural sector as a whole.

One theme relates to New Zealanders' engagement in cultural activities – as participants, consumers and creators – and explores their access to cultural activities and the extent to which these are valued.

The report shows that buying books, using public libraries and purchasing recorded music are some of the most popular cultural activities. It also shows that between 1996 and 2001 the cultural workforce grew at a faster rate than the total workforce – 17 percent compared with 6 percent.

Cultural Indicators for New Zealand: 2006 is part of an initiative to make statistics available over a range of cultural sector areas. The report was produced together with the Ministry for Culture and Heritage as part of a joint cultural statistics programme.

Source: Statistics New Zealand

Table 12.01

Government funding for the arts, culture and heritage sector
Year ending 30 June 2007

	Government funding $(000)
Broadcasting Commission (NZ On Air)	106,671
National Library of New Zealand	53,266
Television New Zealand Ltd	22,051
Museum of New Zealand Te Papa Tongarewa	20,574
Archives New Zealand	19,751
Museum of New Zealand Te Papa Tongarewa (capital contribution)	15,500
Ministry for Culture and Heritage	15,511
Arts Council of New Zealand Toi Aotearoa (Creative New Zealand)	15,452
New Zealand Symphony Orchestra	12,346
New Zealand Film Commission	10,111
New Zealand Historic Places Trust	9,903
Regional museums (for construction projects)	6,489
Royal New Zealand Ballet	3,534
National Pacific Radio Trust	3,390
Commonwealth War Graves Commission	2,330
Radio New Zealand International	1,900
New Zealand Memorial in London	1,323
Te Matatini	1,248
New Zealand Music Commission	1,156
New Zealand Historic Places Trust (capital contribution)	850
New Zealand Film Archive	670
Broadcasting Standards Authority	609
Maintenance of war graves, historic graves and monuments	516
Antarctic Heritage Trust	356
Treaty of Waitangi celebrations	288
New Zealand Archaeological Association	150
Gallipoli memorial projects	48
Regional museums (for advice on antiquities)	19
Kerikeri heritage bypass	15

Source: Ministry for Culture and Heritage

Art from junk

DarzArt is a mobile art factory with a programme that teaches children the importance of recycling while helping them discover their own artistic ability. DarzArt is dedicated to showing participants that through art, they may be able to express themselves more easily than they can verbally.

Resene Paints Ltd is DarzArt's main sponsor. The company recycles by donating mistinted paints that are not able to be used, and would otherwise be dumped. Resene also donates test pots for children to decorate their recycled constructions with bright bold colors.

A number of other manufacturers throughout the Auckland region have also donated materials that would otherwise be heading for the landfill. Thanks to them, children have cardboard, rubber scraps, cork tiles, pieces of leather, fabrics, ropes and twine, and polystyrene scraps to work with.

As well as teaching children the value of recycling scrap materials, DarzArt gives back to the community through the art pieces that have been donated to schools and hospitals around Auckland.

DarzArt has also created art classes for older people in a number of retirement homes.

Source: Resene

Creative New Zealand

Creative New Zealand, the main arts development organisation in New Zealand, was established as a Crown entity under the Arts Council of New Zealand Toi Aotearoa Act 1994. It works to develop and promote New Zealand arts and artists, both at home and internationally.

All Creative New Zealand's work is guided by its strategic plan, *Te Mahere Rautaki 2007–2010*. Its four strategic priorities are to ensure: New Zealanders are engaged in the arts, high-quality New Zealand art is developed, New Zealanders have access to high-quality arts experiences, and New Zealand arts gain international success.

Creative New Zealand's work includes arts advocacy, funding programmes, special initiatives and research. It works in partnership with the arts sector, central and local government, the business sector, and communities to achieve its vision, 'a flourishing arts environment in which New Zealanders value, support and are inspired by the arts'.

The governing body is the New Zealand Arts Council and its three funding decision-making bodies are the Arts Board, Te Waka Toi (the Māori Arts Board) and the Pacific Arts Committee.

Staff in Wellington, Christchurch and Auckland offer services which include funding advice, professional development opportunities, arts advocacy, research, communications and information services.

Creative New Zealand's funding comes from the government through the Vote Arts, Culture and Heritage allocation and from the New Zealand Lottery Grants Board.

Advocacy Arts advocacy underpins all Creative New Zealand's work. The organisation works in partnership with other organisations, to promote the benefits of the arts and artists to New Zealand society as an integral part of everyday life. Creative New Zealand supports several awards to acknowledge contributions to the arts, for example, Te Waka Toi Awards, Arts Pasifika Awards, the Prime Minister's Awards for Literary Achievement, and the Montana New Zealand Book Awards.

Arts infrastructure and development Creative New Zealand supports 36 professional arts organisations on an annual or multi-year basis. It monitors their funding, and works with them to provide capability-building opportunities so they can take a leadership role for the arts sector. These organisations include the New Zealand String Quartet; the New Zealand International Arts Festival; national advocacy and service organisations such as Arts Access Aotearoa, Toi Māori Aotearoa and the New Zealand Book Council; regional theatre companies and orchestras; galleries and opera companies. These organisations were offered $15,186,780 for their activity programmes in 2008.

Project funding, residencies, fellowships, partnerships and audience work by Creative New Zealand all contribute to arts development. The organisation receives 1,500 applications a year for grants through two project funding rounds. It supports approximately 500 of these through three funding

Recipients of the Arts Pasifika Awards 2007. From left, Pele Walker (Creative New Zealand), Sale Pepe (visual artist), Nina Nawalowalo (theatre director), Iga Olivia Muliaumaseali'i (for opera singer Sani Muliaumaseali'i), Justine Simei-Barton (film company owner and director), and Dr Okusitino Mahina (academic and writer).

The Dominion Post

Members of Taki Rua Productions, a national theatre company that provides Māori drama to audiences around New Zealand, here present Strange Resting Places, *a play based on the Māori Battalion's role in Italy during World War II.*

bodies – the Arts Board, Te Waka Toi and the Pacific Arts Committee. Creative New Zealand's work in audience and market development focuses on increasing audiences and markets, and on professional development opportunities for artists and arts organisations – both in New Zealand and internationally. Test Drive the Arts was a recent initiative led by four theatre companies and designed to build new audiences. Creative New Zealand also published *Full House: Turning Data into Audiences*, a ticketing and marketing manual to assist arts organisations maximise the value of customer data for marketing and audience development.

Special initiatives Creative New Zealand identifies opportunities and responds by developing appropriate initiatives. These include fellowships, such as their annual Craft/Object Art Fellowship, and the Michael King Writers' Fellowship. Another initiative is the Smash Palace Fund, a partnership between Creative New Zealand and the Ministry of Research, Science and Technology aimed at encouraging and supporting collaborations between the arts and sciences as a building block for innovation and creativity. This has the potential to increase public understanding of these two disciplines. The registered trademark toi iho™, denoting authenticity and quality of Māori arts, was launched in 2002. This initiative was developed by Creative New Zealand through Te Waka Toi.

The organisation offers a range of international residencies, which provide opportunities for New Zealand artists to develop their practice, build international networks and enhance their careers.

Research Creative New Zealand's research programme identifies key questions about the role the arts play in the lives of New Zealanders, and provides answers and insights through rigorous research projects. Research activities inform Creative New Zealand's strategic planning and policy development, support advocacy work and provide valuable information to the wider arts sector. In 2006, Creative New Zealand, Auckland City Council and the ASB Community Trust jointly commissioned market research for the project 'Asian Aucklanders and the Arts: Attitudes, attendance, and participation'. The qualitative study explored the perceptions, experiences, and attitudes towards the arts held by Chinese, Japanese, Korean and Indian families, community leaders and artists.

Regional arts development Support for regional arts development is delivered through Creative New Zealand's partnerships, funding programmes, initiatives and advocacy work. The Creative Communities Scheme, a long-standing partnership with all local authorities, distributes grants from the Far North to Southland and the Chatham Islands. Established in 1995, the scheme is administered by local authorities and funded by Creative New Zealand. Every year, approximately 2,600 grants are allocated and distributed to local arts projects by assessment committees of representatives from iwi (tribes) and the local arts sector, including community arts councils and local government.

Contributors and related websites

Archives New Zealand – www.archives.govt.nz

Book Publishers Association of New Zealand – www.bpanz.org.nz

Booksellers New Zealand – www.booksellers.co.nz

Chamber Music New Zealand – www.chambermusic.co.nz

Copyright Licensing Ltd – www.copyright.co.nz

Creative New Zealand – www.creativenz.govt.nz

Hocken Collections – www.library.otago.ac.nz

Library and Information Association of New Zealand Aotearoa – www.lianza.org.nz

Ministry for Culture and Heritage – www.mch.govt.nz

Ministry of Economic Development – www.med.govt.nz

Motion Pictures Distributors' Association of New Zealand – www.mpda.org.nz

Museum of New Zealand Te Papa Tongarewa – www.tepapa.govt.nz

National Library of New Zealand – www.natlib.govt.nz

New Zealand Drama School – www.toiwhakaari.ac.nz

New Zealand Film Archive – www.filmarchive.org.nz

New Zealand Film Commission – www.nzfilm.co.nz

New Zealand Historic Places Trust – www.historic.org.nz

New Zealand Music Commission – www.nzmusic.org.nz

New Zealand Opera Company – www.nzopera.com

New Zealand School of Dance – www.nzschoolofdance.co.nz

New Zealand Society of Authors – www.authors.org.nz

New Zealand Symphony Orchestra – www.nzso.co.nz

Office of Film and Literature Classification – www.censorship.govt.nz

Parliamentary Library – www.parliament.nz

Royal New Zealand Ballet – www.nzballet.org.nz

Statistics New Zealand – www.stats.govt.nz

The Rangimarie Kapa Haka group performed a traditional Māori dance at the opening of the giant rugby ball in Paris, kicking off New Zealand's Rugby World Cup 2011 campaign.

13 | Leisure and tourism

Physical recreation and sport

Physical recreation and sport play a huge part in the lives of most New Zealanders. They impact positively on the nation's health and well-being and create a sense of community and nationhood. Sport and physical recreation provide opportunities for New Zealanders to express and reinforce their cultural identity. They also contribute to the development of communities and to economic growth.

Outdoor physical recreation is very popular in New Zealand's scenic natural environment. Ensuring it remains popular, and sustainable, is part of the broad mandate of Sport and Recreation New Zealand (SPARC). SPARC works with partners in the sector to help create opportunities for all New Zealanders to be active, and to reach their potential in their chosen sport or physical activity.

Sport and Recreation New Zealand

SPARC aims to get more New Zealanders more active more often. That means everything from supporting elite athletes, to encouraging people to get active in their local communities.

SPARC's vision is for New Zealand to be a nation inspired to be active, participate, and win.

To realise this vision SPARC aims to foster an environment where more New Zealanders will:

- be physically active in sport and recreation
- participate in supporting and delivering sport and recreation
- win on the world stage.

SPARC invests in organisations that contribute to achieving this vision, and partners with national sport organisations, national recreation organisations, regional sports trusts and many other organisations that have the capability to get people and programmes moving in their areas.

SPARC provides specialist services and programmes for coaches and elite athletes, as well as developing programmes aimed at getting ordinary New Zealanders to be more active.

SPARC represents the sport and physical recreation sector to government and provides a research base for the sector.

Measuring physical activity rates The New Zealand Sport and Physical Activity Survey is the key measure of participation in sport, recreation and physical activity for New Zealanders aged 16 years and over. The survey collects data from each participant on their involvement in sport, recreation, and physical activity over the previous 12 months, over the past four weeks and over the past seven days. The survey asks respondents if they are members of clubs, participate in organised competitions, receive coaching, or are involved in sport and recreation volunteering. This provides national and regional sport organisations with important information.

The 2007/08 survey was extensively re-designed to improve the quality of the information. In particular, each participant completes a seven-day physical activity recall diary. This recall diary collects in-depth information on physical activity (sport and recreation, active transport, occupational physical activity, unpaid work and other physical activities), and sedentary behaviour (TV/DVD/video use, and computer use). Participants record the physical activities they undertook each day and the associated intensity and duration of that activity.

Measuring the broader aspects of physical activity provides a comprehensive picture of total physical activity patterns and the proportion of New Zealand adults who are active to a level that maintains good health.

New Zealand Academy of Sport (NZAS) The academy provides a comprehensive network of world-class expertise, services and facilities for New Zealand's best athletes, promising young athletes, and their coaches.

The NZAS provides technical support for high-performance programmes at national sporting organisations. It also provides support services in sports science, sports medicine, and athlete and career education to eligible national sports organisations, athletes, and coaches.

To access services, athletes are recognised at one of four levels – world, international, development, and junior. Athletes at one of these levels receive a card and are entitled to access services from the academy in accordance with their sport's service agreement.

Tai chi classes improve stability

The Aucklander

The Accident Compensation Corporation (ACC) funds tai chi classes for older people – to help prevent falls. Tai chi is a gentle form of exercise that builds up strength and balance, so even people who suffer from arthritis, or have already had a fall, can participate.

The worry of falling can cause people to become inactive, which is a danger to their overall health. Tai chi builds confidence as well as physical mobility, allowing people to feel safer about being active at home.

ACC studies show that one in three people aged over 65, and half of those over 80 years, will fall each year. Falls caused the greatest number of ACC claims from July 2006 to June 2007, and 150 people aged 65 or over died as a result of a fall. More than 46,000 people aged 65 and over were injured.

Research shows that a 16-week course of tai chi can reduce falls by older adults by 47.5 percent. ACC's modified tai chi classes run for 20 weeks and focus on exercises that improve lower limb strength and balance.

ACC-funded tai chi classes are available for people:

- aged 65 years or older (55 years if Māori or Pacific peoples)
- living independently in the community
- who have had a fall in the previous 12 months, or are at high risk of a fall.

Source: Accident Compensation Corporation

In 2007, there were approximately 800 carded athletes in New Zealand representing 35 sports. The NZAS is funded by the government, with SPARC spending approximately $33 million in 2006/07 on high-performance sport.

There is also a separate Prime Minister's Athlete Scholarship fund, managed by SPARC and administered by the NZAS. The $4.25 million programme enables talented New Zealanders to study at tertiary level while developing skills that contribute to sporting performance at the elite level. The scholarships are available to athletes, coaches, support team members and officials, to help them with professional development. In 2008, 300 athletes, 27 coaches, 34 support team members and 16 officials received scholarships across national sport organisations and NZAS regional operations.

New Zealanders at the Olympics

New Zealanders first competed in the Olympic Games at London in 1908, combining with Australians to compete as Australasia until 1920 in Antwerp. New Zealand has been represented at each Olympic Games since then.

New Zealand's Olympic gold medal roll of honour

Year	Venue	New Zealand gold medal winners	Sport	Event
1908	London	–		
1912	Stockholm	Malcolm Champion	swimming	4 x 200m freestyle relay as member of Australasian team
1916	Berlin	–		
1920	Antwerp	–		
1924	Paris	–		
1928	Amsterdam	Ted Morgan	boxing	welterweight
1932	Los Angeles	–		
1936	Berlin	Jack Lovelock	athletics	1,500m
1948	London	–		
1952	Helsinki	Yvette Williams	athletics	long jump
1956	Melbourne	Peter Mander, Jack Cropp	yachting	sharpie
1960	Rome	Peter Snell	athletics	800m
		Murray Halberg	athletics	5,000m
1964	Tokyo	Helmer Pedersen, Earle Wells	yachting	flying dutchman
		Peter Snell	athletics	800m and 1,500m
1968	Mexico City	Simon Dickie (cox), Warren Cole, Ross Colinge, Dick Joyce, Dudley Storey	rowing	coxed fours
1972	Munich	Simon Dickie (cox), Trevor Coker, Athol Earle, John Hunter, Tony Hurt, Dick Joyce, Gary Robertson, Wybo Veldman, Lindsay Wilson	rowing	eights
1976	Montreal	Paul Ackerley, Jeff Archibald, Thur Borren, Alan Chesney, John Christensen, Greg Dayman, Tony Ineson, Alan McIntyre, Barry Maister, Selwyn Maister, Trevor Manning, Arthur Parkin, Mohan Patel, Ramesh Patel	hockey	
		John Walker	athletics	1,500m
1980	Moscow	–		
1984	Los Angeles	Grant Bramwell, Ian Ferguson, Paul MacDonald, Alan Thompson	canoeing	K4 1,000m
		Russell Coutts	yachting	finn
		Ian Ferguson	canoeing	K1 500m
		Ian Ferguson, Paul MacDonald	canoeing	K2 500m
		Shane O'Brien, Les O'Connell, Conrad Robertston, Keith Trask	rowing	coxless fours
		Rex Sellers, Chris Timms	yachting	tornado
		Alan Thompson	canoeing	K1 1,000m
		Mark Todd (on Charisma)	equestrian	individual three-day event
1988	Seoul	Ian Ferguson, Paul MacDonald	canoeing	K2 500m
		Bruce Kendall	yachting	boardsailing
		Mark Todd (on Charisma)	equestrian	individual three-day event
1992	Barcelona	Barbara Kendall	yachting	boardsailing
1996	Atlanta	Danyon Loader	swimming	200m and 400m freestyle
		Blyth Tait (on Ready Teddy)	equestrian	individual three-day event
2000	Sydney	Rob Waddell	rowing	single sculls
2004	Athens	Hamish Carter	triathlon	individual men
		Sarah Ulmer	cycling	individual pursuit
		Georgina Evers-Swindell, Caroline Evers-Swindell	rowing	double sculls

Symbol: – none

Source: New Zealand Olympic Committee

Oamaru cricket coach Lachlan Kingan, 12 (right) gives his team some catching practice.

Changes in 2006/07 mean the academy now operates from two bases. The Auckland base delivers performance services across the North Island, and the Dunedin base delivers across the South Island.

Physical recreation and sport in the community

Active Communities SPARC supports local government's community development, and recreation and transportation planning. SPARC's Active Communities initiative provides investment which enables communities to become more active, more often. Nearly 70 local authorities receive investment and services from SPARC.

Green Prescriptions (GRx) This SPARC programme encourages general practitioners and practice nurses to give 'green prescriptions' – written advice for a patient to be physically active as part of the patient's health management – to patients whose health could benefit from increased physical activity.

In 2006/07, 20,211 patients were referred to regional sports trusts and primary health organisations (PHOs) for GRx support, up from 16,100 in 2005/06 and 14,600 in 2004/05.

GRx is increasingly being integrated into the health system. A survey in November 2007 showed 99 percent of general practitioners were aware of GRx, and 87 percent have used them. In 2007, more PHOs had become involved by:

- integrating GRx into training for general practitioners and practice nurses (40 PHOs)
- including GRx in plans and policies (31 PHOs)
- investing in GRx (26 PHOs).

Most GRx referrals are in response to patients' weight and obesity issues, diabetes and cardiovascular disease. However, a survey of patients showed that the rewards go far beyond weight alone – 74 percent reported other positive health benefits.

Informing and supporting general practitioners is key to the success of GRx. Seventeen GRx area managers perform this vital role by visiting practitioners, advising on how to integrate the electronic GRx script into the practice system, and offering ongoing information and support.

The 2007 General Practitioner Survey showed that 72 percent of general practitioners were satisfied with GRx as a whole, while 79 percent were satisfied with the support delivered to patients.

Coaching Quality coaches have a positive impact on their communities. Their work has a huge influence on the lives and values of those they come into contact with.

The New Zealand Coaching Strategy was developed by coaches to meet the needs of coaches as well as athletes. It delivers a coordinated coaching approach that links regional and national activities and outcomes. SPARC creates opportunities for coaches at all levels of experience to develop and share their knowledge. This includes supporting coach and athlete development by establishing coaching communities and flexible learning opportunities.

CoachForce is a nationwide programme that provides the 'workforce' to support coaches and regional coach development and education programmes. There are now 107 full-time CoachForce officers across New Zealand who implement SPARC's coaching strategy.

CoachCorp is a SPARC programme that gets employees out of the office and into volunteering, as coaches, managers and officials, with the support of their employers (who provide flexitime). CoachCorp aims to increase the number and quality of coaches, and to get more people into sport and physical recreation, by building relationships between companies and community sport. During 2006/07 approximately 50 companies and over 230 employees were involved in CoachCorp.

Mission-On for young Kiwis is a set of initiatives from SPARC and the Ministries of Education, Health, and Youth Development that aim to improve the lifestyles of young New Zealanders through improved nutrition and increased physical activity.

The Mission-On target audience is children and young people aged 0–24 years. Strategies to improve nutrition and increase physical activity include 'lifestyle ambassadors' promoting healthy messages, a website for 5–12 year olds rewarding those who get active, and the Weird World of Sport competition challenging people to invent a new sport and become a world champion.

Mission-On was launched in September 2006. It has gained strong awareness and positive feedback from children, young adults, parents and schools. SPARC is the lead agency and is responsible for delivering six of Mission-On's 10 initiatives.

No Exceptions is intended to guide and coordinate the strategies and actions of all agencies involved in providing physical recreation and sports opportunities for disabled people. It aims to increase their participation in sports and physical recreation by making more activities inclusive and accessible for disabled people.

The No Exceptions strategy comes with responsibilities for many organisations, many of which have identified the strategies and actions they will implement. At November 2007, nine national sporting organisations had committed to disability action plans and policies. Of these, five had begun developing planning and policy templates.

Push Play is SPARC's national physical-activity campaign to encourage more New Zealanders to be more active. While primarily targeting adults, there are components of the campaign that are designed to improve outcomes for children.

Push Play Nation is an initiative under the Push Play brand that ran from 17 September 2007 through to Push Play Day on 3 November 2007. The campaign included television commercials, featuring five high-profile New Zealanders, who encouraged people to get active. Viewers could download an activity programme from SPARC's website.

Forty thousand New Zealanders registered, choosing one of the 'celebrities' and their preferred month-long activity programme (options included walking, running, cycling, swimming or gym). To keep them motivated, participants received an email message from their celebrity.

SPARC's survey results show a positive change in attitude, with 19 percent of New Zealand adults saying they had started to be more active as a result of the campaign, and another 23 percent were thinking about it.

Te Roopu Manaaki is an advisory board of national and regional representatives, who provide strategic advice to the SPARC board about Māori issues. It also provides assistance to He Oranga Poutama (Steps to health), a SPARC programme targeted at increasing physical activity levels among Māori.

The functions of Te Roopu Manaaki are to:

- ensure all SPARC activities are culturally appropriate to Māori
- provide strategic advice to SPARC to increase Māori participation in the sports and recreation sector
- help communicate with iwi (tribes), hapū (subtribes) and individual Māori, and encourage interested groups to participate.

Other central government bodies are also involved in sport and physical recreation. SPARC has close relationships with the Ministry of Health and the Ministry of Education, who share the objective of helping New Zealanders to be healthy and physically active.

Push Play Parents

The inaugural Push Play Parents campaign that ran from February to June 2007 set out to motivate and inform parents about how important it is to be active with children, and what they could do to help.

In support of television advertising, around 150,000 printed activity brochures with ideas on how to Push Play as a family were given out free through regional sports trusts.

Push Play Parents also had another angle – sponsorship of the SPARC Real Women's Duathlon series, held at 10 venues around the country. A key audience for Push Play is those who are busy and stressed, and many of those people are working mothers. Sponsoring the duathlons was a great way to motivate these women to get active, enjoy it, and be great role models for their children.

In SPARC surveys, 19 percent of New Zealanders who had seen the Push Play Parents television commercials said they had changed their behaviour and were more active with their children.

Source: SPARC

Outdoor leisure activities

Physical recreation

Cycling Many New Zealanders incorporate cycling into their lifestyles, whether they are going cross country through national parks, bunch riding through the city, down at the local BMX park with the kids, or competing on the world stage.

The New Zealand landscape creates some of the world's most outstanding mountain bike rides, including Woodhill Forest near Auckland, Whakarewarewa in Rotorua, the Karapoti Classic near Wellington, the Otago Central Rail Trail from Clyde to Middlemarch, and the tracks around Lake Wanaka.

Bike NZ Inc represents the interests of several cycling organisations, including Cycling New Zealand, Mountain Bike NZ, BMX New Zealand, Cycling Advocates Network, and the New Zealand Schools Cycling Association. Bike NZ Inc has about 8,000 members and is affiliated to international cycling body International Cycling Union.

Mountaineering New Zealand provides a superb environment for mountaineering. The mountains are a dominant feature of the New Zealand landscape, with both islands providing opportunities for climbers of all abilities. The South Island is well known for the spectacular Southern Alps, forming the backbone of the island. They offer an impressive selection of challenging climbs, with 19 peaks over 3,000 metres high, including the well known Aoraki-Mt Cook, New Zealand's highest mountain.

Most tracks are accessible year-round, although some of the high-altitude tracks in the South Island are restricted by winter weather. Commercial guides are available and specialist companies run courses covering a range of climbing experiences. The climbing season is generally November to March, but for experienced climbers this can extend into winter, where there can be extended calm, fine spells. However the New Zealand climate can be changeable, with winds and storms picking up extremely fast.

Skiing and snowboarding The skiing and snowboarding season extends from June to late October/early November, with many ski areas in both the North and South Islands having snow-making equipment to ensure reliable snow depth and quality. New Zealand has 13 commercial ski areas, 11 club ski fields, one commercial cross-country ski area, and a commercial indoor ski slope in Auckland.

In the North Island, the main snow sports centre is Mt Ruapehu in the Tongariro National Park. There are two commercial ski areas, Whakapapa and Turoa, and one club field at Tukino. The Maunganui Ski Club operates on Mt Egmont/Taranaki.

In the South Island, the commercial ski areas are in the Queenstown/Wanaka area at Coronet Peak, the Remarkables, Cardrona, Treble Cone, Snow Park and Snow Farm; in the Aoraki/McKenzie area at Ohau, Mt Dobson and Round Hill; and in Canterbury at Porters, Mt Hutt and Mt Lyford. There are nine club fields in the South Island.

The Snow Farm, on the Pisa Range near Queenstown/Wanaka, offers 50 kilometres of cross-country skiing. Glacier skiing on the Tasman and Fox Glaciers is accessible by ski-plane and helicopter. Guided heli-skiing and ski touring give access to the Ben Ohau Ranges, the Harris Mountains, the Two Thumb Range, the Aoraki-Mt Cook/Tasman Glacier area, Mt Hutt and Queenstown.

The International Ski Federation has authorised annual international snow sports competitions at Whakapapa, Mt Hutt, Turoa, Coronet Peak, Cardrona, Snow Park, Snow Farm and Treble Cone.

Tramping/hiking The closeness of mountains and forests to urban centres gives New Zealanders the opportunity to get away from the cities and enjoy nature. There are many tracks through beautiful scenery, from the Waitakere and Hunua Ranges near Auckland, to the many national and forest parks and reserves of the North Island, and through to the extensive parks and protected natural areas of the South Island. Tramping tracks range from half-day, family-oriented walks to challenging tramps in back-country and alpine isolation.

The Great Walks are New Zealand's most famous tramping tracks. They include Lake Waikaremoana in Urewera National Park, Tongariro northern circuit in Tongariro National Park, Abel Tasman Coastal Track in Abel Tasman National Park, Heaphy Track in Kahurangi National Park, Routeburn Track in Mt Aspiring and Fiordland National Parks, Milford and Kepler Tracks in Fiordland National Park, and Rakiura Track in Rakiura National Park.

Most of these tracks take two to four days to complete and are well marked. Huts and campsites are provided for overnight accommodation. The Abel Tasman Coastal Track is the most popular, with about 30,000 overnight visitors a year. Information on tramping is available through commercial guiding companies and the Department of Conservation.

Walking Government agencies and local authorities develop and maintain public walking tracks throughout New Zealand. The walkways system offers walking opportunities over primarily private land, and complements the network of back-country tramping tracks. Walkways vary from half-hour walks, to four or five days for the St James Walkway in North Canterbury.

Fishing and hunting

Big-game fishing The warm waters off the east coast of the North Island provide some of the best surf, line and spear fishing in the world. The main bases for line fishing from charter boats are at Whangaroa, Bay of Islands (Russell, Otehei Bay and Waitangi), Tutukaka, Mercury Bay (Whitianga) and Tauranga (Mayor Island).

The most-prized catches are broadbill, black marlin, striped marlin and blue marlin, while other types of big-game fish found in New Zealand waters are tiger shark, hammerhead shark, mako shark, thresher shark, kingfish (yellow tail) and tuna. Best catches are usually made in February, but fishing is good from December to April.

Freshwater fishing Rainbow and brown trout are found in most lakes and rivers of both the North Island and South Island. The South Island also has sea-run brown trout in western coastal rivers, sea-run quinnat salmon in eastern coastal rivers, and land-locked salmon in several waterways. Average trout size varies depending on environment, climate, food and the number of anglers.

Shooting and hunting New Zealand's principal game birds are duck, swan, pheasant, quail, geese and chukors. The season traditionally starts on the first weekend in May and extends for six

Gottlieb Braun-Elwert

A group of climbers descend the Hooker Valley after crossing Ball Pass in the Aoraki-Mount Cook National Park.

to eight weeks for most species, depending on the region. Special seasons for paradise shelduck and geese are run on a regional basis. Daily bag limits apply in most regions.

Deer of several species, chamois, tahr, wild pigs, goats and wallabies are numerous in several areas. There are few restrictions on big game hunting and there is generally no limit on the number of big game animals that can be taken. The season is open for most species all year round. For tourists and inexperienced hunters, the service of an experienced guide is recommended.

Fish and Game New Zealand is responsible for protecting, managing and enhancing freshwater sport fishing and gamebird hunting on behalf of anglers and hunters.

With the exception of the Lake Taupo fishery, which is managed by the Department of Conservation, all trout and salmon fisheries are managed by Fish and Game New Zealand. A licence is required for all sport fishing and game bird hunting, and permits are required to hunt big game in some areas.

Public conservation land

The Department of Conservation (DOC) is charged with fostering and promoting recreation, and making areas of public conservation land accessible for the enjoyment and appreciation of all.

This involves providing and maintaining tracks, huts and other amenities for visitors. The department is responsible for 12,900 kilometres of walking tracks, 938 huts, 1,710 toilets, 665 car parks, 420 amenity areas, 13,600 bridges, boardwalks and other structures, 17,400 signs and 323 campsites.

It is estimated that, currently, at least 20 percent of New Zealand residents visit one or more national parks in a year. Thirty percent of international visitors to the country visit at least one national park during their stay.

The nine Great Walks – all of which are located within national parks – are some of the highest profile tracks in the country. In 2006/07, 58,000 people stayed overnight on these tracks, 60 percent of whom were overseas visitors. During the 2006/07 walking season, which started in late October 2006 and finished in April 2007, hut occupancy on the Milford track was 97 percent, while occupancy for the busiest huts on the Abel Tasman was 90 percent, and on the Routeburn, 82 percent. There is slightly less demand for the Kepler, where the busiest hut had a 74 percent occupancy rate, while the huts on the Heaphy Track had an occupancy rate of just over 50 percent.

Commercial operations exist on some of the Great Walks and at many other DOC-managed locations as well. Commercial tourism operators work hand-in-hand with the department, enabling a wider range of recreational opportunities to be enjoyed. The department regards public enjoyment of national parks, other conservation areas, historic reserves, and marine reserves as a key part of its conservation role.

Racing and gaming

Racing

The New Zealand racing industry is a major contributor to the country's economy and to local communities. Racing generates more than $1.4 billion each year, and creates the equivalent of 18,300 full-time jobs. Accommodation, travel, fashion and entertainment providers also benefit from the industry. In 2007, more than 1 million people attended race meetings across New Zealand, spending more than $55 million on bets, food, beverages, transport and accommodation.

A major source of funding for the racing industry is the returns from betting on racing and sports, which is administered by the New Zealand Totalisator Agency Board (TAB), the retail arm of the New Zealand Racing Board.

There are 69 thoroughbred, 51 harness and 12 greyhound clubs licensed to race in New Zealand, with racecourses situated in 59 locations. In the racing year, from August 2006 to July 2007, 8,969 races were held throughout the country.

The bloodstock industry is of international importance to New Zealand, with the sale of horses for export – mainly to Australia and Asia – generating more than $120 million a year. New Zealand-bred runners compete very well overseas and regularly win major races.

New Zealand Racing Board The board facilitates all racing and sports betting in New Zealand. Under the Racing Act 2003, the New Zealand Racing Board is responsible for facilitating and promoting racing and sports betting to maximise profits for the long-term benefit of New Zealand racing and those who derive their livelihood from the industry.

The board coordinates:

- the TAB – which runs all betting on racing and sport in New Zealand
- the three racing codes – New Zealand Thoroughbred Racing (gallops), Harness Racing New Zealand (trotting and pacing) and New Zealand Greyhound Racing (greyhounds)
- the Judicial Control Authority – the legal body that administers the rules of racing and conducts inquiries into breaches of the rules for all three codes.

Totalisator Agency Board (TAB) The New Zealand Racing Board's income comes from betting revenue from the TAB. There are 750 TAB outlets throughout New Zealand, as well as on-course tote terminals, Internet, Phonebet, Touch Tone and SKYbet betting channels. More than 100,000 TAB account holders use the TAB's electronic Touch Tone, Phonebet and Internet services.

The TAB offers a wide range of totalisator and fixed-odds betting products. Just over 80 percent of the betting dollar is returned to the customer. The rest goes to the racing and sporting codes, after tax and New Zealand Racing Board costs.

In 2006/07, $112.7 million was returned to the New Zealand racing codes and more than $2 million was returned to sporting bodies.

Trackside Television and Radio Trackside The New Zealand Racing Board owns Trackside Television and Radio Trackside which have a combined audience of more than 250,000. Trackside Television broadcasts every race the TAB takes bets on and has the highest amount of home-grown content of any channel in New Zealand. Trackside Live broadcasts live action and race information 12 hours a day, seven days per week, 363 days a year.

Table 13.01

Non-inflation adjusted gambling statistics					
By gambling outlet					
Year ending 30 June[1]					
	1980	1990	2000	2005	2006
Gambling outlet			$million		
Racing[2]					
Expenditure[3]	96	230	227	247	258
Dividends	408	815	931	1,026	1,106
Turnover[4]	504	1,045	1,158	1,273	1,364
New Zealand Lotteries Commission					
Expenditure[3]	22	252	277	280	321
Prizes	32	292	348	350	398
Turnover[4]	54	544	625	630	719
Gaming machines (outside casinos)					
Expenditure[3]	...	...	450	1,027	906
Casinos					
Expenditure[3]	...	...	343	472	493
Total expenditure[5]	**118**	**482**	**1,297**	**2,027**	**1,977**

(1) The balance dates for different gaming operators can differ from 30 June – no adjustment has been made for this. (2) Racing data for 2000 and onwards is not strictly comparable with previous years. (3) Expenditure is the amount lost or spent by players, or the gross profit of the gaming operator. (4) Turnover is the total gross amount wagered by punters. It includes re-investment where the same dollar is counted more than once. Turnover is not an indicator of the amount spent by players or of the profit of the operator. (5) Figures may not add up to stated totals due to rounding.
Symbol: ... not applicable

Source: Department of Internal Affairs

To celebrate Lotto's 20th birthday on 25 August 2007, extra prizes worth $5.5 million were available, the largest ever bonus prize offer.

Lotteries and gaming

The Gambling Act 2003 aims to minimise or prevent harm or distress of any kind, including personal, social or economic harm that is caused, or exacerbated by, a person's gambling. Its purpose is to:

- control the growth of gambling
- prevent and minimise the harm caused by gambling, including problem gambling
- authorise some gambling and prohibit the rest
- facilitate responsible gambling
- ensure the integrity and fairness of games
- limit opportunities for crime or dishonesty
- ensure profits from gambling benefit the community
- facilitate community involvement in decisions about the provision of gambling.

The Act's risk-based approach to gambling regulation makes it harder to get licences to operate more harmful forms of gambling, and imposes additional obligations on those forms.

City and district councils control the number of gaming machines in their area and decide the location of gambling venues. The Department of Internal Affairs is responsible for licensing, auditing, reporting, and other controls on gaming machines in pubs and clubs to ensure that profits go to community groups.

Problem gambling is a public health issue and the gambling sector is required to pay a levy to cover the cost of a problem gambling strategy. The Gambling Act established the Gambling Commission, which has an appeal function and a role in regulating casinos. The Act prohibits any new casino licences being issued and prevents existing casinos from expanding their gambling operations.

New Zealand Lotteries Commission (NZ Lotteries) is responsible for promoting and conducting New Zealand lotteries. Net profits from NZ Lotteries' games are distributed to arts, sports, charitable and community causes by the New Zealand Lottery Grants Board.

In the year ending 30 June 2007, NZ Lotteries' sales were $744.8 million, of which $147.5 million was transferred to the Lottery Grants Board. This compares with sales of $719.2 million and a transfer of $138.6 million in the previous year. For every dollar spent on lotteries, 56 cents is paid in prizes, 20 cents is transferred to the Lottery Grants Board, 10 cents is paid in taxes, seven cents is paid in retail commission, and seven cents covers operating costs.

New Zealand Lottery Grants Board Te Puna Tahua is responsible for distributing profits from lotteries run by the New Zealand Lotteries Commission for the benefit of the New Zealand community. It is governed by the Gambling Act 2003.

The board has six members: three community members appointed by the governor-general, representatives of the prime minister and the leader of the opposition, and the Minister of Internal Affairs who chairs the board.

Social, community, arts, heritage, sport, recreation, and health research services and projects are funded through 20 lottery distribution committees and three statutory bodies – Creative New Zealand, the New Zealand Film Commission, and Sport and Recreation New Zealand.

Table 13.02

Allocation of lottery profits					
By organisation					
Year ending 30 June					
	2003	2004	2005	2006	2007
Recipient	$(million)				
Sport and Recreation New Zealand	24.7	24.7	24.7	28.2	30.9
Creative New Zealand	18.6	18.6	18.6	18.6	21.3
NZ Film Commission	8.0	8.0	8.0	8.1	9.0
NZ Film Archive	0.6	0.6	0.6	0.6	0.7
Total	**56.3**	**56.3**	**55.4**	**55.5**	**61.9**
Regional community committees	0.0	0.0	15.0	17.8	22.1
National community committee	0.0	0.0	10.8	10.8	11.9
Environment and heritage	5.5	5.5	6.6	7.4	8.4
Outdoor safety committee	0.0	0.0	6.0	6.7	7.3
Marae heritage and facilities	4.1	4.1	5.0	5.5	7.0
Individuals/disabilities	3.0	3.0	3.2	3.6	6.0
Health research	1.9	1.9	2.3	2.6	2.8
Lottery community PPDF[1]	0.0	0.0	0.0	0.2	0.4
Minister's fund	0.1	0.2	0.2	0.2	0.3
Total	**43.7**	**39.7**	**49.1**	**54.6**	**66.2**
Grand total	**100.0**	**96.1**	**104.5**	**110.1**	**128.2**

(1) Pacific Provider Development Fund.

Note: Figures may not add up to stated totals due to rounding.

Source: New Zealand Lottery Grants Board

Gambling Commission is an independent statutory decision-making body established under the Gambling Act 2003. The commission:

- specifies, varies and revokes casino licence conditions
- decides on applications by the Secretary for Internal Affairs to suspend or cancel casino licences
- decides on applications for casino operator's licences, and the renewal of casino venue licences
- determines appeals against regulatory and licensing decisions made by the Department of Internal Affairs in respect of some classes of gambling
- hears complaints about the way the department has handled complaints in relation to gambling activities
- advises ministers and facilitates consultation on the setting of the problem gambling levy
- advises the Minister of Internal Affairs on matters relating to the performance of the commission's functions and the administration of the Gambling Act 2003.

Problem gambling is a significant social and health issue. New Zealand has seen a marked increase in the consumption of gambling products and in player losses in the past decade. There has also been an increased awareness of the risk of gambling-related harm to various population groups. The Ministry of Health is responsible for funding and coordinating services and activities pertaining to gambling-related harm. The *Preventing and Minimising Gambling Harm Strategic Plan 2004–10* includes primary prevention and population approaches, and more selected intervention services for individuals and their families. The ministry funds problem gambling services through a Vote Health appropriation, and the Crown then recovers these costs through a levy on gambling operators.

Tourism

Situated at the edge of the Pacific Ocean, New Zealand's attractions have made tourism one of the country's largest foreign-exchange earners. Traditionally, international tourists have been drawn to New Zealand to experience unpolluted air and water, open spaces, and unique flora and fauna. Today, as well as these traditional attractions, the international traveller is looking for adventure, sophistication and cultural activities. New Zealand tourism has developed to meet these needs.

The tourism market New Zealand tourism caters for international visitors, and New Zealanders, travelling for pleasure, business or education. The tourism industry meets their needs by providing accommodation, food, tours, activities and transport.

Tourism is an important source of income for New Zealand, so it is important that industry members work together to provide a rewarding experience for travellers. New Zealand has two government-funded tourism organisations: the Ministry of Tourism and Tourism New Zealand. Tourism New Zealand is the marketing agency, and works with the tourism industry to take a cohesive, coordinated approach to marketing New Zealand overseas.

Attractions It is not only New Zealand's landscape, but its distinctive culture, people and sense of adventure that attract overseas visitors. New Zealand culture is reflected in its distinctive stamp on world cuisine, sport, fashion, film-making, and contemporary and wearable art.

SKYCITY

SkyJump® is a 192 metre fall from Auckland's iconic Sky Tower in the central business district.

Catching tourists with technology

With travellers researching and making bookings online, and laptops, mobile phones and personal digital assistants making their way into backpacks and carry-on luggage, the tourism industry is looking at more modern, technologically-advanced marketing tools.

Tourism New Zealand research shows that the more planning visitors do before arriving, the more they enjoy their trips. Travellers were asked what they wanted online, the answer was maps, planning tools and ways to collect ideas and send them to travel agents and airlines.

In response, Tourism New Zealand developed an interactive travel planning feature on its website that allows visitors to organise material, put together an itinerary, plot it on a map and export it to travel agents and friends.

The interactivity of the Internet means websites can be much more than an online version of the printed brochure. High-speed connections give potential visitors the ability to 'experience' destinations before they visit.

A wide range of technology is now available to tourists. With video streaming, guests can use operators' websites to share experiences with friends overseas. They can hook up a video camera to broadcast jumps or jetboat rides, and text message their friends back home to tune in and watch them in real time. Blogs in the form of online diaries and photo repositories allow travellers to share their experiences with the world.

Operators like Whale Watch Kaikoura lead the way in the use of animation and multimedia, helping to educate and broaden the experience of visitors. Web-based applications will soon let clients 're-experience' their visit when they are back home – even logging in to find out where the whales they spotted are swimming now.

Source: Tourism New Zealand

New Zealanders themselves complete the visitor experience. Ingenious, passionate, inspiring yet straightforward people, New Zealanders are famous for looking at things in new ways and doing things with an attitude and an eye for adventure. Combining a breathtaking landscape and an adventurous soul, 'Kiwis' explore nature by extremes – inventing the ski-plane and the jetboat, and popularising bungy jumping.

Events Sporting and cultural events, such as wine, food, art and flower festivals, Māori cultural competitions, triathlons, fashion events, and rugby matches put New Zealand in the international spotlight. Together with conferences and conventions, these events help to promote New Zealand as a tourist destination.

New Zealand Tourism Strategy 2015 Recognising the importance of sustainability and that New Zealand is a small player in the global tourism market, a group representing the tourism industry, local and central government, Māori, and conservation interests, joined together to review the New Zealand Tourism Strategy 2010 (released in 2001). The result is the *New Zealand Tourism Strategy 2015* (2007). This document has far-reaching implications for the structure of the tourism industry and should ensure the industry's sustainability.

The strategy looks at how the tourism sector can deliver sustainable tourism that provides the maximum economic, social, cultural and environmental benefits, with the least negative effects possible. Kaitiakitanga (guardianship) and manākitanga (hospitality) are important values that underpin the strategy.

The strategy's vision is that, in 2015, tourism is valued as the leading contributor to a sustainable New Zealand economy. The sector faces a number of challenges in achieving this, including the impact of climate change on worldwide travel patterns, exchange rate fluctuations, restricted aviation capacity, and the availability of appropriately qualified and skilled staff.

The strategy sets out four outcomes to guide the industry towards its vision:

- New Zealand delivers a world-class visitor experience
- New Zealand's tourism sector is prosperous and attracts ongoing investment
- the tourism sector takes a leading role in protecting and enhancing New Zealand's environment
- the tourism sector and communities work together for mutual benefit.

The updated strategy was released in November 2007, following input from the tourism industry, local and central government, the education and training sector and related organisations, who will work together to deliver on this strategy.

Uniquely New Zealand

The '100% Pure New Zealand' global marketing campaign showcases what visitors to New Zealand can experience while in the country. It is about more than the environment – it is about New Zealand's landscapes, its young and vibrant culture, the openness of its people, and the activities that combine to create a holiday that is uniquely New Zealand.

The 100% Pure New Zealand message is infused throughout everything Tourism New Zealand does, including training the overseas travel trade, developing the www.newzealand.com website, hosting international media in New Zealand, and working with national and international events to promote all that New Zealand has to offer. As a targeted campaign, 100% Pure New Zealand aims to attract visitors who are environmentally-aware, who tend to stay longer and travel out to the regions, and who spend more while they are on holiday.

Tourism is now the world's largest industry, with more than 650 million people travelling globally on holiday each year. It is increasing by 3 percent annually. This growth environment means increased competition for New Zealand as a visitor destination. The 100% Pure New Zealand campaign has made New Zealand stand out from the crowd. The number of annual visitors to the country has increased by nearly 900,000 since it launched.

The first major rethink of the campaign was launched in September 2007. The revised campaign centres on the message that New Zealand is the world's youngest country, and is where visitors can experience life as it should be.

Source: Tourism New Zealand

Tourism organisations

Tourism New Zealand is responsible for coordinating overseas marketing and promotion of New Zealand as a tourist destination. Its objective is to ensure that New Zealand is marketed as a tourism destination to maximise the long-term benefits to the country.

The '100% Pure New Zealand' marketing campaign, introduced in 1999, works on the basis of a single, concise brand position across all its offshore markets. Tourism New Zealand works with the tourism industry to develop quality systems and new tourism products, and on international marketing, to encourage international visitors to 'come now, do more and tell others'.

Tourism New Zealand maintains offices in Wellington, Auckland, Sydney, Bangkok, Mumbai, London, Los Angeles, New York, Tokyo, Osaka, Singapore, Seoul and Shanghai, and has general service agents in Taipei and Johannesburg.

Tourism Industry Association New Zealand (TIA) is the largest representative body of tourism operators in the country. It is a private sector, membership-based organisation that represents around 2,000 businesses and organisations – from small owner-operator businesses through to large stock-exchange-listed companies – who collectively represent 85 percent of the country's tourism turnover.

TIA advocates to central and local government, and other decision makers, for the interests of those who deliver the visitor experience in New Zealand. It provides information, advice and tools to help members run successful businesses, and organises major tourism industry events each year. These include the international business-to-business trade shows, TRENZ (Tourism Rendezvous New Zealand) and PURE LUXURY New Zealand, the Tourism Industry Awards and the Tourism Industry Conference.

Established in 1953 as the New Zealand Travel and Holiday Association, the functions of TIA have evolved as the New Zealand tourism industry has increased in economic importance.

Other agencies with tourism functions are involved in the tourism sector. The New Zealand Customs Service and the Ministry of Agriculture and Forestry's quarantine service screen all visitors entering New Zealand to ensure that no prohibited or restricted materials are brought into the country. New Zealand Police investigate crimes committed by or against visitors. Statistics New Zealand is a key provider of data needed for the management of tourism, and the Foundation for Research, Science and Technology allocates funds for tourism research.

International tourism

Tourism is an important industry throughout the world. The World Tourism Organisation reported that the total number of international visitor arrivals reached 898 million in 2007. New Zealand has hosted more than 2 million international visitors annually since March 2003.

Reasons for visiting New Zealand have changed. In the 20 years to 2007, the proportion of international visitors travelling to New Zealand for a holiday dropped – from 53 percent in 1988 to 49 percent in 2007. The proportion of visitors coming to stay with friends and relatives increased in the same period, up from 23 to 29 percent.

The Dominion Post

Karen Funnell (left) from CentrePort talks with cruise-ship passengers, Gert and Elke Vogt, in Wellington.

Table 13.03 shows the number of international visitors to New Zealand, by their main reason for visiting.

Tourism is an important foreign exchange earner for New Zealand, with international tourism revenue rising from $5.0 billion in 1999 to $8.3 billion in 2006 (19.2 percent of total export earnings). Direct tourism contributed $6.9 billion, or 4.8 percent, to gross domestic product. The indirect value-added of industries supporting tourism generated an additional $5.9 billion.

An estimated 108,600 full-time equivalent employees were directly engaged in producing goods and services purchased by tourists in the year ending 31 March 2006. This is equal to 5.9 percent of total employment in New Zealand.

Total tourism expenditure in New Zealand increased from $12.4 billion in 1999 to $18.6 billion in 2006.

International visitors Over 2.4 million international visitors arrived in New Zealand in the year ending 31 March 2007, an increase of 3 percent from the previous year.

Australia was the largest source of visitors, accounting for 37 percent of all visitors in 2007. The top seven visitors source countries – Australia, the United Kingdom, the United States, Japan, China, Korea and Germany – contributed three-quarters of all visitor arrivals to New Zealand.

Table 13.05 shows the country or region of last permanent residence of New Zealand's international visitors.

Accommodation A wide range of accommodation is available for visitors. Qualmark New Zealand Ltd has developed an independent and comprehensive rating system for assessing hotels, self-contained and serviced accommodation, holiday parks, and backpacker accommodation.

In August 2007, 37 percent of travellers stayed in motels, motor inns or apartments; 37 percent in hotels and resorts; 13 percent in backpacker accommodation or hostels; 12 percent in caravan parks or camping grounds; and 1 percent in hosted accommodation.

Table 13.03

International visitors
By main reason for visit
Year ending 31 March

Reason for visit	1997	2004	2005	2006	2007
Holiday	860,208	1,105,344	1,208,329	1,183,028	1,205,315
Visit friends and relatives	354,226	601,803	676,027	672,384	700,822
Business	163,976	224,061	249,164	264,812	270,191
Other[1]	172,931	230,091	233,871	242,067	259,340
Total[2]	**1,551,341**	**2,163,427**	**2,387,663**	**2,378,797**	**2,445,130**

(1) Includes conferences and conventions, education, medical, stopover and unspecified reasons. (2) Totals are actual counts and may not equal the sum of figures, which are derived from samples.

Source: Statistics New Zealand

Table 13.04

International visitor spending
By country of last permanent residence
Year ending 31 December 2006

Country/region of last permanent residence	Average expenditure per person per day	per visit ($)	Total foreign exchange earnings[1]
Japan	188	3,739	475,475,989
People's Republic of China	186	3,341	325,996,797
United States	184	3,513	696,503,688
Republic of Korea	176	3,458	327,274,561
Thailand	168	5,802	82,554,153
Singapore	162	2,608	60,508,576
Australia	161	1,795	1,466,918,197
Canada	133	4,312	178,262,975
Netherlands	131	3,859	112,797,839
United Kingdom	125	3,534	946,930,863
Switzerland	121	5,415	82,179,475
Taiwan	119	3,862	98,383,634
Hong Kong (SAR)[2]	116	3,173	71,539,554
Nordic countries	112	3,893	104,690,568
Germany	110	4,753	266,733,345
Malaysia	96	2,922	54,252,671
Other Central Europe	143	3,746	240,377,012
Other South-East Asia	72	2,456	32,643,617
Other countries	107	3,049	753,096,651
Total	...	...	**6,377,120,166**

(1) Excluding international airfares. (2) Special Administrative Region.
Symbol: ... not applicable

Source: Ministry of Tourism

Tourism STARs

The Sustainable Tourism Advisors in Regions (STAR) project funds a number of regions to employ local advisers to help tourism businesses become more environmentally sustainable. Protecting the natural environment is a key aim of the *New Zealand Tourism Strategy 2015* as international visitors demand a more environmentally friendly experience.

The STAR project is working in regions to influence sustainable business practices in the tourism industry. The project provides the necessary assistance to equip individual businesses with the knowledge and capability needed to operate in a sustainable way.

The tourism industry is largely made up of small and medium-sized businesses so the STAR project has been designed to provide on-the-ground and practical advice, tailored to the business and situation. Businesses are encouraged to monitor their progress on areas such as waste management and minimisation practices, workplace practices that encourage sustainability, community involvement, supply chain management and sustainable design.

Source: Ministry of Tourism

Table 13.05

International visitors[1]
By country of last permanent residence
Year ending 31 March

Country	2005	2006	2007
Australia	875,337	870,731	913,994
United Kingdom	293,554	306,608	302,812
United States	220,004	219,882	222,454
Japan	163,293	153,208	130,121
People's Republic of China	84,226	90,774	114,364
Republic of Korea	112,676	107,422	111,676
Germany	57,233	57,466	58,790
Canada	41,627	43,277	46,680
Singapore	32,586	29,365	27,744
Taiwan	27,562	28,616	27,647
Netherlands	25,916	26,406	27,380
Hong Kong (SAR)[2]	28,006	24,502	23,844
Fiji	18,149	21,078	22,113
India	16,359	17,909	20,706
Ireland	18,204	21,441	20,335
Malaysia	24,508	22,662	19,917
South Africa	15,848	17,329	19,617
France	16,367	17,949	19,109
Thailand	20,337	18,810	18,313
Samoa	14,710	16,695	17,707
French Polynesia	17,541	17,840	16,626
Switzerland	14,974	13,898	14,688
Tonga	10,495	10,383	12,026
Sweden	13,014	12,203	11,979
New Caledonia	10,323	10,524	11,398
Denmark	9,461	9,821	11,029
Cook Islands	8,968	10,570	10,595
Brazil	6,252	7,762	9,282
Spain	6,334	7,393	8,130
Italy	7,346	7,848	7,912
Philippines	5,666	6,041	7,343
Indonesia	7,855	7,061	7,198
Austria	6,665	6,196	6,464
Israel	6,888	6,543	5,985
Belgium	4,711	4,313	4,718
United Arab Emirates	4,273	4,344	4,527
Argentina	2,734	3,439	4,363
Chile	2,422	3,116	4,111
Other[3]	114,967	100,866	111,971
Total[4]	**2,387,663**	**2,378,797**	**2,445,130**

(1) Intended length of stay in New Zealand less than 12 months. (2) Special Administrative Region. (3) Includes unspecified. (4) Totals are actual counts. They may differ from the sum of individual figures for different countries, which are derived from samples.

Source: Statistics New Zealand

Transport In the year ending 31 March 2007, at some stage of their New Zealand visit, an estimated 44 percent of all international visitors aged 15 and over used a private car or van; 31 percent took a domestic air trip; 31 percent used a scheduled bus service; 29 percent used a rental car/van; 21 percent used a ferry or boat; and 20 percent took a bus tour.

Managing the effects of tourism

The increasing importance of tourism has led to a strong interest in sustainable tourism, both internationally and within New Zealand.

In order to be sustainable, tourism must provide satisfying and distinctive experiences for visitors and reasonable returns for investors, and be acceptable to host communities – providing them with real economic and social benefits. But it must also protect and develop the environmental, cultural and social values on which tourism depends.

Local government plays an important role in creating an environment for sustainable tourism. It contributes to the marketing of the region as a tourist destination and is responsible for enforcing laws and rules associated with managing the effects of tourism. It must also plan for, and in some cases fund, much of the infrastructure on which tourism depends, ensuring that water supply and sewerage systems, roads and car parks can cope with additional demands.

The Department of Conservation (DOC) manages many of the natural areas enjoyed by visitors. Private sector firms provide a variety of facilities or services for visitors, including ski fields, scenic flights, and guiding services, to complement those provided by the department. These firms must comply with strict statutory procedures, strategies, and plans introduced to protect the natural and historical features of conservation areas and the recreational experiences of other visitors. Firms also pay concession fees, which help DOC protect conservation values.

The New Zealand Herald

Tourism company Stray runs its Auckland-orientation tour bus on 100 percent recycled cooking oil. Managing director Neil Geddes says this produces cleaner emissions and lower running costs, and attracts environmentally conscious travellers.

Table 13.06

Commercial accommodation use[1][2]
By accommodation type
Year ending 31 March

Accommodation type	Number of establishments	Capacity (stay unit nights)[3] (000)	Guest nights (000)	Occupancy rate (percent)	Average stay (nights)
Hotels/resorts					
2004	547	10,155	9,341	56.2	1.8
2005	567	10,358	9,861	58.2	1.8
2006	574	11,124	9,896	55.2	1.8
2007	568	11,283	10,147	55.7	1.8
Motels/motor inns/apartments					
2004	1,630	8,990	10,336	56.1	1.8
2005	1,683	9,230	10,677	56.7	1.8
2006	1,717	9,487	10,554	55.0	1.8
2007	1,769	9,762	10,842	54.9	1.8
Hosted accommodation[4]					
2004	519	990	538	30.4	1.9
2005	626	1,037	564	29.5	1.8
2006	659	1,141	561	26.1	1.8
2007	679	1,177	587	26.6	1.9
Backpackers/hostels					
2004	343	6,702	3,693	49.7	2.0
2005	410	7,687	4,057	47.2	1.9
2006	441	8,637	4,208	43.6	1.9
2007	445	8,881	4,370	44.3	1.9
Caravan parks/camping grounds					
2004	399	18,350	6,078	14.3	2.1
2005	411	18,762	6,360	14.6	2.0
2006	419	18,735	6,071	14.0	2.0
2007	416	18,415	6,298	15.1	2.1
Total					
2004	3,438	45,187	29,986	37.6	1.9
2005	3,697	47,075	31,519	38.1	1.9
2006	3,810	49,124	31,288	36.7	1.9
2007	3,877	49,518	32,244	37.7	1.9

(1) Establishments that are temporarily closed for more than 14 days during a month are excluded from the results. (2) Establishments primarily offering accommodation for periods of one month or more are excluded. (3) An establishment's accommodation capacity is measured by multiplying the number of units in the establishment by the number of nights in the period. (4) Hosted accommodation includes private hotels, guest houses, bed and breakfasts, and farmstays.

Source: Statistics New Zealand

Contributors and related websites

BikeNZ Inc – www.bikenz.org.nz

Department of Conservation – www.doc.govt.nz

Department of Internal Affairs – www.dia.govt.nz

Fish and Game New Zealand – www.fishandgame.org.nz

Gambling Commission – www.gamblingcom.govt.nz

Ministry of Health – www.moh.govt.nz

Ministry of Tourism – www.tourism.govt.nz

New Zealand Lotteries Commission – www.nzlotteries.co.nz

New Zealand Olympic Committee – www.olympic.org.nz

New Zealand Racing Board – www.nzracingboard.co.nz

New Zealand Snowsports Council – www.gosnow.co.nz

Qualmark New Zealand Ltd – www.qualmark.co.nz

Sport and Recreation New Zealand – www.sparc.govt.nz

Statistics New Zealand – www.stats.govt.nz

Totalisator Agency Board – www.tab.co.nz

Tourism Industry Association of New Zealand – www.tianz.org.nz

Tourism New Zealand – www.tourismnewzealand.com

Tourism Research Council of New Zealand – www.trcnz.govt.nz

Department of Conservation biosecurity ranger David Wilson replaces fairy tern eggs at Pakiri Beach on the east coast north of Auckland. There were 2,222,000 people in New Zealand's labour force in the March 2008 quarter, 67.7 percent of the working-age population.

14 | Labour market

Labour relations

New Zealand has a range of legislation dealing with employment relations, with the main framework being set out in the Employment Relations Act 2000. Other employment legislation sets out minimum statutory conditions of employment, including minimum entitlements to wages and leave. These laws are administered by the Department of Labour.

Employment Relations Act 2000

The Employment Relations Act 2000 has good faith as its central principle, requiring employers, employees and unions to deal with each other honestly and openly. Specifically, the Act:

- promotes good employment relations and mutual respect and confidence among employers, employees and unions
- sets the environment for individual and collective employment relationships
- sets out requirements for negotiation of collective and individual employment agreements
- provides prompt and flexible options for resolving problems in employment relationships.

The key objective of the Act is to build productive employment relationships through promotion of mutual trust and confidence in all aspects of the employment environment and the employment relationship. In particular, the Act aims to promote productive employment relationships by:

- recognising that employment relationships must be built on good faith
- acknowledging and addressing the inherent inequality of bargaining power in employment relationships
- promoting collective bargaining
- protecting the integrity of individual choice
- promoting mediation as the primary problem-solving mechanism, reducing the need for judicial intervention.

The Act also aims to promote observance in New Zealand of the principles underlying International Labour Organization Convention 87 on freedom of association, and Convention 98 on the right to organize and bargain collectively.

The Act affirms the right of employees to have the freedom to choose whether or not to form a union, or be a member of a union, for the purpose of advancing their collective employment interests.

Labour market organisations

New Zealand is a member of two major international organisations involved in studying the labour market – the International Labour Organization (ILO) and the Organisation for Economic Co-operation and Development (OECD). New Zealand provides statistics to both organisations.

ILO – New Zealand is a founding member of the ILO, which dates from 1919. It maintains a keen interest and close involvement in ILO activities, and has a special relationship with Pacific and Asian members. Currently, the ILO has 181 member states.

A tripartite delegation from New Zealand has attended every International Labour Conference since 1936. New Zealand representatives – including government, employer and worker delegations – have been active in the ILO and held many senior offices. The New Zealand Government has also been an elected deputy member of the ILO's Governing Body (1990–96, and 1999–2005), representing the Far East and Pacific subgroup of the Asia-Pacific regional group.

One of the ILO's major roles is to set international labour standards. Agreed standards are either legally binding (conventions) or voluntary (recommendations). Of the 188 current ILO conventions, New Zealand has ratified 51. In 2007, New Zealand ratified ILO Convention 155 on occupational health and safety.

All member states have their application of ratified conventions, and of 'core' conventions deemed to represent fundamental standards by the ILO, whether ratified or not, scrutinised. For example, the principles of freedom of association and the promotion of collective bargaining are an important part of the ILO's constitution. Complaints can be made against members even if they have not ratified the relevant conventions, as occurred with New Zealand in 1993 in respect of the Employment Contracts Act. New Zealand has since ratified ILO Convention 98 on the right to organise and bargain collectively.

OECD – The OECD is a Paris-based body that has promoted economic cooperation and development among industrialised countries since 1961. Thirty countries are currently OECD members (talks are underway to expand membership). New Zealand has been a member since 1973.

The OECD brings together the governments of countries committed to democracy and the market economy to: support sustainable economic growth, boost employment, raise living standards, maintain financial stability, assist other countries' economic development, and contribute to growth in world trade.

The OECD prepares regular reports on individual member countries, to assess economic conditions and offer policy advice. It collects a range of labour statistics used in producing statistical comparisons and labour market analyses. Labour market conditions, particularly unemployment, are prominent in this analysis.

New Zealand attends meetings of the OECD ministerial council, and its working groups and committees, which cover a range of economic, social and development-related issues. It also contributes data to *Annual Labour Force Statistics* and *Quarterly Labour Force Statistics*, the main OECD labour statistics publications. New Zealand information is also used in other OECD publications, including the annual *Employment Outlook*.

Source: Department of Labour

Unions are legally recognised by the Act, and collective agreements can be negotiated only between unions and employers. In formally recognising the unions' role in promoting their members' collective employment interests, the Act views unions as providing a counterbalance to power differences in direct bargaining between employees and employers.

Minimal barriers to the formation of unions allow employees to form their own unions to represent their collective interests when bargaining, and provide protection to union and non-union members.

In relation to an employment issue, no one may give any preference or apply any undue influence on another because that person is or is not a member of a union.

Union representatives are entitled to enter a workplace, within certain limitations, for purposes related to the employment of union members, or the union's business.

The Act recognises that despite the requirement for all parties to an employment relationship to act in good faith, certain employment relationship problems require specialised assistance and institutions to promote and restore productive employment relationships.

An underlying assumption of the Employment Relations Act 2000 is that if problems in employment relationships are to be resolved promptly, expert problem-solving support, information and assistance needs to be available at short notice. The Act accordingly established mediation services and the Employment Relations Authority, while maintaining the Employment Court.

Mediation Services are provided by the Department of Labour to parties with an employment relationship problem. The services are professional, impartial, and provided by experienced mediators who offer responsive problem-solving assistance to parties. This assistance is available at short notice and at no cost. Mediation services are provided from offices in Auckland, Hamilton, Napier, Palmerston North, Wellington, Christchurch and Dunedin. Staff involved can provide services in other locations, including workplaces. Mediation focuses on providing a balanced and fair environment, empowering parties to solve their own problems.

Once parties reach a settlement in mediation, they can agree to ask the mediator to sign it. Once signed, the settlement cannot be challenged and is enforceable in the Employment Relations Authority or the district court. If the employer and employee cannot reach agreement in mediation, they can agree, in writing, to the mediator making a final and binding decision, which is also enforceable in the authority or the court. If either or both parties do not want the mediator to make a decision, the problem may be taken to the Employment Relations Authority for determination.

Employees and employers can reach a settlement without using mediation, and make it binding by having the written settlement signed by a mediator. Once the settlement is certified, it is enforceable in the authority or the court.

In the year ending 30 June 2007, the department completed 7,216 requests for mediation, and 2,338 recorded settlements were completed. Of the settlements achieved in mediation, 59 percent of complaints involved unjustified dismissal, while 33 percent involved disadvantage.

How New Zealand measures up – unemployment

Organisation for Economic Co-operation and Development (OECD) employment statistics define the labour force as civilian employees, the self-employed, unpaid family workers, professionals, conscripted members of the armed forces, and the unemployed.

The unemployed are defined as those people of working age (15 years and over) who, in a specified period, are without work and are both available for and actively seeking employment, or have a job to start. Between

1999 and 2006, New Zealand's unemployment rate fell from 6.8 percent to 3.8 percent. This was well below the OECD's 6.1 percent average unemployment rate for 2006.

Japan, the United States, Australia, the United Kingdom, Canada, Italy, France and Germany all had higher unemployment rates than New Zealand, while Korea's rate was lower.

OECD standardised unemployment rates
Selected averages for year ending 31 December

Country	1999	2000	2001	2002	2003	2004	2005	2006
Korea	6.6	4.4	4.0	3.3	3.6	3.7	3.7	3.5
New Zealand	6.8	6.0	5.3	5.2	4.6	3.9	3.7	3.8
Japan	4.7	4.7	5.0	5.4	5.3	4.7	4.4	4.1
United States	4.2	4.0	4.7	5.8	6.0	5.5	5.1	4.6
Australia	6.9	6.3	6.7	6.4	5.9	5.4	5.1	4.8
United Kingdom	5.9	5.3	5.0	5.1	4.9	4.7	4.8	5.3
OECD average	6.7	6.2	6.4	6.9	7.1	6.9	6.7	6.1
Canada	7.6	6.8	7.2	7.7	7.6	7.2	6.8	6.3
Italy	10.9	10.1	9.1	8.6	8.4	8.0	7.7	6.8
France	10.5	9.1	8.4	8.7	9.5	9.6	9.7	9.5
Germany	8.2	7.5	7.6	8.3	9.3	9.8	10.6	9.8

Source: OECD *Factbook 2007*

Herald on Sunday

Seventeen-year-old supermarket worker Adam Frain is supported by 69-year-old manager Eileen Herbert. Since April 2008, there has been no specific minimum wage for those under 18 years. More people are now staying in work beyond 65 years.

Employment Relations Authority The authority makes decisions on employment relations problems by establishing facts and considering the merits of a case without being bound by technicalities. It sits between mediation services offered by the Department of Labour and more formal court procedures. As such, the authority is the first judicial intervention for employment relations problem resolution.

The authority has exclusive jurisdiction to make decisions about employment relationship problems generally. Its work includes resolving disputes about the interpretation of employment agreements, matters relating to the breach of those agreements, and personal grievances. It also makes decisions relating to the recovery of wages and other monies, including the recovery of penalties incurred for breaches of employment agreements and minimum employment codes. In addition the authority decides matters relating to good faith bargaining, the registration of unions, union rules, and proceedings about strikes and lockouts.

The authority operates from offices in Auckland, Wellington and Christchurch, although it can travel to other locations. The Department of Labour provides administrative support to the authority, which currently has 17 members including the Chief of the Employment Relations Authority.

In the year ending 30 June 2007, the authority received 2,304 applications for problem resolution. Fifty-five percent of employment complaints involved unjustified dismissal, while 39 percent involved disadvantage.

Minimum entitlements

Statutory minimum entitlements apply to all employees. These include:

- an adult minimum wage for employees aged 18 and over. Since 1 April 2008, there has been no specific minimum wage for youth – instead, there is a new entrant minimum wage, which applies to some 16 and 17-year-old workers
- protection from unlawful deductions from wages
- 11 paid public holidays, if the holidays fall on days that would otherwise be working days for the employee
- time-and-a-half payment for all employees who work on public holidays and, if the day would otherwise be a working day for the employee, they are entitled to a whole day's alternative holiday
- four weeks paid annual holiday after 12 months employment – the minimum entitlement increased from three to four weeks on 1 April 2007
- paid parental leave, and employment protection for employees on parental leave
- equal pay for men and women doing substantially the same work.

Minimum wage The Minimum Wage Act 1983 determines national minimum wages for adults and young people, below which wages cannot generally fall. Since 1 April 2008, the minimum wage for people aged 16 years and over has been $12.00 per hour before tax, $96.00 for an eight-

Table 14.01

Movable public holidays

Holiday	2009	2010	2011
Good Friday	10 Apr	2 Apr	22 Apr
Easter Monday	13 Apr	5 Apr	25 Apr
Queen's Birthday[(1)]	1 Jun	7 Jun	6 Jun
Labour Day	26 Oct	25 Oct	24 Oct

(1) The Queen's actual birth date was 21 April 1926.

Source: Department of Labour

Older New Zealanders keep working

Otago Daily Times

Dave Peters is an 85-year-old worker at a Central Otago fruit packing house. By choosing to remain employed beyond the age of superannuation entitlement, he also helps to ease a shortage of seasonal workers.

A growing number of New Zealanders remain in the labour force beyond the age of superannuation entitlement, according to *New Zealand's 65+ Population: A statistical volume (2007)*, a report that brings together statistics on older New Zealanders – those aged 65 years and over.

More than two-fifths of men aged 65–69 years, and one-fifth of those aged 70–74 years were in full-time or part-time employment at the time of the 2006 Census, as were over a quarter of women aged 65–69 years.

New Zealanders are also living longer. Between 1950–52 and 2004–06, the proportion of New Zealand men living to age 65 increased from 68 percent to 86 percent. Women made even greater gains – about 90 percent are now likely to live to 65, and about half to 85 years.

Population ageing is more pronounced in the South Island than in the North Island, and also in some cities and districts. In 2006, the 65+ group was over 20 percent of all residents in four areas (compared with 12 percent nationally) – Thames Coromandel, Kapiti Coast, Horowhenua and Waitaki.

Source: Statistics New Zealand

hour day, and $480.00 for a 40-hour week. The new entrant rate for those entering the labour market for the first time is $9.60 an hour before tax. The minimum training wage is $9.60 an hour before tax.

Those not entitled to the minimum wage are those under the age of 16, people doing recognised industry training (involving at least 60 credits a year), holders of minimum wage exemptions (issued by the Department of Labour to those with recognised disabilities who are incapable of earning the minimum wage), and employees with disabilities in sheltered workshops. People doing recognised industry training are paid the minimum training wage.

Legislative changes A review of the Holidays Act 1981 resulted in new legislation governing minimum entitlements to annual, sick and bereavement leave; arrangements for those who work on public holidays; and the calculation of holiday pay entitlements. The new legislation also introduced a minimum of four weeks annual leave for all employees, effective from 1 April 2007. For further information, see 'Holidays' below.

A review of the Employment Relations Act's operation led to the Employment Relations Law Reform Bill, which aims to strengthen the Act's key objectives of promoting good faith collective bargaining and effective resolution of employment relationship problems.

Hours of work Working hours are generally negotiated into employment agreements. However, the employer may not unilaterally impose more than 40 hours of work (exclusive of overtime) a week.

Holidays

The Holidays Act 2003 contains minimum rights and obligations concerning annual leave, public holidays, sick leave and bereavement leave. These apply to employees whether they are full time, part time, permanent, casual or temporary. Employers and employees cannot contract out of the Act, but can agree to better terms and conditions.

Public holidays Legislation ensures that all employees receive 11 paid public holidays, as of right, if they fall on days which would otherwise be their working days. The statutory and public holidays are New Year's Day (1 January), 2 January, Waitangi Day (6 February), Anzac Day (25 April), Good Friday, Easter Monday, Queen's Birthday, Labour Day, Christmas Day (25 December), Boxing Day (26 December), and the anniversary day of a province or the day observed locally as that day.

Where employees work on a public holiday, and that day falls on one they would normally work, they are entitled to be paid at time-and-a-half for the hours they work, and to a whole day's alternative holiday. If the employee works on a public holiday and that day is one they would not normally work, the employee is entitled to time-and-a-half pay for the hours they work, but is not entitled to an alternative holiday. Where the Christmas/New Year period falls on either a Saturday or Sunday, the holidays are transferred to a Monday or Tuesday.

Annual holidays Under the Holidays Act 2003, employees are entitled to a minimum of four weeks annual holiday after the first year of employment. The minimum entitlement increased from three to four weeks on 1 April 2007. On each anniversary of the date of starting employment, on or after 1 April 2007, the employee is entitled to four weeks paid annual holiday. The leave can be taken at any time agreed between the employer and employee. Employees must be given the opportunity to take at least two of the four weeks leave in a continuous period, if they wish to.

Parental leave Eligible employees are entitled to up to 52 weeks parental leave, including 14 weeks of paid parental leave. There are several types of parental leave, each with its own entitlements and eligibility requirements. Eligible self-employed parents are entitled to 14 weeks paid parental leave. To be eligible, employees and self-employed people and their partners (including same-sex partners) must be expecting a baby, or adopting a child not more than five years old. Evidence of the pregnancy or adoption may be required by the employer to ensure eligibility for leave. Self-employed people must attach this evidence to their application for paid parental leave. Employees must have worked at least an average of 10 hours a week for the same employer for the six or 12 months preceding the expected date of delivery or adoption. Self-employed people must have been self-employed for at least an average of 10 hours a week for the six or 12 months preceding the expected date of delivery or adoption. In most cases, applications for parental leave should be made in writing to employers at least three months before the expected date of delivery. Following approval from their employer, an employee can apply for paid parental leave from Inland Revenue. Self-employed people apply for paid parental leave directly from Inland Revenue.

Sick and bereavement leave Employees are entitled to sick and bereavement leave whether they are full time, part time, permanent, casual or temporary. After six months with an employer, an employee is entitled to five days sick leave on pay for each subsequent 12 months of employment. Unused sick leave can be carried over, to a maximum of 20 days. Sick leave can be taken if an employee is sick, or if their spouse, dependent child, or a dependent parent of an employee or their spouse is sick. In addition, after six months employment, an employee is entitled to paid bereavement leave. On the death of an employee's spouse, parent, child, sibling, grandparent, father-in-law or mother-in-law, the employee is entitled to three days paid leave. The employee is also entitled to one day's paid leave when the employer accepts that due to the death of any person, an employee has suffered bereavement.

Equal employment opportunities

An equal employment opportunities (EEO) environment helps ensure employers tap the full potential of a diverse workforce. EEO principles are supported in New Zealand by anti-discrimination legislation.

Under the Human Rights Act 1993, an employer cannot discriminate in hiring, training, promoting or dismissing because of an employee's sex, marital status, religious or ethical belief, colour, race, ethnic or national origin, disability, age, political opinion, employment status, family status or sexual orientation.

Discrimination in terms and conditions of employment, training, promotion and dismissal because of an employee's colour, race, ethnic or national origin, sex, age, marital status, or religious or ethical belief, and sexual harassment, are grounds for taking a personal grievance under the Employment Relations Act 2001.

The Equal Pay Act 1972 provides that employers cannot differentiate in pay rates between employees on the basis of their sex.

Employees may make a complaint under the Human Rights Act, or may use personal grievance procedures under the Employment Relations Act, to enforce their rights in cases of alleged discrimination or sexual harassment.

New Zealand Council of Trade Unions

The New Zealand Council of Trade Unions Te Kauae Kaimahi (CTU) is the national voice and advocate for worker interests.

The CTU is made up of unions representing workers in all sectors of the workforce and unites private and public sector unions. It has active local and representative structures and represents New Zealand workers internationally.

The council promotes a wide economic and social development agenda, as well as organising around core issues such as collective bargaining, and health and safety.

Business New Zealand

Business New Zealand is New Zealand's largest business advocacy body, representing the combined members of five regional business organisations and more than 60 industry associations.

Business New Zealand promotes public policy that supports an open, competitive economy and private enterprise. The organisation resulted from a merger between the New Zealand Employers' Federation and the New Zealand Manufacturers' Federation.

Work stoppages

Work stoppage information is used as an indicator of the state of industrial relations in New Zealand. It focuses particularly on the economic impact of events such as strikes and lockouts, but does not cover stop-work meetings, strike notices, protest marches and public rallies. Demarcation and coverage disputes are included only where participants are on strike or locked out.

Trade union membership

For the year to December 2006, there was modest growth in union membership of 5,190 (1.4 percent), to reach 382,538 members. This indicates a slowing in growth during 2006, after a 23,290 (6.6 percent) increase in 2005. Overall, there has been a 25 percent increase in New Zealand union membership since 1999.

Due to a significant 2.6 percent increase in the number of wage and salary earners in 2006 (up from 1,719,500 to 1,764,500) there was a fall in overall union density (the proportion of wage and salary earners who are union members). This figure fell from 21.9 percent in 2005, to 21.7 percent in 2006. Overall union density has been 21–22 percent since 1998, following a rapid decline earlier in the 1990s.

The table below summarises current union membership in New Zealand.

Trade unions, membership and union density
Year ending December 1991–2006

Year	Number of unions	Union membership	Number of wage and salary earners	Union density (%)
1991	66	514,325	1,196,100	43.0
1992	58	428,160	1,203,900	35.6
1993	67	409,112	1,241,300	33.0
1994	82	375,906	1,314,100	28.6
1995	82	362,200	1,357,500	26.7
1996	83	338,967	1,409,300	24.1
1997	80	327,800	1,424,000	23.0
1998	83	306,687	1,399,100	21.9
1999	82	302,405	1,435,900	21.1
2000	134	318,519	1,477,300	21.6
2001	165	329,919	1,524,900	21.6
2002	174	334,783	1,566,400	21.4
2003	181	341,631	1,598,700	21.4
2004	170	354,058	1,676,200	21.1
2005	175	377,348	1,719,500	21.9
2006	166	382,538	1,764,500	21.7

Sources: Statistics New Zealand, Victoria University of Wellington

Table 14.02

EEO groups represented in the Public Service and the employed labour force

EEO group		2000	2001	2002	2003	2004	2005	2006	2007
		Percent							
Ethnicity[1]									
Māori	Public Service[2][3]	16.9	17.0	17.6	17.6	17.4	17.5	16.7	16.8
	Employed labour force	8.9	8.8	9.5	9.4	8.7	8.8	9.0	9.2
Pacific peoples	Public Service[2][3]	6.6	6.6	6.8	7.1	7.1	7.3	7.4	7.6
	Employed labour force	4.0	4.0	4.5	4.4	4.4	4.0	4.4	3.8
People with disabilities[4]	Public Service	..	18.5	..	..	..	..	..[5]	..
	Employed labour force	..	14.6	..	..	..	..	..[5]	..
Women	Public Service[2]	56.2	56.5	57.5	57.8	59.0	59.1	59.4	59.2
	Employed labour force	45.1	45.7	45.7	45.8	45.3	46.2	46.2	46.2

(1) Public Service ethnicity data double-counts people with more than one ethnicity, so a person who is Māori and Samoan is counted as both Māori and Pacific peoples. The labour force figures are sourced from Statistics New Zealand's Household Labour Force Survey and use a priority reporting system that slightly reduces the Pacific peoples' figure. The figures are the percentage of people whose ethnicity is known, not the total population. (2) Data from the State Services Commission's Human Resource Capability Survey of Public Service Departments, at 30 June each year. (3) Ethnicity data from 2000 to 2004 was revised in 2005 due to substantial amendments made to data by one department. (4) Disability data comes from the five-yearly Statistics New Zealand Disability Survey. Disability statistics are no longer collected in the Human Resource Capability survey because of concerns about data quality. The 2005 Career Progression and Development Survey indicated that the proportion of people who self-identified as having a disability was 7 percent, compared with 8 percent in the 2000 survey. These figures are not comparable with Statistics New Zealand's figures because of different definitions and collection methods. (5) Disability rates for those in the labour force were not published as part of the initial release from the 2006 survey.
Symbol: .. figure not available

Source: State Services Commission

Conservation in the workplace

Workplace advocacy groups have teamed up with the Energy Efficiency and Conservation Authority to promote energy saving in the workplace.

The New Zealand Council of Trade Unions and Business New Zealand have formed a partnership to raise awareness among workers about steps they can take to reduce greenhouse gas emissions and promote energy efficiency.

The first initiative is a basic brochure with a checklist to use in the workplace, and information about energy efficiency in the home and with transport options. A website is being established and an interactive education programme developed.

Many suggestions seem obvious – turn off equipment not in use, make the most of natural light, use energy intensive equipment in off-peak hours, use timers and thermostats to regulate energy use, install energy-efficient light bulbs, investigate car pooling, and use public transport and cycle options. But the main aim of the partnership is to encourage workers and managers to discuss the best options for energy efficiency – and for this information to flow into the home.

The New Zealand Energy Efficiency and Conservation Strategy, announced in October 2007, supports the programme to encourage participation in workplace energy management.

Although emissions trading will put a price on greenhouse gases, the partners in this project recognise it will also take concerted and cooperative action to change behaviour. Raising awareness is a good start but the real test will be when workplaces take active steps on energy management.

Source: Council of Trade Unions

The New Zealand Herald

Waterside workers picket the entrance at Auckland's container wharf in October 2007. They were on a 48-hour strike over award negotiations. Since 1986 the number of work stoppages has fallen to levels last seen in the 1930s.

For statistical purposes, work stoppages are defined not only as those disputes which result in the complete withdrawal of labour by workers, or a lockout by employers, but also disputes in which there is an organised 'go-slow', refusal to work overtime, or another method of passive resistance.

Table 14.03 shows that since 1986 the number of work stoppages has fallen to levels last recorded in the early 1930s.

There were 42 work stoppages in the year ending 31 December 2006, compared with 71 in 1991 and 215 in 1986 (before the Employment Contracts Act 1991). The number of employees involved in work stoppages has also decreased. In 2006, 10,079 people were involved; fewer than the 23,309 people in 2002 and considerably lower than the hundreds of thousands involved in stoppages during the 1970s and 1980s.

The manufacturing industry accounted for around 31 percent of the 42 stoppages in 2006. However, the health and community services industry had the greatest number of employees involved (3,495), the greatest number of days lost (11,562) and the greatest estimated loss in wages and salaries ($2,726,000).

Table 14.03

			Work stoppages		
			Year ending 31 December		
Year	Stoppages	Employees involved	Total person days of work lost	Average person days of work lost per employee involved	Estimated loss of wages/ salaries
			Number		$(000)
1921	77	10,433	119,208	11.4	180
1926	59	6,264	47,811	7.6	65
1931	24	6,356	48,486	7.6	89
1936	43	7,354	16,980	2.3	26
1941	89	15,261	26,237	1.7	69
1946	96	15,696	30,393	1.9	80
1951	109	36,878	1,157,390	31.4	6,223
1956	50	13,579	23,870	1.8	168
1961	71	16,626	38,185	2.3	299
1966	145	33,132	99,095	3.0	878
1971	313	86,009	162,563	1.9	2,109
1976	487	201,085	488,441	2.4	10,840
1981	291	135,006	388,086	2.9	20,411
1986	215	100,633	1,329,054	13.2	119,496
1991	71	51,962	99,032	1.9	11,577
1996	72	42,307	69,514	1.6	9,768
2001	42	22,022	54,440	2.5	7,682
2002	46	23,309	34,398	1.5	4,979
2003	28	5,098	19,463	3.8	4,250
2004	34	6,127	6,162	1.0	1,025
2005	60	17,752	30,028	1.7	4,813
2006	42	10,079	27,983	2.8	5,211

Sources: Department of Labour, Statistics New Zealand

Labour force

The Household labour Force Survey (HLFS) produces estimates on statistics relating to the New Zealand labour market. Each quarter the HLFS publishes statistics on employment, unemployment and people not in the labour force, for the working-age population – the usually resident, non-institutionalised, civilian population aged 15 years and over.

In general terms, the labour force includes those in the working-age population who are either 'employed' or 'unemployed'.

The employed category includes all people in the working-age population who work for one hour or more a week for pay or profit, either as an employee or self-employed, or who work without pay for one hour or more in a family business.

The unemployed category includes all people in the working-age population who are without a paid job, are available for work and have either actively sought work in the past four weeks, or have a new job to start within the next four weeks.

These definitions are used by Statistics New Zealand's quarterly HLFS and conform closely to standard definitions of the International Labour Organization.

Table 14.04 shows that between September 2004 and September 2007, the number of people in employment increased by 127,700. At the same time, the number of people unemployed decreased by 800.

Table 14.04

Labour force[1]
By sex
Quarterly, 2004–2007

Quarter		Employed	Unemployed	Total labour force	Not in the labour force	Working-age population[2]	Labour force participation rate	Unemployment rate
		(000)					Percent	
Male								
2004	Sep	1,089.5	38.7	1,128.3	395.8	1,524.1	74.0	3.4
	Dec	1,119.4	37.2	1,156.7	373.5	1,530.2	75.6	3.2
2005	Mar	1,112.4	45.5	1,157.9	378.6	1,536.6	75.4	3.9
	Jun	1,105.3	40.4	1,145.7	395.3	1,541.0	74.3	3.5
	Sep	1,116.7	36.8	1,153.5	391.3	1,544.7	74.7	3.2
	Dec	1,139.2	35.1	1,174.3	376.8	1,551.1	75.7	3.0
2006	Mar	1,138.5	45.6	1,184.2	374.3	1,558.5	76.0	3.9
	Jun	1,138.5	37.1	1,175.6	387.5	1,563.1	75.2	3.2
	Sep	1,136.1	41.2	1,177.4	390.7	1,568.1	75.1	3.5
	Dec	1,158.1	40.7	1,198.8	376.0	1,574.8	76.1	3.4
2007	Mar	1,158.4	45.3	1,203.7	377.6	1,581.3	76.1	3.8
	Jun	1,155.5	37.8	1,193.3	391.8	1,585.1	75.3	3.2
	Sep	1,158.0	38.0	1,196.0	393.1	1,589.1	75.3	3.2
Female								
2004	Sep	925.0	37.6	962.5	648.9	1,611.4	59.7	3.9
	Dec	954.4	37.7	992.1	625.9	1,618.0	61.3	3.8
2005	Mar	942.4	44.2	986.6	636.8	1,623.5	60.8	4.5
	Jun	947.3	35.7	983.0	644.5	1,627.5	60.4	3.6
	Sep	961.9	38.9	1,000.7	630.6	1,631.3	61.3	3.9
	Dec	966.4	40.4	1,006.8	630.6	1,637.4	61.5	4.0
2006	Mar	969.4	49.7	1,019.1	625.3	1,644.4	62.0	4.9
	Jun	977.0	39.2	1,016.2	632.7	1,648.9	61.6	3.9
	Sep	973.6	38.4	1,012.1	641.7	1,653.8	61.2	3.8
	Dec	977.4	38.4	1,015.8	644.7	1,660.6	61.2	3.8
2007	Mar	985.8	48.5	1,034.3	631.9	1,666.3	62.1	4.7
	Jun	992.5	39.4	1,031.9	637.6	1,669.5	61.8	3.8
	Sep	984.1	37.6	1,021.7	651.2	1,672.9	61.1	3.7
Total								
2004	Sep	2,014.5	76.3	2,090.8	1,044.7	3,135.5	66.7	3.6
	Dec	2,073.8	75.0	2,148.8	999.4	3,148.2	68.3	3.5
2005	Mar	2,054.8	89.7	2,144.6	1,015.5	3,160.1	67.9	4.2
	Jun	2,052.6	76.2	2,128.7	1,039.8	3,168.5	67.2	3.6
	Sep	2,078.6	75.6	2,154.2	1,021.8	3,176.0	67.8	3.5
	Dec	2,105.6	75.5	2,181.1	1,007.4	3,188.5	68.4	3.5
2006	Mar	2,107.9	95.3	2,203.3	999.6	3,202.8	68.8	4.3
	Jun	2,115.5	76.3	2,191.8	1,020.1	3,212.0	68.2	3.5
	Sep	2,109.8	79.7	2,189.4	1,032.5	3,221.9	68.0	3.6
	Dec	2,135.5	79.1	2,214.7	1,020.7	3,235.4	68.5	3.6
2007	Mar	2,144.2	93.8	2,238.0	1,009.5	3,247.5	68.9	4.2
	Jun	2,148.1	77.2	2,225.2	1,029.4	3,254.6	68.4	3.5
	Sep	2,142.2	75.5	2,217.7	1,044.3	3,262.0	68.0	3.4

(1) Unadjusted figures. (2) The civilian, non-institutionalised, usually resident New Zealand population aged 15 and over.

Source: Statistics New Zealand

Table 14.05

Labour force participation rates[1]
By sex and age group
Average for year ending 30 Sep 2007

Age group (years)	Male	Female	Total
		Percent	
15–19	55.5	57.2	56.3
20–24	80.6	68.0	74.4
25–29	91.5	72.9	82.0
30–34	92.3	72.8	82.1
35–39	93.3	72.4	82.4
40–44	92.7	79.2	85.7
45–49	92.8	81.2	86.9
50–54	91.1	79.4	85.2
55–59	86.8	72.2	79.4
60–64	75.7	52.9	64.2
65+	19.5	9.3	14.0
All ages	**75.7**	**61.5**	**68.4**

(1) Unadjusted figures.

Source: Statistics New Zealand

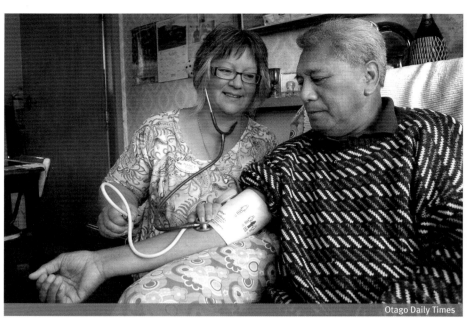
Otago Daily Times

Nancy Todd, a nurse with a Dunedin mobile nursing service for Māori and Pacific people, attends to patient John Whatuira in his home. For the year ending September 2007, the labour force participation rate for females was 61.5 percent.

The total labour force grew by 126,900 (6.1 percent) in the three years, to reach 2,217,700 in the September 2007 quarter. The working-age population increased by 126,500 (4.0 percent) in the same period.

Between the September 2004 and September 2007 quarters, the male labour force increased 6.0 percent, while the female labour force increased 6.2 percent. Both male and female unemployment rates decreased between the quarters.

Labour force participation rates by sex

Labour force participation rates for both males and females increased in the four years ending 30 September 2007.

The female rate increased more than the male rate, but there was still a large gap between them. For the year ending 30 September 2007, the overall labour force participation rate for males was 75.7 percent and for females it was 61.5 percent.

Table 14.05 shows female participation in the labour force is lower than male participation for every age group, except the 15–19-year group. This trend was most marked in the 25–39-year group, which includes the main childbearing ages.

Employment

For the year ending 30 September 2007, there were 1,664,000 people employed in full-time work and 478,500 in part-time work. (Full-time work involves working 30 or more hours a week.)

Table 14.06 shows that between the years ending 30 September 1991 and 2007, part-time employment growth was stronger than full-time employment growth. Full-time employment increased by 37.9 percent and part-time by 50.0 percent.

In 2007, there were 347,900 women in part-time work and 130,600 men. For the same period there were 1,026,900 men and 637,100 women in full-time work.

Status in employment

Table 14.07 shows that the majority of employed people (82.7 percent) were employees (wage or salary earners) in their main job in the year ending 30 September 2007. Those who were self-employed (and not employing others) were the next largest group – at 10.9 percent of the employed population.

While the number of employees is similar for males and females, males dominated the employer (72.0 percent) and self-employed (67.2 percent) categories in the year ending 30 September 2007. The 'unpaid relative assisting' category is dominated by females, who make up 64.7 percent of this group.

Table 14.06

Full-time and part-time employment[1]
By sex
Average for year ending 30 September

Year	Employed full time			Employed part time			Employed total		
	Male	Female	Total	Male	Female	Total	Male	Female	**Total**
					(ooo)				
1991	774.0	432.4	1,206.4	79.4	239.5	318.9	853.4	671.9	**1,525.3**
1996	865.6	491.7	1,357.3	98.4	287.4	385.8	964.0	779.1	**1,743.2**
2001	887.8	539.4	1,427.2	113.7	302.5	416.1	1,001.5	841.8	**1,843.3**
2002	912.7	549.1	1,461.8	118.6	316.7	435.3	1,031.3	865.8	**1,897.1**
2003	935.3	564.9	1,500.2	115.8	322.5	438.4	1,051.1	887.5	**1,938.6**
2004	964.8	590.3	1,555.1	118.3	321.8	440.1	1,083.1	912.0	**1,995.2**
2005	996.3	613.8	1,610.1	117.1	337.7	454.9	1,113.5	951.5	**2,064.9**
2006	1,021.8	629.8	1,651.6	116.3	341.8	458.1	1,138.1	971.6	**2,109.7**
2007	1,026.9	637.1	1,664.0	130.6	347.9	478.5	1,157.5	984.9	**2,142.5**

(1) Unadjusted figures.
Note: Figures may not add up to stated totals due to rounding.

Source: Statistics New Zealand

Table 14.07

People employed in 2002 and 2007[1][2]
By employment status and sex

Status	Male			Female			Total		
	2002	2007	Change	2002	2007	Change	2002	2007	Change
	(ooo)		Percent	(ooo)		Percent	(ooo)		Percent
Employee	778.0	910.4	17.0	749.4	859.9	14.7	1,527.4	1,770.3	15.9
Employer	93.2	79.5	-14.7	38.5	30.9	-19.6	131.7	110.5	-16.1
Self employed	154.2	157.1	1.9	68.5	76.6	11.9	222.7	233.8	5.0
Unpaid relative assisting	5.7	9.0	56.4	9.3	16.5	77.1	15.0	25.5	69.2
Not specified	--	1.5	--	--	1.0	--	--	2.5	--
Total	**1,031.3**	**1,157.5**	**12.2**	**865.8**	**984.9**	**13.8**	**1,897.1**	**2,142.5**	**12.9**

(1) Average for year ending 30 September. (2) Unadjusted figures.
Note: Figures may not add up to stated totals due to rounding.
Symbol: -- estimates are fewer than 1,000 and subject to sampling error too great for most purposes.

Source: Statistics New Zealand

There were a number of shifts in employment status between 2002 and 2007, when the total number of employed people increased by 245,400 (12.9 percent). The number of employees rose by 242,900 (15.9 percent), and the number of employers fell by 21,300 (16.1 percent). There was an 11,100 increase (5.0 percent) in the number who were self-employed (and not employing others), while the number of unpaid relatives assisting grew by 10,400 (69.2 percent).

Industry structure of the labour force

More people are employed in the services sector (wholesale and retail trade, restaurants and hotels; finance and insurance, property and business services; education, health and community, and other services) than manufacturing. Table 14.08 (overleaf) shows the average number of employed people by industry and by sex in the year ending 30 September 2007.

The largest number of employed people worked in the education, health and community, and other services area (27.7 percent); followed by wholesale and retail trade, restaurants and hotels (22.4 percent); and finance and insurance, property and business services (14.7 percent). Industries that employed the least number of people were mining; and electricity, gas and water supply; each with less than 1.0 percent of the total employed.

Male employment was highest in wholesale and retail trade, restaurants and hotels (which employed 20.3 percent of males), followed by manufacturing (17.3 percent), and education, health and community, and other services (16.4 percent). Combined, those industries accounted for 54.0 percent of male employment.

Female employment was highest in education, health and community, and other services (41.1 percent), and wholesale and retail trade, restaurants and hotels (24.7 percent).

Apprentice numbers continue to rise

More than 10,000 'modern apprentices' were involved in structured workplace learning programmes at 30 June 2007 – a 12.2 percent increase since 30 June 2006.

The Modern Apprenticeship Scheme aims to increase the number of young people in systematic industry training, which leads to national qualifications.

The scheme began nationally on 1 January 2001, following passage of the Modern Apprenticeship Training Act 2000. By 30 June 2007 there were 49 modern apprenticeship coordinators throughout New Zealand, covering 32 broad industry groups.

The Tertiary Education Commission arranges for coordinators to provide a range of services to employers, and to 16–21-year-old employees seeking to achieve national certificates at levels 3–4 on the National Qualifications Framework.

Coordinators assist employers with recruitment, provide support and mentoring for apprentices, and liaise with industry training organisations and education providers to help apprentices achieve their qualifications. Some modern apprenticeships are also available to older people wanting to start new careers.

Of the 10,289 modern apprentices in workplace learning at 30 June 2007, 77.0 percent were European, 15.0 percent were Māori, 3.4 percent were Pacific peoples, with the rest from other ethnic groups. Over 8.0 percent were women.

Industries providing modern apprenticeships at 30 June 2007 were: aeronautical engineering, agriculture, architectural aluminium joinery, baking, boat building, building and construction, contracting, dairy manufacturing, electricity supply, electrotechnology, engineering, extractives, flooring, food processing, forest industries, furniture, horticulture, hospitality, joinery, motor engineering, painting and decorating, plastics, plumbing, printing, public sector, retail, road transport, seafood, sports turf, telecommunications, tourism, and water.

Source: Tertiary Education Commission

Table 14.08

People employed in 2007[1]
By sex and industry
Average for year ending 30 September

Industry group	Number			Proportion of total		
	Male	Female	Total	Male	Female	Total
	(000)			Percent		
Agriculture, forestry and fishing	104.0	49.3	153.4	9.0	5.0	7.2
Mining	5.6	1.2	6.9	0.5	0.1	0.3
Manufacturing	199.9	74.2	274.1	17.3	7.5	12.8
Electricity, gas and water supply	6.8	1.9	8.7	0.6	0.2	0.4
Construction	164.2	21.2	185.5	14.2	2.2	8.7
Wholesale and retail trade, restaurants and hotels	235.5	243.3	478.9	20.3	24.7	22.4
Transport, storage and communications	83.6	33.5	117.1	7.2	3.4	5.5
Finance and insurance, property and business services	162.4	152.0	314.4	14.0	15.4	14.7
Education, health and community, and other services	189.4	404.5	593.9	16.4	41.1	27.7
Not specified	6.0	3.6	9.6	0.5	0.4	0.4
Total	**1,157.5**	**984.9**	**2,142.5**	**100.0**	**100.0**	**100.0**

(1) Unadjusted figures.
Note: Figures may not add up to stated totals due to rounding.

Source: Statistics New Zealand

Occupational structure of the labour force

Statistics New Zealand classifies occupations into nine major groups for the purpose of statistical collection and reporting.

Table 14.09 shows the spread of employed people across these groups. In the year ending 30 September 2007, the proportions of people in each occupation remained relatively constant compared with previous years. The largest occupational groups in the September 2007 year were service and sales workers, and professionals. Together, these groups accounted for 31.5 percent of all employed people.

The smallest occupation group was elementary occupations, accounting for 5.5 percent of all employed people. The largest group for males was trades workers, where 18.3 percent of males were employed. The largest group for females was service and sales workers, accounting for 21.6 percent of female employment.

Traditional 'male' and 'female' occupations continue to exist in the New Zealand labour force. Men are over-represented as trades workers, and plant and machine operators and assemblers. Women are over-represented in the service and sales, and clerk occupations.

Table 14.09

People employed in 2007
By sex and occupation
Average for year ending 30 September

Major occupation group	Number			Proportion of total		
	Male	Female	Total	Male	Female	Total
	(000)			Percent		
Legislators, administrators, managers	166.4	111.0	277.3	14.4	11.3	12.9
Professionals	166.6	187.4	354.1	14.4	19.0	16.5
Technicians and associate professionals	116.6	141.3	257.9	10.1	14.3	12.0
Clerks	58.5	201.4	259.9	5.1	20.4	12.1
Service and sales workers	109.0	212.3	321.3	9.4	21.6	15.0
Agriculture and fishery workers	107.0	43.4	150.4	9.2	4.4	7.0
Trades workers	212.2	9.5	221.6	18.3	1.0	10.3
Plant and machine operators and assemblers	145.2	29.9	175.1	12.5	3.0	8.2
Elementary occupations	72.1	45.9	118.0	6.2	4.7	5.5
Not specified	3.9	2.8	6.7	0.3	0.3	0.3
Total	**1,157.5**	**984.9**	**2,142.5**	**100.0**	**100.0**	**100.0**

Note: Figures may not add up to stated totals due to rounding.

Source: Statistics New Zealand

Unemployment

The official measure of unemployment in New Zealand comes from the Household Labour Force Survey. Unemployed people are defined as those in the working-age population (the usually resident, non-institutionalised civilian population aged 15 years and over) who, during the reference week, were without a paid job, were available for work and had actively sought work in the past four weeks, or had a new job to start within four weeks.

A person whose only job search method in the previous four weeks had been to look at job advertisements in newspapers is not considered to be actively seeking work.

Apprentice Kevin Young (right) achieved a national certificate in flat glass glazing. Watching are industry and training representatives Bill Cubitt, John Lister and Deborah Paul. More than 10,000 'modern apprentices' were in structured workplace learning in 2007.

Demographic and social characteristics of the unemployed

An average 81,400 people (3.7 percent of the labour force) were estimated to be unemployed in New Zealand in the year ending 30 September 2007. The male unemployment rate was 3.4 percent and the female rate 4.0 percent.

Table 14.10 shows the average number of unemployed in the year ending 30 September 2007 by sex and educational attainment. The unemployment rate is highest for those with no qualifications (6.2 percent), and lowest for those with post-school and school qualifications (2.3 percent).

Table 14.11 (overleaf) compares the number of unemployed people by educational attainment for census years 1991, 1996 and 2001, and in the years ending 30 September 2002 to 2007.

Helping communities build work skills

Enterprising Community grants help not-for-profit community organisations create community-based enterprises that provide employment opportunities for people who are finding it hard to get work.

Funding is available for a maximum of three years and projects must be financially independent once the funding ceases.

Projects must target one or more of the priority groups identified by Work and Income. These groups include: long-term unemployed, Māori, Pacific peoples, youth, mature workers, sole parents, people with disabilities, refugees and migrants.

Projects need to contribute to supporting:

- community-owned businesses which generate assets and work opportunities to address the needs of the local community
- community-owned businesses providing employment opportunities and work experience for those who are disadvantaged in the labour market
- initiatives that lead to environmentally-based employment opportunities
- projects that work with identified migrant communities to develop skills needed to access the labour market.

Funding is provided for 12 months at a time, with further funding dependent on projects achieving their objectives.

Source: Ministry of Social Development

Figure 14.01

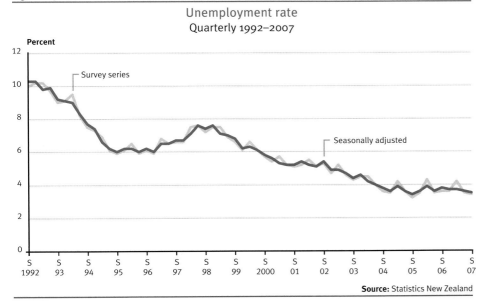

Unemployment rate
Quarterly 1992–2007

Source: Statistics New Zealand

Table 14.10

People unemployed in 2007
By sex and educational attainment
Average for year ending 30 September

Educational attainment	Number (000)			Unemployment rate (percent)		
	Male	Female	Total	Male	Female	Total
No qualifications	13.7	11.6	25.4	6.0	6.5	6.2
School qualification	10.7	11.4	22.1	4.2	4.4	4.3
No school but post-school qualification	4.6	4.2	8.8	3.3	5.0	3.9
Post-school and school qualification	11.0	13.2	24.2	2.0	2.7	2.3
Not specified	--	--	--	--	--	--
Total	**40.4**	**41.0**	**81.4**	**3.4**	**4.0**	**3.7**

Note: Figures may not add up to stated totals due to rounding.

Symbol: -- estimates are fewer than 1,000 and subject to sampling errors too great for most purposes.

Source: Statistics New Zealand

Table 14.11

People unemployed 1991–2007[1]
By educational attainment

Year	No qualification	School qualification	No school but post-school qualification	Post-school and school qualification	Not specified	Total unemployed
			(000)			
1991	68.5	42.5	17.7	35.7	1.6	**166.0**
1996	44.3	28.8	11.5	29.1	--	**114.1**
2001	34.0	28.1	10.1	31.6	--	**104.1**
2002	33.0	27.4	13.2	31.3	--	**105.5**
2003	28.1	25.5	11.6	30.3	--	**96.0**
2004	25.9	22.4	10.3	27.6	--	**86.4**
2005	24.8	21.1	8.6	24.3	--	**79.1**
2006	24.3	22.8	8.9	25.2	--	**81.7**
2007	25.4	22.1	8.8	24.2	--	**81.4**

(1) Averages for census years 1991, 1996, and 2001, then for year ending 30 September.
Note: Figures may not add up to stated totals due to rounding.
Symbol: -- estimates are fewer than 1,000 and subject to sampling errors too great for most purposes.

Source: Statistics New Zealand

Table 14.12

People unemployed in 2007
By sex and age group
Average for year ending 30 September

Age group (years)	Number (000)			Unemployment rate (percent)		
	Male	Female	Total	Male	Female	Total
15–19	13.5	12.1	25.7	15.1	13.8	14.4
20–24	7.1	7.0	14.1	5.9	7.2	6.5
25–29	4.4	4.3	8.7	3.8	4.4	4.1
30–34	2.9	3.0	5.9	2.4	2.9	2.6
35–39	2.5	3.3	5.8	1.8	2.9	2.3
40–44	2.2	3.9	6.1	1.6	3.0	2.3
45–49	2.9	3.6	6.5	2.1	2.8	2.4
50–54	1.9	1.7	3.6	1.6	1.6	1.6
55–59	1.7	1.2	2.9	1.7	1.3	1.5
60–64	--	--	1.5	--	--	1.3
65+	--	--	--	--	--	--
Total	**40.4**	**41.0**	**81.4**	**3.4**	**4.0**	**3.7**

Note: Figures may not add up to stated totals due to rounding.
Symbol: -- estimates are fewer than 1,000 and subject to sampling errors too great for most purposes.

Source: Statistics New Zealand

Table 14.13

Proportions of people unemployed[1]
By age group (years)
1991–2007[2]

Year	15–19	20–24	25–29	30–34	35–39	40–44	45–49	50–54	55–59	60–64	65+
						Percent					
1991	21.1	20.4	14.8	12.2	8.8	7.8	5.7	4.7	3.4	--	--
1996	21.7	17.4	12.1	10.8	10.2	9.3	7.6	5.2	3.7	1.5	--
2001	22.2	16.7	10.2	10.0	9.4	9.7	6.7	6.8	5.2	2.9	--
2002	22.4	16.1	11.1	10.3	9.8	9.3	6.7	6.6	3.9	3.1	--
2003	23.6	15.0	10.4	10.9	9.9	9.2	5.2	6.1	5.3	3.9	--
2004	24.1	16.6	10.4	10.0	9.0	8.0	6.3	5.9	5.8	3.3	--
2005	26.6	17.8	10.9	8.8	8.6	6.9	6.1	6.3	4.8	2.4	--
2006	26.9	17.1	9.8	8.3	7.7	8.5	7.5	5.3	4.9	2.8	1.2
2007	31.5	17.3	10.7	7.2	7.1	7.5	8.0	4.4	3.5	1.9	--

(1) Number of unemployed in each age group divided by total unemployed. (2) Averages for years ending 30 September.
Symbol: -- estimates are fewer than 1,000 and subject to sampling errors too great for most purposes.

Source: Statistics New Zealand

Table 14.12 shows that unemployment was highest in the younger age groups of the working-age population in the year ending 30 September 2007. The unemployment rate for the 15–19-year group was 14.4 percent, compared with the overall rate of 3.7 percent. The lowest unemployment rate (1.3 percent) was for the 60–64-year group.

Table 14.13 shows the proportions of the total unemployed represented by each age group. The trend in recent years has been for the highest proportion to be in the 15–19-year group. In general, the older the age group the less it contributes to total unemployment. The 15–19-year group has shown increases in its proportion over time, while most other age groups have shown decreases.

Table 14.14

People unemployed in 2007
By sex and ethnicity[1]
Average for year ending 30 September

Ethnicity	Number (000)			Unemployment rate (percent)		
	Male	Female	Total	Male	Female	Total
New Zealand European	23.1	20.6	43.7	2.6	2.7	2.6
Māori	7.5	9.6	17.2	6.6	8.8	7.7
Pacific peoples	3.4	3.6	7.0	6.1	8.2	7.1
Other	6.4	7.2	13.5	4.8	6.6	5.6
Not specified	--	--	--	--	--	--
Total	**40.4**	**41.0**	**81.4**	**3.4**	**4.0**	**3.7**

(1) Ethnicity is self-determined. Respondents choose up to three ethnicities, which are then prioritised.

Note: Figures may not add up to stated totals due to rounding.

Symbol: -- estimates are fewer than 1,000 and subject to sampling errors too great for most purposes.

Source: Statistics New Zealand

The unemployment rate for New Zealand Europeans is lower than for all other ethnic groups. Table 14.14 shows that the average unemployment rate for the year ending 30 September 2007 was 2.6 percent for New Zealand Europeans, 7.7 percent for Māori, 7.1 percent for Pacific peoples, and 5.6 percent for the Other ethnic group.

Employment assistance

One of the roles of the Ministry of Social Development is to provide employment assistance to New Zealanders. These services are supplied from more than 190 locations throughout the country, including seven contact centres and 11 regional offices.

Decreasing use of employment assistance in recent years largely reflects the lower number of registered job seekers.

Work and Income offers a range of services to assist job seekers into paid employment – including job search skills and work confidence programmes.

- Information services and work confidence – programmes which help with motivation and confidence when seeking paid work, and supply information on job search techniques and resources. In the year ending June 2007, clients participated in information services

Easing into employment

Transition to Work assistance is available to help people make a successful transition from benefit to paid employment, or to remain in paid employment.

Transition to Work assistance consists of work start and transition to work grants, pathways payments, new employment transition grants, and seasonal work assistance.

Work start and transition to work grants meet the costs of attending a job interview, or taking up paid work, for recipients who are unlikely to do either without receiving the grant. In the year ending June 2007, 54,800 grants were provided, 5,602 more than in the previous year.

Pathways payments help people entering paid work with living costs, for the time between their benefit stopping and receiving their first employment payment. Recipients must have a dependent child or children, and have received a benefit for 12 months or more before entering paid employment. In the year ending June 2007, 6,673 payments were provided, 261 fewer than in 2006.

New employment transition grants compensate people for loss of income arising from sickness (their own or that of a family member), or the need to care for a child. Recipients must have a dependent child or children, and have cancelled a benefit in the previous six months to start paid work. In the year ending June 2007, 702 grants were provided, 167 more than in the previous year.

Seasonal work assistance compensates people in seasonal employment for loss of income resulting from bad weather. Recipients must be working in an approved seasonal industry, and have cancelled a benefit in the previous six months to start paid seasonal work. In the year ending June 2007, 1,130 payments were provided, 362 fewer than in 2006.

Source: Ministry of Social Development

ZooDoo is produced by Second Chance Enterprises on the condition that all money made goes back to people with disabilities. The scheme takes manure from city zoos, then composts and bags it for sale, employing over 60 people and at the same time saving ratepayers' money in dumping fees.

Table 14.15

Personal income group[1] by sex
Year ended 30 June 2007

| Income group | People aged 15 years and over | | |
| | Male | Female | Total |
		(000)[2]	
Under $800[3]	146.4	181.4	327.7
$800–8,999	125.5	196.6	322.1
$9,000–13,599	132.3	188.4	320.7
$13,600–18,399	121.8	206.4	328.2
$18,400–25,399	116.8	210.5	327.4
$25,400–32,899	142.6	183.6	326.2
$32,900–41,299	157.2	165.6	322.8
$41,300–50,499	183.0	141.9	324.8
$50,500–65,999	219.7	105.2	324.9
$66,000 +	226.3	97.5	323.8
All income groups	**1,571.6**	**1,677.1**	**3,248.7**

(1) Income is before tax, from regular recurring sources only, for those aged 15 years or over. Income groups are deciles (to the nearest $100) of personal income. Deciles are formed by dividing the population into 10 groups, by ranking individuals according to the income they receive. The bottom decile (decile 1) is the 10 percent of the population with the lowest income, while the top decile (decile 10) is the highest 10 percent of the population. (2) People counts are rounded to the nearest hundred. Figures may not add up to stated totals due to rounding. (3) This decile includes loss from investment or self-employment income, or no source of income received.

Source: Statistics New Zealand

programmes 2,726 times, compared with 3,711 in the June 2006 year. Clients also took part in work confidence courses 4,936 times in the June 2007 year, compared with 4,322 times in 2006.

- Work experience – programmes providing unpaid experience in a workplace or in a situation resembling work that help develop or maintain self-esteem, motivation, work discipline, work ethic and dignity. In the year ending June 2007, clients took part 761 times, compared with 1,162 times in the previous year.
- Wage subsidies – subsidies act as incentives for employers to provide work for job seekers. In the year ending June 2007, 11,078 subsidies were paid, compared with 12,300 in the June 2006 year.
- Skills training – programmes which aim to improve job-related skills, to increase the client's chance of finding employment. In the year ending June 2007, clients participated in these programmes 1,593 times, down from 1,676 in the previous year.
- Self-employment assistance – programmes which offer financial help and advice for long-term unemployed people moving into self-employment. In the year ending June 2007, clients participated in these programmes 2,065 times, compared with 2,181 in 2006.
- Innovation and market responsiveness – programmes developed by Work and Income to respond to local labour markets, to meet the emerging needs of job seekers, employers and communities, to trial employment services, and to promote learning and awareness of best practice in the design and delivery of work services. In the year ending June 2007, clients participated in these programmes 29,768 times, up from 27,831 in the June 2006 year.
- Job search skills – programmes to assist clients to develop skills required to seek paid work, and identify types of work they may find most suitable. In the year ending June 2007, clients participated in these programmes 19,132 times, well down from 41,126 in 2006.

In addition to providing the above programmes, Work and Income undertakes intensive case management – to assist clients to identify, apply for, and take up suitable work opportunities. This case management is available to a wide range of clients, including many who are not registered as job seekers.

Income

Income strongly influences people's well-being and life circumstances. It is a means for people to achieve many economic and social objectives. Information on sources of income and distribution trends, for both individuals and households, is vital for monitoring social change.

Personal income

Personal income is an individual's pay, profit, or other receipts received on an occasional or regular basis. People receive personal income from sources such as wages and salaries, self-employment, investments, government transfers and private superannuation.

Table 14.15 shows the distribution of income, by sex, for the year ended 30 June 2007. More males than females were at the highest income level ($66,000 or more). There were more males in the top decile than in any other decile. By contrast, the $18,400–$25,399 group (decile 5) contained the most females.

Table 14.16

Average weekly earnings
By sex
Year ending 31 March

| Year | Males | | | Females | | | Total | | |
| | Ordinary time | Overtime | Total | Ordinary time | Overtime | Total | Ordinary time | Overtime | **Total** |
					$				
1993	607.15	40.20	647.35	468.66	11.68	480.33	545.06	27.41	**572.47**
1994	615.24	39.05	654.29	474.58	11.72	486.30	551.98	26.76	**578.73**
1995	631.12	41.65	672.77	485.48	12.26	497.75	565.67	28.44	**594.11**
1996	652.55	40.00	692.55	500.35	11.15	511.49	583.70	26.95	**610.65**
1997	676.18	38.01	714.18	521.88	11.13	533.02	606.66	25.90	**632.56**
1998	689.12	35.82	724.94	536.06	11.09	547.15	619.19	24.52	**643.71**
1999	711.94	31.85	743.79	554.04	9.69	563.73	638.79	21.59	**660.38**
2000	725.19	31.74	756.93	563.05	11.03	574.07	649.46	22.07	**671.53**
2001	751.71	31.65	783.36	574.57	10.82	585.40	667.95	21.80	**689.75**
2002	776.57	32.85	809.42	614.09	10.78	624.87	700.80	22.56	**723.36**
2003	802.93	35.91	838.84	633.20	11.16	644.36	722.64	24.20	**746.84**
2004	827.77	33.99	861.76	657.62	11.74	669.36	747.44	23.48	**770.93**
2005	853.82	35.33	889.15	676.33	12.03	688.36	770.44	24.38	**794.83**
2006	882.04	34.88	916.92	712.25	10.99	723.24	802.40	23.67	**826.08**
2007	927.76	35.26	963.02	747.90	12.24	760.14	843.71	24.50	**868.21**

Note: Figures may not add up to stated totals due to rounding.

Source: Statistics New Zealand

The median annual gross personal income for all those aged 15 years and over was $25,400 – that is, half received more, and half received less than this amount. Overall, more males than females received income of $41,300 or over, and more females than males received less than $41,300.

Earnings

The major component of an individual's income is what they earn from employment. In the 10 years ending 31 March 2007, Statistics New Zealand recorded a 37.3 percent increase in average weekly earnings, up from $632.56 to $868.21.

Table 14.16 shows that male average weekly earnings increased to $963.02 (up 34.8 percent), while female earnings rose to $760.14 (up 42.6 percent). At 31 March 2007, female average weekly earnings were 78.9 percent of male average weekly earnings, compared with 74.6 percent in March 1997.

Income by region

Table 14.18 shows that according to the 2006 Census of Population and Dwellings, people in the Wellington region had the highest median annual income ($28,000), followed by the Auckland ($26,800) and Waikato ($24,100) regions.

Wellington region had the highest proportion of people (24 percent) earning an annual income above $50,000.

Household income

Table 14.19 (overleaf) shows the distribution of household income by the composition of the household, for the year ending 30 June 2007. The median annual gross household income was $55,800 – that is, half the households received more, and half received less than this amount. Almost 87 percent of 'one parent with dependent child(ren) only' households had an income below the median amount.

Most 'couple only' households had an income of $68,000–$80,899 (decile 7) for the June 2007 year, while most 'couple with one dependent child' households received $98,800–$131,299 (decile 9). In contrast, the greatest number of 'one person' households received under $17,600 (decile 1).

Salary and wage rates

Surveyed salary and wage rates (including overtime) for the June 2007 quarter were 3.2 percent higher than a year earlier, as shown in table 14.20 (overleaf). This followed an annual increase of 3.1 percent in the year to the March 2007 quarter.

Pay rates for the private sector for the year to the June 2007 quarter increased 3.2 percent, the largest annual increase in salary and wage rates (including overtime) for the private sector since the series began in the December 1992 quarter. The increase for the public sector was 3.0 percent.

Table 14.17

Median weekly earnings
Full-time wage/salary workers
By sex and age
Quarter ending 30 June 2007

Age group (years)	Males	Females	Difference
		$	
15–19	516	499	17
20–24	650	608	42
25–29	798	767	31
30–34	959	863	96
35–39	997	849	148
40–44	978	784	194
45–49	997	780	217
50–54	1,016	754	262
55–59	959	729	230
60–64	923	710	213
65+	730	620	110
All ages	**882**	**750**	**132**

Source: Statistics New Zealand

Table 14.18

Median personal income[1]
By region
2006 Census

Regional council area	Median income ($)
Wellington	28,000
Auckland	26,800
Waikato	24,100
Canterbury	23,500
Marlborough	23,300
Taranaki	23,200
Southland	23,200
Nelson	23,100
Bay of Plenty	22,600
Hawke's Bay	22,600
Manawatu-Wanganui	21,600
Tasman	21,600
Otago	21,600
Northland	20,900
Gisborne	20,600
West Coast	20,400
Area outside region	S
Total	**24,400**

(1) Personal income is for the year ending 31 March 2006, and includes income from all sources.
Symbol: S suppressed

Source: Statistics New Zealand

Waves of SoFIE

The Survey of Family, Income and Employment (SoFIE) aims to interview the same group of individuals over eight years to show how New Zealanders' income, family type and employment changes over time. The survey began with a sample of 22,200 individuals in 11,500 households in 2002.

Data has so far been collected for the first four interview cycles ('waves'). Each wave runs from 1 October, to 30 September the following year. Wave one ran from October 2002 to September 2003, while wave four finished in September 2006.

SoFIE provides information on changes in employee earnings between wave one and wave four of the survey. All people aged 15 years and over at wave four, who were in the longitudinal population and received employee earnings at any time during their first and fourth years in the survey, are included (representing 1,990,800 individuals).

To make comparison between years easier, data is presented in quintiles. Each quintile contains 20 percent of paid employees, ranked by the average weekly earnings received over the weeks in which they were employed.

The earnings' boundaries for wave one and wave four quintiles are different, due to movement in average earnings between waves one and four.

Quintile boundaries for weekly employee earnings

Quintile	Wave one	Wave four
	Average weekly employee earnings	
1	less than $275	less than $310
2	$275 to less than $486	$310 to less than $552
3	$486 to less than $675	$552 to less than $760
4	$675 to less than $930	$760 to less than $1,047
5	$930 +	$1,047 +

Over half (54.0 percent) the people receiving employee earnings in both waves were in the same quintile in both years – although their actual earnings may have changed, their position, relative to other paid employees, remained the same. A further 29.6 percent had moved up one or more quintiles, and 16.4 percent moved down

one or more quintiles. Of those in the top quintile in their first year in the survey, 71.6 percent were also in the top quintile in their fourth year.

Of those who received employee earnings in both the first and fourth years of the survey, 307,000 (21.1 percent) had moved up one quintile by the fourth wave. One quarter (24.7 percent) of those in quintile 3 in their first year moved into quintile 4 in the fourth wave. There were similar movements in the other quintiles.

A total of 352,900 people who were not employed[1] at the end of the first wave were employed three years later – most (263,800) had not been seeking work when first interviewed. Of those who had been seeking work at the end of the first wave, 9.8 percent were in the same position three years later, while 60.9 percent were employed.

(1) Includes those not employed and seeking work, not employed and not seeking work, and those turning 15 between waves one and four.

Source: Statistics New Zealand

World-wide contact

New Zealanders are among the world's greatest travellers. Many go overseas for short holidays but it is estimated that nearly 25 percent of the country's skilled workforce now resides offshore. Over 77,000 Kiwis left for the long term in 2007.

Larger salaries are part of the pull, but the lure of the overseas experience (OE) is bred into New Zealand culture. The difference now is that New Zealanders are not staying for two years – they are staying longer, buying property, and settling into careers, often in large companies and financial institutions.

Two New Zealand-based websites work to keep those abroad in touch with the New Zealand workplace.

Kea, started in 2001, is a global community of professional people who use their passion for New Zealand to help each other achieve, wherever they are based.

By connecting around 23,000 Kiwis and other 'friends of New Zealand' in more than 170 countries, Kea links with international markets – promoting trade, attracting investment and migration to New Zealand, and stimulating business activity and innovation.

But for many it's the thought of bringing up children in London, Singapore or Sydney that makes them decide to return 'home'. Their decision can be enhanced by more information and better communication around the opportunities and career prospects which exist in New Zealand.

Track Me Back is a website offering New Zealand employers direct communication with offshore Kiwi talent, and providing the infrastructure to manage this communication. It has a searchable database, offering open communication which is purely career related. Launched in November 2007, by early 2008 it had 2,500 people interested in returning home to New Zealand.

Sources: Kea, Track Me Back

Otago Daily Times

Business owner Emily Cooper works with Catherine Broad and Janelle Quigley to reuse packaging available through the Dunedin City Council's waste exchange initiative. The service helps businesses connect their unwanted materials and recyclables with new owners.

Fifty-eight percent of surveyed salary and ordinary time wage rates increased in the year ending 30 June 2007. Twenty-seven percent of these reported an increase of more than 3 percent, but not more than 5 percent, the highest proportion recorded since the survey began.

Labour costs

The labour cost index measures movements in base salary and ordinary time wage rates, overtime wage rates, and non-wage labour costs.

The index began in the December 1992 quarter and is a quality-controlled measure, meaning it reflects only changes in salary and wage rates for the same quality and quantity of work. Increases due to service increments and merit promotions are excluded.

Each quarter, businesses in the sample are asked to provide information about wage and salary costs for specific job descriptions in a variety of occupations. Businesses are also asked to provide information on non-wage labour costs in the June quarter of each year.

Table 14.19

Household income group[1] by household composition
Year ended 30 June 2007

	Household composition										
Income group	Couple only	Couple with one dependent child	Couple with two dependent children	Couple with three or more dependent children	All other 'couple with child(ren) only' households[2]	One parent with dependent child(ren) only	All other 'one parent with child(ren) only' households[3]	Other one-family households[4]	One-person household	All other households[5]	Total[6]
	Number of households (000)[7]										
Under $17,600[8]	19.3	3.6	S	3.3	S	9.7	3.6	S	110.7	S	154.7
$17,600–25,799	37.8	6.0	7.7	S	S	17.9	3.5	S	79.2	S	160.1
$25,800–33,399	54.7	10.1	2.4	3.9	S	26.5	8.6	5.7	38.9	3.4	155.5
$33,400–44,899	39.2	9.0	6.7	10.0	7.4	14.8	5.9	13.0	37.1	14.9	158.0
$44,900–55,799	36.1	18.0	21.4	13.5	10.2	9.4	3.6	8.3	29.7	6.5	156.7
$55,800–67,999	39.8	16.5	19.7	11.4	17.5	6.6	2.2	12.3	20.7	9.8	156.5
$68,000–80,899	58.1	18.2	21.8	5.2	13.5	S	3.8	11.3	12.4	12.0	158.0
$80,900–98,799	39.9	14.8	20.3	14.9	26.1	2.1	4.1	11.9	5.4	17.0	156.5
$98,800–131,299	45.8	21.2	27.9	8.3	17.6	S	S	11.7	6.1	13.5	157.2
$131,300 +	42.4	13.1	19.7	6.0	32.9	S	4.2	15.6	3.6	18.0	156.1
All income groups	**413.1**	**130.3**	**149.0**	**76.9**	**130.5**	**90.3**	**43.4**	**94.4**	**343.8**	**97.5**	**1,569.2**

(1) Income is before tax, from regular and recurring sources only, for those aged 15 years or over. Income groups are deciles (to the nearest $100) of household income. Deciles are formed by dividing the population into 10 groups by ranking households according to the income they receive. The bottom decile (decile 1) is the 10 percent of the population with the lowest income, while the top decile (decile 10) is the highest 10 percent of the population. (2) Includes couple with adult children only, as well as couple with adult and dependent children. (3) Includes one parent with adult children only, as well as one parent with dependent and adult children. (4) Contains all one-family households where 'other people' are present who are related or unrelated to the family nucleus. (5) This category is an aggregation of: two-family households, three-or-more-family households or any other multi-person household. (6) Total includes the 'not specified' category. (7) Household counts are rounded to the nearest hundred. Figures may not add up to stated totals due to rounding. (8) This decile includes loss from investment or self-employment income, or no source of income received.

Symbol: S suppressed, for confidentiality and quality reasons.

Source: Statistics New Zealand

The majority of labour costs come from salaries and wages. Labour costs increased by 3.9 percent overall from the June 2006 quarter to the June 2007 quarter. This increase was due to rises in salary and wage rates (including overtime) of 3.2 percent, and 8.1 percent in non-wage labour costs.

The rise in non-wage labour costs was due to increases in the cost of annual leave and statutory holidays, superannuation, workplace accident insurance, and other non-wage labour costs.

The cost to employers of annual leave and statutory holidays rose 9.3 percent from the June 2006 quarter to the June 2007 quarter, the largest annual increase since the series began in the December 1992 quarter. In the same period, salary and wage rates (including overtime) increased 3.2 percent.

Workplace accident insurance costs increased 9.3 percent from the June 2006 quarter to the June 2007 quarter and employer superannuation costs increased 4.2 percent. The superannuation increase was influenced by a 3.1 percent rise in salary and ordinary time wage rates.

The other surveyed non-wage costs (which include motor vehicles available for private use, medical insurance and employer-related low interest loans) are subject to fringe benefit tax. These costs rose 1.8 percent from the June 2006 quarter to the June 2007 quarter. The cost of providing motor vehicles for private use and medical insurance rose, while the cost of providing low interest loans fell.

Table 14.20

Salary and wage rates index (including overtime)[1]
By sector

Quarter		Local government sector	Central government sector	Total public sector	Private sector	All sectors combined
2005	Sep	1106	1129	1126	1103	1108
	Dec	1122	1141	1139	1112	1117
2006	Mar	1130	1146	1144	1119	1125
	Jun	1137	1157	1155	1126	1132
	Sep	1145	1174	1170	1136	1143
	Dec	1152	1184	1180	1146	1153
2007	Mar	1160	1190	1187	1153	1160
	Jun	1168	1193	1190	1162	1168
Percentage change from same quarter of previous year						
2005	Sep	2.5	3.9	3.6	2.8	3.1
	Dec	3.7	4.0	3.9	2.9	3.0
2006	Mar	3.9	4.0	4.0	3.0	3.3
	Jun	3.9	4.1	4.1	2.9	3.2
	Sep	3.5	4.0	3.9	3.0	3.2
	Dec	2.7	3.8	3.6	3.1	3.2
2007	Mar	2.7	3.8	3.8	3.0	3.1
	Jun	2.7	3.1	3.0	3.2	3.2

(1) Base: December 1992 quarter (=1000).

Source: Statistics New Zealand

Table 14.21

Labour cost index[1]
By type of cost

June quarter	Salary and ordinary time wage rates	Overtime wage rates[2]	All salary and wage rates[3]	All non-wage labour costs[4][5]	All labour costs[5][6]
1999	966	975	967	962	966
2000	983	983	983	978	982
2001	1000	1000	1000	1000	1000
2002	1021	1023	1021	1005	1018
2003	1044	1048	1044	1019	1040
2004	1068	1077	1068	1013	1059
2005	1096	1109	1097	1043	1088
2006	1132	1141	1132	1108	1128
2007	1167	1185	1168	1198	1172
Percentage change from previous June quarter					
1999	1.5	0.1	1.4	-4.0	0.5
2000	1.7	0.9	1.6	1.6	1.6
2001	1.8	1.7	1.8	2.3	1.9
2002	2.1	2.3	2.1	0.5	1.8
2003	2.3	2.4	2.3	1.4	2.2
2004	2.3	2.8	2.3	-0.6	1.8
2005	2.6	3.0	2.7	3.0	2.7
2006	3.3	2.9	3.2	6.2	3.7
2007	3.1	3.9	3.2	8.1	3.9

(1) Base: June 2001 quarter (=1000). (2) Measures changes in rates paid for actual hours worked as overtime in the base period. Some of these pay rates have fallen to ordinary time levels in subsequent quarters. (3) Including overtime. (4) Measures changes in all surveyed non-wage labour costs (ie annual leave and statutory holidays, superannuation, workplace accident insurance, medical insurance, motor vehicles available for private use and low interest loans). (5) Measures changes in all surveyed labour costs (ie all salary and wage rates and all non-wage labour costs). (6) Revisions to series were made in the June 2005 quarter as the result of quality improvement to the non-wage labour cost indexes.

Source: Statistics New Zealand

Contributors and related websites

Business New Zealand – www.businessnz.org.nz

Department of Labour – www.dol.govt.nz

Employment Relations Service – www.ers.dol.govt.nz

Equal Employment Opportunities Trust – www.eeotrust.org.nz

Industrial Relations Centre, Victoria University of Wellington – www.victoria.ac.nz

Ministry of Social Development – www.msd.govt.nz

New Zealand Council of Trade Unions – www.union.org.nz

State Services Commission – www.ssc.govt.nz

Statistics New Zealand – www.stats.govt.nz

Tertiary Education Commission – www.tec.govt.nz

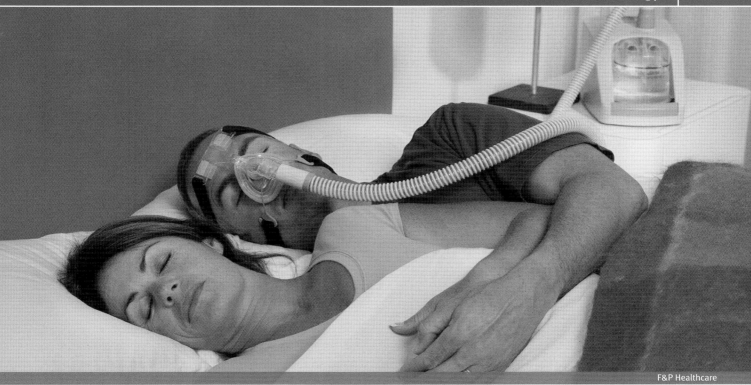

F&P Healthcare

Fisher and Paykel Healthcare's portable monitoring machine allows home diagnosis of obstructive sleep apnoea (OSA), a disorder which disrupts breathing during sleep. The company had strong growth in international demand for its OSA, respiratory, and acute medical care products in 2007. Their products are sold in more than 110 countries.

15 | Science and technology

New Zealand's science sector has many organisations with specialised roles. These include a policy agency, research-funding agencies, and organisations that carry out research. Research organisations include universities and polytechnics, Crown research institutes, private companies and research associations.

Ministry of Research, Science and Technology

The Ministry of Research, Science and Technology Te Manatū Pūtaiao (MoRST) is the main policy agency for research, science and technology (RS&T) in New Zealand. MoRST's major planned outcome for the next 10 to 15 years is, 'Science and technology transforming New Zealanders' lives'. The ministry's main role is to:

- provide policy advice to the government on RS&T, including investment priorities, science matters and international science issues
- apply RS&T policies for sustainable development and economic growth
- manage contracts with agencies that directly invest in RS&T on behalf of the Minister of Research, Science and Technology
- evaluate how various funding schemes are performing
- promote positive relationships between the RS&T sector, the business community and others, so that ideas generated by researchers are passed on to those who can use them to generate new products, services and processes
- promote New Zealand RS&T internationally
- raise the profile of RS&T with those making career choices, and with the social, environmental and business sectors in New Zealand.

Crown Company Monitoring Advisory Unit

The Crown Company Monitoring Advisory Unit (CCMAU) provides ownership monitoring advice to, and manages issues on behalf of, shareholding ministers of Crown research institutes, state-owned enterprises and other Crown companies. In addition, CCMAU is responsible for ensuring the best qualified candidates are recommended to ministers for appointment as directors of these companies.

Total research and development (R&D) expenditure in New Zealand in 2006 was $1,826 million, according to the Research and Development Survey. This is a 10.0 percent increase from $1,660 million in 2004.

Business sector R&D expenditure was $763 million in 2006, up 12.7 percent from 2004. The key drivers of business R&D growth were the manufacturing sector, up 18.5 percent, and the services sector, up 19.6 percent.

R&D expenditure in the university sector grew 13.6 percent to reach $593 million, while the government sector R&D expenditure was up 1.8 percent, to $469 million.

The major funding for R&D in New Zealand was from government and business sources. Government funded $785 million worth of R&D, up 8.0 percent from 2004. Businesses funded $763 million, which was up 18.6 percent. Ninety-five percent of all R&D was domestically funded in 2006.

The Research and Development Survey 2006 was a joint survey between the Ministry of Research, Science and Technology and Statistics New Zealand.

Source: Statistics New Zealand

Research and development expenditure
Percentage of GDP
2005

Country	Percent
Sweden	3.89
Finland	3.48
Japan	3.33
Korea	2.98
Switzerland[1]	2.90
Iceland	2.78
United States	2.62
Germany	2.48
Denmark	2.45
Austria	2.41
OECD	**2.25**
France	2.13
Canada	1.98
Belgium	1.86
United Kingdom	1.78
Australia[1]	1.78
Netherlands	1.73
Luxembourg	1.61
Norway	1.52
Czech Republic	1.41
Ireland	1.26
New Zealand	**1.17**
Spain	1.12
Italy	1.10
Hungary	0.94
Portugal	0.81
Turkey	0.79
Poland	0.57
Greece	0.51
Slovak Republic	0.51
Mexico	0.50

(1) Figures are for 2004.

Source: OECD

Investment in research, science and technology

Research and development (R&D) in New Zealand is funded by the government, universities and the private sector. Total 2005/06 government funding of R&D, including general university funds and local government funding, was estimated to be $785 million, which is 0.50 percent of gross domestic product (GDP). Government funds provided 43 percent of total R&D funding. Major government R&D funding sources in 2006/07 included Vote Research, Science and Technology ($570 million) and Vote Education ($218 million).

Budget 2007 included a 15 percent tax credit for eligible business R&D, applying from 1 April 2008. Estimated to indirectly fund $630 million of R&D over the first four years, it is hoped this initiative will significantly increase the level of business R&D in New Zealand, which is low by international standards. In 2005/06, New Zealand businesses carried out $763 million of R&D (0.49 percent of GDP), which is approximately one-third of the OECD average (1.53 percent of GDP).

Vote Research, Science and Technology

Vote Research, Science and Technology invests in four major goal areas: economic, knowledge, environmental and social. These proportions are illustrated in figure 15.01.

Economic ($262 million in the 2007/08 financial year). The goal is to increase the contribution that knowledge and technology make to the competitiveness of New Zealand enterprises.

- *Research for Industry* aims to increase the competitiveness of sectors such as the food and fibre industries, manufacturing and services industries, and infrastructures such as communications, energy, water and waste. An example is the Algal Technologies programme at the Cawthron Institute. This aims to understand micro-algal biotoxins, and to benefit New Zealand through the 'quality/safe food' brand of seafood products, ensuring access to desired markets. Knowledge of toxins, and development of rapid molecular and chemical detection systems, will enable government and industry end-users to carry out informed risk analysis and make regulatory decisions about public health standards. The budget was $200.7 million in 2007/08.

- *Technology New Zealand* supports businesses by improving their ability to adopt and use new technology and innovation. For example, it helped Surveylab to develop its handheld data-capture tool known as Ike (I know everything). Ike's unique point-and-shoot technology combines a global positioning system, compass, inclinometer, laser distance meter and digital camera facility into a geographic information system database. It can capture data accurately at approximately one kilometre from a target, making it ideal for dangerous or inaccessible environments – from rivers to busy street intersections. The budget was $47.2 million in 2007/08.

- *The Pre-Seed Accelerator Fund* aims to increase the commercialising of innovations from publicly-funded research done by public research providers. It assists Crown research institutes and tertiary education institutes to develop a discovery to the point where its commercial potential is apparent, and private-sector investors are willing to invest the funds required for full commercialisation. For example, this fund helped Otago Innovation Ltd advance their research on blood-borne bone markers to where a potentially valuable licence agreement was signed with Biosite, a leading provider of rapid diagnostic products and antibody development. The fund was $8.3 million in 2007/08.

- *National Measurement Standards* funds the Measurement Standards Laboratory, to provide specified national measurement standards and the related services needed to satisfy accurate measurement and internationally accepted standards for New Zealand products, processes and services. It meets the obligations of the Minister of Research, Science and Technology under the Measurement Standards Act 1992. In 2007/08, funding was $5.8 million.

Knowledge ($189 million in 2007/08). The goal is to accelerate knowledge creation and develop people, learning systems and networks to enhance New Zealand's capacity to innovate.

- The *Marsden Fund* encourages excellence in the advancement of knowledge by supporting research that explores the frontiers of new knowledge. It has supported research that has opened new insights in the physical, life, mathematical and social sciences, and the humanities. For example, it supported geological projects that will provide further understanding of destructive natural processes. Marsden funding was critical in New Zealand's involvement in the international ANDRILL Project which successfully obtained the deepest-ever Antarctic sedimentary core. This will enable future behaviour of the Antarctic ice sheets to be more accurately predicted. The fund also contributed to the collection and analysis of the most comprehensive dataset yet for a lahar – that from Ruapehu in March 2007. The budget was $35.9 million in 2007/08.

- The *New Economy Research Fund* develops research capability and knowledge in areas of science and technology where new industries and enterprises are emerging. For example, the fund is supporting the development of a computational bioengineering software package called CMISS. CMISS models biological processes using anatomically-based geometric models and biophysically-based tissue and cell models. Medical and health applications currently being developed with CMISS include the diagnosis and treatment of diseases of the heart, lungs, digestive system, musculo-skeletal system and lymphatic/immune system. The fund had a $65.8 million budget in 2007/08.

- The *Crown Research Institute Capability Fund* helps Crown research institutes (CRIs) retain and develop research programmes that they identify as important, including new areas of science. For example, HortResearch has used this fund to minimise the environmental footprint of New Zealand's horticulture industry. In collaboration with other CRIs and universities, they have built capability that will allow greater investigation of greenhouse gas flow in soils, efficient water allocation, and carbon sequestration in production soils such as vineyards. A budget of $50.6 million was available in 2007/08.

- *Supporting Promising Individuals* (SPI) supports people in research, science and technology and contributes to their development with knowledge, skills and ideas. SPI consists of a large number of schemes and funding and investment agents, with $18.7 million available in 2007/08. For example, a Te Tipu Pūtaiao Fellowship was awarded by the Foundation for Research, Science and Technology to Dr Bronwyn Lowe from the University of Otago for the study of a unique collection of harakeke and wharariki (New Zealand flax) growing in the Dunedin Botanic Garden. The study aims to establish where the Dunedin collection came from, describe the plants' botanic, textile science and traditional weaving properties, and determine their relationship with other harakeke.

- *Development of International Linkages* promotes and supports New Zealand RS&T internationally by accessing and using the best global ideas, and encouraging New Zealanders to use international linkages to enhance knowledge and innovative capacity. It funds activities that access large funding pools and international expertise. For example, in 2007 New Zealand gained access to the Human Frontier Science Programme, which promotes basic life science research that is innovative, interdisciplinary and requires international collaboration. As a result of membership, New Zealand researchers gained funding for two projects, partnering with researchers in Germany, the United States and the Czech Republic. Funding of $3.2 million was available in 2007/08.

- *International Investment Opportunities Fund* supports research providers and funders in international research collaborations and the recruitment of highly experienced researchers from overseas. This fund enabled the Carbohydrate Chemistry Team at Industrial Research, led by Drs Richard Furneaux and Peter Tyler, to work with researchers from Singapore's Institute of Molecular and Cell Biology on the factors that control the differentiation of stem cells. There was $9.6 million funding available in 2007/08.

Environmental ($93 million in 2007/08). The goal is to increase understanding of the environment and factors that affect it in order to establish and maintain a healthy environment.

- *Environmental Research* builds understanding of the environment through research on New Zealand's ecosystems, and the biophysical and human environments, and in sustainable management of the environment by the production sector. For example, the fund supports

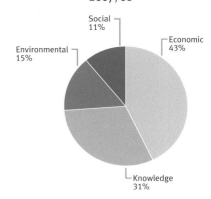

Figure 15.01

Investment in research and technology
2007/08

Social 11%
Economic 43%
Environmental 15%
Knowledge 31%

Source: MoRST

Breaking research boundaries

Modern scientific research is increasingly sophisticated in the range and complexity of the problems and questions it deals with, and in the equipment and facilities required to answer those questions and solve those problems.

There is also a trend towards a multi-disciplinary approach to science and technology – for example, mathematicians may work with biologists, chemists with physicists, and engineers with geologists. These collaborations may be on a national level, but increasingly they bring together scientists living in different countries, all in search of a common goal.

For New Zealand, this has meant ensuring adequate investment in facilities and equipment and taking advantage of opportunities that allow scientists and technologists to access very large (and very expensive) assets, nationally and internationally. One major project that promises to greatly enhance New Zealand scientific research is the Kiwi Advanced Research and Education Network (KAREN). This next-generation, ultra-high-speed broadband Internet connects universities, libraries, research institutions and firms that are collaborating on research in New Zealand with each other, and with similar organisations overseas.

KAREN promises to revolutionise the amount of data that can be transferred between researchers and educationalists working in different parts of the country and around the world. It also allows them to share computing power, for scientific and technological problems that require massive amounts of computer memory and operating capacity. This will result in greatly enhanced capacity to confer and educate at a distance.

As well as aiding collaboration and data-sharing, KAREN is opening new science frontiers. For example, researchers can develop three-dimensional, real-life models of whatever they are studying and share them with colleagues at other research centres. They can also monitor events such as a volcanic eruptions or geological activity deep beneath the world's ocean in real time without having to leave their desks.

Source: MoRST

Graham Leonard

GNS Science geodesic surveyor Neville Palmer uses a global positioning system receiver to record the location and size of the Mt Ruapehu lahar, following the September 2007 eruption.

a project that aims to improve the water quality of New Zealand's largest lake, Lake Taupo. Lake Taupo's water quality is declining due to nitrogen run-off from surrounding farmland. Funding of $93.4 million was available in 2007/08.

Social ($65 million in 2007/08). The goal is to increase knowledge of what constitutes well-being, in order to build a society in which all New Zealanders enjoy health and independence and a strong sense of belonging, identity and partnership.

- *Health Research* supports public-good RS&T to improve the health of New Zealanders. For example, the Health Research Council is supporting a project at the University of Auckland to develop and test the potential effectiveness of a community-based childhood nutrition intervention. The intervention will focus on the role of micronutrients – such as vitamins, minerals and amino acids – in early-childhood nutrition. A key goal is to reduce the number of children who contract pneumonia or gastroenteritis and require hospital admission. Funding of $59 million was available in 2007/08.

- *Social Research* supports public-good RS&T to improve social well-being. For example, it supports Auckland University of Technology's Pacific Islands Families study. This longitudinal study is aimed at providing information on Pacific people's health, and cultural, economic, environmental and psycho-social factors that are important influences on child health and development and family functioning. There was $5.9 million available in 2007/08.

Shaping the system About 5 percent ($35 million in 2007/08) of the government's total investment is spent on 'shaping the system'. This funding supports agencies that advise the government on policies for innovation, and provides management and monitoring of the government's investment in RS&T. It also allows the Minister of Research, Science and Technology to take a wider view across the entire RS&T system.

Foundation for Research, Science and Technology

The Foundation for Research, Science and Technology Tūapapa Rangahau Pūtaiao is a Crown entity with an independent board reporting to the Minister of Research, Science and Technology. The Foundation for Research Science and Technology Act 1990 governs its operations.

It is responsible for: investing in research, science and technology on behalf of the government in order to enhance the wealth and well-being of New Zealanders; providing independent policy advice on science and technology to the government; encouraging technological innovation through the Technology New Zealand suite of schemes; and administering various scholarship schemes.

'Investing in innovation for New Zealand's future' is the mission statement of the foundation, which considers innovation a key to a prosperous and productive future for New Zealand.

'Royal' support for students

Gordon Lawrence

Pakuranga College science students Jenny Suo (left) and Anna Devathasan.

The Royal Society of New Zealand (RSNZ) is involved in a variety of initiatives aimed at developing a scientifically and technologically literate society through education. Examples include:

Realise the Dream

Realise the Dream, sponsored mainly by Genesis Energy, supports students who have carried out excellent pieces of technological or scientific practice.

The students' 2007 research projects netted them more than $20,000 worth of prizes as well as trips to science fairs and youth conferences around the world. The winning projects included: 'don't squash the kid', a road-safety study; methods of controlling facial eczema in farm animals; night vision goggles; and a 'tyre-less' silage cover.

Science and technology fairs

Each year, the RSNZ supports regional science and technology fairs around New Zealand.

Pakuranga College students Anna Devathasan and Jenny Suo made headlines after testing the amount of vitamin C in fruit juice for their 2004 science fair project. When they found Ribena blackcurrant juice contained almost no vitamin C, contradicting the manufacturer's claims, they challenged the makers. Three years later, GlaxoSmithKline admitted they had misled customers. They paid a fine and ran media advertisements to correct their claims.

Chief Executive of the Royal Society of New Zealand, Dr Di McCarthy, said "Following the remarkable research of students into fruit drinks and other issues, the commercial world has developed a new respect for the ingenuity and ability of our students."

BP Challenge

The BP Challenge is a fun team event, challenging students to design and develop solutions to problems using common materials. Each challenge has several viable solutions. Problems are made more challenging by having the 'adult-world' constraints of materials, tools and time.

Challenges are 'environmentally friendly' with most materials being biodegradable or recyclable – newspaper is the main material.

CREST Award Scheme

CREST (Creativity in science and technology) is an international awards scheme to encourage student projects in creativity and problem solving. It has four levels: first (years 7–8 students), bronze (years 9–10) and silver and gold for senior students. CREST is renowned for creating links between school students and researchers and technologists.

BIG Science Adventures

BIG Science Adventures is a DVD competition for senior school students. Sponsored by Freemasons New Zealand, it offers big prizes to the winning teams. In August 2007, students and a teacher from Dunedin visited the east coast of Greenland and made a documentary about the effects of climate change.

Source: RSNZ

The foundation receives applications from Crown research institutes, research associations, government departments, incorporated societies, non-profit private trusts, private individuals, private companies, state-owned enterprises and universities to undertake agreed research programmes which contribute to the achievement of the government's science goals.

Royal Society of New Zealand

The Royal Society of New Zealand is an independent, statutory body incorporating the National Academy of Sciences and scientific and technological societies. It encourages professional development through research grants, fellowships, communication courses, awards and prizes.

The society advances and promotes science and technology in New Zealand, recognises and encourages excellence in research, establishes ethical standards, supports science and technology education and publishes scientific journals, reports and educational resources.

Established in 1867 as the New Zealand Institute, the society is incorporated under The Royal Society of New Zealand Act 1997. It takes responsibility for fostering a culture supportive of science and technology in New Zealand and of initiating appropriate international linkages. It also provides expert advice on important public issues to the government and the community.

Membership includes elected fellows, regional branches, constituent scientific and technological societies and more than 15,000 professional people in New Zealand and overseas.

New Zealand Venture Investment Fund Ltd

The New Zealand Venture Investment Fund (NZVIF) was established as part of the Government's 2001 Budget and on 1 July 2002 it became a Crown-owned company, the New Zealand Venture Investment Fund Ltd. The fund administers two equity investment programmes on behalf of the New Zealand Government: the VIF Venture Capital Fund and, more recently, the Seed Co-investment Fund.

The Venture Capital Fund is a $160–$200 million investment programme to accelerate development of the venture capital market in New Zealand. NZVIF invests its capital, alongside private investors, in selected venture capital investment funds operated by professional fund managers. Each fund operates for 10 years, investing in a portfolio of New Zealand companies with high growth potential and assisting those companies to build and develop successful commercial strategies. The programme targets early-stage venture capital investment, and a buy-out option for investors is an integral aspect of the programme.

The Seed Co-investment Fund provides seed funding for early stage businesses with strong potential for high growth. The fund is managed by NZVIF and has $40 million of seed funding available for co-investment alongside selected private investor groups. There is an upper funding cap of $250,000 per investment, with a requirement for at least 50:50 matching funding from private investors.

University funding

In 2005, expenditure by New Zealand universities on research and development (R&D) was estimated at $593 million – 32 percent of New Zealand's total expenditure on R&D. Of this, $105 million (ex-GST) was general university funds from Vote Education, $241 million was from government research contracts, and $157 million came from universities' own funds (which include student fees). The remainder came from business, overseas and other sources.

Figure 15.02

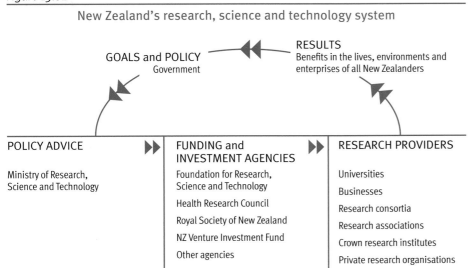

New Zealand's research, science and technology system

Source: MoRST

Environment research

New Zealand's natural environment underpins our lifestyle and is key to how we view ourselves as a nation. The environment is also a vital component of our prosperity, as the base of many of our primary industries and a crucial component of our tourism industry.

Environmental science has two main roles: providing solutions to the increasing economic and social demands we are placing on the environment, and developing opportunities for sustainable environmental, economic and social outcomes. Although New Zealand research is linked to and informed by international research, our country's distinct environment requires New Zealand-based research to develop local solutions, opportunities and understanding.

Through the Vote Research, Science and Technology allocation, the government invests around $150 million annually in environmental research. The Ministry of Research Science and Technology's (MoRST) *Roadmap for Science: Environment Research*, published in May 2007, looks forward to 2017 and provides long-term direction for the development of key environmental science capabilities. It also aligns New Zealand's science with government strategies to manage the environment.

Environmental management decisions increasingly require understanding of the whole environmental system and its processes, and a multidimensional approach which links biophysical, socio-economic and health research.

A crucial task is to create a New Zealand science environment within which systems-based approaches can develop and flourish, while acknowledging that small-scale studies are important to underpin these approaches. With this intent, MoRST worked with interested parties during the development of the environment 'roadmap' and identified three overarching themes to focus on.

- Systems understanding and integration – understanding environmental systems requires more effective integration across multiple disciplines.
- Transfer and uptake – addressing this need requires greater focus on predictive science and solution-oriented research, improved use of management initiatives to help advance scientific understanding, and better communication techniques such as visualisation.
- Information systems – improved integration across disciplines and improved transfer and uptake of research cannot occur unless data management is improved. This includes databases, collections, data accessibility and using new data collection technologies.

The roadmap identified six broad environmental research areas:

- global environment change
- land, water and coasts
- urban design and hazards
- biosecurity
- biodiversity
- oceanic systems.

Source: MoRST

The Australian synchrotron – the Australian synchrotron, located near Monash University in Victoria, is the first synchrotron to be built in the southern hemisphere. It was officially opened in July 2007. Synchrotron light is the electromagnetic radiation emitted when electrons, moving at velocities close to the speed of light, are forced to change direction under the influence of a magnetic field. It can be used to determine the structure of proteins and other biomolecules, for drug design, for the analysis of advanced materials, and for pure spectroscopy of novel molecules.

Access to world-class facilities and equipment is important for researchers, so New Zealand's investment (which includes contributions from central government, Crown research institutes and universities) in the Australian synchrotron ensures they can undertake leading-edge research and development using specialised technology. As a foundation investor, New Zealand has specific access rights and will help determine the strategic direction of the facility.

Tax credit for research and development – from 1 April 2008, New Zealand businesses can claim a 15 percent tax credit on eligible research and development (R&D) expenditure. The credit encourages New Zealand businesses to invest more in R&D and, as a result, to increase innovation. This will have significant benefits for the New Zealand economy, particularly through increased productivity and international competitiveness. The credit is one of the business tax reforms that form a substantial part of the government's economic transformation agenda. The aim of this agenda is a sustainable economy – built on innovation and quality – that produces products for which other countries will pay a premium. More information is available on the Ministry of Research, Science and Technology (MoRST) or Inland Revenue websites.

Roadmaps for Science – are designed to guide New Zealand's science activity, with each strategy document providing broad context and high-level direction on a particular area of science. MoRST has developed roadmaps in four areas: energy research, nanoscience and nanotechnology, biotechnology research and environment research. A food research roadmap is under development. The *Roadmap for Science: Biotechnology Research*, published in March 2007, reflects the importance of biotechnology research for New Zealand. Biotechnology is a mainstay of growth for New Zealand's predominantly biological economic base, providing new knowledge to maintain and build our competitive advantages. It will transform our primary sector into one that is both environmentally sustainable and producing increasingly value-added products and processes. Biotechnology research is fuelling industry and enterprises, including drug development and medical-device companies linked to global research partners and markets. It also underpins biosecurity and biodiversity management in New Zealand. The importance of biotechnology research to New Zealand is reflected in the 25 percent of total government R&D investment (around $195 million annually) it receives – proportionally the highest share of government-funded biotechnology research in the OECD. Information on the roadmaps is available at: www.morst.govt.nz/current-work/roadmaps.

Source: MoRST

Research agencies

Margaret Low

Scientist Uwe Morgenstern prepares to determine the age of some water samples. In 2007, the GNS Science laboratory came top in a test of 70 water-dating labs around the world, a result which is likely to secure more business from overseas for the lab. Water-dating uses tritium, a rare isotope of hydrogen that occurs naturally in rain and snow, to determine when water fell to earth.

Crown research institutes

There are nine autonomous Crown research institutes (CRIs). Government-owned, they are collectively New Zealand's largest science enterprises. Each manages its own assets and has its own independent board of directors reporting to shareholding ministers.

Their purpose is to do research of benefit to New Zealand, while remaining financially viable. The government is represented by two shareholding ministers, the Minister of Research, Science and Technology and the Minister of Finance.

CRIs employ more than 4,230 staff and directly generate revenues of more than $625 million, gained by competing for public and private sector business. Additionally, their research and commercial activity underpins the economic, environmental and social values being created by businesses, departments, and central and local government agencies.

CRIs returned an after-tax and non-operating items surplus of $17.2 million for the year ending 30 June 2007, and paid dividends of $835,000.

Science New Zealand coordinates policy and advocacy on matters of shared interest among members and liaises with other science enterprises, such as businesses and universities.

Scion, formerly the Forest Research Institute, has been recognised as a leader in plantation forestry research and development since its inception in 1947.

In 2003, Scion extended its expertise in forestry to meet the growing consumer demand for renewable materials and products. The organisation is now a leader in the development of next-generation plant-based biomaterials and solutions that utilise the single largest source of renewable industrial materials – forestry.

Research is centred on:

- biomaterials – for example, alternatives to plastics and other oil-based materials
- bioenergy – for example, biofuels and cleaner, healthier heating alternatives created from wood processing residues
- sustainable building practices – for example, warmer, energy-efficient housing.

Forestry research remains a key component of Scion's operation. This is carried out through Ensis, a collaborative agreement between Scion and Australia's Commonwealth Scientific and Industrial Research Organisation. The partnership delivers the largest research and development capability to the forestry, wood and fibre industries in Australasia.

Scion is committed to developing innovative global and local partnerships that provide local benefit, particularly by partnering with Māori to unlock the innovation potential of Māori knowledge, resources and people.

With approximately 350 staff, Scion has its headquarters in Rotorua and offices in Auckland, Wellington and Christchurch.

AgResearch (AgResearch Ltd) is New Zealand's largest Crown research institute. It has a number of farms and renowned research centres: Ruakura, Grasslands, Lincoln and Invermay, and most importantly, teams of scientists, engineers, technicians and support staff. Their work targets the key opportunities and issues faced by the farming, food, textiles and biotechnology sectors, and leads to innovative products and knowledge that benefit all New Zealanders. AgResearch's mission is to create sustainable wealth in the pastoral and biotechnology sectors through science and technology.

The pastoral sector is the backbone of New Zealand's economy and its continued success is essential to the living standard of all New Zealanders. AgResearch was established in 1992 as a government-owned company charged with operating on a full commercial basis. The company has about 1,050 permanent staff members, nearly 300 of whom hold a doctorate. It uses a range of vehicles to commercialise its technologies, including subsidiary companies, associate companies, unincorporated joint ventures, incorporated joint ventures and partnerships.

HortResearch (Horticultural and Food Research Institute of New Zealand) is a New Zealand-based science company which is a world leader in integrated fruit research. Using unique resources in fruit, plants and sustainable production systems, HortResearch provides novel technologies, and innovative fruit and food products with high consumer appeal.

Home to leading-edge scientific capability in plant breeding, and tree, vine and fruit physiology, HortResearch has developed the trademarked Zespri gold kiwifruit and ENZA jazz apples, and other successful cultivars including blueberries, peaches and pears.

The company also developed the world's first intelligent fruit labelling system – which changes colour as the fruit ripens.

HortResearch is enhancing its commercial science capability in plant molecular biology, nutrigenomics, food chemistry and human physiology, to find new ways to improve health, well-being and performance. This includes meeting emerging markets for functional foods and naturally-produced flavours and fragrances.

HortResearch employs more than 400 scientists throughout New Zealand as well as business leaders in international markets such as Australia, Europe and the United States.

Crop & Food Research (New Zealand Institute for Crop and Food Research Ltd) is a New Zealand-based biological science company that carries out both government-funded research and work for commercial clients. Research is around five centres of innovation: sustainable land and water use, high performance plants, personalised foods, high value marine products, and biomolecules and biomaterials.

To promote the application of science, the company undertakes research in partnership with a range of national and international industry and government clients. Many research collaborations are commercialised with business partners. Employing 360 staff, the Crown research institute is based at Lincoln, Canterbury, with research stations in Auckland, Hawke's Bay, Palmerston North, Nelson, Dunedin, Invermay, Gore, and Albury in Australia.

Landcare Research (Landcare Research New Zealand Ltd Manaaki Whenua) is an independent Crown research institute, with approximately 400 staff at nine locations in New Zealand. As New Zealand's foremost environmental research organisation, research and technology development is focused on enhancing the sustainable management of resources in the natural, primary-producing, urban and business environments. Because research is directed towards sustaining the environment, the company is conscious of managing and mitigating any adverse impact of its activities.

The cornerstones of activity are:

- generating and sharing new knowledge from scientific research
- integrating environmental, social and economic sciences to maximise valuable outcomes
- proactively working in partnership with government, business, communities and Māori
- practising the sustainability principles the company espouses.

Research is strongly aligned to key terrestrial environmental issues that New Zealand and many other countries face, which are:

- conserving and restoring biodiversity and the healthy resilience of natural ecosystems
- reducing pest, disease and weed impact on the natural and managed environments
- understanding, mitigating and adapting to the impact of climate change

Spud and onion research

With 2008 being declared International Year of the Potato, New Zealand's Crop & Food Research scientists continue to breed healthier and longer-lasting potatoes for world consumption.

Having the United Nations declare this special event recognises the role potatoes can play in defeating world hunger. Crop & Food Research nutritional expert Dr Carolyn Lister says the potato is an efficient crop since much of what the plant produces can be eaten, compared with about 50 percent in cereal crops. It is also good quality nutrition in terms of cost.

"As potatoes contain a diversity of nutrients and phytochemicals, there is potential to breed to enhance these levels and select those with greater health benefits," she says.

New Zealand's commercial potato breeding started well before World War II. In the past 10 years, Crop & Food Research's potato breeding programme has become self-sustaining through royalties paid on cultivars. Their varieties are being trialled in Europe and Africa.

Potatoes are one of New Zealand's most valuable vegetable export crops – worth $70.8 million in 2006.

Another important crop being worked on by Crop & Food Research is the onion. Dr Colin Eady has been working on a 'tearless' onion – using gene-silencing technology to stop sulphur compounds converting to a tearing agent, and instead make them available for compounds known for flavour and health properties.

The tearless onion is still under development, but if research progresses well, they should be the market norm within a decade.

Dr Eady is also keen to ensure the onion can be produced sustainably and efficiently. In many countries onions already contribute a significant proportion of daily fibre needs. "They are such a versatile and nutritious vegetable ... more people cooking and eating fresh onions has to be a positive outcome," he says.

Source: Crop & Food Research

Riding the waves

A newly-developed experimental wave energy converter was successfully launched in 2007 in Lyttelton harbour as part of a four-year wave energy project involving Industrial Research, the National Institute of Water and Atmospheric Research and energy industry consultants Power Projects Ltd.

New renewable energy resources are needed in response to increasing energy demand, depletion of conventional resources, and global warming – to which exploitation of fossil fuels is a major contributor. In recent years, wave energy conversion has attracted significant interest from governments and developers looking for alternative carbon-free energy resources.

The project team aims to have a pre-commercial wave energy device completed and demonstrated in open sea conditions by early 2009. It will have controls that forecast incoming waves and adjust the response to changing wave patterns, and a modular generation capability of up to 500kW.

The new device seeks to directly harness both kinetic and potential energy from passing waves. It will be largely sub-surface to allow as much of the converter as possible to interact directly with the wave energy.

The key to success is to extract as much energy as possible from more than one type of motion. This is the aim of the development team, alongside keeping the size and cost of the converter within reason.

Source: Industrial Research

- sustaining the long-term health of soils, waterways and landscapes for the continued viability of rural environments
- enhancing urban biodiversity and developing low-impact approaches for built environments
- fostering environmentally sustainable and globally competitive business practices.

While Landcare Research has 10 teams working across the biological systems, and environment and society portfolios, staff can also work across teams to provide the best multi-disciplinary capability to address particular issues.

GNS Science (Institute of Geological and Nuclear Sciences Ltd) is New Zealand's leading supplier of earth and isotope scientific research and consultancy services. As well as public-good research, activities include: resource evaluation for the petroleum exploration industry; assessment and mitigation of natural hazards; geological mapping; engineering geology; geophysical surveys; assessment and development of geothermal fields; assessment of groundwater quality and quantity; environmental chemistry; marine geology; and the application of isotope sciences to age dating and to the medical, environmental and manufacturing industries.

GNS Science has a 130-year history in earth sciences. It has 330 staff, with offices in Wellington, Wairakei and Dunedin. The library, databases and fossil collections are of national importance.

GNS Science has 11 science sections: mapping; earthquakes, volcanoes, tectonics; geohazard monitoring; geohazard solutions; volcanology; environmental isotopes; isoscan; ocean exploration; hydrocarbons; geothermal, minerals and groundwater; and paleontology.

Industrial Research (Industrial Research Ltd) is a technology company based on world-class science and engineering capability, with the New Zealand Government as a shareholder. The company has an emphasis on manufacturing, processing, biopharmaceutical, medical and energy industries. Technologies are also developed which benefit the horticultural, agricultural and forestry sectors, and defence and security.

Industrial Research engages with industry through research and development, pilot scale production, consultancy services, and sales and licensing. The company is also active in commercialising technology-based innovation.

Industrial Research focuses on biochemistry, physics, mathematics, mechanical engineering, chemical and biological engineering, organic and inorganic chemistry, electrical and electronic engineering, metrology, and information science and technology. The company has nine key technology platforms: carbohydrate chemistry, integrated bioactive technologies, assistive devices, imaging and detecting, high temperature superconducting (HTS), hydrogen and distributed energy, photonics, nanotechnology, and measurement for industry.

HTS-110 Ltd is a subsidiary company of Industrial Research. It designs and manufactures HTS-based magnet solutions, including current leads, magnets and coils, and offers a range of HTS-support services including modelling, development, fabrication and testing.

As a Crown research institute, Industrial Research is a stand-alone company with its own board of directors. It employs approximately 350 staff in Auckland, Wellington and Christchurch.

NIWA The National Institute of Water and Atmospheric Research Ltd Taihoro Nukurangi (NIWA) is an environmental science research organisation creating and delivering science-based products and services that enable people and businesses to make the best use of the natural environment and its living resources, and to derive benefit from them in a sustainable manner.

NIWA's science provides the basis for sustainable resource management, and its consultancy services help clients solve problems relating to:

- aquaculture and marine natural products – all species breeding, early life history, growth and survival, hatchery technology, and other research designed to lead to commercial development; biotechnology; bioactive compounds including anti-inflammatories, anti-cancer; probiotics; skincare; anti-fouling
- aquatic biodiversity and biosecurity – biodiversity surveys, aquatic pests, introduced species, toxic algae, ecosystems including seamounts, DNA analysis
- climate change – the physical and chemical processes affecting the atmosphere and climate, including global effects, stratospheric research and atmosphere-ocean interactions; greenhouse gases; sea-level rise; glaciers; adaptation to climate change; ozone; UV
- coasts and oceans – the geological, biological and physical properties of oceans, coastal waters, estuaries and harbours; seafloor mapping; coastal development and pollution; sediment; wave forecasting, tides, currents; continental shelf, submarine volcanoes; algal blooms
- energy – renewable energy, energy efficiency, vehicle emissions, air quality, hydro inflows
- fisheries – fisheries stock assessment, fisheries modelling and population dynamics; fish biology, ecology, genetics and pathology
- fresh water – the chemistry, physics and biology of lakes, rivers and wetlands; complex interactions influencing ecosystems and their response to environmental disturbances; water quality and quantity, algal blooms
- natural hazards – floods and droughts, extreme weather, coastal erosion, undersea earthquakes and landslides, tsunamis.

Keeping time

New Zealand's official timekeeper is Dr Tim Armstrong (left), director of the New Zealand Time Service at Industrial Research in Lower Hutt.

Atomic clocks invented in the 1950s help him keep time standard, to the nanosecond (a billionth of a second). Precise time and frequency standards are needed for modern electronics such as cellphones and computers.

About 100 times a day time checks are sent from Industrial Research's three caesium-atom clocks to Paris, France where the world time standard is set. The international 'second', based on the unchanging vibration of caesium atoms, was set in 1968.

Source: Industrial Research

NIWA was established in 1992 as a stand-alone company with its own board of directors. In 2007, NIWA had 667 staff at 15 sites around New Zealand, and 15 staff in Perth, Australia; with revenue of $114 million, and assets of $78 million.

The corporate office is in Auckland; the main research campuses are in Auckland, Hamilton, Wellington, Nelson, Christchurch and Lauder (Central Otago), and there are field offices in smaller centres. The company has subsidiaries in Australia and the United States, and a vessel company which owns and operates the deepwater research vessel *Tangaroa* and the coastal research vessel *Kaharoa*.

ESR (Institute of Environmental Science and Research Ltd) provides science-related research and consulting services in public health, environmental health and forensic sciences to the public and private sectors in New Zealand and the Asia-Pacific region. ESR employs about 400 staff at: Mt Albert Science Centre in Auckland, Kenepuru Science Centre in Porirua (head office), the National Centre for Biosecurity and Infectious Disease in Wallaceville, Upper Hutt, and Christchurch Science Centre. Each centre has advanced technologies and information systems to support teams of nationally and internationally-recognised scientists.

Other research organisations

Cawthron Institute The Cawthron Institute, a private scientific research centre with 150 staff, was established in 1924. Operations are based in Nelson, with an aquaculture research field station near the city. Its testing laboratories are International Accreditation New Zealand registered, and accredited by the United States Food and Drug Agency for biotoxin monitoring of shellfish.

The institute undertakes research into marine and freshwater biology and ecology, with much of the work being funded by government. Research interests include aquaculture (particularly shellfish), shellfish selective breeding and husbandry, microalgae culturing, and biochemistry.

Biosecurity is another area of interest, with invasions by foreign marine organisms representing a threat to New Zealand's biosecurity. Joint projects with other laboratories and shipping companies examined the efficiency of ballast water exchange practices, and methods of treatment to remove unwanted organisms. Recent work has centred on hull fouling as a source of introduction and dispersal.

The institute also provides commercial services to industry, specialist scientific advice on environmental issues to resource managers and users, and analytical laboratory testing services for New Zealand clients. This includes resource surveys and impact assessments – such as the effects of discharges and land use on the aquatic environment – baseline surveys, monitoring of coastal and freshwater environs, and oil spill contingency planning.

Cawthron Institute scientists work closely with other research organisations and have good links with overseas groups. Research on toxic algal blooms resulted in a close relationship with researchers in Japan, the United States and Ireland.

BRANZ Ltd is an independent and impartial research testing, consulting and information company, based near Wellington, which provides resources for the building industry. BRANZ has two principal areas of responsibility: to research and investigate the technical aspects of construction and buildings which impact on the built environment in New Zealand, and to enable the transfer of knowledge from the research community to the building and construction industry.

Government departments Several government departments carry out R&D to support their own activities, including development and implementation of policy. Departments with a substantial research interest include the Ministry of Fisheries, Ministry of Social Development, Department of Conservation, Ministry of Agriculture and Forestry (in particular, Biosecurity New Zealand), Ministry of Education, Ministry of Health, Ministry of Justice, and the Museum of New Zealand Te Papa Tongarewa. Government agencies such as the Accident Compensation Corporation, the Earthquake Commission, and Land Transport New Zealand are other important funders of research. In local government, regional councils contract significant amounts of environmental research as part of their role in managing the environment.

Higher education sector Universities, polytechnics and wānanga (Māori tertiary education institutions) offer a broad range of tertiary education services that include science in all cases, and aspects of technology in most. As well as this education and training function, these institutions carry out basic and strategic research and make substantial contributions in applied science and technology – they carry out one-quarter of the research funded by Vote Research, Science and Technology. The majority of this work is performed by the eight universities. Several universities have formal links with Crown research institutes.

Centres of research excellence were introduced during 2002/03 and are funded through Vote Education to encourage development of world-class research in New Zealand. There are seven centres, each hosted by a university and having a number of partner organisations, including other universities, Crown research institutes and wānanga (Māori tertiary education institutions). They cover fields as diverse as bio-protection, Māori development, nanotechnology and molecular ecology.

Research consortia funding was introduced in 2002/03 to bring researchers and end users closer together and promote collaboration among universities, Crown research institutes and businesses. There are 10 research consortia, many carrying out research related to New Zealand's primary production sector.

Research associations are non-government, industry-linked institutions that provide research and technology transfer capabilities that may be beyond the reach of individual companies. Major research associations include: Building Research, Dairy NZ, CRL Energy, the Heavy Engineering Research Association, the New Zealand Fertiliser Manufacturer's Research Association, Leather and Shoe Research Association of New Zealand, and Meat and Wool New Zealand.

Other research associations are private-sector organisations that focus on specific areas of expertise. These include the Malaghan Institute (medical research), New Zealand Council for Educational Research, and the New Zealand Institute for Economic Research. Research is also carried out by commercial market-research firms, private research consultancies and research or analysis units within private enterprises, and voluntary agencies.

Technology services

Patents, trademarks and designs

Intellectual Property Office of New Zealand (IPONZ) is a business unit of the Ministry of Economic Development and operates under the Patents Act 1953, the Trade Marks Act 2002, the Designs Act 1953 and the Plant Variety Rights Act 1987. These acts place statutory obligations on IPONZ and the Commissioner of Patents, Trade Marks, Designs and Plant Varieties in relation to the filing, examination, registration, granting and renewal of intellectual property rights. IPONZ also maintains registers of these rights and interests for clients to search. IPONZ is a receiving office for applications filed under the Patent Cooperation Treaty (PCT), administered by the World Intellectual Property Organisation (WIPO).

Patents The owner of an invention may apply to IPONZ to patent it under the New Zealand Patents Act 1953. A patent grants the owner the exclusive right to exploit the invention commercially in New Zealand for a maximum of 20 years. After the patent expires, anyone may make use of the invention.

The Patents Act 1953 has been reviewed, and a new Patents Bill drafted, to ensure that New Zealand's patent legislation reflects developments in international patent practice, and continues to promote innovation and competition within New Zealand. IPONZ holds a comprehensive collection of patent specifications from other countries.

IPONZ receives newly-published patents from New Zealand and other industrialised countries on CD-ROM. These patents, available to the public, describe the latest advances worldwide in every field of manufacture and have the potential to save New Zealand manufacturers substantial time and money in research and development. In the year ending 30 June 2007, letters patent were sealed on 3,607 applications. The total number of patents on the register is 34,394. The IPONZ patent database is at www.iponz.govt.nz.

Trademarks The owner of a trademark may apply to register it under the New Zealand Trade Marks Act 2002. Once the trademark is registered, the owner has the exclusive right to use it in New Zealand for the goods or services covered by the registration. If anyone else copies a registered mark without permission, the owner has a legal remedy.

Trademarks may remain registered indefinitely by the payment of a renewal fee every 10 years. Anyone may search the online trademark database at www.iponz.govt.nz. Anyone planning to apply to register a trademark may request IPONZ to (for a fee) conduct a search of its records and report if a similar mark has already been registered, or request an official opinion on whether the mark is eligible for registration. There were 13,027 trademarks (22,996 classes) registered in the year ending 30 June 2007. The total number of trademarks on the register is 196,790.

Designs The owner of an industrial design (a novel shape or surface pattern on a manufactured article) may apply to register it under the New Zealand Designs Act 1953. Registration protects the design from unauthorised copying in New Zealand for a maximum of 15 years. The Intellectual

The Dominion Post

Karori scouts Andrew Dewar and Ashleigh Dale explore Island Bay's inter-tidal zone. A month-long marine bioblitz, carried out in Wellington's southern waters in October 2007, uncovered great diversity and richness in the marine environment. Professional and amateur scientists identified 551 species, including four new ones. Six others that are potentially new will be examined in more detail before experts decide if they are indeed new species.

In 2007 New Zealand Post celebrated a group of inventive New Zealanders by issuing their Clever Kiwis stamp series – Bill Gallagher launched his electric fence in 1969 and now it is commonly used around the world; jet boats are too, thanks to Bill Hamilton's invention of the waterjet; spreadable butter was developed in the 1970s, reaching the market 15 years later; from 1992, the mountain buggy began to change the way babies travelled; and Colin Murdoch's 1950s invention, the tranquilliser gun, has saved the lives of countless animals.

Source: NZ Post

Property Office of New Zealand (IPONZ) maintains a public register of designs, which anyone may search. There were 1,227 designs registered in the year ending 30 June 2007. The total number of designs on the register is 8,411.

Table 15.01

Applications for patents, trademarks, designs and plant varieties
Year ending 30 June

Year	Patents	Trademarks[1]	Designs	Plant varieties
1999	5,725	17,364	887	155
2000	6,269	22,771	967	185
2001	6,622	22,620	886	160
2002	6,718	19,173	937	165
2003	6,632	21,256	919	193
2004	6,334	16,604 (25,687)[1]	1,366	143
2005	6,397	16,641 (27,937)[1]	1,321	148
2006	7,526	17,754 (30,691)[1]	1,448	99
2007	8,558	20,173 (35,730)[1]	1,487	157

(1)The Trade Marks Act 2002, which came into force in August 2003, introduced a provision for filing multi-class applications. The trademark statistics from 2003 onward reflect these changes.

Source: Intellectual Property Office of New Zealand

Other intellectual property rights

Plant variety rights are intellectual property rights provided under the Plant Variety Rights Act 1987. This right gives the breeder of a new plant variety the exclusive right to sell, or license others to sell, reproductive material of the variety. During the year ending 30 June 2007, 104 grants were issued and 95 grants were terminated. The total number of valid grants on the register is 1,304. Applications for ornamental varieties are the largest group (71 percent of all applications) followed by fruit varieties (14 percent), crop varieties (8 percent), pasture varieties (5 percent) and varieties of fungi (2 percent).

Patent, trademark, design and plant variety applications are shown in table 15.01. Not all applications result in registration.

Copyright is granted automatically upon the creation of any original literary, dramatic, musical or artistic work, sound recording, film, broadcast, cable programme or published edition. The Copyright Act 1994 is administered by the competition, trade and investment branch of the Ministry of Economic Development.

Layout designs The Layout Designs Act 1994 provides protection for the designs of integrated circuits. The Act protects layout designs from unauthorised copying in New Zealand for up to 15 years. The Act is administered by the competition, trade and investment branch of the Ministry of Economic Development.

Telarc SAI Ltd

Telarc SAI Ltd is a registered company owned by the Testing Laboratory Registration Council. Telarc SAI provides recognition and assessment services for management systems, and operates from Auckland, Hamilton, Tauranga, Wellington and Christchurch.

Recognition services Telarc SAI Ltd provides recognition of achieving the standards below.

- Quality management systems certification to ISO 9001 standard – Telarc SAI has provided the ISO 9000 certification service since 1983, being the first organisation in New Zealand to achieve formal accreditation by the Joint Accreditation System of Australia and New Zealand (JAS-ANZ).

- Telarc Q-Base – a basic, entry-level management system based on the ISO 9001 standard, that identifies the basic quality management disciplines essential for managing the quality of small to medium enterprises.

- Environmental management systems certification to ISO 14001 standard – Telarc SAI has provided this service since 1994, and in 1996, was the first organisation in New Zealand to be accredited by JAS-ANZ to certify ISO 14001.

- Certification of health and disability service providers to meet the requirements of the Ministry of Health – this recognition service is provided by Quality Health New Zealand, a division of Telarc SAI.

- Customer 1st – for approving an organisation's commitment to its customers.

Assessments Telarc SAI Ltd provides assessment services for a wide range of management systems, including occupational health and safety, Accident Compensation Corporation workplace safety management practices, product certification, and rail safety.

Training Telarc SAI works closely with the New Zealand Quality College to provide training courses to promote excellence in management system practices.

International Accreditation New Zealand

International Accreditation New Zealand (IANZ) is the national body for the accreditation of testing and calibration laboratories, radiology services and inspection services. It is part of the Testing Laboratory Registration Council, a user-funded Crown entity established by an act of Parliament in 1972. IANZ's functions include:

- laboratory and calibration accreditation – assessing the technical competence of testing, measurement and calibration laboratories in all fields of science and technology, including biological, chemical, dairy, water, electrical, gas cylinder, mechanical, medical, physical and wool testing; and metrology and calibration. All categories are accredited to NZS ISO/IEC 17025 standard, except medical testing, which is accredited to NZS/ISO 15189

- inspection body accreditation – providing formal recognition that an inspection body or food safety assessment body is capable of meeting standards of quality, performance, technical expertise and competence. Accreditation is to AS/NZS ISO/IEC 17020 standard

- radiology service accreditation – providing radiology services with formal recognition of their skills, expertise, competence, systems, procedures and facilities, based on independent peer group assessment. Accreditation is to the New Zealand Code of Radiological Management Practice

- OECD good laboratory practice – IANZ is the compliance monitoring authority in New Zealand for the Organisation for Economic Co-operation and Development's principles of good laboratory practice. This programme is relevant to research laboratories undertaking non-clinical safety trials for new veterinary pharmaceuticals and agricultural chemicals

- CE marking – IANZ is the designating authority for conformity assessment bodies approved to undertake testing or inspection against European directives for CE product standard marking purposes. This appointment is under the New Zealand/European Union Governmental Mutual Recognition Agreement

- meat industry laboratory approval – IANZ accredits meat industry testing laboratories under the New Zealand Food Safety Authority Laboratory Approval Scheme

- building consent authorities – are assessed by IANZ against the requirements of the Building (Accreditation of Building Consent Authorities) Regulations 2006 on behalf of the Department of Building and Housing.

International arrangements IANZ represents New Zealand at international conformity assessment forums and maintains mutual recognition arrangements with other national laboratory and inspection body accreditation authorities. The economies involved include: Argentina, Australia, Austria, Belgium, Brazil, Canada, People's Republic of China, Cuba, Czech Republic, Denmark, Egypt, Estonia, Finland, France, Germany, Greece, Hong Kong China, India, Indonesia, Ireland, Israel, Italy, Japan, Republic of Korea, Latvia, Lithuania, Malaysia, Mexico, the Netherlands, Norway, Philippines, Poland, Portugal, Romania, Singapore, Slovak Republic, Slovenia, South Africa, Spain, Sweden, Switzerland, Chinese Taipei, Thailand, Turkey, United Kingdom, United States and Viet Nam.

Training The New Zealand Quality College is the training division of IANZ and provides training in association with IANZ and Telarc SAI. Topics cover laboratory management, inspection body management, quality and environmental management, health and safety management, food safety management and auditing skills.

Experienced staff from IANZ and Telarc SAI, and others who are national experts in their fields, present these courses. The college is registered as a private training establishment with the New Zealand Qualifications Authority.

Standards New Zealand

Standards New Zealand is the operating arm of the Standards Council, an autonomous Crown entity under the Standards Act 1988. The Standards Council, an appointed body with representatives from a wide range of community sectors, is the governing body for Standards New Zealand.

Standards New Zealand is the country's leading developer of standards and standard-based solutions, providing solutions in areas such as health and disability, environmental management, legal risk, information technology, sport and recreation, and fertility services.

There are 60 full-time staff, supported by more than 2,000 New Zealanders who voluntarily serve on boards and committees. Revenue comes from contracts with industry and government organisations for development and support of standards, and from the sale of standards and standards-related publications.

The majority of standards are developed in partnership with Standards Australia. As New Zealand's representative for the International Organization for Standardization (ISO) and the International Electrotechnical Commission (IEC), Standards New Zealand ensures New Zealand has a voice in the international community.

Standards New Zealand is the enquiry point for the World Trade Organization and supplies specialist advice on overseas standards, regulations, codes of practice, and testing and approval procedures in foreign markets.

Contributors and related websites

AgResearch Ltd – www.agresearch.co.nz

BRANZ Ltd – www.branz.co.nz

Cawthron Institute – www.cawthron.org.nz

Crown Company Monitoring Advisory Unit – www.ccmau.govt.nz

Foundation for Research, Science and Technology – www.frst.govt.nz

GNS Science – www.gns.cri.nz

Health Research Council of New Zealand – www.hrc.govt.nz

HortResearch – www.hortresearch.co.nz

Industrial Research Ltd – www.irl.cri.nz

Institute of Environmental Science and Research Ltd – www.esr.cri.nz

Intellectual Property Office of New Zealand – www.iponz.govt.nz

International Accreditation New Zealand – www.ianz.govt.nz

Landcare Research New Zealand Ltd – www.landcareresearch.co.nz

Ministry of Economic Development – www.med.govt.nz

Ministry of Research, Science and Technology – www.morst.govt.nz

National Institute of Water and Atmospheric Research Ltd – www.niwa.cri.nz

New Zealand Institute for Crop and Food Research – www.crop.cri.nz

New Zealand Post – www.nzpost.co.nz

New Zealand Venture Investment Fund Ltd – www.nzvif.com

Plant Variety Rights Office – www.pvr.govt.nz

Royal Society of New Zealand – www.rsnz.org

Science New Zealand – www.sciencenewzealand.org

Scion – www.scionresearch.com

Standards New Zealand – www.standards.co.nz

Statistics New Zealand – www.stats.govt.nz

Telarc SAI Ltd – www.telarcsai.co.nz

Kennedy Lange

Lake Roundabout near Ashburton in the South Island. Wetlands create a rich and diverse habitat for native plants and animals. They filter water, reduce the severity of floods, and contribute generally to the health of the environment. Wetlands are also among the world's most threatened habitats. In New Zealand only about 10 percent of wetlands remain.

16 | Land and environment

Land, freshwater, and sea resources are core to New Zealand's valuable primary industries and are a large part of the life and culture of New Zealanders. But New Zealand, like every other country, has environmental issues to address. Decades of human activity – production, consumption and growth – have impacted dramatically on the environment. This has increased the need to measure the effect of human activities and to protect the environment in order to secure a sustainable future.

New Zealand's low population and limited industrial base means that its environmental issues are generally less severe than those of many other industrialised countries. Using water more sustainably, managing marine resources, reducing waste, and improving energy efficiency are all essential for a secure economy and quality of life, as well as for environmental sustainability.

New Zealand's big export earners – agriculture, horticulture, forestry and tourism – rely on a stable, predictable climate. International scientists now agree the global climate is changing. It is projected that the world's average temperature could rise by 0.2 degrees Celsius over each of the next two decades.

New Zealand is not immune to the effects of global climate change and the country's climate patterns are changing. The latest forecasts are for more frequent droughts and floods (drier in the east and wetter in the west), rising sea and snow levels, and changing rainfall patterns.

Biodiversity

New Zealand's unique biodiversity – the variety of all biological life, which includes plants, animals, micro-organisms and fungi, the genes they contain, and the ecosystems on land or in water where they live – results from geographic isolation of more than 80 million years. There are an estimated 80,000 native animal, plant, and fungi species in New Zealand.

Biologically diverse ecosystems provide important resources such as clean air and water, help to decompose wastes and recycle nutrients, maintain healthy soils, aid pollination, regulate local climates, and reduce flooding. Protection from pests, weeds and diseases is important for New Zealand's natural resources and for the introduced species on which our primary industry depends.

In the past 700–800 years, two-thirds of New Zealand's land has been extensively modified. Humans and their accompanying animals and pests have caused the extinction of 31 percent of indigenous land and freshwater bird species, 18 percent of endemic seabird species, three of seven species of frogs, and at least 12 invertebrate species (such as snails and insects). Today, almost 2,500 native land-based and freshwater species are listed as threatened.

Figure 16.01

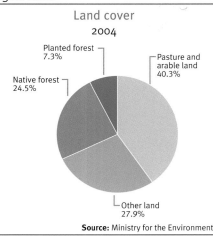

Land cover
2004

Planted forest
7.3%

Native forest
24.5%

Pasture and
arable land
40.3%

Other land
27.9%

Source: Ministry for the Environment

About 44 percent of New Zealand's land area is covered by native vegetation, most of which is in hill country and alpine areas. Little forest remains intact in lowland areas, where the predominant land cover is pastoral or urban open space. It is estimated that wetland areas have reduced by 90 percent from their original area.

Weeds and introduced animals, particularly those that have become feral (for example stoats, deer and rats), pose the greatest threats to remaining native species and ecosystems.

About 31 percent of New Zealand's land area is legally protected for conservation purposes, either as public conservation land or through conservation initiatives on private land. Most of this land is in upland areas and mountains. Lowlands, river margins, wetlands, dune lands and coastal areas remain under-represented in the protected areas network.

A new national statement of priorities for biodiversity has been established to help local authorities make decisions when trying to regenerate or protect biodiversity on private land. A government fund is also provided to support the protection of the country's biodiversity by individuals and communities.

Air quality

Compared with other countries, New Zealand has relatively good air quality because of its small population, its limited heavy industry, its distance from other countries, and regular westerly winds in most places.

Nevertheless, air pollution gets high enough to cause health problems in many urban areas. About 1,100 New Zealanders die prematurely each year from exposure to air pollution. Common pollutants are fine particles (PM10), sulphur dioxide, nitrogen oxides, carbon monoxide, and ground level ozone. The main contributions to air pollution are from transport and home heating (coal and wood fires).

New Zealand's small and dispersed population relies heavily on private transport. Motor vehicle emissions are a significant source of air pollution, emitting pollutants such as carbon monoxide, dioxins, nitrogen oxides, volatile organic compounds and fine particles. Increased vehicle numbers, larger average engine sizes, and traffic congestion all put increasing pressure on air quality.

Three new skink species identified

Department of Conservation

A Fiordland skink, in the Fiordland National Park.

During February–March 2007, Landcare Research herpetologist, Trent Bell, ventured into Fiordland's Sinbad Valley and up Barrier Knob in search of a skink first discovered by rock climbers in 2004. Bell ended up finding three new species.

The Sinbad Valley is a deep, very steep-sided basin that was carved out during the last ice age and Barrier Knob is an inaccessible peak 1,800 metres above sea level. The inaccessible terrain, combined with the remote locations and extraordinary environmental climate, has largely protected the lizards from invasive pests to date, and given the skink species a chance to evolve in isolation.

Finding the skinks raises questions as to what other undiscovered species could still be out there in the alpine areas of Fiordland. These discoveries have led to new expeditions led by Landcare Research into the Fiordland wilderness to search for other possible new species.

Skinks are one of two families known as lizards (the other family is geckos), both of which are important to New Zealand's endemic biodiversity. Lizards act as pollinators and seed dispersers, and also as medium-level predators – roles that are important in maintaining natural ecosystems. More than half of New Zealand's lizard species are classified as rare, threatened or endangered, through habitat loss and introduced predators.

Source: Landcare Research

In the winter, home heating is the main cause of air pollution in populated areas. Wood and coal used in home heating are major sources of air pollution in the form of fine particles and sulphur dioxide. In New Zealand, 45 percent of households burn wood or coal for home heating.

The main focus for improving air quality is to reduce PM10 particles from home heating and traffic. In September 2005, national environmental standards were set for five commonly recognised air pollutants: PM10 particles, nitrogen dioxide, carbon monoxide, sulphur dioxide, and ground-level ozone. Regional councils are required to measure air quality and publicly report whenever pollution levels exceed standard limits.

Through the Warm Homes project, central and local government are working together to help New Zealanders stay warm while reducing the pollution effects of home heating. The number of households with open fires has decreased in recent years, while the number of homes with more efficient slow-combustion fires, such as wood burners, has increased.

Climate change

Atmospheric gases such as carbon dioxide, methane, and nitrous oxide keep the temperature near the earth's surface within a stable range – around 30 degrees Celsius higher than it would be without them – providing climate conditions suitable for humans.

Air pollution increases the concentration of these greenhouse gases, and temperatures rise as more heat from solar energy is trapped in the earth's atmosphere than before – this is the 'greenhouse effect'. Air pollution increasing the concentrations of these greenhouse gases is thought to play a major role in climate change. The result is more extreme weather events – floods, storms, cyclones, droughts and slips – and rising sea levels and coastal erosion.

In 2005, total emissions of greenhouse gases in New Zealand were 77.2 million tonnes of carbon dioxide equivalents. Between 1990 and 2005, total greenhouse gas emissions increased by 25 percent, reflecting the growing population and economy. While New Zealand's greenhouse gas emissions represent much less than 1 percent of global emissions, New Zealand has the 12th highest rate of emissions per head of population.

New Zealand has a unique profile of greenhouse gas emissions for a developed nation, with the agricultural sector contributing nearly 50 percent of total emissions. Carbon dioxide emissions, largely from energy generation and transport, contribute most of the other 50 percent.

Between 1990 and 2005, carbon dioxide removed from the atmosphere by forest growth (forest sinks) increased by 29 percent, largely because of increases in plantation forestry in the mid 1990s.

Figure 16.02 shows changes in levels of greenhouse gas emissions in New Zealand.

The effects of climate change are potentially far-reaching. In New Zealand, climate change is likely to bring about rising sea levels, increase floods and droughts, change wind and rainfall patterns, increase temperatures, reduce frosts, put pressure on ecosystems, and increase the threat of pest species becoming established.

There is global consensus on the urgent need to respond to climate change, both in terms of reducing greenhouse gas emissions and in preparing for its impact. In response to this, the New Zealand Government has programmes already in place to reduce emissions and is developing more.

To ensure New Zealand meets its Kyoto Protocol commitments, the Government has introduced legislation for a carbon emissions trading scheme and has implemented a moratorium on new fossil-fuelled thermal electricity generation, to create a preference for renewable electricity generation. It has also proposed initiatives for environmentally-friendly land management. An existing programme, the New Zealand Energy Efficiency and Conservation Strategy, also addresses the drive to reduce energy use by developing new sources of renewable energy that are less polluting, and by using energy more efficiently.

Ozone layer

The ozone layer, between 15 and 30 kilometres above the earth's surface, shields the earth from the sun's ultraviolet radiation. In the 1980s, a hole in the ozone layer over Antarctica was identified. A reducing ozone layer has serious implications for New Zealand, as ultraviolet radiation can cause skin cancer, damage the marine environment, and distort plant growth.

Depletion of the ozone layer has been caused primarily by emissions of gases containing chlorine and bromine (chlorofluorocarbons or CFCs). These chemicals were used widely in the past as refrigerants, and in some industrial processes. The identification of the ozone hole over Antarctica led to international agreements to control the use of ozone-depleting substances.

Atmospheric ozone levels over Antarctica are now reducing more slowly than they were during the 1980s and 1990s, and ozone measured over Central Otago has stabilised since the late 1990s. Monitored summer-time levels of ultraviolet radiation in New Zealand have also improved.

Many ozone-depleting gases are also greenhouse gases. Reducing the use of ozone-depleting gases can both protect the ozone layer and reduce climate change.

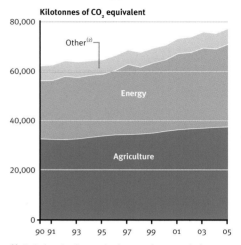

Figure 16.02

Greenhouse gas emissions
By greenhouse gas source[1]
Year ending 31 December

Kilotonnes of CO$_2$ equivalent

(1) Excludes land use, land use change and forestry.
(2) Includes industrial processes, solvent and other product use, waste and other sources.

Source: Ministry for the Environment

Figure 16.03

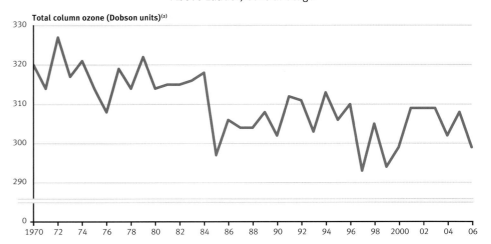

Mean levels of ozone[1]
Above Lauder, Central Otago

(1) Shows annual mean total of column ozone at Lauder, in Central Otago (latitude 45.0S, longitude 169.7E). (2) Figures are based in Dobson spectrophotometer measurements and are supplemented with satellite measurements standardised to the Dobson measurements. One Dobson unit is 0.01mm of ozone layer thickness at zero degrees Celsius at sea level.

Source: NIWA

Figure 16.03 shows changes in the level of ozone measured in Lauder, Central Otago, which is considered to be representative of the ozone layer above New Zealand.

Water quality

By international standards, fresh water in New Zealand is both clean and plentiful. Most areas of New Zealand have between 600 and 1,500 millimetres of rainfall a year. However, availability varies significantly between regions, with higher annual rainfall levels on the western side and generally decreasing levels towards the east coast of both the North and South Islands.

The demand for water is increasingly putting pressure on both the availability and quality of the resource. In areas that are dominated by intensive land use, some aspects of water quality are declining. Urban development, clearance of land and intensification of agriculture have increased sedimentation, nutrients and harmful micro-organisms in rivers and streams. As a result, water quality in many lowland streams and rivers has been affected.

Coastal water quality Over the 2006/07 summer, 80 percent of the 380 monitored beaches had safe levels of bacteria almost all the time. Only 1 percent of sites breached bacterial guidelines regularly.

Common sources of coastal water contamination include sewage and stormwater outfalls, septic tanks, sanitation discharges from boats, and effluent run-off from agricultural areas. Generally, concentrations of contaminants are lower at sites on the open coastline than at inland freshwater sites, with coastal beaches more frequently flushed by tides and currents.

Freshwater quality Fresh water is one of New Zealand's most valuable natural assets and is a vital part of the economy. It is used to irrigate crops and pastures, dispose or dilute trade wastes and sewage, and produce hydroelectric energy.

New Zealand has 425,000 kilometres of rivers and streams. When compared internationally, New Zealand's rivers have very high quality water because they contain low concentrations of dissolved material and nutrients. Rivers in catchments that have little or no farming or urban development make up about half of the total length of New Zealand's rivers and have good water quality.

Water quality is generally poorest in rivers and streams in urban and farmed catchments. Until the 1970s, the major cause of deterioration in water quality in New Zealand was the discharge of poorly treated sewage, stock effluent, and other organic wastes directly into water bodies from sources such as wastewater treatment stations, meat works and dairy factories. However, this type of river pollution has reduced over the past 30 years, as a result of improved management.

Today, the most serious pollutants of fresh water come from diffuse sources. In recent years, the impact of agricultural land use on water quality has grown as a result of increased stocking rates and use of nitrogen fertilisers. Both nitrogen and phosphorus levels in rivers have increased over the past two decades. Excessive levels of these nutrients in waterways can cause algal blooms and degrade water quality. However, even in the most polluted rivers for which data is available, the level of nutrients is only about half the average for all rivers reported by Organisation for Economic Co-operation and Development (OECD) countries.

Of the ground waters that are monitored, 61 percent have normal nitrate levels and only 5 percent have nitrate levels that make the water unsafe for infants to drink. However, it is not known how many of these monitored ground waters are used to supply human drinking water.

Marine environment

New Zealand's marine area is about 14 times bigger than its land area. At more than 4.4 million hectares, New Zealand's marine environment supports a diverse range of ecosystems, plants, animals and food resources, and is immensely valuable. New Zealand's marine environment is home to a large number of species found nowhere else in the world.

The marine area is used for a range of purposes, including transportation, fisheries, recreation, and tourism. New Zealand's marine industries are worth an estimated $3.3 billion (about 3 percent of gross domestic product), including $1.3 billion in fisheries exports in 2007.

Fishing activities are widespread throughout New Zealand and take place in virtually every habitat type, except the deepest sea floor. A quota management system is used in New Zealand to ensure fishing activity is sustainable. The system sets catch limits for each species, based on their abundance and characteristics.

Regional councils manage marine farming in coastal areas under the Aquaculture Reform Act 2004, and the discharge of contaminants into coastal marine areas under the Resource Management Act 1991.

Most of New Zealand's population lives close to the coast. Construction, land reclamation, drainage, urban infrastructure and shoreline developments affect the coastal environment, through the alteration of physical characteristics of shorelines and the discharge of pollutants into the sea. The impact on the marine environment has been less than in other developed countries because of New Zealand's small population and abundant marine resources offshore, where much of the environment is not easily accessible.

Marine reserves are expected to play a significant role in protecting New Zealand's marine biodiversity. Currently, 31 marine reserves cover 7 percent of New Zealand's marine territory. Nearly half these reserves have been established since 2000, and the area designated as marine reserves has almost doubled in that period. However, 99 percent of the area protected is in only two offshore marine reserves, and some key habitats remain unprotected.

Energy

New Zealand has access to a wide range of energy sources, both renewable (hydro, geothermal, wood, wind, biogas and solar) and non-renewable (oil, gas and coal). Energy is an essential element of life, but its production, distribution and use can have an adverse impact on the environment.

New Zealand's total primary energy supply is growing to meet increased consumer demand. Between 1996 and 2006, New Zealand's total primary energy supply increased by 6 percent. In 2006, 70 percent of this supply came from fossil-fuel-based oil, natural gas, and coal. The remaining 30 percent came from renewable sources.

Renewable energy resources, such as hydro, geothermal, wind, and wood, accounted for approximately 66 percent of electricity generation in New Zealand in 2006. Of this, hydro generation was the major supplier of electricity, producing about 56 percent.

The largest energy consumer is the transport sector. Oil accounted for about 51 percent of New Zealand's consumer energy demand in 2006, and the transport sector used approximately 86 percent of this oil. New Zealand's heavy use of oil in transport can largely be attributed to its small and sparsely-distributed population. Although self-sufficient in electricity, gas and coal, New Zealand relies on imported oil to meet most of its domestic oil demand.

While New Zealand's energy needs are increasing, they are not increasing as fast as the economy is growing. Statistics New Zealand's energy account measures energy intensity – the amount of energy needed to produce goods and services. In the 1997–2005 period, energy intensity decreased by nearly 5 percent at a national level. This indicates that New Zealand's economy has become more efficient in its use of energy.

New Zealand's growth in greenhouse gas emissions is largely attributable to two sectors: agriculture and energy. In the energy sector, the growth is associated with increased electricity generation (from coal), and increased use of transport fuels. The *New Zealand Energy Strategy* (2007) and the *New Zealand Energy Efficiency and Conservation Strategy* (revised 2007) include policies to encourage an increasing role for renewable resources in energy supply, and improved energy efficiency in energy demand, in order to help reduce greenhouse gas emissions.

Minerals

New Zealand has a large variety of mineral deposits and is well known for its production of gold and coal.

The mineral industry is a significant contributor to the New Zealand economy, not only in terms of export revenues, but also as a substantial employer of a highly skilled workforce.

Some minerals are also of cultural importance to New Zealanders. For example, pounamu, or New Zealand greenstone, is of particular significance to Māori, specifically Ngai Tahu who have ownership of the resource.

Figure 16.04

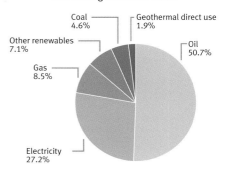

Energy used by consumers
By fuel type
Year ending December 2006

Coal 4.6%
Geothermal direct use 1.9%
Other renewables 7.1%
Oil 50.7%
Gas 8.5%
Electricity 27.2%

Source: Ministry of Economic Development

Powelliphanta snails

Powelliphanta are giants of the snail world. They can reach up to 90 millimetres across, about the size of a man's fist. Their oversized shells come in an array of colours and patterns, ranging from hues of red and brown to yellow and black. Unfortunately, they are also one of the most threatened of New Zealand's invertebrates. A total of 40 species or subspecies are ranked as being of national conservation concern.

Powelliphanta snails are named after Dr A W B Powell, a former scientist at Auckland Museum who studied the snails during the 1930s and 1940s. They are quite different from common garden snails, which are a European import and an unwanted garden pest. Powelliphanta snails are unlikely to be found in domestic gardens as most favour living in the forest.

Powelliphanta snails are carnivores and particularly like to eat earthworms but they are also known to eat slugs. For the most part, they live buried in leaf mould or under logs, only coming out at night to forage and to mate.

Powelliphanta snails are hermaphrodites, meaning they possess both male and female reproductive organs and therefore can mate with any other adult Powelliphanta. Powelliphanta snails lay about 5–10 large eggs a year. Each egg is up to 12–14 millimetres long, pearly pink and hard-shelled – like a small bird's egg.

These meat-eating giants of the forest floor are true biological oddities. They are as representative of New Zealand's unique evolutionary history as the kakapo, moa or kiwi.

Source: Department of Conservation

Gold was first discovered in New Zealand in the 1850s and was retrieved either by washing alluvial gravels, silts and sands, by crushing gold-bearing veins of quartz, or by hydraulic sluicing. In 1881, the first dredge was used to work riverbeds to recover gold.

There are three large open-cast goldmines in New Zealand, with a number of medium and small-sized mines. Mining is subject to strict environmental standards.

Coal is New Zealand's largest energy resource, with recoverable reserves of approximately 8.6 billion tonnes, most of which is lignite. Some New Zealand coals have special properties, which make them valuable for steel making and other specialist uses.

While coal has a long history of use in New Zealand, quantities exported have increased markedly in the past decade, with Japan, India, China and South Africa the main markets. The largest domestic users of coal are the electricity and steel production industries.

Tools for mineral exploration and mine design and measurement include aerial photography, photogrammetric mapping and the use of geographic information systems (GIS) in digital terrain modelling, and three-dimensional modelling of subsurface ore bodies. Remote sensing is being used to provide high-resolution images of the earth's crust, which, when combined with other information, can identify targets for detailed ground investigation. Advances in technology have meant that minerals that were once inaccessible now have the potential to be extracted.

Soil quality

Soils play an integral part in supporting one of New Zealand's top export earners – primary production. In 2007, agriculture, forestry, horticulture, and viticulture generated $16.1 billion, $3.6 billion, $2.5 billion, and $662 million, respectively, in export earnings.

New Zealand soils are naturally acidic, with low levels of nitrogen, phosphorus and sulphur. Soils used to grow crops and pasture need to be developed and maintained with nitrogen-fixing plants (such as clover), fertilisers, and often lime, to sustain high-yield plant growth. As a result, farmed soils today have different biological, chemical and physical properties than soils farmed by early settlers.

Monitoring New Zealand's soils by major land-use types (for example, livestock farming, cropping, forestry) and soil orders (soil groups) helps primary producers and resource managers to understand how different soils respond to different land uses. Maintaining healthy soils is fundamental to maintaining sustained productive land use.

Soil health and intactness Soils underpin food, fibre, and timber production in New Zealand. Soils also protect the environment by:

- acting as buffers and filters to reduce nutrient loss
- limiting the need for irrigation
- breaking down pollutants
- regulating gas emissions
- being a fundamental part of the water cycle.

Landcare Research soil scientist Dr Les Basher assesses the colour of soil in Motupiko valley, Nelson. Results of soil health monitoring provide the opportunity to evaluate and redesign land management systems to increase sustainability.

'Soil health' (or soil quality) is the biological, chemical and physical condition of different soil types under specific land uses. 'Soil intactness' is the ability of soils to stay in place. The Ministry for the Environment's core set of national environment indicators includes two indicators for soils: soil health, and the soil intactness of erosion-prone hill country.

To monitor soil health, the government has encouraged the development of practical indicators of soil quality, as well as techniques and monitoring tools that farmers can use to measure sustainable land management. For example, the 500 Soils Project monitored seven key measures of soil quality across seven major land-use categories and New Zealand's 15 soil orders. Monitoring soil health identifies whether soils are degraded.

Land and resource managers are primarily concerned with soil erosion caused by human activity (induced erosion), rather than natural erosion processes. Human induced hill-country erosion has been estimated to cost New Zealand between $100 million and $150 million each year through: loss of soil and nutrients; loss of production; damage to houses, fences, roads, phone and power lines; damage to waterways and aquatic habitats.

With 30 percent of New Zealand's land being hilly (slope of 25 degrees or more) and 10 percent of this classed as severely erodible, soil intactness on erosion-prone hill country is important. The removal of native forest for pastoral land use between the 1880s and 1920s increased erosion rates. Monitoring changes in land cover can be used to assess changes in pasture on erosion-prone hill country.

Environmental and resource management

Land cover

New Zealand's 26.9 million hectares are predominantly mountainous and hilly. More than two-thirds (18.5 million hectares) of the land slopes at greater than 12 degrees and nearly half at greater than 28 degrees. Nearly three-fifths of the country (16 million hectares) is more than 300 metres above sea level, with one-fifth above 900 metres.

Extensive changes have occurred in New Zealand's land cover since human occupation. The cover of indigenous forest has declined to 29 percent of its former extent and scrub and tussock have nearly doubled in area. Greatest losses of land cover have occurred in warm, dry environments, particularly those with soils and landforms suited to intensive agriculture.

Table 16.01 shows the major types of land use and land cover in New Zealand.

Bioethics Council

The Bioethics Council Toi te Taiao was established in October 2002 as a ministerial advisory committee, following recommendations from a Royal Commission of Inquiry into Genetic Modification. The goal of the council is to enhance New Zealand's understanding of the cultural, ethical and spiritual aspects of biotechnology and to ensure that the use of biotechnology has regard for values held by New Zealanders. The council provides information, promotes and participates in public discussion and gives advice to the government.

Environmental planning framework

The Resource Management Act 1991 (RMA) provides one of the key means through which the people of New Zealand plan and decide how to use, distribute, or protect natural and physical resources.

Resources include rivers, lakes, coastal and geothermal areas, land, (including soils) forests and farmlands, the air, and the built environment, such as buildings, bridges and other structures in cities and towns.

The purpose of the RMA is to promote sustainable management of natural and physical resources. This means local authorities look at the environment as a whole when planning and making decisions. The focus of the legislation is on the effects that proposed activities will have on the environment.

Local authorities prepare plans to help them manage natural and physical resources. While these plans are being formed, members of the community have the opportunity to say what they want to happen in their communities, during public consultation, or through making submissions and attending public hearings.

National policies In preparing plans to manage natural and physical resources under the RMA, local authorities must recognise and provide for matters of national importance by protecting the following from inappropriate subdivision, use and development:

- the natural character of the coastal environment, wetlands, lakes and rivers, and their margins
- outstanding natural features and landscapes
- areas of significant indigenous vegetation, and significant habitats of indigenous fauna
- heritage areas.

Table 16.01

Dominant land use and selected land cover

2004

Land use/cover	Hectares
Land use	
Dairy farming	1,879,600
Intensive sheep and beef farming	3,841,100
Hill-country sheep and beef farming	4,023,200
High-country sheep and beef farming	48,900
Deer farming	249,700
Other animal farming	64,900
Ungrazed	659,800
Urban	203,600
Planted forest	1,957,000
Arable crops	1,200
Vegetables	2,200
Berry fruit	1,200
Pip fruit	10,200
Grapes	18,800
Summer fruit	1,800
Tropical fruit	1,600
Kiwifruit	6,400
Flowers	57
Other land cover	
Tussock	2,645,200
Native forest	6,567,200
Rivers, lakes, snow, and ice	2,094,200
Scrub	2,543,600
Total	**26,821,500**

Note: Figures may not add up to stated totals due to rounding.

Source: Ministry for the Environment

Local authorities must maintain and enhance public access to the coastal marine area, and to lakes and rivers. They must also recognise and provide for the relationship of Māori and their culture and traditions with their ancestral lands, water, sites, wāhi tapu (sacred places) and other taonga (treasures).

Plans must include national policy made under the RMA. A national policy can relate to any matter that is of national significance and is relevant to achieving sustainable management of natural and physical resources.

The RMA requires decision makers to consider:

- kaitiakitanga, the ethic of stewardship
- efficient use and development of natural and physical resources
- maintenance and enhancement of amenity values
- intrinsic values of ecosystems
- maintenance and enhancement of the quality of the environment
- any finite characteristics of natural and physical resources
- protection of the habitat of trout and salmon.

Sustainable management Under the RMA, sustainable management involves managing natural and physical resources in a way that enables people to provide for their own well-being, while sustaining the potential of natural and physical resources to meet the foreseeable needs of future generations. This involves safeguarding the life-supporting capacity of air, water, soil and ecosystems, and avoiding, remedying or mitigating any adverse effects of human activities on the environment.

Regional policies and plans Regional councils have an important role in managing natural and physical resources. Regional councils must each prepare a regional policy statement that provides an overview of the resource management issues in their region, and the policies and methods that will be used to achieve the integrated management of natural and physical resources. Regional and district plans must put the regional policy statement into effect.

Regional councils are responsible for managing water, soil, and geothermal resources; pollution control; and strategic integration of infrastructure with land use. Regional, city, and district councils are jointly responsible for natural hazard mitigation; hazardous substances; contaminated land; and maintaining indigenous biodiversity. Regional councils and the Minister of Conservation are responsible for the coastal marine area. A regional council may produce one or more regional plans to assist them in managing these matters. Such plans contain rules that determine whether a resource consent is required. Regional councils are required to produce one or more regional coastal plan to help them manage the coastal marine area of their region.

District planning District and city councils are responsible for land use management. District and city councils also manage noise and activities on the surface of water. Each district and city council must prepare a district plan, which includes rules that allow, manage or prohibit activities.

Ministry of Agriculture and Forestry

Department of Conservation staff help clean cars and boats, and promote didymo awareness, at the 2007 Jet Boat Marathon held in Canterbury. The invasive alga was first discovered in Southland rivers in 2004.

Resource consents

A resource consent gives permission to use or develop a natural or physical resource and/or carry out an activity that affects the environment in some way. Rules in regional plans or district plans determine when a resource consent is required. There are five types of resource consent described in the RMA: land use (granted by district, city and, sometimes, regional councils); subdivision (district councils); water permit (regional councils); discharge permit (regional councils); and coastal permit (regional councils).

Applicants for consents need to assess potential impacts that the proposal is likely to have on the environment and submit this assessment to the authority responsible for consents. The applicant must also explain what consultation, if any, has taken place with anyone who may be affected by the proposal. Some resource consent applications require the public to be notified, giving them a chance to consider the application and make submissions.

Decisions to grant or decline resource consent applications are usually made by local authorities. If an applicant or submitter disagrees with the decision, they can appeal to the Environment Court.

Around 50,000 resource consent applications are made to local authorities each year. Of these applications, around 6 percent are normally notified, less than 1 percent declined, and around 1 percent appealed to the Environment Court.

Public involvement The RMA provides for members of the public to take part in managing the resources of their area. They can make submissions on proposed regional policy statements and regional and district plans, and on any changes to these.

Members of the public can also make submissions on publicly-notified applications for resource consents. The Environmental Legal Assistance fund was established in 2001 to provide community, environmental, and iwi (tribe) and hapū (subtribe) groups with financial assistance to participate in the environment court and other courts.

Use of land The RMA requires councils to address effects of activities rather than the activity itself. People can generally use their land in the way they wish, provided there are no adverse environmental effects, unless there is a rule in the plans that constrains that use. Constraints must be clearly identified in policy statements and plans.

Hazardous substances and new organisms

The Hazardous Substances and New Organisms Act 1996, protects the environment and the health and safety of people and communities by preventing or managing adverse effects of hazardous substances and new organisms. The Act is administered by the Environmental Risk Management Authority (ERMA). Hazardous substances managed under the Act are substances that are explosive, flammable, oxidising, corrosive, toxic or eco-toxic. Radioactive substances are managed under the Radiation Protection Act 1965. Controls are contained in a set of regulations that ERMA uses to set requirements for specific substances or groups of substances.

The controls are designed to set consistent national standards for resource consents involving hazardous substances. In addition, the controls are designed to provide consistent standards in workplace and transport legislation relating to hazardous substances. The Act is also designed to work closely with regulations for specific use, for example when hazardous substances are also medicines, agricultural components or veterinary medicines. The Act covers deliberate introduction of new species, such as for primary production or for biological control of pests, and development of genetically-modified organisms.

The development, testing, and release of genetically-modified organisms require separate approvals. This part of the Act stands alongside the Biosecurity Act 1993, which aims to prevent unintended introduction of unwanted species into New Zealand. Principles of the new legislation require that all hazardous substances and new organisms are assessed before they are introduced, developed or manufactured in New Zealand, and that they all follow a similar assessment process. Most assessments are publicised and open to public comment, and the final decision is also made public.

Mineral exploration and development

Exploration of Crown-owned minerals is governed by the Crown Minerals Act 1991, administered by the Ministry of Economic Development. Under the Act, the Minister of Energy is required to establish policies, procedures and provisions for managing Crown minerals.

The Minerals Programme for Minerals (Excluding Petroleum) 2008 came into effect on 1 February 2008, and replaced the Minerals Programme for Coal 1996, and the Minerals Programme for Minerals Other than Coal and Petroleum 1996.

The Minister of Energy issues permits allocating Crown-owned minerals, or the rights to search for them. Permits have conditions relating to managing the mineral resource and royalties. The Act provides that anyone prospecting, exploring or mining Crown minerals must also make land access arrangements with the surface landowner or tenant.

Environment vulnerable to new pests and diseases

New Zealand has abundant food, a healthy environment (including fresh, clean water), and a strong productive sector. But New Zealand is vulnerable to introduced pests and diseases, which could seriously damage our precious natural resources and threaten our economy.

MAF Biosecurity New Zealand (MAFBNZ) leads efforts to prevent unwanted pests and diseases from arriving in the country and to control, manage, or eradicate these pests if they do get into the country.

Pests that MAFBNZ is currently responding to are:

- Sea squirt *Styela clava* – an invasive sea squirt, the clubbed tunicate, has been found in parts of New Zealand. It competes for space and food with shellfish and can blanket oyster and mussel lines, suffocating shellfish. Sea squirts are usually club-shaped with tough, leathery skin and can grow up to 16 centimetres long. Colours vary from brownish-white, to yellowish-brown or reddish-brown. People are asked to regularly clean their boat hulls to help control this pest.

- Didymo *Didymosphenia geminata* – an invasive freshwater algae was first found in the Lower Waiau and Mararoa Rivers in Southland in October 2004. It has since been found in other rivers in the South Island, and a controlled area notice has been put in place. Didymo has been declared an unwanted organism under the Biosecurity Act 1993. Under the Act, those knowingly spreading an unwanted organism can be liable for up to five years imprisonment and/or a $100,000 fine. People are asked to 'check, clean and dry' boats and equipment if they are moving between waterways.

- Red imported fire ants – are tiny, but aggressive, reddish-brown ants with a fierce sting. Following the initial discovery of a single nest, in the grounds of Pan Pac Forest Products plant at Whirinaki in June 2006, MAFBNZ has maintained an active surveillance programme. This campaign includes a social marketing programme encouraging public surveillance and reporting. Fire ants are considered to be the worst invasive ant species worldwide because of the harmful effects they have on people, infrastructure, agriculture, flora and fauna, and recreational activities.

Source: MAFBNZ

The Crown issues three types of permits:

- prospecting permits for identifying land likely to contain mineral, coal or petroleum deposits. Permitted activities are very low impact, such as geological mapping, literature search, hand sampling and aerial surveys
- exploration permits for identifying mineral, coal or petroleum deposits and evaluating the feasibility of mining. Permitted activities include drilling, bulk sampling, trenching and mine feasibility studies
- mining permits for the economic recovery of an identified resource.

The environmental impact of prospecting, exploration and mining of minerals, whether Crown or private, is controlled through the RMA by local authorities. The Act controls the environmental impact of all mining activities, including the rehabilitation of land.

Water and soil management

New Zealand's water and soil resources are managed according to the RMA, with maintenance and construction of flood protection structures and soil conservation measures covered by the Soil Conservation and Rivers Control Act 1941. Both acts are administered by the Ministry for the Environment.

Under the RMA, regional councils are responsible for managing, monitoring and controlling wetlands and freshwater bodies, and issuing permits for extraction, discharge and damming of water. Regional councils also develop policies and plans which prevent erosion, landslip and flooding, and protect scenic and recreational waterways.

Water resources New Zealand's consumption of water is estimated at about 2 billion cubic metres a year, with households using 210 million cubic metres, industry 260 million cubic metres, livestock 350 million cubic metres and irrigation 1.1 billion cubic metres. About 87 percent of the population is supplied from public water supply systems, while the rest rely on independent domestic supplies, such as rainwater collection or aquifer bores. Industry obtains about 33 percent of its requirements from public supply systems and 66 percent from its own sources. These figures do not include water for hydroelectric generation, which exceeds 100 billion cubic metres a year. Water flowing through hydro station turbines can be used again. On the Waikato River, including its tributaries, 10 State-owned hydroelectric stations, and a number owned by local authorities, use and reuse a flow, which, at Karapiro (the final station), is more than 7 billion cubic metres a year.

In terms of total water resources, New Zealand has an estimated 300 billion cubic metres available annually, although this is by no means evenly distributed. High mountains, especially in the South Island, create substantial rain-shadow areas (relatively dry areas sheltered by hills from rain-bearing winds). In a few areas, such as Milford Sound, annual rainfalls of more than 10,000 millimetres have been measured, while in others, such as Alexandra, as little as 340 millimetres may fall in a year.

In some parts of New Zealand, including the Canterbury Plains, the Heretaunga Plains in Hawke's Bay, and the Waimea Plain near Nelson, underground water is an important resource. The cities of Christchurch, Lower Hutt, Napier and Hastings, draw at least some of their domestic and industrial supplies, as well as irrigation water, from underground sources. Management of underground water, and its protection from contamination, is an increasing concern for regional councils in these areas.

Water quality Under the RMA, maintaining water quality is the responsibility of regional councils. The RMA controls discharges into waterways through resource consents. Regional policy statements and regional plans are the statutory vehicle for water quality policies, objectives and rules.

The RMA continues earlier legislation, which provided for water conservation orders to be placed over rivers, streams, wetlands and lakes that have outstanding amenity or intrinsic value. An order can preserve a water body in its natural state, or it can protect certain features by placing restrictions on the future issue of water permits.

River control River control projects carried out by local authorities are usually designed to prevent damage by erosion and protect property from flood damage. River training is designed to give the river channel a stable alignment to prevent bank erosion. Stopbanks are constructed to provide flood protection for communities, infrastructure, and low-lying and highly-productive agricultural lands.

A catchment-wide approach to water and soil problems is encouraged. District councils control subdivision and other urban development in designated flood hazard zones. Increasingly, flood plain management planning is being adopted to identify and mitigate the risks associated with flooding.

Soil conservation The change from forest cover to pastoral land use in many parts of New Zealand has resulted in changed soil conditions over time. The protective, stabilising and water-controlling combination of vigorous native vegetation, litter, and spongy soil has given way to a shallow-rooted, less protective, carpet of grass growing in compacted soils.

Natural erosion, caused by climatic factors such as intense rainfall and the inherent instability of surface rock types for much of the country, has been aggravated by human activities. Nearly 10 percent of land is classified as having severe to extreme erosion problems.

Successful techniques that have reduced the frequency and the severity of erosion include control of tussock burning and animal pests, over-sowing, topdressing, strict grazing control, soil conservation, fencing and gully control, tree planting, and permanently retiring land from productive uses.

Pollution and waste

Water pollution Problems of water pollution are addressed by regional councils under the RMA. Pollution of rivers and lakes is caused by soil erosion, farm run-off, industrial waste, domestic sewage, and urban run-off. The RMA provides for the control of waste discharges through resource consents and rules in plans. These include conditions ensuring that the discharge is of a sufficient quality not to harm the receiving river, lake or ocean. Pollution, such as erosion and farm run-off, requires different approaches, such as changing land-use practices or fencing streams.

The Ministry for the Environment has developed a sustainable land management strategy which addresses, in part, the impact of agriculture on aquatic ecosystems and water quality.

Regulations under the RMA control dumping of waste and other materials, and the discharge of contaminants from ships and offshore installations within the coastal marine area (12 nautical mile limit). Ballast water discharges are controlled by the Biosecurity Act 1993.

NIWA staff measure river flow on a South Island river during a didymo investigation.

Waste and landfills The Ministry for the Environment's New Zealand Waste Strategy includes targets for central government, local government and industry to reduce waste and improve waste management. The majority of solid waste in New Zealand has been disposed of in historically poorly-managed 'rubbish tips'. However, many of the substandard landfills of the past have now closed, and there is a move towards landfills that are appropriately sited, designed and operated.

In many areas, regional landfills have been developed with a variety of ownership arrangements, ranging from full local authority ownership to fully commercial operations. In working to reduce waste, the Ministry for the Environment is:

- working with producers and importers of used oil and tyres to identify appropriate solutions for collecting and managing these wastes
- identifying and implementing ways to divert organic waste from landfills
- supporting businesses to implement eco-efficiency concepts into everyday business
- funding specific waste minimisation projects in the construction, demolition and agricultural sectors.

Contaminated sites A total of 1,238 sites have been reported as contaminated. Of these sites, 545 have been cleaned up, and 301 are being managed to make sure they do not significantly affect the environment. The remaining 392 sites have not yet been dealt with.

Land may be contaminated from historical activities or existing activities that use hazardous substances. The RMA provides controls on existing activities that could contaminate land.

The Ministry for the Environment is working with other government departments, local government, and industry to develop guidelines and standards for managing and cleaning up contaminated land. Guidelines have been produced to cover hazardous substances found on sawmills and timber treatment sites, petrol stations and oil storage depots, and old gasworks sites. Guidance is also provided on how to report, identify, collect and manage information, and investigate contaminated land.

The Contaminated Sites Remediation Fund was established in 2003 to help regional councils investigate and clean up contaminated sites. Over $10 million has been awarded to 33 projects since the fund was established. Funding for 2006–09 was increased to $3.7 million per year. High-profile projects include assisting Tasman District Council to clean up the former Fruitgrowers Chemical Company site at Mapua. The site is heavily contaminated with the organochlorine pesticides DDT and dieldrin, and has adversely affected the marine environment nearby. Environment Waikato is being assisted to clean up the historical Tui mine site on Mt Te Aroha, which is leaching contaminants into local rivers and streams.

International environmental coordination

The coordination of New Zealand's international response to environmental issues is carried out by the environment division of the Ministry of Foreign Affairs and Trade.

The division manages New Zealand's participation in the work of a number of international forums, including United Nations (UN) organisations such as the Framework Convention on Climate Change, the Commission on Sustainable Development, the Informal Consultative Process on Oceans and the Law of the Sea, the Convention on Biological Diversity, the Global Environment Facility, and the International Whaling Commission.

The division is responsible for coordinating the international aspects of issues such as sustainability, climate change, biodiversity, biosafety, oceans, atmosphere, and the transboundary movement of hazardous substances.

It provides leadership and support for New Zealand's participation in international discussions on these issues at regional and international meetings, and for negotiations on related international legal instruments. It also works closely with other government departments and domestic agencies to identify, protect and advance New Zealand's interests in these negotiations.

In addition, the division consults with a large number of other interest groups, including Māori, public interest groups, non-government organisations, and businesses, as it seeks to promote environmental values held by New Zealanders, such as the conservation of whales.

Global environmental issues

Some of the most pressing environmental problems extend beyond national borders. Two of these issues are climate change, and ozone depletion.

Under international law, the main method available for countries to work together on global environmental issues is through multilateral environmental agreements. These formal agreements can be non-legally-binding principles that parties will regard when considering actions that affect particular environmental issues, or specific legally-binding actions required to be taken, which work towards an environmental objective. New Zealand is a signatory to many multilateral environmental agreements and its interest in international environmental work is wide ranging.

Priority issues in recent years have included sustainable development, biodiversity, ocean management and protection of marine mammals, South Pacific environmental issues, climate change, ozone depletion, and hazardous substances.

New Zealand is also involved in the work of international institutions on environment issues. These issues are considered in New Zealand's trade policies, and in delivery of overseas development assistance.

International environmental policy The development of international environmental policy involves a wide range of government agencies. The environment division of the Ministry of Foreign Affairs and Trade advises the government on international aspects of global environmental issues.

The Ministry for the Environment provides advice on domestic environmental matters and is responsible for the implementation of several multilateral environment agreements that New Zealand has ratified, including the UN Framework Convention on Climate Change, the Montreal Protocol on Substances that Deplete the Ozone Layer, and the Stockholm Convention on Persistent Organic Pollutants. The Ministry for the Environment is also responsible for implementing environment cooperation agreements as part of New Zealand's free trade agreements with Thailand, and with Chile, Singapore and Brunei.

The ministry also works closely with the Department of Conservation on aspects of the UN Convention on Biological Diversity.

Climate change The 1992 UN Framework Convention on Climate Change (UNFCCC) developed a global response to stabilising greenhouse gas concentrations in the atmosphere. New Zealand ratified the UNFCCC in 1993 and, in December 2002, ratified the Kyoto Protocol, which builds on the concerns of the UNFCCC and makes new commitments that are stronger and more detailed. Having ratified the UNFCCC and the Kyoto Protocol, New Zealand has an obligation to reduce its greenhouse gas emissions and to protect and enhance forest sinks (forest growth that removes carbon from the atmosphere).

During 2005, the Government carried out a review of climate change policies. The review concluded that the existing policy package would not significantly reduce New Zealand's carbon dioxide emissions and announced that no broad-based tax would be introduced before 2012, which is the final year of the first commitment period under the Kyoto Protocol.

The Government is now exploring a number of policy options that may reduce greenhouse gas emissions. These options include:

- alternative measures to the carbon tax (for example, emissions trading, a narrow carbon tax and voluntary agreements)
- incentives for renewable energy
- ways to manage deforestation and encourage reforestation
- links between forestry and agriculture policies
- incentives or disincentives for purchase and use of transport modes and vehicle efficiency.

The Government is also looking at the need for, and future shape of, cross-sector incentive programmes.

Current policies also support the government's climate change objectives, such as the National Energy Strategy, the National Energy Efficiency and Conservation Strategy (to promote energy efficiency, energy conservation and renewable energy), and waste and transport strategies. New Zealand remains committed to meeting its international obligations under the Kyoto Protocol.

Biodiversity New Zealand ratified the Convention for Biological Diversity in 1994 and produced the National Biodiversity Strategy in 2000. A new statement of national priorities was prepared in 2006, which is being developed further at a regional level.

New Zealand has also ratified several conventions that aim to protect specific animals, plants and ecosystems, including the Convention on International Trade in Endangered Species of Wild Fauna and Flora, the Ramsar Convention, and the Convention on the Conservation of Migratory Species of Wild Animals. New Zealand has five sites on the Ramsar list of wetlands of international importance. New Zealand has also ratified the Agreement on the Conservation of Albatrosses and Petrels, which came into force in 2004. This agreement focuses on the effects of incidental capture in fishing operations.

New Zealand has signed the Cartagena Protocol on Biosafety, which aims to protect biodiversity and human health from potential risks arising from the import and export of living modified organisms developed by modern biotechnology.

Ocean management New Zealand actively participated in the negotiations to amend the London Convention on the Prevention of Marine Pollution by Dumping of Wastes 1972, and ratified the Basel Convention on the Control of Transboundary Movements of Hazardous Wastes and their Disposal in 1995.

The Ministry of Foreign Affairs and Trade (MFAT) plays an important role in continuing New Zealand's strong international advocacy for implementing environmentally sustainable policies. New Zealand strongly supports multilateralism and generally works within the broad mainstream of international opinion.

Since the Earth Summit in 1992, New Zealand has been engaged in international efforts to support global sustainability, including the World Summit on Sustainable Development in 2002. On 5 June 2008, New Zealand hosted World Environment Day, with the theme of "Kick the (carbon) habit" – transitioning towards a low carbon economy and lifestyle.

New Zealand is actively working in the World Trade Organization (WTO) to free up trade in environmental goods and services. New Zealand also seeks to incorporate environmental considerations into its bilateral and free trade agreements to ensure trade serves the overarching objective of promoting sustainable development.

New Zealand has ratified and implemented a number of multilateral environment agreements, including the Kyoto Protocol, the United Nations Framework Convention on Climate Change, the Convention on Biological Diversity, and the Cartagena Protocol on Biosafety.

On 6 March 2008, New Zealand signed the International Tropical Timber Agreement 2006. The agreement underpins the governance of the International Tropical Timber Organisation, which promotes conservation and sustainable management, use, and trade of tropical forest resources. New Zealand has been a 'consumer' member of the organisation since 1992.

MFAT's environment division works actively with New Zealand's International Aid and Development Agency, in regional and international forums, to help our developing-country partners realise their environmental development goals.

Source: Ministry of Foreign Affairs and Trade

New Zealand was active in the UN Conference on Straddling Fish Stocks and Highly Migratory Fish Stocks, which, in 1995, resulted in a new convention to complement existing provisions of the United Nations Convention on the Law of the Sea. The convention contains innovative provisions on enforcement of conservation and management measures on the high seas. New Zealand has an active conservationist role in the International Whaling Commission. The Ministry of Foreign Affairs and Trade cooperates closely with the Department of Conservation to develop policy on whale conservation.

New Zealand played a major role in founding the UN Informal Consultative Process on Oceans and the Law of the Sea. The Government has been reviewing the management of New Zealand's oceans within the exclusive economic zone and extended continental shelf, to improve and integrate decisions about the use of marine space and resources.

South Pacific environment issues New Zealand recognises that South Pacific countries are especially vulnerable to global environmental problems. New Zealand has sought to support Pacific island countries, and to ensure their concerns are heard through the South Pacific Environment Programme, the South Pacific Forum and other international environmental negotiations.

New Zealand was involved in the Global Conference on the Sustainable Development of Small Island Developing States in Barbados in 1994, and in the 1999 United Nations special session to review the Barbados Programme of Action. In 1995, New Zealand signed the Waigani Convention to ban imports of hazardous and radioactive wastes into South Pacific Forum countries, and to control transboundary movement and management of hazardous wastes within the South Pacific region.

International environmental institutions

New Zealand participates in the governance and operation of several international environmental bodies. New Zealand is a member country of the UN Environment Programme and was a member of the governing council from 2000–03. New Zealand attends the Global Ministerial Environmental Forum, where environmental assessments, issues and actions are discussed by environment ministers from around the world.

The Global Environmental Facility (GEF) is an international body that provides finance to developing countries to help them address critical threats to the global environment. New Zealand is a donor country and a member of one of the constituencies of the GEF Council. New Zealand has contributed about $27.5 million since 1994 and pledged $8.4 million to the fourth replenishment of the facility from 2006–10. New Zealand is also involved in the South Pacific Regional Environment Programme and the Environment Policy Committee and various working groups (nanotechnology, climate change, trade and environment) of the Organisation for Economic Co-operation and Development.

Trade and the environment

The New Zealand Government includes environment and labour elements in all bilateral and regional trade agreements. The Ministry for the Environment works with the Ministry of Foreign Affairs and Trade to negotiate for environmental provisions in these agreements.

New Zealand has environmental cooperation agreements with Thailand, and with Chile, Singapore and Brunei. The Ministry for the Environment works closely with counterpart agencies in Thailand under a bilateral trade agreement, and with agencies in Chile, Singapore, and Brunei under a regional trade agreement. Environmental cooperation involves sharing knowledge and expertise, and building capacity to address common environmental challenges.

The Ministry for the Environment encourages new government, research, and business partnerships with our trade agreement partners by promoting New Zealand's expertise in the environment and in sustainability.

The World Trade Organization's (WTO) Doha Development Agenda continues to be the government's top trade priority. The government aims to harmonise its objectives for trade and for the environment through the WTO to achieve the overarching goal of promoting sustainable development worldwide.

The Ministry for the Environment works with the Ministry of Foreign Affairs and Trade to promote New Zealand's interests in the following areas:

- The relationship between trade provisions contained in multilateral environment agreements and WTO rules – New Zealand promotes an approach that ensures policy is implemented in a manner consistent with both sets of rules.
- Liberalising market access for environmental goods and services – New Zealand promotes sustainable development through better access to goods and services that prevent, minimise or clean up environmental damage, including cleaner technologies.
- Labelling for environmental purposes – New Zealand's approach aims to balance legitimate environmental objectives with principles of transparency, non-discrimination and equal participation in standards-setting and access to labelling schemes.

Land resources and ownership

Land Information New Zealand

Land Information New Zealand (LINZ) provides New Zealand's authoritative land and seabed information. It advises the government on land-related laws and policies, and administers the government's land interests and regulations on foreign investment in New Zealand. It also provides a secure environment for buying or selling property, and ensures New Zealand has high quality core geographic information.

LINZ's day-to-day business includes:

- providing policy advice to government
- overseeing survey infrastructure
- maintaining up-to-date topographic and hydrographic information
- issuing, and registering land titles
- setting standards for rating valuation
- Crown property acquisition, management, and disposal
- assisting the government to address land-related aspects of Treaty of Waitangi issues
- administering and monitoring significant foreign investment into New Zealand and assessing applications by foreigners to make significant investments
- processing and approving survey plans
- providing search services for titles and survey plans.

Acts administered by LINZ include the Cadastral Survey Act 2002, Crown Grants Act 1908, Deeds Registration Act 1908, Land Act 1948, Land Transfer Act 1952, New Zealand Geographic Board Act 1946, Public Works Act 1981, Rating Valuations Act 1998, the Unit Titles Act 1972 and various reserves and other lands disposal acts.

The chief executive has statutory functions under the Public Works Act 1981 relating to disposal of surplus land. More than 450 other statutes give LINZ specific responsibilities for land transactions.

Surveying, mapping and land information

Surveying infrastructure The New Zealand survey system provides a national spatial reference framework to accurately locate land and seabed rights and resources. The spatial reference framework is based on a national network of survey control marks, including trigonometrical stations, which are connected to tidal gauges and to the global reference framework.

Land Information New Zealand (LINZ) administers the survey system, primarily to provide reliable identification and definition of land boundaries for recording land rights for Crown, Māori, leasehold and freehold tenures.

Supporting these systems is a database of all land parcels, together with street addresses and place names. The database can be used for:

- defining electoral and other administrative boundaries
- determining New Zealand's national and economic zone boundaries
- land development
- resource management
- granting mining and marine licences
- locating utilities
- engineering and construction
- topographic mapping and hydrographic charting
- scientific studies
- locating marine and air navigation aids.

The locations of boundaries and interests in land are defined and documented by licensed cadastral surveyors, mainly in the private sector. The surveyors submit surveys to LINZ to be validated against existing records. LINZ maintains registers of rights and interests in land, and checks to ensure new rights do not conflict with existing rights. This ensures certainty and security about the extent of land rights and interests.

Landonline is New Zealand's only authoritative titles and digital survey register, and is maintained by LINZ. Landonline enables professionals to access the New Zealand land titles system, and surveyors to digitally prepare and submit cadastral surveys directly with LINZ. Since 1 September 2007, it has been mandatory for all cadastral survey plans to be lodged electronically through Landonline.

Topography and hydrography National topographic information provides a reliable and authoritative record of New Zealand's land form and its features. The information includes 1:50,000 and other core topographic maps (including maps of the Pacific and the Antarctic), the

Danny Thornburrow

Tracking giant wetas

Giant weta are iconic New Zealand insects and the biggest – generally weighing up to 35 grams, although the heaviest recorded giant weta weighed 71 grams. Most species on the mainland became extinct because of introduced mammal predators and habitat destruction, but successful recovery programmes are underway for some species.

Cook Strait giant weta became extinct on mainland New Zealand over 100 years ago. However, weta from Matiu-Somes Island were released into the Karori Wildlife Sanctuary, a fenced protected area on the edge of Wellington. In February 2007, 20 of these Cook Strait giant weta were fitted with miniature radio transmitters before being released. Landcare Research scientists and sanctuary staff tracked each of these insects for 50 days, the first study of its kind in New Zealand, and one of only a few such studies in the world.

On average, male giant weta walked 96 metres per night, while the females moved only 33 metres. Landcare Research scientist Dr Corinne Watts believes the males walked further as they were looking for females to mate with. The most mobile weta regularly walked at least 250 metres per night, often moving faster through the dense vegetation than his trackers. By the end of the study, he was one kilometre from the original release point, a staggering effort for an insect that can only walk. It's likely the actual distances covered were considerably further as the measurements were only the start and finish points, not the route taken.

The weta feed mainly on native plants but also eat some introduced plants such as clover and dandelion. All of the tiny one gram transmitters were removed at the end of the study.

Other recovery programmes are focusing on translocating the Mahoenui giant weta (discovered in 1962 in a small area of the King Country where gorse appears to have provided protection from predators), and captive breeding and translocating the Middle Island tusked weta (a giant weta species restricted to the Mercury Islands, off the Coromandel Peninsula).

Source: Landcare Research

Table 16.02

Land transfer documents processed
Year ending 30 June

Year	Instruments[1] received	Certificates of title	Plans lodged	Guaranteed searches[2]	Title searches	Document searches
1996	925,263	50,665	16,462	182,394	1,048,717	287,394
1997	859,162	63,012	18,995	184,995	948,565	257,638
1998	799,370	56,643	16,866	183,275	861,720	226,624
1999	777,236	53,143	13,610	195,974	862,449	195,088
2000	759,003	52,983	13,455	195,125	838,453	197,993
2001	662,945	46,803	11,700	181,618	824,708	179,417
2002	705,590	41,897	10,016	215,337	968,391	194,737
2003	818,225	45,571	10,836	195,791	1,317,569	268,501
2004	931,734	51,219	11,489	229,304	1,671,056	312,709
2005	891,778	54,510	12,809	260,609	2,066,238	351,197
2006	877,815	59,548	13,296	295,660	2,511,502	453,019
2007	886,377	53,459	13,025	297,672	2,642,396	581,468

(1) An electronic document or plan relating to dealings with land. (2) Provides security to a property purchaser that the title will remain for a defined period as it appears in the land register at the time of the search. This is backed by a State guarantee.

Source: Land Information New Zealand

digital topographic database, and Crown copyright aerial photographs. The National Topographic/ Hydrographic Authority of Land Information New Zealand regulates information about national topography and hydrography.

This information is used for planning, construction, development, environmental assessment, local government administration, emergency services, search and rescue, and defence. Commercial ships navigating New Zealand waters must carry hydrographic charts and s. This is a statutory requirement contributing to safety at sea. Recreational boaters are encouraged to use the information for small craft navigation. Charts range from detailed representations of harbours and their entrances to depictions of deep-sea passages.

Land title registration services Nearly all privately-owned land in New Zealand is held under the land title system, under the authority of the Land Transfer Act 1952. Registered land ownership details are a public record. The primary objective of the system is to provide State-guaranteed certainty of title to land.

The register provides ownership details for a piece of land and a record of any registered interests. Most land is defined in reference to a survey plan. Documents listed on a computer register may include mortgages, leases, various types of charges, and rights and restrictions that affect the land in some way.

LINZ provides land title registration services. Most of LINZ's professional customers access this information through the Landonline system, which allows title transactions to be submitted electronically for registration. Electronic registration through Landonline became mandatory in October 2008.

Table 16.03 lists sales of freehold rural land for each half year from 31 December 1997 to 30 June 2007.

Jacek Drecki

A mountaineer stands on one of the peaks of Mt Ruapehu's crater rim, in the Tongariro National Park, reading the 1:80000 Tongariro National Park Map 273-04.

Table 16.03

Market sales of freehold rural land[1]
Half years ending 30 June and 31 December

Half year ending	Number of sales	Total sales $(million)	Index number[2]	Change from previous half year (percent)
1997 December	1,023	411.5	671	...
1998 June	1,160	559.2	648	-3.4
December	718	299.0	657	+1.4
1999 June	1,347	701.9	663	+0.9
December	952	438.0	666	+0.5
2000 June	1,298	720.4	670	+0.6
December	1,192	737.8	700	+4.5
2001 June	1,712	1,179.4	726	+3.7
December	1,534	1,036.6	780	+7.4
2002 June	1,484	1,118.7	802	+2.8
December	1,235	883.3	835	+4.1
2003 June	1,442	1,215.8	906	+8.5
December	839	645.4	1000	+10.4
2004 June	1,677	1,672.6	1117	+11.7
December	1,323	1,451.3	1228	+9.9
2005 June	1,622	2,175.9	1324	+7.8
December	1,099	1,329.5	1552	+17.2
2006 June	1,184	1,687.9	1483	-4.4
December	1,018	1,279.4	1522	+2.6
2007 June	1,323	2,012.2	1549	+1.8

(1) From the June 2000 half year onwards, sales are collated by sale date. Prior to that, sales are collated by the date the sale notice was received by Quotable Value. (2) Base 1000 for half year ending 31 December 2003.

Symbol: ... not applicable

Source: Quotable Value

Acquisition of New Zealand land by overseas parties

Under the Overseas Investment Act 2005, consent is required for a transaction if it will result in an overseas investment in sensitive land, an overseas investment in significant business assets if the value exceeds NZ$100 million, or an overseas investment that concerns fishing quota.

The overseas investment office, within Land Information New Zealand, administers the legislation. The Minister of Finance is the minister responsible for the Act.

Consent is required for an overseas person to purchase or acquire an interest (for more than three years) in land that:

- is more than five hectares in area (and is not urban land)
- includes part of the foreshore or seabed or is more than 2,000 square metres and adjoins the foreshore
- includes an island (other than the North or South Island, or certain specified islands).

Consent is also needed for an overseas person to purchase or acquire an interest (for more than three years) in land greater than 4,000 square metres that:

- is held for conservation purposes
- is provided as a reserve, a public park for recreation purposes, or as a private open space
- is subject to a heritage order or a requirement for a heritage order
- is a registered historic place, historic area, wāhi tapu (sacred place), or for which there is an application or proposal to be registered as such
- includes the bed of a lake
- includes part of certain specified islands
- adjoins the bed of a lake, a regional park, or certain other classes of land
- adjoins land that exceeds 4,000 square metres and: is held for conservation purposes, or is provided as a scientific, scenic, historic or nature reserve; is subject to a heritage order or a requirement for a heritage order; is a registered historic place, historic area, wāhi tapu (sacred place) or area for which there is an application or proposal for registration as such; adjoins the sea or lake and is an esplanade reserve or strip, recreation reserve, a road or Māori reservation.

Most land investment applications by overseas people are decided by the Minister of Finance and the Minister for Land Information. In considering whether or not to grant consent to an investment transaction, ministers must have regard to relevant criteria and factors in the Act and regulations. The Act also provides for conditions to be imposed on any consent granted and for those conditions to be monitored and enforced.

Table 16.04

Land administered by Māori Land Court

By land court district
At 22 November 2007

District	Number of blocks administered	Total area (hectares)
Tai Tokerau	5,376	151,785
Waikato	3,811	136,140
Waiariki	5,371	348,022
Tai Rāwhiti	5,442	285,804
Aotea	3,972	415,631
Tākitimu	1,369	88,848
Te Wai Pounamu	1,908	103,247
Total	**27,249**	**1,529,479**

Source: Ministry of Justice

Māori land

Before European settlement, all land was held by various groups and tribes of Māori in accordance with traditional customs and usage. Land remaining in this tenure is termed 'Māori customary land'. The right to purchase land from Māori was reserved to the Crown by the Treaty of Waitangi. Most of what had been Māori customary land was converted to other forms of title by one or other of the following processes:

- purchase or other acquisition by the Crown, from whom European settlers obtained land
- issue of a Crown grant to a Māori owner on recommendation of the Māori Land Court
- issue of a freehold order by the Māori Land Court in favour of the Māori individual found to be entitled to the land after investigation.

Freehold orders were used instead of Crown grants after the land transfer system was introduced.

Land in the titles issued under the latter two processes became known as 'Māori freehold land.' Māori can buy or otherwise acquire land which is not Māori freehold land, so there is a considerable amount of general land owned by Māori in addition to holdings of Māori freehold land. Māori freehold land is subject to jurisdiction of the Māori Land Court, under the Te Ture Whenua Māori Act 1993. Some general land owned by Māori is also subject to certain provisions of that Act.

Māori Land Court The purpose of the Māori Land Court Te Kooti Whenua Māori is to help administer Māori land and preserve taonga Māori (Māori treasures), and to help owners manage Māori land. The court maintains records of title and ownership of Māori land, provides accurate and accessible information from court and Crown records, and provides support and services.

One of the strategic goals of the court is to make its services, in particular, title and ownership information, easily accessible to Māori. The court's website provides email access to all court offices and answers to frequently-asked questions about succession, trusts, Māori reservations and court processes. An online search tool provides title and ownership details. Table 16.04 lists the blocks of land administered by the Māori Land Court in each district.

Crown-owned land

Before 1987, Crown-owned land was administered by various Crown agencies under the Public Works Act 1981, the Land Act 1948, the Reserves Act 1977, the National Parks Act 1980 and the Forests Act 1949. After the reconstruction of the public sector, which began in 1987, most of the Crown's commercial or productive land was subsequently transferred to state-owned enterprises.

Land remaining in Crown ownership includes land administered by service delivery departments that use the land in the running of their business. The Department of Conservation administers reserves and Land Information New Zealand (LINZ) administers the remaining Crown-owned land.

Land administered by Land Information New Zealand LINZ oversees the management and disposal of the Crown's interest in land and property outside the conservation estate. LINZ administers 3 million hectares of Crown land including:

- unalienated Crown land (2,860 properties), under the Land Act 1948 and various endowment acts
- approximately 2.1 million hectares of South Island high country Crown pastoral leasehold land (303 properties), under the Crown Pastoral Land Act 1998
- Crown forest licence land over which Crown forestry licences have been issued (71 licences), under the Crown Forest Assets Act 1989
- land no longer required to be held by the Crown for the public work purpose for which it was acquired (105 properties), under the Public Works Act 1981
- land no longer required for railway operations (772 properties), under the Railways Corporation Restructuring Act 1990.

LINZ manages the process and policy for reviewing South Island high country Crown pastoral leasehold land. This tenure review process provides the opportunity for land to be used in a better way and for sustainable land management. All Crown forest licence land administered by the department is retained by the Crown until the Crown has resolved Māori land claims lodged under the Treaty of Waitangi Act 1975.

LINZ also administers around 350 Crown land-related liabilities, such as contaminated sites and subsidence areas, as well as issues concerning the Treaty, Crown land, and historical claims that have arisen from actions of previous agencies. LINZ also controls pest plants and animals on its land and on Crown-owned river and lake beds.

Land administered by service delivery Crown agencies This land is held for government works under the Public Works Act 1981 and other legislation, including education, defence, and law and order legislation.

Land administered by the Department of Conservation The Department of Conservation administers public conservation land, which includes national and forest parks, world heritage areas, wilderness areas, marginal strips around lakes and rivers, and more than 1,000 other reserves. It also protects privately-owned land under special arrangements with landowners. The department is responsible for conservation in New Zealand's subantarctic islands.

Landcorp Farming Ltd

Landcorp Farming Ltd (Landcorp) is New Zealand's largest agricultural enterprise, farming nearly 950,000 animals on 108 farming units totalling 370,738 hectares. Its activities are pastoral livestock farming of beef cattle, sheep, dairy cattle, and deer; development and marketing of livestock genetics and systems; and the development of land for more productive and profitable agriculture.

Landcorp is a State-owned enterprise and a company formed and registered under the Companies Act 1993. Among assets purchased from the Crown following establishment in 1987 were 177 farms, along with about 20,000 leases, licences and loans. All of the leases and licences have now been purchased by the lessees and licencees, and all of the loans have been repaid, or otherwise disposed of by the company.

Landcorp manages a sustainable and profitable farming business and its continued development and growth. It sells land that has been identified as having a higher value for uses other than farming, subject to the provisions of the Protected Land Agreement with the Crown and the Crown's policies on sale of sensitive land.

Landcorp Group is structured into a parent company, Landcorp Farming Ltd, with four wholly-owned subsidiaries:

- Landcorp Developments Ltd and Landcorp Pastoral Ltd – lease and develop former forestry land in the central North Island
- Landcorp Estates Ltd – develops and sells land suitable for higher-value use than farming
- Landcorp Holdings Ltd – holds land protected from sale.

Valuation of land

Fair land values are needed to decide rating levies across contributing local authorities. Land values are also used for assessing stamp, estate and gift duties, and for fixing prices for transfers of land to or from the Crown.

Valuers compete to gain contracts with local authorities to assess values of real estate for local rating purposes. The valuer-general audits the work of the valuers.

Valuers are required to determine the value of the land as if it were vacant, the capital value of the whole property (land and buildings, plus improvements), and the value of improvements (if any) on the land.

Valuation rolls show ownership, and a description and valuation of each property. District valuation rolls are revised at least once every three years. Objections can be lodged against revaluations and taken to the Land Valuation Tribunal.

Rating valuations The Local Government (Rating) Act 2002 provides for real estate valuations to be used as a basis for fair adjustment of rates and levies across a number of local authorities, or between parts of a district, city or region if they have been re-valued at different times.

Valuers' Registration Board This board is chaired by the valuer-general and sets standards of education and practical experience required for registration. The board maintains a register of valuers who meet required standards and issues annual practising certificates to public valuers.

The New Zealand Geographic Board

The New Zealand Geographic Board Ngā Pou Taunaha o Aotearoa is responsible for naming places in New Zealand, its offshore islands, and in the Ross Sea Dependency region of Antarctica. Naming responsibility also extends to undersea features within a 12 nautical mile limit.

The board, chaired by the surveyor-general, adopts naming rules, examines cases of doubtful spelling, investigates and determines the priority of discovery, collects original Māori place names for recording on official maps, encourages the use of original Māori place names, determines what foreign names should be replaced by Māori or English names, and investigates any proposed alteration of a place name or any proposed new name. The board also provides advice to the Office of Treaty Settlements on Māori place names included in Treaty of Waitangi settlements.

The process for assigning a new place name or changing an existing name is determined by the New Zealand Geographic Board Act 1946, with rules of nomenclature and guiding principles for naming developed by the board over time. Consultation with the general public and with Māori is an essential part of the process.

When objections are received to a publicly-notified intention to assign a new name or change an existing name, the final decision is made by the minister responsible for the legislation. Time frames for assigning or changing place names vary, but on average the process takes about a year.

Bird of the year – grey warbler

Otago Daily Times

With its subtle charms, the grey warbler/riroriro won the 'Bird of the Year' title in the Royal Forest and Bird Protection Society 2007 popularity poll.

Found throughout New Zealand, the grey warbler (*Gerygone igata*) measures 11 centimetres in length and is New Zealand's lightest bird (equal with the rifleman) weighing just 6.5 grams – one-third the weight of a mouse.

The grey warbler's tiny size and inconspicuous grey feathers mean the grey warbler is heard more often than seen – its beautiful rising and falling song is often noted as a sign of the arrival of spring. Only the male birds sing this song. The song traditionally served as a reminder to Māori to plant their crops.

In his 1910 book *Birds of the Water, Wood and Waste*, natural history writer Herbert Guthrie described the charm of the grey warbler's song, "Presently, from some manuka thicket, a sombre plumaged little bird will emerge, light on some topmost twig, and pour forth to three-quarters of the globe – for in his ecstasy he nearly sings a circle – this faint sweet trill that heralds fuller spring."

The grey warbler's light weight enables it to hover momentarily as it pursues its diet of insects – something few birds can do.

Grey warblers often inadvertently become parents to shining cuckoos, as the adult cuckoos lay their eggs in grey warbler's nests. The unwitting grey warbler parents raise the cuckoo chick as their own, after the cuckoo chick pushes the warblers' own eggs and chicks out of the nest.

The top 10 birds of the year in 2007:

1 Grey warbler/riroriro
2 Kererū/wood pigeon
3 Tui
4 Black-fronted tern
5 Kakapo
6 Fantail/piwakawaka
7 Kea
8 Pukeko
9 Morepork/ruru
10= Kokako, kiwi

Source: Royal Forest and Bird Protection Society

Hawke's Bay Today

Council workers put up a sign for the longest place name in the world, which names a hill near Poranagahau, in Central Hawke's Bay.

Public conservation land

The Department of Conservation administers the majority of publicly-owned land in New Zealand that is protected for scenic, scientific, historic and cultural reasons, or set aside for recreational purposes. The department administers more than 8 million hectares – approximately 30 percent of New Zealand's total land area.

New Zealand has 14 national parks, covering more than 3 million hectares; nearly 170 conservation parks, covering about 1.3 million hectares; and about 3,500 reserves, including marine reserves. More than 61,000 hectares of protected private land and covenants have been set aside for scenic, scientific or ecological reasons.

The department is responsible for preserving and managing wildlife, and has a role in managing the coastal marine area. It is responsible for fire control in State areas, which include national parks and reserves, forest parks and unalienated Crown land, together with a one-kilometre fire safety margin adjoining all these lands.

National parks

The National Parks Act 1980 provides for national parks to be established in areas where the scenery is of such distinctive quality, or the natural features or ecological systems are so scientifically important, that their preservation is in the national interest.

The Act also provides for public access to the parks, though this is subject to conditions and restrictions necessary for preservation of native plants and animals, or for the welfare of the parks in general. Specially protected areas, which total 55,000 hectares, are accessible by permit only.

National parks are maintained, as far as possible, in their natural state so that their value as soil, water, and forest conservation areas is maintained. Native plants and animals are preserved, and introduced plants and animals are removed if their presence conflicts with aims of the Act.

Development in wilderness areas within national parks is restricted to foot tracks and huts essential for wild animal control or scientific research. The Act allows the Department of Conservation to provide houses for park staff, accommodation and other buildings, hostels, huts, camping grounds, ski tows and similar facilities, parking areas, and roads and tracks within the parks.

Accommodation, transport, and other services at entry points to parks are provided by the department, other government agencies, voluntary organisations and private enterprise. Some services within parks, such as guided walks and skiing instruction, are provided by private firms with permission from the department.

World heritage areas

New Zealand has three sites in the United Nations Economic, Scientific and Cultural Organisation's World Heritage List. They are Te Wahipounamu (south-west New Zealand), Tongariro National Park and New Zealand's subantarctic islands.

As of November 2007, the World Heritage List contained 851 world heritage properties in 141 states. These properties have been recognised as the most outstanding natural and cultural places on earth.

Te Wahipounamu is one of the world's great forest and mountain wildernesses. It consists of 2.6 million hectares (10 percent of the area of New Zealand) of the south-west of the South Island. It includes Fiordland, Mt Aspiring, Westland Tai Poutini and Aoraki-Mt Cook national parks, and the coastal swamp kahikatea forests of south Westland.

Tongariro National Park is one of a limited number of sites accorded World Heritage status for both its natural and cultural values. It contains some of the most continuously active strato-volcanoes in the world, and was the first national park in the world to be freely gifted to the nation by an indigenous people, the Ngāti Tūwharetoa, to whom the mountains are sacred.

New Zealand's subantarctic islands consist of five island groups (the Snares, Bounty Islands, Antipodes Islands, Auckland Islands and Campbell Island) in the Southern Ocean south-east of New Zealand. The wildlife on the islands – birds, plants and invertebrates – have high productivity, biodiversity, population density and are highly endemic.

They are particularly notable for the large number and diversity of pelagic seabirds and penguins that nest there. There are 126 bird species in total, including 40 seabirds, of which five breed nowhere else in the world. The islands are major breeding places for several species of birds and animals, including the yellow-eyed penguin, the royal albatross and the Hooker's sea lion. The threat of rats or other predatory animals accidentally being introduced to the islands has led the Department of Conservation to only allow access by permit.

National parks of New Zealand

Wilsons Abel Tasman

Abel Tasman National park.

Te Urewera National Park – 212,675 hectares, established 1954 – together with neighbouring Whirinaki Forest Park, is the largest remaining area of native forest in the North Island. It includes Lake Waikaremoana, noted for its scenic shoreline.

Tongariro National Park – 79,598 hectares, established 1887 – is New Zealand's first national park. It includes three active volcanoes, Ruapehu, Ngauruhoe and Tongariro.

Egmont National Park – 33,534 hectares, established 1900 – comprises all the land within a nine-kilometre radius of the Mt Egmont/Taranaki summit and some outlying areas to the north. The symmetrical cone of the dormant volcano is a provincial landmark. The park is also noted for its green forest, its waterfalls and wetlands.

Whanganui National Park – 74,231 hectares, established 1986 – borders the Whanganui River. It incorporates areas of Crown land, former State forests and a number of former reserves. The river itself is not part of the park.

Kahurangi National Park – 452,002 hectares, established 1996 – is situated in the north-west of the South Island. It consists of spectacular and remote country, and includes the Heaphy Track. It has ancient landforms, with wild rivers and unique flora and fauna. It is New Zealand's second-largest national park.

Abel Tasman National Park – 22,530 hectares, established 1942 – has numerous tidal inlets and beaches of golden sand along the shores of Tasman Bay. As well as its beaches, it is renowned for its sculptured granite cliffs and its world-famous coastal track. It is New Zealand's smallest national park.

Nelson Lakes National Park – 101,753 hectares, established 1956 – is a rugged, mountainous area in Nelson province. It extends southwards from the forested shores of Lakes Rotoiti and Rotoroa to the Lewis Pass National Reserve.

Paparoa National Park – 30,560 hectares, established 1987 – is on the west coast of the South Island between Westport and Greymouth. It includes the pancake rocks at Punakaiki.

Arthur's Pass National Park – 114,500 hectares, established 1929 – is a rugged and mountainous area straddling the main divide of the Southern Alps. It features high mountains with large scree slopes, along with wide, braided rivers and steep gorges.

Westland Tai Poutini National Park – 117,547 hectares, established 1960 – extends from the highest peaks of the Southern Alps to a wild, remote coastline. It incorporates glaciers, scenic lakes, dense rainforests and, along the coast, remains of old gold mining towns.

Aoraki-Mt Cook National Park – 70,696 hectares, established 1953 – is an alpine park containing New Zealand's highest mountain, Aoraki-Mt Cook (3,754 metres), and its longest glacier, Tasman (29 kilometres). A focus for mountaineering, ski touring and scenic flights, the park is an area of outstanding natural beauty. The Aoraki-Mt Cook, Westland Tai Poutini, Mt Aspiring and Fiordland National Parks have together been declared a world heritage area.

Mt Aspiring National Park – 355,543 hectares, established 1964 – is a complex of impressively glaciated mountain scenery centred on Mt Aspiring (3,036 metres), New Zealand's highest peak outside Aoraki-Mt Cook National Park.

Fiordland National Park – 1,251,924 hectares, established 1952 – is the largest national park in New Zealand and one of the largest in the world. The grandeur of Fiordland National Park's scenery, with its deep fiords, lakes of glacial origin, mountains and waterfalls, has earned it international recognition as a world heritage area.

Rakiura National Park – 163,000 hectares, established 2002 – is New Zealand's newest national park. It covers about 85 percent of Stewart Island/ Rakiura. It is one of the most pristine areas of New Zealand wilderness, containing unspoiled native ecosystems, from scrub-covered mountain tops to wild coastline.

Source: Department of Conservation

Figure 16.05

New Zealand conservation areas

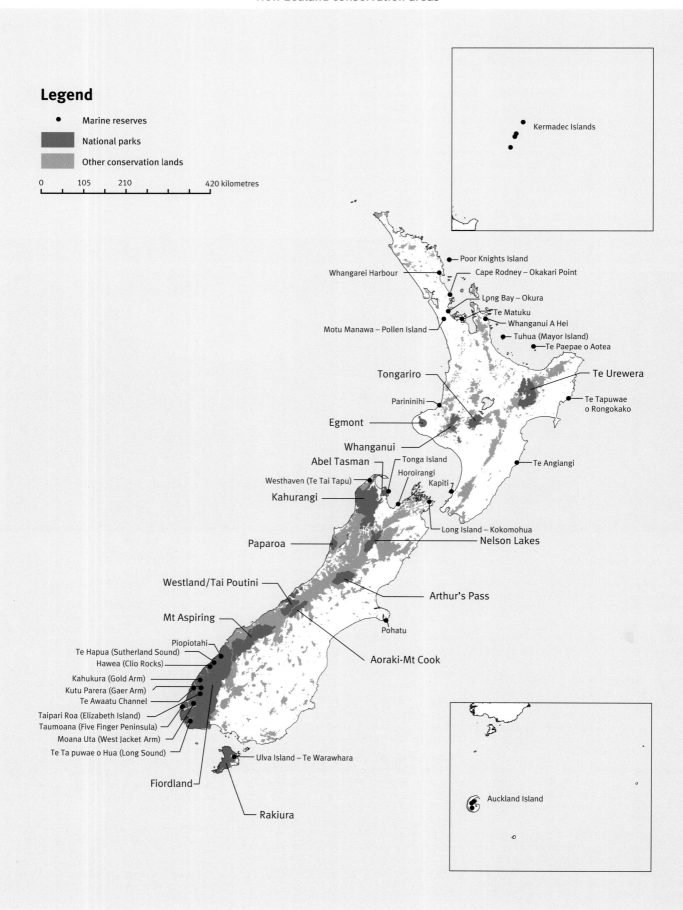

Legend

● Marine reserves

▮ National parks

▮ Other conservation lands

0   105   210   420 kilometres

Kermadec Islands

Poor Knights Island
Whangarei Harbour
Cape Rodney – Okakari Point
Long Bay – Okura
Te Matuku
Whanganui A Hei
Motu Manawa – Pollen Island
Tuhua (Mayor Island)
Te Paepae o Aotea

Tongariro
Te Urewera
Parininihi
Te Tapuwae o Rongokako
Egmont

Whanganui
Te Angiangi
Abel Tasman
Tonga Island
Horoirangi
Westhaven (Te Tai Tapu)
Kapiti
Kahurangi
Long Island – Kokomohua
Paparoa
Nelson Lakes

Westland/Tai Poutini
Arthur's Pass
Mt Aspiring
Pohatu
Piopiotahi
Te Hapua (Sutherland Sound)
Aoraki-Mt Cook
Hawea (Clio Rocks)
Kahukura (Gold Arm)
Kutu Parera (Gaer Arm)
Te Awaatu Channel
Taipari Roa (Elizabeth Island)
Taumoana (Five Finger Peninsula)
Moana Uta (West Jacket Arm)
Te Ta puwae o Hua (Long Sound)
Ulva Island – Te Warawhara
Fiordland
Auckland Island
Rakiura

Source: Department of Conservation

Conservation parks

Conservation parks protect natural and historic resources and provide a space for public recreation and enjoyment. They provide a less restricted range of recreational activities than national parks and reserves; allowing tramping, camping, fishing and shooting for a variety of game.

There are nearly 50 conservation parks, covering coastal areas, forests, lakes, mountains, tablelands and tussock grasslands, with an approximate total area of more than 1.9 million hectares.

Reserves

Reserve land includes scenic, nature, scientific, historic, national and recreational reserves, wildlife reserves, protected private land and land protected under various conservation and open space covenants.

Scenic reserves include areas of scenic interest, such as native forests, limestone and glow worm caves, thermal areas, coastal areas, lakes, rivers, waterfalls and scenic vantage points. About 382,000 hectares are classified scenic reserves.

Nature reserves preserve native plants and animals. They generally consist of areas where rare plants are growing or which supply a suitable habitat for rare birds or other animals. There are 109,400 hectares of nature reserves, some are on the mainland, but most are on offshore or outlying islands.

National reserves protect areas of outstanding natural beauty or scientific or ecological importance. They offer the second highest degree of protection, next to national parks. Total area of national reserves is 96,300 hectares.

Scientific reserves are generally smaller areas reserved to protect examples of rare or endangered plants, animals or unique geographical features for scientific research or education. Entry may be prohibited if it is considered necessary to prevent disturbance. Their total area is 15,200 hectares.

Historic reserves include sites with Māori rock drawings, sites of prehistoric fortifications, landing places of Captain Cook, sites of engagements during the New Zealand wars, and buildings of historic importance. The Department of Conservation and the New Zealand Historic Places Trust cooperate in investigating and administering reserve sites and buildings. There are 16,122 hectares of historic reserves.

Recreation reserves include public domains, camping grounds and other public recreational areas administered by the Department of Conservation. Their total area is 60,261 hectares.

Wildlife reserves can be on land of any tenure. Certain actions are prohibited in respect of wildlife, but land ownership is not affected. Their total area is just over 19,000 hectares.

Whale sanctuaries

Thirty-five species of whales and dolphins have been recorded in New Zealand waters, and four of the largest whale species – sperm, humpback, Bryde's, and southern right whale – are regular visitors.

New Zealand has been actively promoting a South Pacific whale sanctuary to provide long-term protection for the breeding grounds of the region's great whales. The proposal has regularly received the support of a significant majority of members of the International Whaling Commission (IWC), but has not achieved the 75 percent majority required to establish a sanctuary under IWC rules.

Figure 16.06

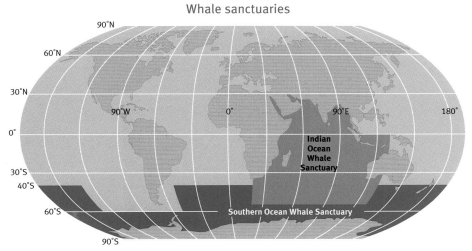

Whale sanctuaries

Source: Department of Conservation

Wetlands

Wetlands are among the world's most productive environments. Examples of wetlands include streams, swamps, bogs, lakes, lagoons, estuaries, mudflats and flood plains. Wetlands are cradles of biological diversity, providing the water and resources that countless species of plants and animals depend for survival. Many of these plants and animals have specially adapted to living in wet places.

Wetlands are important for flood control and water purification. They absorb water during heavy rain, releasing it gradually so flooding is reduced. As water moves into a wetland, the flow rate decreases, allowing particles to settle out. Plant surfaces filter and absorb solids and add oxygen to the water. This cleansing protects downstream environments.

Unfortunately only 45,600 hectares of wetlands remain in New Zealand, which is 9.4 percent of their original extent. The reclamation of wetlands for farming and other development has been the main cause of wetland loss. Because of this, a number of wetland species have become uncommon or endangered.

Whangamarino Wetland is a rich native water bird fauna area in demand for birdwatching tourism. An estimated 20 percent of bittern/matuku numbers in New Zealand resides at Whangamarino. Other uncommon or threatened bird species include spotless crake/puweto, marsh crake/koitareke, fernbird/matatā, and New Zealand dabchick/weweia. The swamp helmet orchid is endemic to Whangamarino. Native fish include the black mudfish. The area is a traditional source of eels/tuna for tangata whenua (people of the land). Whangamarino is part of a substantial and effective flood control scheme on the Lower Waikato River.

Ashburton Lakes/Upper Rangitata River lie between mountains in inland South Canterbury. Around 12 lakes generally drain into the south branch of the Ashburton River. The lakes are bordered by glacial ridges, and sand and gravel left by meltwater streams, or are kettle holes in former glacial surfaces. The smallest lakes freeze over in winter. The Upper Rangitata is one of few braided river habitats in New Zealand largely free of invasive weeds. Living here are native fish, trout/salmon, native water birds, and diverse threatened native plants and aquatic and terrestrial invertebrates. The area is of cultural value to tangata whenua as there are historical seasonal camps and trails, and mahinga kai (food gathering areas).

Waituna Lagoon/Awarua wetland complex The wetland comprises a wetland/peat bog complex, including wirerush, manuka, flax/harakeke swamps, cushion bogs, red tussock, forest, estuary margins, rivers, lakes and tarns. Also important are the ecological gradients between habitat types. The area is frequented by migrating and wading bird species, as well as threatened plant and insect species, including subalpine species. The wetlands face ongoing decline with the intensification of land use and the conversion of wetland to dairying considered the primary threats to water quality and ecosystems.

Source: Department of Conservation

Conservation organisations

New Zealand Conservation Authority provides advice to the Minister of Conservation on departmental policy development, including customary Māori use, Treaty of Waitangi issues, and other conservation matters of national importance.

The authority approves conservation management strategies and maintains close involvement in ecosystem protection, including animal and weed pest control, and in developing strategies and plans to protect New Zealand's biodiversity.

Under the National Parks Act 1980, the authority approves national park management plans and investigates new national parks and additions to existing parks.

Conservation boards are statutory bodies that provide advice on conservation areas, policies, activities and responsibilities of the department. They ensure the community has a voice in conservation management and they represent the long-term public interest in conservation.

Queen Elizabeth II National Trust promotes and enables private conservation of open space in New Zealand, including natural features, landscapes and cultural and historic sites. Landowners voluntarily protect features on their land through the trust's open space covenants or protection agreements.

The land remains in private ownership but, once the covenant is registered on the land title, existing and subsequent landowners are bound by the covenant's protection requirements. The trust acts as trustee.

At 30 June 2007, there were 2,630 registered covenants protecting over 83,610 hectares of land throughout New Zealand and a further 623 covenants covering 19,169 hectares had been approved for registration. The average covenant size is 32 hectares, with the largest being over 6,500 hectares.

The trust also owns properties, most of which have been gifted or bequeathed, where a range of natural, cultural, scientific and aesthetic values are protected. In the year ending 30 June 2007, the trust received a base funding grant of $1.319 million and a biodiversity funding grant of $1.555 million from the Government. It also generated funds from its own activities and investments.

New Zealand Historic Places Trust is a non-profit organisation that identifies, records and preserves New Zealand's historic buildings, archaeological sites and wāhi tapu (sacred places), and encourages public interest in the nation's past.

Waitangi National Trust Board administers the Waitangi National Reserve, which includes the Treaty House at Waitangi. The reserve was gifted to the nation in 1932 by the Governor-General of New Zealand Viscount Bledisloe.

Boards with specific responsibilities have been set up to help the government and the Department of Conservation administer specific responsibilities. These include: the Lakes Rotoiti and Okataina Scenic Reserve Boards; Taupo Fishery Advisory Committee, Guardians of Lakes Manapouri, Monowai and Te Anau; Guardians of Lake Wanaka; and the Archaeological Advisory Committee.

New Zealand Game Bird Habitat Trust Board administers and distributes funds derived from the sale of habitat stamps and artwork, to improve game bird habitat and the habitat of other wildlife.

Sources: Department of Conservation, Queen Elizabeth II National Trust

Two whale sanctuaries have been established by the IWC in the southern hemisphere, the Indian Ocean Sanctuary (established in 1978), and the Southern Ocean Sanctuary (1994). All New Zealand waters south of 40 degrees are included within the Southern Ocean Sanctuary.

New Zealand sponsored a regional workshop in Apia, Samoa, in April 2001, to promote a South Pacific whale sanctuary. The meeting, attended by 15 Pacific island nations and territories, strongly endorsed the sanctuary proposal. Since then, approximately 11 million square kilometres of the South Pacific have been declared whale sanctuaries by the governments of French Polynesia, Cook Islands, Niue, Fiji, New Caledonia, Samoa and American Samoa.

Figure 16.06 shows the Indian Ocean and the Southern Ocean whale sanctuaries.

Marine reserves and parks

There are more than 1,200 different fish species in the waters around New Zealand, as well as various species of seal, whale, dolphin and seabird. More species of albatross breed in New Zealand than anywhere else in the world.

New Zealand has 27 marine reserves, with the Kermadec Islands Reserve the largest at 748,000 hectares. The Cape Rodney–Okakari Point Marine Reserve (547 hectares) was the first marine reserve, in 1975, followed by the Poor Knights Islands Reserve (1,990 hectares) in 1981.

New Zealand has four marine parks – Mimiwhangata, Tawharanui, Sugar Loaf Islands and the Hauraki Gulf Marine Park. New Zealand also has two marine mammal sanctuaries, Auckland Islands and Banks Peninsula.

Forest funds

The Nature Heritage Fund and Ngā Whenua Rahui fund were established as part of New Zealand's indigenous forest policy. Both funds aim to permanently protect conservation-value forest on general and Māori land. The Nature Heritage Fund, works through land being gifted, covenanted, or purchased by the fund.

Ngā Whenua Rahui fund uses a range of mechanisms to achieve protection, with covenanting being the most suitable. Iwi perceive covenants as more acceptable as they lessen the sense of alienation from the land.

Both funds are contestable. Anyone can apply to the Nature Heritage Fund, but Ngā Whenua Rahui is restricted to Māori landowning interests. Applications for funds are considered by advisory committees, who make recommendations to the Minister of Conservation.

Contributors and related websites

Bioethics Council – www.bioethics.org.nz

Department of Conservation – www.doc.govt.nz

Land Information New Zealand – www.linz.govt.nz

Landcare Research – www.landcareresearch.co.nz

Landcorp Farming Ltd – www.landcorp.co.nz

Ministry for the Environment – www.mfe.govt.nz

Ministry of Agriculture and Forestry – www.maf.govt.nz

Ministry of Economic Development – www.med.govt.nz

Ministry of Foreign Affairs and Trade – www.mfat.govt.nz

Ministry of Justice – www.justice.govt.nz

National Institute of Water & Atmospheric Research – www.niwa.co.nz

Queen Elizabeth II National Trust – www.openspace.org.nz

Quotable Value New Zealand – www.qv.co.nz

Royal Forest and Bird Protection Society – www.forestandbird.org.nz

Statistics New Zealand – www.stats.govt.nz

The New Zealand Herald

Walter Fielding-Cotterill rows out on Canterbury's Lake Ellesmere to go fishing in the spring of 2007, making use of two of New Zealand's natural resources. Environmental accounts for the country's natural resources, including fresh water and fish, measure the interaction between the environment and the economy in both monetary and physical terms.

17 | National economy

New Zealand has a mixed economy that operates on free market principles. It has a sizeable service sector, which complements a highly efficient agricultural sector and related manufacturing industries. The economy is strongly trade oriented, with exports of goods and services accounting for just under one-third of expenditure on gross domestic product (GDP).

From around 1984, the direction of economic policy in New Zealand turned away from government intervention towards the removal of many forms of government assistance. On the macroeconomic level, policies were aimed at achieving low inflation and a sound fiscal position, while microeconomic reforms were introduced to open the economy to competitive pressures and world prices.

Reforms included: floating the exchange rate, abolishing controls on capital movements, ending industry assistance, removing price controls, deregulation across a number of sectors of the economy, corporatising and privatising State-owned assets, and labour market legislation aimed at facilitating more flexible patterns of wage bargaining. More recently, the reform process has shifted from one of rapid change to one of fine-tuning.

After a period of weak growth in the late 1980s, New Zealand's economic performance improved significantly during the 1990s. From late 1992 the economy grew strongly, with particularly strong output growth from 1993–96. Annual average growth in real GDP peaked at 6.8 percent in June 1994.

Growth slowed during 1997 and 1998, due to a slowdown in key Asian trading partner economies, together with a drought that affected large parts of the country in the summers of 1997/98 and 1998/99.

Since these twin 'shocks', the New Zealand economy has experienced its strongest period of growth in three decades. The years 2001 and 2002 saw two good agricultural seasons, relatively high world prices for New Zealand's export commodities, a low exchange rate, and a robust labour market. These factors boosted annual average GDP growth from 1.9 percent in June 2001 to 5.2 percent in December 2002.

Over the period 2002–04, annual average GDP growth was 3.5–4.5 percent. Growth then eased as a result of high oil prices, interest rate increases, and slowing permanent and long-term migration. The economy's output was flat in the second half of 2005.

Gross national income

Gross national income (GNI) is defined as gross domestic product (GDP) plus net receipts of wages and salaries, and property income, from overseas.

GNI is a better measure of New Zealanders' income, as it excludes income sent overseas (dividends, interest and other transfers) and includes similar income earned by New Zealanders from overseas investments.

Although GNI per person can be seen as a more accurate indicator of income or welfare, it is less commonly used than GDP per person.

Since the year ending March 1972 GNI has consistently increased for New Zealand, with the exception of 1993, which recorded a decline of 4.1 percent.

Over the most recent 10 years the major driver has been the compensation of employees, reflecting wage and employment increases. These have in part been offset by an increasing deficit in net investment income from overseas.

Gross national income[1] per person
2006

	US$
Luxembourg	63,945
Norway	51,915
United States	44,055
Switzerland	41,226
Netherlands	37,149
Canada	36,539
Denmark	35,704
Austria	35,241
Ireland	35,072
Sweden	35,023
Belgium	33,937
United Kingdom	33,424
Finland	32,906
Japan	32,826
Iceland	32,662
Australia	32,617[2]
Germany	32,255
France	31,288
Spain	28,882
Italy	28,788
Greece	26,735
New Zealand	23,105[2]
Korea	23,038
Czech Republic	20,821
Portugal	20,170
Slovak Republic	17,051
Hungary	16,852
Poland	13,112[2]
Mexico	10,364[3]
Turkey	8,758

(1) Based on current prices and purchasing power parities (common currency). (2) 2005 figure. (3) 2004 figure.

Source: OECD *Factbook 2008*

Recent developments

Growth recovered slightly during 2006, helped by a rebound in domestic demand and exports. The resurgence in growth continued into the first half of 2007, with growth of 0.7 percent in the June 2007 quarter taking the annual average to 2.2 percent in the year to 30 June 2007.

Strong household spending was supported by renewed strength in house prices, a fall in petrol prices, and increases in export commodity prices. In addition, a growing labour market, low unemployment, and government spending provided continuing support for the economy, outweighing the impact of tighter monetary conditions.

Depreciation in the New Zealand dollar over the first half of 2006 and improved agricultural production helped to increase exports, although the exchange-rate depreciation proved to be short-lived. The terms of trade increased sharply in the December 2006 quarter, and continued to increase further during 2007, supporting export receipts in 2007. Dairy prices, which were 6 percent higher in the June 2007 quarter than the June 2005 quarter (despite the higher exchange rate) provided the largest contribution to the increase in the terms of trade.

Higher export receipts contributed to a fall in New Zealand's annual current account deficit – down to 8.2 percent of GDP in the year to June 2007, from 9.3 percent of GDP in the year to 30 September 2006.

Annual inflation, as measured by the consumers price index (CPI), fell to 1.8 percent in the September 2007 quarter, from 2.0 percent in June. The decrease was primarily due to increased government subsidies for medical visits, pharmaceuticals, and child care, which lowered prices to the consumer.

There were diverging trends between tradable and non-tradable inflation. Strength in the domestic economy, particularly in the housing market, resulted in an increase in non-tradable inflation, with an annual 3.7 percent recorded in the September 2007 quarter. In contrast, strength in the currency has resulted in relatively low tradable inflation, with tradable prices recording an annual decrease of 0.3 percent in the September 2007 quarter.

Fiscal policy

The fiscal responsibility provisions of the Public Finance Act 1989 promote consistent, good-quality fiscal management, enabling the government to make a major contribution to the economic health of the country and be better positioned to provide a range of services on a sustained basis.

The Act requires the Crown's financial reporting to be in accordance with New Zealand generally accepted accounting practice (GAAP).

The primary fiscal indicators are the operating balance, gross sovereign-issued debt, net debt and net worth.

The government is required to apply the principles of responsible fiscal management set out in the Act. These include:

- reducing debt to prudent levels to provide a buffer against future adverse events
- maintaining operating balances once prudent debt levels are reached – the government is to live within its means over time, with some scope for flexibility through the business cycle
- achieving and maintaining levels of net worth to provide a buffer against adverse events

The New Zealand Herald

Jo Le Grouw, a founder of Lockwood, in front of the company's new environmentally friendly EcoSmart home in Rotorua in March 2008. Strength in the housing market during 2007 contributed to an increase in non-tradable inflation in the September 2007 quarter.

- managing risks facing the Crown
- following policies that are consistent with a reasonable degree of predictability about the level and stability of future tax rates.

Primary fiscal indicators

Operating balance Following a prolonged period of fiscal deficits, New Zealand achieved surpluses in 1993/94. The initial improvement in the operating balance from 1993/94 onwards reflected a growing economy, increasing tax revenues, and firm expense control. Reductions in the operating balance in the late 1990s largely reflected two rounds of tax reductions, and lower economic growth, which reduced tax revenue growth. Strong growth in the past few years has seen operating balances recovering.

The operating balance, excluding revaluations and accounting policy changes, reached $8.7 billion in 2006/07. Government operating expenses (core Crown) have been reduced as a percentage of GDP, from around 40 percent in 1992/93 to 32 percent in 2006/07. Core Crown expenses as a percentage of GDP are expected to rise to around 33 percent by 2010/11. Operating surpluses are expected to continue. Forecasts for 2008/09, 2009/10 and 2010/11 are $5.6 billion, $5.3 billion and $5.4 billion, respectively.

Net debt Net core Crown debt fell from 49 percent of GDP in 1992/93 to 2.1 percent in 2006/07. Debt repayments were financed from asset sales proceeds (during the 1990s) and operating surpluses. Net debt is projected to stay around 3.0 percent of GDP between 2007/08 and 2010/12. However, surpluses are also being used to build up financial assets in the New Zealand Superannuation Fund (NZSF) to partly pre-fund future superannuation costs, rather than solely paying off debt. These assets do not form part of reported net debt. The NZSF is forecast to contain assets worth around 13.8 percent of GDP by 2010/11.

Net worth In 2006/07, net worth was $95.8 billion. With operating surpluses forecast to continue, net worth is projected to reach $112.4 billion in 2010/11.

Public debt

Before March 1985, the government was borrowing externally to finance the balance of payments deficit and maintain a fixed exchange rate.

Since adoption of a freely floating exchange rate, the government has borrowed externally only to finance foreign-exchange reserves. All other borrowing has been in the domestic market.

Net foreign-currency debt was eliminated in September 1996, largely through proceeds from asset sales and, since 1994, sizeable fiscal surpluses.

Proceeds from the 2005/06 domestic bond programme were used to finance maturing domestic term debt and to partly pre-fund the 2006/07 borrowing requirement. Gross sovereign-issued debt amounted to 21.7 percent of GDP in the year ending 30 June 2007.

Monetary policy

Objectives The Reserve Bank of New Zealand Act 1989 requires the Reserve Bank of New Zealand to formulate and implement monetary policy with the objective of achieving and maintaining stability in the general level of prices. The policy targets agreement (PTA) between the Minister of Finance and the Governor of the Reserve Bank specifies the objective more precisely. Initially, the agreement required the bank to maintain CPI inflation in the range of 0–2 percent in any 12-month period. This changed to 0–3 percent in December 1996. In September 2002, a new PTA was signed requiring the bank to keep inflation within the 1–3 percent range 'on average over the medium term'.

The requirement to deliver price stability 'on average over the medium term' means monetary policy can be a little more flexible than previously. The medium-term target allows inflation to be briefly above or below the target range. In certain circumstances, this allows a more gradual policy response, but in others a more pre-emptive approach is still necessary. A more gradual approach may help in situations where the effects of interest rate changes are uncertain, or where sharp changes in interest rates (to bring inflation back quickly within the target range) would be economically disruptive.

A more pre-emptive approach may be helpful in circumstances where the bank is reasonably confident that the economy has passed a turning point in terms of inflation pressures. Then, even if inflation is still comparatively high or low, an early change to policy settings can help the economy return to more normal conditions. This flexibility is expected to help the bank meet a requirement in the agreement that, in aiming to deliver price stability, it should 'seek to avoid unnecessary instability in output, interest rates and the exchange rate'. The ability to use this extra flexibility depends on expectations of inflation remaining at low levels.

The Act contains provisions that allow the government to override the price stability objective and the PTA, although this can be done initially for a maximum of 12 months only (but can be further extended) and must be disclosed in parliament and publicly.

Jarrad Mapp

In May 2008, the cost of petrol to consumers passed $2 a litre, leading many to look to other forms of transport. Prices are a factor of supply and demand – when a commodity is limited in supply, or demand increases, the price to be paid rises. Petrol is sensitive to such fluctuations.

Implementation Under the Reserve Bank Act, there is a considerable degree of autonomy for the Reserve Bank in formulating and implementing monetary policy. The bank controls the cost of liquidity by setting the official cash rate (OCR). The bank can lend cash overnight at 50 basis points above the OCR and will take deposits at the OCR. By controlling the cost of liquidity for financial institutions, the bank has leverage over interest rates faced by households and firms.

There are eight pre-announced dates each year at which the bank reviews the OCR. Four coincide with publication of the bank's monetary policy statements, which contain projected paths for future conditions and the bank's policy response.

Both interest rates and the exchange rate can influence New Zealand's economic activity and inflation. The Reserve Bank takes the influence of both of these into account when setting the OCR. Other important factors considered include credit conditions, inflation expectations, and external conditions. The bank is generally looking at the inflation outlook up to three years ahead when forming policy response.

Prices

Prices are a key factor in the operation of the New Zealand economy. The prices that consumers pay for goods and services affect their purchasing power – the quantity of goods and services they can buy. They also influence choices consumers make about which goods and services they buy.

Prices are a factor of supply and demand. If a commodity is limited in supply, the price to be paid will increase. Examples of commodities that are often limited in supply include petrol, property, and construction trade services.

Similarly, if demand for commodities increases, due, for example, to population growth or higher disposable income, prices will also generally rise. In general, population and incomes do rise, and so demand for goods and services increases. This leads to inflation, or the upward movement of prices over time.

Price indexes provide a measure of inflation by presenting relative changes in prices. They can be constructed for any given commodity or group of commodities.

Consumers price index

The consumers price index (CPI) is the highest profile measure of inflation in the New Zealand economy and is widely used. The CPI measures changes in the prices of goods and services purchased by private New Zealand households. It is the best available measure of how changes in retail prices affect the average household budget.

Statistics New Zealand endeavours to keep the 'basket' of goods and services, for which prices are regularly surveyed, constant in quantity and quality over time, so that only 'pure' price movements are recorded.

The CPI is reviewed regularly to ensure the basket of goods and services is current and relevant. The last review was in 2006, when goods and services, and the retail outlets where these prices are collected, were reselected. In addition, the index was re-expressed, with a new baseline of 1000 for June 2006.

Price collection More than 120,000 individual prices are collected each quarter. Prices are gathered by collectors in the field and through the Internet, postal and email surveys. How often prices are collected for each item depends on how volatile the price of that item is. For example, petrol prices can rise and fall quite significantly from week to week, so petrol prices are collected weekly. Prices are collected monthly for food items and quarterly for most other commodities.

A weighted average of all the prices collected within the quarter is calculated. Index values are constructed for each item, then compared against the previous period's index value. The change in the index value reflects the change in the average price of the items.

Expenditure weights Each item in the CPI is given an expenditure weight, reflecting the percentage of total spending by private New Zealand households on that item. For example, the expenditure weight given to petrol is 5.37, meaning that 5.37 percent of total household spending is on petrol. By comparison, the expenditure weight given to milk is 0.74 percent. A change in the average price of petrol will have a greater impact on households than a change in the price of milk, and this is reflected in the CPI.

Expenditure weights are reviewed about every three years, to ensure that changes in consumer spending and consumption behaviours are accurately reflected in the CPI basket.

At this time, the basket of goods and services is also reviewed, to ensure that new items are added, or superseded items removed. New items, such as DVD recorders and MP3 players, are included in the CPI basket when they become available to consumers, while items no longer purchased in significant quantities by private households, such as video cassette recorders, are removed. The outlets that are surveyed are also reviewed every six years. Item expenditure weights are derived from the Household Economic Survey (HES), which is conducted every three years.

The 2006 CPI review saw items and outlets reweighted, based on HES information, which was supplemented by market research information.

Table 17.01 (overleaf) shows the June quarter expenditure weights assigned to the CPI's 11 groups, as derived from the HES.

Uses of the consumers price index

The main uses of the CPI include indexation of contracts, setting of monetary policy, and as a deflator of other economic series.

Indexation of contracts There are a number of situations where indexes are used to adjust payments. The following indexation arrangements can apply to both the public and private sectors.

- Adjusting for changes in the cost of living – Many public sector arrangements are based on ensuring people have a sufficient level of income to enable them to continue to buy a range of goods and services. In the context of income support (benefits), much depends on whether the objective is to maintain the spending power of a benefit, or to match changes in the average wage. In the first case, the CPI is used to adjust payments, while in the latter it is more useful to use a measure of an average wage.

- Compensating businesses for costs beyond their control – Commonly, in business contracts, service providers want to be compensated for changes in input costs that they have little or no control over. In determining which index to use to adjust a contract, firms typically use either an index that is closely related to the cost concerned, or they use a more general measure that the parties agree gives a picture of relevant price pressures.

- Ensuring that regular payments maintain their value – A range of regular payments, for example rents, need to be adjusted from time to time. Adjustment methods used involve a wide variety of indexation practices.

Monetary policy Maintaining a stable general level of prices is seen as fundamental to a well-performing economy. The government aims to avoid large increases in the overall level of prices, because this causes erosion in the value of money, and consequently in consumers' purchasing power.

In the context of the CPI, this means maintaining inflation within a defined range. The Reserve Bank of New Zealand has a formal agreement with the government that it will use monetary policy to maintain inflation between 1–3 percent over the medium term. The bank uses the official cash rate (OCR) mechanism to achieve this outcome.

The OCR is the benchmark interest rate from which all borrowing and savings interest rates in New Zealand are set. By adjusting the OCR up or down, the Reserve Bank influences the cost to consumers of borrowing money for goods and services. The higher the OCR, the greater is the cost of borrowing money. An increased cost results in a reduction in consumer demand for goods and services, lessening inflationary pressures. Conversely, if inflation pressures are low, the bank can lower the OCR, reducing the cost to consumers of borrowing money. This has an upward influence on demand and inflation. The bank reviews the OCR approximately every six weeks to ensure that the cost of consumer borrowing is having the desired influence on demand and inflation.

Between December 2005 and December 2007 the bank made four upward adjustments to the OCR. These took the OCR from 7.25 percent in December 2005 to 8.25 percent in December 2007. The OCR was unchanged for all of 2006; the four increases were made from early to mid 2007.

Reserve Bank Governor Alan Bollard announced there was no change to the official cash rate (OCR) in September 2007, following four increases between March and July 2007. The bank uses the OCR to maintain inflation between 1–3 percent over the medium term, as formally agreed with the government.

Deflator Many economic series, such as the value of retail sales, can be deflated using relevant indexes from the CPI to produce 'constant' price series. The purpose of a constant price series is to compare values between different periods, without the effect of price changes. For example, if the total value of retail sales increased 10.6 percent between the June 2005 and June 2007 quarters, some of this increase could be due to price changes. If, after deflation, the total value of retail sales increased 7.3 percent over this same period, then this is the change in the volume of retail sales. That is, 7.3 percent of the increase is due to changes in the number of sales transactions and the remaining 3.3 percent is due to price changes. Other economic series that are deflated using price indexes include gross domestic product (GDP), business investment, and household consumption expenditure.

Organisation of the consumers price index

A new classification system has been adopted for the CPI and Household Economic Survey. Based on the United Nations Classification of Individual Consumption by Purpose, it allows for better cross-country comparisons.

The CPI is divided into 11 groups of items, each weighted according to the expenditure on those items by private New Zealand households. Each group is made up of one or more subgroups which, in turn, are made up of sections, subsections and, finally, individually priced items. The expenditure weight assigned to each group is equivalent to the sum of the expenditure weights for all the items in that group.

- Housing and household utilities – The largest group in the CPI, the housing group includes rents, the cost of purchasing and constructing new dwellings, and home maintenance costs. Housing prices rose consistently between 1999 and 2005, except for a slight decline in the March 2001 quarter. The group has risen an average of 5.2 percent a year since the June 2005 quarter.

  The weight of this group fell from 21.52 percent in 2002 to 20.02 percent in 2006.

- Food – All items within the food group are priced monthly. Items are mostly available in supermarkets, grocery, and convenience stores, and include: fruit, vegetables, meat, fish, poultry, grocery foods, and non-alcoholic drinks. Prices for restaurant meals and ready-to-eat food are also collected. Food is the second-largest group in the CPI. Food prices rose an average of 3.2 percent a year between the June 2000 and June 2003 quarters – with annual changes of 0.0 percent in the year to June 2000, 6.7 percent for the year to December 2001, then 0.0 percent in the year to June 2003. Prices rose 1.1 percent a year from the September 2003 quarter to the June 2006 quarter, and 3.8 percent a year from the September 2006 to 2007 quarters.

- Transport – This group includes public and private transportation costs, including taxi, bus, train and ferry fares, the purchase of vehicles, and motor vehicle running and maintenance costs. Transport prices have been volatile historically. Significant increases were recorded between the June 1999 and December 2000 quarters, and between the March and December 2005 quarters. Prices have increased 3.8 percent a year since the June 2005 quarter.

- Recreation and culture – This group includes stationery, books, magazines and newspapers, leisure and recreation supplies and services, accommodation and board, tuition and exam fees, and child care costs. The group rose fairly consistently between the June 1999 and December 2005 quarters. It has increased, on average, 0.7 percent a year since the June 2005 quarter.

- Alcoholic beverages and tobacco – This group includes cigarettes, tobacco, beer, spirits, liqueurs and wine. From September 2006 to March 2008, the average yearly increase for the alcoholic beverages and tobacco group was 3.4 percent.

Table 17.01

Consumers price index
Expenditure weights[1]
Quarter ending 30 June

Group	2002	2006
Housing and household utilities	21.52	20.02
Food	17.21	17.38
Transport	15.51	17.24
Recreation and culture	9.73	10.21
Alcoholic beverages and tobacco	8.72	7.20
Household contents and services	5.13	5.49
Health	4.83	5.23
Clothing and footwear	4.77	4.75
Communication	2.92	3.26
Education	1.65	2.08
Miscellaneous goods and services	8.01	7.13
All groups	**100.0**	**100.0**

(1) Values may not add up to stated totals due to rounding.

Source: Statistics New Zealand

- Household contents and services – This group includes electricity, household appliances, furnishings, household supplies and services, and water and refuse charges. Household operation prices have historically been stable. Prices fell slightly between the June 2000 and June 2001 quarters and then, except for two quarters, rose slightly to the December 2005 quarter. Since then, prices have fallen and risen, resulting in an average increase of 0.2 percent a year for the group.
- Health – The health group includes medical supplies and services. It has increased by an average of 3.4 percent a year since the June 2005 quarter.
- Clothing and footwear – This group has shown little movement since the June 2005 quarter, increasing just 0.3 percent.
- Communication – The communication group includes postal services, but consists largely of telecommunication services and equipment. It has increased 1.2 percent a year, on average, since the June 2005 quarter.
- Education – The education group includes pre-school, primary, secondary and tertiary education. It has increased by an average of 3.9 percent a year since the June 2005 quarter. This is the smallest group.
- Miscellaneous goods and services – This group includes personal care and effects, as well as credit charges and various professional services. It has increased 3.2 percent a year, on average, since the June 2005 quarter. The weight of this group fell from 8.01 percent in 2002 to 7.13 percent in 2006, due largely to the insurance subgroup falling from 3.71 percent to 1.70 percent.

Retail prices of selected items

Table 17.02 shows weighted average retail prices of goods and services in the June quarters (or months) 2005–07. These weighted average prices of selected items are used in the calculation of the CPI and provide reliable indications of movements in price levels when compared with average prices for earlier periods. The quantity and price of any goods or service differs from shop to shop, and over time, so these prices are not designed to give a statistically accurate measure of absolute transaction prices.

Table 17.02

Retail prices of selected items[1]
June quarter or month[2]
2005–07

Item	Unit	2005	2006	2007
		$		
Apples	1kg	1.61	1.89	1.89
Bananas	1kg	1.88	1.66	2.29
Potatoes	1kg	0.97	1.11	1.22
Beef – mince	1kg	8.33	8.54	9.24
Lamb – chops	1kg	10.90	10.81	10.21
Bread – white sliced loaf[3]	700g	1.37	1.30	1.22
Cheese – mild cheddar[3] (supermarket only)	1kg	6.87	6.77	6.60
Milk – standard homogenised[3]	2 litres	3.05	3.05	2.60
Fish and chips	1 fish/chips	4.20	4.38	4.62
Beer – bottles (supermarket & liquor store)	1 dozen	18.63	18.27	18.25
Beer – glass (licensed premises)	400ml	3.93	4.07	4.26
Whisky (liquor store)	1,000ml	37.87	38.23	39.09
Panty-hose – 15 denier, average size (supermarket)	pair	4.41	4.48	4.84
Socks – men's (clothing store & department store)	pair	9.61	9.35	9.56
Dry cleaning – men's 2-piece, woollen suit	each	19.88	20.00	21.96
Concrete blocks – 390mm x 190mm x 190mm	per 100	303.05	312.48	318.89
House paint – acrylic, white	10 litres	134.72	143.77	146.07
Spouting/guttering – plastic	per 3m	27.48	28.93	29.57
Bleach (supermarket)	2.5 litres	3.34	3.42	3.58
Clothes washing powder – concentrate (supermarket)	1kg	4.48	4.31	4.39
GP visit – consultation, adult without community services card	each	43.18	43.31	37.18
Diesel	10 litres	8.60	12.55	9.93
Petrol – 91 octane	10 litres	12.67	16.79	15.38
Warrant of fitness – private car	each	38.92	41.05	42.42
Postage – standard, medium-size envelope	each	0.45	0.45	0.47
CD – top 10 album (record store & department store)	each	27.91	28.30	27.91
DVD hire – overnight Friday, new release	1 movie	7.28	7.37	7.37
Envelopes – medium-size (supermarket)	pk of 20	1.61	1.64	1.65
Hairdressing – women's, shampoo, cut & blow wave	each	44.91	48.43	50.78
Bathroom soap – cake, 100g (supermarket)	pk of 4	3.39	3.18	3.33
Shampoo (supermarket)	400ml	5.73	6.64	6.40
Toilet paper (supermarket)	4 rolls	2.91	2.79	2.75

(1) Calculated by applying index movements to weighted average prices for the June 2006 quarter or month. These are not statistically accurate measures of average transaction price levels, but do provide a reliable indicator of percentage changes in prices. (2) Items within the food group (apples to fish and chips within table) are for the June month. (3) Based on the cheapest available brand or variety in each retail outlet at the time of price collection.

Source: Statistics New Zealand

Figure 17.01

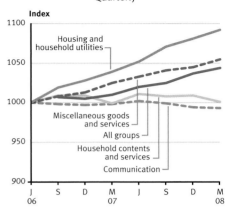

Consumers price index groups
Base: June 2006 quarter (=1000)
Quarterly

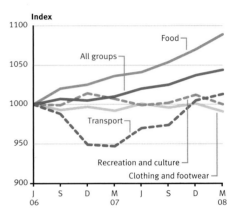

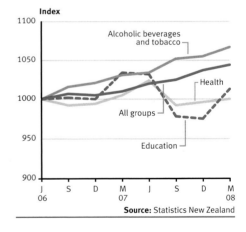

Source: Statistics New Zealand

Figure 17.02

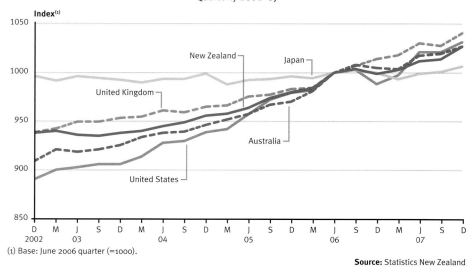

Consumers price index international comparisons
Excludes housing and credit services
Quarterly 2002–07

(1) Base: June 2006 quarter (=1000).

Source: Statistics New Zealand

International comparisons

Inflation, as measured by each country's CPI, rose in 29 of the 30 Organisation for Economic Co-operation and Development (OECD) countries in 2006.

Japan was the only country in the OECD to experience minimal price change between December 2002 and 2007. For this period the increase in New Zealand's CPI (13.9 percent) was marginally ahead of that for the OECD as a whole (13.3 percent). New Zealand's CPI rose 3.1 percent in 2007, compared with 2.6 percent in 2006 and 3.2 percent in 2005.

Figure 17.02 compares New Zealand's CPI with that of its major trading partners, Australia, the United States, the United Kingdom and Japan. For the period September 2002 to December 2007, New Zealand's rate of price change was less than that for the United States, Australia and the United Kingdom.

Figure 17.03

Consumers price index inflation 1977–2007
Percentage change from previous June quarter[1]

(1) Calculated from June quarter index value.

Source: Statistics New Zealand

Producers price index

The producers price index (PPI) is a series of quarterly economic indicators designed to measure price changes in the production sector of the economy. The consumers price index (CPI), in comparison, measures price changes in the household sector of the economy.

The PPI has two types of indexes: outputs and inputs. 'Outputs' measures changes in prices received by producers for the products and services they provide, while 'inputs' measures changes in the costs of production (excluding capital and labour costs).

Uses of the PPI The PPI can be used in the analysis of inflationary trends and in economic forecasting. It is a key input for the calculation of national accounts and gross domestic product – measuring changes in production at a constant price. The indexes that form the PPI are also widely used to determine increases allowable under escalation clauses and in commercial contracts.

Influences on the PPI In recent years, the two key influences on the PPI have been changes in electricity prices and wholesale trade prices.

Producers' output prices rose 3.7 percent during 2005, 4.1 percent during 2006, and 4.0 percent during 2007. Input prices also had three years of consecutive rises: 6.4 percent in 2005, 5.2 percent in 2006 and 3.4 percent in 2007. Several commodities significantly influenced these figures, including:

- Electricity – The direction of significant price movements for electricity generation and supply varied from 2005–07. Prices for electricity generation and supply rose 28.9 percent for the year ending December 2005, to be followed by two annual falls for the years ending December 2006 (down 6.0 percent), and 2007 (down 0.8 percent). Fluctuation in spot market prices for electricity was the main reason for these movements.

- Wholesale trade – The wholesale trade sector had continuous price increases from 2005–07. Higher prices in the mineral metal and chemical wholesaling sector (caused by increased energy prices) were the main contributors to the increases. Prices for the wholesale trade sector rose 5.9 percent for the year ending December 2007, after rises of 6.6 percent in 2006, and 3.8 percent for the year ending December 2005.

- Dairy product manufacturing – Prices for dairy product manufacturing rose significantly in the year ending December 2007 (up 33.9 percent), and during 2005 (up 8.4 percent), driven mainly by higher prices for milk powder and butter. This compares with a fall of 1.1 percent for the year ending December 2006.

- Construction – The construction sector recorded price increases from 2005–07 (up 5.0 percent during 2007, up 5.9 percent for 2006, and up 5.8 percent for the year ending December 2005). Increasing raw material and component prices, and the cost of labour, were the major contributors to rising output prices.

- Livestock and cropping farming – Prices for livestock and cropping farming had mixed movements between 2005 and 2007. Falls were recorded during 2007 (down 4.3 percent), and 2005 (down 3.9 percent), while there was a 5.2 percent rise for the year ending December 2006. The main contributor to the price falls was lower farm-gate prices for livestock.

National accounts

Numerous transactions take place within the New Zealand economy every day. Businesses and individuals buy and sell goods and services, the government collects taxes and pays beneficiaries, and individuals are paid for their labour and buy groceries or pay the rent. Measuring all these transactions is a complex task, but it is essential to understanding how the economy operates.

In New Zealand, as in most other countries, myriad transactions are classified, measured and recorded in the national accounts, which provide a convenient summary of key economic and financial flows. Moreover, they provide a framework in which to analyse and compare important economic variables, such as household consumption and savings.

The national accounts capture all types of transactions, for the economy as a whole, or for certain groups or sectors within it, such as business, government or households.

Gross domestic product (GDP) represents income earned from production in New Zealand, whether that is carried out by New Zealanders or foreign firms operating within New Zealand. It does not measure the final incomes that New Zealand residents earn.

Gross national income is a better measure of New Zealanders' income, as it excludes income sent abroad (dividends, interest and other transfers) and includes similar income earned by New Zealanders from overseas investments. Further adjustments to take account of depreciation and transfers from the rest of the world give an even better measure of income (national disposable income).

In the year ending 31 March 2007, GDP in current prices rose 5.4 percent. When the effects of inflation are removed, there was an increase of 1.6 percent in real GDP for the March 2007 year, compared with 2.7 percent in the March 2006 year. The 2007 increase was the lowest level of economic growth since 1999 when the economy grew by 0.5 percent. Increased spending (final consumption) by general government and the private sector, in volume terms, was partly offset by falling business investment in fixed assets.

The main contributors to the lower rate of economic growth during the year ending March 2007 were goods producing industries. Measured in volume terms, construction (down 3.6 percent),

Table 17.03

Principal aggregates 1998–2007
Year ending 31 March

Year	Gross domestic product	Gross national income[1]	National disposable income[2]	GDP in chain-volume series[3]
	\$(million)			
1998	101,604	95,205	81,630	98,323
1999	103,381	98,402	84,062	98,775
2000	109,629	103,024	87,975	104,041
2001	115,906	108,339	92,366	106,551
2002	124,632	117,549	100,545	110,554
2003	130,996	123,950	106,168	116,143
2004	139,754	132,426	113,871	120,220
2005	149,153	139,687	119,859	125,069
2006	156,849	145,593	124,239	128,428
2007	165,379	153,516	130,573	130,442

(1) GNI = GDP plus net investment income from the rest of the world. (2) NDI = GNI less consumption of fixed capital plus net current transfers from the rest of the world. (3) Chain-volume series expressed in 1995/96 prices. Chain-volume series are not additive.

Source: Statistics New Zealand

Otago Daily Times

Coila Marr from Dunedin buys 10 cent ice creams from Jolani Ferguson. The Outram dairy had been selling so many ice creams that the manufacturer chose to subsidise their \$1.50 product. Service-based industries, including retail trade, account for about two-thirds of all economic activity in New Zealand.

and machinery and equipment manufacturing (down 7.0 percent), recorded large decreases. The construction industry contribution fall was due to a decrease in non-residential building activity and construction trade services. Several large-value non-residential building projects by government had been driving steady growth in previous periods. Rough weather also hampered the primary producing industries, with severe wet weather and snow in the 2006 winter being followed by high winds in autumn.

Consolidated accounts of the nation

The consolidated accounts of the nation consist of four accounts:

Gross domestic product and expenditure account GDP is a measure of the value added from all economic activity in New Zealand. The account shows the various forms of income generated by production, and the categories of final expenditure on available goods and services.

National income and outlay account National disposable income is the value of income available to New Zealanders, and consists mainly of incomes generated in New Zealand. Adjustments are

Table 17.04

Gross domestic product and expenditure account
Year ending 31 March

Item	2003	2004	2005	2006	2007
	\$(million)				
Compensation of employees	55,222	59,484	64,005	68,542	73,875
Gross operating surplus	59,342	62,738	66,524	68,483	70,511
Taxes on production and imports	16,845	17,972	19,115	20,406	21,591
Less subsidies	413	440	491	582	598
Gross domestic product	**130,996**	**139,754**	**149,153**	**156,849**	**165,379**
Final consumption expenditure					
Private households	75,192	80,226	85,750	91,552	96,510
Private non-profit organisations serving households	1,676	1,826	1,917	2,013	2,113
Central government	19,909	21,525	23,195	25,140	27,158
Local government	2,630	2,862	3,067	3,276	3,480
Change in inventories	1094	1,329	1,650	828	-317
Gross fixed capital formation	28,025	31,583	34,965	37,743	38,099
Gross national expenditure	**128,526**	**139,351**	**150,533**	**160,552**	**167,043**
Exports of goods and services	42,565	40,658	43,354	43,786	48,198
Less imports of goods and services	40,095	40,254	44,513	47,444	50,528
Balance on external goods and services	2,471	403	-1,159	-3,858	-2,330
Expenditure on gross domestic product	**130,996**	**139,754**	**149,385**	**156,894**	**164,714**
Statistical discrepancy[1]	0	0	-232	-45	665

(1) Production and expenditure measures of GDP are estimated independently, from diverse data sources. Combining survey and other measurements, and timing errors in various components, results in a difference between the estimates – the statistical discrepancy. This discrepancy does not occur after the two measures have been reconciled.

Note: Figures may not add up to stated totals due to rounding.

Source: Statistics New Zealand

made for income paid to, and received from, the rest of the world. The account also shows the part of disposable income spent by New Zealanders on current consumption, and the portion of income that was saved.

Table 17.05

National income and outlay account
Year ending 31 March

Item	2003	2004	2005	2006	2007
	\$(million)				
Use of income					
Final consumption expenditure					
Private households	75,192	80,226	85,750	91,552	96,510
Private non-profit organisations serving households	1,676	1,826	1,917	2,013	2,113
Central government	19,909	21,525	23,195	25,140	27,158
Local government	2,630	2,862	3,067	3,276	3,480
Total final consumption expenditure	99,407	106,440	113,928	121,981	129,261
Saving	6,761	7,431	5,930	2,258	1,312
Use of national disposable income	**106,168**	**113,871**	**119,859**	**124,239**	**130,573**
Income					
Compensation of employees	55,222	59,484	64,005	68,542	73,875
Compensation of employees from the rest of the world (net)	0	0	0	0	0
Gross operating surplus	59,342	62,738	66,524	68,483	70,511
Taxes on production and imports	16,845	17,972	19,115	20,406	21,591
Less subsidies	413	440	491	582	598
Investment income from the rest of the world (net)	-7,046	-7,328	-9,466	-11,256	-11,863
Gross national income	123,950	132,426	139,687	145,593	153,516
Current transfers from the rest of the world (net)	113	237	318	372	671
Gross national disposable income	**124,063**	**132,663**	**140,005**	**145,965**	**154,187**
Less consumption of fixed capital	17,895	18,792	20,146	21,726	23,614
National disposable income	**106,168**	**113,871**	**119,859**	**124,239**	**130,573**

Note: Figures may not add up to stated totals due to rounding.

Source: Statistics New Zealand

National capital account The national capital account records capital expenditure. The difference between the accumulation of capital assets and the sources of funds (mainly savings and the income set aside for the replacement of capital equipment) gives a residual to be borrowed from (or lent to) the rest of the world.

The two key components of national income – employment income and business profits – both increased in the March 2007 year, with the largest contributor being compensation of employees. National disposable income, which measures the income available to New Zealand residents for current consumption or saving, rose 5.1 percent.

Final consumption expenditure (private and government) increased 6.0 percent, while national saving decreased from \$2.3 billion to \$1.3 billion. As a proportion of national disposable income, saving was 1.0 percent in the March 2007 year, down from the 1.8 percent recorded in the March 2006 year.

Table 17.06

National capital account
Year ending 31 March

Item	2003	2004	2005	2006	2007
	\$(million)				
Change in inventories	1,094	1,329	1,650	828	-317
Gross fixed capital formation					
Private	21,744	25,023	28,090	29,684	29,988
Central government[1]	3,188	3,881	4,642	5,444	5,628
Local government[1]	3,093	2,678	2,233	2,616	2,483
Purchase of non-produced non-financial assets from the rest of the world (net)	-47	3	-6	2	5
Net lending to the rest of the world	-2,877	-5,965	-10,199	-14,869	-13,983
Capital accumulation	**26,195**	**26,949**	**26,411**	**23,704**	**23,805**
Saving	6,761	7,431	5,930	2,258	1,312
Consumption of fixed capital	17,895	18,792	20,146	21,726	23,614
Capital transfers from the rest of the world (net)	1,538	726	102	-325	-457
Finance of capital accumulation	**26,195**	**26,949**	**26,179**	**23,660**	**24,469**
Statistical discrepancy[2]	0	0	232	45	-665

(1) Includes all government-owned producer enterprises. (2) Production and expenditure measures of GDP are estimated independently, from diverse data sources. Combining survey and other measurements, and timing errors in various components, results in a difference between the estimates – the statistical discrepancy. This discrepancy does not occur after the two measures have been reconciled.

Note: Figures may not add up to stated totals due to rounding.

Source: Statistics New Zealand

Environmental accounts

Statistics New Zealand produces environmental accounts for a number of New Zealand's natural resources, including energy, fish, forests, and fresh water. Environmental accounts measure the interaction between the environment and the economy – in both monetary and physical terms. They measure both the value and volume of natural resources, and which industries are using them.

Environmental accounts are compiled using the United Nations Integrated System of Environmental and Economic Accounting framework, which is an extension of the System of National Accounts, the framework used to measure transactions in the economy.

There are two types of accounts – stock accounts and flow accounts. Stock accounts measure the absolute level of natural resources at a point in time. Flow accounts show how the resource has been supplied and used, and by which industries.

Environmental accounts provide information that complements traditional measures of economic activity such as gross domestic product (GDP). Producing environmental information on an accounting framework allows direct comparison between environmental and economic information. For example, comparing energy demand with measures of economic growth provides measures of energy efficiency.

The environmental account for fish uses quota trade information to estimate the asset value of New Zealand's commercially exploited fish stocks. At September 2006, the value was \$3.8 billion, a 40 percent increase since 1996. The commercial fish resource is dominated by five major species: hoki, rock lobster, pāua, arrow squid, and orange roughy. Together they contributed about 55 percent of the total asset value in 2006.

The *Water Physical Stock Account 1995–2005* reports the amount of water coming into New Zealand (inflows), the amount leaving (outflows), and changes in the amount of water held in soil, lakes and glaciers, and as snow and groundwater – on a national and regional basis. In addition, the account presents limited information on water abstraction.

For the June 2005 year, the total volume of precipitation (rainfall, snow, sleet, and hail) was 505,194 million cubic metres – enough to fill Lake Taupo eight times over.

During the period 1995 to 2005, a yearly average of 2.1 metres (depth) of precipitation fell in New Zealand. The West Coast received the greatest amount (an annual average of 5.5 metres) while Otago received the least (an average of 1.2 metres).

Source: Statistics New Zealand

Figure 17.04

National saving and net overseas borrowing
Year ending 31 March

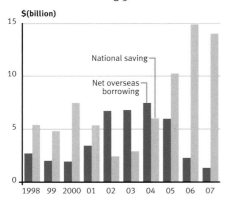

Source: Statistics New Zealand

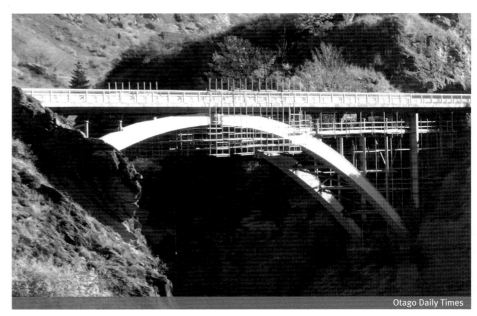

Otago Daily Times

Cracks in the Kawarau Bridge near Queenstown are under repair. In the year ending 31 March 2007, in real terms, investment in fixed assets fell 2.3 percent, although there was increased investment in infrastructural assets such as bridges, roads and dams.

Investment in fixed assets, measured in current prices, rose 0.9 percent in the year ending 31 March 2007, to reach $38.1 billion. Increased investment in residential buildings, plant machinery and equipment, as well as infrastructural assets (such as roads, bridges and dams) was partly offset by falling investment in transport equipment. Measured in real terms, investment in fixed assets fell 2.3 percent in the year ending 31 March 2007.

Funds set aside for the replacement of capital (consumption of fixed capital) rose from $21.7 billion in the year ended March 2006 to $23.6 billion in the year ended March 2007. Net borrowing from the rest of the world decreased from $14.9 billion (9.5 percent of GDP) to $14.0 billion (8.5 percent of GDP) over the same period.

Table 17.07

External account
Year ending 31 March

Item	2003	2004	2005	2006	2007
	\$(million)				
Current					
Income from the rest of the world					
Exports of goods	30,648	29,054	31,114	31,580	35,633
Exports of services	11,917	11,604	12,240	12,206	12,565
Compensation of employees	0	0	0	0	0
Investment income	2,576	2,694	2,848	2,046	2,851
Current transfers	1,376	1,431	1,555	1,664	1,956
Total	**46,518**	**44,782**	**47,757**	**47,496**	**53,006**
Payments to the rest of the world					
Imports of goods	29,982	30,246	33,344	35,685	38,464
Imports of services	10,113	10,009	11,169	11,759	12,064
Compensation of employees	0	0	0	0	0
Investment income	9,622	10,022	12,314	13,302	14,714
Current transfers	1,263	1,194	1,237	1,292	1,285
Balance on the external current account	-4,462	-6,688	-10,307	-14,542	-13,521
Total	**46,518**	**44,782**	**47,757**	**47,496**	**53,006**
Capital					
Capital transfers from the rest of the world	2,337	1,774	1,347	997	957
Less capital transfers to the rest of the world	799	1,047	1,244	1,322	1,414
Capital transfers from the rest of the world (net)	1,538	726	102	-325	-457
Balance on the external current account	-4,462	-6,688	-10,307	-14,542	-13,521
Capital receipts	**-2,924**	**-5,962**	**-10,205**	**-14,867**	**-13,978**
Purchase of non-produced non-financial assets from the rest of the world (net)	-47	3	-6	2	5
Net lending to the rest of the world	-2,877	-5,965	-10,199	-14,869	-13,983
Capital disbursements	**-2,924**	**-5,962**	**-10,205**	**-14,867**	**-13,978**

Note: Figures may not add up to stated totals due to rounding.

Source: Statistics New Zealand

External account The deficit balance on the external current account, which had increased consistently since the year ended March 2003, decreased from $14.5 billion (9.3 percent of GDP) in the year ended March 2006 to $13.5 billion in the March 2007 year (8.2 percent of GDP). This narrowing of the deficit could mainly be attributed to the increased value of exports of goods (up 12.8 percent). Depreciation of the New Zealand dollar against the currencies of most of the country's major trading partners, combined with higher international prices for New Zealand's main export commodities, pushed merchandise export prices higher. In addition, the volume of goods exported over the same period also rose.

Dairy export values rose 24.4 percent, mainly due to higher volumes (up 22.3 percent). A rise in export prices was the main reason behind higher export values of metal products, machinery and equipment, and other food, beverages and tobacco.

The weaker New Zealand dollar also lifted merchandise import prices in the year ending 31 March 2007. Consequently, payments for imported goods and services rose 6.5 percent, despite a decrease in the volume of goods and services imported (down 1.7 percent) in the March 2007 year.

Gross domestic product by industry

The 'value added' component of industrial production is measured by taking the value of goods and services produced by an industry (output) and deducting the cost of goods and services used by the industry in the production process (intermediate consumption). GDP is then obtained by totalling the value added for all industries.

GDP by industry is calculated annually in current prices and volume terms, and quarterly in volume terms. Industries are combined to form the following broad groupings:

- primary industries (agriculture; fishing; forestry; mining and quarrying)
- goods-producing industries (manufacturing; electricity, gas and water; construction)
- service industries (wholesale trade; retail trade, accommodation and restaurants; transport and communications; finance, insurance, real estate and business services (including owner-occupied dwellings); government administration and defence; personal and community services).

Service-based industries account for about two-thirds of the activity within the New Zealand economy, and therefore tend to dominate the contribution to GDP growth. For the year ending 31 March 2007, service industries grew 2.9 percent, while primary and goods-producing industries declined 0.2 and 1.7 percent, respectively.

Tables 17.08 and 17.09 (overleaf) detail production-based GDP statistics. The decrease in both residential and non-residential building investment was reflected in the drop in the construction industry, which was down 3.6 percent in the March 2007 year. The growth in household expenditure was also evident in the increased activity in service-based industries, with the finance, insurance and business services, and the retail trade, accommodation and restaurant sectors being major contributors.

Are we saving enough?

New Zealand's household saving rate has been declining in the past 20 years. The rate is consistently one of the lowest in the Organisation for Economic Co-operation and Development (OECD), and has fallen quite rapidly in the last five years. This has led to debate on the adequacy of saving, especially in the context of retirement income policy.

Given the critical role investment plays in economic development, discussions on growth and economic welfare have also focused on the declining saving levels.

Saving is a 'flow' concept and is measured as a residual, being the difference between some measure of income less some measure of expenditure or consumption. Saving is measured after deducting the consumption of fixed capital, because the cost of using up capital assets should be deducted from both income and saving.

In the national accounts, national saving (S) is defined as national disposable income (NDI) less private and government consumption expenditure (C):

$$S = NDI - C$$

At the national level, saving is a key source of investment funds. Net investment (capital accumulation less consumption of fixed capital) must be funded from either national saving or from overseas borrowing (or foreign saving). New Zealand's national saving rate

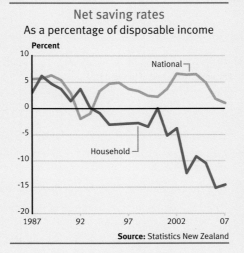

Net saving rates
As a percentage of disposable income

Source: Statistics New Zealand

rose after 2001, on the back of increasing government surpluses, but it has fallen since 2004, largely due to a continuing fall in household saving. As a result, more of New Zealand's investment has been financed by borrowing overseas, as reflected in a higher current account deficit.

Saving can also be broken down by the institutional sectors in the economy, such as financial institutions, government and households. At the household level, saving is defined as disposable income less household consumption expenditure. Household saving as a percentage of disposable income has declined over the last 20 years, and since 1994, has been negative. After 2003, the saving rate has fallen markedly.

In recent years household net wealth has increased significantly, due largely to the rapid rise in house prices. This has led to an apparently paradoxical situation of household wealth increasing, despite the saving rate being negative and declining. Wealth is a 'stock' measure, and each year it changes, due to additions (deductions) from annual saving (dis-saving) and also any revaluations of existing assets. Recently, the capital gain households have made on their properties has completely swamped any wealth decline that may have come from falling saving, resulting in the overall net wealth of households increasing.

In discussing future income adequacy, it is important to distinguish between saving – the current flow, and savings – the wealth stock measure. Although closely related, their effect on the well-being of different household groups may be quite different.

Source: Statistics New Zealand

Figure 17.05

Business activity by broad industry group

Contribution to annual change in GDP in real terms
Year ending 31 March

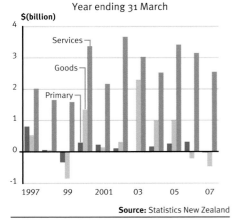

Source: Statistics New Zealand

Table 17.08

Gross domestic product by broad industry group
Chain-volume series expressed in 1995/96 prices[1]

	Primary industries		Goods-producing industries		Service industries		Gross domestic product	
	$(million)	Percentage change	$(million)	Percentage change	$(million)	Percentage change	$(million)	Percentage change
Year			**Actual annual change from previous March year**					
2004	8,774	1.8	26,871	3.8	79,801	3.3	120,220	3.5
2005	9,019	2.8	27,868	3.7	83,205	4.3	125,069	4.0
2006	9,320	3.3	27,657	-0.8	86,340	3.8	128,428	2.7
2007	9,300	-0.2	27,194	-1.7	88,876	2.9	130,442	1.6
Quarter			**Seasonally adjusted change from previous quarter**					
2003 Jun	2,141	0.8	6,490	-1.0	19,610	0.5	29,451	0.3
Sep	2,195	2.5	6,668	2.7	19,782	0.9	29,868	1.4
Dec	2,198	0.1	6,759	1.4	20,082	1.5	30,185	1.1
2004 Mar	2,232	1.6	6,930	2.5	20,346	1.3	30,722	1.8
Jun	2,245	0.6	6,965	0.5	20,487	0.7	31,024	1.0
Sep	2,254	0.4	7,022	0.8	20,632	0.7	31,214	0.6
Dec	2,261	0.3	6,946	-1.1	20,918	1.4	31,284	0.2
2005 Mar	2,255	-0.2	6,899	-0.7	21,173	1.2	31,557	0.9
Jun	2,289	1.5	6,972	1.1	21,404	1.1	31,997	1.4
Sep	2,328	1.7	6,908	-0.9	21,559	0.7	32,131	0.4
Dec	2,351	1.0	6,850	-0.8	21,595	0.2	32,019	-0.3
2006 Mar	2,350	0.0	6,904	0.8	21,792	0.9	32,297	0.9
Jun	2,309	-1.8	6,808	-1.4	21,865	0.3	32,286	0.0
Sep	2,288	-0.9	6,745	-0.9	22,102	1.1	32,427	0.4
Dec	2,358	3.1	6,776	0.4	22,327	1.0	32,668	0.7
2007 Mar	2,347	-0.5	6,842	1.0	22,586	1.2	33,060	1.2
Jun	2,373	1.1	6,844	0.0	22,786	0.9	33,326	0.8
Sep	2,466	3.9	6,748	-1.4	22,955	0.7	33,503	0.5

(1) Chain-volume series are not additive.

Source: Statistics New Zealand

Table 17.09

Gross domestic product by industry
Chain-volume series expressed in 1995/96 prices[1]
Year ending 31 March

Year	Agriculture	Fishing, forestry & mining	Manufacturing	Electricity, gas & water	Construction	Wholesale trade	Retail, accommodation & restaurants	Transport & communication	Finance, insurance & business services	Government administration & defence	Personal & community services	Gross domestic product
						$(million)						
1998	5,496	2,877	16,166	2,230	4,290	7,577	7,119	8,385	24,710	4,305	11,435	**98,323**
1999	5,221	2,824	15,599	2,289	3,928	7,726	7,173	8,894	25,060	4,295	11,999	**98,775**
2000	5,379	2,951	16,369	2,189	4,605	8,542	7,557	9,785	26,062	4,233	12,439	**104,041**
2001	5,526	3,013	16,794	2,210	4,293	8,892	7,704	10,450	26,618	4,312	12,912	**106,551**
2002	5,589	3,042	16,941	2,132	4,531	9,347	8,000	11,160	28,232	4,417	13,444	**110,554**
2003	5,559	3,078	18,398	2,315	5,180	9,025	8,419	11,696	29,719	4,641	14,045	**116,143**
2004	5,920	2,793	18,892	2,370	5,604	9,195	8,866	12,139	30,432	4,885	14,557	**120,220**
2005	6,151	2,782	19,324	2,478	6,030	9,823	9,406	12,836	31,346	5,174	14,988	**125,069**
2006	6,488	2,698	19,012	2,338	6,305	10,082	9,830	13,193	32,718	5,478	15,361	**128,428**
2007	6,491	2,668	18,667	2,402	6,080	10,069	10,111	13,440	33,814	5,765	15,927	**130,442**

(1) Chain-volume series are not additive.

Source: Statistics New Zealand

Expenditure on gross domestic product

Another way of measuring GDP is to total all final domestic expenditure on goods and services, add the value of exports, and subtract the value of imports.

There are three broad categories of final domestic expenditure:

- final consumption expenditure of households, private non-profit institutions serving households, and general government
- gross fixed capital formation by producers
- change in inventories, which consists of increases/decreases in producers' stockholdings of raw materials, work in progress, and finished goods.

Conceptually, both the production and expenditure-based GDP series are the same. However, as each series uses independent data and estimation techniques, some differences between the alternative measures do arise.

Expenditure on GDP is calculated annually and quarterly in current prices and in volume terms. It is summarised in table 17.10.

Table 17.10

Expenditure on gross domestic product
Year ending 31 March

Year	Private final consumption expenditure	General government final consumption expenditure	Change in inventories	Gross fixed capital formation	Gross national expenditure	Exports of goods & services	Less imports of goods & services	Expenditure on gross domestic product
					$(million)			
Current prices								
1998	60,567	18,380	817	21,408	101,172	28,531	28,099	**101,604**
1999	63,463	18,602	270	20,742	103,078	30,394	30,091	**103,381**
2000	65,987	20,062	1,537	22,888	110,474	33,526	34,371	**109,628**
2001	68,692	20,262	1,419	23,595	113,967	41,159	39,219	**115,906**
2002	72,163	21,698	1,886	25,969	121,717	43,694	40,778	**124,632**
2003	76,868	22,539	1094	28,025	128,526	42,566	40,095	**130,997**
2004	82,052	24,387	1,329	31,583	139,351	40,658	40,254	**139,754**
2005	87,666	26,262	1,650	34,965	150,533	43,353	44,512	**149,384**
2006	93,565	28,416	828	37,743	160,552	43,786	47,444	**156,893**
2007	98,623	30,638	-317	38,099	167,043	48,199	50,528	**164,713**
Chain-volume series expressed in 1995/96 prices								
1998	58,276	17,911	682	21,690	98,573	29,505	28,776	**99,256**
1999	60,044	17,822	393	21,180	99,449	30,356	29,367	**100,399**
2000	61,998	18,845	1,576	23,417	105,716	32,591	32,694	**105,564**
2001	62,885	18,474	1,207	23,504	106,032	34,649	32,478	**108,136**
2002	64,636	19,205	1,268	25,097	110,131	35,702	33,784	**111,942**
2003	67,914	19,466	1,174	27,058	115,442	38,503	36,216	**117,657**
2004	72,239	20,355	1,382	30,540	124,115	38,851	40,827	**122,093**
2005	76,064	21,158	1,764	32,867	131,428	40,663	45,911	**126,496**
2006	79,560	22,216	1,009	34,567	136,831	40,609	47,773	**130,206**
2007	81,640	23,192	-137	33,772	138,158	41,869	46,950	**133,303**

Note: Figures may not add up to stated totals due to rounding. Chain-volume series are not additive.

Source: Statistics New Zealand

Growth in the economy for the year ending 31 March 2007 was driven by domestic demand. Both private and general government consumption grew for the year, as did exports. The increase in exports was dominated by increased volumes of dairy product exports.

Investments in fixed assets, measured in volume terms, decreased in the year ending 31 March 2007. This was due largely to decreased expenditure on transport equipment, residential buildings, and non-residential buildings.

Household sector

Households consist of New Zealand-resident individuals and families. Income is earned from businesses, as wages and salaries and entrepreneurial income, or from investments, as interest and dividends.

The Aucklander

Adam checks a packet of butter and finds it 35 grams underweight while conducting a survey of the weights of packaged butter. During 2007 and 2008, dairy product prices soared, mainly due to a strong rise in global commodity prices. Consumer spending on goods and services is the largest part of a household's spending.

Table 17.11

Household consumption expenditure
By purpose
Year ending 31 March

Year	Food & beverages	Clothing & footwear	Housing	Household goods & services	Health & medical	Transport	Recreation & education	Hotels & restaurants	Other goods & services	Net tourist expenditure	Total household consumption
						$(million)					
					Current prices						
1995	8,843	2,511	10,313	5,932	1,646	7,712	5,344	3,810	5,339	-1,245	**50,206**
2000	10,939	3,038	13,925	6,982	..	9,167	..	4,945	7,215	-2,009	**64,458**
2005	15,108	3,981	16,641	9,682	..	12,798	..	6,786	9,553	-4,019	**85,749**
2006	16,068	4,307	17,286	10,322	..	13,685	..	7,342	10,093	-3,515	**91,552**
2007	17,226	4,492	17,885	10,996	..	13,931	..	7,748	10,732	-3,518	**96,510**
			Actual chain-volume series expressed in 1995/96 prices								
1995	8,952	2,486	11,083	5,913	1,723	7,934	5,553	3,908	5,472	-1,386	**51,614**
2000	10,263	2,977	11,969	7,029	..	9,517	..	4,561	7,125	-2,075	**60,501**
2005	12,712	3,824	12,966	9,502	..	12,360	..	5,338	8,212	-2,826	**74,168**
2006	13,374	4,137	13,188	10,039	..	12,598	..	5,585	8,529	-2,186	**77,601**
2007	13,909	4,326	13,380	10,537	..	12,319	..	5,687	8,772	-2,264	**79,636**

Note: Figures may not add up to stated totals due to rounding.

Symbol: .. figure not available

Source: Statistics New Zealand

Figure 17.06

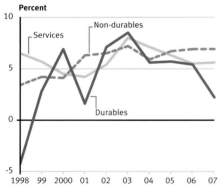

Household spending by type[1]
Annual percentage change
Year ending 31 March

(1) Calculated from current price series.

Source: Statistics New Zealand

Households buy goods and services from businesses and incur interest charges to service borrowing. Consumer spending on goods and services (such as motor vehicles, food, recreation, health and education) is by far the largest part of household outlay.

Following an increase of 6.8 percent in the March 2006 year, household consumption expenditure increased by 5.4 percent in the year ending 31 March 2007. A contributing factor was increased household income from both higher employment levels and higher earnings for paid employees.

Table 17.11 shows household spending, by the type of goods and services purchased. A mixture of goods and services may be combined in a single category. For example the hotel and restaurants item includes expenditure on food, alcohol and accommodation.

As figure 17.06 shows, the increase in household spending was most noticeable in purchases of non-durable or consumable goods, which rose 6.9 percent in the year ending 31 March 2007. Spending by households on services rose 5.6 percent while spending on durable goods increased 2.2 percent.

There has been consistent positive growth in the volume of household consumption spending since the year ending 31 March 1993.

Gross fixed capital formation

Table 17.12 records producers' outlay on durable real assets such as buildings, motor vehicles, plant and machinery, roading, and improvements to land.

Table 17.12

Gross fixed capital formation
By asset type
Year ending 31 March

Year	Residential buildings	Non-residential buildings	Other construction	Land improvements	Transport equipment	Plant machinery & equipment	Intangible assets	Total
				$(million)				
			Current prices					
1995	4,815	2,502	1,226	221	2,473	6,106	1,011	**18,355**
2000	6,222	2,736	2,807	319	2,444	6,506	1,854	**22,888**
2005	10,291	4,450	4,088	491	3,913	9,187	2,545	**34,965**
2006	10,531	5,485	4,528	582	4,465	9,492	2,661	**37,743**
2007	10,812	5,307	4,977	616	3,866	9,735	2,786	**38,099**
			Chain-volume series expressed in 1995/96 prices					
1995	5,158	2,574	1,245	222	2,443	5,913	1,006	**18,543**
2000	5,839	2,700	2,703	308	2,525	7,277	2,085	**23,417**
2005	7,503	3,663	3,291	372	3,787	11,476	3,117	**32,867**
2006	7,165	4,330	3,447	410	4,281	12,189	3,285	**34,567**
2007	6,973	3,963	3,627	414	3,669	12,354	3,464	**33,772**

Note: Figures may not add up to stated totals due to rounding. Chain-volume series are not additive.

Source: Statistics New Zealand

In measuring outlay, sales of similar goods are deducted. Land is excluded from gross fixed capital formation, but the value of construction work done by a firm's own employees is included. The term 'gross' indicates that consumption of fixed capital (economic depreciation) has not been deducted from the value of the outlay.

Measured in volume terms, capital investment fell 2.3 percent in the year ending 31 March 2007. In the previous March year, capital investment rose 5.2 percent. Investment in aircraft and military equipment, which caused a strong increase in the volume measure of transport equipment in the March 2006 year, was not repeated in the March 2007 year. In addition, investment in non-residential buildings fell 8.5 percent in the March 2007 year.

Capital stock statistics

Statistics New Zealand produces two measures of capital stock:

- net capital stock is a wealth measure of the current value of the stock of fixed assets still in use in New Zealand
- productive capital stock is a volume measure of the stock of fixed assets in New Zealand, adjusted for the decline in efficiency as the assets age.

The capital stock series, shown in table 17.14, are calculated using a perpetual inventory model. Briefly, this involves progressively building up capital stock estimates using the following equation:

opening stock + acquisitions − disposals − consumption of fixed capital = closing stock

Consumption of fixed capital at replacement cost, which is represented as economic depreciation in the national accounts, is an important output from the model.

External trade

Exports Table 17.13 records the export values and volumes of goods and services. The value of exports of goods and services rose 10.1 percent in the year ending 31 March 2007, compared with a 1.0 percent rise in the preceding year. A higher volume of dairy exports (up 22.3 percent) was the largest contributor to this increase. In addition, export prices increased as a result of the weaker New Zealand dollar and higher international prices for New Zealand's main export commodities.

Imports The value of imports of goods and services rose 6.5 percent in the year ending 31 March 2007. An increase in merchandise import prices, due mainly to a weaker New Zealand dollar, was partly offset by decreasing import volumes. Import volumes, which had been rising consistently since the March 2002 year, fell 1.7 percent in the year ending March 2007. Imports of services (down 4.3 percent) and capital equipment (down 3.2 percent) were the main contributors to the fall in import volumes.

Annual percentage changes in the current price value of exports and imports since 1997 are shown in figure 17.07.

Table 17.14

Capital stock
Year ending 31 March

Year	Net capital stock[1]	Productive capital stock[2]
	$(million)	
2003	359,054	390,901
2004	393,484	404,559
2005	432,793	419,254
2006	468,962	434,772
2007	504,233	448,703

(1) Current prices (replacement cost). (2) Chain-volume series expressed in 1995/96 prices.

Source: Statistics New Zealand

Figure 17.07

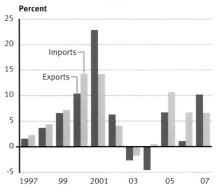

Imports and exports
Annual percentage change in value
Year ending 31 March

Source: Statistics New Zealand

Table 17.13

Exports of goods and services
Year ending 31 March

Year	Agriculture & fishing primary products	Forestry primary products	Coal, crude petroleum & ores, minerals & gases	Meat products	Dairy products	Other food, beverages & tobacco	Textiles, apparel & leather products	Wood & paper products	Chemicals, rubber, plastic & other non-metallic products	Metal products, machinery & equipment	Total exports of goods	Exports of services	Total
						$(million)							
					Current prices								
2003	2,899	750	764	4,404	6,002	3,027	1,704	2,956	2,712	5,430	30,648	11,917	**42,566**
2004	2,944	627	580	4,378	5,836	2,852	1,609	2,495	2,285	5,447	29,054	11,604	**40,658**
2005	2,987	414	727	4,872	5,784	3,369	1,593	2,839	2,561	5,967	31,114	12,240	**43,353**
2006	2,802	450	1,018	4,611	5,993	3,685	1,494	2,692	2,549	6,286	31,580	12,206	**43,786**
2007	C	640	C	5,037	7,455	C	C	C	C	C	35,633	12,565	**48,199**
					Chain-volume series expressed in 1995/96 prices								
2003	2,611	1,011	464	2,978	6,875	2,482	1,855	2,987	2,116	4,990	28,318	10,112	**38,503**
2004	2,749	907	391	3,212	7,230	2,631	1,827	2,867	1,771	5,402	28,919	9,886	**38,851**
2005	3,060	650	396	3,323	6,547	3,168	1,898	3,253	1,957	5,903	30,401	10,235	**40,663**
2006	3,357	631	427	3,250	6,392	3,365	1,878	3,237	1,819	6,015	30,601	10,015	**40,609**
2007	3,282	751	342	3,468	7,815	3,275	1,849	3,246	1,902	6,019	32,102	9,859	**41,869**

Note: Figures may not add up to stated totals due to rounding. Chain-volume series are not additive.

Symbol: C confidential

Source: Statistics New Zealand

Table 17.15

Imports of goods and services
Year ending 31 March

Year	Motor spirit	Passenger motor cars	Military & other goods	Consumption goods[1][2]	Inter-mediate goods[2]	Capital equipment[1]	Total goods	Total services	Total imports of goods & services
				$(million)					
Current prices									
2003	471	2,881	49	7,620	13,291	5,669	29,982	10,113	**40,095**
2004	478	3,111	221	7,650	12,586	6,199	30,246	10,009	**40,254**
2005	636	3,125	319	8,125	14,531	6,607	33,344	11,169	**44,512**
2006	931	2,964	64	8,703	15,720	7,301	35,685	11,759	**47,444**
2007	1,088	2,786	109	9,543	17,716	7,223	38,464	12,064	**50,528**
Chain-volume series expressed in 1995/96 prices									
2003	250	2,925	36	6,858	11,551	6,703	28,001	8,338	**36,216**
2004	261	3,347	218	7,568	12,221	8,755	31,719	9,268	**40,827**
2005	284	3,573	309	8,363	13,630	10,227	35,539	10,535	**45,911**
2006	315	3,552	61	9,041	13,402	11,897	36,924	11,014	**47,773**
2007	313	3,276	93	9,566	13,090	11,520	36,597	10,544	**46,950**

(1) Excludes imports of passenger motor vehicles, which are recorded separately. (2) Excludes imports of motor spirit, which are recorded separately.

Note: Figures may not add up to stated totals due to rounding. Chain-volume series are not additive.

Source: Statistics New Zealand

International accounts

New Zealand's international accounts consist of statistics on the balance of payments (BOP) and international investment position (IIP).

BOP statistics are statements of New Zealand's transactions in goods, services, income, and transfers with the rest of the world, net flows of foreign investment in New Zealand, and New Zealand investment abroad. IIP statistics show the value of foreign investment in New Zealand, and the value of New Zealand investment abroad at specific points in time.

The IIP statement includes statistics measuring New Zealand's gross and net overseas debt for both the government and private sectors.

Statistics New Zealand publishes BOP and IIP statements for each quarter. The level of detail in the quarterly series provides a useful basis for analysing and assessing the country's external financial situation.

Annual BOP and IIP statements are published using a March reference period and show the source of foreign investment into New Zealand, and destinations of New Zealand investment abroad.

BOP statistics are presented in a set of accounts consisting of two main groups: the current account, and the capital and financial account. Each of the BOP accounts is further subdivided into major components and balances. The balance of each component is the inflows (credits) less the outflows (debits).

Jarrad Mapp

Exchange rates for the New Zealand dollar in May 2008 are shown in a bank's window. In the year to 31 March 2007, a weaker New Zealand dollar and increased world commodity prices contributed to higher export and import prices. In the March 2008 year an appreciating New Zealand dollar had a downward impact on export and import prices.

Table 17.16

Balance of payments – major components[1]
Year ending 31 March

	2003	2004	2005	2006	2007
	\$(million)				
Current account summary					
Balance on goods	667	-1,192	-2,230	-4,105	-2,831
Exports (free on board)	30,648	29,054	31,114	31,580	35,633
Imports (free on board)	29,982	30,246	33,344	35,685	38,464
Balance on services	1,804	1,595	1,071	447	501
Exports	11,917	11,604	12,240	12,206	12,565
Imports	10,113	10,009	11,169	11,759	12,064
Balance on income	-7,046	-7,328	-9,466	-11,256	-11,863
Income from investment abroad	2,279	2,406	2,513	1,657	2,607
Income from foreign investment in New Zealand	9,325	9,734	11,979	12,913	14,470
Balance on current transfers	113	237	318	373	671
Inflow	1,376	1,431	1,555	1,664	1,956
Outflow	1,263	1,194	1,237	1,292	1,285
Current account balance	-4,462	-6,688	-10,307	-14,542	-13,521
Capital account summary					
Balance on capital account	1,585	723	108	-327	-462
Inflow	2,384	1,774	1,354	998	958
Outflow	799	1,051	1,246	1,325	1,420
Financial account summary					
New Zealand investment abroad	4,699	8,371	3,057	-4,090	10,912
Direct investment	255	2,442	230	-4,070	1,907
Portfolio investment	1,319	2,979	1,425	-377	3,808
Other investment	529	623	2,315	-4,494	-1,548
Reserve assets	2,596	2,327	-913	4,851	6,744
Foreign investment in New Zealand	6,352	13,781	13,841	10,584	23,781
Direct investment	3,322	4,018	3,826R	2,683	12,449
Portfolio investment	6,659	7,414	3,839	2,843	3,839
Other investment	-3,629	2,349	6,176	5,059	7,492
Net errors and omissions	1,224	555	-585	195	1,114

(1) Tables presented in general accordance with principles laid down by the International Monetary Fund in the fifth edition of the *Balance of Payments Manual* (1993).

Note: Figures may not add up to stated totals due to rounding.

Source: Statistics New Zealand

The current account

The current account records New Zealand's transactions in goods, services, income, and current transfers.

For goods, the balance on goods is the value of exports, less the value of imports. The primary source of data is export and import entry documents lodged with the New Zealand Customs Service by importers, exporters and their agents.

Services include: transportation of exports and imports of goods, passenger airfare revenue and expenditure, spending by New Zealand tourists abroad and foreign tourists in New Zealand, telecommunications, insurance and financial services, and other business services. Royalties and licence fees are also included.

Income encompasses income earned by foreign investors from their investments in New Zealand, and that earned by New Zealand investors from their investments abroad. Income from investments includes operating profits and losses, earnings retained in the business or distributed as dividends, and interest on debt instruments.

Current transfers include benefits and pensions received and paid, foreign aid, and withholding tax. Transfers are classified into either current transfers (which affect the level of disposable income of the donor and recipient), or capital transfers (which involve transfers in ownership of fixed assets or forgiveness of financial liabilities, and are included in the capital account).

Goods dominate New Zealand's current account. Exports of goods accounted for approximately 68 percent of total current account inflows (credits), and imports accounted for approximately 58 percent of total current account outflows (debits) for the year ending 31 March 2007.

Table 17.17 (overleaf) presents New Zealand's international trade in services for the five March years to 2007, and shows that the surplus balance on services has decreased to less than one-third of that recorded in 2003.

The balance on services moved from a surplus of \$1,804 million in the year ending 31 March 2003 to a surplus of \$501 million in the March 2007 year. Exports of services rose \$648 million (5.4 percent) between 2003 and 2007, but this was more than offset by a \$1,951 million (19.3 percent) increase in imports of services.

Growth in imports of transportation, travel and other business services were the key influences in the decrease of the balance on services.

Investing for the future

The New Zealand Superannuation Fund (NZSF), established under the New Zealand Superannuation and Retirement Income Act 2001, began investing in September 2003 with \$2.4 billion in cash. At 30 April 2008, the fund's assets totalled \$14.3 billion.

The NZSF was created to partly pre-fund the country's tax-payer funded 'pay-as-you-go' retirement income system – New Zealand Superannuation (NZS), under which eligible residents over 65 years receive a pension, regardless of their income or assets.

The system requires that current pensions are paid by those currently in work. At present, about one person in eight is over 65 years, but by 2030 the ratio of people in this age group will be one in four. The cost of providing NZS in 2030 will be around 5.6 percent of gross domestic product, compared with 3.4 percent in 2008.

The purpose of the fund is to build up a portfolio of Crown-owned financial assets while the cost of NZS is relatively low. When payments become much greater, the assets can be drawn on to supplement the Crown's annual budget.

Each year until around 2028, the NZSF will invest around \$2 billion of Crown funds, available from general taxes. Under law, no capital withdrawal is allowed before 1 July 2020. The investments are required to maximise returns over the long term, without undue risk and while avoiding prejudice to New Zealand's reputation.

The fund has holdings in both New Zealand and international companies. Through its investments in various asset types, currencies and countries overseas, the fund contributes towards the stock of New Zealand's international assets.

At 31 December 2007, New Zealand's total international assets were 45 percent of its total international liabilities. Income generated by the overseas part of the NZSF's investments helps offset the large investment income imbalance in the current account of New Zealand's balance of payments statistics. Due to the significant ownership of New Zealand firms by non-residents, a large part of the income generated by these firms is repatriated overseas. However the income derived by the NZSF on overseas investments partly offsets the large investment income outflow from New Zealand.

The NZSF is governed by the Guardians of New Zealand Superannuation, a Crown entity overseen by a board whose members are selected by the Minister of Finance for their skills and experience. Although accountable to the government, the guardians operate independently from the Crown.

Sources: New Zealand Superannuation Fund; Statistics New Zealand

A group of Swiss tourists camp out at a holiday park in Paihia in Northland, in early spring. New Zealand's current account records transactions in services, which include spending by foreign tourists in New Zealand and New Zealand tourists abroad.

Table 17.17

	2003	2004	2005	2006	2007
Trade in services Year ending 31 March					
			$(million)		
Exports					
Transportation	2,470	2,234	2,231	2,382	2,673
Travel	7,076	7,178	7,486	7,271	7,387
Business	737	660	704	721	746
Personal	6,339	6,518	6,783	6,550	6,641
Education	1,693	1,892	1,874	1,691	1,550
Health	11	11	11	11	11
Other	4,633	4,614	4,897	4,847	5,079
Communication	465	328	331	361	224
Construction	52	54	87	63	27
Insurance	38	43	44	39	41
Financial	38	60	108	123	114
Computer & information	256	221	265	272	281
Royalties & licence fees	181	191	146	153	184
Other business services	970	914	1,089	1,158	1,253
Personal, cultural & recreational	234	252	310	235	231
Government services not included elsewhere	139	129	142	149	149
Total exports of services	**11,917**	**11,604**	**12,240**	**12,206**	**12,565**
Imports					
Transportation	3,516	3,470	3,926	3,951	4,039
Travel	2,892	2,900	3,479	3,818	3,935
Communication	417	319	344	417	304
Construction	11	7	30	42	85
Insurance	285	316	339	350	325
Financial	131	99	158	152	126
Computer & information	258	231	324	381	398
Royalties & licence fees	774	807	790	778	762
Other business services	1,547	1,565	1,571	1,662	1,875
Personal, cultural & recreational	128	135	66	57	64
Government services not included elsewhere	155	159	143	149	150
Total imports of services	**10,113**	**10,009**	**11,169**	**11,759**	**12,064**
Balance on services	1,804	1,595	1,071	447	501

Note: Figures may not add up to stated totals due to rounding.

Source: Statistics New Zealand

The capital account

The capital account records debt forgiveness, migrant transfers, and sales and purchases of intangible assets, such as licences, patents, copyrights and franchises.

The financial account

The financial account records investment transactions between New Zealand residents and the rest of the world. These transactions increase or decrease the level of foreign investment in New Zealand, and the level of New Zealand investment abroad.

Investment instruments include equity capital (such as shares in companies), and debt instruments (such as bonds and notes), money market instruments, loans, deposits, and trade credits and debits).

Figure 17.08 shows that net inwards investment has consistently outweighed net outwards investment, reflecting New Zealand's dependency on foreign capital to finance its current account deficits.

Classification of investment categories in the financial account is further determined by the relationship between transactors, and is presented as direct, portfolio and other investment.

Direct investment is all financial capital transactions occurring between parties where there is an ownership relationship of 10 percent or more. For example, where a foreign investor owns 10 percent or more of the equity capital of a New Zealand company, then all the financial capital transactions between the New Zealand company (the direct investee) and the overseas investor (the direct investor) are classified as direct investment. These transactions increase or decrease the level of foreign direct investment in New Zealand.

Direct investment transactions include transactions in equity capital and debt instruments, including bonds, loans, trade credits and debits. Income from the foreign direct investor's investment in New Zealand is recorded in the current account as income from foreign investment in New Zealand – direct investment income.

Portfolio investment includes transactions in equity and debt instruments, where the ownership relationship between the transactors does not meet the criteria for direct investment. Therefore, in addition to equity securities, this category includes marketable debt instruments – bonds and notes, and money market instruments.

Banking sector funding transactions in marketable debt instruments between direct investors and direct investees are included within portfolio investment where these transactions are defined as being in the nature of usual banking business (financial intermediation), rather than transactions aimed at increasing or decreasing the direct investor's ownership role.

The main contributors to New Zealand portfolio equity investment abroad are New Zealand-resident fund managers. Foreign portfolio equity investment in New Zealand is dominated by investment into New Zealand companies through New Zealand-resident nominees.

New Zealand portfolio investment abroad, in the form of debt securities, is dominated by banks and fund managers. This form of foreign portfolio investment in New Zealand is spread more widely across the domestic sectors, with banks and government contributing significantly.

Other investment is a residual component within the financial account, and consists of financial assets and liabilities not classified as either direct or portfolio investment. Other investment includes loans, deposits, trade finance (trade credits and debits), and other instruments transacted with an unrelated party abroad.

Figure 17.08

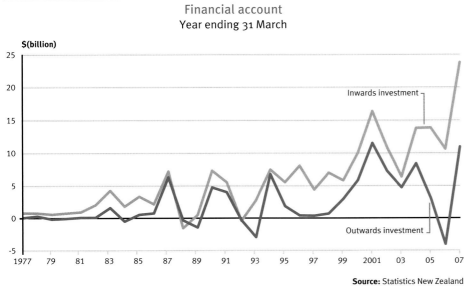

Financial account
Year ending 31 March

Source: Statistics New Zealand

Figure 17.09

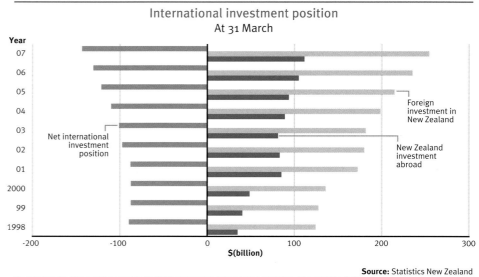

Source: Statistics New Zealand

International investment position

The international investment position (IIP) records the level of an economy's international financial assets and liabilities (the balance sheet) at a particular point in time. These are shown in figure 17.09.

The balance of payments (BOP) financial account and IIP statistics are closely related, with BOP measuring investment flows and IIP measuring stock positions. The New Zealand IIP statement

Table 17.18

International investment position[1]
At 31 March

	2003	2004	2005	2006	2007
	\$(million)				
New Zealand investment abroad					
Direct	17,747	18,389	20,134	17,960	18,635
Equity capital & reinvested earnings	15,970	16,362	16,420	15,331	16,366
Other capital	1,778	2,027	3,714	2,629	2,269
Claims on affiliated enterprises	4,720	5,109	C	5,673	C
Liabilities to affiliated enterprises	-2,942	-3,083	C	-3,044	C
Portfolio	24,289	31,771	33,596	42,072	44,223
Equity securities	13,637	22,570	24,566	33,217	33,876
Debt securities	10,652	9,201	9,031	8,854	10,347
Other	22,875	22,206	25,373	22,458	21,355
Trade credits	2,934	C	C	2,974	3,755
Loans	16,378	17,080	19,502	10,685	10,767
Currency & deposits	2,964	2,533	3,065	7,241	5,710
Other assets	599	C	C	1,559	1,122
Financial derivatives	6,781	6,081	5,347	7,486	6,411
Reserve assets	9,115	10,093	8,828	14,596	20,381
Total	**80,808**	**88,540**	**93,278**	**104,572**	**111,005**
Foreign investment in New Zealand					
Direct	58,347	68,898	73,571	78,265	90,691
Equity capital & reinvested earnings	39,854	45,529	46,991	47,707	53,051
Other capital	18,493	23,369	26,580	30,558	37,640
Claims on direct investors	-8,786	-7,258	-8,612	-7,288	-5,857
Liabilities to direct investors	27,279	30,626	35,192	37,846	43,496
Portfolio	65,177	73,226	77,495	83,117	83,564
Equity securities	11,251	14,700	16,631	17,435	17,033
Debt securities	53,926	58,526	60,864	65,682	66,531
Other	49,115	47,592	57,048	65,834	72,590
Trade credits	2,388	2,.193	1,832	2,085	1,740
Loans	33,604	30,481	38,178	43,382	47,363
Currency & deposits	12,715	14,568	16,490	19,291	22,051
Other liabilities	407	350	547	1,077	1,436
Financial derivatives	8,774	8,544	6,089	7,503	7,235
Total	**181,414**	**198,260**	**214,203**	**234,720**	**254,080**
Net international investment position	-100,606	-109,720	-120,925	-130,148	-143,075

(1) Data may not add up to stated totals due to rounding.
Symbol: C confidential

Source: Statistics New Zealand

includes position data on financial derivatives. Since no transaction data is collected for these, they do not appear in the BOP statistics.

The difference in the level of international financial assets and liabilities between two points in time is due to BOP financial account transactions and other non-transaction changes that occur during the reference period.

Non-transaction changes are revaluations of assets and liabilities, changes arising from translation of overseas assets and liabilities in foreign currencies into New Zealand dollars, changes in market prices, and other adjustments such as write-offs.

Table 17.18 shows New Zealand's IIP at 31 March 2003–07. The value of New Zealand investment abroad (assets) is lower than the value of foreign investment in New Zealand (liabilities). At 31 March 2007, the net IIP (assets less liabilities) was negative $143.1 billion. This net debtor position is a reflection of the long-running current account deficits, which are financed by a net inflow of capital into New Zealand, recorded in the financial account.

Deficits and surpluses

The balance on the current account is the sum of the balances on goods, services, income, and current transfers. Because they involve the exchange of resources, current account surpluses and deficits have financial implications. Surpluses (net outflows of resources) result in increases in New Zealand's net financial claims over the rest of the world. Conversely, deficits (net inflows of resources) translate into decreases in New Zealand's net financial claims over the rest of the world.

Figure 17.10 shows the current account balance as a proportion (ratio) of gross domestic product (GDP), 1957–2007. This ratio measures New Zealand's net provision or acquisition of resources, to or from abroad, as a proportion of the value of New Zealand's annual output. The use of the ratio is an indication of the ability of the economy to sustain a current account imbalance.

Figure 17.10

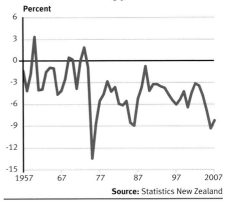

Current account balance
As a proportion of GDP
Year ending 31 March

Source: Statistics New Zealand

Table 17.19

Direct investment[1][2]
By regional groupings and selected countries
At 31 March

Grouping/country	2003	2004	2005	2006	2007
	\$(million)				
New Zealand's direct investment abroad					
APEC	13,805	14,271	16,728	14,443	16,302
ASEAN	879	564	594	493	316
EU	420	565	278	1,969	2,085
OECD	10,212	11,456	13,138	12,776	14,982
Australia	8,960	9,825	11,321	9,468	10,915
Bermuda	610	C	758	98	C
Canada	C	C	38	72	73
Germany	C	C	C	C	C
Hong Kong	347	34	C	102	267
Japan	71	C	C	C	C
Netherlands	C	C	C	C	C
Singapore	495	209	C	C	C
United Kingdom	555	885	C	918	897
United States	686	954	1,348	1,174	1,778
Total	**17,747**	**18,389**	**20,134**	**17,960**	**18,635**
Foreign direct investment in New Zealand					
APEC	34,034	44,780	51,722	56,075	66,801
ASEAN	961	1,082	1,087	1,082	1,514
EU	11,637	10,483	11,627	11,160	11,161
OECD	41,765	51,082	58,941	62,864	73,040
Australia	21,189	29,438	34,274	39,467	47,358
Bermuda	C	C	C	C	C
Canada	C	889	1,100	1,000	1,282
Germany	C	C	C	605	440
Hong Kong	772	757	778	585	724
Japan	1,292	1,532	1,700	1,652	1,819
Netherlands	3,632	3,453	4,230	4,216	4,918
Singapore	986	1,226	1,176	1,194	1,636
Switzerland	190	161	114	52	75
United Kingdom	6,370	5,032	4,439	4,864	3,974
United States	5,967	7,837	9,397	8,844	10,492
Total	**58,347**	**68,898**	**73,571**	**78,265**	**90,691**

(1) Only a limited country breakdown is shown in this table, therefore data does not add up to stated totals. (2) Published under section 37(4)(a) of the Statistics Act 1975 with the consent of all significant contributors.

Note: APEC Asia-Pacific Economic Cooperation. ASEAN Association of Southeast Asian Nations, EU European Union, OECD Organisation for Economic Co-operation and Development.

Symbol: C confidential

Source: Statistics New Zealand

For example, an increasing current account deficit has different implications for a growing economy than for an economy in which GDP is static or falling.

New Zealand has incurred persistent current account deficits since the mid 1970s. These have ranged between -13.4 percent of GDP in 1975 (at the height of the 1970s' oil crisis), to -0.7 percent in 1989. More recently, the ratio has generally risen – from -3.1 percent for the March 2002 year, to -8.2 percent for the March 2007 year.

International investment

Table 17.19 (previous page) shows the main countries, economic groupings and regions that are the sources of foreign direct investment into New Zealand, and the destinations of New Zealand direct investment abroad. Direct investment occurs where there is an ownership relationship of 10 percent or more.

Australia is New Zealand's single most important direct investment partner country in terms of both the country's direct investment abroad, and foreign direct investment in New Zealand. The United States and the United Kingdom are significant sources of foreign direct investment in New Zealand.

New Zealand's most significant regional or group partners are the Asia-Pacific Economic Cooperation economies, the Organisation for Economic Co-operation and Development countries, and the European Union.

Table 17.20 shows New Zealand industries that hold international assets, and those in which foreign investors have invested (New Zealand's international liabilities) at 31 March 2005–07.

Table 17.20

International assets and liabilities By industry[1] At 31 March	2005	2006	2007
	\$(million)		
New Zealand's international assets			
Agriculture, forestry & fishing	C	C	C
Mining	C	C	C
Manufacturing	16,456	14,287	13,798
Electricity, gas & water supply	C	C	C
Construction	166	213	201
Wholesale trade	4,341	4,511	3,797
Retail trade	400	618	953
Accommodation, cafes & restaurants	C	C	C
Transport & storage	82	144	C
Communication services	C	C	C
Finance & insurance	63,694	75,054	81,135
Property & business services	664	714	854
Government administration & defence	7,641	10,336	11,003
Education	C	--	--
Health & community services	--	--	--
Cultural & recreational services	C	C	C
Personal & other services	C	C	C
Unallocated to industry	2,731	3,099	2,245
Total	**105,571**	**116,192**	**119,809**
New Zealand's international liabilities			
Agriculture, forestry & fishing	2,923	3,354	4,744
Mining	C	C	2,414
Manufacturing	22,410	23,449	26,728
Electricity, gas & water	4,996	4,871	4,158
Construction	575	669	702
Wholesale trade	9,888	10,868	10,998
Retail trade	3,668	6,886	6,130
Accommodation, cafes & restaurants	924	934	872
Transport & storage	2,816	3,520	4,614
Communication services	C	C	C
Finance & insurance	124,812	139,323	151,133
Property & business services	3,260	3,602	6,854
Government administration & defence	15,998	15,637	14,716
Education	C	C	--
Health & community services	C	C	657
Cultural & recreational services	3,511	4,478	3,943
Personal & other services	C	C	C
Unallocated to industry	10,125	10,838	10,226
Total	**226,495**	**246,340**	**262,884**

(1) These tables are prepared on a balance sheet basis.

Symbols: C confidential -- figure too small to be expressed

Source: Statistics New Zealand

The finance and insurance industry accounts for the largest proportion of New Zealand's international assets and liabilities. At 31 March 2007, this industry held 67.7 percent of the country's international assets. The main contributions were from banks and funds invested abroad by fund managers on behalf of individuals.

The finance and insurance industry was the recipient of 57.5 percent of total funds invested in New Zealand by overseas investors (New Zealand's international liabilities).

The government administration and defence industry and the manufacturing industry each made significant contributions to New Zealand's international assets and liabilities.

The international investments held by the government administration and defence industry (9.2 percent of New Zealand's total international assets) are predominantly reserve assets held by The Treasury and the Reserve Bank of New Zealand. The manufacturing industry held 11.5 percent of New Zealand's total international assets, and received 10.2 percent of total foreign investment in New Zealand.

Business statistics

Annual and quarterly surveys conducted by Statistics New Zealand provide comprehensive information about businesses in New Zealand.

The Annual Enterprise Survey, which covers most industries, collects information on the financial performance and position of New Zealand businesses.

Quarterly business surveys, such as the Economic Survey of Manufacturing, provide information on short-term activity, while the Employment Survey offers a broad picture of employment across the economy.

In addition to these financial surveys, Statistics New Zealand also produces business demographic statistics, based on a recently developed statistical resource – the Longitudinal Business Frame. Business demographic statistics provide an annual snapshot (at February) of the structure and characteristics of New Zealand businesses.

Table 17.21 (overleaf) shows the number of employees and separate businesses (geographic units) for the different industry groups in New Zealand.

The New Zealand Herald

Glenda Keegan of WAS Ltd, with bags made of PVC vinyl from recycled billboards that were originally destined for the dump. The Longitudinal Business Frame database allows an annual snapshot of the characteristics of New Zealand businesses to be produced.

Table 17.21

Geographic units[1] and employee count[2] by industry
In economically significant enterprises[3]
2007

Industry	Number of geographic units	Employee count
Manufacturing	24,810	258,370
Property & business services	153,834	245,990
Retail trade	46,853	240,000
Health & community services	18,727	187,070
Education	8,540	155,620
Construction	50,136	121,840
Accommodation, cafes & restaurants	14,443	119,010
Wholesale trade	22,021	116,970
Agriculture, forestry & fishing	81,537	115,760
Transport & storage	14,442	76,080
Government administration & defence	1,865	72,880
Personal & other services	18,020	69,250
Finance & insurance	25,770	54,920
Cultural & recreational services	13,966	52,080
Communication services	3,891	24,660
Electricity, gas & water supply	437	7,680
Mining	648	5,020
Total	**499,940**	**1,923,190**

(1) A geographic unit (business location) in New Zealand is a separate operating unit engaged in one, or predominantly one, kind of economic activity from a single physical location. (2) The employee count is the number of salary and wage earners, sourced from taxation data. (3) This generally includes all enterprises with GST turnover greater than $30,000 a year.

Note: Figures may not add up to totals due to rounding.

Source: Statistics New Zealand

Contributors and related websites

New Zealand Superannuation Fund – www.nzsuperfund.co.nz

Reserve Bank of New Zealand – www.rbnz.govt.nz

Statistics New Zealand – www.stats.govt.nz

The Treasury – www.treasury.govt.nz

Wheat farmer Simon Bathgate examines his plants after rain brought the wheat plants into head in December 2007. Farmers are particularly affected by climate change and extreme weather events, although a changing climate may provide opportunities for new crops and faster growth in some regions of New Zealand.

18 | Agriculture

Farming, forestry, and horticulture continue to be significant export-earning industries for New Zealand. In the year ending 31 March 2007, the agricultural, horticultural and forestry sectors provided about two-thirds of New Zealand's export earnings. The primary industries and downstream manufacturing contributed nearly 13 percent to GDP (gross domestic product). In the past few years, dairy and wine have been New Zealand's fastest growing industries.

Dairying has been expanding since 1996 in response to commodity price signals. Many farms have converted to dairying, especially in Canterbury and Southland, and dairy farms across New Zealand have increased in size.

While the number of traditional sheep and cattle farms has decreased, through conversion and amalgamation, the productivity of remaining sheep and cattle farms has increased. Improvements have been achieved by farmers through improving management practices, introducing new livestock sires, and the use of better plant cultivars.

Cereal crops and horticultural products were traditionally grown mainly for the home market, but the horticulture industry and various seed crops are now important export earners.

New Zealand has considered the strategic opportunities offered by genetic modification. Following a Royal Commission of Inquiry, the government accepted the commission's recommendation to proceed with caution, and preserve those opportunities. New Zealand researchers have developed genetically-modified potatoes that are resistant to pests, and genetically-modified cattle (to produce therapeutic proteins in their milk).

Current situation and trends

Rural produce from farming and horticulture makes up more than half of New Zealand's merchandise exports. Uniquely among developed countries, New Zealand farmers are almost totally exposed to world market forces. They receive no subsidies from the government, and have to compete with subsidised production from other countries.

The agreement on agriculture from the General Agreement on Tariffs and Trade (GATT) Uruguay Round imposes progressive reductions on subsidies that other countries can give to agricultural production and exports. One effect of this has been to increase access opportunities for New Zealand's exports into overseas markets. The current Doha Development Round, under the auspices of the World Trade Organization (WTO), will eventually deliver further trade benefits to New Zealand.

Table 18.01

Farm types
By number and area
At 30 June 2005

Farm type	Number	Area (hectares)[1]
Sheep	13,905	8,128,914
Dairy cattle	12,786	2,113,692
Forestry	4,581	2,043,921
Beef cattle	13,254	1,476,129
Sheep/beef	1,614	654,835
Deer	1,617	218,155
Mixed livestock	855	178,080
Grain/sheep and grain/beef	324	73,460
Vegetables	1,524	69,484
Services to agriculture nec	1,062	63,304
Grain	486	58,570
Grapes	1,416	35,918
Crop and plant nec	525	30,904
Kiwifruit	2,172	24,737
Apples and pears	894	20,935
Other fruit nec	2,298	20,592
Livestock nec	633	17,880
Pigs	264	12,831
Plant nursery	1,095	8,726
Stone fruit	351	7,149
Berry fruit	231	4,220
Cut flowers and flower seeds	756	4,098
Citrus	291	2,698
Other	1,563	36,246
Total	**64,491**	**15,305,478**

(1) Figures may not add up to totals due to rounding.
Note: nec not elsewhere classified.

Source: Statistics New Zealand

Alex Hallatt

Customers buy cheese and free-range eggs at the Lyttelton Farmers Market in Canterbury. The market is open every Saturday to sell produce that also includes fruit, vegetables, meat, bread and plants. It is one of a growing number of farmers markets around New Zealand, which offer direct contact between producers and consumers.

New Zealand's total milk production (including domestic-market milk) for the season to 31 May 2007 was 1.314 billion kilograms of milk solids – from nearly 15 billion litres of milk. This was up 3.4 percent on the previous season, due to good climatic conditions. The number of dairy milking cows was estimated at 4.17 million at 30 June 2007, up 0.7 percent from the previous year.

The cooperatively-owned dairy company Fonterra collected 94.8 percent of available milk solids from New Zealand dairy farms. About 2.8 percent of milk collected was made available to other dairy manufacturers, to meet regulatory requirements under the Dairy Industry Restructuring Act 2002, to foster competition in New Zealand.

Payment for milk is by kilogram of milk solids (kgMs). The average dairy company payout for the year ending 31 May 2007 rose 9.7 percent from the previous year, to $4.47 per kgMS (net of 'industry good' levy), due to rising international prices and favourably-hedged exchange rates. (The industry good levy funds research and development in the dairy industry, and is administered by DairyNZ.)

Total sheep numbers were estimated at 38.5 million at 30 June 2007 (down from 40.1 million the previous year), and sheep meat production for the year ending 30 September 2007 was 573,000 tonnes, up 5.7 percent from the previous September year. The quantity of wool sold fell 4.0 percent, to 164,000 clean tonnes for the year ending 30 June 2007.

The New Zealand beef cattle herd was estimated at 4.44 million at June 2006 (up from 4.42 million the previous year). Beef and veal production fell by 3 percent, to 623,000 tonnes for the year ending 30 September 2007.

After two decades of strong growth to 30 June 2004, deer numbers fell to an estimated 1.59 million at 30 June 2006, because high domestic slaughtering weakened international prices.

Agricultural organisations

New Zealand remains a world leader in agricultural research, reflecting the importance of agriculture to the country. A broad range of administrative and special interest organisations are found in the sector.

Ministry of Agriculture and Forestry Te Manatū Ahuwhenua Ngāherehere (MAF) has a mission to 'enhance New Zealand's natural advantage'. Its purpose is to lead the protection and sustainable development of biological resources for all New Zealanders. The organisation employs about 1,600 staff nationally.

MAF's key operational areas include:

- MAF Policy – provides policy advice and delivers services to help create prosperous, sustainable and innovative agriculture, food and forestry sectors, which support a vibrant and healthy New Zealand society, environment and economy.
- Biosecurity New Zealand – leads New Zealand's biosecurity system. It identifies and manages any potential biosecurity risks at the border, and provides domestic and offshore technical inspection and clearance services. It also has international trade and animal welfare responsibilities.
- Crown Forestry – manages the Crown's interest in a number of commercial forests and forestry-related leases.

AsureQuality Ltd was formed in October 2007 by the merger of two state-owned enterprises, Asure New Zealand Ltd and AgriQuality New Zealand Ltd. AsureQuality is now one of the world's leading providers of food quality assurance and biosecurity services. More than 1,700 staff are employed at 140 sites around New Zealand and Australia.

New Zealand Food Safety Authority Te Pou Oranga Kai o Aotearoa (NZFSA) has operated as a stand-alone government department since its separation from MAF in July 2007. It has two key functions:

- to protect and promote public health and safety
- to facilitate market access for New Zealand's food and food-related products.

To achieve these, NZFSA must implement a food regulatory programme that meets New Zealand's needs for the foreseeable future – accounting for rapidly shifting consumer behaviour and expectations, changing food production and distribution systems, and dealing with new and emerging pathogens and risks.

NZFSA administers the Food Act 1981, the Agricultural Compounds and Veterinary Medicines Act 1997, the Animal Products Act 1999, and the Wine Act 2003. It is the controlling authority for imports and exports of food and food-related products. The authority employs about 500 people, and has an operating budget of $90 million (of which $55 million is recovered from industry).

Pastoral agriculture

Pastoral agriculture is practised throughout New Zealand. In the North Island, beef cattle farming dominates in Northland, dairying in the Waikato and Taranaki, and sheep farming (with cattle in the hills) in Gisborne and Hawke's Bay, and in the southern part of the North Island.

In the South Island, sheep farming (both intensive and extensive) is the main form of pastoral agriculture, with a sprinkling of beef cattle farmed in the high and hill country, and on wetter flat areas. An increasing amount of dairying is carried out on the flat land of Canterbury, Otago and Southland, particularly in areas where irrigation is available.

New Zealand livestock are predominantly grass-fed, but feeding of natural grass-based and maize supplements, such as hay (from pasture) and silage (from grass and maize), occurs in winter and during very dry periods. Grass growth is seasonal, is largely dependent on location and climatic fluctuations, peaks in the spring, and is at a minimum in winter.

Feed surpluses are harvested and stored for feeding-out during winter or in times of feed shortages. In recent years, intensive dairy farms have increased their use of protein-rich palm kernel imports, to supplement pasture during the milking season.

Livestock are grazed in paddocks, often with movable electric fencing, which allows rotation of grazing. Lambing and calving are carefully managed to take full advantage of spring grass growth.

Livestock numbers and types

Probably New Zealand's best known statistic is that it once had more than 20 times as many sheep as people. However, by 30 June 2007 the ratio was nine sheep for every person.

Climatic conditions, soil type, type of stock carried, and land contours determine stocking rates for New Zealand farms. Finishing sheep and beef land in both islands carry around 11–12 stock units per hectare, while South Island high country farms average around one stock unit per hectare. An average dairy farm carries 2.8 cows per hectare at peak milk production.

Trends in livestock numbers are largely determined by world market prices for farm products, including meat, wool, and dairy.

The sheep population has declined from 70.3 million at 30 June 1982 to 38.5 million at 30 June 2007. The beef cattle population fell 10 percent in the same period, to reach 4.39 million. The number of dairy cattle at 30 June 2007 was 5.26 million, up 2.26 million on the 30 June 1982 total. The total deer number was 1.37 million at 30 June 2007, compared with just 0.15 million in 1982.

Bio-control beetle fights pest

Landcare Research

A green thistle beetle checks out a Californian thistle.

Californian thistle *(Cirsium arvense)* is one of New Zealand's most persistent and destructive weeds. In the Otago and Southland regions alone, this thistle is estimated to cost farmers around $32 million each year in chemical control, harmful effects on sheep and wool, and reduced production from pasture loss.

The thistle is difficult to control with chemicals, as the weed spreads and forms dense patches through an extensive root system that extends several metres from a single plant. The thistles can re-grow from any piece of the root system.

In November 2007, green thistle beetles *(Cassida rubiginosa)* – a new biological control agent for Californian thistle – were released at two sites in Otago and Southland by the community-based Californian Thistle Action Group and Landcare Research.

The green thistle beetles are the latest in a long line of biological control agents imported and tested by Landcare Research scientists. This beetle could potentially have a major impact on Californian and other thistles because both adult beetles and grubs consume so much leaf material. Research shows that removing thistle foliage also reduces the amount of root material growing below ground.

Bio-control research

The New Zealand Government funds research to improve the effectiveness and safety of biological control. However, end-user groups working with Landcare Research fund other parts of the research process, such as finding suitable new control agents overseas, extensive safety-testing, quarantining in New Zealand, mass rearing and distribution. The collaborative approach was pioneered 20 years ago, and is a significant reason for New Zealand's high success rate in establishing biological control agents.

By November 2007, 45 different control agents had been released against 15 of the country's most widespread or intransigent weeds. Other new weed control agents are being investigated.

Source: Landcare Research

Table 18.02

Sheep categories
At 30 June

Year	Breeding ewes and hoggets	Other sheep	Total[1]
1994	35,754	13,618	**49,466**
1995	34,999	13,818	**48,816**
1996	34,392	13,002	**47,394**
1999[2]	32,234	13,446	**45,680**
2002	29,159	10,413	**39,572**
2003	29,358	10,194	**39,552**
2004	29,405	9,866	**39,271**
2005	29,549	10,330	**39,880**
2006	29,928	10,154	**40,082**
2007	28,588	9,872	**38,460**

(1) Figures may not add up to totals since estimates for sheep categories are calculated independently from total estimates.
(2) Use caution when making comparisons using 1999 data. In this year, the survey population was drawn from a different sample.
Note: Sheep numbers were not counted in 1997, 1998, 2000, and 2001.

Source: Statistics New Zealand

Sheep Lamb and wool prices have fallen 35 percent in real terms since 2002, as a consequence of reduced international prices and adverse exchange rates. Since 2002, New Zealand farmers have increased meat production per ewe, have higher lambing percentages, and also have higher lamb slaughter weights. Many farmers use newly introduced breeds to achieve hybrid vigour and better meat production characteristics. Coarse wool has become a by-product of meat production.

The tariff-free quota New Zealand has with the European Union (EU) underpins the sector, while the People's Republic of China has emerged as a high-volume, low-value market for the cheapest lamb cuts.

In the year ending 30 September 2007, lamb exports amounted to 331,000 tonnes of product, valued at $2.08 billion. The export value of mutton was $283 million for the same period. Chilled lamb contributed 31 percent of the export value.

New Zealand lamb is exported to 99 overseas markets, with the highest-returning markets being the United Kingdom, Germany, France, and the United States.

Dairy cattle Livestock Improvement Corporation data shows that the main dairy cow breed in New Zealand is the Holstein-Friesian, followed by the Holstein-Friesian/Jersey cross, and the Jersey. The North Island carries 80 percent of dairy herds, with 48 percent of these located in the Waikato and Taranaki regions. The South Island has 20 percent of dairy herds, and 28 percent of all dairy cows.

Dairy exports include whole milk powder, skim milk powder, cheese, casein, butter, and other manufactured products. In the year ending 30 June 2007, the export value of dairy products to 154 countries was $8.38 billion. Exports to the United States, Japan, the EU, China, and the Philippines accounted for 38 percent of this export value. Whole milk powder was the largest contributor, making up 26 percent of dairy export value.

Beef cattle The major traditional beef cattle breeds in New Zealand are the Angus and the Hereford. However, around 26 percent of adult cattle slaughtered come from bull beef finishing farms, where cattle primarily originate from dairy calves of Holstein-Friesian and cross-breeds. Approximately 73 percent of beef cattle are located in the North Island, with about 25 percent of the beef herd being run on small-scale farms. In the year ending 30 September 2007, the export

Table 18.03

Cattle categories
At 30 June

Category	2003	2004	2005	2006	2007
Dairy cows/heifers in milk or in calf	3,928,140	4,103,318	4,120,176	4,137,696	4,167,121
Dairy cows/heifers not in milk and not in calf but intended for milk production	149,190	174,124	212,042	234,880	305,727
Dairy heifer yearlings and calves (including bobby)	980,566	830,389	716,423	751,790	734,671
Dairy bulls to be used for dairy breeding	43,707	44,661	38,536	45,190	53,331
Subtotal – dairy cattle	5,101,603	5,152,492	5,087,176	5,169,557	5,260,850
Beef cows and heifers	2,391,779	2,326,624	2,332,037	2,324,900	2,267,636
Bulls – all ages	1,046,411	911,055	869,757	915,590	871,685
Other beef cattle	1,188,427	1,209,720	1,221,831	1,198,645	1,254,296
Subtotal – beef cattle	4,626,617	4,447,400	4,423,626	4,439,136	4,393,617
Total cattle	**9,728,220**	**9,599,892**	**9,510,802**	**9,608,693**	**9,654,467**

Source: Statistics New Zealand

Otago Daily Times

Dairy cows wait for milking time on a South Otago dairy farm. The South Island has 20 percent of New Zealand's dairy herds, and 28 percent of the dairy cows.

volume of beef and veal was 352,000 tonnes, valued at $1.64 billion. A special quota arrangement ensures the United States takes 50 percent by volume, and 45 percent by value, of all beef and veal exports. The main export category is manufacturing beef (that not sold as prime table cuts – it is used for further processed products). Other significant destinations are the Republic of Korea, Japan, Taiwan and Canada, which together account for 37 percent of the value of beef and veal exports.

Deer Since the early 1970s, New Zealand deer farming has developed to become an important livestock industry. New Zealand is the world's largest exporter of farmed venison. In the year ending 30 June 2007, the product weight of exported chilled and frozen venison was 24,200 tonnes, valued at $252 million. New Zealand has more than 30 export markets, with the highest returning ones being Germany, Belgium, France, and the United States. Deer farming is generally permitted in most regions, but some species may be farmed in specified areas only. Red, wapiti, and fallow deer are the main farmed species.

Goats In New Zealand goats are farmed commercially for their milk, mohair, and meat, as well as for weed control. Goat numbers have declined in recent years, but niche markets have been developed for milk products and fibres.

Table 18.04

Distribution of livestock
By region
At 30 June 2007

Region	Dairy cattle	Beef cattle	Sheep	Deer	Pigs
Northland	367,183	495,833	534,452	7,566	3,959
Auckland	113,344	156,787	287,589	12,304	C
Waikato	1,669,472	676,584	2,660,145	116,554	46,666
Bay of Plenty	299,013	119,743	385,373	54,296	6,949
Gisborne	7,891	287,296	1,825,496	26,694	1,857
Hawke's Bay	80,200	438,366	3,624,018	88,408	7,889
Taranaki	589,573	136,715	656,144	4,456	18,031
Manawatu-Wanganui	393,453	680,960	6,746,989	103,908	23,358
Wellington	92,787	155,910	1,822,057	15,985	C
Subtotal – North Island	3,612,916	3,148,194	18,542,263	430,171	135,793
Tasman	63,849	51,428	348,485	20,632	322
Nelson	1,862	1,298	7,639	C	C
Marlborough	23,899	65,768	578,805	C	C
West Coast	152,481	30,275	54,094	41,755	210
Canterbury	754,937	584,806	7,166,822	394,833	202,008
Otago	218,264	292,355	6,031,166	188,103	18,709
Southland	432,642	207,588	5,662,387	307,524	4,303
Chatham Islands	0	11,905	68,816	0	C
Subtotal – South Island	1,647,934	1,245,423	19,918,214	965,852	230,878
Total New Zealand	**5,260,850**	**4,393,617**	**38,460,477**	**1,396,023**	**366,671**

Note: Figures may not add up to stated totals due to rounding.
Symbol: C confidential

Source: Statistics New Zealand

Meat

Meat products are New Zealand's second-largest export income earner after dairy products, accounting for 14 percent of total New Zealand exports in the year ending 30 September 2007.

New Zealand's main meat exports are lamb, mutton and beef. In the year ending 30 September 2006, New Zealand exported 91 percent of its lamb, 89 percent of its mutton, and 79 percent of its beef production. The domestic market takes all the pigmeat and poultry produced.

New Zealanders ate an average of 105 kilograms of meat per person in the year ending 30 September 2006, 4.8 percent more than in 1996. Between 1996–2006, lamb maintained its share of total consumption, while mutton and beef consumption declined. Red meat consumption, at 47 kilograms per person, dropped 17.5 percent during the decade. Consumption of poultry increased 47.0 percent, to 39 kilograms, while pigmeat consumption increased 18.8 percent, to 19 kilograms.

New Zealand Meat Board

The New Zealand Meat Board is empowered by the Meat Board Act 2004 to establish and operate meat export quota management systems. Its responsibilities involve administration of the beef and veal tariff rate quotas granted to New Zealand as a result of the General Agreement on Tariffs and Trade (GATT) Uruguay Round. This includes sheepmeat, goatmeat, and high quality beef in the European Union (EU), and beef and veal in the United States.

Figure 18.01

Proportion of total meat consumption
Year ending 30 September

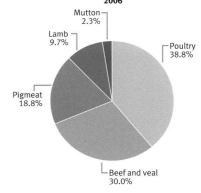

2006

- Mutton 2.3%
- Lamb 9.7%
- Poultry 38.8%
- Pigmeat 18.8%
- Beef and veal 30.0%

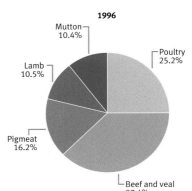

1996

- Mutton 10.4%
- Lamb 10.5%
- Poultry 25.2%
- Pigmeat 16.2%
- Beef and veal 37.4%

Source: Meat & Wool New Zealand

Schedule prices

Some meat processors publish their schedules for stock purchase prices in the weekly Agrifax publication, daily newspapers, and in company newsletters. Producers can sell their stock on schedule, on a pool account system, on the hoof, on contract, or by auction.

Season average net schedules are compiled by Meat and Wool New Zealand and are shown in table 18.05. Schedule prices quoted are inclusive of pelt, slipe wool (wool retrieved from sheepskins at an abattoir or freezing works), and hide payments. The New Zealand production season runs from 1 October to 30 September.

Table 18.05

Average net schedule prices for meat										
Classification	1997/98	1998/99	1999/00	2000/01	2001/02	2002/03	2003/04	2004/05	2005/06	2006/07
Lamb	($)/animal[1]									
YL (9.1–13.2kg)	27.85	25.98	33.50	41.94	43.88	42.73	39.81	43.63	35.52	34.50
YM (13.3–17.0kg)	39.91	41.00	47.48	61.99	66.76	59.93	59.15	62.68	53.27	52.14
YX (17.1–21.3kg)	49.57	54.00	57.93	70.17	79.26	71.73	72.76	75.19	61.00	58.70
Mutton	($)/animal[1]									
MX1 (< 23kg)	28.29	23.54	25.56	39.60	47.65	43.21	41.98	42.92	36.74	34.00
MX2 (> 23kg)	33.57	27.91	29.92	47.61	57.90	54.16	52.76	54.57	47.67	42.81
Beef	cents/kilogram									
P2 Steer (270.5–295kg)	214.3	248.8	311.6	367.3	384.6	306.3	313.1	328.1	319.3	332.9
M Cow (170.5–195kg)	185.6	206.2	267.4	331.5	312.5	211.7	212.2	236.5	242.6	211.4
M Bull (270.5–295kg)	229.0	262.6	325.0	372.7	382.5	277.1	288.2	309.4	304.3	308.0

(1) Includes skin and one kilogram wool pull.

Source: Meat & Wool New Zealand

Meat production

New Zealand accounts for 1 percent of global beef and veal production, and 6 percent of global lamb and mutton production. Table 18.06 shows New Zealand's meat production volumes over the decade to 2007.

Table 18.06

Meat production[1] Year ending 30 September										
Carcass type	1996	1998	2000	2001	2002	2003	2004	2005	2006	2007
	Tonnes (000)									
Beef	606	609	552	570	554	633	686	629	620	601
Veal	27	25	20	20	22	27	24	23	23	23
Mutton	134	129	106	129	107	113	107	105	104	120
Lamb	375	416	433	434	414	433	411	438	438	453
Pigmeat	50	48	46	44	45	47	52	50	51	51
Deer	18	20	25	27	25	28	35	40	39	36
Poultry	91	99	110	119	135	143	154	163R	155	153
Total	**1,301**	**1,346**	**1,292**	**1,343**	**1,302**	**1,424**	**1,469**	**1,448**	**1,430**	**1,437**

(1) Inspected meat production at meat export works and abattoirs.

Sources: Ministry of Agriculture and Forestry; Deer Industry New Zealand

Meat & Wool New Zealand

Meat & Wool New Zealand is a levy-funded organisation that furthers the interests of New Zealand red meat and wool producers. It works to ensure that New Zealand farmers obtain the best possible long-term return on their investment.

The organisation is involved in market access, market services, and international promotion, providing market support through offices in Wellington, Brussels, London, Tokyo, Washington and Seoul. It also commissions or funds research and development activities, with a major focus on on-farm activities designed to help livestock farmers increase the profitability of their farms.

Meat & Wool New Zealand provides funding for a number of organisations, including the beef, sheep, and goat councils, and provides partial funding for the New Zealand Beef and Lamb Marketing Bureau. The funding for Meat & Wool New Zealand comes from all New Zealand beef, sheep, goat, and wool producers, who pay a levy on all stock slaughtered and on every kilogram of wool harvested.

Auctioneer Peter Grieve takes bids during a Balclutha store lamb sale in December 2007. New Zealand exported 331,030 tonnes of lamb in the 2006/07 season.

Sheepmeat

Lamb exports totalled 331,030 tonnes (shipped weight) in the 2006/07 season, an increase of 19,389 tonnes on the previous season.

Sheepmeat exports to the EU were 192,768 tonnes (shipped weight) in the 2006/07 season, making it New Zealand's largest market, followed by North Asia (50,985 tonnes), North America (50,883 tonnes), the Middle East (32,840 tonnes), and the Pacific (26,592 tonnes).

Under a World Trade Organization (WTO) agreement, New Zealand's sheepmeat exports to the EU in 2008 were subject to a tariff rate quota of 227,854 tonnes carcass weight equivalent.

Mutton exports in the 2006/07 season totalled 69,518 tonnes and were up 22.0 percent on the previous year. The largest markets for mutton were the United Kingdom (15.6 percent), Taiwan (13.7 percent), and Germany (11.3 percent).

Classification of sheepmeat Sheepmeat is classified in the following way:

- lamb – a sheep under 12 months, or one that does not have permanent incisor teeth
- hogget – a young male sheep or maiden ewe that has no more than two permanent incisors
- mutton – a female (ewe) or castrated male (wether) with more than two permanent incisors; a wether must not show any ram characteristics
- ram – an adult uncastrated male sheep that has more than two permanent incisors.

Beef and veal

New Zealand's largest market for beef and veal is North America, which took 203,616 tonnes in the 2006/07 season, down 8.1 percent on the previous year. Beef and veal exports to the United States were down 14,808 tonnes on the previous year, to 178,033 tonnes.

In 2006/07, beef and veal exports to North Asia, the second-largest market region, fell 4.8 percent on the previous season, to 99,999 tonnes.

Under WTO agreements, 213,402 tonnes (product weight) of New Zealand beef and veal may be exported to the United States annually at a tariff rate of US4.4c/kg on most beef products. Also under the agreements, 1,300 tonnes (product weight) of New Zealand high-quality beef may be exported to the EU annually, at a 20 percent *ad valorem* duty.

Classification of beef Beef is classified as follows:

- steers, heifers, cows and bulls – a steer is a male bovine castrated when young. A heifer is a female bovine, with no more than six permanent incisors. Cows have more than six permanent incisors. A bull is an entire (uncastrated) bovine with masculine characteristics
- bobby calves – bobby veal carcasses are derived from milk-fed bovine calves, generally less than two weeks old
- veal – maiden female, castrated male, or entire male (not showing masculine characteristics) up to 14 months old.

Table 18.07

Lamb exports to EU
Year ending 30 September

Year	($) per shipped tonne
1998	5,701
1999	5,869
2000	6,461
2001	7,581
2002	8,330
2003	8,211
2004	8,280
2005	8,859
2006	8,283
2007	8,057

Source: Meat & Wool New Zealand

Table 18.08

United States beef prices
At mid March

Year	Manufacturing bull	Manufacturing cow
	US cents/kilogram	
1998	198.3	182.8
1999	198.3	184.0
2000	215.9	202.7
2001	229.1	207.1
2002	245.6	239.0
2003	211.5	193.9
2004	257.8	235.7
2005	295.2	282.0
2006	273.2	260.0
2007	297.4	275.4

Source: Meat & Wool New Zealand

Meat prices

Lamb exports to Europe accounted for 50 percent of total lamb exports in the 2006/07 season. Table 18.07 shows the dollar value per shipped tonne of lamb exports to the EU. In 2006/07, the value per shipped tonne was $8,057.

Table 18.08 gives a measure of New Zealand export beef prices derived from Meat and Wool New Zealand's weekly price series for imported manufacturing beef in the United States.

Meat exports

New Zealand beef and lamb is exported to more than 100 countries. The country is a major exporter of sheepmeat, accounting for 55 percent of the world export trade. New Zealand's major sheepmeat markets are the EU, North America, and the Middle East.

Compared with sheepmeat, New Zealand is a smaller – but significant – player in the global market for beef, accounting for 8 percent of all world export beef trade. North America and North Asia are New Zealand's major markets for beef.

Table 18.09

Livestock slaughter
At meat export works and abattoirs
Year ending 30 September

Animal	2002	2003	2004	2005	2006	2007
	Number of animals (000)					
Lambs[1]	24,703	25,693	23,833	25,053	25,795	26,948
Sheep[1]	4,653	4,880	4,446	4,312	4,279	5,070
Adult cattle[1]	2,177	2,486	2,668	2,422	2,338	2,292
Calves and vealers[1]	1,356	1,607	1,460	1,380	1,389	1,369
Pigs[1]	709	748	786	765	756	741
Deer[2]	465	550	678	762	711	607

(1) Includes condemned carcasses. (2) Excludes condemned carcasses.

Sources: Ministry of Agriculture and Forestry; Deer Industry New Zealand

Table 18.10

Export meat production
Year ending 30 September

Meat	2002	2003	2004	2005	2006	2007
	Shipping weight (tonnes)					
Lamb	286,556	297,527	294,642	301,759	311,641	331,030
Mutton	52,635	56,981	57,034	59,156	57,004	69,518
Beef	331,623	361,607	407,584	374,264	361,089	340,825
Bobby veal	11,997	12,632	17,249	15,943	11,891	11,521
Goat	1,224	1,184	1,266	1,152	1,079	985
Variety meats[1]	54,121	61,460	71,913	67,872	64,612	65,650
Inedible meats and offal	2,449	4,266	...	...	...	...
Total	**738,491**	**831,470**	**849,688**	**820,146**	**807,316**	**819,529**

(1) From 2004, variety meats and inedible meats and offal were combined into one category.
Symbol: ... not applicable

Sources: New Zealand Meat Board; Meat & Wool New Zealand

Wool

New Zealand sheep are largely dual-purpose, wool/meat animals, and their wool is predominantly strong wool.

New Zealand is the world's largest producer of crossbred (strong) wool, used mainly for interior textiles such as carpets, upholstery, furnishings, bedding and rugs. It is also used for hand-knitting yarn, knitwear and blankets. It is estimated that 42 percent of New Zealand wool is used in machine-made carpets, and 10 percent in hand-knotted and hand-tufted carpets. The rest is used primarily for upholstery and bedding. Uses vary markedly among importing countries.

Net domestic consumption of wool in New Zealand is among the highest in the world on a per person basis.

Wool production

Although New Zealand's sheep flock ranks fifth-largest in the world, the country's total wool fibre production is second only to Australia on a clean mass basis. This is due to the high clip yield per head, and lower quantities of grease and other contaminants in New Zealand wool.

Table 18.12

					Shorn
	Flock size	Slipe[1] greasy	Shorn greasy	Total greasy	greasy yield
Year	Million		Tonnes (000)		Kg/sheep
2003	39,572	32.2	197.4	229.6	4.99
2004	39,552	25.9	191.8	217.7	4.85
2005	39,271	28.4	187.1	215.5	4.76
2006	39,880	25.7	198.9	224.6	4.99
2007	40,098	30.0	186.3	216.3	4.65

Wool production
Year ending 30 June

(1) Slipe is the wool retrieved from sheepskins.

Source: Meat & Wool New Zealand

Jordan Fitzgibbon picks up a fleece during the sheep shearing contest at the Cheviot Agricultural and Pastoral (A&P) Show, in March 2008. Most of New Zealand's wool is crossbred (strong), which is used mainly for interior textiles such as carpets.

Wool marketing

In the year ending 30 June 2007, the proportion of shorn wool production sold at auction was 47 percent, while 53 percent was sold by private treaty.

On a clean basis, shorn wool sales totalled 138,999 tonnes (excluding slipe, the wool retrieved from sheepskins) in the year ending 30 June 2007. Sales consisted of 89 percent crossbred wool, 5 percent merino, 4 percent mid-micron wool, and 2 percent dag wool (wool clotted with dung, shorn from the hindquarters).

The shorn wool price for 2006/07 was up 1.4 percent on the previous year. This increase was driven by a sharp 28 percent price rise for fine wool and a 9 percent rise for mid-micron wool, while strong wool prices fell 3 percent. In 2006/07, Australia's drought reduced sheep numbers to 94 million, the lowest level since 1925, which reduced the wool supply and subsequently affected fine and mid-micron wool prices. Mid-micron prices followed the finer end of these clips because this wool is used as a substitute for fine wools when they are in short supply.

About 79 percent of the New Zealand wool clip leaves the country in greasy or scoured form. Of the 21 percent of the clip processed in New Zealand, roughly half is exported in product form, mainly as carpet yarn, carpets, or knitted jerseys.

Wool export earnings

Raw wool and wool product export receipts decreased from $997 million in the year ending 30 September 2006 to $938 million in the 2007 year.

Raw wool exports decreased from $685 million to $655 million, the result of a 5 percent fall in the volume of exports.

Table 18.11

Region	2003	2004	2005	2006	2007
			Clean tonnes		
European Union	56,369	57,270	57,705	59,219	57,666
Northern Asia	36,532	37,768	35,651	43,508	38,550
Southern Asia	18,481	18,271	19,805	20,318	21,627
Pacific	11,486	9,557	8,489	6,590	6,296
Mediterranean	4,113	3,964	3,272	4,742	5,511
Middle East	5,543	5,153	4,950	5,209	4,579
North America	6,072	6,177	5,470	4,723	3,984
Eastern Europe	134	187	558	1,663	1,308
Africa	612	421	967	900	690
South America	559	487	129	94	209
Western Europe	365	294	161	351	166
Total	**140,266**	**139,549**	**137,157**	**147,317**	**140,586**

Export destinations for New Zealand wool
Year ending 30 September

Source: Meat & Wool New Zealand

Breakthrough in methane research

In June 2008, the Pastoral Greenhouse Gas Research Consortium (PGGRC) announced that scientists had mapped the genetic sequence of a microbe that produces methane from the rumen of cattle and sheep.

This breakthrough will help scientists find ways to reduce the amount of methane that farm animals produce – around 32 percent of total greenhouse gas emissions.

Although a solution is probably still five years away, and implementation may be 10 years away, consortium chairman Mark Leslie says that closing the genomic sequence (for methanogens) is an important piece of the complex puzzle.

The breakthrough may also have commercial implications. "There are more than a billion domestic farm animals in the world. If we can win the worldwide race to find a practical, cost-effective solution for reducing agricultural emissions, we can not only help reduce our Kyoto Protocol liabilities, but also commercialise and export the technology to the world," Mr Leslie says.

The PGGRC is a joint government and industry group partnership, set up in 2002 to develop mitigation for agricultural greenhouse gases before New Zealand signed the Kyoto Protocol. The programme is the most comprehensive of its kind in the world. It has six themes for its research: rumen ecology, methanogen genomics, the development of a methane vaccine, animal selection, farms systems and adoption, and nitrous oxide mitigation.

The consortium has enabled initial validation of nitrous oxide mitigations, through the use of feed pads in the winter and nitrification inhibitors. Nitrous oxide is about 16 percent of New Zealand's greenhouse gas emissions, most of which comes from agriculture.

Also, by adding data to the New Zealand's greenhouse gas inventory, the PGGRC has helped improve the accuracy of the country's Kyoto Protocol accounting.

Source: Pastoral Greenhouse Gas Research Consortium

For the year ended 30 September 2007, the European Union took 41 percent of New Zealand's wool exports, a decrease of 2.6 percent. Northern Asia was the second-largest destination region, taking 27 percent, with the majority (22 percent) destined for China. In 2007, exports to China were down 13 percent on the previous year. India accounted for 11 percent of all wool exports in 2007, which was up 11 percent on the previous year.

Table 18.13

	Wool export earnings Year ending 30 September				
	2003	2004	2005	2006	2007
Product	$(million) fob[1]				
Raw wool	817.4	726.1	662.9	685.4	655.1
Tops, yarns and sliver	131.5	131.1	137.2	141.2	131.0
Carpets and rugs	155.3	138.0	132.6	129.9	108.8
Other final woollen products	42.4	46.4	43.7	40.8	43.3
Total	**1,146.5**	**1,041.6**	**976.4**	**997.3**	**938.2**

(1) Free on board at point of loading.
Note: Figures may not add up to stated totals due to rounding.

Source: Meat & Wool New Zealand

Dairy produce

Dairy products, at $8.6 billion, made up 23.6 percent of the value of New Zealand's total merchandise exports in the year ending 31 December 2007. With the exception of the milk and other dairy products used for domestic local consumption, the dairy industry is primarily geared towards overseas markets, which account for more than 90 percent of all milk produced.

There are four major product groups manufactured from liquid whole milk by New Zealand dairy factories:

- milk powders, such as whole milk powder, skim milk powder, and buttermilk powder
- cream products, such as butter, anhydrous milkfat and ghee
- cheese
- milk protein products, such as casein and caseinates.

Liquid whole milk can be broken down into three chief components: milkfat, solids-non-fat (principally protein), and water. Whole milk powder is manufactured directly from the liquid whole milk, without separation of the cream. Skim milk powder is made from skim milk after the cream (milkfat) has been separated from the liquid whole milk. Buttermilk powder is made from buttermilk, a by-product of the butter manufacturing process.

Most butter produced is of a 'sweet cream' type, and anhydrous milkfat and ghee are further refinements of butter.

The predominant cheese variety manufactured in New Zealand is cheddar or cheddar type, although the manufacture of speciality cheese types has shown considerable growth in recent years.

Milk proteins are derived from the by-products of skim milk, and also from the by-products of other dairy product manufactures such as cheese.

Dairy organisations

At the end of the 2006/07 dairy season (31 May 2007), collection and processing of most of New Zealand's milk was being carried out by three cooperative dairy manufacturing companies, operating from 24 sites. However, one independent dairy processor had established itself on a small scale.

Cooperative dairy companies are governed by boards of directors elected by supplying farmers, with provision for the appointment of a small number of non-farmers noted for their commercial expertise. The cooperatives use funds supplied as share capital by their farmers.

The cooperative dairy companies produce nearly all dairy products manufactured in New Zealand. The companies convert approximately 15 billion litres of milk into nearly 2 million tonnes of dairy products annually. More than 90 percent of this is exported. The balance is consumed in the domestic market.

In addition to the three cooperatives, about 20 smaller private dairy companies produce up to 20,000 tonnes of cheese a year. There are also several ice cream manufacturers.

Dairy Companies Association of New Zealand was formed in 2003 by New Zealand's leading dairy companies. Its membership includes Fonterra Co-operative Group, Tatua Co-operative Dairy Company, Westland Milk Products, Goodman Fielder, Open Country Cheese, New Zealand Dairies, and Gisborne Milk. It represents the joint interests of New Zealand dairy companies on domestic and international policy issues, a role previously undertaken by the New Zealand Dairy Board, before deregulation of the industry and the formation of Fonterra in 2001. The general activities of the association are funded by membership subscription, with special activities funded according to a proportional formula.

Fonterra Co-operative Group is New Zealand's largest company, earning revenues of $13.9 billion in the year ending 31 May 2007 from national and international sales of dairy commodities, specialty ingredients, food service products, and branded consumer products.

It is the fifth-largest dairy company in the world by turnover. The cooperative has assets of $12.6 billion, and is owned by nearly 11,000 New Zealand dairy farmers, who supplied nearly 15 billion litres of milk in the 2006/07 season. Payment for milk is made on a per kilogram of milk solids (kgMS) basis. For the 2006/07 year, Fonterra paid out $5.6 billion ($4.47 per kgMS) to farmers, made up of $4.8 billion in the milk price, and $728 million in value returns. A further $52 million was paid in premium payments for the supply of autumn milk, organics, stolle (milk obtained from cows that are immunised to induce the formation of antibodies in their milk), colostrum (milk taken from the first four milkings after calf birth), and winter milk.

In the 2006/07 year, Fonterra earned $9.8 billion from dairy commodities and ingredients, and $4.0 billion from consumer sales. The cooperative manufactured 2 million tonnes of dairy commodities in New Zealand for international sale, and sold 2.8 million tonnes – including product sourced in other regions (Australia, South America, North America and Europe).

Fonterra has four sales channels:

- Fonterra Global Trade – is the world's largest supplier of bulk dairy commodities to the globally traded markets, with sales primarily to Asia, the Middle East, Africa, Latin America, and Oceania

- Fonterra Ingredients – sells dairy ingredients in the United States, Western Europe, Japan, and the Republic of Korea. Sales include dairy products as well as more specialised ingredients. It also sells solutions for largely dairy-based food applications, drawing on the work of Fonterra's research and development programmes, and its technical teams

- Fonterra Brands – produces, markets, and sells dairy products to consumers in 40 countries, with around half of its business concentrated in Australia and New Zealand. Its $1.1 billion brand portfolio includes Anchor™, Anlene™, Anmum™, Mainland™, Tip Top™, Peters & Brownes™ and Soprole

- Fonterra Foodservices – meets the needs of food service customers around the world for branded consumer goods, as well as core ingredients and ready-to-use products. The business has a geographic focus in Asia-Pacific and has many leading fast-food chains as customers.

In addition to its sales channels, the cooperative includes:

- Fonterra Group Manufacturing – is responsible for all of Fonterra's New Zealand and global manufacturing sites

- Fonterra Milk Supply – is the interface with shareholders and suppliers, including milk collection and payment

- Fonterra Shared Services – handles human resource, strategy, finance, legal, and communications functions.

Fonterra has a number of global joint ventures and investments. These include joint ventures with Arla in Europe, Nestlé in South America, Dairy Farmers of America in the United States, and Campina in DMV Fonterra Excipients, a global manufacturer of pharmaceutical lactose. Fonterra's investments include a 43 percent shareholding in one of China's leading dairy companies, San Lu, and a majority shareholding in Chile's leading consumer dairy business, Soprole.

Fonterra has around 16,000 global employees and represents 20 percent of New Zealand's total exports.

Westland Milk Products is an independent cooperative dairy company owned by 327 farmer shareholders. It is located in Hokitika, on the west coast of the South Island. The company processes more than 450 million litres of milk annually into a diverse range of dairy ingredients for nutritional, food, and beverage applications. The products include milk powders, milkfat products (butter and anhydrous milkfat), and milk protein products (casein, milk protein concentrate, and whey protein concentrate), as well as colostrum powder. The products are marketed both nationally and internationally.

Tatua Co-operative Dairy Co Ltd is an autonomous, independent dairy company in the Waikato and is owned entirely by 112 farmer shareholders. The company was established in 1914 and is the only dairy cooperative remaining in New Zealand that has never been part of an amalgamation. Tatua's factory is located at Tatuanui, 35 kilometres east of Hamilton. The company has four divisions:

- Tatua Foods – makes ultra-heat-treated (UHT) sterilised liquid food products. These include aerosol-canned cream, bag-in-box whipping cream, cheese sauce, liquid pre-mixes (for milkshakes and sundaes) and UHT chocolate milk

- Tatua Nutritional Ingredients – makes products that include a variety of proteins, protein hydrolysates, and bioactive peptides, which are suitable for applications in specialist nutrition and healthcare products

Fonterra and the environment

Demand for dairy products is increasing as consumers around the world recognise the nutritious benefits of dairy food. At the same time, people are becoming more aware of the impact of food production on the environment, and making their preferences clear by demanding environmentally-sustainable products.

To meet the challenge posed by these parallel demands, Fonterra has implemented widespread measures to improve the environmental performance of its operations. It has also set clear targets to monitor progress and be more accountable.

Fonterra is making considerable efforts to inform its dairy farmers about ways to reduce their environmental impact. Improving the quality of water in New Zealand's waterways and reducing the volume and intensity of greenhouse gas emissions are the two main focuses of Fonterra's farmer education programmes.

Fonterra has also taken a leadership role in working with government and industry groups to minimise the impact of dairying on the environment. Fonterra has a significant investment in climate change research through the Pastoral Greenhouse Gas Research Consortium. This is a joint government and industry body, which aims to find solutions for reducing the greenhouse gases produced by grazing animals. At November 2007, more than $15 million had been invested in this project, with commitment for a further $25 million over the next five years.

Improving environmental performance throughout all stages of its manufacturing operations underpins Fonterra's commitment to ensuring all practices and processes are sustainable.

Reducing water and energy use, cutting the volume of waste sent to landfill, finding environmentally sound packaging solutions, using less harmful and more cost-effective chemicals for cleaning plants, and reducing the quantity of chemicals used are among the projects that have significantly reduced the environmental footprint of Fonterra's manufacturing business.

Initiatives in transport, energy efficiency, and the use of renewable energy at sites have resulted in a 28 percent reduction in carbon dioxide emissions per tonne of product since 1990. Fonterra is researching the full life-cycle carbon impact of its products – from cow to customer, and right through to packaging disposal.

Source: Fonterra

- Tatua Bionutrient Ingredients – specialises in the manufacture of purified proteins and peptones, customised for biopharmaceutical applications
- Tatua Flavour Ingredients – focuses on the production of specialist dairy flavour ingredients for the global food and beverage industry.

Open Country Cheese Ltd is an independent public company with more than 300 shareholders that was set up following deregulation of the New Zealand dairy industry in 2001. It produces quality semi-hard to hard dry-salted cheeses for domestic and world markets at its state-of-the-art plant at Waharoa. High quality milk is sourced from 140 farms, located in the intensive dairy farming area of the eastern Waikato.

Open Country Cheese produces around 20,000 tonnes of cheese, including cheddar, colby, gouda, edam, havarti, kahui and goya. The company also produces WPC34 (whey protein concentrate), anhydrous milkfat, and skim milk powder. A whole milk powder plant is under construction, and it will produce 30,000 tonnes of whole milk powder a year.

The company's export markets include Australia, Asia, Latin America, the United Kingdom, North Africa and the Middle East.

Overseas marketing

New Zealand's dairy industry is primarily geared towards overseas markets, which account for more than 90 percent of all milk solids produced. However, the international market for dairy products is characterised by its small size, relative to total world milk production. Less than 10 percent of total world production is traded internationally.

Because of this, the market is especially vulnerable to shifts in climatic, commercial, and political forces. Marginal production changes by major producers can trigger major shifts in supplies of, and prices for, products on the international market.

The major dairy exporters are the European Union (EU), New Zealand, Australia and, to a lesser degree, the United States and Canada. These five exporters supply about 90 percent of dairy products traded on the international market.

In the year ending 31 December 2007, the United States, Japan, Australia, the EU, and South-East Asia were New Zealand's most valuable destination markets for dairy produce.

Pigs, poultry, eggs and bees

Pigs

In the year ending 30 September 2007, domestic pork production, in terms of the number of pigs slaughtered, was 741,046 pigs. There was an increase in kill weight, with the average carcass weighing 67.7 kilograms, compared with 67.0 kilograms in the 2006 year. The per-person consumption of pork reached 21.4 kilograms in the 2007 year, an increase of 0.8 kilograms on the previous year.

The demand for 90,617 tonnes of pork in the domestic market in 2007 (up 6 percent on the previous year) was fulfilled by the supply of 50,183 tonnes of domestic pork, and 40,434 tonnes of imported pork.

New Zealand Pork Industry Board is a statutory body operating under the Pork Industry Board Act 1997. The board's mission is to help producers make 'More Profit from Pork'. In delivering on this mission, the board focuses its investments in five key areas: increasing demand for New Zealand pork, increasing supply while reducing the cost of production, improving value chain effectiveness, securing industry sustainability, and developing industry capability and profile.

Board funds come from a levy on pigs slaughtered at licensed premises. The board has five directors – four elected by producers and one appointed by the government.

Poultry

New Zealanders now consume more chicken than any other type of meat. In 2006, consumption of poultry was 36.5 kilograms per person. Production has increased to meet this demand – in 2006, the New Zealand poultry industry produced just over 145,000 tonnes of chicken meat from 84.1 million chickens. Over three-quarters (78.3 percent) of all chicken sold is fresh chicken, with the remainder being frozen. It is expected that current poultry production and consumption levels will continue.

The four largest poultry meat producers in New Zealand, producing over 99 percent of poultry meat, are: Tegel Foods Ltd, Inghams Enterprises (NZ) Pty Ltd, PH van den Brink Ltd, and Turks Poultry Ltd.

Egg Producers Federation of New Zealand

Free-range chickens enjoy the sunshine and the freedom to scratch in the soil. There is an increasing demand for free-range poultry products.

Table 18.14

	Pig numbers		
	At 30 June		
Year	Breeding sows and mated gilts	Other pigs of all ages (including boars)	**Total pigs**
1994	58,065	364,701	**422,766**
1995	59,250	371,755	**431,005**
1996	57,065	367,009	**424,074**
1999(1)	60,626	308,261	**368,887**
2002	46,706	295,309	**342,015**
2003	49,381	327,868	**377,249**
2004	48,453	340,187	**388,640**
2005	42,598	298,867	**341,465**
2006	43,306	312,195	**355,501**
2007	46,911	319,760	**366,671**

(1) Use caution when making comparisons using 1999 data. In this year, the survey population was drawn from a different sample.

Note: Pig numbers were not counted in 1997, 1998, 2000 and 2001.

Sources: Statistics New Zealand; NZ Pork Industry Board

Table 18.15

	Chicken production			
	Year ending 31 December			
Year	Birds (number)	Dressed weight (tonnes)	Fresh	Frozen
			Percent	
1997	60,749	88,904	66.2	33.8
1998	64,667	97,120	64.6	30.2
1999	63,945	100,085	70.7	29.3
2000	67,067	108,929	71.2	29.0
2001	69,361	115,786	73.7	26.3
2002	77,357	130,519	73.4	26.6
2003	80,728	138,697	75.4	24.6
2004	87,570	151,497	77.1	22.9
2005	88,766	154,982	80.0	20.0
2006	83,214	144,634	78.3	21.7

Source: Poultry Industry Association of New Zealand

The New Zealand poultry industry is unique in that it is largely dominated by chicken. Other countries have a heavier emphasis on other poultry species, such as turkey or duck, but chicken's market share in New Zealand has not slipped below 98 percent in the decade to 2006.

The Poultry Industry Association of New Zealand (PIANZ) represents the interests of the poultry processing and breeding companies in New Zealand. Membership is voluntary, but over 99 percent of the country's production is represented by PIANZ.

PIANZ promotes and protects the interests of its members by liaising with government and government departments, and securing representation before boards, committees, and commissions constituted under acts or regulations of the government. Other roles of PIANZ include: coordinating research and development relating to the industry, generic promotion of poultry meat, livestock breeding and development, technical training related to the industry, collection and circulation of technical information and statistics, and general public relations.

Eggs

New Zealand currently has around 130 commercial egg producers, with the largest 20 producers accounting for over 75 percent of total production. With an estimated flock of 3.1 million laying hens, 75 million dozen eggs were produced in 2006 – 900 million eggs in total.

Total egg production in New Zealand has slowly risen over the past decade, due to an increase in demand. In 2006, New Zealanders consumed an average of 218 eggs per person – higher than Australia, Canada, Brazil, and the United Kingdom.

The Egg Producers Federation of New Zealand represents the interests of all commercial egg producers in New Zealand. Membership is mandatory under the Commodity Levies (Eggs) Order 2004 – any person or organisation purchasing 100 or more day-old layer chicks automatically becomes a member. The federation is funded by a levy incorporated into the price of the chicks, and is payable on chicks up to five days old when sold for the first time.

The majority of the federation's levy (75 percent) goes towards funding Eggs Inc – an organisation responsible for the promotion of eggs.

Bees and beekeeping

Honey bees have been kept in New Zealand for nearly 170 years, and in that time beekeeping has moved from being a home craft to a progressive industry. New Zealand is now recognised as one of the most advanced beekeeping countries in the world.

Mary Bumby, the sister of an English missionary, was the first person to successfully ship honey bees to New Zealand when she brought two basket hives (skeps) of bees into Northland in 1839. More than 100 years later, in 1950, beekeeper numbers peaked at 7,000, although they collectively owned only about 150,000 hives, or less than half of today's number.

Beekeeper John Graham checks his hives at Bennies Honey, in Ranfurly. In January 2008, queens and brood bees were stolen from his hives in Central Otago by modern-day rustlers.

During the late 1970s and early 1980s, there were large changes in the beekeeping industry. The centralised Honey Marketing Authority ceased operation, and private individuals and companies began exporting honey products. The number of hives increased by more than 50 percent to 335,000, spurred on by the demand for paid pollination services, especially from the kiwifruit industry. However, since then the number of beekeepers and hives has decreased to the point where, in 2007, there were 2,602 registered beekeepers owning 313,399 hives (see table 18.16). The trend for fewer beekeepers to own more hives continues.

Increases in the price of honey and other bee products, live bees, and pollination services have helped many beekeepers cope with increased costs and the loss of hives due to the varroa pest (see below). AsureQuality Ltd assessed the total saleable honey crop for 2007 at 9,666 tonnes (30.8 kilograms per hive), compared with the six-year average of 9,267 tonnes (30.6 kilograms per hive). Both the best and the worst honey seasons in recent history have occurred since varroa arrived in New Zealand.

Other products such as deer velvet, bee venom, dried fruit, pollen, and royal jelly can be blended with honey to add value.

All operators who handle, process, or store bee products, and who wish to export with an official assurance (export certificate), or supply product to an exporter, must operate under a risk management programme. Such programmes help assure customers that the products are fit for the purpose, and meet importing country requirements.

The industry also markets beeswax, propolis (an antibiotic gum or resin from plants), pollen, and live bees, which include package bees and queen bees. Package bees are ventilated containers with around 1 kilogram of bees, a queen bee, and a food supply. The spread of bee pests and diseases, as well as the aggressive Africanised honey bee, throughout other bee-keeping countries, has increased the demand for bees from New Zealand. Annual exports of live bees are around 20,000–25,000 queen bees, and 20,000kg of package bees, mainly to Canada.

New Zealand beekeepers provide a commercial pollination service to growers of tree and berry fruit, kiwifruit, cucurbits (squash and melons), and small seeds. About 100,000 hives are moved for pollination each season, and this business is becoming more important each year as feral (wild) hives are reduced or eliminated by the varroa mite (see below). The real value of beekeeping is now in pollinating plants rather than producing apiculture products.

Manuka honey In 1992, Waikato University researchers confirmed that manuka honey was unusually effective as an antiseptic dressing for wounds and burns. As a result, both the demand and the price for manuka honey have risen dramatically. Some beekeepers are 'renting' large tracts of land with manuka on it, while others have entered into profit sharing arrangements with landowners. In addition some large exporting companies are buying beekeeping operations and even planting manuka to secure their supply lines.

Varroa In April 2000, the serious bee mite *Varroa destructor* was found in Auckland and has since spread throughout the North Island. Attempts were made to keep it out of the South Island, but in June 2006 the mite was found in Nelson. The mite, if left untreated, kills honey bee colonies. While it can be controlled using miticides and some organic acids, these can be expensive to buy or apply. Many hobby beekeepers have decided not to continue.

After varroa became established in Nelson, the Varroa Agency Incorporated revoked the varroa pest management strategy. Movement controls remain in place for risky goods from the North Island to the South Island, and also out of the Nelson-Blenheim region. These controls are now administered by MAF Biosecurity New Zealand.

The National Beekeepers' Association This voluntary organisation is supported by fee-paying members. It represents the interests of beekeepers to government, and coordinates a national response on issues affecting their industry. The association also levies all beekeepers under the Biosecurity Act 1993, to pay for its American foulbrood pest management strategy. Another organisation, the Bee Industry Group, is a member of New Zealand Federated Farmers, and also represents beekeeping interests.

Table 18.16

	Bee-keepers	Apiaries	Hives	Honey production
Honey production				
Year ending 31 December				
Year	Number			Tonnes
1998	5,356	23,027	298,921	8,081
1999	4,914	21,793	302,988	9,069
2000	4,956	22,443	320,113	9,609
2001	4,539	21,304	314,094	9,144
2002	3,973	20,258	305,152	4,682
2003	3,596	20,153	300,841	12,252
2004	3,211	19,592	292,530	8,888
2005	2,743	19,115	297,605	9,689
2006	2,694	18,954	300,728	10,423
2007	2,602	19,228	313,399	9,666

Source: AsureQuality Limited

Horticulture

Although pastoral farming dominates land use in New Zealand, there have been significant increases in areas planted in horticulture and crops. Major crops for the export market include kiwifruit, pipfruit, stone fruit, onions, squash, flowers and berry fruit. Increasing volumes of grapes are grown for the rapidly-expanding export wine market.

Grain, vegetable and seed crops

Stock feed Animals can be grazed in open pasture in New Zealand for the full 12 months of the year. The winter growth of grass, except in certain favoured localities, needs to be supplemented in order to keep stock in good condition during the colder months, and in some districts, supplementary feed is necessary in the drier summer months.

Hay and silage crops are grown almost exclusively on the farms where they are consumed, and some districts specialise in growing other supplementary feed crops, such as maize in the Waikato

Table 18.17

Horticultural exports
By value and as a proportion of total
Year ending 30 June

Type	2003	2004	2005	2006	2007	2003	2004	2005	2006	2007
	\$(million)					Proportion of total (percent)				
Fresh fruit	1,019	1,233	1,189	1,140	1,200	58.7	63.5	63.6	61.3	60.6
Processed fruit	80	89	102	100	105	4.6	4.6	5.4	5.4	5.3
Fresh vegetables	246	217	199	204	260	14.2	11.2	10.7	11.0	13.1
Processed vegetables	275	285	257	285	297	15.8	14.7	13.7	15.3	15.0
Seeds and bulbs	54	56	60	71	63	3.1	2.9	3.2	3.8	3.2
Cut flowers and foliage	40	39	38	39	43	2.3	2.0	2.1	2.1	2.2
Plants and sphagnum moss[1]	23	23	24	19	12	1.3	1.2	1.3	1.0	0.6
Total horticultural exports	**1,737**	**1,943**	**1,871**	**1,858**	**1,981**	**100.0**	**100.0**	**100.0**	**100.0**	**100.0**

(1) Value excludes confidential data for latest period.
Note: Figures may not add up to stated totals due to rounding.

Source: Statistics New Zealand

and Manawatu-Wanganui regions. The bulk of supplementary food, other than grass and clover, hay and silage, and maize, is grown in the South Island, since the colder climate necessitates more extensive supplementary feeding there than is needed in the North Island.

Wheat New Zealand wheat is primarily grown for domestic human consumption. The best quality wheat is milled into flour for breadmaking. Other wheat grain is milled for biscuit manufacturing and similar uses. The by-products of flour milling, bran and pollard, are used for stock feed. Most wheat is grown in the Canterbury region.

Barley Most barley grown in New Zealand is used for the manufacture of stock feed and for malting. Exports of malting and feed barley fluctuate in response to price changes, which reflect international supply and demand.

Maize Primarily grown in the Waikato and eastern North Island, maize grain is used as poultry feed and, increasingly, as a supplementary feed for pigs and other livestock, such as dairy cattle. Maize silage and green feed are also used as supplementary feed for cattle.

Oats Grown mainly for threshing and green feed, oats are also used to produce milled rolled-oats, oatmeal, and other oaten foods. The main growing areas for oats are Canterbury and Southland.

Vegetables More than 50 different types of vegetables are grown in New Zealand for fresh consumption or for processing. In recent years there has been an increase in the range and volume of Asian vegetable varieties for local consumption.

Vegetable growers in New Zealand farm over 50,000 hectares and employ 25,000 people. The fresh vegetable sector has about 1,450 growers whose crops had an estimated farmgate value of over \$400 million in 2007. There are also around 750 growers who grow vegetables for processing in New Zealand. They produced crops worth more than \$100 million in 2007.

In 2007, fresh vegetables with a value of \$260 million, and processed vegetables worth \$297 million, were exported to 76 countries. Onions and squash dominated fresh vegetable exports, with sales values of \$121 million and \$66 million, respectively. Potatoes, sweetcorn and peas were the main exports of processed and frozen vegetables.

Seed certification AsureQuality Ltd operates a seed certification scheme covering all main herbage and arable species, and participates in the Organisation for Economic Co-operation and Development's seed scheme. New Zealand-certified seed is exported to European Union countries, countries of the Pacific Basin, and North and South America.

Fruit

Stone fruit Fruit in this category includes apricots, cherries, peaches, nectarines, and plums. The New Zealand summer fruit (stone fruit) industry consists of around 400 growers on 3,000 hectares. The main production areas are Hawke's Bay and Central Otago. While Hawke's Bay produces the bulk of the summer fruit consumed on the New Zealand market, the export crop is almost exclusively produced in Central Otago.

The New Zealand market consumes 75 percent of the summer fruit product. With the continued shrinking of production in Marlborough, Hawke's Bay is now emerging as the main producer of pre-Christmas cherries for consumption in New Zealand.

Key export markets are Taiwan, Australia, and the United States, with the Republic of Korea and Thailand emerging as promising markets for cherries. On average, apricots account for 50–60 percent of exports, and cherries for around 45 percent. Very few peaches, nectarines and plums are exported. Processing of peaches and apricots accounts for approximately 5 percent of the market.

Summerfruit New Zealand This organisation is funded predominantly by a commodity levy. The levy funds used in research and development are targeted towards eliminating waste from production and developing sustainable systems for producing quality fruit.

Pipfruit In January 2003, New Zealand's largest exporter, ENZA, merged with Turners and Growers to create a produce marketer of global significance. While the company retains the Turners and Growers name, exports remain under their own distinctive brands. Turners and Growers exports to more than 50 countries, with most of its product going to Europe, the United Kingdom, and the United States. About 30 varieties of apples and pears are sold under the ENZA brand.

Table 18.18

	Pipfruit exports				
	Year ending 30 September				
	2003	2004	2005	2006	2007
Fruit	Tray carton equivalents (18kg)				
Apples	17,766,789	17,899,150	18,482,245	14,767,113	16,371,630
Pears	300,000	292,816	298,503	264,335	308,691
Total pipfruit	**18,066,789**	**18,191,966**	**18,780,748**	**15,031,449**	**16,680,321**

Sources: New Zealand Customs Service; Pipfruit New Zealand

Kiwifruit This fruit is New Zealand's most important horticultural export earner. New Zealand is a major world supplier of kiwifruit and has led the development of the global industry.

ZESPRI International Ltd is a consumer-driven, grower-owned company, dedicated to the global marketing of kiwifruit. It is one of New Zealand's leading exporters, earning in excess of $1 billion in 2006. With global headquarters in New Zealand and a network of offices in Europe, North America, Asia, and the Pacific, ZESPRI is the biggest marketer of kiwifruit in the world and is acknowledged as the world leader in innovation, quality and marketing. ZESPRI sold more than 80 million trays of New Zealand kiwifruit in around 60 countries in 2006. Sales were focused in five major markets: Europe (56 percent), Japan (20 percent), East and South-East Asia (13 percent), North America (5 percent), and developing markets – which include the domestic market, as well as Australia, the Middle East, the Indian Ocean region, and Far East Russia.

While New Zealand growers supply about one-quarter of world production, kiwifruit generally accounts for less than 1 percent of world fresh fruit production. Kiwifruit is produced in many regions of New Zealand's North Island, as well as in the north of the South Island. The Bay of Plenty, with more than 82 percent of production, is the major growing area. There are about 2,700 kiwifruit growers in New Zealand, and a further 1,273 around the world. Annual kiwifruit plantings and sales since 1997 are shown in table 18.20.

Willing workers on organic farms

Willing Workers on Organic Farms – WWOOF – is a worldwide network where volunteers (WWOOFers) live and learn on organic properties. Originally called Working Weekends on Organic Farms, it started in the United Kingdom in 1971.

The WWOOF movement took off in New Zealand in 1974, and there are now WWOOF organisations in more than 70 countries.

These organisations link individuals wanting to volunteer on organic farms or smallholdings with people who are looking for volunteer help.

In return for volunteer help, WWOOF hosts offer food, accommodation, and opportunities to learn about organic lifestyles. No money changes hands between volunteers and hosts.

Many WWOOFing opportunities exist, ranging from large working farms to small lifestyle or homesteading properties where people are trying to be as self-sufficient as possible. WWOOF New Zealand also offers a variety of hosts, including permaculture enthusiasts, eco-builders, renewable energy users, vineyards, breweries, an organic bakery, willow weavers and other craft makers, and Rudolf Steiner homes.

Volunteering as a WWOOFer is a great way to become immersed in the daily life of others, and learn about organics.

The opportunity to meet people and learn about different cultures is also an important part of a WWOOF exchange. Because it brings together such a diverse range of people and requires trust and respect from everyone involved, it actively promotes cultural awareness and understanding.

Northvalley Organics

WWOOFers Tyler (left), Taylor, and Raphaela harvesting salad greens at Northvalley Organics, near Whangarei. The produce is destined for the local growers market on Saturday mornings.

WWOOF New Zealand has around 1,000 hosts, who accommodate between 4,000–5,000 volunteers every year. Worldwide there are about 6,000 hosts and about 35,000 people volunteer each year.

While some countries allow WWOOFing as a tourist activity, New Zealand requires WWOOFers to have a working holiday visa.

Source: Willing Workers on Organic Farms

Table 18.20

| | | Trays | |
| | Area | submitted[1] | Trays sold |
Year	(hectares)	Million	
1997	10,243	60.6	56.2
1998	10,015	60.3	59.7
1999	10,234	52.3	51.8
2000	10,159	63.7	61.5
2001	10,100	66.3	65.1
2002	10,376	62.2	61.3
2003	10,580	65.1	64.6
2004	10,934	81.5	79.7
2005	11,464	84.7	82.3
2006	11,967	81.1	80.1

Title: **Kiwifruit production** — Year ending 31 March

(1) This is the number of trays received from registered suppliers; 'trays sold' is the final sales number. The difference is the fruit loss in transit.

Source: ZESPRI International

Nine-year-old William Craig, a pupil at Ponsonby Primary School, takes a closer look at the new fruit sensation, the Flatto. The flat peach was grown in Central Otago by the Yummy Fruit Company in the summer of 2007/08.

Grape growing and wine production The area planted in production grapevines increased from 11,648 hectares in 2001, to 25,355 hectares in 2007. The major grape-producing areas are Marlborough (11,488 hectares), Hawke's Bay (4,346 hectares), and Gisborne (1,913 hectares). The 2007 season produced 205,000 tonnes of grapes, the most popular varieties being sauvignon blanc (102,426 tonnes), chardonnay (38,792 tonnes), and pinot noir (20,699 tonnes). The number of wineries in New Zealand increased from 262 in 1997, to 543 in 2007.

Table 18.19

Area planted in fruit[1]

At 30 June

Fruit	1994	1995	1996	2000[2]	2002	2003	2005	2007	Main regions
				Hectares					
Citrus									
Grapefruit/goldfruit	116	117	115	117	82	71	48	41	Auckland, Bay of Plenty
Lemons	263	S	330	339	364	362	334	332	Northland
Mandarins	619	654	637	946	911	832	675	691	Northland, Gisborne
Oranges	789	757	607	597	573	S	541	681	Gisborne, Northland
Tangelos	295	316	230	167	163	129	103	89	Gisborne
Pipfruit									
Apples	15,257	15,916	15,819	14,114	11,717	12,150	10,982	9,247	Hawke's Bay, Tasman
Pears	1,279	1,266	1,151	958	952	906	719	694	Hawke's Bay, Tasman
Nashi (Asian pears)	418	413	313	185	119	128	S	97	Waikato, Tasman
Stone fruit									
Apricots	844	831	735	759	636	597	480	457	Otago
Nectarines	667	705	559	618	528	503	433	377	Otago, Hawke's Bay
Peaches	714	738	756	725	808	730	547	527	Hawke's Bay
Plums	342	336	303	408	394	S	333	413	Hawke's Bay
Cherries	274	353	339	535	550	569	524	520	Otago, Marlborough
Berry fruit									
Blackcurrants	720	714	614	834	1,308	S	1,311	1,275	Tasman
Blueberries	357	377	280	348	450	449	567	522	Waikato
Boysenberries	231	222	227	263	239	238	196	334	Tasman
Raspberries	199	S	S	254	302	204	190	150	Tasman, Canterbury
Strawberries	331	S	S	384	311	S	219	216	Auckland
Subtropicals									
Avocados	1,375	1,588	1,573	2,646	3,106	3,235	3,400	4,004	Bay of Plenty, Northland
Feijoas	161	S	138	217	198	S	181	251	Auckland
Kiwifruit	12,174	11,873	11,640	12,184	11,841	12,271	12,071	13,250	Bay of Plenty
Tamarillos	299	249	188	297	270	S	206	194	Northland, Bay of Plenty
Passionfruit	54	54	41	66	70	S	66	47	Bay of Plenty
Grapes (outdoor)[3]	7,160	7,382	7,627	12,665	17,300	19,646	24,793	29,616	Marlborough, Hawke's Bay, Gisborne
Persimmons	412	428	361	384	282	S	195	180	Auckland

(1) Area planted in fruit was not counted in the 1997, 1998, 1999, 2001, 2004 and 2006 agricultural surveys. (2) Use caution when making comparisons using 2000 data, as a different survey population was used. (3) Areas of grapes planted for activities classified to winemaking are not included.
Symbol: S suppressed due to poor statistical quality.

Source: Statistics New Zealand

Exports of wine increased from 22.3 million litres (worth $246 million) in 2002, to 76.0 million litres (worth $698 million) in 2007. The United Kingdom, which imported 27.6 million litres of wine (worth $227 million) in the year ending 30 June 2007, was New Zealand's major export market. The United States and Australia are vying for second place. The United States imported 18.7 million litres (worth $176 million) and Australia imported 18.6 million litres (worth $180 million) in the June 2007 year.

Table 18.21

Wine industry statistics
Year ending 30 June

	1998	1999	2000	2001	2002	2003	2004	2005	2006	2007
Number of wineries	293	334	358	382	398	421	463	516	530	543
Producing area (hectares)	7,580	9,000	10,197	11,648	13,787	15,800	17,809	20,002	22,616	25,355
Average yield (tonnes per hectare)	10.3	8.9	7.8	6.1	8.6	4.8	9.1	6.9	8.2	8.3
Crushed (tonnes)	78,300	79,700	80,100	71,000	118,700	76,400	165,500	142,000	185,000	205,000
Total production (million litres)	60.6	60.2	60.2	53.3	89.0	55.0	119.2	102.0	133.2	147.6
Domestic sales (million litres)	38.2	38.4	41.3	36.2	32.6	35.3	35.5	45.0	50.0	51.0
Consumption per person (litres NZ wine)[1]	10.1	10.1	10.6	9.3	8.3	8.8	8.8	11.2	12.1	12.2
Export volume (million litres)	15.2	16.6	19.2	19.2	23.0	27.1	31.1	51.4	57.8	76.0
Export value ($million)	97.6	125.3	168.6	198.1	246.4	281.9	302.6	434.9	512.4	698.3

(1) Total domestic sales of New Zealand-made wine divided by the total population of New Zealand.

Source: New Zealand Winegrowers

Contributors and related websites

AsureQuality Ltd – www.asurequality.com

Dairy Companies Association of New Zealand – www.dcanz.com

Egg Producers Federation of New Zealand (Inc) – www.eggfarmers.org.nz

Fonterra – www.fonterra.com

Meat & Wool New Zealand – www.meatandwoolnz.com

Ministry of Agriculture and Forestry – www.maf.govt.nz

National Beekeepers' Association of New Zealand – www.nba.org.nz

New Zealand Food Safety Authority – www.nzfsa.govt.nz

New Zealand Meat Board – www.nzmeatboard.org

New Zealand Pork Industry Board – www.pork.co.nz

New Zealand Winegrowers – www.nzwine.com

Open Country Cheese Company Ltd – www.opencountry.co.nz

Poultry Industry Association of New Zealand – www.pianz.org.nz

Statistics New Zealand – www.stats.govt.nz

Summerfruit New Zealand – www.summerfruitnz.co.nz

Tatua Co-operative Dairy Company Ltd – www.tatua.com

Turners and Growers – www.turnersandgrowers.com

Varroa Agency Inc – www.varroa.org.nz

Westland Milk Products – www.westland.co.nz

ZESPRI International – www.zespri.com

Seafood Industry Council

The Marlborough Mussel Company's Intrepid *harvests mussels from a farm in Kenepuru Sound. Shellfish are grown using either suspended long-line ropes, inter-tidal trays, or baskets. The high quality of New Zealand's coastal waters and an abundance of plankton, along with sheltered harbours and inlets, create ideal conditions for shellfish aquaculture.*

19 | Forestry and fishing

Forestry

Forests cover around 30 percent, or 8 million hectares, of New Zealand's land area. Of this, about 6.2 million hectares are indigenous forests and 1.8 million hectares are planted production forests. In addition to tall forests, there are 2.7 million hectares of shrublands, some of which are reverting to indigenous forest.

Of the total planted production forest estate, 89 percent is radiata pine *(Pinus radiata)* and 6.3 percent is Douglas fir *(Pseudotsuga menziesii)*.

Hardwoods make up 2.7 percent of planted production forests, with eucalyptus species being the most important.

Although radiata pine is the principal plantation species, its properties make it is unsuitable for some uses, especially where decorative features, dimensional stability and surface hardness are important. Coupled with the declining supply of timber from indigenous forests, this has resulted in special-purpose species such as blackwood *(Acacia melanoxylon)*, macrocarpa *(Cupressus macrocarpa)* and black walnut *(Juglans nigra)* being established to meet specialist markets.

The average annual new planting rate in the 30 years to 2006 was 42,000 hectares. Between 1992 and 1998, new planting rates were high, averaging 69,000 hectares a year. However, since 1998 new planting has declined, with the 5,000 hectares planted in 2006 being the lowest amount since 1959.

Resources

Indigenous forests New Zealand's 6.2 million hectares of indigenous forests are mainly in mountain lands, particularly on the West Coast of the South Island. The forests contain more than 2,450 species of trees, shrubs and smaller plants. Tree species in these complex forests are beech, rimu, kauri, taraire and tawa.

Indigenous forests harbour about 330 species of native birds (some classed as endangered or threatened), two species of bat, reptiles, freshwater fish, amphibians and invertebrates – most notably land snails and giant weta. The forests are notable for their recreational, scientific, historical and scenic value, as well as for being a key part of New Zealand's ecological environment. The main threats to the forests are introduced animals and plants, and an increasing demand for access and recreational opportunities.

Offsetting greenhouse gas emissions with native forest regeneration

Growing trees and shrubs absorb carbon dioxide from the air, storing the carbon as wood and other biomass, and helping to offset greenhouse gas emissions. Much atte its. The programme is called EBEX21 (Emissions-Biodiversity-EXchange for the 21st century).

EBEX21 regeneration sites generally cover large land areas (over 100 hectares) of privately owned marginal land that has been retired from agricultural production. Rainfall, topography, and soil fertility must be adequate for natural regeneration. 'Shutting the gate' in perpetuity and allowing scrub and bush to develop into native forest has multiple environmental and economic benefits, including reducing soil erosion, protecting catchments, enhancing biodiversity, and helping to slow climate change. In addition, the farmer gets some financial return from the sale of carbon credits.

However, in return the farmer must sign a formal agreement ensuring:

- farm animals are removed and stray grazing is prevented
- weeds and pests are controlled
- no trees are harvested
- the landowner does not sell more carbon credits than are available.

Landcare Research scientists inspect the regenerating forest at all EBEX21 sites to quantify the carbon credits and biodiversity gains. Verification measurements are repeated every 5–10 years. The audited credits are then sold to businesses or individuals wanting to offset their greenhouse gas emissions. All revenue, after costs are subtracted, goes back to the landowner to help with ongoing maintenance of the carbon sink.

The land must also meet the Kyoto Protocol afforestation definitions, such as not being forested at 31 December 1989, and comply with the Permanent Forest Sink Initiative.

How natural regeneration works

In the early stages of forest regeneration, shrubs and small trees such as manuka and kanuka naturally populate the land. This shrub cover acts as a 'nurse' crop for other tree seedlings to establish, and at the same time accumulates carbon credits through carbon storage in the stems, roots, and leaf litter. As the seedlings grow bigger and emerge above the nurse crop, the nurse species decline in importance. The emerging trees continue to grow, eventually becoming a mature forest.

Source: www.ebex21.co.nz, Landcare Research

The Aucklander

Students at Auckland's Sunderland Primary School, Kylan Phillips (left), Jonathan Boulter, and Samuel Dobrec, have propagated kahikatea seedlings which they will donate back to New Zealand forests. Less than 1 percent of New Zealand's total forest production is from indigenous forests.

The Crown owns about 83 percent of indigenous forests, with the rest in private hands.

The Forest Act 1949, amended in 1993, promotes sustainable management of privately-owned indigenous forests. This means the forests are managed in a way that provides products and amenities in perpetuity. The Act does this by requiring private owners to have sustainable management plans and permits, by controlling indigenous timber input to sawmills, and by prohibiting indigenous woodchip and log exports.

Less than 1 percent of New Zealand's total forest production is from indigenous forests. Harvesting timber from State-owned indigenous forests, which was confined to the West Coast of the South Island, stopped in 2002, in line with government policy.

The 130,000 hectares of State-owned indigenous production forests on the West Coast are now conservation forests, administered by the Department of Conservation. A further 12,000 hectares in Southland, set aside for production and managed by State-owned enterprise Crown Forest Management Ltd, were transferred to the Waitutu Incorporation in 1996. These forests are managed under an approved sustainable forest management plan.

Harvesting and milling of 'salvage' timber from areas of farmland and non-natural forest, along with windblown and naturally dead trees from indigenous forests not being managed under an approved sustainable forest management regime, is permitted.

Approval is needed for a landowner to harvest and mill for personal use.

Figure 19.01

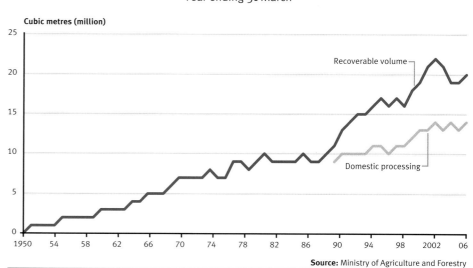

Wood supply
Year ending 31 March

Source: Ministry of Agriculture and Forestry

All sawmills milling timber from indigenous forests must be registered, and they are restricted to processing timber from approved sources.

Exports of indigenous forest products are limited to those sourced from an area managed under an approved sustainable forest management plan or permit, or where the product is manufactured to a finished form.

Planted production forests Trees planted in the second boom of afforestation (1970 through to the mid 1980s) are now a valuable resource for large-scale use, providing opportunities to maximise the economic return from tree growing. Special-purpose plantation species are being planted by small-scale forest growers on suitable sites. Uses for specialist timbers include furniture, cabinet work, turnery, joinery, veneers and boat-building.

Forest ownership

Many early plantation forests were developed by the State, but ownership has since moved increasingly to the private sector. Today, approximately 92 percent of New Zealand's plantation resource is owned by private or publicly-listed companies.

Central government owns 2 percent of the forest area, managed primarily by the Ministry of Agriculture.

Local authorities own a further 3 percent of the area, while the remainder is owned by a large number of private owners, including Māori trusts. Small private investors and landowners continue to develop an expanding area of planted production forests.

An agreement among the Crown, the Māori Council, and the Federation of Māori Authorities provides security of tenure for buyers of State plantations, and protects the interests of Māori with claims before the Waitangi Tribunal.

Purchasers have the right to use the land for the time it takes for any existing tree crop to reach maturity and be harvested. The right to use the land is automatically extended by one year each year, unless notice of termination is given.

If a termination notice is given, the buyer has time to harvest tree crops planted before the notice was given.

In the event of a successful Māori claim to the Waitangi Tribunal, the government will give a termination notice to the purchaser, and compensate the claimant for the rights the purchaser retains until the end of the termination period.

Table 19.01

Forest planting and production
Year ending 31 March

Year	New area planted State	New area planted Private	Production Rough-sawn timber	Production Wood pulp[1]	Production Paper and paperboard
	Hectares (000)		Cubic metres (000)	Tonnes	
1930	22	15	668	..	..
1935	5	7	575	..	..
1940	2	..	793	221	13,079
1945	..	0	803	15,681	20,949
1950	2	1	1,131	21,781	22,136
1955	3	2	1,453	53,016	40,917
1960	4	2	1,638	221,408	164,255
1965	8	5	1,739	370,499	316,104
1970	15	11	1,803	521,654	445,976
1975	22	23	2,086	843,244	546,834
1980	17	21	2,000	1,122,456	673,853
1985	18	30	2,306	1,144,911	770,098
1990	0	16	2,121	1,233,809	757,371
1995	0	74	2,955	1,360,389	876,187
2000	0	34	3,806	1,527,565	829,812
2001	0	30	3,848	1,572,277	871,607
2002	0	22	3,864	1,523,730	846,727
2003	0	20	4,436	1,512,602	851,663
2004	0	11	4,209	1,462,656	845,422
2005	..	6	4,407	1,586,790	921,339
2006	..	5 P	4,215	1,561,173	940,460
2007	..	..	4,369	1,528,991	871,946

(1) Chemical and mechanical wood pulp.

Symbols: P provisional .. figure not available

Source: Ministry of Agriculture and Forestry

Footprint for forestry

In December 2007, the Crown research institute Scion was awarded a contract to measure greenhouse gas (GHG) emissions, or the carbon footprint, of the entire forestry industry supply chain.

The year-long project involves analysing GHG emissions from initial forest plantings and management through the timber manufacturing and distribution stages. It also incorporates the end-of-life scenarios when carbon is potentially released back into the atmosphere.

By working with industry partners such as the Wood Processors Association, Scion can develop case studies to provide the methodology for measuring across a range of products – including particleboard and rough-sawn timber.

Scion had already conducted life-cycle assessment research in forest plantation operations, which has provided data, models and tools from that end of the forestry life cycle. Senior scientist Dr Barbara Nebel says Scion's focus has moved to what happens from the moment the timber is harvested, to when it is disposed of.

"We are also including the carbon footprint created from the use of biomass to create bioenergy; for example, the use of timber waste residues to create alternatives to coal for heating systems," Dr Nebel says.

"We have an absolute commitment to ensure that any bio-based alternatives do not create as many problems as they resolve."

This research provides the type of information a company can use to improve their 'bottom line'. By giving end-users clear information on the 'greenness' of products, New Zealand wood can gain a competitive advantage in the tight global market.

[Scion is also contributing to a project to determine the carbon footprint of an office building, along with the University of Canterbury.]

Source: Scion

New Zealand has 8 million hectares of forest, 1.8 million of which are planted production forest. Of this, 89 percent is radiata pine. Purpose-grown softwood forests could provide the feedstock to produce ethanol and make New Zealand more self-sufficient in transport biofuel.

Forest products and timber

Forest products

Pulp and paper The pulp and paper industry is concentrated mainly near large production forests on the North Island's volcanic plateau. All eight pulp and paper plants are located in the North Island and four of them are integrated with sawmills to make full use of the wood.

There are four main pulp and paper companies:

- Norske Skog Tasman Ltd operates the Tasman pulp and paper mill at Kawerau, in the Bay of Plenty. The plant produces mechanical pulp, newsprint and directory paper.
- Carter Holt Harvey operates pulp and paper plants in New Zealand. The Penrose plant in south Auckland produces corrugated medium paper from recycled waste paper. At the large Kinleith site, near Tokoroa, bleached and unbleached market kraft pulp, linerboards and corrugated paper mediums are produced. A plant at Whakatane produces paperboard from mechanical pulp, outsourced kraft pulp, and waste paper-based pulps. A tissue plant at Kawerau has a chemical thermo-mechanical pulp mill that manufactures a wide range of tissue, towelling and speciality grades.
- Pan Pac Forest Products operates an integrated sawmill and thermo-mechanical pulp mill at Whirinaki, near Napier.
- Winstone Pulp International has a chemical thermo-mechanical pulp mill at Karioi, near Waiouru. The plant uses wood from surrounding forests, as well as sawmill residues.

Recent annual production volumes of pulp and paper products are shown in table 19.02, while table 19.04 shows production volumes of wood panel products.

Table 19.02

Pulp and paper production						
Year ending 31 March						
	Wood pulp		Paper and paperboard			
	Chemical[1]	Mechanical[2]	Newsprint	Other printing and writing paper	Other paper and paperboard	**Total**
Year				Tonnes		
1998	675,453	736,712	393,545	13,556	472,475	**879,576**
1999	645,032	755,707	383,372	11,586	419,356	**814,314**
2000	753,885	773,680	360,623	10,285	458,904	**829,812**
2001	744,991	827,286	380,614	4,155	486,838	**871,607**
2002	723,054	800,676	334,058	0	512,669	**846,727**
2003	684,187	828,415	355,569	0	496,094	**851,663**
2004	654,291	808,365	368,421	0	477,001	**845,422**
2005	727,309	859,481	379,628	0	541,711	**921,339**
2006	742,800	818,373	367,064	0	573,396	**940,460**
2007	784,995	743,996	292,015	0	579,931	**871,946**

(1) Includes semi-chemical pulp. (2) Includes groundwood pulp, thermo-mechanical and chemithermo-mechanical pulp.

Source: Ministry of Agriculture and Forestry

Overseas trade in forest products

Exports of forest products were valued at $3,436 million in the year ending 30 June 2007, up from $2,957 million in 2006. The last trade year to show a higher value was 2003. Australia was the main destination for New Zealand's forest product exports (22.2 percent of the total), followed by the People's Republic of China (14.9 percent) and Japan (14.8 percent).

Table 19.03 shows the annual volumes of timber exports since 1998, while figure 19.02 indicates the proportions of exports going to different countries in 2007.

Table 19.03

Timber exports						
By volume						
Year ending 30 June						
	Sawn timber					Logs and poles
	From natural forest	Radiata pine	Douglas fir	Other	**Total**	
Year	Cubic metres (000)					
1998	1	1,105	16	30	**1,152**	4,657
1999	1	1,216	61	21	**1,299**	5,194
2000	1	1,400	26	55	**1,482**	6,179
2001	1	1,353	35	103	**1,492**	6,177
2002	1	1,595	32	96	**1,724**	7,604
2003	1	1,661	18	129	**1,809**	8,423
2004	1	1,556	32	99	**1,689**	6,298
2005	1	1,701	43	91	**1,836**	5,077
2006	1	1,707	62	65	**1,835**	5,198
2007 P	1	1,814	70	49	**1,934**	6,267

Symbol: P provisional

Source: Ministry of Agriculture and Forestry

Imports of forest products were valued at $1,442 million in the year ending 30 June 2007, compared with $1,393 million in 2006. New Zealand's imports are split between softwoods (55 percent) and hardwoods (45 percent).

Sawn timber imports are mainly tropical hardwoods, Australian hardwoods, and North American softwoods. Imported sawn timbers generally have specialist applications, such as weatherboards with a natural finish, decorative furniture, panelling and boat-building.

Durable Australian hardwoods are imported for use as large poles, cross-arms, and wharf, bridge and construction timbers. Oregon pine, redwood and western red cedar are imported from North America for structural uses, exterior joinery and weatherboards.

Paper, paperboard, and manufactured articles of paper and paperboard accounted for nearly 70 percent of the total forestry product imports (by value) in the year ended June 2007. Of the many paper or paperboard products, one of the largest groups was nappies, sanitary towels and similar products, with $73 million worth of imports.

Table 19.05 shows annual volumes of timber imported into New Zealand since 1998.

Logs are stacked at Wellington's CentrePort, ready to be loaded for export. Exports of forest products were valued at nearly $3.5 billion in the year to June 2007.

Table 19.04

Panel production				
Year ending 31 December				
	Veneer	Plywood(1)	Particle-board	Fibre-board
Year	Cubic metres			
1998	292,171	189,447	196,395	613,345
1999	285,825	192,445	169,569	600,673
2000	378,282	239,947	188,054	744,879
2001	401,590	243,702	204,524	801,493
2002	460,619	263,332	198,347	821,994
2003	601,600	321,655	209,977	883,117
2004	628,747	345,102	230,378	873,112
2005	694,301	408,635	229,971	845,663
2006	655,206	403,808	238,205	906,938
2007	688,312	421,794	256,239	836,755

(1) Includes laminated veneer lumber.

Source: Ministry of Agriculture and Forestry

Figure 19.02

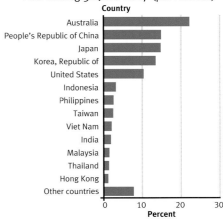

Forestry exports
Year ending 30 June 2007 (provisional)

Country: Australia, People's Republic of China, Japan, Korea, Republic of, United States, Indonesia, Philippines, Taiwan, Viet Nam, India, Malaysia, Thailand, Hong Kong, Other countries

Percent (0, 10, 20, 30)

Source: Ministry of Agriculture and Forestry

Table 19.05

Timber imports				
By volume				
Year ending 30 June				
	Hard-woods	Soft-woods	**Total**	Logs and poles total
Year	Cubic metres (000)			
1998	11	19	**30**	3
1999	12	15	**27**	4
2000	13	20	**33**	4
2001	14	15	**29**	6
2002	17	13	**30**	6
2003	17	17	**34**	5
2004	20	21	**41**	3
2005	22	30	**52**	3
2006	23	26	**49**	6
2007 P	23	28	**51**	5

Symbol: P provisional

Source: Ministry of Agriculture and Forestry

Table 19.07

Overseas trade in forest products
Year ending 30 June

Year	Wood and wood products	Wood pulp	Paper and paper products	Total
	$(000)			
Imports[1]				
1998	202,980	8,880	666,511	**878,371**
1999	217,648	18,710	738,154	**974,512**
2000	263,995	7,596	832,263	**1,103,854**
2001	272,003	10,491	909,663	**1,192,157**
2002	276,676	12,327	933,806	**1,222,809**
2003	308,889	6,654	924,097	**1,239,640**
2004	343,694	3,701	934,183	**1,281,578**
2005	671,146	3,707	657,769	**1,332,622**
2006	707,023	6,799	679,641	**1,393,463**
2007 P	742,166	7,820	691,492	**1,441,478**
Exports[2]				
1998	1,501,981	351,850	489,971	**2,343,802**
1999	1,571,928	370,892	535,816	**2,478,636**
2000	2,104,442	609,798	631,579	**3,345,819**
2001	2,289,699	620,349	695,957	**3,606,005**
2002	2,491,276	518,188	685,278	**3,694,742**
2003	2,475,122	433,449	597,446	**3,506,017**
2004	2,155,889	476,515	591,607	**3,224,011**
2005	2,184,239	477,610	280,056	**2,941,905**
2006	2,182,719	472,867	300,950	**2,956,536**
2007 P	2,468,456	621,785	345,562	**3,435,803**

(1) Imports valued cif (costs including insurance and freight). (2) Exports valued fob (free on board) at New Zealand ports, re-exports included.

Symbol: P provisional

Source: Ministry of Agriculture and Forestry

Timber

Logs (roundwood) In the year ending 31 March 2007, logs from planted production forests supplied 20.0 million cubic metres (99.9 percent) of total roundwood removals.

Approximately 264 sawmills, and 11 veneer, seven plywood, and six fibreboard mills were supported during the year. Roundwood production does not include firewood.

Sawn timber Radiata pine accounts for about 95 percent of the total cut of exotic timber, Douglas fir for 3.5 percent, and other conifers for most of the remainder. Less than 1 percent of New Zealand's sawn timber production comes from indigenous forests, and this proportion has reached the point where only a small, sustained yield in native timber is possible for special purposes.

Table 19.06

Overseas trade in pulp and paper
By volume
Year ending 30 June

Year	Wood pulp	News-print	Other paper and paperboard[1]
			Tonnes
Imports			
1998	11,209	128	247,463
1999	21,662	105	302,973
2000	6,895	467	339,924
2001	8,654	105	311,400
2002	12,543	321	379,506
2003	6,501	4,296	421,618
2004	4,030	8,686	441,894
2005	3,397	10,470	480,576
2006	6,104	5,410	481,290
2007 P	7,332	16,361	466,464
Exports			
1998	626,579	262,060	171,422
1999	622,636	246,386	201,648
2000	687,624	228,022	252,070
2001	728,501	216,494	244,744
2002	783,891	205,227	293,039
2003	708,298	213,374	254,433
2004	787,644	219,720	323,366
2005	857,203	47	350,688
2006	794,822	19	378,070
2007 P	842,979	29	379,916

(1) Products manufactured from paper and paperboard are excluded.

Symbol: P provisional

Source: Ministry of Agriculture and Forestry

Otago Daily Times

Dunedin wood fuel and garden landscaping supplier Rodney Hogg in one of his wood drying hot houses. Dry wood burns more efficiently than damp. Wood heats many New Zealand homes, although some urban areas are now regulating against wood burners to limit air pollution.

Table 19.08

Roundwood removals from New Zealand forests
Year ending 31 March

| Year | Natural forest removals | Planted production forest removals | | | | | Total removals |
		Saw logs	Pulp logs	Export logs	Other[1]	Total	
1998	75	5,810	3,152	5,594	2,074	16,630	**16,705**
1999	125	5,865	2,971	4,803	2,050	15,689	**15,814**
2000	76	6,985	3,049	5,806	2,280	18,120	**18,196**
2001	55	7,221	3,566	5,917	2,528	19,232	**19,287**
2002	57	7,326	3,504	7,382	2,671	20,883	**20,940**
2003	38	8,349	3,288	8,087	2,689	22,413	**22,451**
2004	31	7,718	3,057	7,313	2,767	20,855	**20,886**
2005	26	8,041	3,287	5,123	2,783	19,234	**19,260**
2006	24	7,607	3,234	5,067	2,859	18,767	**18,792**
2007	18	7,891	3,284	5,973	2,872	20,020	**20,038**

(1) Includes peeler logs, small logs and export chips.

Source: Ministry of Agriculture and Forestry

Table 19.09

Sawn timber production
By species
Year ending 31 March

| Species | 1998 | 1999 | 2000 | 2001 | 2002 | 2003 | 2004 | 2005 | 2006 | 2007 |
	Cubic metres (000)									
Natural forest										
Rimu and miro	28	30	22	17	13	5	5	5	0	3
Kauri	2	1	1	1	1	1	1	1	0	0
Tōtara	1	0	0	0	1	1	0	0	0	0
Kahikatea	0	0	1	0	0	1	0	0	0	0
Tawa	1	1	1	1	0	0	0	0	0	0
Beech	5	4	6	8	13	10	8	7	0	6
Other	1	2	0	1	1	2	1	0	0	0
Total	**38**	**38**	**30**	**28**	**28**	**19**	**16**	**13**	**0**	**9**
Planted production forest										
Radiata pine	2,995	2,996	3,583	3,625	3,678	4,214	3,980	4,193	4,018	4,171
Douglas fir	105	143	134	136	124	164	178	167	156	155
Eucalypts	2	3	4	3	3	3	4	3	5	3
Other	56	47	54	56	31	36	32	30	25	30
Total	**3,157**	**3,188**	**3,776**	**3,820**	**3,836**	**4,417**	**4,194**	**4,394**	**4,203**	**4,360**
Total all species	**3,195**	**3,226**	**3,806**	**3,848**	**3,864**	**4,436**	**4,209**	**4,407**	**4,215**	**4,369**

Note: Figures may not add up to stated totals due to rounding.

Source: Ministry of Agriculture and Forestry

Biosecurity

MAF Biosecurity New Zealand is the part of the Ministry of Agriculture and Forestry which leads the country's biosecurity system. It facilitates international trade, protects the health of New Zealanders, and ensures the welfare of the environment, flora and fauna, marine life, and Māori resources.

There are around 1,000 full-time and part-time staff based across New Zealand and overseas. MAF Biosecurity gathers and exchanges information about emerging risks around the world, manages risk before and at the border (including export trade inspection), and manages animal welfare and the risks and impacts of pests and diseases that are already established in New Zealand.

Fisheries

Fishery resources

New Zealand's exclusive economic zone (EEZ) is one of the largest in the world. At 1.3 million square nautical miles, it covers an area nearly 15 times New Zealand's landmass. In spite of the size of the zone, the waters are relatively deep and are not particularly rich in nutrients. Because of this, the average productivity of fishery resources tends to be low.

Less than one-third of New Zealand's EEZ is shallower than 1,000 metres, the area where most fish resources occur. Only 5 percent is coastal water shallower than 200 metres.

There are more than 8,000 described marine species in New Zealand waters, about 100 of which are commercially significant. Species include shallow water shellfish, open water migratory pelagic fish, and deepwater species living more than a kilometre below the surface.

Seeking a methyl bromide replacement

Methyl bromide is used as a quarantine fumigant around the world and has been important in maintaining biosecurity. But it is also an ozone-depleting gas and, while quarantine and pre-shipment use of methyl bromide is allowed under the Montreal Protocol, countries are being encouraged to reduce use.

The Ozone Layer Protection Act 1996 restricts the use of ozone-depleting chemicals in New Zealand. From January 2008, there have been no methyl bromide imports for non-quarantine use.

About 73 percent of methyl bromide imported is used to treat logs and sawn timber. Fumigating with methyl bromide is a market access requirement for $350–450 million of logs and sawn timber exports each year. New Zealand's own biosecurity status also relies significantly on fumigating infested imports with methyl bromide.

Research into finding cost effective alternatives to methyl bromide is being carried out in New Zealand and overseas but progress has been slow. However, New Zealand would be using twice as much gas were it not for a breakthrough with an alternative being used to fumigate logs to China, along with a reduction negotiated in the fumigation rate of sawn timber to Australia. Negotiations are also underway with India to replace methyl bromide for two-thirds of the log shipments going there.

In February 2008, 28 possible alternatives to methyl bromide came under scrutiny when over 90 government and industry representatives met in Wellington to review options for use at the border. Most possibilities are not currently registered for use in New Zealand.

Advice came from United States and Australian experts, but there is no 'one-stop shop' to replace methyl bromide. Possible options are a 'toolbox' of tailored treatments. Any treatment advances need to be specific to New Zealand's commodities and exports – which require the treatment to be acceptable to trading partners.

Any replacement must: be cost effective, not be detrimental to the health and safety of operators and the public, have equivalent effectiveness to methyl bromide, not have a detrimental effect on the environment, be internationally accepted by trading partners, and be effective over a range of commodities.

A working group, formed to ensure industry and government coordination, and the development of a comprehensive response strategy, has implemented a voluntary levy on each kilogram of gas used – to help fund research for alternatives. And MAF Biosecurity New Zealand is collaborating internationally to investigate other treatments.

Source: MAF Biosecurity New Zealand

Plastic protects Fiordland

In winter 2007, divers braved the port of Bluff's chilly waters to wrap wharf piles and structures in plastic sheeting – not to keep them warm, but to protect Fiordland's precious marine environment from invasive pests.

The plastic contains and suffocates fouling pests such as the seaweed *Undaria*, already found in the harbour. This prevents them attaching to boat hulls and being transported from Bluff to Fiordland.

Where marine pests become established outside of their native range they can reduce the biodiversity of the local marine environment by displacing native plant and animal species.

MAF Biosecurity New Zealand (MAFBNZ) hopes that the wrapping treatment, combined with encouraging boat owners to keep their vessels clean, will prevent *Undaria* reinfection and also prevent other pests catching a ride.

MAFBNZ has already used this technique with some success in the Marlborough Sounds. By collaborating with the local marine farming industry and local authorities, they are using it to help control the spread of the sea squirt *Didemnum vexillum* which threatens the environment and mussel farms.

Source: MAFBNZ

Commercial fish resource valued at $3.8 billion

The asset value of New Zealand's commercial fish resource, as managed under the quota management system (QMS), is estimated to be $3.8 billion. This information comes from the *Fish Monetary Stock Account 1996–2007*, released in 2008.

From 1996 to 2007, New Zealand's commercial fish resource is estimated to have increased in value by nearly 40 percent, up from $2.7 billion in 1996 to $3.8 billion in 2007. Although the number of species managed under the QMS has also increased over this period, from 32 to 96, 20 species are responsible for the majority of the total value. These 20 species contributed 90 percent of the asset value of the commercial fish resource in 2007.

Due to data limitations, this valuation currently excludes recreational or customary catch, species reared under aquaculture conditions, and commercial species not managed under the QMS. These are areas for future development within the report.

The *Fish Monetary Stock Account 1996–2007* is part of an environmental series measuring the reliance of New Zealand's economy on natural resources.

Source: Statistics New Zealand

Otago Daily Times

Second mate Jacinda Fowler tastes one of the first oysters brought into Bluff at the start of the 2007 oyster season. Oysters are one of about 100 commercially significant marine species.

Fisheries range from numerous, but mostly small, resources of subtropical species in the north, through moderate resources of many temperate species on the shelves around the main islands, to large resources of a few cool water species on the extensive plateau to the south-east and east of the country.

Fisheries management

Fisheries within New Zealand's EEZ are a 'common property' resource and the government has an important role in ensuring their use is sustainable. In practice, this means ensuring the fisheries are not overfished, while balancing the competing demands of user groups.

Most New Zealanders use the fisheries as a source of food, a place of work, or for relaxation at some time. This places increasing demands on the fisheries. For example, in less than 30 years the commercial fishing industry has expanded from a small, domestic industry to a $1.5 billion-a-year export business.

New Zealand commercial fisheries are managed under a quota management system (QMS) where individual transferable quota for fish stocks are owned by commercial fishers. Under the QMS a total allowable commercial catch (TACC) is set annually for each fish stock and a commercial fisher's catch is balanced against their annual catch entitlement (ACE) holding. ACE is generated annually from the number of quota shares held by an individual. ACE can also be traded.

The main goals of the QMS are to set sustainable total allowable catches (TACs) and TACCs, and to improve economic efficiency in the fishing industry. The QMS also provides security for participants in the fishing industry, enabling them to invest in harvesting and processing capacity.

The QMS applies throughout New Zealand's EEZ for almost all commercial species. Catch limits (TACs), and TACCs are reviewed regularly to see if the TAC or TACC for a fish stock needs to change. The review process involves considering the latest fisheries research and stock assessments, and consulting with representatives from the commercial fishing industry, Māori, recreational fishing groups and environmental organisations.

Table 19.10 shows TACCs for all fish stocks for the 2007/08 fishing year.

Customary fishing regulations

The Fisheries Claims Settlement Act 1992 provided a legislated settlement of fishing claims with two main impacts. First, it addressed the right of Māori to a commercial stake in New Zealand's fishing industry and a role in its management. The second part of the settlement is less well known – it addressed claims to a non-commercial, customary fishing right and provided an input into fisheries management.

As a result of the second part of the settlement, customary fishing regulations were developed by the Crown and Māori. The regulations aim to provide effectively for customary non-commercial fishing, while ensuring sustainability of the resource.

Those given permission to take fish under the customary fishing regulations cannot trade the fish, exchange the fish for money, or accept any other form of payment.

The definition of customary food-gathering in the regulations refers to traditional rights confirmed by the Treaty of Waitangi and the 1992 Settlement Act. Regulations for the South Island were effective from April 1998, and in the North and Chatham Islands from February 1999.

The regulations cover non-commercial customary fishing only, and do not remove the right of tangata whenua ('people of the land') to catch recreational limits under amateur fishing regulations. They do not provide for commercial fishing. In the North and Chatham Islands, fish taken in fresh water are not covered by the regulations, but they are in the South Island, provided the species is managed under the Fisheries Act.

The establishment of mātaitai reserves is also covered by the regulations. These reserves provide a tool for tangata whenua to manage all non-commercial fishing in some of their traditional fishing-grounds. Generally, there is no commercial fishing within mātaitai reserves.

The regulations apply only where Māori have appointed tangata tiaki for South Island areas, and tangata kaitiaki for the North and Chatham Islands. These individuals, or office-holders, can authorise customary fishing within their area/rohe moana, in accordance with tikanga Māori. They are chosen by the area's tangata whenua and, following a submission process and if necessary a dispute resolution process, their appointments are confirmed by the Minister of Fisheries.

In the regulations, tangata whenua is defined as the whānau (family), hapū (sub-tribe) or iwi (tribe) that hold manawhenua manamoana (status and rights) over a particular area.

By 31 December 2007, 107 tangata tiaki had been appointed in the South Island and 214 tangata kaitiaki in the North Island.

Guide to buying fish

When Forest & Bird updated its *Best Fish Guide* in November 2007 seven more fish species joined the red list of unsustainable fisheries, but several also came close to earning a sustainability tick.

The guide aims to help consumers make the best choices for the sustainability of the marine environment when they buy fish.

Kina, anchovies, pilchards, sprats and blue mackerel were within 1–2 points of making it into the green list of fisheries – those that are sustainable. No species ranked as sustainable, but with improvements to fisheries management some could make the green list in future.

Since the previous guide in 2005/06, seven more fish species have joined the list of fisheries that are environmentally unsustainable – red snapper, moonfish, striped marlin, blue shark, mako shark, porbeagle shark and lookdown dory.

Orange roughy was again ranked as the worst fishery for environmental sustainability. Years of over-fishing

have taken orange roughy populations to the point of collapse, and the method used to catch orange roughy inflicts severe damage on the marine ecosystem.

Fisheries are ranked in the *Best Fish Guide* according to management of fish stocks, levels of habitat damage, by-catch of marine mammals and seabirds, and adequacy of monitoring.

Worst 10	Best 10
Orange roughy	Kina
Southern bluefin tuna	Anchovy
Oreo	Pilchards
Porbeagle shark	Sprats
Mako shark	Blue mackerel
Pacific bluefin tuna	Skipjack tuna
Blue shark	Garfish
Hoki	Yellow-eyed mullet
Snapper	Cockles
Swordfish	Kahawai

Source: Forest & Bird

Table 19.10

Total allowable commercial catch
2007/08 fishing year

Species	Sum of TACCs[1] (tonnes)	Number of stocks
Arrow squid	127,332	4
Hoki	90,010	2
Jack mackerel	60,547	4
Southern blue whiting	36,948	5
Barracouta	32,672	5
Ling	21,977	8
Oreo	18,610	5
Orange roughy	13,612	8
Hake	13,211	4
Spiny dogfish	12,660	7
Blue mackerel	11,550	5
Silver warehou	10,380	4
Red cod	8,278	5
Tarakihi	6,439	8
Snapper	6,357	6
Flatfish	5,419	5
Stargazer	5,411	8
Gurnard	5,047	6
Blue warehou	4,512	6
Frostfish	4,019	10
Trevally	3,933	5
Cardinalfish	3,751	10
White warehou	3,735	9
School shark	3,436	8
Bluenose	3,233	6
Other (71 species)	59,630	474
Total	**572,712**	**627**

(1) Total allowable commercial catch.

Source: Ministry of Fisheries

Table 19.11

Registered commercial fishing vessels
At 30 September

Year	Foreign licensed	Foreign chartered	Domestic
1993	25	167	2,707
1994	32	63	2,569
1995	32	54	2,575
1996	22	55	2,458
1997	16	59	2,170
1998	17	52	1,965
1999	10	46	1,861
2000	0	37	1,752
2001	0	36	1,688
2002	0	37	1,674
2003	0	37	1,565
2004	0	35	1,474
2005	0	32	1,381
2006	0	30	1,335

Source: Ministry of Fisheries

Seafood Industry Council

New Zealand's fish stock assessment process is the basis for reviewing catch limits for species subject to quota. Safe fishing levels are worked out by using the concept of maximum sustainable yield – the largest average annual catch that can be taken over time without reducing the stock's productive potential.

The quantity of fish that can be taken for each fish stock by both commercial and non-commercial fishers is the total allowable catch (TAC). An allowance is made to provide for recreational fishing and customary Māori uses, then the remainder is available to the commercial sector as the total allowable commercial catch (TACC). This defines the total quantity of each fish stock that the commercial fishing industry can catch that year.

The Minister of Fisheries sets the TAC and TACC for all fish stocks, based on information supplied by the Ministry of Fisheries and other interest groups, such as the commercial fishing industry, recreational fishers, Māori and conservation groups.

The 96 species or species groups managed under the quota management system (QMS) in 2007, consist of 618 different stocks. TACs and TACCs for these stocks are regularly reviewed.

Working groups convened by the Ministry of Fisheries assess individual species, or groups of species. Their main task is to estimate the sustainable yield from each fish stock, and to determine whether current TACs/TACCs and actual catch levels are sustainable. They may also deal with more general issues, such as marine recreational fishing, or the impact of fishing on non-fish species such as marine mammals or seabirds.

The groups prepare an assessment report for each stock in the QMS. When new information results in substantial changes to previous assessments, the report is referred to the Fishery Assessment Plenary for further consideration. All group members can take part, giving those with an interest in New Zealand's fisheries direct input. The outcome is a document summarising the state of each stock.

From here, economic, social and environmental considerations are added to the scientific assessments to determine whether TACs or TACCs should be adjusted and, if so, how quickly. Once adjustments are made, the process starts again.

Source: Ministry of Fisheries

Māori Fisheries Trust Te Ohu Kaimoana

The Māori Fisheries Act, passed in September 2004, provides a way fisheries assets handed to Māori to settle Treaty of Waitangi commercial fishing claims can be returned to iwi (tribes). The Act put in place the allocation model devised by the former Treaty of Waitangi Fisheries Commission (Te Ohu Kai Moana) through almost 12 years of discussion and consultation with iwi.

Te Ohu Kai Moana Trust (Te Ohu) was created to hold the assets until allocation and transfer to iwi. The Act also provided for the creation of Aotearoa Fisheries Limited (AFL) as the commercial entity for those assets retained and managed centrally. The commercial fishing activities previously owned by the commission were transferred to AFL when the Act took effect.

The model allocates inshore fish stocks, deepwater fish stocks, income shares in AFL, and cash previously held by the commission to iwi. Each iwi's share of the Māori fisheries settlement is calculated according to the length of coastline each iwi has within its rohe (tribal district), and the size of its population.

Under the Act, iwi must meet certain structural and constitutional requirements before becoming eligible to receive assets. Once these requirements are met, an iwi organisation is approved as a mandated iwi organisation and becomes entitled to receive assets.

Two other trusts also form part of the settlement model – Te Putea Whakatupu Trust, to promote educational advancement of Māori in the fishing industry and wider community, and Te Wai Māori Trust, to advance Māori interests in freshwater fisheries.

Te Ohu provides an advisory and policy-making role on behalf of iwi, on marine and freshwater environment matters. Te Ohu also administers the Māori Commercial Aquaculture Settlement Trust (Takutai Trust). The aquaculture settlement provided for iwi with a coastal rohe to receive up to 20 percent of new marine farming space approved, from September 1992. Takutai Trust holds and distributes to iwi the aquaculture assets transferred to it in accordance with the aquaculture settlement.

Since 2004, Te Ohu has facilitated the transfer of more than $400 million worth of fisheries settlement assets to 46 mandated iwi organisations.

New Zealand control

New Zealanders and New Zealand companies have held control of New Zealand's fisheries resources since introduction of the quota management system in 1986.

At 30 September 2006, there were 1,335 domestic-registered commercial fishing vessels. There were also 30 foreign-registered vessels working under charter to New Zealand companies. This charter fleet participates in high-volume seasonal fisheries such as southern blue whiting, jack mackerel and squid.

The New Zealand Herald

Most of the salmon farmed at Mount Cook Salmon in Central Otago are exported. The floating farm, in a canal that is part of the local hydro electricity scheme, holds around 200,000 salmon, which are harvested at about three years. Each day passing tourists buy 60–90 fish, which are sold on-site.

Seafood industry

Exports

The seafood industry generated more than $1.25 billion in export receipts in the year ending 31 December 2007.

The top export species were squid, mussels, hoki and rock lobster. Squid catch and its unit price have both gone up, and the New Zealand squid fishery is experiencing significant growth. It is currently the most valuable export species.

Mussels have had significant growth in export receipts since 2003, to become the second most-valuable export species as a result of stronger market prices. Hoki has shown a downward trend, following reductions in the total allowable commercial catch in 2003 and 2004.

The value of seafood exports has decreased since 2002, largely due to a resurgent New Zealand dollar. On 23 July 2007, the US dollar reached its highest rate in more than 20 years, at US80 cents to NZ$1. A stronger New Zealand dollar means that sales denominated in US dollars are worth less when the proceeds are repatriated in New Zealand dollars. The United States is New Zealand's fourth biggest market after Australia, the European Union and Hong Kong.

Table 19.12

Seafood exports[1]
By principal species
Year ending 31 December

Species	2002 Quantity Tonnes (000)	2002 Value $ (million)	2003 Quantity Tonnes (000)	2003 Value $ (million)	2004 Quantity Tonnes (000)	2004 Value $ (million)	2005 Quantity Tonnes (000)	2005 Value $ (million)	2006 Quantity Tonnes (000)	2006 Value $ (million)	2007[2] Quantity Tonnes (000)	2007[2] Value $ (million)
Squid	41.4	86.2	36.0	68.6	69.8	171.8	70.9	168.1	56.8	118.0	69.9	196.7
Mussels	28.8	185.4	28.0	133.3	30.3	141.4	34.0	166.6	35.1	181.7	36.1	174.5
Hoki	77.2	314.7	64.3	230.0	51.0	174.1	42.8	152.1	41.6	155.5	40.1	141.3
Rock lobster	2.1	128.0	2.2	113.0	2.1	101.6	2.4	114.0	2.4	127.1	2.3	121.7
Abalone/pāua	0.8	63.0	0.7	54.5	0.8	52.4	0.7	50.2	0.8	54.3	0.9	58.1
Orange roughy	8.2	127.2	5.9	78.5	6.0	89.9	5.0	70.0	7.3	83.9	6.9	56.6
Ling	7.9	65.7	9.0	51.7	9.0	47.5	8.1	47.3	6.9	51.0	6.6	54.4
Hake	6.4	35.8	6.1	32.4	8.4	44.8	5.8	31.7	6.3	41.7	6.2	38.1
Salmon	6.0	43.7	4.8	39.3	4.5	35.9	3.3	27.6	4.6	42.5	3.3	36.1
Warehou	5.5	23.3	7.1	22.4	8.7	21.3	8.2	22.7	8.7	29.8	10.0	34.8
Jack mackerel	19.6	19.6	20.3	18.2	25.3	22.3	30.3	31.4	27.8	35.7	25.2	32.5
Snapper	4.0	34.0	3.8	28.8	4.2	29.0	4.1	25.9	4.2	29.4	3.6	30.2
Tuna	8.5	42.4	10.3	32.2	15.1	35.9	12.1	27.1	10.9	28.4	13.3	30.0
Barracouta	9.9	10.9	11.1	10.8	10.7	10.8	15.3	16.3	16.4	19.0	17.8	23.1
Oreo dory	5.1	27.8	4.3	20.6	4.6	21.8	4.5	19.4	4.8	20.4	5.8	19.5
Southern blue whiting	4.7	7.2	6.4	12.8	7.2	11.9	13.6	21.1	9.4	18.8	9.4	14.2
Blue mackerel	8.2	8.5	9.7	9.3	8.1	8.4	6.9	8.1	7.7	11.7	7.5	10.0
Scampi	0.9	26.0	0.7	19.9	0.5	11.9	0.7	20.9	0.5	12.6	0.3	4.2
Gemfish	0.2	2.5	0.3	2.6	0.5	3.1	0.6	3.1	0.4	2.2	0.4	2.3
Scallops	0.3	5.9	0.3	5.9	0.1	2.6	0.1	2.6	0.1	1.1	0.1	1.5

(1) Valued free on board at New Zealand ports. (2) Figures are final figures to 2006. The 2007 figures are provisional.

Source: New Zealand Seafood Industry Council

Table 19.13

Seafood exports[1]
By top 5 destinations
Year ending 31 December

Destination	2002 Value $(million)	2002 Proportion of total (Percent)	2003 Value $(million)	2003 Proportion of total (Percent)	2004 Value $(million)	2004 Proportion of total (Percent)	2005 Value $(million)	2005 Proportion of total (Percent)	2006 Value $(million)	2006 Proportion of total (Percent)	2007[2] Value $(million)	2007[2] Proportion of total (Percent)
Australia	200.9	13.1	197.5	16.4	195.5	15.4	189.0	15.0	219.9	16.3	233.4	18.6
European Union	267.1	17.5	220.2	18.2	250.1	19.7	260.9	20.7	252.6	18.7	211.3	16.9
Hong Kong	175.2	11.5	138.1	11.4	135.4	10.6	137.5	10.9	165.7	12.3	173.2	13.8
United States	315.7	20.6	211.9	17.5	208.4	16.4	196.7	15.6	209.9	15.5	158.9	12.7
Japan	265.4	17.3	186.5	15.4	167.2	13.1	136.6	10.8	143.1	10.6	121.4	9.7
Other markets	305.7	20.0	253.7	21.0	315.3	24.8	341.4	27.1	359.9	26.6	355.1	28.3
Total	**1,530.0**	**100.0**	**1,207.9**	**100.0**	**1,271.9**	**100.0**	**1,262.1**	**100.0**	**1,351.1**	**100.0**	**1,253.3**	**100.0**

(1) Valued free on board at New Zealand ports. (2) Figures are final figures to 2006. The 2007 figures are provisional.

Source: New Zealand Seafood Industry Council

Table 19.14

Seafood exports
By volume and value[1]
Year ending 31 December

Species group	2002		2003		2004		2005		2006		2007[2]	
	Quantity Tonnes (000)	Value $ (million)	Quantity Tonnes (000)	Value $ (million)	Quantity Tonnes (000)	Value $ (million)	Quantity Tonnes (000)	Value $ (million)	Quantity Tonnes (000)	Value $ (million)	Quantity Tonnes (000)	Value $ (million)
Finfish (wetfish)	242.2	1,005.9	228.6	785.4	229.3	751.8	220.5	698.8	219.8	811.7	215.0	775.0
Shellfish	74.1	362.2	67.9	280.3	105.0	393.2	110.4	417.9	98.0	390.0	97.4	345.4
Rock lobster	2.2	128.0	2.2	113.0	2.1	101.6	2.4	113.9	2.4	127.0	2.3	121.7
Other crustacea	1.9	33.9	1.8	29.7	1.5	25.4	1.8	31.4	1.4	22.4	0.9	11.3
Total	**320.4**	**1,530.0**	**300.6**	**1,208.4**	**337.9**	**1,272.0**	**335.1**	**1,262.1**	**321.6**	**1,351.1**	**315.6**	**1,253.5**

(1) Valued free on board at New Zealand ports. (2) Figures are final figures to 2006. The 2007 figures are provisional.

Source: New Zealand Seafood Industry Council

Contributors and related websites

Ministry for the Environment – www.mfe.govt.nz

Ministry of Agriculture and Forestry – www.maf.govt.nz

Ministry of Fisheries – www.fish.govt.nz

New Zealand Seafood Industry Council – www.seafood.co.nz

Scion – www.scionresearch.com

Statistics New Zealand – www.stats.govt.nz

Te Ohu Kaimoana Māori Fisheries Trust – www.teohu.maori.nz

Genesis Energy

Wind turbines at Hau Nui in southern Wairarapa. First commissioned in 1997, the site now has 15 turbines with a total capacity of 8.65 megawatts, and supplies enough power for around 4,200 local homes. The use of wind for electricity generation is growing – the 2006 figure of 2.2 petajoules is a 440 percent increase since 2001.

20 | Energy and minerals

Building a sustainable energy future

New Zealand, like the rest of the world, faces two major energy challenges – to deliver secure energy at affordable prices to support economic development, while also being environmentally sustainable by reducing carbon emissions from energy production and use.

New Zealand's energy use is dominated by electricity and transport. Current reliance is on primary energy from oil, water, natural gas, coal and geothermal energy. Energy prices have historically been low by international standards, and there has been relatively little investment in energy efficiency for homes, shops, light industry and transport. In the transport sector, there is a high level of car ownership, a high proportion of imported used vehicles, low but increasing public transport use, and a limited rail network due to geography and a small population.

While total greenhouse gas emissions are only about 0.3 percent of global emissions, New Zealand has the 12th highest level of emissions per person in the world. *New Zealand's Energy Outlook to 2030* projects that, without a change in direction, energy-related greenhouse gas emissions will rise 39 percent by 2030. This includes a 40 percent rise in transport emissions.

New Zealand's energy strategy

New Zealand's response to the long-term challenges of energy security and climate change is set out in the *New Zealand Energy Strategy*. Released in October 2007, it indicates the Government's vision for a sustainable, low emissions energy system, and an action plan to make that vision a reality.

Key actions include:

- a target for 90 percent of generated electricity to be from renewable sources by 2025
- limiting new base-load fossil fuel electricity generation for 10 years
- policy guidance on renewable energy, and electricity transmission, for local authorities
- relaxing restrictions on electricity generation and retailing by line companies to increase market competition
- using a lower discount rate to assess the net benefits of energy efficiency initiatives
- a target to halve domestic transport emissions per person by 2040, relative to 2007 levels
- an in-principle decision to be one of the first countries to widely deploy electric vehicles

- establishing an expert group to consider implications of higher levels of biofuel, and the introduction of plug-in electric vehicles
- a minimum biofuels sales obligation to encourage the use of alternative fuels
- establishing a Low Carbon Energy Technologies Fund, providing $12 million over three years from July 2008 to support sustainable energy technologies
- a Marine Energy Fund to deploy marine energy technologies
- initiatives to help low and modest income households through the transition to a sustainable low emissions energy system.

More information on the *New Zealand Energy Strategy* is at: www.med.govt.nz/nzes.

Energy efficiency and conservation strategy

The Government's Energy Efficiency and Conservation Strategy (NZEECS) was prepared alongside the *New Zealand Energy Strategy*. It sets the direction for better energy choices through detailed action plans for energy efficiency and conservation, and renewable energy programmes across all sectors of the economy. The NZEECS sits under the policy framework of the *New Zealand Energy Strategy*, as well as meeting the requirements of the Energy Efficiency and Conservation Act 2000.

Revised and released in October 2007, the NZEECS covers five programmes to support reaching high-level targets. These include residential, business, transport, and renewable electricity system programmes, and government leading the way.

Highlights include having:

- up to 180,000 insulation, clean heat, or solar water heating upgrades
- more work to improve the efficiency of appliances, to gain $2.7 billion in savings for consumers by 2025
- over $8 million for energy efficiency programmes to improve the competitiveness of business, including the primary production and tourism sectors, and to boost the use of wood for heating

Primary supply and renewable energy

'Total primary energy supply' per person is a common, though imperfect, measure of a country's energy efficiency. The impact of climate on energy use is not considered, and neither is a country's size or density of population when comparing countries. But its use is widespread in OECD countries.

'Tonnes of oil equivalent' per person consists of primary energy production which is adjusted for net trade and stock changes. Secondary energy production (eg electricity from fossil fuels) is not included since the energy equivalent of the primary fuel (eg coal) used to create the secondary energy (eg electricity) has already been counted.

Countries with small populations, such as Iceland and Luxembourg, often have high ratios. Iceland has a cold climate and cheap, non-polluting thermal energy. Luxembourg has a low petrol tax which brings buyers from neighbouring countries. New Zealand's ratio was just below the OECD average in 1996, with a wider gap in 2006.

The renewables category includes the primary energy equivalent of hydro (excluding pumped storage), geothermal, solar, wind, tide and wave. It also includes solid biomass, biogasoline, biodiesel, other liquid biofuels, biogas, industrial waste and municipal waste. Municipal waste is that produced by the residential, commercial and public service sectors, and collected by local authorities for disposal in a central location – to produce heat and/or power.

In OECD countries total renewable energy supply grew at a faster rate (2.3 percent annually) than the total primary supply (1.4 percent) between the 1970s and 2006. Hydro growth was less than for geothermal and combustible renewables, and where policy support for solar and wind power exists, these sources had rapid growth.

In 2006, the renewables' contribution varied greatly, from 78 percent in Iceland, 38 percent in Norway and 30 percent in New Zealand, down to 1–2 percent in Korea and the United Kingdom.

Total primary energy supply per person
Tonnes of oil equivalent
OECD countries, 2006

Contribution of renewables in OECD countries
As a percentage of total primary energy supply
1976 and 2006

	1976	2006
Australia	8.0	5.2
Austria	11.2	21.3
Belgium	0.1	3.1
Canada	14.3	16.1
Czech Republic	0.3	4.5
Denmark	2.0	15.6
Finland	18.6	22.6
France	7.2	6.3
Germany	1.3	6.3
Greece	4.6	5.8
Hungary	2.2	4.3
Iceland	51.3	77.6
Ireland	0.7	2.9
Italy	4.9	6.8
Japan	2.2	3.4
Korea	0.5	1.3
Luxembourg	..	1.7
Mexico	12.9	9.4
Netherlands	0.3	3.6
New Zealand	**29.5**	**30.0**
Norway	46.2	38.5
Poland	1.3	5.2
Portugal	12.3	16.9
Slovak Republic	2.0	4.8
Spain	2.9	6.6
Sweden	19.2	29.3
Switzerland	13.1	17.0
Turkey	26.7	12.2
United Kingdom	0.2	2.1
United States	3.9	5.0
OECD total	4.7	6.5

Symbol: .. figure not available

Source: OECD *Factbook 2008*

- a target to improve the fuel economy of vehicles entering the fleet by around 25 percent, saving 441 million litres of fuel by 2015
- increased emphasis on transport management, with priority given to public transport, walking and cycling
- support for the target of having 90 percent of electricity generated from renewable sources by 2025.

The final NZEECS is a 'call to action' and seeks to demonstrate Government's commitment to greater energy efficiency and conservation, and renewable energy, as ways to address climate change concerns and progress broader sustainability objectives. Investment and involvement from all New Zealanders is needed to make the most of the potential savings.

Emissions trading scheme The *New Zealand Energy Strategy* and the NZEECS both complement the Government's in-principle decision to introduce an emissions trading scheme to reduce greenhouse gas emissions and develop the path to sustainability.

Energy intensity and efficiency

New Zealand's consumer energy demand was 499 petajoules in the year ending 31 December 2006, up 11.5 percent since 2001. The industrial and transport sectors recorded the greatest increases in energy use over this period (18 and 15 percent, respectively).

The domestic transport sector is the largest energy-consuming sector, accounting for 44 percent of total consumer energy use. Its growth was nearly 56 percent of total growth between 2001 and 2006.

Transport energy use continues to be driven by many factors – including rapidly increasing vehicle numbers, larger vehicles, vehicles with more features, and increased demand for mobility and freight haulage.

The residential sector consumed 63 petajoules in 2006 – 13 percent of national consumed energy and up 5 percent from 2001. In recent years, New Zealanders have increased their level of indoor comfort through additional space and water heating, electrical appliances and lighting.

The commercial sector consumed 46 petajoules – 9 percent of total national consumed energy. Between 2001 and 2006, commercial sector energy use was down by about 10 percent.

The industrial sector uses around 30 percent of consumer energy, with a few large users dominating this sector – in particular the basic metals, food, and paper products subsectors. Industrial sector energy use grew 18 percent between 2001 and 2006, to reach 150 petajoules.

The agriculture sector includes farming, other agriculture, hunting and fishing. In 2006, it consumed 21 petajoules – about 5 percent of the nation's energy. This sector has shown a 4 percent increase in energy consumption since 2001.

The following points relate to table 20.01 (overleaf), which shows the balance between energy supply and demand.

- Supply data is compiled from monthly returns. Figures for geothermal energy are estimated. Approximately 80 percent of geothermal is used for electricity power generation, while 20 percent is used directly for heat. Liquefied petroleum gas production is included in indigenous oil production.

Otago Daily Times

Water crashes down the spillway from Lake Dunstan at the Clyde dam hydro-generation site on the Clutha River in Otago. Renewable hydro electricity supplied 55 percent of New Zealand's total electricity demand in 2006.

Table 20.01

Energy supply and demand balance
Year ending 31 December 2006

Supply/demand	Coal	Oil	Gas	Hydro	Geo-thermal	Renew-ables	Other electricity	Waste heat	Total
					Petajoules				
Supply									
Indigenous production	153.0	46.8	152.5	84.4	89.0	46.7	0.0	1.1	573.8
+ imports	28.4	311.4	0.0	0.0	0.0	0.0	0.0	...	339.7
− exports	85.2	38.1	0.0	0.0	0.0	0.0	0.0	...	123.4
− stock change	3.7	-2.2	0.0	0.0	0.0	0.0	0.0	...	1.4
− international transport	0.0	47.4	0.0	0.0	0.0	0.0	0.0	...	47.4
Total supply	**92.4**	**274.8**	**152.5**	**84.4**	**89.0**	**46.7**	**0.0**	**1.1**	**741.3**
Transformation									
Electricity generation	-51.0	0.0	-61.3	-84.4	-71.8	-3.4	144.9	...	-127.0
Co-generation	-0.7	0.0	-21.4	0.0	-1.5	-8.4	9.7	-1.1	-23.3
Liquid fuels production	0.0	-5.3	0.0	0.0	0.0	0.0	0.0	...	-5.3
Other transformation	-18.6	...	-2.1	...	...	...	2.1	...	-18.6
Losses and own use	0.0	-1.6	-4.7	0.0	-6.0	0.0	-15.8	...	-28.2
Total transformation	**-70.3**	**-6.9**	**-89.5**	**-84.4**	**-79.3**	**-11.7**	**140.9**	**-1.1**	**-202.4**
Non-energy use	...	-13.5	-23.2	0.0	0.0	0.0	0.0	...	-36.7
Consumer energy (calculated)	**22.1**	**254.4**	**39.8**	**0.0**	**9.7**	**35.2**	**140.9**	**0.0**	**502.2**
Demand									
Agriculture	2.0	12.1	1.9	0.0	0.0	0.0	5.4	...	21.4
Industrial	16.4	17.0	28.4	0.0	5.8	26.9	55.4	...	149.9
Commercial	3.8	4.6	5.0	0.0	3.9	0.3	28.0	...	45.6
Residential	0.7	2.6	6.9	0.0	0.1	8.1	44.4	...	62.8
Domestic transport	0.1	216.8	0.2	0.0	0.0	0.0	2.4	...	219.5
Consumer energy (observed)	**22.9**	**253.2**	**42.4**	**0.0**	**9.7**	**35.2**	**135.6**	**0.0**	**499.2**
Discrepancies	-0.8	1.2	-2.6	...	0.0	0.0	5.3	0.0	3.1

Note: Figures may not add up to stated totals due to rounding.
Symbol: ... not applicable

Source: Ministry of Economic Development

- Total primary energy supply is the energy available for use in New Zealand – for energy conversion and end use.
- Transformation of energy from one form to another always results in conversion losses, which are shown as negative entries in the table. Efficiencies for electricity generation are assumed to be 35 percent for coal plants, 50 percent for gas, and 30 percent for co-generation. Hydro and wind are taken as being 100 percent efficient, and geothermal as 15 percent.
- Consumer energy (calculated) = total primary energy supply – total transformation – non-energy used (primary energy used for other purposes, for example bitumen for roads, and natural gas as feedstock to produce methanol and ammonia/urea).
- Energy demand consumption (observed) data is estimated from information about where and how energy is used. Domestic transport refers to domestic road, rail and air transport. Observed values are used as they provide more detail of energy use by each sector.

Energy

The efficiency with which New Zealand produces and uses energy directly affects its international competitiveness, economic growth, and the quality of its environment.

New Zealand is self-sufficient in all energy forms apart from oil. Some coal is imported for electricity generation, but coal exports are about 300 percent greater.

In 2006, New Zealand was 65 percent self-sufficient in its total primary energy needs, and 17 percent self-sufficient in oil. Total primary energy supply from different sources, from 1985 to 2006, is shown in table 20.02.

Environmental impact The Resource Management Act 1991 ensures that environmental costs are recognised in the energy production planning process, and that local impact is avoided, remedied or mitigated.

Amendments in 2004 required that particular regard be paid to the efficiency of the end use of energy, the effects of climate change, and the benefits to be derived from the use and development of renewable energy.

New Zealand is a signatory to the Kyoto Protocol under which emission levels of greenhouse gases during 2008–12 are required to be reduced to levels prevailing in 1990.

Table 20.02

Primary energy supply
Year ending 31 December

Year	Coal	Imported oil and oil products	Indigenous oil (net)	Gas	Hydro	Geothermal	Other renewables	Waste heat	Total
				Petajoules (gross)					
1985	45.6	115.4	31.4	140.6	70.2	78.9	29.3	..	**511.3**
1990	52.6	141.1	46.9	180.9	82.6	92.6	33.4	..	**630.2**
1995	48.8	189.4	31.2	179.2	98.1	93.3	34.5	..	**674.5**
2000	49.3	222.3	26.4	235.2	88.7	114.3	37.8	..	**773.9**
2001	55.5	232.9	19.4	247.1	81.4	111.4	38.2	1.2	**787.0**
2002	51.3	234.5	21.1	234.9	90.8	81.5	40.7	1.0	**755.8**
2003	81.6	256.3	15.2	179.3	85.3	78.8	41.2	3.7	**741.4**
2004	82.4	258.0	17.6	160.5	97.9	79.9	43.8	2.2	**742.3**
2005	97.5	259.6	20.0	148.6	84.0	89.2	47.3	1.1	**747.2**
2006	92.4	261.9	13.0	152.5	84.4	89.0	47.0	1.1	**741.3**

Symbol: .. data not available

Source: Ministry of Economic Development

Greenhouse gas emissions Gross carbon dioxide equivalent emissions from energy sources and industrial processes were about 38 million tonnes in 2006, compared with about 27 million tonnes in 1990.

National transport contributed the largest proportion of energy emissions (42 percent in 2006). Growth in this sector was largely due to greater use of the two major liquid fuels, petrol and diesel, as well as increased aviation fuel use.

The second-largest source of emissions was thermal electricity generation (24 percent in 2006), which had the largest increase in percentage terms since 1990. However, within this general increasing trend in emissions there are strong annual variations, reflecting the availability of hydro generation for each year.

The manufacturing industries category (15 percent in 2006) has showed a decline in emissions, after a peak in 2002. A large part of this fall resulted from Methanex scaling back methanol production, historically a significant source of emissions, after 2002. A reduction in coal consumption in manufacturing also contributed to the emissions decline.

Other greenhouse gases emitted from energy sources include nitrous oxide and methane, although the agriculture sector is the main contributor to these emissions.

Energy research and development The Foundation for Research, Science and Technology is the main funding body for energy-related research and development, investing about $16.7 million a year. Current work includes research that supports the implementation of the *New Zealand Energy Strategy* and the New Zealand Energy Efficiency and Conservation Strategy.

Electricity

Depending on demand, rainfall, and lake storage conditions, about 70 percent of New Zealand's electricity need is met by traditional renewable resources, with hydro contributing 55 percent in 2006 and geothermal 8 percent.

More than two-thirds of hydroelectricity is generated in the South Island, with all geothermal generation being in the North Island.

Most of the balance of electricity demand in 2006 was met by generation from natural gas (22 percent), followed by coal (12 percent) and a small but increasing contribution from renewables such as wind, wood, and landfill gas (3 percent).

Table 20.03 (overleaf) shows electricity generation in gigawatt hours, by fuel type.

Generation For 2006, five electricity generators provided 91 percent of total New Zealand electricity generation. Meridian provided 29 percent, Contact Energy 27 percent, Genesis 19 percent, Mighty River Power 12 percent and TrustPower 4 percent. The remainder came from on-site co-generation, and other independent generators.

Transmission Transpower is New Zealand's national grid company. A state-owned enterprise, Transpower is the owner and system operator of New Zealand's high-voltage electricity transmission grid, linking generators to distribution companies and major industrial users.

Conveyance New Zealand is fully reticulated through a national high-voltage transmission network, and local low-voltage distribution networks largely operated by electric power companies. Power transmission between the North and South Islands is through a high-voltage direct current

Table 20.03

Electricity generation
By fuel type
Year ending 31 December

Year	Hydro	Geo-thermal[1]	Oil[2]	Coal[1][3]	Gas[1]	Biogas[1]	Waste heat[1][3]	Wood[1]	Wind	All fuels
					Gigawatt hours					
1994	25,579	2,140	10	639	5,137	162	0	336	1	**34,005**
1995	27,259	2,049	47	840	4,539	172	0	336	1	**35,244**
1996	25,713	2,020	15	795	6,493	146	0	310	8	**35,500**
1997	23,594	2,130	-14	1,615	8,074	139	0	312	13	**35,863**
1998	24,165	2,386	0	1,524	8,086	137	0	409	22	**36,728**
1999	23,221	2,636	0	1,767	8,941	116	0	392	39	**37,112**
2000	24,387	2,756	0	1,533	8,941	103	0	447	119	**38,285**
2001	22,391	2,678	0	1,838	10,882	101	47	361	138	**38,436**
2002	24,970	2,704	0	1,744	9,530	120	40	412	154	**39,674**
2003	23,455	2,612	0	3,421	9,597	132	145	372	146	**39,879**
2004	26,932	2,597	19	4,433	6,711	114	85	403	354	**41,648**
2005	23,099	3,007	4	5,401	8,859	165	42	484	609	**41,670**
2006	23,220	3,210	21	5,119	9,181	157	43	486	617	**42,056**

(1) These fuels also include generation from co-generation plants. (2) Negative generation by oil-fired plants implies a net import into the station to maintain station viability and system voltage stability. (3) To better align with international reporting, generation from industrial waste heat where the primary energy source is a fossil fuel is now entered under the primary source (principally coal). Revisions have been made back to 1974.

Note: Figures may not add up to stated totals due to rounding.

Source: Ministry of Economic Development

link from the Benmore power station in the South Island to Haywards substation just north of Wellington. Part of this link is a submarine cable under Cook Strait, which allows surplus power generated in the South Island to be transmitted to the North Island, where demand is greatest. It also allows transmission from north to south.

Distribution Most line companies are owned by local communities, either through trust arrangements or local bodies (while electricity generation and retailing is largely controlled by three government-owned and two privately-owned integrated energy companies). The Energy Companies Act 1992 required electric power boards and the municipal electricity departments of local authorities to become independent commercial companies. The result included municipal companies, consumer/community trusts, and private owners. Subsequently, the Electricity Industry Reform Act 1998 required all distribution companies to separate the ownership and control of line businesses from energy retailing and generation activities. Before this, line companies were rapidly emerging as major investors in new and renewable generation – accounting for two-thirds of load growth between 1996 and 1999.

Technicians fix powerlines brought down by gale-force winds, which cut power to Central Otago in 2007. Local communities are responsible for electricity distribution through their line companies.

Distribution companies, along with the government-owned transmission company Transpower, must meet price thresholds set by the Commerce Commission, which also regulates distribution quality standards. A separate regulator, the Electricity Commission, oversees aspects of distribution pricing, and also approves new transmission investments and other transmission functions. There have been several reforms since 2001 aimed at attracting distributors into investing in generation involving renewable resources. However, few line companies are involved in generation today.

Other recent distribution reforms have included standard requirements for connecting small distributed-generation ventures to networks, and modified requirements to offer a volume-linked pricing option to households, in place of fixed line charges. Distributors are required to offer rural customers line charges that are comparable with urban ones, and must also maintain supply to connected customers. A cut-off date for the obligation to supply uneconomic rural customers until 2013 is under review.

Consumption The industrial sector, which includes an aluminium smelter, iron and steel works, several pulp and paper mills and large dairy factories, is the largest electricity-using sector in New Zealand. The sector accounted for 45 percent of electricity consumption in the year ending 31 December 2006, followed by the household sector (33 percent) and commercial applications (22 percent).

Electricity Commission

The Electricity Commission is a Crown entity established under the Electricity Act 2003 to oversee New Zealand's electricity industry operations and markets. The commission is an independent regulatory body whose role is to oversee the governance, operations and development of New Zealand's wholesale and retail electricity markets, and review and approve, if appropriate, Transpower's proposed investments in the national grid. The commission was established after the industry was unable to reach agreement on self-governance arrangements in early 2003.

The commission's principal objective is to promote and facilitate the efficient use of electricity, and to ensure that electricity is produced and delivered to all classes of consumers in an efficient, fair, reliable and environmentally sustainable manner. It is also required to promote and facilitate the efficient use of electricity.

The commission administers the rules and regulations that govern the electricity industry, enforces them, and recommends changes where necessary.

The commission's key areas of responsibility are:

- operating, overseeing and developing the wholesale and retail electricity markets and the rules that govern them
- managing security of supply and reserve generation
- reviewing and approving proposals by Transpower for investment in the transmission grid
- ensuring disputes that arise in operating the system and the markets are managed effectively
- promoting efficient use of electricity.

A number of organisations are contracted to the commission to provide services necessary to administer the electricity markets on a daily basis. It is responsible for the management of these contractors and services: clearing manager, information system, market administration, pricing manager, reconciliation manager, registry, and system operator.

Replacing the light bulb

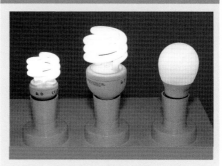

Examples of energy-efficient light bulbs that will meet the new standards.

In June 2008, the Government launched a strategy to phase out 'old-style' incandescent light bulbs and, by 2015, reduce the amount of energy used for lighting by 20 percent.

Incandescent bulbs are inefficient, with only about 5 percent of the energy they use producing light and the rest being wasted as heat. More efficient bulbs last eight times longer and use only a fifth of the power.

The strategy will phase out the bulbs from late 2009. Once new standards are introduced, no new stocks of the incandescent bulbs will be imported for sale.

The strategy aims to achieve the 20 percent goal through more efficient affordable lighting, phasing out inefficient products, and setting minimum energy performance standards. New Zealand spends about $660 million on electricity for lighting a year, at the same time generating about 2.65 million tonnes of greenhouse gas emissions.

According to the Government, almost $500 million could be saved by 2020, just by changing the lights.

The Efficient Lighting Strategy was developed by the lighting industry, the Energy Efficiency and Conservation Authority, and the Electricity Commission.

Source: Energy Efficiency and Conservation Authority

Table 20.04

Electricity consumption
By sector
Year ending 31 March

| | Residential | | | Commercial | | | Industrial | | | |
| | Consumption | Number of consumers | Average price (excl GST) | Consumption | Number of consumers | Average price (excl GST) | Consumption | Number of consumers | Average price (excl GST) | **Total consumption** |
Year	GWh	(000)	cents/kWh	GWh	(000)	cents/kWh	GWh	(000)	cents/kWh	**GWh**
1994	10,256	1,343	9.70	5,580	146	11.04	13,392	132	5.99	**29,228**
1995	10,416	1,356	10.24	5,675	139	10.86	13,834	132	5.84	**29,925**
1996	10,584	1,371	10.73	5,595	141	11.12	14,342	131	6.33	**30,522**
1997	10,959	1,377	11.45	6,101	138	10.99	14,200	136	6.12	**31,260**
1998	10,824	1,418	12.08	7,173	137	9.98	13,937	125	7.01	**31,934**
1999	11,290	1,423	11.61	7,334	140	9.72	14,010	127	6.98	**32,634**
2000[1]	11,057	1,444	11.87	6,919	138	10.11	14,759	112	5.94	**32,735**
2001[1][2]	11,306	1,472	11.76	6,899	137	10.31	15,142	110	6.31	**33,348**
2002[1]	11,660	1,501	12.86	6,964	129	10.16	14,525	102	6.71	**33,150**
2003	11,723	1,543	13.82	7,734	138	10.79	15,431	107	7.23	**34,889**
2004	12,255	1,567	14.84	7,389	138	12.01	16,151	106	8.10	**35,795**
2005	12,161	1,586	16.68	7,975	137	12.35	16,190	104	7.56	**36,326**
2006	12,231	1,603	17.29	8,383	155	13.53	16,780	113	9.13	**37,394**

(1) Inter-year movements of prices between 2000 and 2002 may not be reliable. (2) The number of residential consumers for 2001 has been estimated.
Note: Figures may not add up to stated totals due to rounding.

Source: Ministry of Economic Development

Fuel from home-grown biomass is feasible

New Zealand could be self-sufficient in transport biofuel by using purpose-grown energy forests, helping the country to meet the low-carbon transport vision of the 2007 *New Zealand Energy Strategy*.

Research by Crown research institutes Scion and AgResearch, pulp and paper manufacturer Carter Holt Harvey, and US-based Verenium Corporation found there are no significant technical or supply barriers to producing ethanol from New Zealand's softwood feedstock. Additionally, there is sufficient wood and wood residue to supply a commercial-scale ethanol refinery, and a large enough domestic market to support it.

In contrast to concerns about producing ethanol from grain or grass crops – where the fuel may be produced at the expense of food supplies – biofuel produced from wood is a sustainable and environmentally beneficial option, according to Scion's chief executive, Dr Tom Richardson. New Zealand has an abundant softwood resource.

"We could also plant purpose-grown energy plantations on marginal land to increase that resource further without placing pressure on land for food. This would also alleviate concern around deforestation while providing forest carbon sinks," he said.

Results of the study suggest the country's entire vehicle fleet could run on nationally-grown and manufactured wood-derived biofuels.

"A facility in the central North Island producing 90 million litres of ethanol each year could fulfil the petrol part of the Government's 2007 Biofuels Sales Obligation – by supplying a 10 percent ethanol-petrol blend to the North Island," says research partner and Carter Holt Harvey project manager James Flexman.

The project now requires additional investment for the research to become a reality.

Source: Scion

The commission is governed by a non-executive chair and five other members appointed by the Minister of Energy. It is funded by an appropriation from Parliament, recovered by a levy on generators, retailers and some large industrial consumers, distributors, and Transpower.

Oil

Consumption of energy in New Zealand is dominated by oil liquids, which accounted for 253 petajoules (51 percent) of total consumer energy in the year ending 31 December 2006.

Oil liquids (which include condensate, crude oil, naptha and liquid petroleum gas) also accounted for 275 petajoules (37 percent) of primary energy supplied to New Zealand markets.

Table 20.05 shows reserves at 1 January 2007 and production figures for the year ending 31 December 2006.

Reserves Total remaining reserves of crude oil, condensate and liquid petroleum gas from New Zealand's producing fields at 1 January 2007 were 599 petajoules (97 million barrels) – 21 percent of this from the Maui field. Condensate is reservoir gas that at atmospheric pressure condenses into liquid form. It is typically refined into transport fuels and can be sold at a premium above conventional crude. Four offshore fields are at varying stages of development.

- The condensate-rich Pohokura field, which began production in August 2006, contains recoverable liquid reserves of 43 million barrels.
- The Tui field, discovered in 2003, has 28 million barrels of recoverable oil reserves. First production was in late July 2007.
- The Maari field, discovered in 1983, contains recoverable reserves of 49 million barrels.
- The Kupe field, discovered in 1986, has liquid reserves of 19 million barrels. First production is expected in mid 2009.

Production from these fields is expected to more than double New Zealand's production, and contribute to increased self-sufficiency in the short to medium term. The Maui, Kapuni, Rimu/Kauri and McKee fields dominate remaining current reserves.

Production New Zealand's production of crude oil, condensate and naphtha was 38.9 petajoules (6.8 million barrels) in the year ending 31 December 2006, all from onshore and offshore fields in the Taranaki region.

About 56 percent of total production (3.8 million barrels) came from the offshore Maui field. About 63 percent of total oil production is in the form of condensate, with 21 percent being crude oil and 16 percent naphtha. Average daily production of crude oil and condensate during 2006 was about 18,650 barrels, the lowest level since 1984. About 86 percent of local production was exported – the remainder being used as domestic refinery feedstock.

Liquid petroleum gas (LPG) production totalled 7.6 petajoules (1.8 million barrels) in 2006. Production was dominated by the Maui field (59 percent), with substantial production from the

Table 20.05

Oil, condensate, naphtha and liquid petroleum gas
Reserves and production

Field	Reserves[1] at 1 January 2007 Barrels (million)	Petajoules	Production for year ending 31 Dec 2006 Barrels (million)	Petajoules
Maui	22.15	123.85	4.88	26.28
Kapuni	4.79	22.20	1.24	5.46
Pohokura	43.10	282.31	0.94	6.16
Kaimiro/Moturoa	1.44	8.94	0.08	0.43
Ngatoro[2]	4.53	28.35	0.23	1.13
Tariki/Ahuroa	1.71	10.47	0.27	1.26
Waihapa/Ngaere	0.48	2.94	0.08	0.46
Rimu[3]	8.73	53.41	0.35	1.90
McKee	1.56	10.17	0.37	2.13
Others[4]	8.65	56.26	0.19	1.22
Total	**97.15**	**598.92**	**8.62**	**46.44**
Estimated recoverable reserves				
Kupe	19.17			
Maari	49.00			
Tui	27.90			
Urenui/Ohanga	0.30			
Radnor	0.18			
Total	**96.55**			

(1) Reserves are estimated as 'proven and probable' or P50 by field operators. (2) Includes Goldie well. (3) Includes Kauri well. (4) Includes Mangahewa, Cheal, Turangi and Surrey fields.

Source: Ministry of Economic Development

The New Zealand Herald

The New Zealand Refining Company site at Marsden Point, at the entrance to Whangarei harbour, is the country's only refinery. It supplies petroleum products to the Auckland region through a pipeline to Wiri in south Auckland, and to the rest of the country mainly by coastal tanker.

Table 20.06

Crude oil and condensate
Production and trade
Year ending 31 December

Year	New Zealand production	Imports	Refinery intake	Exports
	Gross petajoules			
1994	81.51	175.84	202.02	51.35
1995	68.33	169.37	196.28	44.12
1996	90.74	165.55	189.61	56.83
1997	120.56	168.30	212.29	77.70
1998	95.67	202.51	217.72	70.97
1999	84.36	198.77	212.72	63.45
2000	74.96	203.30	221.03	55.07
2001	70.02	191.46	208.93	58.12
2002	63.55	205.29	219.92	50.50
2003	49.21	217.66	220.10	41.85
2004	42.56	200.89	214.02	33.45
2005	39.87	204.03	217.07	28.11
2006	38.90	208.34	219.00	33.51

Source: Ministry of Economic Development

onshore fields at Kapuni (26 percent) and Tariki/Ahuroa (9 percent). Average daily production of LPG during 2006 was 4,900 barrels.

Total crude oil, condensate, naphtha and LPG production in the year ending 31 December 2006 was 46.5 petajoules (8.6 million barrels).

Imports In 2006, New Zealand imported crude oil from the Middle East, Australia, and South-East Asia. To meet demand, oil wholesalers also imported refined petroleum.

Exports New Zealand exported about 86 percent of its crude oil and condensate production in the year ending 31 December 2006. In addition, about 2 percent of refined product was exported, while 15 percent was used for international transport, and the remainder consumed within New Zealand's domestic market. Production and trade figures are shown in table 20.06.

Self-sufficiency New Zealand's primary self-sufficiency in oil depends on both local oil production and demand. Self-sufficiency increased dramatically during 1974–86, from below 5 percent to more than 50 percent. In the 1990s, as demand grew faster than production, the figure fell to 30–40 percent. With production declining in a number of fields, self-sufficiency was down to 17 percent in the year ending 31 December 2006. Self-sufficiency is expected to return to the 50 percent range – a result of expected production from four offshore fields at varying stages of development.

Refinery New Zealand's only oil refinery is at Marsden Point, near Whangarei. The main feedstock is imported crude oil (about 93 percent), with local crude oil and condensate making up the rest. The refinery produces petrol, diesel, premium kerosene, jet-A1, fuel oils and bitumen.

Distribution A refinery-owned pipeline transports about one-third of Marsden Point's refined production to Wiri (South Auckland) to supply the Auckland area. The rest of New Zealand is mostly delivered by coastal tankers supplying port depots, which, in turn, supply road tankers, which then distribute stocks to retailers. Imported refined production is shipped directly to coastal ports.

Retailing Four major oil suppliers, BP, Caltex (Chevron), Mobil and Shell, have been the dominant fuel retailers in New Zealand for many years. In 1998, Australian independent Gull began retailing operations. Another independent company, Challenge, was bought by Caltex in 2001.

End use New Zealand's consumer energy is dominated by oil, which was 253 petajoules of the total 499 petajoules of consumer energy used in the year ending 31 December 2006. National transport dominates consumer energy use of petroleum products, with 86 percent of oil consumption being used for transport. Annual end use of petroleum products is about 1,550 litres (10 barrels) per person.

Unleaded petrol Unleaded regular grade petrol, introduced into New Zealand in 1987, was about 79 percent of the total demand for unleaded petrol in the year ending 31 December 2006. Premium unleaded petrol made up the rest. The sale of leaded petrol was banned in October 1996.

Gas

New Zealand's known gas resources are undergoing major changes, with the offshore Maui field, for so long a dominating presence on the local energy scene, now approaching economic depletion. At 1 January 2007, remaining reserves from the Maui field were 439 petajoules (390 billion cubic feet), 21.2 percent of the national total, by volume.

In 2006, joint venture operators of the Maui field completed drilling further production wells from the Maui A platform, originally commissioned in 1979.

Excluding Maui, total remaining gas reserves from producing fields were 1,513 petajoules (1,452 billion cubic feet) at 1 January 2007.

The Pohokura gas-condensate field, discovered offshore near New Plymouth in 2000, is now the largest single reserve of gas, with an estimated 779 billion cubic feet of gas regarded as being economically recoverable. Pohokura went into production in August 2006.

The offshore Kupe field, containing a recoverable reserve of 188 petajoules (203 billion cubic feet), is also being developed. First production from the field, off the south coast of Taranaki, is expected during the second half of 2009.

Onshore Taranaki gas fields such as Kapuni, TAWN (the collective name for Tariki, Ahuroa, Waihapa and Ngaere), McKee, Mangahewa and Rimu/Kauri will also play important roles in gas supply.

Exploration and production Increased demand for natural gas, combined with declining supply, has stimulated an increase in exploration to help fill the gap left by the depletion of the Maui field. Strong oil prices have also led many permit operators to revise their exploration programmes.

In the year ending 31 December 2006, 30 wells (not including wells for coal bed methane exploration) were drilled to a total depth of 112,369 metres. This was a substantial increase on 2001 drilling activity, when 17 wells were drilled to a total depth of 48,541 metres.

During 2005, 34 wells were drilled to a combined depth of 87,533 metres. Increased drilling activity has included a large increase in seismic data acquisition, which is a precursor to drilling.

In the year ending 31 December 2006, $133.0 million was spent on activities in exploration permits, compared with $185.5 million in the previous year.

With the development of multiple offshore fields, and numerous exploration campaigns being planned, rates of expenditure and activity are expected to rise in the short to medium term. Most planned exploration is on and offshore in Taranaki and the Great South Basin (the southern oceans off Southland).

There has been increased permit interest in the Canterbury Basin. Many permits have been granted for exploration of coal bed methane resources over Waikato and West Coast coal fields, and Otago and Southland lignite fields. Substantial areas of offshore Northland, the North Island's east

Table 20.07

Natural gas
Reserves and production

Field	Reserves[1] at 1 January 2007[3]		Production (net)[2] for year ending 31 Dec 2006	
	Cubic feet (billion)	Petajoules	Cubic feet (billion)	Petajoules
Maui	390.2	438.7	74.64	87.14
Kapuni	348.5	263.0	32.25	24.35
Pohokura	779.2	884.8	11.99	14.00
Kaimiro/Moturoa	16.9	16.7	0.00	0.00
Ngatoro[4]	13.3	13.9	0.01	0.01
Tariki/Ahuroa	23.6	26.4	4.55	5.03
Waihapa/Ngaere	0.2	0.3	0.17	0.19
Rimu[5]	48.6	57.0	3.80	4.46
McKee	51.5	60.9	6.00	6.92
Others[6]	170.0	190.3	5.83	6.46
Total	**1,842.05**	**1,951.88**	**139.24**	**148.50**
Estimated recoverable reserves				
Kupe	203.0	188.1		
Urenui/Ohanga	10.0	10.5		
Radnor	6.0	5.0		
Windsor	0.7	0.8		
Total	**219.7**	**204.4**		

(1) Reserves are estimated as 'proven and probable' or P50 by field operators. (2) Excludes gas flared, gas reinjected, LPG extracted, and own use (fuel) and losses. (3) Excludes LPG. (4) Includes Goldie well. (5) Includes Kauri well. (6) Includes Mangahewa, Cheal, Turangi and Surrey fields.

Note: Figures may not add up to stated totals due to rounding.

Source: Ministry of Economic Development

Table 20.08

Gas production and demand
Year ending 31 December

Year	Total natural gas production	Gas reinjected	LPG extracted	Flared	Losses and own use	Net natural gas production	Direct sales (est)	Reticulated sales (est)[1]
	Petajoules							
1994	227.84	28.66	8.14	1.85	4.77	184.41	142.07	41.89
1995	207.67	19.41	7.61	1.24	4.72	174.68	132.03	42.18
1996	243.62	27.67	8.94	2.48	5.43	199.10	154.02	44.50
1997	253.43	20.48	9.78	3.97	5.76	213.43	161.23	51.65
1998	226.85	21.12	9.54	3.09	5.57	187.53	131.15	55.93
1999	253.47	17.74	10.02	1.94	5.56	218.21	157.00	60.57
2000	254.17	6.85	10.47	1.64	5.51	229.70	170.24	58.88
2001	265.25	3.59	11.54	2.59	5.83	241.70	177.53	63.11
2002	248.80	0.50	11.40	1.61	5.67	229.62	165.15	63.51
2003	189.74	0.01	9.10	1.16	5.68	173.80	106.87	65.93
2004	171.30	0.62	9.13	0.90	4.78	155.86	90.37	64.66
2005	159.41	1.22	8.76	0.82	4.25	144.37	74.97	68.58
2006	162.69	1.45	7.83	0.87	3.98	148.55	84.48	63.31

(1) Reticulated sales (calculated) include on-site co-generation.

Source: Ministry of Economic Development

coast, and western Taranaki have been offered as blocks for competitive bidding by exploration companies. Future offerings are scheduled for the Great South Basin and onshore Taranaki.

In July 2007, five permits were awarded to explorers after a 'blocks' offer in the Great South Basin. Consortiums for Exxon Mobil, Todd Energy OMV, PTTEP, Mitsui E&P, and New Zealand explorers Greymouth Gas are all putting their efforts into discovering the potentially large resources in the basin. These companies are expected to spend around $1.2 billion on the exploration, where discoveries would strengthen New Zealand's energy supply.

Table 20.07 shows natural gas reserves at 1 January 2007 and production figures for the year ending 31 December 2006.

End use Around 56 percent of natural gas production was used for electricity generation, including co-generation, in the year ending 31 December 2006. The petrochemical industry used 15 percent of gas production, mainly for chemical methanol and ammonia/urea plants. The remaining 29 percent was reticulated to industry, commercial, and domestic gas users. In 2006, annual end use of gas was about 248 cubic metres per person, up about 4.5 percent on the December 2005 year.

Petrochemicals About 15 percent of New Zealand's natural gas production in the year ending 31 December 2006 was used to produce petrochemicals and chemical methanol at the Waitara methanol plant in Taranaki. The Motunui (Taranaki) methanol plant was closed in November 2004 as a consequence of natural gas supply restraints, and the Waitara methanol plant operates when economically priced gas is available.

Table 20.08 shows natural gas production and demand figures from 1994 to 2006.

Coal

Coal is New Zealand's most abundant fossil fuel. The main coalfields are in the Waikato and Taranaki (both sub-bituminous) regions of the North Island, and the West Coast (bituminous and sub-bituminous), Otago (sub-bituminous and lignite), and Southland (sub-bituminous and lignite) regions of the South Island.

The total in-ground coal resource for New Zealand is estimated at more than 15 billion tonnes, of which 80 percent is South Island lignite. The technically recoverable quantity in the 10 largest lignite deposits is over 6 billion tonnes, equivalent to 72,000 petajoules.

Sub-bituminous and bituminous in-ground resources are approximately 3.5 billion tonnes, but the recoverable quantity of these coals is uncertain. It is dependent on market conditions, ongoing exploration, and feasibility studies to convert resources to reserves.

Production National coal production increased by 47 percent between 2001 and 2006. A record 5.8 million tonnes was produced in 2006, over half a million tonnes more than in the previous year. This was mainly due to increased bituminous coal production (512,000 tonnes), and a smaller increase in sub-bituminous production (77,000 tonnes) – mainly from the Waikato region – offset by a slight fall in lignite production. Almost all production is of bituminous and sub-bituminous coals, in approximately equal quantities.

Coal production centres on the Waikato and the West Coast. Four underground and 22 open-cast mines were operating in 2006. Over 60 percent of national production was from two large open-cast operations, at Rotowaro (Waikato) and Stockton (West Coast). A further 16 percent came from

Powered by landfill gas

Nelson Marlborough District Health Board (DHB) is using waste gas extracted from the local landfill to fuel a steam boiler at Nelson Hospital. The process supplies about 15 percent of the hospital's steam requirements – for space and water heating, sterilisation and laundry operations.

Raw gas, extracted from the landfill, is piped to the gas treatment plant to be filtered, compressed, cooled to remove liquids, and reheated, before being transported down the two-kilometre pipeline to the hospital.

Burning landfill gas saves the DHB around 1,720 tonnes of coal annually, and means around 3,470 tonnes less of carbon dioxide entering the atmosphere. For the city council, it's a practical and strategic use of an otherwise wasted energy resource – providing long-term revenue and helping to reduce local air pollution.

The project was developed and constructed by Energy for Industry (a Meridian Energy business), along with the Nelson City Council.

In 2007, Christchurch City Council celebrated the opening of the Burwood Landfill Gas Utilisation Project. This project uses methane from the landfill to help heat and power the Queen Elizabeth II Park complex, replacing around 1.5 million litres of LPG, and 'removing' an equivalent of 200,000 tonnes of carbon dioxide from the air over the next five years. It also provides carbon credits for the city to sell.

Under the Government's 2004 environmental standards for landfills, those that produce more than one million tonnes of refuse must collect their greenhouse gas emissions – together, these 17 landfills take 70 percent of New Zealand's waste.

Gas also produces energy at plants in Auckland, Rotorua, Palmerston North, and Wellington.

Source: Meridian Energy

Contractors work on a large drilling rig inside the Pike River coal mine on the South Island's West Coast in the Paparoa Range. Production is scheduled to start from the underground mine in 2008, with much of the premium hard-coking coal being for export.

New Zealand's two largest underground mines at Huntly East in the Waikato, and Spring Creek at Greymouth.

Export production for New Zealand coal reached 2.7 million tonnes in the year ending 31 December 2006. Most exports are of premium coking and thermal bituminous coal from the Buller and Greymouth fields on the West Coast. A large underground mine was to start production during 2008, mining bituminous coal for export from the Pike River coal field on the West Coast.

End use Proven indigenous coal resources and dwindling gas supplies mean coal is playing an increasingly important role in New Zealand's energy mix. Coal mines in the Waikato supply New Zealand Steel's Glenbrook mill, as well as the Huntly power station and several other major industrial users. Otago/Southland coals mainly supply local industrial and domestic markets, while most of the output from West Coast mines is exported. The main end use of coal for the year ending 31 December 2006 was for electricity generation (including co-generation), which took 55 percent of production. Other end users were the basic metals industry (20 percent),

Table 20.09

	Coal type				Mining method		
	Bituminous	Sub-bituminous	Lignite	Total	Open-cast	Undergound	Total
Region	Tonnes				Tonnes		
2006							
Waikato	0	2,289,809	0	2,289,809	1,849,290	440,519	2,289,809
West Coast	2,863,029	136,351	0	2,999,380	2,338,268	661,112	2,999,380
Canterbury	0	4,017	0	4,017	4,017	0	4,017
Otago	0	53,904	3,333	57,237	57,237	0	57,237
Southland	0	169,435	248,033	417,468	417,468	0	417,468
Total	**2,863,029**	**2,653,516**	**251,366**	**5,767,911**	**4,666,280**	**1,101,631**	**5,767,911**
2005							
Waikato	0	2,119,909	0	2,119,909	1,758,831	361,078	2,119,909
West Coast	2,543,404	112,194	0	2,655,598	2,267,126	388,472	2,655,598
Canterbury	0	3,929	0	3,929	3,929	0	3,929
Otago	0	54,602	1,584	56,186	56,186	0	56,186
Southland	0	186,678	244,862	431,540	426,655	4,885	431,540
Total	**2,543,404**	**2,477,312**	**246,446**	**5,267,162**	**4,512,727**	**754,435**	**5,267,162**
2004							
Waikato	0	2,053,707	0	2,053,707	1,611,739	441,968	2,053,707
West Coast	2,526,613	100,175	0	2,626,788	2,359,212	267,576	2,626,788
Canterbury	0	3,722	0	3,722	3,722	0	3,722
Otago	0	57,051	1,853	58,904	58,904	0	58,904
Southland	0	174,698	237,576	412,274	394,988	17,286	412,274
Total	**2,526,613**	**2,389,352**	**239,429**	**5,155,394**	**4,428,564**	**726,830**	**5,155,394**

Coal production
By region, coal type and mining method
Year ending 31 December

Note: Figures may not add up to stated totals due to rounding.

Source: Crown Minerals

Table 20.10

	Coal production and exports[1]			
	Year ending 31 December			
	Total production	Exports[1]	Total production	Exports[1]
Year	Gross petajoules		Tonnes (000)	
1994	77.39	32.74	3,033.20	1,043.62
1995	91.47	42.71	3,445.04	1,333.75
1996	96.21	50.90	3,610.55	1,589.53
1997	94.49	38.90	3,664.03	1,243.57
1998	85.25	34.18	3,303.88	1,092.79
1999	92.14	42.27	3,505.73	1,332.70
2000	95.79	48.48	3,585.64	1,528.51
2001	103.79	56.85	3,911.40	1,792.38
2002	119.32	61.02	4,458.94	1,931.69
2003	135.49	69.46	5,179.91	2,210.07
2004	136.98	60.13	5,155.39	1,908.42
2005	139.43	73.45	5,267.16	2,331.06
2006	152.99	85.24	5,767.91	2,719.80

(1) Exports data is based on information from Statistics New Zealand. Coal exports are mainly bituminous rank.

Source: Ministry of Economic Development

other industry (mainly cement, lime and plaster, meat, dairy products, and forestry and timber products), which took 18 percent, commercial (4 percent), and others – mainly agriculture and residential (3 percent).

Solid Energy New Zealand Ltd State-owned enterprise Solid Energy is a major energy producer, and a leading producer of high-quality coal for export and the domestic market. The company also invests in research and the commercialising of new sustainable forms of energy that use coal, and in renewable energy such as biomass, biodiesel and solar power.

The company is committed to achieving a net positive effect on the environment across its businesses, and to high levels of health and safety performance in the workplace. The target is zero injuries for the 728 employees and 555 staff employed by contractors across New Zealand.

Solid Energy produced 4.80 million tonnes of coal in the year ending 30 June 2007 – around 82 percent of New Zealand's total production. Nearly half (2.19 million tonnes, or 45.6 percent) of the coal produced by the company was exported.

Renewables

Renewables are a major part of New Zealand's total primary energy supply, contributing over 220 petajoules in the year ending 31 December 2006. Hydro (84 petajoules) and geothermal (89 petajoules) production dominated.

Derek Ackroyd at home in Rotorua. Energy from the geothermal bore in his driveway heats his water, the steam cooker and his home. The Government has a target for 90 percent of generated electricity to be from renewable sources by 2025.

Carbon credits for sale

In September 2007, the first household parcel of voluntary carbon credits of 20 units (equivalent to 20 tonnes of carbon dioxide emissions) was sold on the online auction site Trade Me for $3,000.

The credits were created by Te Apiti wind farm in 2006 – because it reduced thermal generation of electricity. They were sold by Meridian Energy, in partnership with the Marketplace Company (M-co) and Landcare Research's carboNZero programme. The credits are registered by the Swiss-based Gold Standard Foundation and can be traded globally in the voluntary carbon market.

The auction aimed to get people talking about their carbon footprint and how to reduce it, determine interest in small parcels of credits, and find the price people were willing to pay. Interest was high, with over 35,000 website hits, hundreds of questions and more than 300 bids – but Meridian says it's unlikely this sale has set the future price of carbon credits.

Carbon credits are a 'currency' which can be traded. Trading often takes place when the amount of carbon dioxide emissions produced (by a household, business, country) is greater, or less than, the amount absorbed.

Households can work out their emissions by using the calculator on Landcare Research's website (www.carbonzero.co.nz).

Source: Meridian Energy

Total biomass and waste (wood and wood products) provided 44 petajoules (42 petajoules from woody biomass and animal products, and about 2.3 petajoules from biogas and landfill gas).

The use of wind for electricity generation is growing, with the 2006 figure of 2.2 petajoules being an increase of 440 percent since 2001.

Table 20.11 shows renewable energy supply and consumption figures from 1999 to 2006.

Electricity generation The main use of renewable energy resources in New Zealand is for electricity generation. In the year ending 31 December 2006, about 66 percent of New Zealand's electricity was generated from renewable resources, predominantly hydro (55 percent) and geothermal (7.6 percent). The contribution from wind energy, while growing, is still at a low level (1.5 percent). A further 1.5 percent came from woody biomass, biogas and landfill gas.

Direct use As well as providing electricity, the direct use of renewables supplies 9 percent (45 petajoules) of consumer energy. This is mainly from wood (35 petajoules a year). Direct geothermal use for heating contributes 10 petajoules, with biogas and landfill gas providing 0.3 petajoules. Non-traditional renewable sources such as micro-hydro, wind, and solar schemes make a small contribution to overall consumer energy supply.

Landfill gas is used to produce energy at plants in Auckland, Rotorua, Palmerston North, Wellington, Nelson and Christchurch.

Wind energy

New Zealand has one of the best wind resources of any country in the world and is consequently well suited to wind energy development. It lies across an area long referred to by sailors as the 'Roaring Forties', with prevailing westerly winds.

The wind resource is enhanced by the country's oceanic location and a fairly steady succession of troughs and depressions passing to the east. Each weather system induces a pressure pattern over mountains which can lead to almost continual winds in some parts of the country.

While wind energy developments began in New Zealand with a few tentative projects, installation rates are growing rapidly. The first wind turbine (generating 225 kilowatts (kW)), now owned by Meridian Energy, has been operating successfully in Brooklyn, Wellington, since 1993.

Table 20.11

Renewable energy supply and consumption
Year ending 31 December

	1999	2000	2001	2002	2003	2004	2005	2006
				Petajoules				
Primary energy supply								
Hydro	83.73	88.67	81.41	90.79	85.28	97.92	83.99	84.43
Geothermal[1]	84.31	114.25	111.40	81.49	78.77	79.85	89.16	89.03
Solar	..	..	..	0.16	0.19	0.20	0.23	0.24
Wind	0.14	0.43	0.50	0.56	0.53	1.31	2.19	2.22
Biomass and landfill gas	1.63	1.47	1.48	1.73	1.87	1.57	2.34	2.30
Woody biomass and animal products[2]	34.94	35.88	36.21	38.22	38.58	40.70	42.58	42.21
Total	**204.74**	**240.71**	**231.00**	**212.95**	**205.23**	**221.55**	**220.50**	**220.43**
Energy transformation (including losses)								
Hydro	83.73	88.67	81.41	90.79	85.28	97.92	83.99	84.43
Geothermal[1]	70.00	104.80	101.86	71.78	69.19	70.31	79.49	79.30
Wind	0.14	0.43	0.50	0.56	0.53	1.31	2.19	2.22
Biogas and landfill gas	1.49	1.32	1.30	1.54	1.69	1.46	2.12	2.02
Woody biomass and animal products[2]	6.04	6.88	5.56	6.35	5.73	6.21	7.46	7.49
Final consumption								
Geothermal[3]	14.31	9.45	9.54	9.72	9.58	9.54	9.67	9.73
Solar	..	..	..	0.16	0.19	0.20	0.23	0.24
Biomass and landfill gas	0.14	0.15	0.18	0.19	0.18	0.11	0.22	0.28
Woody biomass and animal products[2]	28.90	29.00	30.64	31.87	32.86	34.49	35.13	34.72
Total	**43.35**	**38.60**	**40.36**	**41.94**	**42.81**	**44.34**	**45.25**	**44.97**

(1) Efficiency of geothermal plants for electricity generation is assumed to be 10 percent prior to 2000. From 2000, it is assumed to be 15 percent. (2) Before 2004, the residential firewood use figure was based on a 4.3GJ per household average. After 2004, results from the Household Energy End-use Project (HEEP), carried out by BRANZ, were used. HEEP monitored actual use, reporting annual average use of 13.7GJ. (3) 2000 figures were based on: *An Assessment of Geothermal Direct Heat Use in New Zealand*, by Brian White of the New Zealand Geothermal Association.

Note: Figures may not add up to stated totals due to rounding.

Symbol: .. figure not available

Sources: Ministry of Economic Development, Statistics New Zealand

Hau Nui, in the Wairarapa and owned by Genesis Energy, was first commissioned in 1997 and now has a total capacity of 8.65 megawatts (MW).

In 1999, TrustPower commissioned stage one of the Tararua wind farm near Palmerston North – 48 wind turbines rated at 660kW each. The second stage was completed in May 2004, and brought the total capacity to 68MW from 103 turbines.

A 500kW Windflow Technology turbine at Gebbies Pass near Christchurch was commissioned in July 2003. Meridian Energy's Te Apiti wind farm, near Palmerston North, began supplying electricity to Transpower's national grid in August 2004, with a total generating capacity of 91MW.

In March 2005, Energy3 commissioned a 100kW pilot project in Southbridge, Canterbury.

The first stage of Te Rere Hau wind farm in the Tararua Ranges was commissioned in September 2006. Te Rere Hau is the first wind farm in New Zealand to be built using New Zealand designed and manufactured turbines. Stage I is five turbines with a total generating capacity of 2.5MW.

Two new large wind projects were commissioned in 2007. Meridian Energy opened the first South Island wind farm in July 2007, in Southland, with a total capacity of 58MW. In September 2007, stage three of TrustPower's Tararua wind farm opened, increasing capacity from 68MW to 161MW by adding 31 extra 3MW turbines.

At mid 2007, the total wind generating capacity in New Zealand was 322MW, almost double the capacity from the previous year.

Solar energy

Solar energy is available throughout the country, although amounts vary according to a region's sunshine hours. On average, New Zealand has about 2,000 hours of sunshine each year, making the solar energy resource plentiful.

The performance of a solar heating system is determined by the collector area, the hot water storage tank size, the amount of hot water used and whether boosting is controlled by electricity, gas or wetback. For 2006–07, an average of 4,000 solar water-heating systems were installed each year, mainly on private residences and commercial buildings. There are two main types of solar collectors for water heating – flat plate panels, and evacuated tubes. In New Zealand's temperate climate both types are equally efficient. During 2006, there were 4,060 water heating systems with 12,320 square metres of collector area installed.

Minerals

New Zealand has a wide variety of minerals, reflecting its diverse geology and dynamic tectonic history.

While it is best known for gold production (10,617 kilograms in the year ending 31 December 2006), there is also production of silver, ironsand, coal, aggregate, limestone, clay, dolomite, pumice, salt, serpentine, zeolite and bentonite. In addition, there are resources, or potential deposits, of titanium (ilmenite beachsands), platinum, sulphur, phosphate, silica and mercury.

Mineral legislation The Crown owns all of New Zealand's petroleum, gold and silver, along with approximately half of in-ground coal, metallic and non-metallic minerals, industrial rocks, and building stones. Permits to prospect, explore or mine Crown-owned minerals are issued under the Crown Minerals Act 1991. The relevant minerals programme and regulations are administered

Hukanui School

Students from Hamilton's Hukanui School look over the open pit of Martha's gold mine at Waihi near Coromandel. The mine, which began operating in 1987, produced more than 4,800 kilograms of gold in 2006. Waihi also has an underground mine at Favona.

Cleaning up after mining

The Golden Cross mine in the Coromandel area produced 20.5 tonnes of gold and 52 tonnes of silver between 1991 and 1998. It is the first modern mine to close. But before mining started, it had a long-term rehabilitation plan, which was updated while it operated.

Today, mining is regarded as a temporary use for land. It is the responsibility of the mine operator to plan and put in place environmental programmes during the operation of the mine and at closure. Mining companies must hold significant bonds (usually millions of dollars for large mines) with local authorities to guarantee the closure plan will be completed.

The Resource Management Act 1991 (RMA) regulates the use of land, lake and river beds, and water, and also the discharge of contaminants into the environment. Resource consents granted under the RMA are to ensure the effects of mining on the area or the natural environment are controlled. This includes plans for both concurrent and post-closure rehabilitation of the land.

Operational issues such as noise, dust, and surface and groundwater quality are regularly monitored. Any waste rock and tailings must be contained within an engineered embankment, which becomes part of the rehabilitation on closure. Landforms left must be safe, stable and self-sustaining.

Regional and district councils monitor operations throughout the life of the mine, to ensure compliance with the consents granted. Final rehabilitation is completed when all the original consent conditions have been satisfied and the area is again a safe landform. The mining company's bond ensures no ratepayer funds are needed to rehabilitate the site.

In 2008, site rehabilitation at Golden Cross mine was complete – the land returned to pasture and native trees, and walking paths established. A small volume of water from the underground mine, partly related to century-old mine workings, continues to be treated.

The tailings pond, which once contained waste slurry and the unrecycled part of the cyanide used to extract the gold and silver, is now home to wading birds and waterfowl. The site is used for recreation and education, while the office provides accommodation.

Source: New Zealand Minerals Industry Association

by Crown Minerals, a group within the Ministry of Economic Development. The government sees the development of petroleum and mineral resources as a significant contributor to national and regional economic development. A permit from Crown Minerals does not give land access, which is negotiated with each landowner and occupier. Environmental impact is regulated under the Resource Management Act 1991, with resource consents granted by district or regional councils.

Metals

Gold is present in New Zealand in quartz veins. It is finely dispersed through host rocks, and as alluvial gold in river gravels. The majority of gold production during 2006 came from two hard-rock mines, Macraes mine in east Otago, the largest mine in New Zealand, and the Martha mine at Waihi, in the Coromandel area. Macraes mine produced more than 5,000 kilograms in 2006, while the open-pit Martha mine, which began operating in 1987, produced more than 4,800 kilograms.

There has been an increased level of exploration for hard-rock gold in recent years, with permit interests and drilling activity around the country. Three new projects are under development. In the Reefton area, the Globe Progress mine will be an open-pit operation, and the Blackwater mine will be underground – targeting the deep Birthday Reef, originally mined in the first half of the 20th century. An underground resource at Favona, near Waihi and the Martha mine, started production in 2006.

Alluvial gold mining continues in the South Island, mainly on the West Coast and in Otago. Extraction methods range from sole-operator plants, to medium and large floating or skid-mounted plants fed by hydraulic excavators.

In 2006, production from outside the two major gold mining operations totalled almost 500 kilograms.

Silver was historically produced mainly in the Coromandel area and is almost always associated with gold in various proportions. Production in recent years has been mostly from the Martha mine at Waihi, although production from the Macraes mine has increased sharply. In the year ending 31 December 2006, national silver production totalled 27,220 kilograms.

Iron ore is a large resource found in the black sands of the North Island's west coast beaches, especially between Muriwai and Wanganui. Two deposits of titanomagnetite (ironsand) are mined by Bluescope Steel Ltd. At Waikato North Head, mining has been carried out since 1969 using two bucket-wheel excavators which convey the ore to concentration plants. The titanomagnetite concentrate slurry is then pumped through an 18-kilometre pipeline to the Glenbrook steel mill. Here it is reduced in a solid state process, and smelted with scrap in an electrical arc furnace to produce a range of steel products. The operation at Taharoa, which started in 1972, pumps titanomagnetite concentrate slurry to ships moored offshore for export to Japan, the Republic of Korea and China.

In the year ending 31 December 2006, ironsand production totalled 2,146,496 tonnes. Production from the Waikato North Head operation remained high as a result of strong local demand for steel. Production from the Taharoa operation, exclusively for export, was 921,191 tonnes in 2006.

Ilmenite is found in sands along 320 kilometres of the South Island's west coast. The largest known ilmenite resource is at Barrytown, where exploration has defined a 50-million-tonne resource. South of Westport, another quantity of 17–30 million tonnes contains ilmenite. Ilmenite is a source of titanium dioxide, used as a pigment in paint, paper, plastics, cloth and rubber, and to make them opaque. Garnet is a major component of the sand and zircon a minor component.

Platinum group metals are being sought in a number of areas in the South Island. The Longwood Range, in western Southland, which consists of a layered gabbro (dark, granular, plutonic, crystalline rock) complex, is the only site in New Zealand where platinum has been produced – in association with alluvial gold.

Other metallic minerals are found in small deposits in many localities. Some areas of Northland, Coromandel, Nelson, and Westland have potential for base metals (copper, lead and zinc), but there is little prospecting. Iron ore, stibnite (antimony), orpiment (arsenic), chromite, monazite (rare earths), nickel, and rutile have all been mined in the past. Cassiterite (tin) is known in Stewart Island. Bauxite is present in Northland, where 20 million tonnes of reserves have been identified. Cinnabar, the principal ore of mercury, was historically produced in limited quantities from sinter deposits in Northland.

Non-metallic minerals

In the year ending 31 December 2006, 46.12 million tonnes of non-metals (industrial minerals) were quarried in New Zealand.

This was made up of: the production of limestone for marl and cement (1.76 million tonnes), rock, sand and gravel for roading (24.1 million tonnes), rock, sand and gravel for building (8.6 million tonnes), rock, sand, gravel and clay for fill (4.4 million tonnes), silica sand (58,824 tonnes), pumice (305,659 tonnes), decorative pebbles including scoria (131,074 tonnes), perlite (3,552 tonnes), bentonite (3,028 tonnes), building and dimension stone (22,880 tonnes), dolomite for industry (1,626 tonnes), limestone for industry and roading (948,366 tonnes), limestone for agriculture (2.3 million tonnes), sand for industry (2.4 million tonnes), and serpentine (41,000 tonnes).

Aggregates are produced from a variety of rocks, gravels and sands and are used in road construction and concrete manufacture. Suitable rocks for aggregate production are found throughout New Zealand.

Clays found throughout New Zealand include bentonite, halloysite and kaolinite. They are used in the manufacture of sanitary ware, ceramics, bricks, tiles, pipes and pottery; as fillers in the manufacture of paper, paint, pharmaceutical and animal health products; and as pelletising agents. White halloysite from Northland's Matauri Bay is exported for the manufacture of fine ceramics and porcelain. Bentonite, found in substantial quantities in Hawke's Bay and Canterbury, is used as a bonding agent and for specialist drilling products. Although bentonite is still imported for drilling operations, because long-established overseas sources are commonly preferred, New Zealand bentonite is increasingly being used.

Dolomite rock, used in agriculture, glassmaking and for harbour protection blocks, is produced near Collingwood in Golden Bay.

Greenstone is also called nephrite and bowenite, and popularly known as pounamu. It is found in Westland and northern Fiordland. A deposit of nephrite boulders in a tributary of the Arahura River has been the main source of greenstone. Best known occurrences of bowenite, the serpentine variety of greenstone, are in the Griffin range in Westland and in Fiordland. Boulders of greenstone are reduced in size using a portable diamond saw, and airlifted by helicopter. Ownership of pounamu was returned to Ngāi Tahu, the South Island's largest Māori iwi (tribe) as part of its Treaty of Waitangi settlement.

Limestone is found throughout New Zealand and is used in cement manufacture, roading, industry and agriculture. High quality limestone from Te Kuiti in the North Island, and Nelson in the South Island, is processed for export. Limestone is also used in New Zealand as a filler in the paint, glass, rubber, plastic and paper industries. A crystallised form of limestone, marble, is mined in Nelson and used as a filler and in building construction.

Salt is produced by the solar evaporation of sea water at Lake Grassmere, in Marlborough. Low rainfall, long hours of sunlight and the right wind conditions make this locality the most suitable in New Zealand for salt production. About 60,000 tonnes are produced each year for the domestic market.

Serpentine is a magnesium-rich rock which is used as a fertiliser additive, and in the manufacture of decorative tiles. Deposits are mined at Piopio, near Hamilton, and at Greenhills in Southland.

Silica sand deposits are found in Northland and Canterbury, and mined for use in glass manufacture, foundry moulds, and in the building industry.

Sulphur is used mainly in the production of agricultural fertiliser, and is mined at Tikitere, near Rotorua.

Zeolite is mined at Ngakuru, in the central North Island near Rotorua. It is used in horticulture, and as animal litter.

Other non-metallic minerals, some of which have been mined in the past, are also present in New Zealand. They include: diatomite (used for industrial filtration), barite (industrial uses include glassmaking and fillers), asbestos (building material), feldspar (glassmaking, ceramics and enamels), magnesite (agriculture), mica (electronics), phosphate (fertiliser), talc (cosmetics) and wollastonite (paper, asbestos substitute, ceramics, adhesives and plastics).

Putting clay on the table

The source of an ingredient in some of the world's finest porcelain and bone china is Northland's Matauri Bay. The china isn't manufactured here, but the halloysite clay mined is the whitest clay in the world and is valued by tableware manufacturers in 24 countries.

The very white clay deposits in Northland were formed through the alteration of volcanic rocks. Weathering over millions of years has 'rotted' the rocks into clay minerals and residual silica. The raw material is 50 percent halloysite clay and 50 percent silica. It is the low level of iron that makes the clay so white.

The purity and microscopic structure of the clay also adds translucency to ceramic ware.

The raw material from the quarries is crushed, milled, separated, filtered, dried, and packaged for export. Processing removes most of the silica from the clay, making it available locally for concreting, plastering, and general construction.

A small but increasing amount of halloysite is also used for hi-tech ceramics. Honeycomb catalyst support units are placed in vehicle exhaust systems to clean up exhaust gases.

Almost all the white clay is exported. But eventually some does return to New Zealand – as elegant tableware, with labels such as Noritake (from Japan), Duraline (England), Monno (Bangladesh), Limoges (France) and Llandro (Spain).

Source: New Zealand Minerals Industry Association

Merv Dickey, supervisor of the gold room at the Macraes mine in Otago, holds a 25-kilogram bar containing the two-millionth ounce of gold produced at the mine (in late 2005). In 2006, Macraes produced more than 5,000 kilograms from its large open-pit mine.

Contributors and related websites

Crown Minerals, Ministry of Economic Development – www.crownminerals.govt.nz

Electricity Commission – www.electricitycommission.govt.nz

Energy Efficiency and Conservation Authority – www.eeca.govt.nz

Foundation for Research, Science and Technology – www.frst.govt.nz

Genesis Energy – www.genesisenergy.co.nz

GRD Ltd – www.grd.com.au

Meridian Energy – www.meridianenergy.co.nz

Ministry of Economic Development – www.med.govt.nz

New Zealand Minerals Industry Association – www.minerals.co.nz

Newmont Waihi Gold – www.marthamine.co.nz

Scion – www.scionresearch.com

Solid Energy New Zealand Ltd – www.coalnz.com

Transpower New Zealand Ltd – www.transpower.co.nz

TrustPower – www.trustpower.co.nz

The Buy Kiwi Made campaign stall at the Auckland Food Show in August 2007 featured New Zealand manufacturers and their products.

21 | Manufacturing

The future of New Zealand manufacturing depends on the sector's ability to innovate and service global markets. To excel in the rapidly evolving global environment, manufacturers have to create and capitalise on their own initiatives, and distinguish themselves from their competitors. Firms have to be innovative, enterprising and able to respond swiftly to the market.

To achieve this, successful manufacturers encourage high levels of quality in both their operations and their management. The need to remain ahead of the competition has also resulted in increased emphasis on productivity and technology innovation.

Most countries in the Organisation for Economic Co-operation and Development (OECD) have strong policies of increasing innovation to remain competitive. The aim is to create new products and services, maximise the resulting economic returns, and move into new products, before they become 'standardised' or 'commoditised'. To achieve this, the manufacturing sector needs to be aware of, and closely aligned with, market trends.

New Zealand's business environment provides a strong framework for manufacturers to create and capitalise on opportunities. However, the sector needs to continue to respond to the constantly changing global environment.

The government, through New Zealand Trade and Enterprise (NZTE), provides a range of export development services and programmes to manufacturing firms. NZTE targets firms that produce low-volume, high-value niche export-market goods. It works with these firms to develop manufacturing clusters, long-term growth strategies, and access to export markets.

Targeted niche manufacturing areas have included engineering, marine manufacturing, plastics and electronics, and the food and beverage sector.

Table 21.01 (overleaf) shows contributions to gross domestic product (GDP) made by the manufacturing sector.

Tariffs

Approximately 95 percent of imports (by value) enter New Zealand free of duty, and most other imports face low tariffs of 5–7 percent.

Following a tariff review in 2003 by the Ministry of Economic Development, the government decided on the gradual reduction of *ad valorem* tariffs – tariffs that are calculated as a percentage of the goods' total value (rather than per item) – finishing in 2009.

Table 21.01

Manufacturing sector contribution to GDP

Year ending 31 March

Year	Contribution to GDP[1] (million)	Change from previous year (percent)	Total GDP[1] ($million)
2000	16,369	4.9	104,041
2001	16,794	2.6	106,551
2002	16,941	0.9	110,554
2003	18,398	8.6	116,143
2004	18,892	2.7	120,220
2005	19,324	2.3	125,069
2006	19,012	-1.6	128,428
2007	18,667	-1.8	130,442

(1) Chain-volume series expressed in 1995/96 prices.

Source: Statistics New Zealand

The highest *ad valorem* tariff rate of 15 percent (applying to carpet, clothing, headgear, footwear, ambulances and motor homes) was reduced to 12.5 percent on 1 July 2008 and will be further reduced to 10 percent on 1 July 2009. Tarrif rates on all other goods were reduced to 5 percent by July 2008.

Free trade agreements

Bilateral and regional free trade agreements (FTAs) play an increasingly important role in international trade.

In FTA negotiations, New Zealand seeks reciprocal removal of tariffs on all goods.

New Zealand's Closer Economic Partnership Agreement with Thailand came into force in 2005. By November 2006, the Trans-Pacific Strategic Economic Partnership, an FTA with Chile, Brunei and Singapore, had come into force for all partners. An FTA with China was signed in April 2008.

Negotiations for further agreements with Malaysia, and the Association of Southeast Asian Nations (ASEAN) are continuing. Negotiations with the Gulf Cooperation Council (involving Saudi Arabia, Bahrain, United Arab Emirates, Oman, Qatar and Kuwait) commenced in July 2007.

Ministry of Economic Development

The Ministry of Economic Development Manatū Ōhanga works cooperatively with businesses, regions, local government, iwi (tribes) and other state sector agencies, on activities that stimulate economic development.

The government's economic transformation agenda aims to move New Zealand's economy towards greater productivity and higher value activity. The ministry is working to ensure that New Zealand's business environment actively promotes and enables a higher rate of sustainable economic development. The ministry leads and coordinates policy advice related to economic, regional and industry development. It also works with New Zealand Trade and Enterprise to design and implement programmes to deliver the government's economic development policies.

The ministry is also the government's primary advisor on the operation and regulation of specific markets and industries, including energy and telecommunications.

The ministry is focused on providing a legal framework that protects intellectual property, ensures appropriate rights for consumers and investors, allows markets to function effectively, and helps New Zealand businesses to compete effectively in the international arena.

New Zealand Trade and Enterprise

New Zealand Trade and Enterprise (NZTE) works to stimulate economic growth by helping to boost export earnings, strengthen regional economies, and deliver economic development assistance to industries and individual businesses. NZTE uses its knowledge and contacts in overseas markets to connect New Zealand businesses with trade and investment opportunities.

Buy Kiwi Made – Buy Kiwi Mad

Buy New Zealand Made

The 2007 'Buy Kiwi Made' media campaign promoted consumer awareness of locally-made products, encouraged domestic producers to label their goods "New Zealand made", and urged retailers to stock and promote New Zealand-made goods. It also encouraged manufacturers to become members of Buy NZ Made Campaign Ltd, the membership organisation that licenses the use of the kiwi in a triangle logo.

The $6.3 million Buy Kiwi Made campaign involved a nationwide newspaper and magazine insert, *New Zealand We've Got it Made*, which celebrated the story of New Zealand manufacturing and the more than 250,000 people working in the industry. After five months, the membership of Buy NZ Made had increased by more than 50 percent. Consumers were the focus of newspaper, magazine, television, radio and outdoor advertising.

Research showed that where price and quality were the same, nine out of 10 consumers preferred to purchase New Zealand-made goods and nine out of 10 retailers preferred to stock them. About one-third of manufacturers whose goods could qualify to be labelled as "New Zealand made" said they were not labelling them.

The Government's programme also included a sector and regional initiatives fund of $3 million, and government leadership through public sector procurement policies. In February 2008, the Government agreed to transfer $2 million from the Buy Kiwi Made sector and regional initiatives fund to enable the media campaign to be extended.

April 2008 was 'Buy Kiwi Mad' month. It celebrated 100 years of manufacturing, with advertising, events and promotions encouraging consumers to look for New Zealand-made goods.

Source: Ministry of Economic Development

The New Zealand Herald

Brad Lathorpe, a technician at Nautech Electronics, fits out a new police car. The company has a contract to outfit cars for the Queensland police in Australia.

Companies just starting-up, through to established groups of exporters, can use NZTE services and programmes. These include advice, training, mentoring, funding, and business and market development assistance. Some services are provided directly by NZTE and others are provided through external organisations funded by NZTE.

Business incubators are designed to help businesses become established and sustainable during their start-up phase. Incubators typically do this by providing shared premises, business advice and services, networking, mentoring, and a full-time manager. The incubation period for an individual business is normally one to three years. NZTE's Incubator Awards provide financial support to approved New Zealand incubators. At June 2007, $14.8 million had been awarded since the programme was established in 2001.

Enterprise Training Programme is aimed at upskilling the owners and operators of small and medium enterprises to help them develop and grow their businesses. The programme is delivered by specialist training providers throughout New Zealand. It offers training for managing a business, complemented by follow-up coaching that is designed to help business owners implement what they have learned.

Business Information Zone is a specialist business information and referral service for small to medium businesses. The service helps New Zealanders to identify organisations, people, training programmes and resources that can help them to develop their business. It also provides contacts and information on government and non-government services. Online information about running a business is available at www.business.govt.nz. This is a free and independent business resource, and a convenient way to find tools and information to help start, manage, and grow a business.

Escalator Service provides specialist skills and assistance to raise equity funding or consolidate a strategic relationship that may help a business expand, diversify, or market a product or service.

Enterprise Development Grants Programme aims to help New Zealand businesses and entrepreneurs gain the additional skills and abilities that they need to pursue their business development goal. The programme builds capability and supports development initiatives.

Industry Capability Network encourages major purchasers in the New Zealand and Australian markets to use competitive local products instead of imported products. The major focus of this activity is on large projects that provide clear opportunities for import substitution, and benefit local industry. The Australasian Industry Capability Network ensures opportunities for import substitution are coordinated within the wider New Zealand and Australian market.

E-business Guide provides information and practical advice to help businesses grow by using information technology and the Internet. The self-service guide allows businesses to work through e-business development at their own pace, while an adviser is also available to talk them through the process.

Business mentors are funded by NZTE, through Business Mentors New Zealand. Their programmes are provided by people with proven business skills and experience. Businesses can also use the enterprise development grants to employ mentors, get specialist advice, and engage a small-business advisory board.

International services help New Zealand businesses with their international market development plans. The services include generic market information and more specific customised research for New Zealand businesses that are considered capable of succeeding overseas. Some services are provided directly by NZTE and others are from external organisations.

Exporter Education Programme is designed to provide existing and new exporters with the skills and advice to help them increase exports. Services offered include an export assessment, export workshops, follow-up coaching, and one-to-one business support training.

Beachheads Programme gives companies with high-growth potential faster access to better international networks. The programme is designed around a unique partnership between NZTE and successful executives who are willing to share their experience, skills and business networks. These executives help New Zealand businesses accelerate their market entry and growth in key export markets.

Market intelligence and news comes from NZTE's network of offices in New Zealand and around the world. The offices provide practical information on New Zealand's top international markets. NZTE's online trade enquiry system also enables businesses with proven export capability to profile their products and services to an international business audience, and receive trade enquiries, through www.marketnewzealand.com.

Manufacturing groups

Some of the major secondary industries in New Zealand are briefly described below.

Food The New Zealand food manufacturing industry produces high-quality products for both the domestic and export market. This industry enjoys the advantages of a natural environment that is highly conducive to pastoral agriculture, a disease-free status, the potential for year-round production, and an international reputation for excellence.

The industry had sales of over $28 billion in the year ending 2007, including more than $20 billion for meat and dairy. Meat and dairy exports of $13.5 billion brought total food manufacturing exports to $17.5 billion.

During the 2005/06 financial year the food manufacturing industry invested $94 million in research and development. At February 2007, more than 75,000 people were employed in the industry.

Plastics The New Zealand plastics industry, excluding composites, had an annual turnover of more than $2.5 billion for the year ending December 2007, and at February 2007 employed 10,670 people in 575 enterprises.

A major use of plastics is in the packaging industry, which supports New Zealand's agriculture, horticulture and aquaculture sectors. Other significant end users of plastics include home appliance manufacturers, the information technology industry, and the building and construction sector.

Growth in this competitive and highly technical industry is being driven globally by the increasing substitution of plastics for other less versatile, more expensive materials. The New Zealand industry keeps up with world growth through innovation in process, design, and customer service.

Sustainable business of the year

Float – a bed design by David Trubridge for Design Mobel.

The top award at the 2007 NZI National Sustainable Business Awards went to Design Mobel, a designer and manufacturer of slat beds, mattresses and bedroom furniture.

Design Mobel has been committed to sustainable business practices in resource use, product design, and the manufacturing process, since its establishment 20 years ago.

The Tauranga-based company assesses the life cycle of its products – from raw materials to manufacturing, and including waste by-product. Wood is sourced from sustainable forests and, wherever possible, Design Mobel uses natural products – including bamboo, cotton, natural latex and wool. Their timber waste is formed into briquettes before being sold as fuel. Design briefs are created with sustainability in mind.

Design Mobel has achieved international environmental and quality standard certification (ISO14001 and ISO9001). Their next goal is to achieve zero waste.

The awards celebrate businesses that are making outstanding progress towards sustainability. Other category winners in 2007 were Contact Energy, Bees Online, YHA Wellington City, Starfish, and Fumes TV.

Sources: Sustainable Business Network and Design Mobel

The New Zealand Herald

Canvasland managing director Brendan Duffy in the general production area of his Levin factory. The company makes a range of innovative canvas and PVC products including bouncy castles, trampolines and goal post protectors and is a member of DesignTex, an industry group given $2 million by the Government to develop the textile industry in the lower North Island.

Better by Design

Mastering design and innovation principles is translating into increased exports for the more than 100 companies participating in the Better by Design programme.

Better by Design helps New Zealand companies increase their international competitiveness by integrating design principles right across the business – into their production and manufacturing processes, branding and communications, leadership, and company culture. Better by Design is part of New Zealand Trade and Enterprise, with an independent advisory board made up of leading private sector business people.

Independent research in 2007 found that on average, Better by Design companies have grown their export revenues by more than 20 percent after one year in the programme. They have also made changes to ensure sustainable, long-term growth, such as increasing research and development to rates higher than the national average, and hiring in-house industrial designers.

The programme's results mean it is well on the way to achieving the target of having its top 50 companies growing at five times targeted gross domestic product (currently around 3 percent) after five years in the programme, and adding hundreds of millions of dollars to the economy.

Companies across all sectors are represented in the programme. Specialised manufacturing companies such as Design Mobel, phil&teds, and timber products company Key Lumber are among those making changes. Key Lumber was named the fastest-growing agriculture company in New Zealand in the 2007 Deloitte Fast 50, after it began focusing on outdoor landscaping solutions and manu-factured products.

The role of design in improving New Zealand exports was highlighted by a government-appointed taskforce as part of the growth and innovation framework. It showed that well-designed products gain a bigger market share, demand premium prices, and are more efficient to produce. A culture of design and innovation in a company paves the way for future breakthroughs.

Companies selected for the programme work through a six-stage design integration programme, which starts with a 360-degree assessment, and includes the development of a plan outlining opportunities and potential projects.

Better by Design also works as an advocate for education, by running workshops and conferences and offering design internships for leading design graduates.

Source: New Zealand Trade and Enterprise

Figure 21.01

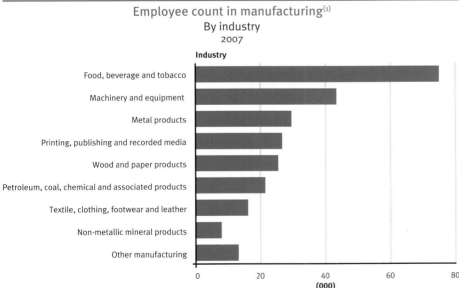

Employee count in manufacturing[1]
By industry
2007

(1) The employee count is a head count of salary and wage earners, sourced from taxation data.

Source: Statistics New Zealand

Marine New Zealand's marine industry has built its profile on the back of sporting success in international yachting regattas such as the Olympics and the America's Cup. This has led to a worldwide reputation for excellence in the design and construction of top level racing yachts and super yachts.

Figure 21.01 shows the total employee count for the different industry groups, while table 21.02 (overleaf) shows employment numbers by industry and region.

The New Zealand Herald

Ingrid Jagersma, general manager of JJ Wafer Biscuits, inspects sheets of wafer biscuits as they come off the production line. More than 75,000 people were employed in food manufacturing in 2007.

New Zealand has set benchmark standards for high performance and advanced technology in the areas of racing technique, boat building and design, refits, sails, spars, electronics, technology, software and systems.

Annual turnover for boat and ship manufacturing in the year ending 31 December 2007 was $770 million. Exports totalled $287 million, including re-exports of $66 million. In February 2007, 750 companies were engaged in ship and boat building, employing around 4,420 people.

Textiles The New Zealand textiles industry consists of four interrelated sectors – textiles, carpet, footwear, and apparel – and has a reputation for innovative technology and quality products. New Zealand produces some of the finest quality wool and fibre in the world. Local producers' and exporters' knowledge of sheep and wool fibre is backed by an international reputation for innovation in manufacturing processes and products.

Table 21.02

Regional employee count in manufacturing[1]
By industry
2007

Region	Food, beverage & tobacco	Textile, clothing, footwear & leather	Wood & paper products	Printing, publishing & recorded media	Petrol, coal, chemical & associated products	Non-metallic mineral products	Metal products	Machinery & equipment	Other manufacturing	**Total employed 2007**	Total employed 2006
Northland	1,560	110	1,410	350	550	390	570	1,140	310	**6,370**	6,580
Auckland	15,380	6,130	5,090	11,270	10,750	3,430	12,590	17,200	6,050	**87,900**	89,910
Waikato	7,700	500	3,720	1,470	1,550	650	3,180	4,080	640	**23,490**	24,000
Bay of Plenty	3,280	330	3,930	770	980	320	1,400	2,360	710	**14,070**	14,360
Gisborne	1,140	140	450	160	12	85	110	190	30	**2,320**	2,230
Hawke's Bay	6,110	1,070	1,120	410	380	250	680	890	500	**11,380**	12,060
Taranaki	4,440	90	690	560	430	100	1,360	1,220	180	**9,070**	8,820
Manawatu/Wanganui	4,370	1,510	1,230	1,180	600	290	1,150	1,620	640	**12,590**	12,780
Wellington	3,150	1,120	1,550	3,670	1,940	400	2,030	2,570	1,200	**17,650**	18,650
Tasman	840	25	900	25	70	100	180	160	75	**2,370**	2,430
Nelson	1,740	160	330	460	140	30	230	430	95	**3,590**	3,580
Marlborough	2,100	55	290	300	110	60	240	510	140	**3,810**	4,170
West Coast	640	18	290	100	15	170	35	180	90	**1,550**	1,610
Canterbury	11,450	3,640	2,570	3,700	3,560	1,160	3,240	8,490	2,060	**39,870**	40,330
Otago	5,390	890	1,040	1,560	240	330	960	1,730	310	**12,450**	12,520
Southland	5,650	270	760	620	80	140	1,560	670	90	**9,820**	9,460

(1) Employee count is a head count of all salary and wage earners, including working proprietors who also pay themselves a taxable salary or wage.
Note: Figures may not add up to totals due to rounding.

Source: Statistics New Zealand

The industry is a significant contributor to the New Zealand economy, with an annual turnover of nearly $2.5 billion in the year ending December 2007. Exports totalled around $1.7 billion, including re-exports of $0.2 billion. New Zealand apparel, from high-performance sportswear to children's clothing and designer fashion, is exported around the world.

In February 2007, the industry employed about 16,000 people in more than 1,750 businesses. The textiles industry invested $25.9 million in research and development in the 2005/06 financial year.

Manufacturing statistics

Statistics New Zealand's Quarterly Economic Survey of Manufacturing gives a representative estimate of economic activity for 17 groups within the manufacturing sector.

The survey asks for information about operating income, purchases and operating expenditure, salaries and wages, closing stocks of materials and finished goods, and additions to and disposals of fixed assets.

Table 21.03 presents economic activity results for recent years, and table 21.04 shows manufacturing sector contributions, by industry group.

Table 21.03

Manufacturing economic activity
Year ending 31 March

Year	Operating income	Purchases & operating expenditure	Salaries & wages	Stock of raw materials for use in production	Finished goods, work in progress & trading stocks	Additions to fixed assets	Disposal of fixed assets
				$(million)			
2000	54,146	39,103	8,582	9,289	15,309	2,314	0
2001	60,537	43,698	8,796	10,037	17,101	1,949	0
2002	63,364	47,077	8,961	10,289	18,578	2,806	336
2003	65,069	47,612	9,539	10,538	23,743	2,392	327
2004	66,232	48,163	10,300	10,523	25,763	2,698	380
2005	69,555	51,325	10,843	11,537	26,631	2,685	450
2006	70,261	51,657	11,048	11,736	28,590	2,678	502
2007	74,412	53,710	11,498	11,625	28,860	2,598	480

Source: Statistics New Zealand

Table 21.04

Manufacturing sector contributions
By industry group
Year ending 31 March 2007

Industry group	Operating income	Purchases & operating expenditure	Salaries & wages	Stock of raw materials for use in production	Finished goods, work in progress & trading stocks
			$(million)		
Dairy and meat products	19,809	15,889	1,893	1,000	10,138
Other food	7,531	5,692	1,031	1,083	2,562
Beverages, malt and tobacco	3,540	2,313	385	851	2,436
Textile and apparel	2,500	1,651	573	720	1,229
Wood products	4,636	3,389	766	637	1,809
Paper and paper products	2,805	2,196	365	454	916
Printing, publishing and recorded media	3,833	2,112	931	394	414
Petroleum and industrial chemicals	2,629	1,848	253	757	825
Rubber, plastic and other chemical products	5,176	3,688	936	1,172	2,508
Non-metallic mineral products	2,705	1,826	403	239	666
Basic metal products	2,579	1,865	368	502	715
Structural, sheet and fabricated metal products	5,138	3,449	1,038	928	1,054
Transport equipment	2,339	1,487	642	777	700
Machinery and equipment	7,058	4,852	1,468	1,590	2,398
Furniture and other manufacturing	2,128	1,446	440	513	483

Source: Statistics New Zealand

Powering manufacturing

In the year ending 31 March 2006, the manufacturing industry used 151.97 petajoules of energy. This is roughly equivalent to the total electricity that would be used by 5.3 million households in one year.

The wood and paper product manufacturing industry was the largest user of energy, accounting for 38 percent of the total used. Half the energy used by this industry group came from wood and wood-waste products, such as shavings, sawdust and bark.

The food, beverage and tobacco industry was the second-largest user of energy, accounting for almost 24 percent of the total energy used by the manufacturing industry. This was followed by the metal product manufacturing industry, at 20 percent of the total. The remaining industry groups collectively used just under 18 percent of the total.

Electricity was the energy type used in greatest quantity, at almost 35 percent of total energy use. This was followed by wood and wood waste, and natural gas, each at 19 percent.

Fifty-seven percent of businesses reported that they actively recorded and monitored their energy use in the March 2006 year. Nine percent of businesses had a formal energy policy and 37 percent had an informal energy policy.

Sources: Statistics New Zealand and Ministry of Economic Development

Contributors and related websites

Buy Kiwi Made – www.buykiwimade.govt.nz

Design Mobel – www.designmobel.co.nz

Ministry of Economic Development – www.med.govt.nz

New Zealand Trade and Enterprise – www.nzte.govt.nz

Statistics New Zealand – www.stats.govt.nz

Sustainable Business Network – www.sustainable.org.nz

Lloyd McGinty, from the 'Energy Doctor' service, checks the insulation in the roof space of a Titahi Bay house near Wellington. Energy doctors visit homes to advise homeowners on how to improve their energy efficiency.

22 | Housing and construction

Housing

A house provides shelter and security for both the family and the individual. A home can fulfil social requirements as well as physical needs, allowing individuals the opportunity to express aspirations and tastes.

Housing is a central part of the domestic economy, since it is a major source of investment for many New Zealanders and provides employment and livelihood for a variety of trades.

Home ownership is seen as a form of investment savings, an expression of independence and a way to achieve security and self-determination. While home ownership is still the main form of tenure, the proportion of households that do not own the house they live in has been increasing in New Zealand. In the 2006 Census, 33.1 percent of privately occupied dwellings were not owned by the household, compared with 29.3 percent in the 1996 Census.

The 2006 Census also revealed that the average number of usual residents per household has decreased marginally in the last 10 years – from 2.8 in 1996 to 2.7 in 2006.

House prices The average sale price for houses in the year ending 31 December 2006 was $362,501, as shown in table 22.01. This was 11.3 percent higher than the average price for the previous year ($325,678) and 99.9 percent higher than that recorded nine years previously in 1997 ($181,372).

Table 22.01

Average sale price of property By property type Year ending 31 December					
	2002	2003	2004	2005	2006
Property type			$		
Section (bare land)	99,309	114,971	144,172	170,827	193,944
House	226,941	249,039	285,158	325,678	362,501
Owner-occupier flat	190,137	214,479	238,100	251,062	296,642

Source: Quotable Value

NOW Homes® are live research projects that demonstrate how environmentally sustainable, affordable, and desirable houses can be built by using design concepts, products and materials that are available now. NOW Homes aim to balance environmental, social and economic gains.

The houses are designed and built to maximise the sun's warmth, retain heat while allowing summer cooling, reduce water use, and provide a dry, healthy indoor environment.

Each NOW Home is different and has been designed to make the most effective use of its site and location, and to fit in with existing houses in the neighbourhood. After construction is complete, the house is tenanted and its performance is monitored.

The first live project, the Waitakere NOW Home in Auckland, was constructed with modern, readily available materials and design methods, and cost just $220,000 to build. A family has been living in the house since performance monitoring began and, after the first 12 months, the house is exceeding expectations.

A solar hot water heating system provides for more than half of the household's water heating needs – equivalent to an annual saving of 1,620 kWh or about $275.

The highly-insulated, north-facing house retains solar warmth for space heating. An insulated, polished concrete floor absorbs the sun's heat then releases it when temperatures cool, and double glazing prevents further heat loss.

The tenants report feeling very warm, and have only used electric heating a few times during the year. Overall, the house used 7,400 kWh for the year or 30 percent less than similar households in the area.

A rainwater tank supplies all non-drinking water to the house, the toilets are dual-flush, and the showers and taps have flow-restrictors. Together these features have saved the tenants 40 percent of the average Waitakere household water bill.

Results from the Waitakere NOW Home are feeding into the larger-scale NOW 100 Project, which aims to build 100 new houses.

The NOW Homes project is run by research consortium Beacon Pathway Limited. The Foundation for Research, Science and Technology matches funding from Beacon's shareholding partners: a unique mix of industry, local government and research organisations – Building Research, Scion, New Zealand Steel, Waitakere City Council and Fletcher Building.

Source: Beacon Pathways Limited

Quotable Value's residential house price index measures changes in the average level of prices paid for residential properties during each quarter. Table 22.02 shows changes in recent years.

Table 22.02

Location	House price index[1][2] December quarter				
	2002	2003	2004	2005	2006
Whangarei district	852	1000	1194	1577	1715
Auckland[3]	798	1000	1057	1184	1273
Hamilton city	859	1000	1164	1477	1663
Tauranga district	801	1000	1204	1342	1365
Rotorua district	895	1000	1142	1510	1709
Gisborne district	887	1000	1338	1817	2047
Napier city	759	1000	1174	1342	1352
Hastings district	754	1000	1215	1385	1439
New Plymouth district	767	1000	1303	1550	1662
Wanganui district	888	1000	1379	1814	2043
Palmerston North city	844	1000	1151	1385	1567
Masterton district	860	1000	1138	1340	1542
Wellington[4]	861	1000	1114	1273	1443
Nelson city	703	1000	958	1017	1086
Christchurch city	778	1000	1176	1375	1512
Timaru district	771	1000	1291	1599	1725
Dunedin city	671	1000	1214	1349	1435
Invercargill district	733	1000	1118	1270	1499
All New Zealand	**801**	**1000**	**1122**	**1294**	**1420**

(1) Base: December 2003 quarter = 1000. (2) Variations in the average age of properties, as an indicator of the average quality of such properties, are eliminated in the index methodology in order to arrive at a valid index of price level changes. (3) Includes North Shore city, Waitakere city, Manukau city, Papakura district, and Auckland city. (4) Includes Porirua city, Upper Hutt city, Wellington city, and Hutt city.

Source: Quotable Value

House sales In the year ending 31 December 2006, Quotable Value was notified of 90,457 freehold open market house sales, a 2.5 percent decrease from the 92,747 sales recorded in the previous year. Freehold open market sales cover about 80 percent of all house sales, but exclude forced sales, sales between family members with a gift element, and sales of leasehold and mixed-tenure properties.

Housing loans

There were an estimated 1.45 million privately-owned non-farm residential dwellings in New Zealand at 31 December 2006. An estimated 800,000 of these dwellings had a loan or loans secured by mortgage (including residential rental properties and second homes). The average outstanding debt secured on residential dwellings at 31 December 2006 was estimated to be in the $140,000 – $150,000 range.

The value of private non-farm residential dwellings doubled to more than $500 billion in the four years to 31 December 2005. Total debt secured on these dwellings increased by 70 percent, or $50 billion. During this period of rising prices, annual sales turnover averaged around 10 percent of the total private sector housing stock.

Figure 22.01 shows mortgages registered and discharged between 1920 and 2007.

Figure 22.01

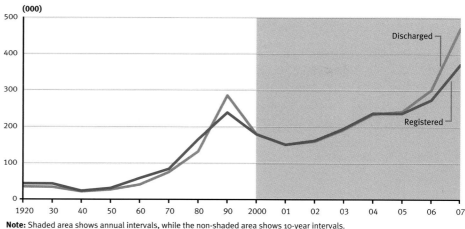

Mortgages
Registered and discharged
Year ending 31 March

Note: Shaded area shows annual intervals, while the non-shaded area shows 10-year intervals.

Source: Land Information New Zealand

Auctioneer Warwick Grimmer sells a house built by Otago Polytechnic students.

Mortgage interest rates Since inflation fell to a low rate in the early 1990s the average annual rate of interest on new floating-rate mortgages has been considerably lower than it was for the previous two decades, as figure 22.02 shows. In the mid 1990s, and again recently, rising interest rates for floating-rate mortgages have reflected tightening monetary policy in response to inflationary pressures.

Fixed-rate mortgages have been widely available in New Zealand since the mid 1990s and most home borrowers have not relied on floating-rate mortgages, tending to borrow for relatively short terms (three years or less) at fixed rates. By the end of 2007, more than 85 percent of all mortgage loans by value were at fixed rates, up from 60 percent in the late 1990s. This occurred because, for most of the period since then, fixed interest rates have been lower than floating rates. While the average floating interest rate during 2007 was over 9.75 percent, weighted fixed interest rates averaged close to 8.00 percent.

Table 22.03 shows household borrowing for housing and other purposes, from a monthly Reserve Bank of New Zealand survey. Registered banks are the source of more than 90 percent of the total household borrowing surveyed.

Table 22.03

		Household borrowing By reason for borrowing Quarterly		
Quarter		Housing	Other purposes	**Total**
			$(million)	
2001	Mar	66,770	7,096	**73,866**
	Jun	68,023	7,235	**75,258**
	Sep	68,964	7,444	**76,407**
	Dec	70,349	7,821	**78,170**
2002	Mar	72,021	7,836	**79,858**
	Jun	73,622	7,961	**81,583**
	Sep	74,983	8,286	**83,269**
	Dec	77,166	8,721	**85,887**
2003	Mar	79,746	8,774	**88,519**
	Jun	82,576	8,977	**91,552**
	Sep	85,763	9,294	**95,057**
	Dec	89,589	9,645	**99,234**
2004	Mar	93,185	9,670	**102,854**
	Jun	96,767	9,777	**106,544**
	Sep	100,025	9,970	**109,994**
	Dec	103,861	10,241	**114,102**
2005	Mar	107,927	10,483	**118,410**
	Jun	112,028	10,529	**122,557**
	Sep	116,142	10,665	**126,807**
	Dec	120,537	11,312	**131,848**
2006	Mar	124,436	11,343	**135,779**
	Jun	128,565	11,306	**139,870**
	Sep	132,375	11,314	**143,688**
	Dec	137,002	11,917	**148,919**
2007	Mar	142,197	11,949	**154,147**
	Jun	147,129	11,945	**159,073**
	Sep	150,654	12,075	**162,729**

Note: Figures may not add up to stated totals due to rounding.

Source: Reserve Bank of New Zealand

Figure 22.02

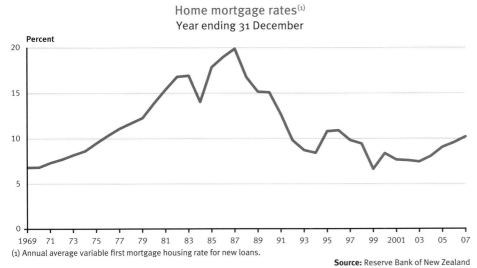

Home mortgage rates[1]
Year ending 31 December

(1) Annual average variable first mortgage housing rate for new loans.

Source: Reserve Bank of New Zealand

Housing New Zealand Corporation

Housing New Zealand Corporation is a Crown entity, established under the Housing Corporation Act 1974 and the Housing Corporation Amendment Act 2001, that provides housing and services related to housing. The corporation also ensures that the Minister of Housing receives appropriate policy advice and information on housing issues.

The corporation owns or manages more than 68,000 rental properties nationwide for people on low incomes or who are in need of housing assistance, and also offers a range of home ownership options.

Helping New Zealanders have smarter homes

A Department of Housing and Building website is helping New Zealanders create homes that are healthier, cheaper-to-run and kinder to the environment.

The Smarter Homes website, at www.smarterhomes. org.nz, gives clear and objective advice on how to design, build and renovate homes that are 'smarter' in every sense of the word. For people who are not building or renovating, the site gives tips on how to be more energy and water efficient at home.

A smart home creates less waste, uses less energy, costs less to run, and is warmer, drier and healthier to live in. Smart homes have higher capital value and will last well into the future while being kind to the environment.

Smart homes need not cost more or be less comfortable. For example, orienting a new home to capture the free heat and light of the sun is simple and cost-free to do in the design and construction phase. Adding insulation when re-lining walls during renovation adds little to the total cost of the work, but reduces annual heating bills and increases the warmth of a home for years to come. With features like heat pumps, double-glazing and solar hot water systems, costs can be recovered through lower energy bills over time.

Visitors to the website can find out how to have a healthier house that has lower energy bills each month, what appliances are the most energy and water efficient, the best heating systems to choose, and how to reduce moisture (mould and mildew) in the home.

The site also gives advice on selecting building materials, construction methods, and landscaping. Tips include simple things people can do to improve their home at little or no cost, easy fixes, and worthwhile investments that need the input of building professionals.

Source: Department of Housing and Building

Housing New Zealand Corporation

Housing New Zealand Corporation's apartment block in Talbot Park, Auckland, took top honours at the regional New Zealand Institute of Architects Resene Awards.

A social allocation system is used to ensure that those with the greatest need are given priority for housing. In 2006/07, the corporation assisted 10,313 people into state housing, bringing the number of people living in state houses to almost 198,000. At 30 June 2007, 9,837 applicants were on waiting lists for state houses.

Housing New Zealand Corporation provides ongoing support for households with complex housing and other needs. It provides income-related rents (where eligible tenants pay no more than 25 percent of their income), tenancy debt management, modified housing for people with disabilities, localised tenant newsletters, and support work with migrant communities.

The corporation has about 1,500 properties available for use by community groups, and organisations that offer residential support services. The groups renting these properties offer services for people with special health or welfare needs.

The corporation increased the number of properties in its housing portfolio by almost 1,000 during 2006/07, bringing the total of state-owned or leased rental units to 68,128. At 30 June 2007, property assets were valued at more than $15 billion, and the corporation returned a surplus of $13 million for the 2006/07 year.

Table 22.04 details Housing New Zealand Corporation's activity in recent years.

Healthy Housing is a joint initiative with district health boards that targets overcrowded state houses in Northland, and south and central Auckland, to reduce the risks of disease. During 2006/07, 1,067 households had their living standards improved through the Healthy Housing project, at a cost of more than $8 million.

Community Renewal Programme operates in areas with both high concentrations of state housing and high levels of disadvantage. The main aims are to address social exclusion, foster strong and sustainable communities, and improve the neighbourhood's physical assets and appearance.

The Community Renewal Programme began in July 2001 and is currently underway in seven areas: Otangarei in Whangarei, Northcote central in North Shore City, Talbot Park in central Auckland, Clendon in south Auckland, Fordlands in Rotorua, eastern Porirua near Wellington, and Aranui in Christchurch.

Major achievements in 2006/07 included completion of the Talbot Park Community Renewal project in Tamaki, Auckland. The six-year project involved refurbishing 108 units and building 111 new state houses using good quality urban design; improving the amenity and safety of the local residential environment through better landscaping and lighting; redesigned roads and safer

Table 22.04

Housing New Zealand Corporation statistics
Year ending 30 June

	2003	2004	2005	2006	2007
Total rental units[1]	64,543	65,448	66,498	67,117	68,128
Number of allocations (new tenancies)	9,885	9,453	10,093	10,326	10,313
Number of new tenancies for priority customers	8,031	7,977	8,428	8,504	8,775
Allocation to low-income households (%)[2]	97.0	98.3	98.0	98.8	98.4
Property disposals[3]	420	563	510	573	596
Properties acquired or contracted (gross)[4]	2,941	1,466	1,560	1,616	1,452

(1) Includes relocatable and non-relocatable units, garages and carparks. (2) Figures denote percentage of new tenancies receiving an income-related rent. (3) Figures are for all property disposals, including sales to non-tenants and lease terminations. (4) Includes transfer of properties to Community Housing Ltd.

Source: Housing New Zealand Corporation

parks; and incorporating new sustainability initiatives, such as solar hot water systems and on-site stormwater treatment devices.

Rural Housing Programme aims to address substandard housing in rural parts of New Zealand, particularly Northland, the eastern Bay of Plenty and the East Coast.

Welcome Home Loan aims to bring home ownership within the reach of modest income earners. Housing New Zealand Corporation provides mortgage insurance support to lenders to facilitate lending to low-income households.

In 2006/07, Housing New Zealand Corporation responded to the changing housing market and housing needs by expanding the Welcome Home Loan scheme. Four new lenders came on board, helping a further 1,070 people – including 13 state housing tenants – buy their own home. Loan criteria were amended in September 2006, with the maximum no-deposit loan increasing from $150,000 to $200,000 – better reflecting house price growth since the scheme was launched in 2003. These changes resulted in a 35 percent increase in the number of loans underwritten in 2006/07 compared with the previous year.

Low Deposit Rural Lending is targeted at low to modest income earners who want to buy or build in rural areas. Applicants must complete a home ownership course and meet the Housing New Zealand Corporation's lending criteria before becoming eligible for loan assistance.

Table 22.05 details Housing New Zealand Corporation's loan approvals in recent years.

Housing assistance

The Accommodation Supplement is available for low to middle income households, irrespective of whether they are renters, mortgagees or boarders, but is not available to people living in Housing New Zealand Corporation accommodation.

The Accommodation Supplement is administered by Work and Income New Zealand and takes account of high housing costs in main urban centres. The low-income threshold depends on circumstances, and is subject to an asset test. Table 22.06 (overleaf) shows trends in recent years in the number of clients receiving accommodation assistance.

Reintroduction of income-related rents for Housing New Zealand Corporation tenants in 2000 resulted in a large number of people losing eligibility for the Accommodation Supplement because of lower rent levels. Increases between 2004 and 2006 in the number of people receiving the supplement coincided with the broadening of eligibility to include more working families, part of the Government's Working for Families package.

At the end of June 2007, there were 243,433 people receiving an Accommodation Supplement, 5,945 fewer than at the end of June 2006. This decrease reflects a decrease in the number of people on main benefits. During the year ending June 2007, there were 214,219 applications for the supplement granted, 10,053 fewer than during the year ending June 2006.

Table 22.06 shows the number of people receiving assistance and the total value of payments.

Department of Building and Housing

The Department of Building and Housing provides information and guidance on building law and compliance. It also provides services, including advice for tenants and landlords, and guidance on how to keep homes weathertight.

The department is responsible for:

- making sure the laws and standards that govern the building and housing sector are effective
- providing good information, advice and dispute resolution services (for tenancy and weathertightness issues)
- working with the building and housing sector to develop better professional standards, skills and behaviours

Table 22.05

Housing New Zealand Corporation loan approvals
Year ending 30 June

Programme	2003 Number	2003 Value $(m)	2004 Number	2004 Value $(m)	2005 Number	2005 Value $(m)	2006 Number	2006 Value $(m)	2007 Number	2007 Value $(m)
Papakāinga[1]	2	0.09	1	0.18	2	0.14	4	1.60	4	0.93
Low Deposit Rural Lending	264	19.80	224	17.45	90	6.83	70	6.00	25	2.89
Suspensory[2]	280	4.26	388	5.13	429	6.75	396	7.39	405	7.55
General[3]	11	0.37	6	0.45	5	0.33	1	0.60	1	0.03
Welcome Home Loan[4]	..	..	367	40.20	597	73.60	791	110.90	1,070	180.70

(1) Mortgage finance to build on multiple-owned Māori land. (2) Loans to cover the cost of urgent and essential repairs and the cost of installing infrastructure services to new homes. (3) Borrower has to meet Housing New Zealand Corporation's lending conditions and have a deposit of at least 20 percent of the purchase price. (4) Before 1 July 2005 was called Mortgage Insurance Scheme.

Symbol: .. figure not available

Source: Housing New Zealand Corporation

Table 22.06

Accommodation assistance[1]

Year	Benefits at 30 June Number	Annual payment, year ending June $(million)
2000	315,988	867.0
2001	265,882	795.1
2002	258,034	719.6
2003	251,941	706.0
2004	236,695	702.1
2005	242,612	749.7
2006	249,378	843.2
2007	243,433	877.0

(1) Supplement from Work and Income.

Source: Ministry of Social Development

Eco Design Advisors

Currently operating out of nine city and district councils, Eco Design Advisors give free, customised advice to homeowners, the building industry, and community groups. The advice covers the whole building life cycle – from concept design, construction, and renovation, to eventual demolition. The advisors recommend environmental construction solutions for energy use, water conservation, waste management, and selecting materials with low environmental impacts.

The advisory service grew from a need to address key barriers to sustainable home construction and renovation in New Zealand – it ensures that home-owners and the building industry have access to free and independent advice on products and services. The advisors pass on technical knowledge about environmental building and act as consumer advocates by promoting smart and practical environmental building solutions.

Two research programmes ensure that the advisory service is well targeted and delivers significant behavioural and physical changes to building practices in New Zealand. The building industry and the public have so far responded very positively to the advisors. Home-owners appreciate getting immediate, clear, and site-specific information that is free from sales and marketing pitches.

The Eco Design Advisor service is in its second year of operation and aims to double in size by 2010. Although currently funded by Building Research, the Energy Efficiency Conservation Authority, the participating councils, and the Ministry for the Environment's Sustainable Management Fund, the service aims to be self-funded by 2011.

Source: BRANZ Ltd

- providing policy advice to the government on the building sector and residential tenancy market, including emerging trends and issues
- providing purchase and monitoring advice to the government on the Housing New Zealand Corporation, and administering the State Housing Appeal Authority.

The department works with Housing New Zealand Corporation on government outcomes for the building and housing sector by defining outcomes; analysing the housing environment, including monitoring the supply, quality and affordability of housing; influencing and working with the wider government and other agencies to ensure it meets the government's goals for housing; and undertaking specific initiatives under the New Zealand Housing Strategy Programme of Action.

Building and housing sector and regulatory policy The Department of Building and Housing provides policy advice to government on regulating and monitoring the building and housing sectors, and provides a regulatory framework for the building industry.

In the year ending 30 June 2007, the department drafted 114 responses to parliamentary questions, 494 responses to Ministerial correspondence, and responded to 122 Official Information Act requests.

State Housing Appeals Service The Department of Building and Housing is responsible for the State Housing Appeals Service. In the year ending 30 June 2007, the department received four applications to this authority.

Residential Tenancies Act 1986 This Act sets out the rights and obligations of landlords and tenants, and covers issues such as payment of rent, bonds, property repairs and giving notice.

A comprehensive review of the Act that began in 2004 addresses the impact of societal changes in the residential rental market, including changes in rental demographics since 1986, and increased private investment in rental properties.

Proposed changes seek to balance the rights of landlords and tenants and the needs of a changing society. They include plans to:

- extend the Act's coverage to boarding houses and to some rented accommodation where services such as meals or cleaning are provided
- increase the jurisdiction of the Tenancy Tribunal and penalties for breaching the Act
- limit tenant liability for damage to their rental premises under specific circumstances
- clarify responsibility for expenses such as such as rates, insurance and water use
- allow tenant breaches such as subletting to be subject to exemplary damages, as an alternative to eviction
- clarify the status of body corporate rules.

In the year ending 30 June 2007 the department received 237,744 telephone requests for tenancy advice and 213,150 telephone requests for tenancy bond advice. The department received 217,329 bond lodgements, made 211,049 bond refunds and scheduled 24,297 Tenancy Tribunal hearings.

Retirement Villages Act 2003 This Act aims to strengthen consumer protection offered to residents and potential residents of retirement villages. It includes a system for registering retirement villages. Regulations and a code of practice came into force in 2006 and 2007.

Retirement village operators are required to disclose specific information about the village, the fee structure, and termination agreements to residents and intending residents. The regulations provide for a disputes resolution process.

The Department of Building and Housing provides education and information on retirement village issues and works with the retirement commissioner, who is responsible for monitoring the effect of the Act and regulations, and appointing the panel members for the dispute resolution process. The Ministry of Economic Development is responsible for registration-related matters, which include acting as the registrar for retirement villages.

Unit Titles Act 1972 This Act governs building developments where multiple owners hold a type of property ownership known as a unit title. Such building developments may be apartment blocks, townhouses, office blocks, or industrial or retail complexes. Unit owners own a defined part of the building, such as an apartment, and have shared ownership in common areas such as lifts, lobbies or driveways.

Collectively, the unit owners make up a body corporate, which is responsible for matters relating to the common property and to the building as a whole.

Since the Act came into force there have been major changes in the number, scale, and nature of property developments in New Zealand. After extensive public consultation, the department has been working to update the Act.

Proposals include:

- clarifying the rights and responsibilities of unit owners, the body corporate, developers and tenants
- amendments to voting provisions to make joint decision-making by the body corporate easier

- introducing disclosure requirements for vendors and developers
- establishing dispute resolution mechanisms
- broadening the role of the body corporate in maintaining and managing the building
- providing for bodies corporate to have legal ownership of common property
- streamlining survey and title processes
- allowing for large, staged or complex unit-title developments to be set up and managed more easily.

Weathertight Services The Weathertight Homes Resolution Service was established by the Weathertight Homes Resolution Services Act 2002 in response to the emerging 'leaky buildings' problem. A major review undertaken in 2005 resulted in the new Weathertight Homes Resolution Services Act 2006, which came into force on 1 April 2007.

The new Act gives leaky-home owners access to speedy, flexible and cost-effective procedures for assessing and resolving their claims. A new Weathertight Services group, together with the Weathertight Homes Tribunal, replaced the resolution service.

Claimants can bring a claim under the Act by applying to Weathertight Services for an assessor's report. If the claim is found to be eligible the claimant can proceed to the resolution process. The claims process offers access to negotiation or mediation for claims where estimated or actual repair costs total $20,000 or less. All other standard claims can apply to the Weathertight Homes Tribunal for adjudication, which includes an opportunity for mediation.

Progress to 30 June 2007:

- 752 new claims received
- 933 assessments completed
- 345 addenda or revisions completed
- 168 claims commencing dispute resolution received
- 134 claims ready for mediation or adjudication hearings
- 155 claims resolved.

Building and construction

Building and construction is an important part of the New Zealand economy.

For the year ending 31 March 2007, gross fixed capital investment on building and other construction totalled $21.1 billion, compared with $20.5 billion in the previous year and $18.8 billion in 2005.

The number of people engaged in the building and construction industry at February 2007 was 121,840, or 6.3 percent of those in all industries. Thousands more were employed supporting the industry in manufacturing, material supplies and transport.

The share of New Zealand's gross domestic product contributed by the industry (in constant prices) was 4.7 percent in the year ending 31 March 2007, compared with 4.9 percent in the March 2006 year.

Building apprentice Sheree Young works on hard-lining the interior walls of the Cromwell Swim Centre.

Five stars for green offices

Meridian Energy

Meridian's new building in Wellington.

Two new office buildings have received New Zealand's first five-star green ratings from the New Zealand Green Building Council (NZGBC).

The Meridian building on Wellington's waterfront, owned by Dominion Funds, and 80 Queen Street in Auckland's central business district, were involved in the NZGBC's pilot programme and received their five-star certification in late 2007.

To receive certification, buildings must score well in eight key areas: management, indoor environment quality, energy, transport, water, materials, land use and ecology, and emissions. Innovative solutions in these areas are encouraged. Four stars rates a building as 'best practice', five stars means 'New Zealand excellence', and six stars gives a building as 'world leadership' rating.

Buildings and the building industry use a significant proportion of raw materials, land, water, and energy and they create solid waste. The green star ratings allow the industry to measure the environmental impact and quality of the work space environment, and create economic, social and environmental benefits for the building's occupants and owners.

Green star ratings aim to enhance building value and encourage a market shift towards ecologically sustainable building. At 31 December 2007, 25 buildings were registered in the green star programme and more than 600 professionals had completed green star training. Government is supporting these ratings and now requires new buildings that will house government employees to achieve four or five star ratings.

The NZGBC was founded in 2005 and joined the World Green Building Council in 2006. The other members are Australia, Canada, India, Japan, Mexico, Taiwan, the United States, the United Arab Emirates and the United Kingdom.

The NZGBC works to involve all parts of the building and construction production process, and create transparency in the industry – to reduce the environmental impact of buildings and create more efficient, more flexible, healthier buildings. The NZGBC will continue to develop customised rating tools within the green star system for all building types, including retail, health, education, residential, and industrial, as the market demands and with industry support.

Source: New Zealand Green Building Council

Builders work on a two-storey structure in the Chinese Garden, behind the Otago Settlers Museum.

The most common construction systems used in New Zealand are light timber framing for housing, reinforced concrete (pre-cast and cast on-site) for multi-storey buildings, and light steel framing for industrial buildings. With shortages of timber on the domestic market, light steel framing is becoming more common.

With the introduction of a performance-based building code, traditional systems are slowly being replaced with new methods and products.

New Zealand has particular expertise in the design of earthquake-resistant structures, and in other specialist areas such as hydro and geothermal power station design and construction.

Construction law

The Department of Building and Housing is responsible for administering the New Zealand Building Code as part of its management of building controls. The code specifies essential requirements for building performance that provide for: the health and safety of building users, the protection of other people's property, the well-being and physical independence of people using buildings, and sustainable development.

The department writes technical documents (known as the New Zealand Building Code Handbook and compliance documents) that provide methods for satisfying code requirements. Solutions and methods published in these documents are not mandatory, and the building industry is encouraged to develop new materials and systems as alternatives to conventional methods.

Day-to-day administration of building controls is the responsibility of city and district councils, which must confirm that building projects satisfy code provisions.

Building consents are required for all new buildings and for alterations to existing buildings. Any such work must also comply with city and district council district plans prepared under the Resource Management Act 1991. For completed buildings, the requirement for regular maintenance of essential systems, such as fire alarms, lifts and air conditioning, is covered by the compliance schedule of the Building Act 2004 and in the provisions of the annual building warrant of fitness.

In November 2007, the department reported to the Government on a comprehensive review of all aspects of the code, as required by the Building Act.

The department's building controls activities are funded by a building consent levy of $1.97 for every $1,000 of building work for projects exceeding $20,000.

Building Act 2004 The department's administration of the Building Act 2004 includes responsibility for implementing various building sector reforms that require buildings to be designed and built right the first time. These reforms include:

- the licensing of building practitioners, which began in November 2007 with licensing available for carpentry, and for three classes of site management and three classes of design (licence classes for other building professionals such as brick and blocklayers and those undertaking concrete and steel construction are being introduced)

- the accrediting and registering of local authorities as building consent authorities, to strengthen the decision-making processes at the critical building consent and inspection stages. All local authorities were required to be accredited and registered by 30 June 2008, or to transfer their building control obligations to an accredited and registered local authority

- a full review of the New Zealand Building Code, to ensure it meets current needs and those of the foreseeable future
- introducing a product certification scheme for manufacturers and distributors to get independent confirmation that their products comply with the code.

Building statistics

New Zealand's main official building statistics are Statistics New Zealand's monthly compilation of building authorisations, and its quarterly survey of the value of building work put in place.

Building authorisations indicate future building work to be put in place. These statistics are sourced from building consents issued by territorial authorities.

Published figures on the number and value of building authorisations are of particular interest to economists and the government. The Reserve Bank of New Zealand uses the figures to predict the inflationary pressures within the building and construction industry, and its contribution to overall inflation.

Table 22.07 shows the number and value of building authorisations by region for the years ending 31 March 2006 and 2007.

Table 22.07

Building authorisations[1]
By region
Year ending 31 March

Region	New dwellings 2006	New dwellings 2007	Residential value 2006	Residential value 2007	Non-residential value 2006	Non-residential value 2007	All buildings value 2006	All buildings value 2007
	Number		$(million)					
Northland	1,354	1,341	333	361	82	119	415	480
Auckland	7,199	6,769	1,949	2,080	1,348	1,457	3,297	3,536
Waikato	3,230	3,583	798	949	533	379	1,331	1,328
Bay of Plenty	2,028	1,899	544	559	241	287	785	846
Gisborne	139	166	37	50	26	27	62	77
Hawke's Bay	1,017	830	262	258	126	113	388	372
Taranaki	566	603	159	184	83	80	242	264
Manawatu-Wanganui	1,007	1,068	265	301	161	180	426	481
Wellington	1,964	1,844	551	580	563	364	1,114	944
Tasman	264	304	71	96	37	23	107	119
Nelson	226	318	62	82	31	44	93	126
Marlborough	463	434	114	120	50	61	164	181
West Coast	199	284	48	65	36	49	85	114
Canterbury	3,901	4,435	980	1,154	440	519	1,420	1,673
Otago	1,472	1,497	430	465	233	197	663	662
Southland	373	363	100	111	69	71	169	182
Area outside regions	4	2	0	0	0	0	1	1
Total New Zealand	**25,406**	**25,740**	**6,703**	**7,415**	**4,059**	**3,972**	**10,762**	**11,387**

(1) Values include new buildings plus alterations and additions.
Note: Figures may not add up to stated totals due to rounding.

Source: Statistics New Zealand

Table 22.08

Building authorisations
Value by building type[1]
Year ending 31 March

Building type	2003	2004	2005	2006	2007
	$(million)				
Domestic dwellings	5,240	6,484	6,833	6,451	7,153
Domestic outbuildings	185	224	237	252	262
Total residential buildings	**5,425**	**6,707**	**7,070**	**6,703**	**7,415**
Hostels and boarding houses	130	63	279	345	119
Hotels and other short-term accommodation	144	238	182	186	311
Hospitals and nursing homes	221	208	230	315	230
Education buildings	415	425	445	489	378
Social, cultural and religious buildings	206	235	291	298	288
Shops, restaurants and taverns	393	500	588	671	637
Offices and administration buildings	304	443	737	647	842
Storage buildings	265	297	413	403	463
Factories and industrial buildings	352	391	537	428	456
Farm buildings	162	165	175	190	209
Miscellaneous buildings	25	32	33	86	41
Total non-residential buildings	**2,617**	**2,998**	**3,910**	**4,059**	**3,972**
All buildings	**8,042**	**9,705**	**10,981**	**10,762**	**11,387**

(1) Values are for new buildings plus alterations and additions.
Note: Figures may not add up to stated totals due to rounding.

Source: Statistics New Zealand

Rating the bricks and mortar of sustainability

Materials are often the most important aspect of sustainable building – from the nuts and bolts, to the trusses, to the choice of flooring. The Greenbuild™ website provides a place to list and assess New Zealand's building products, with a particular emphasis on their sustainability.

Until recently, it was difficult to judge how environmentally sustainable a building product was. There are many trade-offs when considering the environmental characteristics of a building product. Rather than giving a pass/fail, the Greenbuild assessment process rates the properties of similar products in categories ranging from toxicity, to the degree of recycled material content, to the use of fossil fuel in production.

By having their product environmentally assessed and posted on the site, manufacturers gain exposure to everyone in the building industry. Website users gain access to an independent environmental assessment of the product.

With around 12,000 building products on the New Zealand market, independently assessing each product is a big task. Although the majority of these products are already listed on the website, it will be some time before they are all assessed. The Greenbuild site aims to be New Zealand's national database of building products.

Greenbuild is a joint venture of Masterspec, Building Research, and Warren and Mahoney. Masterspec, in turn, is owned by the New Zealand Institute of Architects, Registered Master Builders Federation and Building Research.

Source: Greenbuild

Authorisation values usually represent the contract price or the estimated cost of the building before starting construction. The finished cost may be higher or lower due to changes in wage rates, material prices and design. Table 22.08 (on the previous page) shows the value of building authorisations by building type. Authorisations cover alterations and additions, as well as new buildings.

Residential and non-residential building authorisations are listed in table 22.09, while figure 22.03 shows the number of new dwelling units authorised from 1977 to 2007. Authorisations for new dwellings totalled 25,740 units and $6.1 billion in the year ending 31 March 2007. Compared with the previous March year, the number of new dwellings authorised rose by 1.3 percent while the value rose by 12 percent.

Table 22.09

Residential and non-residential building authorisations
Annual values
Year ending 31 March

| Year | New dwellings | | | Residential buildings[1] | Non-residential buildings[2] | All buildings |
	Number of units	Value $(million)	Floor area sq m (000)	$(million)		
2000	25,858	3,533	4,261	4,263	2,206	6,468
2001	19,370	2,833	3,382	3,544	2,478	6,022
2002	21,262	3,353	3,876	4,111	2,666	6,777
2003	28,320	4,549	4,983	5,425	2,617	8,042
2004	31,823	5,657	5,814	6,707	2,998	9,705
2005	30,255	5,896	5,465	7,070	3,910	10,981
2006	25,406	5,461	4,894	6,703	4,059	10,762
2007	25,740	6,104	4,983	7,415	3,972	11,387

(1) Includes alterations and additions, and domestic outbuildings. (2) Includes alterations and additions.
Note: Figures may not add up to stated totals due to rounding.

Source: Statistics New Zealand

Figure 22.03

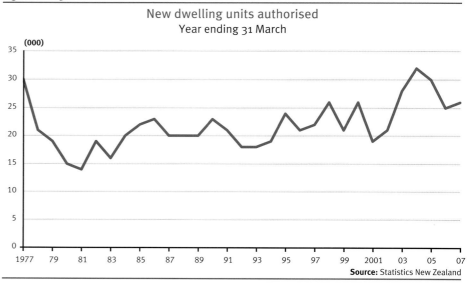

New dwelling units authorised
Year ending 31 March

Source: Statistics New Zealand

Figure 22.04 shows how the average floor area of new dwellings has changed since 1992. These figures include garages that are built into dwellings.

Work put in place Surveys of building work put in place show the gross value of actual building work done, excluding GST. There can be varying time lags between issue of a building authorisation and commencement of building, depending largely on the amount of work that builders have. Table 22.10 shows the value of building work put in place, while figure 22.05 compares the value of residential and non-residential work put in place.

Building and construction price indexes Price indexes for buildings and construction are contained within Statistics New Zealand's capital goods price index. During the year ending March 2007 the building and construction indexes recorded increases of 5.1 percent for residential buildings, 5.0 percent for non-residential buildings, 4.1 percent for other construction, and 5.5 percent for land improvement.

There has been strong growth in recent years in the price of constructing residential buildings. The 5.1 percent increase for residential buildings for 2007 contributed to an overall increase of 36.2 percent for the five-year period ending 31 March 2007.

The price of renting houses has not increased as quickly as the price of building houses. The 'dwelling rentals' component of the consumers price index increased by 3.0 percent from the

March 2006 quarter to the March 2007 quarter, and by a total of 14.7 percent for the five-year period ending 31 March 2007.

Figure 22.04

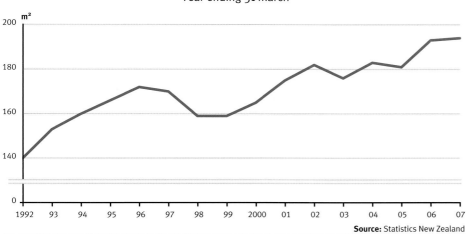

Average floor area of new dwellings
Year ending 31 March

Source: Statistics New Zealand

Table 22.10

Value of work put in place[1]
By building type
Years ending 31 March

Building type	2003	2004	2005	2006	2007
	\$(million)				
New government dwellings	7	33	56	52	78
Other new dwellings	4,322	5,467	6,265	6,256	6,271
Alterations, additions and outbuildings	859	1,022	1,075	1,193	1,341
Total residential buildings	**5,188**	**6,522**	**7,396**	**7,501**	**7,690**
Accommodation and outbuildings	242	298	522	907	691
Hospitals and nursing homes	333	330	313	318	418
Factories and industrial buildings	388	451	467	564	423
Commercial buildings[2]	853	929	1,285	1,574	1,491
Education buildings	469	540	514	615	556
Miscellaneous buildings[3]	921	831	1,126	1,228	1,464
Total non-residential buildings	**3,206**	**3,380**	**4,227**	**5,206**	**5,042**
Total all buildings	**8,394**	**9,902**	**11,624**	**12,707**	**12,732**

(1) Values exclude GST. Consents below \$5,000 are excluded. (2) Includes shops, restaurants, taverns, offices, and administration buildings. (3) Includes social, cultural, religious, recreational, storage, and farm buildings.

Note: Figures may not add up to stated totals due to rounding.

Source: Statistics New Zealand

Figure 22.05

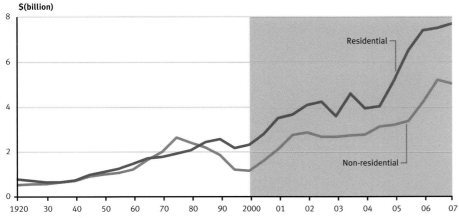

Building work put in place
Residential and non-residential, by value
Year ending 31 March

Note: Shaded area shows annual intervals, while the non-shaded area shows 10-year intervals.

Source: Statistics New Zealand

Contributors and related websites

Beacon Pathways Ltd – www.beaconpathway.co.nz

BRANZ Ltd – www.branz.co.nz

Department of Building and Housing – www.dbh.govt.nz

Greenbuild – www.greenbuild.co.nz

Housing New Zealand Corporation – www.hnzc.co.nz

Land Information New Zealand – www.linz.govt.nz

Ministry for the Environment – www.mfe.govt.nz

Ministry of Social Development – www.msd.govt.nz

New Zealand Green Building Council – www.nzgbc.org.nz

New Zealand Institute of Architects – www.nzia.co.nz

Quotable Value New Zealand – www.qv.co.nz

Reserve Bank of New Zealand – www.rbnz.govt.nz

Statistics New Zealand – www.stats.govt.nz

Land Transport NZ

These Churton Park School students in Wellington are part of a walking school bus movement, joining thousands of primary school children who walk to school along designated routes, supervised by volunteer 'school bus drivers'.

23 | Transport

New Zealand's geographic isolation means that there is a heavy reliance on sea transport for the bulk of the country's imports and exports, and international travel is dominated by air services. Road, rail, air and shipping services are the main ways people and goods move within New Zealand, a long, thin island country.

The New Zealand transport sector has been subject to ongoing change since the late 1970s. Major regulatory changes have encouraged competition within the industry and allowed introduction of a wide range of new technologies. Organisational changes have brought about greater use of commercial structures for publicly-owned transport systems, with some of these being transferred to the private sector.

Since the late 1990s, transport policy has evolved beyond economic and safety issues, and now includes environmental, social and public health aspects of transport. This approach was reflected in the Government's *New Zealand Transport Strategy*, published in 2002. An update of this strategy will be published in 2008.

This update will:

- provide direction for the transport sector until 2040 in the context of the Government's sustainability agenda and other Government strategies in the areas of energy and energy efficiency
- translate that direction into high-level targets for the transport sector and intermediate targets for sub-sectors (air, sea, road, vehicle fleet, rail, freight, public transport, walking and cycling) to help achieve the high-level targets.

Shipping

Over 99 percent of both New Zealand's exports (23 million tonnes) and imports (around 19 million tonnes) are carried by sea. By value, this represents about 85 percent of exports and 75 percent of imports. It is therefore important that New Zealand has access to efficient and cost-competitive international shipping services, especially considering the country's distance from overseas markets. Within New Zealand, coastal shipping provides intra- and inter-island links, and plays a key role in the distribution of petroleum products and cement.

Comprehensive reforms of New Zealand's waterfront since 1988 have resulted in cost savings and efficiency improvements. Thirteen port companies were established in 1988 to take over

Finding out what happened

The Transport Accident Investigation Commission Te Komihana Tirotiro Aitua Waka is an independent Crown entity. It was established in 1990 under the Transport Accident Investigation Act to investigate accidents and incidents, and determine their circumstances and causes. In doing this, the commission's purpose is to avoid similar occurrences in the future, rather than to ascribe blame to any person.

The commission is made up of three commissioners, each of whom is appointed by the governor-general on the recommendation of the Minister of Transport.

The commission is supported by an administration made up of the chief executive of the Crown entity, an investigative team, administrative staff, and assessors appointed to assist the commission in its determinations.

For the year ending June 2007, the commission launched investigations into seven marine, three air, and five rail accidents or incidents. Investigations in the previous June year totalled 13, 11 and 29, respectively. The commission issued 26 safety recommendations in 2007 (77 in 2006).

Crown funding for 2006/07 was $2.616 million, the same as for 2005/06.

Source: Transport Accident Investigation Commission

Ports of Auckland Limited

The Port of Auckland is New Zealand's largest international container port and a major gateway for trade for the North Island's east coast, west coast (Port of Onehunga), and two inland Auckland ports.

ownership and operation of commercial port facilities, and waterfront labour was reformed in 1989. This reform saw the end of the government-managed labour pool system and introduced direct employment and enterprise bargaining to the waterfront.

Since the 1990s, shipping policy has shifted to reflect New Zealand's status as a ship-using, rather than a ship-operating nation. For New Zealand exporters and shippers, this policy seeks to ensure unrestricted access to the carrier of their choice, and to the benefits of fair competition among carriers.

The Maritime Transport Act 1994 regulates ship safety, maritime liability and marine environmental protection. The Act also made Maritime New Zealand, a Crown entity, responsible for maritime safety and marine pollution prevention, and for response functions.

There were 820 employees were engaged in international sea transport, 1,270 in coastal water transport, and 940 in inland water transport in February 2007. Equivalent employee figures for February 2006 were 900, 1,210 and 1,040, respectively.

Overseas lines

Major trading routes for New Zealand include the United Kingdom and Europe; Africa, India and the Middle East; North Asia, East Asia and South-East Asia; North America, Central America and South America; trans-Tasman and the Pacific.

New Zealand is well provided with international shipping services, with more than 30 global and New Zealand-based international shipping lines represented. Among them are Maersk Line, Mediterranean Shipping Company, Contship Containerlines, CMA CGM Group, Hamburg Süd, Hapag-Lloyd, Wallenius Wilhelmsen, Malaysia International Shipping Corporation Berhad, China Ocean Shipping Company, Orient Overseas Container Line, Nippon Yusen Kaisha, Mitsui OSK Lines, Pacific International Lines, Australia New Zealand Direct Line, Chief Container Service, Tasman Orient Line, Pacific Forum Line, Sofrana Unilines and Pacific Direct Line.

Conference lines and vessel sharing agreements (VSAs) are involved in much of New Zealand's overseas shipping. Conferences are associations among shipping companies to provide joint services on several trade routes. VSAs are more limited arrangements than conferences, involving separate services jointly scheduling the same vessels to make better use of vessel capacity.

Increased competition in the shipping industry in recent years, however, has seen greater participation in New Zealand trade by independent carriers.

Inter-island shipping services

Interisland Line provides rail and road ferry services across Cook Strait, transporting passengers, vehicles and freight between Wellington and Picton.

Lyttelton-based Pacifica Shipping operates two cargo vessels, which link Auckland, Tauranga, Wellington, Nelson, Lyttelton and Timaru.

Strait Shipping operates livestock and roll-on roll-off freight services between Wellington, Picton, Nelson and Napier; and the Bluebridge passenger and vehicle service between Wellington and Picton.

Auckland-based Sea-Tow operates tugs and barges on tramp (non-liner) services around the New Zealand coast.

Black Robin Shipping operates a general cargo and livestock service between the North Island, the South Island and the Chatham Islands.

Since 1995, coastal shipping services have also been provided by foreign ships transiting the New Zealand coast in the course of their international voyages.

Bulk shipping

Overseas trade New Zealand's bulk shipping needs are mainly served by a mix of vessels, few of which operate fixed services. Imported bulk cargoes include crude oil, phosphate rock, bauxite and petroleum coke. Bulk exports include ironsand, coal, forest products and methanol. Sea-Tow provides tug and barge services to Australia and the South Pacific.

Coastal Bulk cement distribution is handled by three small cement vessels, two operated by Holcim New Zealand and one by the Golden Bay Cement Company. Two tankers operated by Silver Fern Shipping Ltd distribute petroleum products from the Marsden Point oil refinery.

Domestic sea freight strategy In November 2007 the Minister of Transport, Hon Annette King, launched 'Sea Change' for public consultation. Sea Change is a draft strategy setting out proposed actions to help industry and government to transform the domestic sea freight sector, so that it can play its part in the overall New Zealand transportation system. Sea Change is about contributing to an integrated transport network that meets both present and future needs, and it is aligned to the overall *New Zealand Transport Strategy*.

The draft strategy proposes that New Zealand will move 30 percent of its inter-regional domestic freight by sea by 2040 (compared with about 15 percent at present). This is a realistic target, but it assumes that there will be some changes within the overall transport sector to allow this to happen. The development of Sea Change follows the New Zealand Shipping Federation's report *Roadways to Waterways* in September 2006, and the *Shipping Industry Review* in December 2000.

Services to shipping

Ports Port companies established under the Port Companies Act 1988 operate New Zealand's 13 commercial ports. These companies are predominantly owned by local authorities, although four are partly privatised and listed on the New Zealand Stock Exchange. Two of the port companies, Northland Port Corporation and Port of Tauranga Ltd, have established a deep-water port (Northport Ltd) at Marsden Point, in Northland. In addition to the 13 commercial ports, there are smaller ports at Greymouth, Westport, Wanganui and Taharoa.

Ship registration At 31 December 2006, there were 2,532 ships on the New Zealand Register of Ships, with total gross tonnage of 267,454 and net tonnage of 125,462. This compares with 2,465 ships, with a gross tonnage of 258,952 and net tonnage of 121,640, at 31 December 2005. Under the provisions of the Ship Registration Act 1992, ships not exceeding 24 metres registered length are not required to have tonnages registered.

New registrations during 2006 included the passenger vessel *Monte Stello*. Vessels removed from the New Zealand register during 2006 included the fishing vessel *Independent 1*, the cargo vessel *Southern Tiare* and the passenger vessel *Purbeck*.

Table 23.01 shows the number and capacity of registered vessels involved in overseas and domestic trade.

Seafarer qualifications Maritime New Zealand is the administrative and licensing body for all New Zealand Merchant Navy, super yacht, fishing, and all other commercial maritime qualifications. After obtaining suitable qualifying sea service, further approved training and examinations at teaching institutions are undertaken. Successful seafarers are issued with certificates of competency as master, mate or engineer, as well as deck and engine room ratings.

There are different classes of certificates of competency for foreign-going, offshore, fishing or restricted-limit ships. Foreign-going certificates and endorsements for service on special types of ships meet the requirements of relevant United Nations conventions and may be accepted for use in other countries. All certificate of competency holders are required to meet minimum medical standards, including eyesight.

The Royal New Zealand Coastguard Federation is the organisation that caters for pleasure-boat mariners on a voluntary basis. The federation holds courses and conducts examinations for day skipper, boat master, coastal skipper and ocean yacht-master certificates. The Royal New Zealand Coastguard Federation is also accredited to conduct Royal Yachting Association (UK) certificates.

Maritime safety The New Zealand Government is a signatory to many International Maritime Organisation and International Labour Organization conventions that specify safety standards for international ships, and health and safety standards for crews. Maritime New Zealand is responsible for administering these conventions, and for inspecting foreign and New Zealand ships to ensure they meet required standards.

Marine safety services There are 142 navigational aids, owned and maintained by Maritime New Zealand, on headlands, capes, reefs and shoals around 5,400 nautical miles (9,000

Keeping it clean

Maritime New Zealand's Marine Pollution Response Service team deploy a boom to contain an oil spill in the Whangarei harbour during a test scenario in May 2007. The exercise started with a response to a small localised oil spill, before 'escalating' to a large, national response to a tanker spill at Marsden Point oil refinery.

Source: Maritime New Zealand

Table 23.01

Registered vessels involved in overseas and domestic trade
At 31 December

Year	Vessels	Net tonnage	Crew[1]
Overseas			
1996	8	59,006	153
1997	7	54,711	115
1998	7	43,763	111
1999	4	32,543	42
2000	3	29,484	23
2001	3	29,484	40
2002	..	..	..
2003	3	23,686	48
2004	3	23,272	40
2005	3	23,272	40
2006	3	23,272	40
Domestic			
1996	12	26,048	302
1997	12	26,048	302
1998	8	16,875	200
1999	8	16,875	200
2000	8	14,580	145
2001	9	14,406	158
2002	..	..	..
2003	11	21,673	205
2004	9	18,203	171
2005	13	24,182	171
2006	12	25,684	178

(1) Crew figures are not necessarily up-to-date.

Symbol: .. figure not available

Source: Maritime New Zealand

Figure 23.01

Marine accidents

Year ending 30 June[1]

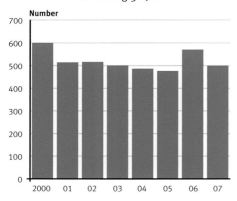

By month[1]

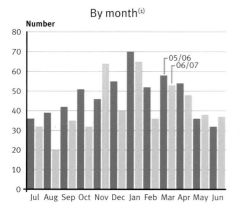

By ship category[2]

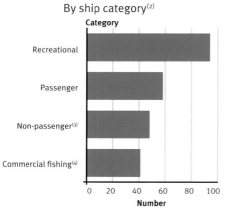

By type of accident[2][4]

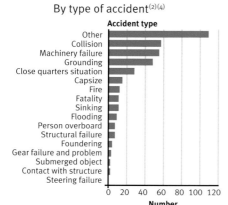

(1) Includes reported commercial, recreational and mishap (injury) accidents. (2) Year ending 30 June 2007. (3) Mishap (injury) accidents are not included unless fatal. (4) Mishap (injury) accidents are not included.

Source: Maritime New Zealand

kilometres) of New Zealand coastline. The aids consist of 97 automatic lights, 40 day beacons and five navigational buoys. There are no staffed lighthouses in New Zealand. Maritime New Zealand also provides a distress and safety radio communication system for mariners. Radio frequencies dedicated to distress messages are monitored 24-hours a day in the very high, high, and medium frequency bands.

The system also broadcasts weather reports and warnings of maritime hazards, and assists during search and rescue operations and medical emergencies at sea. The cost of providing navigation aids and the distress and safety radio system is met from a marine safety charge levied on all commercial ships (New Zealand and foreign). The government also contributes on behalf of the recreational boating sector.

Wrecks Where ships are wrecked on the New Zealand coast or in lakes and rivers, the director of Maritime New Zealand has powers for preserving life and protecting property. A wreck or an article belonging to it remains the property of the owner, and it is illegal for others to take any items of wreckage. People finding or taking possession of wrecks, or articles from wrecks, must notify the police, who may take custody until ownership is resolved.

Maritime accidents Maritime New Zealand investigates maritime accidents and incidents to identify their cause, analyses trends, and makes recommendations for preventing similar occurrences. Investigators also assess whether there has been any breach of law.

Marine pollution Maritime New Zealand is required to promote a clean marine environment and is responsible for developing and implementing New Zealand's marine oil spill response strategy.

The strategy sets out principles to ensure that New Zealand is prepared for, and can respond to, marine oil spills. A tiered planning and response system for dealing with oil spills has been established at local, regional, national and international levels. While New Zealand's equipment, trained personnel and services are designed to respond to a one in 100-year spill, arrangements are in place to use international assistance if needed.

The National Oil Spill Service Centre, at Te Atatu, Auckland, houses equipment that can be mobilised immediately in the event of an oil spill. This national stockpile complements equipment Maritime New Zealand stores in key locations throughout New Zealand.

Figure 23.01 shows marine accidents by: June year; month; ship category; and type of accident.

Civil aviation

Due to its island status and its distance from other countries, New Zealand is one of the most aviation-oriented nations in the world. In a population of 4.2 million, there were 9,361 pilot licences on issue at 30 June 2007 and 4,105 registered aircraft – one pilot licence per 450 people and one aircraft per 1,000 people. The 4,105 aircraft in the New Zealand civil fleet is an increase of 114 from the previous June year. The number of licensed aircraft engineers also increased, from 2,114 at 30 June 2006 to 2,181 a year later.

The rate of increase in the total number of hours flown by New Zealand registered aircraft (excluding sport aircraft) in the five years to 30 June 2007 averaged 2.5 percent a year.

There were 8,930 employees working in civil aviation at February 2007. Of these, 4,120 were employed in scheduled international air transport and 4,810 in scheduled domestic air transport. There were also another 2,190 employees working in other air transport services.

Civil Aviation Authority

The Civil Aviation Authority (CAA) is New Zealand's aviation safety regulator, with the prime function of promoting civil aviation safety and security, and contributing to an integrated, responsive and sustainable transport system.

Specific functions include: establishing safety and security standards relating to entry into, and exit from, the civil aviation system; monitoring adherence to safety and security standards within the civil aviation system; ensuring regular review of the civil aviation system to promote improvement and development of its safety and security; investigating and reviewing civil aviation accidents and incidents; providing civil aviation safety and security policy advice to the Minister of Transport; promoting safety and security in the civil aviation system through information, advice and education programmes; and maintaining the New Zealand Register of Aircraft, the Civil Aviation Registry, and other records and documents relating to activities within the civil aviation system.

The CAA also acts on behalf of the Crown in respect of the International Civil Aviation Organisation (ICAO). As part of ICAO responsibilities, the CAA is designated the Aviation Security Authority, the Air Traffic Services Authority, the Personnel Licensing Authority, the Meteorological Authority and the Dangerous Goods Authority, as well as meeting New Zealand's ICAO obligations for aeronautical information. It also undertakes ICAO technical and safety regulation responsibilities that are associated with the ICAO Air Navigation Bureau and Technical Assistance Bureau.

The CAA is funded from a number of sources – a domestic passenger levy ($1.77 plus GST per passenger, per sector); an international departing passenger levy ($0.89 plus GST per passenger); a participation levy based on aircraft weights; an aeronautical information services levy; and fees for services, such as certification, licensing, rules development and policy advice to the government.

In the year ending 30 June 2007, the CAA received $27.465 million in income and spent $28.475 million, resulting in a deficit of $1.010 million (against a budgeted deficit of $1.579 million). Levies totalled just under 75 percent of income.

Figure 23.02 shows the number of notifiable aircraft accidents in New Zealand from 1997 to 2007.

Airways New Zealand

Airways New Zealand (Airways) provides air navigation services for the aviation industry within New Zealand's domestic and oceanic airspace. Established in 1987 as a State-owned enterprise, Airways was the first fully-commercialised air navigation services organisation in the world.

Airways provides air traffic services, including flight information, to civil and military air traffic, and is responsible for the planning, provision and maintenance of radar, navigational aids and communications. Air navigation facilities provided in New Zealand include electronic aids, such as non-directional medium frequency beacons (NDB), Doppler very high frequency omni-directional radio ranges (DVOR), instrument landing systems (ILS), primary surveillance radar equipment (PSR), secondary surveillance radar (SSR), distance measuring equipment (DME), and very high frequency direction-finding equipment (VDF).

Airways aims to ensure the safe, orderly and efficient flow of air traffic within the 37 million square kilometres of Pacific airspace assigned to New Zealand by the International Civil Aviation Organisation (ICAO).

Aircraft operators and pilots pay Airways for the services they use. These include radar control, landing charges, and aeronautical charts and publications. Its technicians install and maintain technical facilities, including runway lighting and navigation aids, for airport companies in New Zealand and overseas.

Airways assists in discharging operational and technical commitments arising from New Zealand's membership of ICAO. All military air traffic control and radar surveillance is

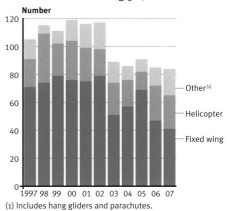

Figure 23.02

Notifiable aircraft accidents
Year ending 30 June

(1) Includes hang gliders and parachutes.

Source: Civil Aviation Authority

Aircraft accidents and deaths

There were 84 aircraft accidents reported to the Civil Aviation Authority in the year ending 30 June 2007, compared with 85 in the previous June year. The 2007 total included two fatal accidents in which four people died. In the June 2006 year, there were eight fatal accidents in which 12 people died. Accidents include events where the aircraft sustains damage that affects its structural strength, performance or flight characteristics, or where someone is seriously injured or killed.

Number of aircraft accidents
Year ending 30 June

Aircraft category	1997	1998	1999	2000	2001	2002	2003	2004	2005	2006	2007
13,608kg and above	1	0	0	1	1	0	2	1	0	0	0
5,670 to 13,607kg	2	0	0	1	1	1	0	0	1	3	1
2,721 to 5,669kg	4	3	2	2	4	5	4	3	1	3	3
Below 2,721kg	40	40	43	50	45	47	23	33	38	21	21
Helicopters	20	35	23	27	24	19	23	19	13	25	24
Sport	25	31	34	24	25	26	23	20	29	20	16
Unknown	2	0	0	2	0	0	3	3	0	0	0
Total	**94**	**109**	**102**	**107**	**100**	**98**	**78**	**79**	**82**	**72**	**65**
Hang gliders	7	6	6	10	15	16	9	6	9	11	12
Parachutes	4	1	3	2	1	3	3	1	0	2	7
Total	**11**	**7**	**9**	**12**	**16**	**19**	**12**	**7**	**9**	**13**	**19**

Fatal aircraft accidents and fatalities[1]
Year ending 30 June

Aircraft category	1997	1998	1999	2000	2001	2002	2003	2004	2005	2006	2007
13,608kg and above	0	0	0	0	0	0	0	1 (2)	0	0	0
5,670 to 13,607kg	0	0	0	0	0	0	0	0	1 (2)	0	0
2,721 to 5,669kg	0	0	1 (5)	0	1 (1)	0	2 (11)	2 (3)	0	0	0
Below 2,721kg	4 (9)	4 (7)	7 (18)	4 (11)	2 (5)	5 (11)	3 (4)	5 (6)	5 (9)	5 (7)	1 (2)
Helicopters	3 (5)	2 (3)	2 (6)	6 (15)	4 (6)	2 (4)	3 (3)	4 (6)	0	0	1 (2)
Sport	3 (4)	3 (6)	6 (9)	2 (2)	2 (3)	2 (2)	6 (9)	2 (3)	2 (2)	3 (5)	0
Unknown	0	0	0	0	0	0	0	0	0	0	0
Total	**10 (18)**	**9 (16)**	**16 (38)**	**12 (28)**	**9 (15)**	**9 (17)**	**14 (27)**	**14 (20)**	**8 (13)**	**8 (12)**	**2 (4)**
Hang gliders	1 (1)	1 (1)	0	1 (1)	2 (2)	0	1 (1)	0	0	0	0
Parachutes	3 (4)	0	1 (1)	0	0	1 (1)	0	0	0	0	1 (1)
Total	**4 (5)**	**1 (1)**	**1 (1)**	**1 (1)**	**2 (2)**	**1 (1)**	**1 (1)**	**0**	**0**	**0**	**1 (1)**

(1) Figures in brackets indicate the number of fatalities.

Source: Civil Aviation Authority

Air New Zealand takes part in biofuel research initiative

Air New Zealand will play a world-leading role in the development of more environmentally friendly fuel for commercial aircraft. The airline has signed a memorandum of understanding with aircraft manufacturer Boeing and engine maker Rolls-Royce to work together on projects aimed at making commercial aviation more environmentally sustainable.

The first step will be the first commercial trial of a biofuelled, Rolls-Royce-powered, Boeing aircraft toward the second half of 2008 or in early 2009. The Boeing 747 flight, which is likely to depart Auckland, will not carry customers and will be conducted under strict safety standards.

Only one engine will run on a blended biofuel/kerosene mix, and the remaining three will be powered by regular aviation fuel. An announcement on the source and mix of the blended fuel will be made closer to the time of the flight.

The test flight is another step in Air New Zealand's plan to lead the global aviation industry in developing environmentally responsible airline practices and be an environmentally responsible airline.

Air New Zealand would like to progress to an all-New Zealand biofuel for future test flights, but sourcing the quantity necessary may be a challenge in the short term.

Air New Zealand has already made significant steps towards becoming one of the world's most environmentally responsible airlines through a large fleet investment programme.

The Boeing 787 Dreamliner, due to come into Air New Zealand service in 2010, will use 20 percent less fuel than similar aircraft, through a combination of new technology and weight reduction.

Source: Air New Zealand

supplied on contract to the Royal New Zealand Air Force. Specialised divisions of Airways provide a range of related aviation services. Aviation Publishing is responsible for producing aeronautical charts and manuals on behalf of the CAA.

The Airways Training Centre, in Christchurch, conducts courses in air traffic services and telecommunications for New Zealand and international students. Airways International has applied expertise gained in New Zealand in the provision of air navigation services solutions internationally, and has provided technical and training solutions to more than 65 countries.

Airports

New Zealand has 24 airports certificated by the Civil Aviation Authority (CAA) to receive regular air services by aircraft of 30 or more passenger capacity. There are several other airports with regular scheduled services by smaller aircraft, as well as numerous aerodromes and airstrips.

Airport ownership is mixed, with Crown, local (or territorial) authority and private interests, or a combination of these. The major international and regional airports are operated by airport companies. The chief international airports are Auckland (which is listed on the New Zealand Stock Exchange), Wellington (co-owned by a listed company and the local authority) and Christchurch (jointly owned by the local authority and the Crown). Hamilton, Dunedin and Queenstown airports also receive trans-Tasman services.

Airport safety standards, certification and inspection are addressed by the CAA. The Aviation Security Service provides airport security and passenger and baggage screening at major airports (typically those handling jet passenger aircraft). Air traffic control services are supplied to most airports by Airways New Zealand.

Domestic air services

Domestic air services were economically deregulated between 1984 and 1990, with deregulation including a policy allowing 100 percent foreign ownership of domestic airlines. Air New Zealand is the major domestic operator and has regional connections through the three branded Air New Zealand Link commuter airlines (Air Nelson, Mount Cook Airline and Eagle Airways). Qantas and Pacific Blue provide jet services on the main trunk routes.

Qantas, Air New Zealand and Korean Airlines planes at Christchurch Airport.

International air services

International air services are operated under formal agreements between governments. New Zealand has 40 such agreements (with another two still to be signed) and a non-government agreement with Taiwan. Agreements outline routes by which airlines can operate to and from New Zealand and, in some cases, capacity that can be used on those routes. One agreement, the Multilateral Agreement on the Liberalisation of International Air Transportation, covers New Zealand's air services arrangements with Brunei Darussalam, Chile, the Cook Islands, Samoa, Singapore, Tonga and the United States. New Zealand's international air transport policy is to maximise economic benefit to New Zealand, including trade and tourism, consistent with foreign policy and strategic considerations.

Air New Zealand operates services to six gateways in Australia (Sydney, Melbourne, Adelaide, Brisbane, Perth and Cairns). In the Pacific, Air New Zealand operates services to the Cook Islands, Samoa, Fiji, Vanuatu, Tonga, Tahiti, Niue, Norfolk Island and New Caledonia. Services to Europe are offered on both an own-aircraft basis (London) and a code-share basis.

Air New Zealand code-shares with Austria, Belgium, Germany, Ireland, the Netherlands and the United Kingdom. Air New Zealand operates to China, Japan (Tokyo and Osaka) and Hong Kong, and offers code-share services to Ho Chi Minh City, Beijing, Shanghai, Bangkok and Kuala Lumpur.

Own-aircraft services are also operated to Honolulu, Los Angeles, San Francisco and Vancouver. Code-share services are offered to a variety of other points in the United States and Canada. Code-share services are also offered to Guadalajara and Mexico City.

Pacific Blue Airlines (NZ) Ltd, a subsidiary of Australian-based Virgin Blue Airlines, offers budget services across the Tasman.

A number of foreign airlines offer services to New Zealand on a code-share basis only – Air Canada, Air China, American Airlines, Austrian Airlines, British Airways, Japan Airlines, KLM Royal Dutch Airlines, Lufthansa, Mexicana, Shanghai Airlines and United Airlines.

Railways

The New Zealand railway network spans 3,898 kilometres, from Otiria in the north to Bluff in the south, with 2,559 kilometres of track in the North Island and 1,515 kilometres of track in the South Island. The network includes 150 tunnels, which collectively measure over 87 kilometres, and 2,174 bridges (including culverts), measuring nearly 85 kilometres in total length. More than 500 kilometres of the North Island network is electrified. The track is narrow gauge – 1,067 millimetres.

Since 1962, the network has included inter-island rail ferries connecting the North Island and South Island rail networks.

The Railways Department was reorganised in 1982 to become a government-owned corporation with a commercial mandate.

Travellers on the rise

The New Zealand Customs Service checks and clears all international travellers and crews entering or leaving New Zealand by air or sea. This includes control of transit passengers and crews, and associated craft and vessels.

During the year ending 30 June 2007, 4,715,148 people arrived in New Zealand by air. This was an increase of 114,468 (2.49 percent) on arrivals in the June 2006 year. In the year ending 30 June 2007, 4,705,665 travellers departed New Zealand by air, an increase of 102,454 (2.23 percent) on the previous June year.

The annual average growth rate for travellers arriving in New Zealand is 4 percent.

The number of passengers travelling by air continues to increase year on year, with around a 60 percent increase in passengers since the year ending June 2000.

In the year ending 30 June 2007, the number of air travellers processed on arrival and on departure increased by 2.5 percent and 2.2 percent, respectively. This continued the trend of passenger increases since 2000, although the increases were at a slower rate than

in the years ending June 2004 (14.1 percent) and 2005 (10.1 percent). The number of arriving and departing aircraft has increased marginally from the June 2006 year, reversing the marginal decrease in the previous June year.

In 2007 the number of vessels arriving increased (2.2 percent) – the first increase since the June 2003 year. However, the number of departing vessels decreased (1.7 percent), continuing the trend of the past three years.

Movement of people and craft to and from New Zealand ports and airports
Year ending 30 June

	2000	2001	2002	2003	2004	2005	2006	2007
Air travellers processed								
On arrival	2,989,486	3,251,349	3,536,932	3,627,389	4,138,873	4,557,317	4,600,680	4,715,148
On departure	2,986,587	3,238,822	3,248,445	3,366,516	4,139,018	4,528,969	4,603,211	4,705,665
Aircraft numbers								
Arriving	21,666	23,492	22,815	24,803	28,189	30,994	30,800	30,979
Departing	21,996	24,204	23,680	25,563	29,328	31,410	31,209	31,305
Vessel numbers								
Arriving direct	3,731	3,294	3,428	3,542	3,154	3,146	3,087	3,154
Departing direct	3,779	3,283	3,458	3,488	3,209	3,205	3,083	3,031

Source: New Zealand Customs Service

More Wellingtonians use public transport to get to work

The Wellington region leads the nation in using public transport to travel to and from work. Figures from the 2006 Census show that 16.9 percent of Wellington commuters use public transport (7.3 percent train and 9.5 percent bus) as their main means of travel to work. This figure is significantly higher than for other regions in New Zealand and is 2.6 percent higher than in 1996. Wellington's train network linking the city with neighbouring Lower Hutt, Upper Hutt, South Wairarapa, Porirua, and the Kapiti Coast, is largely responsible for this high usage. Between 10.2 and 12.4 percent of people living in these areas use the train network as their main means of travel to work.

Public transport use in all other areas of New Zealand is significantly less, particularly in major regions such as Auckland and Canterbury. Public transport is used by 6.9 percent of commuting Aucklanders (5.8 percent bus and 1.1 percent train), and just 3.7 percent of Cantabrians (3.7 percent bus and a negligible percent train). As a nation, use of public transport as a means of travel to work has increased slightly over the past 10 years, from 4.8 percent in 1996 to 5.2 percent in 2006.

Aucklanders also fall behind the rest of New Zealand when it comes to biking, walking or jogging to work, with 5.9 percent using this option, compared with 9.5 percent for all of New Zealand. The Nelson region had the highest proportion biking, walking or jogging, with 17.5 percent. Of the territorial authorities, the Mackenzie District and Wellington City had the highest proportion biking, walking or jogging, with 30.1 percent and 21.3 percent, respectively.

In 2006, 77.0 percent of individuals drove a car to work, an increase from 73.9 percent in 1996. This rise is a result of a number of factors, some of which can be associated with the development of road infrastructure.

Factors such as age, sex, ethnicity, income, hours worked, and proximity to work all have an effect on whether people decide to bike, walk or jog to work, catch public transport or drive a car. The most significant of these is age, with 8.9 percent of 20–24-year-olds using public transport, compared with 3.4 percent of 50–54-year-olds. Similarly, as people age they tend to move towards driving to work, with 83.2 percent of 50–54-year-olds driving to work, compared with 64.7 percent of 20–24-year-olds.

Source: Statistics New Zealand

The same year, the government began deregulation of the transport industry, removing the statutory protections rail had against competition by road.

In 1990, the operating assets of the Railways Corporation were transferred to a limited liability company under government ownership, New Zealand Rail Ltd. In 1993, the company was sold to a private consortium made up of Wisconsin Central Transportation Corporation and two investment groups. Three years later, the new owners made a public offering of shares in Tranz Rail Holdings, listing the company on the New Zealand Stock Exchange and the NASDAQ market in the United States.

The process of deregulation, commercialisation and privatisation saw a reduction in the number of employees, from 21,000 with the Railways Department in 1982 to 3,757 with Tranz Rail in 2002.

After the sale in 1993, the Railways Corporation continued as a residual government body with two principal activities: to manage all known litigation, contingent issues and statutory obligations; and to manage the rail corridor lease with Tranz Rail and the lease of other Crown land held for operational rail purposes.

During the 1990s, Tranz Rail expanded into new markets, including movement of bulk milk to dairy processing plants and establishment of New Zealand's first inland port at Wiri south of Auckland. The port, a joint development with the Port of Tauranga, is connected by train with Tauranga, creating a significant line of containerised freight business. A second inland port at East Tamaki has been operating since 2002.

In 2003, Toll Holdings Ltd, an Australian-based transportation and logistics operator, acquired approximately 85 percent of Tranz Rail's shares. As a result of Toll's offer for shares in Tranz Rail becoming unconditional, an agreement between Toll and the Crown was triggered, a key feature of which was the buy-back of track and associated infrastructure by the Crown.

The Crown undertook to invest $200 million in improving rail infrastructure, while Toll undertook to invest $100 million in new rolling stock.

In September 2004, ownership and management of the network and its assets was vested in the existing Railway Corporation, which adopted the trading name ONTRACK.

Under the agreement, Toll retained exclusive rights to the network for freight purposes, subject to meeting minimum tonnage levels annually. ONTRACK is responsible for managing and developing the network, controlling track access to rail operators, and providing advice to the government on railway matters.

In February 2006, ONTRACK took back control of maintaining the infrastructure, which had been contracted out. As a result, its staff increased from 150 to approximately 700. In 2007, ONTRACK employed approximately 850 staff. ONTRACK is currently a State-owned enterprise, but will become a Crown entity once enabling legislation is passed by Parliament.

The Government purchased Toll NZ's rail and ferry operations in May 2008 for $665 million.

Passenger services Toll NZ operates four long distance passenger trains, as well as commuter services linking central Wellington with Johnsonville, Paraparaumu, the Hutt Valley, Palmerston North and Masterton.

The four long distance passenger trains are: the Overlander between Auckland and Wellington; the Capital Connection between Palmerston North and Wellington; the Tranz Coastal between Picton and Christchurch; and the Tranz Alpine between Christchurch and Greymouth. It was the 20th anniversary of the Tranz Alpine in 2007, a year in which record passenger numbers were carried (in excess of 200,000 people).

Table 23.02

New Zealand railways
Locomotives, passengers and freight
At 30 June

	1998	1999	2000	2001	2002	2003	2004	2005	2006	2007
Locomotives										
Diesel/diesel-electric	218	188	187	184	131	131	144	168	168	168
Electric	27	27	27	27	23	14	17	17	17	17
Rolling stock										
Freight	6,382	6,004	5,948	5,606	4,321	4,048	4,176	4,180	4,166	4,166
Passenger (including motorised)	328	321	321	314	177[1]	177[1]	177[1]	198	196	196
Passengers carried										
Long distance[2]	458,000	466,400	465,800	513,500	..	..	560,000	520,000	520,000	520,000
Wellington commuter trains	11,293,000	11,422,000	12,118,000	12,577,000	12,300,000	12,300,000	11,000,000	11,100,000	11,200,000	11,200,000
Auckland commuter trains[3]	..	..	..	..	..	..	..	3,600,000	5,000,000	5,600,000
Freight carried										
Tonnes	11,706,000	12,900,000	14,699,000	14,461,000	14,330,000	14,822,000	14,800,000	14,500,000	14,800,000	14,800,000

(1) Excludes the Auckland region. (2) Includes the Capital Connection between Palmerston North and Wellington. (3) Figures for Auckland commuter trains are for 2004/05, 2005/06 and 2006/07.
Symbol: .. figure not available

Source: Toll NZ

Jarrad Mapp

Wellington is the commuting capital, with the highest proportion of people using public transport to travel to work. On census day (7 March) in 2006, 7.3 percent of people in the Wellington region took the train to work and 9.5 percent travelled by bus.

Since August 2004, commuter services in Auckland have been provided by Connex Auckland, which was re-branded as Veolia Transport Auckland in March 2006. Veolia Transport operates on three lines – the southern, eastern and western lines – and in 2007 carried just over 6 million passengers.

Freight transport Toll NZ's freight business is carried out under the brand name Toll TranzLink. In 2006/07 overall trading revenue for Toll NZ was $725 million. The bulk of freight revenue was from agriculture and food products, followed by revenue from manufactured products, forest products and coal.

Table 23.02 provides locomotive, passenger and freight details about New Zealand railways.

Road transport

Central government invests more than $2 billion in land transport each year, mostly through the National Land Transport Fund. Regional and territorial authorities invest a further $400 million, mainly funded from rates.

There are about 93,500 kilometres of formed roads and streets and, as at 30 June 2007, about 3.8 million registered motor vehicles.

In February 2007, there were 9,750 employees engaged in road passenger transport and 24,440 employees engaged in road freight transport.

Commercial road users are regulated through a system of quality controls that focus primarily on safety regulation, although there is an increasing emphasis on environmental performance.

Land Transport New Zealand

On 1 December 2004, the Land Transport Management Amendment Act 2004 disestablished Transfund New Zealand and the Land Transport Safety Authority, and created Land Transport New Zealand (Land Transport NZ) to take responsibility for land transport funding and to promote land transport safety and sustainability.

Land Transport NZ is charged with helping deliver the government's vision, as set out in the *New Zealand Transport Strategy*, for "an integrated, safe, responsive and sustainable transport system".

Alongside the promotion of land transport safety and sustainability, Land Transport NZ's functions include managing access through licensing and regulation, monitoring and communicating information, and funding development and operation.

Land Transport NZ works in partnership with the transport sector and other organisations – including industry and other interest groups – to develop an integrated approach to land transport.

TravelWise is run by the Auckland Regional Transport Authority (ARTA) in partnership with Auckland Regional Council, Land Transport NZ, Ministry of Health, RoadSafe Auckland, and city and district councils within the greater Auckland region.

TravelWise aims to reduce people's dependency on cars and persuade them to choose sustainable travel alternatives, such as travelling by public transport, cycling and walking. Auckland's TravelWise team works with communities, schools, tertiary organisations and workplaces to develop travel plans that make it easier for people to get out of the car and into public transport, biking or walking.

School travel plans are active in 171 schools across the Auckland region, covering a school population of over 90,000 children. Walking school buses are a popular part of the programme – with over 4,200 children walking on 237 'bus routes' in primary schools throughout the Auckland region in early 2008, supported by over 1,800 adult volunteers.

But it is not only children who are being encouraged to use more sustainable forms of transport – over 80,000 Aucklanders were participating in a workplace or tertiary travel plan in early 2008. ARTA's original target was 90,000 Aucklanders by 2016.

Source: TravelWise

Travel to work

Main means of travel to work[1]
Employed people aged 15 and over
2006 Census

Drove a private car, truck or van	951,477
Drove a company car, truck or van	212,211
Did not go to work today	203,880
Worked at home	163,977
Walked or jogged	105,462
Passenger in a car, truck, van or company bus	91,071
Public bus	59,481
Bicycle	38,091
Train	19,707
Motorcycle or power cycle	19,695
Other	14,535
Response unidentifiable	33,270
Not stated	72,921
Total	**1,985,778**

(1) Employed people who usually lived in New Zealand were asked about the main means they used to travel to work on census day, Tuesday 7 March 2006.

Source: Statistics New Zealand

Cycle lanes offer improved safety to cyclists and encourage people to travel by bike. This cyclist is using part of the extensive network of cycling lanes in Christchurch.

Land Transport NZ receives funding from the government's National Land Transport Fund for the National Land Transport Programme (NLTP). The NLTP is the mechanism through which Land Transport NZ allocates funds to: renewal, improvement and maintenance of state highways and local roads; passenger transport; rail freight and barging; travel behaviour change; transport demand management; walking and cycling; projects that support regional development; administration activities; research, education and training; and New Zealand Police land transport activities.

Changes in the government land transport sector

In May 2007, a review of the government land transport sector found transport agencies needed to work more collaboratively and with a common purpose. The review recommended a package of changes designed to support a cohesive and efficient sector, including the merger of Transit New Zealand and Land Transport NZ, and the establishment of a short- to medium-term funding and investment priority.

In July 2008, a new Crown entity was formally established and named the New Zealand Transport Agency. A new planning and funding structure was also established, with the release of the first three-yearly government policy statement, detailing short- to medium-term funding and planning priorities.

Land transport network

New Zealand's land transport network is managed by the New Zealand Transport Agency (formed in July 2008 when Transit New Zealand and Land Transport New Zealand merged), 12 regional councils, and 74 provincial road-controlling authorities (territorial authorities).

As table 23.05 shows, there were 17,251 kilometres of urban roads, 65,432 kilometres of rural roads and 10,893 kilometres of state highways, with a total of 93,576 kilometres of developed roading at 30 June 2007.

Table 23.03

Expenditure on state highways
Year ending 30 June

Class of expenditure	1998	1999	2000	2001[1]	2002	2003[2]	2004	2005	2006	2007
					$(000)					
Construction and improvement	199,237	246,355	302,864	265,151	280,259	268,886	351,164	438,696	618,217	719,844
Bridges	13,898	6,587	6,999	10,952	3,879	7,960	7,241	8,157	15,152	25,671
Maintenance, repairs, etc[3]	256,643	262,742	283,270	272,447	278,503	299,267	329,310	362,474	374,865	422,446
Total	**469,778**	**515,684**	**593,133**	**548,550**	**562,641**	**576,113**	**687,715**	**809,327**	**1,008,233**	**1,167,961**

(1) From the year ending 30 June 2001, public roading expenditure includes the funding of public transport and alternative-to-road projects. (2) From the year ending 30 June 2003, public roading expenditure includes the funding of walking and cycling projects. (3) Includes the cost of flood damage repairs.

Source: Land Transport NZ

Table 23.04

Expenditure on public roads
Year ending 30 June

Class of expenditure	1998	1999	2000	2001[1]	2002	2003[2]	2004	2005	2006	2007
					$(000)					
State highway	469,778	515,684	593,133	548,550	562,641	576,113	687,715	809,327	1,008,233	1,167,961
Local authority roading[3]	287,570	297,889	290,926	297,788	319,163	371,839	423,992	497,309	513,487	713,736
Total	**757,348**	**813,573**	**884,059**	**846,338**	**881,804**	**947,952**	**1,111,707**	**1,306,636**	**1,521,720**	**1,881,697**

(1) From the year ending 30 June 2001, public roading expenditure includes the funding of public transport and alternative-to-road projects. (2) From the year ending 30 June 2003, public roading expenditure includes the funding of walking and cycling projects. (3) Expenditure is the Land Transport NZ contribution and does not include the local authority contribution. The rate of assistance to local authorities for construction work ranges from 43 to 83 percent.

Source: Land Transport NZ

Table 23.05

Maintained roads and streets
By type of seal
At 30 June

Year/nature of surface	Local authority roading		State highways and motorways	Total
	Urban roads	Rural roads		
		Kilometres		
1998				
Paved or sealed	15,238	30,764	10,500	56,502
Metal or gravel	442	35,127	71	35,640
Total	**15,680**	**65,891**	**10,571**	**92,142**
1999				
Paved or sealed	15,520	30,968	10,540	57,028
Metal or gravel	442	34,540	65	35,047
Total	**15,962**	**65,508**	**10,605**	**92,075**
2000				
Paved or sealed	15,590	31,474	10,707	57,771
Metal or gravel	419	33,809	54	34,282
Total	**16,009**	**65,283**	**10,761**	**92,053**
2001				
Paved or sealed	15,708	31,762	10,716	58,186
Metal or gravel	414	33,549	58	34,021
Total	**16,122**	**65,311**	**10,774**	**92,207**
2002				
Paved or sealed	15,809	32,017	10,736	58,562
Metal or gravel	418	33,354	47	33,819
Total	**16,227**	**65,371**	**10,783**	**92,381**
2003				
Paved or sealed	15,929	32,258	10,750	58,937
Metal or gravel	409	33,107	41	33,557
Total	**16,338**	**65,365**	**10,791**	**92,494**
2004				
Paved or sealed	16,166	32,539	10,798	59,503
Metal or gravel	402	32,816	39	33,257
Total	**16,568**	**65,355**	**10,837**	**92,760**
2005				
Paved or sealed	16,423	32,819	10,838	60,080
Metal or gravel	397	32,615	56	33,068
Total	**16,820**	**65,434**	**10,894**	**93,148**
2006				
Paved or sealed	16,644	33,167	10,838	60,649
Metal or gravel	403	32,351	57	32,811
Total	**17,046**	**65,519**	**10,895**	**93,460**
2007				
Paved or sealed	16,869	33,439	10,837	61,146
Metal or gravel	382	31,993	56	32,431
Total	**17,251**	**65,432**	**10,893**	**93,576**

Source: Land Transport NZ

For many New Zealanders living near busy roads or railways, a broken night's sleep is just one of the many side-effects of land transport noise. This form of pollution is generated in a number of ways – by increased traffic flows, by changes in infrastructure and land use planning controls, and by the noise of individual vehicles.

The government has been addressing the effects of transport noise for some time. An objective noise test, which uses scientific procedures to measure noise levels, has been part of the warrant of fitness (WoF) and certificate of fitness (CoF) tests since July 2008. Cars and light trucks that have entered the New Zealand vehicle fleet since July 2008 have needed to comply with a reduced noise limit of 90 decibels.

To address broader transport noise issues, a proposed national environmental standard for land transport noise, covering both road and rail, is being investigated by the Ministry of Transport, along with the Ministry for the Environment, and Transit New Zealand, ONTRACK, Land Transport NZ, the Ministry of Health and local government.

The Ministry of Transport heads a strategic policy review considering all aspects of land transport noise, such as road surface and construction, and the proximity of sensitive land uses (for example residential housing) to existing roads and railways. Standards New Zealand is managing a project to develop an acoustic road emissions standard, with good progress to date developing the public comment draft for this standard.

Source: Ministry of Transport

Transport licensing

The Transport Services Licensing Act 1989 contains provisions for transport licensing, which assesses licensees on a qualitative basis – for goods, passenger, rental and vehicle recovery services. The Act uses the concept of 'a fit and proper person' as the principal criterion for road transport operators. Anyone who enters the industry needs to meet certain minimum fitness standards.

Railway operator licensing requirements are now contained in the Railways Act 2005, which recognises changes in the operation and ownership of rail in New Zealand.

All railway operators, as well as rail access providers, are required to develop a safety case to cover standards, practices and procedures. These safety cases are approved by rail regulator Land Transport NZ.

Registration and licensing of vehicles

All vehicles using public roads in New Zealand are required to be registered. An annual relicensing charge is payable, which includes a licence fee, accident compensation levy, administration and label fee, goods and services tax and, in some cases, a transport licence fee.

The country's vehicles are relicensed progressively throughout the year.

Annual relicensing charges for petrol-powered vehicles for the year ending 30 June 2007 were:

- motorcars, $183.22
- motorcycles (private use – 60cc or less), $213.03
- motorcycles (more than 60cc), $224.28
- rental cars and taxis, $208.71
- trucks, vans and utilities (private passenger), $183.22 to $184.71
- trucks, vans and utilities (subject to transport licence fee), $207.21 to $208.71
- tractors (non-exempt), $73.22.

Motor vehicles exempted from the annual licence fee include a variety of machines, such as vehicles used in a declared road construction zone, and vehicles used on a road that is not a public highway. These vehicles are still required to be registered.

Table 23.06 shows registrations of new commercial vehicles from 1996 to 2006. New tractors are not included in this table.

Table 23.07 shows registrations of new cars, station wagons and motorcycles from 1996 to 2006.

Table 23.08 shows the number of licensed motor vehicles by vehicle type for the years 1998 to 2006.

Motor vehicle registers

The Ministry of Economic Development operates two registers specifically concerned with motor vehicles – the Personal Property Securities Register (PPSR) under the Personal Property Securities Act 1999, and the Motor Vehicle Traders Register (MVTR) under the Motor Vehicle Sales Act 2003.

In May 2002, the PPSR was implemented in New Zealand. This register amalgamated the four previous registers of securities over personal property into one wholly-electronic noticeboard. The registers replaced included the Motor Vehicle Securities Register and the Chattels Register. Buyers of motor vehicles can search the PPSR to see whether a security interest has been registered (indicating whether money is owed) in respect of a vehicle. There are two ways to search the PPSR for security interests over motor vehicles – by searching online at www.ppsr.govt.nz or by texting the registration, VIN and/or chassis number to the PPSR.

Table 23.06

Registration of new commercial vehicles
By gross weight
Year ending 31 December

Year	2,500kg or less	2,501 to 4,500kg	4,501 to 9,000kg	9,001 to 14,500kg	14,501kg and over	Bus services	Total
1996	10,859	12,702	2,654	882	1,747	1,000	**29,844**
1997	9,005	9,718	2,549	866	1,566	816	**24,520**
1998	6,301	9,456	2,038	781	1,184	780	**20,540**
1999	5,737	11,290	2,036	865	1,566	834	**22,328**
2000	4,859	13,375	1,738	674	1,881	764	**23,291**
2001	4,439	14,133	1,504	771	1,777	839	**23,463**
2002	4,729	18,256	1,929	1,040	2,245	1,120	**29,319**
2003	4,813	20,851	2,355	1,160	2,747	1,093	**33,019**
2004	4,669	23,997	3,140	1,566	3,168	1,329	**37,869**
2005	4,140	25,363	2,945	1,492	3,140	1,325	**38,405**
2006	3,097	23,239	2,683	1,277	2,587	1,318	**34,201**

Source: Land Transport NZ

In 2006, 393,648 people in the Auckland region drove a private or company car to work on census day (7 March). Government initiatives and programmes such as TravelWise aim to get more people out of their cars and into using public transport, or biking, walking or jogging to work.

By December 2006, over 8 million searches had been conducted on the PPSR, with around 67 percent of them relating to motor vehicles.

The PPSR includes private and commercial motor vehicles, motorcycles, trucks, trailers, caravans, farm vehicles and aircraft. Security interests in boats, except those exceeding 24 metres, can also be registered on the PPSR.

The MVTR contains essential information about whether someone is a registered motor vehicle trader. Buying a motor vehicle from a registered motor vehicle trader provides improved protection for consumers.

Table 23.07

Registrations of new[1] cars, station wagons and motorcycles
Year ending 31 December

| | Cars and station wagons | | | | | | | | New |
Year	850cc and under	851 to 1,300cc	1,301 to 1,600cc	1,601 to 2,000cc	2,001 to 5,000cc	5,001cc and over	Total	Vehicles previously registered overseas[2]	motorcycles
1996	586	3,799	56,066	67,402	47,829	496	**177,678**	111,764	3,812
1997	694	2,680	45,275	58,379	48,256	315	**157,281**	97,041	4,078
1998	608	2,685	41,669	59,868	48,932	332	**155,760**	99,937	4,067
1999	118	3,949	48,418	76,899	59,208	721	**190,591**	131,118	3,849
2000	120	4,120	41,114	69,834	57,146	1,408	**174,334**	116,124	3,598
2001	73	4,070	41,622	76,744	62,498	1,848	**187,008**	128,693	3,575
2002	33	4,459	41,110	76,268	76,214	2,420	**200,086**	136,418	4,118
2003	106	5,790	43,228	82,869	91,752	3,680	**225,748**	156,972	4,967
2004	213	5,786	41,138	79,879	98,096	3,685	**227,116**	154,042	6,341
2005	129	6,869	42,561	84,801	92,874	3,079	**229,239**	152,488	7,654
2006	168	7,020	40,817	73,247	75,863	3,079	**199,121**	123,390	9,596

(1) Includes cars and station wagons previously registered overseas. (2) Included in 'Total'.

Source: Land Transport NZ

Table 23.08

Licensed motor vehicles
At 30 June

Type of vehicle	1998	1999	2000	2001	2002	2003	2004	2005	2006
Cars	1,762,813	1,868,297	1,886,982	1,916,685	1,970,403	2,036,804	2,118,240	2,189,187	2,232,915
Rental cars	13,154	15,117	18,022	17,178	18,119	19,775	22,128	22,604	21,754
Taxis	6,572	7,280	7,588	7,108	7,507	7,795	8,089	8,172	8,011
Trucks	359,411	371,365	368,624	363,166	366,918	374,361	386,295	399,843	408,757
Buses and coaches	10,950	11,748	12,397	12,709	13,379	14,107	14,932	15,671	16,486
Trailers	308,751	339,325	354,487	362,225	373,940	386,005	397,113	408,982	420,289
Motorcycles	38,151	40,664	37,794	35,939	36,045	33,601	34,873	37,717	43,513
Mopeds	8,034	7,495	7,253	7,364	7,395	7,881	8,617	10,282	14,171
Tractors	19,492	19,669	20,369	21,229	22,756	24,016	25,279	26,521	27,124
Exempt vehicles	6,348	6,628	7,369	7,706	8,195	8,825	9,708	10,328	11,130
Miscellaneous	14,119	15,090	15,096	15,225	16,644	17,557	19,206	20,946	22,464
All vehicles	**2,547,795**	**2,702,678**	**2,735,981**	**2,766,534**	**2,841,301**	**2,930,727**	**3,044,480**	**3,150,253**	**3,226,614**

Source: Land Transport NZ

Table 23.09

Licensed vehicles by population[1]
At 30 June

Year	People per licensed car[2]	People per licensed motor vehicle[3]
1998	2.15	1.71
1999	2.04	1.63
2000	2.03	1.62
2001	2.01	1.62
2002	1.99	1.61
2003	1.96	1.59
2004	1.91	1.55
2005	1.87	1.51
2006	1.86	1.50

(1) Based on estimated resident population (2006 base).
(2) Includes cars and rental cars. (3) Excludes trailers, caravans and exempt vehicles.

Sources: Land Transport NZ, Statistics New Zealand

The MVTR holds information about who is registered and details of each trader's business, such as its physical address. The MVTR includes a list of banned motor vehicle traders. The MVTR was established by the Motor Vehicle Sales Act 2003 (which replaced the Motor Vehicle Dealers Act 1975) on 15 December 2003.

A wider definition of 'motor vehicle trader' means more traders must register under the new law. People who import more than three vehicles, or who sell more than six vehicles in a 12-month period, must be registered.

Table 23.09 shows the number of people in New Zealand per licensed car and per licensed motor vehicle. Figure 23.03 plots new tractor registrations since 1950, while figure 23.04 shows cars previously registered in another country.

Road safety

Land Transport NZ is charged with helping deliver the Government's vision, as set out in the *New Zealand Transport Strategy*, for "an affordable, integrated, safe, responsive and sustainable transport system".

Land Transport NZ advises the government on land transport safety and sustainability, and suggests policy, develops standards and reviews land transport safety systems in consultation with industry groups.

Road laws are enforced by the New Zealand Police, who investigate serious and fatal accidents, enforce laws regarding heavy traffic and allowable weights of vehicles and loads, and assist with licensing of road transport services, such as taxis, buses and tow trucks.

Figure 23.03

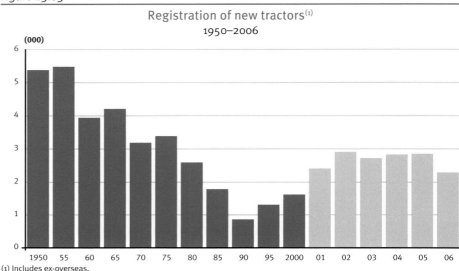

Registration of new tractors[1]
1950–2006

(1) Includes ex-overseas.
Note: Colour change represents change from 'five-year' to 'one-year' intervals.

Source: Land Transport NZ

Figure 23.04

Registration of ex-overseas cars[1]
1950–2006

(1) Ex-overseas cars are those that have been registered in another country before entry into New Zealand.
Note: Colour change represents change from 'five-year' to 'one-year' intervals.

Source: Land Transport NZ

In 2007, New Zealand's road toll was 423, an increase of 30 from 2006 when road deaths reached the lowest level since 1963. To minimise the road toll, police are continuing to target speed, alcohol, driver fatigue, restraint use and failure to give way.

Driver licensing A New Zealand driver licence is valid for up to 10 years. A graduated system for obtaining a driver licence involves a number of restrictions on learner drivers to ensure they are protected from high-risk situations until they have obtained experience on the road. Incentives to attend driver education courses are available to all first applicants for licences. The system has three stages: learner, restricted and full licence. A test must be passed in order to graduate to a full licence. At ages 75 and 80, and every two years thereafter, the licence holder is required to undergo a medical check. The mandatory older driver test was discontinued at the end of 2006.

Inspection of motor vehicles All vehicles using New Zealand roads must be inspected regularly to ensure mechanical and structural fitness. They are inspected every six months, except for vehicles that are less than six years old – these are inspected every 12 months. Most lightweight vehicles require a warrant of fitness, which can be issued at approved garages.

All heavy vehicles, with minor exceptions, undergo a more exacting examination for a certificate of fitness, which, in respect of passenger service buses, has special regard for the safety and comfort of passengers. Taxis and rental vehicles also require a certificate of fitness, which can be issued by approved testing agencies only.

Table 23.10 shows the age of major motor vehicle types in New Zealand at 31 December 2006.

Safety belts Wearing safety belts is compulsory in New Zealand for drivers and front-seat passengers in most classes of light vehicles registered after January 1955. It is compulsory for rear-seat passengers to wear safety belts in all cars. All children under five years of age must be properly restrained by an approved child restraint when travelling in cars and vans.

Drivers must make sure that children between the ages of five and seven years are safely restrained if there is a child restraint or safety belt in the vehicle. If no restraint is available, children must be seated in the rear of the car. Drivers are also responsible for making sure children between the ages of eight and 14 use safety belts when available.

Helmets All motorcyclists and pillion riders must wear safety helmets at all speeds. Bicycle helmets are also compulsory for cyclists.

Table 23.10

Age profile of major vehicle types
At 31 December 2006

Age in whole years	Cars	Trucks	Buses	Motor caravans	Motor-cycles	Mopeds	Trailers
Under 1 year	76,483	21,063	761	538	5,789	4,148	25,932
1	79,783	23,456	624	625	6,202	4,645	25,693
2	76,828	23,203	668	896	4,814	1,993	24,541
3	76,650	20,601	524	735	3,828	1,151	21,366
4	73,396	18,848	556	422	3,374	727	19,314
5	75,822	16,904	625	792	3,007	626	18,092
6	84,834	17,773	568	494	2,849	469	18,042
7	104,074	15,985	707	606	2,851	452	16,323
8	130,580	15,653	655	329	2,890	432	15,830
9	195,291	20,385	856	329	2,578	301	14,940
10	253,931	22,785	1,099	627	2,020	289	15,035
11	196,352	20,705	971	708	1,635	323	14,959
12	189,968	22,985	913	967	1,546	263	12,742
13	153,880	19,743	738	787	1,390	184	11,128
14	167,894	20,438	819	874	1,611	413	10,847
15	142,723	21,405	981	951	2,140	337	10,224
16	136,458	27,004	981	1,201	2,477	527	16,896
17	115,495	23,205	913	975	2,880	462	12,950
18	77,651	19,019	751	893	3,495	537	12,052
19	55,692	16,275	694	791	3,555	576	10,994
20	43,367	14,103	705	855	3,346	638	11,439
21	35,247	13,373	506	1,219	2,182	418	14,712
22	26,558	11,416	430	627	1,802	274	11,112
23	15,380	7,328	309	545	1,668	216	8,905
24	12,150	6,736	239	371	1,746	350	9,434
25	9,701	5,146	224	294	1,687	268	8,837
26	8,016	4,309	190	276	1,553	339	15,622
27	6,917	3,438	223	234	1,282	217	10,720
28	6,385	2,785	217	221	768	98	12,794
29	4,704	2,473	155	250	619	94	12,923
30	4,651	2,203	148	275	718	78	15,049
31 to 40	53,894	10,886	434	2,049	5,069	703	71,957
41 to 50	19,832	3,449	121	939	1,419	313	18,483
51 and over	15,816	3,631	48	417	2,933	100	3,796
Total vehicles	2,726,403	498,711	19,353	23,112	87,723	22,961	553,683
Mean age (years)	**12.10**	**12.71**	**13.34**	**17.72**	**14.98**	**8.90**	**17.03**

Source: Land Transport NZ

Government action on transport

Transport strategy

The *New Zealand Transport Strategy* outlines the Government's strategic framework for achieving the vision that "by 2010 New Zealand will have an affordable, integrated, safe, responsive, and sustainable transport system" (Ministry of Transport, 2002). This strategy will be updated in 2008.

National walking and cycling strategy

In February 2005, the Government launched a national strategy to encourage walking and cycling: Getting There – on foot, by cycle (Ministry of Transport, 2005). Funding for walking and cycling initiatives was boosted by $1.15 million at this time.

Mandatory vehicle fuel economy labelling

In 2007, a mandatory vehicle fuel economy labelling scheme was approved for both new and used vehicles. The labelling scheme will apply at the point of sale for later model vehicles for which fuel economy information is available.

The label will have a comparative 'star rating', allowing buyers to compare fuel economy ratings across vehicles. The label will also show the annual fuel cost for a typical driver. The scheme will increase consumer information about fuel economy and encourage people to buy more fuel-efficient vehicles. (Energy Efficiency and Conservation Authority, 2007)

Fuel $aver website

The Fuel $aver website (www.fuelsaver.govt.nz) was launched in 2006. The website provides up-to-date information about the fuel efficiency of vehicles sold in New Zealand. This information lets consumers assess different vehicles on the basis of fuel consumption.

Biofuels Sales Obligation

The Government has announced a Biofuels Sales Obligation, which requires companies that sell petrol or diesel in New Zealand to also sell biofuels. The amount of biofuels they will have to sell will be a percentage of their total combined petrol and diesel sales each year, measured in petajoules and based on the volumetric energy content of each fuel. The amount has been set at a minimum of 0.53 percent for year one (2008) and will increase each subsequent year. By 2012, at least 3.4 percent of all fuel that oil companies sell in New Zealand will have to be biofuels.

Public transport

Investment in public transport has also increased. In 2006/07, the Government committed $301 million to fund public transport and buy back the nation's rail tracks. The 2006/07 National Land Transport Programme allocated $136 million to passenger transport community services and almost $160 million to passenger transport infrastructure. In May 2008 the Government purchased Toll NZ's rail and ferry operations.

Government funding for passenger transport services increased 16 percent between 2005/06 and 2006/07. In addition, the Government committed $600 million over four years to upgrade the Auckland rail network.

Source: Ministry for the Environment

A police officer uses a hand-held speed camera to target speeding vehicles in heavy traffic.

Alcohol impairment Police have several tests available to test whether drivers are affected by alcohol. Any driver may be required to give a passive test at any time. A breath-screening test may be administered after a police officer has detected alcohol on a driver's breath using a passive alcohol detector.

If this screening test is positive, the person may be required to give an evidential breath test. If this is also positive, the person has the option of either accepting the breath test reading or providing a blood sample for analysis.

A driver commits an offence and is liable for prosecution if either:

- breath-alcohol concentration as recorded on an evidential breath-testing device exceeds 400 micrograms of alcohol per litre of breath, or 150 micrograms of alcohol per litre of breath in the case of a person under the age of 20
- blood-alcohol concentration exceeds 80 milligrams of alcohol per 100 millilitres of blood, or 30 milligrams of alcohol per 100 millilitres of blood in the case of a person under the age of 20.

Speed limits New Zealand's roading network is primarily a two-way system with one lane each way. Management of speed is, therefore, a critical aspect of traffic safety.

Maximum speed limits for highways and motorways are: 100 kilometres per hour (km/h) for cars, motorcycles, vans and light vehicles; and 90km/h for vehicles towing trailers and all heavy vehicles, including buses. A general speed limit of 50km/h is fixed in all urban traffic areas.

Cost of running a car falls in 2007

On average in 2007, it cost 48.2 cents per kilometre to own and operate a car up to 1,300 cc. That gave a total annual cost of $6,755, or $130 a week, if the car was driven 14,000 kilometres a year, the New Zealand average.

For 1,601–2,000 cc cars, the average cost per kilometre was 70.3 cents, $9,847 a year or $189 a week.

The overall cost of running a car in 2007, compared with 2006, was down by 1.9 percent, on average.

In 2007, fixed costs increased due to a slight increase in new car prices. However, a drop in fuel prices from 2006 and reduced service costs made vehicle ownership more affordable, on average.

Cost of running a car in 2007

	Up to 1,300 cc	1,601–2,000 cc
	$	
Average price of new car, including registration	21,417	37,976
Average value at start of third year	14,032	25,442
Fixed costs: relicensing, insurance, warrant of fitness	685	807
Interest on outlay (9.5 percent)	1,395	2,488
Depreciation at third year	2,385	3,685
Fixed cost total	**4,465**	**6,981**
Running costs: petrol, oil, tyres, repairs, maintenance	2,289	2,697
Total operating costs (fixed and running)	**6,755**	**9,847**
Divided by 14,000km	48.2 cents/km	70.3 cents/km
Operating costs in 2006	50.2 cents/km	72.9 cents/km
Change from 2006	Down 3.9 percent	Down 3.5 percent

Note: Rounding may affect some calculations. This table gives running costs for selected car types only.

Source: Automobile Association

In recent years, road controlling authorities have been given more flexibility in setting speed limits and may set limits from 10 to 100km/h provided they are safe and appropriate for particular roads.

Speed cameras, radars and lasers Under the 'anywhere/anytime' policy adopted in December 2003, mobile and fixed speed cameras can be located in any place and at any time, with all signage removed (this excludes the use of hidden or camouflaged cameras).

Police also use mobile mode radar and laser speed measuring equipment to supplement speed cameras. The laser equipment is particularly useful in heavy traffic and multi-lane situations, where its ability to isolate and measure individual vehicles permits the targeting of speeding vehicles in traffic.

Traffic offences Penalties are imposed by courts for driving and other offences under the Transport Act 1962, the Land Transport Act 1998, and accompanying regulations. Breaches of certain laws are dealt with under an infringement system, where a driver may pay an infringement fee within a specified time to avoid court proceedings.

There is also a system whereby demerit points are automatically registered, according to a fixed scale, against people convicted of driving offences, or people who pay certain infringement fees.

The director of Land Transport NZ may suspend a driver's licence for three months when 100 or more demerit points are received within two years. Demerit points for speeding are awarded on a graduated scale, based on the speed a driver is detected travelling at.

Table 23.11 shows the number of traffic offences and infringements in New Zealand for the years 2002–07. Figure 23.05 shows the rate of traffic convictions per 10,000 people.

Figure 23.05

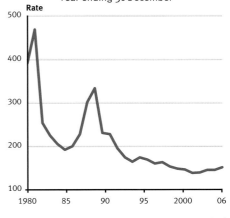

Traffic convictions
Rate per 10,000 people
Year ending 31 December

Sources: Ministry of Justice, Statistics New Zealand

Table 23.11

			Traffic offences and infringements[1]				
			Year ending 30 June				
Category	2002	2003	2004	2005	2006	2007	Change from 2006 (percent)
Drink/drive offence	25,348	24,744	25,496	26,697	27,408	30,796	11.0
Dangerous/reckless driving offence	4,586	5,159	6,162	6,602	7,570	8,166	7.3
Unsafe use of vehicle	20,675	23,805	26,522	25,206	24,583	25,772	4.6
Careless/inconsiderate driving or overtaking offence	12,249	11,993	11,411	11,397	11,527	12,098	4.7
Speeding – general[2]	249,133	349,469	394,940	363,949	299,427	291,194	-2.8
Speeding – trailer, towing, heavy motor vehicle	11,650	14,710	13,177	14,167	10,073	10,488	4.0
Speeding – speed camera	458,622	488,714	479,164	416,492	394,585	439,497	10.2
Failure to stop/give way	31,396	36,054	49,165	44,840	39,704	42,105	5.7
Failure to obey officer/fulfill duty	18,322	18,746	19,549	17,956	18,558	20,330	8.7
Vehicle licence infringement	19,092	19,069	18,375	18,742	17,044	15,908	-7.1
Driving while disqualified	8,213	8,217	8,653	9,061	9,788	10,736	8.8
Certificate of fitness infringement	94,260	100,761	107,898	107,265	113,878	127,613	10.8
Driver licence and vehicle registration infringement	222,907	255,933	283,555	281,381	269,481	277,634	2.9
Driver hours/log book infringement	3,626	3,783	4,594	3,375	3,117	2,647	-17.8
Seat belt	40,224	66,977	89,671	77,897	64,257	64,441	0.3
Safety helmet	414	532	631	676	946	973	2.8
Passenger/recovery/rental service vehicle	2,055	1,813	1,726	2,206	1,863	1,329	-40.2
Vehicle condition	16,281	21,173	26,410	26,888	21,238	19,624	-8.2
Vehicle noise/loading	5,488	6,280	6,468	5,606	4,976	4,912	-1.3
Bicycle infringement	2,148	2,774	3,142	3,012	2,617	2,118	-23.6
Cycle helmet	5,399	8,673	10,038	9,551	8,305	7,118	-16.7
Pedestrian and other	391	597	758	850	1,002	1,322	24.2
Stock and vehicle bylaws offence	234	237	82	56	44	162	72.8
Local body bylaw infringement	804	1,105	1,368	958	242	430	43.7
Other transport offence	8,744	10,391	8,130	6,151	6,094	5,831	-4.5
Total	**1,253,517**	**1,471,318**	**1,588,955**	**1,474,830**	**1,352,233**	**1,417,413**	**4.6**

(1) Data as published in police annual reports. (2) Speeding – general is a new category. It was previously split into two categories (under 100 km/h and over 100 km/h).

Source: New Zealand Police

Contributors and related websites

Airways New Zealand – www.airways.co.nz

Civil Aviation Authority of New Zealand – www.caa.govt.nz

Land Transport New Zealand – www.landtransport.govt.nz

Maritime New Zealand – www.msa.govt.nz

Ministry for the Environment – www.mfe.govt.nz

Ministry of Economic Development – www.med.govt.nz

Ministry of Justice – www.justice.govt.nz

Ministry of Transport – www.transport.govt.nz

Motor Vehicle Traders Register – www.motortraders.med.govt.nz

New Zealand Automobile Association – www.aa.co.nz

New Zealand Police – www.police.govt.nz

New Zealand Railways Corporation – www.ontrack.govt.nz

Personal Property Securities Register – www.ppsr.govt.nz

Statistics New Zealand – www.stats.govt.nz

Toll NZ – www.tollnz.co.nz

Transit New Zealand – www.transit.govt.nz

Transport Accident Investigation Commission – www.taic.org.nz

TravelWise – www.travelwise.org.nz

Jarrad Mapp

Reusable shopping bags are becoming a popular environmentally-friendly option for consumers, instead of single-use plastic shopping bags.

24 | Commerce and services

In recent years, New Zealand's industries have had to compete in the international marketplace. There has also been emphasis on competitiveness within the New Zealand economy, with the government encouraging structural change through deregulation.

The past two decades have seen across-the-board tariff reductions, the disappearance of import licensing, removal of restrictions on the operation of financial markets, and reorganisation of State trading enterprises to be more competitive. Specific sectors that were deregulated to allow greater competition include the telecommunications, transport and petroleum industries.

The withdrawal of subsidies and import controls exposed large areas of the domestic economy to new levels of competition. The result has been reorganisation and, in some cases, attrition, especially in manufacturing.

These policy changes have made it necessary to review the legal environment in which business is conducted. Like virtually every developed market economy, New Zealand has laws aimed at protecting the competitive process.

The Commerce Act 1986, the Fair Trading Act 1986 and the Electricity Industry Reform Act 1998 are New Zealand's main competition laws. In general terms, they are based on the premise that open and competitive markets will ensure the efficient allocation of economic resources. The Commerce Act was reviewed in 1992 to ensure its provisions were consistent with other Government policies promoting economic growth. Several amendments have been made to the Act since then, including the prohibition of business acquisitions that substantially lessen competition in any market.

As the economy has become more market-oriented, traditional controls in the retail sector have also been reviewed. Laws controlling shop trading hours and the sale of liquor have been reviewed, and relaxed in some areas, to encourage competition, and to provide structures for businesses to compete with imported products, and to meet consumer demand.

Commercial framework

Companies and partnerships

Individuals wishing to start a business can do so by forming a company under the Companies Act 1993, by trading in their own name, or by trading in partnership under the Partnership Act 1908, which covers ordinary partnerships and the lesser-used special partnerships.

Table 24.01

Company registrations
Year ending 30 June

Year	New companies registered	Companies dissolved or struck off	Companies on register
1997	23,172	7,936	192,224
2000	33,234	20,255	230,359
2001	35,254	20,045	249,047
2002	41,996	15,509	275,813
2003	41,457	17,223	307,461
2004	53,900	19,185	345,702
2005	59,744	23,037	388,846
2006	65,590	28,719	428,697
2007	74,247	35,292	474,212

Source: Ministry of Economic Development

Companies are by far the most usual form of business operation in New Zealand. Incorporating a limited liability company under the Companies Act 1993 limits an individual's liability for any losses the business may suffer. Companies are founded on three concepts:

- shareholders have limited liability, meaning that their liability is limited to the amount they have agreed to pay for their shares, so that if the company should fail owing money, their other assets are protected from seizure to pay the outstanding debts
- shares in the company are transferable
- the company is a separate legal entity from the shareholders.

Companies in which shareholders have limited liability have names ending in 'Limited' or 'Tapui' (Limited).

Table 24.01 shows the number of new companies registered, companies dissolved or struck off, and the number of registered companies.

Partnerships are defined in the Partnership Act 1908 as the relationship between people carrying on a business in common, with a view to profit. Partnerships are started by mutual agreement, which can be informal, however, terms are normally contained in a written agreement.

Characteristics of a partnership are that each partner is usually under a joint liability for all partnership debts, a partnership will as a rule be dissolved by the death or retirement of a partner, partnership interests are not usually capable of being assigned or transferred, and control and management of a partnership's affairs are (subject to the partnership agreement) vested in all partners. Lastly, a partner is ostensibly an agent for the other partners, and can commit the partnership to binding arrangements.

Commerce Commission

The Commerce Commission enforces a number of general and specific regulatory regimes set out in the Commerce Act 1986, the Fair Trading Act 1986, the Electricity Industry Reform Act 1998, the Dairy Industry Restructuring Act 2001, the Telecommunications Act 2001, and the Credit Contracts and Consumer Finance Act 2003.

The commission, a Crown entity established under the Commerce Act 1986, consists of up to five members appointed by the governor-general on the recommendation of the Minister of Economic Development. Associate members may also be appointed. A Telecommunications Commissioner was established in 2001.

The commission's revenue is derived mainly from the Crown, supplemented by fees from parties seeking adjudication decisions. In addition, the commission receives some revenue from court costs awarded, and from interest. New responsibilities in the electricity, telecommunications and dairy industries are, for the most part, funded by government-imposed industry levies.

The commission's budget increased to $31 million for 2006/07, up from $23 million in 2005/06. The commission had 149 staff at December 2007, compared with 130 staff at December 2005. It operates from a head office in Wellington, and has offices in Auckland and Christchurch that deal with Fair Trading Act responsibilities.

Commerce Act 1986 The aim of this Act is to promote efficient operation of markets by promoting competition for the long-term benefit of consumers. The Act is designed to prevent or deter abuses of market power, collusion, and anti-competitive mergers. The Act applies to all individuals and commercial organisations, including local government, State-owned enterprises, and government departments.

The Act prohibits restrictive trade practices, such as substantially lessening competition, excluding competitors, price fixing, taking advantage of market power, and arranging prices between manufacturers and resellers. Parties planning to enter arrangements that may include restrictive trade practices can apply to the commission for authorisation. The commission will authorise the arrangement if it is satisfied that the public will ultimately benefit from the business practice, even though there is a lessening of competition.

The Act prohibits the acquisition of assets or shares in a business if the acquisition results in a substantial lessening of competition in a market. Under the Act, those acquiring assets or shares can apply to the commission for clearance or authorisation. The commission will grant a clearance if it is satisfied an acquisition will not substantially lessen competition. Even if the acquisition results in the acquiring or strengthening of a dominant position in a market, the commission will grant an authorisation if there is sufficient public benefit to outweigh the detriment to competition. Clearance or authorisation exempts the business practice or acquisition from the Act's prohibitions, and protects the business from action by the commission and private individuals.

The Act gives the Minister of Economic Development the power to set regulatory control for goods or services. Regulatory control may be imposed only where there is limited competition in the market for particular goods or services, and control is seen as necessary or desirable in the interests of consumers or suppliers.

Penalties for breaching the Act are fines up to $500,000 for individuals, and up to the greater of either $10 million or three times the value of any commercial gain resulting from the breach (or 10 percent of the turnover of the business if the commercial gain is unknown) for companies.

Electricity Industry Reform Act 1998 The purpose of this Act is to separate electricity distribution from electricity generation and retailing, to ensure that costs and prices in the electricity industry are subject to sustained downward pressure. Businesses generating or selling more than a specified amount of electricity cannot also own power lines. Businesses can apply to the Commerce Commission for exemptions from the Act.

Dairy Industry Restructuring Act 2001 This Act provides for regulatory and structural reform of the New Zealand dairy industry. The Act authorised the amalgamation of New Zealand's two largest dairy cooperatives, the New Zealand Cooperative Dairy Company Ltd and Kiwi Cooperative Dairies Ltd, into Fonterra Co-operative Group Ltd, and the resulting ownership by Fonterra of all the shares in the New Zealand Dairy Board.

The resulting cooperative has significant power in New Zealand's dairy markets. The Act provides for measures to mitigate the risks of that market power. The commission continues to monitor developments in competition in the dairy market, and to consider the implications in terms of the Act.

Telecommunications Act 2001 This Act aims to reform the telecommunications industry to deliver a better deal for consumers, by providing greater certainty, investment, competition, opportunity and consumer benefit. Under the Act, the Commerce Commission:

- resolves access disputes between carriers
- oversees telecommunications service obligations
- divides the annual net cost between Telecom and liable carriers
- monitors the regulatory regime
- recommends changes to the list of regulated services to the Minister of Communications.

The Telecommunications Act was amended in December 2006. The amendment gives the commission scope to set access terms and conditions without having to wait for an access dispute to be referred to the commission. The access terms set by the commission apply to all players in the market, not merely the parties involved in the access dispute.

Takeovers Panel

The Takeovers Panel is a body corporate established by the Takeovers Act 1993. The panel has between five and 11 members, who are appointed by the Minister of Commerce. At least one member must be a barrister or solicitor of the High Court of New Zealand with at least seven years experience.

The law relating to takeovers of specified companies is kept under review by the panel, which recommends any changes it considers necessary to the government. Practices relating to takeovers of specified companies are also kept under review.

In exercising its powers, the panel investigates any act or omission, or practice. Determinations, orders and applications to the court are made under the enforcement provisions of the Takeovers Act 1993.

The panel cooperates with overseas regulators by providing information that may be useful to that regulator. The panel also promotes public understanding of the law and practice relating to takeovers.

In exercising its functions and powers, the panel is required to comply with the principles of natural justice.

Stock exchange

New Zealand Exchange Ltd is a public company trading as NZX. NZX is now a company listed on one of its own markets, the NZSX (stock) market. NZX operates and regulates markets in New Zealand for entities to raise capital (for example by issuing shares or debt securities), and for the trading of listed securities. The trading markets are the NZSX, which had 223 quoted securities at 31 December 2007; the NZDX (debt market), where companies and the government list bonds and other fixed-interest securities; and the NZAX (alternative market), for small-to-medium-sized and non-standard entities. There were 152 New Zealand entities and 26 overseas entities listed on NZX's markets at 31 December 2007.

Table 24.02 (overleaf) shows the number of companies listed on the New Zealand stock exchange, and the share price index.

Investors can trade derivatives based on New Zealand securities at the Sydney Futures Exchange (SFE). Called NZFOX, they are futures and options products listed on the SFE. Futures and options allow investors to hedge against risk, or speculate (take on extra risk in the hope of making a profit).

NZX firms are accredited to provide investment advice and to buy and sell securities on NZX's markets on behalf of clients. NZX firms also advise entities on listing, and assist entities to raise capital by issuing securities. NZX is responsible for regulating the conduct of those who participate in its market, including NZX firms, other market participants, and listed issuers.

Corruption perceived to be low

Transparency International, a non-government organisation based in Berlin, issues a corruption perception index each year.

The index assesses the impact of perceived corruption on commercial and social life in each country – as reported by people working for multinational firms and institutions. It is not an assessment of the actual level of corruption.

New Zealand is consistently perceived as being one of the least corrupt countries in the world.

The index allocates a country a score out of 10, with 10 indicating a country is perceived as having a negligible level of corruption and zero seen as highly corrupt.

In 2007, New Zealand ranked first-equal with Denmark and Finland with a score of 9.4. Myanmar and Somalia, each with scores of 1.4, were ranked lowest on the 2007 Corruption Perception Index.

Countries perceived as least corrupt
By score
2006, 2007

Country	Score 2006	Score 2007
New Zealand	**9.6**	**9.4**
Finland	9.6	9.4
Denmark	9.5	9.4
Singapore	9.4	9.3
Sweden	9.2	9.3
Iceland	9.6	9.2
Switzerland	9.1	9.0
Netherlands	8.7	9.0
Norway	8.8	8.7
Canada	8.5	8.7
Australia	8.7	8.6

Source: Transparency International

Table 24.02

	Stock exchange statistics		
	Year ending 31 December		
	Number of companies listed on New Zealand stock exchange markets		Share price
Year	Overseas	New Zealand	index[1]
1930	..	..	309
1935	..	..	341
1940	..	..	306
1945	..	..	413
1950	..	..	506
1955	..	..	554
1960	..	..	854
1965	..	..	1060
1970	83	300	1361
1975	79	305	1159
1980	75	275	1599
1985	81	316	4964
1990	74	171	514
1995	60	145	1287
1996	65	136	1527
1997	79	146	1572
1998	83	146	1520
1999	84	134	1778
2000	77	144	1616
2001	71	149	1886
2002	69	151	1966
2003	60	169	2487
2004	57	195	3184
2005	44	194	3469
2006	31	151	4118
2007	26	152	4107

(1) Until 1966, Department of Statistics Index; from 1967 to 1986, Reserve Bank of New Zealand Share Price Index; from 1987, New Zealand Stock Exchange Gross Index; from 2003, NZX all index. Base: July quarter 1986 (= 1000).

Symbol: .. figure not available

Source: New Zealand Exchange Ltd

Contractors watch trends on a NZX stock exchange display board in the foyer of Quay Towers in central Auckland.

Under listing rules, listed issuers are required to disclose any information that is relevant for investors. NZX publishes these disclosures of information as market announcements, which ensures the market is kept informed. There are also listing rules relating to the appointment of directors, disclosure of financial results, and general conduct.

NZX generates revenue from listing fees paid by listed issuers, accreditation fees paid by NZX advisors and NZX firms, fees for trading activity, and from the sale of market data, such as trading statistics and prices. Revenue is also earned from the sale of exchange-traded funds, a type of investment product.

At 31 December 2007, NZX managed five exchange-traded funds: the NZX 10 Fund (smartTENZ); the NZX MidCap Index Fund (smartMIDZ); the NZX 50 Portfolio Index Fund (smartFONZ); NZX Australian MidCap Index Fund (smartMOZY); and NZX Australian 20 Leaders Fund (smartOZZY).

Securities trading is facilitated through the new Trayport Globalvision Exchange Trading System, implemented in July 2007. Orders to buy and sell securities are placed into the system by NZX brokers, and are matched according to price and time priority. After orders are matched, securities and payment are delivered, and securities are registered in the name of the new owner. The new technology platform includes a trade reporting system for the electronic communications network being established in Australia by NZX and five major banks.

NZX calculates a number of share price indexes, including the NZX50. This index tracks the collective movement in market value of the 50 largest listed issuers on the NZSX market. In 2006, NZX launched the Sci-Tech Index to highlight the performance of companies listed with NZX that have significant business interests in developing and commercialising new technologies. The index acts to promote and raise the profile of listed tech companies.

Figure 24.01 shows movement of the NZX all index from 1986 to 2006.

Securities Commission

The purpose of the Securities Commission is to strengthen investor confidence in New Zealand by promoting the efficiency, integrity, and cost-effective regulation of the securities markets.

The commission, New Zealand's main regulator of investments, is an independent Crown entity formed under the Securities Act 1978.

The law relating to bodies corporate, securities, and unincorporated issuers of securities is kept under review by the commission, which recommends changes to the Minister of Commerce. Practices relating to securities and the activities of securities markets are also kept under review.

The commission promotes understanding of the law and practice of securities, and cooperates with overseas securities commissions.

To help perform these functions, the commission has the power to:

- suspend or cancel a registered prospectus
- prohibit advertising of any securities
- enforce insider-trading and substantial security holder law
- administer the law relating to futures contracts
- recommend approval of electronic systems for the transfer of securities.

Figure 24.01

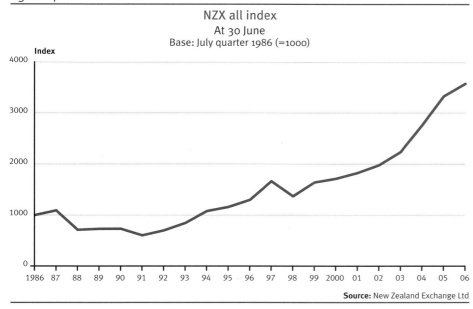

NZX all index
At 30 June
Base: July quarter 1986 (=1000)

Source: New Zealand Exchange Ltd

Insolvency

Bankruptcy Insolvency of individuals is referred to as bankruptcy. The main laws that relate to bankruptcy are the Insolvency Act 2006, the Insolvency Regulations 2007, and the High Court Amendment Rules (No. 2) 1999. Bankruptcy matters come under the jurisdiction of the High Court of New Zealand.

Bankruptcy can be initiated in two ways:

- a debtor can file a completed 'statement of affairs' and application for bankruptcy with the official assignee. Upon acceptance of the statement of affairs being a true and correct representation of the debtor's affairs and application, the debtor is made bankrupt
- a creditor can file a petition seeking a debtor's bankruptcy in the High Court.

At least $1,000 must be owed by a debtor seeking to make themselves bankrupt, or where a creditor is seeking to make a debtor bankrupt.

The official assignee administers the insolvency. The official assignee investigates the bankrupt's financial affairs, and follows up on matters likely to result in the recovery of funds for the creditors. They have the power to sell the bankrupt's property, enforce debts due to the bankrupt's estate, or carry on the business of the bankrupt so far as it is necessary or expedient for its disposal or conclusion.

When all assets have been converted to cash, the official assignee deducts expenses incurred, pays any debts that have statutory priority, and then divides the proceeds among creditors. Secured creditors are paid from the proceeds of their security and other creditors are paid proportionally.

Bankruptcies are generally automatically discharged after three years. Where the debtor has initiated the bankruptcy, the three years start from the adjudication. Where the creditor has initiated the bankruptcy, the three years start from when the debtor has filed a satisfactory statement of affairs with the official assignee.

Alternatives to bankruptcy A debtor may apply for an alternative to bankruptcy such as a 'summary instalment order' or seek admission to the 'no asset procedure' if their debts total $40,000 or less.

A summary instalment order involves paying creditors in part or in full over a period of up to three years. While the summary instalment order is in force, creditors included in the order cannot seek to enforce their debt. The period for repayment of debt can be extended to five years under special circumstances.

The no asset procedure is designed for consumer debtors with no assets, no means of repaying any of their debts, debts of $40,000 or less, and who have not been previously bankrupt or entered

Table 24.03

Bankruptcies Year ending 30 June	
Year	Number
1997	2,458
2000	2,675
2001	2,859
2002	2,811
2003	2,800
2004	2,791
2005	2,995
2006	3,087
2007	3,593
Source: Ministry of Economic Development	

a no asset procedure. Unlike bankruptcy, the no asset procedure lasts for only 12 months. It can be terminated by the official assignee if it is found that the debtor has misled the official assignee about their affairs when applying for the procedure. Creditors cannot pursue the debtor for debts included in the no asset procedure.

Creditors may accept a composition (an agreement among all creditors of a debtor to accept a percentage of the amount due as full payment) in satisfaction of the debts due to them.

Table 24.03 shows the number of bankruptcies in New Zealand and figure 24.02 shows the bankruptcy rate per 100,000 people.

Figure 24.02

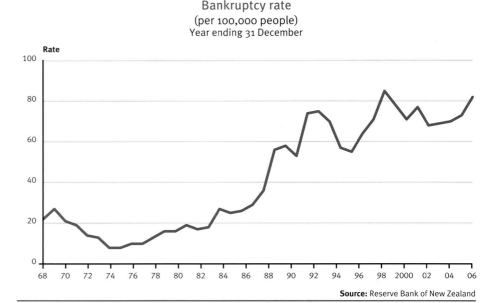

Bankruptcy rate
(per 100,000 people)
Year ending 31 December

Source: Reserve Bank of New Zealand

Company liquidation Liquidation, sometimes called winding up, is the legal process by which a company's life is ended. The company's assets are converted to cash, creditors are paid as far as possible, any surplus is distributed to shareholders, and the company is then removed from the register, after which it ceases to exist. Companies are liquidated according to provisions in the Companies Act 1993.

Company receivership Companies with heavy debt loads and cash-flow problems can have a receiver appointed over their assets, either by the court, or, more commonly, under a clause in a security. Securities often contain a detailed statement of events that will enable the holder to recover the loan if the borrower gets into financial difficulties. One of these provisions is the power of the security holder to appoint a receiver.

The function of a receiver is to sell what is necessary to recover the amount owed to the holder (plus costs), or to manage the company's business for this purpose, and then retire as receiver. No property of the company is actually vested in the receiver. Although the directors remain in office, the receiver's power supersedes theirs. The receiver is an agent for, not an officer of, the company. Receivership is quite distinct from liquidation, as a receiver acts only for the benefit only of the debenture-holder who appointed him or her, whereas a liquidator acts for unsecured creditors.

Voluntary administration A procedure called voluntary administration provides an alternative to liquidation for companies in financial distress. It is intended to be a relatively short-term measure that freezes the company's financial position while the administrator and the creditors determine the company's future.

Controls on trading

The two overarching pieces of legislation setting out consumer rights and protections are the Fair Trading Act 1986 and the Consumer Guarantees Act 1993.

Fair Trading Act

The aim of the Fair Trading Act 1986 is to promote product safety and ensure customers receive accurate information about goods and services. The Act protects consumers from unfair business practices and protects businesses that comply with the legislation from unfair competition. The Act covers all advertising and selling of goods and services, but does not cover private sales.

The Act prohibits misleading and deceptive conduct, false representation and unfair practices by people in trade. These include false statements that goods or services:

- are a particular price or involve particular savings
- are of a particular kind, standard, quality, grade or origin
- are endorsed by an organisation or sponsor
- are supplied with particular warranties or guarantees
- have particular uses or benefits.

The Act makes it a criminal offence to engage in certain unfair or misleading practices. These include:

- offering free gifts or prizes when supplying goods or services if those involved do not intend to award the gift or prize
- 'bait' advertising, such as advertising 'specials' or 'loss leaders' to attract customers into a shop if the advertiser does not intend making the goods or services available for a reasonable time and in reasonable quantities
- demanding or accepting payment without intending to supply the goods or services ordered
- making misleading representations about profitability, risk or other matters affecting a business run from a home
- use of physical force, harassment or coercion when supplying goods or services
- pyramid selling schemes.

The Act gives the Minister of Consumer Affairs the power to ban and recall unsafe products and to make consumer information and product safety standards mandatory.

Consumer information standards cover:

- used motor vehicles
- country-of-origin labelling of clothing and footwear
- care labelling for textile goods (such as dry-cleaning, washing and ironing instructions)
- fibre content labelling of textile goods.

Product safety standards cover:

- baby walkers
- toys for children aged up to three years
- children's nightwear
- cigarette lighters
- bicycles.

The Commerce Commission is responsible for enforcing the Act, but anyone – consumers and businesses alike – can take legal action under the Act. Criminal court action may result in fines of up to $60,000 for individuals and $200,000 for companies. Both a company and individuals involved in a breach can be prosecuted by the commission.

Consumer Guarantees Act

The Consumer Guarantees Act 1993 covers consumer protection in the period after a purchase is made. Statutory guarantees are automatically conferred whenever a consumer purchases goods or services from a trader. As with the Fair Trading Act 1986, the Consumer Guarantees Act 1993 protects consumers from unfair business practices, and protects businesses that comply with the legislation from unfair competition. The Act also covers items given away by a trader or manufacturer when goods are purchased.

Under the Act, a trader must have the right to sell the goods, and have spare parts and repair facilities available. All goods must:

- be of acceptable quality
- be fit for their particular purpose
- match their description
- match a sample or demonstration model
- be a reasonable price.

The Act also ensures consumer rights when services paid for are not carried out properly. Services must be:

- provided with reasonable care and skill
- fit for their particular purpose
- completed within a reasonable time
- provided at a reasonable price.

If a guarantee is not met, consumers may have rights against the trader (or in some cases the manufacturer) for a remedy to put the problem right. If a problem is major, a consumer can reject

Eco-labels

Cert.TM

New Zealand Ecolabelling Trust

Eco-labels have been around for almost three decades but have proliferated in recent years. They range from strictly-regulated labels verified by an independent third party, through to relatively meaningless self-declared labels created by companies for their own products.

Many commonly-used claims such as 'environmentally-friendly', 'biodegradable' 'ozone-friendly' can be misleading. 'CFC-free' labels are particularly meaningless as the use of chlorofluorocarbons has been banned since 1993 under the Montreal Protocol.

Certified eco-labels have much greater credibility as they indicate compliance with a set of standards that have been developed through an independent, multi-stakeholder process, and compliance with the standard is audited.

Eco-labelling can be grouped into several broad categories.

- Comparative labels – show how efficient a product is in comparison with other similar products. To qualify for the label, products must meet efficiency standards that are generally administered by a national authority. An example is Energy Star labelling for electrical appliances.
- Production labels – indicate a product or service is produced in accordance with legally established and audited standards. The most familiar examples are for organic food production and carbon-neutrality.
- End-of-life labels – show the recycled content of materials, or the potential to recover or recycle resources at the end of a product's life.
- Source or origin labels – highlight sustainable resource management and the traceability ('chain-of-custody') for products. For example, paper made from wood harvested from sustainably-managed forests.
- Comprehensive labels – evaluate the overall environmental impact of the product against a set of criteria based on life-cycle assessments. Because of the stringent criteria, comprehensive labels have high credibility but relatively slow uptake. The most well-known New Zealand example is the Environmental Choice label.
- Other labels (social and 'wider world') – address specific ethical or environmental issues associated with the places products are sourced from. These are concerned with the behaviour of traders (offering a fair price and payment conditions for the product), and the behaviour of producers (minimum standards for treatment of workers). The best known example is the Fair Trade label.
- Environmental management system standards (eg ISO 14001) – do not indicate that the product meets an environmental standard but only refer to the management practices of the company.

Source: Landcare Research

the goods and choose a replacement, or keep the goods and seek compensation for the reduction in the value of the goods. Since July 2003, the Consumer Guarantees Act 1993 also applies to electricity, gas, water, and computer software.

Online trading

The same rules that apply when shopping at stores also apply to Internet sales.

Online traders must comply with the Fair Trading Act 1986, which prohibits misleading claims or false representations about goods and services for sale. Private sales are not covered by the Fair Trading Act 1986 or Consumer Guarantees Act 1993, but may be covered by the Contractual Remedies Act 1979 or the Sale of Goods Act 1908.

Auctions and competitive tenders are not covered by the Consumer Guarantees Act 1993. Likewise, winning bids for items on Internet sites are not protected. Items bought at a 'buy now' price, however, are covered – these purchases are similar to buying in a shop, as there is no negotiation or competition on price.

Other legislation covering consumer law

Auctioneers Act 1928 requires all auctioneers to be licensed. Entry to the occupation depends on applicants being able to satisfy a district court judge that they are 'fit and proper' and financially secure. This is in accordance with the Act's primary objective to protect consumers from reckless or incompetent auctioneers and financial loss.

Credit Contracts and Consumer Finance Act 2003 regulates consumer credit, including home loans, personal loans, credit sales/hire purchase, credit cards, long-term leases and housing buy-back schemes. The Act requires disclosure of key information to the debtor, prohibits unreasonable fees, allows for contracts to be varied in cases of hardship, and provides for re-opening of oppressive contracts.

The Credit Contracts and Consumer Finance Act 2003 replaces the Credit Contracts Act 1981 and the Hire Purchase Act 1971. These acts still apply to credit contracts and hire purchase agreements entered into before 1 April 2005. The Credit Contracts and Consumer Finance Act is enforced by the Commerce Commission.

Credit (Repossession) Act 1997 standardises procedures relating to the repossession of goods under a security agreement. The Act covers the repossession process that a creditor (or agent) must follow for all secured loans, and hire purchase agreements over consumer goods.

Door to Door Sales Act 1967 regulates agreements for the sale of goods and the provision of services on credit, entered into at places other than appropriate trade premises.

Layby Sales Act 1971 sets out rules for layby sales – where the goods being bought are not available to the buyer until the purchase price is paid off by instalment. The Act does not apply to layby sales over $7,500, or to a motor vehicle being sold by a licensed dealer.

Motor Vehicle Sales Act 2003 requires that all motor vehicle traders are registered on the Motor Vehicle Traders Register (including car market operators and vehicle auctioneers). Traders are required to display a supplier information notice, in the form prescribed under the Fair Trading Act, with all used motor vehicles for sale. The register is administered by the Ministry of Economic Development, with enforcement carried out by the ministry's national enforcement unit. The supplier information notice is enforced by the Commerce Commission.

Unsolicited Goods and Services Act 1975 provides protection for people who receive unsolicited goods or invoices for unordered goods or services.

Weights and Measures Act 1987 protects New Zealand's system of metric weights and measures, and prescribes their use in the marketplace. It ensures that goods sold by weight, measure or number are traded fairly and in accordance with internationally recognised principles. The Act is enforced by the Ministry of Consumer Affairs.

Ministry of Consumer Affairs

The Ministry of Consumer Affairs Manatū Kaihokohoko is part of the Ministry of Economic Development. The Ministry of Consumer Affairs' primary role is to create an environment that promotes accurate information flows between suppliers and consumers, so that consumers can purchase with confidence.

The ministry's work includes:

- developing consumer policy including consumer protection, product safety, and weights and measures
- providing appropriate, accurate and accessible information, education and advice for consumers and businesses on consumer law and issues
- investigating unsafe consumer products
- providing advice on consumer representation, including a nomination service to government departments and agencies

- administering a range of consumer legislation
- enforcement the Weights and Measures Act 1987.

Consumer NZ

The principal aim of Consumer NZ is to collect and disseminate information of benefit to consumers, to advance the interests of its subscribing members and those of consumers generally. This is done through research, publishing *Consumer* magazine and www.consumer.org.nz, and public advocacy on behalf of all New Zealand consumers.

Consumer NZ's work includes:

- comparative tests and surveys of consumer goods and services
- research into and advice on financial, food, health, safety, welfare and environmental matters
- representation at parliamentary committees and public inquiries
- liaison with government, business, trade and safety organisations
- consumer education
- complaints advisory work for members.

Consumer magazine covers a wide range of consumer information and protection material, including results of tests on home appliances and other products. The website supplements the magazine, and runs exclusive online tests and features. It also hosts a register of product safety recalls.

Funded through membership subscriptions, the sale of publications, and contract research, Consumer NZ is independent and impartial. It has no financial ties with any commercial organisation. It does, however, have a good relationship with most traders and liaises with trade and professional associations, as well as government departments, safety organisations and special-interest groups.

Shop trading hours

Shops in New Zealand can open every day of the year, 24 hours a day, except on Christmas Day, Good Friday, Easter Sunday and before 1pm on Anzac Day. Exceptions allow dairy/mixed businesses, service stations, takeaway outlets, souvenir and duty-free shops, shops at public passenger transport terminals, and genuine exhibitions and shows to open on any day. Garden centres have a specific exemption allowing them to open on Easter Sunday.

Sale of liquor

Under the Sale of Liquor Act 1989, 18 years is the minimum legal age at which a person may purchase liquor, or be on licensed premises in certain circumstances. A person aged under 18 years may have access to any licensed premises (other than restricted areas), and be supplied with liquor, providing he or she is accompanied by a parent or legal guardian and liquor is supplied by the parent or guardian.

All on and off-licence premises are permitted to sell liquor any day of the week. However, hotels, taverns and off-licences are prohibited from selling, supplying or delivering liquor on Good Friday, Easter Sunday, Anzac Day (before 1pm) and Christmas Day. The law does not apply to people living in a hotel or tavern, or people dining on the premises. Wineries may sell or deliver wine on Easter Sunday if it is made on their premises or from grapes or fruit harvested from land on which the premises are situated.

Supermarkets and grocers may be licensed to sell beer, wine, and any food condiment containing liquor if the food condiment has been prepared for culinary purposes and rendered unsuitable for drinking.

The sale of liquor to any member of the public requires one of four types of licence:

- On-licences authorise the sale and supply of liquor to any person on the premises or conveyance (such as a ship or aircraft) for consumption on the premises only. Examples include taverns, licensed restaurants and nightclubs.
- Off-licences authorise the sale or delivery of liquor on or from the premises to any person for consumption off the premises. Examples are wine resellers, supermarkets and bottle stores.
- Club licences authorise the sale and supply of liquor on the premises for consumption on the premises by a club member or guest of a member, or members of a club who have reciprocal visiting rights. (A 'club' means a chartered club, a club that participates in or promotes any sporting or other recreational activity other than for gain, or any group of people combined for any purpose other than gain.)
- Special licences authorise the sale and supply of liquor on the premises or conveyance to any person attending any occasion or event.

Hours of sale The hours during which liquor is allowed to be sold, delivered or consumed are a condition of the licence and are not set out in legislation. Each application is dealt with on its merits.

Using fewer plastic bags

Even though plastic shopping bags are often 'free' they are a cost to the retailer and to the environment. Plastic shopping bags are made from fossil fuels and often end up as litter. It is estimated that they take 500 years to break down in landfills. Plastic shopping bags are sometimes ingested by marine animals and other wildlife.

The volume of lightweight plastic shopping bags used in New Zealand in 2006 was 8,000 tonnes, or approximately 1 billion bags. The Packaging Accord 2004–2009 aims to reduce that by at least 20 percent.

The accord is signed by the Ministry for the Environment, New Zealand Packaging Council, Recycling Operators of New Zealand and Local Government New Zealand. The accord recognises that the brand owner and retailer/importer have the greatest control over material selection and product design (rather than the manufacturer).

The New Zealand Retailers Association believes the target can be reached, with usage reduced by 17 percent so far, saving 115 million bags (1,200 tonnes of plastic).

The owners of the main supermarket chains in New Zealand have initiatives to reduce plastic bag use. Foodstuffs has introduced reusable cloth bags into all PAK'nSAVE and New World stores, and check-out staff are asking customers whether they really need a plastic bag or if they would like a reusable one. In Countdown, Foodtown and Woolworths stores, Progressive Enterprises sell reusable bags and chiller bags for cold items and aim to pack more items in plastic bags. In Christchurch, Progressive Enterprises is working with a recycling company, Terranova, to collect and recycle clean plastic bags.

A variety of groups have been working towards reducing the use of plastic shopping bags. Kiwi PlasticBag Concern started in February 2007 to encourage the use of reusable bags. The group includes the Golden Bay Bag Ladies, Wanaka Wastebusters, Community Recyclers of Otago, Green Teens, BagsNOT group and individuals.

In 2005, Collingwood in Golden Bay became the first town in New Zealand to be plastic bag free. Kaikoura is aiming to be the first region to be plastic bag free, and gave away free reusable bags to every household in December 2007. Auckland councils have been working together, and with stockists, to develop affordable New Zealand-made and imported reusable bags.

Other countries have been working towards reducing the use of plastic shopping bags. The Australian environment minister, Hon Peter Garrett, aims to make the whole country plastic bag free. In China, production of ultra-thin plastic bags and giving out free plastic bags are banned. In Ireland, a levy was placed on plastic bags in 2002, and the cost had to be passed onto the consumers.

Sources: Kiwi PlasticBag Concern, Ministry for the Environment

Drinking responsibly

Hunters Inn in Papatoetoe has been encouraging patrons to choose low-alcohol beer as part of a trial initiated by Manukau City Council to reduce drink driving and alcohol-related violence.

The pub used t-shirts and beer mats with the slogan "Good friends. Good food. Good times. Drink responsibly." to advertise Amstel Light beer, which has an alcohol content of 2.5 percent, compared with 4–5 percent for standard beers. The low-alcohol beer was priced at $7 a jug, cheaper than the $8.50 standard beer.

In the year before the trial, seven violent offences were linked to people who had been drinking at Hunters Inn by the Police Alcolink system. Since the campaign started in November 2007, through to April 2008, there were no violent offences. The number of drink driving offences linked to the pub dropped from 26 to two.

Northern Hospitality, which manages the pub, is now running the campaign in two of its other pubs, encouraged by the improved atmosphere of well-behaved drinkers, and an increase in customers.

Source: The New Zealand Herald

Liquor licensing New Zealand's central liquor licensing body is the Liquor Licensing Authority, consisting of a district court judge as chairperson, together with three or four members appointed by the governor-general on the recommendation of the Minister of Justice. The authority considers and determines opposed applications for on, off and club licences, and for manager's certificates referred to it by district licensing agencies. It also decides on appeals against decisions by district licensing agencies and considers the suspension and cancellation of licences.

There are 74 district licensing agencies, which are essentially the city or district authority. District licensing agencies receive applications for liquor licences, gather reports, and determine all unopposed applications. Opposed applications are forwarded to the Liquor Licensing Authority. District licensing agencies grant special licences and temporary authorities, whether opposed or not.

Retail trade and services

Retailing involves retail businesses, accommodation, restaurants, and businesses providing household and personal services. Retail trade statistics are important indicators of economic activity, as retail trade constitutes a large proportion of personal expenditure on consumer goods and services. Table 24.04 shows annual retail sales from 2003 to 2007.

Retail sales trends

Total actual retail sales increased 4.7 percent in the year ending 31 March 2007 to reach $62,305 million, compared with $59,511 million in the previous March year. Almost all industries recorded sales increases in 2007 compared with the previous year.

Supermarket and grocery stores had the largest dollar-value increase, up $840 million or 7.0 percent. Their volume of sales rose 4.8 percent in the year ended March 2007. The automotive fuel retailing industry had the second-largest sales increase in 2007, up $426 million or 7.8 percent, despite a 2.0 percent fall in the volume of sales.

The largest decrease in sales value was in motor vehicle retailing, down $171 million or 2.1 percent. Sales volumes fell for the second successive year, down 0.6 percent compared with the year ended March 2006.

The value of retail sales per head of population was $15,000 in the year ended 31 March 2007, 3.6 percent higher than in the previous March year.

Table 24.04

Retail sales[1][2]					
By industry					
Year ending 31 March					
Industry	2003	2004	2005	2006	2007
	\$(million)				
Supermarkets and grocery stores	10,052	10,794	11,325	11,965	12,805
Fresh produce	700	787	832	899	921
Liquor	899	951	1,010	1,052	1,112
Other food	631	659	750	827	881
Takeaway food	697	801	922	1,047	1,162
Department stores	2,924	3,263	3,382	3,482	3,623
Furniture and floor coverings	1,246	1,264	1,376	1,493	1,539
Hardware	919	1,029	1,141	1,309	1,395
Appliances	1,870	1,954	2,196	2,334	2,499
Recreational goods	1,953	2,025	2,123	2,135	2,258
Clothing and softgoods	1,878	1,995	2,165	2,413	2,482
Footwear	259	295	319	354	398
Chemist retailing	1,297	1,407	1,563	1,626	1,747
Household equipment repair services	299	315	301	310	321
Other retailing	2,559	2,449	2,520	2,610	2,718
Accommodation	1,931	2,056	2,283	2,387	2,490
Bars and clubs	1,063	1,070	1,084	1,117	1,155
Cafes and restaurants	2,768	2,865	3,099	3,449	3,638
Personal and household goods hiring	168	188	213	214	245
Other personal services	1,243	1,337	1,478	1,541	1,662
Subtotal	**35,355**	**37,505**	**40,079**	**42,564**	**45,053**
Motor vehicle retailing	7,598	8,006	8,349	8,211	8,040
Automotive fuel retailing	3,762	3,866	4,633	5,430	5,855
Automotive electrical services, smash repairing and tyre retailing	1,166	1,259	1,346	1,432	1,494
Automotive repair and services nec[3]	1,471	1,634	1,659	1,875	1,862
Total	**49,352**	**52,269**	**56,066**	**59,511**	**62,305**
			(\$)		
Sales per head of population	12,465	12,985	13,764	14,478	15,000

(1) Figures are exclusive of goods and services tax. (2) The Retail Trade Survey was redesigned in October 2003. (3) nec: not elsewhere classified.
Note: Figures may not add up to stated totals due to rounding.

Source: Statistics New Zealand

The New Zealand Herald

Chilled-food manager, Sam Chawla, stacks trim milk at a New World supermarket in Auckland. Some supermarkets are choosing to stock healthier foods at eye level to be more noticeable to consumers.

Eco-fashion label recognised by the United Nations

New Zealand luxury clothing brand Untouched World is the first New Zealand company and first fashion company in the world to be invited to use an exclusive United Nations sustainability logo on all its garments and products. Only a few organisations worldwide are allowed to use the special United Nations Decade of Education logo.

One percent of every Untouched World sale goes to Untouched World Charitable Trust's youth leadership programmes: Blumine Island Conservation and Restoration; Tiromoana "there's no such place as away"; Ruapehu Kiwi Forever; and Sustainable Cities – Auckland. These programmes focus on developing leadership in environmental, social and cultural sustainability.

Untouched World clothing is made from organic cotton, organic merino wool, organic denim and possum-fibre blends. The company has implemented innovative initiatives aimed at reusing and recycling.

Untouched World is one of six organisations globally that are developing a strategy with the United Nations Educational, Scientific and Cultural Organisation (UNESCO) to further engage the corporate sector in sustainability education. UNESCO is also using Untouched World as a case study in sustainable business practice.

Source: Untouched World

Regional sales

Retail sales in the year ending 31 March 2007 increased 4.7 percent in the North Island and 4.6 percent in the South Island, compared with the previous year. The Waikato region recorded the largest percentage increase in sales, up 8.9 percent or $465 million. Table 24.05 shows the value of sales by region.

Table 24.05

Retail sales[1][2]
By region
Year ending 31 March

Region	2003	2004	2005	2006	2007
	$(million)				
Auckland	16,287	17,627	19,153	20,037	20,952
Waikato	4,717	4,744	4,962	5,243	5,707
Wellington	5,565	5,733	5,950	6,285	6,642
Remainder of North Island	10,692	11,427	12,525	13,518	13,911
Total North Island	**37,261**	**39,531**	**42,590**	**45,082**	**47,212**
Canterbury	6,656	6,762	6,869	7,431	7,767
Remainder of South Island	5,436	5,975	6,608	6,998	7,326
Total South Island	**12,091**	**12,738**	**13,476**	**14,429**	**15,093**
Total New Zealand	**49,352**	**52,269**	**56,066**	**59,511**	**62,305**

(1) Figures are exclusive of goods and services tax. (2) The Retail Trade Survey was redesigned in October 2003.

Note: Figures may not add up to stated totals due to rounding.

Source: Statistics New Zealand

Table 24.06

Credit card use
Year ending 31 December

	Advances	Billings[1]			Average monthly retail sales (excluding motor vehicle retailing)[2]	Card spending in New Zealand as proportion of retail sales
	Total outstanding	New Zealand cardholder spending in New Zealand	Overseas cardholder spending in New Zealand	**Total**		
Year	$(million)					Percent
1998	2,067	498	108	**606**	2,721	22
1999	2,403	656	119	**775**	2,871	27
2000	2,904	900	142	**1,042**	3,046	34
2001	3,390	1,150	165	**1,315**	3,219	41
2002	3,768	1,312	199	**1,511**	3,429	44
2003	3,956	1,438	217	**1,655**	3,615	46
2004	4,210	1,585	235	**1,820**	3,914	47
2005	4,533	1,738	240	**1,978**	4,208	47
2006	4,856	1,899	250	**2,149**	4,447	48
2007	5,208	2,067	262	**2,329**	4,713	49

(1) Credit card spending includes services and other purchases not included in retail sales. (2) Figures are monthly averages over the complete year.

Source: Reserve Bank of New Zealand

Credit cards

The value of purchases using credit cards continues to rise, although less strongly since 2002, while the growth in borrowing on credit cards has eased from 2003. The relative increase in the use of credit cards as a means of payment is partly due to the wider acceptance of the card in supermarkets and over the Internet, and also for services such as doctors and dentists, and power and phone bills. Loyalty schemes introduced in the late 1990s influenced this growth. Growth in credit card use is shown in table 24.06 (previous page).

Insurance and superannuation

The insurance industry

The insurance industry in New Zealand has a number of characteristics that make international comparison difficult. These include the fact that work-cover products are all supplied by the government Accident Compensation Corporation scheme; up to 80 percent of general insurance products are sold by Australian owned or controlled companies; and the majority of the products sold are short-tail – notified and settled quickly – by nature.

The life insurance industry has changed considerably in recent years through demutualisation, takeovers and restructuring. Statistics New Zealand's business demographic statistics recorded 41 life insurance enterprises at February 2007, down from 45 in February 2006.

The non-life insurance market was divided among 159 enterprises (150 in 2006): 63 health (57 in 2006) and 96 general (93 in 2006) insurance enterprises at February 2007. These statistics include life companies doing non-life business that have made deposits under the Insurance Companies' Deposits Act 1953. Many of these companies are not active in the New Zealand market.

Some New Zealand insurance business is placed directly offshore. The ability to spread risk through international reinsurance markets has allowed New Zealand insurers to absorb large increases in business.

The number of direct underwriters has been reducing, with amalgamations and withdrawals, and this has been accompanied by a decrease in the number of reinsurers establishing a place of business in New Zealand. While the overall number of enterprises in the insurance and superannuation industries has generally been on the decrease (768 in 2007, 947 in 2006 and 920 in 2005), the number of employees has been increasing (9,330 in 2007, 8,570 in 2006 and 8,030 in 2005).

Government involvement

Some classes of insurance that make a substantial contribution to overseas markets do not feature in New Zealand because of the different legal climate and background. The accident compensation scheme effectively removed many classes of liability insurance. Historically, the government had also been involved in both fire and general, and life insurance through government-backed life insurance and mutual funds, but in recent years it has withdrawn from these activities. Fire services in New Zealand are funded through a levy on all fire insurance policyholders.

Regulation The Insurance Companies' (Ratings and Inspections) Act requires fire and general insurance companies to obtain, register and disclose a claims-paying ability rating. The requirement also applies to any non-life business of life insurance companies, such as disability products. Some insurers not providing property or disaster insurance can apply for an exemption. The legislation effectively introduces a form of market regulation that allows consumers to judge the financial strength of their insurers.

The Insurance Companies' Deposits Act 1953 requires any person or company providing insurance in New Zealand to lodge approved securities with a market value of not less than $500,000 with the Public Trustee. Insurance companies are also required to provide detailed annual reports and statements of financial condition to the Ministry of Economic Development.

Life and general insurance companies are required to comply with consumer protection legislation, such as the Fair Trading Act 1986 and the Consumer Guarantees Act 1993. Regulation of the New Zealand insurance industry has developed through a combination of loose government supervision and self-regulation. Competition has also been an important factor in regulating all parts of the insurance market.

Natural disaster insurance New Zealand is susceptible to damage caused by earthquakes and other geophysical events. The Earthquake and War Damage Commission was established in 1944 to provide a government-guaranteed fund for damage caused by war and earthquakes. The fund was created with premiums collected from fire insurance policyholders. The original Act was replaced by the Earthquake Commission Act 1993, which dropped war damage and non-residential property from the cover.

The Earthquake Commission (EQC) is a Crown entity responsible to the Minister of Finance. It provides cover for a single house (up to $112,500 including GST), its contents (up to $22,500

The Gisborne Herald

MP Moana Mackey, Mayor Meng Foon and MP Hon Rick Barker inspect property damage from the earthquake that hit Gisborne on 20 December 2007.

including GST), and land under and surrounding the house based on valuation, subject to limits. It covers damage caused by earthquake, natural landslip, volcanic eruption, hydrothermal activity, tsunami, residential land in the case of storm or flood, and fire caused by any of these. Cost of cover is five cents a year for every $100 value of property insured. The maximum premium for one year is $67.50 (including GST).

Table 24.07 shows the number and value of claims made to the EQC in 2006 and 2007.

EQC premium income for the June 2007 year was $83.8 million ($82.4 million in 2006) and investment income was $46.7 million ($691.0 million in 2006).

Table 24.07

Earthquake Commission claims By event type				
	2006		2007	
Event type	Number of claims	Value $(million)	Number of claims	Value $(million)
Landslip/storm/flood	810	11.08	1,848	32.14
Earthquake	662	1.14	1,522	2.67
Hydrothermal	1	0	0	0
Volcanic	0	0	0	0
			Source: Earthquake Commission	

Loss prevention

Much of New Zealand's effort in loss prevention has traditionally been organised and financed through the insurance industry – in areas such as electrical safety and registration, research into fire prevention and fire safety equipment, and approval of passive fire protection and alarm systems.

Other organisations that work in loss prevention:

- the Insurance Council of New Zealand, along with the Fire Service Commission, is active in fire prevention and fire safety education
- BRANZ Ltd undertakes work in assessing building materials and methods of construction
- the Earthquake Commission advises how to minimise the impact of potential earthquakes
- the New Zealand Automobile Association and similar organisations are active in the prevention of motor vehicle accidents
- the Accident Compensation Corporation and the Department of Labour promote occupational safety and accident prevention, and this activity has had some indirect benefit to the insurance industry
- most other activity in the field of loss prevention and accident prevention is undertaken by the government or by other organisations that are wholly or partly public funded.

Insurance and Savings Ombudsman

The Office of the Insurance and Savings Ombudsman (ISO) provides an independent service for consumers to resolve their dispute with an insurance or savings company. Free to consumers, the service is funded by levies on the service providers who participate in the scheme.

The ISO can investigate complaints relating to personal, domestic and small business claims. The service must have been provided within New Zealand by a company that is a participant in the scheme.

The ISO cannot consider complaints that relate to:

- insurance provided for business or commercial purposes, except small business claims
- claims for more than $150,000, or disability benefits providing for regular payments above $1,000 a week, unless the insurance or savings company agrees
- claims made by an uninsured third party
- proceedings in another forum, such as a court
- a company's commercial decision-making – for example renewal of a policy, underwriting practices, conditions imposed on insurance cover, premiums, charges, returns, earning rates and investment practices.

A complaint can be taken to the ISO only after the internal complaints procedure of the insurance or savings company has been exhausted. The ISO's approach is inquisitorial, rather than adversarial. Hearings are not held and legal representation is not required.

The ISO may resolve a complaint by preparing an assessment. If there is relevant new evidence or proper grounds on which to make a request, the parties can accept or reject the decision made in the assessment and request a recommendation. The ISO's ruling is binding on the insurance company, but not on the complainant, who may reject it and take the matter to court or any other authority.

Complaints received By sector Year ending 30 June				
Sector	2004	2005	2006	2007
Fire and general	106	97	109	110
Health	12	26	24	39
Life and savings	54	44	58	52
Total	**172**	**167**	**191**	**201**

Complaint outcomes Year ending 30 June				
Complaint outcome	2004	2005	2006	2007
Upheld	30	36	25	28
Partly upheld	12	6	5	3
Withdrawn	4	0	0	0
Not upheld	177	119	131	141
Settled	17	17	12	37
Total	**240**	**178**	**173**	**209**

Source: Office of the Insurance and Savings Ombudsman

Contributors and related websites

Commerce Commission – www.comcom.govt.nz

Consumer NZ – www.consumer.org.nz

Department of Labour – www.dol.govt.nz

Earthquake Commission – www.eqc.govt.nz

Insurance Council of New Zealand – www.icnz.org.nz

Kiwi PlasticBag Concern – www.plasticshoppingbagfree.org.nz

Landcare Research – www.landcareresearch.co.nz

Ministry for the Environment – www.mfe.govt.nz

Ministry of Consumer Affairs – www.consumeraffairs.govt.nz

Ministry of Economic Development – www.med.govt.nz

Ministry of Justice – www.justice.govt.nz

New Zealand Exchange Limited – www.nzx.com

Office of the Insurance and Savings Ombudsman – www.iombudsman.org.nz

Reserve Bank of New Zealand – www.rbnz.govt.nz

Securities Commission – www.seccom.govt.nz

Statistics New Zealand – www.stats.govt.nz

Sustainable Business Network – www.sustainable.org.nz

Takeovers Panel – www.takeovers.govt.nz

Transparency International – www.transparency.org

Untouched World – www.untouchedworld.com

Landcare Research

The New Zealand Wine Company, producer of Grove Mill wines, gained carboNZero certification through measuring, managing and mitigating their greenhouse gas emissions. The first winery in the world to gain certified carbon-neutral status, their wines are now sought after in the United Kingdom.

25 | Overseas trade

Development and administration of trade

New Zealand Trade and Enterprise

New Zealand Trade and Enterprise (NZTE) is the government's national economic development agency. NZTE works to stimulate economic growth by helping to boost export earnings, strengthen regional economies, and deliver economic development assistance to industries and individual businesses.

As a global organisation, NZTE uses knowledge and contacts in overseas markets to connect New Zealand businesses with trade and investment opportunities.

NZTE's focus is on industries and sectors where New Zealand has a long-term competitive advantage in the world market, and on businesses with high-growth potential. Their strategic goals are:

- increasing international connections for New Zealand business
- helping businesses build their capability
- improving the environment for enterprise and growth.

NZTE services and programmes can be used by start-up companies and established groups of exporters. Services include advice, training, mentoring, funding, and business and market development assistance. Some services are provided directly by NZTE, while others come from external organisations funded by NZTE.

Services in New Zealand NZTE has staff in nine offices around New Zealand. Staff work in sector-specific teams that reflect the focus on industries in which New Zealand has a long-term sustainable advantage. These include the biotechnology and agritech; creative; information and communication technology; food and beverages; wood, building and interiors; specialised manufacturing; education; and tourism industries.

Services available to start-up clients include training, investment facilitation, and business incubation – to help them become established. For new exporters, a free-phone business consultancy line is available, along with mentoring, 'how to' guides, networking events, and seminars. For high-growth businesses and exporters, client managers provide customised services, such as business appraisals and help with applications for financing, export market consultancy, and access to NZTE's international network of trade commissioners.

Customs control and duty collection

The *Working Tariff Document of New Zealand* provides the framework for the New Zealand Customs Service to control goods coming into the country, and to collect duty on them. The tariff is enacted through the Tariff Act 1988, which implements the International Convention on the Harmonized Commodity Description and Coding System.

Part I classifies goods that can be imported or exported – it identifies commodities in broad categories, which are further refined into more detailed and specific classifications.

The tariff shows the duty that is payable on each imported item. The amount depends on the country of origin – some goods have preferential rates when they originate in a country with which New Zealand has a trade agreement (eg Australia). Types of duty include: *ad valorem* duties (a percentage of the goods' value), specific duties (a fixed amount for a given quantity, irrespective of value), or a combination of the two.

Part II of the tariff sets out the categories under which duty may be reduced or waived. For example, there are categories for passengers' baggage and effects. There is also a general category under which concessions can be approved by the Minister of Commerce. Concessions are frequently approved for goods that are not manufactured locally.

Excise duty is a tax levied on locally manufactured goods. Beer, wine, spirits and other alcoholic beverages, alcoholic food preparations, tobacco and cigarettes, and some petroleum products all attract excise duty. The same goods, when imported, are subject to an excise-equivalent duty.

All goods imported into New Zealand are liable for goods and services tax (GST). This tax is in addition to any customs duty, excise-equivalent duty, and any other levies. The GST rate is 12.5 percent.

Source: New Zealand Customs Service

Services overseas NZTE has 36 offshore offices, with staff who understand local business cultures, speak the local language, and provide hands-on assistance to New Zealand exporters. They conduct market and product research, identify suitable business partners, and arrange visitor programmes, interpreters, and trade fair promotions. Staff also provide information to international buyers, importers, and distributors on New Zealand's business capability, enabling them to source quality New Zealand products and services.

Brand New Zealand This 'visual identity' for marketing the country is jointly owned by NZTE and Tourism New Zealand. Brand New Zealand's stories and values are shared by both organisations at events where there is a New Zealand focus.

'New Zealand New Thinking' is the concept for NZTE's offshore marketing campaign. Its key objective is to accelerate global awareness of New Zealand as being innovative, technologically-advanced, creative and successful. NZTE is involved with events and activities to deliver and develop the New Zealand New Thinking campaign.

World Customs Organization

The New Zealand Customs Service is a fully participating member of the World Customs Organization (WCO), established (as the Customs Co-operation Council) in 1952.

The WCO is an intergovernmental organisation of 173 member countries with headquarters in Brussels. Its mission is to ensure customs administrations are effective and efficient.

To do this the WCO:

- develops and administers international instruments that uniformly apply effective customs procedures – these govern the movement of commodities, people and goods across customs frontiers
- develops international standards to secure the movement of goods, such as the SAFE Framework of Standards
- assists members in their efforts to modernise, by building their capacity
- encourages cooperation between customs administrations, and between customs administrations and the trading community – to improve communication, notably around trade security and the fight against fraud
- organises training for the private sector – to deal with technical and operational problems that result from strategies that are implemented in response to challenges in the international customs environment.

Border operations

The New Zealand Customs Service (NZCS) provides protection at the border by managing the import and export of goods, and the movement of international passengers, aircraft and vessels. It does this in accordance with customs, immigration, quarantine and other statutory requirements.

NZCS seeks to ensure a safe and secure border, with minimum intervention to legitimate trade and travel. It achieves this by employing risk management techniques to monitor and assess the level of risk of arriving and departing people, craft and goods.

Border operations involve checking and clearing passengers and craft at airports and seaports, surveillance and search for prohibited items, and investigation of customs offences and related issues.

Underpinning these activities is the collection and processing of intelligence on potential breaches of the legislation that NZCS enforces.

Overseas trade statistics

Overseas merchandise trade statistics measure the value (in New Zealand dollars) and volume of New Zealand's exports, imports and overseas cargo.

The monthly statistics are based on export and import entries lodged with the NZCS. The data is processed by NZCS and passed to Statistics New Zealand for further editing and compilation.

Where a commodity is traded by only a few businesses, there is the potential for disclosure of confidential information. On request by an affected business, commodity data can be suppressed by merging it with other confidential data. In the following overseas trade statistics, confidential data may have been removed from detailed commodity figures but is included in the totals (table 25.02 is an example).

Exports (including re-exports) are valued 'fob' (free on board), which is the value of goods at New Zealand ports before export. It includes the value added in bringing goods to the port, but excludes international freight and associated insurance. Re-exports are included, unless otherwise specified, while goods for repair are excluded.

Imports, which also exclude goods for repair, are valued 'cif' (cost, including insurance and freight) and 'vfd' (value for duty). The cif value is the market value of goods at the New Zealand port of unloading. It includes the value added for the cost of international freight and associated

Table 25.01

Overseas merchandise trade[1]
Year ending 30 June

Year	Exports (fob)	Imports (cif)	Trade balance (fob - cif)
	\$(million)		
1998	21,941	22,589	-648
1999	22,582	24,248	-1,667
2000	26,111	29,193	-3,082
2001	32,000	31,927	73
2002	32,332	31,811	521
2003	29,291	32,161	-2,869
2004	29,864	33,378	-3,514
2005	30,618	35,793	-5,175
2006	32,430	39,040	-6,609
2007	34,939	41,165	-6,226

(1) Exports valued fob (free on board) at New Zealand ports. Imports valued cif (cost, including insurance and freight).

Note: Figures may not equate to stated balances due to rounding.

Source: Statistics New Zealand

A Ministry of Agriculture and Forestry quarantine officer inspects imported wood for unwanted wood-borer insects – if allowed through, they could put New Zealand's biosecurity status and international trade at risk. Along with the New Zealand Customs Service, MAF helps protect the country's borders.

insurance. The vfd value is the value assessed for duty. It is a close approximation of the fob value at the overseas port of loading. Unless otherwise stated, all import values quoted in this chapter are cif values.

Balance of merchandise trade

The balance of merchandise trade is an important analytical indicator of New Zealand's overseas trade. It is calculated by deducting the merchandise imports value from the merchandise exports value, for the same period.

An excess of export values over import values is a surplus, which is treated as a positive number. Conversely, an excess of import values over export values is a deficit, which is treated as a negative number.

In the year ending June 2007, New Zealand's balance of merchandise trade was a deficit of \$6.2 billion, compared with a deficit of \$6.6 billion in the June 2006 year.

Table 25.01 provides overseas merchandise trade figures from 1998 to 2007.

Exports

Export values include re-exports, which are goods imported into New Zealand and then exported later without being significantly altered. Typical re-exports are aircraft and heavy machinery.

Exports in the year ending June 2007 totalled \$34.9 billion, a 7.7 percent increase on the June 2006 year. Milk powder, butter and cheese, and meat and edible offal were New Zealand's two major export commodity groups in the June 2007 year, contributing 18.5 percent and 13.2 percent of total exports, respectively.

Table 25.02 (overleaf) lists major commodities exported for 2003–07. The groupings in this table match those published monthly by Statistics New Zealand. Further detail on some commodity groups is provided in the sections that follow (some groups are aggregated).

Food miles – from the field to the table

Global demand for urgent action on climate change has fuelled publicity about 'food-miles' – the distance food travels from production to the consumer. In New Zealand, this measure is seen as being a possible trade barrier, through placing climate taxes on primary exports.

While the concept of food miles is simple, it may be a misleading surrogate for greenhouse gas (GHG) emissions. In reality, the debate is about more than GHG emissions. It is part of wider discussion about global versus local, and about sustainable systems of production and consumption.

New Zealand exporters need to develop proactive strategies, to bring the debate into a context that explores the interrelated environmental, social and economic impact along the whole value chain.

"Rather than just focusing on the distance travelled, 'life-cycle thinking' with a carbon emissions profile for each step along the supply chain, provides a more accurate and holistic approach. It often reveals that New Zealand goods are produced more efficiently than many in the northern hemisphere," say Landcare Research scientists Professor Ann Smith and Cerasela Stancu.

"We can do nothing about our distance from markets, but businesses can reposition themselves, and even create an advantage, by recognising what their emissions are and addressing them before goods go to market."

The researchers advise exporters to thoroughly research their customers' specific concerns regarding energy use and emissions generation, and to investigate environmental improvement schemes.

A good example of a business putting climate change issues to work for them is the New Zealand Wine Company (NZWC), which gained carboNZero certification through measuring, managing and mitigating their emissions. NZWC was the first winery in the world to gain certified carbon-neutral status, and as a consequence, their Grove Mill and Sanctuary wines are particularly sought after in the United Kingdom.

More information about food-miles, including practical steps for New Zealand exporters, is available on the Landcare Research website.

Source: Landcare Research

Table 25.02

Major export commodities[1]
Year ending 30 June

Commodity group	2003	2004	2005	2006	2007
	$(million)				
Milk powder, butter and cheese	4,679	5,115	4,924	5,762	6,455
Meat and edible offal	4,111	4,479	4,577	4,500	4,609
Logs, wood and wood articles	2,386	2,071	1,984	1,960	2,203
Mechanical machinery and equipment	1,356	1,470	1,628	1,791	1,879
Aluminium and aluminium articles	980	1,008	1,053	1,261	1,565
Fruit	1,032	1,254	1,212	1,161	1,227
Fish, crustaceans and molluscs	1,215	1,111	1,134	1,146	1,153
Electrical machinery and equipment	938	963	1,004	1,045	1,105
Iron, steel and articles	589	625	761	747	860
Beverages, spirits and vinegar	417	463	569	652	858
Casein and caseinates	959	782	651	660	818
Miscellaneous edible preparations	421	469	564	634	700
Textile and textile articles	629	652	645	657	675
Wood pulp and waste paper	461	507	512	509	663
Wool	801	740	666	689	655
Petroleum and products	524	355	439	596	557
Preparations of cereals, flour and starch	159	155	388	529	555
Paper and paperboard and articles	610	601	402	443	506
Optical, medical and measuring equipment	393	398	384	394	498
Raw hides, skins and leather	638	551	471	431	479
Other commodities	5,993	6,096	6,199	6,207	6,147
Confidential data	0	0	453	656	774
Total	**29,291**	**29,864**	**30,618**	**32,430**	**34,939**

(1) Exports valued free on board at New Zealand ports.

Note: Figures may not add up to stated totals due to rounding.

Source: Statistics New Zealand

Dairy product exports

The export value of all dairy products in the year ending June 2007 was $7.3 billion, up 13.3 percent on the previous June year and 30.5 percent higher than the year ending June 2005. Dairy produce made up 20.8 percent of New Zealand's total merchandise trade export value in the year ended June 2007.

Main dairy products exported were milk powder ($3.3 billion), cheese ($1.2 billion), butter ($1.1 billion), and casein and caseinates ($818 million).

The United States remained the largest dairy product export market ($842 million) in the June 2007 year, followed by the Philippines ($428 million), and Japan ($423 million).

Table 25.03 lists the main dairy products exported for 2003–07, while table 25.04 shows New Zealand's main dairy export markets for the same period.

Table 25.03

Dairy product exports[1]
Year ending 30 June

Product	2003	2004	2005	2006	2007
	$(million)				
Milk powder	2,571	2,785	2,482	2,944	3,318
Cheese and curd	1,001	1,035	1,052	1,147	1,232
Butter and dairy spread	922	1,076	858	1,032	1,063
Casein and caseinates	959	782	651	660	818
Whey and other products	27	44	349	437	598
Buttermilk, curdled milk, yoghurt, etc	81	96	101	123	158
Milk and cream	77	78	82	79	86
Total	**5,638**	**5,897**	**5,575**	**6,421**	**7,273**
Percentage of all exports	19.2	19.7	18.2	19.8	20.8

(1) Exports valued free on board at New Zealand ports.

Note: Figures may not add up to stated totals due to rounding.

Source: Statistics New Zealand

Table 25.04

Dairy product exports[1]
By destination
Year ending 30 June

Destination	2003	2004	2005	2006	2007
			$(million)		
United States	679	630	691	715	842
Philippines	320	345	369	310	428
Japan	314	320	363	379	423
People's Republic of China	316	373	296	396	351
Mexico	310	340	254	289	339
Australia	253	231	259	299	307
Saudi Arabia	171	205	300	304	305
Indonesia	201	154	199	223	291
Malaysia	262	283	212	211	275
Thailand	182	204	155	171	246
Venezuela	89	137	104	151	244
Sri Lanka	117	142	162	189	193
Algeria	77	106	100	153	191
Taiwan	191	180	184	174	187
Singapore	96	104	129	143	178
Belgium	356	331	166	189	176
Egypt	100	101	74	114	166
Viet Nam	102	95	73	127	135
Canada	176	112	116	127	128
Germany	168	116	100	103	114
Other countries	1,158	1,390	1,269	1,653	1,755
Total	**5,638**	**5,897**	**5,575**	**6,421**	**7,273**

(1) Exports valued free on board at New Zealand ports.

Note: Figures may not add up to stated totals due to rounding.

Source: Statistics New Zealand

Meat and edible offal exports

The export value of all meat and edible offal in the year ending June 2007 was $4.6 billion, up 2.4 percent on the previous June year and 0.7 percent higher than in 2005. Meat and edible offal made up 13.2 percent of the total merchandise trade export value in the year ended June 2007.

The main meat and edible offal products exported were sheep ($2.4 billion), beef ($1.7 billion), venison ($258 million), and offal ($168 million).

The United States ($1.0 billion) and the United Kingdom ($645 million) remained the two largest export markets in the June 2007 year.

Table 25.05 lists the main meat and edible offal commodities exported over the five years to 2007, while table 25.06 (overleaf) shows New Zealand's main export markets for the same products.

Table 25.05

Meat and edible offal exports[1]
Year ending 30 June

Product	2003	2004	2005	2006	2007
			$(million)		
Sheep	2,257	2,259	2,305	2,279	2,439
Beef	1,554	1,827	1,801	1,786	1,710
Venison	165	182	206	225	258
Offal	108	172	240	183	168
Poultry	3	4	9	9	8
Goat	6	5	5	7	6
Other	19	30	11	11	20
Total	**4,111**	**4,479**	**4,577**	**4,500**	**4,609**
Percentage of all exports	14.0	15.0	14.9	13.9	13.2

(1) Exports valued free on board at New Zealand ports.

Note: Figures may not add up to stated totals due to rounding.

Source: Statistics New Zealand

Table 25.06

Meat and edible offal exports[1]
By destination
Year ending 30 June

Destination	2003	2004	2005	2006	2007
	\$(million)				
United States	1,149	1,250	1,048	1,069	1,026
United Kingdom	539	580	557	594	645
Germany	369	352	421	386	423
Japan	163	298	409	370	294
Republic of Korea	111	203	233	225	251
France	261	234	249	209	239
Belgium	182	193	189	210	197
Taiwan	134	203	193	206	181
Canada	242	184	211	183	175
Netherlands	51	47	69	71	94
Indonesia	28	45	57	74	87
Saudi Arabia	62	52	55	48	77
Mexico	72	71	76	66	63
People's Republic of China	60	61	45	54	59
Switzerland	63	61	56	51	59
Italy	57	50	51	58	55
Hong Kong (SAR)	46	48	42	54	47
French Polynesia	50	51	50	45	43
Sweden	27	20	24	26	35
Greece	40	31	40	38	35
Other countries	403	446	504	462	526
Total	**4,111**	**4,479**	**4,577**	**4,500**	**4,609**

(1) Exports valued free on board at New Zealand ports.
Note: SAR Special Administrative Region. Figures may not add up to stated totals due to rounding.

Source: Statistics New Zealand

Forest product exports

The export value of all forest products in the year ending June 2007 was \$3.4 billion, up 15.8 percent on the previous June year and 16.4 percent higher than for 2005. Forest products made up 9.7 percent of New Zealand's total merchandise trade export value in the year ended June 2007.

The main forest product exports were sawn wood, at \$784 million, rough wood at \$681 million, and wood pulp at \$663 million.

Australia (at \$732 million) remained the main forest products export market in the 2007 June year, with the People's Republic of China (\$512 million) becoming an increasingly large market over the five years to 2007.

Table 25.07 lists the main forest products exported for 2003–07, while table 25.08 shows New Zealand's main export markets for forest products.

Table 25.07

Forest product exports[1]
Year ending 30 June

Product	2003	2004	2005	2006	2007
	\$(million)				
Wood (sawn)	855	725	781	746	784
Wood (rough)	722	565	396	476	681
Wood pulp	461	507	512	509	663
Paper and paperboard	610	601	402	443	506
Board (fibre, veneer, plywood)	545	527	570	483	446
Other	265	253	236	254	292
Total	**3,457**	**3,178**	**2,898**	**2,913**	**3,373**
Percentage of all exports	11.8	10.6	9.5	9.0	9.7

(1) Exports valued free on board at New Zealand ports.
Note: Figures may not add up to stated totals due to rounding.

Source: Statistics New Zealand

Table 25.08

Forest product exports[1]
By destination
Year ending 30 June

Destination	2003	2004	2005	2006	2007
			$(million)		
Australia	907	866	651	641	732
People's Republic of China	347	358	314	345	512
Japan	674	632	610	511	510
Republic of Korea	431	394	300	345	463
United States	521	378	440	395	345
Indonesia	74	75	75	113	111
Philippines	125	84	109	89	88
Taiwan	73	69	64	67	87
Viet Nam	20	26	36	46	73
India	35	28	30	55	65
Malaysia	43	44	29	37	52
Thailand	32	29	31	38	49
United Arab Emirates	8	8	17	18	40
Saudi Arabia	9	10	8	19	30
Fiji	20	21	26	27	27
French Polynesia	8	14	16	13	19
Hong Kong (SAR)	41	51	33	31	18
Singapore	20	14	10	11	15
Kuwait	1	0	3	9	14
Western Samoa	9	9	11	12	14
Other countries	59	70	88	91	109
Total	**3,457**	**3,178**	**2,898**	**2,913**	**3,373**

(1) Exports valued free on board at New Zealand ports.

Note: SAR Special Administrative Region. Figures may not add up to stated totals due to rounding.

Source: Statistics New Zealand

Mechanical and electrical machinery exports

The export value of all mechanical and electrical machinery in the year ending June 2007 was $3.0 billion, up 5.2 percent on the June 2006 year and 13.4 percent higher than the year ending June 2005. Mechanical and electrical machinery exports made up 8.5 percent of New Zealand's total merchandise trade export value in the year ending June 2007.

In the year ending June 2007, the largest group of products exported was refrigerators, freezers and other refrigeration equipment, but, as seen in table 25.09, these are only about 5 percent of the total, and there are many other products exported in this commodity group.

Table 25.10 (overleaf) shows New Zealand's main mechanical and electrical machinery export markets for 2003–07; in the June 2007 year the largest export market for these products was Australia ($1.2 billion).

Table 25.09

Mechanical and electrical machinery exports[1]
Year ending 30 June

Product	2003	2004	2005	2006	2007
			$(million)		
Refrigerators, freezers and other refrigeration equipment	156	145	142	143	157
Equipment for washing, filling, sealing, labelling, etc.	108	141	143	146	149
Automatic data processing machines	57	60	86	127	138
Insulated wire, cable and other electric conductors	62	53	72	89	133
Diodes, transistors and similar semiconductor devices	51	49	66	77	102
Household or laundry-type washing machines	59	87	91	101	92
Telephones	75	46	43	40	86
Electric transformers, converters and inductors	43	62	84	69	82
Parts and accessories for automatic data processing machines	108	94	77	81	78
Equipment for electricity control and distribution	139	111	89	90	76
Other	1,436	1,585	1,740	1,874	1,891
Total	**2,294**	**2,433**	**2,631**	**2,836**	**2,984**
Percentage of all exports	7.8	8.1	8.6	8.7	8.5

(1) Exports valued free on board at New Zealand ports.

Note: Figures may not add up to stated totals due to rounding.

Source: Statistics New Zealand

Table 25.10

Mechanical and electrical machinery exports[1]
By destination
Year ending 30 June

Destination	2003	2004	2005	2006	2007
			$(million)		
Australia	961	1,043	1,063	1,135	1,234
United States	454	452	515	568	528
United Kingdom	126	161	149	136	134
Fiji	43	48	60	74	78
Singapore	68	57	75	65	78
People's Republic of China	40	52	50	60	77
Japan	33	39	50	51	61
Canada	57	46	67	82	52
Germany	45	38	31	37	44
Taiwan	44	28	29	42	44
Hong Kong (SAR)	45	30	35	36	43
Republic of Korea	11	12	29	33	39
South Africa	20	27	34	38	33
Malaysia	21	22	26	30	32
France	13	13	26	30	32
India	12	15	14	21	30
Netherlands	17	23	20	30	29
Denmark	12	13	17	21	26
Thailand	17	23	20	21	23
Western Samoa	23	25	28	24	21
Other countries	231	265	293	303	348
Total	**2,294**	**2,433**	**2,631**	**2,836**	**2,984**

(1) Exports valued free on board at New Zealand ports.

Note: SAR Special Administrative Region. Figures may not add up to stated totals due to rounding.

Source: Statistics New Zealand

Fruit, nut and vegetable exports

The value of all fruit, nut and vegetable exports in the year ending June 2007 was $1.7 billion, up 7.4 percent on the previous June year and 5.7 percent higher than for 2005. Fruit, nut and vegetable exports made up 4.7 percent of the total merchandise trade export value in the year ended June 2007.

Kiwifruit ($767 million) and apples ($343 million) remained the two largest export products from this group in the June 2007 year.

The main fruit, nut and vegetable export markets were Japan ($357 million), and 'destination unknown – European Union (EU)', ($247 million). The reason the second figure is large is that much of the fruit exported to the EU is known to be sold on from the original destination point. Therefore, at the time of export, the final country of destination within the EU is unknown. In the June 2007 year, all exports to this destination were fruit (with kiwifruit being nearly 80 percent of the total).

Table 25.11 lists the main fruit, nut and vegetable products exported for 2003–07, while table 25.12 shows the main export markets.

Table 25.11

Fruit, nut and vegetable exports[1]
Year ending 30 June

Product	2003	2004	2005	2006	2007
			$(million)		
Kiwifruit	539	661	722	702	767
Apples	394	486	387	330	343
Onions, leeks etc	103	93	63	79	122
Legumes	72	68	62	75	76
Squash and gourds	68	54	72	56	66
Berries and cherries	34	44	44	43	46
Corn	52	49	44	47	39
Capsicum	24	24	26	29	34
Avocados	26	27	29	54	29
Potatoes, carrots, root vegetables	29	24	19	19	21
Other vegetables	72	70	65	73	68
Other fruit	39	38	30	32	42
Total	**1,451**	**1,638**	**1,563**	**1,540**	**1,653**
Percentage of all exports	5.0	5.5	5.1	4.7	4.7

(1) Exports valued free on board at New Zealand ports.

Note: Figures may not add up to stated totals due to rounding.

Source: Statistics New Zealand

Customers in a German supermarket sample and buy New Zealand kiwifruit. The European Union is a strong market for New Zealand's fruit exports, particularly kiwifruit.

Table 25.12

Fruit, nut and vegetable exports[1] By destination Year ending 30 June					
Destination	2003	2004	2005	2006	2007
	$(million)				
Japan	366	355	418	343	357
Destination unknown – EU[2]	235	328	240	245	247
Australia	121	143	144	193	174
United Kingdom	133	149	120	111	124
United States	119	142	82	99	123
Republic of Korea	34	49	69	76	94
Taiwan	75	69	72	82	79
Netherlands	54	81	95	66	75
Spain	47	63	81	58	73
Hong Kong (SAR)	30	26	25	31	39
Italy	20	30	32	24	29
Malaysia	27	24	18	18	24
Germany	44	28	34	29	23
Fiji	17	18	17	18	22
People's Republic of China	9	9	10	19	20
Singapore	25	18	14	16	16
Belgium	9	10	7	8	14
Canada	9	10	7	9	10
Thailand	10	5	4	8	10
France	6	8	10	8	10
Other countries	61	71	64	78	90
Total	**1,451**	**1,638**	**1,563**	**1,540**	**1,653**

(1) Exports valued free on board at New Zealand ports. (2) Final destination point in EU is unknown at time of export.
Note: EU European Union, SAR Special Administrative Region. Figures may not add up to stated totals due to rounding.

Source: Statistics New Zealand

Fish, crustacean and mollusc exports

The value of all fish, crustacean and mollusc exports in the year ending June 2007 was $1.3 billion, up 2.5 percent on the previous June year and 3.7 percent higher than for the June 2005 year. Fish, crustaceans and molluscs made up 3.6 percent of New Zealand's total merchandise trade export value in the year ended June 2007.

The main fish, crustacean and mollusc exports were frozen fish ($345 million), molluscs and aquatic invertebrates ($290 million), and fish fillets and other fish meats ($263 million).

The largest export market in the 2007 June year was Australia ($235 million).

Table 25.13 (overleaf) lists the main fish, crustacean and mollusc exports for 2003–07, while table 25.14 shows New Zealand's main markets for the same products.

Table 25.13

Fish, crustacean and mollusc exports[1]
Year ending 30 June

Product	2003	2004	2005	2006	2007
	\$(million)				
Frozen fish	266	259	283	315	345
Molluscs and aquatic invertebrates	251	316	340	327	290
Fish fillets and other fish meat	452	317	301	274	263
Crustaceans	146	127	126	141	153
Fresh or chilled fish	89	80	75	81	93
Fish, dried, salted or smoked; edible fish meal	10	10	7	6	7
Live fish	2	2	2	2	2
Subtotal	1,215	1,111	1,134	1,146	1,153
Extracts and preparations					
Prepared or preserved molluscs and crustaceans	60	64	60	64	70
Prepared or preserved fish, including fish eggs	37	36	32	31	48
Fish or crustacean extracts and juices	1	5	4	3	3
Subtotal	98	104	95	97	121
Total	**1,314**	**1,216**	**1,230**	**1,243**	**1,275**
Percentage of all exports	4.5	4.1	4.0	3.8	3.6

(1) Exports valued free on board at New Zealand ports.

Note: Figures may not add up to stated totals due to rounding.

Source: Statistics New Zealand

Table 25.14

Fish, crustacean and mollusc exports[1][2]
By destination
Year ending 30 June

Destination	2003	2004	2005	2006	2007
	\$(million)				
Australia	206	202	184	193	235
United States	248	203	208	206	184
Hong Kong (SAR)	153	138	138	150	172
Japan	234	168	158	131	133
People's Republic of China	56	69	109	96	93
Spain	58	105	88	77	85
Republic of Korea	36	42	37	66	49
Germany	67	35	41	42	35
Singapore	29	28	27	24	27
France	31	23	25	31	26
South Africa	5	5	7	10	18
United Kingdom	23	13	20	16	17
Canada	14	12	13	13	12
Belgium	12	12	11	12	12
Russia	2	5	9	16	12
Italy	14	15	17	18	11
Greece	15	13	21	14	11
Thailand	12	12	11	10	11
Georgia	0	1	3	7	10
Taiwan	17	28	19	16	10
Other countries	82	89	84	95	110
Total	**1,314**	**1,216**	**1,230**	**1,243**	**1,275**

(1) Exports valued free on board at New Zealand ports. (2) Includes extracts and preparations of fish, crustaceans and molluscs.

Note: SAR Special Administrative Region. Figures may not add up to stated totals due to rounding.

Source: Statistics New Zealand

Imports

Imports are valued in New Zealand dollars. Foreign currency values are converted to New Zealand dollars when import documents are processed by the New Zealand Customs Service, which sets exchange rates each fortnight.

Imports for the year ending June 2007 were valued at \$41.2 billion, an increase of 5.4 percent on the previous June year. As table 25.15 shows, the largest import values were for petroleum and products, with \$5.8 billion worth of imports, mechanical machinery and equipment (\$5.2 billion), and vehicles and accessories (\$4.9 billion).

The groupings in this table match those published monthly by Statistics New Zealand. Further detail on some commodity groups is provided in the following sections (some groups have been aggregated).

Table 25.15

Major import commodities[1]
Year ending 30 June

Commodity group	2003	2004	2005	2006	2007
			$(million)		
Petroleum and products	3,071	3,026	4,019	5,240	5,785
Mechanical machinery and equipment	4,333	4,529	4,906	5,150	5,230
Vehicles, parts and accessories	4,985	5,347	5,463	5,006	4,854
Electrical machinery and equipment	2,701	3,116	3,223	3,340	3,693
Textiles and textile articles	1,641	1,599	1,652	1,768	1,877
Plastic and plastic articles	1,279	1,230	1,382	1,432	1,567
Iron, steel and articles	981	1,062	1,335	1,273	1,490
Aircraft and parts	804	1,131	705	1,889	1,186
Optical, medical and measuring equipment	967	1,034	1,094	1,159	1,177
Pharmaceutical products	747	788	875	965	989
Paper and paperboard and articles	924	935	942	972	988
Furniture, furnishings and light fittings	399	447	505	565	600
Inorganic chemicals	429	435	438	494	575
Ships, boats and floating structures	185	159	140	259	565
Rubber and rubber articles	393	408	432	439	471
Other chemical products	380	361	382	436	463
Miscellaneous edible preparations	350	359	383	420	459
Books, newspapers and printed matter	386	375	383	393	437
Fertilisers	315	330	450	341	423
Beverages, spirits and vinegar	354	367	373	397	422
Other commodities	6,493	6,284	6,635	6,992	7,696
Confidential data	40	57	77	109	218
Total	**32,161**	**33,378**	**35,793**	**39,040**	**41,165**

(1) Imports valued cif (cost, including insurance and freight).

Note: Figures may not add up to stated totals due to rounding.

Source: Statistics New Zealand

Mechanical and electrical machinery imports

The imports value of all mechanical and electrical machinery in the year ending June 2007 was $8.9 billion, up 5.1 percent on the previous June year and 9.8 percent higher than for 2005. Mechanical and electrical machinery imports made up 21.7 percent of New Zealand's total merchandise trade imports value in the year ended June 2007.

The main mechanical and electrical machinery imports were automatic data processing machines (computers and similar) at $1.1 billion, telephones at $514 million, and transmission apparatus at $439 million.

The main source of mechanical and electrical machinery imports in the June 2007 year was the People's Republic of China ($1.8 billion). Since 2003, the People's Republic of China has more than doubled its market share for this commodity group.

Table 25.16

Mechanical and electrical machinery imports[1]
Year ending 30 June

Product	2003	2004	2005	2006	2007
			$(million)		
Automatic data processing machines	929	1,023	1,069	1,182	1,081
Telephones	315	292	343	332	514
Transmission apparatus	310	469	531	542	439
Parts and accessories for automatic data processing machines	449	465	416	436	382
Monitors and projectors	193	221	247	296	343
Bulldozers, graders, levellers, etc	269	253	326	320	294
Printing machinery	90	102	122	99	222
Electric heaters and driers	129	139	143	149	179
Taps, cocks, valves, etc.	132	136	148	156	174
Parts and accessories for earthworking and manual handling machinery	96	81	112	110	163
Other	4,122	4,463	4,671	4,867	5,134
Total	**7,034**	**7,645**	**8,129**	**8,491**	**8,923**
Percentage of all imports	21.9	22.9	22.7	21.7	21.7

(1) Imports valued cif (cost, including insurance and freight).

Note: Figures may not add up to stated totals due to rounding.

Source: Statistics New Zealand

Free trade agreements

On 7 April 2008, New Zealand signed a free trade agreement (FTA) with the People's Republic of China. The FTA liberalises and facilitates the trade in goods and services, seeks to improve the business environment, and promotes cooperation between the two countries in a broad range of economic areas.

FTAs are negotiated with individual or groups of countries as a way to improve access for New Zealand exporters and investors to overseas markets, reduce barriers to trade, and ensure current access is maintained. In return, New Zealand makes access commitments to the other parties of an FTA.

An FTA must be mutually beneficial to the countries involved. Countries considering an FTA look to determine whether it would bring them economic benefit. The rationale behind FTAs is not exclusively economic – it is often underpinned by political and strategic considerations.

Negotiating a successful FTA can take years. Potential FTA partners initiate study to determine the possible economic benefit. If demonstrable benefit exists, then negotiation rounds may start.

In early rounds, participants will build confidence in each other, with negotiators bringing ideas about their intentions for the deal. In later rounds this switches to discussions on specific text, and requests and offers for market access commitments, such as tariff cuts.

Currently New Zealand has completed five FTAs:

- 1983 – Australia and New Zealand Closer Economic Relations
- 2001 – New Zealand and Singapore Closer Economic Partnership
- 2005 – New Zealand and Thailand Closer Economic Partnership
- 2006 – Trans-Pacific Strategic Economic Partnership (Brunei, Chile, New Zealand, Singapore)
- 2008 – New Zealand and China Free Trade Agreement.

New Zealand is in the process of negotiating other FTAs:

- New Zealand and the Gulf Cooperation Council Free Trade Agreement (Bahrain, Kuwait, Oman, Qatar, Saudi Arabia and the United Arab Emirates)
- ASEAN and New Zealand/Australia Free Trade Agreement
- New Zealand and Malaysia Free Trade Agreement
- New Zealand and Hong Kong Closer Economic Partnership (currently on hold).

New Zealand is also conducting joint economic studies with Japan, the Republic of Korea, and India, with the hope of progressing to formal FTA negotiations.

Source: Ministry of Foreign Affairs and Trade

Table 25.17

Mechanical and electrical machinery imports[1]
By country of origin
Year ending 30 June

Origin	2003	2004	2005	2006	2007
			$(million)		
People's Republic of China	708	900	1,164	1,518	1,845
United States	1,316	1,352	1,133	1,135	1,103
Australia	822	953	956	938	921
Japan	818	845	958	1,049	858
Germany	496	463	536	519	583
Malaysia	303	337	345	359	415
Republic of Korea	261	313	345	309	318
Singapore	235	237	281	302	316
Italy	294	314	317	307	304
Taiwan	267	260	272	284	262
United Kingdom	223	238	248	262	241
Thailand	121	125	159	195	222
Denmark	53	132	93	59	196
France	131	141	153	172	184
Sweden	116	120	122	119	132
Canada	81	88	103	118	110
Hong Kong (SAR)	50	67	76	91	100
Indonesia	56	51	54	70	78
Netherlands	68	59	76	56	66
Switzerland	60	56	83	49	61
Other countries	555	596	657	580	609
Total	**7,034**	**7,645**	**8,129**	**8,491**	**8,923**

(1) Imports valued cif (cost, including insurance and freight).

Note: SAR Special Administrative Region. Figures may not add up to stated totals due to rounding.

Source: Statistics New Zealand

Mineral fuel imports

The import value of all mineral fuels in the year ending June 2007 was $5.9 billion, up 9.9 percent on the June 2006 year and 41.4 percent higher than for the year ending June 2005. Mineral fuels accounted for 14.2 percent of the total merchandise trade import value in the year ended June 2007.

The two main types of mineral fuel imported were crude oil ($3.0 billion), which was almost half the total, and diesel ($802 million).

Australia and Singapore were New Zealand's two main sources of mineral fuel imports in the June 2007 year ($1.4 billion and $1.1 billion, respectively).

Table 25.18

Mineral fuel imports[1]
Year ending 30 June

Product	2003	2004	2005	2006	2007
			$(million)		
Crude oil	1,939	1,617	2,080	2,876	2,980
Diesel	147	292	484	571	802
Regular petrol (fully refined)	381	359	425	473	723
Partly refined petroleum	213	239	347	339	355
Premium petrol (fully refined)	113	127	156	296	253
Jet fuel and aviation spirit	84	139	207	267	234
Coal, coke, tar, etc	128	142	164	142	122
Lubricating preparations	74	71	76	91	109
Premium petrol (partly refined)	13	57	97	118	106
Other petroleum oils	31	51	74	118	80
Other	28	35	39	43	102
Total	**3,152**	**3,129**	**4,149**	**5,335**	**5,865**
Percentage of all imports	9.8	9.4	11.6	13.7	14.2

(1) Imports valued cif (cost, including insurance and freight).

Note: Figures may not add up to stated totals due to rounding.

Source: Statistics New Zealand

Table 25.19

Mineral fuel imports[1]
By country of origin
Year ending 30 June

Origin	2003	2004	2005	2006	2007
			$(million)		
Australia	944	777	1,267	833	1,408
Singapore	172	394	609	1,061	1,098
Qatar	124	46	101	228	526
United Arab Emirates	333	384	363	454	508
Saudi Arabia	151	93	177	390	423
Indonesia	82	57	177	219	324
Republic of Korea	79	128	114	135	316
Japan	1	33	2	258	252
Brunei Darussalam	216	275	160	330	250
Papua New Guinea	59	86	9	84	130
Other countries	991	856	1,171	1,344	629
Total	**3,152**	**3,129**	**4,149**	**5,335**	**5,865**

(1) Imports valued cif (cost, including insurance and freight).

Note: Figures may not add up to stated totals due to rounding.

Source: Statistics New Zealand

Passenger vehicle imports

The value of all passenger vehicles imported in the year ending June 2007 was $3.1 billion, down 1.5 percent on the 2006 June year and 10.2 percent lower than the year ending June 2005. Passenger vehicle imports made up 7.5 percent of New Zealand's total merchandise trade imports value in the year ended June 2007. Japan was by far New Zealand's main source of imported passenger vehicles, supplying 45.1 percent by value, and 64.2 percent by number, during the June 2007 year. Australia and Germany remain the second and third-largest countries of origin, while the Republic of Korea is an increasingly popular source.

Table 25.20

Passenger vehicle imports[1]
By country of origin
Year ending 30 June

Origin	Value $(million)					Quantity				
	2003	2004	2005	2006	2007	2003	2004	2005	2006	2007
Japan	1,711	1,761	1,656	1,489	1,384	177,230	184,422	177,818	153,712	132,591
Australia	566	575	628	498	466	19,061	18,729	20,233	16,708	14,195
Germany	394	472	434	405	462	12,654	16,497	16,968	17,415	20,763
Republic of Korea	51	49	93	164	203	3,772	4,053	7,172	9,112	10,621
United States	136	110	129	121	141	7,061	6,499	9,403	9,263	9,525
United Kingdom	131	141	151	131	114	4,733	5,871	5,616	4,421	2,987
France	63	44	58	51	52	2,743	2,108	2,550	2,490	2,495
Belgium	83	58	58	47	51	3,655	2,731	2,736	2,166	2,271
Austria	17	15	20	30	41	363	394	540	732	904
South Africa	37	26	59	74	38	677	549	1,669	2,485	1,063
Other countries	100	107	129	106	117	4,808	5,350	9,823	7,589	9,125
Total	**3,289**	**3,360**	**3,416**	**3,115**	**3,068**	**236,757**	**247,203**	**254,528**	**226,093**	**206,540**

(1) Imports valued cif (cost, including insurance and freight).

Note: Figures may not add up to stated totals due to rounding.

Source: Statistics New Zealand

Imported cars are parked alongside logs waiting for export at Wellington's CentrePort.

Trading partners

New Zealand has the same top four trading partners for both exports and imports, with Australia being the largest for both. The following sections provide a breakdown of trade with these main four countries – Australia, the United States, Japan, and the People's Republic of China.

Table 25.21

	Merchandise exports[1] Main destination countries Year ending 30 June				
	2003	2004	2005	2006	2007
Destination	$(million)				
Australia	6,050	6,332	6,507	6,797	7,203
United States	4,366	4,297	4,295	4,354	4,522
Japan	3,354	3,283	3,446	3,303	3,496
People's Republic of China	1,457	1,617	1,587	1,740	1,877
United Kingdom	1,361	1,449	1,436	1,554	1,682
Republic of Korea	1,178	1,112	1,080	1,160	1,405
Germany	855	710	793	831	797
Taiwan	667	661	688	800	795
Indonesia	400	373	455	534	652
Malaysia	564	533	488	465	584
Philippines	490	478	543	465	584
Hong Kong (SAR)	582	556	532	544	578
Canada	605	477	526	546	518
Singapore	347	331	418	493	514
Belgium	651	638	475	585	502
Italy	452	453	438	458	484
Thailand	325	346	348	384	474
Mexico	421	434	427	429	463
Saudi Arabia	267	282	386	395	437
Netherlands	253	300	324	344	432
Other countries	4,646	5,203	5,428	6,249	6,941
Total	**29,291**	**29,864**	**30,618**	**32,430**	**34,939**

(1) Exports valued free on board at New Zealand ports.
Note: SAR Special Administrative Region. Figures may not add up to stated totals due to rounding.

Source: Statistics New Zealand

Table 25.22

	Merchandise imports[1] Main countries of origin Year ending 30 June				
	2003	2004	2005	2006	2007
Origin	$(million)				
Australia	7,278	7,364	7,933	7,600	8,664
People's Republic of China	2,687	3,066	3,673	4,443	5,274
United States	4,067	3,930	3,641	4,755	4,295
Japan	3,876	3,849	3,924	3,994	3,688
Singapore	610	828	1,120	1,602	1,928
Germany	1,713	1,736	1,848	1,765	1,898
Republic of Korea	832	897	1,018	1,068	1,310
United Kingdom	1,120	1,090	1,190	1,164	1,106
Thailand	559	590	819	1,007	1,050
Malaysia	864	764	740	1,276	948
Italy	826	810	877	824	881
Taiwan	700	734	876	721	835
Indonesia	420	395	529	576	737
France	700	1131	927	1013	680
Canada	382	732	447	581	675
Saudi Arabia	233	195	313	491	601
United Arab Emirates	357	417	402	512	568
Qatar	126	61	154	241	556
Netherlands	308	279	300	385	471
Sweden	319	344	374	349	344
Other countries	4,181	4,168	4,687	4,673	4,657
Total	**32,161**	**33,378**	**35,793**	**39,040**	**41,165**

(1) Imports valued cif (cost, including insurance and freight).
Note: Figures may not add up to stated totals due to rounding.

Source: Statistics New Zealand

Australia

Australia is New Zealand's main trading partner, receiving 20.6 percent (by value) of New Zealand's merchandise exports, and supplying 21.0 percent of merchandise imports in the year ending June 2007. The value of exports to Australia increased 6.0 percent in the year ending June 2007, while imports rose 14.0 percent from the previous year.

In the June 2007 year, New Zealand's balance of merchandise trade with Australia was a deficit of $1.5 billion, compared with a deficit of $803 million in the June 2006 year.

In the year ending June 2007, Australia received $7.2 billion of New Zealand's merchandise exports. The main commodities exported were mechanical machinery and equipment ($823 million), textiles and textile articles ($469 million), and petroleum and products ($445 million).

Table 25.23

Trade with Australia[1]
By main commodities exported
Year ending 30 June

Commodity group	2003	2004	2005	2006	2007
	\$(million)				
Mechanical machinery and equipment	669	740	731	761	823
Textiles and textile articles[2]	472	498	467	470	469
Petroleum and products	359	256	332	455	445
Electrical machinery and equipment	292	303	332	374	411
Logs, wood and wood articles	412	399	376	334	343
Precious metals, jewellery and coins	279	312	337	357	335
Iron, steel and articles	261	283	323	274	307
Milk powder, butter and cheese	239	217	248	289	292
Beverages, spirits and vinegar	135	158	172	216	290
Plastic and plastic articles	254	270	288	285	286
Paper, paperboard and articles	386	376	180	217	283
Miscellaneous edible preparations	138	166	165	201	188
Fish, crustaceans and molluscs	175	170	153	159	185
Preparations of cereals, flour and starch	85	100	120	136	157
Vehicles, parts and accessories	112	159	137	153	137
Optical, medical and measuring equipment	108	116	119	109	115
Preparations of vegetables, fruit and nuts	84	100	103	99	114
Aluminium and aluminium articles	113	106	104	90	111
Ships, boats and floating structures	46	148	32	47	110
Wood pulp and waste paper	109	91	95	90	106
Other commodities	1,323	1,362	1,480	1,450	1,491
Confidential data	0	0	213	231	206
Total	**6,050**	**6,332**	**6,507**	**6,797**	**7,203**

(1) Exports valued free on board at New Zealand ports. (2) Excluding wool.
Note: Figures may not add up to stated totals due to rounding.
Source: Statistics New Zealand

New Zealand imported goods worth $8.7 billion from Australia in the year ending 30 June 2007. The two main commodities imported were petroleum products ($1.4 billion), and vehicles, parts and accessories ($643 million). While the value of vehicles, parts and accessories imports fell from the June 2006 year, imports of petroleum products rose 70.1 percent in value.

Table 25.24

Trade with Australia[1]
By main commodities imported
Year ending 30 June

Commodity group	2003	2004	2005	2006	2007
	\$(million)				
Petroleum and products	883	740	1,233	822	1,398
Vehicles, parts and accessories	761	796	853	718	643
Mechanical machinery and equipment	509	586	553	530	499
Iron, steel and articles	340	389	454	426	464
Electrical machinery and equipment	312	367	403	408	422
Inorganic chemicals	286	303	285	337	392
Paper, paperboard and articles	425	435	390	385	379
Plastic and plastic articles	266	282	305	317	333
Pharmaceutical products	210	236	211	251	319
Beverages, spirits and vinegar	183	189	184	196	202
Textiles and textile articles	232	234	214	208	201
Preparations of cereals, flour and starch	152	161	161	177	198
Miscellaneous edible preparations	163	169	162	170	192
Books, newspapers and printed matter	186	185	191	184	192
Copper and copper articles	84	80	88	140	186
Aluminium and aluminium articles	149	145	144	152	172
Optical, medical and measuring equipment	110	136	140	149	155
Sugars and sugar confectionery	133	104	127	142	148
Cereals	136	114	124	118	142
Tanning extracts, dyes, paints and putty	106	104	105	102	119
Other commodities	1,648	1,592	1,579	1,640	1,850
Confidential data	4	17	26	28	58
Total	**7,278**	**7,364**	**7,933**	**7,600**	**8,664**

(1) Imports valued cif (cost, including insurance and freight).
Note: Figures may not add up to stated totals due to rounding.
Source: Statistics New Zealand

Table 25.25

Trade with Australia[1]
Year ending 30 June

Year	Exports (fob)	Imports (cif)	Trade balance (fob - cif)
	\$(million)		
1998	4,589	5,579	-990
1999	4,857	5,367	-510
2000	5,528	6,843	-1,316
2001	6,083	7,010	-927
2002	6,326	7,188	-862
2003	6,050	7,278	-1,228
2004	6,332	7,364	-1,032
2005	6,507	7,933	-1,426
2006	6,797	7,600	-803
2007	7,203	8,664	-1,460

(1) Exports valued fob (free on board) at New Zealand ports. Imports valued cif (cost including insurance and freight).
Note: Figures may not equate to stated balances due to rounding.
Source: Statistics New Zealand

Table 25.26

Trade with United States[1]
Year ending 30 June

Year	Exports (fob)	Imports (cif)	Trade balance (fob - cif)
		$(million)	
1998	2,589	3,974	-1385
1999	2,995	4,283	-1,288
2000	3,733	5,127	-1,394
2001	4,651	5,298	-647
2002	4,922	4,777	145
2003	4,366	4,067	299
2004	4,297	3,930	368
2005	4,295	3,641	655
2006	4,354	4,755	-401
2007	4,522	4,295	228

(1) Exports valued fob (free on board) at New Zealand ports. Imports valued cif (cost including insurance and freight).

Note: Figures may not equate to stated balances due to rounding.

Source: Statistics New Zealand

United States

The United States is New Zealand's second main trading partner, receiving 12.9 percent (by value) of New Zealand's merchandise exports, and supplying 10.4 percent of merchandise imports in the year ending June 2007. The value of exports to the United States rose 3.9 percent in the year ending June 2007 while imports fell 9.7 percent over the same period.

The balance of merchandise trade with the United States returned to a surplus in the June 2007 year after being in deficit in the June 2006 year.

In the year ending June 2007, the United States received $4.5 billion of New Zealand's merchandise exports. The main commodities exported were meat and edible offal ($1.0 billion); milk powder, butter and cheese ($479 million); and casein and caseinates ($363 million).

New Zealand imported goods worth $4.3 billion from the United States in the year ending 30 June 2007. The main commodities were aircraft and parts ($892 million), including three large aircraft which accounted for more than three-quarters of this total, and mechanical machinery and equipment ($790 million).

Table 25.27

Trade with United States[1]
By main commodities exported
Year ending 30 June

Commodity group	2003	2004	2005	2006	2007
			$(million)		
Meat and edible offal	1,149	1,250	1,048	1,069	1,026
Milk powder, butter and cheese	221	265	402	417	479
Casein and caseinates	458	365	289	299	363
Mechanical machinery and equipment	258	266	326	394	334
Logs, wood and wood articles	496	359	420	377	331
Miscellaneous edible preparations	89	121	147	168	213
Electrical machinery and equipment	196	186	189	174	194
Beverages, spirits and vinegar	81	95	127	155	193
Fish, crustaceans and molluscs	245	199	202	201	179
Aluminium and aluminium articles	67	93	123	119	168
Optical, medical and measuring equipment	124	118	95	112	160
Iron and steel and articles	73	70	106	120	111
Fruit	102	129	72	86	98
Aircraft and parts	45	12	60	31	87
Textiles and textile articles[2]	48	43	45	51	68
Albumins, gelatin, glues and enzymes	57	42	34	33	45
Ships, boats and floating structures	43	130	54	43	40
Other animal originated products	40	44	38	37	34
Metal tools, implements and cutlery	33	30	33	40	31
Plastics and plastic articles	34	25	30	36	31
Other commodities	504	456	453	386	335
Confidential data	0	0	1	7	3
Total	**4,366**	**4,297**	**4,295**	**4,354**	**4,522**

(1) Exports valued free on board at New Zealand ports. (2) Excluding wool.

Note: Figures may not add up to stated totals due to rounding.

Source: Statistics New Zealand

Rodger Whitson, president of the New Zealand Paeony Society, cuts paeony buds for export. Japan is the most significant market for New Zealand-grown cut flowers, which include calla lilies, orchids and hydrangeas as well as paeonies.

Table 25.28

Trade with United States[1]
By main commodities imported
Year ending 30 June

Commodity group	2003	2004	2005	2006	2007
			$(million)		
Aircraft and parts	586	457	361	1,371	892
Mechanical machinery and equipment	908	904	810	817	790
Optical, medical and measuring equipment	268	277	304	340	361
Vehicles, parts and accessories	297	289	306	315	326
Electrical machinery and equipment	408	448	324	318	313
Plastic and plastic articles	205	191	192	181	184
Other chemical products	117	109	104	122	130
Pharmaceutical products	82	81	70	78	78
Essential oils, perfumes and toiletries	67	64	64	68	76
Textiles and textile articles	62	54	58	66	62
Books, newspapers and printed matter	68	59	59	61	60
Fruit	39	49	50	54	60
Petroleum and products	56	75	42	60	59
Organic chemicals	85	88	82	63	55
Iron, steel and articles	39	39	46	48	52
Food residues, wastes and fodder	57	70	48	65	51
Paper, paperboard and articles	56	47	46	50	49
Miscellaneous edible preparations	34	36	40	43	48
Toys, games and sports requisites	55	47	47	60	42
Rubber and rubber articles	42	39	42	42	40
Other commodities	535	507	544	531	549
Confidential data	1	1	2	3	15
Total	**4,067**	**3,930**	**3,641**	**4,755**	**4,295**

(1) Imports valued cif (cost, including insurance and freight).

Note: Figures may not add up to stated totals due to rounding.

Source: Statistics New Zealand

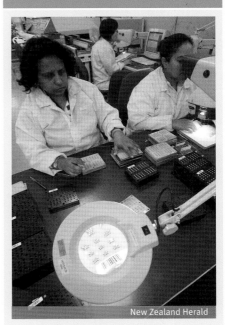

Workers at Rakon's manufacturing plant in Auckland. The company makes crystals and oscillators used in global positioning products, supplying over 50 percent of the frequency control devices used by the GPS industry. Rakon is a multinational company and a global leader in the essential electronics industry. The Asian region is a major market for the company.

Japan

Japan is New Zealand's third main trading partner for merchandise exports and the fourth-largest supplier of merchandise imports. The value of exports to Japan in the year ending June 2007 was up 5.8 percent from the previous June year, while imports fell 7.7 percent. In the June 2007 year New Zealand's balance of merchandise trade with Japan was a deficit of $192 million, compared with a deficit of $690 million in the June 2006 year.

In the year ending June 2007, Japan received $3.5 billion of New Zealand's merchandise exports. The main commodities exported were aluminium and aluminium articles ($895 million); logs, wood and wood articles ($427 million); and milk powder, butter and cheese ($309 million).

Table 25.29

Trade with Japan[1]
By main commodities exported
Year ending 30 June

Commodity group	2003	2004	2005	2006	2007
			$(million)		
Aluminium and aluminium articles	553	582	565	703	895
Logs, wood and wood articles	578	546	513	432	427
Milk powder, butter and cheese	232	237	263	276	309
Meat and edible offal	163	298	409	370	294
Fruit	184	216	267	217	235
Miscellaneous edible preparations	138	108	138	133	134
Fish, crustaceans and molluscs	229	164	155	127	131
Vegetables	182	139	151	126	122
Casein and caseinates	82	83	100	102	114
Wood pulp and waste paper	94	85	97	79	82
Petroleum and products	138	86	67	55	82
Albumins, gelatin, glues and enzymes	38	38	33	36	40
Iron, steel and articles	22	40	35	46	35
Electrical machinery and equipment	16	22	29	35	32
Cocoa and cocoa preparations	31	36	29	30	30
Meat and fish preparations	19	14	18	25	30
Trees, plants, bulbs and cut flowers	44	37	32	34	30
Mechanical machinery and equipment	17	17	21	16	28
Preparations of vegetables, fruit and nuts	23	22	23	24	27
Other animal-originated products	33	37	40	34	23
Other commodities	539	477	384	271	205
Confidential data	0	0	77	132	190
Total	**3,354**	**3,283**	**3,446**	**3,303**	**3,496**

(1) Exports valued free on board at New Zealand ports.

Note: Figures may not add up to stated totals due to rounding.

Source: Statistics New Zealand

Table 25.30

Trade with Japan[1]
Year ending 30 June

Year	Exports (fob)	Imports (cif)	Trade balance (fob - cif)
	\$(million)		
1998	3,038	2,539	499
1999	2,894	3,056	-162
2000	3,382	3,474	-93
2001	4,314	3,427	887
2002	3,732	3,618	115
2003	3,354	3,876	-522
2004	3,283	3,849	-566
2005	3,446	3,924	-479
2006	3,303	3,994	-690
2007	3,496	3,688	-192

(1) Exports valued fob (free on board) at New Zealand ports. Imports valued cif (cost including insurance and freight).

Note: Figures may not equate to stated balances due to rounding.

Source: Statistics New Zealand

New Zealand imported goods worth \$3.7 billion from Japan in the year ending 30 June 2007. More than half the total imports were vehicles, parts and accessories (\$1.8 billion) – Japan is the most common source for imports of passenger vehicles (see table 25.20). Mechanical machinery and equipment (\$564 million), and electrical machinery and equipment (\$294 million) were the next-largest commodity groups imported from Japan.

Table 25.31

Trade with Japan[1]
By main commodities imported
Year ending 30 June

Commodity group	2003	2004	2005	2006	2007
	\$(million)				
Vehicles, parts and accessories	2,293	2,321	2,264	1,963	1,863
Mechanical machinery and equipment	561	505	590	639	564
Electrical machinery and equipment	257	341	368	411	294
Petroleum and products	1	33	2	258	252
Iron, steel and articles	118	106	134	142	140
Optical, medical and measuring equipment	150	142	133	125	89
Rubber and rubber articles	80	83	87	88	88
Plastic and plastic articles	79	63	82	81	83
Photographic films, papers and chemicals	56	44	46	55	68
Paper, paperboard and articles	28	31	33	37	46
Inorganic chemicals	21	14	19	20	23
Organic chemicals	19	15	20	23	21
Tanning extracts, dyes, paints and putty	22	16	14	15	18
Other chemical products	15	11	11	12	10
Precious metals, jewellery and coins	1	1	1	2	9
Textiles and textile articles	22	13	11	12	9
Metal tools, implements and cutlery	8	8	8	7	7
Toys, games and sports requisites	39	7	4	8	7
Aircraft and parts	5	5	3	4	6
Pharmaceutical products	7	6	6	7	6
Other commodities	95	83	86	80	78
Confidential data	0	0	1	6	8
Total	**3,876**	**3,849**	**3,924**	**3,994**	**3,688**

(1) Imports valued cif (cost, including insurance and freight).

Note: Figures may not add up to stated totals due to rounding.

Source: Statistics New Zealand

People's Republic of China

The People's Republic of China became New Zealand's fourth-largest trading partner in the year ending June 2001, displacing the United Kingdom. In the year ending June 2007, the value of exports to the People's Republic of China increased 7.9 percent, while imports rose 18.7 percent compared with the previous June year.

In the year ending June 2007, New Zealand's balance of merchandise trade with the People's Republic of China was a deficit of \$3.4 billion. With the exception of the June 2002 year, this deficit has increased every year since 1998.

New Zealand's Minister of Trade Phil Goff, and his Chinese counterpart Commerce Minister Chen Deming, sign the New Zealand and China free trade agreement in Beijing in April 2008.

Table 25.32

Trade with People's Republic of China[1]
By main commodities exported
Year ending 30 June

Commodity group	2003	2004	2005	2006	2007
	\$(million)				
Milk powder, butter and cheese	302	358	280	372	328
Logs, wood and wood articles	220	187	137	186	270
Wood pulp and waste paper	78	140	145	128	207
Wool	150	165	132	183	168
Raw hides, skins and leather	117	88	88	64	96
Fish, crustaceans and molluscs	55	67	109	96	93
Preparations of cereals, flour and starch	12	8	38	77	84
Other animal-originated products	76	84	88	86	78
Animal or vegetable fats and oils	48	61	53	60	73
Meat and edible offal	60	61	45	54	59
Electrical machinery and equipment	27	33	28	35	53
Copper and copper articles	6	13	15	39	42
Paper, paperboard and articles	50	30	33	32	35
Ores, slag and ash	5	21	54	50	31
Aluminium and aluminium articles	24	29	18	28	27
Food residues, wastes and fodder	37	32	32	27	27
Mechanical machinery and equipment	12	19	22	24	24
Casein and caseinates	14	15	16	23	23
Albumins, gelatin, glues and enzymes	0	3	6	18	23
Fruit	6	5	7	15	19
Other commodities	158	201	216	123	72
Confidential data	0	0	27	20	45
Total	**1,457**	**1,617**	**1,587**	**1,740**	**1,877**

(1) Exports valued free on board at New Zealand ports.
Note: Figures may not add up to stated totals due to rounding.

Source: Statistics New Zealand

Table 25.34

Trade with People's Republic of China[1]
Year ending 30 June

Year	Exports (fob)	Imports (cif)	Trade balance (fob - cif)
	\$(million)		
1998	614	1,107	-493
1999	626	1,234	-608
2000	766	1,630	-864
2001	1,126	2,149	-1,024
2002	1,434	2,371	-937
2003	1,457	2,687	-1,231
2004	1,617	3,066	-1,449
2005	1,587	3,673	-2,087
2006	1,740	4,443	-2,703
2007	1,877	5,274	-3,398

(1) Exports valued fob (free on board) at New Zealand ports. Imports valued cif (cost, including insurance and freight).
Note: Figures may not equate to stated balances due to rounding.

Source: Statistics New Zealand

In the June 2007 year, the People's Republic of China received \$1.9 billion of New Zealand's merchandise exports, up 7.9 percent from the June 2006 year. The main commodities exported were milk powder, butter and cheese (\$328 million); logs, wood and wood articles (\$270 million); and wood pulp and waste paper (\$207 million).

In the year ending June 2007, New Zealand imported goods worth \$5.3 billion from the People's Republic of China, up 18.7 percent on the June 2006 year. The main commodities imported were textiles and textile articles (\$1.1 billion), mechanical machinery and equipment (\$943 million), and electrical machinery and equipment (\$902 million).

Table 25.33

Trade with People's Republic of China[1]
By main commodities imported
Year ending 30 June

Commodity group	2003	2004	2005	2006	2007
	\$(million)				
Textiles and textile articles	731	769	834	953	1,067
Mechanical machinery and equipment	309	410	579	793	943
Electrical machinery and equipment	399	490	585	725	902
Furniture, furnishings and light fittings	107	140	194	240	278
Toys, games and sports requisites	146	176	177	198	228
Iron and steel and articles	80	101	143	157	220
Footwear	132	141	155	180	194
Plastic and plastic articles	78	83	106	134	163
Paper, paperboard and articles	33	32	38	69	94
Optical, medical and measuring equipment	76	75	79	100	89
Articles of leather and animal gut	59	64	70	80	88
Vehicles, parts and accessories	41	47	61	73	83
Glass and glassware	31	36	38	59	71
Inorganic chemicals	43	41	48	46	62
Ceramic products	38	34	36	43	50
Organic chemicals	25	27	38	42	48
Rubber and rubber articles	20	25	29	38	47
Metal tools, implements and cutlery	33	35	39	41	46
Miscellaneous metal products	20	23	26	32	39
Preparations of vegetables, fruit and nuts	9	16	21	26	35
Other commodities	278	302	375	408	513
Confidential data	0	1	3	5	14
Total	**2,687**	**3,066**	**3,673**	**4,443**	**5,274**

(1) Imports valued cif (cost, including insurance and freight).
Note: Figures may not add up to stated totals due to rounding.

Source: Statistics New Zealand

Country groupings

Table 25.35 shows New Zealand's trade with selected geographical and economic country groups. Both exports and imports increased for all groups in the year ending June 2007. For Asia, Europe, ASEAN, the European Union, and the OECD the increase in exports exceeded the increase in imports. This resulted in reduced trade deficits for these groups. APEC was the only group to show a larger trade deficit than in the year ending June 2006.

Table 25.35

		\multicolumn{5}{c}{Merchandise trade[1]}
		\multicolumn{5}{c}{By country grouping}
		\multicolumn{5}{c}{Year ending 30 June}
		2003	2004	2005	2006	2007
	Grouping	\multicolumn{5}{c}{$(million)}
Exports	Asia	9,930	9,870	10,229	10,893	12,028
	Europe	4,941	5,230	5,138	5,336	5,629
	APEC	21,219	21,334	21,763	22,684	24,273
	ASEAN	2,291	2,221	2,401	2,659	3,082
	EU	4,744	4,999	4,850	5,057	5,303
	OECD	20,792	21,037	21,263	21,747	23,050
Imports	Asia	11,401	12,053	13,598	15,852	16,907
	Europe	6,612	7,028	7,296	7,200	7,300
	APEC	23,209	24,227	25,667	28,808	30,645
	ASEAN	2,859	3,057	3,592	5,029	5,233
	EU	6,261	6,690	6,950	6,876	6,975
	OECD	23,310	23,971	24,554	25,507	26,251
Trade balance	Asia	-1,471	-2,183	-3,369	-4,959	-4,878
	Europe	-1,671	-1,798	-2,158	-1,864	-1,671
	APEC	-1,990	-2,893	-3,904	-6,124	-6,372
	ASEAN	-568	-836	-1,191	-2,370	-2,151
	EU	-1,517	-1,691	-2,099	-1,820	-1,671
	OECD	-2,517	-2,934	-3,291	-3,760	-3,201

(1) Exports valued free on board at New Zealand ports. Imports valued cif (cost, including insurance and freight).

Note: APEC Asia-Pacific Economic Cooperation. ASEAN Association of Southeast Asian Nations. EU European Union. OECD Organisation for Economic Co-operation and Development.

Source: Statistics New Zealand

Overseas cargo

Overseas cargo statistics record all goods (by value and gross weight) loaded or unloaded at New Zealand's seaports and airports. Overseas cargo statistics, like overseas merchandise trade statistics, are sourced from New Zealand Customs Service entries.

However, there are some conceptual differences between overseas trade statistics and overseas cargo statistics.

Some items are included in overseas cargo statistics, but not in trade statistics. These include goods on short-term loan or lease, service transactions (such as computer data tapes and drawings), goods consigned for modification or repair, and returnable containers and samples.

Overseas cargo statistics exclude large self-propelled items, such as aircraft and ships that arrive in or depart from New Zealand using their own power.

Overseas cargo loaded

Overseas cargo loaded at New Zealand ports in the year ending 30 June 2007 weighed 22.9 million tonnes, up 5.2 percent on the previous June year. The value of cargo loaded was $30.3 billion, up 9.1 percent.

By both weight and value, the main seaport was Tauranga. It handled 26.3 percent by weight, and 24.9 percent by value, of all overseas cargo loaded at New Zealand seaports.

By weight, air cargo was only 0.5 percent of cargo loaded, but by value it was 15.1 percent, reflecting the comparatively high value of much air cargo.

Table 25.36 gives a breakdown of other New Zealand seaports (and airports) by weight and value of cargo loaded.

Overseas cargo unloaded

Overseas cargo unloaded at New Zealand ports in the year ending 30 June 2007 weighed 18.4 million tonnes, up 2.1 percent on the June 2006 year. The value of cargo unloaded was $31.5 billion, up 7.4 percent.

Table 25.36

Overseas cargo loaded at New Zealand ports[1]
Year ending 30 June

	Value $(million)			Gross weight (tonnes)		
	2005	2006	2007	2005	2006	2007
Seaport						
Tauranga	7,060	7,259	7,538	6,256,421	6,051,907	6,011,423
Auckland	5,700	6,526	7,348	1,987,714	2,228,129	2,509,929
Port Chalmers	3,032	3,254	4,130	1,107,764	1,203,237	1,530,062
Lyttelton	2,263	2,608	2,624	3,086,659	3,583,293	3,273,370
Napier	2,256	2,268	2,253	1,794,905	1,743,720	2,078,729
New Plymouth	1,965	1,778	1,848	1,889,505	1,304,226	1,374,886
Bluff	817	1,009	1,230	518,557	606,689	648,011
Timaru	1,014	1,185	1,116	398,816	543,331	517,266
Wellington	922	807	917	761,049	705,671	818,456
Nelson	699	703	849	1,187,575	1,135,477	1,243,839
Whangarei	284	250	273	941,038	900,550	1,156,500
Gisborne	98	80	119	423,450	388,809	589,041
Picton	33	32	40	387,295	367,149	377,947
Taharoa	17	19	14	991,385	943,544	682,200
Other	5	4	8	58,000	27,600	49,990
Seaport subtotal	26,165	27,783	30,306	21,790,133	21,733,333	22,861,648
Airport						
Auckland	4,080	4,142	4,403	86,804	89,572	86,837
Christchurch	991	985	964	16,245	16,210	16,698
Wellington	27	28	34	990	729	575
Other	1	1	0	4	17	7
Airport subtotal	5,100	5,158	5,401	104,043	106,528	104,116
Parcel post	12	8	8	16	24	40
Total cargo	**31,277**	**32,948**	**35,715**	**21,894,191**	**21,839,885**	**22,965,804**

(1) Includes merchandise freight, goods for repair, loaned and leased goods, military and diplomatic goods, and returnable containers and samples.

Note: Figures may not add up to stated totals due to rounding.

Source: Statistics New Zealand

By cargo weight, the main seaport was Whangarei (which handled 28.5 percent of the total unloaded), followed by Tauranga (21.1 percent), and Auckland (21.1 percent). By value, the main seaport was Auckland, handling 49.7 percent of the total unloaded at seaports.

By weight, air cargo was only 0.6 percent of cargo unloaded, but by value it represented 21.0 percent of the total. By value, Auckland airport handled nearly 20 percent of all cargo unloaded at New Zealand ports.

Table 25.37

Overseas cargo unloaded at New Zealand ports[1]
Year ending 30 June

	Value $(million)			Gross weight (tonnes)		
	2005	2006	2007	2005	2006	2007
Seaport						
Auckland	14,776	15,339	15,663	3,783,654	3,718,952	3,875,889
Tauranga	3,521	3,850	4,660	3,535,992	3,830,744	3,878,849
Whangarei	2,817	3,689	3,692	5,651,163	5,707,633	5,242,347
Lyttelton	2,304	2,266	2,613	1,500,907	1,139,596	1,344,764
Wellington	2,127	1,970	2,208	1,388,228	1,002,735	1,217,135
Napier	655	649	585	745,873	547,480	484,236
Bluff	356	413	553	1,147,312	1,109,811	1,125,054
New Plymouth	275	219	452	462,693	347,028	488,717
Timaru	362	369	382	336,612	246,790	314,696
Port Chalmers	332	344	350	336,477	263,990	264,727
Nelson	222	223	327	139,461	79,942	124,273
Other	4	3	11	29,134	18,581	33,873
Seaport subtotal	27,752	29,334	31,498	19,057,505	18,013,282	18,394,560
Airport						
Auckland	7,006	7,446	7,827	94,226	95,541	94,419
Christchurch	483	469	503	10,212	8,985	8,967
Wellington	97	117	72	1,650	1,577	1,059
Other	0	1	0	0	2	1
Airport subtotal	7,587	8,032	8,403	106,089	106,104	104,446
Parcel post	27	25	21	91	67	108
Total all cargo	**35,366**	**37,392**	**39,922**	**19,163,684**	**18,119,453**	**18,499,114**

(1) Includes merchandise freight, goods for repair, loaned and leased goods, military and diplomatic goods, and returnable containers and samples.

Note: Figures may not add up to stated totals due to rounding.

Source: Statistics New Zealand

Voluntary or mandatory labelling of origin?

There has been recent debate about whether food imports should be required to have their country of origin specified on a label, to help consumers make a choice to buy or not. The Government sees this issue as a commercial and trade matter, not a food safety issue, and that any labelling should therefore be voluntary not mandatory.

New Zealand's Food Safety Authority promotes and protects public health and safety. It argues food should be safe before it enters the marketplace, and checks imports by using pre-market assessment of foods such as additives and processing aids, novel foods, and genetically modified foods.

When a problem occurs, food can be recalled by using more accurate, and mandatory, information than the name of the country – for example a producer's identity or production batch number.

The authority also helps exporters access markets for New Zealand food and food-related products. New Zealand exports 80–90 percent of the food it produces and needs to be flexible in its marketing around the world. The authority argues that mandatory labelling would add trade costs without any easily quantifiable consumer benefit.

Source: New Zealand Food Safety Authority

Contributors and related websites

Landcare Research Ltd – www.landcareresearch.co.nz

New Zealand Customs Service – www.customs.govt.nz

New Zealand Trade and Enterprise – www.nzte.govt.nz

Statistics New Zealand – www.stats.govt.nz

The New Zealand Herald

Silver coin project manager Alan Brandon among $575,000 of old coins being prepared for export at the Reserve Bank in Wellington. The coins were exported to South Korea, where, because of their metal content, they were melted down, and will most likely be made into new coins.

26 | Money and banking

Financial institutions

Unlike most other countries, New Zealand has no specific restrictions on the provision of financial services, such as deposit taking. Only financial institutions wishing to use the word 'bank' (or one of its derivatives) in their name or title are required to obtain authorisation to operate as registered banks.

Nevertheless, in terms of volume, registered banks dominate financial intermediation in New Zealand, although there are a substantial number of small, non-bank financial institutions, such as finance companies, credit unions and building societies.

The majority of New Zealand's registered banks are subsidiaries or branches of overseas banks. Only two of the 17 banks registered at 31 December 2007 were wholly New Zealand owned.

Reserve Bank of New Zealand

The Reserve Bank of New Zealand is New Zealand's central bank. It has three main functions: operating monetary policy to maintain price stability; promoting the maintenance of a sound and efficient financial system; and meeting the currency needs of the public.

The bank is required to manage monetary policy independently to maintain overall price stability. Price stability is defined (in an agreement between the bank's governor and the Minister of Finance) as keeping inflation between 1 and 3 percent, on average, over the medium term. This is achieved through influencing short-term interest rates, which, in turn, influence longer-term interest rates and therefore the spending, saving and borrowing by the public and businesses.

The bank is also responsible for the registration and prudential supervision of registered banks, and for overseeing payment systems, to help ensure a sound and efficient financial system. In future, all finance companies, building societies and credit unions, or non-bank deposit-takers (NBDTs) will be required to be licensed by the Reserve Bank.

The bank issues New Zealand's currency, manages foreign exchange reserves, and provides cash and debt management services to the government.

The Reserve Bank of New Zealand Act 1989 defines the bank's duties and governance arrangements, but makes the bank operationally independent. The bank's chief executive officer, or governor, is accountable for the bank's actions. The bank's performance is monitored by a board of directors on behalf of the Minister of Finance.

Owners of New Zealand's major banks

There were 17 registered banks operating in New Zealand at 31 December 2007, the largest of which (by total reported assets) were ANZ National Bank Ltd, Bank of New Zealand, ASB Bank Ltd, and Westpac New Zealand Ltd.

The banks and their parent companies:

New Zealand bank	Parent company
ANZ National Bank Ltd	Australia and New Zealand Banking Group Ltd
ASB Bank Ltd	Commonwealth Bank of Australia Ltd
Bank of New Zealand	National Australia Bank Ltd
Westpac New Zealand Ltd	Westpac Banking Corporation

The assets of these banks range from $46 billion to $108 billion and, across all four banks, total approximately $260 billion.

Concentrations of credit risk by industry (as a demonstration of business positioning) for the banks vary by profile, but all have significant concentrations of credit risk in real estate mortgages. This demonstrates the significant investment New Zealanders have in property, compared with other investment vehicles, for example, financial investment products.

The other main concentrations of credit risk are in finance, insurance, investment, agriculture, forestry, fishing and mining.

Source: Reserve Bank of New Zealand

Bank registration and supervision

The Act requires the bank to maintain a sound and efficient financial system, and to avoid significant damage to the financial system that could result from the failure of a registered bank. Accordingly, the bank's supervision and registration framework does not aim to protect depositors or individual banks from loss. Instead, the main focus is on the efficient and effective operation of the banking system as a whole.

A major disruption in the provision of financial services, or lack of efficiency in the delivery of services, could potentially impose significant costs on other sectors of the economy.

In the event that a bank does fail, the Reserve Bank has crisis management powers that allow it to take steps to minimise any flow-on effects to the rest of the financial sector.

There is no upper limit on the number of banks that can be registered in New Zealand. The policy behind this is based on the belief that competitive forces encourage efficiency and innovation, and that overseas banks coming to New Zealand can bring valuable expertise to the local market.

Nevertheless, all applicants for registration must satisfy the Reserve Bank that they can meet minimum prudential requirements. Applicants must satisfy the bank that they are primarily involved in providing financial services.

In addition, when considering an application for registration, the Reserve Bank is required to have regard to:

- incorporation and ownership structure
- size and nature of the proposed business
- standing of the applicant in financial markets
- suitability of directors and senior managers for their positions
- standing of the owner in financial markets
- ability to carry on business in a prudent manner.

If the applicant is an overseas bank, the following are also examined:

- the amount and frequency of disclosure in their home jurisdiction
- the law and regulatory requirements in the home jurisdiction relating to: bank registration or authorisation; the priority of claims of creditors in an insolvency; the duties and powers of the applicant's directors; accounting and auditing standards; and disclosure of financial and other information.

As at 31 December 2007, there were 17 registered banks. Only two were not wholly overseas owned – TSB Bank Ltd and Kiwibank Ltd (a subsidiary of state-owned enterprise New Zealand Post Ltd).

One of several amendments to the Reserve Bank of New Zealand Act in 2003 was the introduction of a requirement that the Reserve Bank's consent be obtained before any significant change in bank ownership takes place. This was in recognition of the influence that a bank's owners can have on the operations and health of a bank. The power of the Act was exercised in October 2003, when the Australia and New Zealand Banking Group applied to purchase the National Bank of New Zealand – at the time the largest commercial transaction in New Zealand's history.

The Reserve Bank's supervision framework focuses primarily on public disclosure and director attestation requirements. Each bank must publish a quarterly disclosure statement containing a comprehensive range of financial information on the bank, the banking group it heads and, where applicable, the parent company. The bank's directors are required to sign each disclosure statement and a number of attestations about key prudential matters, including one relating to the adequacy of the bank's systems and controls.

The disclosure and attestation requirements strengthen market disciplines on banks and sharpen incentives for directors to take appropriate responsibility for the prudent operation of their bank. The disclosure regime also provides depositors and other creditors with the information they need to make informed decisions on where to place their money.

Banks are also required to meet regulatory requirements covering several areas, including:

- the internationally-agreed minimum capital adequacy ratio of 8 percent
- exposure to connected persons
- the scope of non-banking business the bank can undertake
- provisions in the bank's constitution.

The Reserve Bank has a wide range of powers to respond to a bank in distress or failure, including the power to give directions to the bank and the ability to recommend to the Minister of Finance that a bank be placed under statutory management.

Tables 26.01 and 26.02 list assets and liabilities of the Reserve Bank.

Registered banks

At 31 December 2007, there were 17 registered banks in New Zealand. The number of banks per capita is still relatively high by international standards. In part, this reflects the open nature of the registration regime.

Registered banks operating in New Zealand at 31 December 2007 were: ABN AMRO Bank NV; ANZ National Bank Ltd; ASB Bank Ltd; Bank of New Zealand; Bank of Tokyo-Mitsubishi Ltd; Citibank NA; Commonwealth Bank of Australia; Deutsche Bank AG; JP Morgan Chase NA; Kiwibank Ltd; Kookmin Bank; Rabobank Nederland; Rabobank New Zealand Ltd; The Hong Kong and Shanghai Banking Corporation Ltd; TSB Bank Ltd; Westpac Banking Corporation; and Westpac New Zealand Ltd.

Table 26.01

Assets of the Reserve Bank of New Zealand
At 30 June

	Denominated in foreign currency				Denominated in New Zealand dollars							
						Advances		Investment in New Zealand		Fixed assets		
Year	Current account advances[1]	Marketable securities[2][3]	IMF holdings of SDRs[4]	Foreign assets[5]	Settlement institutions[6]	Crown settlement account[7]	Advances to Treasury[8]	Government securities[9]	Other[10]	and other inventories[11]	Other assets[12]	Total assets[13]
					$(million)							
1997	1,133	3,340	0	0	750	0	1,236	2,041	0	58	8	8,566
1998	1,860	4,490	2	1	1,059	0	1,204	2,149	0	58	6	10,829
1999	2,283	3,602	0	0	3,064	0	0	2,256	1	56	6	11,268
2000	2,020	4,109	0	0	1,600	0	0	2,492	0	48	5	10,274
2001	1,810	4,056	0	0	2,517	0	0	2,708	0	44	4	11,139
2002	2,763	2,825	0	4	2,819	0	0	3,002	0	35	6	11,454
2003	2,938	3,137	0	-4	2,120	0	0	3,300	10	36	2	11,539
2004	2,057	2,824	0	0	1,454	0	0	3,323	0	36	4	9,698
2005	3,855	4,108	0	93	265	0	0	4,601	0	40	2	12,964
2006	7,611	4,011	0	117	123	0	0	4,912	0	63	18	16,855
2007	4,025	12,526	0	97	16	0	0	4,342	0	85	4	21,095

(1) Foreign-currency-denominated current accounts, reverse repurchase and secured/unsecured short-term advances to foreign banks and financial institutions. (2) Foreign-currency-denominated sovereign and non-sovereign securities. (3) Prior to August 2004, short sales of bonds were netted off against the bonds in marketable securities. From August 2004, short sales are reported as liabilities denominated in foreign currency. (4) International Monetary Fund (IMF) holdings of SDR-denominated foreign currency assets. (5) Sundry foreign assets. (6) Repurchase advances, secured loans, overnight advances and accrued interest owing from settlement institutions. (7) Net overdrawn balances in the Crown settlement account. (8) Fixed term deposits with the Treasury. (9) Government stock investment portfolio. (10) New Zealand denominated marketable securities held for trading purposes. (11) Land, buildings, plant, machinery, motor vehicles and inventories. (12) Accounts receivable and sundry assets. (13) The sum of the above-defined foreign currency and New Zealand dollar assets.

Note: SDR refers to special drawing rights.

Source: Reserve Bank of New Zealand

Table 26.02

Liabilities of the Reserve Bank of New Zealand
At 30 June

	Denominated in foreign currency			Denominated in New Zealand dollars							
			IMF allocations of SDRs[4]	Reserve Bank bills[5]	Deposits			Currency in circulation[9]	Other liabilities[10]	Capital reserves[11]	Total liabilities[12]
Year	Current[1][2]	Long-term[3]			Government[6]	Settlement institutions[7]	Other[8]				
					$(million)						
1997	595	3,586	292	1,236	608	1	46	1,665	143	394	8,566
1998	1,266	4,714	370	1,203	957	2	25	1,733	158	401	10,829
1999	1,474	4,405	0	0	2,881	1	55	1,885	13	554	11,268
2000	1,541	4,589	0	0	1,328	49	36	2,160	14	557	10,274
2001	963	4,756	0	0	2,250	66	70	2,463	166	405	11,139
2002	1,047	4,192	0	0	2,947	4	15	2,659	10	580	11,454
2003	892	4,069	0	0	3,143	2	24	2,806	7	596	11,539
2004	945	3,828	0	0	1,243	71	70	2,920	8	613	9,698
2005	3,220	4,057	0	0	668	57	64	3,183	161	1,554	12,964
2006	1,783	5,342	0	0	2,248	2,177	103	3,348	433	1,421	16,855
2007	901	3,962	0	0	3,152	7,810	47	3,360	284	1,579	21,095

(1) Foreign-currency-denominated repurchase, secured loan, and credit line financing provided by foreign counterparties. (2) Prior to August 2004, short sales of bonds were netted off against the bonds in marketable securities. From August 2004, short sales are reported as liabilities denominated in foreign currency. (3) Foreign-currency-denominated financing provided by the Treasury (and the Earthquake Commission up to 3 June 1998). (4) SDR-denominated financing provided by the International Monetary Fund (IMF). In December 1998, SDR assets and liabilities were transferred to the Treasury. SDRs are now directly accounted for on the Crown balance sheet. (5) Short-term discount securities issued by the Reserve Bank. The bank ceased issuing Reserve Bank bills on 5 February 1999. All Reserve Bank bills and related advances to the Treasury were repaid by 9 April 1999. (6) Net in-funds balance in the Crown settlement and other government accounts held at the Reserve Bank. (7) Balances in the exchange settlement accounts held at the Reserve Bank. (8) IMF No. 1 account, other central bank accounts, staff deposits and other sundry deposits. (9) The face value of notes and coins issued into circulation. (10) Creditors and accounts payable. (11) Retained earnings, revaluation reserves and current period accumulated income. (12) The sum of the above-defined foreign currency and New Zealand dollar liabilities.

Note: SDR refers to special drawing rights.

Source: Reserve Bank of New Zealand

The number of ways to pay for goods and services is on the rise. In some cities you can now pay for parking by cash, text message, or credit card. These solid aluminium machines are vandal-resistant and run on solar/battery power.

Jarrad Mapp

Table 26.03 lists the liabilities and assets of M3 financial institutions (a group of 13 financial institutions surveyed by the Reserve Bank when compiling monetary aggregates).

Access to branches and services The first automated teller machines (ATMs) were introduced to New Zealand in mid-1979, and by the end of 1982 all major trading banks offered ATM services.

Table 26.03

Liabilities and assets of M3 financial institutions
At 30 December

Item	1997	1998	1999	2000	2001	2002	2003	2004	2005	2006	2007
						$(million)					
Liabilities											
New Zealand dollar funding											
New Zealand residents	86,096	89,370	94,831	95,638	103,558	112,161	121,893	127,834	139,699	154,747	168,616
Non-residents	12,759	13,597	14,079	18,535	24,481	28,468	26,404	31,228	31,072	42,977	40,840
Total	98,856	102,967	108,909	114,173	128,039	140,628	148,297	159,062	170,771	197,724	209,456
Foreign currency funding											
New Zealand residents	2,806	4,198	2,521	3,296	3,194	2,638	4,667	5,620	7,769	8,011	9,876
Non-residents	16,507	21,568	31,915	37,066	39,162	32,642	34,594	40,372	45,437	52,862	65,990
Total	19,314	25,766	34,436	40,362	42,356	35,279	39,260	45,992	53,206	60,873	75,866
Capital and reserves	7,262	8,224	9,848	10,685	11,790	14,022	17,803	18,396	19,063	20,355	20,719
Other liabilities[1]	8,296	5,636	4,714	15,397	6,508	11,268	14,845	12,735	9,279	14,349	21,742
Total liabilities	**133,726**	**142,593**	**157,907**	**180,617**	**188,693**	**201,198**	**220,205**	**236,185**	**252,320**	**293,300**	**327,782**
Funding from associates[2]	13,935	23,389	28,148	29,735	33,659	31,008	31,001	29,191	30,795	43,933	48,806
Assets											
Government securities	3,572	4,384	6,921	7,149	5,818	8,183	7,920	5,601	5,034	2,221	2,052
New Zealand notes and coin	409	448	1,050	818	907	941	908	930	974	896	896
Claims on the Reserve Bank[3]	1,164	1,057	542	0	1	4	1	80	245	8,917	8,006
New Zealand dollar claims											
New Zealand residents (M3)	9,044	11,883	11,721	10,601	12,734	10,920	10,968	12,870	14,083	14,573	12,811
New Zealand residents (non-M3)	101,500	107,900	118,140	124,303	132,173	143,470	156,728	176,873	203,143	229,880	260,978
Non-residents	2,869	4,359	6,550	9,011	12,926	14,034	13,950	14,945	8,744	8,266	7,553
Total	113,413	124,141	136,411	143,915	157,833	168,424	181,645	204,687	225,970	252,719	281,342
Foreign currency claims											
New Zealand residents	3,268	3,716	3,431	4,671	5,123	3,852	3,793	3,872	4,262	3,488	4,290
Non-residents	389	974	3,102	7,726	10,546	10,563	8,535	7,390	3,295	5,449	7,117
Total	3,657	4,690	6,533	12,398	15,669	14,416	12,328	11,262	7,557	8,937	11,407
Foreign currency fixed assets and equity investment	34	36	41	57	87	77	75	79	83	228	94
Shares (in New Zealand companies)	421	509	312	326	522	458	2,111	45	258	214	240
Other assets[1]	11,055	7,329	6,095	15,954	7,857	8,695	15,217	13,502	12,197	19,169	23,746
Total assets	**133,726**	**142,593**	**157,907**	**180,617**	**188,694**	**201,198**	**220,205**	**236,185**	**252,320**	**293,300**	**327,782**
Financial claims on associates[2]	1,164	3,093	4,745	9,612	12,543	13,267	12,198	10,502	4,751	4,323	5,145

(1) Includes trade creditors/debtors, accounts payable/receivable, and items in transit, timing and statistical adjustments. (2) Any two entities, that is companies, organisations or individuals, with the same shareholders and/or any company that holds 20 percent or more of the paid-up capital of another company (the associated). A subsidiary is an associate. (3) This series shows a large decline from 1999 until 2006. In early 1999, the Reserve Bank of New Zealand discontinued the issuance of Reserve Bank bills when it implemented the overnight cash rate regime for monetary policy implementation. In 2006, the Reserve Bank made changes to its domestic liquidity management regime, which resulted in a significant increase of overnight settlement cash balances.

Note: Figures may not add up to stated totals, due to rounding.

Source: Reserve Bank of New Zealand

New Zealanders use EFTPOS to conduct many of their day-to-day transactions. There were 125,008 EFTPOS terminals in New Zealand in 2006, with 2.54 million credit cards and 5.07 million debit cards on issue.

Online banking booms

Online banking has experienced rapid growth, with the proportion of users doubling in the past three years. The Nielsen Company interviewed 3,600 people about their online banking habits in the December 2007 quarter.

Online banking has become mainstream, with frequently used sites receiving more than half a million unique browsers a month. Once they use the Internet, people of all ages adopt online banking with enthusiasm. For younger people with Internet access, online banking is the norm. Eighty percent of those under 40 used online banking, and it was becoming more common practice for older people, with 62 percent of those over 55 logging on in the month prior to being surveyed.

On their last visit to an online banking site, 90 percent of customers checked their account balances and about half transferred money or made payments online. On the whole, customers are very happy with the online banking sites they use – around 8 in 10 rate their experience as 'very good' or 'excellent'.

ASB had the highest proportion of customers (85 percent) who used online banking in the month prior to being surveyed, followed by Kiwibank (81 percent) and Westpac (77 percent).

There are risks associated with online banking and customers are encouraged to run up-to-date anti-virus programs and regularly change passwords. Most banks employ two-factor online authentication – generally a user name and a password. National Bank, ANZ, ASB, Kiwibank and BNZ all offer reimbursement for online banking fraud on a case-by-case basis. Westpac guarantees cover for all online banking fraud losses.

Source: The Nielsen Company

Table 26.04

Bank branches and automated teller machines (ATMs)
At 31 December

Year	Bank branches	Bank-owned ATMs
2000	849	1,692
2001	832	1,830
2002	1,098	1,889
2003	1,103	1,889
2004	1,124	2,019
2005	1,148	2,289
2006	1,155	2,321

Source: New Zealand Bankers' Association

Table 26.05

Number of EFTPOS terminals
Year ending 31 December

Year	Terminals
2000	84,351
2001	92,840
2002	95,221
2003	98,474
2004	118,174
2005	119,651
2006	125,008

Source: New Zealand Bankers' Association

Electronic funds transfer at point of sale (EFTPOS) was introduced to New Zealand in 1984 as a means of paying for retail goods and services. Banks agreed in 1990 to integrate their EFTPOS services, and growth of the network has been rapid since then.

Table 26.05 shows the number of EFTPOS terminals in New Zealand supermarkets, service stations, liquor markets and other retail outlets.

Electronic card transactions There were 973 million electronic transactions in the year ended January 2008, with a value of $53.7 billion. This compares with 889 million transactions with a value of $49.4 billion in the January 2007 year.

For the year ended January 2008, debit transactions made up 53 percent of all electronic transactions by value (credit made up 47 percent).

Figure 26.01

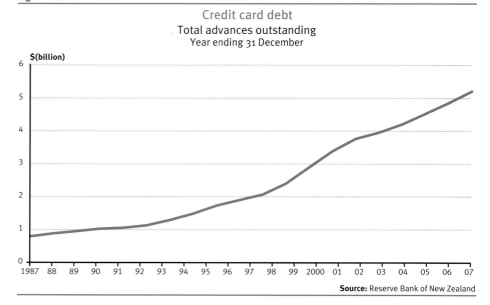

Credit card debt
Total advances outstanding
Year ending 31 December

Source: Reserve Bank of New Zealand

Credit cards are popular for the purchase of goods and services. At 31 December 2006 there were 2.54 million cards on issue nationally, up from the 2.36 million on issue two years earlier.

Industry self-regulation The New Zealand Bankers' Association is a professional industry association established in 1891. The association represents and promotes the interests of the banking industry and delivers to its members those services that can be undertaken effectively on an industry basis.

The association introduced a Code of Banking Practice in 1992, which established minimum standards of practice to be observed by banks in their dealings with personal customers. The most recent edition of the code was published in 2007, following a comprehensive public consultation process.

The code is linked to an independent external complaints review process, the Banking Ombudsman Scheme, established in July 1992.

Towards a cashless society

New Zealand is a world leader in the transition towards a cashless society, as online banking, credit cards, EFTPOS (electronic funds transfer at point of sale), and telephone banking transform the way people pay for goods and services.

While EFTPOS use is growing, the use of cheques is decreasing. When the New Zealand Bankers' Association started keeping records in 1993, cheques accounted for 54 percent of all transactions. That has now fallen to less than 10 percent (see the category 'MICR' in the table below).

Growth in the number of automated teller machines (ATMs) and EFTPOS terminals reflects the increased use of plastic cards to conduct transactions.

Number of ATM and EFTPOS terminals and credit and debit cards on issue

	2004	2005	2006
ATM terminals	2,019	2,289	2,321
EFTPOS terminals	118,174	119,651	125,008
Credit cards on issue	2,360,777	2,408,051	2,537,074
Debit cards on issue	4,701,569	4,743,785	5,072,252

Transaction types

Payment type	2004 volume	%	2005 volume	%	2006 volume	%
MICR[1]	192,072,405	10	185,505,307	9	171,709,374	8
Electronic credits[2]	309,553,531	17	329,606,602	16	326,086,382	16
Direct debits						
Credit card[3]	94,930,874	5	96,160,238	5	94,922,600	5
Credit card[4]	179,226,205	10	194,033,729	10	213,365,169	10
Credit card[5]	180,575,950	10	191,611,088	10	218,138,379	10
ATM	208,386,529	11	212,112,905	11	208,683,516	10
EFTPOS[6]	694,534,599	37	800,233,024	40	857,033,727	41
Total transactions	**1,859,280,093**	..	**2,009,262,893**	..	**2,089,939,147**	..

(1) Magnetic ink character recognition (MICR) refers primarily to the use of cheques. (2) Automatic payments and direct credits. (3) Includes EFTPOS-initiated transactions. (4) Transactions on credit cards issued by banks located in New Zealand and transactions generated within and outside New Zealand. (5) Credit card transactions generated at New Zealand merchants, including credit cards issued by banks located in and outside New Zealand. (6) Debit card transactions on current account.

Note: Figures may not add up to stated totals, due to rounding.

Symbol: .. not applicable

Source: New Zealand Bankers' Association

Other deposit-taking financial institutions

Although banks are the dominant financial institutions in New Zealand, there are more than 70 smaller deposit-taking financial institutions in New Zealand and 50 credit unions. These include a medium-sized, nationwide, cooperative savings institution, and a large, regionally-based building society that continues to specialise in housing finance. There are also nine smaller building societies, most of which have diversified their lending portfolios away from reliance on lending for housing since deregulation. Credit unions have total loans to members of less than $700 million, or less than 0.5 percent of all loans to households.

Total loans of finance companies nearly trebled in the five years ending 31 December 2006. In the latter part of the period, lending for property development contributed strongly to loan growth, but it was nonetheless spread across hire purchase for cars and consumer goods, for business leasing and plant and machinery purposes, and for commercial and residential property development.

More recent developments in the 'other financial institution' market include the growth of residential mortgage managers – lenders who fund their loans via securitisation in wholesale markets – and the emergence of several 'non-conforming' personal lenders. In addition, several retail groups have stepped up their involvement in personal finance, for example by issuing a credit card or offering direct personal loans in addition to providing hire purchase finance.

Since the late 1990s, banks' share of the personal lending market has declined slightly, as other institutions have developed a range of niche markets.

Money

Currency

One of the key statutory obligations of the Reserve Bank is to provide New Zealand's currency. The total face value of currency in circulation (bank notes and coins) was $3.5 billion at 31 October 2007. Of this, $3.0 billion is held by the public, with the balance being held by banks and other financial institutions.

New Zealand's decimal currency system was introduced in 1967 when dollars and cents replaced pounds, shillings and pence as monetary units. The Reserve Bank initially issued 1, 2, 5, 10, 20 and 50 cent coins, and $1, $2, $5, $10, $20 and $100 bank notes. In 1983 the Reserve Bank started issuing a $50 bank note. In 1989 it stopped issuing 1 and 2 cent coins, and in 1991 it started issuing $1 and $2 coins to replace the corresponding bank notes.

A substantial change to New Zealand's bank notes occurred in 1992 when a new series was issued. These notes included images of New Zealanders and contained new security features. Portraits on the new notes were: $5, Sir Edmund Hillary; $10, Kate Sheppard; $20, Queen Elizabeth II; $50, Sir Apirana Ngata; and $100, Ernest, Lord Rutherford of Nelson. Queen Elizabeth II features on the watermark of all notes. Rare New Zealand birds are featured on the backs of the notes.

New rules for non-bank deposit takers

In September 2007, Cabinet announced its decision on a new regulatory framework for non-bank deposit-takers (NBDTs), including finance companies, building societies, and credit unions. Consequently, the Reserve Bank of New Zealand Amendment Bill (No. 3) was introduced to Parliament in November 2007.

This bill will require all NBDTs to obtain and disclose a credit rating, and to comply with minimum prudential requirements, such as minimum capital, capital adequacy, limits on exposures to related parties, and liquidity. The Reserve Bank will become the single prudential regulator for New Zealand, and trustee corporations will continue to be the front-line supervisors of deposit-takers. It is expected that this bill will be enacted in 2008.

NBDTs provide a valid option for investors and are an important part of the financial sector. However, there has been concern that the retail investor may not be adequately aware of the risk profile of their investment. This was highlighted with the collapse of several finance companies in 2007.

One of the main requirements under the new regime is that NBDTs will be required to obtain and publicly disclose a credit rating from a rating agency approved

by the Reserve Bank. Ratings, a relatively simple metric summarising the risk of a NBDT defaulting on its financial obligations, would provide the most cost-effective means of enabling depositors to distinguish between higher and lower risk NBDTs, and thereby make better-informed investment decisions.

Trustees will continue to play an important role, as with the current supervision model. Their functions will include establishing a trust deed for particular offers of securities, prescribing the financial, reporting and other covenants in the trust deed, enforcing trust deed covenants, and supervising and monitoring NBDTs. Trustees will be subject to greater oversight by the Securities Commission under the new regulatory arrangements, and there will be a minimum set of requirements for the content of trust deeds.

A second bill, to be introduced later in 2008, will contain all the remaining matters required to implement the NBDT regime, including licensing and fit and proper requirements.

It is likely that a transition period will apply after the commencement date to provide existing NBDTs with sufficient time to come into compliance with the new regulatory requirements.

Source: Reserve Bank of New Zealand

Facilitation enhances resolution of banking complaints

The Banking Ombudsman Scheme is independent of banks. It resolves disputes between banks and their customers about banking services, at no cost to complainants.

Only disputes that have been through a bank's internal complaints process may be investigated by the Banking Ombudsman, who conducts investigations in an impartial, informal and non-adversarial manner, on the basis of an examination of all relevant information.

The Banking Ombudsman Scheme, established in 1992, distinguishes between enquiries, complaints, disputes, and facilitations. Disputes are cases that have been considered through a bank's internal complaints procedure, without agreement being reached. Complaints are cases that have not been through a bank's internal complaints procedure, and enquiries lie outside the terms of reference of the ombudsman. Facilitations are the growing proportion of disputes that are quickly settled by agreement between the bank and the complainant, with a minimum of procedural formality and complexity.

In recent years, the pattern of disputes has changed significantly, partly in response to the economic buoyancy of recent years, and partly as a consequence of the rapid introduction of Internet banking. Complaints relating to Internet or e-banking have accordingly increased, while there has been a marked decline in the number and proportion of cases relating to mortgages.

If the ombudsman finds that a bank is at fault and is unable to settle the matter on a voluntary basis, compensation may be awarded to cover direct losses of up to $200,000, and some incidental expenses. Compensation for amounts up to $6,000 may also be awarded for inconvenience.

A five-member board guarantees the independence and efficiency of the Banking Ombudsman Scheme. While the board is responsible for the governance of the scheme, it has no influence over the everyday investigative work of the banking ombudsman.

Liz Brown, the current Banking Ombudsman, has been in office since 1995.

All banks that provide services to the public and are members of the New Zealand Bankers' Association (NZBA) are participants in the scheme, as is Rabobank, which is not a member of the NZBA.

Source: Office of the Banking Ombudsman

2008 – International Year of the Frog

In 2008, New Zealand Post released a legal tender Hamilton's frog coin (with a $5 denomination) as part of its endangered New Zealand native animal series.

With an estimated 300 adults living in the wild, the Hamilton's frog *(Leiopelma hamiltoni)* is New Zealand's rarest native frog and possibly the world's. The land-loving Hamilton's frog is found only in the wild on Takapourewa Island (Stephens Island) in the Marlborough Sounds of New Zealand, and has unique characteristics.

Having adapted to living in rocky surroundings, this frog has almost no webbing on its hind feet and the young do not go through a tadpole stage. The Hamilton's frog is said to descend from one of the most ancient amphibian lineages and still has a tail bone (but no tail), as well as undeveloped vocal and hearing capabilities.

Source: New Zealand Post

Polymer notes

Bundles of processed $100 polymer notes in cages at the Reserve Bank, ready for reissue to the banks. Polymer notes have transparent windows, which allow you to see right through the bank note, making forgery difficult. Compared with paper notes, polymer bank notes are stronger and non-porous, don't get dirty and tatty, and need to be replaced less often. Old polymer bank notes can be recycled economically into manufactured items.

Source: Reserve Bank of New Zealand

Until 1999, New Zealand's bank notes were printed on paper made from cotton. On 3 May 1999, the Reserve Bank started circulating polymer (plastic) bank notes. The main reasons to change to polymer were:

- the average polymer note lasts four times as long as a paper note, which keeps the cost of producing money down
- polymer notes are stronger and non-porous, so they do not get as dirty as paper
- the polymer notes incorporated new security features that are difficult to counterfeit, including a transparent 'window'.

The design of these new notes changed slightly to incorporate the new security features, but the size and colours stayed the same as the paper notes.

In July 2006, the Reserve Bank introduced new, smaller 10, 20 and 50 cent coins. The 5 cent coin was withdrawn from circulation. The new 20 and 50 cent coins are made from nickel-plated steel. The new 10 cent coin is made from copper-plated steel. The one and two dollar coins were retained unchanged, as were the images on the lower value coins. All coins continue to feature the Queen on the back.

The main reason for the withdrawal of the 5 cent coin was that it had little purchasing power. It was worth less than what a half a cent would have been worth when decimal currency was introduced in 1967. The great increase in the use of electronic methods of payment also reduced the need for the 5 cent coin.

New Zealand's old 20 and 50 cent coins were extremely large by international standards. The 50 cent coin, with a diameter of 31.75mm, was one of the largest circulating coins in the world. Those old coins were inconvenient to carry in purses and pockets, and for employees to handle.

The old 'silver' coins were demonetised (declared no longer legal tender) three months after the new coins were issued. This meant that shops and other businesses were no longer obliged to accept them as payment for goods and services. However, the Reserve Bank will always pay face value for the coins – as it does for pre-decimal currency.

Monetary policy

Monetary policy is implemented by the Reserve Bank under the terms of the Reserve Bank of New Zealand Act 1989.

The government has given the bank responsibility for keeping average inflation between 1 and 3 percent a year over the medium term. The specific details of the target are set out in a written agreement – between the Governor of the Reserve Bank and the Minister of Finance – called the policy targets agreement (PTA).

The bank changed the way it implements monetary policy in March 1999, when the settlement cash target system, used since the mid-1980s, was replaced by an implementation system based on an official cash rate (OCR).

Previously, the bank relied on adjustments to the quantity of settlement cash in the banking system to ensure monetary conditions were appropriate. These adjustments were relatively rare, however, as financial markets generally adjusted monetary conditions in response to the bank's quarterly inflation projections and to emerging economic data.

Under the OCR system, the Reserve Bank influences short-term interest rates by being prepared to lend an unlimited amount of cash overnight, or borrow an unlimited amount of cash overnight, at the OCR itself. This influences other interest rates, affecting demand within the economy and therefore inflationary pressures.

The Act stipulates that the bank must publish policy statements that specify how it intends to achieve the inflation target defined in the PTA, the reasons for choosing the policies, and the means it intends to use to achieve the target. The policy statements must also provide a medium-term policy outlook, and must review and assess the implementation of monetary policy since the previous policy statement.

To meet these requirements, the bank publishes monetary policy statements which provide the economic projections and rationale underpinning its monetary policy decisions, and also assess the implementation of monetary policy since the previous publication.

The OCR is reviewed eight times a year – at each of the bank's quarterly monetary policy statements, and approximately halfway between each quarterly statement.

Government securities market

The government sells three types of debt instruments to meet its financing requirements:

- *Government bonds* are a medium-term instrument (usually with maturity of one to around 10 years), paying a fixed-coupon interest rate and aimed at the wholesale market (mainly institutional investors). Since September 1983, government bonds have been sold through regular, competitive tenders.

Figure 26.02

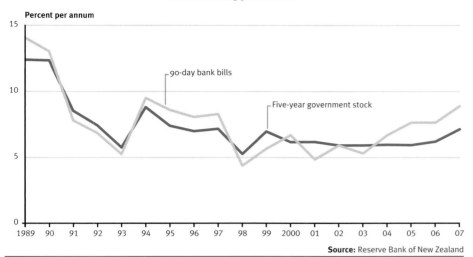

Key market rates
Average wholesale interest rates
Quarter ending 31 December

90-day bank bills

Five-year government stock

Source: Reserve Bank of New Zealand

- *Treasury bills* are short-term wholesale debt instruments (usually with maturity of up to around 12 months). Since January 1985, bills have been sold through regular weekly tenders to meet the government's ongoing funding requirements. They are also used to meet the government's seasonal financing needs. Bills do not pay interest, but rather are sold (and subsequently traded) at a discount to their par (maturity) value, producing an effective yield for the holder.

- *Kiwi Bonds*, introduced in 1985, are aimed at retail investors. These bonds are fixed-interest instruments issued on demand in six-month, one-, two- and four-year maturities. On issue, Kiwi Bond interest rates are related to the current market yields on wholesale government bonds (of comparable maturities). They are transferable and may be sold by the holder to another party.

The Reserve Bank maintains registers of government securities (and those of local authorities and other public bodies and of several state-owned enterprises). At 31 December 2006, the value of total government securities registered was $29.3 billion, with treasury bills accounting for $2.4 billion of this. Kiwi Bonds to the value of $315 million were also on issue at this date. (These figures exclude securities issued by state-owned enterprises.)

Table 26.06

Foreign exchange rates[1]
Trade-weighted index (TWI) percentage change

Month	USA mid-rate US$/NZ$[1]	UK mid-rate Stg/NZ$[1]	Australia mid-rate A$/NZ$[1]	Japan mid-rate Yen/NZ$[1]	Euro mid-rate E$/NZ$[1]	TWI-base June 1979=100	Percentage change Monthly	Annual
September								
1999	0.5224	0.3221	0.8053	56.05	0.4978	55.70	-1.9	-1.0
2000	0.4188	0.2922	0.7546	44.69	0.4805	48.30	-4.5	-13.0
2001	0.4198	0.2869	0.8280	49.86	0.4605	49.60	-2.8	3.0
2002	0.4699	0.3022	0.8587	56.74	0.4793	53.80	1.3	9.0
2003	0.5838	0.3627	0.8831	67.21	0.5202	62.20	-0.8	16.0
2004	0.6588	0.3674	0.9384	72.49	0.5392	67.1	0.9	8.0
2005	0.6995	0.3867	0.9144	77.68	0.5708	70.3	0.6	5.0
2006	0.6547	0.3469	0.8655	76.68	0.5140	65.7	4.0	-7.0
2007								
January	0.6953	0.3550	0.8883	83.75	0.5353	69.1	1.5	-2.0
February	0.6939	0.3542	0.8865	83.65	0.5303	68.8	-0.4	-1.0
March	0.6982	0.3585	0.8815	81.91	0.5271	68.6	-0.3	5.0
April	0.7347	0.3697	0.8880	87.35	0.5440	71.3	3.9	12.0
May	0.7325	0.3692	0.8885	88.43	0.5419	71.3	0.0	14.0
June	0.7559	0.3806	0.8980	92.66	0.5634	73.6	3.2	18.0
July	0.7858	0.3864	0.9065	95.58	0.5729	75.4	2.5	22.0
August	0.7285	0.3622	0.8766	85.16	0.5347	70.2	-6.9	11.0
September	0.7171	0.3554	0.8492	82.48	0.5162	68.3	-2.6	4.0

(1) All average exchange rates use representative 11.10am market mid-rates.

Source: Reserve Bank of New Zealand

KiwiSaver

The Dominion Post

Wellington couple Megan Rose and Jules van Cruysen sign up eight-month-old son Remy to the KiwiSaver scheme. Remy became the 500,000th KiwiSaver and poster boy for the scheme after his parents signed him up.

KiwiSaver is a savings initiative introduced by the Government on 1 July 2007. Its purpose is to make it easy for New Zealanders to save for their retirement.

Key features of the initiative:

- employees aged between 18 and 65 who are starting a new job are automatically enrolled in the scheme in most cases, and have eight weeks to decide if they want to opt out

- contributions are deducted from an employee's first pay at a before-tax rate of either 4 or 8 percent – employees choose the rate

- savings cannot be withdrawn until the member is eligible for New Zealand Superannuation – currently at age 65 – except in cases of financial hardship, serious illness, death, or permanent emigration

- after 12 months, members can take 'contribution holidays' of up to five years at a time

- employers have to make compulsory contributions, starting at 1 percent on 1 April 2008, and rising to 4 percent in 2011 (employers get a tax credit to help offset this)

- member benefits include a $1,000 government kick-start and matching contributions up to $1,040 each year

- after three years' saving, a first-home deposit subsidy is available for people who meet the criteria, up to a maximum of $5,000 for five years.

KiwiSaver is predominantly a work-based initiative, but is open to anyone aged under 65, including those who are self-employed or beneficiaries. Children can also join.

More than 500,000 people had joined KiwiSaver by the end of March 2008.

Source: The Treasury

Figure 26.03

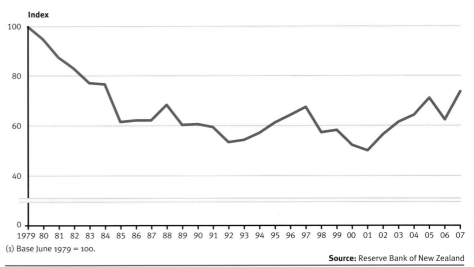

(1) Base June 1979 = 100.

Source: Reserve Bank of New Zealand

Foreign exchange

New Zealand has had a floating exchange rate since 1985. The value of the New Zealand dollar against other currencies is set solely by the market. However, the Reserve Bank retains the capacity to intervene in the foreign exchange market either to counter disorderly conditions in that market or for monetary policy purposes.

Intervention would involve buying or selling New Zealand dollars in exchange for other currencies, with the aim of restoring a smoothly-functioning private market. To maintain a capacity to do this, the Reserve Bank holds and manages the government's foreign exchange reserves, invested in a diversified portfolio of liquid foreign currency assets of about $7 billion.

Contributors and related websites

New Zealand Bankers' Association – www.nzba.org.nz

Office of the Banking Ombudsman – www.bankombudsman.org.nz

Reserve Bank of New Zealand – www.rbnz.govt.nz

Statistics New Zealand – www.stats.govt.nz

The Treasury – www.treasury.govt.nz

The Dominion Post

Wellington parents Josephine Kent and Danny Clark, and their children Michael (left), Samantha, Joshua, and baby Flynn. The Working for Families tax credit provides financial help for low- to middle-income families with children under 18 years who are living at home.

27 | Public sector finance

Central government finance

The New Zealand public sector management system is concerned with, and seeks to bring together, both the financial and non-financial aspects of public sector performance. Each element of the system is intended to reinforce other elements, in order to provide a comprehensive approach to implementing the government's strategy, facilitating high-quality decision making by management, and enabling effective scrutiny by Parliament.

The system is designed to help the government translate strategy into action, to promote informed decision making and accountability, and to encourage the state sector to be responsive and efficient.

The system achieves these aims through: planning, decision-making and scrutiny processes that culminate in passing of the government's budget; incentives for managing efficiently; and reporting and feedback processes. The system emphasises expected performance within the control of managers, delegating authority to achieve high-quality performance, providing incentives to perform to expected levels, and measuring achievements in a timely and consistent manner.

The system is continually examined and refined to meet emerging needs. A number of policy projects and pilots are underway that seek to improve areas such as Crown entity governance and accountability, departmental accountability and reporting, public service senior leadership and management talent, collaboration among departments, and relationships with non-government organisations.

Roles and responsibilities

The State Sector Act 1988 sets out the general duties and responsibilities of public service chief executives, and processes for their appointment and reappointment. Chief executives have contracts of up to five years, with tenure based on performance. They are recommended, appointed, employed, and reviewed by the independent State Services Commissioner, though Cabinet (operating through the governor-general in council) may veto the commissioner's appointment recommendation. As the legal employer of staff in their departments, public service chief executives have the power, within the bounds of general employment law, to hire and fire, set salaries, and negotiate conditions of employment.

Cabinet ministers are formally responsible for specifying performance expectations of departments. Departmental chief executives are, in turn, responsible to relevant ministers for delivering expected services (sometimes referred to as the government's 'purchase' interest), and maintaining the department's ability to keep delivering effectively, efficiently and economically (the 'ownership' interest). Services are placed firmly in the context of government policy goals. For these purposes, chief executives are given appropriate managerial decision-making authority. There are incentives to perform, and requirements for the presentation of performance information as a basis for monitoring and assessment. The chart below summarises this.

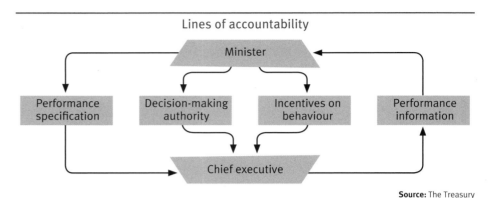

Lines of accountability

Source: The Treasury

Purchase and ownership interests The government's interest in the performance of a department is twofold:

- as the owner, seeking efficient stewardship of its resources
- as the purchaser of services, provided directly to the government or to third parties.

This distinction is made in the annual performance agreements for chief executives. The government looks for a balance between strong, healthy departments and value for money in their operations.

Setting objectives Setting objectives within the public service focuses mainly on outputs, rather than inputs or outcomes. With this focus, chief executives are responsible for the delivery of services – rather than any ultimate consequences (outcomes) of that service delivery. Outputs are placed firmly in the context of government policy goals.

The budget process

The fiscal responsibility provisions of the Public Finance Act 1989 require clear formulation and reporting by the government on its fiscal policy objectives. Using generally accepted accounting practice (GAAP), the following principles have been formulated to define responsible fiscal management:

- debt should be reduced to prudent levels
- operating expenses should not exceed operating revenues over a reasonable period
- Crown net worth should be maintained at sufficient levels to counter adverse events
- fiscal risks facing the government should be managed prudently
- fiscal policies should be consistent with predictable, stable tax rates.

As part of the budget process, the Minister of Finance must report on the government's long-term fiscal objectives and short-term fiscal intentions, and on the extent to which these are consistent with the above principles, and must provide justification for any inconsistencies.

These fiscal objectives must be presented to Parliament by 31 March – three months before the start of the financial year – in the Budget Policy Statement. In practice, the objectives are usually presented in the previous December, allowing debate on them to take place well before the budget is introduced.

The government maintains a baseline budget, projecting policies forward four years. Baseline updates occur regularly as the government makes adjustments in accordance with its strategic and fiscal objectives. Outside these budget update processes, amendments to the baseline are usually permitted only for fiscally-neutral adjustments, unavoidable or uncontrollable expenses, natural disasters or civil emergencies, recognition of existing liabilities, and capital investments supported by business plans and a sound business case.

The budget must be introduced to Parliament by the end of July and the associated appropriation legislation must be passed by the end of October.

Revised economic and fiscal forecasts are published half-yearly and immediately before a general election. These forecasts must be prepared on a GAAP basis and must include a statement of specific fiscal risks, including contingent liabilities, which describe, and quantify if possible, all specific and general fiscal risks associated with the forecasts.

The Minister of Finance, Dr Michael Cullen, giving his Budget 2007 speech in the media lock-up at Parliament.

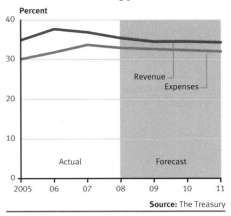

Figure 27.01

Government revenue and expenses
As a proportion of GDP
Year ending 30 June

Source: The Treasury

Accrual-based appropriations Parliament authorises expenditure of public money by ministers, departments, and offices of Parliament, through the appropriation process. Appropriations are made separately for expenses incurred on each class of outputs: benefits or other unrequited expenses, borrowing expenses, other expenses, capital injections, the purchase or development of capital assets, and the repayment of debt. This gives Parliament control over: outputs purchased from departments and others; what size balance sheets it thinks are needed to produce those outputs; and what resources (that do not involve production of outputs) it wants transferred among different groups in the community.

Charging for capital A common weakness in government financial management systems is the incentive for budget maximisation and for accumulating assets of low utility. To counter this, the government charges departments for the capital they use.

Cost allocations Focusing on outputs requires cost accounting systems that allocate costs, including the capital charge, to those outputs. Costs can then be compared with similar costs that would be incurred by other suppliers, both in the public and private sectors. These costing systems help ministers reprioritise and choose the appropriate mix of outputs in order to achieve desired outcomes. The systems also identify opportunities to improve output performance and to facilitate cost recovery where there are recognisable recipients of the service or output.

Cash management Before the start of every year, each department negotiates with the Treasury a profile of cash payments to the department during the year (updated as needs change). The Treasury operates a central cash management system that sweeps all departmental bank accounts each night and invests spare funds in the overnight money market.

Table 27.01 (overleaf) shows actual government expenses for the year ending June 2006 and 2007 using old GAAP (generally accepted accounting practice), and forecasts for 2007–11 using new GAAP.

Parliamentary scrutiny

Parliament's scrutiny of the government's financial performance involves the budget, and several reporting events through the year. Budget documents incorporate:

- the government's budget speech and fiscal strategy for the medium term (10 years)
- an economic and fiscal outlook, including the government's forecast financial statements
- estimates of the appropriations ministers seek from Parliament
- statements of intent for each government department.

Progress against the budget is reported monthly from the end of the first quarter. These reports are prepared on a GAAP basis, consistent with the forecasts, and must be published within six weeks of the end of the month. Annual financial statements must be prepared and audited within three months. Parliament and its committees scrutinise financial management of the executive, comparing actual performance with planned performance, in three ways:

- scrutiny of the government's intentions for the current year, as expressed in its budget proposals, and scrutiny of its actual performance, reported in the financial statements of the government
- examination of the actual performance of departments, as reported in their annual reports and financial statements, compared with plans laid a year earlier
- examination of the performance of state-owned enterprises and other non-departmental government entities.

New Zealand's foreign currency credit rating

Before 1983, New Zealand enjoyed a foreign currency credit rating of Triple A, which was at the top of international agencies Moody's, and Standard and Poor's, rating scales, and which put New Zealand in the same category as the United States, the United Kingdom, Japan, Germany, and France.

Deteriorating economic and fiscal conditions resulted in a series of downgrades over the next eight years to the point where New Zealand was at the bottom of the Double A rankings from both agencies.

During 1994, and again in 1996, New Zealand's credit rating was upgraded by both agencies in recognition of the improving economic and fiscal position.

During the early part of 1998, Moody's became increasingly concerned about the balance of payments position and the effects of the Asian financial crisis. These concerns culminated in a downgrade to Aa2 in September 1998. Standard and Poor's shared these concerns, but did not implement a downgrade, instead changing the outlook from stable to negative.

In March 2001, Standard and Poor's reviewed the rating and confirmed it as AA+ with a stable outlook, while in October 2001 Moody's upgraded its rating to Aaa.

Both ratings were unchanged at 31 December 2006.

Source: The Treasury

Table 27.01

Government expenses
Year ending 30 June

	Actual (Old GAAP)		Forecast (New GAAP)				
Expenses	2006	2007	2007	2008	2009	2010	2011
			$(million)				
Crown							
Depreciation & amortisation	2,708	3,144	3,023	3,296	3,417	3,579	3,696
Future new spending	..	..	..	..	1,908	3,838	5,786
Insurance	1,321	1,020	954	994	1,027	1,115	1,160
Interest	2,241	2,265	2,780	2,748	2,705	2,643	2,766
New operating, up to Budget 2008	..	..	80	314	329	398	460
Operating	26,731	28,634	28,132	28,997	29,471	30,030	30,408
Personnel	15,395	15,647	15,084	15,657	15,787	15,950	16,006
Social & official development assistance	16,688	18,307	18,300	19,908	20,975	22,095	23,190
Top-down adjustment	..	..	(500)	..	..	..	..
Total Crown	65,084	69,017	67,853	71,914	75,619	79,648	83,472
Subsidies & transfers							
Social assistance grants							
ACC payments	1,708	1,967	1,781	2,016	2,235	2,369	2,537
Domestic purposes benefit	1,493	1,468	1,467	1,456	1,454	1,467	1,491
Family support	1285	1,699	1,779	1,964	1,998	1,995	1,989
New Zealand Superannuation	6,414	6,810	6,807	7,292	7,605	7,998	8,440
Official development assistance	330	356	348	401	432	498	567
Other social assistance grants	4,392	5,012	5,118	5,880	6,373	6,874	7,255
Other transfer payments							
Student allowances	354	382	385	402	407	410	411
Unemployment benefit	712	613	615	497	471	484	500
Total subsidies & transfers	16,688	18,307	18,300	19,908	20,975	22,095	23,190
Personnel							
Defined benefit retirement plan[1]	1,392	1,222	192	214	230	248	247
Defined contribution retirement plan	206	227	654	637	596	558	534
Other personnel	279	..	334	311	318	335	358
Wages & salaries	13,518	14,198	13,904	14,495	14,643	14,809	14,867
Total personnel	15,395	15,647	15,084	15,657	15,787	15,950	16,006
Depreciation & amortisation							
Depreciation expense (by class of asset)							
Aircraft (ex-SME[2])	102	173	203	215	202	189	170
Buildings	880	940	929	989	1,017	1,039	1,044
Electricity distribution network	109	110	87	87	90	93	97
Electricity generation assets	198	229	248	276	324	380	388
Other assets	75	46	108	115	121	123	122
Other plant & equipment	905	954	685	739	772	788	795
Rail network	..	155	152	177	184	189	194
Specialist military equipment (SME)	187	238	239	286	310	335	445
State highways	252	299	242	255	270	286	302
Total depreciation	2,708	3,144	2,893	3,139	3,290	3,422	3,557
Amortisation & impairment on intangible assets	..	..	130	157	127	157	139
Total depreciation, amortisation & impairment on intangible assets	2,708	3,144	3,023	3,296	3,417	3,579	3,696
Other operating expenses							
Grants	1,578	1,688	1,936	2,085	2,222	2,259	2,269
Impairment on financial assets	1,925	2,885	1,439	133	101	103	104
Inventory expensed during period	..	..	211	231	230	229	239
Lottery prize payments	398	414	397	412	429	446	464
Other operating costs	21,682	22,272	22,749	24,795	25,123	25,593	25,895
Rental & leasing costs	820	887	812	823	841	853	869
Write-down on initial recognition of loans	328	488	588	518	525	547	568
Total other operating expenses	26,731	28,634	28,132	28,997	29,471	30,030	30,408

(1) Excluding actuarial gains/losses. (2) Specialist military equipment.
Note: GAAP is generally accepted accounting practice.
Symbol: .. figure not available

Source: The Treasury

Line-by-line consolidation of Crown financial statements

Changes to accounting standards introduced from Budget 2002 meant changes to the way Crown financial statements are prepared. The changes were required for consistency with GAAP and did not affect fiscal policy. Crown financial statements now record the revenues, expenses, assets and liabilities of all Crown-controlled entities (eg departments, State-owned enterprises and Crown entities) except tertiary educational institutions. Previously, only the net surplus, net investment and net worth of state-owned enterprises and Crown entities were recorded. Goods and services tax (GST) on Crown expenses has also been removed. Net worth and the operating balance are largely unaffected.

The Crown publishes fully consolidated ('total Crown') accounts as described above, but splits out 'core Crown' information. Core Crown revenues and expenses are similar to the previous presentation of the accounts, except that they remove GST on Crown expenses. This change results in some of the historical data contained in this yearbook being restated from data in previous yearbooks. This is because, where possible, historical data has been recast to be consistent with current treatment.

New Zealand international accounting standards

From 1 July 2007, the financial statements of the government must be prepared in accordance with New Zealand International Financial Reporting Standards (NZ IFRS). The fiscal forecast presented in Budget 2007 was prepared on an NZ IFRS basis. This means some data in the tables are not comparable with historical data published in previous yearbooks.

External reporting

The *Financial Statements of the Government of New Zealand* include the following key statements: financial performance; financial position; movements in equity; cash flows; borrowings; commitments; contingent liabilities; and unappropriated expenditure, expenses or liabilities.

Departmental financial statements contain the same key statements, as well as a statement of objectives, and a statement of service performance. An important feature of the New Zealand financial management system is the publication of financial statements for the whole of government, with an audit opinion attached, within three months of the end of the financial year. Very few countries account for government operations under accrual accounting rules.

Valuation problems are generally dealt with in conventional and pragmatic ways that provide a good estimate of net current value by using a realisable value, or a depreciated replacement cost approach. The underlying information systems provide new and superior information to the national statistical data collection for the System of National Accounts. The balance sheet can also indicate movements in net worth caused by the relationship between capital consumption and new investment. It can provide an indicator of whether the government is running down its estate to maintain current consumption.

In a real economic sense, the power of the government to tax its citizens provides a guarantee of revenue that is not available to a private sector company. This power can, however, be viewed as comparable with mutual or cooperative organisations that levy their members.

The levy is not treated as an asset, as members want to know the financial position of the organisation before exercise of the power to levy. Further, it is impossible to value this 'asset' with sufficient reliability, and any attempt to do so would drown other information in the balance sheet.

On the liabilities side, the value of future social welfare obligations is a similarly large item over which the government has significant discretion, and which is very difficult to quantify.

Figure 27.02 shows operating balances and forecasts, table 27.02 (overleaf) shows the Government's statement of financial performance and forecasts, while table 27.03 shows the Government's statement of financial position and forecasts. Table 27.04 shows the Government's statement of cash flows and forecasts.

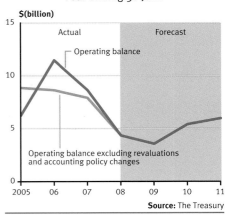

Figure 27.02

Operating balance
Year ending 30 June

Source: The Treasury

In June 2008, the Government finalised the purchase of Toll NZ's rail and ferry operations. This train was newly branded for the launch of KiwiRail on 1 July 2008.

Table 27.02

Statement of financial performance
Year ending 30 June

Revenue/expenses	Actual (Old GAAP)		Forecast (New GAAP)			
	2006	2007	2008	2009	2010	2011
	$(million)					
Crown revenue						
Taxation	51,973	52,938	54,173	55,691	58,269	61,351
Other sovereign revenue	3,411	3,568	3,693	3,757	3,846	3,931
Total levied through the Crown's sovereign power	55,384	56,506	57,866	59,448	62,115	65,282
Sales of goods & services	13,337	13,085	13,253	13,870	14,431	14,790
Interest revenue & dividends	5,828	5,819	3,366	3,585	3,636	3,756
Other	2,032	2,156	2,387	2,673	2,996	2,991
Total earned through Crown operations	21,197	21,060	19,006	20,128	21,063	21,537
Total revenue	76,581	77,566	76,872	79,576	83,178	86,819
Crown expenses						
Social security & welfare	18,969	20,239	21,271	22,025	22,888	23,768
Government superannuation fund	1,671	302	629	587	549	525
Health	9,262	9,932	11,699	11,987	12,290	12,287
Education	10,430	9,836	10,321	10,460	10,561	10,671
Core government services	2,046	4,088	2,132	2,158	2,236	2,501
Law & order	2,420	2,825	3,076	3,055	3,088	3,084
Defence	1,339	1,557	1,597	1,641	1,729	1,838
Transport & communications	5,986	7,473	7,671	7,759	7,841	7,782
Economic & industrial services	6,334	5,324	5,879	6,468	7,022	7,375
Primary services	1,219	1,265	1,319	1,314	1,314	1,316
Heritage, culture & recreation	2,361	2,036	2,218	2,174	2,207	2,240
Housing & community development	758	889	961	972	977	958
Other	48	66	79	77	66	73
Finance	2,652	3,069	2,748	2,705	2,644	2,808
Net foreign-exchange gains (losses)	(411)	116	..	..	..	..
New operating spending for Budget 2008	..	..	314	329	398	460
Future new spending	..	..	..	1,908	3,838	5,786
Top-down adjustment	..	..	..	..	..	..
Total expenses	65,084	69,017	71,914	75,619	79,648	83,472
Operating balance before gains (losses)	11,497	8,549	4,958	3,957	3,530	3,347
Net gains (losses) on financial instruments	..	..	1,377	1,516	1,684	1,922
Net gains (losses) on non-financial instruments	..	..	..	..	..	..
Net surplus (deficit) from associates & joint ventures	54	120	96	96	96	97
Gain (loss) from discounted operations	..	..	..	..	..	..
Operating balance from continuing activities	11,551	8,669	6,431	5,569	5,310	5,366
Gain (loss) attributed to interest in Air New Zealand	(78)	(6)	..	..	..	..
Operating balance	**11,473**	**8,663**	**6,431**	**5,569**	**5,310**	**5,366**

Symbol: .. figure not available

Source: The Treasury

Table 27.03

Statement of financial position
At 30 June

Assets	Actual (Old GAAP)		Forecast (New GAAP)			
	2006	2007	2008	2009	2010	2011
	$(million)					
Assets						
Cash & bank balances	4,168	4,629	3,196	3,435	3,319	3,272
Marketable securities, deposits & equity investments	27,668	33,270	32,885	32,203	31,468	34,008
Advances	9,099	10,266	15,087	16,798	17,362	17,920
Receivables	14,053	13,193	12,547	13,262	13,390	13,413
Inventories	907	992	982	1,046	1,071	1,080
Share investments	15,834	18,219	17,273	20,179	23,330	26,722
Prepayments & other assets	1,463	951	1,205	1,209	1,218	1,224
Property, plant & equipment	78,974	96,543	95,950	97,667	99,675	101,846
Equity accounted investments (including TEI[1])	5,475	6,305	6,647	6,812	6,914	7,003
Intangible assets (including goodwill)	630	608	1,555	1,529	1,456	1,392
Forecast new capital spending	..	..	184	751	1,557	2,460
Top-down capital adjustment	..	..	-200	-200	-200	-200
Total assets	158,271	184,976	187,311	194,691	200,560	210,140
Liabilities						
Deferred revenue	..	..	845	850	855	857
Defined benefit retirement plan	15,231	14,311	8,414	8,402	8,331	8,224
Insurance	12,715	13,735	19,011	20,042	21,162	22,328
Issued currency	3,362	3,360	3,730	3,914	4,110	4,316
Other borrowings	37,463	41,385	38,841	39,527	38,999	42,168
Payables	12,469	12,451	9,036	9,002	8,737	8,491
Provisions	3,664	3,898	3,850	3,786	3,819	3,812
Settlement deposits with the Reserve Bank	1,964	..	7,523	7,523	7,523	7,523
Total liabilities	86,868	89,140	91,250	93,046	93,536	97,719
Total assets less total liabilities	**71,403**	**95,836**	**96,061**	**101,645**	**107,024**	**112,421**

Table 27.03 continued

Statement of financial position
At 30 June

	Actual (Old GAAP)		Forecast (New GAAP)			
	2006	2007	2008	2009	2010	2011
			$(million)			
Net worth						
Taxpayer funds	33,477	42,140	48,239	53,844	59,236	64,630
Revaluation reserve	37,633	53,327	47,402	47,406	47,409	47,412
Cash flow hedge reserve	..	..	97	72	56	56
Financial asset reserve available for sale	..	..	13	13	13	13
Foreign exchange translation reserve	..	..	17	17	17	17
Total net worth attributable to the Crown	71,110	95,467	95,768	101,352	106,731	112,128
Net worth attributable to minority interest in Air New Zealand	293	369	293	293	293	293
Total net worth	**71,403**	**95,836**	**96,061**	**101,645**	**107,024**	**112,421**

(1) Tertiary education institutions.

Symbol: .. figure not available

Source: The Treasury

Table 27.04

Statement of cash flows
Year ending 30 June

	Actual (Old GAAP)		Forecast (New GAAP)			
	2006	2007	2008	2009	2010	2011
Revenue/expenses			$(million)			
Cash flows from operations						
Cash provided from						
Tax receipts	49,706	52,138	54,266	55,048	58,099	61,252
Other sovereign receipts	3,246	3,418	3,472	3,607	3,728	3,825
Interest	1,622	2,241	2,256	2,395	2,305	2,293
Dividends	117	435	504	586	676	772
Sales of goods & services	13,457	13,515	13,394	13,935	14,501	14,832
Other operating receipts	1,919	2,147	2,302	2,609	2,880	2,908
Total cash from operations	**70,067**	**73,894**	**76,194**	**78,180**	**82,189**	**85,882**
Cash disbursed to						
Subsidies & transfer payments	16,944	18,509	19,529	20,130	20,960	21,870
Personnel & operating payments	38,964	40,261	44,025	45,030	46,107	46,543
Interest expenses	2,047	2,504	2,530	2,610	2,622	2,667
Forecast for new spending	..	..	314	2,306	4,391	6,508
Top-down cash adjustment	..	..	..	..	..	..
Total cash to operations	**57,955**	**61,274**	**66,398**	**70,076**	**74,080**	**77,588**
Net cash flows from operations	**12,112**	**12,620**	**9,796**	**8,104**	**8,109**	**8,294**
Net cash flows from investing activities						
Sale/(purchase) of share investments & other securities	(5,859)	(8,273)	(4,491)	(1,155)	(983)	(4,289)
Sale/(purchase) of physical assets	(4,044)	(5,531)	(6,661)	(5,363)	(5,675)	(6,024)
Sale/(purchase) of intangible assets	..	..	(144)	(101)	(84)	(75)
Repayment/(issue) of advances	(1,637)	(1,791)	(1,628)	(1,449)	(59)	18)
Disposal/(acquisition) of investment in associates	..	..	(95)	(68)	(7)	(2)
Forecast for new capital spending	..	..	(184)	(567)	(806)	(903)
Top-down capital adjustment	..	..	..	..	..	..
Net cash flows from investing activities	**(11,540)**	**(15,595)**	**(13,203)**	**(8,703)**	**(7,614)**	**(11,275)**
Net cash flows from operating & investing activities	**572**	**(2,975)**	**(3,407)**	**(599)**	**495**	**(2,981)**
Net cash flows from financing activities						
Cash was provided from						
Issue of circulating currency	165	81	178	186	196	206
Issue/(repayment) of government stock	151	-334	2,223	(714)	(956)	2,159
Issue/(repayment) of other New Zealand-dollar borrowing	1,856	4,009	2,225	1,865	474	215
Repayment/(issue) of other New Zealand-dollar borrowing	(2,300)	(219)	(1,130)	(499)	(325)	354
Net cash flows from financing activities	**(128)**	**3,537**	**3,496**	**838**	**(611)**	**2,934**
Net increase/(decrease) in cash & cash equivalents	**444**	**562**	**89**	**239**	**(116)**	**(47)**
Opening cash equivalents	**3,710**	**4,168**	**3,107**	**3,196**	**3,435**	**3,319**
Foreign-exchange gain on opening cash	14	(101)	..	..	..	..
Closing cash balance	**4,168**	**4,629**	**3,196**	**3,435**	**3,319**	**3,272**

Symbol: .. figure not available

Source: The Treasury

Taxation

The New Zealand tax year is from 1 April to 31 March. Inland Revenue administers three principal acts: the Income Tax Act 2004, the Tax Administration Act 1994, and the Goods and Services Tax Act 1985. The Income Tax Act 2007 came into effect on 1 April 2008, with application to the 2008/09 and subsequent tax years.

Individuals

The New Zealand Government deducts taxes at income source, with a graduated-scale, pay-as-you-earn (PAYE) tax deducted from salaries and wages, and withholding tax deducted from various other specified categories of income.

The tax system has been simplified for most individual taxpayers – those who earn income solely from salary, wages, dividends and interest – by removing the requirement to file annual income tax returns. In certain circumstances, taxpayers receive a personal tax summary showing whether they have tax to pay or will receive a refund. Taxpayers are also able to request a personal tax summary.

The PAYE system requires employers to provide Inland Revenue with a monthly schedule detailing each employee's salary or wage income, PAYE deductions, and other information, such as student loan or child support payments.

Tax rates

Income tax is deducted under the Income Tax Act 2004 (Income Tax Act 2007 for income earned during the 2008/09 and subsequent tax years) and is charged on most income, including business profits, employment income, royalties, interest, dividends and pensions.

Rates of income tax for individual taxpayers in the 2006/07 tax year were:

- income up to and including $38,000 – 19.5 cents for every dollar of taxable income
- income over $38,000 and not exceeding $60,000 – 33 cents for every dollar of taxable income
- income over $60,000 – 39 cents for every dollar of taxable income.

The tax rates used for assessment are based on annual income (normally from 1 April to 31 March).

Resident withholding tax

Resident withholding tax (RWT) is tax deducted from interest and dividend income. For example, when banks pay interest, they deduct RWT before paying the recipient.

A flat RWT rate of 33 percent applies for dividends. Individual taxpayers receiving interest can elect to have RWT deducted at a rate of 19.5 percent, 33 percent or 39 percent.

If the recipient does not provide the interest payer with a taxpayer identification number, a non-declaration rate of 39 percent applies. Certain recipients of interest or dividends (such as charitable or non-profit organisations, sports clubs and others) may apply for exemption from RWT.

Imputation credits

Dividends received from a New Zealand company may have imputation credits and/or withholding payment credits attached. An imputation credit is a tax credit received from a company for tax it has already paid on its profits. It therefore avoids the double payment of tax (by the company and its shareholders) on the same income.

Withholding payment credits arise when a New Zealand company has paid dividend withholding payments on foreign dividends received.

The imputation system integrates personal and business tax for company income distributed as dividends, and allows the benefit for tax paid by the company to be passed on to the shareholder.

Since April 2003, eligible Australian companies are able to elect to be a New Zealand imputation credit account company; since October 2003, New Zealand shareholders in these Australian companies are able to claim imputation credits allocated for their share of New Zealand tax paid by the company.

Rebates

Rebates are reductions from the amount of tax to be paid. Inland Revenue administers several types of rebates for personal taxpayers. These include:

- a rebate for low-income New Zealand resident taxpayers
- a transitional tax allowance for certain full-time employees
- a child rebate for taxpayers aged 18 or under, provided they turned 18 after 1 January of the preceding tax year and that they attended school

- a housekeeper/childcare rebate for working parents who pay for childcare, or for disabled people who pay for help with childcare or housekeeping – the maximum rebate is $310
- a rebate for charitable donations, which is 33.3 percent of all qualifying donations (the minimum qualifying charitable donation is $5).

Company taxation

Company taxation is deducted under the Income Tax Act 2004. (Income Tax Act 2007 for income earned during the 2008/09 and subsequent tax years). The company rate of taxation differs from that of individuals, in that a company does not get any of the exemptions or rebates individuals are entitled to, and a flat tax rate applies.

From the 2008/09 income year, the company tax rate reduced from 33 percent to 30 percent.

Certain companies can get a rebate for gifts of money to charitable organisations, but there is a threshold to the amount they can claim.

Company taxation in the year ending 30 June 2007 produced $9.622 billion.

A company resident in New Zealand is assessable on all income, whether earned in New Zealand or elsewhere. A company is a New Zealand resident if one or more of the following applies:

- it is incorporated in New Zealand
- its head office is in New Zealand
- its centre of management is in New Zealand
- control of the company by its directors is exercised in New Zealand.

Companies that maintain imputation accounts receive a tax credit when they pay tax on their taxable income, under the Income Tax Act 2004, and these credits are attached to dividends paid to shareholders.

A company not resident in New Zealand is liable for tax only on income earned in New Zealand. Non-resident companies are taxed at 33 cents in the dollar for any activity they conduct in New Zealand. For most non-residents who simply earn interest or dividend income, non-resident withholding tax is the final New Zealand tax on that income.

Fringe benefit tax

Fringe benefit tax (FBT) is a tax on certain non-monetary benefits employees receive from their employer as part of their employment, for example, a company car. It is payable at the rate of 64 percent. However, employers have the option of using the multi-rate calculation process, which reflects the remuneration level of those employees receiving benefits. FBT is payable by the employer on an annual or quarterly basis.

Taxable fringe benefits include private use of a motor vehicle by an employee; low-interest loans; free, subsidised or discounted transport and other goods and services; and the employer's contribution to accident, sickness, or death benefit fund and insurance policies.

Total FBT collected in the year ending 30 June 2007 was $467.7 million.

The Dominion Post

Wine is one of the goods on which excise duty is levied. Excise duty is a tax imposed by the government on certain products such as alcoholic beverages, tobacco products, and fuels.

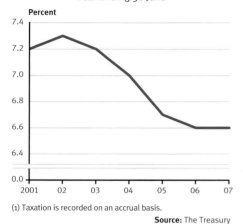

Figure 27.03

Customs and excise receipts
As a proportion of total consolidated account taxation[1]
Year ending 30 June

(1) Taxation is recorded on an accrual basis.

Source: The Treasury

Goods and services tax

Goods and services tax (GST) is a value-added tax charged at 12.5 percent on supplies of most goods and services provided in New Zealand. GST was introduced at a rate of 10 percent in 1986 and increased to 12.5 percent in 1989.

All companies and individual traders with an annual turnover of $40,000 or more must register for GST.

People registered for GST must charge GST on the goods and services they supply. GST-registered suppliers of goods and services pay GST on purchases made and expenses incurred in the course of their business, but may claim it back later. Registered people must pay the GST they have collected, less that on their purchases, to Inland Revenue.

Some activities, such as salaries and wages, hobby activities, and private sales of personal and domestic items, are not taxable supplies.

GST is not charged on exempt supplies. Exempt supplies include residential property rentals, the sale of donated goods, and services by non-profit organisations.

Total GST collected in the year ending 30 June 2007 was $9.71 billion.

Excise duty

The Customs and Excise Act 1996 provides for the imposition of excise duty on alcoholic beverages, tobacco products, super and regular grade petroleum, liquefied petroleum gas, and compressed natural gas (when compressed by a natural gas fuelling facility for use as a motor vehicle fuel). Similarly, excise-equivalent duty is levied on the same goods when they are imported into New Zealand.

The excise regime is dependent on the licensing of areas within which excisable goods may be manufactured or stored, and within which customs powers may be exercised. These customs-controlled areas – including manufacturing areas, off-site storage areas, export warehouses, and duty-free shops – may be licensed for the purpose of:

- the manufacture of excisable goods (for example breweries, wineries, tobacco manufacturing plants, distilleries, petrol refineries)
- the deposit, keeping or securing of imported goods, without payment of duty on the goods, pending export of those goods (for example ships' provedores)
- storage by, or for, the manufacturer or the first owner of wine manufactured in New Zealand, where the wine cannot physically be accommodated within the area in which it was manufactured (that is, off-site storage of wine)
- storage of imported goods, or goods manufactured in a manufacturing area, of a kind that are subject to duty and on which duty has not been paid, pending the sale of those goods to people departing to, or arriving from, a country outside New Zealand, or to people who are entitled to the supply of goods free of duty. These premises are usually duty-free shops.

Excise duty must be paid when the excisable product is removed from the place of manufacture or, in the case of wine, from the off-site storage area, other than to an export warehouse or to another customs-controlled area for further manufacture. Liability for excise-equivalent duty is triggered by importation of the goods.

Excise-equivalent duty must be paid in accordance with the customs-deferred payment system, or before the goods are delivered from customs control.

Rates of excise duty and excise-equivalent duty are contained in the third schedule to the Act. The legislation provides discretionary authority for the government to apply increases to the rates of excise and excise-equivalent duties on alcoholic beverages and tobacco products, in accordance with movement in the consumers price index. Adjustments may be made to alcoholic beverage rates on 1 July of any year, and to rates of duty on tobacco products on 1 January in any year. Excise-equivalent duty rates are similarly adjusted.

Similar provision exists for the rates of excise and excise-equivalent duty on petroleum, with adjustments in accordance with movement in the consumers price index able to be applied on 1 April of any year.

Figure 27.03 shows customs and excise receipts for the year ending June 2001–07 as a proportion of consolidated account taxation.

Fuel excise and road user charges

Excise and excise-equivalent duty is paid on all purchases of petrol, liquid petroleum gas (LPG) and compressed natural gas (CNG). The excise and excise-equivalent duty is incorporated into the pump price of fuel on a per-litre basis.

In 2008, the excise duty on petrol was 42.5 cents per litre (excluding GST). The duty on LPG was 10.4 cents per litre and the duty on CNG was 10.5 cents per litre.

The Road User Charges Act 1977 requires all vehicles that are powered by diesel or that weigh over 3.5 tonnes to purchase a road user charge licence, depending on the gross weight of the vehicle and the distance to be travelled. Road user charges are based on the wear and tear that a vehicle causes to the land transport network. The cost for a road user charge licence varies, depending on the number of axles, the number of wheels and the weight of the vehicle.

At May 2008, 23.8 cents per litre of petrol excise duty, and the total excise duty for LPG and CNG, was paid into the National Land Transport Fund (NLTF). From 1 July 2008, all excise collected from petrol has gone to the NLTF. Already, all road user charges and motor vehicle registration fees are paid into the NLTF. Since 2004, appropriations have also been made to the NLTF from general Crown revenue, on a case-by-case basis, to enable the land transport network to meet user demand.

The Customs and Excise Act 1996 was amended to allow the annual option of increasing, by any rate up to the rate of inflation, the road user charges for 1- to 6-tonne vehicles, and that portion of petrol excise duty that is paid into the NLTF. The first increase took place on 1 April 2006. The NLTF portion of petrol excise and 1- to 6-tonne road user charge rates were indexed to the movement of inflation on 1 April 2007. At this time, for vehicles weighing over 6 tonnes, rates were increased by an average of 11 percent, the first increase in 17 years.

The NLTF fund contributes to the maintenance and construction of New Zealand's land transport network, alternatives to roading such as public transport, administration, traffic enforcement, and road safety education and publicity.

Gift duty

Gift duty is payable by a person giving a gift to another. It is charged at a progressive rate, according to the total value of gifts given by a donor within a 12-month period. Dutiable gifts with a total combined value of $27,000 in any 12-month period do not have gift duty charged on them. From there, the rate rises from 5 percent, to a top rate of 25 percent on gifts exceeding $72,000 in any 12-month period. Dutiable gifts include the transfer of property such as company shares or land, any form of payment, and forgiveness or reduction of debt.

A gift duty statement must be provided to Inland Revenue when the value of the gift exceeds $12,000, or when the value of gifts within the previous 12 months exceeds $12,000.

Stamp duty

Stamp duty was abolished from 21 May 1999, but remains payable on the sale and lease of commercial land by transfer, or by lease if the transaction was completed before that date.

Cheque duty

Cheque duty is payable, with exceptions, on all cheques and other bills of exchange made or drawn. Licensed banks are required to forward quarterly statements containing particulars of all bill-of-exchange forms to Inland Revenue. Licensed printers who print prepaid bills of exchange are required to forward statements to Inland Revenue monthly.

Cheque duty is set at the rate of 5 cents per bill of exchange, or 5 cents per form when the duty is prepaid.

The Dominion Post

The National Land Transport Fund contributes to traffic enforcement. Here, Police launch their first checkpoint and booze bus patrols of the 2007 Christmas season in Wellington.

Otago Daily Times

Gaming machine operators pay a levy to Inland Revenue to contribute to the costs of developing, managing, and delivering an integrated problem-gambling strategy.

Gaming duty

Gaming duty consists of totalisator duty, lottery duty, gaming machine duty, and casino duty.

Totalisator duty is payable at the rate of 4 percent of the betting profits for all racing betting (horses and greyhounds), sports betting, and fixed-odds racing betting. The New Zealand Racing Board must forward a statement to Inland Revenue by the 20th of each month.

Lottery duty is payable at the rate of 5.5 percent of the nominal value of all tickets in the drawing of a lottery, including instant games, lotteries, and prize competitions promoted by the New Zealand Lotteries Commission. Organisers of a lottery are required to supply Inland Revenue with a statement of lottery duty payable, and pay it within 14 days of drawing the lottery.

Gaming machine duty is payable at the rate of 20 percent of profits from dutiable games played on gaming machines. Gaming machine operators are required to send a statement to Inland Revenue each month, setting out the gaming machine duty, and must pay the duty by the due date.

Casino duty is payable at the rate of 4 percent on the casino wins of any casino. Casino operators are required to send a statement of the casino wins to Inland Revenue and pay casino duty on a monthly basis.

Total gaming duties assessed in the year ending 30 June 2007 were $271.2 million.

Problem gambling levy

The Government introduced a levy on player expenditure from 1 October 2004. The purpose of the levy is to recover the cost of developing, managing, and delivering an integrated problem-gambling strategy.

The levy is payable on gaming profits and is collected through monthly returns. The following levy rates (GST exclusive) applied from 1 July 2007, and will be reviewed every three years:

- casino operators – 0.72 percent
- non-casino gaming machine operators – 1.70 percent
- New Zealand Racing Board – 0.55 percent
- New Zealand Lotteries Commission – 0.20 percent.

The levy rate takes account of the level of attributable harm and total revenue for each sector. Revenue collected for the year ending 30 June 2007 was nearly $15.0 million, made up of levies from:

- casino operators – $2,387,422
- non-casino gaming machine operators – $10,624,655
- New Zealand Racing Board – $1,531,760
- New Zealand Lotteries Commission – $440,083.

International tax

Non-residents are taxed in New Zealand only if their income is from a New Zealand source. If the income is interest, dividends or royalties, a person is liable for non-resident withholding tax (NRWT). NRWT is deducted by a payer of non-resident withholding income.

Provided certain criteria are met, the resident payer of interest can seek registration as an approved issuer and pay an approved issuer levy of 2 percent. The non-resident may be able to claim NRWT as a credit in the country of residence – subject to the tax regime in that country. However, the approved issuer levy cannot be claimed as a credit as it is not a tax and has not been deducted from the interest.

For tax purposes, individuals are considered to be resident in New Zealand when they fulfil one or more of the following criteria:

- they have an enduring relationship with New Zealand, that is, strong financial, personal or other ties with New Zealand – each case is considered on its facts
- they have been in New Zealand for more than 183 days in any 12-month period
- they are away from New Zealand in the service of the New Zealand Government.

Individuals cease to be New Zealand residents if they are absent from New Zealand for more than 325 days (about 11 months) in any 12-month period, and they do not have an enduring relationship with New Zealand during that time.

Pensions New Zealand residents who receive a pension from a foreign country, including those with which New Zealand has a double tax agreement, are generally subject to tax in New Zealand. If the person receiving the pension is taxed in the country of origin, credit is generally allowed against New Zealand income tax for the overseas tax paid, up to the amount of New Zealand tax on that income.

The Dominion Post

Eric King-Turner and his wife Doris arrived from England in February 2008 to start a new life in Wellington. At 102 years, Eric is New Zealand's oldest immigrant. New Zealand has double tax agreements with 34 countries, including the United Kingdom. This means that a person receiving a pension taxed in the country of origin is generally allowed a credit against New Zealand income tax for the overseas tax paid.

Double tax agreements New Zealand has agreements to avoid double taxation with the following countries: Australia, Austria, Belgium, Canada, Chile, the People's Republic of China, Denmark, Fiji, Finland, France, Germany, India, Indonesia, Ireland, Italy, Japan, the Republic of Korea, Malaysia, Mexico, the Netherlands, Norway, the Philippines, Poland, the Russian Federation, Singapore, South Africa, Spain, Sweden, Switzerland, Taiwan, Thailand, the United Arab Emirates, the United Kingdom, and the United States.

A visitor from one of these countries who has received income from New Zealand sources should refer to the relevant agreement at the following link: www.taxpolicy.ird.govt.nz/international/DTA.

Social assistance

Working for Families is a package designed to help make it easier to be in paid work and raise a family. Entitlement is based on combined family income and the number and age of children.

The Working for Families package has three components: Working for Families Tax Credits (administered jointly by Inland Revenue and the Ministry of Social Development), Childcare Assistance, and the Accommodation Supplement (administered solely by the Ministry of Social Development).

Other forms of social assistance include child support and student loans for tertiary students.

Working for Families tax credits are paid to families with children aged 18 years or under, to help with the cost of raising a family. There are four types of payments: family tax credit, parental tax credit, in-work tax credit, and minimum family tax credit. If the family receives an income-tested benefit, family tax credit can be paid by the Ministry of Social Development. If the family receives an income-tested benefit they are not entitled to the other three credits.

Family tax credit – is the main part of the Working for Families initiative and involves a payment to eligible families for each child living at home, up to the age of 18. How much is paid depends on how many children are living at home and how old they are, and on the combined family income.

In-work tax credit – from the 2006/07 tax year, child tax credits were gradually phased out and replaced by the in-work tax credit. However, in some circumstances, families that do not qualify for the in-work tax credit may continue to receive child tax credits, until they no longer meet the eligibility requirements. The in-work tax credit is $60 per week for up to three children and a further $15 for each additional child.

Parental tax credit – provides extra financial support, to a maximum of $150 per child per week, for the first eight weeks after a child is born.

Minimum family tax credit – tops up a family's total income to at least $22,119 a year before tax – $347 after tax each week (2007/08 year). If either partner has been injured and is receiving accident compensation payments, but would usually be working, they may still be eligible for the minimum family tax credit.

For the minimum family tax credit, and the in-work tax credit, at least one parent must be in paid work. For the minimum family tax credit this must be work for salary or wages. The combined weekly hours of work in a two-parent family must be at least 30 hours; in a single-parent family, it is at least 20 hours.

Child support – Inland Revenue administers the Child Support Act 1991. Child support is money paid by parents not living with their children to help financially support those children. To qualify for child support, the child must be under the age of 19, be a New Zealand citizen or 'ordinarily resident' in New Zealand, be not married or in a civil union or in a de facto relationship, and be financially dependent.

The person caring for the child (the custodian) generally applies for child support. Custodians are sometimes people other than parents, such as grandparents, a member of the whānau or extended family, or Child Youth and Family. In these cases, both parents may be required to pay child support. Custodians receiving a sole-parent benefit must apply for child support.

The Child Support Act 1991 sets a minimum annual rate of child support, and a maximum income amount taken into account in calculating an assessment. The paying parent must pay the rate calculated under the child support formula, within these minimum and maximum limits.

A three-step calculation (the child support formula) is used to work out how much child support a paying parent needs to pay. The formula uses the paying parent's taxable income, less a set living allowance (the amount of which depends on their living arrangements, eg whether they have a partner and/or children living with them), and multiplies the result by a percentage – based on the number of children the paying parent pays child support for.

Inland Revenue collects payments from the paying parent and passes them on to the custodian to assist with care of the child, or to the government to help offset the cost of the benefit, if the custodian is receiving a sole-parent benefit. The payment is passed on only when it has been received from the paying parent.

Otago Daily Times

Students attend a first-year physics lecture at Otago University. Since 1 April 2006, student loans for borrowers living in New Zealand for 183 consecutive days or more have been interest-free, whether they are still studying or not.

In 2007, there were approximately 174,000 paying parents, 177,000 custodians and 285,000 children for whom child support was paid. The overall debt collection rate (excluding penalties) is approximately 88.5 percent. In the year ending 30 June 2007, Inland Revenue collected $346.6 million from paying parents, of which $173.0 million was paid to custodians and $173.6 million was paid to the Government.

Student loans The Ministry of Education manages policy aspects of the student loan scheme, and StudyLink processes loan applications and administers payments to borrowers. Loans are transferred to Inland Revenue on 28 February following the end of the calendar year in which a borrower was studying.

Inland Revenue assesses and collects loan repayments until the loan is repaid. Interest rates and repayment thresholds are reviewed annually, and are effective from 1 April to 31 March.

The student loan total annual interest rate for the 2007/08 financial year was 6.8 percent and the repayment threshold for the 2007/08 tax year was $17,784. Borrowers earning over the repayment threshold are legally required to repay 10 cents in the dollar of every dollar earned over the repayment threshold. Those on a salary or wages generally have their loan repayments deducted at source, along with PAYE deductions.

Since 1 April 2006, student loans for borrowers living in New Zealand for 183 consecutive days or more (with some exceptions to this requirement) have been interest free.

Government statistics

Table 27.06 (overleaf) is from the Government's accounts. As well as taxes and duties collected by Inland Revenue, the accounts also include taxes and duties collected by the New Zealand Customs Service. It shows tax revenue for the 2006 and 2007 June years, and forecasts for 2008–11.

Taxation review authorities

The Taxation Review Authorities Act 1994 established taxation review authorities. There are two authorities, each consisting of one person who is either a district court judge, or a barrister or solicitor of the High Court with no fewer than seven years practice. The authorities are appointed by the Governor-General on recommendation of the Minister of Justice.

The authorities sit as judicial authorities for hearing and determining objections and challenges to assessments of tax, or to decisions or determinations of the Commissioner of Inland Revenue.

Table 27.05

Public account taxation and national disposable income[1][2][3]
Year ending 30 June

Year	National disposable income	Public account taxation — Total	National disposable income Percent
	$(million)	$(million)	Percent
1997	77,918	30,546	39.2
1998	81,630	31,511	38.6
1999	84,062	30,525	36.3
2000	87,975	32,248	36.7
2001	92,366	34,995	37.9
2002	100,545	36,459	36.3
2003	106,168	40,168	37.8
2004	113,871	43,008	37.8
2005	119,859	47,118	39.3
2006	124,239	52,444	42.2
2007	130,573	53,411	40.9

(1) Data from 1997 to 2005 has been revised. (2) Accounts prepared on an accrual basis. (3) The public account taxation series includes the removal of goods and services tax (GST) on Crown expenses.

Source: Statistics New Zealand

Table 27.06

Breakdown of tax revenue
Year ending 30 June

Revenue/expenses	Actual (Old GAAP) 2006	2007	Forecast (New GAAP) 2008	2009	2010	2011
	$(million)					
Direct income						
Individuals						
Source deductions	19,985	21,085	22,334	23,695	25,094	26,619
Other persons	5,075	4,440	4,553	4,774	5,169	5,529
Refunds	(953)	(1,080)	(1,102)	(1,130)	(1,205)	(1,260)
Fringe benefit tax	451	468	474	498	519	546
Total individuals	**24,558**	**24,913**	**26,259**	**27,837**	**29,577**	**31,434**
Corporate tax						
Gross companies tax	9,439	8,618	8,222	7,469	7,765	8,190
Refunds	(270)	(296)	(255)	(260)	(260)	(260)
Non-resident withholding tax	1,096	1,189	1,005	1,002	1,020	1,009
Foreign-source dividend withholding payments	160	149	102	86	86	86
Total corporate	**10,425**	**9,660**	**9,074**	**8,297**	**8,611**	**9,025**
Other income tax						
Resident withholding tax on interest income	1,880	2,227	2,340	2,441	2,362	2,376
Resident withholding tax on dividend income	74	89	92	114	249	296
Estate & gift duties	3	2	2	2	2	2
Total other	**1,957**	**2,318**	**2,434**	**2,557**	**2,613**	**2,674**
Total direct income tax revenue	**36,940**	**36,891**	**37,767**	**38,691**	**40,801**	**43,133**
Indirect income						
Goods & services tax						
Gross goods & services tax	18,367	19,527	19,726	20,704	21,729	22,844
Refunds	(7,664)	(8,325)	(8,231)	(8,711)	(9,396)	(9,948)
Total indirect	**10,703**	**11,202**	**11,495**	**11,993**	**12,333**	**12,896**
Other indirect taxation						
Petroleum fuels excise	852	819	903	921	938	955
Tobacco excise	834	238	148	150	152	154
Customs duty	1,083	1,836	1,865	1,849	1,873	1,921
Road user charges	731	786	877	933	988	1,043
Alcohol excise	516	553	586	614	641	670
Gaming duties	275	245	215	214	212	212
Motor vehicle fees	221	222	219	228	233	239
Energy resources levies	73	54	34	34	34	64
Approved issuer levy & cheque duty	83	92	64	64	64	64
Total other indirect	**4,668**	**4,845**	**4,911**	**5,007**	**5,135**	**5,322**
Total indirect taxation	**15,371**	**16,047**	**16,406**	**17,000**	**17,468**	**18,218**
Total tax revenue collected	**52,311**	**52,938**	**54,173**	**55,691**	**58,269**	**61,351**

Source: The Treasury

Assets and liabilities

Public debt management

The New Zealand Debt Management Office (NZDMO) is responsible for managing the government's New Zealand-dollar and foreign-currency debt, some liquidity assets, and overall net cashflows within an appropriate risk management framework.

Principal risks managed are market, credit, liquidity, funding, concentration, and operational risk.

In 1988, NZDMO introduced reforms to public sector cash management, involving the centralisation of surplus cash funds for investment and cash management, and decentralisation of responsibility for payments and other banking operations to departments.

Separation of the government's financial management from monetary policy implementation, which is the responsibility of the Reserve Bank of New Zealand, enables NZDMO to focus on defining a low-risk net liability portfolio for the government and implementing it in a cost-effective manner.

Before March 1985, the government borrowed externally to finance the balance of payments deficit and maintain a fixed exchange rate. Since the adoption of a freely floating exchange rate, the government has borrowed externally only to finance foreign-exchange reserves. All other borrowing has been in the domestic market.

Net foreign-currency debt was eliminated in September 1996 through the proceeds from asset sales and, since 1994, fiscal surpluses.

Debt record

New Zealand has always paid, when due, the full amount of principal, interest and amortisation requirements on its external and internal debt, including guaranteed debt. The government's long-term fiscal objectives include running operating surpluses, on average, over the economic cycle, to allow a build-up of assets to meet future New Zealand Superannuation costs.

Total debt is to be managed at prudent levels, with gross sovereign-issued debt broadly stable at around 20 percent of GDP over the next 10 years. Quantifiable contingent liabilities of the Government, including the Reserve Bank of New Zealand, state-owned enterprises and Crown entities, amounted to approximately $5.2 billion at 30 June 2007. Figure 27.04 shows gross and net public debt as a proportion of GDP for June 1977–2007.

Table 27.07 is one of the key statements from the Government's financial statements, the statement of borrowings for the 2006–07 June years, and forecasts for 2008–11.

Table 27.08 shows central government debt from June 1991–2007.

Table 27.09 (overleaf) shows the maturity profile of New Zealand Government debt at 30 June 2007.

Table 27.08

Gross sovereign-issued debt
At 30 June

Year	Amount $(million)	Per head of population $
1997	35,972	9,513
1998	37,892	9,932
1999	36,712	9,573
2000	36,041	9,342
2001	36,761	9,473
2002	36,202	9,169
2003	36,086	8,961
2004	35,527	8,692
2005	35,045	8,477
2006	35,461	8,474
2007	36,150	8,550

Source: Statistics New Zealand

Table 27.07

Statement of borrowings
Year ending 30 June

	Actual (Old GAAP)		Forecast (New GAAP)			
	2006	2007	2008	2009	2010	2011
	$(million)					
Borrowings						
Government retail stock	532	471	358	358	358	358
Settlement deposits with the Reserve Bank	1,964	7,507	7,523	7,523	7,523	7,523
Derivatives in loss	..	..	300	186	174	154
Finance lease liabilities	..	..	958	949	941	937
Other borrowings	8,651	27,772	16,707	18,548	19,119	20,150
Total borrowings	**11,147**	**35,750**	**25,846**	**27,564**	**28,115**	**29,122**
Foreign-currency debt						
United States dollars	14,430	(3,937)	..	..	..	..
Japanese yen	404	(603)	..	..	..	..
European & other currencies	3,898	(857)	..	..	..	..
Total foreign currency debt	18,732	(5,397)	7,321	4,745	3,132	4,187
Borrowings – sovereign guaranteed	**29,879**	**30,353**	**33,167**	**32,309**	**31,247**	**33,309**
Borrowings – non-sovereign guaranteed						
Non-sovereign guaranteed debt						
New Zealand	7,198	8,900	..	..	..	..
United States dollars	1,794	1,564	..	..	..	..
Japanese yen	279	133	..	..	..	..
European & other currencies	277	435	..	..	..	..
Total non-sovereign guaranteed debt	**9,548**	**11,032**	**13,197**	**14,741**	**15,275**	**16,382**
Total borrowings (gross debt)	**39,427**	**41,385**	**46,364**	**47,050**	**46,522**	**49,691**
Less						
Financial assets[1]						
Marketable securities, deposits & equity investments.						
New Zealand dollars	8,003	44,554	..	..	..	..
United States dollars	11,080	(10,860)	..	..	..	..
Japanese yen	615	(286)	..	..	..	..
European & other currencies	7,970	(191)	..	..	..	..
Reserve position at International Monetary Fund	458	183	..	..	..	..
New Zealand equity investments	2,721	3,598	..	..	..	..
Foreign equity investments	12,673	14,491	..	..	..	..
Total marketable securities, deposits & equity investments	**43,520**	**51,489**	**..**	**..**	**..**	**..**
Advances & cash		..	..	..	..	..
Student loans	5,569	6,011	..	..	..	..
Other advances	3,189	4,255	..	..	..	..
Cash	4,168	4,629	..	..	..	..
Total advances & cash	12,926	14,895	..	..	..	..
Total financial assets	**56,446**	**66,384**	**..**	**..**	**..**	**..**
Borrowings less financial assets	**(17,019)**	**(24,999)**	**..**	**..**	**..**	**..**
Net New Zealand-dollar (assets)/debt	(5,569)	(18,829)	..	..	..	..
Net foreign currency (assets)/debt	(11,450)	(6,170)	..	..	..	..
Borrowings less financial assets	**(17,019)**	**(24,999)**	**..**	**..**	**..**	**..**

(1) Includes restricted assets.
Symbol: .. figure not available

Source: The Treasury

Figure 27.04

Public debt
As a percentage of GDP
Year ending 30 June

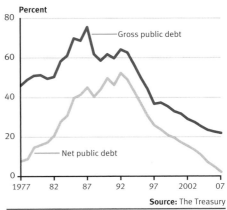

Source: The Treasury

Table 27.09

Refinancing/repricing risk[1]
Periods within which assets and liabilities will mature or reprice
At 30 June 2007

Asset/liability	Total	0–12 months	1–2 years	2–5 years	5–10 years	10+ years
				$(million)		
Domestic assets						
Cash & deposits	**3,618**	0	0	0	0	0
Marketable securities	**25,005**	20,235	1,879	1,073	869	949
Others	**3,642**	2,890	618	1	0	133
Domestic liabilities						
Government stock	**16,834**	0	2,571	6,135	5,608	2,520
Treasury bills	**2,080**	2,080	0	0	0	0
Retail stock	**471**	430	33	8	0	0
Others	**25,266**	30,257	(1,195)	(1,270)	(1,328)	(1,198)
Foreign assets						
Cash & deposits	**1,098**	1,098	0	0	0	0
Marketable securities	**6,952**	4,684	184	490	1,122	472
Others	**15,803**	15,799	0	0	0	4
Foreign liabilities						
Foreign currency debt	**(3,266)**	(5,774)	354	837	940	377

(1) Refinancing/repricing risk refers to the risk that maturing debt is refinanced, maturing assets are reinvested, or instruments repriced are at an acceptable yield.

Source: The Treasury

Contributors and related websites

Accident Compensation Corporation – www.acc.co.nz

Inland Revenue – www.ird.govt.nz

KiwiSaver – www.kiwisaver.govt.nz

Land Transport New Zealand – www.landtransport.govt.nz

Local Government New Zealand – www.localgovtnz.co.nz

Ministry of Social Development – www.msd.govt.nz

Ministry of Transport – www.transport.govt.nz

New Zealand Customs Service – www.customs.govt.nz

Reserve Bank of New Zealand – www.rbnz.govt.nz

State Services Commission – www.ssc.govt.nz

Statistics New Zealand – www.stats.govt.nz

The Treasury – www.treasury.govt.nz

Work and Income New Zealand – www.winz.govt.nz

Glossary

Abortion Fetal loss excluding stillbirths, usually during the first 20 weeks of gestation. 'Induced' abortions are those initiated voluntarily with the intention of terminating a pregnancy. All other abortions are called 'spontaneous', even if an external cause such as injury or high fever is involved. All abortion statistics and derived abortion rates are based on the number of legally-induced abortions. No information is available on spontaneous or illegal abortions.

Accreditation The process by which a State (eg Canada) formally agrees to accept a head of mission from a second State (eg New Zealand) as that country's representative, with authority to act on the second State's behalf. A head of mission can be cross-accredited to act in a third State (eg Jamaica) while living outside its border (eg in Canada).

***Ad valorem* duty** A type of duty that is paid as a percentage of the imported goods' value.

Additions to fixed assets Purchases of new and second-hand fixed assets, and the cost of work done by a firm's employees in producing, constructing and installing fixed assets for its own use.

ANZSIC06 The Australia New Zealand Standard Industry Classification is a hierarchical industrial classification that groups businesses based on the types of economic activities they carry out.

Assumption A statement about a future course of behaviour from which demographic projections are derived.

Baby boom Usually the period 1946–65, which is associated with high fertility rates and high numbers of births.

Balance of payments (BOP) A statistical statement that systemically summarises, for a specific time period, the economic transactions of an economy with the rest of the world.

Balance of payments conceptual adjustments Adjustments to international trade statistics to bring the value of exports and imports into line with balance of payments concepts. Imports are adjusted to free on board (fob) value. Exports are adjusted for goods shipped and sold on consignment.

Balance on current account A balance of payments statement is presented as a series of accounts – current, capital and financial. The current account records the export and import of goods and services, income earned and paid and, under current transfers, offsetting entries to resources supplied or received from non-residents. The sum of the exports of goods and services, earnings and resources received (inflows), less imports of goods and services, income paid and resources supplied (outflows) is the balance on current account. The account is usually in either surplus (inflows exceed outflows) or deficit (outflows exceed inflows).

Balance on current transfers This is calculated by deducting total debit entries from total credit entries for all current transfers components, for example, income tax and international aid.

Balance on goods This is calculated by deducting the total imports of goods from the total exports of goods. The balance is a surplus when exports of goods exceed imports.

Balance on income This is calculated by deducting the total income accruing to foreign investors from their investments in New Zealand, from the total income earned by New Zealand investors from their investments abroad. Income includes profits, dividends and interest.

Balance on services This is calculated by deducting total imports of services from total exports of services. Services include transportation, travel and insurance.

Balance on the external current account (national accounts) This is the residual item for the external account – the excess of income from the rest of the world over payments to the rest of the world. A negative value indicates payments exceed income.

Banking sector All units engaging in financial intermediation as a principal activity and having liabilities in the form of deposits or financial instruments.

Birth rate (crude) The number of live births per 1,000 mean estimated population.

Births Includes live births and stillbirths.

Bonds and notes Financial instruments that give the holder the unconditional right to a fixed money income, or a contractually-determined variable money income.

Capital account This account records all transactions that involve the receipt or payment of capital transfers, and acquisition or disposal of non-produced, non-financial assets such as patents and copyrights. The balance is equal to debit entries (inflows) minus credit entries (outflows).

Capital transfers to/from the rest of the world (national accounts) This is the excess of capital transfers by non-residents to New Zealand residents, over the value of similar transfers by residents to non-residents. Capital transfers are unrequited transfers in cash or in kind, which are not considered by the recipient as adding to current income, nor by the donor as reducing current income. Examples are unilateral transfers of capital goods, legacies, investment grants, and transfers of migrants' funds.

Census A survey of the total population of interest. New Zealand's Census of Population and Dwellings, carried out at five-yearly intervals, is an example of a census.

Census night population count A count of all people present in a given area on a given census night. The census night population count of New Zealand includes visitors from overseas, but excludes residents who are temporarily overseas on census night. For a subnational area, the count includes visitors from overseas and elsewhere in New Zealand (people who do not usually live in that area), but excludes residents of that area who are temporarily absent on census night.

Census undercount/overcount Census undercount is the number of people missed by a census who were meant to be counted. Census overcount is the number of people counted by a census who should not have been counted, or who were counted more than once. Net census undercount is the difference between the under- and overcount, usually expressed as a percentage of what the complete count should have been, rather than as a percentage of what was counted.

Census usually resident population count A count of all people who usually live in a given area, and are present in New Zealand, on a given census night. This count excludes both visitors from overseas and residents who are temporarily overseas on census night. For a subnational area, this count excludes visitors from overseas and elsewhere in New Zealand (people who do not usually live in that area), but includes residents of that area who are temporarily elsewhere in New Zealand on census night.

Chain-volume series Chain-volume measures express gross domestic product and its components with price effects removed. To do this involves revaluing a current price time series (of components) in the price of a chosen base period. Since chain-volume measures are done at component level, the components are not additive.

Change in inventories (national accounts) This consists of changes in:

- stocks of outputs that are held by the units that produced them before the stocks are further processed, sold or delivered to other units

- stocks of products acquired from other units that are intended to be used for intermediate consumption, or for resale without further processing.

They are measured by the value of the entries into inventories, less the value of withdrawals, and the value of any recurrent losses of goods held in inventories. Work in progress is included.

cif (cost, including insurance and freight) A basis for valuation of merchandise imports, representing the cost to the importer of buying the goods and bringing them to the wharf or airport in New Zealand.

Compensation of employees (national accounts) Total remuneration, in cash or in kind, payable to employees by enterprises. As well as salaries and wages, it includes contributions paid on an employee's behalf to a superannuation fund, a private pension scheme, the Accident Compensation Corporation, a casualty and life insurance scheme, and other fringe benefits.

Compensation of employees to/from the rest of the world (national accounts) In principle, these items cover the compensation that residents of one country earn from employment in another, where they are classed as non-residents (because their stay is for less than 12 months). In practice, data available does not permit estimates of these items.

Consensual union/de facto union Two people usually living in the same dwelling, but not in a registered marriage to each other, who share mutual concern for each other, have a degree of economic, social and emotional interdependence, and consider their relationship to be akin to marriage.

Constant price estimate This is an estimate in which the portion of the sales movement caused by a price change has been removed.

Consulate-general (foreign affairs) A country's office in a second country, which provides the full range of consular functions, and may also offer non-commercial trade or tourism activities. A consul-general is usually authorised to cover one large or significant consular district, or several smaller ones. A consulate (headed by a consul or honorary consul) provides only consular functions. An honorary consul is usually a national of the host country who performs consular duties on behalf of the foreign country.

Consumers price index (CPI) The official measure of inflation in the New Zealand economy. The CPI measures changes in the prices of goods and services purchased by New Zealand households.

Consumption of fixed capital (national accounts) This represents the reduction in the value of fixed assets used in production, during the accounting period, that results from physical deterioration, normal obsolescence, or normal accidental damage. It is valued at replacement cost.

Crown entity A body established by law in which the government has a controlling interest, but which is separate from the Crown. Control can be through owning a majority of the voting shares or by having the power to appoint and replace a majority of the governing members.

Crown research institute A government-owned business with a scientific purpose. There are nine institutes, each based around a productive sector of the economy or a grouping of natural resources.

Current account This account records all transactions (other than those in financial items) that involve economic values and occur between New Zealand-resident and non-resident entities. Also recorded are offsets to current economic values provided

or acquired without a quid pro quo. The major classifications are goods, services, income and transfers.

Current transfers to/from the rest of the world (national accounts) These refer to current transfers that take place between residents in New Zealand and non-residents. Examples include government aid in the form of food, clothing and medical supplies; social contributions and/or benefits; and personal transfers such as gifts.

Death rate (crude) The number of deaths per 1,000 mean estimated population.

Density (of population) The average number of people per square kilometre (or hectare) in a particular locality.

Depreciation Lowering of value, as charged in books of account, on fixed tangible assets.

Direct investment Investments made to acquire a lasting interest in an enterprise located in an economy other than the resident economy of the investor. The investor's purpose is to have a significant influence in the management of the enterprise. The International Monetary Fund defines 'significant influence' in the direct investment enterprise as the investor holding at least 10 percent of the voting capital of the enterprise. Once the relationship is established, all forms of financial capital investment between the direct investor and direct investment enterprise are classed as direct investment, that is, equity and debt.

Direct investment income Income earned by investors from their direct investment relationship with an enterprise. The income includes dividends (including bonus issues of shares), interest, earnings of branches, and direct investors' share of the earnings of direct investment enterprises that are not distributed.

Domestically-issued securities These securities are domestically-issued bonds and notes, taken up directly by non-resident organisations and individuals, or through New Zealand organisations acting as nominees.

Dwelling A structure, part of a structure, or a group of structures used, or intended to be used, as a place where people live.

Economically-significant enterprise An enterprise meeting at least one of the following criteria:

- greater than $30,000 annual GST expenses or sales
- at least three for its rolling mean employment (the average employee count over the previous 12 months)
- in a GST-exempt industry, except residential property leasing and rental
- part of a group of enterprises
- a new GST registration that is compulsory, special or forced (ie the business is expected to exceed the $30,000 limit)
- registered for GST and involved in agriculture or forestry.

Employed All people in the working-age population who, during the reference week: worked for one hour or more for pay or profit, in the context of an employee/employer relationship or self-employment; or worked without pay for one hour or more in work that contributed directly to the operation of a farm, business or professional practice owned or operated by a relative; or had a job but were not at work due to various factors (own illness or injury, personal or family responsibilities, bad weather or mechanical breakdown, direct involvement in an industrial dispute, or leave, or holiday).

Employee count (EC) The count of all people who are paid a salary or wages, and pay tax on this payment. The EC refers mostly to employees, but includes a small number of working proprietors who also pay themselves a taxable salary or wage. The EC data is derived from the Employer Monthly Schedule, provided by employers to Inland Revenue.

Employer contributions Payments by employers to superannuation, pension and welfare schemes, and accident compensation levies.

Employment status This describes a person's employment status within the labour force. Employed people aged 15 years or over are classified according to whether they work for themselves or other people either in full- or part-time employment. Employment status categories are: paid employee, self-employed and without employees, employer, and unpaid family worker.

Enterprise A business or service entity operating in New Zealand. It can be a company, a partnership, a trust, an estate, an incorporated society, a local or central government organisation, a voluntary organisation, or a self-employed individual.

Estimated resident population An estimate of all people who usually live in a given area at a given date. The estimated resident population of New Zealand includes all residents present in New Zealand and counted by the census (census usually resident population count), residents who are temporarily overseas (who are not included in the census), and an adjustment for residents missed or counted more than once by the census (net census undercount). Visitors from overseas are excluded. For a subnational area, the estimate includes residents of that area who are temporarily absent on census night but excludes visitors from elsewhere in New Zealand (people who do not usually live in that area). The estimated resident population at a given date after census includes births, deaths and net migration (arrivals less departures) of residents during the period between census night and the given date.

Ethnicity An ethnic group is made up of people who have some or all of the following characteristics: a common proper name; one or more elements of common culture, which need not be specified but may include religion, customs or language; unique community of interests, feelings and actions; a shared sense of common origin or ancestry; and a common geographic origin. Ethnicity is self-perceived and people can belong to more than one ethnic group. People can identify with an ethnicity even though they may not be descended from ancestors with that ethnicity. Conversely, people may choose to not identify with an ethnicity even though they are descended from ancestors with that ethnicity.

Excise A duty or tax on goods produced or sold within the country of origin.

Exports of goods and services All goods and services produced by New Zealand residents and purchased by non-residents.

External migration The short-term and long-term movement of overseas and New Zealand travellers in to and out of New Zealand. External migration statistics are compiled from individual migration forms filled in by passengers arriving in and departing from New Zealand. The classes of arrival and departure are: overseas visitor, New Zealand resident departing from New Zealand or returning after a short-term absence, permanent and long-term arrival, permanent and long-term departure.

Family A couple, with or without children, or one parent with one or more children, usually living together in a household.

Fertility The actual level of reproduction of a population, based on the number of live births that occur. Fertility is normally measured in terms of women of childbearing age.

Fertility rate (total) The average number of live births that a woman would have during her life, if she experienced the age-specific fertility rates of a given period (usually a year). It excludes the effects of mortality.

Final consumption expenditure (national accounts) Expenditure, including imputed expenditure, on goods and services according to which sector (private and government) actually pays for the goods and services, and therefore makes the decision on the expenditure.

Financial account This account records transactions associated with changes in ownership of the foreign financial assets and liabilities of an economy. For example, foreign investors' purchases and sales of equity (shares) issues by New Zealand-resident companies, and the borrowing and lending overseas by New Zealand entities.

Financial derivatives Financial derivatives are financial instruments that derive their value by reference to an underlying product or index. Financial derivatives involve:

- future delivery, receipt or exchange of financial items such as cash or another derivative instrument
- future exchange of real assets for financial items where the contract may be tradable and have market value.

Financial derivatives include, for example, currency swaps, interest rate swaps, futures, forward foreign exchange contracts, options (contracts), and warrants.

Financial performance The broad heading for variables that measure the financial performance of a unit or group of units. This includes, for example, variables for income, expenditure, profit and stocks.

Financial position The broad heading for variables that measure the financial position of a unit or group of units. Previously called the balance sheet, it includes assets, liabilities, equity, and investment in fixed assets.

First marriage rate First marriages per 1,000 never-married women.

fob (free on board) The current market value of goods in the country of origin, including all costs necessary to get them on board a ship or aircraft, but excluding freight, insurance, and other costs involved in transporting them to New Zealand.

Foreign direct investment in New Zealand Investment in New Zealand-located enterprises by non-resident investors that meets the direct investment criteria. The financial account measures transactions that increase and decrease these investments. The international investment position statement measures the value of this investment at points in time.

Full-time employed People working 30 hours or more a week.

Full-time equivalent employees (FTEs) The number of FTEs equals the number of full-time employees, plus half the part-time employees.

General government sector Central and local government units, other than the Reserve Bank of New Zealand.

Geographic unit A separate operating unit engaged in one, or predominately one, kind of economic activity from a single physical location or base in New Zealand.

Gross (national accounts) Used to denote values before deducting consumption of fixed capital.

Gross domestic product (GDP, national accounts) The total market value of goods and services produced in New Zealand, after deducting the cost of goods and services used in the process of production, but before deducting allowances for the consumption of fixed capital.

Gross fixed capital formation (national accounts) Measured by the total value, less disposals, of a producer's purchases of fixed assets, plus certain additions to the value of non-produced assets (such as subsoil assets or major improvements in the quantity, quality or productivity of land) realised by the productive activity of institutional units. The term 'gross' indicates that consumption of fixed capital has not been deducted from the value of the outlays.

Gross national expenditure (national accounts) The total expenditure by New Zealand residents, within a given period, on final goods and services. This excludes goods and services used up during the production process.

Gross national income (GNI, national accounts) The income accruing to New Zealand residents, within a given period, from their services in supplying factors of production in New Zealand and overseas, plus net taxes on production and imports, and before the deduction of allowances for the consumption of fixed capital. Previously referred to as gross national product.

Gross operating surplus (national accounts) The surplus or deficit accruing from production. The residual item to the gross domestic product and expenditure account, obtained after deducting compensation of employees and taxes on production, less subsidies, from the value-added component.

Gross reproduction rate The average number of daughters that a woman would have during her life if she experienced the age-specific fertility rates of a given year. It excludes the effect of mortality.

Gross tonne The unit of actual weight of cargo, including packaging, but not including the weight of reusable containers.

Hapū Subtribe.

Harmonised system The New Zealand Harmonised System Classification is used for processing customs entries and publishing statistics on external trade.

Household Either one person usually living alone, or two or more people usually living together and sharing facilities, in a private dwelling.

Imports of goods and services All goods and services produced by non-New Zealand residents and purchased by New Zealand residents.

Indexes An index is used to measure the total impact of changes in the attributes of commodities that cannot be compared directly. In New Zealand, the most common use of index numbers is to measure changes in prices, volumes, or money values over time. When calculating a price index, the type, quantity and quality of each commodity is held constant so that the price movement can be measured. The most frequently quoted index in New Zealand is the consumers price index, which reports quarterly changes in price levels of goods and services purchased by New Zealand households during a specified period. By expressing the changes in index form, price changes in commodities as diverse as beef, hairdressing and club subscriptions can all be aggregated to produce a measure of overall price change.

Indirect taxes Taxes assessed on producers in respect of the production, sale, purchase, and use of goods and services, and which add to the market price of those goods and services. They include: sales tax, local authority rates, import and excise duties, fringe benefit tax, and registration fees (such as motor vehicle registration) paid by producers.

Inflation An increase in the general or average level of prices of goods and services over a period of time.

Insurance (balance of payments) This covers the provision of various types of insurance by non-residents to residents, and vice versa.

All types of insurance and reinsurance are included: freight insurance on goods, reinsurance, and other forms of direct insurance (such as life, marine, general and fire, and accident). Also included are commissions related to insurance transactions earned by agents.

Intermediate consumption (national accounts) The value of goods and services used as inputs in production.

International investment position A statistical statement of the:

- value and composition of the stock of an economy's financial assets, or the economy's claims on the rest of the world

- value and composition of the stock of an economy's liabilities to the rest of the world.

Investment income Income earned by foreign investors from their equity and financial assets invested in New Zealand (the debit or expenditure item), and the income New Zealand investors earn from their equity and financial assets invested abroad (the credit or income earned item).

Investment income to/from the rest of the world (national accounts) This consists of:

- Investment income, which represents transfers of income accruing to the owners of financial assets (mainly from earning interest and dividends) and tangible non-produced assets (from owning natural assets such as land, subsoil assets and water resources). This now includes reinvested earnings on overseas direct investment, where the retained earnings of a direct foreign investment enterprise are treated as if they were distributed and remitted to foreign direct investors in proportion to their ownership of the equity of the enterprise, and then reinvested by them in the enterprise.

- Entrepreneurial income, which refers to actual withdrawals of income from enterprises operating overseas, such as branches of foreign companies.

Iwi Tribe.

Kind of activity unit A subdivision of an enterprise, consisting of one or more activity units for which a single set of accounting records is available.

Labour force The labour force consists of people aged 15 and over who regularly work for one hour or more a week for financial gain, or who work without pay in a family business, as well as those who are not working, but are actively seeking and are available for work.

Labour force participation rate The total labour force expressed as a percentage of the working-age population.

Labour income (total) Before-tax income that people aged 15 and over receive in a financial year from all sources. This includes wages, salary, government benefits, interest, dividends, commission, and pre-tax business or farming income (less expenses).

Life expectancy at birth The average length of life of a newborn baby, assuming they experience the age-specific mortality rates of a given period throughout their life. Life expectancy represents the average longevity of the whole population and does not necessarily reflect the longevity of an individual.

Loans (balance of payments) Direct agreements between borrowers and lenders that involve the transfer of funds to the borrower, and the repayment to the lender over time. Loans include: secured and unsecured loans, trade-related loans, overdrafts, roll-over loans, revolving-credit advances, advances from overseas parent and/or subsidiary companies, the use of credit facilities, and non-market debentures and notes.

Long term Refers to financial instruments with an original maturity of more than one year.

Marriage (registered) The act, ceremony or process by which the legal relationship of husband and wife is constituted. In New Zealand, marriage must be solemnised by a celebrant or before a registrar of marriages.

Maturity profile The residual maturity profile is based on the time remaining to scheduled maturity.

Mean population The average number of people in an area during a given period, usually a year. This measure may be estimated in terms of a simple or weighted arithmetic mean of monthly or quarterly population during the reference period.

Median A value with an equal number of items on either side of it.

Median age Half the population is younger, and half older, than this age.

Merchandise exports Goods of domestic origin, and re-exports, sent from New Zealand to other countries. This includes goods leased for a year or more, but excludes goods for repair.

Merchandise imports Goods from other countries landed in New Zealand, including goods leased for a year or more, but excluding goods for repair.

Merchandise trade All goods that add to or subtract from the stock of material resources in a country, as a result of their movement in to or out of it. This includes goods leased for a year or more, but excludes goods for repair.

Monetary authority The Reserve Bank of New Zealand.

Money market instruments Securities generally giving the holder the unconditional right to receive a stated fixed sum of money on a specified date. These instruments are usually traded at a discount in organised markets. The predominant money market instruments in New Zealand are treasury bills, Reserve Bank bills, bills of exchange, and certificates of deposit.

National disposable income (national accounts) The total income of New Zealand residents, from all sources, that is available for either final consumption (current spending) or saving.

Natural increase The excess of live births over deaths. When deaths exceed births, this is described as a natural decrease, or a negative natural increase.

Net errors and omissions This is a balancing item. The balance of payments statement employs a double entry system and so, in the accounting sense, it should always balance. In practice, this seldom occurs, due to factors such as the variety of data sources used, the probability that some transactions will not be captured, and the possibility of errors in reporting and compilation. Net errors and omissions (or the residual) is used to balance the accounts.

Net lending to the rest of the world (national accounts) The residual item for the national capital account. If the nation's savings are insufficient to pay for all capital investment needed for production, the shortfall must be borrowed from overseas. Net lending to the rest of the world is then a negative item.

Net reproduction rate The average number of daughters that a woman would have during her life if she experienced the age-specific fertility and mortality rates of a given year. A net reproduction rate of one means a woman would exactly replace herself.

New Zealand direct investment abroad Investment by New Zealand investors in overseas-located enterprises that meets the direct investment criteria. The balance of payments financial account measures transactions that increase and decrease these investments. The international investment position statement measures the value of this investment at points in time.

New Zealand residents departing temporarily or returning after a short-term absence A New Zealand resident whose absence from New Zealand is intended to be, or was, less than 12 months.

Not in the labour force Any person in the working-age population who is neither employed nor unemployed. This residual category includes: retired people; those with personal or family responsibilities such as childcare and unpaid housework; people attending educational institutions; those permanently unable to work due to physical or mental disabilities; people who were temporarily unavailable for work in the survey reference week; and those not actively seeking work.

Operating expenditure Expenditure from the main activities of an economic unit, usually directly incurred from sales of goods and services. Salaries and wages, interest, donations, and unusual expenditure (such as valuation changes) are excluded.

Operating income Income from the main activities of an economic unit, usually from the sales of goods and services. Generally it excludes unusual expenditure (such as valuation changes), interest, dividends and subsidies.

Operating surplus (financial accounts) Surplus or deficit of total income less total expenditure, before direct tax, payments to owners, and stock change.

Other investment A residual category covering all forms of financial capital not included elsewhere (under direct, portfolio or reserves). Types of capital include trade finance (trade creditor and debtor accounts), loans, and deposits.

'Other' sectors (balance of payments) Includes non-financial corporations, insurance companies, pension funds, other non-depository financial intermediaries, private non-profit institutions and households.

Output (national accounts) Output represents the value of total production, including intermediate inputs. Deducting intermediate inputs from output gives the value-added component.

Overseas trade – exports and imports New Zealand Customs Service entries relating to goods cleared. Overseas trade statistics show exports valued free on board (fob), and imports valued cost, including insurance and freight (cif) and value for duty (vfd).

Paid employees People who have an employment agreement and who receive payment for their work in the form of wages, salary, commission, tips, piece rates, or pay in kind.

Part-time employed People who usually work fewer than 30 hours a week.

Permanent and long-term arrivals People who have spent the previous 12 months or more overseas and who arrive in New Zealand intending to stay 12 months or more.

Permanent and long-term departures People who have spent the previous 12 months or more in New Zealand and who depart for an intended absence of 12 months or more.

Population estimate Data from the most recent Census of Population and Dwellings, updated with estimates of births, deaths and net migration since the census.

Population projection Indication of the future demographic characteristics of a population, based on an assessment of past trends and assumptions about the future course of demographic behaviour – fertility, mortality and migration.

Portfolio investment Investment in equity securities of less than 10 percent of the voting stock of an enterprise; and investment in debt securities, such as bonds and notes, and money market instruments.

Provisional (statistics) Statistics derived using preliminary or incomplete data, which are released before final data becomes available.

Purchase of non-produced non-financial assets to/from the rest of the world net (national accounts) This refers to assets (tangible and intangible) that come into existence other than through production processes. Also included are the costs of ownership transfer on, and major improvements to, such assets.

Random rounding Random rounding to base 3, as used in a census, means that all table cell values, including totals, are rounded as follows: zero and numbers that are already multiples of three are not changed. Other numbers are randomly rounded to one of the two nearest multiples of three, using fixed probabilities. For example, a nine is left unchanged, while eight could be rounded to either six or nine. Because rounding is done separately for each cell, rows and columns do not necessarily add up to the published totals.

Re-exports Merchandise exports that were earlier imported into New Zealand and contain less than 50 percent New Zealand content by value. Examples are computer hardware, machinery and aircraft.

Re-imports Goods, materials or articles imported in the same condition as they were exported from New Zealand. (One-third of New Zealand's re-imports are live animals, principally racehorses and dogs).

Replacement level fertility The average number of children a woman needs to have to produce one daughter who survives to childbearing age. (Also described as the total fertility rate required for the population to replace itself, without migration.) The internationally accepted replacement level is 2.1 births per woman. This allows for females dying between birth and childbearing, and for the fact that on average, 105 boys are born for every 100 girls. The actual replacement level varies slightly among countries, depending on child mortality rates. In countries with high child mortality, the rate will need to be higher than 2.1 births per woman to achieve replacement level.

Reserve assets External financial assets denominated in foreign currencies that are readily available to, and controlled by, monetary authorities.

Resident population In census statistics, a resident is a person who self-identifies that they usually live in an area. In external migration statistics, a resident is a person who self-identifies on a departure card that they have lived in New Zealand for 12 months or more. On an arrival card, a resident identifies that they live in New Zealand, have been away for less than 12 months, and intend to stay in New Zealand for 12 months or more.

Resident population concept A statistical basis for a population in terms of those who usually live in a given area at a given time. The census usually resident population count is a census measure, and the estimated resident population is a demographic measure, of the resident population concept.

Residents and non-residents An individual or enterprise is a resident of New Zealand when their centre of economic interest is in New Zealand. Broadly, an individual is resident in New Zealand if they live in New Zealand for one year or more and their general centre of interest is New Zealand. This can apply to people who spend much of their time outside New Zealand, but still retain 'permanent' links with New Zealand. Resident individuals include: people whose usual place of living is New Zealand; New Zealanders living, travelling or working abroad for less than a year; New Zealanders living abroad studying; and New Zealand diplomatic or military personnel. An entity is resident in New Zealand if it engages in production of goods or services in New Zealand. Resident entities include New Zealand-located subsidiaries of overseas companies, and New Zealand-located branches or partnerships of overseas entities. Individuals and entities not regarded as residents of New Zealand are defined as non-residents. Non-resident entities include overseas-located subsidiaries, associates, and branches of New Zealand companies.

Rounding Rounding of numbers involves replacing a given number with another one – the rounded number. In tables, rounding can create a discrepancy between a total shown and the total of individual cells in the table. Data may be rounded for ease of use, or for confidentiality reasons. Numbers are rounded when making statistical calculations, where it might not be possible, practical, or reasonable to record numbers to the last digit. Published statistics are often rounded to make them easily understood and readily comparable with other data. Such practices are quite acceptable, providing an adequate level of accuracy is retained.

Rural areas Those areas not specifically designated as 'urban'. Rural areas include towns with a population of fewer than 1,000 people, plus an administrative district (where this is not included in an urban area). Rural areas include offshore islands.

Salaries and wages Gross earnings during the accounting year of all paid employees (full time, part time and casual). Included are: overtime, sick and holiday pay, bonuses, payments under penal-rate schemes, severance pay, value of free supplies, and sales commission paid to employees. Payments for working proprietors or partners are excluded.

Sample survey A type of survey in which only a representative part of the population of interest provides information. The sample statistics are summarised and used to estimate statistics for the full population.

Saving (national accounts) The residual item in the national income and outlay account. It is the amount of national disposable income left after current spending.

Seasonal adjustment Adjustment made to statistical time series (usually monthly or quarterly) to provide a refined series in which the estimated fluctuations due to seasonal variations are removed.

Short term Refers to financial instruments with an original maturity of less than one year.

Statistical discrepancy In the New Zealand System of National Accounts, items making up gross domestic product (GDP) and expenditure on GDP are estimated independently, using diverse data sources. The combination of survey and other measurement and timing errors in the various components results in a difference between the estimates, which is the statistical discrepancy.

Stocks Materials such as components, stores, fuels, containers and other packaging materials, as well as finished goods and work in progress, such as goods purchased for resale without further processing.

Subnational Geographical units of a country (eg area units, territorial authorities, and regional council and urban areas) whose boundaries are defined for administrative, legal or statistical purposes.

Subsidies (national accounts) Current unrequited payments made by governments to enterprises on the basis of the levels of their production activities, or the quantity or value of the goods and services that they produce, sell or import.

Taonga Treasure.

Taxes on production and imports (national accounts) Taxes payable on goods and services when they are produced, delivered, sold, transferred, or otherwise disposed of by their producers. Also included are taxes and duties on imports that become payable when goods enter New Zealand, or when services are delivered to resident units by non-resident units. They also include other taxes on production, which consist mainly of taxes on the ownership or use of land, buildings or other assets used in production, or on the labour employed, or compensation of employees paid.

Tenure (of household) Tenure refers to the nature of the occupancy of a private household in a home – whether the household rents or owns the home, and whether payment is made

for that right. It does not refer to the tenure of the land on which the home is situated.

Terms of trade The ratio of goods export prices to goods import prices. Measures the purchasing power of New Zealand's merchandise exports in terms of its merchandise imports.

Trade credits Accounts payable to, and prepayments received from, non-residents for imports and exports of goods and services.

Transfers (balance of payments) Special counter-entries for one-sided transactions such as gifts of goods, services, and financial assets.

Transportation (balance of payments) Exports and imports of services associated with the international carriage of goods and passengers. Services include freight, air fares, freight insurance, port services, and stevedoring.

Travel (balance of payments) Expenditure by foreign travellers in New Zealand and New Zealanders travelling overseas.

Unemployed All people in the working-age population who, during the reference week, were without a paid job, were available for work, and had either actively sought work in the past four weeks or had a new job to start within the next four weeks.

Unemployment rate The number of unemployed people expressed as a percentage of the labour force.

Urban areas Non-administrative areas with urban characteristics and a high to moderate concentration of population. Main, secondary, and minor urban areas are differentiated by population size. Urban areas are currently defined as: main urban areas – centres with populations of 30,000 or more; secondary urban areas – 10,000–29,999 people; minor urban areas – 1,000 or more people, and not already classified as urban.

Value added (national accounts) The value added to goods and services by the contributions of capital and labour (ie, after the costs of bought-in materials and services have been deducted from the total value of output).

vfd (value for duty) The assessed value of merchandise imports on which duty is based. It approximates the current domestic value of goods in the exporting country.

Visitor from overseas In census statistics, a visitor from overseas is a person who self-identifies that they usually live overseas. In external migration statistics, a visitor from overseas is a person who self-identifies on an arrival card that they intend to stay in New Zealand less than 12 months.

Vital statistics Statistics for events such as births, deaths and marriages.

Wāhi tapu Sacred place.

Whānau Family.

Working-age population Generally refers to the population aged 15 years and over.

Abbreviations

ACC Accident Compensation Corporation

ANZSCO Australian and New Zealand Standard Classification for Occupations

ANZSIC Australian and New Zealand Standard Industry Classification

APEC Asia-Pacific Economic Cooperation

ASEAN Association of Southeast Asian Nations

ATM automated teller machine

BPM5 Balance of Payments Manual, edition 5

CCMAU Crown Companies Monitoring Advisory Unit

cif cost, including insurance and freight

CNZM Companion of the New Zealand Order of Merit

CPI consumers price index

CRI Crown research institute

CTU Council of Trade Unions

DHB district health board

DOC Department of Conservation

EC employee count

EECA Energy Efficiency and Conservation Authority

EEO equal employment opportunities

EFTPOS electronic funds transfer at point of sale

ESR Institute of Environmental Science and Research

EU European Union

fob free on board

FRST Foundation for Research, Science and Technology

FTA free trade agreement

FTE full-time equivalent employee

GAAP generally accepted accounting practice

GATT General Agreement on Tarrifs and Trade

GDP gross domestic product

GST goods and services tax

HLFS Household Labour Force Survey

HMNZS Her Majesty's New Zealand ship

ICT information and communications technology

IMF International Monetary Fund

ISO International Organization for Standardization

ISP Internet service provider

LINZ Land Information New Zealand

MAF Ministry of Agriculture and Forestry

MFAT Ministry of Foreign Affairs and Trade

MoRST Ministry of Research, Science and Technology

MP Member of Parliament

NCEA National Certificate of Educational Achievement

NGO non-government organisation

NIWA National Institute of Water and Atmospheric Research

NQF National Qualifications Framework

NZCS New Zealand Customs Service

NZQA New Zealand Qualifications Authority

NZSNA New Zealand System of National Accounts

NZTE New Zealand Trade and Enterprise

OCR official cash rate

OECD Organisation for Economic Co-operation and Development

PCNZM principal companion of the New Zealand Order of Merit

PHARMAC Pharmaceutical Management Agency of New Zealand

PHO primary health organisation

QC Queen's Council

QSO Queen's Service Order

R&D research and development

RMA Resource Management Act 1991

RNZ Radio New Zealand

RNZAF Royal New Zealand Air Force

RS&T research, science and technology

SOE state-owned enterprise

SPARC Sport and Recreation New Zealand

SSC State Services Commission

TAB Totalisator Agency Board

TUANZ Telecommunications Users' Association of New Zealand

TVNZ Television New Zealand

UN United Nations

UNESCO United Nations Educational, Scientific and Cultural Organisation

vfd value for duty

WCO World Customs Organization

WTO World Trade Organization

Weights and measures

All statistics in this publication are in metric units.

Metric to imperial

Length

1 millimetre (mm)	= 0.04 inches
1 centimetre (cm)	= 0.39 inches
1 metre (m)	= 39.37 inches
	= 1.09 yards
1 kilometre (km)	= 0.62 miles

Area

1 square metre (m²)	= 10.76 square feet
	= 1.20 square yards
1 hectare (ha)	= 2.47 acres
1 square kilometre (km²)	= 247 acres
	= 0.39 square miles

Volume and capacity

1 cubic centimetre (cm³)	= 0.06 cubic inches
1 cubic metre (m³)	= 35.31 cubic feet
	= 1.31 cubic yards
1 litre (l)	= 1.76 pints
	= 0.22 gallons

Mass (weight)

1 gram (g)	= 0.04 ounces
1 kilogram (kg)	= 2.20 pounds
1 tonne (t)	= 2,204.62 pounds
	= 0.98 tons

Velocity

1 kilometre per hour (km/h)	= 0.62 miles per hour

Pressure

1 kilopascal (kPa)	= 0.15 pounds per square inch
1 megapascal (MPa)	= 0.07 tons per square inch

Temperature

Degrees Fahrenheit (°F) $°F = °C \times \dfrac{9}{5} + 32$

Degrees Celsius (°C) $°C = (°F - 32) \times \dfrac{5}{9}$

Energy

1 kilojoule (kJ)	= 0.95 British thermal units
	= 0.24 calories

Power

1 kilowatt (kW)	= 1.34 UK horsepower

Metric multiples

Length

1 centimetre	= 10 millimetres
1 metre	= 100 centimetres
1 kilometre	= 1,000 metres

Area

1 hectare	= 10,000 square metres
1 square kilometre	= 100 hectares

Volume and capacity

1 cubic metre	= 1 million cubic centimetres
1 litre	= 1,000 millilitres
1 millilitre (ml)	= 1 cubic centimetre
1 cubic metre	= 1,000 litres

Mass (weight)

1 kilogram	= 1,000 grams
1 tonne	= 1,000 kilograms

Pressure

1 megapascal	= 1,000 kilopascals

Energy

1 megajoule (MJ)	= 1,000 kilojoules
1 kilowatt hour (kWh)	= 3.6 megajoules
1 gigajoule (GJ)	= 1,000 megajoules
1 terajoule (TJ)	= 1,000 gigajoules
1 petajoule (PJ)	= 1 million gigajoules

Power

1 kilowatt	= 1,000 watts
1 megawatt (MW)	= 1,000 kilowatts
1 gigawatt (GW)	= 1,000 megawatts

Index

In all cases the word New Zealand has been abbreviated to NZ to save space in the index.

Names of organisations starting with NZ may also be found in an inverted form (eg String Quartet, NZ) and organisations may found in a relevant subject area (eg Department of Conservation, listed under the main heading: Conservation).

Ministries, departments, government agencies and other organisations cited in the Yearbook with a Māori name may be accessed by that name.

Acts of Parliament are included in the index when there is a major reference.

A

Abortion, 161–2

Abuse of children, 137, 138

Academy of Sport, NZ, 260–2

Access PHOs, 148

Access radio stations, 232

Accident Compensation Corporation, 167–8, 260, 455

Accident insurance, 167–8

Accidents
air, 429
collection of injury statistics, 170
external causes, 166
marine, 428
occupational safety and health, 170–1
prevention, 166–7
road crashes, 162–4
water, 165

Accommodation
see also Housing
employee count in sector, 356
GDP by industry, 344
use, 271, 273

Accounts *see* International accounts; National accounts

Accreditation services *see* Standards and accreditation services

Administration of estates, Public Trust, 51

Administrative boundaries of NZ, 1

Adopt a Stream programme, 179

Adoption, 139–40

Adult education, 186

Advanced network, 228, 295

Advertising industry, 235–6

Advertising Standards Authority, 236

Advisory Committee on Assisted Human Reproduction, 143

Afghanistan, deployment in, 64, 79, 218

Africa
development assistance, 66
relationship with, 63–4

Age
abortion by, 162
deaths from external causes by, 166
first marriage, median age, 98
labour force participation by, 282

population
age-sex profile, 103–4
Asian peoples, 106, 124, 125
European, 106
Māori, 106, 117
mortality, 100–1
Pacific peoples, 106, 121–2
projections, 84–9
prisoners, 212, 213
unemployment by, 286
weekly earnings by, 289

Aged residential care, 154, 155

Aggregates, 403

AgResearch Ltd, 299

Agricultural compounds, regulation of, 154

Agricultural sector
bees and beekeeping, 369–70
biosecurity, 381
Crop & Food Research, 299
cropping farming prices, 339
crops, 370–1
current situation and trends, 357–8
dairy industry *see* Dairy industry
eggs, 369
employee count in sector, 356
energy use, 389
exports
dairy products, 360, 366, 367, 368, 408, 460–1
horticultural, 371
meat, 360–1, 363–4, 408, 461–2
wine, 374
wool, 365–6
farm types by number and area, 358
GATT Uruguay Round, 357
GDP by industry, 343, 344
generally, 357
genetic modification, 357
horticulture, 370–4
livestock *see* Livestock
MAF, 358–9
meat products, 361–4
methane research, 366
organic farming, WWOOF movement, 372
organisations, 358–9
pastoral agriculture, 359–61
research consortia, 302
water quality in farmed catchments, 310
wool *see* Wool

Agriculture and Forestry, Ministry of, 358–9

Aid *see* Defence and security; Emergency and disaster relief; International development assistance

AIDS Foundation, NZ, 155

Air Force, Royal NZ, 76–7

Air NZ Ltd, 45

Air pollution and health study, 144

Air quality, 308–9

Air Training Corps, 79

Air transport *see* Civil aviation

Airports
generally, 430
overseas cargo loaded and unloaded, 476–7

Alcohol
see also Sale of liquor
consumption, 151
CPI group, 336, 337
driving and, 440, 441
excise, 458, 498, 504
public health, 151
responsible drinking, 452
wine industry, 373–4

Alexander Turnbull Library, 243, 244

Allowances
see also Work and Income
disability, 133
Student allowance, 134, 181, 182
Training Incentive Allowance, 135

Animal products, regulation of, 154

Animal species, 12, 13

Annual holidays, employee entitlements, 278

Antarctica
cooperation with US, 62
Defence Force assistance, 80
fisheries, 71
Operation Antarctica, 80
Ross Dependency, 1, 70–1
treaty system, 71

Anthems, national, 55

Antiquities, protection of, 242–3, 255

ANZAC, 19, 72

ANZUS Treaty, 78

Aoraki/Mt Cook, 2

Aotearoa Fisheries Ltd, 384

APEC
generally, 62
value of trade with APEC countries, 476

Apiata, Corporal Willie, 64

Apparel, CPI group, 337

Apparel industry, 410

Apples, 372, 373

Apprenticeships, 283

Approved issuer levy, 504

Aquaculture, management of, 311

Arabian Gulf, deployment in, 79

Arab-Israeli conflict, 64, 78

Archaeological sites, protection of, 242–3

Architecture awards, 417

Archives
    Archives NZ, 243
    Cartoon Archive, NZ, 243
    Film Archive, 251
    Hocken Collections, 245
    Sound Archives, 232

Area of NZ, 1–2

Argentina, relationship with, 62

Armed forces see NZ Defence Force

Armed offenders squads, 216

Arms convictions, 206

Army, NZ, 75–6

Arrivals and departures, 101–2

Art galleries, 241

Artefacts, protection of, 242–3, 255

Arts and cultural heritage
    administration, 254–7
    Archives NZ, 243
    art galleries, 241
    Cartoon Archive NZ, 243
    censorship, 251–3
    contribution to GDP, 239
    copyright, 253–4
    CPI group, 336, 337
    Creative NZ
        Authors' Fund, 246
        generally, 256–7
        Māori arts, 240
    Cultural Indicators for NZ: 2006, 255
    employee count in sector, 356
    employment in sector, 239
    film and video, 250–3
    generally, 239
    government expenditure, 239
    Historic Places Trust, 241–2, 330
    library services, 243–6
    literature, 245, 246–7
    Living Heritage, 242
    Ministry for Culture and Heritage, 254–5
    museums, 241
    performing arts, 247–50
    regional development, 257
    research, 257
    taonga tuku iho, 239–40
    Te Papa Tongarewa, 241

ASEAN, 61–2, 77

ASEAN countries, value of trade with, 476

ASEAN Regional Forum, 62

ASEAN-Australia/NZ free trade negotiations, 61, 467

Asia
    'Boxing Day' tsunami, 6
    defence and security, 62
    development assistance, 61, 66
    relationship with, 61–2
    Seriously Asia Fund, 61
    trade, value of, 473–6
    trade with, 61, 62

Asia NZ Foundation, 61

Asia Pacific Economic Cooperation
    generally, 62
    value of trade with APEC countries, 476

Asian population
    age distribution, 106, 124, 125
    ethnicities, 124
    fertility rate, 97
    growth, 105, 106
    links with Asia, 61
    migration to NZ, 124
    proportion of total, 87
    regional distribution, 125

Asia-Pacific Regional Interfaith Dialogue, 67

Assaults
    convictions, 202
    on Police, 216

Assets
    international, 354–5
    privatisation of state assets, 20

Assisted reproductive technology see
    Human assisted reproductive
    technology

Association of NZ Advertisers, 236

Association of South-East Asian Nations,
    61–2, 77

AsureQuality Ltd, 359, 371

Attorney-general
    generally, 200
    reporting function under Bill of Rights
        Act, 49

Auahi Kore programme, 150

Auctioneers Act 1928, 450

Auditor-general, 44, 46

Australia
    ASEAN-Australia/NZ free trade
        negotiations, 61, 467
    business law coordination, 60
    CER agreement, 60
    CPI comparison, 338
    defence relationship, 60, 77–8
    FRANZ arrangement, 59
    'open skies' aviation market
        agreement, 60
    relationship with, 60
    social security agreement, 136
    synchrotron facility, 298
    trade with, 60, 470–1
    trans-Tasman travel arrangement, 60, 101

Australia NZ Food Standards Code, 60

Australia NZ Leadership Forum, 60

Australian and NZ Army Corps, 19, 72

Authors' Fund, NZ, 246

Automobile Association, NZ, 455

Automobiles see Motor vehicles

Avian influenza, pandemic planning, 159

Aviation see Civil aviation

Awards
    architecture, 417
    books, 245, 246
    bravery, 48
    EEO Trust, 126
    exporters, 463
    gallantry, 48
    honours system, 48
    sustainable business, 408

B

Bachelor degrees, sex ratio of, 188

Backpacker, accommodation use, 271, 273

Balance of payments, 348–55

Ballet, Royal NZ, 249

Bankers' Association, NZ, 484

Banking Ombudsman Scheme, 484, 485

Bankruptcy, 447–8

Banks and banking see Financial
    institutions; Reserve Bank of NZ

Barley, 371

Beef cattle
    breeds, 360
    classification, 363
    farming, 359
    Meat & Wool NZ, 362
    meat exports, 360–4, 461, 462
    meat production prices, 362
    meat production volumes, 362
    meat products, 361
    methane, 366
    numbers
        by category, 360
        by region, 361
        total population, 358, 359
    tariff rate quotas, administration of, 361
    veal, 358, 360–1, 362, 363, 364

Bees and beekeeping, 369–70

Benefits and pensions see Unemployment
    Benefit; Work and Income

Bereavement leave, employee entitlements,
    278

Best Fish Guide (Forest & Bird), 383

Bestselling books, 246

Better by Design programme, 409

Bibliography, National, 243

Biketawa Declaration, 60

Bill of Rights Act 1990, 49, 50

Biodiversity, 307–8, 319

Bioethics Council, 313

Bio-fuel research (aviation industry), 430

Biogas, 400

Biomass and waste, 400

Biosecurity
    see also Pests and diseases
    bio-control research, 359
    MAF Biosecurity NZ, 315, 358–9, 381, 382
    services, 358–9

Bird flu, pandemic planning, 159

Birds
    grey warbler as 'Bird of the Year', 325
    wetlands, 329

Births see Childbirth

Births, Deaths and Marriages registers, 99

Blood Service, NZ, 143

Boarding school bursaries, 180

Boarding schools, 185

Boards of trustees, schools, 177

Boat design and construction, 409–10

Bonded Merit scholarships, 181

Books, 246–7

Booksellers NZ, 246–7

Border security
counter-terrorism, 77
Defence Force assistance, 80
operations, 458

Borrowing
credit cards, 453–4, 484
credit charges, CPI group, 337
credit contracts and consumer finance,
450
government securities, 486–7
housing loans and mortgages, 414–5
public debt, 333, 504–5

Bougainville, deployment in, 60, 218

'Boxing Day' tsunami, 6

Brand NZ, 458

BRANZ, 302, 455

Bravery awards, 48

Brazil, relationship with, 62

Breast screening programme, 157

British sovereignty, 17

Broadband, 219, 220, 227–8

Broadcasting
Broadcasting Commission (NZ On Air),
223
Broadcasting Standards Authority,
223–4
Māori, 224, 240
parliamentary proceedings, 36
policy, 222–3
racing, 230, 266
radio, 230–2
television, 222–3, 228–30

Brunei, free trade agreement with,
61, 406, 467

Buddhist faith, 108

Budget, 490–2

Building and construction
awards, 417
building authorisations, 421–2
building code, 420
building products, Greenbuild website,
421
construction systems, 420
Department of Building and Housing,
417–9, 420
economic growth, 339–40
employee count in sector, 356
GDP by industry, 344, 419
gross fixed capital investment, 419
legislation, 420–1
new dwellings
average floor area, 423
units authorised, 422
NZ Green Building Council, 419
people engaged in industry, 419
price indexes, 422–3
prices, 339
regulatory policy, 418
work put in place, 422, 423

Burials, natural, 100

Business
see also Commerce and services
advocacy, 279
business law coordination with Australia,
60
e-commerce, 222
indexation of contracts, 335
NZDipBus, 191
services
employee count by industry, 356
GDP by industry, 344
statistics, 355–6
Sustainable Business Awards, 408
visas, long-term, 116

Business NZ, 279

Butter, 366

Buy Kiwi Made, 406

C

CAB, 140

Cabinet, 37, 39

Cabinet Office, 37

Cadet forces, 79

Cafes see Restaurants and cafes

Campbell Island, 1

Canada
relationship with, 62
social security agreement, 136

Cancer
Cancer Control Council, 143
cervical cancer vaccine, 157
control of, 154
deaths, 154, 160–1
screening programmes, 157
smoking-related deaths, 151
SunSmart campaign, 150

Capital account see International accounts;
National accounts

Capital formation, 346–7

Capital stock, 347

Caravan park/camping ground use, 271, 273

Carbon emissions see Climate change

Carbon footprint of forestry industry, 378

Care and protection services, 137–8

Caregiver-provided education, 184

Cargo, overseas, 476–7

Caribbean, relationship with, 62

Carpet industry, 410

Cars see Motor vehicles

Cartoon Archive, NZ, 243

Casein, 366

Casino duty, 500

Casinos, 266, 267, 268

Cattle see Beef cattle; Dairy industry

Caves, 2, 3

Cawthron Institute, 301

CCMAU, 45, 293

Cellular service providers, 224–5, 226–7

Censorship, 251–3

Census of Population and Dwellings
see also Population
counting the population, 86
ethnicity definition, 106
identification as 'New Zealander', 107
online option, 104
population growth, 1858–2006, 85
rounding and random rounding, 87

Central government see Government

Centres of research excellence, 302

CER agreement, 60

Cervical cancer vaccine, 157

Cervical screening, 157

Chamber Music NZ, 248

Chatham Islands
Chatham Islands Council, 52
land area, 1

Cheese, 366

Cheque duty, 499, 504

Chicken production, 368–9

Chief executives, government departments,
45, 489–90

Chief Justice of NZ
generally, 196
salary and allowances, 197

Child abuse, 137, 138

Child and Youth Mortality Review Committee,
142

Child Disability Allowance, 133

Child sex offenders, extended supervision,
209

Child support, 135, 502–3

Child, Youth and Family
adoption services, 139–40
care and protection, 137–9
community services funding, 140
establishment of, 137
guiding principles, 137
youth justice services, 138–9

Childbirth
birth rate, 103
fertility rate, 84, 95–7
Human Assisted Reproductive
Technology register, 96
median age of childbearing, 97
registration, 99
vital statistics, 99

Childcare centres, 182–4

Childcare Subsidy, 132

Children and young people
adoption, 139–40
age of population, 104
care and protection, 137–8, 139
child abuse, 137, 138
family group conferences, 138
family/whānau agreements, 137
health services, 157–8
immunisation, 153, 157
literacy, international comparisons, 174
minimum wage, 277–8
Mission-On healthy lifestyles campaign,
154, 263
names, 98

obesity prevention, 142, 150
offenders *see* Young offenders
oral health services, 158–9
physical activity, 263

Chile
free trade agreement with, 406, 467
relationship with, 62

China
free trade agreement with, 61, 467
trade, value of, 474–5

Chiropractors, 147

CHOGM, 68

Choral Federation, NZ, 248

Christian denominations, 108

Christian missionaries, 16–7

Chronology of events, c1300–2007, 22–7

Chunuk Bair, 72

Churches, religious affiliation and, 108

Cigarettes *see* Tobacco

Cinema *see* Film and video

Citizens Advice Bureaux, 140

Citizenship, 109–10

Civil aviation
aircraft, number of, 428
airports, 430
Airways NZ, 429–30
bio-fuel research, 430
Civil Aviation Authority, 428–9
domestic air services, 430
employee count in sector, 428
generally, 428
international air services, 431
International Civil Aviation
Organisation, 428
jet fuel imports, 468
'open skies' agreement with Australia,
60
Pacific airspace capacity, 429
pilot licences, 428
traveller arrivals and departures, 431

Civil Defence and Emergency
Management, Ministry of, 168

Civil legal aid, 199

Civil unions
celebrants, 99
generally, 99
Property (Relationships) Act 1976, 127

Clark, Helen, 38

Clays, 403

Clerk of the Executive Council, 37

Clerk of the House of Representatives, 34

Climate
climate norms, 7, 9
extremes, 11
flooding, 11
hail, 11, 341
rain days, 9
rainfall, 9, 11, 341
sunshine hours, 9, 11
temperatures, 8, 9, 10, 11
tornadoes, 11
weather in 2007, 10–11
wind, 8, 11

Climate change
effects, 309
emissions trading scheme, 309, 389
food miles, 460
Framework Convention, 318, 319, 320
generally, 8, 10, 307, 309
'Greenhouse effect', 309
greenhouse gas emissions *see* Greenhouse
gas emissions
Intergovernmental Panel on Climate
Change, 8
international environmental work, 318–9
Kyoto Protocol
generally, 319, 320
NZ initiatives to meet commitments, 309
methane research, 366
World Environment Day, 39, 320

Clinical dental technicians, 145

Closer Economic Relations, 60

Clothing
CPI group, 337
household expenditure, 346

Clothing industry, 410

Cluster munitions treaty, 73

Clutha River, 2

Coaching, sports, 262–3

Coal, 312, 315, 390, 391, 397–9

Coalition government, 33

Coastal environment
conservation parks, 329
discharges into water, 317
length of coastline, 2
management of activities, 311
water quality, 310

Coastal shipping, 425, 426–7

Coat of arms, NZ, iv

Coins, 486

Colleges of education, enrolments,
193, 194

Colonial government, 17

Commerce and services
Auctioneers Act 1928, 450
cheque duty, 499
Commerce Act 1986, 443, 444
Commerce Commission, 444–5
companies, 443, 444
Consumer Affairs, Ministry of, 450–1
Consumer Guarantees Act 1993,
449–50
controls on trading, 448–52
corruption, international comparisons,
445
Credit (Repossession) Act 1997, 450
Credit Contracts and Consumer
Finance Act 2003, 450
Dairy Industry Restructuring Act 2001,
445
Door to Door Sales Act 1967, 450
Electricity Industry Reform Act 1997,
443, 445
energy use, 389
Fair Trading Act 1986, 443, 444,
448–9
insolvency, 447–8
insurance industry, 454–5
Layby Sales Act 1971, 450
legal environment, generally, 443

Motor Vehicle Sales Act 2003, 450
NZX all index, 447
online sales, 450
partnerships, 443, 444
sale of liquor, 451–2
Securities Commission, 446–7
shop trading hours, 451
stock exchange, 445–6
Takeovers Panel, 445
Telecommunications Act 2001, 445
Unsolicited Goods and Services Act
1975, 450
Weights and Measures Act 1987, 450

Commercial fishing *see* Fishing and fisheries

Commissioner of Police, 215

Commodities, exports and imports *see*
Exports; Imports

Commonwealth, 68–9

Commonwealth Heads of Government, 68

Commonwealth of Independent States,
relationship with, 63

Communicable disease control, 153

Communication Agencies Association of NZ,
235

Communications
advertising, 235–6
broadcasting policy, 222–3
CPI group, 337
Digital Strategy, 219, 220
employee count in sector, 356
GDP by industry, 344
generally, 219
ICT surveys, 219
magazines, 233
newspapers, 233–4
postal services, 236–8
radio, 230–2
telecommunications
relay service, 226
television, 222–4, 228–30

Community and voluntary sector
conservation work, 133
employee count in sector, 356
Family and Community Services, 138
GDP by industry, 344
Office for the Community and Voluntary
Sector, 130
Police and, 218
public health services, 155
social services funding, 150

Community boards, 53

Community education, 186

Community law centres, 199–200

Community Oral Health Service, 158

Community policing, 217

Community Probation and Psychological
Services, 208–9

Community Services Card, 133

Community support groups, 218

Community-based sentences, 209

Commuting, 432–3, 434

Companies
generally, 443, 444
liquidation, 448
receiverships, 448

registrations, 444
taxation, 497, 504
voluntary administration, 448

Comprehensive Nuclear Test-Ban Treaty
Organisation, 67

Computers
see also Internet; Telecommunications
high performance computing centres, 228

Conservation
see also Environment; Resource
management
biodiversity, 308, 319
community contribution, 133
Department of Conservation
administration of public conservation
land, 265, 324, 326–30
conservation boards, 330
recreation promotion, 265
forest funds, 330
heritage collections, 244
history, 27
organisations, 330
protected areas, 308
tourism and, 272
workplaces, 280

Conservation Authority, NZ, 330

Conservation parks, 327

Consolidated accounts see National accounts

Constables, community, 217

Constitution
see also Parliament
British sovereignty, 17
constitutional monarchy, 29
Declaration of Independence, 1835, 29
electoral system, 30–1
Executive, role of, 37
governor-general, 29–30
history, 29
Judiciary, role of, 29
nature of, 29
Parliament, role of, 30
parliamentary democracy, 29
parliamentary tradition, 30
premiers and prime ministers, 38
Queen of NZ, 29
separation of powers, 29
sources of, 29

Construction see Building and construction

Consular representation see Diplomatic
and consular representation

Consumer Affairs, Ministry of, 450–1

Consumer finance, regulation of, 450

Consumer Guarantees Act 1993, 449–50

Consumer NZ, 451

Consumers price index see Prices

Contaminants, discharge into water, 316–7

Contaminated sites, 318

Controller and auditor-general, 44, 46

Convention on Biological Diversity, 318, 319,
320

Convention on the Conservation and
Management of Highly Migratory Fish
Stocks in the Western and Central
Pacific Ocean, 59

Convictions see Criminal justice

Cook Islands
citizenship of NZ, 109
migration to NZ from, 122
special relationship with, 59

Cook, James, 16, 22, 27

Cook Strait inter-island ferries, 426

Copyright, 253–4, 304

Copyright Tribunal, 254

Coronial Services of NZ, 198

Corrections system
Community Probation and Psychological
Services, 208–9
community-based sentences, 209
courtroom custodial services, 208
Department of Corrections, 208
extended supervision orders, 209
home detention, 209
parole, 209, 212
Prison Services, 210–1
prisoner escort, 208
prisoners, 212–3
proceeds of crime, 206–7
restorative justice scheme, 202
sentence of imprisonment, 205–6, 211,
212, 213
victims' rights, 211–2

Correspondence School, 185

Corruption, international comparisons, 445

Council for International Development, 66

Council of Trade Unions, NZ, 279

Counter-terrorism, 77

Court of Appeal
generally, 197
judicial salaries and allowances, 197

Courtroom custodial services, 208

Courts system, 196–8

CPI see Prices

Craft/Object Art Fellowship, 257

Creative Communities Scheme, 257

Creative NZ
Authors' Fund, 246
generally, 256–7
Māori arts, 240

Crèches, 183–4

Credit cards, 453–4, 483–4

Credit charges, CPI group, 337

Credit Contracts and Consumer Finance
Act 2003, 450

Credit rating, foreign currency, 492

Credit Reporting Privacy Code 2004, 47

Credit (Repossession) Act 1997, 450

Crime
prevention and reduction, 207–8
proceeds of, 206–7

Criminal Investigation Branch, NZ Police, 217

Criminal justice
see also Corrections system
convictions, 201–5
arms, 206

by offence type, 201–5
dog control, 204, 206
drug offences, 203
fisheries, 206
local liquor bans, 204, 206
minors drinking in public place, 206
miscellaneous, 204, 206
motor vehicle conversion, 204
offences against administration of
justice, 204, 205
offences against good order, 204, 205
other offences against the person, 203
property offences, 203–4
sale of liquor, 204, 206
tax-related, 206
traffic offences, 204, 441
violent offences, 201–2
DNA profiles, 217
duty solicitor scheme, 199
fines, enforcement of, 206
fingerprints, 217
legal aid, 199–200
offences recorded and resolved, 201
proceeds of crime, 206–7
protection orders, 204
Public Defence Service, 200
sentences and sentencing, 205–6, 209, 211
serious fraud, 200–1
Victim Support, 207
young offenders see Young offenders

Crop & Food Research, 299

Cropping farming prices, 339

Crown Company Monitoring Advisory Unit,
44, 45, 293

Crown entities, 44

Crown forests, MAF's role, 359

Crown Law, 200

Crown Research Institute Capability Fund,
295

Crown research institutes, 44, 298–301

Crown-owned land, 324

Crown-owned minerals, 401–2

Crustacean exports, 465–6

Cultural heritage see Arts and cultural
heritage

Cultural Indicators for NZ: 2006, 255

Culture and Heritage, Ministry for, 254–5

Culture Online, NZ, 255

Currency, 485–6
see also Money

Current account see International
accounts

Curriculum, school, 173

Customary fishing regulations, 383

Customs and excise, 458, 498, 499, 504

Customs Service, NZ
border security, 458
censorship law enforcement, 253
traveller arrivals and departures, 431

Cycle helmets, 439

Cycling, 263, 433

D

Dairy cattle
  breeds, 360
  farming, 357, 359
  methane, 366
  numbers
    by category, 360
    by region, 361
    total population, 359

Dairy industry
  cooperative dairy companies, 366
  Dairy Companies Association of NZ, 366–7
  dairy company payout, 358
  exports, 360, 366, 368, 408, 460–1
  Fonterra, 366, 367
  milk production and processing, 358, 366–8
  Open Country Cheese Ltd, 368
  prices for dairy product manufacturing, 339
  Tatua Co-operative Dairy Co Ltd, 367–8
  Westland Milk Products, 367

Dairy Industry Restructuring Act 2001, 445

Dance, 249

Daylight saving, 14

De facto relationships, Property (Relationships) Act 1976, 127

Deaths
  see also Mortality
  abortion, 161–2
  air accidents, 429
  cancer, 154, 160–1
  Defence Force personnel in UN missions, 78
  drownings, 165
  earthquakes, 4
  eco-coffins, 100
  external causes, 166
  major causes, 160
  natural burials, 100
  number, 99
  road accidents, 162–4
  suicide, 155–6
  volcanic areas, 6
  workplace fatalities, 171

Debt
  see also Borrowing
  public, 333, 504–5

Debt instruments, 486–7

Declaration of Independence, 1835, 29

Deep sea volcanoes, 7

Deer, 358, 359, 361

Defence and security
  Africa, 64
  ANZUS treaty, 78
  Asia, 61
  Australia, relationship with, 60, 77
  cluster munitions treaty, 73
  Corporal Willie Apiata, 64
  counter-terrorism, 77
  disarmament, 73
  employee count in sector, 356
  expenditure, 72
  Five Power Defence Arrangements, 72, 77
  GDP by industry, 344
  generally, 71

intelligence and security, 81–2
  Middle East, 64
  NZ Defence Force see Defence Force
  Pacific region, 60, 77–8
  personnel, number of, 72
  policy, 72–3
  United Nations, involvement in, 67
  United States, relationship with, 62, 78

Defence Force
  Air Force, 76–7
  Army, 75–6
  casualties, overseas, 79
  community assistance, 79–80
  emergency and disaster relief, 79–80
  gallantry awards, 48
  hydrographic survey work for, 75
  international relationships, 77–8
  Limited Service volunteer training courses, 79
  locations, NZ, 73
  mutual assistance programme, 77, 78
  Navy, 74–5
  Operation Antarctica, 80
  personnel constituting, 71

Defence, Ministry of, 71

Demography
  see also Māori population; Population
  Asian population, 124–5
  Māori, 116–7
  Pacific peoples, 121–4

Denmark, social security agreement with, 136

Dental decay prevention, 159

Dental health services, 158

Dental research, 159

Dentists and other oral health practitioners, 145

Department of Building and Housing, 417–9, 420

Department of Conservation see Conservation

Department of Corrections, 208

Departments, generally see State sector

Departures and arrivals, 101–2

Deportation, 116

Depression era, 18

Design
  Better by Design programme, 409
  Design Mobel, 408, 409
  urban design, 53

Design registration, 303–4

Designated character schools, 186

Development assistance (aid) see International development assistance

Development Resource Centre, 66

Dictionary of NZ Biography, 255

Didymo, 315

Diesel imports, 468

Dietitians, 147

Digital rights protection, 253

Digital Strategy, 219, 220

Diplomatic and consular representation
  Asia, 61
  European Union, 62–3
  generally, 59
  Middle East, 63
  military representatives, 78
  North Africa, 63
  Pacific region, 59
  Russia and CIS, 63

Director of Human Rights Proceedings, 50, 126

Disabled people
  advisory committees, 142
  Child Disability Allowance, 133
  code of health and disability services consumers' rights, 146
  Disability Allowance, 133
  equipment and modifications services, 148
  ethics committees, 143
  Invalid's Benefit, 131, 132
  Office for Disability Issues, 130, 133
  special education, 176, 179
  sport and physical recreation, 263
  support services, 156
  telecommunications relay service, 226

Disarmament, 73

Disaster insurance, 454–5

Disaster relief see Emergency and disaster relief

Discovery of NZ, 15–7

Discrimination, 49, 50, 126, 279

Disease
  communicable disease control, 153
  immunisation, 153, 157

Dispensing opticians, 147

Disputes tribunals, 198

District courts
  generally, 197
  judicial salaries and allowances, 197

District health boards, 141–2

DNA Profile Databank, 217

Doctors, 145

Dogs
  dog control, offence convictions, 204, 206
  Police, 217

Doha Development Round, 68, 320, 357

Dolomite, 403

Dolphins, 12

Domain name registration, 220

Domestic air services, 430

Domestic Purposes Benefit, 132
  expenditure on, 135
  number of people receiving, 134
  weekly rates, 131

Domestic retail trade see Retail trade and services

Domestic violence
  immigration and, 113
  legislation, 127

Door to Door Sales Act 1967, 450

Double tax agreements, 501, 502

DPB *see* Domestic Purposes Benefit

Drama School, NZ, 249

Drinking water, 149–50

Driving
  see also Motor vehicles; Road transport
  alcohol impairment, 440
  licences, 439
  motor vehicle running costs, 440
  safety belts, 439
  sentenced prisoners by offence and
    sex, 213
  speed cameras, 216–7, 441
  speed limits, 440
  traffic offences and convictions, 204, 441

Drownings, 165

Drug Intelligence Bureau, 216

Drugs
  misuse, 150–1
  National Drug Policy, 150–1
  offences, 203
  prescription charges, 148, 149
  seizures, 216
  sentenced prisoners by offence and
    sex, 213

Duties (tax), 458, 498, 504

Duty solicitor scheme, 199

Dwellings *see* Housing

E

EAB, 82

Early childhood education
  10-year strategic plan, 183
  attendance, 183
  enrolments, 193, 194
  food and nutrition guidelines, 154
  full-time equivalent teaching staff, 192
  funding, 178–9
  generally, 182–3
  institutions, number of, 193
  licensing, 183
  Māori language, 183
  Pacific children, 183
  providers, 183–4

Earthquake Commission, 5, 6, 454–5

Earthquakes, 3, 4–5

East Asia Summit, 62

East Timor, deployment in, 62, 78, 218

EBEX$_{21}$ regeneration sites, 376

Eco-coffins, 100

Eco-fashion label, 453

E-commerce, 222

Economic Development, Ministry of, 406

Economic science research, 294

Economy
  business statistics, 355–6
  exchange rates, 332, 334, 487–8
  fiscal indicators, 333
  fiscal policy, 332–3
  foreign currency credit rating, 492
  generally, 331
  growth, 331, 332, 339–40
  inflation rate, 332, 338
  inflation target, 333

interest rates
  key market rates, 487
  monetary policy and, 334, 486
  mortgages and, 415
international accounts *see*
  International accounts
monetary policy, 333–4, 335, 486
national accounts *see* National
  accounts
net debt, 333
net worth, 333
official cash rate, 334, 335, 486
operating balance, 333
prices *see* Prices
public debt, 333, 504–5
recent developments, 332
reforms of mid-1980s, 331

Education
  administration of, 175–7
  advanced computing network (KAREN),
    295
  boards of trustees, 177
  compulsory schooling *see* Schools
  CPI group, 337
  curriculum, 173
  early childhood education *see* Early
    childhood education
  Education Review Office, 176
  employee count in sector, 356
  funding, 178–82
  high performance computing centres,
    228
  international students, 191–2
  Learning Media Ltd, 178
  literacy, international comparisons,
    174
  Māori, 182
  National Qualifications Framework,
    174–5
  NCEA, 175, 185, 186
  NZ Qualifications Authority, 176–7
  NZ Scholarship, 175, 185, 187
  NZ Teachers' Council, 177
  Pacific peoples' qualifications, 122
  Rural Education Activities Programme,
    182
  school-age population, 87, 176
  special education
    funding, 179
    policy, 176
    schools, 186
  transport assistance, 179
  teacher registration, 177
  tertiary councils, 177
  tertiary education *see* Tertiary education
  unemployment by level of attainment,
    285, 286

Education and care services, 183–4

Education, Ministry of, 175–6

Education Review Office, 176

EEO Trust, 126

EFTPOS, 483, 484

Eggs, 369

E-government Strategy, 220–1

Elderly people *see* Older people

Elections
  local government, 54
  observer missions overseas, 69
  parliamentary *see* Parliamentary
    elections

Electrical machinery
  exports, 463–4
  imports, 467–8

Electricity
  consumption, 393
  distributed generation, 391
  distribution, 392–3
  employee count in sector, 356
  GDP by industry, 344
  generally, 391
  generation, 391, 392
  prices, 339
  renewable resources, 400
  transmission, 391–2

Electricity Commission, 393–4

Electricity Industry Reform Act 1998,
  443, 445

Electronic commerce, 222

Electronic waste recycling, 222

Elizabeth II, Queen, 29

Email *see* Internet

Embassies, overseas *see* Diplomatic and
  consular representation

Emergency and disaster relief
  civil defence, 5, 168
  Defence Force assistance, 79
  insurance, 454–5
  overseas
    NZAID programmes and expenditure, 66
    Pacific region, 59

Emergency hospital treatment, 159

Emergency Maintenance Allowance, 131

Emissions *see* Air quality; Greenhouse gas
  emissions

Emissions trading scheme, 309

Employment
  see also Labour force; Labour market;
    Unemployment
  arts and cultural heritage, 239
  assistance, 287–8
  bereavement leave, 278
  civil aviation sector, 428
  discrimination, 279
  EEO Trust, 126
  employee count by sector, 356
  employment survey, 355
  equal employment opportunities, 279
  flexible working arrangements, 277
  holidays, 278
  hours of work, 278
  insurance industry, 356, 454
  KiwiSaver, 487
  labour relations, 275–7, 280
  legal framework, 275–80
  manufacturing sector, 356, 408, 409, 410
  minimum entitlements, 277–8
  minimum wage, 277–8
  modern apprenticeships, 283
  parental leave, 278
  PAYE system, 496
  safety and health, 170–1
  seasonal work assistance, 287
  sick leave, 278
  smoke-free workplaces, 153
  teaching staff, 192
  Transition to Work assistance, 287
  union membership, 279
  work permits, 114–6

work stoppages, 279–80
workers' advocacy, 279
working-age population, 87

Employment courts
generally, 197
judicial salaries and allowances, 197

Employment Relations Act 2000, 275–6

Employment Relations Authority, 277

Encyclopedia of NZ (Te Ara), 20, 255

Energy
biofuel research, aviation industry, 430
biogas, 400
biomass and waste, 400
coal, 390, 391, 397–9
consumption, 311
agricultural sector, 389
commercial sector, 389
households, 389
industry, 389
manufacturing, 411
transport sector, 311, 387, 389
electricity, 387
consumption, 393
distributed generation, 391
distribution, 392–3
employee count in sector, 356
GDP by industry, 344
generally, 391
generation, 391, 392
prices, 339
renewable resources, 400
transmission, 391–2
energy efficiency and conservation
strategy, 309, 311, 388–9
energy strategy, 311, 387–8
environment and, 390–1
environmental accounts, 341
gas, 390, 391, 396–7
generally, 387
geothermal, 390, 391, 399
greenhouse gas emissions, 311, 387, 391
hydro, 390, 391, 399
hydrogen fuel gas, 391
landfill gas, 397, 400
minerals exploration and mining see
Minerals
oil, 390, 391, 394–5
primary energy supply, 391
prisons, 211
renewable resources, 311, 390, 391,
399–401
research and development, 391
self-sufficiency, 390, 395
solar energy, 401
sources, 311
supply, 311
supply and demand balance, 389–90
use by fuel type, 311
wave energy converter, 300
wind energy, 400–1
workplace conservation measures, 280

Energy resources levies, 504

Enterprising community grants, 134, 285

Environment
see also Conservation; Resource
management; Sustainability
Adopt a Stream programme, 179
air pollution and health study, 144
air quality, 308–9
biodiversity, 307–8, 319
climate change see Climate change

coastal see Coastal environment
conservation parks, 329
energy see Energy
erosion, 313, 317
Fonterra's initiatives, 367
forest protection funds, 330
generally, 307
genetic modification, 357
hazardous substances, 315
international coordination, 318
international environmental institutions,
320
international work, 318–20
land cover, 308, 313
land use, 313, 315
marine environment, 311, 330, 427, 428
MFAT, role of, 318, 320
minerals see Minerals
mining cleanup, 402
national parks, 326, 327, 328
new organisms, 315
overseas trade and, 320
ozone layer depletion, 309–10, 319
Parliamentary Commissioner for the
Environment, 44, 50
plastic shopping bags, 451
Powelliphanta snails, 312
radioactive substances, 315
research, 295–6, 297
reserves, 329
soil quality, 312–3, 316–7
television programmes, 230
tourism and, 269, 272
Volunteer Service Abroad, 60
water quality, 310
wetlands, 329
whale sanctuaries, 329–30
World Heritage Areas, 326–7

Environment Court
generally, 198
judicial salaries and allowances, 197

Environmental accounts, 341

Environmental Risk Management Authority,
315

Environmental Science and Research,
Institute of, 301

Environmental support services for disabled
people, 156

Enviroschools Foundation, 185

Equal employment opportunities, 279

Equal Employment Opportunities
Commissioner, 126

Equal Employment Opportunities Trust, 126

ERMA, 315

ERO, 176

Erosion, 313, 317

ESR, 301

Estate duty, 504

Ethics Committee on Assisted Reproductive
Technology, 143

Ethnic Affairs, Office of, 113

Ethnic groups
age distribution, 106
Asian see Asian population
census definition, 106
composition of population, generally,
87–9, 105–6

convicted offenders, 205
country of birth, 107
European see European ethnic group
fertility rate, 97
fetal and infant mortality rate, 161
life expectancy, 100
Māori see Māori
modern apprenticeships, 283
Pacific peoples see Pacific peoples
population projections, 88–9
school leavers
attainment levels, 185
by year level, 186
unemployment, 287

European ethnic group
convicted offenders, 205
population
age distribution, 106
census of 1871, 18
decrease, 105, 106
fertility rate, 97
projections, 88–9
proportion of total, 87
unemployment, 287

European Union relationship with, 62–3
trade with, 476

Events, c1300–2007, 22–7

E-waste recycling, 222

Exchange rates, 332, 334, 487–8

Exchange reserves financing, 333

Excise and excise-equivalent duty, 458, 498,
499, 504

Exclusive economic zone, 80, 381

Executive government
Cabinet, 37, 39
composition of, 39
Executive Council, 37, 39
function, 195
ministers, appointment of, 37

Exercise see Sport and physical recreation

Exports
see also Overseas trade
annual percentage change in value, 347
Asia, 61
Australia, 60, 471
award winners, 463
balance of merchandise trade, 459
balance of payments, 348–51
boat and ship manufacturing, 410
book publishing, 247
China, 474–5
coal, 399
dairy products, 360, 366–8, 408, 460–1
excise-equivalent duty, 458, 498, 499, 504
food miles, 460
forest products, 379, 380, 462–3
fruit, 371, 464–5
horticultural exports, 371
ICT goods and services, 222
iron ore, 402
Japan, 473–4
machinery, 463–4
main destination countries, 470
major commodities, 459–60
marine industry, 410
meat, 360–1, 363–4, 408, 461–2
merchandise trade by country grouping,
476
nuts, 464–5

oil, 395
Pacific region, 59
re-exports, 458, 459
seafood, 385–6, 465–6
seeds, 371
textiles, 411
United States, 472
valuation of, 458
values and volumes of goods and
    services, 347
vegetables, 371, 464–5
white clay, 403
wine, 374
wool, 365–6

External Assessments Bureau, 82

External migration, 101–2
    see also Immigration

External trade see Exports; Imports;
    Overseas trade

Extinct species, 12, 13

F

Fair Trading Act 1986, 443, 444, 448–9

Families
    health of, 156
    issues, 127

Family and Community Services, 138

Family assistance provisions, 132–3

Family Benefit, 134, 135

Family courts
    generally, 197
    judicial salaries and allowances, 197

Family group conferences, 138, 139

Family Planning Association, NZ, 155

Family tax credits, 132, 502

Family/whānau agreements, 137

Farming see Agricultural sector

Fatalities see Deaths

Feeding our Futures programme, 150

Ferries, inter-island, 426–7

Fertility rate
    generally, 84, 95–7
    Māori, 117

Fetal mortality rates, 161

Fiji
    migration to NZ from, 123
    Police deployment in, 218

Film and Literature Board of Review, 252

Film and video
    censorship, 251–3
    cinema admissions, 251
    distribution and exhibition, 250
    Film and Video Labelling Body, 252
    Film Archive, 251
    Film Commission, 250
    screen industry businesses, 250
    screen industry revenue, 250
    top NZ films at box office, 251

Finance
    GDP by industry, 344
    local government, 54–5
    public sector see Government finance

Finance sector
    employee count, 356

Financial account see International
    accounts

Financial institutions
    Banking Ombudsman Scheme, 484, 485
    banking services, 482–4
    cashless society, 484
    EFTPOS, 483, 484
    generally, 479
    online banking, 483
    other deposit-taking institutions, 485
    ownership of banks, 480
    registered banks, 479, 481–4
    regulation, 480, 484, 485
    Reserve Bank of NZ see Reserve Bank
        of NZ

Fines, 206

Fingerprints, 217

Fire ants, 315

Fire brigades, incidents attended by, 169

Fire Service, 169–70

Fire Service Commission, 169, 455

Firearms, convictions for offences, 206

First past the post voting system, 32

Fiscal indicators, 333

Fiscal policy, 332–3

Fish, 12

Fish and game councils, 44

Fish and Game NZ, 265

Fish exports, 465–6

Fishing and fisheries
    Antarctica, 71
    commercial catch limits, 382–3, 384
    convictions for offences, 206
    customary fishing regulations, 383
    employee count in sector, 356
    energy use, 389
    environmental accounts, 341
    exclusive economic zone, 381
    fish buying guide, 383
    fish stock assessment process, 384
    GDP by industry, 344
    NZ control, 384
    Pacific region, 59
    protection, Defence Force assistance, 80
    quota management system, 311, 382–4
    recreational fishing, 264
    registered commercial vessels, 383, 384
    resources, 381–2
    seafood exports, 385–6, 465–6
    sustainability, 311, 383

Five Power Defence Arrangements, 72, 77

Fixed capital formation, 346–7

Flag, NZ, iv

Flag, first, iv, 31

Flooding, 11

Fluoridation of water, 159

Fonterra Co-operative Group, 366, 367

Food and Agricultural Organization (UN), 67

Food and beverages
    see also Alcohol
    CPI group, 336

exports see Exports
    household expenditure, 346
    safety and quality, 153–4

Food manufacturing industry, 408

Food miles, 460

Food Safety Authority, NZ, 153–4, 359

Food Standards Australia and NZ, 154, 460

Footwear, CPI group, 337

Footwear manufacturing industry, 410

Foreign Affairs and Trade, Ministry of
    see also International relations
    disarmament division, 73–4
    environment division, 318, 320
    functions, 57–8
    NZAID, 59–60, 65–6

Foreign aid see International development
    assistance

Foreign currency credit rating, 492

Foreign exchange rates, 332, 334, 487–8

Foreign investment in NZ
    generally, 348, 351–5
    land, 323

Foreign pensions, taxation of, 501

Foreign-born residents, 107

Foreign-exchange reserves financing, 333

Forests and forestry
    biosecurity, 381
    carbon footprint, 378
    carbon sinks, 319
    conservation
        forest funds, 330
        parks, 329
    Crown forestry licences, 324
    Crown forests, MAF's role, 359
    $EBEX_{21}$ regeneration sites, 376
    employee count in sector, 356
    environmental accounts, 341
    exports and imports, 379–80, 462–3
    generally, 375
    Māori interests, 377
    ownership, 376, 377
    panel production, 379
    planting and production, 377
    pulp and paper, 378, 380
    resources, 12, 375–7
    Scion, 298–9
    timber, 379, 380–1
    wood supply, 376

Forum Fisheries Agency, 59

Foundation for Research, Science and
    Technology, 296–7

FPP voting system, 32

France, Australia, NZ arrangement, 59

Franz Josef Glacier, 2

Fraud, 200–1

Free trade agreements, 59, 61, 68, 406, 467

Freeview satellite service, 222–3, 228

Freight see Rail transport; Shipping

Fresh water
    environmental accounts, 341
    quality, 310
    sport fishing, 265

Fringe benefit tax, 497

Fruit
apples, 372, 373, 464
area planted by region, 373
exports, 371, 464–5
kiwifruit, 372, 373, 464
pears, 372, 373
pipfruit marketing, 372
stone fruit, 371, 373
Summerfruit NZ, 371
ZESPRI International Ltd, 372

Fuel excise, 458, 498, 499, 504

Fuels *see* Energy; Mineral fuel imports; Oil; Petroleum

G

Gallantry awards, 48

Galleries, art, 241

Gallipoli, 19, 72

Gambling Commission, 268

Gambling, problem, 151, 268, 500

Game Bird Habitat Trust Board, NZ, 330

Game fishing, 264

Game hunting, 264–5

Gaming, 266, 267

Gaming duty, 500, 504

Gas, 390, 391, 396–7

GATT Uruguay Round, 68, 357

GCSB, 81–2

GDP *see* Gross domestic product

General elections *see* Parliamentary elections

General practitioners *see* Doctors; Primary Health Organisations

Genetic modification, 357

Genetic origins, information about, 96

Geographic Board, NZ, 325

Geography
climate *see* Climate
earthquakes, 3, 4–5
extremes, 2
geology, 3–7
landscape, 3–4
physical features, 1–3
place names, 325
vegetation, 12–3
volcanoes, 3, 4, 6–7
wildlife, 12, 13

GeoNet, 5, 7

Geothermal energy, 390, 391, 399

Giant weta, 321

Gift duty, 499, 504

Gift options for international development assistance, 65

Glaciers, 2

Global Environmental Facility, 320

Global warming *see* Climate change

GNI *see* Gross national income

GNS Science, 5, 300

Goats
farming, 361
meat exports, 364, 461

God Defend NZ (national anthem), 55

God Save the Queen (national anthem), 55

Gold
discoveries, 19th century, 18
generally, 312, 402

Goods and services tax, 498, 504

Goods, exports and imports *see* Exports; Imports

Government
see also Constitution; Parliament
administration
employee count, 356
GDP by industry, 344
departments, generally *see* State sector
Executive
Cabinet, 37, 39
composition of, 39
Executive Council, 37
function, 193
ministers, appointment of, 37
finance *see* Government finance
information matching programmes, 221
local *see* Local government
national anthems, 55
securities market, 486–7
state sector *see* State sector

Government bonds, 486

Government Communications Security Bureau, 81–2

Government finance
accounting practice, 492–3
Budget, 490–2
chief executives, duties and responsibilities, 489–90
external reporting, 493–5
foreign currency credit rating, 492
generally, 489
government expenses, 492
operating balance, 493
public account taxation and national disposable income, 504
public debt, 333, 504–5
revenue and expenses as proportion of GDP, 491
statement of cash flows, 495
statement of financial performance, 494
statement of financial position, 494–5
tax revenue, 503, 504

Government works, land held for, 324

Governor-general
former representatives, 30
functions and powers, 29–30, 36, 37
Satyanand, Judge Anand, 30
Royal Assent, 36

Grain crops, 370–1

Grapes, 373, 374

Greece, social security agreement with, 136

Green Building Council, NZ, 419

Green Cabs fleet, 439

Green Party, cooperation agreement with government, 33

Greenbuild, 421

'Greenhouse effect', 309

Greenhouse gas emissions, 8, 309
agricultural sector, 366
by source, 309
$EBEX_{21}$ regeneration sites, 376
energy sector, 311, 387, 391
food miles, 460
household purchase of carbon credits, 400
methane research, 366
ozone-depleting gases, 309
reduction initiatives, 309, 311

Greenstone, 311, 403

Grey warbler, 325

Gross domestic product
arts and cultural heritage sector and, 239
building and construction industry, 419
by industry, 343–4
definition, 339
expenditure on, 344–5
GDP and expenditure account, 340
government revenue and expenses as proportion of, 491
growth, 331, 339–40
manufacturing sector and, 406
principle aggregates, 340
research and development expenditure and, 294

Gross fixed capital formation, 346–7

Gross national income
definition, 339
per person, 332
principle aggregates, 340

Ground water quality, 310

Guardian visas, 114

Guardians of NZ Superannuation, 349

Gulf Cooperation Council, free trade negotiations, 406

H

Hail, 11, 341

Hay and silage crops, 370–1

Hazardous substances, regulation of, 315

Health
accidents *see* Accidents
CPI group, 337
death, causes of *see* Deaths
household expenditure, 346
occupational safety and health, 170–1
problem gambling, 151, 268
public health *see* Public health
research, 143–4, 296
services *see* Health services

Health and Air Pollution in NZ study, 144

Health and Disability Commissioner, 145, 146

Health and Disability Ethics Committees, 143

Health Information Privacy Code 1994, 47

Health Information Strategy Action Committee, 143

Health, Ministry of, 141

Health Research Council of NZ, 143–4, 296

Health services
advisory committees, 142–3
benefits and subsidies, 148–9

Blood Service, 143
code of health and disability services
    consumers' rights, 146
complaints, 145, 146
CPI group, 337
district health boards, 141–2
employee count in sector, 356
expenditure, 144
hospital services, 148, 159
mental health, 155
Ministry of Health, 141
organisation of, 141–6
Primary Health Organisations, 148
professionals, regulation of, 145–7
public health see Public health

Health Sponsorship Council, 150

HealthPAC, 148–9

Healthy Eating – Healthy Action strategy, 142

Hector's dolphins, 12

Herald of Arms, NZ, 46

Heritage see Arts and cultural heritage

Heritage areas, world, 326–7

High Court of NZ, 197

High performance computing centres, 228

Highways and motorways, 435

Hiking, 264

Hillary, Sir Edmund, 21

Hindu faith, 108

Hire purchase, 450

Historic Places Trust, NZ, 241–2, 330

Historic reserves, 329

History
    20th century, 18–20
    British sovereignty, 17
    Christian missionaries, 16–7
    chronology of events, c1300–2007, 22–7
    conservation, 27
    discovery, 15–6
    economic depression, 18
    Labour governments, 19, 20
    National governments, 19–20
    politics, 18–20

History Online, NZ, 255

Hocken Collections, 245

Holidays, employee entitlements, 278

Home detention, 209

Home nursing and home help, 148

Home ownership see Housing

Home-based early childhood care, 183, 184

Home-based schooling, 185–6

Honey bees and production, 368–9

Honours system, 48

Horticulture, 370–4

HortResearch Ltd, 299

Hospital services, 148, 159

Hostel accommodation use, 271, 273

Hotels
    employee count in sector, 356
    household expenditure, 346
    use, 271, 273

House of Representatives see Parliament

Household Labour Force Survey
    definitions used, 281
    unemployment, measurement of, 284

Households
    borrowing, 415
    carbon credit purchase, 400
    consumption expenditure, 346
    contents and services, CPI group, 337
    energy use, 389
    home heating
        emissions, 309
        insulation, 167
    income, 289, 345
    telecommunications services, access to,
        225

Housing
    accommodation assistance, 417, 418
    construction see Building and construction
    CPI group, 336, 337
    Department of Building and Housing,
        417–9
    home ownership
        generally, 413
        number of privately-owned dwellings,
            414
    house prices
        generally, 336, 413–4
        inflation pressures, 332
    house sales, 414
    household expenditure, 346
    Housing NZ Corporation, 415–7
    loan approvals by Housing NZ, 417
    loans and mortgages, 414–5
    new dwellings
        average floor area, 423
        units authorised, 422
    NOW Homes project, 414
    residential tenancies, 418
    retirement villages, 418
    Smarter Homes website, 416
    State Housing Appeals Service, 418
    unit titles, 418–9
    Weathertight Homes Resolution Service,
        419

Human assisted reproductive technology
    advisory committee, 143
    ethics committee, 143
    HART register, 96

Human rights
    complaints, 50, 126
    national action plan, 49, 127
    UN reporting requirements, 67
    UN resolutions, support of, 67
    unlawful discrimination, 49, 126, 279

Human Rights Commission, 49, 50, 126, 127

Human Rights Review Tribunal, 50, 126, 198

Humanitarian Action Fund, 66

Humanitarian assistance, 66

Hunting and shooting, 264–5

Hydro energy, 390, 391, 399

Hydrogen fuel gas, 391

Hydrographic survey work for Defence Force,
    75

Hydrography, national, 322

I

ICT goods and services, sales of, 222

ICTs, 219–22

Ilmenite, 402

ILO, 67, 276

Immigration
    Asian population, 124
    citizenship
        approvals by country of birth, 111
        granting of, 109–10
        legislation and policy, 109
    domestic violence policy, 113
    family-sponsored residence stream, 112–3
    international/humanitarian residence
        stream, 113
    legislation and policy, 101, 110
    net migration, 101–2
    overseas-born residents, 107
    Pacific access, 113
    Pacific peoples, generally, 121–4
    partnership policy, 113
    refugees, 101, 113
    removal and deportation, 116
    residence streams, 110
    Samoan quota, 113
    skilled/business stream, 110, 112
    skills shortage lists, 115
    sources of migration, 114
    temporary entry, 114–6

Immigration NZ, 110

Immunisation, 153, 157

Imports
    see also Overseas trade
    annual percentage change in value, 347
    Australia, 471
    balance of merchandise trade, 459
    balance of payments, 348–9
    China, 474–5
    forest products, 379, 380
    Japan, 473–4
    machinery, 467–8
    main countries of origin, 470
    major commodities, 466–7
    merchandise trade by country grouping,
        476
    mineral fuels, 468–9
    oil, 395
    Pacific region, 59
    passenger vehicles, 469
    United States, 472, 473
    valuation of, 458–9, 466
    values of goods and services, 347, 348

Imprisonment see Prisons

Income
    annual, 288, 289
    by region, 289
    household, 289
    personal income, 288–9
    salary and wage rates, 289–90, 291
    taxation see Taxation
    weekly earnings, 288, 289

Income support, 130–2

Independent Police Conduct Authority, 216

Independent schools, 185

Independent Youth Benefit, 131

Indexation of contracts, 335

Indonesia, police deployment in, 218

Industrial designs, registration of, 302–4

Industrial Research Ltd, 300

Industry
    energy use, 389, 411
    fatal accidents, 171
    manufacturing sector *see* Manufacturing
        industry
    modern apprenticeships, 283
    national certificates and diplomas, 174–5
    research associations, 302
    service industries *see* Service industries
    Straight2Work partnerships, 134
    training
        programmes, 186–7
        vocational qualifications, 174, 190–1

Infant mortality rates, 158, 161

Inflation
    see also Prices
    rate, 332, 338
    target, 333

Influenza, pandemic planning, 159

Information and communication technologies,
    219–22

Information matching programmes, 47, 221

Information privacy principles, 47

Information technology goods and services,
    sales of, 222

Injuries
    see also accidents
    accident insurance, 167–8
    prevention, 166–7, 170–1

Inland Revenue
    child support payments, collection of, 135,
        502
    student loan repayments, administration
        of, 503
    taxation, generally *see* Taxation

Inmates *see* Prisons

Insects, 12

Insolvency, 447–8

Inspector-general of intelligence and security,
    81

Institute of Environmental Science and
    Research Ltd, 301

Insulation of houses, 167

Insurance, accident, 167–8

Insurance and Savings Ombudsman, 455

Insurance Council of NZ, 455

Insurance industry
    employee count in sector, 356, 454
    GDP by industry, 344
    generally, 454–5

Integrated circuits, layout designs, 304

Integrated schools, 185

Intellectual Property Office of NZ, 302

Intellectual property rights, 253–4, 302–4

Intelligence and security agencies, 81–2

Intensive supervision, sentence of, 209

Interest rates
    key market rates, 487

monetary policy and, 333–4, 335, 486
mortgages, 415

Interfaith and inter-cultural dialogue, 67

Intergovernmental Panel on Climate Change, 8

Inter-island ferries, 426

International accounts
    balance of payments, 348–51
    capital account, 350
    current account
        balance as proportion of GDP, 353
        deficits and surpluses, 332, 353–4
        generally, 348, 349
        trade in services, 350
    financial account, 351
    generally, 348
    international assets and liabilities, 354–5
    international investment position, 348,
        352–3
    sources of international investment, 353

International Accreditation NZ, 305

International air services, 431

International Atomic Energy Agency, 67

International Civil Aviation Organisation, 428

International copyright agreements, 254

International Court of Justice, 67

International development assistance
    see also Emergency and disaster relief
    Afghanistan, 64
    Africa, 64, 66
    Asia, 61, 66
    gift options, 65
    humanitarian assistance, 66
    international agencies, 66
    Iraq, 64
    Latin America, 66
    NZ non-government organisations, 66
    NZAID, 59–60, 65–6
    Pacific region, 59–60, 65–6, 70
    UN Relief and Works Agency, 64

International Energy Agency, 69

International environmental coordination, 318

International environmental institutions, 320

International environmental work, 318–20

International investment, 348

International Labour Organization, 67, 276

International relations
    see also Defence and security
    Africa, 63, 64
    Asia, 61–2
    Australia, 60
    Canada, 62
    Caribbean, 62
    development assistance *see* International
        development assistance
    diplomatic and consular representation,
        58, 59
    European Union, 62–3
    generally, 57–8
    interfaith and inter-cultural dialogue, 67
    international organisations, 67–9
    Latin America, 62
    Middle East, 63–4
    NZ territories, 69–71
    Pacific region, 59–60
    United States, 62

International Security Assistance Force
    (Afghanistan), 64

International students
    generally, 191–2
    visas, 114

International tourism, 270–2

International Whaling Commission, 318, 320

Internet
    see also Telecommunications
    access and use, 219–22
    activities, 221
    advanced network, 228
    broadband, 219, 220, 227–8
    dial-up access, 219
    Digital Strategy, 219, 220
    domain name registrations, 220
    e-commerce, 222
    e-government strategy, 220–1
    ICT surveys, 219
    InternetNZ, 220
    Māori presence, 220
    sales, 450
    service providers, 224–5, 226–7
    spam email, 222
    subscribers, 220
    travel planning and experience sharing,
        269

Invalid's Benefit, 131, 132, 134, 135

Investment, international, 348, 351–5

In-work tax credits, 132, 502

IPONZ, 302

Iraq, deployment in, 64, 79

IRD *see* Inland Revenue

Ireland, social security agreement with, 136

Iron ore, 402

Islamic faith, 108

Islands
    conservation in subantarctic islands, 327
    outlying, 1

ISO certification service, 304–5

Israeli-Arab conflict, 64, 78

J

Japan
    CPI comparison, 338
    value of trade with, 473–4

Jersey and Guernsey, social security
    agreement with, 136

Jobs *see* Employment; Labour force

Judges
    appointment, 195
    complaints against, 195
    removal from office, 195
    role, 195
    salaries and allowances, 197

Judicial Committee of the Privy Council, 196

Jury service, 200

Justice, Ministry of, 196

Justice system
    see also Police
    corrections *see* Corrections system

courts system, 196-8, 199-200
criminal justice *see* Criminal justice
young offenders *see* Young offenders

Justices of the Peace, 197

K

KAREN, 295

Kindergartens, 183

Kingitanga, 117

Kiwi Bonds, 487

Kiwifruit, 372, 373, 464

KiwiSaver, 487

Knowledge creation funding, 294-5

Kōhanga reo, 120-1, 183

KOHA-PICD, 66

Kosovo, deployment in, 79

Kupe, 15

Kura kaupapa Māori, 120, 185

Kyoto Protocol
generally, 319, 320
NZ initiatives to meet commitments, 309

L

Labour force
definition of, 281
employment status, 282-3
full- and part-time employment, 283
growth, 282
industry structure, 283-4
modern apprenticeships, 283
occupational structure, 284
older people, 278
participation rates by sex and age, 281, 282
unemployment, 284-7

Labour governments, 19, 20, 33

Labour market
discrimination, 279
employers' advocacy, 279
employment assistance, 287-8
equal employment opportunities, 279
income, 288-90
international organisations, 276
labour costs, 290-1
labour force *see* Labour force
labour relations, 275-80
minimum entitlements, 277-8
unemployment, 284-7
union membership, 279
work stoppages, 280
workers' advocacy, 279

Labour Party, minority coalition government, 33

Labour relations, 275-80

Lahar risk, 5, 6

Lakes, 2, 3

Lamb
exports, 360, 361, 363, 364
meat production volumes, 362

Land
see also Conservation; Resource management

area, 1-2
Crown-owned, 324
erosion, 313, 317
land cover, 308, 313
Landcorp, 325
Māori land, 324
number of land transfer documents processed, 322
NZ Geographic Board, 325
overseas parties, acquisition by, 323
rural sales, 323
soil quality, 312-3, 316-7
stamp duty, 499
survey system, 321-2
title registration, 322
use, 313, 315
valuation, 325

Land Information NZ
generally, 321
land administered by, 324

Land transport *see* Rail transport; Road transport

Land Transport NZ, 433-4

Land wars, 19th century, 17

Landcare Research NZ Ltd, 299-300

Landcorp Farming Ltd, 325

Landfill gas, 397, 400

Landfills, 318

Landonline, 321

Landscape, 3-4

Language
languages spoken, 109
official, 120
Pacific peoples, 122

Latin America
development assistance, 66
relationship with, 62

Law centres, 199-200

Law Commission, 199

Lawyers, duty solicitor scheme, 199

Layby Sales Act 1971, 450

Layout designs, 304

Leader of the Opposition, 34

Learning Media Ltd, 178

Lebanon, deployment in, 64

Legal aid, 199

Legal deposit system, 243

Legal Services Agency, 199-200

Legal system
see also Corrections system; Criminal justice
attorney-general, 196
Chief Justice of NZ, 196
salary and allowances, 197
community law centres, 199-200
courts system, 196-9
Crown Law, 200
Judges *see* Judges
jury service, 200
Justices of the Peace, 197
Law Commission, 199
legal aid, 199
Legal Services Agency, 199-200
Ministry of Justice, 196

Queen as source of legal authority, 195
separation of powers, 195
solicitor-general, 200
tribunals, 198-9

Leisure
gaming, 266, 267
lotteries, 266, 267-8
racing, 266
sport *see* Sport and physical recreation

Liabilities, international, 354-5

Liberal governments, 18-9

Library services
conservation, 244
Hocken Collections, 245
legal deposit system, 243
National Library, 243-4
NZ National Bibliography, 243
Parliamentary Library, 244-5
public libraries, 245
specialist library and information centres, 246
universities, 245

Life expectancy, 101

Life insurance, 454

Limestone, 403

Limited Service volunteer training courses, 79

LINZ
generally, 321
land administered by, 324

Liquidations, 448

Liquor, sale of
see also Alcohol
convictions for offences, 204, 206
generally, 451-2
licensing, 452

Literacy of students, 174

Literature, 245, 246-7

Livestock
beef cattle *see* Beef cattle
dairy cattle *see* Dairy cattle
deer, 358, 359, 361
goats
farming, 361
meat exports, 364
numbers by category, 360
pigs, 361, 368
poultry
generally, 368-9
meat exports, 461
prices, 339
sheep *see* Sheep
slaughter, 364
stock feed, 359, 370-1
total numbers, 359
types, 360-1

Living Heritage initiative, 242

Lizard species, 308

Loans
see also Borrowing
housing, 414-5
regulation of, 450

Local government
boundaries, 51
categories of local authorities, 51
community boards, 53
decision making, 51
elections, 54

finance, 54–5
functions and powers, 51, 52–3
income, 51
legislation applicable, 51
local bills, 51
new cities, constitution of, 52
organisation of, 51–2
population estimates, 93–4
rates, setting of, 51
regional councils, 52
review authority, 51
sources of power, 51
special purpose local authorities, 53
territorial authorities, 52–3
unitary authorities, 53
urban design, 53

Local Government Commission, 54

Local Government Official Information and
    Meetings Act 1987, 46, 47, 51

Local television services, 230

Lockouts, 280

Lotteries, 266, 267–8

Lottery duty, 500

Lottery Grants Board, NZ, 267–8

M

Machinery and equipment
    economic growth, 340
    exports, 463–4
    imports, 467–8

MAF, 358–9

MAF Biosecurity NZ, 315, 359, 381, 382

Magazines, 233

Mail services, 236–8

Maize, 370, 371

Malaghan Institute of Medical Research, 144,
    302

Malaysia, free trade negotiations, 61, 406

Mana Tohu Mātauranga o Aotearoa (NZQA),
    176–7

Manaaki Whenua (Landcare Research NZ
    Ltd), 299–300

Manatū Kaihokohoko (Ministry of Consumer
    Affairs), 450–1

Manufacturing industry
    Better by Design programme, 409
    business development, 406–8
    contribution to GDP, 406
    economic activity survey, 411
    employment, 356, 409, 410, 411
    energy consumption, 411
    food industry, 408
    GDP by industry, 344
    general environment, 405
    major groups, 408–11
    marine industry, 311, 409–10
    plastics, 408
    tariffs, 405–6
    textiles, 410–1
    wine industry, 374

Manuka honey, 370

Māori
    20th century history, 20–1
    artefacts and traditional sites, 242–3

broadcasting, 224
convicted offenders, 205
cultural heritage, 239–40
customary fishing, 383
Declaration of Independence, 1835, 29
demography, 116–7
discovery and settlement of NZ, 15
early society, 15–6
education
    draft education strategy, 182
    generally, 182
    kōhanga reo, 120–1, 183
    kura kaupapa Māori, 120, 185
    wānanga, 44, 177, 188, 302
    wharekura, 120
fisheries settlement assets, 384
forestry interests, 377
health services, 157
Internet presence, 220
land wars, 17
Māori King movement, 117
organisations, 119–20
physical activity, 263
population see Māori population
religious affiliation, 108
smoking, prevalence of, 152
taonga tuku iho, 239–40
te reo Māori, 120–1, 240
toi iho, 257
unemployment, 287
writers' awards, 245

Māori Appellate Court, 198

Māori Arts and Crafts Institute, 240

Māori Congress, 120

Māori Council, NZ, 119–20

Māori Development, Ministry of, 119

Māori Education Trust, 182

Māori electoral districts, 41, 42

Māori electoral option, 31, 40

Māori Heritage Council, 240

Māori Internet Society, 220

Māori land, 324

Māori Land Court
    generally, 198, 324
    judicial salaries and allowances, 197
    land blocks administered by, 324

Māori Language Commission, 120, 240

Māori population
    age distribution, 106, 117
    female-to-male ratio, 117
    fertility rate, 97, 117
    fetal and infant mortality rates, 161
    growth, 105, 106
    infant mortality rates, 158
    life expectancy, 100
    pre-European contact, 15
    projections, 88–9
    proportion of total population, 87, 116
    regional distribution, 117, 118

Māori Television, 224, 240

Māori Trustee, 119

Māori Women's Welfare League, 120

Mapping services, 321–2

Marine environment, 311, 427, 428

Marine industry, 311, 409–10

Marine pollution, 311, 427, 428

Marine reserves and parks, 311, 330

Maritime NZ, 427–8

Marriages
    celebrants, 99
    first marriage, median age, 98
    generally, 99
    licences, 99
    Property (Relationships) Act 1976, 127
    rate, 98

Marsden Fund, 294

Maternity services, 148

Measures, metric, 450

Meat
    consumption, 361
    exports, 360–1, 363–4, 408, 461–2
    NZ Meat Board, 361
    production volumes, 362
    products, 361–4
    schedule prices, 362
    sheep meat production, 358

Meat & Wool NZ, 362

Mechanical machinery
    exports, 463–4
    imports, 467–8

Mediation of employment relationship
    problems, 276

Medical Council of NZ, 145

Medical education, 145

Medical laboratory scientists and
    technologists, 147

Medical professionals and technologists,
    145–7

Medical radiation technologists, 147

Medicines
    misuse, 150–1
    National Drug Policy, 150–1
    prescription charges, 148, 149

Members of Parliament see Parliament

Men
    see also Sex ratios
    life expectancy, 101
    prisoners, 212

Meningococcal B immunisation, 153

Mental health services, 148, 155

Merchandise trade see Overseas trade

Metals, 402

Methane research, 366

Methanol production, 397

Methyl bromide, 381

Mexico, relationship with, 62

MFAT see Ministry of Foreign Affairs and
    Trade

Michael King Writers' Fellowship, 257

Middle East
    relationship with, 63–4
    UN Truce Supervisory Organization, 64, 78

Midwives, 146, 148

Migration
    see also Immigration
    external, 101–2
    internal, 91

Military *see* Defence Force

Military Police company, 76

Milk production and processing, 358, 366–8

Mineral fuel imports, 468–9

Minerals
coal, 312, 315
Crown Minerals Act 1991, 315
Crown ownership, 401–2
environment and, 311–2
exploration and mining, 312, 315–6, 401–2, 402
exports, 402
generally, 311–2, 401
gold, 312
metals, 402
mining cleanup, 402
non-metallic, 402–3
petroleum, 316

Miner's Benefit, 134, 135

Minimum family tax credits, 502

Minimum wage, 277–8

Mining
see also Minerals
employee count in sector, 356
GDP by industry, 344

Ministries, generally *see* State sector

Ministry for Culture and Heritage, 254–5

Ministry of Agriculture and Forestry, 315, 358–9

Ministry of Civil Defence and Emergency Management, 168

Ministry of Consumer Affairs, 450–1

Ministry of Defence, 71

Ministry of Economic Development, 406

Ministry of Education, 175–6

Ministry of Foreign Affairs and Trade
see also International relations
disarmament division, 73
environment division, 318, 320
functions, 57–8
NZAID, 59–60, 65–6

Ministry of Health, 141

Ministry of Justice, 196

Ministry of Māori Development, 119

Ministry of Research, Science and Technology, 293

Ministry of Social Development *see* Social Development, Ministry of

Ministry of Women's Affairs, 126

Ministry of Youth Development, 127–8, 130

Mission-On campaign, 154, 263

Misuse of drugs, 150–1

MMP voting system, 30–1, 32–3

Mobile phone service providers, 224–5, 226–7

Modern apprenticeships, 283

Mollusc exports, 465–6

Monetary policy, 333–4, 335, 486

Money
cashless society, 484
currency, 485–6

foreign exchange rates, 332, 334, 487–8
interest rates, 334, 486
official cash rate, 334, 335, 486

Moral rights, 254

MoRST, 293

Mortality
by age and sex, 100
Child and Youth Mortality Review Committee, 142
death rate, 103
fetal mortality rates, 161
infant mortality rates, 158, 161
median age at death, 101
Perinatal and Maternity Mortality Review Committee, 143
vital statistics, 99

Mortgages, 414–5

Motel use, 271, 273

Motor Vehicle Sales Act 2003, 450

Motor Vehicle Traders Register, 436–8

Motor vehicles
see also Driving; Road transport
accidents, 162–4
age profile, 439
commuting, 432, 433, 434, 440
conversion, 203, 204
fees, 504
GreenFleet programme, 444
imported passenger vehicles, 469
inspection, 439
registers, 436–8
registration and licensing, 436–8
running costs, 440
safety belts, 439

Motorways, 435

Motu Ihupuku (Campbell Island), 1

Mountaineering, 264

Mountains, 2

Movies *see* Film and video

MPs *see* Parliament

Mt Cook, 2

Mt Ruapehu lahar, 5, 6

Multinational Force and Observers (Sinai), 64, 79

Murder, sentencing for, 211

Museums, 241

Music
Chamber Music NZ, 248
Choral Federation, 248
Māori, 240
National Youth Orchestra, 248
NZ Music Commission, 247
NZ On Air, 223
NZ Opera Ltd, 249–50
Symphony Orchestra, 247–8

Muslim faith, 108

Mutton
exports, 360, 361, 363, 364
meat production volumes, 362

Mutual assistance programme (NZ Defence Force), 77, 78

N

Names, children's, 98

Naming of places, 325

National accounts
capital stock, 347
consolidated accounts
external account, 342–3
GDP and expenditure account, 340
national capital account, 341–2
national income and outlay account, 340–1
environmental accounts, 341
external trade, 347–8
generally, 339–40
gross domestic product
arts and cultural heritage sector, 239
building and construction industry, 419
by industry, 343–4
definition, 339
expenditure on, 344–5
GDP and expenditure account, 340
government revenue and expenses as proportion of, 491
growth, 331, 339–40
manufacturing sector, 406
principle aggregates, 340
research and development expenditure and, 294
gross fixed capital formation, 346–7
gross national income
definition, 339
principle aggregates, 340
household sector, 345–6
national disposable income
definition, 339
national income and outlay account, 340–1
principle aggregates, 340
public account taxation and, 504
national saving and net overseas borrowing, 342

National Advisory Committee on Health and Disability, 142

National Advisory Committee on Health and Disability Support Services Ethics, 142

National anthems, 55

National assets, privatisation of, 20

National Beekeepers' Association, 370

National Bibliography, NZ, 243

National Certificate of Educational Achievement, 175, 185, 186

National certificates and diplomas, 174, 190–1

National Cervical Screening Programme, 157

National disposable income *see* National accounts

National DNA Databank, 217

National Drug Intelligence Bureau, 151, 216

National Drug Policy, 150–1

National environmental standards, air quality, 309

National governments, 19–20

National Heritage Preservation Incentive Fund, 242

National identity, protection of symbols, 255

National immunisation schedule, 153

National Institute of Water and Atmospheric Research Ltd, 7, 300–1

National Land Transport Fund, 434, 499

National Land Transport Programme, 434

National Library of NZ, 243–4

National parks, 326

National Preservation Office, 244

National Qualifications Framework, 174–5

National Radio, 230, 231–2

National reserves, 329

National Topographic/Hydrographic Authority of LINZ, 322

National War Memorial, 255

National Youth Orchestra, 248

Natural burials, 100

Natural disasters, relief for see Emergency and disaster relief

Natural gas, 390, 391, 396–7

Nature Heritage Fund, 330

Nature reserves, 329

Nautical charts, 75

Navigation safety, 75

Navy, Royal NZ, 74–5

NCEA, 175, 185, 186

Neglect of children, 137, 138

Net migration, 101–2

New organisms, regulation of, 315

New Zealanders, identification as, 107

Newspapers, 233–4, 235

Ngā Kaitiaki O Ngā Taonga Whitiāhua (NZ Film Archive), 251

Ngā Pou Taunaha o Aotearoa (NZ Geographic Board), 325

Ngā Taonga Kōrero (Sound Archives), 232

Ngā Whenua Rahui fund, 330

Niue
citizenship of NZ, 109
migration to NZ from, 123
special relationship with, 59

NIWA, 7, 300–1

Non-resident withholding tax, 500, 504

North Island
land area, 1
population, 90, 91

Not for profit sector see Community and voluntary sector

Notifiable diseases, 153

NOW Homes project, 414

Numeracy of students, 174

Nurses, 146

Nursing services, home-based, 148

Nut exports, 464–5

Nutrition
Mission-On campaign, 154
obesity prevention, 142, 150

Nutrition survey, 142

NZ Academy of Sport, 260–2

NZ Agency for International Development, 59–60, 65–6

NZ AIDS Foundation, 155

NZ Army, 75–6

NZ Authors' Fund, 246

NZ Automobile Association, 440, 455

NZ Bankers' Association, 484

NZ Bill of Rights Act 1990, 49

NZ Blood Service, 143

NZ Cadet Forces, 79

NZ Cancer Control Strategy, 154

NZ Cartoon Archive, 243

NZ certificates in engineering, 191

NZ Choral Federation, 248

NZ Conservation Authority, 330

NZ Council of Trade Unions, 279

NZ Culture Online, 255

NZ Customs Service see Customs Service, NZ

NZ Defence Force see Defence Force

NZ Diploma in Business, 191

NZ Drama School, 249

NZ Energy Efficiency and Conservation Strategy, 309, 311, 388–9

NZ Energy Strategy, 311, 387–8

NZ Exchange Ltd, 445–6

NZ Exclusive Economic Zone, 381

NZ Family Planning Association, 155

NZ Film Archive, 251

NZ Film Commission, 250

NZ Fire Service, 169–70

NZ Fire Service Commission, 169

NZ First, confidence and supply agreement, 33

NZ flag, first, 31

NZ Food Safety Authority, 153–4, 359

NZ Game Bird Habitat Trust Board, 330

NZ Geographic Board, 325

NZ Green Building Council, 419

NZ Herald of Arms, 46

NZ Historic Places Trust, 241–2, 330

NZ History Online, 255

NZ Institute for Crop & Food Research Ltd, 299

NZ Lottery Grants Board, 267–8

NZ Māori Council, 119–20

NZ Meat Board, 361

NZ Music Commission, 247

NZ National Bibliography, 243

NZ On Air, 223

NZ Opera Ltd, 249–50

NZ Order of Merit, 48

NZ Parole Board, 212

NZ Police see Police

NZ Police International Service Group, 218

NZ Pork Industry Board, 368

NZ Positive Ageing Strategy, 137

NZ Post Ltd, 236–8

NZ Press Association, 234

NZ Press Council, 234–5

NZ Public Service see State sector

NZ Qualifications Authority, 176–7

NZ Racing Board, 266

NZ Register of Quality Assured Qualifications, 177, 187

NZ Scholarship, 175, 185, 187

NZ School of Dance, 249

NZ Society of Authors, 246

NZ Special Air Service Group, 64

NZ Standard Time, 13–4

NZ String Quartet, 248

NZ Superannuation
generally, 135
number of people in receipt of, 134
portability, 136–7
weekly rates, 131

NZ Superannuation Fund, 349

NZ Symphony Orchestra, 247–8

NZ Teachers' Council, 177

NZ Tourism Strategy 2015, 269

NZ Trade and Enterprise, 58, 405, 406–8, 409, 457–8

NZ Transport Agency, 434

NZ Venture Investment Fund Ltd, 297

NZCE, 191

NZCTU, 279

NZDipBus, 191

NZI National Sustainable Business Awards, 408

NZQA, 176–7

NZSIS, 81

NZX, 445–6

NZX all index, 447

O

Oats, 370

Obesity prevention, 142, 150

Occupational safety and health, 170–1

Occupational therapists, 147

Ocean management, 319–20
see also Fishing and fisheries

OECD see Organisation for Economic Co-operation and Development

Offal exports, 461–2

Offences *see* Criminal justice; Young offenders

Office for Disability Issues, 130, 133

Office for Senior Citizens, 130, 137

Office for the Community and Voluntary Sector, 130

Office of Ethnic Affairs, 113

Office of Film and Literature Classification, 252–3

Office of the Insurance and Savings Ombudsman, 455

Office of Treaty Settlements, 119

Offices of Parliament, 44

Official assignee, duties under Proceeds of Crime Act 1991, 206–7

Official cash rate, 334, 335, 486

Official Information Act 1982, 46, 47

Official languages, 120

Offshore islands, land area, 1

Oil
    generally, 394–5
    imports, 468

Older people
    labour force, 278
    Office for Senior Citizens, 130, 137
    Positive Ageing Strategy, 137
    public health services, 154–5
    residential care, 154, 155

Olympic Games, 261

Ombudsmen, 44, 46–7

Onion crop research, 299

Online banking, 483

Online sales, 450

ONTRACK, 432

Open Country Cheese Ltd, 368

Open Polytechnic of NZ, the, 188

Opera, NZ, 249–50

Operation Antarctica, 80

Opticians, 147

Optometrists, 147

Oral health practitioners, 145–6

Oral health services, 158–9

Oral History Centre, 244

Oranga Pumau (HEHA strategy), 142

Order of NZ, 48

Organic farming, WWOOF movement, 372

Organisation for Economic Co-operation and Development
    energy
        primary supply, 388
        renewables, 388
    Environment Policy Committee, 320
    GNI per person, 332
    infant mortality rates, 161
    inflation rate, 338
    NZ involvement in, 69, 276
    research and development expenditure, 294
    river water quality, 310

student literacy, 174
trade, value of, 476

Orphan's Benefit, 131, 132–3, 134, 135

Osteopaths, 147

Out of School Care and Recreation Subsidy, 132

Outdoor leisure activities, 263–4

Outpatient services, 159

Overseas investment in NZ
    generally, 348, 351–5
    land, 323

Overseas relations *see* International relations

Overseas trade
    Africa, 63–4
    APEC countries, 476
    ASEAN countries, 476
    Asia, 61, 62, 473–6
    Australia, 60, 470–1
    balance of merchandise trade, 459
    Canada, 62
    cargo, 476–7
    Caribbean, 62
    China, People's Republic of 474–5
    Customs Service, 458
    development and administration, 457–9
    environment and, 320
    European Union, 62–3, 476
    exports *see* Exports
    food miles, 460
    free trade agreements, 59, 61, 68, 406, 467
    imports *see* Imports
    Japan, 473–4
    Latin America, 62
    liberalisation, 68
    merchandise exports, main destination countries, 470
    merchandise imports, main countries of origin, 470
    merchandise trade by country grouping, 476
    Middle East, 63–4
    NZ Trade and Enterprise, 457–8
    OECD countries, 476
    Pacific region, 59
    Russia and CIS, 63
    shipping services, 425, 426, 427
    suppression of confidential data in statistics, 458
    trading partners, 470–6
    United States, 62, 472–3
    World Customs Organization, 458
    WTO, 68

Overseas-born residents, 107

Oxfam's gift option, 65

Ozone layer depletion, 309–10, 319

P

Pacific Agreement on Closer Economic Relations, 59

Pacific Forum Line, 59

Pacific Island Countries Trade Agreement, 59

Pacific Islands Forum, 59

Pacific peoples
    convicted offenders, 205
    demography, 121–2

early childhood education, 183
educational qualifications, 122
fetal and infant mortality rate, 161
languages, 122
largest ethnic groups, 122
migrant quota, 113
migration to NZ, 122–4
population
    age distribution, 106, 121–2
    fertility rate, 97
    growth, 105, 106
    projections, 88–9
    proportion of total population, 87
    regional distribution, 122
religious affiliation, 122
smoking, prevalence of, 152
unemployment, 287

Pacific region
    Biketawa Declaration, 60
    defence and security, 60, 77–8
    development assistance, 59–60, 65–6, 70
    diplomatic and consular representation, 59
    disaster coordination, 59
    emergency and disaster relief, 59
    environmental issues, 320
    exports, 59
    imports, 59
    radio broadcasting, 230, 231
    relationship with, 59–60
    social security agreements, 137
    trade with, 59

Pākehā *see* European ethnic group

Palestinian-Israeli conflict, 64, 78

Pandemic planning, 159

Parental leave, 278

Parental tax credits, 502

Parents as First Teachers, 183

Parks
    conservation, 329
    marine, 330
    national, 326–8

Parliament
    see also Constitution; Executive government; Parliamentary elections
    Budget, 490–1
    function, 195
    governor-general *see* Governor-general
    House of Representatives, 32–6
        bills, types of, 36
        clerk, 32, 34, 36
        composition of 48th Parliament, 34–5
        debates, 36
        freedom of speech, 32
        functions, 32
        Leader of the Opposition, 34
        legislative procedure, 36
        salaries and allowances, 33
        select committees, 36
        sessions, 32
        Speakers, 32, 34
        television coverage, 36
    Offices of Parliament, 44
    political parties
        representation, 33
        role, 32–3
        seats held after general elections, 31
    Youth Parliament, 127, 128

Parliamentary Commissioner for the Environment, 44, 50

Parliamentary elections
  2005 election, 40
  electoral boundaries and districts, 40-2
  electoral rolls, 40
  enrolment, 40
  FPP system, 32
  Māori electoral districts, 41, 42
  Māori electoral option, 31, 40
  MMP system, 30-1, 32-3
  voter turnout, 40, 41
  voting patterns, 41
  voting process, 40

Parliamentary Library, 244-5

Parole, 209, 212

Parole Board, NZ, 212

Partnerships, 443, 444

Pasifika Early Childhood Education Services, 183

Passenger vehicle imports, 469

Pastoral agriculture, 359-61

Pastoral Greenhouse Gas Research Consortium, 366

Pastoral leasehold land, 324

Patents, 302-3

PAYE system, 496

Pears, 372, 373

PEN NZ Inc, 246

Penal institutions see Prisons

Pensions
  expenditure on, 135
  foreign pensions, taxation of, 501
  number of people in receipt of, 134
  NZ Superannuation, 131, 134, 135, 136-7

People's Republic of China see China

Performers' rights, 254

Performing arts, 247-50

Perinatal and Maternity Mortality Review Committee, 143

Persistent organic pollutants, 318

Personal computers see Computers; Internet

Personal information, disclosure of, 47

Personal Property Securities Register, 436-7

Personal services
  employee count in sector, 356
  GDP by industry, 344

Peru, relationship with, 62

Pests and diseases
  bio-control, 359
  didymo, 315
  fire ants, 315
  marine pest management, 382
  sea squirt, 315, 382
  thistle control, 359
  varroa mite, 370

Petrochemicals, 397

Petroleum
  distribution, 395
  end use, 395
  exploration and mining, 316
  fuels excise, 458, 498, 499, 504
  imports, 468
  refinery, 395

retailing, 395
  unleaded petrol, 395

PHARMAC, 149

Pharmaceutical benefits, 148

Pharmacists, 147

Physical recreation see Sport and physical recreation

Physiotherapists, 146

Pigs and pigmeat, 361, 362, 368

Pikihuia Awards, 245

Pipfruit
  area planted, 373
  exports, 372
  marketing, 372

Place names, 325

Plant species, 12-3

Plant variety rights, 304

Plastic shopping bags, 451

Plastics industry, 408

Platinum group metals, 402

Playcentres, 183

Playgroups, 184

Plunket Society, 155

Podiatrists, 147

Police
  armed offenders squads, 216
  assaults on, 216
  censorship law enforcement, 253
  Commissioner, 215
  community policing, 217
  community support groups, 218
  complaints against, 216
  Criminal Investigation Branch, 217
  dogs, 217
  drug seizures, 216
  fingerprint processing, 217
  generally, 215
  International Service Group, 218
  operations, 216-8
  overseas deployments, 218
  Police Infringement Bureau, 216-7
  population per sworn officer, 215
  prosecutors, 215
  search and rescue, 216
  Special Tactics Group, 216
  speed cameras, radars and lasers, 216-7, 441
  wiki for new Policing Act, 215
  Youth Education Service, 217

Police detention legal assistance, 199

Political history, 18-20

Political parties
  representation, 33
  role, 32-3
  seats held after general elections, 31

Pollution
  air, 308-9
  air pollution and health study, 144
  marine environment, 311, 428
  water, 317
  water quality, 310

Polynesian discovery and settlement of NZ, 15

Polynesian peoples see Pacific peoples

Polytechnics/institutes of technology
  enrolments, 193, 194
  governance, 177
  list of, 188
  number of, 44
  Open Polytechnic of NZ, 188
  research, science and technology, 302
  vocational qualifications, 174, 190-1

Population
  see also Census of Population and Dwellings
  age-sex profile, 103-4
  Asian see Asian population
  components of change, 95-102
  counting, 86
  country of birth, 107
  distribution, 90-4
  estimated population, 1885-2007, 90
  ethnic composition, 87-9, 105-6
  European
    age distribution, 106
    census of 1871, 18
    decrease, 105, 106
    projections, 88-9
    proportion of total population, 87
  external migration, 101-2
  fertility rate, 84, 95-7
  growth see Population growth
  internal migration, 91
  life expectancy, 101
  local government areas, 93-4
  Māori see Māori population
  mortality, 100-1
  net migration, 101-2
  North Island, 90, 91
  overseas-born, 107
  Pacific peoples
    age distribution, 121-2
    growth, 105, 106
    projections, 88-9
    proportion of total population, 87
    regional distribution, 122
  regional estimates, 93
  rounding and random rounding, 87
  rural, 92-3
  school-age, 87, 176
  South Island, 90, 91
  urban, 92-3
  vital statistics, 99

Population growth
  censuses, 1858-2006, 85
  components of change, 95-102
  ethnic groups, 87-9, 105-6
  future demographic trends, 83-4
  historical and projected, 83, 84
  projections
    age groups, 85, 86-7, 88
    components of population change, 85
    dependency ratio, 86
    educational age groups, 87, 176
    ethnic population, 88-9
    generally, 85
    regional populations, 89

Pork, 361, 368

Pork Industry Board, NZ, 368

Ports
  generally, 427
  overseas cargo loaded and unloaded, 476-7

Positive Ageing Strategy, NZ, 137

Postal services, 236-8

Potato crop research, 299

Pouhere Taonga (NZ Historic Places Trust), 241–2, 330

Poultry industry
  exports, 461
  generally, 368–9

Poultry Industry Association of NZ, 369

Pounamu, 311, 403

Powelliphanta snails, 312

Precipitation, total volume, 341

Premiers, former, 38

Prescription charges, 148, 149

Preservation of heritage collections, 244

Press Association, NZ, 234

Press Council, NZ, 234–5

Preventive detention, 211

Prices
  building and construction indexes, 422–3
  consumers price index
    deflation uses, 336
    expenditure weights, 335, 336
    generally, 334
    groups of items, 336–7
    indexation of contracts, 335
    inflation rate, 332, 338
    inflation target, 333
    international comparisons, 338
    monetary policy, 333–4, 335
    price collection, 335
    retail prices of selected items, 337
  generally, 334
  houses, 413–4
  producers price index, 338–9
  share price movement, 446

Primary Health Organisations, 148

Primary production see Agricultural sector;
  Forests and forestry

Prime ministers
  former, 38
  Helen Clark, 38

Prime Television, 229

Prisons
  energy cost reduction, 211
  inmate employment, 214–5
  inmates per mean population, 210
  new facilities, 210
  NZQA units and credits achieved by
    inmates, 213
  offences against prison discipline, 215
  parole eligibility and final release, 212
  Prison Services, 210
  prisoner escort, 208
  prisoners, 212–4
  sentence of imprisonment, 205–6, 211, 212

Privacy commissioner, 47–8

Private schools, 185

Private training establishments, 180

Privatisation of state assets, 20

Privy Council, 196

Probation services, 208–9

Problem gambling, 151, 268

Problem gambling levy, 500

Producers price index, 338–9

Progressive Party, coalition agreement, 33

Property (Relationships) Act 1976, 127

Property offences, 203–4

Property, school, 180

Property services, employee count in sector, 356

Protected areas network, 308

Protected Disclosures Act 2000, 47

Protected objects, 242–3, 255

Protection orders, 204

Psychologists, 146

Public Advisory Committee on Disarmament
  and Arms Control, 74

Public debt, 333, 504–5

Public health
  alcohol, 151
  cancer control, 154
  child health, 157–8
  communicable disease control, 153
  disability support services, 156
  drinking water, 149–50
  drug misuse, 150–1
  drug policy, 150–1
  family health, 156
  food safety and quality, 153–4
  generally, 149
  immunisation, 153, 157
  Māori health, 157
  marketing healthy lifestyles, 150
  mental health, 155
  not-for-profit organisations, 155
  older people, 154–5
  oral health, 158–9
  pandemic planning, 159
  sexual and reproductive health, 156–7
  suicide prevention, 155–6
  tobacco, 151–3
  women's health, 157

Public holidays, employee entitlements, 278

Public hospitals, 148, 159

Public libraries, 245

Public radio, 230–2

Public register privacy principles, 47

Public sector finance see Government finance

Public Service see State sector

Public transport, commuting, 432–6

Public Trust, 51

Publications and publishing
  books, 245, 246–7
  censorship, 251–3
  magazines, 233, 235
  Māori and Pacific writers, 245
  newspapers, 233–5
  NZ National Bibliography, 243

Pulp and paper industry, 378, 380

Push Play, 263

secondary school leavers, 185
tertiary education
  bachelor degrees, sex ratio of, 188
  completions, 190
  Register of Quality Assured
    Qualifications, 187
  unemployment by educational attainment,
    285, 286
  vocational, 174, 190–1

Quality Improvement Committee, 143

Qualmark NZ Ltd, 271

Quarantine fumigant, 381

Queen Elizabeth II National Trust, 330

Queen of NZ, 29

Queen's Service Medal, 48

Queen's Service Order, 48

R

Race Relations Commissioner, 126

Racing
  broadcasting, 230, 266
  generally, 266

Racing Board, NZ, 266

Radiation Protection Advisory Council, 143

Radiation technologists, 147

Radio
  broadcasting policy, 222–3
  broadcasting standards, 223–4
  commercial radio, 232
  community access, 232
  Māori broadcasting, 224, 240
  NZ On Air, 223
  Pacific region, 230, 231
  public radio, 230
  Sound Archives, 232
  spectrum management, 231

Radio Network of NZ Ltd, 232

Radio NZ, 230, 231–2

Radio Trackside, 266

Radioactive substances, regulation of, 315

Radiocommunications, 231

Rail transport
  commuting, 432, 436
  freight transport, 432, 433
  history, 15, 431–2
  noise reduction, 436
  passenger services, 432–3

Rain days, 9

Rainfall, 9, 11, 341

Rakiura, land area, 1

RAMSI, 60, 79, 218

Raoul Island, land area, 1

Rates
  rating valuations, 325
  setting of, 51

Receivership, 448

Recreation
  see also Arts and cultural heritage; Leisure;
    Sport and physical recreation
  CPI group, 336, 337

Q

Qualifications
  National Qualifications Framework, 174–5
  NCEA, 175, 185, 186
  NZ Scholarship, 175, 185, 187
  quality assurance, 176

employee count in sector, 356
household expenditure, 346

Recreation reserves, 329

Recycling of e-waste, 222

Refugee immigration, 101, 113

Regional Assistance Mission to the Solomon
Islands, 60, 79, 218

Regional councils, 52

Regions
arts development, 257
Asian population, 125
employees in manufacturing, 410
fruit plantings, 373
income by, 289
livestock distribution by, 361
Māori population, 117, 118
Pacific peoples, 122
population estimates, 93
population projections, 89
retail sales by, 453
television services, 230

Registers
births, deaths, marriages and civil unions, 99
Human Assisted Reproductive Technology
Register, 96
motor vehicles, 436–8
public register privacy principles, 47

Registration
banks, 480
companies, 444
health service professionals, 145–7
land titles, 322
motor vehicles, 436–8
ships, 427
teachers, 177

Relationship property legislation, 127

Religious affiliation, 108, 122

Removal from NZ, 116

Renewable energy see Energy

Reproductive health, 156–7

Reproductive technology see Human assisted
reproductive technology

Rescue operations
Defence Force assistance, 80
Police, 216

Research, science and technology
advanced network, 228, 295
Cawthron Institute, 301
CCMAU, 293
centres of research excellence, 302
Crown Research Institute Capability Fund,
295
Crown research institutes, 298–301
economic research, 294
energy sector, 391
environmental research, 295–6, 297
expenditure as proportion of GDP, 294
Foundation for Research, Science and
Technology, 296–7
funding, 294–7
high performance computing centres, 228
intellectual property rights, 302–4
knowledge creation, 294–5
Marsden Fund, 294
MoRST, 293
NZ Venture Investment Fund Ltd, 297
organisation of, 293

polytechnics, 302
potatoes and onions, 299
research agencies, 298–302
research associations, 302
research consortia, 302
Roadmaps for Science, 298
Royal Society of NZ, 296, 297
Smash Palace Fund, 257
standards and accreditation services,
304–5
synchrotron facility, 298
system, 297
tax credits, 298
universities, 297, 302
Vote Research, Science and Technology,
294–6, 297
wānanga, 302
wave energy converter, 300

Reserve Bank of NZ
as part of state services, 44
assets and liabilities, 481
bank registration and supervision, 480
functions, generally, 479
government securities registers, 487
monetary policy, 333–4, 486
regulation of non-bank deposit takers, 485

Reserve boards, 44

Reserves, 329

Resident withholding tax, 496, 504

Residential care
older people, 154, 155
young offenders, 139

Residential sector see Households; Housing

Residential Tenancies Act 1986, 418

Resource management
see also Conservation; Environment
contaminated sites, 318
discharges into water, 317
district planning, 314
land use constraints, 315
mineral exploration and mining, 316, 402
national policies, 313–4
planning framework, 313–4
public involvement, 315
purpose of RMA, 313
regional policies and plans, 314
resource consents, 315
soil management, 312–3, 316–7
sustainable management, 314
waste and landfills, 318
water management, 316, 317

Restaurants and cafes
employee count in sector, 356
GDP by industry, 344
household expenditure, 346

Restorative justice scheme, 202

Retail trade and services
credit cards, 453–4
employee count in sector, 356
GDP by industry, 344
information technology goods and services,
222
plastic shopping bags, 451
prices of selected items, 337
retail sales, 452–4
sales by industry, 452
sales by region, 453

Retirement
KiwiSaver, 487

NZ Superannuation, 131, 134, 135, 136–7
NZ Superannuation Fund, 349
Retirement Commission, 136
Transitional Retirement Benefit, 134, 135

Retirement Villages Act 2003, 418

Rivers
generally, 2
greatest flow, 2
management, 316
water quality, 310

Road transport
see also Driving; Motor vehicles
accidents, 162–4
alcohol impairment, 440
commuting, 432, 433, 434, 436
cycle helmets, 439
cycling, 433, 434
driver licensing, 439
emissions, 308–9
fuel excise, 458, 498, 499, 504
funding, 434
generally, 433
Green Cabs fleet, 439
Land Transport NZ, 433–4
motor vehicle registers, 436–8
National Land Transport Fund, 499
NZ Transport Agency, 434
road user charges, 499, 504
roading network, 434–5
safety, 163, 438–41
safety belts, 439
sentenced prisoners by offence and sex,
213
speed cameras, radars and lasers, 216–7,
441
speed limits, 440–1
traffic offences and convictions, 204, 213,
441
Transit NZ, 434
transport services licensing, 436
vehicle inspection, 439
vehicle registration and licensing, 436–8
walking, 433, 434

Roadmaps for Science, 298

Ross Dependency, 1, 70–1

Rounding and random rounding, 87

Royal Honours, 48

Royal NZ Air Force, 76–7

Royal NZ Ballet, 249

Royal NZ Navy, 74–5

Royal NZ Plunket Society, 155

Royal Society of NZ, 296, 297

Ruapehu eruption, 8

Ruapehu lahar, 5, 6

Rural Education Activities Programme, 182

Rural land sales, 323

Rural population, 92, 93

Russia, relationship with, 63

S

Safety
accident prevention, 166–7
air, 428, 429
civil defence emergency management, 168

fire protection, 169–70
maritime, 427–8
occupational safety and health, 170–1
road, 163, 438–41
water, 165

Salaries and allowances
Judges, 197
parliamentary, 33
salary and wage rates, 289–90, 291

Sale of liquor
see also Alcohol
convictions for offences, 204, 206
generally, 451–2
licensing, 452

Salmon, 265, 384

Salt, 403

Samoa
citizenship of NZ, 109
migrant quota, 113
migration to NZ from, 123

Satyanand, Judge Anand, 30

Save the Children's gift option, 65

Scenic reserves, 329

Scholarship, NZ, 175, 185, 187

Schools
administration of education, 175–8
Adopt a Stream programme, 179
assessment of students, 186
boarding, 185
boarding bursaries, 180
boards of trustees, 177
Community Oral Health Service, 158
Correspondence School, 185
crime prevention programmes, 217
curriculum, 173
designated character schools, 186
enrolments, 193, 194
Enviroschools Foundation, 185
food and nutrition guidelines, 154
full-time equivalent teaching staff, 192
funding, 178–80
generally, 184–5
governance, 177
home-based schooling, 185–6
independent (private) schools, 185
institutions, number of, 193
integrated schools, 185
international students, 191–2
kura kaupapa Māori, 120, 185
literacy, international comparisons, 174
Living Heritage initiative, 242
NCEA, 175, 185, 186
number of days required to be open, 185
NZ Scholarship, 175, 185
property, 180
school leavers
attainment levels, 185
by year level, 186
school-age population, 87, 176
special education
funding, 179
policy, 176
transport assistance, 180
special schools, 186
state schools, 185
structure of system, 184
terms, 185
transport, 180
types, 185–6
wharekura, 120

Science sector see Research, science and
technology

Scientific literacy of students, 174

Scientific reserves, 329

Scion, 298–9, 378

Scott Base, 70

Sculpture, wind-powered, 248

Sea Cadet Corps, 79

Sea squirt, 315, 382

Seafood exports, 385–6, 465–6

Seaports, overseas cargo loaded and
unloaded, 476–7

Search and rescue
Defence Force assistance, 80
Police, 216

Seasonal work assistance, 287

Secretariat of the Pacific Community, 59, 60

Secretary of the Cabinet, 37

Securities Commission, 446–7

Securities market
generally, 445–7
government securities, 486–7

Security see Defence and security

Security Intelligence Service, 81

Security interests in vehicles, registration of,
436–7

Seed certification, 371

Seed exports, 371

Select committees, 36

Senior citizens see Older people

Sentences and sentencing, 205–6, 209, 211

Serious Fraud Office, 200–1

Serpentine, 403

Service industries
see also Accommodation; Communications;
Defence and security; Financial
institutions; Health services; Retail trade
and services; State sector; Transport
employee count in sector, 356
GDP by industry, 343, 344

Services, exports and imports see Exports;
Imports

Sex offences, 202, 213

Sex offenders, extended supervision, 209

Sex ratios
age-sex distribution, 103
employment
by industry, 284
by occupation, 284
labour force participation rates, 281, 282
modern apprenticeships, 283
weekly earnings, 288, 289
Māori, 117
mortality, 100–1
prisoners, 212
school leavers
attainment levels, 185
by year level, 186
tertiary education
bachelor degrees, 188
convicted offenders, 205

deaths from external causes, 166
field of study and level of study, 189
unemployment, 286, 287

Sexual health, 156–7

Share market, 445–6

Sheep
farming, 359
lamb
exports, 360, 362, 363, 364
meat production volumes, 362
Meat & Wool NZ, 362
methane, 366
mutton
consumption, 361
exports, 363, 364
meat production volumes, 362
numbers, 358, 359
by category, 360
by region, 361
total export value, 461
total meat production, 362
wool
exports, 364–6
marketing, 365
prices, 365
production, 358, 364–5
uses, 364

Ship design and construction, 409–10

Shipping
bulk shipping, 427
coastal, 425, 426–7
domestic sea freight strategy, 427
inter-island shipping services, 426
marine pollution, 311, 427, 428
maritime accidents, 428
maritime safety, 427–8
overseas trade, 425, 426, 427
ports, 427
registered vessels, 427
seafarer qualifications, 427
wrecks, 428

Shooting and hunting, 264–5

Shop trading hours, 451

Sick leave, employee entitlements, 278

Sickness Benefit, 131, 132, 134, 135

Silage crops, 370–1

Silica sand, 403

Silver, 402

Sinai, Multilateral Force and Observers,
64, 79

Singapore, free trade agreement with, 61,
406, 467

Single transferable vote system, 54

SIS, 81

Skiing, 264

Skilled migrants, 110, 112

Skills-based work visas and permits, 115

Skink species, 308

SKY Network Television Ltd, 229, 230

Smokefree programme, 150

Smoke-free workplaces, 153

Smoking, prevalence of, 152

Smoking-related deaths, 151–2

Snails, 312

Snowboarding, 264

Social development
see also Social Development, Ministry of
aims, 129
child support payments, collection of, 135
Citizens Advice Bureaux, 140
definition, 129
research, 296
StudyLink, 134–5, 181–2, 503
trans-Tasman travel arrangement, 60
welfare benefits *see* Work and Income

Social Development, Ministry of, 129–40
aims, 129
Child, Youth and Family *see* Child, Youth and Family
functions, generally, 129–30
Ministry of Youth Development, 127–8, 130
Office for Disability Issues, 130, 133
Office for Senior Citizens, 130, 137
Office for the Community and Voluntary Sector, 130
Work and Income *see* Work and Income

Social framework
Asian population *see* Asian population
citizenship, 109–10
ethnicity, generally *see* Ethnic groups
European ethnic group *see* European ethnic group
human rights *see* Human rights
immigration *see* Immigration
languages spoken, 109
Māori *see* Māori
Pacific peoples *see* Pacific peoples
religious affiliation, 108
social welfare *see* Social development

Social security agreements, 136–7

Social welfare benefits *see* Work and Income

SOEs, 44–5

Soil quality and conservation, 312–3, 316–7

Solar energy, 401

Solicitor-general, 200

Solomon Islands, deployment in, 60, 79, 218

Sorted (Retirement Commission's website), 136

Sound Archives, 232

South Africa, 64, 66

South Island
land area, 1
population, 90, 91

South Pacific Applied Geoscience Commission, 59

South Pacific Commission *see* Secretariat of the Pacific Community

South Pacific Forum, 59

South Pacific Regional Environment Programme, 59, 320

South Pacific Regional Trade and Economic Cooperation Agreement, 59

Sovereigns
former, 29
governor-general, appointment of, 30
Queen Elizabeth II, 29

Spam email, 222

SPARC, 259–63

Speaker of the House of Representatives, 32, 34

Special air service group, NZ, 64, 76

Special Benefit, 133

Special education
funding, 179
policy, 176
special schools, 186
transport assistance, 180

Special Needs Grant, 133

Special purpose local authorities, 53

Speed cameras, 216–7, 441

Speed limits, 440

Sport and physical recreation
Academy of Sport, 260–2
Active Communities initiative, 262
coaching, 262–3
Department of Conservation's role, 265
disabled people, 263
generally, 259
Green prescriptions, 262
high-performance athletes, 260–1
Mission-On, 263
No Exceptions strategy, 263
Olympic Games, 261
outdoor activities, 263–4
physical activity rates, 260
Push Play, 263
SPARC, 259–63
tai chi for older people, 260
Te Roopu Manaaki, 263
young people, 263

Stamp duty, 499

Stamp issues, 237, 238, 304

Standards and accreditation services
science and technology sector, 304–5
tourist accommodation, 271

Standards NZ, 305

State and state-integrated schools *see* Schools

State assets, privatisation of, 20

State highways, 435

State Housing Appeals Service, 418

State sector
CCMAU, 45, 293
composition, 42–5
controller and auditor-general, 46
Crown entities, 44
EEO groups, 279
government administration
employee count, 356
GDP by industry, 344
human rights, 49–50
NZ Bill of Rights Act 1990, 49
Offices of Parliament, generally, 44
official information, 46, 47
Ombudsmen, 44, 46–7
parliamentary commissioner for the environment, 50
privacy commissioner, 47–8
Public Trust, 51
public service departments
Budget, 490–2
chief executives, 45, 489–90
full-time equivalent staff employed, 44
list, 43–4
Reserve Bank of NZ, 44

state services, 43–4
State Services Commission, 45
state services commissioner, 45
state-owned enterprises, 44–5
tertiary education institutions, 44

State-owned enterprises, 44–5

Statistical calculations, rounding and random rounding, 87

Step up scholarships, 181

Stewart Island, land area, 1

Stock *see* Livestock

Stock exchange, 445–6

Stockholm Convention on Persistent Organic Pollutants, 319

Straight2Work industry partnerships, 134

Streams, water quality, 310

Streets, 435

Strikes, 280

String Quartet, NZ, 248

Student allowance, 134, 181, 182

Student loan scheme, 134, 181, 503

Students *see* Early childhood education; Schools; Tertiary education

StudyLink, 134, 181–2, 503

Subantarctic islands, conservation in, 327

Sudan, deployment in, 64, 79

Suicide, 155–6

Sulphur, 403

Summerfruit NZ, 371

Sunshine hours, 9, 11

SunSmart campaign, 150

Superannuation Fund, NZ, 349

Superannuation, NZ
generally, 135
number of people receiving, 134
portability, 136–7
weekly rates, 131

Supercomputers, 228

Supervision, sentence of, 209

Supreme Court of NZ
generally, 196
judicial salaries and allowances, 197

Surveying
hydrographic survey work for Defence Force, 75
land, 321–2

Sustainability
eco-fashion label, 453
Enviroschools Foundation, 185
fisheries, 311, 383
Greenbuild website, 421
GreenFleet programme, 444
NOW Homes project, 414
office buildings, 419
prisons' energy use, 211
Smarter Homes website, 416
Sustainable Business Awards, 408
Sustainable Business Network, 444
sustainable management under Resource Management Act 1991, 314
tourism, 269, 272

World Summit on Sustainable Development, 320

Symbols of national identity, protection of, 255

Symphony Orchestra, NZ, 247–8

Synchrotron facility, 298

T

TAB, 266

Tai chi, 260

Taihoro Nukurangi (NIWA), 300–1

Takeovers Panel, 445

Talent-based visas and work permits, 115–6

Tariffs
  see also Free trade agreements
  GATT Uruguay Round, 68, 357
  manufacturing sector, 405–6
  WTO Doha Development Round, 68, 320, 357

Tasman, Abel, 16

Tasman Glacier, 2

Tatua Co-operative Dairy Co Ltd, 367–8

Taupo Fishery Advisory Committee, 330

Taxation
  cheque duty, 499, 504
  companies, 497, 504
  convictions for offences, 206
  double tax agreements, 501, 502
  excise and excise-equivalent duty, 458, 498, 499, 504
  foreign pensions, 501
  foreign-source dividend withholding payments, 504
  fringe benefit tax, 497
  fuel excise, 458, 498, 499, 504
  gaming duty, 500, 504
  gift duty, 499, 504
  goods and services tax, 498, 504
  imputation credits, 496
  income tax, 496–7
  individuals, 496, 504
  international tax, 500–2
  non-resident withholding tax, 497, 500, 504
  non-residents, 500–1
  public account taxation and national disposable income, 504
  rebates, 496–7
  research and development expenditure tax credits, 298
  resident withholding tax, 496, 504
  revenue from, 504
  road user charges, 499, 504
  stamp duty, 499
  tax rates, 496, 497
  taxation review authorities, 503
  Working for Families tax credits, 132, 502

Taxis, green fleet, 439

Te Āhurutanga (NZ Register of Quality Assured Qualifications), 177, 187

Te Aka Matua o te Ture (Law Commission), 199

Te Ara – the Encyclopedia of NZ, 20, 255

Te Hakituatahi o Aotearoa (First Flag of NZ), 31

Te Kāhui Tika Tangata (Human Rights Commission), 49, 50, 126, 127

Te Kaunihera Māori (NZ Māori Council), 119–20

Te Komihana Tirotiro Aitua Waka (Transport Accident Investigation Commission), 426

Te Kooti Whenua Māori (Māori Land Court), 198, 324

Te Kotahitanga Manu Reo o Aotearoa (NZ Choral Federation), 248

Te Kura Toi Whakaari O Aotearoa (NZ Drama School), 249

Te Mana Matapono Matatapu (Office of the Privacy Commissioner), 47–8

Te Manatū Ahuwhenua Ngāherehere (MAF), 358–9

Te Manatū Pūtaiao (MoRST), 293

Te Manatū Whakahiato Taiohi (Ministry of Youth Development), 127–8

Te Māngai Pāho, 224

Te Matatini Society Inc, 240

Te Ohu Kaimoana, 384

Te Papa Tongarewa, 241

Te Pou Oranga Kai o Aotearoa (NZFSA), 359

Te Pou Taki Kōrero (Learning Media Ltd), 178

Te Pouherenga Kaiako o Aotearoa (NZ Teachers' Council), 177

Te Puna Mātauranga o Aotearoa (National Library of NZ), 243–4

Te Puna Tahua (NZ Lottery Grants Board), 267–8

Te Puni Kōkiri, 119

Te Rākau Whakamarumaru (Ministry of Civil Defence and Emergency Management), 168

Te reo Māori, 120–1, 240

Te Reo Whakapuaki Irirangi, 224

Te Roopu Manaaki, 263

Te Rōpū Wāhine Māori Toko i te Ora (Māori Women's Welfare League), 120

Te Rōpū Whakatarairanga Hauora (Health Sponsorship Council), 150

Te Tāhuhu o te Mātauranga (Ministry of Education), 175

Te Tari Hara Tāware (Serious Fraud Office), 200–1

Te Tari Matawaka (Office of Ethnic Affairs), 113

Te Tari Tohu Taonga (National Preservation Office), 244

Te Taura Whiri i te Reo Māori (Māori Language Commission), 120, 240

Te Whakakotahitanga o Ngā Iwi o Aotearoa (Māori Congress), 120

Teacher registration, 177

Teachers' Council, NZ, 177

Teaching staff, 192

Tearfund's gift option, 65

Technology sector *see* Research, science and technology

Telarc SAI Ltd, 304

Telecommunications
  see also Internet
  advanced network, 228
  broadband, 219, 220, 227–8
  generally, 224
  high performance computing centres, 228
  household access, 225
  Kiwi Share TSO, 225–6
  local loop unbundling, 226
  operational separation of Telecom, 226
  regulated services, 225
  regulatory bodies, 225
  relay service, 226
  Telecom NZ Ltd, 224, 226–7
  Telecommunications Act 2001, 445
  Telecommunications Commissioner, 224
  TelstraClear Ltd, 224, 227
  TUANZ, 227
  Vodafone NZ, 224, 227

Television
  broadcasting policy, 222–3
  broadcasting standards, 223–4
  community access, 230
  environmental programmes, 230
  Freeview, 222–3, 228
  local content, 229, 230
  Māori broadcasting, 224, 240
  most popular programmes, 229
  NZ On Air, 223
  parliamentary proceedings, 36
  service providers, 228–30
  TVNZ charter, 222

Television NZ Ltd, 222, 228–9

TelstraClear Ltd, 224, 227

Temperatures, 8, 9, 10, 11

Temporary Additional Support, 133

Tenancies, residential, 418

Tenancy Tribunal, 198

Tenders, 450

Territorial authorities
  generally, 52–3
  population estimates, 94

Terrorism, 77

Tertiary councils, 177

Tertiary education
  accommodation benefit, 181
  administration, 177
  affordability and access, 187
  attendance, 187
  enrolments 1875–2006, 194
    by educational institute, 193
    by field of study, level of study and sex, 189
  full-time equivalent teaching staff, 192
  funding, 180–2, 187
  generally, 186–8
  health professionals, 145–7
  institutions, number of, 44, 193
  international students, 191–2
  library services, 245
  Open Polytechnic of NZ, 188
  polytechnics/institutes of technology, 188
  private training establishments, 180, 189
  qualifications
    bachelor degrees, 187

completions, 190
    Register of Quality Assured
      Qualifications, 187
scholarships, 181, 182
scope of, 186
statement of priorities, 187
student allowance, 134, 181, 182
student loan scheme, 134, 181, 503
StudyLink, 134-5, 181-2, 503
Tertiary Education Strategy, 187
tertiary-age population, 87
universities, 188
vocational qualifications, 174, 190-1
wānanga see Wānanga

Tertiary Education Commission, 187

Textile industry, 409, 410-1

Thailand
  Closer Economic Partnership Agreement,
    406, 467

Thistle control, 359

Timber, 379-81

Time zone, 14

Timor-Leste, deployment in, 62, 78, 218

Tobacco
  cigarette packets, 152
  consumption, 152
  CPI group, 336, 337
  excise, 458, 498, 504
  smoking-related deaths, 151-2

Toi iho, 257

Toi te Taiao (Bioethics Council), 313

Tokelau
  citizenship of NZ, 109
  migration to NZ from, 124
  NZ jurisdiction, 1
  special relationship with, 59, 69-70

Toll Holdings Ltd, 432

Toll NZ, 432-3

Tomb of the Unknown Warrior, 255

Tonga
  migration to NZ from, 124
  Police deployment in, 218

Topography, national, 321-2

Tornadoes, 11

Totalisator Agency Board, 266

Totalisator duty, 500

Tourism
  100% Pure NZ campaign, 270
  accommodation, 271
  attractions, 268-9
  Brand NZ, 458
  events, 269
  generally, 268
  government agencies, 270
  household expenditure, 346
  international visitors, 270-2
  market, 268
  online technologies, 269
  STAR project, 272
  sustainability, 269, 272
  Tourism Industry Association NZ, 270
  Tourism NZ, 270
  Tourism Strategy 2015, 269
  transport, 272

Trackside, 230, 266

Trade
  see also Commerce and services
  domestic retail trade, generally, 452-4
  environment and, 320
  overseas see Exports; Imports; Overseas
    trade

Trade Aid, 66

Trade and Enterprise, NZ, 58, 405, 406-8,
  409, 457-8

Trade union membership, 279

Trademarks, 303

Trade-weighted index, 487, 488

Traditional sites, protection of, 242-3

Traffic offences
  convictions, 204
  number of offences and infringements, 441
  sentenced prisoners by offence and sex,
    213

Training benefit, 134, 135

Training Incentive Allowance, 135

Tramping, 264

Transit NZ, 434

Transition to Work assistance, 287

Transitional Retirement Benefit, 134, 135

Trans-Pacific Strategic Economic Partnership,
  62, 406, 467

Transport
  civil aviation see Civil aviation
  commuting, 432-3, 434
  CPI group, 336, 337
  emissions, 308
  employee count in sector, 356
  energy use, 311, 387, 389
  GDP by industry, 344
  generally, 425
  household expenditure, 346
  international visitors, 272
  rail
    commuting, 432
    freight transport, 432, 433
    history, 15, 431-2
    noise reduction, 436
    passenger services, 432-3
  road transport see Road transport
  school children, 180
  shipping, 425-8

Transport Accident Investigation
  Commission, 426

Transport Agency, NZ, 434

Trans-Tasman travel agreement, 60, 101

Tranz Rail, 432

Treasury bills, 486

Treaty of Waitangi
  claims under, 118-9
  Office of Treaty Settlements, 119
  significance of, 117
  signing of, 17

Tribunals, 198-9

Trout, 265

Trust administration, Public Trust, 51

Tsunami (Boxing Day 2004), 6

Tsunami monitoring network, 6

TUANZ, 227

Turners and Growers, 372

TV see Television

TV3, 229

TVNZ, 222, 228-9

U

Unemployment
  by age, 286
  by educational attainment, 285, 286
  by ethnicity, 287
  by sex, 286, 287
  demographic and social characteristics,
    285-7
  employment assistance, 287-8
  Enterprising Community grants, 134, 285
  rate, 285
  seasonal work assistance, 287
  Straight2Work industry partnerships, 134
  Transition to Work assistance, 287
  Work and Income, 130-3

Unemployment Benefit
  entitlement, 131
  expenditure, 135
  income adjustment, 131
  number of people in receipt of, 131-2, 134
  student hardship, 182
  weekly rates, 131

Union membership, 279

Unit Titles Act 1972, 418-9

Unitary authorities, 53

United Future, confidence and supply
  agreement, 33

United Kingdom
  CPI comparison, 338
  social security agreement with, 136

United Nations
  Alliance of Civilisations, 67
  contributions to, 67
  Convention on Biological Diversity, 318,
    319, 320
  Environment Programme, 320
  Framework Convention on Climate Change,
    318, 319, 320
  generally, 67
  human rights resolutions, 67
  International Court of Justice, 67
  MFAT's role in coordination of international
    environmental work, 318
  specialised agencies, 67
  UN Truce Supervisory Organization, 64, 78
  UNESCO, 67

United States
  CPI comparison, 338
  defence relationship, 62, 78
  relationship with, 62
  trade, value of, 472-3
  trade with, 62

Universities
  bachelor degrees, sex ratio of, 188
  governance, 177
  library services, 245
  list of, 188
  number of, 44
  research funding and activities, 297, 302

University of the South Pacific, 60

Unsolicited Goods and Services Act 1975, 450

Unsupported Child's Benefit, 133, 134, 135
    number of people in receipt of, 134
    weekly rates, 131

Urban design, 53

Urban population, 92–4

Uruguay, relationship with, 62

Uruguay Round, GATT, 68, 357

V

Vaccination, 153, 157

Valuation of land, 325

Valuers' Registration Board, 325

Varroa mite, 370

Vava'u Declaration on Pacific Fisheries
    Resources, 59

Veal, 361, 362, 363

Vegetable exports, 371, 464–5

Vegetation, 12–3

Vehicles see Driving; Motor vehicles; Road
    transport

Venison exports, 361, 461

Venture Investment Fund Ltd, NZ, 297

Veteran's Pension, 131, 134, 135, 136–7

Veterinary medicines, regulation of, 154

Vice-regal representatives, 30

Victim Support, 207

Victims' rights, 211–2

Video see Film and video

Violent offences, 201–2, 213

Visas, 114–6

Visitor's permits, 114

Vital statistics, 99

Vocational qualifications, 174, 190–1

Vodafone NZ, 224, 227

Volcanoes, 3, 4, 6–7

Voluntary administration (insolvency), 448

Voluntary sector see Community and
    voluntary sector

Volunteer Service Abroad, 60, 64, 66

Voting
    local government elections, 54
    parliamentary elections see Parliamentary
    elections

W

Wages
    minimum wage, 277–8
    salary and wage rates, 289–90, 291

Waitangi National Trust Board, 330

Waitangi, Treaty of see Treaty of Waitangi

Waitangi Tribunal, 20, 118–9, 199

Walking and walkways, 264, 265, 433, 434

Wānanga
    enrolments, 193, 194
    generally, 188
    governance, 177
    number of, 44
    research, science and technology, 302

War memorials and graves, 255

War pensions, 134, 135, 136

Wars, involvement in, 19

Waste
    e-waste recycling, 222
    landfill gas, 397, 400
    landfills, 318

Water
    accidents, 165
    drinking water, 149–50
    environmental accounts, 341
    fluoridation, 159
    management, 316, 317
    pollution, 317
    quality, 310–1, 316, 317

Water Safety NZ, 165

Watercare Services' Adopt a Stream
    programme, 179

Wave energy converter, 300

Weapons, convictions for offences, 206

Weather see Climate

Weathertight Homes Resolution Service, 419

Weeds, bio-control, 359

Weights and Measures Act 1987, 450

Welfare benefits see Social development

Westland Milk Products, 367

Weta, 12, 321

Wetlands, 329

Whale sanctuaries, 329–30

Whales, 12

Whaling Commission, 318, 320, 329

Whānau agreements, 137

Whangaehu Valley, lahar risk, 5

Wharekura, 120

Wheat, 371

Wholesale trade
    employee count in sector, 356
    GDP by industry, 344
    prices, 339

Widow's Benefit, 131, 132, 134, 135

Wiki for new Policing Act, 215

Wildlife, 12, 13

Wildlife reserves, 329

Willing Workers on Organic Farms, 372

Wind, 8, 11

Wind energy, 400–1

Wind-powered sculpture, 248

Wine industry, 373–4

Women
    see also Sex ratios
    health services, 157
    issues, 126
    life expectancy, 101
    prisoners, 213, 214

Women's Affairs, Ministry of, 126

Wool
    exports, 365–6
    marketing, 365
    prices, 365
    production, 358, 364–5
    uses, 364

Work and Income
    accommodation assistance, 417, 418
    advance payments, 134
    CPI-related adjustment of payments, 131,
        335
    employment assistance, 130, 131, 287–8
    Enterprising Communities, 134, 285
    family assistance, 132–3
    hospitalisation of income support client,
        135
    income adjustment, 131
    income support, 130–1
    industry partnerships, 134
    NZ Superannuation, 131, 134, 135, 136–7
    other assistance, 133
    seasonal work assistance, 287
    services, 130–7
    social security agreements, 136–7
    Special Needs Grant, 133
    Transitional Retirement Benefit, 134, 135
    Transition to Work assistance, 287
    types of benefits and pensions, 130
    Unemployment Benefit see Unemployment
        Benefit
    Veteran's Pension, 131, 134, 135, 136–7
    war pensions, 134, 135, 136

Work permits, 114–6

Working for Families, 132, 502

Working holiday schemes, 115–6

Working-age population, 87

Workplaces
    see also Employment
    child education and care services, 183–4
    conservation, 280
    EEO Trust, 126
    KiwiSaver, 487
    safety and health, 170–1
    smoke-free, 153
    work stoppages, 279–80

World Customs Organization, 458

World Environment Day, 39, 320

World Health Organization, 67

World heritage areas, 326–7

World Heritage Committee (UN), 67

World Summit on Sustainable Development,
    320

World Trade Organization
    Doha Development Round, 68, 320, 357
    environmental goods and services, 320
    establishment, 68

World wars, involvement in, 19, 72

Wrecks (ships), 428

Writers and writing, 245, 246–7

Writers' Fellowship, Michael King, 257

Y

Young offenders
  convicted offenders, 205
  dealing with, 205
  diversion, 217
  family group conferences, 139
  home-based care, 139
  residential care, 139
  youth justice services, 138–9

Youth aid section, NZ Police, 217

Youth courts, 197–8

Youth Development, Ministry of, 127–8, 130

Youth Development Partnership Fund, 128

Youth Development Strategy Aotearoa, 128

Youth Education Service, 217

Youth Health Action Plan, 158

Youth issues, 127–8

Youth minimum wage, abolition of, 277

Youth Orchestra, National, 248

Youth Parliament, 127, 128

Z

Zeolite, 403
ZESPRI International Ltd, 372